Student's Guide to Using

BEHAVIOR IN ORGANIZATIONS

We have included in this book several key features designed to help students find and understand the most important aspects of the material. To help you get the most out of this book, we thought it would be useful to introduce some of these features here.

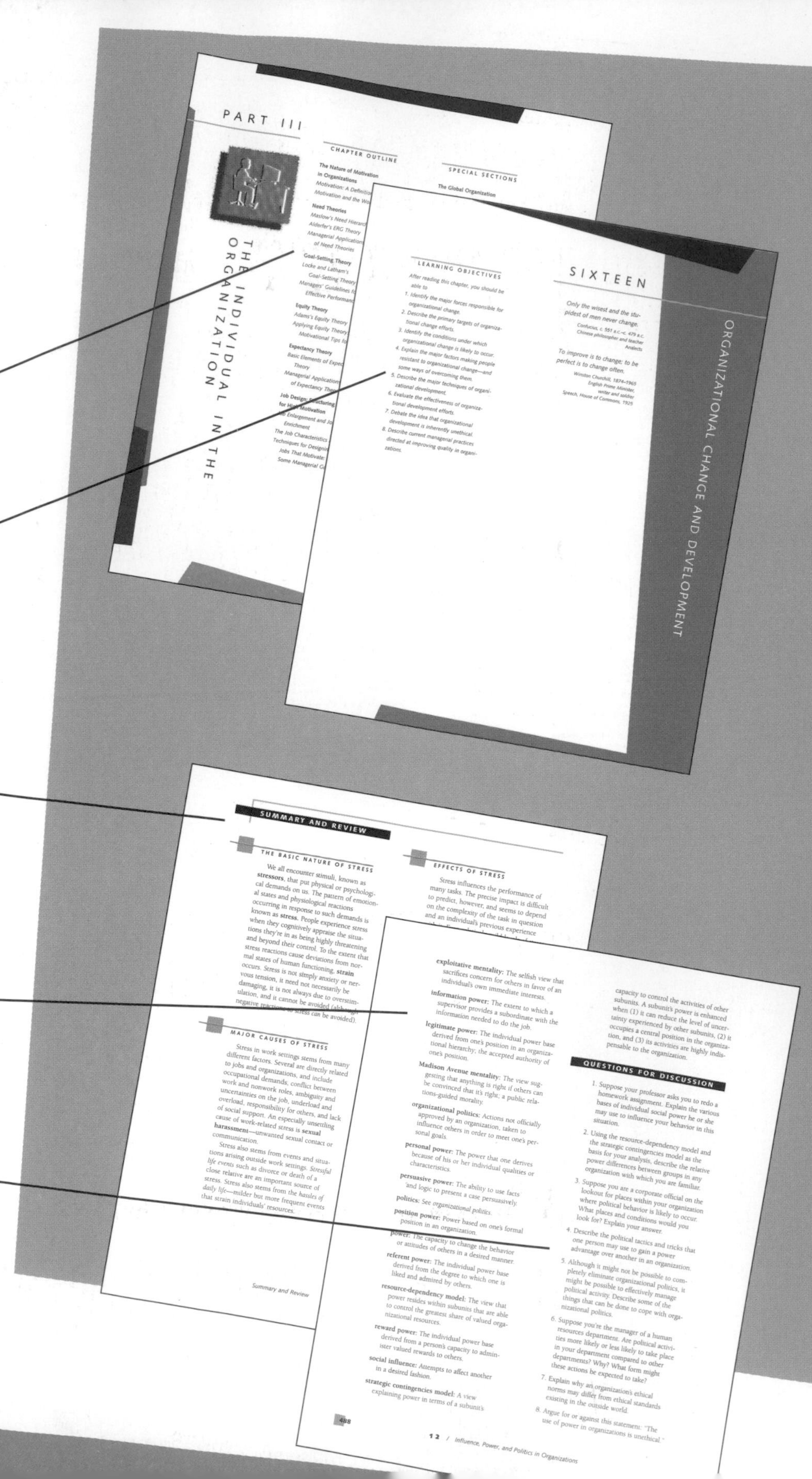

CHAPTER OUTLINE
An outline of major headings to show what's coming ahead and to help you refind material you've already read

LEARNING OBJECTIVES
Your guide to what you should know after reading this chapter

SUMMARY AND REVIEW
A simplified recap of all the most important ideas in the chapter, divided into major headings

KEY TERMS
Definitions of all the most important terms in the chapter—those appearing in boldface type

QUESTIONS FOR DISCUSSION
Useful questions for both reviewing the material and for thinking about it further

fifth edition

SPECIAL SECTIONS

Close-up looks at some of the most fascinating aspects of the field, focusing on such themes as ethics, quality, globalization, and the future of organizations

EXPERIENCING ORGANIZATIONAL BEHAVIOR

Interesting exercises that allow you to experience key ideas first hand, and to learn more about them and yourself as well

CASE STUDIES

To demonstrate how organizational behavior is put to use, each chapter contains two cases describing actual organizations—one to help you understand the importance of the topic (*Preview Case*) and one to highlight how key concepts are used in practice (*Case in Point*).

BEHAVIOR IN ORGANIZATIONS

UNDERSTANDING & MANAGING THE HUMAN SIDE OF WORK

fifth edition

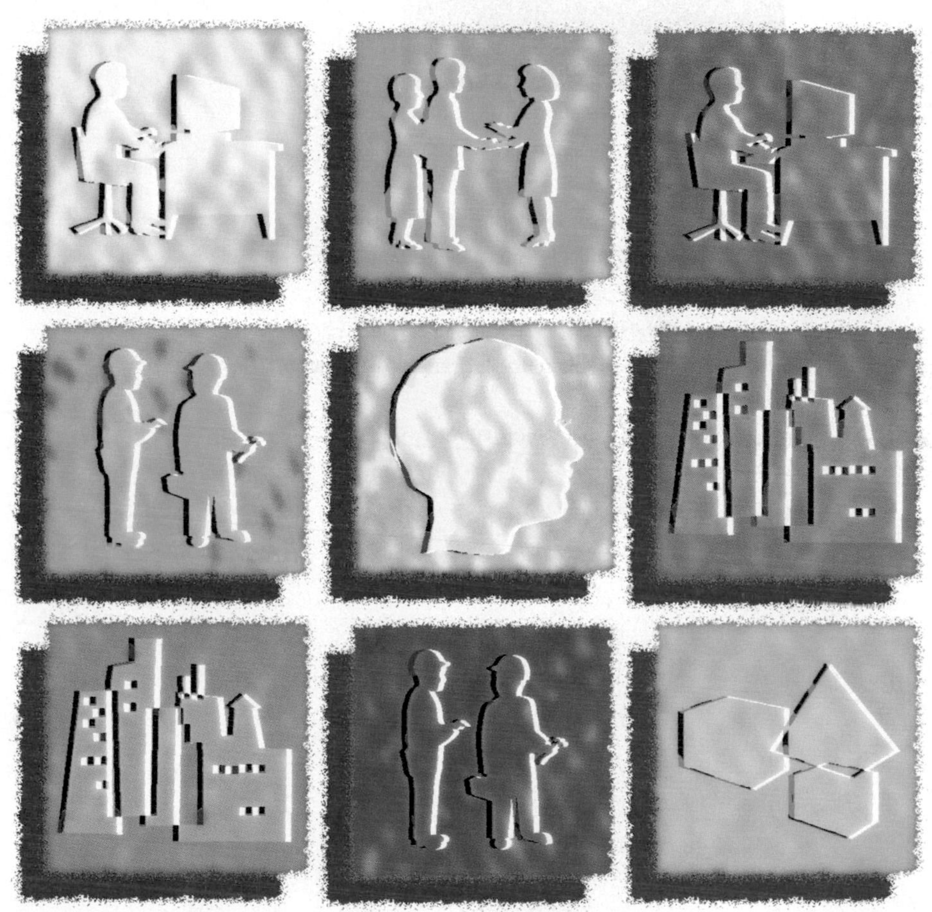

Jerald Greenberg
THE OHIO STATE UNIVERSITY

Robert A. Baron
RENSSELAER POLYTECHNIC INSTITUTE

PRENTICE-HALL INTERNATIONAL, INC.

Printed in the United States of America

10 9 8 7 6 5 4 3 2 1
ISBN 0-13-324930-1

Prentice-Hall International (UK) Limited, *London*
Prentice-Hall of Australia Pty. Limited, *Sydney*
Prentice-Hall Canada Inc., *Toronto*
Prentice-Hall Hispanoamericana, S.A., *Mexico*
Prentice-Hall of India Private Limited, *New Delhi*
Prentice-Hall of Japan, Inc. *Tokyo*
Simon & Schuster Asia Pte. Ltd., *Singapore*
Editora Prentice-Hall do Brasil, Ltda., *Rio de Janeiro*

DEDICATION

To Carolyn—

For teaching me about behavior in organizations.

and

To Birdie and Pepper—

For showing me the power of words.

J. G.

To Sandra—

Who long ago mastered the art of adding quality (in the best sense of this term) to our life.

and

To Jessica—

Who, much more than I, will experience all the changes described on the pages of this book.

R. A. B.

PHOTO CREDITS

Chapter 1: Preview Case, Courtesy of General Motors Europe; Figure 1-5, © Bob Sacha ; Figure 1-6, © Blair Seitz/Photo Researchers; Figure 1-7, © Gordon Feller; Figure 1-8, © Smithsonian Institution, photo no. 80-20573.

Chapter 2: Preview Case, Courtesy of Stihl Company; Figure 2-1, © John Coletti; Figure 2-8, © Richard Sobol/Stock, Boston; Figure 2-12, © Rob Crandall; Figure 2-13, Courtesy of Corning Incorporated.

Chapter 3: Preview Case, © Jeffrey Lowe/ONYX; Figure 3-1, Courtesy of AlliedSignal Inc.; Figure 3-9, © Andy Sacks/Tony Stone Images; Figure 3-11, North Wind Picture Archives.

Chapter 4: Preview Case, Courtesy of United Electric Controls Co.; Figure 4-5, Courtesy of Odetics; Figure 4-9, © Marc Pokemper/Tony Stone Images.

Chapter 5: Preview Case, Courtesy of Manor HealthCare, Division of Manor Care, Inc.; Figure 5-3, Photofest; Figure 5-5, Courtesy of Federal Express; Figure 5-11, Courtesy of Solectron Corporation, Jim Karageorge; Figure 5-14, Courtesy of Digital Equipment Corporation.

Chapter 6: Preview Case, Courtesy of Dabney Resnick Asset Management, Inc.; Figure 6-4, Courtesy of Union Pacific Corporation; Figure 6-7, © Paul Fetters; Figure 6-13, © Alice Q. Hargrave; Figure 6-14, Courtesy of America West Airlines; Figure 6-15, Courtesy of Quad/Graphics.

Chapter 7: Preview Case, © 1987 Matthew Neal McVay/All Stock; Figure 7-5, © John Coletti; Figure 7-9, Charlie Cole/SIPA; Figure 7-12, © Jerry Howard/Stock Boston; Figure 7-14, AP/Wide World Photos.

Chapter 8: Preview Case, Courtesy of XEL Communications, Inc.; Figure 8-4, Gans/Furones/The Stock Market; Figure 8-6, Andy Sacks/Tony Stone Images; Figure 8-14, © James Schnepf.

Chapter 9: Preview Case, Courtesy of General Motors; Figure 9-4, Courtesy of Microsoft Corporation; Figure 9-5, © Chris Corsmeier.

Chapter 10: Preview Case, (top) courtesy of Chrysler Corporation, (bottom) AP/Wide World Photos; Figure 10-3, © Blair Seitz/Photo Researchers; Figure 10-10, David Woo/Stock, Boston.

Chapter 11: Preview Case, Courtesy of SC Johnson Wax; Figure 11-1, © Tom Stewart/The Stock Market; Figure 11-3, Courtesy of Pfizer Inc., Figure 11-11, © Lester Sloan/Woodfin Camp & Associates.

Chapter 12: Preview Case, © Michael Abramson/Woodfin Camp & Associates; Figure 12-2, © Chuck O'Rear/Woodfin Camp & Associates; Figure 12-5, © 1993 Brian Smith; Figure 12-7, (left) © Archive Photos, (right) Courtesy of Microsoft Corporation; Figure 12-11, © Dick Luria/Photo Researchers; Figure 12-14, Courtesy of The Body Shop, Inc.

Chapter 13: Preview Case, Courtesy of Mary Kay Cosmetics, Inc.; Figure 13-1, (left) Courtesy of Chrysler Corporation, (right) © John Marmaras/Woodfin Camp & Associates; Figure 13-6, (left) © Dan Budnik/Woodfin Camp & Associates (right) AP/Wide World Photos; Figure 13-12, © John Abbott.

Chapter 14: Preview Case, Courtesy of United Parcel Service; Figure 14-1, © Alastair Black/Tony Stone Images; Figure 14-4, Courtesy of McDonald's Corporation; Figure 14-9, © Charles Thatcher/Tony Stone Images; Figure 14-12, © Jon Feingersh/Stock Boston; Figure 14-3, (left) © Archive Photos, (right) AP/Wide World Photos.

Chapter 15: Preview Case, Courtesy of Johnson & Johnson; Figure 15-8, (top) UPI/Bettmann Newsphotos, (bottom) AP/Wide World Photos; Figure 15-9, © Gerd Ludwig/Woodfin Camp & Associates; Figure 15-12, AP/Wide World Photos.

Chapter 16: Preview Case, AP/Wide World Photos; Figure 16-1, © Freda Leinwand; Figure 16-3, © Ed Kashi; Figure 16-4, © Erik Hill/Anchorage Daily News; Figure 16-15, © John Abbott.

CONTENTS

PART IV GROUP PROCESSES

CHAPTER 8 GROUP DYNAMICS AND TEAMWORK IN ORGANIZATIONS 282

CHAPTER 9 INTERPERSONAL COMMUNICATION IN ORGANIZATIONS 326

PART V INFLUENCING OTHERS

PART VI ORGANIZATIONAL PROCESSES

PREFACE: THE EVER-CHANGING NATURE OF ORGANIZATIONS—AND THIS BOOK

The world of work has changed a great deal since we wrote the first edition of this book twelve years ago. Today, five editions later, our typewriters have given way to powerful desktop computers, the organizations about which we write have reorganized (including the company that publishes this book!), a more diverse mix of people fills the workforce, and interest in producing high quality goods and services has reached a pinnacle. In short, the nature of organizations, and the work experience itself, has changed. These and many other contemporary trends in the workplace highlight the need to understand how people operate in organizations and how to manage their behavior if individuals and companies are to flourish. In other words, the challenges faced by the field of organizational behavior (OB) today are more important than ever.

OB's dual allegiance to theory and practice makes it well suited to meet these challenges. On the one hand, OB is based on and driven by *research*, a discipline using highly sophisticated techniques and procedures to study the complex interplay between people and the organizations in which they work. On the other hand, it is also an *applications-oriented* field, one deeply concerned with identifying practical means for enhancing the productivity of individuals and the effectiveness of organizations. So, in short, OB perpetually focuses on these two distinct, but complementary, orientations and goals.

The balance between these approaches is a major theme of this new edition. We have tried to continue the strong research tradition that has been so well received by our colleagues in previous editions, while, at the same time, enhancing coverage of the practical, applications-oriented side of OB—that is, the many ways in which its findings and principles are put to use by organizations. In recent years, the balance between OB research and practice has been brought to the forefront by rapid changes in the nature of organizations and their relationships with the people who work within them. As a result, many new topics have become the focus of systematic study, and many well-established ones have received increased attention. We have carefully monitored these changes in the field and have adjusted our coverage accordingly. The result, we believe, is a book that closely reflects the mood of OB as it is studied and practiced today. We will now point out some of the specific improvements that can be found in this edition of the book.

INCREASED ATTENTION TO ORGANIZATIONAL PRACTICES —BUT WITHOUT LOSING THE ESSENTIAL RESEARCH-ORIENTED CHARACTER OF THE BOOK

To reflect the practical value of OB more fully, we have instituted several different changes. Together, these serve to illustrate the applications-oriented approach of modern OB, but without losing sight of the strong research orientation that historically has been found in this book.

Greater Use of Examples From Contemporary Companies. We have liberally seasoned our discussions of various topics in OB with examples from real companies—so many, in fact, that a new *Company Index* has been added to help find them. We refer to a broad range of real organizations—large and small companies, providing both products and services, with domestic and/or international operations. The organizational examples we cite illustrate the principles and findings being discussed and show how they relate to practical problems and issues faced by functioning organizations and those working within them. Highlighting these features are new tables summarizing current organizational practices with respect to various issues, such as promoting autonomy (Table 4-4), mentorship programs (Table 6-2), the effectiveness of work teams (Table 8-6), and culture clashes in mergers and acquisitions (Table 14-2) to name a few.

Expanded Case Materials. Each chapter now has two cases describing real companies, doubling the number appearing in the previous edition. The "Preview Case," which opens each chapter, is designed to highlight the importance of various concepts related to the subject of that chapter by showing how they have been used in a specific company. The "Case In Point," appearing at the end of each chapter, is designed to review and summarize organizational practices that illustrate the application of OB concepts presented in the chapter. All cases deal with a wide variety of companies (e.g., Boeing, Chrysler, and S. C. Johnson & Son) and personalities (e.g., Mary Kay Ash, Richard Branson, and Anita Roddick).

It is important to note that our expanded attention to organizational practices did *not* come at the expense of the focus on research that has been a hallmark of this book over the years. Adopters of earlier editions of this book will find that *we continue our long-standing commitment to chronicling the latest research findings in the field of OB in a lively and understandable manner*. This may be seen not only in the body of the text itself, but also in one of the most popular features of our previous editions, the *annotated data diagrams*. Thus, our emphasis on the scientific side of OB is just as strong as ever. Now, however, we more carefully balance this orientation with the practical, applications-oriented side of OB. The result, we believe, does a better job of capturing the essence of the field of OB today. And this, after all, is what this book is all about.

INCREASED ATTENTION TO GROWING DIVERSITY IN THE WORKFORCE AND THE INTERNATIONAL NATURE OF ORGANIZATIONS

Many of the most pressing issues faced by organizations today center around the growing *internationalization* of all business activities, and the increasing *cultural diversity* of today's work forces. OB, as a field, is deeply concerned with such issues. To reflect this fact, and to illustrate the many ways in which OB can help modern organizations in their efforts to deal with these matters, we have included a special section called **The Global Organization**. A few examples:

- Confronting the Challenge of Free Enterprise in Russian Organizations (Chapter 1)
- Cross-Cultural Differences in Sex-Role Stereotyping (Chapter 2)
- Motivation Makes the World Go 'Round: A Cross-Cultural Investigation of Work Values (Chapter 4)
- Karoushi: The Ultimate Effect of Hard Work in Japan (Chapter 7)
- Where in The World Does Social Loafing Occur? Comparing China, Israel and the United States (Chapter 8)
- Cultural Differences in Approaches to Conflict (Chapter 11)
- Nationality and Leader Behavior: Is there a World of Difference? (Chapter 13)

Matters of cultural diversity within organizations are also addressed throughout the book, such as when introducing the nature of the field of OB (Chapter 1), discussing the nature of attitudes and discrimination in the workplace (Chapter 5), and discussing efforts at managing conflict (Chapter 11).

EXPANDED COVERAGE OF THE GROWING EMPHASIS ON ORGANIZATIONAL QUALITY

Whether it's part of a strategic commitment to a *total quality management* philosophy, or simply an effort to gain a competitive edge, many of today's organizations are more committed than ever to improving the quality of their products and services, and the lives of their employees. Because these efforts are such an important part of organizational life today, we have highlighted them in special sections called **The Quest for Quality**. Some examples include:

- Managing Stress Among Police Officers: Some Lessons From Those Who Do It Best (Chapter 7)
- Boundary Spanning Strategies for Team Effectiveness: What Do Successful Teams Do? (Chapter 8)
- Managing Conflict by Managing Diversity: Was Anything Learned from the Los Angeles Riots? (Chapter 11)
- Achieving Success as a Team Leader: Some Guidelines (Chapter 13)
- Laptop Computers: A Key to Improving the Sales Process (Chapter 14)
- The Baldridge Award: Recognizing the Best in Quality (Chapter 16)

CLOSE ATTENTION TO ETHICAL ISSUES IN ORGANIZATIONS

In this edition we continue to highlight the growing concern over matters of ethical behavior that have permeated the workplace in recent years. Our special section, **The Ethical Workplace**, highlights ethical practices and controversies that have arisen. Some of these include:

- Observers' Reactions to Disciplining Unethical Behavior: The Fairness of Making the Punishment Fit the Crime (Chapter 2)
- The White Collar Criminal: A Personality Profile (Chapter 3)
- Affirmative Action and Presumed Incompetence: The Unequal Impact of "Equal Opportunities" (Chapter 5)
- Married Couples Working Together: Where Do Companies Stand? (Chapter 6)
- Sexual Harassment: Facing The Facts (Chapter 7)
- Employee Communication: Not as Confidential as You Think! (Chapter 9)

EMPHASIS ON FUTURE TRENDS IN ORGANIZATIONAL PRACTICES

Now that we are poised at the threshold of the twenty-first century, it is tempting to consider what organizational life might be like in the future. Our new feature, **The Organization of Tomorrow**, specifically focuses on future trends in the practice of OB. Some examples:

- The Hottest Careers for the Twenty-First Century (Chapter 6)
- Social Facilitation via an "Electronic Presence": Some Experimental Findings (Chapter 8)
- How We Will Be Communicating in the Twenty-First Century—If Not Sooner! (Chapter 9)
- What Will Become of Managerial Power in the Age of the Empowered Employee? (Chapter 12)
- Workflow Automation: Toward the Paperless Office (Chapter 14)
- The Contingency Work Force: Permanent Temporary Employees (Chapter 16)

CHANGES IN CONTENT

At first glance, the Table of Contents for this text appears to be highly similar to that for the preceding edition. Yet, closer examination indicates that in fact, there are major changes in content within each chapter. In fact, literally scores of *new topics* are now included in the text. A small sample of these includes the following:

- Teams
- Total Quality Management
- Diversity Management
- Reengineering
- The Horizontal Organization
- Mintzberg's Organizational Forms
- Computerized Performance Monitoring
- Assistive Technology
- Workflow Automation
- Strategic Alliances

This is in addition to the *expanded coverage* of several topics whose growing popularity has dictated that more space be devoted to them. Some of these include:

- Diversity in the Workforce
- Organizational Commitment
- Culture
- Technology
- Mentoring
- Career Management
- Prejudice and Discrimination in the Workplace

Much of this expanded coverage resulted from reorganizing material into a new chapter (14) on the work environment. This chapter expands our discussion of organizational culture, and introduces new material on the use of—and reactions to—technology in the workplace. In all, these changes reflect our commitment to keeping the text current—reflecting the latest research, findings, and applications in modern OB. The up-to-date nature of the text is illustrated by the fact that the vast majority of our reference materials were published during the last few years.

CHANGES IN MATERIALS ACCOMPANYING THE TEXT

The changes outlined above constitute the key alterations we have made in the text itself. Other changes, however, involve the materials that accompany **Behavior in Organizations (5th edition)**. Foremost among these are the following:

Revised Transparency Masters and Transparency Package. We have extensively revised and expanded the transparency package provided to colleagues who adopt our text. A set of 150 full-color transparencies is available, consisting of art adapted from graphic material appearing in the book but redrawn for clearer classroom use. Lecture notes accompany each transparency. The entire transparency set is also available on diskette (Power Point files in both IBM and Macintosh formats) for those who wish to display them on a computer. These materials are in addition to 80 transparency masters appearing in the *Instructors' Manual.*

A Test Item File. A thoroughly revised and expanded *Test Bank* is available to instructors. It contains 100 items per chapter, including multiple choice, short answer, fill-in, and essay questions. As an aid to item selection, the questions are categorized as being either easy, moderate in difficulty, or challenging. To assist in exam preparation, all test questions are also available in computerized form through Prentice Hall's *Test Manager* software.

An Extensive Instructor's Manual. The *Instructor's Manual* contains a variety of useful features for instructors using this book in their classes. Among these are: course outlines and syllabi, chapter overviews and outlines, learning objectives, answers to review questions, teaching suggestions, skills exercises, additional cases, and notes on the "Case-In-Point" features—including the accompanying videos. In short, it contains many helpful tools for instructors.

A CNN Video Library. A feature that truly brings OB to life is a set of videotapes containing news clips and interviews with business leaders that originally appeared on CNN, including shows such as *Pinnacle*, and *Managing with Lou Dobbs*. There are 16 video segments each ranging from 3 to 10 minutes in length—one coordinated to the "Case in Point" appearing in each chapter. Notes for the cases and the videos appear in the CNN Video User's Guide found inside the *Instructor's Manual*.

Marginal Annotations. To assist instructors using this book, 15 supplemental annotations have been included in the margins of each chapter of the Instructor's Edition. These are of five different types:

- *OB in Action*—Examples of how OB is being applied in organizations
- *Research Finding*—Summary of research findings that supplement the text
- *Teaching Tip*—Suggestions for how to illustrate a point in the classroom
- *Facts and Figures*—Some interesting statistic relevant to the material
- *In Addition . . .*—An interesting tidbit of information that supplements the text

The annotations are positioned in the margins of the text at the points where they apply. For those seeking more information about the points made in the annotations, source materials are cited.

CONCLUSION

Looking back, we can honestly say that we have spared no effort in preparing a book that reflects the current character of the field of OB, with respect to both scientific inquiry and practical application. In so doing, we were inspired by the words of Lord Chesterfield, who wrote:

> *Aim at perfection in everything, though in most things it is unattainable; however, those who aim at perfection and persevere, will come closer to it than those give it up as unattainable...*

Whether, and to what extent, we have reached this goal, however, can only be judged by you—our colleagues. So, as always, we sincerely invite your input. Please let us know what you like about the book, and what features can stand improvement. Such feedback is always welcomed, and does not fall on deaf ears. We promise faithfully to take your comments and suggestions to heart, and to incorporate them into the next edition.

Jerald Greenberg
Abramowitz Professor of Business Ethics and
Professor of Organizational Behavior
Department of Management and Human Resources
Fisher College of Business
The Ohio State University
Columbus, Ohio 43210

Robert A. Baron (seated)
Chair of the Department of Managerial Policy
and Organization
Rensselaer Polytechnic Institute
Troy, New York 12180

ACKNOWLEDGMENTS: SOME WORDS OF THANKS

Writing is a solitary task. Converting authors' words into a book, however, requires the efforts and cooperation of many individuals. In preparing this text, we have been assisted by a large number of dedicated, talented people. Although we cannot possibly thank all of them here, we wish to express our appreciation to those whose help has been most valuable.

First, our sincere thanks to our colleagues who read and commented on various portions of the manuscript. Their suggestions were invaluable, and helped us in many ways. These include:

Royce L. Abrahamson, Southwest Texas State University

Ralph R. Braithwaite, University of Hartford

Roy A. Cook, Fort Lewis College

Cynthia Cordes, State University of New York at Binghamton

Paul N. Keaton, University of Wisconsin at LaCrosse

Daniel Levi, California Polytechnic State University

Jeffrey Lewis, Pitzer College

Charles W. Mattox, Jr., St. Mary's University

James McElroy, Iowa State University

Audry Murrell, University of Pittsburgh

William D. Patzig, James Madison University

David W. Roach, Arkansas Tech University

Terri A. Scandura, University of Miami, Coral Gables

Marc Siegall, California State University, Chico

Patrick C. Stubbleine, Indiana University—Purdue University at Fort Wayne

Philip A. Weatherford, Embry-Riddle Aeronautical University

Richard M. Weiss, University of Delaware

The contributions of these individuals built upon the assistance we received from reviewers of the fourth edition of this book:

Rabi S. Bhagat, Memphis State University

Richard Grover, University of Southern Maine

Ralph Katerberg, University of Cincinnati

Mary Kernan, University of Delaware

Rodney Lim, Tulane University

Richard McKinney, Southern Illinois University

Paula Morrow, Iowa State University

Shirley Rickert, Indiana University—Purdue University at Fort Wayne

Taggart Smith, Purdue University

Paul Sweeney, Marquette University

Second, we wish to express our appreciation to our editor, Suzy Spivey, who saw us through this project. Her enthusiasm was contagious, and her constant support and good humor helped us bring it to completion in a timely and enjoyable manner. Our developmental editor, Judy Fifer, did a terrific job of keeping us focused on all the many details that go into writing a book like this. We also wish to thank our new editor, Natalie Anderson, for sharing her vision of future editions of this book.

Third, our sincere thanks go out to Prentice Hall's outstanding production team for making this book so beautiful—Alana Zdinak, Production Liaison, Linda Fiordilino, Design Director, and Fran Russello, Production Manager. We also worked closely with Laurie Frankenthaler on photo research, Linda Purrington on copy-editing, and Tom Dorsaneo on putting the entire package together. Their diligence and skill with matters of design, permissions, and illustrations—not to mention constant refinements—helped us immeasurably throughout the process of preparing this work. It was a pleasure to work with such kind and understanding professionals, and we are greatly indebted to them for their contributions. With a team like this behind us—a group that can spot an undotted "i" or an uncrossed "t" from forty paces away—authors cannot help but look good.

Third, we wish to thank our colleagues who have provided expert assistance in preparing various features for this book. Suzyn Ornstein diligently researched and wrote the very interesting "Case-In Point" features that end each chapter. Audry Murrell did a terrific job on the *Test Bank*, Lewis Hershey created beautiful art for the transparencies, and Paul Keaton prepared a wonderful *Instructor's Manual*. Lisamarie Brassini helped coordinate these new and improved teaching materials. We also wish to thank Kim Scott and Tom Welchans for their fascinating annotations appearing in the margins of the instructor's edition of this book.

Finally, Jerald Greenberg wishes to acknowledge the family of the late Irving Abramowitz for their generous endowment to the Ohio State University, which provided invaluable support during the writing of this book.

To all these truly outstanding people, and to many others too, our warm personal regards.

BEHAVIOR IN ORGANIZATIONS

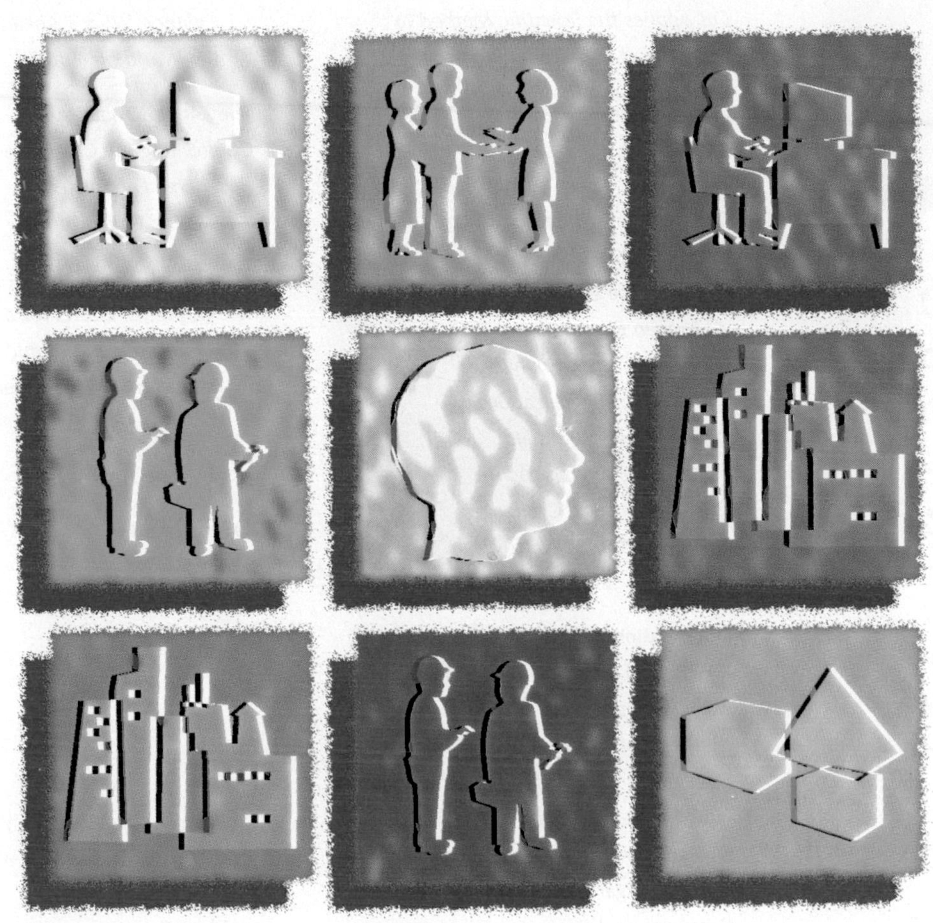

PART I

ORGANIZATIONAL BEHAVIOR: AN INTRODUCTION

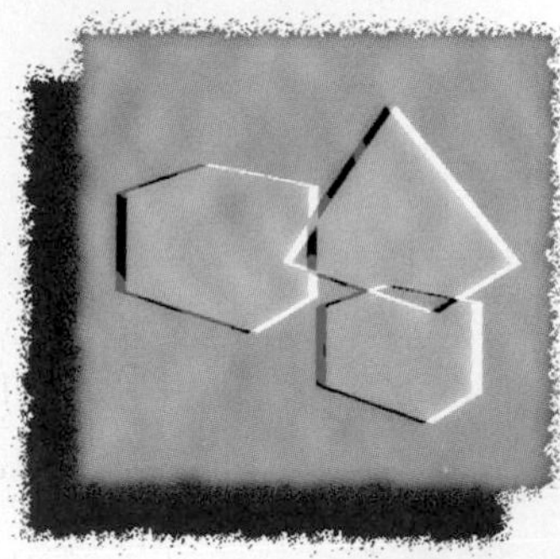

CHAPTER OUTLINE

SPECIAL SECTIONS

ONE

THE NATURE AND STUDY OF ORGANIZATIONS

LEARNING OBJECTIVES

After reading this chapter, you should be able to

1. *Describe the major focus of the field of organizational behavior (OB) including the three basic units of analysis used.*
2. *Characterize the major characteristics of the field of organizational behavior today.*
3. *Explain how the study of organizational behavior is influenced by trends toward workforce diversity and globalization.*
4. *Trace the historical developments and schools of thought leading up to the field of organizational behavior today.*
5. *Explain the importance of the scientific method in learning about behavior in organizations.*
6. *Describe the role of theory in the pursuit of knowledge about organizational behavior.*
7. *Characterize the major approaches to conducting research in the field of organizational behavior, and compare the relative advantages and disadvantages of each.*

There is no animal more difficult to understand than man.

Leonardo Salviati, 1540–1589
Italian humanist
La Spina

First study the science and then practice the art which is born of that science.

Leonardo da Vinci, 1452–1519
Italian artist, inventor, and scientist
Treatise on Painting

PREVIEW CASE

Making Opel the Gem of General Motors Europe

It's clear now to everyone that the management of people is the key to productivity," remarked David Herman, chairman of Opel, General Motors' successful European car line, as he reflected on the task of reorganizing his company's workforce. Organizing the German-based company's 35 thousand hourly employees into teams (Gruppen, as they are called) was going to be no easy feat, especially given the mix of Americans and Germans who worked side by side. Building cars is tough enough even without the added cultural and communication barriers. "We're trying to build new cultures together," Herman said, "but we have a long way to go."

If the past is any indication, however, Herman is up to the task. Before taking over the reins at Opel in November 1992, Herman ran Saab, the Swedish auto company (half of which has been controlled by GM since 1989). While at Saab, Herman helped trim the company's daily absenteeism rate from 12 to 8 percent, and its annual rate of turnover from 16 to 5 percent. Now it was critical for Herman to perform similar magic at Opel. Because the union was successful at getting auto manufacturers to agree to reduce the workweek from 37 to 35 hours, it was more important than ever for employees to be as productive as possible. But how? Herman's strategy has been to use the team approach—organizing almost half of the workers into groups of 5 to 15. Thus far, the teams have been largely successful at figuring out how to do their jobs better and learning how to balance their responsibilities so that jobs get done as efficiently as possible.

GM's real challenge promises to be its new plant in the former East German town of Eisenach, a facility capable of producing as many as 150 thousand cars a year—about 10 percent of GM's total European production capacity. Part of the problem is the fact that employees there earn only 65 percent as much pay as their counterparts in the West—more than they would have earned in the former East Germany, but not enough to keep them satisfied. Although a 26 percent pay increase is in the works, productivity still promises to lag, due to technological changes in auto manufacturing. In the mid-1980s GM used heavily automated plants, sophisticated robotized machines, and expensive motorized platforms that transported parts between workstations. However, having learned that such equipment is expensive to install and maintain, GM Europe has entered a "postautomation stage," reverting to traditional fixed-conveyor assembly lines.

Of course, all the machinery in the world isn't sufficient to help make the company more productive without the help of people. Acknowledging this, GM Europe officials, headed by its 44-year-old president, Louis Hughes, sought to sharpen the company's competitive edge. Their strategy was to get company executives to understand and cooperate with each other. With this in mind, groups of executives were sent on five-day Outward Bound expeditions in the Swiss Alps,

Louis Hughes, president of General Motors Europe, and the Opel Corsa

adventures designed to teach executives how to face challenges as a team and to work together with trust and harmony. To assist further, GM retained scientists specializing in workplace dynamics to study the company's operations and train its officials in ways of improving employee relations. As Hughes put it, "That's what life is all about, having a dream and working together toward it."

GM Europe's most serious challenges all revolve around a common focus—*people*. Corporate officials, trying to keep the large automaker competitive in the face of tough and changing economic conditions, are tinkering with various approaches to dealing with people. They're putting people into teams, raising their pay, changing the way work is done, and training executives in ways that promise to improve and enrich them personally. As you might imagine, all this is much easier said than done—not only for GM, but for all organizations, large and small (see Figure 1-1). In general, how do we learn what makes people more productive and satisfied on their jobs? How can we find out the best ways to organize the way work is done? These questions lie at the heart of the topic of this book—**organizational behavior (OB)**, the field specializing in the study of human behavior in organizations.

If you think about it, you'll probably quickly realize that, in general, "people problems" pose a serious threat to the functioning of many organizations, not to mention the satisfaction and well-being of their employees. There can be no organizations without people. No matter how sophisticated a company's mechanical equipment may be, and how healthy its financial status is, people problems can bring an organization down very quickly. Hence, it makes sense to realize that "the human side of work" (not coincidentally, part of the subtitle of this book) is a crucial element in the effective functioning—and basic existence—of organizations. It is this people-centered orientation that is taken in the field of OB.

FIGURE 1-1

FACING THE CHALLENGE OF MANAGEMENT: GENERAL MOTORS AND ELSEWHERE

Running a large company—or even a small one—is no easy task. The field of organizational behavior provides many helpful insights into understanding the complexities of people's behavior on the job. It may even provide some hints as to what this fellow is thinking! (Source: Estate of Joe Mirachi. From Harvard Business Review, *March–April 1992.)*

"A person should know his own limitations. I wouldn't even attempt to run General Motors."

OB scientists and practitioners study and attempt to solve organizational problems by using knowledge derived from research in the **behavioral sciences**, such as psychology and sociology. In other words, the field of OB is firmly rooted in science. It relies on research to derive valuable information about organizations and the complex processes operating within them. Such knowledge is used as the basis for helping to solve a wide range of organizational problems. In fact, as you will see as you read this book, the problems faced by GM Europe—how to enhance productivity, how to get people to accept changes in the ways work is done, and others—all have been addressed by OB specialists. The scientists hired to analyze the workplace dynamics of GM Europe relied on this knowledge when considering how to handle the situations GM faces.

As you read this text, it will become clear that OB specialists have sought to learn about a large variety of issues involving people in organizations. In fact, over the past few decades OB has developed into a field so diverse that its researchers have examined just about every conceivable aspect of behavior in organizations.[1] The fruits of this labor are already being enjoyed by people who are interested in making organizations not only more productive, but also more pleasant to work in. We are both very impressed by what the field of OB has shown us thus far and highly optimistic about its potential as an applied science. We think you will come to share our enthusiasm as you read this book.

In the remainder of this chapter we will give you the background information you will need to understand the scope of OB research and its potential value to management. This first chapter is designed to formally introduce you to the field of OB—its characteristics, its history, and the tools it uses to learn about the behavior of people in organizations. We will begin by formally defining OB, describing exactly what it is and what it seeks to accomplish. Then we will summarize the history of the field, from its origins to its emergence as a modern science. Finally, we will discuss the methods OB scientists use to add to basic knowledge about the behavior of people in organizations. This background will prepare you for our primary task: enhancing your understanding of the human side of work by giving you a comprehensive overview of the field of OB and its major findings.

ORGANIZATIONAL BEHAVIOR: A WORKING DEFINITION

Having just informally described what the topic of organizational behavior is all about, we are now prepared to define the field more formally and to describe its basic characteristics. Specifically, organizational behavior is *the field that seeks knowledge of behavior in organizational settings by systematically studying individual, group, and organizational processes*. This knowledge is sought as an end in itself by scientists who are interested in basic human behavior, and by practitioners interested in enhancing organizational effectiveness and individual well-being in organizations. Before beginning our examination of this field, it would be useful to further describe some of the key aspects referred to in our definition.

OB APPLIES THE SCIENTIFIC METHOD TO PRACTICAL MANAGERIAL PROBLEMS

Our definition of OB refers to seeking knowledge and to studying behavioral processes. This should not be surprising since, as we noted earlier, OB knowledge is based on the behavioral sciences. Although not as sophisticated as the study of physics or chemistry (nor as mature as these fields), the orientation of the field of OB is still scientific in nature. Thus, like other scientific fields, OB seeks to develop a base of knowledge by using an empirical, research-oriented approach. That is, it is based on systematic observation and measurement of the phenomena of interest. As we will describe later in this chapter—and as you will see for yourself as you read this book—organizational research is neither easy nor foolproof. Yet, it is widely agreed that the scientific method is the best way to learn about behavior in organizations. For this reason, the scientific orientation should be acknowledged as a hallmark of the field of OB.

Why is it so important to learn about behavior in organizational settings? The answer depends on whom you ask. To social scientists, learning about human behavior on the job—"what makes people tick" in organizations—is valuable for its own sake. After all, scientists are interested in the generation of knowledge—in this case, insight into the effects of organizations on people, and the effects of people on organizations. This is not to say, however, that such knowledge has no value outside of scientific circles. Far from it! OB specialists also work hard at applying knowledge from scientific studies, putting it to good practical use. As they seek to improve organizational functioning and the quality of life of people working in organizations, they rely heavily on knowledge derived from OB research. Thus, there are both scientific and applied facets of the field of OB—aspects that not only coexist but also complement each other. Indeed, just as knowledge about physics can be put to use by engineers, and engineering data can be used to test theories of basic physics, so too are knowledge and practical applications closely intertwined in the field of OB.

OB specialists may use their knowledge about behavior in organizations not only to help suggest ways of improving organizational problems in general, but also to conduct research designed specifically to solve problems in a particular organization (such as was done at GM Europe in our Preview Case). In other words, OB specialists use the scientific method to derive both general knowledge about behavior in organizations (referred to as *normal science research*) and specific knowledge used to solve problems in a particular organization (referred to as *action research*).[2] Although the underlying reasons for conducting the research may be different, both approaches share something in common—their reliance on the scientific method. Regardless of one's goals for learning about behavior in organizations—deriving theoretical or practical knowledge of organizational behavior in general, or insight into a specific organization—the scientific approach is a central defining characteristic of modern OB.

OB FOCUSES ON THREE LEVELS OF ANALYSIS: INDIVIDUALS, GROUPS, AND ORGANIZATIONS

To best appreciate behavior in organizations, OB specialists cannot focus exclusively on individuals acting alone. After all, in organizational settings people frequently work together in groups. Furthermore, people—alone and in groups—both influence and are influenced by their work environments. Considering this, it should not be surprising to learn that the field of OB focuses on three distinct levels of analysis—individuals, groups, and organizations. As an example, consider our Preview Case. GM Europe is interested not only in individual reactions to pay and cultural differences between employees, but also in how work teams can help the company be more efficient. At the same time, company officials are also concerned with ways of organizing work that can make the company more competitive in the midst of challenging economic conditions. In other words, the situation at GM Europe cannot be understood from any single perspective alone—be it a focus on individuals, or groups, or organizations as a whole.

The field of OB recognizes that *all three levels of analysis* must be used to comprehend the complex dynamics of behavior in organizations (see Figure 1-2). Careful attention to all three levels of analysis is a central theme of modern OB, and is reflected throughout this text. For example, we will be describing how OB specialists are concerned with individual perceptions, attitudes, and motives. We will also be describing how people communicate with each other and coordinate their activities in work groups. Finally, we will examine organizations as a whole—the way they are structured and operate in their environments, and the effects of their operations on the individuals and groups within them. We're optimistic that by the time you finish reading this book, you will appreciate the value of all three approaches.

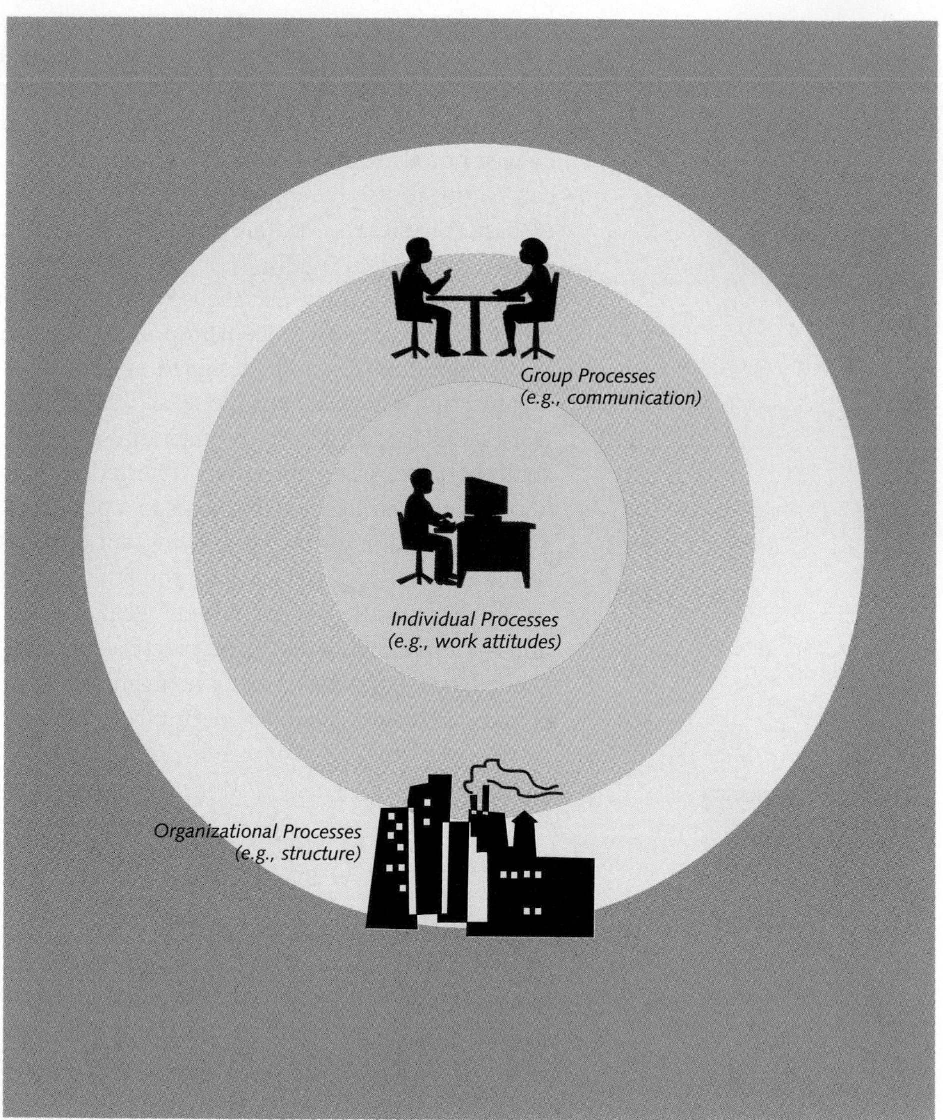

FIGURE 1-2
THREE LEVELS OF ANALYSIS USED IN ORGANIZATIONAL BEHAVIOR
To fully understand organizational behavior, we must consider three levels of analysis: processes occurring within individuals, groups, and organizations themselves.

ORGANIZATIONAL BEHAVIOR TODAY: CHARACTERISTICS OF THE FIELD

Now that we have defined what is meant by organizational behavior, it will be useful to summarize some of the major characteristics of the field today. This overview will help you understand the work of OB scientists that we will be describing in the chapters ahead. We are confident that the better you understand the field's basic approaches, the more you will be able to appreciate its contributions.

OB SEEKS THE BETTERMENT OF HUMAN RESOURCES

In the early part of the twentieth century, as railroads opened up the western portion of the United States and the nation's population rapidly grew (it doubled from 1880 to 1920!), the demand for manufactured products was great. New manufacturing plants were built, attracting waves of new immigrants in search of a living wage and laborers lured off farms by the employment prospects that factory work offered. These early factories were gigantic, noisy, hot, and highly regimented—in short, brutal places in which to work. Bosses demanded more and more of their employees, and treated them like disposable machines, replacing those who quit or who died from accidents with others who waited outside the factory gates.[3] Obviously, the managers of one hundred years ago held very negative views of employees. They assumed that people were basically lazy and irresponsible, and treated them with disrespect. This very negativistic approach, which has been with us for many years, reflects the traditional view of management—what Douglas McGregor called **Theory X**.[4] This philosophy of management assumes that people are basically lazy, dislike work, need direction, and will only work hard when they are goaded into performing (that is, because there is a carrot at the end of the stick).

Today, however, if you asked a diverse group of corporate officials to describe their basic views of human nature, you'd probably find some more optimistic thoughts. Although some of today's managers still believe that people are basically lazy, many others would disagree, arguing that it's not that simple. They would claim that most individuals are at least as capable of working hard as they are of "goofing off." If employees are recognized for their efforts (such as by being appropriately paid) and are given an opportunity to succeed (such as by being well trained), they may be expected to work very hard without being pushed. Thus, employees may put forth a great deal of effort simply because they want to. Management's job, then, is to create those conditions that make people want to perform as desired. The approach that assumes that people are not intrinsically lazy, but are willing to work hard when the right conditions prevail is known as the **Theory Y** orientation. This philosophy assumes that people have a psychological need to work and seek achievement and responsibility. In contrast to the Theory X philosophy of management, which essentially demonstrates distrust for people on the job, the Theory Y approach is strongly associated with promoting the betterment of human resources (for a summary of the differences, see Figure 1-3).

As you might suspect, the Theory Y perspective currently prevails among those interested in organizational behavior. Recognizing that people are capable of performing desirable behaviors under the right working conditions does *not* reflect a Pollyanna-like belief that people always will act responsibly. Rather, it assumes that people are highly responsive to their work environments; how they are treated will

FIGURE 1-3

THEORY X VERSUS THEORY Y: A SUMMARY

The traditional, Theory X orientation toward people is far more negativistic than the more contemporary, Theory Y approach—the one accepted by modern OB. Some of the key differences between these philosophies are summarized here.

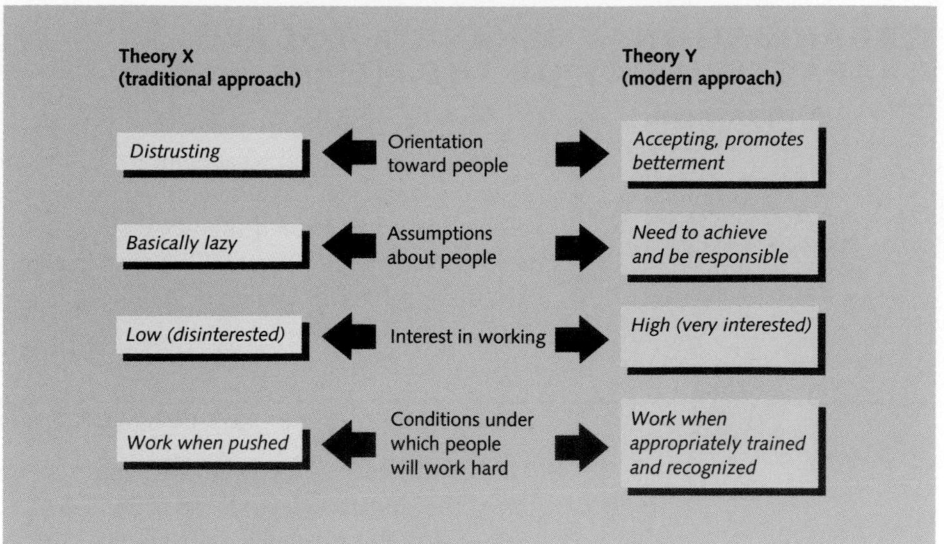

influence how they act. In fact, OB scientists are very interested in learning exactly what conditions will lead people to behave in the most positive ways. As you will learn as you read this book, conditions in which employees are treated favorably will help them become more committed to their organizations and to go above and beyond the call of duty (see Chapters 5 and 11). In contrast, employees who are exploited will act more negatively—slacking off, behaving antisocially (e.g., stealing), or eventually quitting. In short, modern OB assumes that there are no intrinsic reasons why work settings cannot be made both pleasant and productive.

OB RECOGNIZES THE DYNAMIC NATURE OF ORGANIZATIONS

Thus far, our characterization of the field of OB has focused more on individual behavior than on organizations as a whole. Nonetheless, it is important to point out that both OB scientists and practitioners *do* pay a great deal of attention to the nature of organizations themselves. Under what conditions will organizations change? How are organizations structured? How do organizations interact with their environments? Questions such as these are of major interest to specialists in OB. But before we can consider them—as we will later in this book—we must first clarify exactly what we mean by an organization. Although you probably have a very good idea of what an organization is, and would know one if you saw it, you would probably find it difficult to define an organization exactly. Thus, we offer the following definition. An **organization** is *a structured social system consisting of groups and individuals working together to meet some agreed-on objectives*. In other words, organizations consist of structured social units, such as individuals and/or work groups, who strive to attain a common goal, such as to produce and sell a product at a profit.

In studying organizations, OB scientists recognize that organizations are not static, but dynamic and ever-changing entities. In other words, they recognize that organizations are **open systems**—that is, self-sustaining systems that use energy to transform resources from the environment (such as raw materials) into some form of output (for example, a finished product).[5] Figure 1-4 summarizes some of the key properties of open systems. As this diagram makes clear, organizations receive

FIGURE 1-4
ORGANIZATIONS AS OPEN SYSTEMS
The open-systems approach to organizations assumes that they operate in a self-sustaining manner, transforming inputs into outputs in continuous fashion. (Source: Based on suggestions by Katz & Kahn, 1978; see Note 5.)

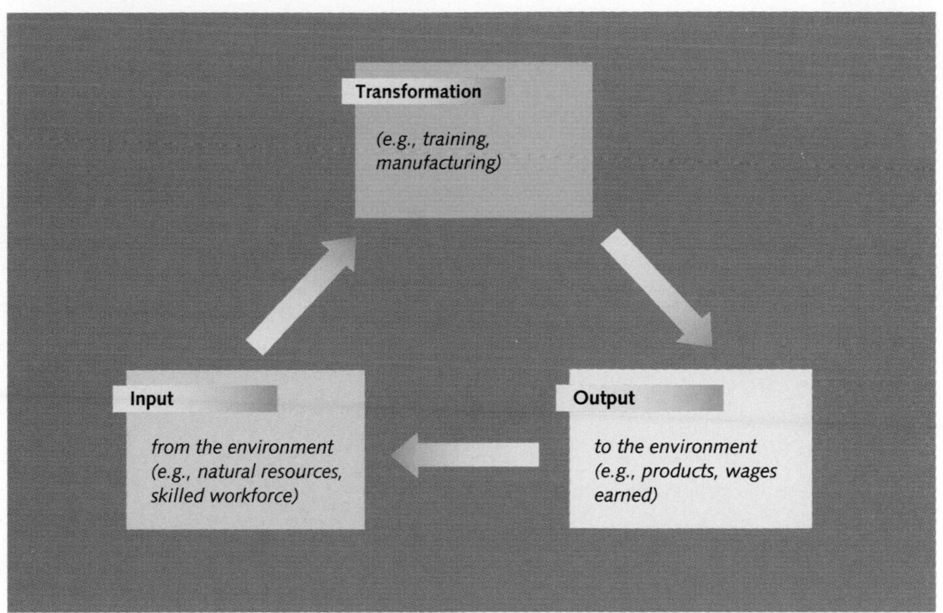

input from their environments and continuously transform it into output. This output gets transformed back to input, and the cyclical operation continues. Consider for example, how organizations may tap the human resources of the community by hiring and training people to do jobs. These individuals may work to provide a product in exchange for wages. They then spend these wages, putting money back into the community, allowing more people to afford the company's products. This, in turn creates the need for still more employees, and so on. If you think about it this way, it's easy to realize that organizations are dynamic and constantly changing. In this way, they are like the operations of the human body. As people breathe, they take in oxygen and transform it into carbon dioxide. This, in turn, sustains the life of green plants, which in turn emit oxygen for people to breathe. The continuous flow of the open system characterizes not only human life but also organizations. (The dynamic nature of organizations is particularly apparent when one considers all the changes in organizations that are likely to occur in the future. For a closer look at some of the key changes in organizations that we may expect to see in the years ahead, refer to the Organization of Tomorrow section on the next page.)

OB ASSUMES THERE IS NO "ONE BEST" APPROACH

What's the most effective way to motivate people? What style of leadership works best? Should groups or individuals be used to make important organizational decisions? Although questions such as these appear to be quite reasonable, there is a basic problem with all of them. Namely, they all assume that there is a simple, unitary answer. That is, they suggest that there is *one* best approach: one best way to motivate, to lead, and to make decisions.

Specialists in the field of OB today agree that there is no one best approach when it comes to such complex phenomena. To assume otherwise is not only overly simplistic and naive, but, as you will see, grossly inaccurate. When it comes to studying human behavior in organizations, there are no simple answers. The processes involved are too complex to permit such a luxury. Instead, OB scholars

THE ORGANIZATION OF TOMORROW

ORGANIZATIONS OF THE TWENTY-FIRST CENTURY: WHAT'S AHEAD IN THE WORLD OF WORK?

Considering the dynamic nature of organizations, the one thing you can be sure of is that they will change. Given current trends, what may we expect the organizations of the future to be like? How will tomorrow's workplaces be different from today's? Looking into their crystal balls, experts have painted some interesting pictures of things to come.[6]

At the heart of the changes we can expect lies the fact that we are currently experiencing a second industrial revolution. During the early twentieth century, there was a shift from an agricultural economy to a manufacturing economy. People left farms and moved into cities so they could work in factories. Now, things are changing again—and, once more, we have technology to thank. This time, it's the computer, rather than the internal combustion engine, that's primarily responsible. Specifically, we're moving from a world in which electromechanical machines dominated into one in which digital signals are created, stored, and transmitted over vast distances. The result is that more and more work can be routinized, freeing people to do more creative jobs, and creating new jobs for people developing and maintaining that equipment.

As we have been implying, the workforce of tomorrow will be more technically skilled. The core of the worker elite will be technicians—people programming and repairing computers and other high-tech equipment—rather than manufacturing operatives. Many people will specialize in technical fields, developing skills needed to support the ever-expanding network of computer-based companies that are developing.

Not only will tomorrow's organizations be more technical in nature, but in many countries, including the United States, they also will be smaller. In fact, up until the 1970s the average company size continued to increase, but it has been decreasing ever since—especially in the area of manufacturing. For example, after a series of layoffs in the late 1980s, by 1993 IBM's workforce was only about 60 percent of the size it was in 1985 (406,000 employees).[7] Similar figures can be cited in the case of other large U.S. companies, such as Xerox and AT&T. This trend is the result not only of the tendency for computers to replace the routine work of some employees, but also of attempts to make companies more creative and responsive to the needs of the marketplace—something that is more likely to be seen in smaller companies (see Figure 1-5). In short, many companies have learned—sometimes the hard way—that when it comes to providing the highest-quality goods and services, generally speaking, smaller is better.

As companies downsize, they are also restructuring. In particular, they are becoming increasingly decentralized, moving decision-making power into the hands of those individuals doing the job (we will have more to say about this in Chapter 15). The result will be that organizational hierarchies will flatten out. What will really matter will be not where you stand on the corporate ladder, but what specialized skills you have. Skills, not position, will be used as the basis for determining who gets to lead. People will be likely to work in teams, and these teams will be empowered to make decisions (we will discuss this further in Chapter 8). Team leaders will be those whose skills best qualify them for the job. As one management expert put it, "A team is not like a pack of sled dogs, with one dog the leader . . . it's more like the flight of wild geese: the leader always changes, but they fly in a flock."[8]

In view of the increasing emphasis on specialized skills and computer technology, it will be possible for vast changes to occur in the way work is done. People will no longer have to live a 9-to-5 workday. In fact, they may not even leave home to "go to work" at all. Already, over 30 million Americans are using high-tech telecommunica-

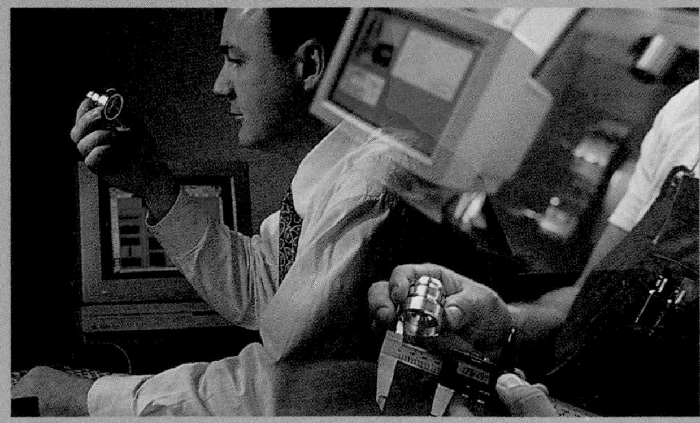

FIGURE 1-5

ORGANIZATIONS OF THE FUTURE: SMALLER AND MORE HIGH TECH

Brian Westcott's company, Westt, Inc. (Menlo Park, California), uses $500,000 worth of advanced equipment and only ten employees to manufacture customized industrial automation equipment.

tion equipment to work from their homes, and the numbers are rapidly growing (see Chapter 14).[9] As people no longer have to flood large cities to do their jobs, we may expect to see shifts in population. For example, Nick Davis, an investment broker, used to commute from his suburban home in Denver to his Paine Webber office downtown. Using user-friendly electronics, he has now set up shop in Bozeman, Montana—a peaceful environment where he prefers to raise his family while still working in the investments field.

Rapidly advancing technology is likely to bring organizational change at such a frantic pace that it will be difficult for people to maintain their jobs for very long—at least not without constant high-level training. Experts believe that people will be "scrambling for footing on a shifting corporate landscape." More traditional employment relationships will become a thing of the past; instabilities in the workplace will make the prospect of job security dim at best. In fact, it has been claimed that the average American will be likely to work in 10 or more different types of jobs in at least five different companies during his or her working years.[10] With such tremendous shifts, it will be difficult for people to have long-lasting careers inside their companies or to develop any meaningful commitment to them.

Tomorrow's workers, although they may not be highly committed to their organizations, may be expected to have a strong commitment to quality. When the United States was the world's major economic power, it was easy for American companies to let work quality slip. "For most of the 20th century, the inefficiencies and foul-ups didn't much matter. Work was done; goods were produced and services provided, often in astonishing quantity."[11] Now, however, international competition has forced organizations to be as efficient and quality conscious as possible. The lesson for the future has been sounded loud and clear: just "OK" quality will not be good enough.[12]

Clearly, the changes we've summarized here will have important implications for the study of behavior in organizations. How can employees be trained to meet the challenges they will face? What needs to be done to motivate people—often working away from corporate offices—to meet the challenge of producing high-quality goods and services? As you will see throughout this book, the field of OB is focused on these and other related questions. And, as the world of work changes, OB scientists and practitioners will be kept very busy updating and applying their knowledge about behavior in organizations to the many new developments in organizations we are likely to see in the future.

recognize that behavior in work settings is the complex result of many interacting forces. This fact is recognized in what is known as the **contingency approach**, an orientation that is a hallmark of modern OB.[13] Consider, for example, how an individual's personal characteristics (e.g., personal attitudes and beliefs) may work in conjunction with situational factors (e.g., an organization's climate or relations between co-workers) which may all work together when it comes to influencing how a particular individual is likely to behave on the job.

When we teach OB to our students, we often find ourselves answering their questions by saying, "It depends." As our knowledge of behavior on the job becomes more and more complex, it becomes difficult, if not impossible, to give "straight answers." Rather, it is usually necessary to report that people will do certain things "under some conditions" or "when all other factors are equal." Such phrases provide a clear indication that the contingency approach is being used. They tell us that a certain behavior is *contingent on* the existence of certain conditions—hence, the name. Although this approach may frustrate and disappoint some because it makes it impossible to use simple cookbook formulas to predict and explain behavior, we believe that such a complaint is unjustified. After all, it is *accuracy*, and not simplicity, that is the ultimate goal of our studies of behavior in organizations. In the chapters that follow, you will see how this approach prevails with respect to various aspects of the field. In presenting this material to you, we will attempt to walk the fine line between being so complex as to be incomprehensible and so simplistic as to be misleading.

OB CONFRONTS THE CHALLENGES OF WORKFORCE DIVERSITY

In the Organization of Tomorrow section on pages 12–13, we noted that the nature of work is changing. Similarly, the field of OB faces challenges created by changes in the workforce itself. Specifically, if we had to characterize today's labor force using only one word, it would be diversity. The demographic characteristics of the workforce have been changing over the past few decades, and such shifts have not gone unnoticed in the field of OB (see Figure 1-6).[14]

For example, there are more women working today than ever before, and they are more highly educated and better trained for a wider variety of positions. However, many women still find that they are victimized by stereotypes and male-dominated corporate cultures that keep them from advancing.[15] Furthermore, because women tend to shoulder a disproportionate share of the responsibility for family care in U.S. society, they frequently face conflicts between their careers and their families. As you will see throughout this book, these and other issues related to gender diversity are of considerable interest to OB scientists and practitioners. Indeed, they are closely connected to such topics as prejudice and stereotypes (Chapter 5), career development (Chapter 6), stress (Chapter 7), and organizational culture (Chapter 14).

In addition to gender diversity, racial and cultural diversity is another potent demographic trend in the workforce. The relative proportion of white Americans in the workforce has been steadily shrinking as growing numbers of African-Americans, Hispanic-Americans, Asian-Americans, and foreign nationals enter the workforce.[16] If you consider that within these cultures there are various subcultures, it is clear that the current level of racial and ethnic diversity encountered in the workforce is considerable. The matter of how this trend affects organizations is of great interest in the field of OB. Some accommodations to cultural diversity may involve simple decisions, such as offering a broader variety of ethnic dishes in the company cafeteria. But it's not always that simple. When people with different habits, values, and worldviews come together, the potential for misunderstanding and conflict rises.

FIGURE 1-6
WORKFORCE DIVERSITY: AN IMPORTANT CONSIDERATION IN OB
As the workforce grows increasingly diverse with respect to both gender and culture, the field of OB considers ways for organizations to tap the richness that diversity can offer while minimizing the prejudice and conflict that sometimes result.

The challenge for the field of OB is easier stated than accomplished: How can organizations tap the rich pool of resources offered by culturally diverse employees in a manner that minimizes interpersonal conflict among them? Although OB provides no easy answers to this question, it does provide some critical insight. As you will see, research on stereotyping (Chapter 5), mentoring (Chapter 6), communication (Chapter 9), and conflict (Chapter 11) has contributed to our understanding of ways to work effectively in a multicultural environment.

OB TAKES A GLOBAL PERSPECTIVE

If you've ever traveled abroad, then you know how different from you people from various cultures can seem. Not only do they dress and speak in a different fashion, but they also may seem to behave and think quite differently. Whether these discrepancies strike you as quaint or curious, there can be little doubt that real differences exist among people of different nations. The idea that culture is an important determinant of people's actions and values is clearly an understatement–and a conclusion that has important implications for the study of organizational behavior.

When the study of behavior in organizations first emerged, the United States was the world's dominant economic power. As a result, much of what was learned about organizations came from a uniquely American middle-class perspective.[17] Today, however, it is clear that the economy is much more global in scope and orientation. There exist strong economic forces all over the world, and organizations operate within many different cultures. Even formerly communist nations, such as Russia, are rapidly developing into strong economic powers with growing organizations of their own (see the Global Organization section on the next page). Moreover, many organizations have operations in several different countries (as evidenced by our Preview Case on GM).

Considering these trends, it would be seriously limiting—not to mention very misleading—to ignore the possibility that behavior in organizations is affected by cultural differences. Indeed, there are clear signs that the field of OB is rapidly becoming increasingly international in its approach to the study of organizations.[18]

Theorists have noted that the international perspective on OB is characterized by its comparative nature—that is, its tendency to examine OB concepts across different nations and cultures.[19] Among the most popular questions asked by scientists in this area are (1) How similar or different are people of various cultures with respect to different types of organizational behavior? and (2) To what extent do OB theories and practices apply across different cultures?

Although it is usually very difficult to isolate the unique effects of culture (relative to other variables that might make a difference) when researching comparative cultural questions, many researchers have attempted to do so.[20] Such efforts have proven worthwhile because they have revealed that theories of OB that are "Made in the U.S.A." may have limited value when it comes to applying them to other cultures. This is not to say that all such theories are useless. They are, in fact, far from it! Our point is that simply assuming a unicultural perspective can be very misleading, and that incorporating cultural differences into OB research is an effective way of learning about the cultural influences on OB.

Throughout this book, wherever relevant, we will highlight international differences in various aspects of organizational behavior. (For a closer look at some of the challenges the field of OB faces as the Russian economy is transformed by capitalism, please see the Global Organization section on the next page.)

THE GLOBAL ORGANIZATION

CONFRONTING THE CHALLENGE OF FREE ENTERPRISE IN RUSSIAN ORGANIZATIONS

It's difficult enough for organizations operating in the international arena to have to face widespread cultural differences and uncertain economies without also being handicapped by a lack of experience in a capitalist, free-enterprise system. Yet, this is exactly the challenge facing organizations in today's Russia. Until the fall of the communist system in the Soviet Union at the close of the 1980s, Russian organizations were huge (averaging 800 employees, compared to only 80 in Western nations), highly centralized (controlled by a single head, known as a *rukovoditei*), very inefficient monopolies that produced generally very poor-quality goods.

When Marxist-Leninist doctrine was overthrown, Russian organizations needed intensive indoctrination in the free-enterprise system—not only techniques of manufacturing and finance, but also ways of managing people. After all, OB concepts such as motivation, career development, teamwork, and participative management (all of which we will discuss in this book) have little meaning in a dehumanizing system such as Soviet communism, in which people are assigned to jobs, treated like machines, and are given absolutely no autonomy to make decisions. In many ways, appreciating the behavior of people in democratic organizations is one of the toughest challenges Russian managers will have to face.

To characterize the difficulties faced by Russian organizations, consider this description of the typical Soviet worker: "He is lazy, doesn't want responsibility, and doesn't want to even be at work. There is no incentive to work and no reason to be a good performer. There is widespread alienation, disaffection, and apathy among workers. Managers have very few solutions that can overcome years of apathy, disgust, and undisciplined practices."[21] Given this state of affairs, the result of decades of communist rule, it certainly will be difficult to turn around the Soviet system—and OB lies at the heart of the situation. In view of this, it is interesting to consider some of the greatest challenges Russian organizations will have to confront with respect to the behavior of people at work.

At the top of the list is the need for people to be given—and for them to accept—opportunities to make decisions themselves, to accept responsibility for their own actions, and to question authority figures if necessary. It will take time for Russian citizens to become comfortable with these practices, which are second nature to people who grew up in democratic cultures. For people who never felt accountable for their actions or the quality of their work, however, the shift to a private market economy, in which success is dictated by individual performance, is most certainly jarring.

Survey research has shown that Soviet managers believe that adaptability and initiative are relatively unimportant among employees.[22] In fact, they are more likely to blame poor product quality on inferior equipment than on their own actions. Not surprisingly, Russia's working people believe that they are powerless to affect change, and are reluctant to work together to make things better. Compared to their U.S. counterparts, who frequently coordinate their efforts by communicating among others at their same levels, Russian employees typically do *not* initiate communication horizontally (we will discuss the topic of communication across different organizational levels in Chapter 9).[23]

In view of the problems faced by Russian companies, it should not be surprising to learn that Russian managers tend to have extraordinarily high stress levels (we will discuss the concept of stress and its measurement fully in Chapter 7).[24] Their stress comes from several sources: high levels of uncertainty (ever-changing rules), strong pressure from above (highly authoritarian superiors), and the frustration of not having the resources needed to respond to their system's woes. Adding to the high stress levels is the fact that workdays of ten or twelve hours are not unusual. And, in factories at least, the workplaces are extremely hazardous. Manufacturing plants tend to be nightmares of unsafe conditions—for example, chemical containers are left open, safety goggles and helmets are rarely used, and people are exposed to hazardous fumes—in the United States, all serious violations of occupational safety and health regulations.

Believe it or not, the bleak picture we've been painting of life in Russian organizations today represents an *improvement* over conditions that existed under commu-

THE GLOBAL ORGANIZATION, Cont.

nist rule. Indeed, in some communities, such as the port city of Kaliningrad, business is thriving, and capitalist business norms are rapidly becoming accepted (see Figure 1-7).[25] Still, management experts believe that until Soviet managers become better equipped to get people to be productive in a free society, it will be impossible for Russian companies to compete successfully in the world market. As you might imagine, the deeply entrenched values of millions of people over decades cannot be altered overnight, and the attitudes of Russians toward work may be expected to change only very gradually.

FIGURE 1-7

KALININGRAD: RUSSIA'S PORT OF ENTRY TO THE FREE-ENTERPRISE SYSTEM

The Russian port city of Kaliningrad is one place where that nation's switch to capitalism is going smoothly. The transformation from communism to the free-enterprise system provides many new opportunities to learn about organizational behavior in a new environment.

ORGANIZATIONAL BEHAVIOR: A HISTORICAL OVERVIEW OF THE FIELD

Although today we take for granted the importance of understanding the functioning of organizations and the behavior of people at work, this was not always the case. In fact, it was not until the early part of the twentieth century that the idea first developed, and only during the last few decades that it gained widespread acceptance. So that you can appreciate how the field of OB got to where it is today, we will now briefly outline its history and describe some of the most influential forces in its development.

SCIENTIFIC MANAGEMENT: THE ROOTS OF ORGANIZATIONAL BEHAVIOR

The earliest attempts to study behavior in organizations came out of a desire by industrial efficiency experts to improve worker productivity. Their central question was straightforward: What could be done to get people to do more work in less time? Attempts to answer this question were made at the turn of the century—a period of rapid industrialization and technological change in the United States. As engineers attempted to make machines more efficient, it was a natural extension of their efforts to work on the human side of the equation—making people more productive too. Given this history, it should not be too surprising that the earliest people we now credit for their contributions to OB were actually industrial engineers.

Frederick Winslow Taylor worked most of his life in steel mills, starting as a laborer and working his way up to the position of chief engineer.[26] In the 1880s, while a foreman at Philadelphia's Midvale Steel Company, Taylor became aware of some of the inefficient practices of the employees. Noticing, for example, that laborers wasted movements when shifting pig iron, Taylor studied the individual components of this task, and established what he believed was the best way—motion by motion—to perform it. A few years later, while a consulting engineer at Pittsburgh's Bethlehem Steel, Taylor similarly redesigned the job of loading and unloading rail cars so they too could be done as efficiently as possible. On the heels of these experiences, Taylor published his groundbreaking book, *Scientific Management*. In this work, Taylor argued that the objective of management is "to secure the maximum prosperity for the employer, coupled with the maximum prosperity of each employee."[27]

Beyond identifying ways in which manual labor jobs can be performed more efficiently, Taylor's **scientific management** approach was unique in its focus on the role of employees as individuals. Taylor advocated two ideas that hardly seem special today, but were quite new eighty-five years ago. First, he recommended that employees be carefully selected and trained to perform their jobs—helping them become, in his own words, "first class" at some task. Second, he believed that increasing workers' wages would raise their motivation and make them more productive. Although this idea is unsophisticated by today's standards—and not completely accurate (as we will see in Chapter 4)—Taylor may be credited with recognizing the important role of motivation in job performance. It was contributions like these that stimulated further study of behavior in organizations and created an intellectual climate that eventually paved the way for the development of the field of OB. Acknowledging these contributions, management theorist Peter Drucker has described Taylor as "the first man in history who did not take work for granted, but who looked at it and studied it."[28]

The publication of *Scientific Management* stimulated several other scientists to pick up and expand Taylor's ideas. For example, psychologist Hugo Münsterberg worked to "humanize" the jobs of people by explaining how the concepts of learning and motivation are relevant to the behavior of people at work.[29] Similarly, management writer Mary Parker Follet claimed that organizations could benefit by attempting to recognize the needs of employees.[30]

The scientists who were closely influenced by Taylor were the industrial psychologists Frank and Lillian Gilbreth. This husband-and-wife team pioneered an approach known as **time-and-motion study**, a type of applied research designed to classify and streamline the individual movements needed to perform jobs with the intent of finding "the one best way" to perform them.[31] Although this approach appears to be highly mechanical and dehumanizing, the Gilbreths, parents of twelve children, practiced Taylorism with a human face in their personal lives. In fact, you may even recall the story of how the Gilbreths applied the principles of scientific management to the operation of their household, as told in their classic film, *Cheaper by the Dozen*. (In addition, as we describe in the Ethical Workplace section on the next page, the Gilbreths worked diligently at applying their craft to an extremely humane goal outside their family—improving the welfare of people with physical handicaps.)

THE ETHICAL WORKPLACE

THE GILBRETHS' EFFORTS FOR THE HANDICAPPED: AN ETHICAL OASIS IN SCIENTIFIC MANAGEMENT

When you think of scientific management, the one word that most certainly comes to mind is "efficient." Indeed, Frederick Taylor and other proponents of scientific management were primarily concerned with developing ways of making people work as efficiently as possible—whatever it took. Often this approach had dehumanizing effects on people, treating them like machines required to move in certain ways and to complete tasks in specified periods of time. For those who suffered physical handicaps that limited their ability to move as required, such an approach was particularly demoralizing. Because they could not perform many jobs in the most efficient manner, people with physical handicaps were considered undesirable employees by most proponents of scientific management.

Fortunately, two pioneers of scientific management, Frank and Lillian Gilbreth, found this rejection of human life to be completely unacceptable (see Figure 1-8).[32] They believed that disabled people should be encouraged to fulfill themselves by working at jobs they are capable of performing. Although this approach sounds perfectly acceptable by today's standards, it was quite unusual given the treatment of handicapped people that prevailed in the early part of the twentieth century. At that time, it was more typical to fit workers with the prosthetic devices necessary to perform jobs at acceptable levels. The Gilbreths believed that this practice was demoralizing, and applied their expertise in scientific management to treating people with handicaps more humanely.

Frank Gilbreth advocated that the U.S. government train the disabled veterans of World War I so they could develop job skills that worked around their limitations. He believed that "handicapped" did not mean helpless, but "capable"—if proper jobs and training were available. In this respect, Gilbreth was decades ahead of his time. To help advance this position, he created a slide presentation illustrating how people with disabilities easily could be incorporated into the workplace. Gilbreth argued that able-bodied people should be required to move to new jobs whenever doing so opens up that job to someone whose physical limitations make it difficult for them to do anything else. In short, Frank Gilbreth became an active spokesperson for vocational rehabilitation efforts.

On Frank's death, his wife Lillian took over much of his work. Among other things, Lillian developed ways of adapting home kitchens for people with physical handicaps. In fact, Lillian Gilbreth worked with General Electric to redesign kitchen appliances with the needs of the handicapped in mind. She also developed ways of redesigning tools and equipment so that people with physical limitations could use them more easily. Interestingly, some of the ideas initially developed to help people with handicaps eventually found their way into widespread use for all (e.g., the automatic paper-feeding mechanism found in typewriters). Among the early pioneers of the study of people at work, Frank and Lillian Gilbreth will be remembered for their then-radical position that the quest for individual dignity and self-respect is as important as the quest for efficiency. As they put it some eighty years ago, "The great need is that everyone shall realize that there is a part in the work for him [or her]. It is the work of the psychologist, of the economist, of the industrial expert—True! It is just as much the work of every man, woman and child in the community. It is active, practical interested cooperation that is needed—and it is needed NOW."[33] Although this position is much better accepted today than it was when originally expressed by the Gilbreths, it is fascinating to note that these words are just as timely today.

FIGURE 1-8

FRANK AND LILLIAN GILBRETH: APPLYING SCIENTIFIC MANAGEMENT TO THE NEEDS OF THE HANDICAPPED

Breaking with traditionally dehumanizing applications of scientific management, Frank and Lillian Gilbreth championed ways of helping people with physical handicaps by redesigning equipment and by promoting policies that gave them chances to succeed on the job.

THE HUMAN RELATIONS MOVEMENT: ELTON MAYO AND THE HAWTHORNE STUDIES

Despite the important contributions of scientific management, this approach did not go far enough in directing our attention to the wide variety of factors that might influence behavior in work settings. The efficient performance of jobs and monetary incentives are very important, to be sure, although emphasizing these factors makes people feel like cogs in a machine. In fact, many employees and theorists alike rejected Taylorism, favoring instead an approach that focused on employees' own views and emphasized respect for individuals. At the forefront of this orientation was Elton W. Mayo, an organizational scientist and consultant widely regarded as the founder of what is called the **human relations movement**.[34] This brand of management philosophy rejects the primarily economic orientation of scientific management, and focuses, instead, on noneconomic, social factors operating in the workplace. Mayo and other proponents of the human relations movement *were* concerned with task performance, but realized that it was greatly influenced by the social conditions that existed in organizations—the way employees were treated by management, and the relationships they had with each other.

In 1927 a series of studies were begun at the Western Electric's Hawthorne Works near Chicago. Inspired by scientific management, the researchers were interested in determining, among other things, the effects of illumination on work productivity. How brightly or dimly lit should the work environment be for people to produce at their maximum level? Two groups of female employees took part in the study. One group, the *control room* condition, did their jobs without any changes in lighting; the other group, the *test room* condition, worked while the lighting was systematically varied, sometimes getting brighter, and sometimes getting dimmer. The results were baffling: productivity increased in *both* locations. Just as surprising, there was no clear connection between illumination and performance. In fact, output in the test room remained high even when the level of illumination was so low that workers could barely see what they were doing!

In response to these puzzling findings, Western Electric officials called in a team of experts headed by Elton Mayo. Attempting to replicate these results, Mayo and his colleagues examined the effects of a wide variety of different variables on productivity. Among these were the length of rest pauses, the duration of the workday and workweek, and the presence or absence of a free mid-morning lunch. How would these factors influence the amount of work performed? To answer this question, Mayo and his colleagues studied female employees working in the company's Relay Room. As shown in Figure 1-9, the results were once again quite surprising: Productivity improved following almost every change in working conditions.[35] In fact, performance remained extremely high even when conditions were returned to normal, the way they were before the study began.

Not all of Mayo's studies showed that Hawthorne employees were highly productive, however. In fact, in another study conducted at the company's Bank Wiring Room, male members of various work groups were observed during regular working conditions, and were interviewed at length after work. In this investigation, no attempts were made to alter the work environment. What Mayo found here also was surprising. Namely, instead of improving their performance, employees deliberately restricted their output. Not only did the researchers actually see the men stopping work long before quitting time, but in interviews the men admitted that they easily could do more if they desired.

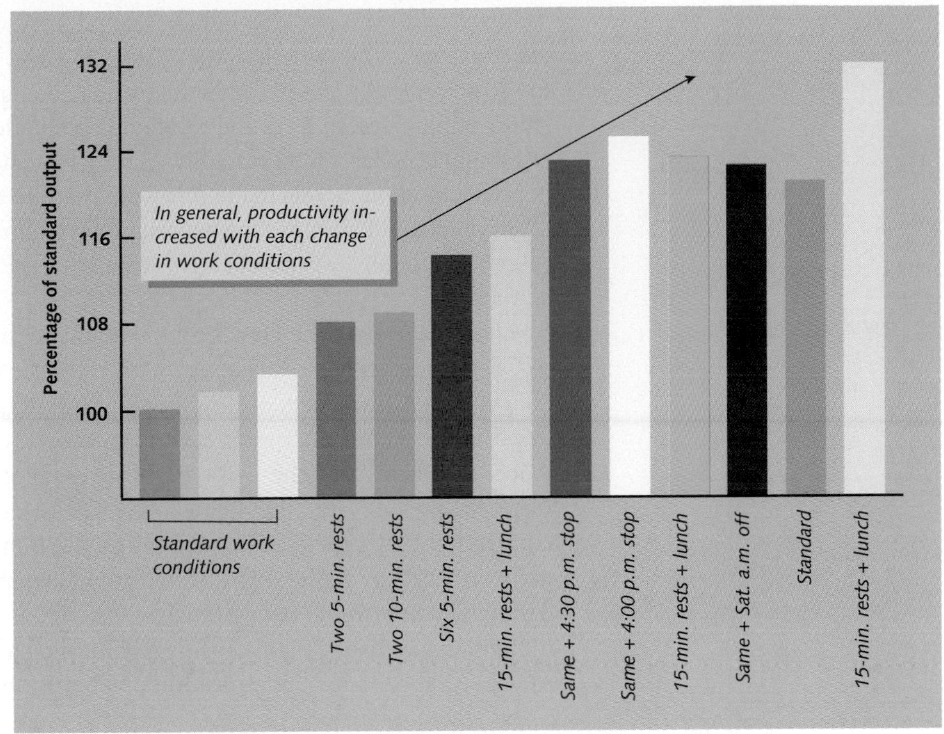

FIGURE 1-9
THE HAWTHORNE STUDIES: SOME PUZZLING RESULTS
In one part of the Hawthorne studies, female employees were exposed to several changes in working conditions. Surprisingly, almost every one of these alterations produced an increase in productivity. (Source: Based on data from Roethlisberger & Dickson, 1939; see Note 35.)

Why did this occur, especially in view of the increased performance noted in the Relay Room studies? Eventually, Mayo and his associates recognized that the answer resided in the fact that organizations are *social systems*. How effectively people worked depended, in great part, not only on the physical aspects of the working conditions experienced, but also the social conditions encountered. In the Relay Room studies, Mayo noted, productivity rose simply because people responded favorably to the special attention they received. Knowing they were being studied made them feel special and motivated them to do their best. Hence, it was these social factors more than the physical factors, that had such profound effects on job performance. The same explanation applied in the Bank Wiring Room study as well. Here, the employees feared that because they were being studied, the company was eventually going to raise the amount of work they were expected to do each day. To guard against the imposition of unreasonable standards (and, thus, to keep their jobs!), the men agreed among themselves to keep output low. In other words, informal rules (known as *norms*) were established about what constituted acceptable levels of job performance (we will discuss this topic more thoroughly in Chapter 8). These social forces at work in this setting proved to be much more potent determinants of job performance than the physical factors studied.

This conclusion, based on the surprising findings of the Hawthorne studies, is important because it ushered in a whole new way of thinking about behavior at work. It suggests that to understand behavior on the job, we must fully appreciate people's attitudes and the processes by which they communicate with each other. This way of thinking, so fundamental to modern OB, may be traced back to Elton Mayo's pioneering Hawthorne studies. In contrast with the scientific management views that prevailed at the time, this perspective was quite novel.

This is not to say, however, that the Hawthorne studies were, by any means, perfect. Indeed, by modern standards, the research was seriously flawed. As we will describe in our presentation of experimentation later in this chapter, the research violated several important rules. For example, no effort was made to assure that the rooms used in the study were identical in every way except for the variables studied (the level of illumination, the scheduling and duration of the rest pauses), making it possible for factors other than those being studied to influence the results. (Interestingly, research on the topic of illumination is still being conducted today, although it is far more carefully conducted and sophisticated.[36]) Furthermore, because no attempt was made to assure that the employees chosen for study were representative of all those in their factory (or all manufacturing personnel generally), it is difficult to generalize the results of the study beyond those individuals studied.

Clearly, although the Hawthorne studies are imperfect, their impact on the field of OB is considerable. This contribution lies *not* with respect to what the research tells us about the effects of illumination, but what it revealed indirectly about the importance of human needs, attitudes, motives, and relationships in the workplace. In this respect, the work established a close link between the newly emerging field of OB, and the behavioral sciences of psychology and sociology—a connection that persists today. Although the human relations approach was gradually replaced by more sophisticated views, several of its ideas and concepts contributed greatly to the development of the field of OB. Little could those workers in that long-vanished plant outside of Chicago have guessed that their contribution to the social science of organizational behavior would be so enduring!

CLASSICAL ORGANIZATIONAL THEORY

During the same time that proponents of scientific management got people to begin thinking about the interrelationships between people and their jobs, another approach to managing people emerged. This perspective, known as **classical organizational theory**, focused on the efficient structuring of overall organizations. This is in contrast, of course, to scientific management, which sought to effectively organize the work of individuals.

Several different theorists are identified with classical organizational theory. Among the first was Henri Fayol, a French industrialist who attributed his managerial success to various principles he developed.[37] Among these are the following:

- A *division of labor* should be used because it allows people to specialize, doing only what they do best.
- Managers should have *authority* over their subordinates, the right to order them to do what's necessary for the organization.
- Lines of authority should be uninterrupted; that is, a *scalar chain* should exist that connects the top management to the lower-level employees.
- There should exist a clearly defined *unity of command,* such that employees receive directions from only one other person, to avoid confusion.
- Subordinates should be given *initiative* to formulate and implement their plans.

Although many of these principles are still well accepted today, it is widely recognized that they should not always be applied in exactly the same way. For example, whereas some organizations thrive on being structured according to a unity of command, still others require that some employees take directions from several different superiors. We will have more to say about this subject when we discuss various types of organizational designs in Chapter 15. For now, suffice it to say that current organizational theorists owe a debt of gratitude to Fayol for his pioneering and far-reaching ideas.

Probably the best-known classical organizational theorist is the German sociologist Max Weber.[38] Among other things, Weber is well known for proposing a form of organizational structure well known today—the *bureaucracy*. A **bureaucracy** is an organizational design that attempts to make organizations operate more efficiently by having a clear hierarchy of authority in which people are required to perform well-defined jobs (see Chapter 15). Weber's idea was that the bureaucracy is the one best way to efficiently organize work in all organizations (much as proponents of scientific management searched for the ideal way to perform a job). The elements of an ideal bureaucracy are summarized in Table 1-1.

When you think about bureaucracies, negative images probably come to mind of lots of inflexible people getting bogged down in lots of red tape. (By the way, the phrase "red tape" is said to have become popular during World War I, when red tape was used on documents from the British government.[39] Given the tendency for national governments to be bureaucratic in structure, it is not surprising that the

TABLE 1-1

Characteristics of an Ideal Bureaucracy

According to Max Weber, bureaucracies must possess certain characteristics. Here is a summary of the major defining characteristics of bureaucratic organizations.

CHARACTERISTIC	DESCRIPTION
Formal rules and regulations	*Written guidelines are used to control all employees' behaviors.*
Impersonal treatment	*Favoritism is to be avoided, and all work relationships are to be based on objective standards.*
Division of labor	*All duties are divided into specialized tasks and are performed by individuals with the appropriate skills.*
Hierarchical structure	*Positions are ranked by authority level in clear fashion from lower-level to upper-level ones.*
Authority structure	*The making of decisions is determined by one's position in the hierarchy; people have authority over those in lower-ranking positions.*
Lifelong career commitment	*Employment is viewed as a permanent, lifelong obligation on the part of the organization and its employees.*
Rationality	*The organization is committed to achieving its ends (e.g., profitability) in the most efficient manner possible.*

term *red tape* came to refer to bureaucratic processes of all types.) Weber's "universal" view of bureaucratic structure lies in contrast to the more modern approaches to organizational design (see Chapter 15), in which it is recognized that different forms of organizational structure may be more or less appropriate under different situations. Although the bureaucracy may not have proven to be a perfect structure for organizing all work, organizational theorists owe a great deal to Weber, many of whose ideas are still considered viable today.

ORGANIZATIONAL BEHAVIOR IN THE MODERN ERA

Based on the pioneering contributions noted thus far, the realization that behavior in work settings is shaped by a wide range of individual, group and organizational factors set the stage for the emergence of the science of organizational behavior. By the 1940s, clear signs appeared that an independent field had emerged. For example, in 1941 the first doctoral degree in OB was granted (to George Lombard at the Harvard Business School).[40] Only four years later the first textbook in this field appeared.[41] By the late 1950s and early 1960s, OB was clearly a going concern. By that time, active programs of research were going on—research into such key processes as motivation and leadership, and the impact of organizational structure.[42] For a summary of some of the major milestones in the development of the field of OB during the modern era, refer to Table 1-2.

Unfortunately—but not unexpectedly, for a new field—the development of scientific investigation into managerial and organizational issues was uneven and unsystematic in the 1940s and 1950s. In response to this state of affairs, the Ford Foundation sponsored a project by economists R. A. Gordon and J. E. Howell in which they carefully analyzed the nature of business education in the United States. They published their findings in 1959, in what became a very influential work known as the *Gordon and Howell report*.[43] This work recommended that the study of management pay greater attention to basic academic disciplines, especially the social sciences. This advice had an enormous influence on business school curricula during the 1960s and promoted the development of the field of organizational behavior.

Observing the effects of these changes in business curricula in the decades following the Gordon and Howell report, Lyman Porter and Lawrence McKibbin *conducted* another influential study on management education.[44] The *Porter and McKibbin report,* as it has come to be known, published in 1988, recognized advances made by incorporating social science notions into business curricula but pushed for further advances in several areas. These include paying greater attention to the effects of the external environment (e.g., society, government, and international developments), intensifying consideration of the international aspects of business, noting the ethical implications of business practices, and increasing attention to the growing service and information sectors of business (in contrast to the traditional manufacturing orientation). Although these recommendations (and other aspects of their report) are considered controversial, it is clearly the case that OB scientists and practitioners are taking many of these suggestions to heart.[45] Indeed, as you continue reading this book, you will see attention paid to topics such as international differences, ethics, the business environment, and the service sector. These clearly represent areas of growing interest in the field of OB—topics that will complement the array of well-established topic areas considered in the field in the years to come.

TABLE 1-2

Some Milestones in the History of Organizational Behavior

Summarized here are some of the major events that have contributed to the development of the field of organizational behavior in the modern era.

YEAR	EVENT	COVERAGE IN THIS TEXT
1943	Lewin's studies of group climate distinguished among various styles of leadership.	Chapter 13
1951	Ohio State leadership studies distinguished among key dimensions of leader behavior.	Chapter 13
1958	Fiedler's leadership theory contributed to the contingency approach to leadership.	Chapter 13
1960	McGregor stated the Theory X and Theory Y approaches to managing people in organizations.	Chapter 1
1964	Vroom developed the expectancy theory of motivation as it applied to people in organizations.	Chapter 4
1967	Lawrence and Lorsch's research examined the relationship between the external environment and organizational structure.	Chapter 15
1979	Pfeffer and Salancik established the resource-dependency perspective of power.	Chapter 12
1987	Schein advanced the conceptual basis for organizational culture.	Chapter 14

Source: Based on suggestions by Lawrence, 1987; see Note 40.

THEORY AND RESEARCH: TOOLS FOR LEARNING ABOUT BEHAVIOR IN ORGANIZATIONS

Because, as we have already noted, organizational behavior is a science, it should not be surprising to learn that the field relies heavily upon the scientific method. As in the case of other scientific fields, OB uses the tools of science to achieve its goals—in this case, to learn about organizations and the behavior of people working in them. With this in mind, it is essential to understand the basic tools scientists use to learn about behavior in organizations. In this section we will briefly describe some of these techniques. Our goal here is not to make you an expert in scientific methodology, but to give you a solid understanding of the techniques you will be encountering as you venture further into this book.

ISN'T IT ALL JUST COMMON SENSE?

Maybe you're not (yet, at least!) a top executive of a large business firm, with decades of experience in the work world. Still, you doubtlessly know *something* about the behavior of people on the job. After all, you already may have learned quite a bit from whatever jobs you had yourself, or from talking to other people about their experiences. This isn't surprising given that we can all observe a great deal about people's behavior in organizational settings just by paying casual attention. So, whether you're the CEO of a *Fortune* 500 firm or a part-time pizza delivery driver, you probably have a few ideas about how people behave on the job. Besides, there are probably some things you just take for granted. For example, would you say that happier employees tend to be more productive? If you're like most people, you would probably say, "Yes, of course." It's logical, right? Well, despite what you may believe, this is generally *not* true. In fact, as we will see in Chapter 5, people who are satisfied with their jobs tend to be no more productive than those who are dissatisfied with their jobs. This contradiction of common sense is not an isolated example. This book is full of examples of phenomena studied in the field of OB that you might find surprising. To see how good you may be at predicting human behavior in organizations, we invite you to take the brief quiz appearing in the Experiencing Organizational Behavior section at the end of this chapter (see pp. 42–43). If you don't do very well, don't despair. It's just our way of demonstrating that there's more to understanding the complexities of behavior in organizations than meets the eye.

So, if we can't trust our common sense, on what can we rely? This is where the scientific method enters the picture. Although social science research is far from perfect, the techniques used to study behavior in organizations can reveal a great deal. Naturally, not everything scientific research reveals contradicts common sense. In fact, a considerable amount of research confirms things we already believe to be true. If this occurs, is the research useless? The answer is emphatically no! After all, scientific evidence often reveals a great deal about the subtle conditions under which various events occur. Such complexities would not have been apparent from only casual, unsystematic observation and common sense. In other words, the field of OB is solidly based on carefully conducted and logically analyzed research. Although common sense may provide a useful starting point for getting us to think about behavior in organizations, there's no substitute for scientific research when it comes to really understanding what happens and why.

Now that you understand the important role of the scientific method in the field of OB, you are prepared to appreciate the specific approaches used to conduct scientific research in this field. We will begin our presentation of these techniques with a discussion of one of the best-accepted sources of ideas for OB research—theory.

THEORY: AN INDISPENSABLE GUIDE TO ORGANIZATIONAL RESEARCH

What image comes to mind when you think of a scientist? Someone wearing a white lab coat surrounded by microscopes and test tubes busily at work testing theories? Although OB scientists typically don't wear lab coats or use microscopes and test tubes, it *is* true that they make use of theories. This is the case despite the fact that OB is, in part, an applied science. Simply because a field is characterized as being "theoretical" does not imply that it is impractical and out of touch with reality. On the contrary, a theory is simply a way of describing the relationship between concepts. Thus, theories help, not hinder, our understanding of practical situations. More formally, we define a **theory** as *a set of statements about the interrelationships among concepts that allow us to predict and explain various processes and events*. As you might imagine, such statements may be of interest to both practitioners and scientists alike. We're certain that as you read this book you will come to appreciate the valuable role that theories play when it comes to understanding behavior in organizations—and putting that knowledge to practical use.

To demonstrate the value of theory in OB, let's consider an example based on a phenomenon we'll describe in more detail in Chapter 4, the effects of task goals on performance. Imagine observing that word processing operators type faster when they are given a specific goal (e.g., 75 words per minute) than when they are told to try to do their best. Imagine also observing that salespeople make more sales when they are given quotas than when they are not given any quotas. By itself, these are useful observations insofar as they allow us to predict what will happen when goals are introduced. In addition, they suggest a way to change conditions so as to improve performance among people in these groups. These two accomplishments—*prediction* and *control*—are major goals of science.

Yet there's something missing—namely, knowing that concrete goals improve performance fails to tell us anything about *why* this is so. What is going on here? After all, this was observed in two different settings, and with two different groups of people. Why is it that people are so productive in response to specific goals? This is where theory enters the picture. In contrast to some fields, such as physics and chemistry, where theories often take the form of mathematical equations, theories in OB generally involve verbal statements of assumptions. For example, in the present case, the assumptions might be stated as follows:

1. When people are given specific goals, they know exactly what's expected of them.

2. When people know what's expected of them, they are motivated to work hard to find ways to succeed.

3. When people work hard to succeed, they perform at high levels.

This simple theory, like all others, consists of two basic elements: concepts (in this case goals and motives) and assertions about how they are related.

In science, the formation of a theory is only the beginning of a sequence of events followed to understand behavior. Once a theory is proposed, it is used to introduce *hypotheses*—-logically derived statements that follow from the theory. In our example, it may be hypothesized that specific goals will only improve performance when they are not so difficult that they cannot be attained. Next, such predictions need to be tested in actual research to see if they are confirmed. If research confirms our hypotheses, we can be more confident about the accuracy of the theory. However, if it is not confirmed after several well-conducted studies are done, our confidence in the theory is weakened. When this happens, it's time to revise the theory and generate new, testable hypotheses from it. As you might imagine, given the complexities of human behavior in organizations, theories are rarely—if ever—fully confirmed. In fact, many of the field's most popular and useful theories are constantly being refined and tested. In Figure 1-10, we have summarized the cyclical nature of the scientific endeavor.

It will probably come as no surprise to you to learn that the process of theory development and testing we have been describing is very laborious. In view of this, why do scientists bother to constantly fine-tune their theories? The answer lies in

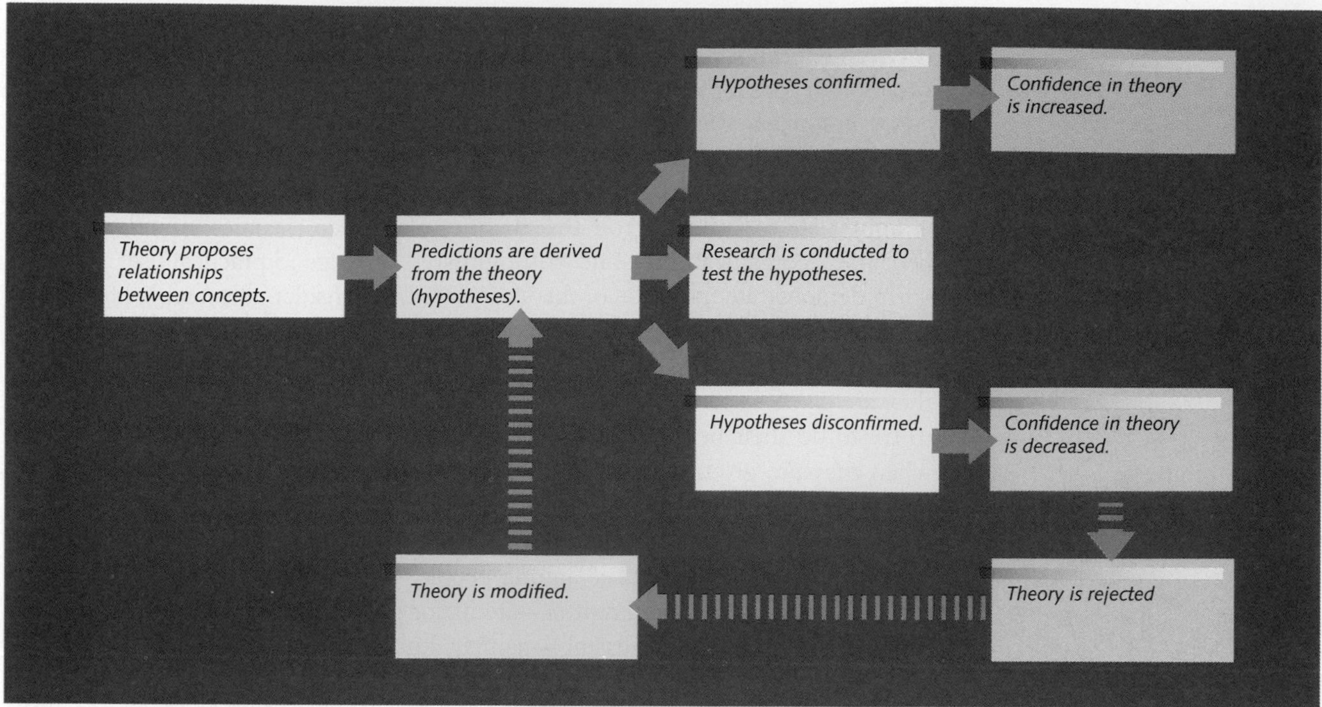

FIGURE 1-10

THEORY TESTING: THE RESEARCH PROCESS

Once a theory has been formulated, predictions derived from it are tested through direct research. If these are confirmed, confidence in the theory is increased. If they are disconfirmed, confidence is diminished. At this point, the theory is either modified and retested, or completely rejected.

the very useful purposes that theories serve. Specifically, theories serve three important functions—organizing, summarizing, and guiding. First, given the complexities of human behavior, theories provide a way of *organizing* large amounts of data into meaningful propositions. In other words, they help us combine information so diverse that it might be difficult to grasp without the help of a theory. Second, theories help us to *summarize* this knowledge by making it possible to make sense out of bits and pieces of information that otherwise would be difficult—if not impossible—to understand. Third, and finally, theories provide an important *guiding* function. That is, they help scientists identify important areas of needed research that would not have been apparent without theories to guide their thinking.

As you read this text, you will come across many different theories attempting to explain various aspects of behavior in organizations. When you do, we think you will appreciate the useful organizing, summarizing, and guiding roles they play—in short, how theories help provide meaningful explanations of behavior. In all cases the usefulness of any theory is based on the extent to which it can be confirmed or disconfirmed. In other words, theories must be *testable*. A theory that cannot be tested serves no real purpose to scientists. Once it's tested, a theory—or, at least part of it—must be confirmed if it is to be considered an accurate account of human behavior. And, of course, that's what the field of OB is all about.

How are theories tested? The answer is, by conducting *research*. Unless we do research, we cannot test theories, and unless we test theories we are greatly limited in what we can learn about behavior in organizations.[46] This is why research is such a major concern of specialists in OB. So, in order for you to fully appreciate the field of OB, it's critical for you to understand something about the techniques it uses—that is, how we come to know about the behavior of people at work. As a result, throughout this book, we will be explaining not only *what* is known about OB, but also *how* that knowledge was derived. We are confident that the better you understand OB's "tools of the trade," the more you will come to appreciate its value as a field. With this in mind, we will now describe some of the major research techniques used to learn about organizational behavior.

SURVEY RESEARCH: THE CORRELATIONAL METHOD

The most popular approach to conducting research in OB involves giving people questionnaires in which they are asked to report how they feel about various aspects of themselves, their jobs, and organizations. Such questionnaires, also known as **surveys**, make it possible for organizational scientists to delve into a broad range of issues. This research technique is very popular because it is applicable to studying a wide variety of topics. After all, you can learn a great deal about how people feel by asking them a systematic series of carefully worded questions. Moreover, questionnaires are relatively easy to administer (be it by mail, phone, or in person), and—as we will note shortly—they are readily quantifiable and lend themselves to powerful statistical analyses. These features make survey research a very appealing option to OB scientists. Not surprisingly, we will be describing quite a few survey studies throughout this text.

The survey approach consists of three major steps. First, the researcher must identify the variables in which he or she is interested. These may be various aspects of people (e.g., their attitudes toward work), organizations (e.g., the pay plans they use), or the environment in general (e.g., how competitive the industry is). They may be suggested from many different sources, such as a theory, previous research, or even hunches based on casual observations. Second, these variables are measured as precisely as possible. As you might imagine, it isn't always easy to tap precisely people's feelings about things (especially if they are uncertain about those feelings or reluctant to share them). As a result, researchers must pay a great deal of attention to the way they word the questions they use. For some examples of questions designed to measure various work-related attitudes, see Table 1-3. Finally, after the variables of interest have been identified and measured, scientists must determine how—if at all—they are related to each other. With this in mind, scientists analyze their survey findings using a variety of different statistical procedures.

Scientists conducting survey research typically are interested in determining how variables are interrelated—or, put differently, how changes in one variable are associated with changes in another variable. For example, let's say that a researcher is interested in learning the relationship between how fairly people believe they are paid and various work-related attitudes, such as their willingness to help their coworkers and their interest in quitting. Based on various theories and previous

TABLE 1-3

Survey Questions Designed to Measure Work Attitudes
Items such as these might be used to measure attitudes toward various aspects of work.

- *Overall, how fairly are you paid?*

Not at all fairly	1	2	3	4	5	6	7	Extremely fairly

- *Imagine that one of your office-mates needs to stay late to complete an important project. How likely or unlikely would you be to volunteer to help that person, even if you would not receive any special recognition for your efforts?*

Not at all likely	1	2	3	4	5	6	7	Extremely likely

- *How interested are you in quitting your present job?*

Not at all interested	1	2	3	4	5	6	7	Extremely interested

research (which we will describe in Chapters 4 and 5), a researcher may suspect that the more people believe they are unfairly paid, the less likely they will be to help their co-workers and the more likely they will be to desire new jobs. These predictions constitute the researcher's **hypothesis**—the as-yet-untested prediction the researcher wishes to investigate. After devising an appropriate questionnaire measuring these variables, the researcher must administer it to a large number of people so that the hypothesis can be tested.

Once the data are collected, the investigator must statistically analyze them and compare the results to the hypothesis. Suppose a researcher obtains results like those shown in the left side of Figure 1-11. In this case, the more fairly employees believe they are paid, the more willing they are to help their co-workers. In other words, the variables are related to each other in such a way that the more one variable increases, the more the other variable also increases. Any variables that increase together are said to have a *positive correlation*.

Now imagine what will be found when the researcher compares the sample's perceptions of pay fairness with their interest in quitting their jobs. If the experimenter's hypothesis is correct, the results will look like those shown on the right side of Figure 1-11. In other words, the more people believe their pay is fair, the less interested they are in looking for a new job. Any such case—in which the more one variable increases, the more another decreases—is said to have a *negative correlation*.

OB scientists are not only interested in the *direction* of the relationship between variables—that is, whether the association is positive or negative—but also, how strong that relationship is. To gauge this, researchers rely on a statistic known as the **correlation coefficient**. This is a number between –1 and +1 used to express the strength of the relationship between the variables studied. The closer this number is to 1 (either –1 or +1), the stronger the relationship is—that is, the more closely the variables are related to each other. However, the closer the correlation coefficient is to 0, the weaker the relationship between the variables—that is, the less strongly they are associated. So, when interpreting correlation coefficients, there are two things to keep in mind: its sign (in keeping with algebraic traditions, positive correlations are usually expressed without any sign), and its absolute value

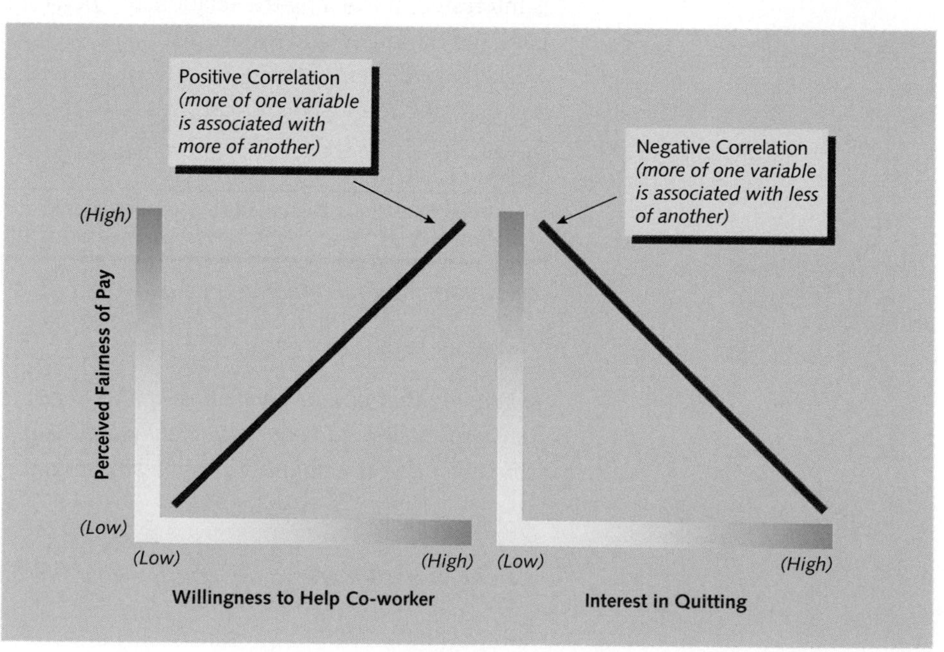

FIGURE 1-11
POSITIVE AND NEGATIVE CORRELATIONS: WHAT THEY MEAN
Positive correlations, such as the one shown on the left, exist when more of one variable is associated with more of another variable. Negative correlations, such as the one shown on the right, exist when more of one variable is associated with less of another variable.

(that is, the size of the number without respect to its sign). For example, a correlation coefficient of –.92 reflects a much stronger relationship between variables than one of .22. The minus sign simply reveals that the relationship between the variables being described is negative (more of one variable is associated with less of another variable). The fact that the absolute value of this correlation coefficient is greater tells us that the relationship between the variables is stronger.

When variables are strongly correlated, scientists can make more accurate predictions about how they are related to each other. So, using our example, a negative correlation between perceptions of pay fairness and intent to quit, we may expect that in general, people who believe they are unfairly paid will be more likely to quit their jobs than those who believe they are fairly paid. If the correlation coefficient were high, say over –.80, we would be more confident that this would occur than if the correlation were low, say under –.20. In fact, as correlation coefficients approach 0, it's impossible to make any accurate predictions whatsoever. In such a case, knowing one variable would not allow us to predict anything about the other. As you might imagine, organizational scientists are extremely interested in discovering the relationships between variables, and rely on correlation coefficients to tell them a great deal.

Although the examples we've been using involve the relationship between only two variables at a time, organizational researchers are frequently interested in the interrelationships among many different variables at once. For example, an employee's intent to quit may be related to several variables besides the perceived fairness of one's pay, such as satisfaction with the job itself, or liking for one's immediate supervisor. Researchers may make predictions using several different variables at once, using a technique known as **multiple regression**. Using this approach, researchers may be able to tell the extent to which each of several different variables contributes to predicting the behavior in question. In our example, they would be able to learn the degree to which the several variables studied, together and individually, are related to the intent to quit one's job. Given the complex nature of human behavior on the job, and the wide range of variables likely to influence it, it should not be surprising to learn that OB researchers use the multiple regression technique a great deal in their work.

Despite the fact that the analysis of surveys using correlational techniques, such as multiple regression, can be very valuable, conclusions drawn from correlations are limited in a very important way. Namely, *correlations do not reveal anything about causation*. In other words, although correlations tell us about how variables are related to each other, they don't provide any insight into their cause-and-effect relationships. So, in our example, although we may learn that the less employees feel they are fairly paid the more interested they are in quitting, we cannot tell *why* this is the case. In other words, we cannot tell whether or not employees to want to quit *because* they believe they are unfairly paid. Might this be the case? Yes, but it also might be the case that people who believe they are unfairly paid tend to dislike the work they do, and it is this that encourages them to find a new job. Another possibility is that people believe they are unfairly paid because their supervisors are too demanding—and it is this that raises their interest in quitting (see Figure 1-12). Our point is simple: although all these possibilities are reasonable, knowing only that variables are correlated does *not* permit us to determine what causes what. Because it is important for researchers to establish the causal relationships between the variables they study, OB researchers frequently turn to another technique that *does* permit such conclusions to be drawn—the experiment.

FIGURE 1-12

CORRELATIONS: WHAT THEY *DON'T* REVEAL ABOUT CAUSATION

Just because there may be a strong negative correlation between perceived pay fairness and the desire to leave one's job, we cannot tell why this relationship exists. As shown here, there are many possible underlying reasons that are not identified by knowledge of the correlation alone.

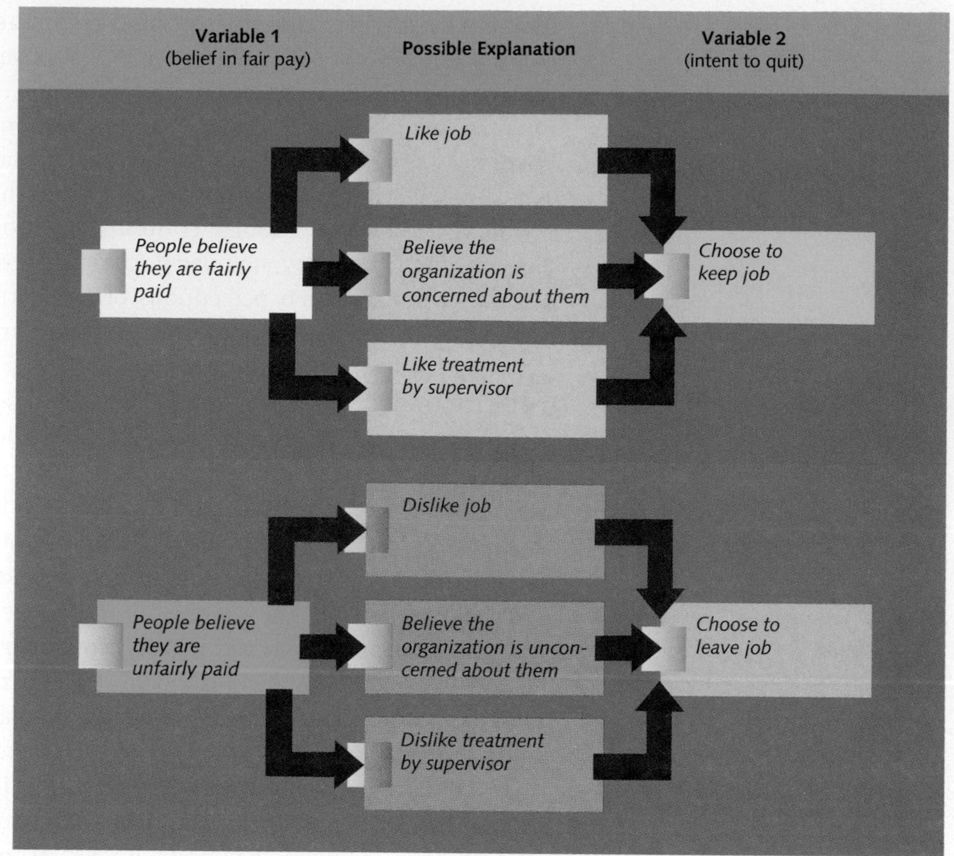

EXPERIMENTAL RESEARCH: THE LOGIC OF CAUSE AND EFFECT

Because both scientists and practitioners want to know not only the degree to which variables are related but also how much one variable causes another, the **experimental method** is popularly used in OB. The more we know about the causal connections between variables, the better we can explain the underlying causes of behavior—and this, after all, is one of the major goals of OB.

To illustrate how experiments work, let's consider an example. Suppose we're interested in determining the effects of social density (the number of people per unit of space) on the job performance of clerical employees—that is, the degree to which the crowdedness of working conditions in an office influence how well word processing operators do their jobs. Although this topic might be studied in many different ways, imagine that we do the following. First, we select at random a large group of word processing operators working in a variety of different organizations—the participants in our study. Then, we prepare a specially designed office, the setting for the experiment. Throughout the study, we would keep the design of the office and all the working conditions (e.g., temperature, light, and noise levels) alike with one exception—we would systematically vary the number of people working in the office at any given time.

For example, we could have one condition—which we could call the "high-density" condition—in which fifty people are put into a 500-square-foot room at once (allowing 10 square feet per person). In another condition—the "low-density" condition—we could put five people into a 500-square-foot room at once (allowing

100 square feet per person). Finally, we can have a "moderate-density" condition in which we put twenty-five people into a 500-square-foot room (allowing 20 square feet per person). Say we have several hundred people participating in the study and we assign them at random to each of these three conditions. Each word processing operator is given the same passage of text to type over two hours. After this period, the typists are dismissed, and the researcher counts the number of words accurately typed by each typist, noting any possible differences between performance in the various conditions. Suppose we obtain the results summarized in Figure 1-13.

Let's analyze what was done in this simple hypothetical experiment to help explain the basic elements of the experimental method and the underlying logic behind it. First, recall that we selected participants from the population of interest and assigned them to conditions on a *random* basis. This means that each of the participants had an equal chance of being assigned to any one of the three conditions. This is critical because it is possible that differences between conditions could result from having many very good operators in one condition and many unproductive ones in another. So, to safeguard against this possibility, it is important to assign people to conditions at random. When this is done, we can assume that the effects of any possible differences between people would equalize over conditions. Thus, by assigning people to conditions at random, we can be assured that there will be just as many fast operators and slow operators in each. As a result, there is no reason to believe that any differences in productivity that may be noted between conditions can be attributed to systematic differences in the skills of the participants. Given "the luck of the draw," such differences can be discounted, thereby enhancing our confidence that differences are solely the result of the social density of the rooms. This is the logic behind random assignment. Although it is not always feasible to use random assignment when conducting experiments in organizations, it is highly desirable whenever possible.

FIGURE 1-13
EXPERIMENTATION IN ORGANIZATIONAL BEHAVIOR: A SIMPLE EXAMPLE
In our hypothetical example, word processing operators were put into rooms that differed with respect to only one variable—social density (i.e., the number of people per unit of space). The results summarized here show that the subjects performed best under the conditions of lowest density, and worst under conditions of highest density.

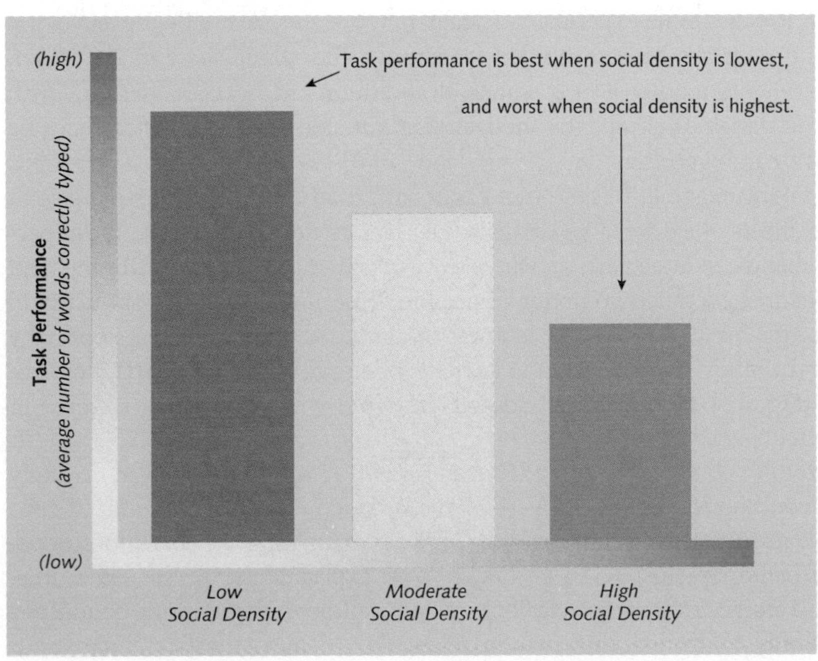

Recall that operators were assigned to conditions that differed with respect to only the variable of interest, in this case, social density. We can say that the experimenter *manipulated* this aspect of the work environment, systematically changing it from condition to condition. A variable altered in this way is called an **independent variable**. An independent variable is that variable which is systematically manipulated by the experimenter so as to determine its effects on the behavior of interest. In our example, the independent variable is social density. Specifically, it may be said to have three different *levels*—that is, degrees of the independent variable: high, moderate, and low. The variable that is measured, the one influenced by the independent variable, is known as the **dependent variable**. A dependent variable is the behavior of interest that is being measured—the behavior that is dependent on the independent variable. In this case, the dependent variable was word processing performance, the quantity of words typed. Besides studying this, we could have studied other dependent variables, such as satisfaction with the work or the perceived level of stress encountered. In fact, it would be quite common for OB researchers to study several dependent variables in one experiment. By the same token, researchers also frequently consider the effects of several different independent variables in a given experiment. The matter of which particular independent variables and dependent variables are studied is one of the most important decisions researchers make. Often they base these decisions on suggestions from previous research (other experiments suggesting that certain variables are important) and existing theory (conceptualizations suggesting that certain variables may be important).

The basic logic behind the experimental method is quite simple. In fact, it involves only two major steps. First, some variable of interest (the independent variable) must be systematically varied. Second, the effects, if any, of such variations must be measured. The underlying idea is that if the independent variable does indeed influence behavior, then people exposed to different amounts of it should behave differently. In our example, we can be certain that social density caused differences in processing performance because when all other factors were held constant, different amounts of density led to different levels of performance. Although our experiment is fabricated, it follows the same basic logic of all experiments—namely, it is designed to reveal the effects of the independent variables on the dependent variables.

For the conclusions of experiments to be valid, researchers must hold constant all factors other than the independent variable. Then, if there are differences in the dependent variable, we can assume that they are the result of the effects of the independent variable. By assigning participants to conditions at random, we already took an important step to ensure that one key factor—differences in the ability levels of the participants—would be equalized. But there are other possible factors that also may affect the results. For example, it is also essential to hold constant any environmental conditions that might influence word processing speed. In this case, more people would generate more heat, so to make sure that the results are influenced only by density—and not heat—it would be necessary to air-condition the work room so as to keep it the same temperature in all conditions at all times. If you think about it, our simple experiment is really not that simple at all—especially if it is conducted with all the care needed to permit valid conclusions to be drawn. Thus, experiments require all experimental conditions to be kept identical with respect to all variables except the independent variable so that its effects can be determined unambiguously.

As you might imagine, this is often easier said than done. How simple it is to control the effects of extraneous variables (i.e., factors not of interest to the experimenter) depends, in large part, on where the experiment is conducted. In the field of OB, there are generally two options available: experiments can be conducted in naturalistic organizational settings referred to as the *field*, or in settings specially created for the study itself, referred to as the *laboratory* (or, *lab* for short). As summarized in Figure 1-14, there are trade-offs involved with conducting research in each setting.

The study in our example was a lab experiment. It was conducted in carefully controlled conditions specially created for the research. The great amount of control possible in such settings improves the chances of creating the conditions needed to allow valid conclusions to be drawn from experiments. At the same time, however, lab studies suffer from a lack of realism. Although the working conditions can be carefully controlled, they may be relatively unrealistic, not carefully simu-

FIGURE 1-14
OB EXPERIMENTATION IN THE LAB AND FIELD: A SUMMARY OF TRADEOFFS
Organizational behavior researchers may conduct experiments in laboratory or field settings—each with its own advantages and disadvantages. As summarized here, the lab offers more control but less realism, whereas the field offers less control but more realism.

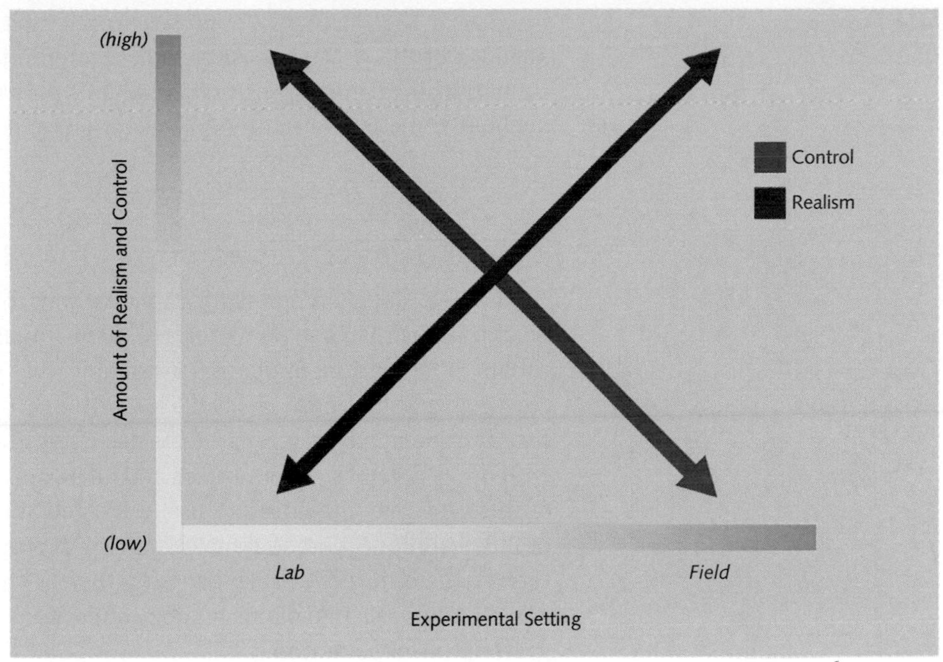

lating the conditions found in actual organizations. As a result, it may be difficult to generalize the findings of lab studies to settings outside the lab, such as the workplace.

However, if we conducted our study in actual organizations, there would be many unknowns, many uncontrollable factors at work. To conduct such a study, we would have to distinguish between those who worked in offices differing with respect to social density and later compare people's performance. If we did this, we would be sure that the conditions studied were realistic. However, there would be so little control over the setting that many different factors could be operating. For example, because people would not be assigned to conditions at random, it might be the case that people work in those settings they most desire. Furthermore, there would be no control over such factors as distractions and differences in environmental conditions (e.g., noise and temperature).

In short, field studies, although strong in the level of realism they offer, are weak with respect to the level of control they provide. By contrast, lab experiments permit a great deal of control, but tend to be unrealistic. In view of these complementary strengths and weaknesses, it should be clear that experiments should be conducted in *both* types of sites. As researchers do so, our confidence can be increased that valid conclusions will be drawn about the effects of variables of interest on behavior.

QUALITATIVE RESEARCH: NATURALISTIC OBSERVATION AND THE CASE METHOD

In contrast to the highly empirical approaches to research we have been describing thus far, we should also note that OB researchers sometimes use a less empirical approach. After all, probably the most obvious ways of learning about behavior in organizations are to observe it firsthand and to describe it after it occurs. Organizational scientists have a long tradition of studying behavior using these nonempirical, descriptive techniques, relying on what is known as *qualitative research*.[47] The qualitative approach to research relies on preserving the natural qualities of the situation being studied, attempting to capture the richness of the context while disturbing natural conditions only minimally, if at all. The two major qualitative methods used by OB scientists are *naturalistic observation* and *the case method*.

NATURALISTIC OBSERVATION

There's probably no more fundamental way of learning about how people act in organizations than simply to observe them—a research technique known as **naturalistic observation**. Suppose, for example, that you wanted to learn how employees behave in response to layoffs. One thing you could do would be to visit an organization in which layoffs will be occurring and systematically observe what the employees do and say both before and after the layoffs occur. Making comparisons of this type may provide very useful insights into what's going on. As a variation of this technique, you could take a job in the organization, and make your observations as an insider actually working there—giving you a perspective you might not otherwise gain. This technique, often used by anthropologists, is known as **participant observation**.

It's not too difficult to think of the advantages and disadvantages of observational research. Its major advantage is that it can be used without disrupting normal routines, allowing behavior to be studied in its natural state. Moreover, almost anyone—including people already working in the host organization—can be trained to use it. Observational research also suffers from several important limitations. First, the potential for subjectivity among researchers is considerable. Even among the most diligent of researchers, it's inevitable that different people will make different observations of the same events. Second, being involved in the daily functioning of an organization will make it difficult for observers to be impartial. Researchers interpreting organizational events may be subject to bias due to their feelings about the people involved. Finally, because most of what goes on in an organization is fairly dull and routine, it's very easy for researchers to place a great deal of emphasis on unusual or unexpected events, possibly leading to inaccurate conclusions. Given these limitations, most OB scientists consider observational research to be more useful as a starting point for providing basic insight into behavior, than as a tool for acquiring definitive knowledge about behavior.

THE CASE METHOD

Suppose that we conducted our hypothetical study of reactions to layoffs differently. Instead of observing behavior directly, we might fully describe the company's history leading up to the event and some statistics summarizing its aftermath (e.g., how long people were unemployed, how the company was restructured after downsizing, and the like). We might even include some interviews with people affected by the event, and quote them directly. The approach we are describing here is known as the **case method**. More often than not, the rationale behind the case method is *not* to teach us about a specific organization per se, but to learn what happened in that organization as a means of providing cues as to what may be going on in other organizations. The case method is similar to naturalistic observation in that it relies on descriptive accounts of events. However, it is different in that it often involves using post hoc accounts of events from those involved as opposed to firsthand observations by scientists.

As you might imagine, a great deal can be learned by detailed accounts of events in organizations summarized in the form of written cases. Especially when these cases are supplemented by careful interviews (in which case the method would be considered quantitative rather than qualitative in nature), cases can paint a particularly detailed picture of events as they unfolded in a particular organization. Of course, to the extent that the organization studied is unique, it may be not be possible to generalize what is learned to others. To get around this limitation, some researchers have recommended that multiple, as opposed to single, cases should be used to test theories.[48] Another problem with the case method—a limitation it shares with naturalistic observation—is that the potential for bias is relatively high. As a result, many scientists believe that while the case method may serve as a valuable source of hypotheses about behavior on the job, testing those hypotheses requires more rigorous research methods.[49]

SUMMARY AND REVIEW

THE FIELD OF ORGANIZATIONAL BEHAVIOR

Organizational behavior (OB) seeks knowledge of all aspects of behavior in organizational settings through the systematic study of individual, group, and organizational processes. It uses this knowledge to promote basic understanding of human behavior and to enhance the effectiveness of organizations and the well-being of individuals working in them. Because it relies on scientific methods, the field of OB provides much more accurate knowledge about work behavior than simply relying on common sense.

In contrast to the traditional view that people are basically lazy and uninterested in working (the **Theory X** approach), modern OB is characterized by the belief that under the right combination of conditions people are responsive to their work environments and are highly committed to work (the **Theory Y** approach). The field also recognizes that organizations are dynamic, self-sustaining units known as **open systems**. In view of the complex nature of human behavior at work, OB generally takes a **contingency approach**, recognizing that behavior depends on the complex interaction of many different variables. OB also confronts various challenges brought on by the growing diversity of today's workforce. Finally, modern OB appreciates the need to adopt a multicultural, global perspective to most fully understand the dynamic nature of behavior in organizations.

HISTORICAL DEVELOPMENT OF THE FIELD OF ORGANIZATIONAL BEHAVIOR

The roots of OB can be traced back to the early twentieth-century work of Frederick W. Taylor, who developed **scientific management**—a management philosophy that attempted to find the most efficient ways for people to perform their jobs. Around this same time, **classical organizational theory** attempted to discover the most effective ways of designing organizations. Among these was the **bureaucracy**—a form of organization identified by Max Weber that advocated clear organizational hierarchies and well-defined jobs.

The field was also greatly influenced by the **human relations approach**, an orientation highlighting the impact of complex social systems on job performance. Elton Mayo's Hawthorne studies represented the pioneering efforts in this area. In the second half of the twentieth century, the field of OB grew dramatically to become the diverse, multidisciplinary field it is today.

RESEARCH METHODS IN ORGANIZATIONAL BEHAVIOR

Although much of what OB studies appears to be commonsensical, casual observations are often misleading and fail to reveal the complex nature of behavior. Accordingly, the field of OB is based on knowledge derived from scientific research. Research is often guided by **theories**, testable explanations as to why various events occur as they do. Correlational research is among the most popularly used techniques in the field. In this approach potentially important variables are identified and then systematically measured using **surveys** to determine how they are related to one another. The **correlation coefficient** is the statistic used to summarize the degree and direction of the relationship between variables.

Because correlational research does not allow us to draw conclusions about cause and effect, scientists often rely on the **experimental method**. Using this approach, researchers systematically alter one or more variables (**independent variables**) while holding other factors constant so as to determine the effects on the behavior of interest (**dependent variables**). In contrast to these empirical techniques, OB researchers often rely on qualitative approaches, such as **naturalistic observation**, in which trained observers make systematic observations of behavior in an organization, and the **case method**, in which detailed accounts are given of events that occurred in a particular organization.

KEY TERMS

behavioral sciences: Fields such as psychology and sociology that seek knowledge of human behavior and society through the use of the scientific method.

bureaucracy: An organizational design developed by Max Weber that attempts to make organizations operate efficiently by having a clear hierarchy of authority in which people are required to perform well-defined jobs.

case method: A qualitative research method in which a particular organization is studied in detail, usually in the hopes of being able to learn about organizational functioning in general.

classical organizational theory: An early approach to the study of management that focused on the most efficient way of structuring organizations.

contingency approach: A perspective suggesting that organizational behavior is affected by a large number of interacting factors. How someone will behave is said to be contingent on many different variables at once.

correlation coefficient: A statistical index indicating the degree to which two or more variables are related.

dependent variable: The variable in an experiment that is measured, affected by the impact of the independent variable.

experimental method: An empirical research method in which one or more variables are systematically varied (the independent variables) to determine if such changes have any impact on the behavior of interest (the dependent variables).

human relations movement: A perspective on organizational behavior that recognizes the importance of social processes in work settings.

hypothesis: An unverified prediction concerning the relationships between variables. These propositions may be derived from previous research, existing theory, or informal observation.

independent variable: The factor in an experiment that is systematically varied by the experimenter to determine its impact on behavior (the dependent variable).

multiple regression: A statistical technique

indicating the extent to which each of several variables contributes to accurate predictions of another variable.

naturalistic observation: A qualitative research technique in which an investigator observes events occurring in an organization while attempting to not affect those events by being present.

open systems: Self-sustaining systems that transform input from the external environment into output, which the system then returns to the environment.

organization: A structured social system consisting of groups and individuals working together to meet some agreed-on objectives.

organizational behavior (OB): The field that seeks increased knowledge of all aspects of behavior in organizational settings through the use of the scientific method.

participant observation: Naturalistic observations of an organization made by people who have been hired as employees.

scientific management: An early approach to management and organizational behavior emphasizing the importance of designing jobs as efficiently as possible.

surveys: Questionnaires designed to measure people's perceptions of some aspect of organizational behavior.

theory: Efforts to explain why various events occur as they do. Theories consist of basic concepts and assertions regarding the relationship between them.

Theory X: A traditional philosophy of management suggesting that most people are lazy and irresponsible, and will work hard only when forced to do so.

Theory Y: A philosophy of management suggesting that under the right circumstances, people are capable of working productively and accepting responsibility for their work.

time-and-motion study: A type of applied research, popular during the early twentieth century, designed to classify and streamline the individual movements needed to perform jobs.

QUESTIONS FOR DISCUSSION

1. How can the field of organizational behavior contribute to both the effective functioning of organizations *and* to the well-being of individuals? Are these goals inconsistent? Why or why not?
2. Explain the following statement: "People influence organizations, and organizations influence people."
3. What is the "contingency approach"? Why is it so popular in the field of OB today?
4. Explain how the field of organizational behavior stands to benefit by taking a multicultural, global perspective. What would you say are the major challenges associated with such a perspective?
5. Kurt Lewin, a famous social scientist, once said, "There is nothing as applied as a good theory." Explain how this statement is applicable to the study of organizational behavior.
6. Explain the relative advantages and disadvantages of conducting survey research and experimental research in the field of organizational behavior.
7. Describe a situation in which an organization might decide to hire an organizational behavior specialist as an outside consultant.
8. The Hawthorne studies inadvertently revealed a great deal about behavior in organizations despite flaws in the way the research was conducted. Using your knowledge of the experimental method, describe some of the weaknesses of the Hawthorne studies and ways they might have been alleviated.

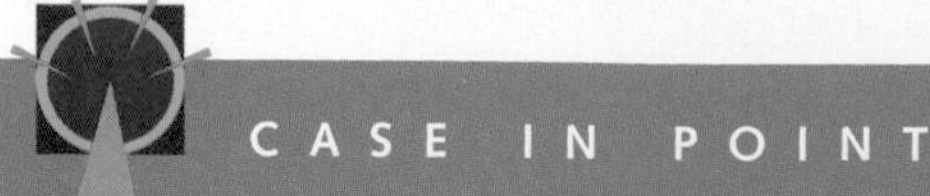

THE LIFE AND TIMES OF ED WAX

Ed Wax looks and sounds like a man who has it all. He has risen to the top of his profession and has achieved great material success. According to Wax, much of his accomplishment can be credited to getting others to work hard.[1] To an outside observer, however, it appears that the real reason for Wax's achievements is his work ethic.

Wax began his career as an engineer with DuPont but soon realized that this wasn't as exciting as he would have liked. After finishing his M.B.A., he began work in the field of advertising with Saatchi and Saatchi Compton Co. His rise through the ranks was direct and rapid. He was promoted through numerous management positions until he was placed in charge of the company's U.S. operations in 1989. This was followed by elevation to the position of chairman of operations of Saatchi and Saatchi Advertising Worldwide (SSAW), a wholly owned subsidiary of Saatchi and Saatchi Company P.L.C. London. SSAW is the second largest advertising agency in the world with 135 offices in 62 different countries and annual billings of over $6 billion.[2]

Wax was promoted to this position with the charge of "rethinking" the traditional workings and structures within an advertising agency. This was necessary because the advertising industry itself was experiencing great turbulence and change. As a result of numerous mergers and acquisitions in which SSAW had participated in the 1970s and 1980s, its leaders felt it was necessary to reorganize the company to avoid duplication of effort as well as to centralize authority. They believed they could achieve great economies of scale, putting together global firms so that advertising could be coordinated worldwide. They also believed that this type of organization could provide consistent services to clients throughout the world.

In order to improve the functioning of the business, Wax found himself in charge of a difficult restructuring. He reports,

Mergers are tough in any business, but in the advertising agency business where it's all people, you're not just merging factories and plants, you're merging living beings. It's not easy because we didn't know each other, you're suspicious of people you don't know, you're afraid to walk down the corridor without looking in a mirror to make sure no one's coming up behind you. Turned out that we were very fortunate, there were terrific people on both sides. Everybody wanted the merger to work and we kept to the promise of taking care of our clients and it worked.[3]

The merger was successful in accomplishing its goals. But the world of advertising hasn't stood still. Consequently, Wax has had to lead the firm in a number of new initiatives. One of these comes as a result of the development of new technologies, creating expanded markets in which advertisers have the opportunity to sell their client's products. SSAW has added the position of "new media specialist" to look into buying time on interactive television channels (e.g., "TV Answer") and on-line computer services (e.g., Prodigy).[4]

Another new direction in which Wax has led the company regards compensation. One goal of this change is to provide incentive to employees to improve their productivity. Another goal is to reduce overall payroll costs while at the same time rewarding top performers. To accomplish these goals, a new pay plan was developed to link top management salaries and bonuses to the performance of local and regional offices as well as to overall company results. Although this new plan meant that some people would receive less money, it was designed so that people who demonstrated more effort and achieved higher levels of performance would be better compensated.[5] Prior to the adoption of this plan, SSAW began a system of paying an "international bonus" to their creative and account workers "based on the quality of their work and its international success." According to Wax, "Agencies of the future really have to not only provide the systems but they have to provide the quality control in the creative area. We don't think it's being done consistently by anyone, including ourselves."[6]

The advertising industry has become so intensely competitive that numerous organizational changes have been implemented by SSAW. The multiple California offices of the company have experimented with various restructuring plans.[7] In addition, SSAW merged with two other large international agencies to form a worldwide network. They did this as a means of re-emphasizing their global marketing strategy and to formalize their working relationships with these other agencies.[8]

CASE IN POINT, Cont.

On his way to the top, Wax emphasized his career over his family. He was concerned with promotions and with working hard. This took a toll on his family that ended in divorce. Although he claims that he was not necessarily ambitious in terms of looking far ahead in his career, he was clearly very focused on his immediate work progress. He also had lots of inner drive and self-confidence developed from years of hard work and handed down from his parents. From his mother he especially learned humor—a characteristic that he credits with helping him weather the storms of failure and success.

Recently remarried, Wax is trying to find ways to balance his commuter marriage. His wife, an executive with Procter & Gamble, works out of the company headquarters in Cincinnati while Wax works from the SSAW main office in New York City. Fortunately, they both travel a great deal for work, so they try to coordinate their business schedules so that they can meet in different cities around the world. Wax admits that it is "a difficult balance," but he maintains that these tradeoffs are necessary for career success. He is happy now to be at the top of his profession and in a new marriage.[9]

QUESTIONS FOR DISCUSSION

1. Identify the elements in this case that have to do with (a) motivation, (b) leadership, and (c) organizational change.
2. Does Ed Wax have a Theory X or a Theory Y orientation toward his employees? What support can you find in the case for your answer?
3. How does open-systems theory account for the many recent changes in the advertising industry?
4. What three major factors seem to impact Wax's managerial philosophy and decision making?

EXPERIENCING ORGANIZATIONAL BEHAVIOR

Organizational Behavior versus Common Sense: A Demonstration

Over the years, we've heard many people remark, "Why do you study that stuff? I knew the answer all along; it's just common sense." Perhaps you're one of these people. If so, take and score the following quiz. We're sure you'll be enlightened.

PROCEDURE

Read each of the statements listed below. For each one, mark whether you believe it is true or false by inserting a *T* (for true) or *F* (for false) in the spaces provided.

____ 1. Relatively few top executives demonstrate the Type A behavior pattern (extreme competitiveness, time urgency, aggressiveness).

____ 2. The proverb, "Two heads are better than one" is generally accurate. That is, groups almost always perform a task better than an individual working alone.

____ 3. The most effective way to combat a rumor is to present convincing evidence against it.

____ 4. When employee morale is high, job performance tends to be high as well.

____ 5. People like being overpaid and work hard to receive more pay than they deserve.

____ 6. When employees are given specific performance goals to shoot for, it tends to interfere with their performance. They generally do better when simply asked to "do your best."

____ 7. The most effective way to get what you want over the long run when negotiating with another is to attempt to defeat your opponent.

____ 8. Most people do their best work under conditions in which they are highly stressed.

____ 9. Effective leaders always act the same way regardless of the situation they face.

____ 10. Most people seek to change the way things are done in their organizations.

POINTS TO CONSIDER

The correct answers to these questions are listed below. How did you do? If you're like most people, you probably missed a few. In fact, you may even be quite surprised at the ones you missed. After all, your own experiences may suggest something other than what we're telling you here.

This leads us to our next point—namely, the answers we provided are really only suggestions. In reality, each of the questions addresses processes so complex that they defy simple "true" or "false" answers. Consider question 4, for example. As we will describe in detail in Chapter 5, although performance *may* be high when morale is high, performance also may be low. In fact, job performance is caused by many factors, and morale alone might contribute very little to how effectively people do their jobs. In other words, because the relationship between morale and performance is so complex, the real answer to the question is, "It depends." In fact, this is really the best answer to all ten questions presented here.

Our intent in presenting this exercise is not to frustrate you, but to demonstrate our main point: where organizational behavior is concerned, there are no simple answers. To rely on what we believe to be true may only be misleading. Systematic scientific inquiries are needed to tap the complexities lying beneath the surface of organizational behavior.

Correct Answers: 1 = T; 2 = F; 3 = F; 4 = F; 5 = F; 6 = F; 7 = F; 8 = F; 9 = F; 10 = F.

PART II

BASIC HUMAN PROCESSES

CHAPTER OUTLINE

SPECIAL SECTIONS

TWO

PERCEPTION AND LEARNING: UNDERSTANDING AND ADAPTING TO THE WORK ENVIRONMENT

LEARNING OBJECTIVES

After reading this chapter, you should be able to

1. *Define* social perception *and indicate its relevance to organizational behavior.*
2. *Explain how we employ* attribution *to understand the causes of others' behavior.*
3. *Describe the process of impression management, and explain how it operates in organizations.*
4. *Indicate how the process of social perception operates in the context of employment interviews and performance appraisals.*
5. *Explain the concept of learning and describe how it operates in organizations.*
6. *Describe the concepts of* operant conditioning *and* observational learning.
7. *Appreciate how principles of learning are involved in organizational programs involving training, organizational behavior management, and discipline.*

Men are born with two eyes, but with one tongue, in order that they should see twice as much as they say.

Charles Caleb Colton, c. 1780–1832
English cleric, sportsman, and wine merchant
Lacon

I praise loudly, I blame softly.

Catherine II ("The Great"), 1729–1796 Empress of Russia
The Complete Works of Catherine II

PREVIEW CASE

Stihl Hones Employees' Skills to the Cutting Edge

At 41 years old, North Carolina native Donald Dowdy saw himself as a "jack of few trades," someone who bounced around from one unskilled, low-paying job to another. A high school graduate who once worked in building maintenance, Dowdy now earns $45,000 a year as a skilled craftsperson at the Virginia Beach, Virginia, plant of Stihl, the German-owned manufacturer of chain saws, lawn trimmers, and blowers. The turnaround in this case is not attributable to anything Dowdy learned while in high school, but rather to Stihl's 8,000-hour work and education program. Combining classroom training at Tidewater Community College (a twenty-eight-credit curriculum in such fields as blueprint reading and industrial mathematics) with intensive shop-floor training by skilled technicians, Stihl has been successful in giving Dowdy—and the others who the company has trained—opportunities to develop valuable new skills.

Stihl's apprentice program was created from a need for skilled labor to help make its high-quality power tools (a chain saw, for example, has as many as 200 parts that are manufactured with tolerances as close as 4 one hundred thousandths of an inch). With difficulty finding enough skilled personnel in Virginia Beach, Stihl decided to "grow its own," and the apprenticeship program was born.

Since the program's inception, the company has been very productive—despite the $500,000 annual cost of training, and a worldwide slump in the sales of chain saws. Specifically, since initiating its apprentice program, Stihl's revenues in the United States have more than doubled (to $200 million), and the annual number of tools produced per employee has risen by over 260 percent (from 800 to 2,100 tools per year). With some 500 employees, compared to only 40 when the plant opened in 1974, Stihl is now Virginia Beach's largest employer. Company officials are convinced that the apprentice program is largely responsible for this growth and success.

An employee in Stihl's apprenticeship program

Stihl has used apprentice graduates to design and build its own custom-made machines (such as a device that automatically assembles lawn trimmers)—manufacturing equipment that is not only easier to use and maintain than off-the-shelf equipment that is retrofitted, but that also requires fewer unskilled laborers to operate. When something goes wrong, Don Dowdy doesn't have to pull out the manual and study a schematic; he helped build the company's machines, so he knows how to fix them. Such expertise doesn't come cheaply, and the program is not without its problems. At an annual cost of $50,000 per employee, Stihl's investment is considerable. Moreover, because there's nothing to stop well-trained employees from leaving Stihl (or being "poached" by competitors), the company's talent pool is quite vulnerable. Another problem is that none of the program's graduates have been women, and only

two have been nonwhite. Justifiably, Stihl officials are concerned that this will tarnish the company's otherwise strong image as an equal opportunity employer.

Completing the program isn't easy for anyone. The courses and the factory work grow tougher and tougher each year, and Stihl officials take no chances that the curriculum will fail to be useful. In fact, they work carefully with the instructors to ensure that trainees are taught exactly what is needed (such as reading blueprints the way it is done in the parent company, Germany's Andreas Stihl, using the metric system). As you might expect, the standards are high. Grades must be kept above C and only one failed course can be made up. Those who flunk out—four so far—usually leave the company out of embarrassment. According to Peter Mueller, Stihl's executive vice president of manufacturing, "It's not the company kicking you out . . . you're kicking yourself out." Clearly, those who don't make it face quite a threat to the way they see themselves. Likewise, those who do make it are viewed quite positively by others, who recognize their considerable achievement. New graduates not only receive a sizable pay raise, but are also rewarded with a college-style ring decorated with the company's logo, a model chain saw, and a stone personalized with their initials. For Don Dowdy, this ring is a clear symbol of his entry into the world of skilled labor.

There can be no doubt that Dowdy's success in Stihl's training program has changed his life. He not only has a new portfolio of job skills, but because of them, he now earns more money and enjoys higher status in the company than he did before. Deep down inside, of course, Don isn't any different. Still, it's likely that he is thought of differently by those who meet him for the first time. What image comes to mind when you think of an unskilled laborer (Don's old position) as opposed to someone in a highly skilled technical position (his new position)? If you don't know someone, you're likely to base your judgments on things you associate with people like them and use these images to create a mental picture of the person in question. In your eyes the unskilled, floundering Don may appear to be quite a different individual than the highly skilled and successful Don. To his friends and family, however, he's probably the same likable guy they knew before—only now full of new technical skills. How is it that different people may see the same person so differently? Clearly, there is an active and complex process going on, a mechanism through which people are able to make sense out of the things they confront in the world around them—the process of **perception**.

Although perception may sound very mysterious, it is really very basic, and extremely valuable when it comes to explaining many different types of situations faced in organizations. For example, think about what goes on when you apply for a job. Your prospective employer attempts to learn about you—based, most likely, on an interview and your résumé—and makes a judgment about what you'd be like as an employee. Will you be lazy or hard working? Do you know how to do the job? At the same time, you are attempting to figure what it would be like to work for that company. Will the boss be pleasant? Will the work be challenging? If hired, you'll be sizing up your new co-workers (Who's nice, and who's going to stab me in the back?) while they do the same to you (What's the new person like?). Then, as time goes on, you'll be evaluated by your superior (How well is this person doing?). Obviously, there's a lot of perceiving going on here. Understanding the complex nature of perceptual processes, basic as they are to human behavior in organizations, is critical to our understanding of OB, and so it will be one of the foci of this chapter.

Equally fundamental is another basic psychological process that is highlighted in our account of Dowdy's experiences at Stihl—**learning**. The apprenticeship program provides a excellent opportunity for Don and Stihl's other trainees to add important new skills to their repertoire. However, learning may involve much more than formally training people in new ways of doing their jobs. The process of learning is also involved in such everyday activities as attaining information about who really has the power in an organization, how to get things done most effectively, who to talk to in the event of a problem, and even what to eat or avoid at the company cafeteria. Principles of learning are also applied in ways designed to help improve the functioning of organizations by systematically doing things that help maintain desirable employee behaviors and reduce undesirable behaviors. In this chapter we will not only explain the psychological processes responsible for learning—that is, how it occurs—but also ways in which these processes are used to improve organizational functioning.

SOCIAL PERCEPTION: THE PROCESS OF UNDERSTANDING OTHERS

There can be no doubt about it—the world around us is a very complex place. At any given moment we are flooded with input from our various senses. Yet we do not respond to the world as a random collection of sights, sounds, smells, and tastes. Rather, we notice order and pattern everywhere. This process of making sense out of the vast array of sensory inputs involves the active processing of information, the process of *perception*. Formally, we may define perception as *the process through which people select, organize, and interpret information.*[1]

To illustrate this process, let's consider an example. Suppose that you meet your new boss. You know her general reputation as a manager, you see the way she looks, hear the words she says, and read the memos she writes. In no time at all, you're trying to figure her out. Will she be easy to work with? Will she like me? Will she do a good job for the company? On the basis of whatever information you have available to you (even if it's very little), you will try to understand her and how you will be affected by her (see Figure 2-1). In other words, you will attempt to combine the various things you learn about her into a meaningful picture. Interestingly, this process is so automatic that we are almost never aware of doing it. Yet it goes on all the time. Clearly, when it comes to understanding the objects and people in our environment, there's a lot more going on than may be obvious.

FIGURE 2-1

MEETING NEW PEOPLE: AN OPPORTUNITY FOR SOCIAL PERCEPTION

Meeting new people presents many opportunities to combine, integrate, and interpret a great deal of information about them—that is, to engage in the process of social perception.

The process of perception is especially important in the field of OB. Indeed, other people—whether they're bosses, co-workers, subordinates, family, or friends—can have profound effects on us. To understand the people around us—to figure out who they are and why they do what they do—may be very helpful to us. After all, you wouldn't want to ask your boss for a raise when you believe he or she is in a bad mood! Clearly, **social perception**—the task of combining, integrating, and interpreting information about others to gain an accurate understanding of them—is very important, especially in organizations.

Several decades of research on social perception suggests that it is a very complex process. One thing we know for certain is that a great deal of the way we perceive other people has to do not only with what those people are actually like, called *subject characteristics*, but also the characteristics and experiences of the people perceiving them, called *perceiver variables*. As an illustration, think about how two people exposed to a person at the same time may form very different impressions. Hearing your new instructor tell lots of funny stories in class, for example, you and a classmate might reach opposite conclusions. You might find him friendly and approachable, whereas your classmate might think he's unprofessional. How can this happen? After all, the instructor is the same person. The answer rests on the fact that our perceptions of other people depend in great part not only on them, but on what we bring to the situation ourselves—our own biases and past experiences (see Figure 2-2).

In the section that follows we will describe two of the most influential perceiver variables: stereotypes and perceptual biases. We will then turn our attention to a critical process involved in social perception—**attribution,** attempts to identify the causes of others' behavior.

PERCEIVER VARIABLES: PERCEPTUAL BIASES AND STEREOTYPES

What predispositions do people have that lead them to perceive others in certain ways? In other words, what is it about perceivers themselves that influences their perceptions of others? Research has shown that two major categories of variables are involved—*perceptual biases*, types of judgment errors that people are prone to make, and *stereotypes*, tendencies to categorize people based on the groups to which they belong.

PERCEPTUAL BIASES: HALO EFFECTS AND SIMILAR-TO-ME EFFECTS

Have you ever heard someone say something like "She's very smart, so she also must be hard working"? Or "He's not too bright, so I guess he's lazy"? If so, then you are already aware of a common perceptual bias known as the **halo effect**. Once

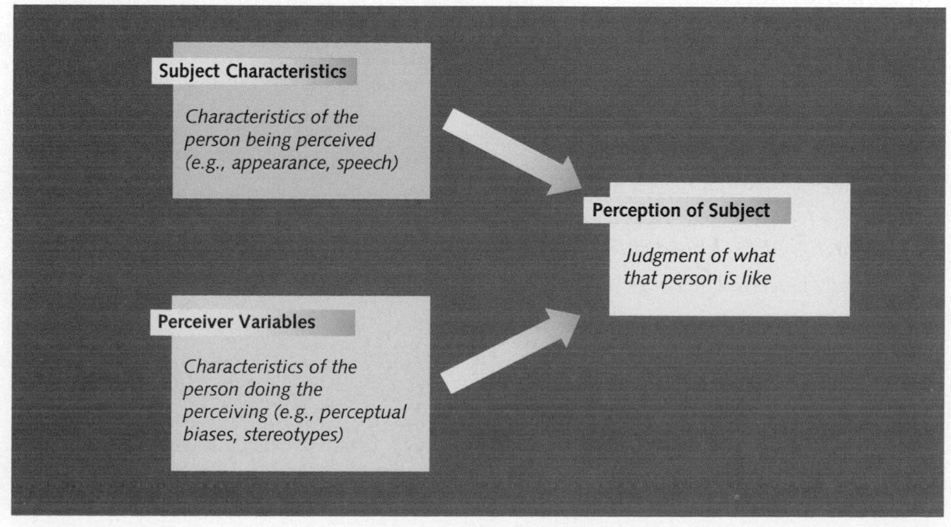

FIGURE 2-2
SOCIAL PERCEPTION: THE RESULT OF SUBJECT CHARACTERISTICS AND PERCEIVER VARIABLES
*Our perceptions of others are based not only on what those people are actually like (*subject characteristics*), but also on our own experiences and characteristics (*perceiver variables*).*

we form a positive impression of someone, we tend to view the things that person does in favorable terms—even things about which we have no knowledge. Similarly, a generally negative impression of someone is likely to be associated with negative evaluations of that person's behavior. Both these tendencies are referred to as halo effects—even the negative case (which is also referred to as the *rusty halo* or *horns* effect). In organizations, the halo effect often occurs when superiors rate subordinates in a formal performance appraisal. In this context, a manager evaluating one of his employees highly on some dimensions may assume that someone so good must also be good at other things, and rate that person highly on other dimensions (see Figure 2-3). Put differently, the halo effect may be responsible for finding high correlations between the ratings given to people on various dimensions.[2] When this occurs, the resulting evaluations lack accuracy, and the quality of the resulting evaluations is compromised.

Another common type of perceptual bias involves the tendency for people to perceive more favorably others who are like themselves than those who are dissimilar. This inclination, known as the **similar-to-me effect**, constitutes a potential source of bias when it comes to judging other people. In fact, research has shown that when superiors rate their subordinates, the more similar the parties are, the higher the rating the superior tends to give.[3] This tendency applies with respect to several different dimensions of similarity—similarity of work values and habits, similarity of beliefs about the way things should be at work, and similarity with respect to demographic variables (such as age, race, gender, and work experience).

This effect appears to be partly the result of the tendency for people to be able to empathize and relate better to similar others, and to be more lenient toward them. However, research by Turban and Jones suggests that more may be involved.[4] Specifically, it appears that subordinates tend to be more trusting and confident in supervisors whom they perceive as similar to themselves than those they perceive as dissimilar. As a result, they may have a more positive relationship, and this may lead superiors to judge similar subordinates in a more favorable light. In other words, similar others may be perceived in a favorable light for several different reasons. Regardless of the underlying explanation for the similar-to-me effect, it is important to recognize its important implications: differences in the way

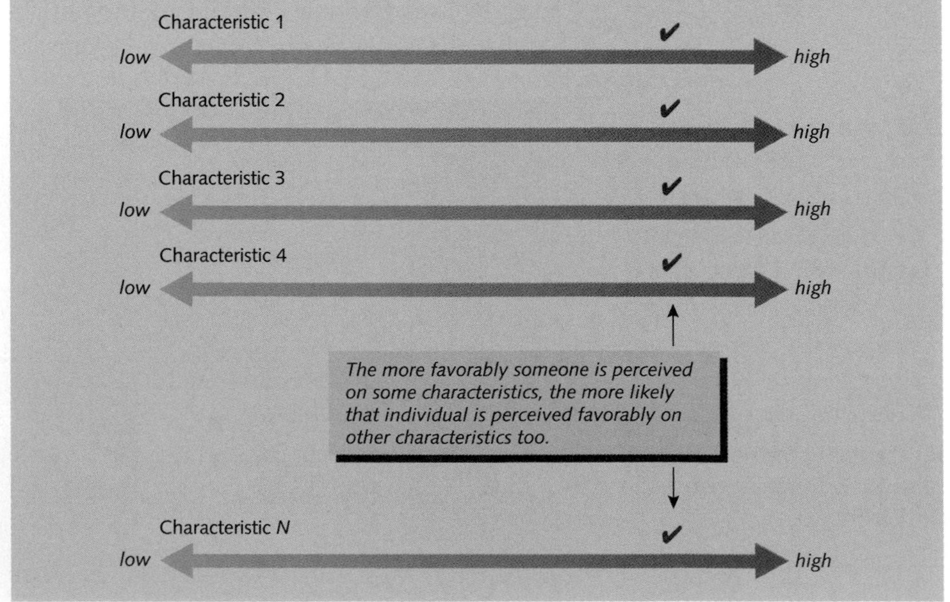

FIGURE 2-3

THE HALO EFFECT: A DEMONSTRATION

One manifestation of the halo effect is the tendency for people rating others to give either consistently high ratings (if the individual is generally perceived in a positive manner), or low ratings (if the individual is generally perceived in a negative manner). Because each rating dimension is not considered independently, inaccurate evaluations may result.

people are perceived are likely to be based in large part on the similarities between the perceiver and the perceived.

STEREOTYPES: FITTING OTHERS INTO CATEGORIES

What comes to mind when you think about people who wear glasses? Are they studious? Eggheads? Although there is no evidence of such a connection, it is interesting to note that for many people, such an image lingers in their minds. Of course, this is only one example. You can probably think of many other commonly held beliefs about the characteristics of specific groups. Such assumptions usually take the form "People from group *X* possess characteristic *Y*." The characteristics described are often quite negative. Assumptions of this type are referred to as **stereotypes**—beliefs that all members of specific groups share similar traits and behaviors.

Deep down inside many of us know, of course, that not all people from a specific group possess the negative characteristics we associate with them. In other words, most of us accept that the stereotypes we use are at least partially inaccurate. After all, not *all X*'s have trait *Y*; there are exceptions (maybe even quite a few!). If so, then why are stereotypes so prevalent? Why do we use them?

To a great extent the answer resides in the fact that people tend to do as little cognitive work as possible when it comes to thinking about others.[5] That is, we tend to rely on mental shortcuts. If assigning people to groups allows us to assume that we know what they are like and how they may act, then we can save the tedious work of learning about them as individuals. After all, we come into contact with so many people that it's impractical—if not impossible—to learn everything about them we need to know. So we rely on readily available information—such as someone's age, race, gender, or job type—as the basis for organizing our perceptions in a coherent way. If you believe that members of group *X* tend to have trait *Y*, then simply observing that someone falls into category *X* becomes the basis for your believing something about that individual (in this case, that he or she possesses trait *Y*). To the extent that the stereotype applies in this case, then the perception will be accurate. However, such mental shorthand often leads us to inaccurate judgments about people—the price we pay for using stereotypes. The problem with our tendency to rely on stereotypes, of course, is that it leads us to judge people prematurely, without the benefit of learning more about them than just the categories into which they fit (see Figure 2-4). Still, we all rely on stereotypes at least sometimes; their temptation is far too great to resist.

It is easy to imagine how the use of stereotypes can have powerful effects on the kinds of judgments people make in organizations. For example, if a personnel officer believes that members of certain groups are lazy, then he purposely may avoid hiring or promoting individuals who belong to those groups. The personnel

FRANK AND ERNEST® by Bob Thaves

FIGURE 2-4
STEREOTYPES: SERIOUS THREATS TO ACCURATE SOCIAL PERCEPTIONS
Our perceptions of others are frequently based solely on knowledge of the groups to which they belong. As the character in this cartoon appears to be aware, such judgments, known as stereotypes, may well be inaccurate. (Source: FRANK AND ERNEST *reprinted by permission of NEA, Inc.)*

officer may firmly believe that he is using good judgment—gathering all the necessary information and listening to the candidate carefully. Still, without being aware of it, the stereotypes he holds may influence the way he judges that person. The result, of course, is that the fate of the individual in question is sealed in advance—not necessarily because of anything he or she may have done or said, but by the mere fact that he or she belongs to a certain group. In other words, even people who are not being intentionally bigoted still may be influenced by the stereotypes they hold.

We realize, of course, that the effects of stereotyping others are not always as profound as they are in our example (in which someone was not hired or promoted). Referring to accountants as "bean counters" and professors as "absent minded" are observations that also reflect stereotypes—ones that appear to be only mildly negative. Still, it must be cautioned that holding stereotypes of people in various groups runs the risk of causing miscommunication and conflict among them (we will say more about this in Chapter 11). Generally speaking, society so strongly disapproves of stereotypes based on some criteria—notably race, gender, religion, physical condition, age, and ethnic identity—that efforts to overcome them in the workplace have been institutionalized in the form of laws.[6] Although stereotypes cannot be outlawed, to the extent that laws can alter behavior, people's attitudes toward various groups may be likely to follow suit (a topic we will consider in more detail in Chapter 5). For example, if because of equal employment laws Americans have increased contact with women in managerial positions, it is possible that they will learn things about females that will weaken the stereotypes they hold. (Because such laws are not in force throughout the world, one may expect that stereotypes about women may be different in various nations. For a closer look at research that illustrates this point, see the Global Organization section below.)

THE GLOBAL ORGANIZATION

CROSS-CULTURAL DIFFERENCES IN SEX ROLE STEREOTYPING

Think about the work-related trait of "initiative." Using a scale ranging from 1 ("not characteristic" to 5 ("characteristic"), how well would you say this describes men in general? How about women in general? How about successful middle managers? Now ask yourself the same three questions with respect to these other characteristics: leadership ability, analytical ability, emotional stablity, aggression, dominance, curiosity, and competence. For some people, the way they think of successful middle managers comes closer to the way they think of men than does the way they think of women. The reason? Sex role stereotypes. Over the years, it has been found that many people—both women and men—think of women as less likely than men to possess the kind of skills needed for managerial success.[7] Not surprisingly, beliefs of this type are considered a barrier to women's entry into management positions. After all, to the extent that people believe women don't "have what it takes" to succeed in management, women are unlikely to be granted admittance to managerial positions. Unfortunately, this barrier is rather strong. But is it universal? That is, does this stereotype hold all over the world?

Attempting to shed light on this question, Schein and Mueller conducted a study much like the exercise just described. In this case, however, people (male and female college students) were asked to consider a much larger number of traits (a total of 92, in fact)—and the judgments were made by people in three countries: Germany, Great Britain, and the United States.[8] In Germany there are fewer women managers than in Great Britain, and in Great Britain, there are fewer women managers than in the United States. Would the participants' different familiarity with female managers make a difference with respect to how women are perceived? To answer this question,

Schein and Mueller compared the correlations between the perceptions of successful managers and men, and those between successful managers and women. The results are summarized in Figure 2-5.

Among Germans, the traditional stereotypical pattern was found—namely, both men and women described men as having characteristics that were closer to those of successful managers than did women. However, the pattern was somewhat different in both Great Britain and the United States. In these nations, men believed that men were more like successful managers than were women, but women did not agree. Although the women in both these nations also closely associated the characteristics of successful managers with men, they closely associated these characteristics with women as well (although not quite as much).

These findings suggest that whereas sex role stereotypes are alive and well among males in all three nations, they appear to be weakening among some women—particularly, among women in nations exposed to female managers (Great Britain and the United States). For these women, the sex role stereotype appears to be breaking down: what it takes to enjoy success as a manager is just about as likely to be recognized among women as it is among men. These findings are both encouraging and discouraging with respect to their implications for breaking down barriers to women in the workplace. Specifically, they show that among men, sex role stereotypes remain alive and well in all three nations. The opportunity to come into contact with female managers has done little to make men in general less sexist in their views toward women. However, women who are exposed to other women in managerial positions (such as in Great Britain and the United States), become *less* stereotyped in their views of women in general. As they see more successful female managers, they describe women and managers using similar terms. However, to the extent that men in power continue to hold these stereotypes, it is possible that barriers to women will remain in organizations.

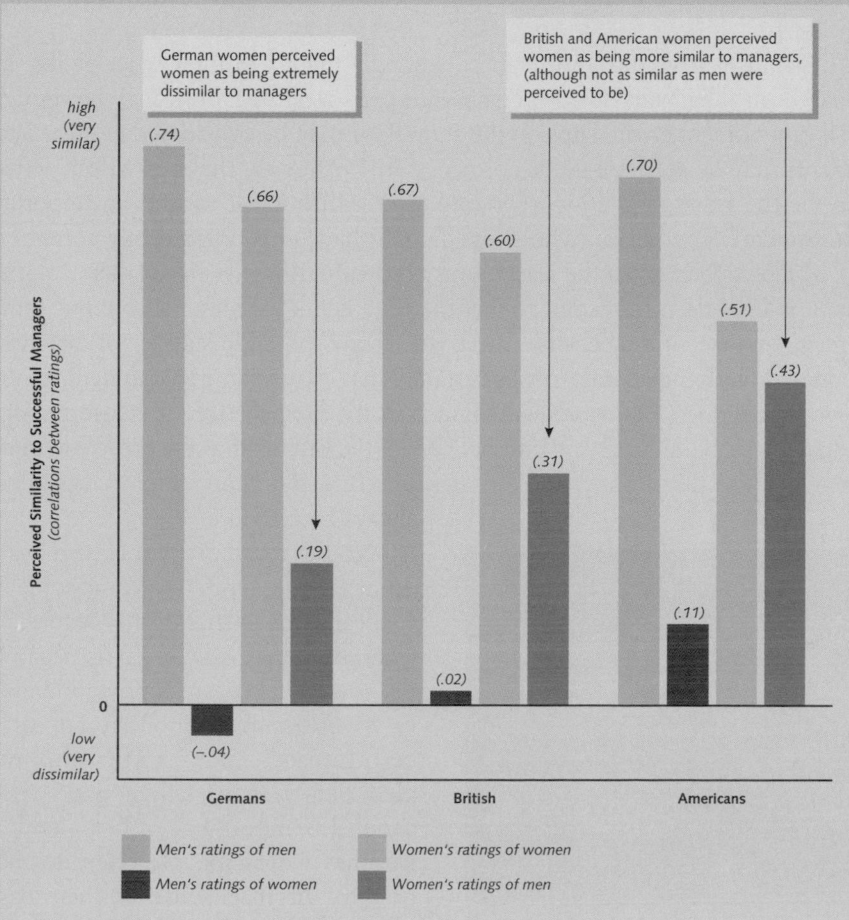

FIGURE 2-5

FEMALE STEREOTYPES: CROSS-CULTURAL DIFFERENCES

Rating men, women, and successful managers, Schein and Mueller found cross-cultural differences in sex role stereotypes. Specifically, whereas German women perceived women in general as being extremely dissimilar to managers, British and American women perceived women as being more similar to managers—although not as similar as men were perceived to be. (Source: Based on data reported by Schein & Muller, 1992; see Note 8.)

ATTRIBUTION: JUDGING THE CAUSES OF OTHERS' BEHAVIOR

A question we often ask about others is "Why?" Why did Ralph goof up the order? Why did the president make the policy he did? When we ask such questions, we're really attempting to get at two different types of information: (1) What is someone really like (that is, what traits and characteristics does he or she possess)? and (2) What made the person behave as he or she did (that is, what accounted for his or her actions)? Research suggests that we attempt to answer these questions in different ways.[9]

MAKING CORRESPONDENT INFERENCES: USING ACTS TO JUDGE DISPOSITIONS

In organizations, situations frequently arise in which we want to know what someone is like. Is your opponent a tough negotiator? Are your co-workers prone to be punctual? The more you know about what people are like, the better equipped you are to know what to expect and how to deal with them. How, precisely, do we go about identifying another's traits? Generally speaking, we do so by observing their behavior and then inferring their traits from this information. The judgments we make about what someone is like based on what we have observed about him or her are known as **correspondent inferences**.[10] Simply put, correspondent inferences are judgments about people's dispositions—their traits and characteristics—that correspond to what we have observed of their actions (see Figure 2-6).

At first blush, it would appear to be a simple matter to infer what people are like, based on their behavior. A person with a disorganized desk may be thought of as sloppy. Someone who slips on the shop floor may be considered clumsy. Such judgments may be accurate—but not necessarily! After all, the messy desk actually may be the result of a co-worker rummaging through it to find an important report. Similarly, the person who slipped could have encountered oily conditions under which anyone, even the least clumsy individual, would have fallen. In other words, it is important to recognize that the judgments we may make about someone may be inaccurate because there are many possible causes of behavior. Someone's underlying characteristics certainly may play a large role in determining what he or she does, but as we will explain in the next section, it is also possible for behavior to be shaped by external forces (in our examples, the co-worker's actions, and the oily floor). For this reason, correspondent inferences may not always be accurate.

FIGURE 2-6
CORRESPONDENT INFERENCES: JUDGING DISPOSITIONS BASED ON BEHAVIOR
One of the ways in which we come to judge what others are like is by making inferences about them that follow from what we have observed of their behavior. Such judgments, known as correspondent inferences, *are frequently misleading. How might the inference summarized here be inaccurate?*

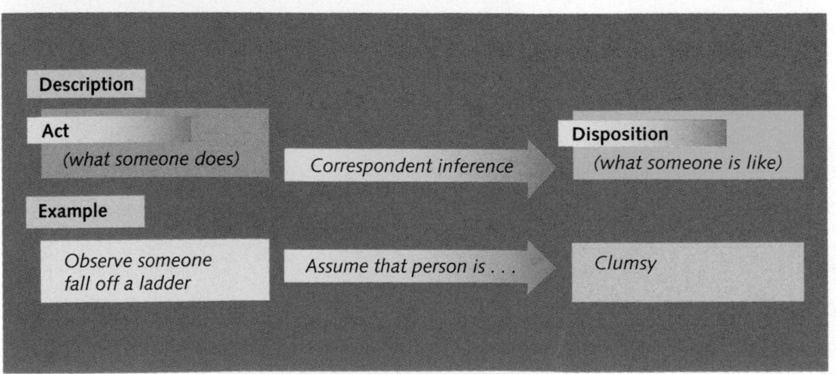

Another reason why this is so has to do with the tendency for people to conceal some of their traits—especially when they may be viewed as negative. So, for example, a sloppy individual may work hard in public to appear to be organized. Likewise, the unprincipled person may talk a good show about the importance of being ethical. In other words, people often do their best to disguise some of their basic traits. In summary, then, due to the facts that (1) behavior is complex and has many different causes, and (2) people sometimes purposely disguise their true characteristics, the making of correspondent inferences is a risky business.

Despite such difficulties, we can use several techniques to help make more accurate correspondent inferences. First, we can focus on others' behavior in situations in which they do not *have to* behave in a pleasant or socially acceptable manner. For example, anyone would behave in a courteous manner toward the president of the company, so when people do so, we don't learn too much about them. However, only those who are *really* courteous would be expected to behave politely toward someone of much lower rank—that is, someone toward whom they don't have to behave politely. In other words, someone who is polite toward the company president, but condescending toward a secretary is probably really arrogant. The way people behave in situations in which a certain behavior is not clearly expected of them may reveal a great deal about their basic traits and motives.

Similarly, we can learn a great deal about someone by focusing on behavior for which there appears to be only one explanation. For example, imagine finding out that your friend accepts a new job. On questioning him, you learn that the position is very high paying, involves interesting work, and is in a desirable location. What have you learned about what's important to your friend? The answer is: not too much. After all, any of these are good reasons to consider taking a position. Now, imagine finding out that the work is very demanding and that the job is in an undesirable location, but that it pays very well. In this case, you're more prone to learn something about your friend—namely, that he or she highly values money. Clearly, the opportunity to make accurate correspondent inferences about people is far greater in situations in which there is only one plausible explanation for their behavior than those in which there are many.

CAUSAL ATTRIBUTION OF RESPONSIBILITY: ANSWERING THE QUESTION "WHY?"

Imagine that it's right before Christmas and your boss just fired one of your fellow employees. Naturally you'd ask yourself, "Why did he do that?" Was it because your co-worker violated a key aspect of the company's code of conduct? Or, was it because the boss is a cruel and heartless person? These two answers to the question "why?" represent two major classes of explanations for the causes of someone's behavior: *internal* causes, explanations based on actions for which the individual is responsible, and *external* causes, explanations based on situations over which the individual has no control. In this case, the internal cause would be the person's violation of the rules, and the external cause would be the boss's cruel and arbitrary behavior.

In this situation, and many others as well, it's important to be able to determine whether an internal or an external cause was responsible for someone's behavior. Knowing why something happened to someone else might better help you prepare for what might happen to you. So, in this case, if you believe that your colleague was fired because of something for which she was responsible herself, such as violating a company rule, then you might not feel as vulnerable as you would if you thought she was fired because of the arbitrary, spiteful nature of your boss. In the latter case, you might decide to take some precautionary actions, to do something to protect yourself from your boss, such as staying on his good side, or even giving up and finding a new job—before you are forced to. The key question of interest to social scientists is: How do people go about judging whether someone's actions were caused by internal or external causes? That is, when do they make internal or external attributions of causality?

An answer to this question is provided by **Kelley's theory of causal attribution**. According to this conceptualization, we base our judgments of internal and external causality on three types of information. First, we consider the extent to which other people behave in the same manner as the person we're judging; this is known as *consensus*. If others do behave similarly, consensus is considered, high; if they do not, consensus is considered low. Second, we consider the extent to which this person acts the same at other times; this is known as *consistency*. If the person acts the same way at other times, consistency is high, if he or she does not, then consistency is low. Third, we consider the extent to which this person behaves in the same manner in other contexts; this is known as *distinctiveness*. If he or she behaves the same way in other situations, distinctiveness is low; if he or she behaves differently, distinctiveness is high. (Keep in mind that a distinctive response is one that is unique, different.) According to the theory, after learning about these three factors, we combine this information to make our attributions of causality.

Here's how. If we learn that other people act like this one (consensus is high), this person behaves in the same manner at other times (consistency is high) and this person does not act in the same manner in other situations (distinctiveness is high), we are likely to conclude that this person's behavior stemmed from external causes. In contrast, imagine learning that other people do not act like this one (consensus is low), this person behaves in the same manner at other times (consistency is high), and this person acts in the same manner in other situations (distinctiveness is low), we will probably conclude that this person's behavior stemmed from internal causes.

Since this explanation was, admittedly, somewhat abstract, let's consider an example that helps illustrate how the process works. Imagine that you're at a business lunch with several of your company's sales representatives when the sales manager makes some critical remarks about the restaurant's food and service. Further, imagine that no one else in your party acts this way (consensus is low), you have heard her say the same things during other visits to the restaurant (consistency is high), and that you have seen her acting critically in other settings, such as the regional sales meeting (distinctiveness is low). What would you conclude in this situation? Probably that her behavior stems from internal causes. In other words, she is a "picky" person, someone who is difficult to please.

Now imagine the same setting, but with different observations. Suppose that several other members of your group also complain about the restaurant (consensus is high), that you have seen this person complain in the same restaurant at other times (consistency is high), but that you have never seen her complain about anything else before (distinctiveness is high). By contrast, in this case, you probably would conclude that the sales manager's behavior stems from external causes: the restaurant really *is* inferior. For a summary of these contrasting conclusions, see Figure 2-7.

A large body of evidence suggests that people really do think about others, and the causes behind their actions, in this way.[11] However, it is important to be aware of two important qualifications. First, people don't always engage in the kind of elaborate thought processes we described here. Instead, they tend to do so only when they are faced with unexpected actions by others—ones they cannot readily explain.[12]

Second, people are not equally predisposed to reach judgments regarding internal and external causality; they are more likely to explain others' actions in terms

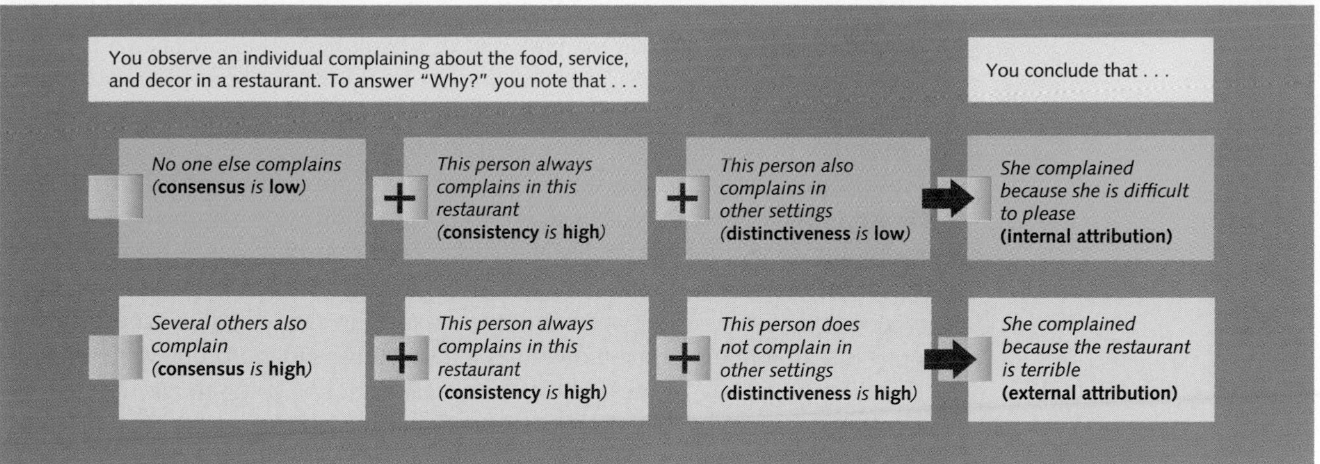

FIGURE 2-7

KELLEY'S THEORY OF CAUSAL ATTRIBUTION: A SUMMARY

In determining whether others' behavior stems mainly from internal or external causes, we focus on the three types of information illustrated here.

of internal rather than external causes. In other words, we are prone to assume that others' behavior is due to the way they are, their traits and dispositions (e.g., "She's that kind of person"). For example, we are more likely to assume that someone who shows up for work late does so because she is lazy rather than because she got caught in traffic. This tendency is so strong that it has been referred to as the **fundamental attribution error**.[13] Its presence derives from the fact that it is easier to explain others' actions in terms of discrete traits than in terms of a complex pattern of situational factors that also may have affected their actions.

Unfortunately, this tendency can be quite damaging in organizations. Specifically, it leads us to prematurely assume that people are responsible for the negative things that happen to them (e.g., "He wrecked the company car because he is careless"), without considering external alternatives, ones that may be less damning (e.g., "Another driver hit the car"). Moreover, because we assume that behavior is based on people's internal characteristics, we are likely to expect greater consistency from them than we should. As a result, we may be unpleasantly surprised when they appear to act "out of character" in some situation, possibly contributing to tension and conflict.

For many years scientists have relied on Kelley's theory of causal attribution as a tool for understanding individual perceptions. Recently, however, Moussavi and Evans expanded this approach to the interorganizational level.[14] Specifically, they theorized that top managers in one organization, termed the *stakeholder organization*, may observe and make attributions about the causes underlying the actions of another organization, termed the *focal organization*. For example, consider how members of a community group (the stakeholder organization in this case) might react when they learn that, after being pressured to do so, a local bank (the focal organization) has committed substantial funds to low-interest housing loans in a poor neighborhood. Moussavi and Evans theorized that top managers from the stakeholder organization would attempt to answer the question "Why did the focal organization behave as it did?" in a manner analogous to the way individual attributions are made.

Specifically, building on Kelley's theory, they postulated that consensus, consistency, and distinctiveness would come into play. For example, they would look for answers to three questions: (1) Have other banks also made low-interest loans available in this neighborhood (consensus)? (2) Has this bank instituted such a program in the past (consistency)? and (3) Has this bank acted in a socially responsible manner in response to other types of demands from the community (distinctiveness)? If all three factors are judged to be high (that is, other banks acted similarly, this bank instituted such programs in the past, and this bank has not established a record of socially responsible lending), then managers of the community group will likely assume that the bank's actions were the results of external factors—in this case, the demands it put on the bank. However, if no other banks took such action (low consensus), this bank acted this way previously (high consistency), and the bank has a record of socially responsible action in other situations (low distinctiveness), then community group leaders are likely to make internal attributions—that is, the bank is concerned about the well-being of the community.

A unique aspect of the attribution process in the case of groups and organizations is that although some individuals may perceive situations one way or another, others may disagree. As a result, if an organization is going to reach a *collective attribution* (that is, a shared explanation about why things occurred as they did) then it is necessary for the group's attribution to be openly discussed—and, if there's disagreement, for it to be negotiated. To the extent that information about consensus, consistency, and distinctiveness are perfectly clear, there are unlikely to be disagreements, and the group's attribution will be identical to the individuals' attributions. However, when the available information is equivocal (as may often be the case), then the most powerful individuals in the group are likely to have the greatest effect on determining the group's attribution (we will have more to say about the use of power in Chapter 12). In short, Moussavi and Evans have encouraged us to think about the attribution process in ways that go beyond the realm of pure cognition, extending into the dynamics of social interaction in organizations.

PERCEIVING OTHERS: ORGANIZATIONAL APPLICATIONS

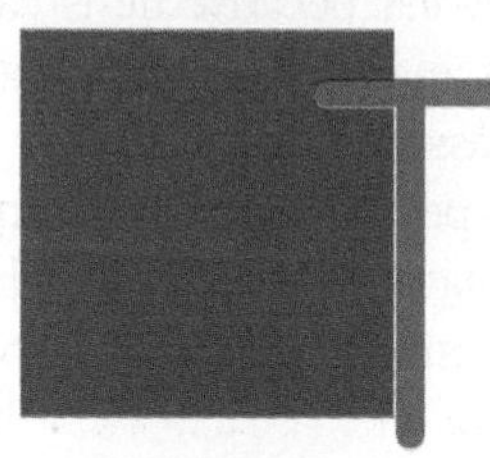

Thus far, we have identified some of the basic processes of social perception, and have referred to them as being critically involved in organizational behavior. Now, in this section we will make explicit some of the ways in which the processes by which we perceive others are involved in arenas of organizational functioning—the employment interview and the performance appraisal.

IMPRESSION MANAGEMENT: MARKETING ONESELF IN THE EMPLOYMENT INTERVIEW AND ELSEWHERE

The desire to make a favorable impression on others is universal. In one way or another, we all do things to attempt to control how other people will see us, often attempting to get them to think of us in the best light possible. The employment interview is one organizational context in which this process, known as **impression management**, is busily at work.[15]

The impressions prospective employers form of us may be based on subtle behaviors, such as how we dress and speak, or more elaborate acts, such as announcing our accomplishments.[16] They may be the result of calculated efforts to get others to think of us in a certain way, or be the passive, unintended effects of our actions.[17] Impression management might involve direct attempts to make ourselves look better—*self-enhancing* behaviors (such as improving one's appearance, and "name dropping," claiming associations with highly regarded others), as well as attempts to make others feel better about themselves—*other-enhancing* behaviors (such as by flattering them, and showing your approval for the things they say).[18] As you might imagine, how effectively people manage impressions not only has a great impact on their success in getting a job, but their entire careers.[19] We will now consider some of the ways in which this occurs.

One thing we know is that the things people do to create favorable impressions also have beneficial effects on their relationships with others. For example, it has been found that supervisors feel better toward those subordinates who are successful at cultivating positive impressions (such as by using self- and other-enhancing tactics) than those who are less skilled at doing so. Not surprisingly, supervisors also enjoy friendlier and more open communication links with such individuals.[20] Similarly, it has been found that subordinates who engage in impression management efforts are more liked by their supervisors, and such liking, in turn, enhances the quality of the social interaction between them.[21]

Attempting to look good to others may take its toll on the accuracy of the information communicated. After all, someone attempting to make a favorable impression on another may refrain from sharing the complete story, especially when doing so threatens to uncover some negative information with which the person may be associated. Fandt and Ferris demonstrated this effect in a study in which customer service employees in a telecommunications company were asked to make decisions about a particular kind of problem they might face—a power failure on a hot summer afternoon.[22] In documenting their actions in such a situation, the employees studied reported significantly more positive and less negative information (that is, information that made them look best) when they believed they were going to be held accountable for the way they chose to solve the problem than when they believed they were not going to be accountable. As you might imagine, such distortions of the facts may have a critical impact on the quality of decisions made in organizations. To summarize, whereas efforts at impression management may improve the quality of social functioning in organizations, such actions may occur at the cost of information accuracy and high-quality decision making (we will more closely examine the process of decision making in Chapter 10).

This is not to say that the effects of all impression management techniques run counter to organizational well-being. Indeed, it is quite possible for some impression management behaviors to have a beneficial impact on both individual employees and their organizations. A good example of this is *feedback seeking*, the soliciting of advice and guidance about one's work, attempting to get answers to the question "How am I doing?" Naturally, efforts at correcting misguided work may be beneficial to organizational functioning (see Chapter 6). What may be less clear, however, is that these same actions also help cultivate positive impressions on one's superiors. In a recent study, Ashford and Northcraft found that people generally were nervous about seeking feedback, and refrained from doing so when they believed others were attempting to discover the kind of people they really were.[23] However, these reactions were not justified. The researchers' follow-up study found that managers held more *positive* impressions of employees—particularly superior ones—who sought feedback regarding their performance than those who did not. Apparently, the act of seeking feedback is perceived as an attempt to improve one's performance, and those who do so are recognized for their efforts in this connection—especially when it involves making a good employee even better.

Thus far, we have focused exclusively on the impressions created by individuals. However, we also may look at the impressions made by organizations as a whole—what has been termed *corporate image*.[24] As you might imagine, the impression an organization makes on people can have a considerable effect on the way they relate to it. In the context of job recruitment, not only do candidates want to make good impressions on prospective employers, but employers want their job offers to be accepted by the best candidates!

The importance of a corporate image in this context has been demonstrated in a recent study by Gatewood, Gowam, and Lautenschlager.[25] These researchers found that a company's image is strongly related to people's interest in seeking employment with it. Specifically, the more favorably a company's reputation was rated (based on a *Fortune* magazine survey), the more interested a group of college seniors was in working there. This is important insofar as organizations must effectively recruit prospective employees to function effectively. Given this important correlate of corporate image, it is worthwhile to consider exactly what factors contribute to a corporate image. Interestingly, Gatewood and his colleagues found that a company's image was positively correlated with the amount of information people had about it (such as from recruitment ads in a college placement guide, and from previous work experiences). In general, longer ads were associated with more positive images. This finding is likely the result of not only what is in the ad but also the mere length of the ad itself. Specifically, because recruitment ads emphasize the benefits of employment with a firm, longer ads describe more benefits than shorter ones, thereby creating even stronger positive images. Moreover, to the extent that people believe that longer ads reflect a company's commitment to obtaining good employees (by their willingness to invest in a large ad), they may be more impressed with a company as a prospective place to work. Regardless of the explanation, the overall conclusion is clear: organizations, just like individuals, stand to benefit by making positive impressions.

PERFORMANCE APPRAISALS: MAKING FORMAL JUDGMENTS ABOUT OTHERS

One of the most obvious instances in which social perception occurs is when someone formally evaluates the job performance of another. This process, known as **performance appraisal**, occurs in organizations—often on an annual or semi-annual basis—for purposes of determining raises, promotions, and training needs.[26] Ideally, this process should be completely rational, leading to unbiased and objective judgments about exactly how well each employee performed, and how he or she should be treated. However, based on what we have said about perception thus far, you're probably not surprised to learn that the performance evaluation process is far from objective. Indeed, people have a limited capacity to process, store and retrieve information, making them prone to bias when it comes to evaluating others (see Figure 2-8).[27]

One such bias is reflected by the tendency for people to evaluate others in terms of their own expectations of their performance. Suppose, for example, you are supervising two individuals who are performing equally well at this point in time. Rationally, you should give them equal performance ratings. However, a study by Hogan suggests that people might not actually do so.[28] The participants in this study were bank managers who completed questionnaires on two occasions four months apart. The first time, they were asked to indicate how well they expected their newest tellers to do on the job. Then, four months later, they were asked to rate the tellers' actual job performance. Managers gave higher ratings to individuals whose performance matched their expectations than to those who did either better or worse than predicted. These effects are unsettling insofar as they suggest that the improved performance of some employees may go unrecognized—or, worse yet, be downgraded! Of course, to the extent that human resource management decisions are made on the basis of several sources of information, besides judgments by a single superior, it is unlikely that such biased judgments may go uncorrected. Nonetheless,

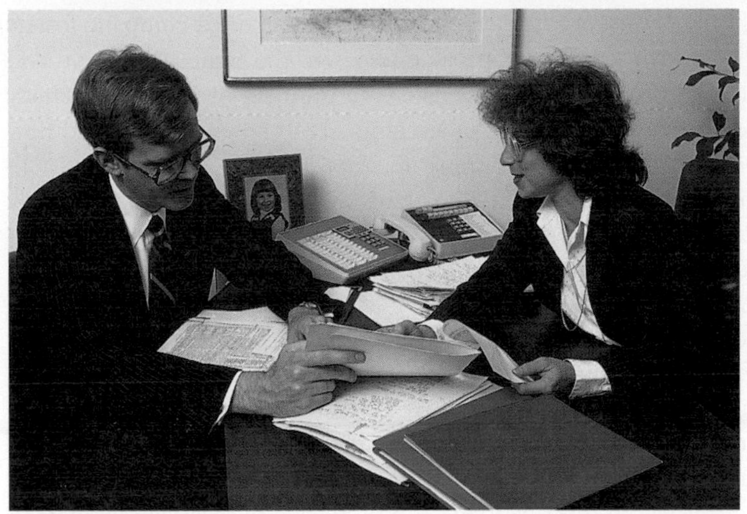

FIGURE 2-8
PERFORMANCE APPRAISAL: CAN IT BE UNBIASED?
Despite people's best efforts at accurately appraising others' performance, various attributional biases are likely to make the process less than objective.

Hogan's findings clearly underscore a point we made earlier—namely, that perceptions are based on characteristics not only of the person being perceived, but on those of the perceiver as well.

This conclusion is supported by research showing several different attribution biases in evaluations of job performance. To illustrate one of these, recall our earlier discussion of the general tendency for people to attribute others' behavior to internal causes, the fundamental attribution error. In the context of performance evaluations, this effect appears to be qualified by the nature of the relationship between the rater (the perceiver, in this case) and the ratee (the person being perceived). Specifically, it has been found that when superiors rate subordinates they like, they are more likely to recognize the internal causes of their behavior (such as effort and ability) than when they rate disliked subordinates.[29] In other words, people are more willing to make flattering attributions (e.g., they did well because they work hard) toward people they like. This reluctance to credit the good performance of disliked others to internal causes (i.e., the unwillingness to flatter them in this way) is particularly distressing when you consider that we rely on internal attributions of performance as the basis for evaluating job performance. For example, research has found that two equally good employees do *not* receive the same performance ratings when different attributions are made about the underlying causes of their performance.[30] Instead, we tend to give higher ratings to individuals whose poor performance we attribute to factors outside their control (e.g., someone who may be trying hard, but who is too inexperienced to perform at an acceptable level) than to those we believe are capable of better performance, but who are purposely holding back (e.g., a highly talented but lazy person). Findings such as these illustrate our point that organizational performance evaluations are far from the unbiased, rational procedures one would hope to find. Instead, they represent a complex mix of perceptual biases—effects that must be appreciated and firmly understood if we are to have any chance of ultimately improving the accuracy of the performance evaluation process.

LEARNING: ADAPTING TO THE WORLD OF WORK

Recall our Preview Case: the story of a man whose image in the eyes of others changed as a result of his successful completion of Stihl's apprentice program. Thus far, we have focused on one of the basic human processes involved in this case—perception, the process of understanding what other people are like. Now we will turn our attention to the other basic psychological process involved in this case—**learning**. Whether we're talking about how a person develops new job skills (in this case, how a technician at Stihl learns to operate new machinery), social skills (such as how to interact with others), or general life skills (such as how to read or write), many of the same basic processes are involved. Clearly, learning is a fundamental process in organizational behavior. In fact, learning has been considered such a critical process in organizations that it has been closely linked to the successful operation of organizations. Specifically, recent research has shown that the more a company fosters an environment in which employees are able to learn, the more productive and profitable it is likely to be.[31] Naturally, scientists in the field of OB are extremely interested in understanding the process of learning—both how it occurs, and how it may be applied to the effective functioning of organizations.

Before we turn our attention to these matters, we should first explain exactly what we mean by learning. Specifically, we define learning as *a relatively permanent change in behavior occurring as a result of experience*.[32] Despite its simplicity, several aspects of this definition bear pointing out. First, it's clear that learning requires that some kind of change occur. Second, this change must be more than just temporary. Finally, it must be the result of experience—that is, continued contact with the world around us. Given this definition, we cannot say that short-lived performance changes on the job, such as those due to illness or fatigue, are the result of learning. Learning is a difficult concept for scientists to study because it cannot be directly observed. Instead, it must be inferred on the basis of relatively permanent changes in behavior.

We will now consider two of the most prevalent forms of learning that occur in organizations—operant conditioning and observational learning.

OPERANT CONDITIONING: LEARNING THROUGH REWARDS AND PUNISHMENTS

Imagine you are a copywriter working at an advertising agency where you are assigned to an important new client. If you can write the perfect radio script for Fluffy Detergent, the company stands a good chance of adding a huge new account. You work hard at doing the best job possible and present your work to the anxiously awaiting client. Now, how does the story end? If the client loves your script, your grateful boss gives you a huge raise and a promotion. If the client hates it, your boss gives you two weeks' notice to vacate your office. Regardless of which of these outcomes occur, one thing is certain: whatever you did in this situation, you will be sure to do it again *if* it was successful, or to avoid doing it again *if* it failed.

This story nicely illustrates an important principle of **operant conditioning** (also known as **instrumental conditioning**)—namely, that our behavior produces consequences and that how we behave in the future will depend on what those consequences are. If our actions have pleasant effects, then we will be more likely to repeat them in the future. If, however, our actions have unpleasant effects, we are less likely to repeat them in the future. This phenomenon, known as the **law of effect**, is fundamental to operant conditioning.[33] Our knowledge of this phenomenon comes from the work of the famous social scientist B. F. Skinner. Skinner's pioneering research (initially with animals, although also with humans—including his own daughter) has shown us that it is through the connections between our actions and their consequences that we learn to behave in certain ways.[34] In Figure 2-9 we summarize this process and give an example of it.

FIGURE 2-9
THE OPERANT CONDITIONING PROCESS: AN OVERVIEW

The basic premise of operant conditioning *is that people learn by connecting the consequences of their behavior with the behavior itself. In this example, the manager's praise increases the subordinate's tendency to perform the job properly in the future. Learning occurs by providing the appropriate antecedents and consequences.*

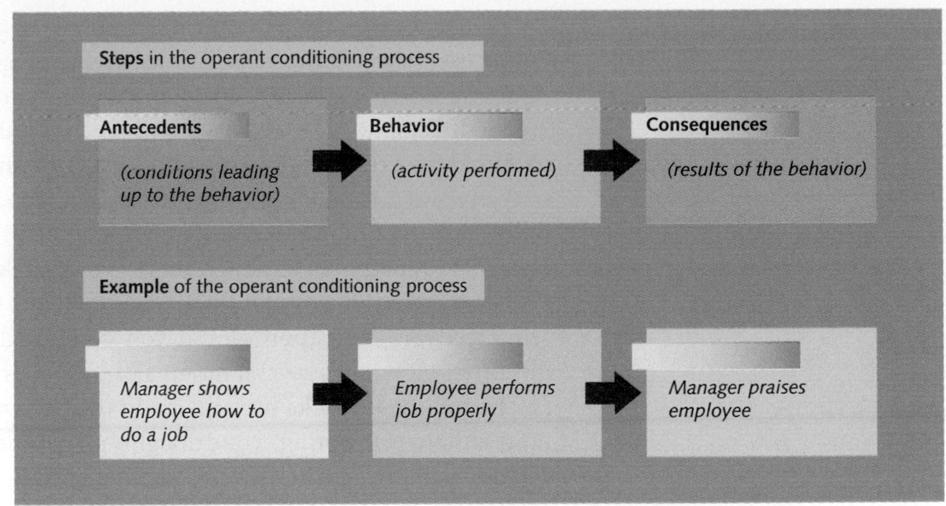

REINFORCEMENT CONTINGENCIES: LEARNING FROM THE EFFECTS OF OUR ACTIONS

As noted above, we learn to engage in behaviors that have positive results, actions leading to pleasurable outcomes. In organizations, for example, people usually find it pleasant and desirable to receive monetary bonuses, paid vacations, and various forms of recognition. The process by which people learn to perform acts leading to such desirable outcomes is known as **positive reinforcement**. Whatever behavior led to the positive outcomes are likely to occur again, thereby strengthening that behavior. For a reward to serve as a positive reinforcer, it must be made contingent on the specific behavior sought. So, for example, if a sales representative is given a bonus after landing a huge account, the bonus will only reinforce the person's actions *if* he or she associates it with the landing of the account. When this occurs, the individual will be more inclined in the future to do whatever it was that helped get the account. Consider the example that opened this section—the one in which you were an advertising copywriter. If your script is well received, you will be inclined to try using the same approach on other campaigns. The fact that it was positively reinforced—that is, linked to desired rewards—"teaches" you to make that same response again.

Sometimes we also learn to perform acts because they permit us to avoid undesirable consequences. Unpleasant events, such as reprimands, rejection, probation, and termination are some of the consequences faced for certain negative actions in the workplace. The process by which people learn to perform acts leading to the avoidance of such undesirable consequences is known as **negative reinforcement**, or **avoidance**. Whatever response led to the termination of these undesirable events is likely to occur again, thereby strengthening that response. For example, you may stay late at the office one evening to revise a sales presentation because you believe that the boss will "chew you out" if it's not ready in the morning.[35] You learned how to avoid this type of aversive situation, and behave accordingly.

Thus far, we have identified responses that are strengthened—either because they lead to positive consequences, or the termination of negative consequences. However, the connection between a behavior and its consequences is not always strengthened; such links also may be weakened. This is what happens in the case of **punishment**. Punishment involves presenting an undesirable or aversive consequence in response to an unwanted behavior. A behavior accompanied by an undesirable outcome is less likely to recur if the person associates the negative consequences with the behavior. For example, if you are chastised by your boss for taking excessively long coffee breaks, you are considered punished for this action. As a result, you will be less likely to take long breaks again in the future.

The link between a behavior and its consequences also may be weakened by withholding a reward—a process known as **extinction**. When a response that was once rewarded is no longer rewarded, it tends to weaken and eventually die out—or be *extinguished*. Let's consider an example. Suppose for many months you brought several boxes of doughnuts to your weekly staff meetings. Your colleagues always thanked you profusely as they gobbled them down. You were positively reinforced by their approval, so you continued bringing the doughnuts to the meetings. Now, after several months of this, your colleagues are beginning to realize the toll these snacks have taken on their waistlines and have begun dieting. So now, although tempting, your doughnuts go uneaten—a testimonial to your colleagues' willpower. After several months of no longer being praised for your generosity, you will be unlikely to continue bringing doughnuts. Your once-rewarded behavior will die out; it will be extinguished.

The various relationships between a person's behavior and the consequences resulting from it—*positive reinforcement, negative reinforcement, punishment,* and *extinction*—are known collectively as **contingencies of reinforcement**. They represent the conditions under which rewards and punishments will either be given or taken away. The four contingencies we discussed are summarized in Table 2-1. As we will see later in this chapter, administering these contingencies can be an effective tool for managing behavior in organizations.

SCHEDULES OF REINFORCEMENT: PATTERNS OF ADMINISTERING REWARDS

Psychologists have identified several different **schedules of reinforcement**—rules governing the timing and frequency of the administration of reinforcement. Thus far, our discussion of whether a reward will be presented or withdrawn has

TABLE 2-1

Contingencies of Reinforcement: A Summary

The four reinforcement contingencies may be defined in terms of the presentation or withdrawal of a pleasant or unpleasant stimulus. Positively or negatively reinforced behaviors are strengthened; punished or extinguished behaviors are weakened.

STIMULUS PRESENTED OR WITHDRAWN	DESIRABILITY OF STIMULUS	NAME OF CONTINGENCY	STRENGTH OF RESPONSE	EXAMPLE
Presented	*Pleasant*	*Positive reinforcement*	*Increases*	*Praise from a supervisor encourages continuing the praised behavior*
	Unpleasant	*Punishment*	*Decreases*	*Criticism from a supervisor discourages enacting the punished behavior*
Withdrawn	*Pleasant*	*Extinction*	*Decreases*	*Failing to praise a helpful act reduces the odds of helping in the future*
	Unpleasant	*Negative reinforcement*	*Increases*	*Future criticism is avoided by doing whatever the supervisor wants*

assumed that the presentation or withdrawal will follow each occurrence of behavior. However, it is not always practical (or, as we will see, advisable) to do this. Rewarding *every* desired response made is called **continuous reinforcement**. Unlike animals performing tricks in a circus, people on the job are rarely reinforced continuously. Instead, organizational rewards tend to be administered following **partial** (or **intermittent**) **reinforcement** schedules. That is, rewards are administered intermittently, with some desired responses reinforced and others not. Four varieties of partial reinforcement schedules have direct application to organizations.[36]

1. **Fixed-interval schedules** are those in which reinforcement is administered the first time the desired behavior occurs after a specific amount of time has passed. For example, the practice of issuing paychecks each Friday at 3:00 P.M. is an example of a fixed-interval schedule insofar as the rewards are administered at regular times. Fixed-interval schedules are not especially effective in maintaining desired behavior. For example, employees who know that their boss will pass by their desks every day at 11:30 A.M. will make sure they are working hard at that time. However, without the boss around to praise them, they may take an early lunch or otherwise work less hard because they know that they will not be positively reinforced for their efforts or punished for not working.

2. **Variable-interval schedules** are those in which a variable amount of time (based on some average amount) must elapse between the administration of reinforcements. For example, consider a bank auditor who pays surprise visits to the branch offices an average of every six weeks (e.g., visits may be four weeks apart one time, and eight weeks apart another time). The auditor may be said to be using a variable-interval schedule. Because the bank managers cannot tell exactly when their branch may be audited, they cannot afford to slack off. Another inspection may be closer than they think! Not surprisingly, variable-interval schedules tend to be more effective than fixed-interval schedules.

3. **Fixed-ratio schedules** are those in which reinforcement is administered the first time the desired behavior occurs after a specified number of such actions have been performed. For example, suppose members of a sales staff know that they will receive a bonus for each $1,000 worth of goods they sell. Immediately after receiving the first reward, performance may slack off. But as their sales begin to approach $2,000, the next level at which reward is expected, performance will once again improve.

4. **Variable-ratio schedules** are those in which a variable number of desired responses (based on some average amount) must elapse between the administration of reinforcements. A classic example may be seen in the behavior of people playing slot machines. Most of the time when people put a coin into the slot they lose. But, after some unknown number of plays, the machine will pay off. Because gamblers can never tell which pull of the handle will win the jackpot, they are likely to keep on playing for a long time. As you might imagine, variable-ratio schedules tend to be more effective than fixed-ratio schedules.

The various schedules of reinforcement we described here have a number of important similarities and differences. We have summarized these in Table 2-2. As you review this table, it is important to keep in mind that these schedules represent "pure" forms. Used in practice, several different reinforcement schedules may be combined, making complex new schedules. Still, whether they operate separately or

TABLE 2-2

Schedules of Reinforcement: A Summary

The four schedules of reinforcement summarized here represent different ways of systematically administering reinforcements intermittently (i.e., according to a partial reinforcement schedule).

SCHEDULE OF REINFORCEMENT	DESCRIPTION	EXAMPLE
Fixed interval	*Rewards given after a constant amount of time has passed*	*Pay check given the same time each week*
Variable interval	*Rewards given after a variable amount of time has passed*	*Bank auditor visits branch offices an average of once every eight weeks, but not on a fixed schedule*
Fixed ratio	*Rewards given after a constant number of actions performed*	*Pay of $1 is given for every five boxes of fruit picked and packed*
Variable ratio	*Rewards given after a variable number of actions performed*	*A slot machine pays a jackpot, on average, one time per million plays*

in conjunction with one another, it is important to recognize the strong influences that schedules of reinforcement can have on people's behavior in organizations.

OBSERVATIONAL LEARNING: LEARNING BY IMITATING OTHERS

Although operant conditioning is based on the idea that we engage in behaviors for which we are directly reinforced, many of the things we learn on the job are *not* directly reinforced. Suppose, for example, on your new job you see many of your co-workers complimenting your boss on his attire. Each time someone says something flattering, the boss stops at his or her desk, smiles, and acts friendly. By complimenting the boss, they are reinforced by being granted his social approval. Chances are, after observing this several times, you too will eventually learn to say something nice to the boss. Although you may not have directly experienced the boss's approval, you would expect to receive it based on what you have observed from others. This is an example of a kind of learning known as **observational learning**, or **modeling**.[37] It occurs when someone acquires new knowledge *vicariously*—that is, by observing what happens to others. The person whose behavior is imitated is referred to as the *model*. For someone to learn by observing a model, several processes must occur. These are summarized in Figure 2-10.

First, the learner must pay careful *attention* to the model—the greater the attention, the more effective the learning will be. To facilitate learning, models sometimes call attention to themselves. This is what happens when supervisors admonish their subordinates to "pay close attention" to what they're doing. Second, people must have good *retention* of the model's behavior. It helps to be able to develop a verbal description or a mental image of someone's actions in order to remember them. After all, we cannot learn from observing behavior we cannot remember. Third,

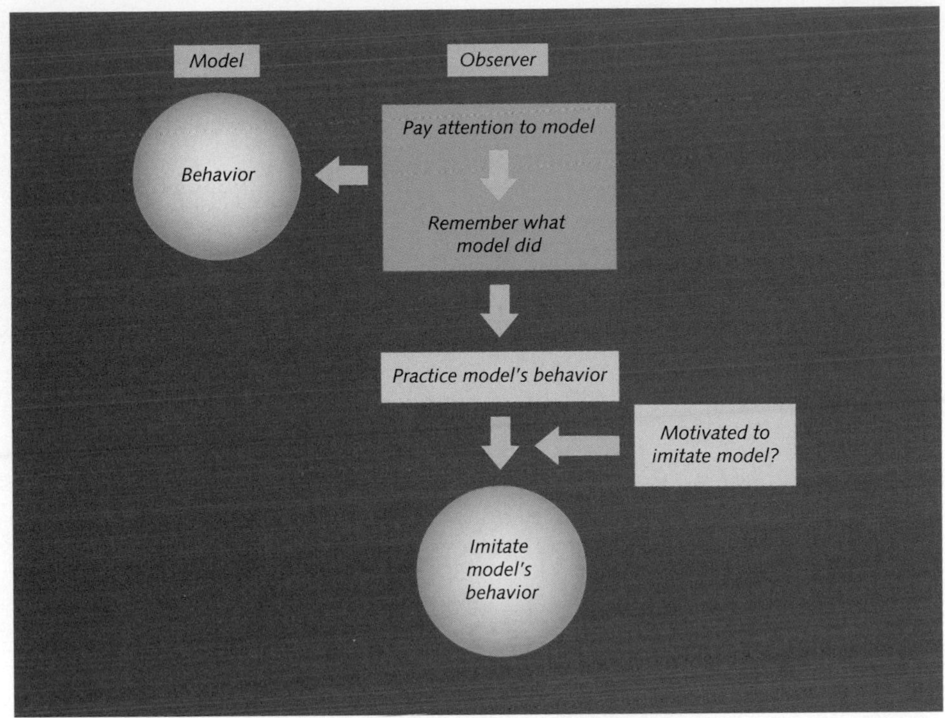

FIGURE 2-10
OBSERVATIONAL LEARNING: AN OVERVIEW
The process of observational learning requires that an observer pay attention to and remember a model's behavior. By observing what the model did and rehearsing those actions, the observer may learn to imitate the model, but only if the observer is motivated to do so (i.e., if the model was rewarded for behaving as observed).

there must be some *behavioral reproduction* of the model's behavior. Unless people are capable of doing exactly what the models do, they will not be able to learn from observing them. Naturally, this ability may be limited at first, but may improve with practice. Finally, people must have some *motivation* to learn from the model. Of course, we don't emulate every behavior we see, but focus on those we have some reason or incentive to match—such as actions for which others are rewarded.

A great deal of what is learned about how to behave in organizations can be explained as the result of the process of observational learning.[38] On the job, observational learning is a key part of many formal job instruction training programs.[39] As we will explain in the next section, trainees given a chance to observe experts doing their jobs, followed by an opportunity to practice the desired skills, and receive feedback on their work, tend to learn new job skills quite effectively. Observational learning also occurs in a very informal, uncalculated manner. For example, people who experience the norms and traditions of their organizations and who subsequently incorporate these into their own behavior may be recognized as having learned through observation (we describe this process of "learning the ropes" in organizations more fully in Chapter 6). It is important to note that people learn not only what to do by observing others, but also what *not* to do. Specifically, research has shown that people observing their co-workers getting punished for behaving inappropriately on the job tend to refrain from engaging in those same actions themselves.[40] As you might imagine, this is a very effective way for people to learn how to behave—and, without ever experiencing any displeasure themselves. (For a closer examination of this process, and evidence regarding the perceived fairness of using discipline to punish unethical behavior, please refer to The Ethical Workplace section beginning on the next page.)

OBSERVERS' REACTIONS TO DISCIPLINING UNETHICAL BEHAVIOR: THE FAIRNESS OF MAKING THE PUNISHMENT FIT THE CRIME

When an employee is disciplined for some wrongdoing, it is not only he or she who is affected, but potentially everyone in the organization who becomes aware of the use of punishment. In fact, general knowledge of an organization's use of discipline may be expected to have a sobering effect on the entire organization—leading in some cases to performance improvements—as employees fear what might happen to them as their employers flex their corporate muscles.[41] Will observers believe their employer acted fairly when someone is punished? This is an important question. After all, using punishment sends a clear message to all about the organization's tolerance for unethical behavior.

A recent study by Trevino and Ball examined how people respond when others are punished for behaving unethically.[42] The major question they asked was this: Will people believe it is fair or unfair for others to be punished for their unethical actions? Trevino and Ball reasoned that the answer would depend on the extent to which the punishment given fit the crime—that is, how appropriate the punishment was believed to be for the infraction committed. To test this idea, they studied a group of MBA students who participated in a laboratory experiment. Participants in the study were asked to respond to a series of memos and letters presented to them in the form of papers appearing in an in-basket. Among these was a company newsletter and a memo to them describing two incidents of unethical behavior that occurred in the company: (1) a case of serious sexual harassment, and (2) a manager's substitution of unsafe, substandard wiring in one of the company's products. Both actions were clearly against company policy.

The company's reaction to these incidents was presented in three systematically different ways, one to each of three randomly selected groups of people from the research sample. In the *appropriate punishment condition* those behaving unethically were described as having been suspended without pay for a period of one week. In the *harsh punishment condition,* the rule violators were said to be dismissed from the company and legal action was taken. Finally, in the *no punishment condition*, participants were informed that the company took no action in response to these unethical behaviors. (In advance of this project the researchers empirically established that a one-week suspension was considered appropriate, whereas the dismissal was considered overly harsh, and no action was considered overly lenient.) Participants were asked to judge how fair it was for the company to punish the individual who acted unethically.

The results, summarized in Figure 2-11, show that in general, the harshest punishment was considered the most fair whereas the most lenient response (no punishment at all) was considered least fair. However, the results were somewhat different depending on the nature of the unethical action. In the case of substandard wiring, people believed it was no less fair to suspend perpetrators than to fire them; both responses were considered fairer than doing nothing. However, when it came to people accused of sexual harassment, participants believed that the harshest response was the fairest. In fact, the "harsh" punishment was judged to be fairer than the "appropriate" punishment in this case. Although one might expect an "appropriate" response to be fairest, it appears that the so-called harsh response used in this study was not really harsh enough to suit those judging someone accused of sexual harassment. The researchers interpret this finding as showing that the type of discipline appropriate for sexual harassment is greater than that needed to fairly punish someone accused of substituting substandard wiring.

Although the participants in this study were responding to hypothetical situations (which lowers the extent to which the results may be generalizable outside the laboratory), the findings are still potentially useful in several ways. First, they underscore the idea that the effects of punishment may be expected to extend beyond those who are directly punished. By punishing unethical acts, organizations are sending clear messages as to how serious they are about not tolerating breaches of ethics. Second, this experiment demonstrates that people are sensitive to the fairness of using different punishment for different ethics violations. Although we cannot say exactly what punishment is believed to be fair for every crime, Trevino and Ball's findings suggest that the perceived fairness of punishment depends on the extent to which it is believed to be appropriate for the crime.

FIGURE 2-11

TAILORING THE PUNISHMENT TO FIT THE CRIME: AN EXPERIMENTAL DEMONSTRATION

Participants in a study by Trevino and Ball judged the fairness of various punishments given to people committing different infractions of company rules. The harshest punishment was considered more fair when given to someone accused of sexual harassment than someone accused of using substandard wiring in a company product. (Source: Based on data reported by Trevino & Ball, 1992; see Note 42.)

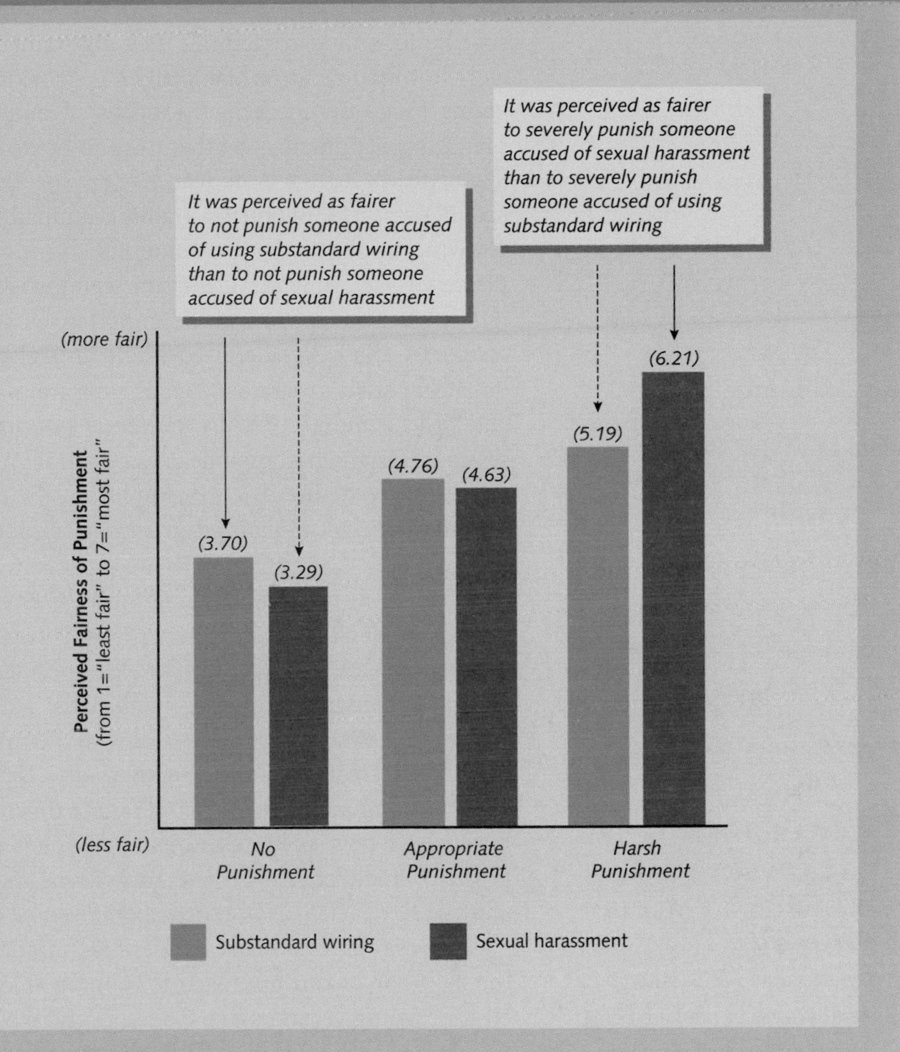

APPLICATIONS OF LEARNING IN ORGANIZATIONS

The principles of learning we have discussed thus far are used in organizations in many different ways. We will now discuss three systematic approaches to incorporating learning in organizations: *training, organizational behavior management,* and *discipline.*

TRAINING: LEARNING AND DEVELOPING JOB SKILLS

Probably the most obvious use to which principles of learning may be applied in organizations is **training**—that is, the process through which people systematically acquire and improve the skills and abilities needed to better their job performance. Just as students learn basic educational skills in the classroom, employees must learn their job skills. Training is used not only to prepare newly hired employees to meet the challenges of the jobs they will face, but also to upgrade and refine the skills of existing employees. Sometimes people are trained to perform specific jobs, and sometimes they are trained in skills that are not used immediately but may prove valuable at some later time. In either case, good training programs focus on meeting the needs of employees and their organizations, and preparing people for jobs that need to be done—both today and tomorrow.

According to the American Society for Training and Development, companies spend over $44 billion on training annually.[43] Such training takes many forms. Growing in popularity are apprenticeship programs (such as used by Stihl in our Preview Case), in which classroom training is systematically combined with on-the-job instruction. In view of the importance of such programs in developing human resources, the U.S. federal government lately has invested hundreds of millions of dollars in such programs, encouraging training partnerships between government and private industry.[44] Also currently popular are executive training programs—sessions in which companies systematically attempt to develop the skills of their top managers, either by bringing in outside experts to train them in-house, or by sending them to specialized programs conducted by colleges and universities (see Figure 2-12).[45] Such programs are especially popular in getting people to be effective leaders in rapidly changing business environments (we will more thoroughly discuss leadership in Chapter 13, and organizational change in Chapter 16).[46] Employees may be trained to develop specific job-related skills, such as how to use computer software, or more general skills, such as how to get along with others.[47,48] The large Japanese firm Sanyo trains new employees in its air-conditioning division to be more creative by showing them how to build a simple clay flute.[49] Of course, most training methods are neither quite this unusual, nor are they always as formal as those we have been describing. Training is also involved in everyday job instruction in which employees are told about the job, instructed how to do it, and allowed to practice as a more experienced co-worker watches on.

Why are there so many different techniques? The answer rests, in large part, on the fact that no one approach to training is ideal. Some techniques are better suited to learning certain skills than are others because they incorporate more principles of learning than do others. Not surprisingly, the best training programs often use many different approaches, thereby assuring that several different learning principles may be incorporated into training.[50] If you recall some of the ways you learned skills such as how to study, drive, or use a word processor, you probably can appreciate some of the principles that help make training effective. Four major principles are most relevant.

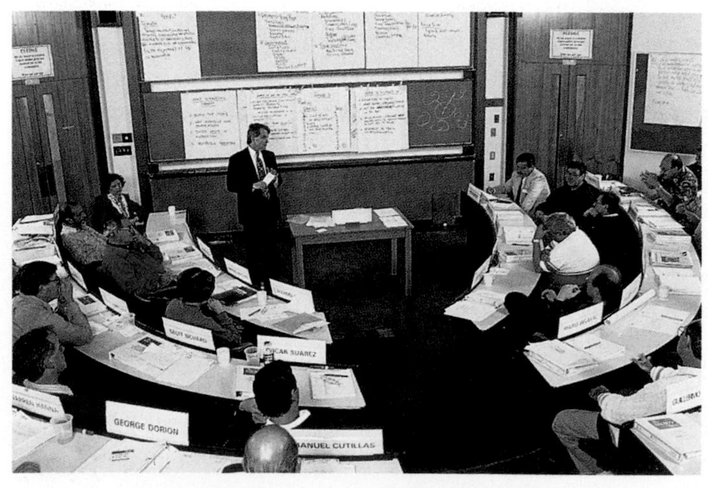

FIGURE 2-12
EXECUTIVE EDUCATION: TRAINING TODAY FOR TOMORROW'S SUCCESS
Top executives at Bacardi, a manufacturer of rum, are being trained by professors at the University of Virginia's Darden School of Business in ways of improving the company's global business strategy.

1. **Participation.** It has been well established that people not only learn more quickly, but also retain the skills longer when they have actively *participated* in the learning process. This applies to the learning of both motor tasks as well as cognitive skills. For example, when learning to swim, there's no substitute for actually getting in the water and moving your arms and legs. In the classroom, students who listen attentively to lectures, think about the material, and get involved in discussions tend to learn more effectively than those who just sit passively.

2. **Repetition.** If you know the old adage "Practice makes perfect," you are already aware of the benefits of repetition for learning. Perhaps you learned the multiplication table, or a poem, or a foreign language phrase by going over it repeatedly. Scientists have not only established the benefits of *repetition* on learning, but have shown that these effects are even greater when practice is spread out over time than when it is lumped together. After all, when practice periods are too long, learning can suffer from fatigue, whereas learning a little bit at a time allows the material to sink in. Although it would be useful to be able to state exactly how long one should practice and how long one should rest in order to learn most effectively, research has shown that a simple answer is not possible; a lot depends on the nature of the task and the skills of the people involved.[51] Despite this complexity, a general conclusion is clear: practice spaced repeatedly over time is more effective in promoting learning over the long term than is practice crammed into short periods without rest.

3. **Transfer of training**. As you might imagine, for training to be most effective, what is learned during training must be applied to the job. In general, the more closely a training program matches the demands of a job, the more effective the training will be.[52] Unfortunately, opportunities for *transfer of training* don't always exist. For example, a recent study in a military organization revealed that only half the skills people learned while training were actually used within the first four months on the job.[53] Still, many training programs are designed so as to provide direct opportunities for learning to transfer from training sessions to actual job situations. A good example is the elaborate simulation devices used to train pilots and astronauts. At a more down-to-earth level is the equipment used in many technical schools for people to learn skilled trades such as welding, computer repair, and radiation technology. Interestingly, transfer of training tends to be more effective among trainees who understand that their job skills may erode if they do not stay current than those have no such knowledge.[54] In sum, for training to be most effective, not only must the opportunities for transfer of training be in place, but the need for training benefits to transfer also must be appreciated.

4. **Feedback**. It is extremely difficult for learning to occur in the absence of *feedback*—that is, knowledge of the results of one's actions. Feedback provides information about the effectiveness of one's training.[55] Of course, unless you learn what you already are doing well and what behaviors you need to correct, you will probably be unable to improve your skills. If you've ever played golf or pitched a baseball, you probably know quite well just how useful feedback can be in helping to correct your actions (e.g., if the ball goes too far to one side or another, you must adjust your grip and stance). Feedback is equally useful on the job. For example, to gauge their improvement it is critical for people being trained as word processing operators to know exactly how many words they correctly entered per minute.

In sum, these four principles—*participation, repetition, transfer of training,* and *feedback*—are the key to the effectiveness of any training program. The most effective training programs are those that incorporate as many of these principles as possible. (Given the importance of training in today's competitive business environment, several companies are going beyond most others in the training they do. For a closer look at some particularly impressive examples, please see the Quest for Quality section beginning on the next page.)

THE QUEST FOR QUALITY

EMPLOYEE TRAINING: COMPANIES AT THE HEAD OF THE CLASS

Despite the obvious importance of training human resources to meet the ever-growing technical demands of today's workplace, job training remains the exception rather than the rule in most organizations. In fact, only five companies out of one thousand (a mere 15,000) account for 90 percent of all the training done in the United States. Among these are several companies, both large and small, that devote considerable resources to training their employees—and that benefit greatly as a result.[56]

At the top of the list is Motorola, a company that spent $120 million on employee education in 1992 alone (a year in which its sales reached a record $13.3 billion). That same year, the company's training arm, known as "Motorola University," delivered 102,000 training days to its employees, customers, and suppliers at its branches in Phoenix, Arizona and Austin, Texas. According to the university's president, William Wiggenhorn, "When you buy a piece of equipment, you set aside a percentage for maintenance. Shouldn't you do the same for people?" Indeed, the company does just that. Motorola uses engineers, scientists, and former managers to teach most of its courses. These range from coverage of people-related skills (e.g., communication and teamwork) to technical skills (e.g., advanced statistical techniques). Company officials credit Motorola's training investment for much of its recent success. Specifically, it has been calculated that each dollar Motorola spends on training brings $30 in increased productivity over three years. In the words of materials manager Karney Yakmalian, "Other companies talk about quality, but Motorola gives you the tools."

Federal Express is another company that has made a sizable investment in employee training. For example, at least once a year, all 40,000 of the company's couriers and customer service agents use interactive computer programs to test their job knowledge. Some employees, such as couriers specializing in handling dangerous goods, are tested every six months to determine if they are up to date on the latest company policies and governmental regulations. Computerized exams containing 90 questions are used to identify areas in which employees need remedial action. A record of employee skills is maintained on the computer, and this information is considered when employees are reviewed for promotion. According to Larry McMahan, Federal Express's vice president of human resources, this training regimen is greatly responsible for improving the company's index of customer complaints (which in 1992 reached its lowest level ever).

A very different, but equally effective approach is taken by Corning at its Erwin, New York, ceramics plant (see Figure 2-13). Here, employees are trained in the classroom and on the job—in formal apprentice programs (similar to the one used by Stihl described in our Preview Case) in which they become certified as specialists in working with Celcor, a clay-based product used in catalytic converters. To reach that stage takes about two years of training (with the equivalent of one day per week in the classroom) and demonstrated competency on a series of tests. On being certified, employees receive increases of 20 percent in their hourly pay. Training director Everett Larson explains that "There's a heavy up-front cost in training, but the payback is quite impressive." That benefit has come to Corning in the form of increased productivity and reduced waste as well as a 38 percent drop in product defects in 1992 alone. Although those trained to work with Celcor are special, they are not unique with respect to Corning's overall commitment to training. In fact all Corning employees are expected to spend 5 percent of their work time in training—averaging 92 hours (almost 2–1/2 workweeks) per employee each year.

Although that figure is high overall, Corning is by no means alone in making such a heavy investment in training. Several other companies are equally involved in training their employees—and not all of them are corporate giants. Consider, for example, Chicago's Wm. Dudek Manufacturing Co., a family-owned business of 35 employees that makes small clips and clasps used in manufacturing appliances and automobiles. Although Dudek employees know how to operate their machines, most of them are immigrants who lack skills in basic English and math. Working with instructors at Northern Illinois University, Dudek began training its workforce to develop these skills so they could learn what they needed to know to meet specifications and fill out order forms. This is clearly a very basic first step toward improving quality. Training, whether it's basic skills or more advanced knowledge, is critical to the success of organizations—especially in these competitive times when resources are tight. In the words of W. J. Conaty, an official at General Electric's Aircraft Engine division, "When an industry is in turmoil, productivity and people become the name of the game. That's where we get our edge." Clearly, training is the steel that hones this edge.

FIGURE 2-13

CLASSROOM TRAINING AT CORNING

Formal training programs help employees of Corning, Inc. develop the skills needed to produce a broad range of new ceramic and glass products. The company's considerable investment in human resources has led to remarkable improvements in productivity.

ORGANIZATIONAL BEHAVIOR MANAGEMENT: POSITIVELY REINFORCING DESIRABLE ORGANIZATIONAL BEHAVIORS

Earlier, in describing operant conditioning, we noted that the consequences of behavior determines whether we repeat it or abandon it. Behaviors that are rewarded tend to be strengthened, repeated in the future. With this in mind, it is possible to administer rewards selectively to help reinforce desirable behaviors. This is the basic principle behind **organizational behavior management** (also known as **organizational behavior modification**, or more simply, **OB mod**). Organizational behavior management may be defined as *the systematic application of positive reinforcement principles in organizational settings for the purpose of raising the incidence of desirable organizational behaviors.*

To be effective in using organizational behavior management programs, managers should follow certain steps.[57] The first step is to *pinpoint the desired behaviors.* That is, they should specify exactly what they want done differently (e.g., saying that they want to answer customers' inquiries 50 percent quicker, instead of saying that they want to improve customer service). Second, *perform a baseline audit.* In other words, they should determine exactly how well people perform the behavior they wish to change (e.g., how quickly do they currently answer calls?). Third, *define a criterion standard.* Exactly what performance goal is being sought? For example, should all calls be answered within the first 30 seconds?

After all this is done, we are ready to begin the reinforcement process. Thus, the fourth step is to *choose a reinforcer*. Exactly how will the desired behavior be rewarded? Will service agents be given a bonus for answering all calls received in a month within 30 seconds? Praise is an effective reinforcer in organizations, and an inexpensive one at that!

Fifth, it is considered useful to *selectively reward desired behaviors that approximate the criterion standard.* In other words, the learning process may be facilitated by rewarding behaviors that come close to the desired level. So, for example, if agents are answering calls within 60 seconds, their progress should be rewarded a little. But after a while, reward should only be given after the 50-second level is reached, then the 40-second level, and so on. The process of selectively reinforcing a behavior that approaches a goal is known as **shaping**. This technique, frequently used in training animals to perform tricks, applies equally well to teaching human beings to perform a desired behavior.

Finally, after the desired goal has been attained, it is considered useful to *periodically re-evaluate the program*. Is the goal behavior still being performed? Are the rewards still working? Changes in these events over time should be expected. As a result, administrators of behavior management programs will carefully monitor the behaviors they worked so hard to develop.

Over the years, organizational behavior management programs have been used successfully to stimulate a variety of behaviors in many different organizations (see summary in Table 2-3).[58,59] For example, a particularly interesting and effective program has been used in recent years at Diamond International, the Palmer, Massachusetts, company of 325 employees that manufactures Styrofoam egg cartons.[60] In response to sluggish productivity, a simple but elegant reinforcement was put into place. Any employee working for a full year without an industrial accident is given 20 points. Perfect attendance is given 25 points. Once a year, the points are totaled. When employees reach 100 points, they get a blue nylon jacket with the company's logo on it and a patch identifying their membership in the "100 Club." Those earning still more points receive extra awards. For example, at 500 points, employees can select any of a number of small household appliances (e.g., a blender, a set of cookware, or a wall clock). Although these are certainly very inexpensive prizes, they go a long way toward symbolizing the company's appreciation for their good work.

This program has helped improve productivity dramatically at Diamond International. Compared to before the reinforcement program began, output improved 16.5 percent, quality-related errors dropped 40 percent, grievances

TABLE 2-3

Organizational Behavior Management Programs: Some Success Stories

Although not all organizational behavior management programs are as successful as the ones summarized here, many have been extremely effective in bringing about improvements in desired behaviors.

COMPANY	REINFORCERS USED	RESULTS
General Electric	*Praise and constructive reinforcement*	*Productivity increased, cost savings resulted*
Weyerhaeuser	*Contingent pay, and praise or recognition*	*Productivity increased in most work groups (by 18–33 percent)*
B. F. Goodrich Chemical	*Praise and recognition*	*Production increased more than 300 percent*
Connecticut General Life Insurance	*Time off based on performance*	*Chronic absenteeism and lateness were drastically reduced*
General Mills	*Praise and feedback for meeting objectives*	*Sales increased*

Sources: Based on material appearing in Hamner & Hamner, 1976, Note 58; and Frederiksen, 1982, Note 59.

decreased 72 percent, and time lost due to accidents was lowered by 43.7 percent. The result of all of this has been over $1 million in gross financial benefits from the company—and a much happier workforce. Needless to say, this has been a very simple and effective organizational behavior management program. Although not all such programs are equally successful, evidence suggests that they are generally quite beneficial.[61]

DISCIPLINE: ELIMINATING UNDESIRABLE ORGANIZATIONAL BEHAVIORS

Just as organizations systematically may use rewards to encourage desirable behavior, they also may use punishment to discourage undesirable behavior. Problems such as absenteeism, lateness, theft, and substance abuse cost companies vast sums of money, situations many companies attempt to manage by using **discipline**—the systematic administration of punishment.[62] By administering an unpleasant outcome (e.g., suspension without pay) in response to an undesirable behavior (e.g., excessive tardiness), companies seek to minimize the undesirable behavior. In one form or another, using discipline is a relatively common practice. Survey research has shown, in fact, that 83 percent of companies use some form of discipline, or at least the threat of discipline, in response to undesirable behaviors.[63] But, as you might imagine, disciplinary actions taken in organizations vary greatly. At one extreme, they may be very formal, such as written warnings that become part of the employee's permanent record. At the other extreme, they may be informal and low key, such as friendly reminders and off-the-record discussions between supervisors and their problem subordinates.

An interesting field study by Beyer and Trice reported the frequency with which different types of disciplinary actions were taken by a large sample of managers in dealing with their problem subordinates (a large proportion of whom had alcohol addiction problems).[64] They found that 95 percent of the managers first discussed the problem informally with their subordinates, with most of the discussions covering both constructive topics (e.g., ways to get help) and confrontational topics (e.g., possible disciplinary actions). More formal, and more punitive, written warnings were given by 49 percent of the managers. Suspension without pay (for an average of 4 days) was used by 27 percent of the managers. Finally, only 3 percent fired the problem workers.

The organization studied in this research used punishment *progressively*—that is, starting mildly, and then increasing in severity with each successive infraction. This is the idea behind **progressive discipline**—the practice of basing punishment on the frequency and severity of the infraction.[65] Let's consider an example of how progressive discipline might work for a common problem such as chronic absenteeism or tardiness. First, the supervisor may give the employee an informal oral warning. Then, if the problem persists, there would be an official meeting with the supervisor, during which time a formal warning would be issued. The next offense would result in a formal written warning that becomes part of the employee's personnel record. Subsequent offenses would lead to suspension without pay. And finally, if all this failed, the employee would be terminated. In the case of more serious offenses—such as gambling, for example—some of the preliminary steps would be dropped, and a formal written warning would be given. For the most serious offenses, such as stealing or intentionally damaging company property, officials would move immediately to the most severe step, immediate dismissal.

Companies with the most effective disciplinary programs tend to make the contingencies clear, such as by publicizing punishment rules in the company handbook. When this is done, employees know exactly what kind of behaviors the company will not tolerate, often minimizing the need to actually use discipline at all. It probably comes as no surprise to you that supervisors do not always punish all inappropriate behaviors they encounter.[66] A key reason for this is that supervisors may feel constrained by limitations imposed by labor unions or by their own lack of formal authority. Also, in the absence of a clear company policy about how to use discipline, supervisors may fear strong negative emotional reactions from the punished individual, if not also revenge and retaliation. As a result, many supervisors may look the other way, and simply do nothing when employees behave inappropriately. Although doing nothing may be easy, in the long run ignoring chronic problems is a way of informally approving of them, leading to increasingly serious problems in the future. With this in mind, companies with the best disciplinary programs make it a practice to take immediate action. At Honda of America, for example, human resource specialist Tim Garrett notes that the company pays very close attention to all infractions of the rules, including ones "that other companies wouldn't think of paying attention to," adding "if there's a problem, we'll pay attention to it right away." [67]

Obviously, it isn't easy to know exactly when and how to administer punishment, and how it can be done in a way that is considered fair and reasonable. Fortunately, research and theory have pointed to some effective principles that may be followed to maximize the effectiveness of discipline in organizations.[68] We will now consider several of these key principles.

1. *Deliver punishment immediately after the undesirable response occurs.* The less time that passes between the occurrence of an undesirable behavior and the administration of a negative consequence, the more strongly people will make the connection between them. When people make this association, the consequence is likely to serve as a punishment, thereby reducing the probability of the unwanted behavior. With this principle in mind, it is best for managers to talk to their subordinates about their undesirable behaviors immediately after committing them (or, at least as soon thereafter as may be practical). Expressing disapproval after several days or weeks have gone by will be less effective, since the passage of time will weaken the association between behavior and its consequences.

2. *Give moderate levels of punishment—nothing too high or too low.* If the consequences for performing an undesirable action are not very severe (e.g., rolling one's eyes as a show of disapproval), then it is unlikely to operate as a punishment. After all, it is quite easy to live with such a mild response. In contrast, consequences that are overly severe might be perceived as unfair and inhumane.[69] When this occurs, not only might the individual resign, but also, a strong signal will be sent to others about the unreasonableness of the company's actions. In either case, the company risks losing its most valuable assets—its human resources.

3. *Punish the undesirable behavior, not the person.* Good punishment is impersonal in nature, and focuses on the individual's actions rather than his or her personality. So, for example, when addressing an employee who is repeatedly caught taking excessively long breaks it is unwise to say, "You're lazy and have a bad attitude." Instead, it would be better to say, "By not being at your desk when expected, you're making it more difficult for all of us to get our work

done on time." Responding in this manner will be less humiliating for the individual, making the discussion far less unpleasant. In addition, focusing on exactly what people can do to avoid such disapproval (taking shorter breaks, in this case) increases the likelihood that they will attempt to alter their behavior in the desired fashion. In contrast, the person who feels personally attacked might not only "tune out" the message, but not know exactly how to improve.

4. *Use punishment consistently—all the time, for all employees*. Sometimes, managers attempting to be lenient turn a blind eye to infractions of company rules. Doing this may cause more harm than good insofar as it inadvertently reinforces the undesirable behavior (by demonstrating that one can get away with breaking the rules). As a result, it is considered most effective to administer punishment after each occurrence of an undesirable behavior. Similarly, it is important to show consistency in the treatment of all employees. In other words, everyone who commits the same infraction should be punished the same way, regardless of the person administering the punishment. When this occurs, supervisors are unlikely to be accused of showing favoritism. Also, if one supervisor is perceived to be very lenient and another very harsh, subordinates simply may learn to avoid the harsh supervisor rather than the undesirable behavior itself!

5. *Clearly communicate the reasons for the punishment given*. Making clear exactly what behaviors lead to what disciplinary actions greatly increases the effectiveness of punishment. Clearly communicated expectations help strengthen the perceived connection between behavior and its consequences. Wise managers use their opportunities to communicate with subordinates to make clear that the punishment being given does not constitute revenge, but an attempt to eliminate an unwanted behavior (which, of course, it is). Communicating information about poor performance in a personal interview is a good idea, but doing so isn't easy. To make such interviews as effective as possible, managers should conduct them systematically, following the steps outlined in Figure 2-14.[70]

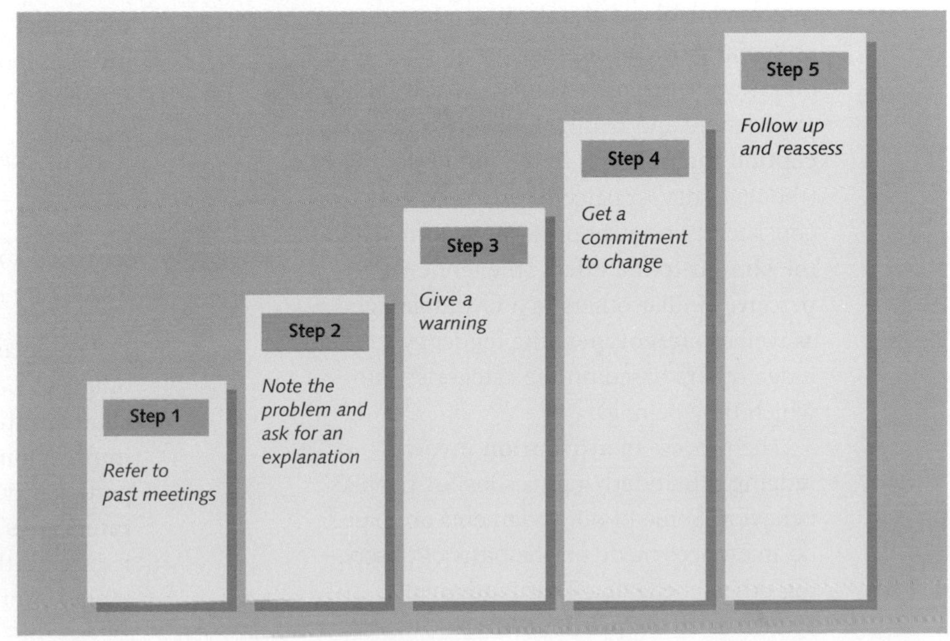

FIGURE 2-14
CONDUCTING A DISCIPLINARY INTERVIEW: SOME VITAL STEPS
It is never easy to communicate a performance problem. Following the steps listed here helps ensure that the problem is identified and that the consequences for failing to improve are made clear. (Source: Based on suggestions by Lussier, 1990; see Note 70.)

6. *Do not follow punishment with noncontingent rewards.* Imagine that you are a supervisor who has just written a formal letter of discipline in reaction to a serious infraction of the rules by a particular subordinate. The disciplined employee is feeling very low, which makes you feel remorseful. Feeling bad, you reduce your guilt by telling the employee that he can take the rest of the day off with pay. Although this may make you feel better, it poses a serious problem: you inadvertently rewarded the person for the unwanted behavior. The serious infraction was punished by the letter, but rewarded by the time off. Consequently, the effect of the punishment may be greatly diminished. More seriously, such an action sends the wrong message to the other employees. Soon they too may learn that you will give them time off if they display the proper degree of dejection. The advice is clear: for punishment to be most effective supervisors should refrain from inadvertently rewarding undesirable behaviors—a suggestion that appears obvious but that is not always followed.[71]

If, after reading all this, you are thinking that it is truly difficult to properly administer rewards and punishments in organizations, you have reached the same conclusion as experts in the field of organizational behavior. Indeed, one of the key skills that makes some managers so effective is their ability to influence others by properly administering rewards and punishments.

SUMMARY AND REVIEW

THE BASIC PROCESS OF SOCIAL PERCEPTION

Perception is the process through which people select, organize, and interpret the information around them. When this process focuses on the interpretation of information about people, it is referred to as **social perception.** Our perceptions of others are largely determined by our own experiences and biases. These include **perceptual biases,** such as the **halo effect** (the tendency to perceive others in either consistently positive or negative terms) and the **similar-to-me effect** (the tendency to perceive similar others in a favorable light), as well as **stereotypes** (the tendency to judge others based on the categories into which they belong).

The process of **attribution** involves judging the underlying reasons for people's behavior. Some of our judgments are based on inferences made on the basis of observing others' behavior. These judgments, known as **correspondent inferences,** are often inaccurate. Our search for explanations about the causes of others' behavior leads us to make either judgments of *internal causality* (the individual is responsible for his or her own actions) or *external causality* (someone or something else is responsible). **Kelley's theory of causal attribution** explains that such judgments will be based on three types of information: *consensus* (whether others act in a similar manner), *consistency* (whether the individual previously acted this way in the same situation), and *distinctiveness* (whether this person acted similarly in different situations).

APPLICATIONS OF SOCIAL PERCEPTION IN ORGANIZATIONS

People are generally interested in getting others to perceive them favorably, and their efforts in this regard are referred to as **impression management**. This process is particularly important in **employment interviews,** although it sometimes interferes with the accuracy of information presented about individuals or companies. An organization's overall impression on people, its *corporate image,* is a determinant of its ability to attract qualified job applicants.

Biased judgments about others sometimes occur during the process of **performance appraisal**. In this context, research has shown that people judge as superior those individuals whose performance matches their expectations, and those whose poor performance is attributable to factors outside their control.

PRINCIPLES OF LEARNING

Learning refers to relatively permanent changes in behavior occurring as a result of experience. In organizations, two approaches are most common. In the **operant conditioning** approach, individuals learn to behave in certain ways based on the consequences of those actions. Stimuli that increase the probability of the behaviors preceding it are known as **reinforcers**. Reinforcement may be either *positive,* if it is based on the presentation of a desirable outcome, or *negative,* if it is based on the withdrawal of an unwanted outcome. The probability of certain responses can be decreased if an unpleasant outcome results **(punishment)**, or if a pleasant outcome is withdrawn **(extinction)**.

Observational learning involves learning by modeling the behavior of others. By paying attention to and rehearsing the behavior of others, we can learn vicariously, that is, through the model's experiences.

APPLICATIONS OF LEARNING PRINCIPLES IN ORGANIZATIONS

Learning is directly involved in efforts to teach people to acquire new job skills, the process of **training.** Training is most effective when people can actively participate in the learning process, repeat the desired behaviors, receive feedback on their performance, and learn under conditions closely resembling those found on the job (allowing *transfer of training*).

Organizational behavior management is a systematic attempt to apply principles of reinforcement to the workplace so as to improve organizational functioning. Studies have shown that reinforcing desired behaviors can greatly improve organizational functioning.

In contrast to applications of reinforcement, **discipline** is the systematic application of punishments so as to minimize undesirable organizational behaviors. The effects of discipline are most effective when punishment is applied immediately after the undesirable activity, moderately severe, focused on the activity rather than the individual, applied consistently over time and for all employees, clearly explained and communicated, and not weakened by the use of inadvertent rewards.

KEY TERMS

attribution: The process through which people attempt to determine the causes of others' behavior.

avoidance: See *negative reinforcement.*

contingencies of reinforcement: The various relationships between one's behavior and the consequences of that behavior—positive reinforcement, negative reinforcement, punishment, and extinction.

continuous reinforcement: A schedule of reinforcement in which all desired behaviors are reinforced.

correspondent inferences: Judgments made about what someone is like based on observations of that person's behavior.

discipline: The process of systematically administering punishments.

extinction: The process through which responses that are no longer reinforced tend to gradually diminish in strength.

feedback: Knowledge of the results of one's behavior.

CASE IN POINT

DIFFERENCES IN UNDERSTANDING

It was the time of year for promotions to be announced, and Ann Hopkins felt confident that her five years of hard work at Price Waterhouse would be rewarded with the announcement of her being made partner in the international accounting and consulting company's Washington, D.C., office. After all, reasoned Hopkins, she was responsible for bringing over $37 million worth of business to the firm.[1] In addition, she knew that clients were pleased with her performance and that fellow staff members had written reviews highly complimentary of her competence.[2]

The partners at Price Waterhouse, however, didn't see Hopkins quite as favorably as she might have liked. They viewed her as arrogant, abrasive, overbearing, insensitive, impatient, and hard-nosed. Of course, these are all legitimate reasons to deny someone a promotion to partnership. However, the partners also claimed that Hopkins should "go to charm school" and learn to "walk more femininely, talk more femininely, dress more femininely . . . wear makeup, have her hair styled, and wear jewelry."[3]

A year after being denied this promotion, Hopkins was not even considered for partner when it again became time to make this determination. At this point she realized that she would never be promoted because she did not conform to the typical partner's stereotype of a female executive. As a result, Hopkins filed suit, alleging that she was denied promotion based on her gender—a charge of sexual discrimination. This allegation was supported by district court, federal court, and the U.S. Supreme Court, which handed down its decision on May 1, 1989. The courts agreed with the firm in maintaining its right to deny promotion based on interpersonal characteristics such as aggression. However, the Supreme Court held that "an employer who objects to aggressiveness in women but whose positions require this trait places women in an intolerable and impermissible Catch-22: out of a job if they behave aggressively and out of a job if they don't."[4] The courts thereby upheld the principle that companies are responsible for developing fair and accurate performance appraisal systems that do not discriminate based on gender.

David Lam, an engineer at Hewlett-Packard, asserts that gender isn't the only basis on which people make judgments based on stereotypes. Lam, an Asian American, believes he was passed over for promotion because of his ethnic heritage. Instead, a Caucasian with less experience—hired by Lam—was given the promotion. Says Lam, "There's strong prejudice prevailing in the corporate world."[5]

Unfortunately, Lam's assertions are given credence by the vice president of a large midwestern company (he requested anonymity), who said he would like to employ many more people of Asian descent because they are "loyal and hard working." He doesn't consider promoting them, however, because they "have to have pats on the back constantly."[6]

Although in Lam's case stereotyping resulted in his being denied a promotion, for many Asian Americans stereotyping also is (paradoxically) responsible for their being hired in the first place. They are viewed as the "model minority,"[7] frequently graduating at or near the top of their college classes and heavily recruited for entry-level technical and professional jobs. Often they perform exceptionally well in these positions. However, suggests Jim Tso, president of the Organization of Chinese Americans, their high level of competence makes companies reluctant to promote them. The rationale for this seems to be that because they have demonatrated such expertise at lower levels, it would be a shame to lose them by promoting them to management."[8]

Stereotypes of Asian Americans as passive and quiet seem to present the biggest obstacle to their fulfilling management roles. On the one hand, if they are in fact quiet, management uses this as proof of their inability to handle managerial responsibilities. On the other hand, if they are aggressive this is taken as evidence that they don't fit in! (This is the same type of Catch-22 that the Supreme Court warned against in its decision for Ann Hopkins.)

Although promotion wasn't at issue, when Terry Koroda worked at Merrill Lynch he experienced these mixed expectations when he took an aggressive stance during the negotiation for a new computer system. The people in the purchasing department were wary of his behavior and attempted to bypass his suggestions. Nonetheless, he prevailed on them to let him manage the bargaining. This resulted in the purchase of a system that saved the company $30,000 a month in computer costs.[9]

Differences in understanding can lead to more problems than discrimination alone. This was proven beyond a shadow of a doubt in the confirmation hearings for U.S. Supreme Court Justice Clarence Thomas. As part of this process, Anita Hill, a woman who had worked with Thomas, was called to testify about her charge that Thomas had sexually harassed her when they worked together. Although it will probably never be proven that Clarence Thomas either did or did not sexually harass Anita Hill, it is obvious to nearly everyone who watched the hearings that Thomas and Hill had very different perceptions about the incidents that took place.

Questions for Discussion

1. What stereotypes did the Price Waterhouse partners appear to hold of women?
2. How did these stereotypes affect the partners' judgment of Ann Hopkins' suitability for promotion?
3. Other than stereotyping, what perceptual biases do you think the Price Waterhouse partners may have held?
4. Why does the prevailing stereotype of Asian Americans result in their being denied management promotions?
5. Why are stereotypes particularly unfair to individuals who are members of a minority group?
6. How do people learn stereotypes? In what ways are these beliefs reinforced or punished?
7. Do you think that training programs can be effective in changing the attitudes and behaviors of people in the workplace toward others who differ from them by gender, race, ethnicity, age, and/or sexual orientation?

EXPERIENCING ORGANIZATIONAL BEHAVIOR

The All-Too-Powerful Impact of Stereotypes

Most people are well aware of the existence of stereotypes. They realize that in the past, negative stereotypes were responsible for unfair treatment of women and minority group members in many work settings. At the same time, though, most people do not recognize the existence and potentially powerful impact of a wide range of other stereotypes. This exercise is designed to demonstrate the fact that your own thinking (enlightened as it may be) can be affected by various stereotypes, even if you think you are an eminently fair-minded and unbiased person. Follow the directions below for some firsthand insights into such effects.

PROCEDURE

Rate the members of the following groups on each of the following dimensions. Circle one number for each characteristic.

Investment Bankers

Liberal						Conservative
1	2	3	4	5	6	7
Intelligent						Unintelligent
1	2	3	4	5	6	7
Greedy						Generous
1	2	3	4	5	6	7
Dull						Interesting
1	2	3	4	5	6	7

Engineers

Liberal						Conservative
1	2	3	4	5	6	7
Intelligent						Unintelligent
1	2	3	4	5	6	7
Greedy						Generous
1	2	3	4	5	6	7
Dull						Interesting
1	2	3	4	5	6	7

Professors

Liberal						Conservative
1	2	3	4	5	6	7
Intelligent						Unintelligent
1	2	3	4	5	6	7
Greedy						Generous
1	2	3	4	5	6	7
Dull						Interesting
1	2	3	4	5	6	7

POINTS TO CONSIDER

Did your ratings of the various groups differ? If you are like most people, they probably did. For example, you probably rated investment bankers as more conservative and less interesting than professors. Moreover—and this is an important point—your ratings may well have differed *even if you do not know members of these various professions personally.*

The point of this exercise is straightforward. We hold stereotypes concerning the supposed traits or characteristics of many different groups. Furthermore, such beliefs are so pervasive that we are often unaware of their existence until, as in this demonstration, they are called to our attention. Given the widespread existence of stereotypes and their potential effects on important organizational processes, it is important to be aware of them and to try to resist their influence. If you choose, instead, to ignore them, you may fall victim to serious errors in perceiving others.

CHAPTER OUTLINE

SPECIAL SECTIONS

THREE

PERSONALITY: INDIVIDUAL DIFFERENCES IN ORGANIZATIONAL BEHAVIOR

We boil at different degrees.

Ralph Waldo Emerson, 1803–1882
American essayist and poet
Literary Ethics

He who knows his own incapacity knows something after all.

Margaret of Anjoulême, c. 1492–1549
Queen of Navarre
Heptameron

LEARNING OBJECTIVES

After reading this chapter, you should be able to

1. *Define personality.*
2. *Identify the interactionist perspective of personality, and describe how it is involved in organizational behavior, especially the idea of person–job fit.*
3. *Identify the "big five" dimensions of personality, and explain how they are related to organizational behavior.*
4. *Explain what is meant by negative affectivity and the Type A behavior pattern.*
5. *Distinguish between self-monitoring, self-esteem, and self-efficacy, and describe how the concept of self-efficacy can be changed.*
6. *Describe the Machiavellian personality, and identify steps that can be taken to protect oneself from such individuals.*
7. *Explain what is meant by achievement motivation, and describe how it is related to the Japanese management philosophy known as kaizen.*
8. *Identify and describe the major approaches to the measurement of personality—objective tests and projective techniques—and explain the importance of reliability and validity in personality testing.*

PREVIEW CASE

An American Success Story Becomes an American Express Story

In July, 1993 Kenneth I. Chenault was named president of U.S. operations of American Express Travel Related Services, the company's flagship credit card division. This was no ordinary executive succession, however, for Chenault was the company's first African-American to rise to this level. In a company with a buttoned-down, "establishment" image and an elitist, patrician culture, the move raised more than a few eyebrows. However, James D. Robinson, III, one of Chenault's predecessors, applauded this appointment as a way of shaking up the elitist culture that pervaded American Express, "If you bring in people from different backgrounds, you're going to wake up the country club that's gotten too comfortable." Among those who really knew the 42-year-old Chenault, such as Robinson, the appointment was not a surprise at all, but precisely the kind of accomplishment they expected of him.

Growing up in Hempstead, New York, the young Kenneth Chenault and his three siblings were raised in a family in which becoming successful was not only encouraged, but an out-and-out necessity. In discussions at the family dinner table, his father, Hortenius Chenault, always stressed the importance of achievement. Focusing on themes ranging from the serious, such as racism and civil rights, to the mundane, such as getting a part in the school play, family conversations emphasized how one can make a difference by working hard. Indeed, the elder Chenault was no stranger to accomplishment, himself. A child whose parents were servants, he was denied opportunities his whole life, but rose to prominence as a dentist and a champion of civil rights in his community. Hortenius expected no less from his own son. "You're equal to the task," he would assure Kenneth as he struggled with life's challenges.

In his position at the helm of American Express, Chenault now faces some of his most serious challenges ever. In the early 1990s many merchants stopped accepting the card (rebelling against the higher fees it charges than competitors, Master Card and VISA) and card membership dropped 6.8%, necessitating large-scale cost-cutting just to keep revenues flat. Given Chenault's history of success at American Express, he has shown he is clearly up to the challenge. In the early 1980s, for example, Chenault was the manager of American Express's merchandise services—a division with low revenues (a mere $100 million) that was slated to be axed, an assignment considered a "graveyard" position. Turning this situation into an opportunity to shine, Chenault convinced then president Louis V. Gerstner to give him $4 million and two months to revive the unit. And, that he did. Reorganizing management structure and introducing new technology, Chenault was able to cut order processing time in half and

Kenneth I. Chenault, President, American Express Travel Related Services.

improve customer service. He also switched to more upscale merchandise that appealed to the affluent cardholders. The result was a turnaround of impressive proportions: by 1986 annual growth increased by over 20 percent, and annual revenues rose to $400 million. Not only did this save the unit from extinction, but it also marked Chenault as a rising star within American Express.

From this platform, Chenault launched still more accomplishments. In 1991, for example, he helped increase card usage by introducing a popular airline-mileage bonus program. He also convinced top executives to lower fees to keep merchants from defecting. On the heels of these accomplishments Chenault was tagged by his predecessor, Harvey Golub, as a prime candidate to succeed him as president.

Chenault credits his will to succeed to his upbringing in a household in which his father was driven to break the color barrier. "My father felt that race was society's biggest problem, but that you couldn't let it beat you down. He felt like we had an obligation to make an impact, and that an individual could make a very strong impact in bringing about change." This emphasis on accomplishment was contagious, leading young Kenneth to be obsessed with leadership (his heroes were W. E. B. DuBois, Winston Churchill, and Frederick Douglass). Not surprisingly, this momentum catapulted Chenault to a record of academic achievement at Bowdoin College and Harvard Law School, before taking on the corporate world. Striving his entire life to be successful at whatever he did, it appears he was advised as follows: "The need to achieve success—don't leave home without it!"

One cannot help but remark at how special Kenneth Chenault is. His constant striving for success is a hallmark of his style, something that sets him apart from others. Clearly, Chenault is a truly unique and distinctive individual. But then, he is certainly not the only person who ever grew up in a household in which striving for success was strongly emphasized. Others exposed to the same pressures may fail to work as hard as him, and not attain the exceptionally high position he did. Of course, a lot has to do with the situation (e.g., where one lives and works, the economy, and so on), but we cannot dismiss the importance of the traits and characteristics that people possess and carry around with them in all situations. It is the particular blend of traits and characteristics that makes us each unique in our own ways (even those of us who are *not* the president of American Express). These distinctive aspects of people, referred to as *personality*, have important effects on the way people behave in organizations. In this chapter we will closely examine the ways in which personality is related to various aspects of behavior in organizations.

Specifically, we will begin by defining the concept of personality more precisely and considering the general role it plays in organizations. We will then review several specific traits that have been found to influence organizational behavior. Finally, we will consider various methods used to measure personality, techniques that are necessary to compare individuals in this regard and to put such knowledge to practical use.

PERSONALITY: ITS BASIC NATURE AND ROLE IN ORGANIZATIONS

If our experience with other people tells us anything, it is that they are all in some way *unique* and, at least to a degree, they are all *consistent*. That is, we each possess a distinct pattern of traits and characteristics not fully duplicated in any other person, and these are generally stable over time. Thus, if you know someone who is dependable, friendly, and optimistic today, he or she probably showed these traits in the past and will likely continue to show them in the future. Moreover, this person will tend to show them in many different situations over time. Together, these two facts form the basis for a useful working definition of **personality:** *the unique and relatively stable pattern of behavior, thoughts, and emotions shown by individuals.*[1] In short, personality is the lasting ways in which any one person is different from all others (see Figure 3-1).

PERSON VERSUS SITUATION: THE CONTROVERSY OVER TWO IMPORTANT DETERMINANTS OF BEHAVIOR

Because we so often think of behavior as the result of stable differences in who we are—that is, personality—you may find it surprising to learn that over the years some social scientists have rejected the notion of personality, arguing instead that how we behave is predominantly determined by the external conditions we face.[2] Indeed, some have gone so far as to claim that what appear to be differences in dispositions between people is really "just a mirage," an illusion stemming from the fact that we *want* to perceive such consistency because it makes it easier for us to predict what others will do.[3]

On the opposite side of the controversy are social scientists who have argued just as strongly that stable traits *do* exist, and that these lead people to behave consistently across a variety of different settings. In support of their claim is evidence showing that when personality variables are measured and remeasured over time and a wide variety of situations, people tend to show the same, stable patterns.[4] Further support is provided by research comparing the personalities of twins who, for one reason or another, were raised in different environments. If personality is more strongly determined by our environments than by our basic predispositions (in great part the result of genetic factors), then there would be no reason to expect that twins reared apart would have any personality variables in common. However, studies have found that twins reared apart tend to be remarkably similar with respect to personality, just as they are in physical characteristics such as hair color and height.[5] Findings such as these strongly suggest that personality is a viable, stable aspect of people.

FIGURE 3-1
PERSONALITY: A DISTINCT ASPECT OF WHO WE ARE
We may be able to see the ways in which people look different from each other, but we cannot see one of the most important ways in which people are unique—their personalities. Yet, these stable patterns of behavior, thoughts, and emotions are greatly responsible for how individuals behave on the job.

If so, then to what extent is personality responsible for how we behave? To consider the impact of personality relative to situational factors, consider the following example. Suppose two stock brokers working for the same firm both discover that by slightly altering a computer program, they could divert large sums of money into their own personal accounts. The two stock brokers are different in an important way: one stock broker strongly endorses high moral standards whereas the other is more lax in this regard. Will they act differently? Although you might expect that the immoral person will behave fraudulently while the highly moral one will not, the situation is not that simple. This *may* happen, but not always. If the funds can be transferred quickly, and the company is believed to use sloppy bookkeeping procedures, the possibility of detection may be low enough to tempt the immoral person to commit a fraudulent act. However, even in this situation the highly moral broker may resist the temptation to make a quick, but illegal, profit. Now, suppose the possibility of detection is made much greater by the use of extremely thorough, unannounced audits. Under this situation, even the immoral individual may refrain from stealing. In other words, the situational constraint was greatly responsible for his or her behavior—so much so, in fact, that it counteracted the influence of personality.

This example demonstrates a fundamental point relevant to our discussion of personality—namely, that *behavior is the result of both an individual's personality and the nature of the situation experienced*. In other words, the way we behave at any given time is likely to be affected by two forces acting together in concert: who we are (i.e., our personality) and the existing context (i.e., the situations in which we find ourselves). This line of thinking reflects what is called the **interactionist perspective**, the position suggesting that thorough understanding of behavior requires appreciation of *both* personality and the environment.[6] As you might imagine, this approach is widely popular among social scientists today, especially those studying complex topics, such as behavior in organizations.[7] The interactionist perspective highlights the importance of personality variables insofar as it suggests that they may qualify any knowledge of behavior in organizations obtained without paying attention to them. At the same time, it suggests that it may be unreasonable to expect personality variables to be completely responsible for human behavior (since, as illustrated by our example, the situation people face may introduce strong forces that shape our behavior) (for a summary of these points, see Figure 3-2).

An interesting implication of the interactionist perspective is that there may be some work environments that more closely match the personalities of some people than others. In other words, we may ask: are there times in which the demands of a job more closely fit the characteristics of one person as opposed to another? And, when such a match occurs, does the person perform the job better than when no such match occurs? Questions such as these have received a great deal of attention lately in the field of organizational behavior.[8] On the basis of what has been found so far, it appears that when someone's personality is particularly well suited to the demands of a job, he or she is, in fact, likely to be more satisfied and productive than someone else who is more poorly equipped to do the job.[9] This concept, known as **person–job fit**, suggests that work-related outcomes will be extremely positive when there is a high correlation between people's characteristics and the requirements of their jobs.

FIGURE 3-2
THE INTERACTIONIST PERSPECTIVE: AN EXAMPLE
The interactionist perspective recognizes that people's behavior is influenced by their personalities in conjunction with the situation encountered. In this example, when situational constraints are weak, the stock broker with weak moral standards will steal, but the one with strong moral standards will not steal (i.e., personality influences will prevail). However, when situational constraints are strong, neither stock broker is likely to steal (situational influences will prevail).

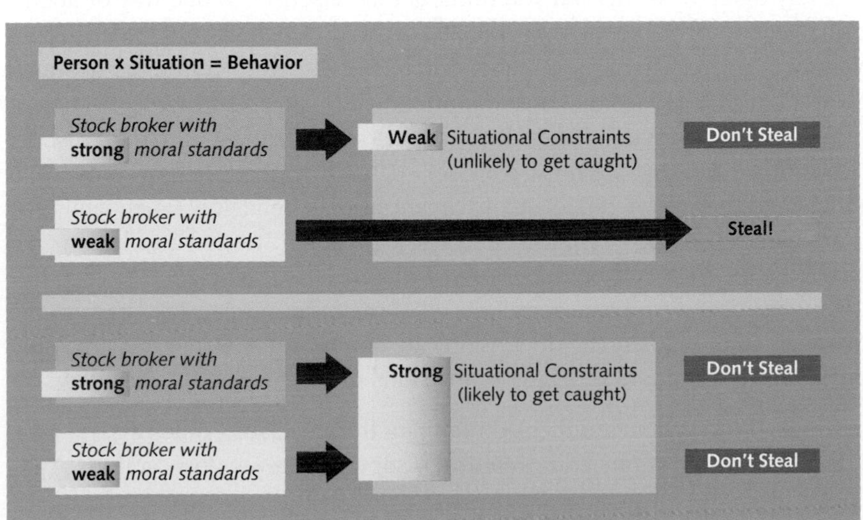

A clear demonstration of this effect may be seen in a series of studies conducted by Caldwell and O'Reilly.[10] Their basic approach was as follows. First, individuals familiar with specific jobs were interviewed to identify the skills and characteristics necessary to perform their jobs well. Next, these lists of competencies were presented to people with expert knowledge about these jobs to make sure the ones identified were indeed required for success (and to reword and clarify these descriptions as needed). Third, the people actually performing the jobs in question were asked to rate how important for good job performance each of the skills and characteristics on the list were, in their opinion. Fourth, another group of people holding these same jobs were asked to rate how much each of the characteristics in question described themselves. In the fifth step, the investigators compared the extent to which the individuals' self-descriptions matched the profile of characteristics required for the job. Then, finally, these matches or mismatches were correlated with measures of job satisfaction and performance.

Caldwell and O'Reilly applied this basic method to a wide variety of jobs and employees. Their samples included production supervisors in a large consumer products company, claims adjustment supervisors, and people in many other types of jobs. As you might expect, a wide range of different characteristics were identified as being crucial for success in these jobs. For example, for managers in a public utility the ability to build trust with subordinates was identified as crucial. However, for computer equipment sales managers, the ability to set challenging personal goals emerged as a key characteristic. Despite such differences, the results were clear: in all cases, the higher the person–job fit, the better their job performance (see Figure 3-3). Among some groups (e.g., secretaries), person–job fit also was highly correlated with job satisfaction.

As noted by Caldwell and O'Reilly, these findings offer support for the importance of considering individual difference variables in efforts to enhance both productivity and job satisfaction. The closer the fit between individuals' personal traits and the requirements of their jobs, the more positive are the results. Insofar as personality may have such profound effects on organizational behavior, we will highlight in this chapter some of the key personality variables at work. By way of introducing this idea, we will begin by describing some basic dimensions of personality relevant to organizations and illustrate how they are related to job performance.

THE "BIG FIVE" DIMENSIONS OF PERSONALITY IN ORGANIZATIONAL BEHAVIOR

How many different words can you think of that describe, in one way or another, a characteristic of someone's personality? Would you believe *17,953*!? That's exactly how many different personality-related words were found in a search through an English language dictionary approximately sixty years ago.[11] Even after combining words with similar meanings, the list shrank to a mere 171 distinct traits. Does this mean that we must consider such a huge list of characteristics to fully understand the role of personality in organizational behavior? Fortunately, the answer appears to be "no." Sophisticated research points to the conclusion that there may be a much smaller number of key dimensions to consider. In fact, five central dimensions now appear to underlie all of the others.[12] Because they emerge in so many different studies, the dimensions are commonly referred to as the **"big five" personality dimensions.** These dimensions may be described as follows:

- *Extroversion–introversion*: a dimension ranging from sociable, talkative, assertive, and active at one end, to retiring, sober, reserved, and cautious at the other

- *Agreeableness*: a dimension ranging from good-natured, gentle, cooperative forgiving, and hopeful at one end, to irritable, ruthless, suspicious, uncooperative, and inflexible at the other
- *Conscientiousness*: a dimension ranging from careful, thorough, responsible, organized, self-disciplined, and scrupulous at one end, to irresponsible, disorganized, lacking in self-discipline, and unscrupulous at the other
- *Emotional stability*: a dimension ranging from anxious, depressed, angry, emotional, insecure, and excitable at one end, to calm, enthusiastic, poised, and secure at the other
- *Openness to experience*: a dimension ranging from imaginative, sensitive, intellectual, and polished at one end, to down-to-earth, insensitive, narrow, crude, and simple at the other

Recently, attempts have been made to examine the relationship between these personality variables and various aspects of organizational behavior.[13,14] For example, reviewing the research on this topic, Barrick and Mount examined the results of over 200 separate studies in which at least one of these dimensions was related to job performance.[15] These studies examined a wide range of professional groups and used a variety of different performance measures.

Several interesting findings were uncovered. First, conscientiousness was found to be a good predictor of performance for all types of jobs. As you might expect, highly conscientious employees were generally more productive than unconscientious ones. However, contrary to the researchers' predictions, emotional stability was not found to be related to performance. This may well be because those who are least stable tend to quit their jobs, leaving a restricted sample of relatively stable individuals in the research. Another interesting finding pertained to people in managerial and sales positions. Among these individuals, extraversion was highly related to job success, consistent with the image of the highly sociable, gregarious salesperson. Interestingly, however, agreeableness was not related to performance within this group. Again, it is possible that the only people who remain on the job are those who are agreeable enough to get by. As a result, there's probably a highly restricted range of scores on this variable, not enough to lead to a significant relationship.

Adding to these findings, Barrick and Mount recently conducted a study in which a sample of civilian managerial and supervisory employees working in U.S. military installations completed a questionnaire that included measures of the "big five" personality variables. Consistent with their earlier review of the literature, Barrick and Mount find that the personality variables of conscientiousness and extroversion were positively correlated with job performance (important characteristics for the jobs of the people in their sample). Interestingly, they also found that these relationships were qualified by perceptions of job autonomy

FIGURE 3-3

PERSON-JOB FIT: A DEMONSTRATION

Caldwell and O'Reilly found that the degree to which people experienced person-job fit (i.e., their characteristics matched the job requirements) was positively correlated with the level of performance demonstrated. The general nature of this relationship is shown here. (Source: Based on Caldwell & O'Reilly, 1990; see Note 10.)

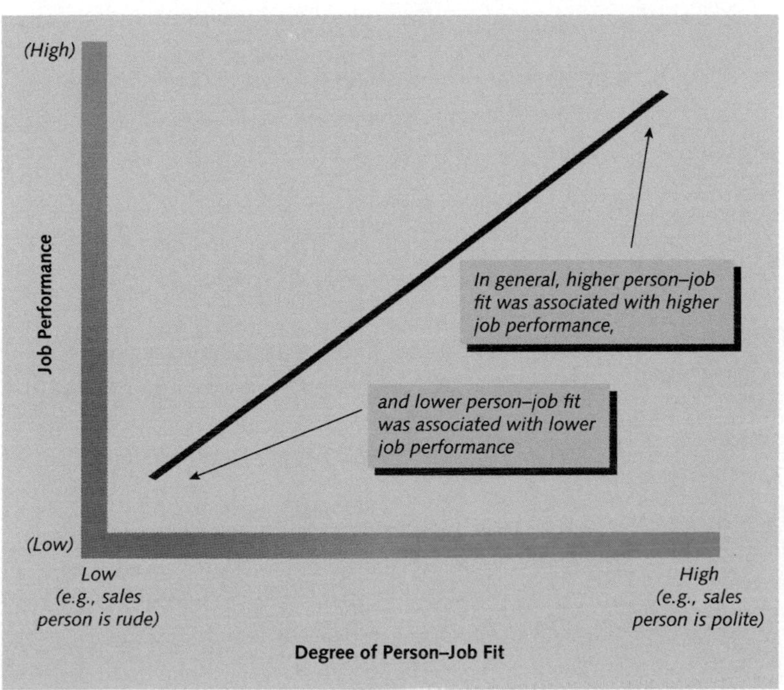

such that the relationship was strongest under conditions in which job autonomy was greatest.[16] In other words, job performance benefits most when people have the freedom to do their jobs in a way that makes it possible for the helpful aspects of their personality to "shine through."

Findings such as these suggest not only that there are many different personality variables related to organizational behavior, but also that such associations may be more complex than is apparent at first blush. They also suggest that various clusters of personality variables may be used to paint some interesting pictures of behavior in organizations. (For a look at the fascinating, and highly useful, knowledge derived from one attempt to study a variety of personality variables, see The Ethical Workplace section below.)

WORK-RELATED ASPECTS OF PERSONALITY

By now we trust you are convinced that individual differences do matter, and that searching for relationships between personality and key aspects of organizational behavior make sense. But *what* facets of personality are most relevant? A great deal of research has focused on this question. In this section, therefore, we will identify several traits or characteristics that have been found to have an important bearing on behavior in work settings.

THE ETHICAL WORKPLACE

THE WHITE-COLLAR CRIMINAL: A PERSONALITY PROFILE

As we go through life, it appears that some people are more ethical than others. In the very same situation one person may lie, cheat, and steal, while another's behavior may be completely virtuous.[17] This observation leads us to ask whether there any systematic differences in personality between individuals who behave ethically and those who do not.

Attempting to answer this question, Collins and Schmidt administered a battery of different personality measures to two large groups of people: federal prison inmates convicted of white-collar crimes (e.g., counterfeiting, fraud, and embezzlement), and a demographically comparable sample of noninmates employed in a wide variety of white-collar positions of authority (e.g., corporate presidents and senior managers).[18] The greatest differences between the samples were found with respect to four personality variables that share a common thread. These were as follows:

- *Performance:* the extent to which someone is dependable, reliable, responsible, motivated to perform well on the job, and abides by work rules
- *Socialization*: the degree to which a person adheres to social norms, that is, behaves in a dependable, honest, way, as opposed to being opportunistic and manipulative
- *Responsibility*: the extent to which a person embraces social, civic, and moral values as opposed to antisocial values
- *Tolerance*: the degree to which people are tolerant and trusting as opposed to suspicious, and judgmental, and believe they cannot depend on others

As you might expect, the offenders scored lower on these dimensions than their non-imprisoned counterparts, painting a picture of a group of people who are essentially immoral and unconcerned with others. Interestingly, they were also more socially extraverted—that is, they tended to be popular with others and highly involved in group activities (not loners, as some criminals are described to be). Collins and Schmidt speculate that extraverts may have considerable opportunities to swindle others, and those who lack a social conscience may succumb to the temptation. It is also possible that the considerable "people skills" of social extraverts may have been used as a potent weapon (e.g., to con others) among those who are lacking in morality. In other words, the particular blend of personality characteristics that distinguish white-collar criminals from noncriminal white-collar personnel predisposes them to their chosen field of criminal activity.

Noting the connections between the various personality dimensions that characterize white-collar criminals, Collins and Schmidt call the composite *social conscientiousness.* This term reflects the tendency for white-collar criminals to be socially active but at the same time self-indulgent and lacking in self-control, social responsibility, and honesty. Although specialists in psychiatry and criminology have yet to determine effective ways of curbing white-collar criminals, it is clear that the snapshot of this group presented by the research described here will provide a good head start. And, given the rash of stories about white-collar criminals that have filled the pages of our newspapers in recent years (e.g., bankers and stock brokers accused of various illegal dealings), such work would appear to come not a moment too soon.[19]

POSITIVE AND NEGATIVE AFFECTIVITY: THE STABLE TENDENCY TO FEEL GOOD OR BAD AT WORK

Moods, as we all know, fluctuate rapidly, and often widely, during the course of a day. Whereas favorable feedback from our bosses may make us feel good, harsh criticism may put us in a bad mood. Such temporary shifts in affective *states*—short-term differences in the way we feel—are only partly responsible for the affect (or, mood) that people demonstrate. Superimposed over these transient conditions are also more stable *traits*—consistent differences between people's predispositions toward experiencing positive or negative affect.[20] If you have ever noticed the tendency for some people to be "up" most of the time, while others tend to be more subdued and depressed, you are already aware of affectivity as a personality variable (see Figure 3-4). People who are high in the trait of **positive affectivity** tend to have an overall sense of well-being, see people and things in a positive light, and tend to experience positive emotional states. By contrast, those high in the trait of **negative affectivity** tend to hold negative views of themselves and others, interpret ambiguous situations negatively, and experience negative emotional states.[21] Do such differences in people's characteristic levels of mood play any role in organizational behavior. Recent research suggests that they do.[22]

FIGURE 3-4
POSITIVE AFFECTIVITY IN ORGANIZATIONS: AN UNLIKELY DEMONSTRATION
Although they may not go so far as to blow bubbles at a business meeting, some people tend to be higher in positive affectivity than others. Such individuals tend to have an overall sense of well-being and see people and situations in a positive light. (Source: Drawing by Frank Modell; © 1975 The New Yorker Magazine, Inc.)

"Obviously, some people here do not appreciate the gravity of our situation."

In what is perhaps one of the most revealing of these investigations to date, Staw and Barsade assessed the positive and negative affectivity of MBA students who participated in a series of exercises simulating business decision making.[23] They used various paper-and-pencil tests to measure the participants' characteristic levels of affectivity (we will describe measures of this type later in this chapter). Several different dependent variables were used—that is, measures of their decision-making performance. These included accuracy of decisions (the number of decisions that yielded the correct response), interpersonal performance (peer rankings of overall performance and contributions to group effectiveness), and managerial potential (ratings by experts of the degree to which participants could succeed as a manager). The results paint a clear picture: with respect to each of these different criteria, people showing positive affectivity were superior to those showing negative affectivity (see Figure 3-5). Specifically, they made more accurate decisions, were judged by their peers to make more important contributions to the group's effectiveness, and were rated by experts as having greater managerial potential.

Not only does affectivity influence individual performance, it also has an impact on group performance. Demonstrating this, George asked salespeople working in a large department store to complete measures of positive and negative affectivity.[24] She then used these scores to determine the *affective tone* of the work groups to which these people belonged (that is, the typical level of affective reactions within the group). George reasoned that affective tone would vary between work groups in large part because people with similar personalities will tend to be attracted to, selected by, and retained by, such groups. Taking this rationale a step further, she also argued that the affective tone of work groups would influence members' willingness to help customers. As expected, she found that work groups in which a highly negative affective tone prevailed did, in fact, offer less assistance to customers than those in which less negative tones existed.

This evidence suggests that affectivity may shape not only the behavior of individuals, but also that of work groups. How does this work? A theory known as the **attraction-selection-attrition framework** provides some insight.[25] According to this conceptualization, people with similar personalities will tend to be attracted to one another and so tend to form groups. These groups then tend to select people whose personality traits match those of the people who are already members ("like

FIGURE 3-5

THE BENEFICIAL EFFECTS OF POSITIVE AFFECTIVITY ON TASK PERFORMANCE: RESEARCH EVIDENCE

Comparing people who are high on positive affectivity to those who are high on negative affectivity, Staw and Barsade found consistent evidence for the superiority of positive affectivity with respect to several different measures of task performance. (Source: Based on data reported by Staw & Barsade, 1993; see Note 23.)

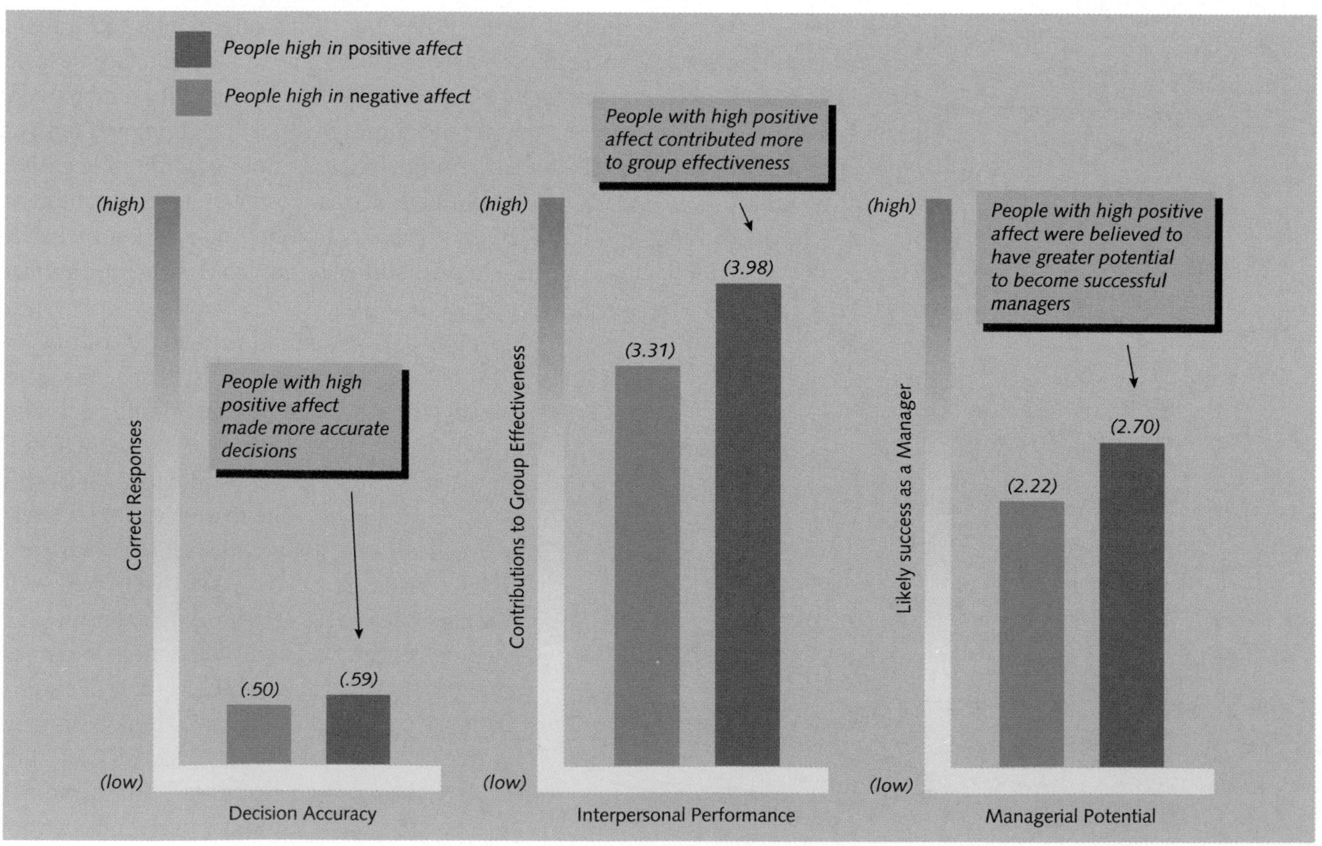

attracts like," or "birds of a feather flock together," as the saying goes). In most cases, only people who share such characteristics will be retained as members. In this manner, aspects of individual personality can, and often do, influence the nature and functioning of groups. Given the wide range of tasks carried out by groups in most organizations, such links between personality and group performance are clearly very important (we will discuss the dynamics of group interaction more thoroughly in Chapter 8).

THE TYPE A BEHAVIOR PATTERN: THE FRENZIED PERSONALITY

Think about the people you know. Can you name one who always seems to be in a hurry, is extremely competitive, and is often irritable? Now, try to name one who shows the opposite pattern—someone who is relaxed, not very competitive, and easygoing. The people you have in mind represent extremes on one key dimension of personality. The first individual would be labeled **Type A**, and the second, **Type B**.[26] People categorized as Type A show high levels of competitiveness, irritability, and time urgency (they are always in a hurry). In addition, they demonstrate certain stylistic patterns, such as loud and exaggerated speech, and a tendency to respond very quickly in many contexts (e.g., during conversations they often begin speaking before others are through). People classified as Type B show the opposite pattern; they are much calmer and laid back. Although there are several different ways used to classify people into Type A or Type B categories, including special structured interviews, paper-and-pencil tests are commonly used—and among these, the *Jenkins Activity Survey* is most popular.[27] For a look at some items similar to those used in this test, see Figure 3-6.

As you can probably guess, the differences between Type A's and Type B's have vital implications for their behavior in work settings. The most important of these involve differences in their personal health, task performance and relations with others.[28] Because we will consider the impact of the Type A behavior pattern on health later in this book (while considering reactions to stress in Chapter 7), we will focus on the remaining two issues here.

First, do people who are Type A's and Type B's differ with respect to job performance? Given their high level of competitiveness, it seems reasonable to expect that Type A's will work harder at various tasks than Type B's and, as a result, will perform at higher levels. In fact, however, the situation turns out to be more complex than this. Type A's *do* tend to work faster on many tasks than Type B's, even when no pressure or deadline is involved. Similarly, they are able to get more done in the presence of distractions.[29] In addition, Type A's often seek more challenges in their work than Type B's (e.g., given a choice, they tend to select more difficult tasks).[30]

Despite these differences, it is important to note that Type A's do not *always* perform better than Type B's. For example, Type A's frequently do poorly on tasks requiring patience or careful, considered judgment. For the most part, they are simply in too much of a hurry to complete such work in an effective manner. A recent study by Jamal and Baba suggests why this may be so.[31] Comparing samples of nurses who were Type A and Type B, an interesting pattern emerged. Specifically, although Type A's were significantly more involved in their jobs and invested greater effort, they were also more overloaded (e.g., took on too much to do) and experienced more conflict with respect to the various aspects of the job required of them. It is easy to understand how differences such as these may well interfere with any possible improvements in performance that may derive from effort alone.

Consistent with this idea are surveys revealing that most top executives are Type B's rather than Type A's.[32] Several factors probably contribute to this pattern. First, it is possible that Type A's simply do not last long enough on their jobs to rise to the highest management levels; the health risks they face (especially coronary heart disease—a serious illness often linked to the Type A behavior pattern) may remove them from contention before they're experienced enough to advance. Second, the impatient, always-in-a-hurry style of Type A's is generally incompatible with the deliberate, carefully studied decision style required of top-level managers. Finally, it is possible that the impatient, hostile style of Type A's may irritate the people around them so much that it interferes with their chances for promotion.

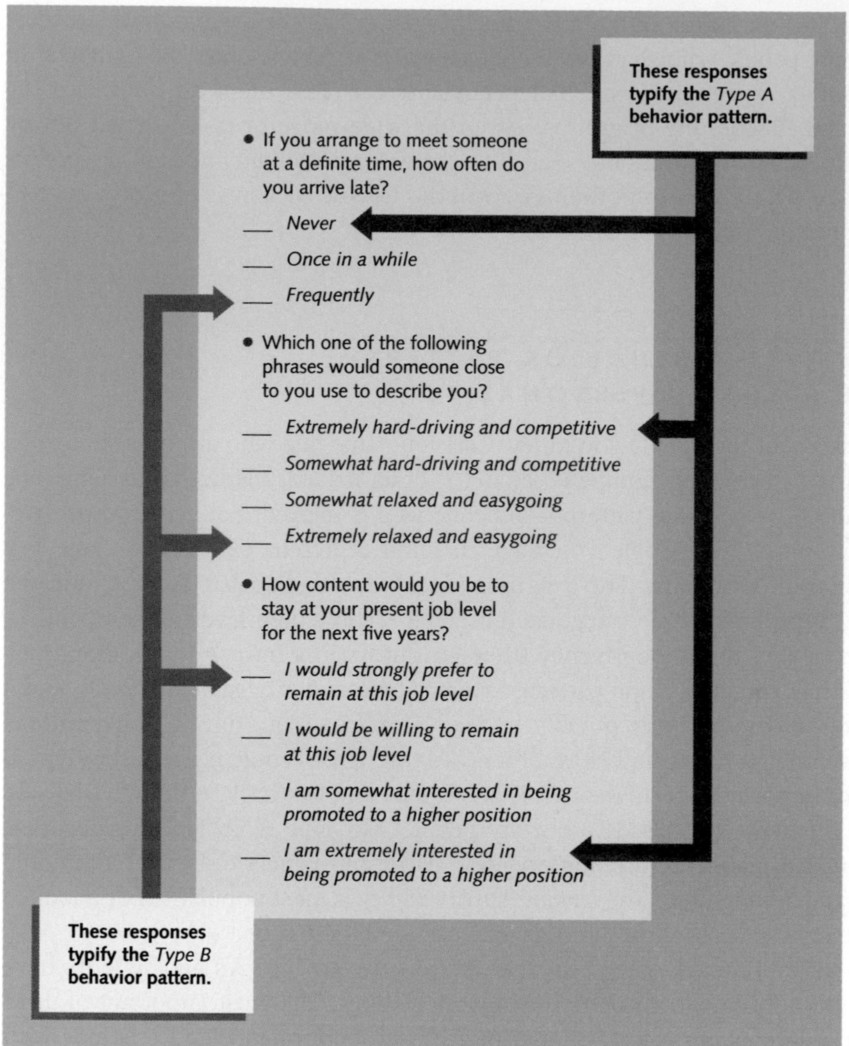

These responses typify the *Type A* behavior pattern.
• If you arrange to meet someone at a definite time, how often do you arrive late?
___ *Never*
___ *Once in a while*
___ *Frequently*
• Which one of the following phrases would someone close to you use to describe you?
___ *Extremely hard-driving and competitive*
___ *Somewhat hard-driving and competitive*
___ *Somewhat relaxed and easygoing*
___ *Extremely relaxed and easygoing*
• How content would you be to stay at your present job level for the next five years?
___ *I would strongly prefer to remain at this job level*
___ *I would be willing to remain at this job level*
___ *I am somewhat interested in being promoted to a higher position*
___ *I am extremely interested in being promoted to a higher position*
These responses typify the *Type B* behavior pattern.

FIGURE 3-6

MEASURING THE TYPE A AND TYPE B BEHAVIOR PATTERNS: AN EXAMPLE

Questions similar to these are included in the Jenkins Activity Survey, a test commonly used to identify people within the Type A and Type B behavior patterns. (Source: Based on Jenkins, 1965; see Note 27.)

Taken together, these findings suggest that neither pattern has the overall edge when it comes to task performance. Although Type A's may excel on tasks involving time pressure or solitary work, Type B's have the advantage when it comes to tasks involving complex judgments and accuracy, as opposed to speed. Further insight into these differences come from studies examining the differences between Type A's and Type B's with respect to interpersonal relations, their dealings with others.[33] Type A's tend to become impatient with people and grow angry if someone delays them in any way. In fact, they are likely to lose their tempers and lash out at others in response to even slight provocations. Fortunately, they also prefer working by themselves as opposed to with others; they are definitely loners instead of team players. Not surprisingly, Type A's tend to become involved in more conflicts at work than Type B's.

In a study examining this issue, Baron asked managers at a large food-processing company to indicate the frequency with which they experienced conflict with subordinates, peers, and supervisors.[34] As you can see from Figure 3-7, people classified as Type A reported a significantly higher frequency of peer conflict and subordinate conflict than those classified as Type B. However, when it came to conflict with superiors Type A's and Type B's were not significantly different from each other. Apparently, although the abrasive style of Type A's was likely to arouse conflict with those at the same or lower organizational levels, they may have kept this aspect of their personality in check when dealing with people at higher levels so as to refrain from creating conflict with them. In sum, several characteristics of Type

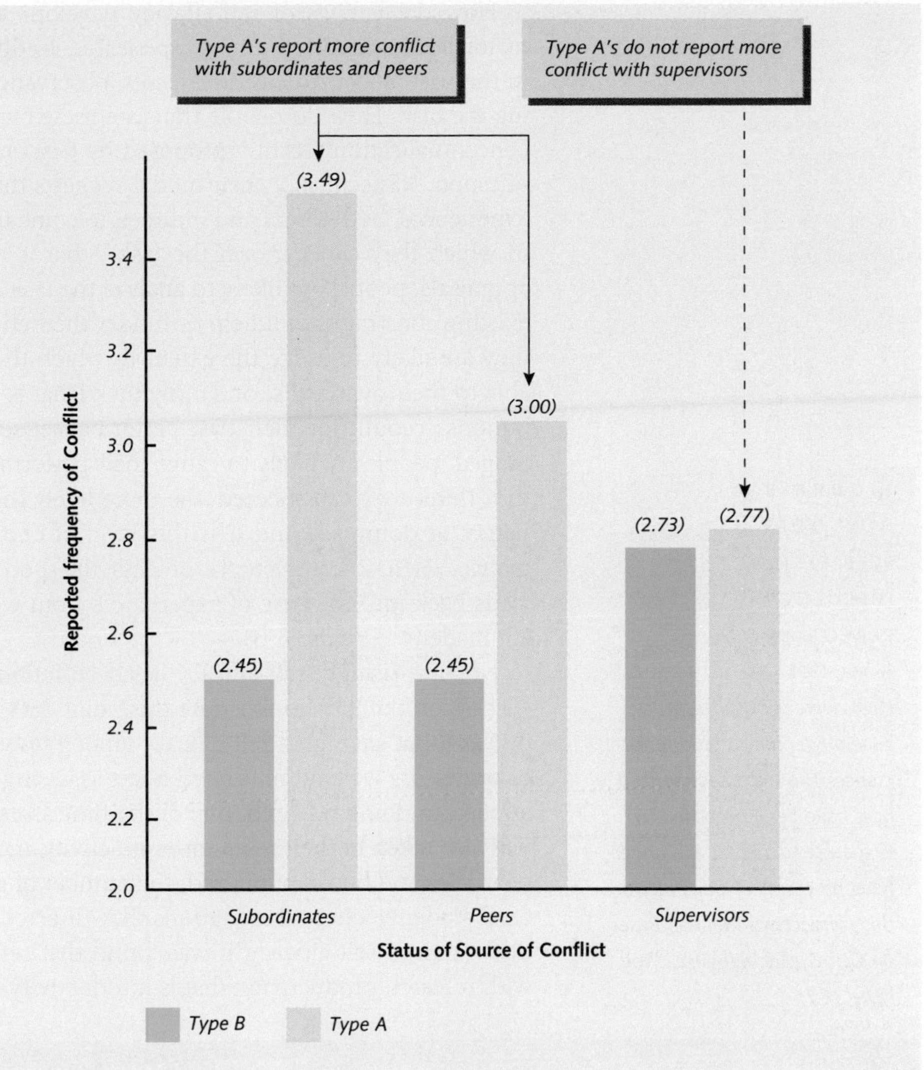

FIGURE 3-7
CONFLICT AND THE TYPE A BEHAVIOR PATTERN
Type A managers reported a higher incidence of conflict with peers and subordinates than did Type B managers, However, they did not report a higher incidence of conflict with supervisors than did Type B managers. (Source: Based on data from Baron, 1989; see Note 34.)

A's seem to get them into more than their share of interpersonal difficulties at work, and these appear to interfere with their performance on jobs in which these skills are vital to success.

SELF-EFFICACY: THE "CAN DO" FACET OF PERSONALITY

Suppose that two individuals are assigned the same task by their supervisor, and that one is confident of her ability to carry it out successfully, whereas the other has some serious doubts on this score. Which person is more likely to succeed? Assuming that all other factors (e.g., differences in their ability and motivation) are held constant, it is reasonable to predict that the first will do better. Such an individual is higher in a personality variable known as **self-efficacy**—the belief in one's own capacity to perform a task.[35] When considered in the context of a given task, self-efficacy is not, strictly speaking an aspect of personality. However, people seem to acquire general expectations about their ability to perform a wide range of tasks in many different contexts. Such generalized beliefs about self-efficacy are stable over time, and these can be viewed as a personality variable.

How do feelings of self-efficacy develop? Theorists agree that there are two major factors involved: *direct experiences*, feedback from performing similar tasks in the past, and *vicarious experiences*, observations of others' experiences performing the task. How do people translate these experiences into task performance? A conceptualization recently proposed by Gist and Mitchell attempts to answer this question.[36] Specifically, their model suggests that people cognitively appraise their experiences, both direct and indirect, to come up with judgments about the extent to which they can perform the task—that is, their self-efficacy. In making such appraisals, people are likely to analyze the task and assess how their resources and existing constraints will help or hinder their chances of success. At the same time, they are likely to judge the extent to which their past outcomes may be attributable to their own skills, or simply luck (that is, whether internal or external attributions account for their past performance; see Chapter 2). Once self-efficacy is judged, people are likely to gauge their performance accordingly. That is, the more they think they can succeed, the more likely they will reach for difficult goals and persist at doing so. And it is this level of effort that will determine task performance. Then, to complete the process, the successfulness of one's task performance feeds back into the base of experiences from which future self-efficacy judgments are made (see Figure 3-8).

Not surprisingly, self-efficacy has been found to be a good predictor of people's success on the job. To illustrate this point, let's consider a recent study conducted by Vasil that examined self-efficacy among university professors .[37] A large sample of professors were administered a test assessing their self-efficacy, particularly as it applied to doing research, one of the professors' key job requirements. A measure was also taken of their research productivity, including such indices as the number of articles and books published, the number of grants received, the number of doctoral students whose dissertations they directed, and the like. Consistent with our discussion of self-efficacy, it was found that self-efficacy was positively correlated with research productivity; that is, productivity increased as self-efficacy increased.

FIGURE 3-8

HOW DOES SELF-EFFICACY INFLUENCE PERFORMANCE? A MODEL

High degrees of self-efficacy generally enhance task performance. The steps summarized here have been proposed by Gist and Mitchell as the underlying processes responsible for this connection. (Source: Based on Gist & Mitchell, 1992; see Note 36.)

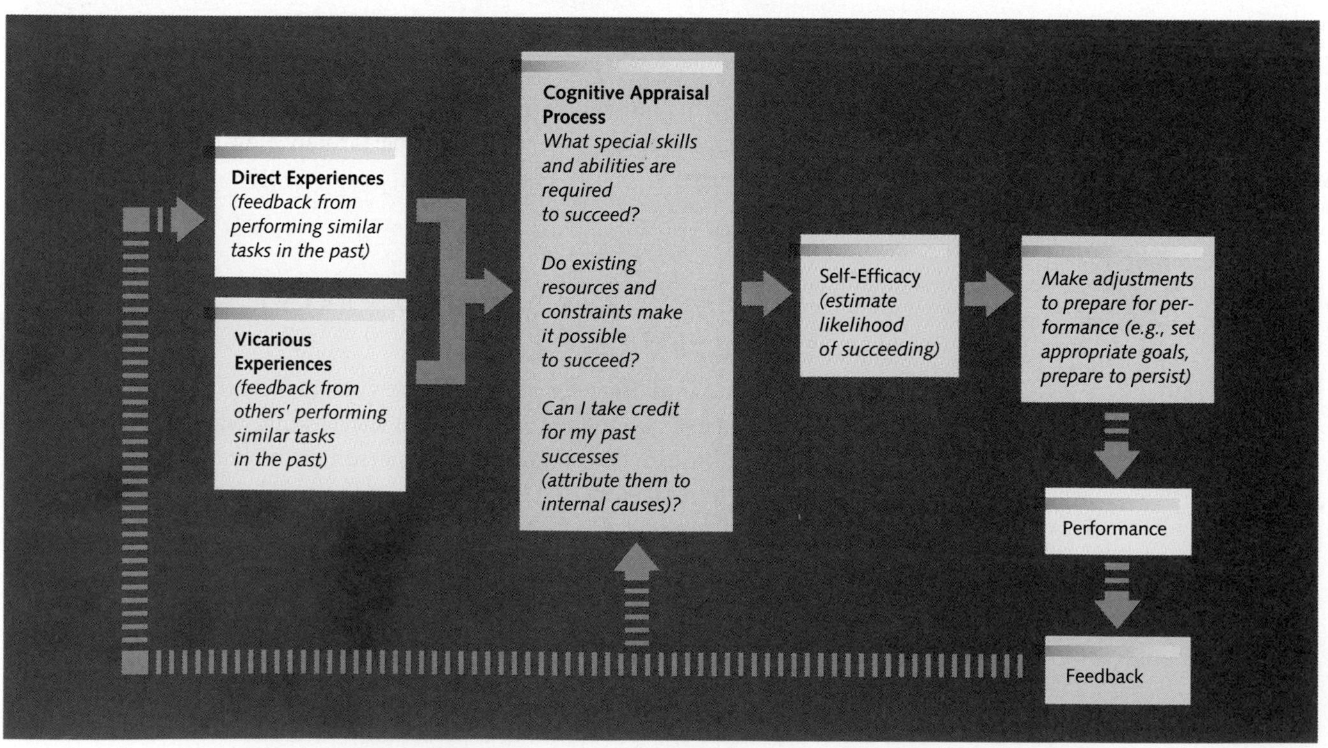

It also was found that this effect was stronger among those who believed that their past success was due to their ability, as opposed to external factors such as luck. Both these findings are completely consistent with the model of the self-efficacy process we have described.

Although self-efficacy is a relatively new topic in the study of organizational behavior, its importance already has been recognized.[38] For example, the idea of self-efficacy has been a central part of attempts to explain how the process of goal setting works to improve motivation and task performance (see Chapter 4). In addition, self-efficacy also may be a useful tool for use in career counseling situations, helping to pinpoint areas in which additional skill development is needed (see Chapter 7). In short, the concept of self-efficacy is involved in several different aspects of organizational behavior. (Most interesting, perhaps, are attempts to change an individual's level of self-efficacy. For a look at how such efforts have been put to use in identifying a promising solution to an important organizational and personal problem, see the Organization of Tomorrow section below.)

THE ORGANIZATION OF TOMORROW

SPEEDING UP RE-EMPLOYMENT WITH SELF-EFFICACY TRAINING: HELPING PEOPLE HELP THEMSELVES

We tend to think of self-efficacy as we do most personality variables: it's just the way you are; some people have more of it, others have less, and there's nothing you can do to change it. But in the case of self-efficacy, because our general expectations about our ability to perform a wide range of tasks is based on our past experiences with success and failure, it is reasonable to consider the possibility that as these experiences change, so too may self-efficacy perceptions. And of course, as they do, behavioral changes may follow. This is the general rationale behind a recent study by Eden and Aviram that has very interesting implications for how unemployed people might become re-employed in tomorrow's organizations.[39]

To appreciate this work, ask yourself why athletes commit themselves to such demanding undertakings as winning a gold medal at the Olympics? In large part, it's because they believe they have "got what it takes" to do it. When we feel optimistic about our capacity to succeed, we are willing to intensify our efforts and persist in the face of long odds and setbacks. However, when we feel we don't stand a chance, we are unlikely to rise to the occasion and simply give up. A process such as this appears to operate when people lose their jobs. Because so much of our self-concepts is tied to our jobs, losing a job can be a devastating blow to the way we think about ourselves, raising doubts about how good we are at what we do.[40] When such thoughts occur, people might be reluctant to look for new jobs, thinking that they don't stand a chance of succeeding. This is a vicious cycle: job loss reduces self-efficacy, which reduces one's effort at searching for a new job, which prolongs unemployment, which lowers self-efficacy still further, and so on (see Figure 3-9).

Realizing the devastating personal toll that this cycle takes on people, Eden and Aviram developed a technique designed to help unemployed people break the cycle and seek re-employment. They reasoned that self-efficacy could be rebuilt in two ways. First, they had to teach people how to be effective as a job seeker (e.g., how to make a convincing presentation of their skills during an interview). Second, they had to be exposed to models of people who searched for and found a good job, giving them a vicarious (i.e., an indirect, or secondhand) experience with success in this arena. To do this, they studied a group of unemployed Israeli vocational workers (unemployed between 2 and 18 weeks) who enrolled in a special workshop conducted to help them seek re-employment. The workshop, conducted over 2–1/2 weeks, began by viewing 4- to 5-minute video tapes showing people successfully performing various job-search behaviors. These behaviors were then discussed by the group, followed by role-playing sessions in which each participant rehearsed the behavior they saw in the tape. Feedback was provided about how effectively the individual practiced the behaviors, and strong verbal encouragement was given. To determine the effectiveness of the workshops, the investigators compared those who were trained to a comparable group of Israeli vocational workers who were not trained, both before the workshops began and after they were over.

Some fascinating results were found. First, the researchers measured self-efficacy using a standardized paper-and-pencil test, and noted that the workshops were, in fact, effective in raising levels of this variable in the participants. Specifically, although the trained and the untrained workers had relatively equal levels of self-efficacy before training occurred, self-efficacy rose dramatically among those who were trained (even as long as two months after it was completed!) whereas it stayed the same among those who were untrained. Clearly, the workshops were successful at raising the self-efficacy of the unemployed. But, the more crucial question remains: does raising self-efficacy help promote job search behavior—and ultimately, getting a new job?

To answer this question, participants in the study were asked to describe their job search behaviors during the two previous days. Each specific episode of job search behavior was counted (e.g., "I visited Factory *X* and filled out an application"). The researchers found that those who scored high in self-efficacy were more actively involved in searching for work than those who scored low. Insofar as low self-efficacy was expected to discourage people from looking for work, this finding is not surprising. But did job searching increase following self-efficacy training? The answer depended on the initial level of self-efficacy people had. Among those who were already high in self-efficacy, training in self-efficacy had a negligible effect on their job search behavior. After all, these individuals were already willing to look for work, so additional training in self-efficacy didn't matter. However, among people with low self-efficacy, training was extremely effective. In fact, it was responsible for getting them to do as much looking for jobs as those who were high in self-efficacy to begin with. By contrast, people with low self-efficacy who were not trained suffered from the vicious cycle described earlier; as time went on, they became even less involved in finding work.

Did the job search behavior pay off? To find out, the researchers recontacted the participants and asked them if they had gotten a job yet. Among those who were initially low in self-efficacy but trained to improve, a far greater percentage of people were found to be re-employed than those who were not trained (62 versus only 23 percent). This success rate was so high that it matched those who were high in self-esteem to begin with. So, not only did self-efficacy training get people to engage in job search behaviors, but these behaviors were effective in getting them re-employed. In other words, among those who stood to benefit most from the training—people with low self-efficacy—the training was remarkably effective.

The findings from Eden and Aviram's study are important for several reasons. From a scientific perspective, they suggest that a fundamental aspect of people's personality can be changed, and in a way that can have beneficial effects on their well-being. From a practical perspective, this means that concrete steps can be taken to help unemployed people become re-employed. Systematic training in self-efficacy appears to be an effective means of helping those individuals who suffer from low self-efficacy take more control over their lives—in short, helping them to help themselves. Although additional research is needed to reveal more about the conditions in which self-efficacy training is most effective, we believe it is a promising technique and are optimistic that it will be used as a key weapon in the arsenal of social scientists attempting to tackle the vexing problem of unemployment.

FIGURE 3-9

THE LINK BETWEEN SELF-EFFICACY AND JOB LOSS: A VICIOUS CYCLE

People's self-efficacy is lowered when they lose their jobs. This discourages them from looking for new jobs, which prolongs their unemployment. Their self-efficacy is further reduced as a result, continuing the cycle. Self-efficacy training is effective at breaking the cycle.

SELF-ESTEEM: THE IMPORTANCE OF SELF-EVALUATIONS

Beliefs about one's ability to perform specific tasks are an important part of the *self-concept*—individuals' conceptions of their own abilities, traits, and skills. Yet they are only a small part. Another important aspect concerns **self-esteem**—the extent to which people hold positive or negative views about themselves. People high in self-esteem evaluate themselves favorably, believing they possess many desirable traits and qualities. In contrast, people low in self-esteem evaluate themselves unfavorably, believing they are lacking in important respects and that they have characteristics that others consider unappealing. Do such feelings affect behavior in organizational settings? Considerable evidence suggests that they do.[41]

To begin with, evidence suggests that people who are low in self-esteem tend to be less successful in their job searches than those who are high in self-esteem. This finding was obtained in an investigation by Ellis and Taylor focusing on the job search behavior of a group of seniors about to graduate from college.[42] Measures of their self-esteem were taken, and these were compared with evaluations by organizational recruiters who had interviewed them. Not surprisingly, compared to candidates with high self-esteem, those with low self-esteem came across as less confident in their abilities and were less likely to receive job offers. Adding to this picture, recent research has found that when people with low self-esteem are eventually employed, they tend to be attracted to positions in larger organizations, ones in which it is more difficult for them to be noticed and call attention to themselves.[43]

Once on the job, what can be expected of people who have low self-esteem? Research has shown that the lower an employee's self-esteem, the less likely he or she is to take any active steps to solve problems confronted on the job (e.g., insufficient time or skill to do a job). As a result, their performance tends to suffer.[44] By contrast, employees with high levels of self-esteem are more inclined to actively attempt to acquire the resources needed to cope with work problems, and to use their skills and abilities to their fullest—and, as a result, to perform at higher levels. Interestingly, people with low self-esteem tend to be aware of their tendency to perform poorly. Research has shown that they are predisposed to evaluate themselves quite negatively (especially when ambiguity exists concerning their performance), and to believe that they are inherently responsible for their poor performance.[45]

Although our comments so far sound somewhat discouraging with respect to the fate of people with low self-esteem, we can conclude on a more positive note: the good news is that low self-esteem can be changed.[46] While formal approaches are available, techniques that require the skills of a trained professional to implement (such as psychiatrists or clinical psychologists) can be very time consuming. Fortunately, there are some things that can be done on an everyday basis in organizations to help minimize the degree to which feelings of low self-esteem may emerge.[47] Here are some suggestions:

1. *Make people feel uniquely valuable*. Everyone has his or her own special contributions that can be made to the company, and these need to be recognized. Leaders should encourage all constructive ideas and behaviors, especially those that reflect the unique differences of individuals.
2. *Make people feel competent*. It is a good idea to recognize the good things that people do and praise them accordingly. That is, "catch someone in the act of

doing something right." Managers who fail to credit their subordinates for their ideas and achievements miss a golden opportunity to build the self-esteem of these individuals.

3. *Make people feel secure.* The less people know about what is going on in an organization, the less likely they are to understand things, and the less likely they are to know what's expected of them. Employees' self-esteem is enhanced when managers make their expectations clear, and are forthright with them.
4. *Make people feel empowered.* People who lack power (even limited power, such as the opportunity to chose among a list of acceptable options) will tend to suffer from low self-esteem. By contrast, employees who are given opportunities to decide how to act will feel better about themselves and their work.
5. *Make people feel connected.* It is important for people to feel that they belong and are appreciated. It is useful to create opportunities for people to feel accepted, even if only during social events, in which they have opportunities to make use of each other's skills and experiences.

Naturally, although these techniques will not change the basic structure of someone's personality, they are bound to go a long way toward alleviating the problems resulting from low self-esteem in organizations. These suggestions are predicated on a very simple but powerful idea: that organizations, often unknowingly, fail to do anything to build and maintain their employees' self-esteem. To the extent that top executives consider the self-esteem of their employees a valuable resource, they would be wise to follow these suggestions as a way of managing this resource and using it to its potential.

SELF-MONITORING: SELF-IMAGE VERSUS PRIVATE REALITY

Imagine that you're a middle manager at a company picnic, going around talking to different groups of people. Would you behave differently when interacting with lower-level employees than when interacting with higher-level employees? Interestingly, there are individual differences with respect to such behavior. In other words, some people readily adjust their behavior to produce the most positive reactions in people. However, others are less aware of, or less concerned about, their impact on others, and simply act in the way that reflects their inner feelings without changing it in each new context. This dimension of behavior is referred to as **self-monitoring**.[48] *High self-monitors* tend to be guided by their efforts to produce positive reactions in others, and are willing to adjust their behavior to do so. At the other end of the range are *low self-monitors*, individuals who are unwilling to make such adaptations; for them, "what you see is what you get."

Differences between people with respect to self-monitoring are related to various aspects of organizational behavior. For example, research has found that high self-monitors think more about quitting their jobs when they are dissatisfied than low self-monitors.[49] In other words, they are willing to make the adjustments in their behavior required to change the unsatisfactory state of affairs. By contrast, low self-monitors are more tolerant of the unsatisfactory conditions and are less likely to think of quitting. The ready adaptability of high self-monitors is manifested in another way as well. Specifically, high self-monitors are often more effective than low self-monitors in jobs that require *boundary spanning*—that is, communicating and interacting with different groups of people from different professional or occupational groups.[50] Since they can readily adjust their actions to the norms, expectations, and styles of each group, high self-monitors are more successful in dealing with them, and this improves their performance. Because boundary-spanning roles are very important in most organizations, it makes good sense to consider assigning people high in self-monitoring to such positions.

The superiority of high self-monitors in communication skills also has been demonstrated in other ways. For example, in a study focusing on this issue, Larkin asked college students to think of the best and the worst instructors they ever had.[51] When they rated these individuals with respect to self-monitoring, clear differences emerged: the best teachers were rated much higher (see the left panel of Figure 3-10). In a follow-up study, Larkin asked participants to imagine that they were going to tutor two students, one very tense and nervous, and the other overconfident. They then rated the extent to which they felt they could change their teaching style to fit the needs of each individual. As predicted, people who were high in self-monitoring reported greater flexibility than those who were low in self-monitoring (see the right panel of Figure 3-10).

Extending these findings is research showing that self-monitoring is also related to the use of several different techniques of *impression management* (recall our discussion of this topic in Chapter 2). In particular, findings reported by Fandt and Ferris indicate that high self-monitors are more likely than lows to create a favorable impression on their managers by selectively picking and choosing, or

FIGURE 3-10

SELF-MONITORING AND TEACHING EXCELLENCE

College students rated their best instructors as higher in self-monitoring than their worst instructors. In addition, students high in self-monitoring reported greater flexibility than students low in self-monitoring in their own teaching styles while serving as tutors. (Source: Based on date reported in Larkin, 1987; see Note 50.)

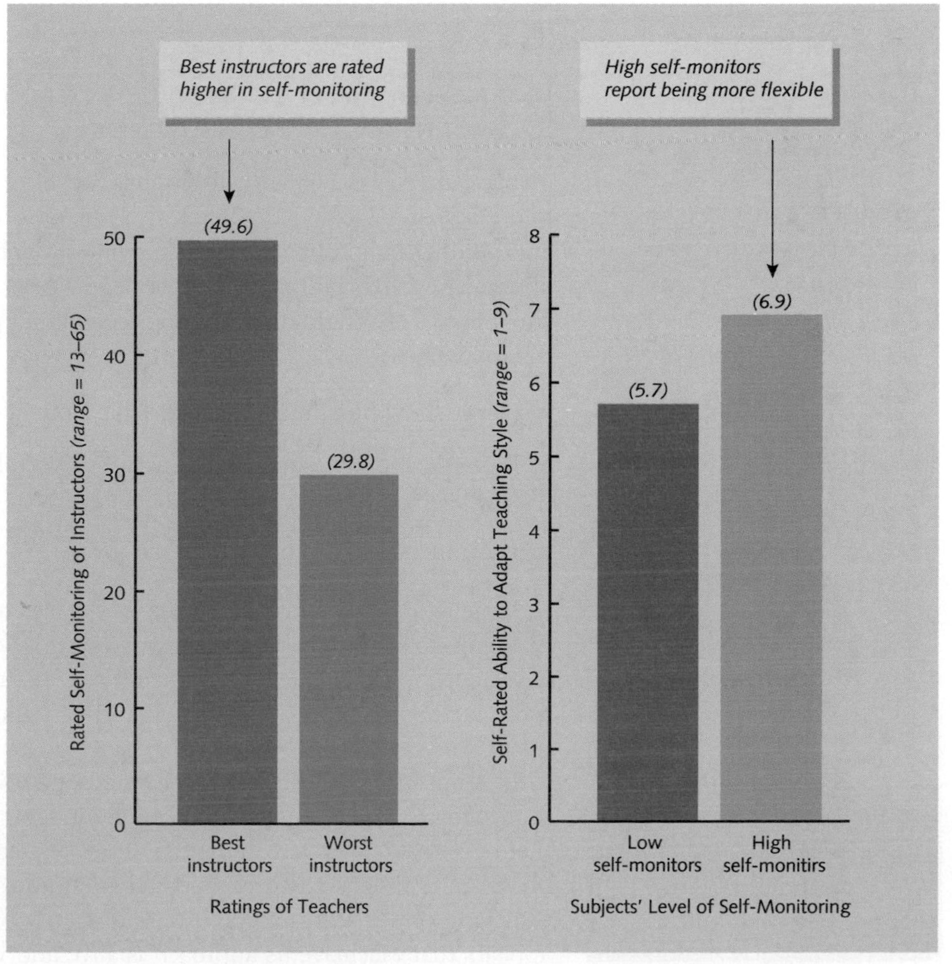

"filtering," the information they transmit to their superiors.[52] As you may recall from Chapter 2, Fandt and Ferris asked customer service employees in a telecommunications corporation to make decisions concerning realistic customer service problems (e.g., power failures on a hot summer afternoon). Participants decided how to proceed in these situations and then wrote a brief report justifying these decisions to their supervisors. Under conditions of high accountability (i.e., when they were responsible for the results of their decisions), subjects high in self-monitoring transmitted more positive information (i.e., information reflecting favorably on their decisions) and more defensive information (i.e., information that shifted the blame for mistakes to others) than people low in self-monitoring. Thus, high self-monitors engaged in impression management to a greater extent than low self-monitors.

On some occasions, high self-monitors' concerns about making a good impression leads them to show concern over others' feelings. For example, when they are in a conflict situation with another, high self-monitors are inclined to resolve these conflicts through collaboration or compromise than through avoidance or competition.[53] That is, they are more conciliatory in their approach, showing greater concern for long-range solutions than low self-monitors. (We will discuss conflict more fully in Chapter 11.) High self-monitors are also less willing than low self-monitors to show outward signs of joy (i.e., to gloat) when they defeat another in a competitive situation.[54] This is an indication of their interest in concealing their true emotions in a situation in which it may be considered inappropriate to reveal them. Taken together, these various findings suggest that self-monitoring is an aspect of personality with important implications for understanding organizational behavior.

MACHIAVELLIANISM: USING OTHERS ON THE WAY TO SUCCESS

Back in 1513 the Italian philosopher Niccolò Machiavelli published a book entitled *The Prince* (see Figure 3-11). In it, he outlined a ruthless strategy for seizing and holding political power now known as **Machiavellianism.** The essence of his approach was straightforward: other people can be readily used or manipulated by sticking to a few basic rules. Among the guiding principles he recommended were the following:

- Never show humility; arrogance is far more effective when dealing with others.
- Morality and ethics are for the weak; powerful people feel free to lie, cheat, and deceive whenever it suits their purpose.
- It is much better to be feared than loved.

FIGURE 3-11
NICCOLO MACHIAVELLI (1469-1527)
People who follow Machiavelli's approach to dealing with others are likely to do whatever it takes to get what they want.

In general, Machiavelli urged those who desired power to adapt a totally pragmatic approach to life. Let others be swayed by considerations of friendship, loyalty, or fair play, he suggested; a truly successful leader should always be above those factors. In short, he or she should be willing to do whatever it takes to get his or her way!

It is unsettling to think that the philosophy Machiavelli promoted almost 500 years ago is still very much with us today. In fact, it is readily visible in many books that have made their way to the top of the best-seller list in recent years—the kind of "get to the top at all costs" books that outline similar self-centered strategies for achieving power and success. If the popularity of such books is any indication, it appears that Machiavelli's approach is alive and well in contemporary society. But are these strategies really put to practical use? In other words, are there really individuals who choose to live by the ruthless, self-serving creed Machiavelli proposed? The answer appears to be yes. When large numbers of people complete a test designed to measure acceptance of Machiavelli's suggestions (the *Mach scale*, as it is called), many receive very high scores.[55] Thus, people with a Machiavellian orientation (referred to as high Machs) are quite common. In fact, you already may have come across such individuals.

If high Machs are willing to do whatever it takes to succeed, you would expect that they would be rather successful at whatever jobs they perform. But, are they? Insight into this issue is provided by a fascinating study recently conducted by Schultz.[56] In planning this investigation, Schultz reasoned that because high Machs would go to just about any lengths to achieve success, they would perform well under loosely structured situations (i.e., those in which there are few rules) because they are well equipped to take advantage of the opportunities existing in such contexts. By contrast, in tightly structured situations the rules regarding expected behavior are clearly spelled out, and people's behavior is highly restricted. In contexts like this, high Machs have little or no opportunities to exercise the skills that make them so unique, leading them to become apathetic and disinterested in their work and to suffer impaired performance as a result.

To test this logic, Schultz compared the performance of sales representatives working in two different settings. One sample worked in a tightly structured situation, a large telephone company in which there was a large number of organizational levels, relatively close supervision, a lengthy set of regulations in which to operate, and no opportunities to "cut deals" or manipulate people in any way. The other sample consisted of sales reps who worked in loosely structured settings—various stock brokerage firms, organizations in which there were relatively few organizational levels, a rather informal style of supervision, fewer regulations, and many opportunities to manipulate sales. Two measures were used to compare sales performance, the amount of commission earned during the six-month study period, and the number of clients maintained. The results supported Schultz's hypotheses. Specifically, stock brokers who were high Machs performed better than those who were low Machs, whereas telephone company sales reps who were high Machs performed worse than those who were low Machs. These findings are consistent with the interactionist perspective discussed earlier in this chapter: the effects of personality depended on the nature of the setting in which people worked.

As you might imagine, high Machs can be very difficult to have around in one's work environment. Because they are attracted to situations in which they can use their devious skills and show little welfare for others, they can be wily adversaries indeed. Although you cannot always restructure work situations so as to stymie high Machs, there are several strategies you can use to protect yourself from them. Here are several that may prove useful.

- *Expose them to others.* One reason high Machs so often get away with breaking promises, lying, and using "dirty tricks" is that in many cases, their victims choose to remain silent. This is hardly surprising inasmuch as few people wish to call attention to the fact that they have been cheated or manipulated. Unfortunately, this understandable desire to protect one's ego plays directly into the high Machs' hands, leaving them to repeat their devious behaviors. One effective means of dealing with high Machs involves exposing their unprincipled behavior. Once their actions are made public within an organization, others may be on guard, making it harder for high Machs to use (and get away with) their manipulative tactics in the future.

- *Pay attention to what others do, not what they say*. High Machs are often masters at deception. They frequently succeed in convincing other people that they have their bests interests at heart, and are at their most convincing when they are busily cutting the ground out from under the unsuspecting person. Although it is often difficult to see through such duplicitous maneuvers, it may help to focus on what others do rather than what they say. If their actions suggest that they are cold-bloodedly manipulating the people around them, even while loudly proclaiming commitment to such principles as loyalty and fair play, chances are good that they are Machiavellian in orientation and should be carefully avoided.
- *Avoid situations that give high Machs an edge*. To assure their success, high Machs prefer to operate in certain types of situations—ones in which others' emotions run high and in which others are uncertain about how to proceed. The reason for this preference is simple: high Machs realize that under such conditions many people will be distracted and less likely to recognize that they are being manipulated for someone else's gain. It is usually wise, therefore, to avoid such situations. And, if this is not possible, you should at least refrain from making important decisions or commitments at that time. Such restraint may make it harder for high Machs to use you for their own benefit.

Together, these suggestions may help you avoid falling under the spell—and into the clutches—of unprincipled, pragmatic high Machs. Given the presence of at least some high Machs in most organizations, and the dangers they pose to the unwary, it is worth keeping these suggestions, and the existence of this unsettling aspect of personality, firmly in mind.

WORK-RELATED MOTIVES: ACHIEVEMENT, POWER, AND AFFILIATION

Some people, such as American Express's new president, Kenneth Chenault (recall our Preview Case), seem to yearn for and focus on success. Others concentrate predominantly on status; they want to be admired and respected by others. Still others seem primarily concerned with friendship or love; having pleasant, satisfying relations with others is what they crave most. Do such differences play a role in organizational behavior? They most certainly do. Differences with respect to several basic motives can affect performance on many tasks, success in leadership roles, and a wide range of other outcomes. We now examine three such motives—*achievement*, *power*, and *affiliation.*

ACHIEVEMENT MOTIVATION: THE QUEST FOR EXCELLENCE

As its name suggests, **achievement motivation** (sometimes termed the *need for achievement*) refers to the strength of an individual's desire to excel—to succeed at difficult tasks and to do them better than anyone else. People high in achievement motivation may be characterized as having a highly task-oriented outlook: they are more concerned with getting things done than they are with having good relationships with others. Also, because they are so interested in achieving success, people who have a high amount of achievement motivation tend to seek tasks that are moderately difficult and challenging.[57] After all, too difficult a task is likely to lead to failure, and too easy a task doesn't offer sufficient challenge. By contrast, people

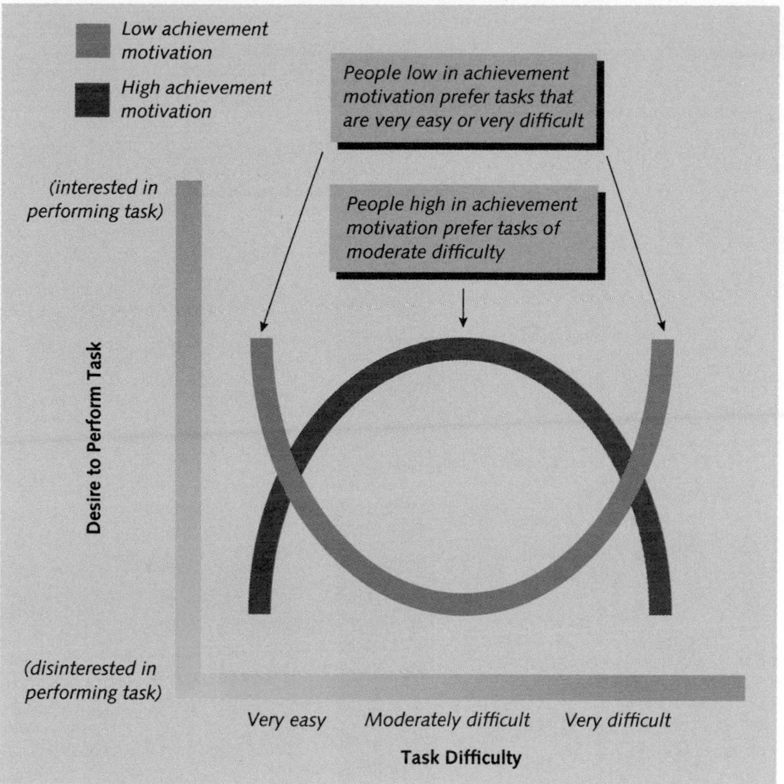

FIGURE 3-12
ACHIEVEMENT MOTIVATION AND ATTRACTION TO TASKS: THE GENERAL RELATIONSHIP
In general, people who are high in achievement motivation are attracted to tasks of moderate difficulty. Too simple tasks don't offer enough challenge, and too difficult tasks are likely to lead to failure. However, people who are low in achievement motivation are attracted to tasks that are either very simple (where success is virtually guaranteed) or very difficult (where failure can be readily excused).

who score low on achievement motivation very much prefer extremely difficult or extremely easy tasks. This is because if the task is easy enough success is almost guaranteed, and if the task is difficult, failure can readily be justified by attributing it to external sources (i.e., the extreme difficulty) (see Figure 3-12).

As you might imagine, people who are high in achievement motivation strongly desire feedback on their performance. This allows them to adjust their aspirations (i.e., to shoot for easier or more difficult goals) and to determine when they have succeeded, allowing them to attain the good feelings about their accomplishments that they crave. As part of this tendency, people who are high and low in achievement motivation are not likely to be attracted to the same kinds of jobs. This idea was demonstrated in a recent study by Turban and Keon.[58] Participants in this research were management students who read descriptions of hypothetical companies that were systematically varied with respect to several factors, including the nature of their pay systems. Some companies were described as having a *merit-based* pay system, one in which pay and promotion was based entirely on the quality of individual performance; others were described as having a *seniority-based* pay system, one in which pay and promotion was determined by the length of time working in the company. After being measured with respect to their level of achievement motivation, participants were asked to read descriptions of the various organizations and to indicate how interested they would be in working for that company. The results showed that although all participants were more attracted to organizations that rewarded merit, this tendency was much greater among people who scored high on achievement motivation (see Figure 3-13). This finding makes a great deal of sense. After all, the more interested people are in achieving success, the more interested they will be in working for a company in which the pay system recognizes their accomplishments.

Given their strong desire to excel, it seems reasonable to predict that people high in achievement motivation will attain greater success in their careers than others. To some extent, this is true. People high in achievement motivation tend to gain promotions more rapidly than those who are low in achievement motivation, at least early in their careers.[59] However, people who are high in achievement motivation are not necessarily superior managers. In part, this might be due to the desire of people who are high in achievement motivation to create situations in which they can receive credit for their performance while carefully monitoring others. As we will see later in this book (Chapter 15), such ways of structuring organizations are not always conducive to high performance. Illustrating this phenomenon, Miller and Droge found that chief executive officers (CEOs) who are high on achievement motivation were more likely to centralize power (i.e., to keep power in the hands of just a few) than CEOs who were low on achievement moti-

FIGURE 3-13
ACHIEVEMENT MOTIVATION AND ATTRACTION TO ORGANIZATIONS

Turban and Keon found that people were more strongly attracted to organizations that used merit-based pay systems (ones that recognize their accomplishments) than organizations using seniority-based pay systems. This attraction was much stronger among individuals who scored high in achievement motivation than those who scored low in achievement motivation. (Source: Based on data reported by Turban & Keon, 1993; see Note 43.)

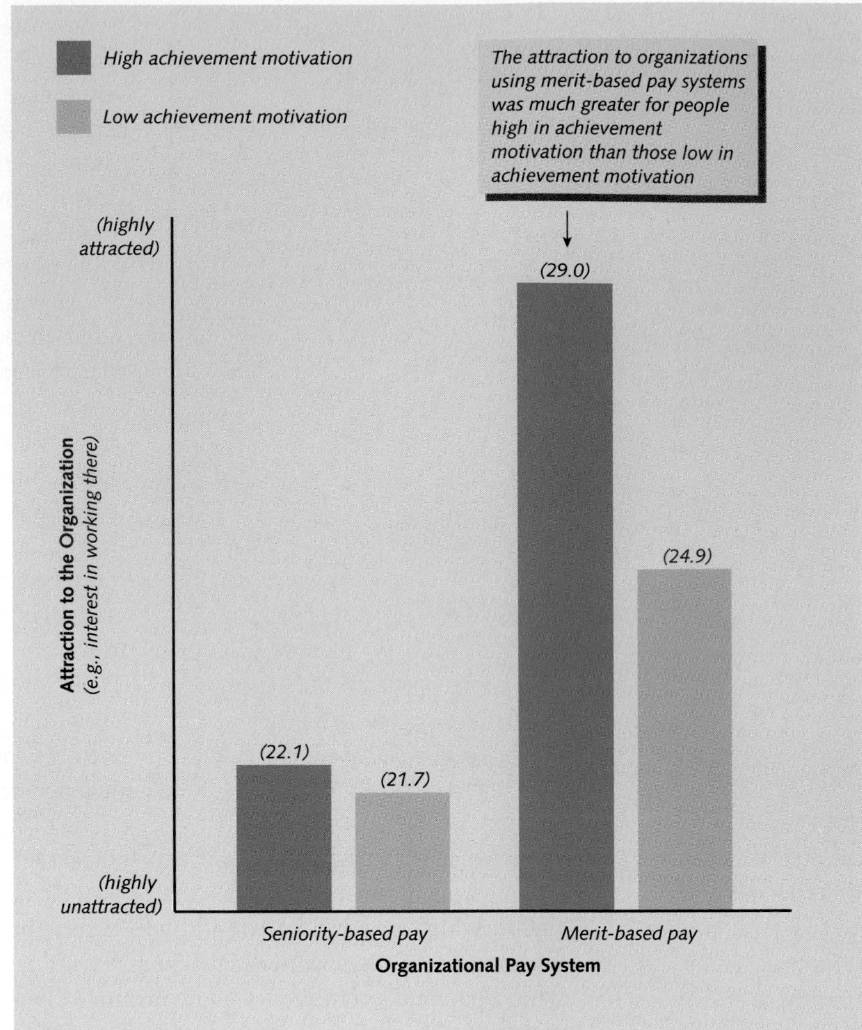

vation.[60] Although such decisions may help tightly control corporate performance, such conditions are not always appropriate nor are they well accepted. As a result, while a high achievement motive may be an important determinant of individual success, there is little reason to believe that it will contribute to organizational success. (This is not to say that the collective impact of achievement motivation cannot have profound effects on society. For a discussion of the effects of achievement motivation in various cultures throughout history, including modern-day Japan, see the Global Organization section on the opposite page.)

AFFILIATION AND POWER MOTIVATION: TWO SIDES OF THE SAME COIN?

At first glance, the desire to be in charge **(power motivation)** and the desire to have close, friendly relations with others **(affiliation motivation)** appear to be unrelated. It is possible to imagine people high on both dimensions, people who are low on both, and people who are high on one and low on the other. Research findings suggest, however, that the two are often linked.

First, consider the matter of managerial success. What kind of individuals are most successful as managers? One possibility, suggested by McClelland and

THE GLOBAL ORGANIZATION

NATIONAL DIFFERENCES IN ACHIEVEMENT MOTIVATION: HISTORICAL ANALYSES, WITH JAPAN AS A MODERN-DAY EXAMPLE

Achievement motivation—the desire to excel, to achieve success. Not only is this a major personality variable, a key difference between individuals, but also a shared cultural value, a fundamental difference between people of various national groups. And, as established in classic research by psychologist David McClelland, the father of achievement motivation, it is responsible for differences among nations with respect to economic development.[61] Although McClelland's research was quite complex, his reasoning was straightforward: members of a society must have sufficiently high amounts of achievement motivation before it can become industrialized.

To test this idea, McClelland analyzed the children's stories from twenty-two different cultures with respect to the degree to which themes of achievement motivation were contained in them (e.g., the classic American story, "The Little Engine That Could," would reflect a great deal of achievement motivation). (As we will describe later in this chapter, analyzing the content of stories is a scientifically established method of measuring achievement motivation.) His analyses covered two years: 1925 and 1950, a period during which the world experienced considerable amounts of industrial growth. McClelland used two different measures of economic development: per capita income, and electrical production per capita. After massive amounts of data had been gathered, the major finding emerged: achievement motivation scores were highly correlated with economic growth. In other words, the greater emphasis that was placed on achievement in the stories told to children in various nations, the more industrialized those nations became as the children grew up. Suggesting that this finding isn't just a fluke, McClelland also went back further in history—much further, in fact—to the period of the Greek empire, between 2,000 and 3,000 years ago.[62] In this investigation, achievement motivation was measured by scoring the literary content of writings by the leading authors of that era. As expected, the period of climax (475 to 362 B.C.) was preceded by the highest achievement scores whereas the period of decline (362 to 100 B.C.) was preceded by the lowest. Findings such as these lend good support to McClelland's claim that a nation's economic success is critically related to the achievement motivation of its people.

A good example of this can be seen in Japan, where in modern times there has existed "a pervasive preoccupation with achievement and accomplishment."[63] With this in mind, it is not surprising that there has emerged in recent years a manifestation of achievement motivation known as *kaizen* (pronounced *ky' zen*).[64] Loosely translated, *kaizen* means improvement—specifically, continuing, ongoing improvement for everyone in an organization, from the president of the company to the lowest-ranking employee. So pervasive is the expectation for change as a continuous process in Japanese life, that the theme can be seen in the ancient Japanese saying, "If a man has not been seen for three days, his friends should take a look at him to see what changes have befallen him." Even in as short a period as three days the Japanese expect some change to occur in people!

Kaizen, the philosophy of achievement that pervades Japanese enterprises (and with increasing frequency, U.S. ones too), runs counter to the traditional wisdom of American business expressed in the phrases: "don't mess with success," "if it ain't broke, don't fix it," and "leave well enough alone." Despite these admonitions, the evidence is clear that companies that don't improve the way they operate on a continuous basis may find it difficult to stay competitive. "Improve or die" appears to be a better slogan in today's era of global competition. In other words, to achieve success today, it is insufficient to rest on one's laurels until it is too late, and only then have top management introduce innovations and sell them to rank-and-file employees. The *kaizen* approach to corporate achievement calls for *everyone* to be involved in the improvement process all the time—what has been called *total quality improvement*.[65] To give you a better idea of how this philosophy of achievement can be implemented, we have summarized some suggestions in Table 3-1. Although *kaizen* is far more complex than outlined here (including specific statistical techniques for ensuring the quality of the manufacturing process), this table provides good guidance as to how the need for achievement can be developed in today's organizations (see Chapter 16).

In summary, it is useful to think of *kaizen* as an institutionalized philosophy of achievement motivation that has proven successful when translated into the management of organizations. Although it originated in Japan (based on approaches suggested by the American W. E. Deming, who helped rebuild Japan's economic base after World War II), the approach is becoming increasingly popular in other nations. However, insofar as it stresses achievement motivation, and this variable is deeply rooted in societal culture, as McClelland demonstrated, it remains an interesting question as to whether or not the approach will catch on in other nations.

TABLE 3-1

Tips for Developing an Achievement Orientation

The notion of total quality improvement, *central to the Japanese management philosophy known as* kaizen, *emphasizes a company-wide achievement orientation. Here are some tips for implementing such a philosophy.*

SUGGESTION	EXPLANATION
Set moderately difficult goals.	*Because goals that are too high cannot be attained, and those that are too low are not very challenging (and tend to lower organizational performance), moderately difficult goals are the most highly motivating.*
Give lots of feedback.	*Not only does feedback provide people with information about how they need to improve, it also encourages very hard work among those who strive to achieve success.*
Let people take responsibility for their work.	*The more everyone feels accountable for producing high-quality goods and services, the more they will strive to achieve perfection.*
Encourage an "action" orientation.	*It is important to encourage people to try out new ideas, and share suggestions for improvement with management. Formal suggestion system systems should be implemented, and all employees should be encouraged to use them.*

Source: Based on suggestions by Holpp, 1989; see Note 65.

Boyatzis, is that it is people who are high in power motivation, but low in affiliation motivation.[66] Such individuals will focus on gaining influence over others while at the same time avoiding the trap of being unduly concerned about being liked by them. In other words, they will seek power and influence, but won't shy away from the tough decisions and actions often required by this quest. (According to McClelland and Boyatzis, another characteristic—a high degree of *self-control*—is also important for managerial success. People who easily lose their tempers or who have a low degree of self-discipline won't succeed as managers even if they possess a high need for power and a low need for affiliation.) Are individuals who possess this combination of traits—known as the **leadership motivation pattern (LMP)** actually more effective than those who do not? Research by McClelland and Boyatzis suggest that this is so.

In this investigation, managers' levels of power motivation, affiliation motivation, and self-control were assessed by means of appropriate tests. On the basis of this information, the managers were then divided into two groups: those who demonstrated the LMP and those who did not. Next the researchers obtained information about these individuals' job levels eight and sixteen years after they joined their organizations. Results offered clear support for the role of the leadership motivation pattern in managerial success, at least for managers who held nontechnical positions. For this group, persons who possessed the LMP were much more likely to be promoted to higher-level jobs than those who did not. (These findings did not hold true for managers holding technical jobs, because for them promotion depended more on technical competence than on the ability to deal effectively with others.)

These findings suggest that individual differences with respect to several motives are closely linked to important aspects of organizational behavior. The nature of this relationship, however, is far from simple. To understand how individuals' motives influence their job performance or careers, we must take into account not only the motives themselves but also the combinations or patterns in which they occur, the specific jobs being performed, and the organizational contexts in which these motives operate. Only when the complex interplay of such factors is given full consideration can knowledge about individuals' motives yield valuable insights into their behavior in work settings.

MEASURING PERSONALITY: SOME BASIC METHODS

hysical traits such as height and weight can be measured quite easily and directly by using simple devices such as a tape measure and a scale. The various aspects of personality, however, cannot be assessed quite so simply. There are no rulers for measuring self-esteem and no thermometers for measuring achievement motivation. How, then, can we quantify differences between individuals with respect to the various personality characteristics we've been describing? Several methods exist for accomplishing this task. In this section, we will describe some of the major techniques used to measure personality, and then consider some of the essential characteristics of such measuring devices.

OBJECTIVE AND PROJECTIVE TESTS: THE MAJOR ASSESSMENT TECHNIQUES

The assessment of personality is a task that occupies a great deal of time among social scientists.[67] As you might imagine, such knowledge may be put to use not only by scientists interested in understanding individual differences in behavior, but also by clinical psychologists and psychiatrists interested in diagnosing various disorders. Because there is such a great demand for information about the extent to which people possess various personality characteristics, scientists have developed a number of useful techniques for accomplishing this task. The most important of these are *objective tests* and *projective tests*.

Objective tests, such as *inventories* and *questionnaires*, are by far the most widely used method for assessing personality. These consist of a series of questions or statements to which individuals respond in various ways. For example, a questionnaire may ask respondents to indicate whether each of a set of statements about themselves is true or false, the extent to which they agree or disagree with various sentences, or which of a pair of named activities they prefer (for some examples, see Figure 3-6 on page 98, and the Experiencing Organizational Behavior section at the end of this chapter). Their answers are then scored by means of special keys and compared with the scores obtained by hundreds, or even thousands, of other people who have taken the test previously. In this way, an individual's relative standing on the trait being measured can be determined. Because

FIGURE 3-14

THE TAT: AN EXAMPLE OF A PROJECTIVE TEST FOR MEASURING PERSONALITY

Drawings similar to this one are used in the Thematic Apperception Test (TAT), a kind of projective test. (Source: From Robert J. Gregory, Psychological Testing: History, Principles, and Applications. *Copyright © 1992 by Allyn & Bacon. Reprinted with permission.)*

such tests can be scored directly, without requiring any special interpretation of the responses (beyond seeing how to count them), they are called *objective*.

Not all techniques used to measure personality are scored and interpreted objectively. As an example, look at the drawing in Figure 3-14. What is happening here? Do you think your response would differ from someone else's? If so, would these differences reveal anything about the differences between your personalities? The answer is "yes." Personality tests of this type are known as **projective tests.** Such tools for assessing personality assume that when different people are exposed to ambiguous stimuli, each will report something different. The pattern of these differences, in turn will reveal much about important aspects of personality. In other words, in giving their answers, people will "project" something about themselves.

Actually, the illustration in Figure 3-14 is similar to the ones contained in a widely used test designed to measure individual differences in achievement and power motivation, the *Thematic Apperception Test* (or,*TAT*).[68] This test consists of a series of ambiguous drawings, and the people completing it are asked to make up a story about each. These are then carefully analyzed for basic themes in accordance with specific scoring procedures (e.g, if you interpret Figure 3-14 as someone who is saddened by learning that he or she didn't pass a test, this may be an indication of the fact that you are highly worried about failing). It is important to point out that the task of scoring and interpreting projective tests is complex, and should only be performed by people who have had extensive training in such procedures. To administer such tests and interpret them based on your intuition or "common sense," would not only lead to erroneous conclusions, but be highly unethical as well. Still, when the task of scoring and interpretation is left in the hands of trained professionals, projective tests, such as the TAT, can provide valuable information about many different personality traits.

As you might imagine, all personality tests, whether objective or projective in nature, are difficult to create, and must meet highly stringent standards if they are to provide meaningful insight into personality. Although there are several desirable characteristics of all tests, two are especially crucial and worthy of describing—*reliability* and *validity*.

RELIABILITY AND VALIDITY: ESSENTIAL CHARACTERISTICS OF ALL PERSONALITY TESTS

Whether we're talking about objective or projective tests, all measures of personality must have two essential qualities: they must be *reliable* and they must also be *valid*.

A test's **reliability** is the degree to which it yields stable, consistent scores over time. Consider, for example, how useless a tailor's measurements of your waist would be if he or she used an elastic tape measure. Each time a measurement was recorded it would be different from the previous occasion—not because you pigged out and gained ten pounds, but because the measuring instrument itself is unreliable. Similarly, measures of personality must yield consistent pictures of the traits and characteristics people hold if they are to be at all useful. Unless it is assumed that the traits being measured changed greatly over time, such consistency is required if the test is not to be rejected as flawed on the grounds of low reliability. Similarly, a test designed to measure a single aspect of personality would be useless if it were found that items on it were unrelated to one another and, in fact, appeared to measure several different traits. Much is known about the factors that determine the reliability of personality tests, so constructing ones with high levels of reliability is usually not a serious problem.

However, just because a test measures something reliably does not ensure that what it *is* measuring is at all close to what it is *supposed* to measure. For example, we can measure someone's waist repeatedly and come up with 32 inches each time, suggesting that the measure is reliable. If, however, what we are really after is something other than waist size, such as hat size, then the mere fact that our measurement is consistent is not enough. We must also measure the right thing! In the case of physical measures, this is rather obvious. But, when it comes to psychological constructs such as personality, it is a lot easier to miss measuring what you really want to measure. In other words, while it is necessary for a test to be reliable, it is not sufficient; it also must be *valid*. A test's **validity** refers to the extent to which it measures what it purports to measure. In other words, *a test designed to measure a given personality variable is considered valid to the extent that it measures all relevant aspects of that variable and nothing else*.

Establishing the validity of a personality variable is a complex matter. It usually involves demonstrating what other measures the scores on a test are related to, or can predict. If a test is valid, we will find that scores on the test are associated with various other characteristics and behaviors that are conceptually related to it. For example, consider a test designed to measure the desire for high levels of excitement or stimulation. If the test is valid, then the higher people score on it, the more likely they would be expected to do such things as drive sports cars, engage in sports such as bungee jumping or skydiving, and seek change and challenge in their careers. If people who score high on the test do indeed engage in these activities to a greater extent than people who score low, we might conclude, albeit tentatively, that the test does measure their desire for excitement.

But which of these activities is most closely related to this aspect of personality? It is difficult to tell, so if high scorers on the test show some of these activities more than others, we are left with a degree of uncertainty concerning the test's validity. Also, all these behaviors may reflect the operation of other variables as well. For example, people might drive sports cars partly because doing so enhances their status. Thus, such behavior may might indicate status-seeking as well as excitement-seeking tendencies. Similarly, individuals may seek challenge in their careers because they are ambitious, not merely out of a preference for high levels of stimulation. Because of these and many other complexities, establishing the validity of any measure of personality is difficult. The conservative rule, then, is to question the validity of *all* measures of personality unless they are accompanied by convincing evidence that they really do measure what they claim to measure.

Having made these points, we should note that all of the traits considered in this chapter are measured by tests known to be both reliable and valid. Thus, you can be confident that the findings we have discussed are based on important dimensions of personality.

SUMMARY AND REVIEW

THE NATURE OF PERSONALITY

Personality is the unique and relatively stable pattern of behavior, thoughts, and emotions shown by individuals. In organizations, both an individual's personality and the demands of the context combine to influence behavior, a viewpoint known as the **interactionist perspective.** For example, work-related outcomes are most positive when there is a match between people's personalities and the requirements of their jobs (known as **person–job fit**). A cluster of characteristics known as the **big five dimensions of personality** is related to a variety of different work behaviors. These include: *extraversion and introversion*, *agreeableness*, *conscientiousness*, *emotional stability*, and *openness to experience*.

WORK-RELATED ASPECTS OF PERSONALITY

Several personality characteristics have been linked to various aspects of organizational behavior. For example, **positive affectivity** and **negative affectivity** (stable predispositions to be either upbeat and positive, or downbeat and negative, respectively) are related to the quality of individual decision making and the willingness to help others.

When working alone, people demonstrating the **Type A** behavior pattern (competitive, irritable, always in a hurry) tend to perform better than those with the **Type B** behavior pattern (the opposite, more relaxed style). However, because they are often impatient with others, Type A's frequently encounter interpersonal conflict, interfering with their performance on tasks involving coordination with others.

Individuals who believe that they possess the capability of performing various tasks—people high in **self-efficacy**—often achieve higher levels of performance than people lacking in such confidence. Individuals high in **self-esteem** have positive feelings about themselves and their characteristics. They often report higher job satisfaction, perform at higher levels, and come across better in job interviews than people who are low in self-esteem.

People high in **self-monitoring** are concerned with making good impressions on others and can adapt their behavior to match the requirements of a given situation. High self-monitors are more effective *boundary spanners* than low self-monitors. They also tend to use various tactics of *impression management* more frequently than low self-monitors.

Individuals who adopt a manipulative approach to their relations with others are sometimes described as being high in **Machiavellianism.** They are not influenced by considerations of loyalty, friendship or ethics. Instead, they simply do whatever is needed to get their way.

People differ with respect to several important *work-related motives*. **Achievement motivation** is the desire to excel. People who are high in achievement motivation seek situations of moderate difficulty (challenging enough to matter, but not so difficult as to make failure inevitable), and gravitate toward positions in which they are recognized for their accomplishments (e.g., jobs using merit-based pay). In Japan, achievement motivation is manifested through the concept of *kaizen*, a concern with continuously striving for improvement in the way work is done. People who are high on **power motivation** (the desire to be in charge) and low on **affiliation motivation** (the desire to have friendly relations with others), while also having a high degree of self-control (i.e., not losing their tempers), possess the **leadership motivation pattern (LMP)**. People who possess this pattern of characteristics tend to be promoted more readily than those who do not.

MEASUREMENT OF PERSONALITY

Personality assessment is typically based either on **objective tests** (paper-and-pencil questionnaires scored using an established key) or on **projective tests** (situations in which people respond to ambiguous stimuli). Responses to projective tests reflect various aspects of people's personalities, and require scoring and interpretation by trained professionals. To be useful, both types of tests must be **reliable** (yield consistent measurements over time) and **valid** (measure what they purport to measure).

KEY TERMS

achievement motivation: The strength of an individual's desire to excel, to succeed at difficult tasks and to do them better than anyone else.

affiliation motivation: The strength of an individual's desire to have close and satisfying relations with others.

attraction-selection-attrition framework: A conceptualization suggesting that people with similar personality traits tend to form groups. The groups then tend to select and retain only those individuals whose personality traits match those of existing group members.

"big five" dimensions of personality: Five basic dimensions of personality that are assumed to underlie many specific traits.

interactionist perspective: The view that behavior is a result of the combined impact of an individual's personality and the nature of the situation experienced.

leadership motivation pattern (LMP): The pattern of personality traits characterized by high power motivation, low affiliation motivation, and a high degree of self-control.

Machiavellianism: A personality trait involving willingness to manipulate others for one's own purposes.

negative affectivity: The tendency to experience negative moods and feelings in a wide range of settings and under many different conditions.

objective tests: Questionnaires and inventories designed to measure various aspects of personality.

person–job fit: The extent to which individuals possess the competencies and traits required to perform specific jobs.

personality: The unique and relatively stable patterns of behavior, thoughts, and emotions shown by individuals.

positive affectivity: The tendency to experience positive moods and feelings in a wide range of settings and under many different conditions.

power motivation: The strength of an individual's desire to be in charge, to be able to exercise control over others.

projective tests: Methods for measuring personality in which individuals respond to ambiguous stimuli. Their responses provide insight into their personality traits.

reliability: The extent to which a test yields consistent scores on various occasions, and the extent to which all of its items measure the same construct.

self-efficacy: Individuals' beliefs concerning their ability to perform specific tasks successfully.

self-esteem: Individuals' evaluations of their own traits and behavior.

self-monitoring: An aspect of personality involving individuals' sensitivity to the reactions of others, their ability to manage their own expressive behavior so as to induce positive reactions in others, and their willingness to serve as the center of others' attention.

Type A behavior pattern: The pattern of behavior involving high levels of competitiveness, time urgency, and irritability.

Type B behavior pattern: The pattern of behavior characterized by a casual, laid-back style; the opposite of the Type A behavior pattern.

validity: The extent to which a test actually measures what it purports to measure.

QUESTIONS FOR DISCUSSION

1. Why might two individuals with the same personality characteristics behave differently in a given situation?
2. What are the implications of the notions of *person–job fit* and the *attraction-selection-attrition framework* for the practice of management?
3. What is the difference between simply being in a bad mood and having the characteristic of negative affectivity?
4. Given the opportunity to hire a Type A or a Type B person for a job, under what conditions would you hire each one?
5. How does someone get to suffer from low self-efficacy, and what can be done to raise it?
6. What are the dangers of interacting with someone who is high in Machiavellianism, and what can one do to protect oneself from such individuals?
7. How do you think the culture in which one is brought up might influence the development of person-ality?
8. What are the advantages and the risks associated with using information about personality as the basis for making important organizational decisions (e.g., hiring and promotion)?

CASE IN POINT

RICHARD BRANSON: NOT YOUR AVERAGE MILLIONAIRE

Most people think of wealthy, successful entrepreneurs as elderly, conservative, quiet, and serious. Richard Branson, chairman of Virgin Group (the parent company of Virgin Atlantic Airways as well as over two hundred other businesses), certainly does not fit this stereotype. He is young (42), dresses casually, pilots hot-air balloons, runs his business from his homes (including a houseboat!), and even dons flight attendant uniforms to serve customers on his planes. Unorthodox in his image, he has even been known to give interviews with his feet propped up on the furniture and pillows under his head.[1]

Despite his laid-back style, Branson is a driven man. He is compelled by his desire to overcome challenges—a desire he claims to have learned from his mother. For example, when he was 6 years old, his mother drove him to his grandparents' house, stopped the car three miles away, and told him to get out of the car and find his way! Although he initially got lost, young Richard eventually reached his destination.[2]

This incident sheds light on Branson's latest challenge—running an airline. As chairman of Virgin Atlantic, a small carrier with a fleet of only eight planes, based in London, Branson has taken on some of the largest airlines in the world. The company's potential for future success was evidently so threatening to their main competitor, British Airways (BA), that BA launched a "dirty tricks" campaign against Virgin in an attempt to drive them out of business. After filing and winning a libel suit against them (Virgin Atlantic was awarded $940,000 in penalties, and $5.4 million in legal fees).[3] Branson is confident that his carrier can continue to grow and increase market share.[4] He persists in this belief despite the fact that the airline business is one of the most competitive and cutthroat industries in the world.

Branson has a history of entrepreneurial ventures. He dropped out of high school to begin a music magazine that quickly found success, earning $1 million within the first year.[5] Soon afterward, he began a mail-order record business. Then, in 1970 he founded Virgin Records, a label that grew to include such pop acts as Boy George, Phil Collins, Janet Jackson, and the Rolling Stones. The company became so successful that in 1992 he sold it for almost $1 billion.[6]

In discussing his successes, Branson is emphatic that people are the most important element. "The most important aspect of running a company is motivating your staff and caring," he says. "You may have no end to important business meetings, your diary might keep getting full up. But you've got to clear the time and space to go out and be with your staff as often as possible."[7] When starting his businesses, he deliberately selected friends to work with him, figuring that if you are working with people you like, you can trust them to be good with their staff and inspire morale in others and confidence in customers.

Branson believes in giving his employees lots of freedom to develop their own best work styles and patterns. He accomplishes this by letting employees wear whatever clothing they choose and by carefully selecting desirable work sites. In this way groups of employees who work in different locations are encouraged to develop their own personalized ways of completing their tasks. And Branson is a big believer in the value of praise. In fact, he took the $940,000 award from BA and distributed a large part of it to employees of the airline.[8]

In addition to his faith in people, Branson values fun. This conviction permeates both his business and personal philosophies. Says Branson, "If you do something for fun and create the best possible product, then profit will come."[9] He seeks fun not only as a means of profit, but as a means of recreation. Richard Branson has garnered much publicity for himself with his pranks. He has disguised a hot-air balloon as a UFO, water-skied from a blimp, and has flown hot-air balloons across both the Atlantic and Pacific oceans. His antics became so well known that even Margaret Thatcher, then Prime Minister of Great Britain, went on a balloon ride with him up the Thames in London.[10]

Branson consciously tries to create a nontraditional climate in his companies. He encourages his employees to take risks. He writes to all employees every few months and requests written replies. He also learns the first names of all his employees—currently about 500 at Virgin Atlantic alone.

His creativity in management also extends to business decisions. After experiencing his first manicure and massage (gifts from his wife), he decided that these services should be offered to all "upper class" passengers aboard Virgin Atlantic flights (equivalent to "business class" on other airlines). His Virgin Megastores—large record stores currently located throughout Europe as well as Australia and Los Angeles—have some unusual twists as well.[11] In the Paris store—a facility that doubled the space for selling music in all of Paris—hours extend until midnight. There is also a café, headphones to sample all music, screens on which to watch videos, places to try the latest computer games, and even a vending machine dispensing condoms—all Branson innovations.[12]

Although Branson's success can clearly be credited to his energy, talent, inspiration, and luck, the one trait of which he has taken greatest advantage is his knowledge of his own strengths and weaknesses. Richard admits, "What I think I'm good at is having the energy to get something up and running and finding good people. That's what I enjoy the most—creating new things."[13] He clearly recognizes his limits and gladly delegates the operational details of management to others. Similarly, he knows that he is driven by challenge, fun, and some risk. Branson views risk, not as a necessary evil with which to reach the greatest returns, but rather as an opportunity for failure from which he can learn. He says, "I think by definition, a failure is somebody that doesn't give something a try, and I think that if somebody gives something a try and fails, that they haven't failed, they've learned lessons which hopefully the next time around that they'll be able to put to good use and be successful."[14]

QUESTIONS FOR DISCUSSION

1. How would you characterize Branson with respect to the "big five" personality dimensions?
2. Do you think Branson is a Type A or Type B personality? What leads you to this assessment?
3. Does Branson demonstrate high or low self-efficacy? What experiences might have led to the development of his self-efficacy?
4. Describe Branson's achievement, power, and affiliation motives.
5. Would you like to work for Branson? Why or why not?

EXPERIENCING ORGANIZATIONAL BEHAVIOR

How's Your Self-Esteem? Take This Test and Find Out

It isn't always east to recognize the extent to which we have certain personality variables, especially ones that have to do with deeply rooted, covert aspects of ourselves, such as self-esteem. Yet, as described in this chapter, the amount of self-esteem people have accounts for much of their behavior in organizations (and their life in general, as you might imagine). To gain some insight into yourself, you may find it valuable to complete this questionnaire. (This scale is based on a scale actually used to measure self-esteem.)

PROCEDURE

A. For each of the following items, indicate whether you *strongly disagree, disagree, agree, or strongly agree.*

1. I believe I am a worthwhile individual who is as good as other people.
2. I have several positive qualitites.
3. Generally speaking, I consider myself a failure.
4. For the most part, I can do things as well as others.
5. There are not many things about myself that I can be proud of.
6. I have very positive feelings about myself.
7. In general, I am very pleased with myself.
8. I really don't have a great deal of self-respect.
9. At times I feel quite useless.
10. Sometimes I don't think I'm very good at all.

B. After completing all ten items, score them by assigning points as follows:

For items 1, 2, 4, 6, and 7	*For items 3, 5, 8, 9, and 10*
strongly disagree = 1 point	strongly disagree = 4 points
disagree = 2 points	disagree = 3 points
agree = 3 points	agree = 2 points
strongly agree = 4 points	strongly agree = 1 point

C. Add your points according to this key. Total scores can range from a low of 10 to a high of 40. Higher scores reflect greater degrees of self-esteem.

POINTS TO CONSIDER

1. How high or low was your self-esteem?
2. Does your score make sense to you? In other words, did this test tell you something about yourself that agrees or disagrees with the way you already think of yourself?
3. Why do you think items 1, 2, 4, 6, and 7 are scored in an opposite manner from items 3, 5, 8, 9, and 10? In other words, how are these two sets of items different from each other?
4. Regardless of what this test reveals about you, keep in mind the following very important words of caution: *assessing personality and interpreting the results of personality tests are complex tasks that require the skills of trained professionals. This test is not a definitive measure of your self-esteem, but a useful way of thinking about your self-esteem and showing how it can be measured.* Realizing that any one measure of personality may be incomplete, scientists often use several different measures of personality before drawing any firm conclusions about what someone is really like.
5. Whatever your level of self-esteem is, what do you think can be done to raise it?

Source: Adapted from Rosenberg, M. (1965). *Society and the adolescent self-image.* Princeton, NJ: Princeton University Press.

PART III

THE INDIVIDUAL IN THE ORGANIZATION

CHAPTER OUTLINE

SPECIAL SECTIONS

FOUR

MOTIVATION IN ORGANIZATIONS

LEARNING OBJECTIVES

After reading this chapter, you should be able to

1. *Define motivation and explain its importance in the field of organizational behavior.*
2. *Describe need hierarchy theory and what it suggests about improving motivation in organizations.*
3. *Identify and explain the conditions under which goal setting can be used to improve job performance.*
4. *Explain equity theory,and describe some of the research designed to test its basic tenets.*
5. *Describe expectancy theory and how it may be applied in organizations.*
6. *Distinguish between job enlargement and job enrichment as techniques for motivating employees.*
7. *Describe the job characteristics model and its implications for redesigning jobs so as to enhance motivation.*

What makes life dreary is the want of a motive.

George Eliot (Marian Evans),1819–1880
English novelist, essayist, and editor
Daniel Deronda

Motivation will almost always beat mere talent.

Norman R. Augustine
President and CEO,
Martin Marietta Corporation
Augustine's Laws *(Penguin, 1987)*

PREVIEW CASE

United Electric Controls: Where Employees Are Involved in Improvement

What do you do when you've been in business for sixty years and realize that your company now represents little more than a symbol of the outmoded U.S. factory? This was the problem faced by David Reis, president of United Electric Controls Company, the Watertown, Massachusetts, manufacturer of industrial temperature and pressure controls. As recently as 1987, United Electric was saddled with antiquated technology and a highly autocratic management structure that led it to problems with poor delivery and high inventory that threatened its financial stability. Today, however, United Electric is a thriving, $36-million company.

David Reis, and his brother and co-owner Robert, are convinced that their company's turnaround was due, in great measure, to a very simple philosophy: if you want to know how people can do their jobs better, just ask them. With this principle guiding them, the Reis brothers set up several programs to collect ideas from their 350 employees. For example, the "Valued Ideas Program" gives financial rewards to employees for submitting usable proposals for improvement. There's also the "Action Center Program," in which groups of employees get together and brainstorm suggestions to pressing company problems.

United Electric's employees actively participate in these programs. As many as forty different action centers were created within the first week after the plan was announced. As for suggestions, in 1990 alone 1,000 were made, two-thirds of which were implemented, netting employees over $50,000 in bonuses. For example, one suggestion for eliminating a single sheet of paper from the materials requisition process now saves the company $6,000 a year—not much for a big company, but a considerable savings for such a simple suggestion.

United Electric Controls Company, Watertown, Massachusetts

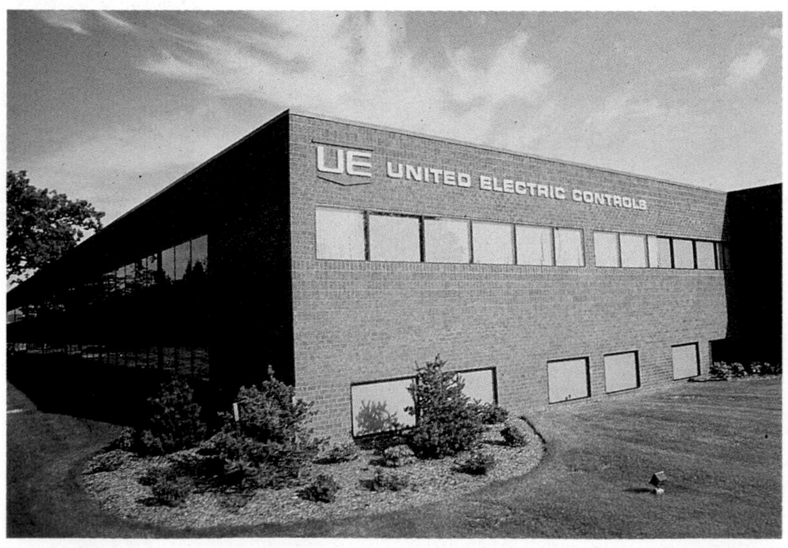

Making these changes wasn't easy for David and Robert, who were used to running United Electric using a highly directive, centralized style. Being able to relinquish control, to let employees get involved in how to do their work, was the hardest thing for them—but, they stuck with it. As David Reis put it, "You reach a point where you can't go back but also don't like where you are. It's scary."

What's not so scary is how successful the approach has been. Today, United Electric buzzes with a sense of excitement and productivity. Its shop floor is a wonderland of home-made technological gadgets the employees created to help them become more productive. Commenting on the joy of contributing to the company's success, twenty-two-year United Electric Controls veteran Gladys Applyby says, "There's always a way to do something better. We always thought of things [before], but there was nobody to listen to our ideas. Now there is."

Apparently, the company is getting an earful, and it's heeding the good advice. Before implementing these programs only 65 percent of the United Electric's deliveries were made on time, and the company was losing money on annual sales of $28 million. Currently, on-time deliveries are up to 95 percent, inventory has been reduced 70 percent, sales have risen by 30 percent, and the company is now highly profitable. On the basis of these improvement, United Electric was selected in 1990 as the winner of the coveted North American Shingo Prize for Excellence in Manufacturing. Today, the improvement continues, as one employee puts it, "because we know we can't sit still, and we know we can be better."

The dramatic turnaround at United Electric Controls is certainly quite impressive. Employees are working harder than ever, and more creatively too. The company now listens to them, incorporates their ideas into the ways work is done, and rewards them for their suggestions. As a result, United Electric's employees now feel that they're an integral part of what it takes to make the company successful—and indeed, they are. How can this process be explained? How can the simple act of involving employees in the company's activities have such profound effects? Put more generally, why is it that some people work hard while others do whatever they can to get out of working at all (see Figure 4-1)? Questions such as these have to do with the process of *motivation*—the theme of this chapter.

As we noted in Chapter 1, the field of OB is concerned with both understanding human behavior in organizations and applying that knowledge toward improving performance and employees' quality of life. Nowhere in the field are these dual interests more clearly realized than in the study of motivation. Indeed, we are interested in asking both theoretical questions, such as "*What* motivates people, and *why*?" and applied questions, such as "*How* can this knowledge be put to practical use?" Hence, our focus in this chapter will be both on theories of motivation and on their practical application. The theories we will consider represent the major approaches to the topic of motivation currently studied.[1] Our look at each one will focus on what the theory says, the research bearing on it, and its practical implica-

FIGURE 4-1
MOTIVATION: AN IMPORTANT ASPECT OF ORGANIZATIONAL BEHAVIOR
It's not difficult to find some people who are highly motivated to perform their jobs well, and others who prefer to get away with as little work as possible. The study of motivation provides insight into the conditions under which each of these outcomes is likely to occur. (Source: Reprinted with special permission of King Features Syndicate.)

tions. We think this approach will help you develop a solid understanding of the importance of motivation as a topic of interest to organizational scientists. However, before turning to these theories and applications, we will begin by taking a closer look at the concept of motivation and the role of motivation in the work ethic.

THE NATURE OF MOTIVATION IN ORGANIZATIONS

On the basis of what we've said so far, you should not be surprised to hear that motivation is one of the most important and widely studied topics in the field of organizational behavior.[2] To begin the process of helping you understand and appreciate what is known in this field, we will define the concept of motivation and explain its role in organizational behavior.

MOTIVATION: A DEFINITION

Although motivation is a broad and complex concept, organizational scientists have agreed on its basic characteristics.[3] We define **motivation** as *the set of processes that arouse, direct, and maintain human behavior toward attaining some goal.* The diagram in Figure 4-2 will guide our explanation as we elaborate on this definition.

The first part of our definition deals with *arousal*. This has to do with the drive, or energy behind our actions. For example, people may be guided by their interest in making a good impression on others, doing interesting work, being successful at what they do, and so on. Their interest in fulfilling these motives stimulates them to engage in behaviors designed to fulfill them. But what will people do to satisfy their motives? Motivation is also concerned with the choices people make, the *direction* their behavior takes. For example, employees interested in cultivating a favorable impression on their supervisors may do many different things: compliment them on their good work, do them special favors, work extra hard on an important project, and the like. Each of these options may be recognized as a path toward meeting the person's goal. The final part of our definition deals with *maintaining* behavior. How long will people persist at attempting to meet their goal? To give up in advance of goal attainment means to not satisfy the need that stimulated behavior in the first place. Obviously, people who do not persist at meeting their goals (e.g., salespeople who give up before reaching their quotas) cannot be said to be highly motivated.

To summarize, motivation requires all three components: the arousal, direction, and maintenance of goal-directed behavior. An analogy may help tie these compo-

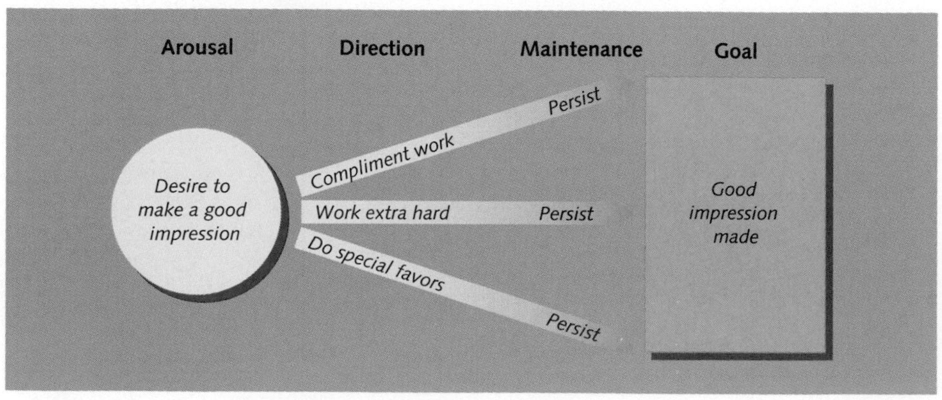

FIGURE 4-2
MOTIVATION: ITS BASIC COMPONENTS
Motivation involves the arousal, direction, and maintenance of behavior toward a goal. An example of this process is shown here.

nents together. Imagine that you are driving down a road on your way home. The arousal part of motivation is like the energy created by the car's engine. The direction component is like the steering wheel, taking you along your chosen path. Finally, the maintenance aspect of the definition is the persistence that keeps you going until you arrive home, reaching your goal.

Now that we have defined motivation, it is time to bring up two important points. First, motivation cannot be seen, but only inferred on the basis of performance. However, *motivation and job performance are not synonymous*. Just because someone performs at a task well does not mean that he or she is highly motivated. This person actually may be very skillful, but not putting forth much effort at all. If you're a mathematical genius, for example, you may breeze through your calculus class without hardly trying. By contrast, someone who performs poorly may be putting forth a great deal of effort, but is falling short of a desired goal because he or she lacks the skill needed to succeed. If you've ever tried to learn a new sport, but found that you couldn't get the hang of it no matter how hard you tried, you know what we mean.

A second key point is that *motivation is multifaceted*. By this we mean that people may have several different motives operating at once. Sometimes these may conflict. For example, a word processing operator might be motivated to please his boss by being as productive as possible. However, being too productive may antagonize one's co-workers, who fear that they're being made to look bad. The result is that the two motives may pull the individual in different directions; the one that wins out is the one that's strongest in that situation.

These examples clearly show that motivation is a complex and important concept in the field of organizational behavior. This complexity creates challenges for the theories of motivation used in the field. Before turning to these theories, however, we will further set the stage for them by examining the role of motivation in the work ethic.

MOTIVATION AND THE WORK ETHIC

Throughout history, views about the meaning and importance of work have shifted dramatically.[4] In ancient Rome, for example, work was considered a vulgar and degrading activity. According to the Roman writer Cato the Elder, "The best principle of management is to treat both slaves and animals well enough to give them the strength to work hard."[5] As civilization developed, so did more positive feelings about work. By the Middle Ages, a tradition espousing the virtues of hard work was firmly established. Following the teachings of Judeo-Christian philosophers (such as Luther and Calvin), beliefs in the value of work eventually became a cherished tradition in American society. Reflecting this view in modern times, former U.S. president Richard M. Nixon once proclaimed during a Labor Day address, "Labor is good in itself. A man or woman at work . . . becomes a better person by virtue of the act of working."[6]

Despite such inspiring words, many observers of American business trends have attributed problems of sagging production to a general lack of motivation within the workforce.[7] However, to claim that today's employees are poorly motivated would be misleading. After all, surveys show that most Americans would continue to work even if they didn't need the money.[8] Although money is certainly important to people, they are motivated to attain many other goals as well. Because of technological advances that took the drudgery out of many jobs, today's workers are motivated by the prospect of performing jobs that are interesting and challenging—not just jobs that pay well. As a result, problems of motivation may be difficult to identify because of the wide variety of work-related goals that people are motivated to achieve on the job. (Although we have been talking about American work values, the Global Organization section below examines how the cultural traditions of various nations are important in influencing work values.)

THE GLOBAL ORGANIZATION

MOTIVATION MAKES THE WORLD GO 'ROUND: A CROSS-CULTURAL INVESTIGATION OF WORK VALUES

What motivates you on the job? What are your most important work-related goals and values? That the answers to these questions would be influenced by one's nationality is an intriguing possibility. After all, if the varied social, political, and religious beliefs of people in different nations influence work values, it follows that people in different countries would be motivated by different aspects of their jobs. Testing this reasoning, Elizur, Borg, Hunt, and Beck conducted a survey among people from eight different nations: China, Germany, Holland, Hungary, Israel, Korea, Taiwan, and the United States.[9] They sampled 2,280 people holding a wide variety of different jobs. Each person was asked to rate the importance to themselves of each of twenty-four different work values, such as achievement, opportunities for advancement, pleasant co-workers, meaningful work, pleasant working conditions, pay, and interesting work.

The results were somewhat surprising (see Figure 4-3). Although you might expect there to be a logical pattern of differences between countries (e.g., people in Eastern countries might be expected to have values that are similar to each other, but different from those in Western countries), this did *not* occur. For example, although achievement is generally regarded as being much more important in the West than in the East, Elizur and his associates found that

FIGURE 4-3

WHAT MOTIVATES EMPLOYEES: AN INTERNATIONAL VIEW

Survey research assesing the predominant work goals of 2,280 people in eight different nations found considerable agreement that the two most important motivating factors were achievement *and* performing interest work *(Source: Based on data reported by Elizur, Borg, Hunt, and Beck, 1991, see Note 9.)*

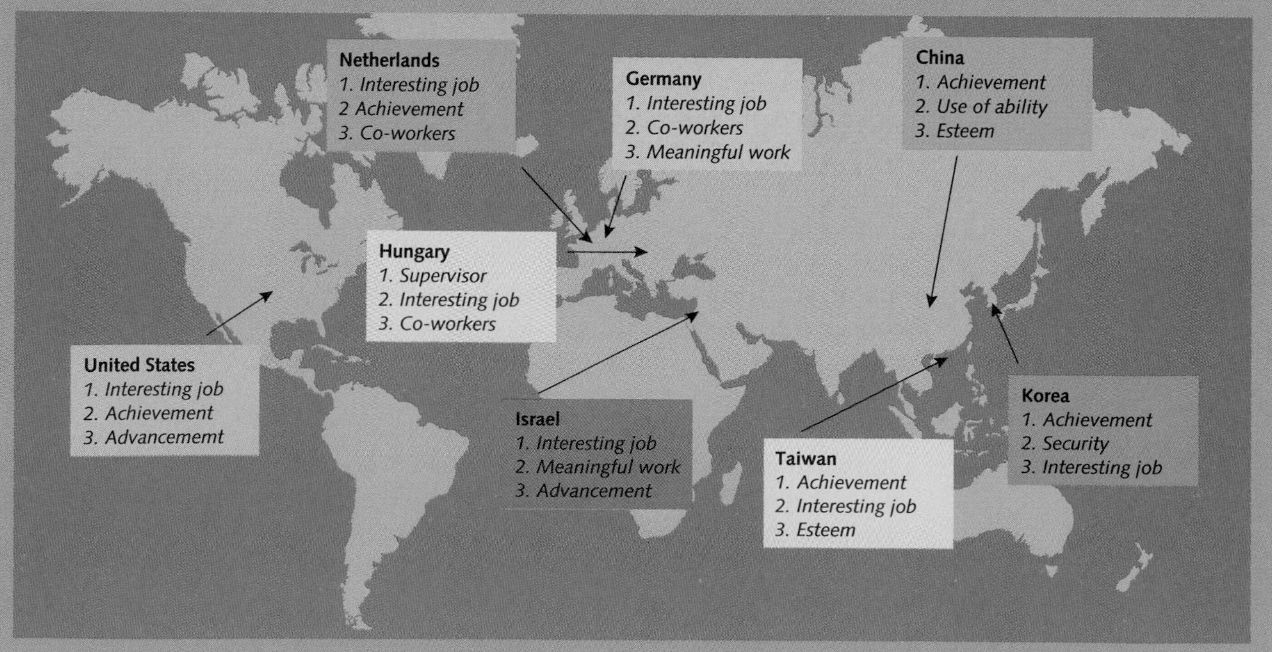

THE GLOBAL ORGANIZATION, Cont.

achievement was very highly rated in almost all countries (where it was ranked either first or second) except Germany (where it ranked ninth). Performing interesting work was another very highly rated value (ranking first or second) among people in all nations except China (where it ranked eighth) and Hungary (where it ranked seventh). Another surprising feature of the results is that in *no* country was pay considered the most important work-related goal: it was most highly rated in Hungary (where it ranked fifth), and least highly rated in China (where it ranked twentieth).

What makes these findings noteworthy is that the goals people are motivated to seek in their jobs are remarkably similar all over the world. This is a particularly impressive finding when you consider that the sample consisted of people from highly industrialized nations from both the East (e.g., Korea) and West (e.g., United States) as well as people from former Eastern Bloc (e.g., Hungary). Despite the extreme differences in the economic and social conditions within countries studied, there was widespread agreement about the importance of various work goals. Given the apparently universal concerns over doing interesting work and achieving success, it is not surprising these variables consistently emerge (in one form or another) as key elements of various theories of motivation in organizations.

NEED THEORIES

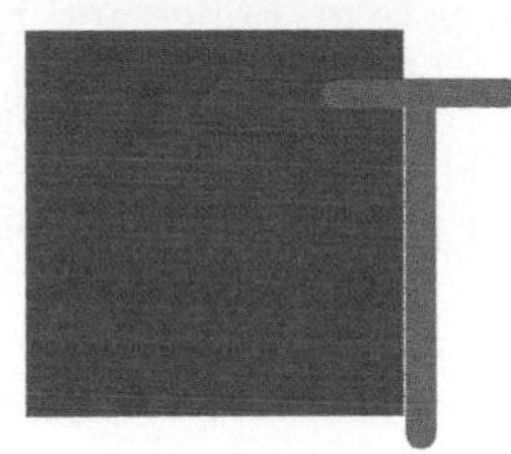

The first conceptualizations of motivation we will consider are the most basic: theories that explain motivation in terms of the satisfaction of basic human needs. Indeed, organizational scholars have paid a great deal of attention to the idea that people are motivated to use their jobs as mechanisms for satisfying their needs. Probably the best-known conceptualization of human needs in organizations has been proposed by Maslow.[10]

MASLOW'S NEED HIERARCHY THEORY

Abraham Maslow was a clinical psychologist who introduced a theory of personal adjustment, known as **need hierarchy theory**, based on his observations of patients seen throughout the years. His premise was that if people grow up in an environment in which their needs are not met, they will be unlikely to function as healthy, well-adjusted individuals. Much of the popularity of Maslow's approach is based on applying the same idea in organizations. That is, unless people get their needs met on the job, they will not function as effectively as possible.

Specifically, Maslow theorized that people have five types of needs, and that these are activated in a *hierarchical* manner. This means that the needs are aroused in a specific order from lowest to highest, and that the lowest-order need must be fulfilled before the next highest-order need is triggered, and so on. The five major categories of needs are listed on the left side of Figure 4-4. As we describe these needs here, please refer to this diagram as a summary.

1. *Physiological needs* are the lowest-order, most basic needs specified by Maslow. These involve satisfying fundamental biological drives, such as the need for food, air, water, and shelter. To satisfy such needs, organizations must provide employees with a salary that allows them to afford adequate living conditions. Similarly, sufficient opportunities to rest (e.g., coffee breaks) and to engage in physical activity (e.g., fitness and exercise facilities) are also important for people to meet their physiological needs. With increasing

frequency, companies (tens of thousands of them, in fact) are providing exercise and physical fitness programs for their employees to help them stay healthy.[11] The rationale is quite simple: people who are too hungry or too ill to work will hardly be able to make much of a contribution to their companies

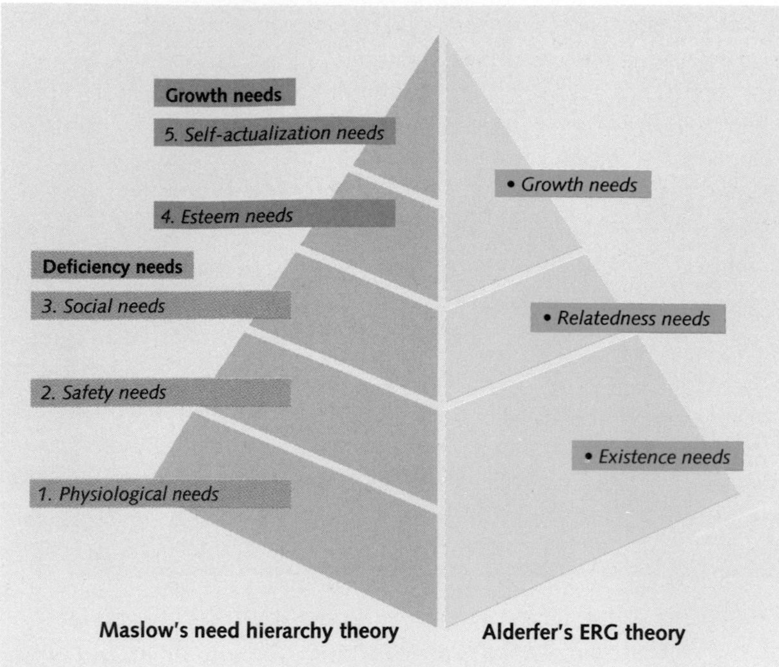

FIGURE 4-4
NEED THEORIES: A COMPARISON
The five needs identified by Maslow's need hierarchy theory correspond to the three needs of Alderfer's ERG theory. However, Maslow's theory specifies that needs are activated in order from lowest level to highest level, whereas Alderfer's theory specifies that needs can be activated in any order.

2. *Safety needs,* the second level of need in Maslow's hierarchy, are activated after physiological needs are met. Safety needs involve the need for a secure environment, free from threats of physical or psychological harm. Organizations can do many things to help satisfy safety needs. For example, they may provide employees with safety equipment (e.g., hard hats and goggles), life and health insurance plans, and security forces (e.g., police and fire protection). Similarly, jobs that provide tenure (such as teaching) and no-layoff agreements provide a psychological security blanket that helps satisfy safety needs. All these practices enable people to do their jobs without fear of harm, and in a safe and secure atmosphere.
3. *Social needs,* Maslow's third level of need, are activated after safety needs have been met. Social needs involve the need to be affiliative—to have friends, to be loved and accepted by other people. To help meet social needs, organizations may encourage participation in social events, such as office picnics or parties. Company bowling or softball leagues, as well as country club memberships, also provide good opportunities for meeting social needs. Not only do such activities help promote physical fitness—helping satisfy physiological needs, as we noted above—but they also give employees a chance to socialize and develop friendships.

   Taken together as a group, physiological needs, safety needs, and social needs are known as deficiency needs. Maslow's idea was that if these needs are not met, an individual will fail to develop into a healthy person—both physically and psychologically. In contrast, the next two highest-order needs, the ones at the top of the hierarchy, are known as *growth needs.* Gratification of these needs is said to help a person grow and to develop to his or her fullest potential.
4. *Esteem needs* are the fourth level of need. These refer to a person's need to develop self-respect and to gain the approval of others. The desire to achieve success, have prestige, and be recognized by others all fall into this category. Companies do many things to satisfy their employees' esteem needs. They may, for example have awards banquets to recognize distinguished achievements. Giving monetary bonuses—even small ones—in recognition of employees' suggestions for improvement helps promote their esteem (as is done at United Electric Controls, described in our Preview Case). Nonmonetary awards, such as trophies and plaques, provide reminders of an employee's important contributions, continuously fulfilling esteem needs.[12]

Including articles in company newsletters describing an employee's success, giving keys to the executive washroom, assigning private parking spaces, and posting signs identifying the "employee of the month" are also examples of things that can be done to satisfy esteem needs.

5. *Self-actualization needs* are found at the top of Maslow's hierarchy. These are the needs aroused only after all the lower-order needs have been met. **Self-actualization** is the need for self-fulfillment—the desire to become all that one is capable of being, developing to one's fullest potential. By working at their maximum creative potential, employees who are self-actualized can be extremely valuable assets to their organizations. Individuals who have self-actualized are working at their peak, and represent the most effective use of an organization's human resources.

Research testing Maslow's theory has supported the distinction between deficiency needs and growth needs. Unfortunately the research has shown that not all people are able to satisfy their higher-order needs on the job. For example, Porter found that whereas lower-level managers were able to satisfy only their deficiency needs on the job, managers from the higher echelons of organizations were able to satisfy both their deficiency and growth needs.[13] An interesting study by Betz also examined the extent to which different groups' needs are met—specifically women who work outside the home, and housewives.[14] Betz found that full-time homemakers had higher levels of deficiency needs than married women employed outside the home. Presumably, this was because they did not have jobs through which these needs could be fulfilled. It was also found that the growth needs of working women were higher than those of full-time homemakers, presumably because their deficiency needs were already satisfied on the job. This evidence is clearly consistent with Maslow's ideas about the tendency to fulfill deficiency needs prior to growth needs.

Despite such evidence, Maslow's theory has not received a great deal of support with respect to the specific notions it proposes—namely, the exact needs that exist and the order in which they are activated.[15] Specifically, many researchers have failed to confirm that there are only five basic categories of need and that they are activated in the exact order specified by Maslow. In response to these criticisms, an alternative formulation has been proposed by Clayton Alderfer.[16]

ALDERFER'S ERG THEORY

Alderfer's approach, known as **ERG theory**, is mush simpler than Maslow's. Alderfer specifies not only that there are only three types of needs instead of five, but also that these are not necessarily activated in any specific order. In fact, Alderfer postulates that any need may be activated at any time. The three needs specified by ERG theory are the needs for *e*xistence, *r*elatedness, and growth. *Existence* needs correspond to Maslow's physiological needs and safety needs. *Relatedness* needs correspond to Maslow's social needs, the need for meaningful social relationships. Finally, *growth* needs correspond to the esteem needs and self-actualization needs in Maslow's theory—the need for developing one's potential. A summary of Alderfer's ERG theory is shown on the right side of Figure 4-4, along with the corresponding needs proposed by Maslow.

Clearly, ERG theory is much less restrictive than Maslow's need hierarchy theory. Its advantage is that it fits better with research evidence, suggesting that although basic needs exist, they are not exactly as specified by Maslow.[17] Despite the fact that need theories are not in complete agreement about the precise number of needs and the relationships between them, they do agree that satisfying human needs is an important part of motivating behavior on the job.

MANAGERIAL APPLICATIONS OF NEED THEORIES

Probably the greatest value of need theories lies in the practical implications they have for management. In particular, the theories are important insofar as they suggest specific things that managers can do to help their subordinates become self-actualized. Because self-actualized employees are likely to work at their maximum creative potential, it makes sense to help people attain this state by helping them meet their needs. With this in mind, it is worthwhile to consider what organizations may do to help satisfy their employees' needs.

Some companies are helping satisfy their employees' physiological needs, by providing incentives to keep them healthy. For example, Hershey Foods Corporation, and Southern California Edison Company, among others, give insurance rebates to employees with healthy lifestyles, while charging extra premiums to those whose habits (e.g., smoking) put them at greater risk for health problems.[18] To the extent that these incentives encourage employees to adapt healthier lifestyles, the likelihood of satisfying their physiological needs is increased.

Financial security is an important type of safety need. In this regard, some companies are going beyond the more traditional forms of payroll savings and profit-sharing plans. Notably, Com-Corp Industries (an auto parts manufacturer based in Cleveland, Ohio) found that its employees had serious financial difficulties when faced with sending their children to college, leading them to offer very low interest loans (only 3 percent annually for ten years) for this purpose.[19] Financial security is a key aspect of job security, particularly in troubled economic times, when layoffs are inevitable. To help soften the blow of layoffs, more and more organizations are providing outplacement services—assistance in securing new employment. In the most extensive of such programs, AT&T and Wang Labs provided extensive career counseling and job search assistance to its laid-off employees.[20] Although it is certainly more desirable not to be laid off at all, knowing that such assistance is available, if needed, helps reduce the negative emotional aspects of job insecurity.

To help satisfy its employees' social needs, IBM each spring holds a Family Day picnic near its Armonk, New York headquarters.[21] Some other companies have incorporated social activities deep into the fabric of its culture. For example, Odetics Inc. (the Anaheim, California manufacturer of intelligent machine systems) not only has its own repertory theater troupe, but also regular "theme" days (e.g., a "sock hop" in the company's cafeteria), athletic teams, and a standing "fun committee," which organized such events as a lunch-hour employee Olympics complete with goofy games (see Figure 4-5).[22]

Recognizing employees' accomplishments is an important way to satisfy their esteem needs. In this connection, GTE Data Services (Temple Terrace, Florida) gives awards to employees who develop ways of improving customer satisfaction or business performance.[23] The big award is a four-day first-class vacation, $500, a plaque, and recognition in the company magazine. Not all such awards are equally extravagant, however. Companies such as American Airlines, Shell Oil, the Campbell Soup Company, AT&T, and each of the big-three automakers (General

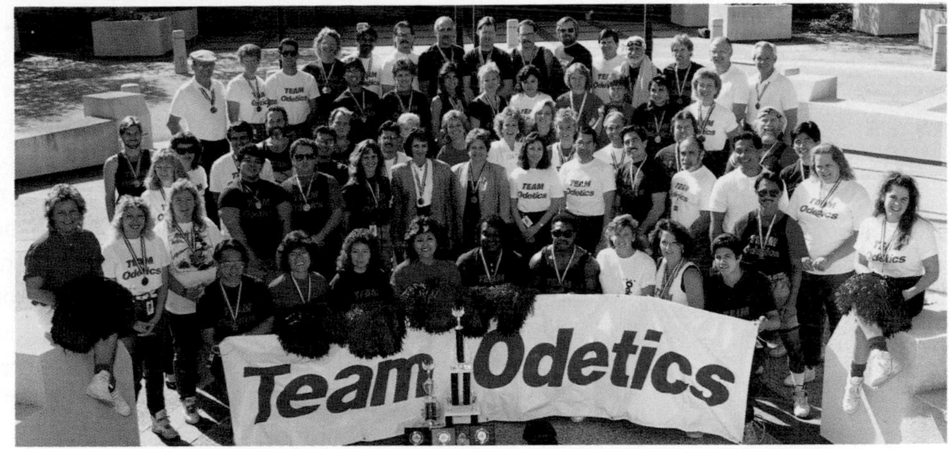

FIGURE 4-5
A FUN APPROACH TO SATISFYING SOCIAL NEEDS
These employees (called "associates") of Anaheim, California-based Odetics Inc., satisfy their social needs by playing together on athletic teams. This Odetics team participated in the most events offered in the City of Anaheim Corporate Challenge, a competition between local businesses.

Motors, Ford, and Chrysler) all offer relatively small nonmonetary gifts (e.g., dinner certificates, VCRs, and computers) to employees in recognition of their accomplishments.[24] Such awards, of course, are only effective at enhancing esteem when they are clearly linked to desired behaviors. Awards that are too general (e.g., a trophy for "best attitude") may not only fail to satisfy esteem needs, but may also minimize the impact of awards that are truly deserved (see Chapter 2).

To conclude, need theories represent a potentially useful approach to understanding motivation in organizations. These theories reflect the major ways in which human needs are involved in explaining motivation in work organizations.

GOAL-SETTING THEORY

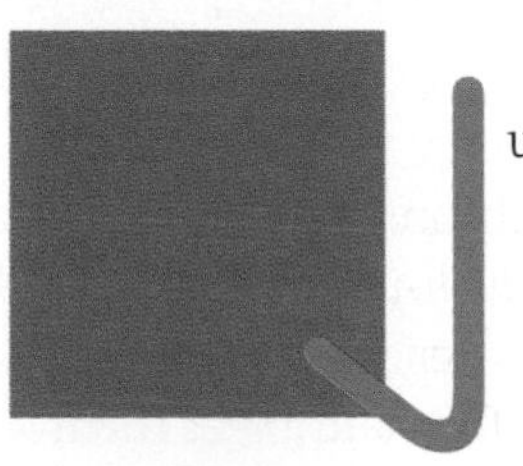

Just as people are motivated to satisfy their needs on the job, they are also motivated to strive for and attain goals. In fact, the process of setting goals is one of the most important motivational forces operating on people in organizations.[25] We will describe a prominent theory of **goal setting** and then identify some practical suggestions for setting goals effectively.

LOCKE AND LATHAM'S GOAL-SETTING THEORY

Suppose that you are doing a task, such as word processing, when a performance goal is assigned. You are now expected, for example, to type 70 words per minute (wpm) instead of the 60 wpm you've been doing all along. Would you work hard to meet this goal, or would you simply give up? Some insight into the question of how people respond to assigned goals is provided by a model proposed by Locke and Latham.[26] These theorists claim that an assigned goal influences people's beliefs about being able to perform the task in question (i.e., *self-efficacy*; see Chapter 3) and their personal goals. Both of these factors, in turn, influence performance.

The basic idea behind Locke and Latham's theory is that a goal serves as a motivator because it causes people to compare their present capacity to perform with that required to succeed at the goal. To the extent that people believe they will fall short of a goal, they will feel dissatisfied, and will work harder to attain it so long as they believe it is possible for them to do so. When they succeed at meeting a goal, they feel competent and successful.[27] Having a goal enhances performance in large part because the goal makes clear exactly what type and level of performance is expected. Goals also help improve performance because they provide information about how well one is performing a task.

The model also claims that assigned goals will lead to the acceptance of those goals as personal goals. In other words, they will be accepted as one's own. Indeed, Klein has shown that people will become more committed to a goal to the extent that they desire to attain that goal and believe they have a reasonable chance of doing so.[28] Likewise, the more strongly people believe they are capable of meeting a goal, the more strongly they will accept it as their own.

Finally, the model claims that beliefs about both self-efficacy and personal goals influence task performance. This makes sense insofar as people are willing to exert greater effort when they believe they will succeed than when they believe their efforts will be in vain.[29] Moreover, goals that are not personally accepted will have little capacity to guide behavior. In fact, research has shown that the more strongly people are committed to meeting goals, the better they will perform.[30] In general, Locke and Latham's model of goal setting has been supported by several studies, suggesting that is a valuable source of insight into how the goal-setting process works.[31]

MANAGERS' GUIDELINES FOR SETTING EFFECTIVE PERFORMANCE GOALS

Because researchers have been actively involved in studying the goal-setting process for many years, it is possible to summarize their findings in the form of principles. These represent very practical suggestions to enhance motivation.

ASSIGN SPECIFIC GOALS

Probably the best-established finding of research on goal setting is that *people perform at higher levels when asked to meet a specific high-performance goal than when simply asked to "do your best" or when no goal at all is assigned.*[32] People tend to find specific goals quite challenging and are motivated to try to meet them—not only to fulfill management's expectations but also to convince themselves that they have performed well.

A classic study by Latham and Baldes conducted at an Oklahoma lumber camp in the early 1970s provides a particularly dramatic demonstration of this principle.[33] The participants in this research were lumber camp crews who hauled logs from forests to their company's nearby sawmill. Over a three-month period before the study began, it was found that the crew loaded trucks to only about 60 percent of their legal capacity, wasting trips that cost the company money. Then a specific goal was set, challenging the loggers to load the trucks to 94 percent of their capacity before returning to the mill. How effective was this goal in raising performance? The results, summarized in Figure 4-6, show that the goal was extremely effective. In fact, not only was the specific goal effective in raising performance to the goal level in just a few weeks, but the effects were long lasting as well. In fact, the loggers were found to sustain this level of performance as long as seven years later! The resulting savings for the company was estimated to be $250,000 in the first nine months alone (an amount that would be considerably higher in today's dollars).

This is just one of many studies that clearly demonstrate the effectiveness of setting specific, challenging performance goals. Other research has found that specific

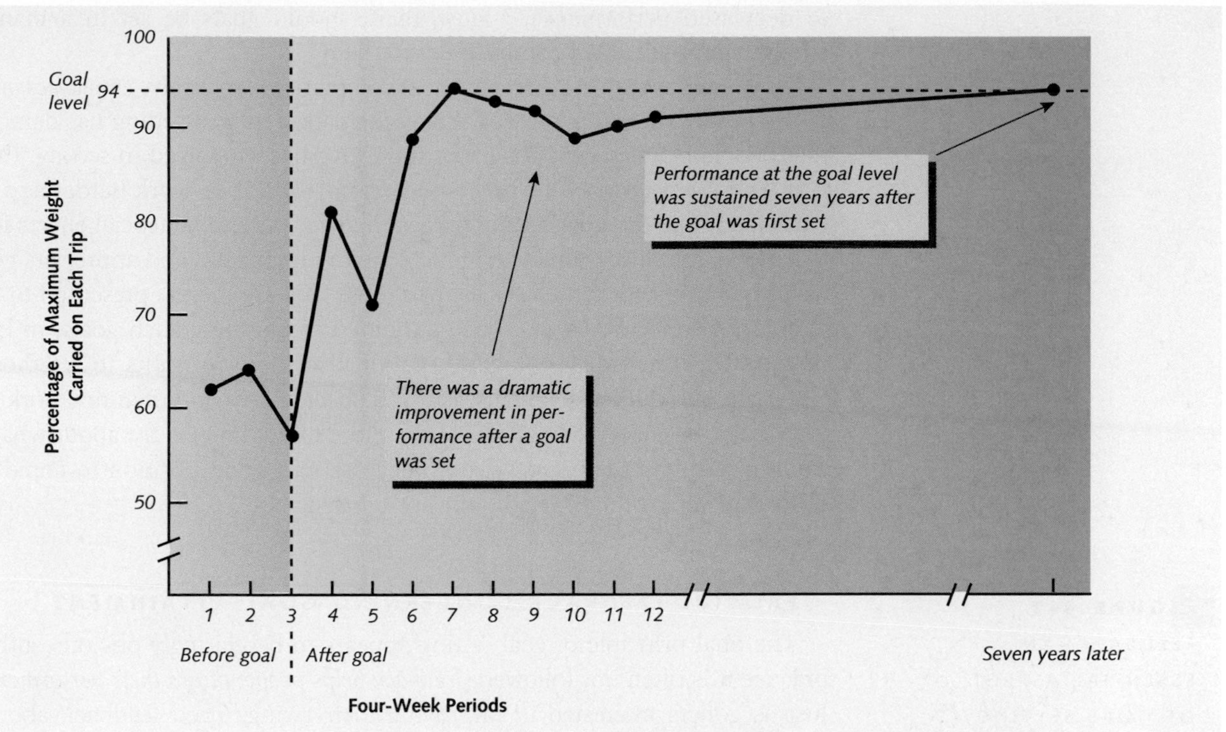

FIGURE 4-6

GOAL SETTING: SOME IMPRESSIVE EFFECTS

The performance of loggers loading timber onto trucks markedly improved after a specific, difficult goal was set. The percentage of the maximum weight of timber loaded onto trucks rose from approximately 60 percent before any goal was set, to approximately 95 percent—the goal level—after the goal was set. Performance remained at this level seven years later. (Source: *Adapted from Latham & Baldes, 1975; see Note 33.)*

goals are also helpful in getting to bring about other desirable organizational goals, such as reducing absenteeism and industrial accidents.[34] Naturally, to reap such beneficial effects, goals must not only be highly specific, but challenging as well.

ASSIGN DIFFICULT, BUT ACCEPTABLE, PERFORMANCE GOALS

The goal set at the logging camp was successful not only because it was specific, but also because it pushed crew members to a higher standard. Obviously, a goal that is too easy to attain will not bring about the desired increments in performance. For example, if you already type at 70 wpm, a goal of 60 wpm—although specific—would probably *lower* your performance. The key point is that *to raise performance a goal must be difficult as well as specific*. At the same time, however, people will work hard to reach challenging goals as long as these are within the limits of their capability. As goals become too difficult, performance suffers because people reject the goals as unrealistic and unattainable.[35] For example, you may work much harder as a student in a class that challenges your ability than in one that is very easy. At the same time, you would probably give up trying if the only way of passing was to get perfect scores on all exams—a standard you would reject as being unacceptable. In short, specific goals are most effective if they are set neither too low nor too high.

The same phenomenon occurs in organizations. For example, Bell Canada's telephone operators are required to handle calls within 23 seconds, and Federal Express's customer service agents are expected to answer customers' questions within 140 seconds.[36] Although both goals were initially considered difficult when they were imposed, the employees of both companies eventually met—or exceeded—these goals, and enjoyed the satisfaction of knowing they succeeded at this task. At a General Electric manufacturing plant, specific goals were set for productivity and cost reduction. Those goals that were perceived as challenging but possible led to improved performance, whereas those thought to be unattainable led to decreased performance.[37] How, then, should goals be set in a manner that strengthens employees' commitment to them?

One obvious way of enhancing goal acceptance is to *involve employees in the goal-setting process*. Research on workers' participation in goal setting has demonstrated that people better accept goals that they have been involved in setting, than goals that have been assigned by their supervisors—and they work harder as a result.[38] Participation in the goal-setting process may have these beneficial effects for several reasons. For one, people are more likely to understand and appreciate goals they had a hand in setting themselves than those that are merely presented to them. In addition, people are likely to be committed to attaining such goals, in large part because they must psychologically rationalize their decisions to set those goals. (After all, one can hardly justify setting a specific goal and then not work to attain it.) Finally, because workers often have more direct knowledge about what it takes to do a job than their supervisors, they are in a good position to come up with goals that are acceptably high, but not unreasonable.

PROVIDE FEEDBACK CONCERNING GOAL ATTAINMENT

The final principle of goal setting appears to be glaringly obvious, although in practice it is often not followed: *feedback helps people attain their performance goals.* Just as golfers interested in improving their swings need feedback about where their balls are going, so do workers need feedback about how closely they are approaching their performance goals in order to meet them (recall our discussion of this topic in Chapter 2).

The importance of using feedback in conjunction with goal setting has been demonstrated in an ambitious study comparing the performance of work crews in the U.S. Air Force.[39] A standardized index of job performance was used to measure five different groups repeatedly over a 2-year period. During the first nine months, a baseline measure of effectiveness was taken that was used to compare the relative impact of feedback and goal setting. Then the groups received feedback for five months (reports detailing how well they performed on various performance measures). After five months of feedback, the goal-setting phase of the study was begun. During this period, the crew members set goals for themselves with respect to their performance on various measures. Then, for the final five months, in addition to the feedback and goal setting, an incentive (time off from work) was made available to crew members who met their goals. The effectiveness of the crews during each phase of the study is summarized in Figure 4-7.

FIGURE 4-7
FEEDBACK: AN ESSENTIAL ASPECT OF GOAL SETTING
Research on U.S. Air Force crews over a two-year period showed that feedback enhanced performance, and that the addition of goal setting enhanced it even more. (Source: Based on data reported by Pritchard, Jones, Roth, Stuebing, & Ekeberg, 1988; see Note 39.)

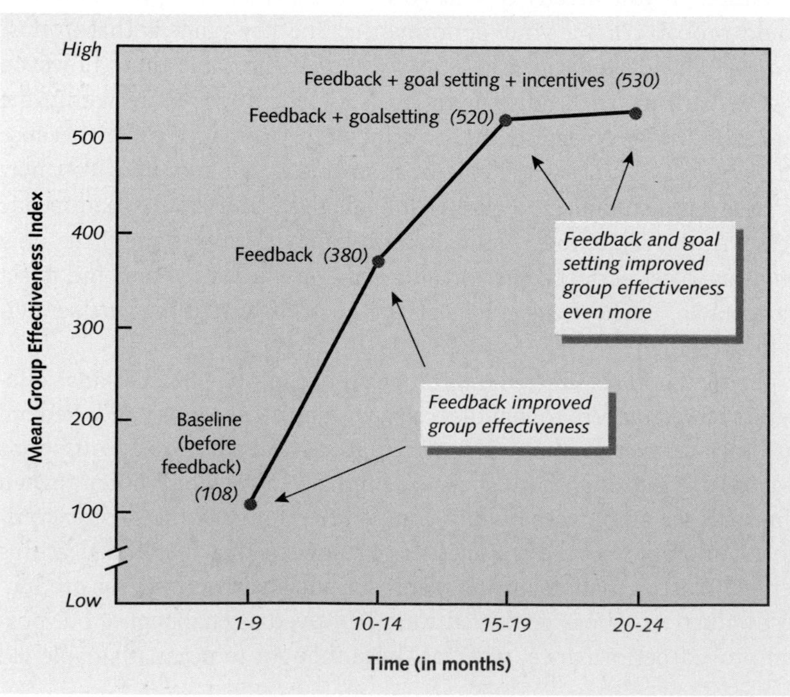

As Figure 4-7 clearly shows, feedback and goal setting dramatically increased group effectiveness. Group feedback improved performance approximately 50 percent over the baseline level. The addition of group goal setting improved it 75 percent over baseline. These findings show that the combination of goal setting and feedback helps raise the effectiveness of group performance. Groups that know how well they're doing and have a target goal to shoot for tend to perform very well. Providing incentives, however, improved performance only negligibly. The real incentive seems to be meeting the challenge of performing up to the level of the goal.

In sum, goal setting is a very effective tool managers can use to motivate people. Setting a specific, acceptably difficult goal, and providing feedback about progress toward that goal greatly enhances job performance.

EQUITY THEORY

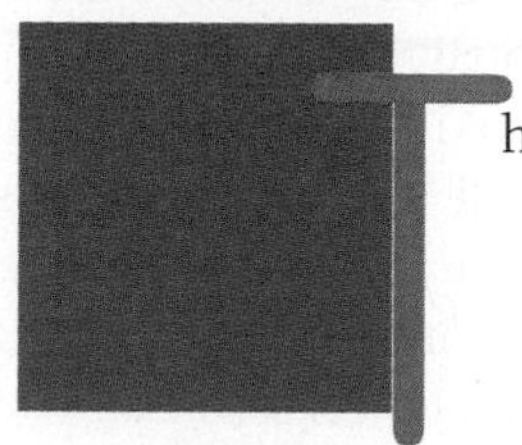

The theories we've described thus far are based on the operation of completely individual processes—the activation of needs, and the responses to goals. The next approach to motivation we will consider, **equity theory**, is also an individual-based theory, but one that adds a social component. Specifically, equity theory views motivation from the perspective of the *social comparisons* people make—that is, what they see when they compare themselves to others.[40] It proposes that individuals are motivated to maintain fair, or *equitable,* relationships among themselves and to avoid those relationships that are unfair, or *inequitable*.[41] The ways in which this is done has been a topic of considerable interest in the field of organizational behavior.

ADAMS'S EQUITY THEORY

Equity theory, introduced by J. Stacy Adams, proposes that people comparing themselves to others focus on two variables, *outcomes* and *inputs*.[42] **Outcomes** are what we get out of our jobs, including pay, fringe benefits, and prestige. **Inputs**, are the contributions made, such as the amount of time worked, the amount of effort expended, the number of units produced, and the qualifications brought to the job. Equity theory is concerned with outcomes and inputs as they are *perceived* by the people involved, not necessarily what they might actually be based on any objective standards. Not surprisingly, therefore, people sometimes disagree about what constitutes equitable treatment on the job.

Equity theory states that people compare their outcomes and inputs to those of others, and judge the equitableness of these relationships in the form of a ratio. Specifically, they compare the ratios of their own outcomes/inputs to the ratios of others' outcomes/inputs. This "other" that serves as the basis of comparison may be someone else in one's work group, another employee in the organization, an individual working in the same field, or even oneself at an earlier point in time—in short, almost anyone against whom we compare ourselves. As shown in Figure 4-8, these comparisons can result in any of three different states: *overpayment inequity*, *underpayment inequity*, or *equitable payment*.

To illustrate these concepts, let's consider an example. Imagine that Jack and Ray work alongside each other on an assembly line doing the same job. Both men have equal amounts of experience, training and education, and work equally long and hard at their jobs—in other words, their inputs are equivalent. But suppose Jack is paid a salary of $500 per week while Ray is paid only $350 per week. In this case, Jack's ratio of outcomes/inputs is higher than Ray's, creating a state of **overpayment inequity** for Jack, but **underpayment inequity** for Ray (since the ratio of his out-

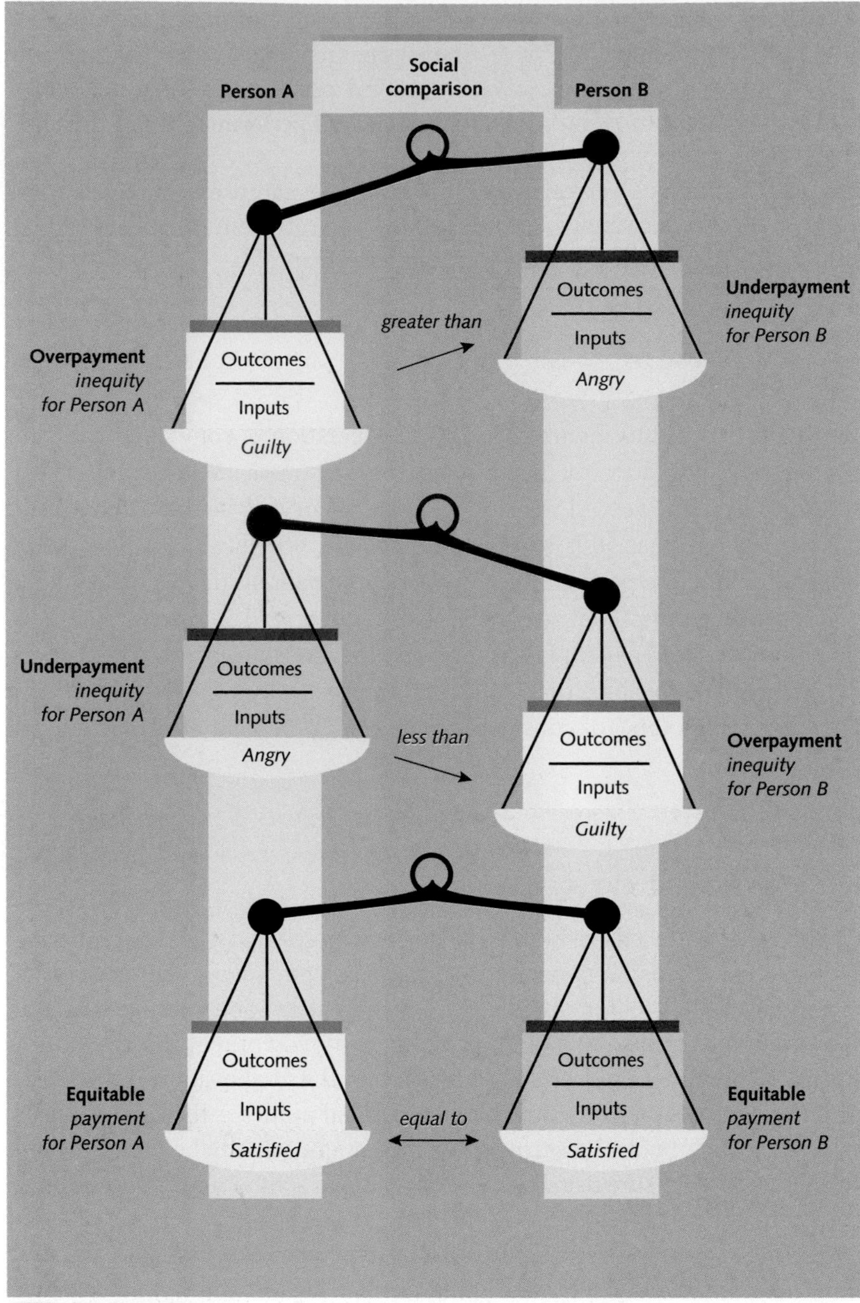

FIGURE 4-8
EQUITY THEORY: AN OVERVIEW
To judge equity or inequity people compare the ratios of their own outcomes–inputs to the corresponding ratios of others (or themselves at an earlier time). The resulting states—overpayment inequity, underpayment inequity, and equitable payment—and their associated emotional responses are summarized here.

comes/inputs is lower). According to equity theory, Jack—realizing that he is paid more than an equally qualified person doing the same work—will feel *guilty* in response to his overpayment. By contrast, Ray, realizing that he is paid less than an equally qualified person for doing the same work, will feel *angry* in response to his underpayment. Feeling guilty or angry are negative emotional states that people are motivated to change. Specifically, they will seek to create a state of **equitable payment** in which their outcome/input ratios are equal, leading them to feel *satisfied*.

How can people change inequitable states to equitable ones? Equity theory suggests several possible courses of action (see Table 4-1). In general, people who are underpaid may either lower their inputs or raise their outcomes. Either action would effectively bring the underpaid individual's outcome/input ratio into line with that of the comparison person. In our example, the underpaid Ray might lower his inputs such as by slacking off, arriving at work late, leaving early, taking longer breaks, doing less work, or lower-quality work—or, in an extreme case, quit his job. He also may attempt to raise his outcomes, such as by asking for a raise, or even taking home company property, such as tools or office supplies. By contrast, the overpaid person, Jack, may do the opposite—raise his inputs or lower his outcomes. For example, he might put forth much more effort, work longer hours, and try to make a greater contribution to the company. He also might lower his outcomes, such as by working through a paid vacation, or not taking advantage of fringe benefits the company offers. These are all specific *behavioral* reactions to inequitable conditions—that is, things people *do* in attempting to change inequitable states to equitable ones.

As you might imagine, people may be unwilling to do some of the things necessary to respond behaviorally to inequities. In particular, they may feel uncomfortable stealing from their employers (as they should), or would be unwilling to restrict their productivity (in fear of getting caught "goofing off"), or uncomfortable asking their boss for a raise. As a result, they may resort to resolving the inequity not by changing their behavior, but by changing the way they think about the situation. Because equity theory deals with perceptions of fairness or unfairness, it is

TABLE 4-1

Possible Reactions to Inequity: A Summary

People can respond to overpayment and underpayment inequities in behavioral and/or psychological ways. A few of these are summarized here. These reactions help change the perceived inequities into a state of perceived equity.

	TYPE OF REACTION	
TYPE OF INEQUITY	BEHAVIORAL (WHAT YOU CAN DO IS . . .)	PSYCHOLOGICAL (WHAT YOU CAN THINK IS . . .)
Overpayment inequity	*Raise your inputs (e.g., work harder), or lower your outcomes (e.g., work through a paid vacation)*	*Convince yourself that your outcomes are deserved based on your inputs (e.g., rationalize that you work harder than others and so you deserve more pay)*
Underpayment inequity	*Lower your inputs (e.g., reduce effort), or raise your outcomes (e.g., get a raise in pay)*	*Convince yourself that others' inputs are really higher than your own (e.g., rationalize that the comparison worker is really more qualified and so deserves higher outcomes)*

reasonable to expect that inequitable states may be redressed by merely altering one's thinking about the circumstances. For example, underpaid people may rationalize that others' inputs are really higher than their own (e.g., "I suppose she really *is* more qualified than me"), thereby convincing themselves that their higher outcomes are justified. Similarly, overpaid people may convince themselves that they really *are* better, and really do deserve their relatively higher pay. So, by changing the way they see things, people can come to perceive inequitable situations as equitable, thereby effectively reducing their inequity distress.[43]

Research has generally supported equity theory's claim that people respond to overpayment and underpayment inequities in the ways described.[44] For example, in a classic study, Pritchard, Dunnette, and Jorgenson found that compared to clerical workers who were equitably paid (paid the amount they expected), those who were overpaid (paid more than they expected) were more productive, and those who were underpaid (paid less than they expected) were less productive.[45] Performance decrements for underpaid people have been found among professional athletes as well. For example, Harder found that professional basketball players who were underpaid (based on objective measures of pay relative to performance) scored fewer points than those who were equitably paid.[46] In the world of baseball, players who are paid less than others who play comparably well tend to change teams or even leave the sport when they are unsuccessful at negotiating higher pay.[47] Not only do underpaid people lower their inputs, but they also attempt to raise their outcomes. For example, Greenberg found that people who were underpaid responded by stealing some of the money they thought they had coming to them.[48] Taken together, these studies provide strong support for equity theory.

APPLYING EQUITY THEORY: SOME MOTIVATIONAL TIPS FOR MANAGERS

Equity theory has some important implications for ways of motivating people. First, it suggests that *underpayment should be avoided*. Companies that attempt to save money by shaving a few dollars off employees' salaries may find that they respond by cutting a few minutes off their workdays, or otherwise withholding production. In recent years, a particularly unsettling form of institutionalizing underpayment has materialized in the form of **two-tier wage structures**—payment systems in which newer employees are paid less than those hired to do the same work at an earlier point in time. Not surprisingly, such systems are considered to be highly unfair, particularly by those in the lower tier.[49] When such a plan was instituted at the Giant Food supermarket chain, two-thirds of the lower-tier employees quit their jobs in the first three months. "It stinks," said a clerk at one Giant store in Los Angeles, "They're paying us lower wages for the same work."[50] A proposal to institute a two-tier wage system at United Airlines in the mid-1980s led its pilots to go on strike (see Figure 4-9).[51] And who can blame them? The plan would have virtually cut in half the amount DC-10 pilots would be earning at the top of their careers—an annual difference of over $64,000. Clearly, the negative reactions to such forms of inequities should make employers think twice before introducing any plan that would compensate employees unfairly.

Although we have been talking about underpayment, we also advise that *overpayment should be avoided*. You may think that because overpaid employees work hard to deserve their pay, it would be a useful motivational technique to pay people more than they merit. There are several reasons why this would not work. First, the increases in performance shown in response to overpayment inequity tend to be only temporary. As time goes on, people begin to believe that they actually deserve the higher pay they're getting, and bring their work level down to normal. A second reason why it is unwise to overpay employees is that when you overpay one employee, you are underpaying all the others. When the majority of the employees feel underpaid, they will lower their performance, resulting in a net *decrease* in productivity—and widespread dissatisfaction. Hence, the conclusion is clear: *managers should strive to treat all employees equitably*.

We realize, of course, that this may be easier said than done. Part of the difficulty resides in the fact that feelings of equity and inequity are based on perceptions, and these aren't always easy to control (as we discussed in Chapter 2). One approach that may help is to *be open and honest about outcomes and inputs*. People tend to overestimate how much their superiors are paid, and therefore tend to feel that their own pay is not as high as it should be.[52] However, if information about pay is shared, inequitable feelings may not result. Finally, we recommend that *managers should present information about outcomes and inputs in a thorough and socially sensitive manner*. Not only may doing so take some of the sting out of receiving undesirable outcomes (such as layoffs), but it also enhances the manager's image as a fair person.[53] (For an example of how this approach can help people accept the fairness of an important organizational policy—a worksite smoking ban—see the Ethical Workplace section on the opposite page.)

FIGURE 4-9
STRIKING: A CLEAR DEMONSTRATION OF INEQUITY
In the mid-1980s pilots from United Airlines went on strike because the company proposed a two-tier wage system *that would have paid new pilots considerably less than those who were already employed. Their strike was a potent response to their strong feelings of inequity.*

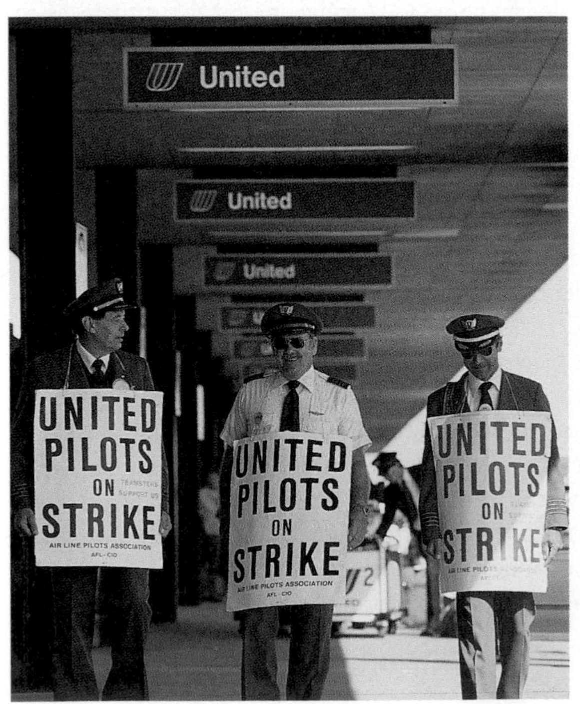

THE ETHICAL WORKPLACE

HELPING EMPLOYEES ACCEPT A CORPORATE SMOKING BAN: A LITTLE FAIRNESS GOES A LONG WAY

When it comes to the ethical treatment of employees, scientists have learned that there's more involved than just the relative balance of outcomes and inputs. People also judge fairness on the basis of the way they are treated. Are you given sufficient information about how important decisions are made? Are you treated with respect when information is shared with you? To believe that we are treated fairly, the answers to these questions must be "yes."[54] Not only does fair treatment make people feel good, but it also helps them accept undesirable situations (even a bitter pill may be easier to swallow if it's sugar-coated, and if you know why it's important to take).

In this regard, consider the very timely issue of work-site smoking bans. In today's society, for people to enjoy a high quality of life at work it is necessary to provide a smoke-free environment. Not only does this reduce the health risks to both smokers and nonsmokers, but it also benefits everyone with reduced insurance costs and increased safety. As a result, many organizations are imposing totally smoke-free environments. As beneficial as this is to everyone, it also creates a terrible imposition on smokers because it forces them to curb their habits. Obviously, this isn't easy to do, and smokers might object on the grounds that the smoking ban infringes on their rights. This is a difficult situation. The challenge, then, is to find a way of getting everyone—including smokers—to believe that a smoking ban is acceptable.

In a recent study, Greenberg reasoned that people would be more willing to accept a work-site smoking ban if they believed it was imposed on them fairly.[55] Specifically, he hypothesized that although smokers might not like a smoking ban, they would be more likely to accept it if they were led to thoroughly understand *why* it was necessary to impose it, and if this information was presented to them in a socially sensitive manner (i.e., by showing concern over to their plight). To test

FIGURE 4-10

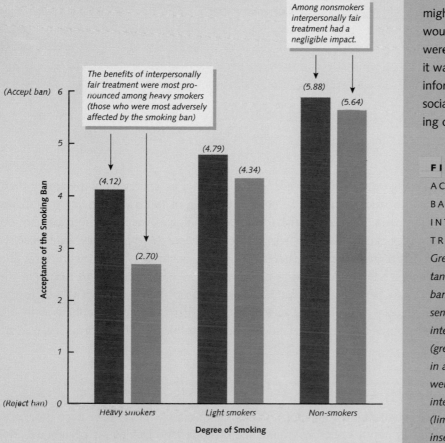

ACCEPTANCE OF A SMOKING BAN: THE BENEFITS OF INTERPERSONALLY FAIR TREATMENT

Greenberg measured employees' acceptance of an impending work site smoking ban as a function of the way it was presented to the workforce. When very interpersonally fair procedures were used (great amounts of information presented in a highly sensitive manner), people were more accepting than when less interpersonally fair procedures were used (limited information presented in an insensitive fashion). These effects were most pronounced among heavy smokers. (Source: Based on data reported by Greenberg, 1994; see Note 54.)

this idea, Greenberg arranged for the president of a large financial services company to address the workforce immediately before a complete ban on smoking was about to be imposed. The employees were randomly assigned to one of four different rooms where they heard one of four different messages by the company president presented via a large-screen television. The messages systematically varied the manner in which the smoking ban was presented. They either presented extremely thorough information justifying the decision (a lot of detailed charts and graphs describing the health and safety risks, and the cost to the company) or very little information (simple statements of the dangers and costs of smoking). In conjunction with this, the president either projected a very high amount of social sensitivity (concern and sympathy over how difficult it will be to stop smoking) or very low social sensitivity (emphasizing the business-related nature of the decision). After these messages were presented, the employees were given a questionnaire to see how much they accepted the smoking ban (i.e., how willing they were to go along with it). The results are summarized in Figure 4-10.

There are several interesting trends in these data. First, all employees were most accepting of the ban when a great deal of information was provided and a great deal of sensitivity was shown. Interestingly, however, not all employees were influenced to the same degree. As you might expect, heavy smokers (those in the group who smoked most) were less accepting of the ban than either light smokers or nonsmokers. Fortunately, heavy smokers—those who stood to be most inconvenienced by the ban—were most positively affected by the highly sensitive and informative explanations. Although they didn't come to accept the ban as much as those who didn't smoke, they showed the greatest increase in acceptance following high amounts of information and sensitivity. Not surprisingly, those who were positively affected by the ban, nonsmokers, accepted it so much that the way the message was presented had only a negligible effect on them.

These findings reveal that treating people in an interpersonally fair manner (i.e., by giving them thorough explanations of important events and presenting these in a socially sensitive manner) can help them accept a change in an important organizational policy. Such changes are inevitable in organizations, and it is unfortunate that some will find them undesirable. Fortunately, in such cases interpersonally fair treatment can be used to help ease the blow.

EXPECTANCY THEORY

Instead of focusing on individual needs, goals, or social comparisons, **expectancy theory** takes a broader approach; it looks at the role of motivation in the overall work environment. In essence, the theory asserts that people are motivated to work when they expect that they will be able to achieve the things they want from their jobs. Expectancy theory characterizes people as rational beings who think about what they have to do to be rewarded and how much the reward means to them before they perform their jobs. But, as we will see, the theory doesn't only focus on what people think. It also recognizes that these thoughts combine with other aspects of the organizational environment to influence job performance.

BASIC ELEMENTS OF EXPECTANCY THEORY

Although slightly different versions of expectancy theory have been proposed—including popular ones by Vroom, and by Porter and Lawler—expectancy theorists agree that motivation is the result of three different types of beliefs that people have.[56,57] These are **expectancy**—the belief that one's effort will result in performance, **instrumentality**—the belief that one's performance will be rewarded, and **valence**—the perceived value of the rewards to the recipient.

Sometimes people putting forth a great deal of effort expect that they will get a lot accomplished. However, in other cases, people do not expect that their efforts will have much effect on how well they do. For example, an employee operating a faulty piece of equipment may have a very low *expectancy* that his or her efforts will lead to high levels of performance. Naturally, someone working under such conditions probably would not continue to exert much effort.

Even *if* an employee works hard and performs at a high level, motivation may falter if that performance is not suitably rewarded—that is, if the performance is not perceived as *instrumental* in bringing about the rewards. So, for example, a worker who is extremely productive may be poorly motivated to perform if he or she has already reached the top level of pay given by the company.

Finally, even *if* employees believe that hard work will lead to good performance *and* that they will be rewarded commensurate with their performance, they still may be poorly motivated *if* those so-called rewards have a low *valence* to them. In other words, someone who doesn't care about the rewards offered by the organization is not motivated to attain them. As an example, a reward of $100 would not be likely to motivate a multimillionaire, whereas it may be a very desirable reward for someone of more modest means. Only those rewards that have a high positive valence to their recipients will motivate behavior.

Expectancy theory claims that motivation is a multiplicative function of all three components. This means that higher levels of motivation will result when expectancy, instrumentality, and valence are all high than when they are all low. The multiplicative assumption of the theory also implies that if any one of these three components is zero, the overall level of motivation will be zero. So, for example, even if an employee believes that her effort will result in performance, which will result in reward, motivation will be zero if the valance of the reward she expects to receive is zero. Figure 4-11 summarizes the definitions of expectancy theory components and shows their relationships.

Figure 4-11 also highlights a point we made in our opening remarks about motivation (see p. 127): that motivation is not equivalent to job performance. Expectancy theory recognizes that motivation is one of several important determinants of job performance. In particular, the theory assumes that *skills and abilities* also contribute to a person's job performance. It's no secret that some people are better suited to performing their jobs than others by virtue of their unique characteristics and special skills and abilities. For example, a tall, strong, well-coordinated person is likely to make a better professional basketball player than a very short, weak, uncoordinated one—even if the shorter person is highly motivated to succeed.

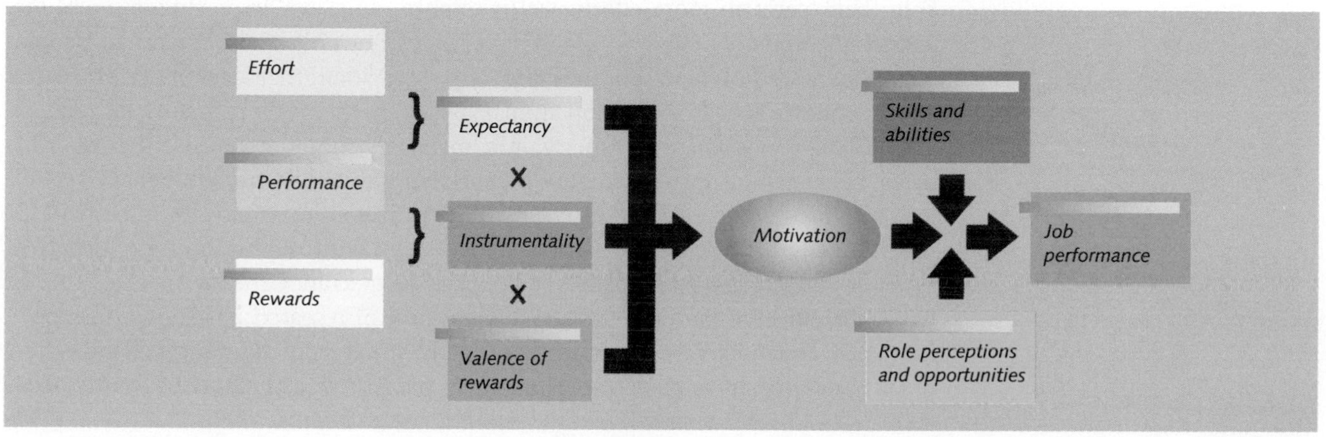

FIGURE 4-11
EXPECTANCY THEORY: AN OVERVIEW
According to expectancy theory, *motivation is the product of three types of beliefs:* expectancy *(effort will result in performance) X* instrumentality *(performance will result in rewards) X* valence of rewards *(the perceived value of the rewards expected). It also recognizes that motivation is only one of several factors responsible for job performance.*

Expectancy theory also recognizes that job performance will be influenced by people's *role perceptions*—in other words, what they believe is expected of them on the job. To the extent that there are disagreements about what one's job duties are, performance may suffer. For example, an assistant manager who believes her primary job duty is to train new employees may find that her performance is downgraded by a supervisor who believes she should be spending more time doing routine paperwork instead. In this case the person's performance wouldn't suffer as a result of any deficit in motivation, but simply because of misunderstandings regarding what the job entails.

Finally, expectancy theory also recognizes the role of *opportunities to perform* one's job. Even the best employees may perform at low levels if their opportunities are limited. For example, a highly motivated salesperson may perform poorly if opportunities are restricted (such as if the territory is having a financial downturn, or if the available inventory is limited).

It is important to recognize that expectancy theory views motivation as just one of several determinants of job performance. Motivation, combined with a person's skills and abilities, role perceptions, and opportunities, influences job performance.

Expectancy theory has generated a great deal of research and has been successfully applied to understanding behavior in many different organizational settings.[58] Although the theory has received only mixed support about some of its specific aspects (e.g., the multiplicative assumption), it is still one of the dominant approaches to the study of motivation in organizations. Probably the primary reason for expectancy theory's popularity is the many useful suggestions it makes for practicing managers.

We will now describe some of the most essential applications of expectancy theory, giving examples from organizations in which they have been implemented.

MANAGERIAL APPLICATIONS OF EXPECTANCY THEORY

Expectancy theory strongly suggests that it is essential to *clarify people's expectancies that their effort will lead to performance*. Motivation may be enhanced by training employees to do their jobs more efficiently (see Chapter 2), thereby achieving higher levels of performance from their efforts. It also may be possible to enhance effort–performance expectancies by following employees' suggestions about ways to change their jobs (as is done at United Electric Controls, described in our Preview Case). To the extent that employees are aware of problems in their jobs that interfere with their performance, attempting to alleviate these problems may help them perform more effectively. In essence, what we are saying is: *make the desired performance attainable*. Good supervisors not only make it clear to people what is expected of them, but they also help them attain that level of performance.

A second practical suggestion from expectancy theory is to *clearly link valued rewards and performance*. In other words, managers should enhance their subordinates' beliefs about instrumentality by specifying exactly what job behaviors will lead to what rewards. To the extent that it is possible for employees to be paid in ways directly linked to their performance—such as through piece-rate incentive systems, sales commission plans, or bonuses—expectancy theory specifies that it would be effective to do so. Indeed, a great deal of research has shown that performance increases can result from carefully implemented merit systems—frequently referred to as **pay-for-performance** plans.[59] Of course, the rewards need not be monetary in nature; even verbal recognition for a job well done can be very effective. In some extreme cases (such as San Diego's Science Applications International Corporation), good performance is rewarded with shares of ownership in the company.[60] Unfortunately, not all incentive plans do as good a job as they should in rewarding desired performance. A recent survey found that only 25 percent of employees see a clear link between good job performance and their pay raises. Obviously many organizations have a long way to go in raising their employees' instrumentality beliefs.[61]

Finally, one of the most obvious practical suggestions from expectancy theory is to *administer rewards that are positively valent to employees*. In other words, the carrot at the end of the stick must be tasty for it to have potential as a motivator. These days, with a highly diverse workforce, it would be erroneous to assume that all employees care about having the same rewards. Some might recognize the incentive value of a pay raise, whereas others might prefer additional vacation days, improved insurance benefits, day care or elder care facilities. With this in mind, many companies have introduced **cafeteria-style benefit plans**—incentive systems allowing employees to select their fringe benefits from a menu of available alternatives. Given that fringe benefits represent almost 40 percent of payroll costs, more and more companies are recognizing the value of administering them flexibly.[62] For example, Primerica has had a flexible benefit plan in use since 1978—one that almost 95 percent of the company's 8,000 salaried employees believe is extremely beneficial to them.[63] Today's companies are doing many creative things to help ensure that its employees can achieve rewards that have value to them (see Table 4-2).[64]

TABLE 4-2

Ensuring Positively Valent Rewards: What Some Companies Are Doing

All companies pay their employees, but a few also provide more creative incentives that help ensure that employees receive rewards that have value to them.

COMPANY	PRACTICE
Calvert Group *(financial management company, located in Bethesda, MD)*	*Company reimburses recruiting expenses for all 190 of its employees.*
ESP Software Services *(computer consultancy firm, located in Minneapolis, MN)*	*Employees can select either a base salary with no hourly pay, or hourly pay based on time spent on assignment, or a blend of the two.*
Rogan *(manufacturer of plastic knobs, located in Northbrook, IL)*	*Employees are not only rewarded for their money-saving contributions, but these also are recognized in the company newsletter.*
Ashton Photo *(photo-image printer, located in Salem, OR)*	*Company rewards employees by allowing them to decide on the skills needed to do their jobs best, and lets them grade their own performance.*

Source: Based on Ehrenfeld, 1993; see Note 64.

JOB DESIGN: STRUCTURING TASKS FOR HIGH MOTIVATION

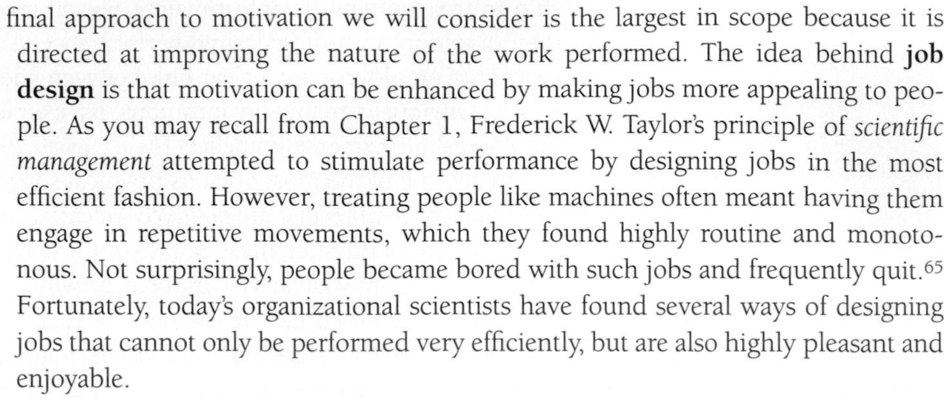

The final approach to motivation we will consider is the largest in scope because it is directed at improving the nature of the work performed. The idea behind **job design** is that motivation can be enhanced by making jobs more appealing to people. As you may recall from Chapter 1, Frederick W. Taylor's principle of *scientific management* attempted to stimulate performance by designing jobs in the most efficient fashion. However, treating people like machines often meant having them engage in repetitive movements, which they found highly routine and monotonous. Not surprisingly, people became bored with such jobs and frequently quit.[65] Fortunately, today's organizational scientists have found several ways of designing jobs that cannot only be performed very efficiently, but are also highly pleasant and enjoyable.

JOB ENLARGEMENT AND JOB ENRICHMENT

Imagine that you have a highly routine job, such as tightening the lugs on the left rear wheel of a car as it rolls down an assembly line. Naturally, such a highly repetitive task would be monotonous and not very pleasant. One of the first modern approaches to redesigning jobs suggested that such consequences could be minimized by having people perform an increased number of different tasks all at the same level. This approach is known as **job enlargement**. To enlarge the jobs in our example, workers could be required to tighten the lugs on all four wheels. As a result of such an action, employees have no more responsibility nor use any greater skills, but perform a wider variety of different tasks at the same level. Adding tasks in this fashion is said to increase the *horizontal job loading* of the position.

Recently, American Greetings Corporation, Cleveland, Ohio's greeting card and licensing concern, enlarged some 400 jobs in its creative division.[66] Now, rather than always working exclusively on Christmas cards, for example, employees will be able to move back and forth between different teams, such as those working on birthday ribbons, humorous mugs, and Valentine's Day gift bags. Employees at American Greetings reportedly enjoy the variety, as do those at RJR Nabisco, Corning, and Eastman Kodak, other companies that have recently allowed employees to make such lateral moves.

Although most reports of the effectiveness of job enlargement have been anecdotal, carefully conducted empirical studies also have examined their impact. For example, Campion and McClelland studied the effects of a job enlargement program instituted at a large financial services company.[67] The unenlarged jobs had different employees perform separate paperwork tasks such as preparing, sorting, coding, and keypunching various forms. The enlarged jobs combined these various functions into larger jobs performed by the same people. Although it was more difficult and expensive to train people to perform the enlarged jobs than the separate jobs, important benefits resulted as well. In particular, employees expressed greater job satisfaction and less boredom. And, because one person followed the whole job all the way through, greater opportunities to correct errors existed. Not surprisingly, customers were satisfied with the result. Unfortunately, in a follow-up investigation of the same company conducted two years later, Campion and McClelland found that not all the beneficial effects continued.[68] Notably, employee satisfaction leveled off, and the rate of errors went up, suggesting that as

FIGURE 4-12
JOB ENLARGEMENT VERSUS JOB ENRICHMENT: TWO WAYS OF DESIGNING JOBS
Designing jobs by increasing the number of tasks performed at the same level (horizontal job loading) is referred to as job enlargement. *Designing jobs by increasing employee's level of responsibility and control (vertical job loading) is referred to as* job enrichment.

employees got used to their enlarged jobs they found them less interesting, and stopped paying attention to all the details. Hence, although job enlargement may help improve job performance, its effects may not be long-lasting.

In contrast to job enlargement, **job enrichment** gives employees not only more jobs to do, but more tasks to perform at a higher level of skill and responsibility (see Figure 4-12). Job enrichment gives employees the opportunity to take greater control over how to do their jobs. Because people performing enriched jobs have increased opportunities to work at higher levels, the job enrichment process is said to increase a job's *vertical job loading*.

Probably the most carefully studied job enrichment program was one developed by Volvo, the Swedish auto manufacturer. In response to serious dissension in its workforce in the late 1960s, the company's then president, Pehr Gyllenhammar, introduced job enrichment in its Kalmar assembly plant.[69] Cars are assembled by 25 groups of approximately twenty workers who are each responsible for one part of the car's assembly (e.g., engine, electrical system). In contrast to the usual

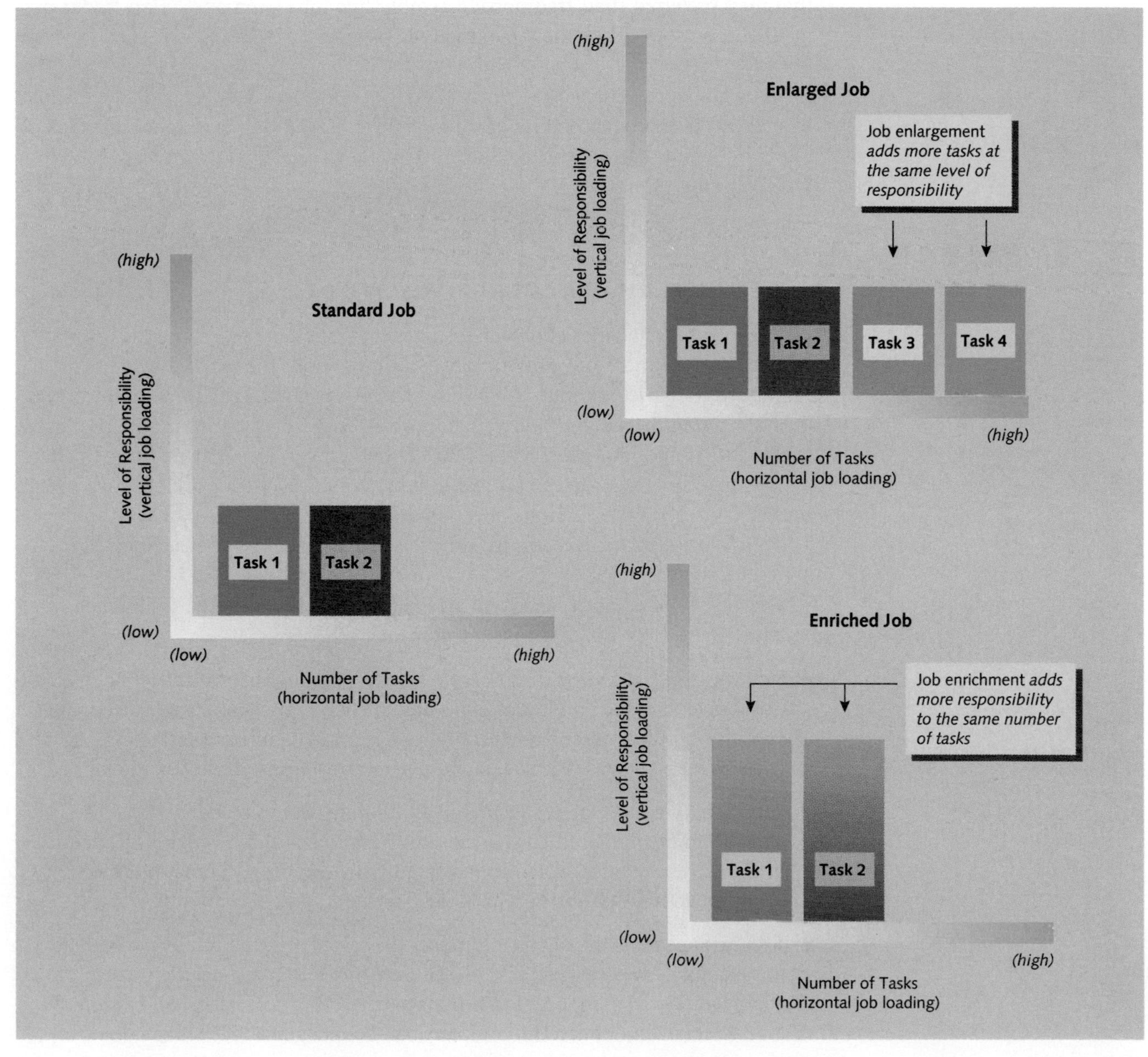

assembly-line method of manufacturing cars, Volvo's work groups are set up so they can freely plan, organize, and inspect their own work. In time, the workers became more satisfied with their jobs and the plant experienced a significant reduction in turnover and absenteeism.

Although evidence suggests that job enrichment programs also have been successful at other organizations, several factors limit their popularity.[70] Most obvious, is the *difficulty of implementation*. To redesign existing facilities so that jobs can be enriched is often prohibitively expensive. Besides, the technology needed to perform certain jobs makes it impractical for them to be redesigned. Another impediment is the *lack of employee acceptance*. Although many relish it, some people do *not* desire the additional responsibility associated with performing enriched jobs. In particular, individuals low in achievement motivation (see Chapter 3) are especially frustrated with enriched jobs.[71] Similarly, people may get used to having to do their jobs in certain ways, and don't like having to change (see Chapter 16). In fact, when a group of U.S. auto workers was sent to Sweden to work in a Saab engine assembly plant where jobs were highly enriched, five out of six indicated that they preferred their traditional assembly-line jobs.[72] As one union leader put it, "If you want to enrich the job, enrich the paycheck."[73] Clearly, enriched jobs are not for everyone.

Thus far, we have failed to specify precisely *how* to enrich a job. *What* elements of a job need to be enriched for it to be effective? An attempt to expand the idea of job enrichment, known as the *job characteristics model*, provides an answer to this important question.

THE JOB CHARACTERISTICS MODEL

The job characteristics approach assumes that jobs can be designed so as to help people get enjoyment out of their jobs, and care about the work they do. The *job characteristics model* identifies how jobs can be designed to help people feel that they are doing meaningful and valuable work. In particular, the model proposed by Hackman and Oldham specifies that enriching certain elements of jobs alters people's psychological states in a manner that enhances their work effectiveness.[74] Specifically, the model identifies five *core job dimensions* that help create three *critical psychological states*, leading, in turn, to several beneficial *personal and work outcomes* (see Figure 4-13).

The five critical job dimensions are *skill variety*, *task identity*, *task significance*, *autonomy*, and *feedback*. Let's take a closer look at these:

- *Skill variety* is the extent to which a job requires a number of different activities using several of the employee's skills and talents. For example, an office manager with high skill variety may have to perform many different tasks (e.g., do word processing, answer the telephone, greet visitors, and file records).
- *Task identity* is the extent to which a job requires completing a whole piece of work from beginning to end. For example, tailors will have high task identity if they do everything related to making a whole suit (e.g., measuring the client, selecting the fabric, cutting and sewing it, and altering it to fit).
- *Task significance* is the degree of impact the job is believed to have on others. For example, medical researchers working on a cure for a deadly disease probably recognize the importance of their work to the world at large. Even more modest contributions to the company can be recognized as being significant to

FIGURE 4-13

THE JOB CHARACTERISTICS MODEL: AN OVERVIEW

The job characteristics model *stipulates that certain* core job dimensions *create* critical psychological states, *which in turn lead to several beneficial* personal and work outcomes. *The model recognizes that these relationships are strongest among individuals who have high levels of* growth need strength. *(Source: Adapted from Hackman & Oldham, 1980; see Note 74.)*

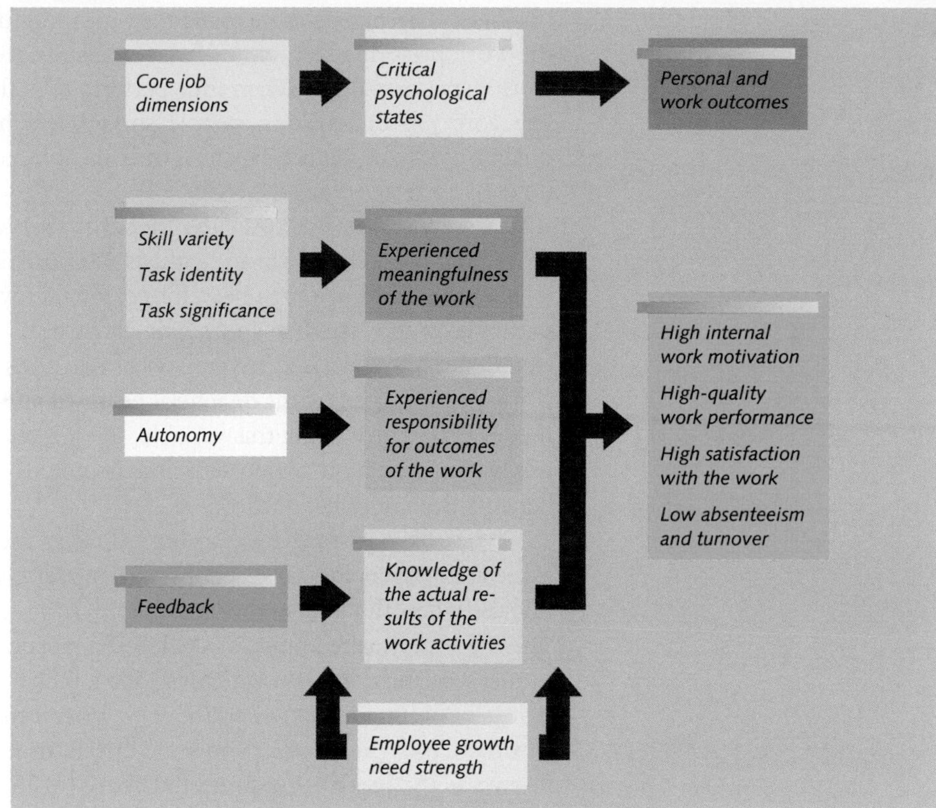

the extent that employees understand the role of their jobs in the overall mission of the organization.

- *Autonomy* is the extent to which employees have the freedom and discretion to plan, schedule, and carry out their jobs as desired. For example, a furniture repair person may act highly autonomously by freely scheduling his or her day's work and by freely deciding how to tackle each repair job confronted.
- *Feedback* is the extent to which the job allows people to have information about the effectiveness of their performance. For example, telemarketing representatives regularly receive information about how many calls they make per day and the number and values of the sales made.

The model specifies that these various job dimensions have important effects on various critical psychological states. For example, skill variety, task identity, and task significance jointly contribute to a task's *experienced meaningfulness*. A task is considered meaningful to the extent that it is experienced as being highly important, valuable, and worthwhile. Jobs that provide a great deal of autonomy are said to make people feel *personally responsible and accountable for their work*. When they are free to decide what to do and how to do it, they feel more responsible for the results, whether good or bad. Finally, effective feedback is said to give employees *knowledge of the results of their work*. When a job is designed to provide people with information about the effects of their actions, they are better able to develop an understanding of how well they have performed—and such knowledge improves their effectiveness.

The job characteristics model specifies that the three critical psychological states affect various personal and work outcomes—namely people's feelings of motivation, the quality of work performed, satisfaction with work, absenteeism, and turnover. The higher the experienced meaningfulness of work, responsibility for the work performed, and knowledge of results, the more positive the personal and work benefits will be. When they perform jobs that incorporate high levels of the five core job dimensions, people should feel highly motivated, perform high-quality work, be highly satisfied with their jobs, be absent infrequently, and be unlikely to resign from their jobs.

We should also note that the model is theorized to be especially effective in describing the behavior of individuals who are high in *growth need strength*—that is, people who have a high need for personal growth and development. People not particularly interested in improving themselves on the job are not expected to experience the theorized psychological reactions to the core job dimensions, nor consequently, to enjoy the beneficial personal and work outcomes predicted by the model.[75] By introducing this variable, the job characteristics model recognizes the important limitation of job enrichment noted earlier—not everyone wants and benefits from enriched jobs.

Given the proposed relationship between the core job dimensions and their associated psychological reactions, the model claims that job motivation will be highest when the jobs performed rate high on the various dimensions. To assess this, a questionnaire known as the Job Diagnostic Survey (JDS) has been developed to measure the degree to which various job characteristics are present in a particular job.[76] Using responses to the JDS, we can make predictions about the degree to which a job motivates people who perform it. This is done by using an index known as the **motivating potential score** (**MPS**), computed as follows:

$$\text{MPS} = \frac{\text{Skill variety} + \text{Task identity} + \text{Task significance}}{3} \times \text{Autonomy} \times \text{Feedback}$$

The MPS is a summary index of a job's potential for motivating people. The higher the score for a given job, the greater the likelihood of experiencing the personal and work outcomes specified by the model. Knowing a job's MPS helps one identify jobs that might benefit by being redesigned.

The job characteristics model has been the focus of many empirical tests, most of which are supportive of many aspects of the model.[77] One study conducted among a group of South African clerical workers found particularly strong support.[78] The jobs of employees in some of the offices in this company were enriched in accordance with techniques specified by the job characteristics model. Specifically, employees performing the enriched jobs were given opportunities to choose the kinds of tasks they perform (high skill variety), do the entire job (high task identity), receive instructions regarding how their job fit into the organization as a whole (high task significance), freely set their own schedules and inspect their own work (high autonomy), and keep records of their daily productivity (high feedback). Another group of employees, equivalent in all respects except that their jobs were not enriched, served as a control group.

After employees performed the newly designed jobs for six months, comparisons were made between them and their counterparts in the control group. With respect to most of the outcomes specified by the model, individuals performing redesigned jobs showed superior results. Specifically, they reported feeling more internally motivated and more satisfied with their jobs. There were also lower rates of absenteeism and turnover among employees performing the enriched jobs. The only outcome predicted by the model that was not found to differ was actual work performance; people performed equally well in enriched and unenriched jobs.

Considering the many factors that are responsible for job performance (as discussed in connection with expectancy theory), this finding should not be too surprising.

TECHNIQUES FOR DESIGNING JOBS THAT MOTIVATE: SOME MANAGERIAL GUIDELINES

The job characteristics model specifies several ways in which jobs can be designed to enhance their motivating potential.[79] In Table 4-3 we present these in the form of general principles.

COMBINE TASKS

Instead of having several workers each performing a separate part of a whole job, it would be better to have each person perform the entire job. Doing so helps provide greater skill variety and task identity. For example, Corning Glass Works in Medford, Massachusetts, redesigned jobs so that people who assembled laboratory hot plates put together entire units instead of contributing a single part to the assembly process.[80]

ESTABLISH CLIENT RELATIONSHIPS

The job characteristics model suggests that jobs should be set up so that the person performing a service (such as an auto mechanic) comes into contact with the recipient of the service (such as the car owner). Jobs designed in this manner will not only help the employee by providing feedback, but also provide skill variety (e.g., talking to customers in addition to fixing cars), and enhance autonomy (by giving people the freedom to manage their own relationships with clients). This suggestion has been implemented at Sea-Land Service, the large containerized ocean-shipping company.[81] Once this company's mechanics, clerks, and crane

TABLE 4-3

Enriching Jobs: Some Suggestions from the Job Characteristics Model

The job characteristics model specifies several ways jobs can be designed to incorporate the core job dimensions responsible for enhancing motivation and performance. A few are listed here.

PRINCIPLES OF JOB DESIGN	CORE JOB DIMENSIONS INCORPORATED
1. Combine jobs, enabling workers to perform the entire job	*Skill variety* *Task identity*
2. Establish client relationships, allowing providers of a service to meet the recipients	*Skill variety* *Autonomy* *Feedback*
3. Load jobs vertically, allowing greater responsibility and control over work.	*Autonomy*
4. Open feedback channels, giving workers knowledge of the results of their work.	*Feedback*

Source: Based on information in Hackman, 1976; see Note 80.

operators started meeting with customers, they became much more productive. Having faces to associate with the once-abstract jobs they did clearly helped them take their jobs more seriously.

OPEN FEEDBACK CHANNELS

Jobs should be designed to give employees as much feedback as possible. The more people know how well they're doing (be it from customers, supervisors, or co-workers), the better equipped they are to take appropriate corrective action (we already noted the importance of feedback in the learning process in Chapter 2). Sometimes cues about job performance can be clearly identified as people perform their jobs (as we noted in conjunction with goal setting). In the best cases, open lines of communication between employees and managers are so strongly incorporated into the corporate culture—as has been reported to exist at Boise Cascade's paper products group—that feedback flows without hesitation.[82]

LOAD JOBS VERTICALLY

As we described earlier, loading a job vertically involves giving people greater responsibility for their jobs. Taking responsibility for and control over performance away from managers and giving it to their subordinates increases the level of autonomy the jobs offer these lower-level employees. (For a look at some of the fascinating things some companies are doing to promote employees' feelings of autonomy, see the Quest for Quality section below).

THE QUEST FOR QUALITY

MOTIVATING WITH JOB AUTONOMY: LESSONS FROM THE BEST

Although there are certainly many elements that go into making a company a great place to work, autonomy is among the most crucial. In fact, when workers responded to a 1991 Gallup poll asking them what they valued most in a job, 64 percent answered "ability to work independently," making it the number one response—even more popular than "high income."[83] In view of this, it is fortunate that a growing number of companies are yielding control and giving employees increasing freedom to do their jobs as they wish (within limits, at least). In a troubled economy, where raises are few and far between, autonomy is something employers can offer employees to reduce their frustration. Besides, since management doesn't always have the answer, it makes sense to look for ways to improve work from those who *really* know best—the people who do the jobs.

Autonomy takes different forms in different organizations. And in many cases its effects are extremely beneficial. The improvements to both the quality of work life and to the quality of corporate performance that result from giving people the freedom to do their jobs as they choose are sometimes quite impressive. Consider, for example, Advanced Network Design Inc. (ADNET), the now-thriving La Mirada, California, telecommunications company that in 1988 was on the verge of shutting down.[84] The main problem, ADNET president Dave Wiegand learned, was his highly demanding managerial style. So, with the help of a consultant, he completely turned around the way he operated. Now, rather than pushing and riding herd on his staff, he very carefully selects staff members for their skills, and once they've shown they can do the job, he turns it over to them. Employees simply report to management either weekly or monthly. No more does Wiegand make decisions for the company; the employees do it—and better than ever. "Before, I'd make a decision and nobody would buy into it," says Wiegand, but now "once a decision is made, it sticks." Although the change was jarring for some (especially Wiegand himself, a self-confessed control freak), the majority find life at work vastly improved. "My supervisor used to dictate all my weekly and monthly goals," says Carmen Pugliese, ADNET's client services supervisor. "Job satisfaction is much stronger now."[85]

As you might imagine, ADNET is not the only company that jumped on the autonomy bandwagon after experiencing problems with more traditional, autocratic management styles (for a summary of what other companies are doing, see Table 4-4). For example, Childress Buick Company, a Phoenix, Arizona, auto dealership suffered serious customer dissatisfaction and employee retention problems before owner Rusty Childress began encouraging his employees to use their own judgment and initiative. Sometimes, previously autocratic managers are shocked when they see how hard people work when they are allowed to make their own decisions. Bob Freese, CEO of Alphatronix Inc., in Research Triangle Park, North Carolina, is among the newly converted. "We let employees tell us when they can accomplish a project and what resources they need, he says. "Virtually always they set higher goals than we would ever set for them."[86]

Naturally, autonomy is not a panacea. If it were *always* effective, all companies would be using it all the time. There are, however, some commonalties among organizations in which it works. First, companies that have successfully given employees autonomy tend to invest a lot of time and effort in making sure they hire people who can do their jobs properly without close supervision. Second, autonomy works in organizations in which high-quality performance is always expected—and, in which it is the performance itself, and not the process, that matters. This is not to say that there are never any boundaries to restrict employees. Indeed, companies that successfully grant autonomy usually provide some guidelines within which employees must operate. But within these boundaries, it's clear that new levels of motivation—and performance—can be evidenced.

TABLE 4-4

Promoting Autonomy: What Some Companies Are Doing

Some organizations go out of their way to allow employees to exercise high amounts of autonomy in the way they work. Here are some particularly interesting examples.

COMPANY	PRACTICE
Avid Technology *(film-editing-system maker, located in Tewksbury, MA)*	*Let its employees make up their own work schedules*
Alphatronix *(optical storage system maker, located in Research Triangle Park, NC)*	*Has employees set their own goals and timetables for completing projects*
Job Boss Software *(developer of factory software, located in Minneapolis, MN)*	*Grants employees wide latitude in doing their jobs; managers only facilitate, do not act as "bosses"*
Action Instruments *(instrument manufacturer, located in San Diego, CA)*	*Urges employees to solve their own problems; openly discloses financial information about the company*

Source: Based on Finegan, 1993; see Note 83.

SUMMARY AND REVIEW

THE NATURE OF MOTIVATION

Motivation is concerned with the set of processes that arouse, direct, and maintain behavior toward a goal. It is not equivalent to job performance, but is one of several determinants of job performance. Today's work ethic motivates people to seek interesting and challenging jobs, instead of just money.

NEED THEORIES

Maslow's **need hierarchy theory** postulates that people have five types of needs, activated in a specific order from the most basic, lowest-level need (physiological needs) to the highest-level need (need for self-actualization). Although this theory has not been supported by rigorous research studies, it has been quite useful in suggesting several ways of satisfying employees' needs on the job.

Alderfer's **ERG theory** is similar, but claims that there are only three basic needs—existence, relatedness, and growth—that can be activated in any order.

GOAL-SETTING THEORY

Locke and Latham's **goal-setting theory** claims that an assigned goal influences a person's beliefs about being able to perform a task (referred to as *self-efficacy*) and his or her personal goals. Both of these factors, in turn, influence performance. Research has shown that people will improve their performance when specific, acceptably difficult goals are set and feedback about task performance is provided. The task of selecting goals that are acceptable to employees is facilitated by allowing employees to participate in the goal-setting process.

EQUITY THEORY

Adams's **equity theory** claims that people desire to attain an equitable balance between the ratios of their work rewards (outcomes) and their job contributions (inputs) and the corresponding ratios of comparison others. Inequitable states of *overpayment* and *underpayment* are undesirable, motivating people to try to attain equitable conditions. Responses to inequity may be either behavioral (e.g., raising or lowering one's performance) or psychological (e.g., thinking differently about work contributions). Research supports equity theory's claim that people will lower their inputs in response to perceived underpayment and will raise their inputs in response to perceived overpayment.

EXPECTANCY THEORY

Expectancy theory recognizes that motivation is the product of a person's beliefs about *expectancy* (effort will lead to performance), *instrumentality* (performance will result in reward), and *valence* (the perceived value of the rewards). In conjunction with skills, abilities, role perceptions, and opportunities, motivation contributes to job performance. Expectancy theory suggests that motivation may be enhanced by linking rewards to performance (as in *pay-for-performance plans*) and by administering rewards that are highly valued (as may be done using *cafeteria-style benefit plans*).

JOB DESIGN

An effective organizational-level technique for motivating people is the designing or redesigning of jobs. **Job design** techniques include **job enlargement** (performing more tasks at the same level) and job enrichment (giving people greater responsibility and control over their jobs). The **job characteristics model**, a currently popular approach to enriching jobs, identifies the specific job dimensions that should be enriched (skill variety, task identity, task significance, autonomy, and feedback), and relates these to the critical psychological states influenced by including these dimensions on a job. These psychological states will, in turn, lead to certain beneficial outcomes for both individual employees (e.g., job satisfaction) and the organization (e.g., reduced absenteeism and turnover).

KEY TERMS

cafeteria-style benefit plans: Incentive systems in which employees have an opportunity to select the fringe benefits they want from a menu of available alternatives.

equitable payment: The state in which one person's outcome-input ratios is equivalent to that of another person with whom this individual compares himself or herself.

equity theory: The theory stating that people strive to maintain ratios of their own outcomes (rewards) to their own inputs (contributions) that are equal to the outcome/input ratios of others with whom they compare themselves.

ERG theory: An alternative to Maslow's need hierarchy theory proposed by Alderfer, which asserts that there are three basic human needs—existence, relatedness, and growth.

expectancy: The beliefs that people hold regarding the extent to which their efforts will influence their performance.

expectancy theory: The theory that asserts that motivation is based on people's beliefs about the probability that effort will lead to performance *(expectancy)*, multiplied by the probability that performance will lead to reward *(instrumentality)*, multiplied by the perceived value of the reward *(valence)*.

goal setting: The process of determining specific levels of performance for workers to attain.

inputs: People's contributions to their jobs, such as their experience, qualifications, or the amount of time worked.

instrumentality: An individual's belief regarding the likelihood of being rewarded in accord with his or her own level of performance.

job characteristics model: An approach taken by organizations toward job enrichment, which specifies that five *core job dimensions* (skill variety, task identity, task significance, autonomy, and job feedback) produce critical psychological states that lead to beneficial outcomes for individuals (e.g., high job satisfaction) and the organization (e.g., high performance).

job design: An approach to motivation suggesting that jobs can be created so as to motivate people. (See *job enlargement, job enrichment,* and the *job characteristics model.)*

job enlargement: The practice of expanding the content of a job to include more variety and a greater number of tasks at the same level.

job enrichment: The practice of giving employees a high degree of control over their work, from planning and organization, through implementing the jobs and evaluating the results.

motivating potential score (MPS): A mathematical index describing the degree to which a job is designed so as to motivate people, as suggested by the *jobs characteristic model.* It is computed on the basis of responses to a questionnaire know as the Job Diagnostic Survey (JDS). The higher the MPS, the more motivating a job is; the lower the MPS, the more the job may stand to benefit from redesign.

motivation: The set of processes that arouse, direct, and maintain human behavior toward attaining some goal.

need hierarchy theory: Maslow's theory that there are five human needs (physiological, safety, social, esteem, and self-actualization) and that these are arranged in such a way that lower, more basic needs must be satisfied before higher-level needs become activated.

outcomes: The rewards employees receive from their jobs, such as salary and recognition.

overpayment inequity: The condition, resulting in feelings of guilt, in which the ratio of one's outcomes-inputs is greater than the corresponding ratio of another person against whom that person compares himself or herself.

pay-for-performance: A payment system in which employees are paid differentially, based on the quantity and quality of their performance (i.e., *merit pay*). Pay-for-performance plans strengthen *instrumentality* beliefs.

self-actualization: The need to discover who we are and to develop ourselves to the fullest potential.

two-tier wage structures: Payment systems in which newer employees are paid less than employees hired at earlier times to do the same work.

underpayment inequity: The condition, resulting in feelings of anger, in which the ratio of one's outcomes-inputs is less than the corresponding ratio of another person against whom that person compares himself or herself.

valence: The value a person places on the rewards he or she expects to receive from an organization.

QUESTIONS FOR DISCUSSION

1. Define the concept of motivation, and describe how this topic is relevant to the field of organizational behavior.
2. Characterize the importance placed on work as a life value at different periods in history. What is the predominant belief about the role of work as a life value in today's society?
3. Maslow's need hierarchy theory specifies several ways to satisfy people's needs on the job. Identify each of the five need categories specified by Maslow, and for each one describe something that can be done on the job to enhance need satisfaction.
4. According to equity theory, how might an individual who is overpaid feel and behave? What might such a person do to alleviate this inequity? How about someone who is underpaid?
5. Imagine a student who performs poorly on an exam and then claims to the instructor, "I tried." According to expectancy theory, what other factors can account for performance besides motivation?
6. Compare and contrast the role of money as a motivator as characterized be need theory, equity theory, and expectancy theory.
7. Imagine that you are establishing a goal-setting program for an organization. Describe the way goals should be set and some of the factors that will make the program effective. What hurdles would have to be overcome?
8. Think of a job with which you are familiar, and describe specific things that can be done to enrich that job using the core job dimensions identified by the job characteristics model. What obstacles would have to be overcome to apply the model to this particular job?

HOG WILD WITH ENTHUSIASM AT HARLEY-DAVIDSON

Harley-Davidson (HD)—the name conjures up images of big gas-guzzling motorcycles, the roar of engines, and the open road. Recently, it also has been associated with movie stars and sports heroes who have made this machine something of a status symbol. Not long ago, however, the "Harley" name, image, and product itself was headed for extinction. Poor-quality craftsmanship and the resultant lack of sales had driven the firm to the brink of bankruptcy.[1]

A change in management philosophy however, brought the company back from the edge and now in the world of business, the Harley-Davidson name connotes an impression of the smart, successful firm of the future. How has this remarkable turnaround been accomplished? In great part, this is a result of management's realization that they had to "be drivers of change. For the business to work, everything must work well and function together—everyone must be excited about going to work in the morning."[2]

To accomplish this, the HD management team implemented two programs to increase employee motivation. The most far-reaching of these initiatives was a total redesign of nearly all jobs at HD. For the people who worked on the line, assembling the motorcycles, this change was radical. Instead of only having responsibility for a limited number of manufacturing operations these employees now design what goes where, who supplies the components, and how quality is evaluated. These same individuals are responsible for selecting their own tools and equipment and bargaining with the salespeople. In addition, they also do their own scheduling and develop and monitor their own budgets.[3]

HD management had two convictions in selecting this approach to job design. The first was that the people who work on the line making the motorcycles are the ones who have the knowledge necessary to be able to make the best, high-quality product in the most cost- and time-efficient manner. The second was that giving people responsibility, autonomy, and built-in feedback would make them more enthusiastic about their work, leading them try to do a better job. As CEO Richard Teerlink says, the survival of HD is based on using the hearts, souls, and minds of everybody and that increasing motivation is the way to accomplish this objective.[4]

Still, shifting to a model of job design in which employees are vested with responsibility for the accomplishment of organization goals hasn't been completely easy. Some people didn't understand this style of work. Similarly, there were managers who felt threatened. To help minimize these problems, HD started the Harley Leadership Institute. The purpose of this group is to provide training for employees so that all will understand their roles and thereby improve their performance.[5]

Another motivational program implemented by HD management is a pay-for-performance system. Teerlink believes that this practice will reinforce employee motivation and performance. He also believes that by paying for improved performance, more and more employees will seek out additional training so that they can improve their work productivity. Claims Teerlink,

> *In the business environment of the future, everyone will be in a leadership role. The only sustainable competitive advantage is your people. . . . An employee must make the decision that he or she wants more training—no one will tap you on the shoulder—but once you are there, we will help you.*[6]

The changes in inspiration of HD employees have helped create a big change in the financial accomplishments of this company. This is indicated by its rise from near bankruptcy to market leader in the heavyweight motorcycle business. The HD market share has risen from 12.5 percent in 1983 to 63 percent in 1993, sales have topped $1 billion, and the stock price has quintupled between 1990 and 1993.[7]

Paradoxically, the success of HD has led to shortages of the product. Frequently, customers have to wait more than six months for their bikes, and dealer showrooms are practically empty. Still, Teerlink insists that production will not be speeded up to meet the increased demand. He claims that an increase in production may lead to poor-quality products which could damage both the prestige HD has worked so hard to build, as well as the enthusiasm among employees.[8]

Although redesigning jobs for increased motivation and performance has been adopted by numerous firms, there are plenty of companies that still provide little inspiration or autonomy for their employees. For example, Sitel

Corporation, a telemarketing firm located in Omaha, Nebraska, schedules everything for its employees. Bathroom breaks must be requested, no food can be brought into the cubicles, the number of phone calls to be made are strictly enforced, and supervisors monitor calls to make sure that their representatives use the pre-approved script. In fact, the management at Sitel Corporation feels so strongly about delineating the activities of their personnel that they wouldn't allow them to be interviewed for a newspaper article on the working conditions at the firm.[9]

The one thing this company cannot schedule, however, is employee turnover, which runs near 100 percent per year. Showing some recognition of the rigidity of this environment, Sitel's chief executive, Jim Lynch, remarks, "It's difficult to have them convinced they should work in a task-oriented environment for any length of time—let alone for the rest of their lives." He acknowledges that employees "don't feel loyalty because the company doesn't give anything back to them. They have a high level of expectation of what a company should provide for them. There's nothing in our power we can do to fulfill those expectations—and therein lies the problem."[10]

QUESTIONS FOR DISCUSSION

1. In what ways is job redesign as practiced at Harley-Davidson similar to or different from job enlargement and enrichment?
2. Use the job characteristics model to analyze the responsibilities of line employees at HD.
3. Do you think that the pay-for-performance program instituted at HD will lead to increases in motivation? How about in performance? Explain your response.
4. If you were hired as a consultant charged with decreasing turnover and increasing motivation and performance at Sitel Corporation, what suggestions would you make? Be specific and be prepared to defend your suggestions.
5. Would you prefer to work at HD or Sitel? What factors influence your preference?

EXPERIENCING ORGANIZATIONAL BEHAVIOR

Goal Setting and Personal Productivity

The effectiveness of goal setting as a motivational technique has been well established. Setting goals that are specific, and difficult but acceptable, and providing feedback on their attainment, improves job performance (see pages 134-137). As this exercise demonstrates, you can apply these same guidelines to improving your own personal productivity.

PROCEDURE

1. Think of a task you need to perform before the next class meeting. The task should be one for which performance can be measured. Some good examples would be studying a certain subject, writing a term paper, or making improvements in your living quarters.
2. Set specific goals for performing this task, goals that challenge you but are possible to achieve. Make sure the goals are such that progress toward attaining them can be measured. For example, it is appropriate to set the goal of studying two chapters in your history text in the next forty-eight hours. However, the goal of "working harder to improve myself" is much too general.
3. Share your goals with your classmates. Through discussion, help everyone set goals that are specific, measurable, and difficult but acceptable.
4. Once it is clear that everyone has set a specific goal, agree to try to meet these goals and report back to the class on your progress at the next class meeting.
5. During the next class session, take turns reporting on your experiences in meeting your goals. Did you meet your goals? Exactly how well did you do? Do you think setting the goals was helpful? What factors interfered with goal setting?

POINTS TO CONSIDER

1. How many students succeeded in meeting their goals? How many failed? What factors do you believe distinguish between those who succeeded and those who failed?
2. What could have been done to make the unsuccessful students more successful? Did the goals they set for themselves prove too easy or too difficult? Was it possible to measure their goal attainment?
3. On what other tasks might you be able to successfully apply goal-setting principles?
4. Do you think people are capable of setting their own performance goals, or should they obtain the help of others?
5. Do you think social approval serves as a reinforcer of behavior in organizations? Explain why or why not.

CHAPTER OUTLINE

SPECIAL SECTIONS

FIVE

WORK-RELATED ATTITUDES: THEIR NATURE AND IMPACT

LEARNING OBJECTIVES

After reading this chapter, you should be able to

1. *Identify and describe the major components of attitudes.*
2. *Define what attitudes are and how they can be changed in others.*
3. *Describe the process of cognitive dissonance and how it leads people to change their own attitudes.*
4. *Identify and describe the major theories of job satisfaction and the techniques used to measure it.*
5. *Explain the major causes and consequences of job satisfaction.*
6. *Describe the major dimensions of organizational commitment, including its foci and bases.*
7. *Describe the major causes and consequences of organizational commitment.*
8. *Distinguish between prejudice and discrimination, and describe various types of prejudice in organizations.*
9. *Describe some of the steps being taken by organizations today to manage diversity in the workforce.*

Nothing is so firmly believed as what we least know.

Michel Eyquem de Montaigne,
1533–1592
French philosopher and essayist
Works

The greater the man, the less he is opinionated; he depends on events and circumstances.

Napoleon Bonaparte, 1769–1821
Emperor of France
Maxims

PREVIEW CASE

A Benefit Plan That Really Benefits Employees: Showing They Care at Manor Care

Any executive will tell you it's difficult, if not impossible, to do any long-term planning when you don't know who will be working for you. Imagine, then, the crisis that must have existed at Manor Care Inc., a provider of health care services, where for several years the entire workforce turned over annually. That was up until November 1991, when Chuck Shields, senior vice president of human resources, implemented a program that really turned things around.

"Benefits of Choice," as they called it, was designed to help build a stable, satisfied, and highly committed workforce. A key to their approach was to get each of Manor Care's 25,000 employees to feel that the company appreciated their contributions and rewarded them for their loyalty. With this in mind, a system was introduced in which greater shares of employees' health care costs are paid and larger contributions are made to their savings plans with each year worked.

Another critical element of the program is centered around communication. Because some of Manor Care's employees are poorly educated and/or illiterate, it was necessary to explain its complex benefit plans very carefully. To help, human resource professionals conducted sessions in which small groups of employees were shown videos and slides describing the plan, all using the most simple language. Employees also were given packets of information to take home that gave clear examples of the various retirement options. In addition, a toll-free telephone hotline was set up to answer employees' questions during the open enrollment period (even during Thanksgiving). The challenge was to get employees to understand the various complex options they had and to educate them about their various benefit choices without steering them in any particular direction.

Although this intensive educational program was expensive (taking into account the costs of producing the video, staffing the hotline, printing literature, and the like), the effort more than paid for itself in lowered turnover. Shields reports that "voluntary turnover across the corporation dropped approximately 15 percent in all classifications"—even more, about 20 percent, among front-line service employees, such as nursing assistants. This comes to approximately 2,000 fewer nursing assistants that do not have to be recruited and trained each year. And at an estimated cost of as much as $2,500 per employee, the savings are considerable.

Manor Care officials are not only pleased at the program's savings, but also the boost to employee morale that lies at the root of the new, higher rate of retention. By making this investment in their employees' well-being, Manor Care created a more loyal workforce—producing a high level of commitment and satisfaction.

A Manor Care employee at work.

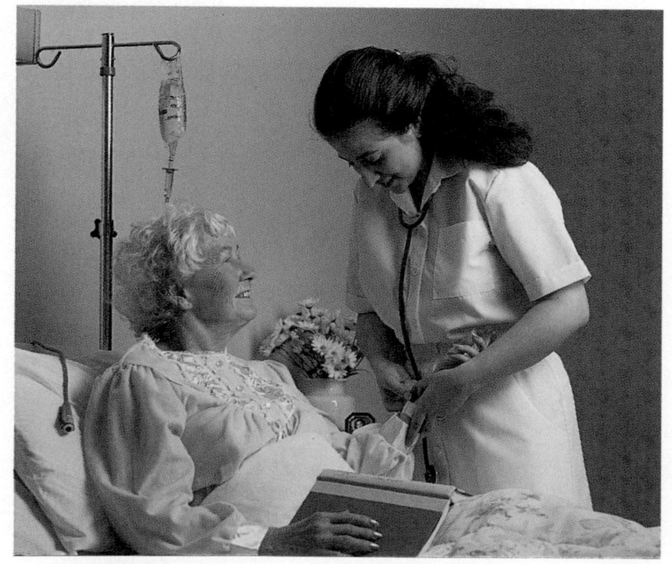

As Shields put it, "If you come to work for us, you're joining the Manor Care family and the longer you stay with us, the more we're going to take care of you." The company that specializes in providing care to others clearly now demonstrates care for its own.

What is responsible for the impressive turnaround in the stability of the workforce at Manor Care? It's probably neither the benefit package per se, nor the care in explaining it that really mattered, but the way the employees felt about the company as a result of these things. In other words, their feelings changed, and with them, came a new willingness to remain on the job. Obviously, such feelings can have a strong impact on the way we behave in organizations. Indeed, such feelings—*attitudes* as they are called—represent an important part of people's lives, particularly on the job. Our attitudes toward our jobs or organizations—referred to as *work-related attitudes*—may not only have profound effects on the way we perform, but also on the quality of life we experience while at work. We will carefully examine these effects in this chapter.

We will begin by describing the general nature of attitudes—what they are and how they change. With this background behind us, we will take a closer look at several specific types of work-related attitudes. We'll start with *job satisfaction*—essentially, people's positive or negative feelings about their jobs.[1] Specifically, we will describe some of the major factors contributing to feelings of satisfaction and dissatisfaction with one's work, and then consider the consequences of such reactions on organizational behavior.

Building on this, we will turn to another important work-related attitude—*organizational commitment*. This has to do with people's feelings about the organizations for which they work—the degree to which they identify with the organizations that employ them.[2] Finally, we will turn to a special type of attitude with which you are probably already somewhat familiar (unfortunately!)—*prejudice*. This involves negative views about others who fall into certain categories, such as women and ethnic minorities, to mention just a few.[3] As we will see, such attitudes can have a seriously disruptive impact on the lives of individuals and the effective functioning of the organizations in which they are employed.

ATTITUDES: WHAT ARE THEY AND WHAT MAKES THEM CHANGE?

Although we often refer to attitudes in our everyday language, such casual use of the concept fails to capture the richness of the concept as it has been applied by social scientists. To help appreciate more precisely what an attitude is, we will formally define the term and describe its role in the study of organizations. Following this, we will identify some of the key considerations involved in changing attitudes, both others and our own.

ATTITUDES: A DEFINITION

If we asked you how you feel about your job, we'd probably find you to be very opinionated. You might say, for example, that you really like it and think its very interesting. Or perhaps, you may complain about it bitterly and feel bored out of your mind. Maybe you'd hold views that are more complex, liking some things (e.g., "my boss is great") and disliking others (e.g., "the pay is terrible"). Regardless of exactly how you might feel, the attitudes you express may be recognized as consisting of three major components: an evaluative component, a cognitive component, and a behavioral component.[4] Because these represent the basic building blocks of our definition of attitudes, it will be useful for us to take a closer look at them (see Figure 5-1).

So far, we've been suggesting that attitudes have a great deal to do with how we feel about something. Indeed, this aspect of an attitude, its *evaluative component*, refers to our liking or disliking of any particular person, item, or event (what might be called the *attitude object*, the focus of our attitude). You may, for example, feel positively or negatively toward your boss, the sculpture in the lobby, or the fact that your company just landed a large contract. But attitudes involve more than feelings; they also involve knowledge—that is, what you believe to be the case about an attitude object. For example, you might believe that one of your co-workers is paid much more than you, or that your supervisor doesn't know too much about the job. These beliefs, whether completely accurate or totally false, comprise the *cognitive component* of attitudes.

FIGURE 5-1
ATTITUDES: THREE BASIC COMPONENTS
Attitudes are composed of the three fundamental components shown here: the evaluative *component, the* cognitive *component, and the* behavioral *component.*

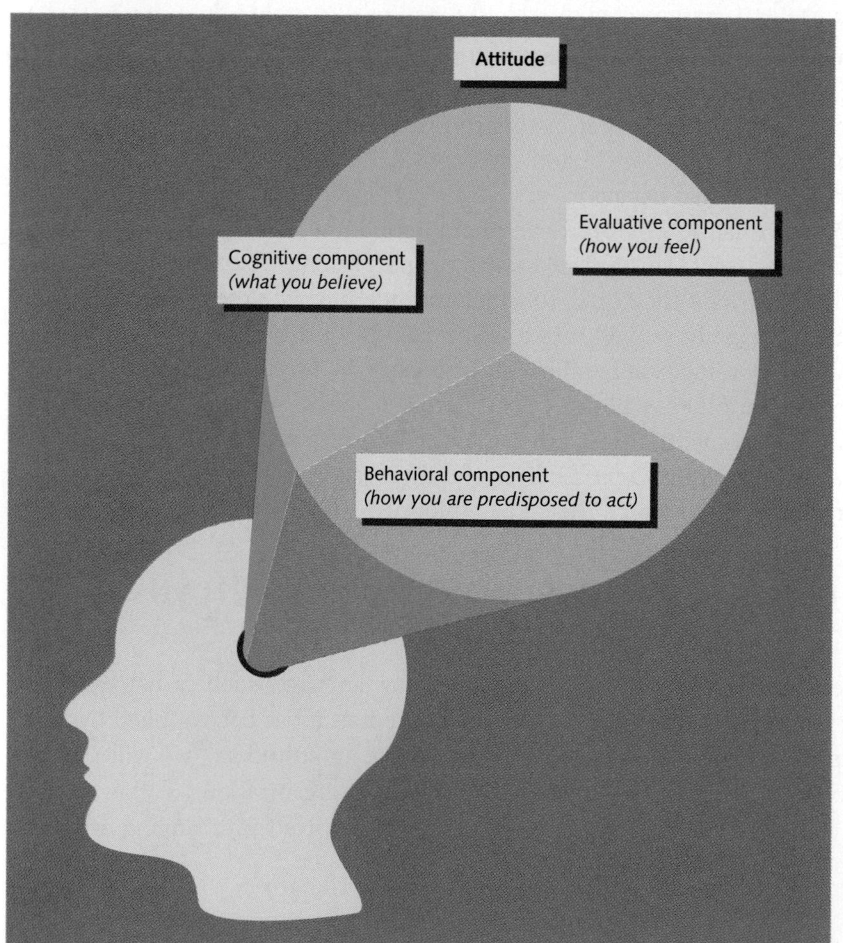

As you might imagine, the things you believe about something (e.g., "my boss is embezzling company funds") and the way you feel about it (e.g., "I can't stand working for him") may have some effect on the way you are predisposed to behave (e.g., "I think I'm going to look for a new job"). In other words, attitudes also have a *behavioral component*—a predisposition to act in a certain way. It is important to note that such a predisposition may not actually be predictive of one's behavior. For example, although you may be interested in taking a new job, you might not actually take one if a better position isn't available, or if there are other aspects of the job you like enough to compensate for the negative feelings. In other words, your intention to behave a certain way may or may not dictate how you will actually behave.

Combining these various components, we can define **attitudes** as *relatively stable clusters of feelings, beliefs, and behavioral predispositions (i.e.,* *intentions) toward some specific object.* By including the phrase "relatively stable" in the definition, we are referring to something that is not fleeting and that, once formed, tends to persist. Indeed, as we will explain in the next section, changing attitudes may require considerable effort. When we speak about **work-related attitudes**, we are talking about those lasting feelings, beliefs, and behavioral tendencies toward various aspects of the job itself, the setting in which the work is conducted, and/or the people involved. As you will discover as you read this chapter, work-related attitudes are associated with many important aspects of organizational behavior, including job performance, absence from work, and voluntary turnover. Such relationships are often very complex, varying across different situations and different people, and cannot be understood without a great deal of carefully conducted systematic research.

CHANGING OUR OWN ATTITUDES: THE PROCESS OF COGNITIVE DISSONANCE

Suppose as your college graduation approaches you receive two job offers. After much agonizing, you finally select one. If you're like most people, you will probably find that your attitudes toward the two companies will change. Specifically, your attitude toward the job you accepted will become more positive ("It's a great place, I'm fortunate to be working there") and your attitude toward the job you did not take will become more negative ("It's really not such a good company, I'm glad I decided against it"). The same process might occur after you select a car to purchase, a school to attend, or any course of action to take. What we are saying, in its most general form, is that people's attitudes toward selected alternatives become more positive, and their attitudes toward rejected alternatives become more negative. Why does this occur? The answer lies in a process known as **cognitive dissonance**.[5]

For the most part, people dislike inconsistencies. When we say one thing but do another (e.g., claim we like job *A* but take job *B*), or when we discover that one attitude we hold is inconsistent with another (e.g., we cherish our health but also enjoy smoking), the unpleasant state known as *cognitive dissonance* arises. We feel uneasy about the inconsistencies between our words and deeds, or between our various attitudes, and are motivated to change our attitudes so as to resolve this dissonance. In our example, the fact that you selected one job may be dissonant with the fact that you once considered the advantages of the other. So, to justify your decision and avoid cognitive dissonance, you simply change the way you feel, bringing your attitudes into line with your feelings. Specifically, you adopt a more positive attitude toward the job you accepted and a less positive attitude toward the job you rejected. Derogating the characteristics of a position you did not take and touting the benefits of the position you took may be understood as attempts to avoid cognitive dissonance.

To show how attempts to avoid cognitive dissonance may be involved in changing our own attitudes, let's consider an example. Suppose that you believe strongly in protecting the physical environment from pollution. At the same time, you also strongly believe in being a loyal employee, doing what your boss asks for the good of the company. No problems arise until one day you are required by your company to do something that you believe pollutes the environment—packing shipments in nonbiodegradable materials. Confronted with this situation, you experience cognitive dissonance: your positive attitude toward protecting the environment is inconsistent with the fact that you contributed to polluting it (which you did because you are such a loyal employee). As a result, your behavior is dissonant with your attitude, prompting you to change your attitude toward protecting the environment—perhaps by rationalizing that protecting the environment really isn't that important after all. By shifting your attitudes in this fashion, your behaviors are no longer inconsistent with your attitudes, thereby resolving cognitive dissonance.

CHANGING OTHERS' ATTITUDES: THE DETERMINANTS OF PERSUASIVENESS

As we have suggested, people sometimes change their own attitudes so as to make them consistent with one another. There are also situations in which we purposely attempt to change others attitudes. In particular, we may be interested in improving people's work-related attitudes because their negative attitudes may be associated with undesirable behavior (e.g., high rates of absenteeism and turnover). Of course, we also may be interested in changing attitudes for its own sake—that is, creating more positive attitudes toward the job just because of the positive feelings that result, helping people enjoy a higher quality of life at work.

Suppose your boss asks you to work late to complete a vital report in time for an important meeting tomorrow morning. Now, imagine watching a TV commercial touting the healthful benefits of a new breakfast cereal. Although these two situations appear to be quite dissimilar, they share an important common element: both are appeals to change your attitudes—to be more willing to work late, in the first case, and to become interested in the cereal in the second. Although you are probably not aware of it much of the time, it's likely that you're constantly bombarded by attempts to change your attitudes—a process known as **persuasion.** In the persuasion process, a target person (the individual whose attitude is to be changed) is given a message (either written or spoken) in which the information presented is designed to change his or her attitude (see Figure 5-2). This process involves two basic elements—the *communicator* (the person doing the persuading) and the *communication* (the specific content of the message itself).[6]

FIGURE 5-2
ATTITUDE CHANGE: ITS MAJOR DETERMINANTS
Several factors make persuasive appeals more effective. These involve characteristics of the communicator *(the person delivering the appeal), and characteristics of the* communication *(the message itself).*

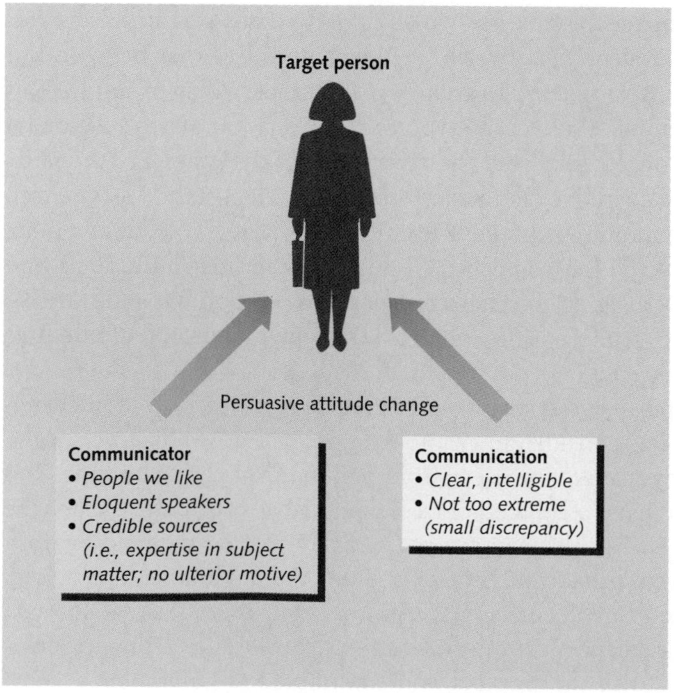

COMMUNICATORS: WHAT MAKES THEM PERSUASIVE?

Research has shown that several factors enhance the persuasiveness of communicators. First, in general we are more highly persuaded by *individuals we like*. Because we tend to ignore those we dislike, such individuals are unlikely to be effective agents of attitude change. Second, people who are *smooth, eloquent speakers* tend to be highly effective at persuading others. By speaking rapidly and without hesitation, eloquent speakers project the image that they know what they're talking about.[7] So, despite popular beliefs to the contrary, fast-talkers are generally very convincing and therefore highly persuasive.

Probably the single most important determinant of persuasiveness is a person's *credibility*, the extent to which an individual appears to be trustworthy or believable. The more credible an individual is believed to be, the more effective he or she will be in changing attitudes. What, then, makes someone appear to be credible? One key factor is *expertise*.[8] Generally speaking, the more someone appears to possess a high level of knowledge about a topic, the more persuasive that individual will be in persuading people on issues relevant to that topic. The persuasive power of expertise appears to be precisely what advertisers of pain medications rely on when they cite the opinions of experts—doctors, in this case—as the basis for their appeals to use their products. But advertisers know as well that credibility also depends on the *communicator's apparent motives*. In particular, someone's credibility will likely be challenged if he or she is expected to derive some gain by changing our attitudes. For this reason, many commercials rely on "hidden camera" scenes in which product testimonials are given by people who are unaware that their remarks are being recorded. The idea is that someone who does not stand to benefit from your behavior would be unlikely to misrepresent himself or herself for purposes of changing your attitudes. Without any reason to discount what they say, individuals lacking ulterior motives may be highly credible, and therefore, highly effective in getting people to change their attitudes.

COMMUNICATIONS: WHAT MAKES A MESSAGE PERSUASIVE?

Persuasiveness, as you might imagine, depends not only on the characteristics of the communicator, but the message itself—that is, the message being communicated. What characteristics of the content of a message make it persuasive? Two particularly important factors have been identified.

First, it is essential for messages to be *clear and intelligible*. Obviously, unless messages are accurately understood, they have little or no chance of changing attitudes. Still, people in business settings often fail to keep this in mind. Consider, for example, a supervisor of a chemical analysis research unit attempting to convince company officials that her division needs a larger budget. If she makes the mistake of "talking over the heads" of her less technologically-oriented colleagues, she won't stand much chance of persuading them to part with funds.

A second determinant of the persuasiveness of messages is how different they are from the views already held by target persons—that is, the *size of the attitude discrepancy*.[9] Sometimes people are asked to change their attitudes a great deal (e.g., from being pro-life to pro-choice on the issue of abortion), whereas other times they are asked to change them only a little (e.g., from being in favor of a $1 million budget for your department, to accepting a $950,000 budget). As you might expect, it's easier to get people to change their attitudes when the position you advocate is only slightly different from their own than when it is extremely different. This occurs, in large part, because people tend to dismiss highly discrepant views as unreasonable and unworthy of their consideration, whereas slightly discrepant views are believed to be more reasonable and acceptable. On this basis, it would appear that attitudes may be more effectively changed by "chipping away" at them a little bit at a time than by attempting to persuade someone to change his or her views more drastically all at once. (Although we have been describing ways of changing the attitudes of people individually, it is possible to use the mass media to change the attitudes of large numbers of people toward companies, or even business in general. For an example of how one popular movie appears to have been very effective in changing attitudes, see the Global Organization section on the following page.)

FIGURE 5-4

ARE PEOPLE SATISFIED WITH THEIR JOBS? A THREE-NATION COMPARISON

A recent survey among working people in the United States, Mexico, and Spain has found that people in all three countries are highly satisfied with their work and the behavior of their supervisors.

(Source: Based on data reported by Page & Wiseman, 1993; see Note 13.)

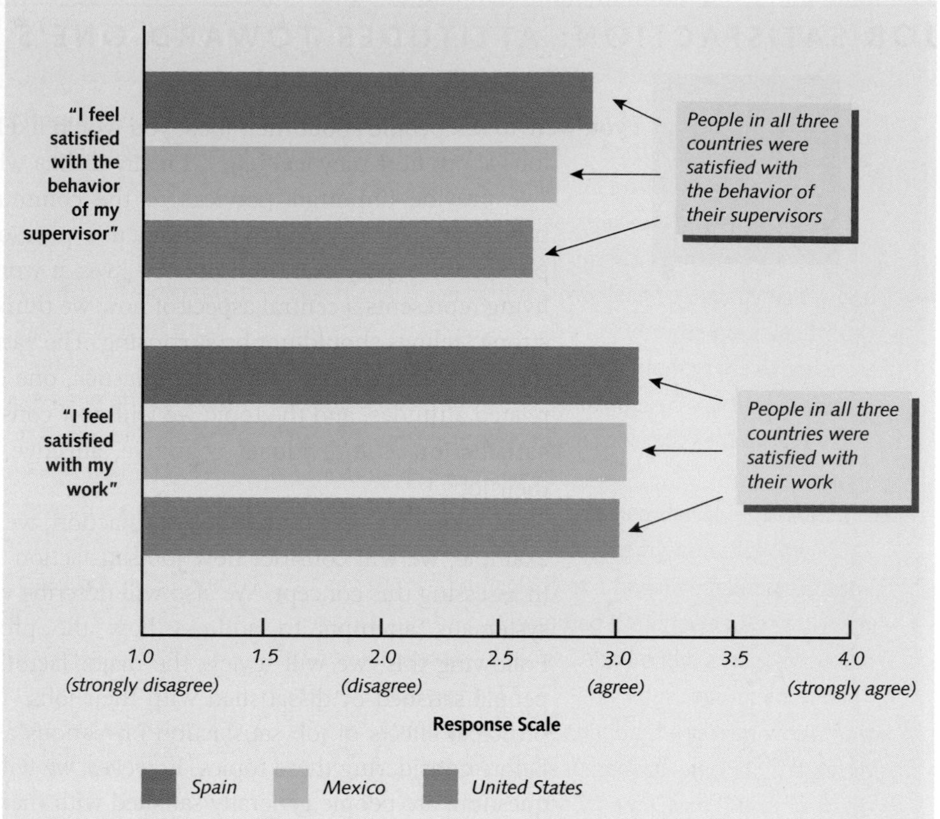

more satisfied with their jobs in their 30s (as they become more successful), level off in their 40s (as they become disenchanted), and become more satisfied again in their late 50s (as they resign themselves to their lot in life).[16]

- People who are more experienced on their jobs are more highly satisfied than those who are less experienced.[17] This shouldn't be too surprising since people who are highly dissatisfied with their jobs may be expected to find new jobs when they can. Moreover, in keeping with the notion of cognitive dissonance described earlier, the longer one stays on a job, the more strongly one is likely to feel compelled to justify his or her tenure by seeing the job in a positive light.
- Women and members of minority groups tend to be more dissatisfied with their jobs than are men and members of majority groups. This appears to be due to the tendency for victims of employment discrimination to be channeled into lower-level jobs, and positions with limited opportunities for advancement.[18]

Not only may certain groups of people be more satisfied with their jobs than others, but in addition, some individuals are likely to be either consistently satisfied or dissatisfied with their jobs. If this idea sounds familiar to you, it may be because it is an extension of the notion of positive and negative affectivity discussed in Chapter 3. The main idea is that job satisfaction is a relatively stable *disposition*, a characteristic of individuals that stays with them across situations. Evidence of this effect was provided in a fascinating study by Staw and Ross.[19] Their survey of over 5,000 men who changed jobs between 1969 and 1971 found that expressions of job satisfaction were relatively stable. In other words, despite the fact that they had different jobs, men who were satisfied or dissatisfied in 1969 were equally satisfied or dissatisfied in 1971. Although some scientists have challenged claims regarding the dispositional stability of job satisfaction, a considerable amount of follow-up research supports Staw and Ross's findings, strengthening the possibility that the tendency to be satisfied or dissatisfied with one's job is a stable disposition.[20]

MEASURING JOB SATISFACTION: ASSESSING REACTIONS TO WORK

Although people have many different attitudes toward various aspects of their jobs, these are not as easy to assess as you might think. Not only can't you directly observe an attitude, but as we noted, you cannot accurately infer their existence on the basis of people's behavior. So, for the most part, to determine people's attitudes, we have to rely on what they tell us. However, people are generally not entirely open about their attitudes, and keep much of what they feel to themselves. Moreover, sometimes our attitudes are so complex that it's difficult to express them in any coherent fashion—even if we are willing to do so. In view of these challenges, social scientists have worked hard over the past sixty years to develop reliable and valid instruments designed to systematically measure job satisfaction.[21] Several useful techniques have been developed, including *rating scales* or *questionnaires*, *critical incidents*, and *interviews*.

RATING SCALES AND QUESTIONNAIRES

The most common approach to measuring job satisfaction involves the use of questionnaires in which highly specialized rating scales are completed. Using this method, people answer questions allowing them to report their reactions to their jobs. Several different scales have been developed for this purpose, and these vary greatly in form and scope (see Table 5-1). One of the most popular instruments is the **Job Descriptive Index (JDI)**, a questionnaire in which people indicate whether or not each of several adjectives describes a particular aspect of their work.[22] Questions on the JDI deal with five distinct aspects of jobs: the work itself, pay, promotional opportunities, supervision, and people (co-workers). Another widely used measure, the **Minnesota Satisfaction Questionnaire (MSQ)** uses a different approach.[23] People completing this scale rate the extent to which they are satisfied or dissatisfied with various aspects of their jobs (e.g., their pay, chances for advancement). Higher scores reflect higher degrees of job satisfaction.

Although the JDI and the MSQ measure many different aspects of job satisfaction, other scales focus more narrowly on specific facets of satisfaction. For example, as its name suggests, the **Pay Satisfaction Questionnaire (PSQ)** is primarily concerned with attitudes toward various aspects of pay.[24] The PSQ provides valid measures of such critical aspects as satisfaction with pay level, pay raises, fringe benefits, and the structure and administration of the pay system.[25]

An important advantage of rating scales is that they can be completed quickly and efficiently by large numbers of people. Another benefit is that when the same questionnaire has already been administered to many thousands of individuals, average scores for people in many kinds of jobs and many types of organizations are available. This makes it possible to compare the scores of people in a given company with these averages, and obtain measures of *relative* satisfaction. This may

TABLE 5-1

Measures of Job Satisfaction: Some Widely Used Scales

The items shown here are similar to those used in three popular measures of job satisfaction.

JOB DESCRIPTIVE INDEX (JDI)	MINNESOTA SATISFACTION QUESTIONNAIRE (MSQ)	PAY SATISFACTION QUESTIONNAIRE (PSQ)
Enter "Yes," "No," or "?" for each description or word below.	*Indicate the extent to which you are satisfied with each aspect of your present job. Enter one number next to each aspect.*	*Indicate the extent to which you are satisfied with each aspect of present pay. Enter one number next to each aspect.*
Work itself:	*1 = Extremely dissatisfied*	*1 = Extremely dissatisfied*
___ *Routine*	*2 = Not satisfied*	*2 = Not satisfied*
___ *Satisfactory*	*3 = Neither satisfied nor dissatisfied*	*3 = Neither satisfied nor dissatisfied*
___ *Good*	*4 = Satisfied*	*4 = Satisfied*
Promotions:	*5 = Extremely satisfied*	*5 = Extremely satisfied*
___ *Dead-end job*	___ *Utilization of your abilities*	*Satisfaction with pay level:*
___ *Few promotions*	___ *Authority*	___ *My current pay*
___ *Good opportunity for promotion*	___ *Company policies and practices*	___ *Size of my salary*
	___ *Independence*	*Satisfaction with raises:*
	___ *Supervision–human relations*	___ *Typical raises*
		___ *How raises are determined*

Source: Based on items from the JDI, MSQ, and PSQ; see Notes 22, 23, and 24.

not only be useful information for scientists interested in studying job satisfaction, but also for companies interested in learning about trends in the feelings of its employees. Federal Express, for example, is so actively interested in tracking the attitudes of its employees that it has instituted a fully automated on-line survey administration process out of its Memphis headquarters.[26] The company uses information about the attitudes of its 68,000 U.S.-based employees as the basis for identifying problems and introducing remedies (see Figure 5-5).

CRITICAL INCIDENTS

A second procedure for assessing job satisfaction is the **critical incident technique**. Here, individuals describe events relating to their work that they found especially satisfying or dissatisfying. Their replies are then examined to uncover underlying themes. For example, if many employees mentioned on-the-job situations in which they were treated rudely by their supervisors, or praised supervisors for sensitivity they showed in a difficult period, this would suggest that supervisory style plays an important role in their job satisfaction.

INTERVIEWS AND CONFRONTATION MEETINGS

A third procedure for assessing job satisfaction involves carefully interviewing employees in face-to-face sessions. By questioning people in person about their attitudes, it is often possible to explore them more deeply than by using highly structured questionnaires. By carefully posing questions to employees and systematically recording their answers, it is possible to learn about the causes of various work-related attitudes. For example, Sutton and Callahan held face-to-face meetings with employees to learn their feelings about their company's recent bankrupt-

FIGURE 5-5
FEDERAL EXPRESS: DELIVERING EMPLOYEE ATTITUDE DATA
To track the attitudes of its 86,000 U.S. employees, Federal Express administers surveys on-line from its Memphis headquarters.

cy filing.[27] Their highly personal approach to data collection was particularly effective in gathering reactions to such a complex and difficult situation.

Sometimes interviews are designed to have employees "lay it on the line" and discuss their major complaints and concerns. Interviews of this type are known as *confrontation meetings*. If such sessions are conducted skillfully, in an environment in which employees feel free to speak out without retaliation, serious problems that adversely affect job satisfaction but that might otherwise remain hidden, can be brought out into the open. This may be a crucial first step toward correcting or eliminating the problems.

As you might imagine, confrontation meetings may only be successful to the extent that people respond honestly and are capable of accurately reporting their feelings. Indeed, the same can be said of *any* of the self-report measures we have described, including questionnaires and reports of critical incidents. One key to collecting valid information about people's attitudes is to gain their cooperation. With this in mind, it is important for researchers collecting information about job satisfaction to keep all individuals' responses completely confidential, and to clearly assure them of this. In fact, it is also useful to keep respondents' identities anonymous, so that it is impossible to identify anything that any one respondent may have said. In short, it is essential for measures of job satisfaction—or any work-related attitudes, for that matter—to carefully safeguard respondents' rights to privacy, not only because doing so helps safeguard the validity of the measures, but also because it is unethical to do otherwise.

THEORIES OF JOB SATISFACTION

What makes some people more satisfied with their jobs than others? What underlying processes account for people's feelings of job satisfaction? Insight into these important questions is provided by various theories of job satisfaction. We will describe two of the most influential approaches—Herzberg's *two-factor theory* and Locke's *value theory*.

HERZBERG'S TWO-FACTOR THEORY

Think about something that may have happened on your job that made you feel especially satisfied or dissatisfied. What were these events? (This is an example of the *critical incident technique* described above.) Over thirty years ago Frederick Herzberg posed this question to more than 200 accountants and engineers, and carefully analyzed their responses.[28] What he found was somewhat surprising: different factors accounted for job satisfaction and dissatisfaction.

Although you might expect that certain factors lead to satisfaction when they are present, and dissatisfaction when they are absent, this was *not* the case. Job satisfaction and dissatisfaction were found to stem from different sources (see Figure 5-6). In particular, dissatisfaction was associated with conditions surrounding the jobs (e.g., working conditions, pay, security, quality of supervision, relations with others) rather than the work itself. Because these factors prevent negative reactions, Herzberg referred to them as *hygiene* (or *maintenance*) *factors*. By contrast, satisfaction was associated with factors associated with the work itself or to outcomes

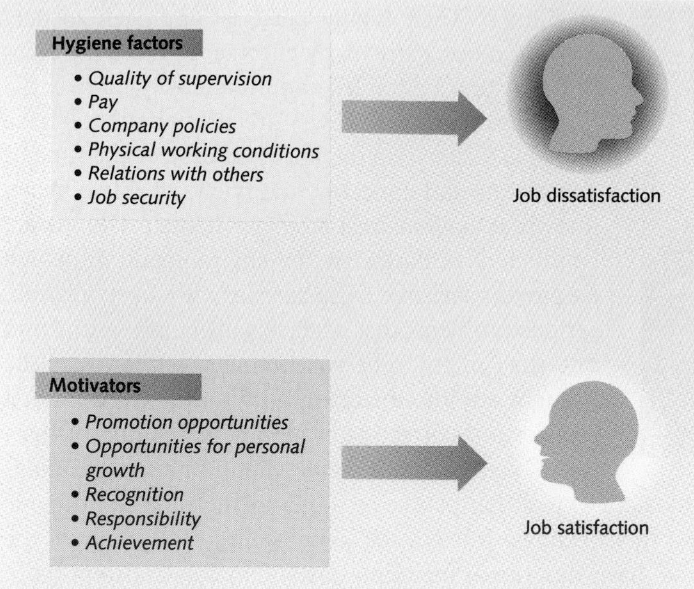

Hygiene factors
• Quality of supervision
• Pay
• Company policies
• Physical working conditions
• Relations with others
• Job security
Job dissatisfaction
Motivators
• Promotion opportunities
• Opportunities for personal growth
• Recognition
• Responsibility
• Achievement
Job satisfaction

FIGURE 5-6
HERZBERG'S TWO-FACTOR THEORY
According to Herzberg's two-factor theory, job satisfaction is caused by a set of factors referred to as motivators, *while job dissatisfaction is caused by a different set of factors, known as* hygiene factors.

directly derived from it, such as the nature of their jobs, achievement in the work, promotion opportunities, and chances for personal growth and recognition. Because such factors were associated with high levels of job satisfaction, Herzberg called them *motivators*. Herzberg's distinction between motivators and hygiene factors is referred to as the **two-factor theory of job satisfaction.**

Research testing Herzberg's theory has yielded mixed results. Some studies have found that job satisfaction and dissatisfaction were based on different factors, and that these are in keeping with the distinction made by Herzberg.[29] Other studies, however, have found that factors labeled as hygienes and motivators exerted strong effects on both satisfaction and dissatisfaction, thereby casting doubt on Herzberg's theory.[30] In view of such equivocal evidence, we must label Herzberg's theory as an intriguing but unverified framework for understanding job satisfaction. Still, the theory is useful for describing the conditions that people find satisfying and dissatisfying on the job. The theory also has been useful in emphasizing the importance of factors such as the opportunity for personal growth, recognition, and increased responsibility. Attention to such variables has stimulated much of the research and theory on job enlargement and job enrichment identified in Chapter 4. In this way, Herzberg's theory has contributed much to the field of organizational behavior, despite the lack of support for some of its key predictions.

LOCKE'S VALUE THEORY

A second important theory of job satisfaction is Locke's **value theory**.[31] This conceptualization claims that job satisfaction exists to the extent that the job outcomes (such as rewards) an individual receives matches those outcomes that are desired. The more people receive outcomes they value, the more satisfied they will be; the less they receive outcomes they value, the less satisfied they will be. Locke's approach focuses on *any* outcomes that people value, regardless of what they are, and not necessarily basic lower-order needs (such as those identified by need theories of motivation discussed in Chapter 4). The key to satisfaction in Locke's theory is the *discrepancy* between those aspects of the job one has and those one wants; the greater the discrepancy, the less the satisfaction.

McFarlin and Rice conducted a study that provides good support for value theory.[32] Using a questionnaire, these investigators measured how much of various job facets—such as freedom to work one's own way, learning opportunities, promotion opportunities, and pay level—a diverse group of workers wanted, and how much they felt they already had. They also measured how satisfied the respondents were with each of these facets and how important each facet was to them. As shown in Figure 5-7, an interesting trend emerged: those aspects of the job about which respondents experienced the greatest discrepancies were the ones with which they were most dissatisfied, and those with which they experienced the smallest discrepancies were the ones with which they were most satisfied. Interestingly,

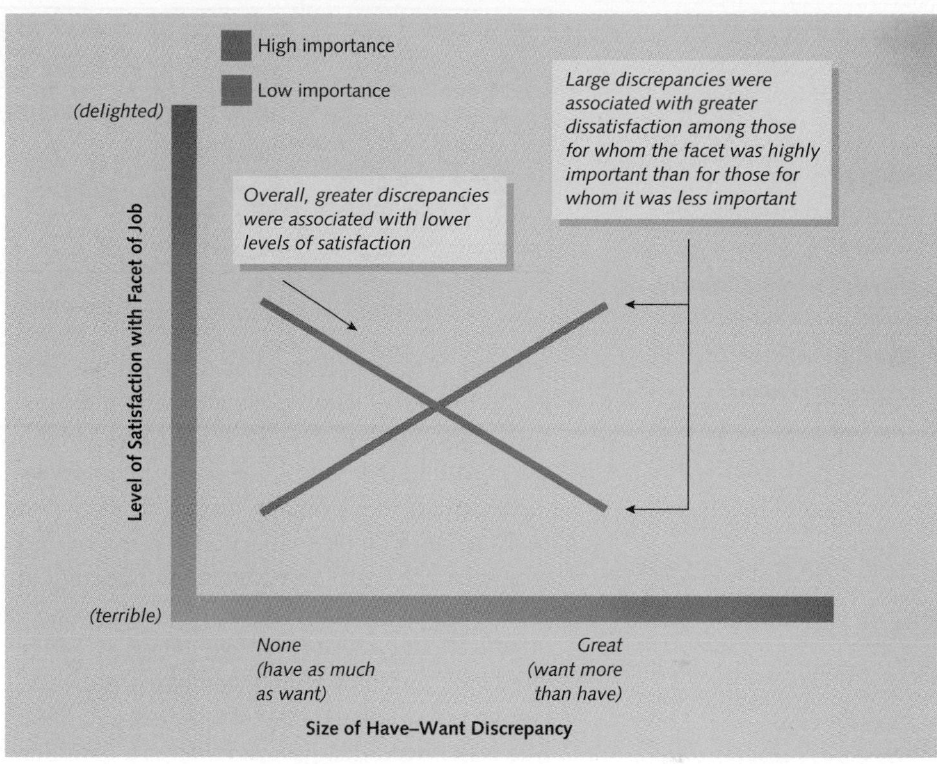

FIGURE 5-7
JOB SATISFACTION: A RESULT OF THE DISCREPANCY BETWEEN WHAT WE WANT AND WHAT WE HAVE
Research has shown that the larger a discrepancy that exists between what people have and what they want with respect to various facets of their jobs (e.g., pay, learning opportunities), the more dissatisfied they are with their jobs. This relationship is greater among those who place a great deal of importance on that facet than among those who consider it less important. (Source: Adapted from McFarlin & Rice, 1992; see Note 32.)

McFarlin and Rice also found that this relationship was greater among individuals who placed a high amount of satisfaction on a particular facet of the job. In other words, the more important a particular facet of the job was believed to be, the less satisfied people were when they failed to get as much of this facet as they wanted.

An interesting implication of value theory is that it calls attention to the aspects of the job that need to be changed for job satisfaction to result. Specifically, the theory suggests that these aspects might not be the same ones for all people, but any valued aspects of the job about which people perceive serious discrepancies. By emphasizing values, Locke's theory suggests that job satisfaction may be derived from many factors. In this respect, it is fully consistent with the findings of research on the causes of job satisfaction—the topic to which we will now turn.

JOB SATISFACTION: ITS PRINCIPAL CAUSES

Over the past seventy years, researchers have conducted virtually thousands of studies dealing with job satisfaction. Many of these have identified factors that lead people to become more satisfied or more dissatisfied with their jobs. Although many such factors have been identified, these fall into two broad categories: those relating to the organization and the job performed, and those relating to the personal characteristics of the employees themselves.

ORGANIZATIONAL DETERMINANTS OF JOB SATISFACTION

What organizational policies and procedures, and what elements of the work itself are related to job satisfaction? Several key determinants have been identified. First, we know that the organization's *reward system* is highly related to job satisfaction (see Figure 5-8). This refers to how pay, benefits, and promotions are dis-

FIGURE 5-8
REWARD: AN IMPORTANT SOURCE OF JOB SATISFACTION
Pay is a key determinant of job satisfaction—although, as shown here, people often cannot agree on what constitutes a fair level of reward. (Source: Reprinted with special permission of King Features Syndicate.)

tributed. Are people paid adequately and fairly relative to others? Research has found that satisfaction is enhanced by the use of pay systems believed to be fair—with respect to both the level of compensation received, and the mechanisms used to determine that pay.[33] For example, interviewing several hundred people about their current levels of job satisfaction, Berkowitz and his associates found that the best predictor of job satisfaction was the belief that one is treated in a fair and equitable manner (recall our discussion of equity in Chapter 4).[34]

Additional recent research has focused on the distribution of another type of organizational reward—fringe benefits. Specifically, in a recent study, Barber, Dunham, and Formisano compared the levels of job satisfaction among 110 employees of a large financial services company both before and after a program was introduced that gave employees a considerable amount of flexibility in selecting their fringe benefits.[35] As you might expect on the basis of value theory, employees were more satisfied with their benefits and their jobs after the plan was introduced. To the extent that flexibility in the selection of outcomes gives employees greater opportunities to receive the rewards they really value, it follows that they will find less discrepancy between the benefits they want and those they receive, enhancing feelings of satisfaction.

A second organization-based determinant of job satisfaction is *perceived quality of supervision*. Specifically, studies have determined that satisfaction tends to be higher when people believe their supervisors are competent, have their best interests in mind, and treat them with dignity and respect than when they are just the opposite.[36] Communication is another aspect of high-quality supervision. In this regard, it has been determined that people are more satisfied with their jobs the more they have opportunities to communicate with their supervisors.[37]

Third, we know what job satisfaction is related to the *decentralization of power*. As we will discuss later in this book—in the contexts of power (Chapter 11), decision making (Chapter 14), and organizational design (Chapter 15)—decentralization is the degree to which the capacity to make decisions resides in many people as opposed to just one, central person. When power is decentralized, many people are allowed to make decisions and can freely participate in decision making. Such situations tend to promote job satisfaction.[38] By contrast, when decision-making authority is concentrated in the hands of just a few, people tend to believe that they are relatively powerless and, not surprisingly, feel dissatisfied.

A fourth determinant of satisfaction is level of *work and social stimulation*. Many people are satisfied with jobs that provide them with an overall workload and level of variety that is not so low as to be boring and not so high as to be overwhelming and overly challenging.[39] This factor applies mostly to individuals who see their jobs as a career as opposed to those who see their positions as temporary, short-term ones.[40] By contrast, those who do not have a career orientation tend to be most satisfied not by aspects of the work, but by pleasant social conditions on the job (e.g., lots of friends). This is not surprising, because only those who really care about their careers would be expected to find satisfaction in the work they do.[41]

A fifth determinant of job satisfaction is *pleasant working conditions*. Research has shown that job satisfaction is reduced by overcrowded conditions, and dark, noisy environments with extreme temperatures and poor air quality.[42] Although these factors are not directly associated with the jobs themselves, but with the context in which the work is performed, unpleasant working conditions have been found to have adverse effects on job satisfaction.

PERSONAL DETERMINANTS OF JOB SATISFACTION

In addition to these organizational determinants of job satisfaction, there are also several different personal factors that influence this important work-related attitude (for a summary of both classes of factors, refer to Figure 5-9).

First, several different *personality variables* have been linked to job satisfaction. Among these are self-esteem[43] and the Type A behavior pattern[44] (both of which were discussed in Chapter 3), and the ability to withstand stress (see Chapter 7).[45] Research has shown that the more of these variables people possess, the more satisfied they will feel about their jobs.

Second, job satisfaction is related to *status and seniority*. Generally speaking, the higher one's position in an organizational hierarchy, the more satisfied that individual tends to be.[46] This satisfaction stems, to some extent, from the fact that higher-level individuals usually enjoy better working conditions and more generous rewards than lower-level individuals. Moreover, people who are satisfied with their jobs tend to remain in them longer than those who are dissatisfied (as we will describe in the next section). Not surprisingly, the most dissatisfied employees probably do not stay long enough to ever reach the highest echelons of their organizations.

Third, job satisfaction is related to the extent to which people are performing jobs *congruent with their interests*. Testing this relationship, Fricko and Beehr measured the job satisfaction levels of 253 full-time employees on several occasions within seven years after graduating from college.[47] They found that the participants' job satisfaction was related to the degree to which they held positions in keeping with their vocational interests and their college majors. The better their positions fit with their interests, the more satisfied they were with their jobs. Not surprisingly, people working in fields that did not interest them expressed considerable dissatisfaction with their positions.

FIGURE 5-9

JOB SATISFACTION: A SUMMARY OF CAUSES

*Based on many research studies, two principal categories of job satisfaction have been found—*organizational causes, *and* personal causes. *Several examples of each are listed here.*

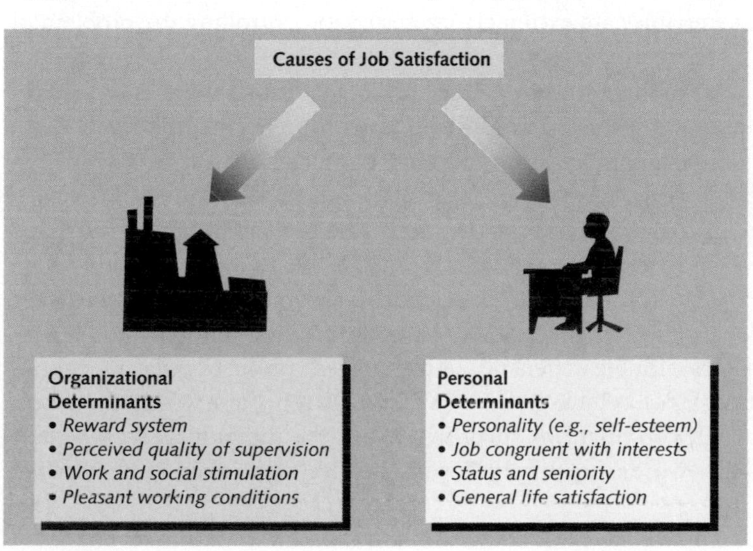

Causes of Job Satisfaction
Organizational Determinants
• Reward system
• Perceived quality of supervision
• Work and social stimulation
• Pleasant working conditions
Personal Determinants
• Personality (e.g., self-esteem)
• Job congruent with interests
• Status and seniority
• General life satisfaction

Fourth, and finally, job satisfaction has been found to be related to one's *general life satisfaction*. The more people are satisfied with aspects of their lives unrelated to their jobs, the more they also tend to be satisfied with their jobs.[48] This effect has been explained, in part, in terms of the tendency for one type of satisfaction to "spill over" into the other.[49] For example, the greater the importance of work in people's lives, the more likely satisfaction with one's job is likely to be associated with satisfaction with one's life in general.[50]

To summarize, a broad array of both personal and job-related variables are associated with job satisfaction. Although some of these variables are consistent with established theories of job satisfaction, others are either at odds with such views or fail to be taken into consideration by them. As a whole, these lines of investigation take a critical step toward the dual goals of studying job satisfaction as well as improving the quality of working life and the functioning of organizations.

JOB SATISFACTION: ITS MAJOR EFFECTS

People talk a great deal about the importance of building employee satisfaction, assuming that morale is critical to the functioning of organizations. As we will see, although job satisfaction does indeed influence organizations, its impact is not always as strong as one might expect. Thus, we might ask: What variables are affected by job satisfaction? Our summary will focus on two main types: employee withdrawal (i.e., absenteeism and turnover) and job performance.

JOB SATISFACTION AND EMPLOYEE WITHDRAWAL

When employees are dissatisfied with their jobs they tend to find ways of minimizing their exposure to them—that is, they *withdraw.* Two main forms of employee withdrawal are absenteeism and voluntary turnover.[51] By not showing up to work and/or by quitting to take a new job, people might be expressing their dissatisfaction with their jobs or attempting to escape from the unpleasant aspects they may be experiencing.

With respect to absenteeism, research has shown that the lower individuals' satisfaction with their jobs, the more likely they are to be absent from work.[52] The strength of this relationship, however, is modest rather than strong. The reason is that dissatisfaction with one's job is likely to be just one of many factors influencing employees' decisions to report or not report to work. For example, even someone who really dislikes her job may not be absent if she believes her presence is necessary to complete an important project. However, another employee might dislike her job so much that she will "play hooky" without showing any concern over how the company will be affected. Thus, although it's not a perfectly reliable reaction to job dissatisfaction, absenteeism is one of its most important consequences. And, it is also a costly one: the average company's annual expenses resulting from unscheduled absences range between $247 and $534 per employee.[53] Not surprisingly, companies are extremely interested in controlling the problem of absenteeism.

Another costly form of withdrawal related to job satisfaction is voluntary turnover. The lower people's levels of satisfaction with their jobs, the more likely they are to consider resigning and to actually do so (recall our Preview Case). As in the case of absenteeism, this relationship is modest, and for similar reasons.[54] Many factors relating to the individuals, their jobs, and economic conditions shape decisions to move from one job to another. For example, in a recent study Judge found that the extent to which dissatisfaction was associated with turnover depended on people's affective dispositions—that is, on their tendency to be generally satisfied (happy with life in general) or dissatisfied (prone to gripe a lot about things) (see Chapter 3).[55] Which group was more likely to quit when they were dissatisfied? Although you might be surprised, it was the individuals with *positive* dispositions. In other words, among those with positive dispositions, the negative

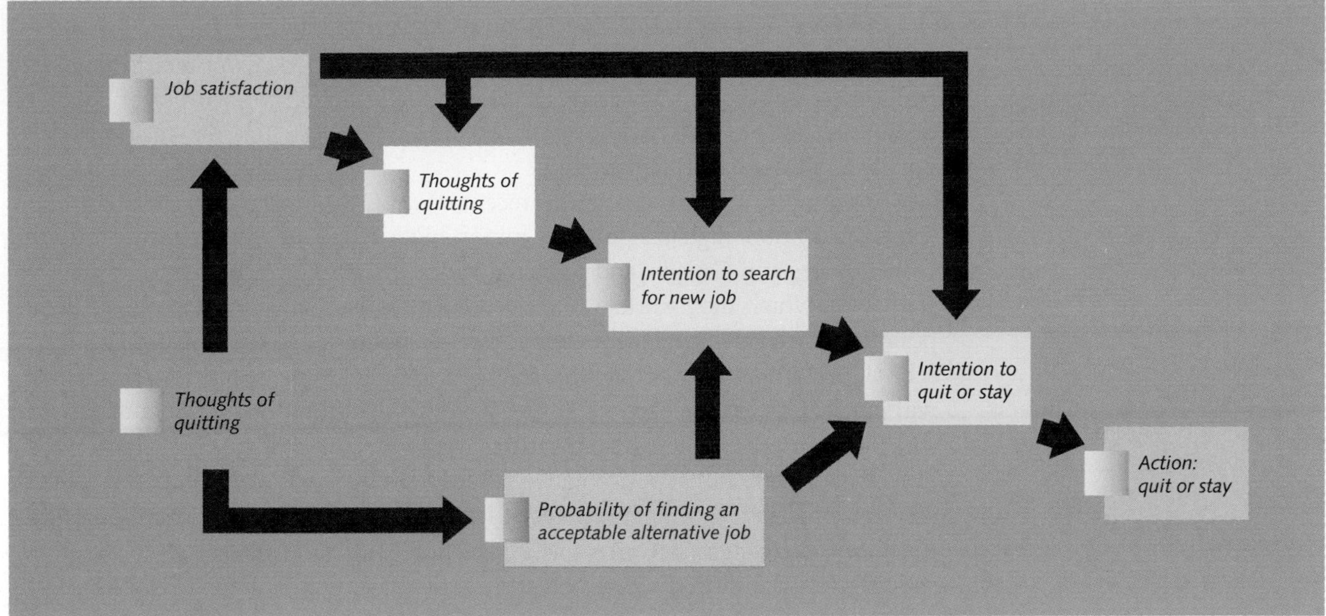

FIGURE 5-10

VOLUNTARY TURNOVER: AN OVERVIEW

According to a model proposed by Mobley and his associates, voluntary turnover is a complex process triggered by low levels of job satisfaction. This leads people to think about quitting, and then to search for another job. Finally, they form intentions to quit or remain on their present jobs. At several steps in this process, the probability of finding an acceptable alternative job plays a key role. (Source: Based on suggestions by Mobley, Horner, & Hollingsworth, 1978; see Note 56.)

correlation between job satisfaction and turnover was much stronger than it was among those with negative dispositions. This may be explained by noting that when someone who is generally positive about things is dissatisfied with his or her job, that reaction is so special that it prompts the individual into taking action—quitting. By contrast, someone who is generally dissatisfied with life is probably also dissatisfied with his or her job, and this reaction is not so unique as to trigger any concrete reaction. Thus, the extent to which dissatisfaction is associated with turnover appears to depend on a key aspect of personality.

As you might imagine, there are many more variables involved in making turnover decisions. Many of these are described in a model of the voluntary turnover process described by Mobley (see Figure 5-10).[56] According to this conceptualization, job dissatisfaction leads employees to think about the possibility of quitting. This, in turn, leads to the decision to search for another job. Then, if the search is successful, the individual will develop definite intentions either to quit or to remain on the job. Finally, these intentions are reflected in concrete actions.

Mobley's suggestion that economic conditions, and hence the success of an initial search for alternative jobs, exert a strong impact on voluntary turnover is supported by the findings of a study by Carsten and Spector.[57] These researchers examined the results of a large number of previous studies concerned with turnover. For each, they contacted the people who had conducted the study and determined the precise dates during which their data had been collected. Then, Carsten and Spector obtained data on the unemployment rates prevailing at those times. They predicted that the relationship between job satisfaction and turnover would be stronger at times when unemployment was low than when it was high. When unemployment was low, they reasoned, people would recognize that they have many other job opportunities, and would be prone to take one when they are highly dissatisfied with their present jobs. By contrast, conditions of high unemployment would limit alternative job options, leading people to stay with their present jobs despite their dissatisfaction with them. This is precisely what they found. The higher the unemployment rates were, the lower was the correlation between job satisfaction and turnover.

JOB SATISFACTION AND TASK PERFORMANCE

Many people believe that "happy workers are productive workers." But is this really the case? *Is* job satisfaction, in fact, directly linked to task performance or organizational productivity? Overall, the results suggest that the relationship is positive, but not especially strong.

For example, in a very ambitious recent study, Ostroff measured the satisfaction levels of 13,808 high school and junior high school teachers throughout the United States and Canada, and collected various indices of performance of the 298 schools in which they worked (e.g., percentage of students graduating, academic performance levels, vandalism expenditures).[58] She found that most measures of school performance were significantly linked to employee satisfaction: schools with more satisfied teachers were more effective than those with less satisfied ones (the mean correlation across all measures was .28). However, this one study, which looked at organizational performance, found a stronger relationship than most others. In fact, after reviewing hundreds of studies on this topic, it has been found that the mean correlation between job satisfaction and performance is considerably smaller—only .17.[59] Why does job satisfaction have such a limited relationship to performance? There are several explanations.

First, in many work settings, there is little room for large changes in performance. Some jobs are structured so that the people holding them *must* maintain at least some minimum level of performance just to remain at their jobs. For others, there may be very little leeway for exceeding minimum standards. Thus, the range of possible performance in many jobs is highly restricted. Moreover, for many employees, the rate at which they work is closely linked to the work of others or the speed at which various machines operate. As such, their performance may have so little room to fluctuate that it may not be highly responsive to changes in their attitudes.

Second, job satisfaction and performance may actually not be directly linked. Rather, any apparent relationship between them may stem from the fact that both are related to a third factor—receipt of various rewards. As suggested by Porter and Lawler, the relationship may work as follows.[60] Past levels of performance lead to the receipt of both extrinsic rewards (e.g., pay and promotions) and intrinsic rewards (e.g., feelings of accomplishment). If employees judge these to be fair, they may eventually recognize a link between their performance and these outcomes (see our discussion of expectancy theory in Chapter 4). This, in turn, may have two effects. First, it may encourage high levels of effort, and thus, good performance. Second, it may lead to high levels of job satisfaction. In short, high productivity and high satisfaction may both stem from the same conditions. These two factors themselves, however, may not be directly linked.

For these and other reasons, job satisfaction may not be directly related to performance in many contexts. However, this conclusion may be true only with respect to "standard" measures of performance, such as quantity or quality of output. It may have stronger influences on other aspects of on-the-job-behavior, including **organizational citizenship behaviors.**[61] These include actions that enhance social relationships and cooperation within an organization (e.g., offering help to co-workers when it is requested, demonstrating a cheerful and cooperative attitude, protecting or conserving the organization's resources, tolerating temporary inconveniences without complaint, and so on). Such actions may contribute to the smooth and effective functioning of organizations without showing up directly in more standard measures (e.g., monthly sales reports). To the extent that your job makes you feel good, you are likely to reciprocate by helping the organization and the others who have contributed to those good feelings. Indeed, research has shown that the more highly satisfied people are with their jobs, the more contributions to organizational citizenship they are recognized as making by their co-workers.[62]

In view of these findings, it is clear that the answer to the question "Are job satisfaction and performance linked?" requires another question: "What kind of performance do you have in mind?" With respect to many traditional indices of job performance, the link to job satisfaction is quite weak. For other aspects of performance, such as organizational citizenship behavior, the relationship appears to be stronger.

ORGANIZATIONAL COMMITMENT: FEELINGS OF ATTACHMENT TOWARD ORGANIZATIONS

Suppose you really enjoy the work you do and are very satisfied with your job. This doesn't necessarily mean that you will feel positively toward your company as well. In fact, you may even despise it and hope to get out as soon as possible. Similarly, it's possible for you to think your company is a wonderful place to work, although you might be terribly displeased about the job you do. The point we are making is that to fully understand people's work-related attitudes we must go beyond the concept of job satisfaction and also consider people's feelings toward their organizations.[63] Such attitudes, referred to as **organizational commitment**, reflect the extent to which people identify with and are involved with their organizations and are unwilling to leave them. As you might imagine, many factors are responsible for organizational commitment, and the impact of such attitudes may be quite serious. Before we consider these various causes and consequences of organizational commitment, we will take a closer look at its basic dimensions.

ORGANIZATIONAL COMMITMENT: ITS BASIC DIMENSIONS

To help understand the complex nature of organizational commitment, theorists have broken it down to its basic components. Recently, for example, Becker has distinguished between the *foci of commitment*, the particular entity, such as group or individual, to which a person is committed; and the *bases of commitment*, the underlying reasons why the commitment occurs.

FOCI OF COMMITMENT

It is important to note that people can be committed to various entities in their organizations. For example, they may have varying degrees of commitment to their co-workers, subordinates, superiors, customers, the union, or top management—in short, any particular individual or group target. In an attempt to categorize some of these various foci, Becker and Billings distinguished between those whose commitment is concentrated at lower organizational levels, such as one's immediate work group and supervisor, and those who are primarily focused on higher levels, such as top management and the organization as a whole.[64] By combining high and low levels of each of these, they identified the four distinct *commitment profiles* summarized in Table 5-2.

TABLE 5-2

Four Different Commitment Profiles

Becker and Billings have distinguished between two major focuses of commitment: the supervisor and the work group, and top management and the organization. By combining low and high levels of each, the four commitment profiles *shown here emerge.*

		ATTACHMENT TO SUPERVISOR AND WORK GROUP	
		LOW	HIGH
ATTACHMENT TO TOP MANAGEMENT AND ORGANIZATION	LOW	*Uncommitted*	*Locally committed*
	HIGH	*Globally committed*	*Committed*

Source: Based on information in Becker & Billings, 1993; see Note 64.

First, individuals who are low in commitment to both their work groups and supervisors as well as low in commitment to top management and the organization are labeled *uncommitted*. In contrast, individuals who are high in commitment to both sets of foci are labeled *committed*. In between are two groups: (1) those who are highly committed to their supervisor and work group but not top management and the organization (known as *locally committed*), and (2) those who are highly committed to top management and the organization, but not to their supervisor and work group (known as *globally committed*).

In a study conducted at a large military supply organization, Becker and Billings found that employees' attitudes differed in ways consistent with their profiles. For example, individuals falling into the uncommitted category (based on their responses to various questionnaire items) were more interested in quitting their jobs and less interested in helping others than those who were in the committed category. Those who were globally committed and locally committed scored in between these two extremes. In conclusion, although this method of distinguishing between various focuses of commitment is still new, it appears to hold a great deal of promise as a tool for understanding a key dimension of organizational commitment.

BASES OF COMMITMENT

To fully understand the concept of commitment, we must not only look at various foci, but also its bases—that is, the motives that people have for being committed. Historically, two different approaches to understanding these bases have dominated—the *side-bets orientation* and the individual–organizational *goal congruence orientation*.[65]

Becker's **side-bets orientation** focuses on the accumulated investments an individual stands to lose if he or she leaves the organization.[66] The idea is that over time, leaving an organization becomes more costly because people fear losing what they have invested in the organization and become concerned that they cannot replace these things. For example, people may be unwilling to leave their jobs because they are concerned about being perceived as "job hoppers" and stake their reputation for stability on remaining in their present jobs (i.e., they make a "side bet" on some aspect of themselves on continued organizational membership).

The individual–organizational **goal-congruence orientation** focuses on the extent to which people identifying with an organization have personal goals that are in keeping with those of the organization. This approach, popularized by Porter and his associates, reflects people's willingness to accept and work toward attaining organizational goals.[67] It views organizational commitment as the result of three factors: (1) acceptance of the organization's goals and values, (2) willingness to help the organization achieve its goals, and (3) the desire to remain within the organization.

As researchers began to study organizational commitment from each of these two perspectives, it became clear that both approaches were necessary to understand organizational commitment.[68] With this in mind, Meyer, Allen, and Gellatly have proposed that there are two distinct bases of organizational commitment—*continuance commitment*, and *affective commitment*.[69] **Continuance commitment**, related to the side bets approach, refers to the strength of a person's tendency to need to continue working for an organization because he or she cannot afford to do otherwise. **Affective commitment**, suggested by the goal-congruence approach, refers to the strength of a person's desire to continue working for an organization because he or she agrees with it and wants to do so. After research had been done on these two forms of commitment, it became apparent that a third type also existed—**normative commitment**.[70] This kind of commitment refers to employees' feelings of obligation to stay with the organization because of pressures from others. Questionnaires measuring these three bases of commitment have been developed, and research using them has confirmed that the three different forms are, in fact, distinct from each other.[71,72] By looking at items similar to those used to measure each kind of commitment, shown in Table 5-3, you will be able to recognize the distinction between the three different forms.

Using measures such as those shown in Table 5-3, researchers have found not only that all three bases of commitment are important, but also that they reflect different aspects of organizational commitment.[73] For example, Allen and Meyer have found that whereas affective commitment was associated with work experiences that make people feel competent, continuance commitment was associated with concern about losing one's job benefits.[74] Overall, many variables have been found

TABLE 5-3

Organizational Commitment: How Is It Measured?

Questionnaire items similar to those shown here are used to measure continuance commitment, affective commitment, *and* normative commitment. *The more strongly people agree with each item, the more strongly they are expressing the type of commitment associated with it.*

CONTINUANCE COMMITMENT ITEMS	AFFECTIVE COMMITMENT ITEMS	NORMATIVE COMMITMENT ITEMS
1. At this point, I stay on my job because I have to more than because I want to. *2. Leaving my job would entail a lot of personal sacrifice.* *3. I don't have any other choice but to stay on my present job.* *4. Too much of my life would be disrupted if I left my present job.*	*1. I feel I strongly belong to my organization.* *2. I feel I am emotionally connected to the organization in which I work.* *3. I feel like I'm part of the family at my organization.* *4. I'd be very pleased to spend the rest of my life working for this organization.*	*1. I am reluctant to leave an organization once I have been working there.* *2. My employer would be very disappointed if I left.* *3. I feel a strong obligation to stay on my job.* *4. I remain on my job because people would think poorly of me of me for leaving.*

Source: Based on items from Meyer & Allen, 1991, see Note 71; and McGee & Ford, 1987, see Note 72.

to be associated with one base of commitment or another—either as its causes or consequences. We will now turn to the task of summarizing some of the major causes and effects of organizational commitment.

FACTORS INFLUENCING ORGANIZATIONAL COMMITMENT

As our discussion has suggested, many possible determinants of organizational commitment exist. We will now review some of the most important ones. First, research has shown that organizational commitment is affected by various *job characteristics*. For example, commitment tends to be greater when people have high levels of responsibility over the jobs they perform, and ample opportunities for promotion.[75] Similarly, organizational commitment tends to be high among individuals whose jobs are highly enriched (along dimensions described in Chapter 4). The more jobs are recognized as having these characteristics (e.g., autonomy, job variety, and so on), the more strongly attached employees are toward them.[76] In view of the fact that these characteristics are typically present in abundance among people who are self-employed, it is not surprising to find that levels of commitment are higher among such individuals than those who are employed by organizations.[77]

Second, an employee's commitment is also likely to be influenced by the *nature of the rewards* he or she receives. For example, recent research has shown that feelings of commitment are enhanced by the use of a profit-sharing plan (an incentive plan in which employees receive bonuses in proportion to the company's profitability), particularly when employees believe the plan is administered in an equitable fashion.[78] To the extent that rewards are believed to be administered fairly, employees believe that the company has made a long-term commitment to treating them in a just manner, paving the way for their increased commitment.[79]

Third, organizational commitment is affected by the existence of *alternative employment opportunities*. As you might expect, the greater the perceived chances of finding another job, the lower an individual's commitment tends to be (particularly continuance commitment).[80]

Fourth, perceptions of commitment are likely to be related to an organization's *treatment of newcomers*. As we will describe in Chapter 6, organizations can do various things to help new employees learn the ropes and become productive members of their organizations. Such treatment also influences organizational commitment. For example, Caldwell, Chatman, and O'Reilly have found that organizational commitment was influenced by the organization's use of rigorous recruitment methods and the communication of strong, clear organizational value systems.[81] These factors make a great deal of sense. After all, the more an organization invests in someone by strongly trying to hire him or her, the more that individual is likely to return the investment of energy by expressing feelings of commitment toward the organization.

The same dynamic applies as well to the return of employees who have been on overseas assignment. Studying this process, Gregersen has found that the more organizations clarify the new roles they expect the returning employees to play and the more appropriately they compensate them for their transition costs, the more highly committed to the organization employees are likely to be.[82] Again, attempts by the organization to demonstrate the depth of its investment in its employees are rewarded by employees' investment of commitment. And, as we will see in the next section, such demonstrations of commitment can have important effects on organizational functioning.

Fifth and finally, various *personal characteristics* also influence organizational commitment. For example, people who have more tenure with their organization are more highly committed to them than those who have been employed for shorter periods of time.[83] This follows from the side-bets approach insofar as the longer one has been working for an organization, the more he or she is likely to have invested in it. Gender is another personal characteristic that has been found to be related to commitment. For many years, researchers found that women were less strongly committed to their jobs than men. This makes sense if you consider that the less involving, lower-level jobs that women have traditionally performed are unlikely to provide any strong sources of attraction. However, women are more likely to work in higher-level, more gratifying jobs. As this trend has unfolded, gender differences in organizational commitment have disappeared.[84] (This is not to say however, that one's gender is unrelated to organizational commitment. As described in the Quest for Quality section below, demographic factors can have a considerable impact on commitment—especially for some groups.)

THE QUEST FOR QUALITY

THE IMPACT OF "BEING DIFFERENT" ON ORGANIZATIONAL COMMITMENT: SOME UNSETTLING EFFECTS OF DIVERSITY

How would you feel about working in an organization in which you are very different from most of the other employees—particularly with respect to your race or gender? Although people generally prefer interacting with others who are similar to themselves, the high level of racial and ethnic diversity found in today's organizations requires people to interact with a wide variety of people who may be considerably different. How does this state of affairs affect people's attitudes toward their jobs? To what extent are people committed to working in organizations in which they represent a demographic minority?

To answer these questions Tsui, Egan, and O'Reilly conducted a survey of over 1,700 employees from 151 work groups within three large organizations.[85] After gathering information about each person's demographic background (e.g., age, race, and gender), the researchers computed a mathematical index of how different each individual was from the others in his or her work group. (For example, an Asian-American woman in a work group in which all others are white men would have a high difference score, whereas an African-American man in a group composed of all other African-American males would have a low difference score.) These scores were then compared to three separate measures of *organizational attachment*: psychological commitment (degree of care about and involvement with the organization), self-reports of absence frequency, and the desire to continue to work for the company. How were demographic differences related to organizational attachment? Several interesting relationships were observed.

Overall, Tsui and her colleagues found that being different was negatively correlated with organizational attachment: the more different people were from their co-workers with respect to gender and race, the less committed they were to their organizations, the less interested they were in continuing to work there, and the more frequently they were absent. They also found different reactions between men and women and between whites and nonwhites with respect to being demographically different. Men working in groups composed primarily of women showed less attachment than men in groups in which males were in the majority. However, the opposite was found among women: the more women were in the minority, the more attached they were to their organizations. The same pattern found among men was also found among whites. Specifically, the more whites were racially different than others in their work groups, the less attached they were to their organizations. However, among nonwhites, being different had no effect on attachment.

Taken together, these results paint a very interesting picture. The lowest levels of organizational attachment were found among men and whites, two groups whose members were not accustomed to being in the minority in their organizations. To the extent that this made them feel uncomfortable, it follows that they were less strongly committed to and involved with the organizations in which these conditions exist, and were more frequently absent from them as well. However, among women and nonwhites, groups whose members were used to being in the minority in their organizations, being different did not take its toll on attitudes toward the organization. In fact, among women, being different meant having the opportunity to work within a group of men (who are often regarded as having higher status), apparently making them feel special, and enhancing their feelings of organizational attachment.

Tsui and her associates interpret their findings as evidence suggesting that the effects of diversity in the workplace may not always be beneficial. Although diverse work groups may enjoy the advantages that follow from having heterogeneous perspectives, this comes at the cost of lowered organizational attachment—especially among men and whites. Building diversity in the workplace is intended to improve the quality of work life for employees by building a "melting pot" in which all people come to accept others as equals. However, the present results suggest that those who over the years have been a demographic majority may be uncomfortable with the erosion of this status. In the future, as the workforce becomes increasingly diverse, men and whites, who have traditionally held dominant positions in organizations, may get used to not always being in the majority, and the negative effects of demographic differences on attachment found in this study may not be replicated. For now, however, as Tsui and her associates put it, "managers face a difficult balancing act, paying attention to the negative effects of diversity on individual attachment and turnover while simultaneously attempting to capture the benefits of heterogeneity."[86]

ORGANIZATIONAL COMMITMENT: ITS MAJOR EFFECTS

The prediction seems reasonable that people who feel deeply committed to their organizations will behave differently from those who do not. And, despite very complex findings, considerable evidence supports this suggestion.[87] Organizational commitment greatly affects several key aspects of work behavior.

First, generally speaking, studies have found that high levels of organizational commitment tend to be associated with *low levels of absenteeism and voluntary turnover*.[88] In most cases, more committed individuals are less likely to look for new jobs than less committed ones. Interestingly, it appears that people enter jobs with a predisposition toward commitment, and this influences their tendency to stick with their organizations. Lee, Ashford, Walsh, and Mowday demonstrated this in a recent survey of dropout rates among cadets in the U.S. Air Force Academy.[89] Specifically, they found that the higher the commitment to the Academy cadets had on entering training, the less likely they were to drop out over the four years it took to earn their degrees.

Second, organizational commitment is associated with *high levels of willingness to share and make sacrifices*.[90] It should not be surprising that these types of organizational citizenship behaviors are related to commitment inasmuch as we can expect those who are most committed to their organizations to be those who give most generously of themselves.

Finally, organizational commitment has *positive personal consequences*. Although one might expect commitment to an organization to detract from one's personal life (because it would be costly in terms of time and emotional investment), research by Romzek suggests otherwise.[91] Her survey of work attitudes among public employees suggests that those who were most strongly attached to their organizations tended to enjoy highly successful careers and pleasant nonwork lives.

Taking all these findings into account, steps designed to generate high levels of organizational commitment among employees seem worthwhile. A committed workforce, it appears, is indeed beneficial to both individuals and organizations.

PREJUDICE: NEGATIVE ATTITUDES TOWARD OTHERS

Don't jump to conclusions. That's advice we often hear. But, when it comes to forming attitudes toward others, it is often ignored. Instead, people frequently do jump to conclusions about others—and on the basis of very limited information. If you have ever made a judgment about someone else on the basis of his or her ethnic background, age, gender, sexual orientation, or physical condition, then you are well aware of this tendency. As we discussed in conjunction with the topic of *stereotypes* (see Chapter 2), such judgments are frequently negative in nature. A negative attitude we hold toward another based on his or her membership in a particular groups is referred to as **prejudice.**[92] Not only might people holding prejudicial attitudes have negative beliefs and feelings, but these may predispose people to behave in ways consistent with these attitudes. For example, it would not be surprising to find that someone who does not like members of a certain minority group refuse to work alongside someone who belongs to that group, or even to sit next to such an individual in the company cafeteria. Such behaviors would be labeled acts of **discrimination** because they treat different groups of people in different ways. The key thing to keep in mind is this: prejudice is a negative attitude, and discrimination is the behavior that follows from it (the behavioral expression of that attitude).

DIVERSITY VERSUS PREJUDICE: COMPETING ORGANIZATIONAL REALITIES

There can be no mistaking the fact that the United States is an ethnically diverse nation—and that it is getting more so. For example, it has been estimated that by the year 2040, half of the U.S. population will be composed of people of African, Latin, Native American, and/or Asian descent. In addition, women—who, for many years only infrequently worked outside the home—are currently filling 65 percent of all new jobs, and by the year 2000 about half of the civilian workforce will be female.[93] For some companies, diversity is already a reality. For example, at the Solectron Corporation, a computer assembly company in Milpitas, California, 30 nationalities can be found speaking 40 different languages and dialects among the company's 3,200 employees (see Figure 5-11).[94]

Interestingly, as this picture of the highly diverse U.S. workforce unfolds, equally real is the unfortunate fact that prejudice against various groups still exists, and these prejudices are likely to have serious consequences. Before describing the nature of such prejudicial attitudes, we will first outline some of the general problems that they create.

First, prejudice can be the source of serious friction or conflict among people. Although a highly diverse workforce can potentially bring the advantage of differing opinions and perspectives (as we will discuss in Chapter 8), this may turn into a disadvantage among individuals who hold prejudicial attitudes. Indeed, if one's group membership causes an underlying current of distrust, then the conflict that results may be disruptive to the organization (Chapter 11) as people fail to cooperate with each other to get their jobs done. In extreme cases, the discriminatory actions that follow from prejudicial attitudes culminate in legal action—be it employees charging their employers with unfair discrimination,[95] or customers charging companies with discriminatory actions.[96]

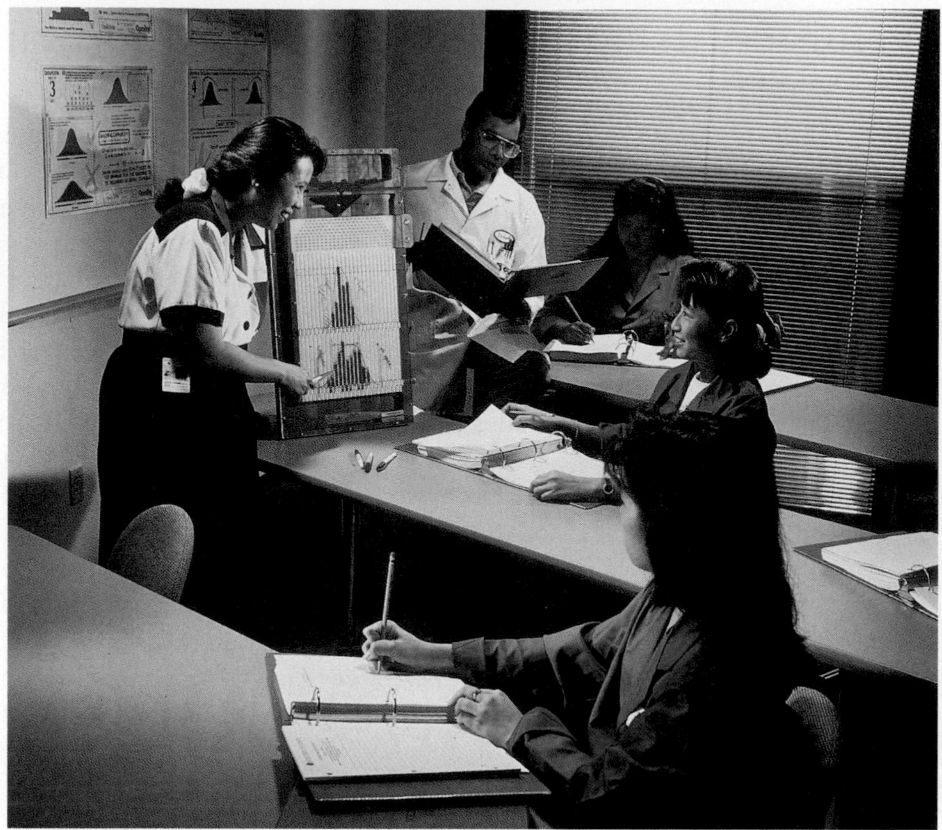

FIGURE 5-11
SOLECTRON CORPORATION: A HIGHLY DIVERSE WORKFORCE
Represented among Solectron Corporation's 3,200 employees are people from 30 different nationalities who speak 40 different languages. Such high levels of diversity are not uncommon among high-tech firms located in California's Silicon Valley.

Second, prejudice may have adverse effects on the careers of people who are the targets of such attitudes. Affected individuals may encounter various forms of discrimination—some very subtle, but others quite overt—with respect to hiring, promotion, and pay. For example, although there are more women than ever in the workforce, they are highly underrepresented in the upper echelons of organizations—in fact, only 3 percent of senior managers and 5.7 percent of corporate directors of Fortune 500 companies are women.[97] Because the discrimination is quite real, but not openly admitted, it is frequently referred to as the *glass ceiling* (i.e., a barrier that cannot be seen).

Third, we cannot overlook the devastating psychological impact of prejudice on victims of discrimination. Not only is the victim penalized, but so too are others who share the same background, in what has been called *covictimization*.[98] To the extent that talented individuals are passed over because of their membership in certain groups, individuals suffer an affront to their self-esteem that can be quite harmful (see Chapter 3). This, of course, is in addition to the loss to the organization of overlooking talented individuals simply because they are not white males. In today's highly competitive global economy, this is a mistake that no companies can afford.[99]

VARIOUS "GROUPISMS": MANIFESTATIONS OF PREJUDICIAL ATTITUDES IN THE WORKPLACE

If there is any one truly "equal opportunity" for people in today's workplace, it is that we all stand a chance of being the victim of prejudice. Indeed, there are many different forms of *groupism*—prejudices based on membership in certain groups—and no one is immune.[100]

PREJUDICE BASED ON AGE

We're all going to get older (if we're lucky), and as people are living longer and the birth rate is holding steady, the median age of Americans is rising all the time.[101] Despite this trend, it is clear that prejudice based on age is all too common. Although laws in the United States and elsewhere have done much to counter employment discrimination against older workers, prejudices continue to exist. Part of the problem resides in stereotypes that people have that older workers are too set in their ways to train and that they will tend to be sick or accident prone. As in the case of many attitudes, these prejudices are not founded on accurate information. Recent survey findings paint just the opposite picture of older workers. Namely, organizations tend to have extremely positive experiences with older workers: they have good skills, are highly committed to doing their jobs well, and have outstanding safety records.[102]

One reason why these negative attitudes persist despite evidence to the contrary is that people often have strongly held beliefs about the activities that are most appropriate at different ages. For example, first-line supervisors are implicitly assumed to be in their late 20s or early 30s, department heads should be in their mid-30s to mid-40s, and vice presidents should be at least 40.[103] Given such beliefs, individuals who attain a given position sooner than expected may profit from an age-related halo, whereas those who attain it later than anticipated may be evaluated negatively. To the extent that people continue to associate certain ages with certain job levels, it should not be surprising to find that age-related prejudices persist.

PREJUDICE BASED ON PHYSICAL CONDITION

If you think about it, every one of us has one physical feature or another that keeps us from doing a certain kind of work. Some people are not strong enough to load heavy packages onto trucks, others are not athletic enough to play professional sports, and still others might lack the agility and stamina needed to be a firefighter. Thus, although we all may be handicapped in some way, certain physical conditions tend to be the focus of widely held prejudicial attitudes. Such conditions (e.g., blindness, disfigurement, physical paralysis) are said to have *stigmas* attached to them—that is, negative aspects of one's identity.[104]

In the early 1990s, legislation known as the Americans with Disabilities Act (ADA) was enacted in the United States for purposes of safeguarding the rights of people with physical and mental disabilities. The rationale behind this law is that just because an employee is limited in some way, it does not mean that accommodations cannot be made to help the individual perform his or her job (you may recall from Chapter 1 that the Gilbreths had this same idea some eighty years ago). Companies that do not comply are subject to legal damages. In fact, the first award under the ADA, $572,000, was presented to an employee fired after missing work while recovering from cancer, and as many as 15,000 discrimination claims were filed in the law's first year alone.[105]

Many companies are finding that it is possible for them to meet the needs of disabled employees quite easily, and with little expense. For example, Greiner Engineering Inc., in Irving, Texas, was able to accommodate its employees in wheelchairs by simply substituting a lighter-weight door on its restrooms, and raising a drafting table by putting bricks under its legs.[106] Although not all accommodations are as easily made, experts are confident that the ADA will be an effective way of minimizing discrimination against employees based on their physical condition.[107]

PREJUDICE BASED ON SEXUAL ORIENTATION

Unlike people with physical disabilities, who are protected from discrimination by federal law, no such protection exists (yet, at least!) for another group whose members are frequently victims of prejudice—gay men and lesbian women. Unfortunately, although more people than ever are tolerant of nontraditional sexual orientations, antihomosexual prejudice still exists in the workplace. Indeed, about two-thirds of CEOs from major companies note that they are reluctant to put a homosexual on a top management committee.[108] Not surprisingly, without the law to protect them, and with widespread prejudices against them, many gays and lesbians are reluctant to openly make their sexual orientations known.[109]

Naturally, fears of being "discovered," exposed as a homosexual, represent a considerable source of stress among such individuals.[110] For example, a gay vice president of a large office equipment manufacturer in Chicago admitted in a magazine interview that he'd like to become the company's CEO, but fears that his chances will be ruined if his sexual orientation becomes known.[111] Although the pressure of having to go through life (or at least an important part of it) with a disguised identity must be extreme, imagine the cumulative effect of such efforts on organizations in which several employees are homosexual. Such misdirection of energy can become quite a serious productivity issue. In the words of consultant Mark Kaplan, "gay and lesbian employees use a lot of time and stress trying to conceal a big part of their identity."[112] To work in an organization with a homophobic culture, to have to endure jokes and slurs on gays and lesbians, can easily distract even the most highly focused employees.

To help avoid these problems—and, out of respect for diverse sexual orientations—many organizations have adopted internal fair employment policies that include sexual orientation. In addition, some companies are actively working to prohibit discrimination on the basis of sexual orientation. Extending this idea, still other companies are now extending fringe benefits, which traditionally have been offered exclusively to opposite-sex partners, to same-sex domestic partners as well (see Table 5-4). Russ Campanello, vice president of human resources for Lotus Development Corporation (the Cambridge, Massachusetts, developer of software

TABLE 5-4

Companies Offering Same-Sex Domestic Partner Benefits

Recognizing the prevalence of nontraditional families in today's society, a growing list of companies—some of which are listed here—are extending benefits to employees and their domestic partners regardless of whether they are of the opposite sex or the same sex. Recognizing diversity in sexual orientation has helped many companies attract and retain personnel.

ORGANIZATION	LOCATION
Ben and Jerry's Homemade Inc.	*Waterbury, VT*
Beth Israel Medical Center	*New York, NY*
Levi Strauss & Company	*San Francisco, CA*
Lotus Development Company	*Cambridge, MA*
MCA Inc.	*Universal City, CA*
Minnesota Communications Group	*St. Paul, MN*
The Village Voice	*New York, NY*

Source: Based on Martinez, 1993; see Note 108.

products) notes that his organization's reputation for having such a program has been an important key to its success in attracting highly talented technical personnel.[113] Clearly, although some companies are passively discouraging diversity with respect to sexual orientation, others, by encouraging diversity, are using it to their own—and their employees'—advantage.

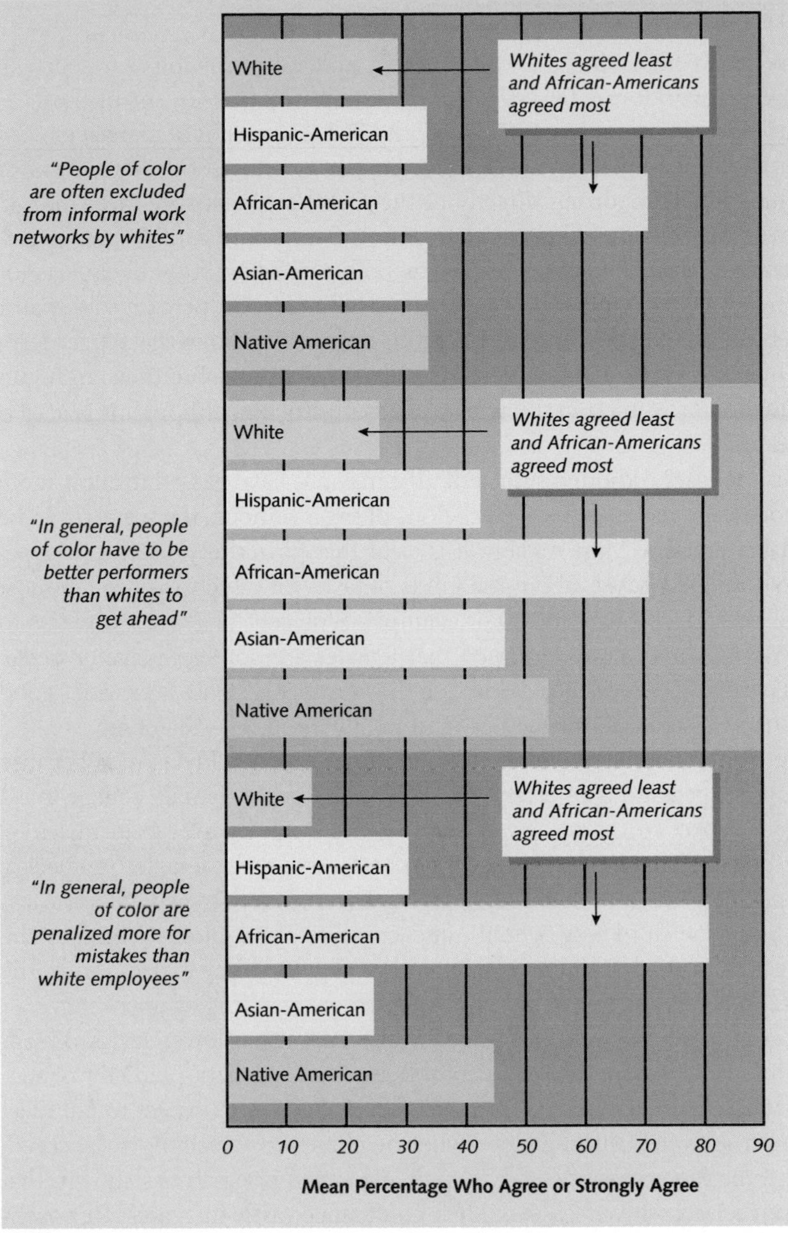

FIGURE 5-12
RACIAL DISCRIMINATION: BELIEFS ABOUT ITS PREVALENCE
A survey of American workers (collected between 1988 and 1992) shows that racial discrimination is believed to be quite prevalent in many forms, and that whites are generally less aware of it than non-whites. (Source: Based on data reported by Fernandez & Barr, 1993; see Note 93.)

PREJUDICE BASED ON RACE AND NATIONAL ORIGIN

The history of the United States is marked by struggles over acceptance for people of various racial and ethnic groups. Although, as we have documented, the U.S. workplace is more diverse than ever, it is also clear that prejudicial attitudes linger on. The survey results summarized in Figure 5-12, based on data collected from a large sample of U.S. workers in the late 1980s and early 1990s illustrate this point.[114]

Members of various minority groups not only believe they are the victims of prejudice and discrimination, they are also taking action. As evidence, consider that there was a 30 percent increase in the number of complaints of discrimination based on national origin filed at the Equal Employment Opportunity Commission (EEOC) between 1989 and 1991. Moreover, discrimination victims have been winning such cases. For example, in 1993 the Supreme Court of the state of Washington upheld a $389,000 judgment against a Seattle bank brought by a Cambodian-American employee fired because of his accent.[115] Outside the courtroom, companies that discriminate pay in other ways as well—notably, in lost talent and productivity. According to EEOC commissioner Joy Cherian, employees who feel victimized "may not take the initiative to introduce inventions and other innovations," adding, "every day, American employers are losing millions of dollars because these talents are frozen."[116]

To help minimize these problems, some companies are taking concrete steps. For example, AT&T Bell Labs in Murray Hill, New Jersey, is working with managers to find ways of helping the company's many ethnic minority employees get promoted more rapidly. Similarly, Hughes Aircraft Company of Los Angeles has been assigning mentors to minority-group employees to help teach them about the company's culture (see Chapter 14) and the skills needed to succeed.[117] Although both examples are only modest steps, they represent very encouraging trends intended to help reduce a long-standing problem.

PREJUDICE AGAINST WOMEN

There can be no mistaking the widespread—and ever-growing—presence of women in today's workforce. In 1991 women composed 46 percent of the U.S. workforce, up from 43 percent in 1981. Also, in 1991 41 percent of managers were women, compared to only 27 percent only ten years earlier. Still, female senior executives (individuals reporting directly to the CEO) are relatively rare—only 3 percent are women.[118] Is this likely to change in the next ten years? When executives completing a recent *Business Week*/Harris poll were asked how likely it is for their company to have a female CEO in the next ten years, 82 percent said that it was not likely, although they were a bit more optimistic about the longer-term prospects. Thus, it appears that "women populate corporations, but they rarely run them."[119] Equality for women in the workplace is improving, although it is a slow victory, to be sure.

Why is this the case? Although sufficient time may not have passed to allow more women to work their way into the top echelons of organizations, there appear to be more formidable barriers. Most notably, it is clear that powerful *sex role stereotypes* persist, narrow-minded beliefs about the kinds of tasks for which women are most appropriately suited (see Chapter 2). For example, 8 percent of the respondents to the *Business Week*/Harris survey indicated that females are not aggressive or determined enough to make it to the top. Although this number is small, it provides good evidence of the persistence of a nagging—and highly limiting—stereotype.

It is also possible that many women do not advance as quickly as men because they have lower expectations of career success. For example, female college graduates generally expect to receive lower starting and peak salaries than males.[120] This may be due to several factors, including the tendency for females to specialize in lower-paying areas, and the observation that women are, in general, paid less than men (about one third less overall), and come to expect less. Whatever the basis, it is a general rule that in life people tend to get what they expect. Thus, the lower expectations held by females may be one factor operating against them.

In addition to lower expectations, women also may have lower levels of self-confidence. This is important insofar as confidence is an excellent predictor of success: people who expect to succeed often do, while those who expect to fail meet this expectation as well. Unfortunately, when it comes to expecting to succeed, women tend to be more pessimistic than men. However, research has shown, that when women receive positive feedback, their confidence vastly increases, approaching the higher levels adopted by men.[121] This is a point managers who wish to foster advancement among women would do well to consider. (Some attempts to make women and members of ethnic minorities more successful at their jobs have focused on broader, society-based initiatives. For evidence regarding the impact of one well-known program, see the Ethical Workplace section on the following page.)

THE ETHICAL WORKPLACE

WHEN AFFIRMATIVE ACTION BACKFIRES: THE UNEQUAL IMPACT OF "EQUAL OPPORTUNITIES"

Affirmative action programs represent one of American society's most cherished tools for ensuring the ethical treatment of women and members of ethnic minorities in the workplace. The rationale is quite reasonable: by encouraging the hiring of women and minority group members into positions in which they have been traditionally underrepresented, exposure to diverse groups will increase and stereotypes of incompetence will crumble, leading to lowered prejudice and the halting of employment discrimination. However, it has been argued that affirmative action policies may backfire because they lead people to believe that job candidates who have been hired to meet affirmative action quotas are really not competent enough to do their jobs.[122] Regardless of a female candidate's actual qualifications, to the extent that people believe she was selected because of who she is as opposed to what she can do, they are likely to discount her qualifications, potentially strengthening the very stereotype that such efforts are attempting to combat.

Heilman, Block, and Lucas recently conducted a study to determine whether affirmative action designations actually backfire in this way.[123] Subjects in their experiment were college students asked to review the hypothetical personnel files of men and women hired as either electricians or lab technicians, and to make judgments about how well they thought the new hirees would do their jobs. A photo included in each file made it possible for participants to identify the hiree's gender. Some participants looking at females' cases had information in their packets indicating that the individual was hired to meet affirmative action quotas (e.g., the phrase "affirmative action hiree" was written on the bottom of the application in a space reserved for processing). The primary measure of interest was the participants' judgments of how competently they expected the individual to perform (ranging from 1, "not

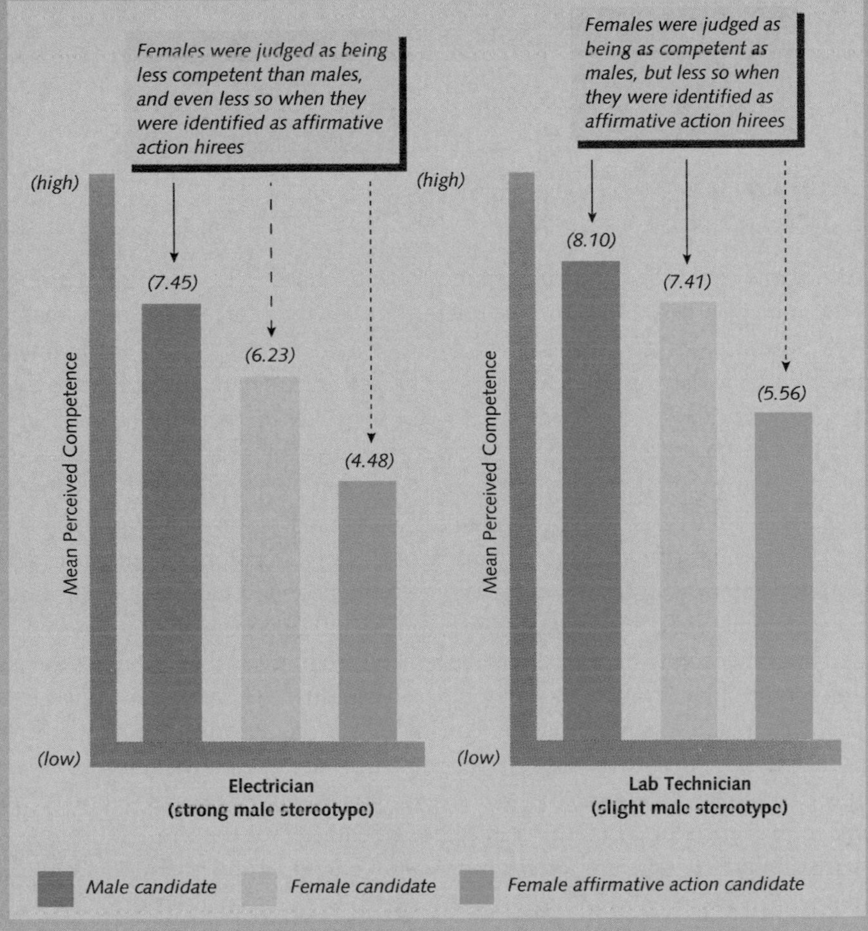
Females were judged as being less competent than males, and even less so when they were identified as affirmative action hirees
Females were judged as being as competent as males, but less so when they were identified as affirmative action hirees
(high)
(low)
Mean Perceived Competence
(7.45)
(6.23)
(4.48)
(8.10)
(7.41)
(5.56)
Electrician
(strong male stereotype)
Lab Technician
(slight male stereotype)
Male candidate
Female candidate
Female affirmative action candidate

FIGURE 5-13
"AFFIRMATIVE ACTION": A LABEL THAT SUGGESTS INCOMPETENCE
When asked to judge the competence of several hypothetical employees, subjects in an experiment by Heilman, Block, and Lucas rated females hired to fulfill affirmative action quotas as being less competent than other women. This occurred even in conditions under which women without the affirmative action designation were judged to be equally competent as men. (Source: Based on data reported by Heilman, Block, & Lucas, 1992; see Note 123.)

at all competently," to 9, very competently). Did the "affirmative action" designation hinder judgments of competence, as suspected? The results shown in Figure 5-13 suggest that the answer is yes.

As Figure 5-13 reveals, women identified as being hired for affirmative action purposes were perceived as being less competent than not only men, but also other women who were not hired in consideration of affirmative action. In other words, the backfire effect suggested did, in fact, materialize. However, there were some interesting differences for each type of job studied. When the position was one in which women were expected, based on stereotypes, to be poorly qualified (because they would be doing a traditionally male-dominated job, such as electrician), they were judged to be less competent than men—even before the affirmative action label was given. When the affirmative action designation was given, it lowered judgments of competence even further. However, for jobs that are less strongly dominated by men (e.g., laboratory technician), women were *not* judged as being any less competent than men—but only when the affirmative action label was not applied. When female hirees were identified as affirmative action candidates, their perceived competence was considerably lower. In other words, in a situation in which women are generally judged to be equally qualified as men, the affirmative action label lowered perceptions of competence when they would not otherwise have been.

These findings are certainly disconcerting. Although affirmative action programs are intended to help eradicate prejudicial attitudes in the workplace, it appears that they may have just the opposite effect. To the extent that people may believe that individuals hired to meet affirmative action regulations are automatically unqualified and would not be hired otherwise (which, of course, is untrue), it is unlikely that the spirit of such programs will be satisfied in actual practice. This is especially problematic insofar as perceptions of incompetence may become self-fulfilling, thereby potentially reinforcing rather than challenging prejudicial beliefs. Although it would be unwise to scrap an important social program on the basis of any single study—especially one conducted in an unrealistic setting—the findings of Heilman and her associates clearly merit further attention, and we suspect this investigation will spawn many follow-up studies.

MANAGING A DIVERSE WORKFORCE: CURRENT PRACTICES

Affirmative action programs, despite problems, have been effective at bringing women and members of minority groups into the workforce. However, many of today's organizations are interested in going beyond affirmative action by not just hiring a wider variety of different people, but also creating an atmosphere in which diverse groups can flourish. They are not merely trying to obey the law or attempting to be socially responsible, but they recognize that diversity is a business issue. As one consultant put it, "A corporation's success will increasingly be determined by its managers' ability to naturally tap the full potential of a diverse workforce."[124] It is with this goal in mind that three-quarters of U.S. organizations are adapting **diversity management programs**—efforts to celebrate diversity by creating supportive, not just neutral, work environments for women and minorities.[125] Simply put, the underlying philosophy of diversity management programs is that breaking the glass ceiling requires that women and minorities are not just tolerated, but valued.[126]

Diversity management programs consist of various efforts to not only create opportunities for diverse groups of people within organizations, but also to train people to embrace differences between them. For example, Xerox's "Step-Up" program, in existence for some thirty years, has been one of the most thorough and sustained efforts to hire minority-group members and train them to succeed.[127] Similarly, Pacific Bell is another company that has made great strides at reaching out to minority-group members (e.g., through internship programs), creating jobs for them in positions that have broad opportunities for advancement.[128] Although they have been highly successful, these efforts have focused more on changing the system so as to give opportunities to a diverse group of individuals than on changing the attitudes of the people involved.

Digital Equipment Corporation (DEC) has extended these initiatives in its "Valuing Differences" program, an approach that focuses on not just accepting people (e.g., giving them opportunities to succeed), but valuing them *because* of their differences.[129] DEC officials provide the following rationale:

> The philosophy is anchored in the conviction that the broader the spectrum of differences in the workplace, the richer the synergy among the employees and the more excellent the organization's performance. It is a belief in the constructive potential of all people. It assumes that each person's differences bring unique and special gifts to the organization.[130]

What does DEC do to capitalize on the differences between its employees? Four specific efforts may be identified. First, DEC invests in special training sessions designed to get employees to understand the diversity in their workplace, examining the cultural norms of the different people who work there. Second, DEC celebrates these differences by sponsoring a calendar of special cultural and educational events designed to provide ways of learning about different people (e.g., Black History Month, Gay and Lesbian Pride Week, and International Women's Month) (see Figure 5-14). Third, they help organize support groups for members of various groups who find it beneficial to meet with others of their own race or nationality who can give them needed emotional support and/or career guidance. Finally, DEC supports an informal network of small ongoing discussion groups referred to as "core groups." These are groups of between seven and nine members who meet monthly to openly discuss their stereotypes and ways of improving relationships with others they regard as different. Although empirical tests of the effectiveness of this four-pronged approach to managing diversity have not been conducted, both DEC officials and employees are convinced that its Valuing Differences program is a huge success.

DEC's efforts at managing diversity represent just one of a broad range of approaches that have been used with by companies in recent years. Pepsi Cola, American Express Travel Related Services, and the accounting firm Coopers & Lybrand, are just a few of the companies that also have been actively engaged in diversity management efforts.[131]

FIGURE 5-14
DIVERSITY MANAGEMENT AT WORK
Digital Equipment Corporation's diversity management program, *"Valuing Differences," has enabled the company to tap the rich resources of its highly diverse pool of employees while maintaining harmonious relationships between them. These Digital employees are celebrating "Native American Awareness Week," one of the special cultural events that makes this program effective.*

Although most companies have been pleased with the ways their diversity management efforts have promoted harmony between employees, some have encountered problems. In the most serious cases, diversity management efforts have backfired, leaving race and gender divisions even greater.[132] The most serious problems have stemmed from the practice of focusing on stereotypes, even positive ones. Thinking of people in stereotypical ways can create barriers that interfere with looking at people as individuals. So, instead of looking at the *average* differences between people (which may reinforce stereotypes), experts recommend that managing diversity demands accepting a *range* of differences between people (a range that promises to become even greater in the years ahead).[133] With this in mind, managers are advised to not treat someone as special because he or she is a member of a certain group, but because of the unique skills, or abilities he or she brings to the job. To the extent that managers are trained to seek, recognize, and develop the talents of their employees regardless of the groups to which they belong, they will help break down the barriers that made diversity training necessary in the first place.

In conclusion, although mistakes have been made in the way some diversity management programs have been implemented, diversity management programs have, in general, greatly helped organizations find ways of tapping the rich pool of talent found in a highly diverse workforce. Fortunately, today's researchers and practitioners are sharing their experiences with diversity management techniques, both successful and unsuccessful, making it easier than ever to learn what others are doing and what works best.[134]

SUMMARY AND REVIEW

ATTITUDES AND HOW THEY CHANGE

Attitudes are the stable clusters of feelings, beliefs, and behavioral tendencies directed toward some aspect of the external world. **Work-related attitudes** involve such reactions toward various aspects of work settings or the people in them. All attitudes consist of a *cognitive* component (what you believe), an *evaluative* component (how you feel), and a *behavioral* component (the tendency to behave a certain way).

When people discover that two attitudes they hold are inconsistent, or that their attitudes and behavior are inconsistent, an unpleasant state of **cognitive dissonance** results. This produces pressure to alter either one's behavior or the attitudes involved. Efforts to change others' attitudes are referred to as **persuasion**. The extent to which one is persuasive depends on his or her own characteristics (e.g. credibility), and the nature of the message itself (e.g., its clarity and the degree to which it is discrepant from currently held views).

JOB SATISFACTION

Job satisfaction involves positive or negative attitudes toward one's work. Such attitudes can be measured by completing rating scales (such as the JDI or the MSQ), conducting interviews, or recounting *critical incidents* (instances found to be especially pleasing or displeasing).

According to Herzberg's **two-factor theory**, job satisfaction and dissatisfaction stem from different factors. Evidence for the accuracy of this theory has been mixed. Locke's **value theory** suggests that job satisfaction reflects the apparent match between the outcomes individuals desire from their jobs (what they *value*) and what they believe they are actually receiving.

Job satisfaction is caused by various organizational factors (e.g., reward system, quality of supervision) and personal factors (e.g., self-esteem, general life satisfaction, status and seniority). When people are dissatisfied with their jobs, they tend to withdraw (i.e., they show high levels of absenteeism and voluntary turnover). Performance quantity and quality are only weakly related to job satisfaction, although they have been shown to be linked to **organizational citizenship behaviors.**

ORGANIZATIONAL COMMITMENT

Organizational commitment deals with people's attitudes toward their organizations. People can have various targets, or *foci* of commitment, such as top managers, or one's work group. Commitment may based primarily on three different *bases*. One is **continuance commitment**—the strength of a person's tendency to continue working for an organization because he or she has to and cannot afford to do otherwise. Another is **affective commitment**—the strength of a person's tendency to continue working for an organization because he or she agrees with its goals and values and desires to stay with it. A third is **normative commitment**—commitment to remain in an organization stemming from social obligations to do so.

Organizational commitment is related to various job characteristics, the nature of the rewards received, treatment of newcomers, and other variables. High levels of commitment have been associated with low levels of absenteeism and voluntary turnover, high levels of willingness to share and make sacrifices, and various positive personal consequences.

PREJUDICE IN WORK SETTINGS

The term **prejudice** refers to negative attitudes toward members of specific groups, and **discrimination** refers to treating people differently because of these prejudices. Today's workforce is characterized by high levels of diversity, with many groups finding themselves victims of prejudicial attitudes and discriminatory behaviors (based on many different factors, including age, sexual orientation, physical condition, racial or ethnic group membership, and gender).

Evidence shows that although people are becoming more tolerant of individuals from diverse groups, prejudicial attitudes persist. To help tap the rich pool of resources available in today's highly diverse workforce, many companies are using **diversity management programs**—techniques for systematically teaching employees to celebrate the differences between people. Typically, these programs go beyond efforts to recruit and hire women and members of minority groups, to creating supportive work environments for them.

KEY TERMS

affective commitment: The strength of a person's desire to work for an organization because he or she agrees with it and wants to do so (see *goal congruence orientation*).

attitudes: Stable clusters of feelings, beliefs, and behavioral intentions toward specific objects, people, or institutions.

cognitive dissonance: An unpleasant state that occurs when individuals notice inconsistencies between various attitudes they hold, or between their attitudes and their behavior.

continuance commitment: The strength of a person's desire to continue working for an organization because he or she needs to do so and cannot afford to do otherwise (see *side-bets orientation*).

critical incident technique: A procedure for measuring job satisfaction in which employees describe incidents relating to their work that they find especially satisfying or dissatisfying.

goal congruence orientation: An approach to organizational commitment according to which the degree of agreement between an individual's personal goals and those of the organization is a determinant of organizational commitment (see *affective commitment*).

discrimination: The behavior consistent with a prejudicial attitude; the act of treating someone negatively because of his or her membership in a specific group.

diversity management programs: Programs in which employees are taught to celebrate the differences between people and in which organizations create supportive work environments for women and minorities.

Job Descriptive Index (JDI): A rating scale for assessing job satisfaction. Individuals respond to this questionnaire by indicating whether or not various adjectives describe aspects of their work.

job satisfaction: Positive or negative attitudes held by individuals toward their jobs.

Minnesota Satisfaction Questionnaire (MSQ): A rating scale for assessing job satisfaction in which people indicate the extent to which they are satisfied with various aspects of their jobs.

normative commitment: The strength of a person's desire to continue working for an organization because he or she feels obligations from others to remain there.

organizational citizenship behaviors: Actions by employees that contribute to the smooth functioning of their organization, but that are not part of their formal job requirements (e.g., helping others, giving advice).

organizational commitment: The extent to which an individual identifies and is involved with his or her organization and/or is unwilling to leave it (see *affective commitment, normative commitment* and *continuance commitment*).

Pay Satisfaction Questionnaire (PSQ): A questionnaire designed to assess employees' levels of satisfaction with various aspects of their pay (e.g., its overall level, raises, benefits).

persuasion: A process in which one or more individuals attempt to alter the attitudes of others.

prejudice: Negative attitudes toward the members of specific groups, based solely on the fact that they are members of those groups (e.g., age, race, sexual orientation).

side-bets orientation: The view of organizational commitment that focuses on the accumulated investments an individual stands to lose if he or she leaves the organization (see *continuance commitment*).

two-factor theory of job satisfaction: A theory, devised by Herzberg, suggesting that satisfaction and dissatisfaction stem from different groups of variables (*motivators* and *hygienes*, respectively).

value theory: A theory, devised by Locke, suggesting that job satisfaction depends primarily on the match between the outcomes individuals value in their jobs and their perceptions about the availability of such outcomes.

work-related attitudes: Attitudes relating to any aspect of work or work settings.

QUESTIONS FOR DISCUSSION

1. How is the process of persuasion used in organizations, and how might it contribute to one's career success?
2. Suppose you just bought an expensive new car, but immediately discovered serious problems with it. According to the process of cognitive dissonance, explain how you might be expected to react?
3. Suppose that as a manager, you wanted to enhance job satisfaction among your subordinates. What steps might you take to accomplish this goal?
4. Most people indicate that they are reasonably satisfied with their jobs. Why? How can we go about determining whether such satisfaction is real or only apparent?
5. Absenteeism and voluntary turnover are costly problems for many companies. What steps can be taken to reduce the incidence of these forms of employee withdrawal?
6. Why might you find an employee who is highly dissatisfied with his or her job and the organization, but simply remains on the job and does not take a new one in another organization?
7. What would you say are the prospects for a prejudice-free workplace? Explain the basis for your optimism or pessimism.

CASE IN POINT

"KILLER" ANTICS AT SOUTHWEST AIRLINES

Look, up in the sky. It's a bird, it's a plane, it's a plane painted to look like a killer whale! Shamu One, the "killer whaleplane" is a Southwest Airlines Boeing 737-300 painted to look like its namesake at San Antonio's Sea World.[1]

Decorating a plane to look like one of the animals at a theme park for which it is the official carrier is only one of the zany antics enjoyed by Herb Kelleher, the CEO of Southwest Airlines. Others include his dressing in clown suits, Elvis costumes, and as the Easter bunny. He also encourages his employees to have fun by holding weekly parties at corporate headquarters and organizing employee trivia contests. So that the customers don't feel left out, these types of clever activities are extended to them as well. Flight attendants have been known to deliver their safety instructions in rap or the voice of Mr. Ed, award prizes for the customer with the biggest holes in their socks, and play "guess the gate agent's weight" to keep passengers amused.[2,3,4]

The purpose of all these endeavors is to create an atmosphere of fun. Says Kelleher, "Fun is a stimulant to people. They enjoy their work more and work more productively."[5] Clearly Kelleher knows what he is talking about. His airline, a relative newcomer to the industry, has grown from 4 aircraft carrying passengers among Dallas, Houston, and San Antonio in 1971, to over 150 planes serving more than 35 cities in 1994. In fact, the Department of Transportation has called the carrier, "the dominant airline in the nation's busiest markets."[6]

Southwest Airlines is the only carrier to post a profit in each of the last twenty-three years of service. Given the massive restructuring and retrenchment in the airline industry this is an incredible accomplishment. Passenger traffic was up 20 percent in 1993,[7] revenues are growing more than 15 percent annually, and more than 200 new employees are being hired every month.[8]

Kelleher claims that the key to his airlines' success is that, "We dignify the customer."[9] He insists that good customer service depends on a high level of *esprit de corps*. This is partly accomplished by the attitude that Kelleher himself shows toward his employees. He values the employees as individuals instead of lumping them together into a group. In addition, to ensure good customer service Southwest is extremely selective in whom it hires. The airline looks for people who like other people, who enjoy providing the best service possible, and who have a real zest for living. According to Kelleher, "We draft great attitudes. If you don't have a good attitude, we don't want you, no matter how skilled you are. We can change skill levels through training. We can't change attitude."[10]

Does this emphasis on hiring people with great attitudes and keeping these people happy pay off? Southwest employees and customers think so. This airline makes more money per revenue dollar earned than any of its competitors. This is in great part a function of the productivity of Southwest employees. Everyone at this company chips in to do whatever needs to be done. Airplanes are cleaned only once per day. Flight attendents and pilots pick up trash between flights and load baggage when necessary. The productivity of its employees has made Southwest the lowest-cost company in the airline industry—15 percent lower than its next-lowest-cost competitor, American Airlines.

Not only is customer satisfaction very high, so is employee job satisfaction. Southwest's relationship with its employee unions are cooperative, and it has one of the lowest rates of employee turnover in the industry. Kelleher accounts for these positive relations with the unions by noting that Southwest's management does not treat unions in a hostile way or think of them as adversaries. Instead, at this airline the unions and management work together to accomplish their mutually agreed-on goals.

Illustrating the high level of employee commitment is the "Fuel from the Heart" program. When Iraq invaded Kuwait in 1990, jet fuel prices skyrocketed. Without Kelleher's knowing anything about it, one-third of Southwest's 8,600 employees volunteered a portion of their pay to buy fuel for the airline. Kelleher first learned of the program when employees presented him with a "Fuel from the Heart" banner signed by all the employees who had contributed.

Not surprisingly, Kelleher also finds ways to give back to the employees. One such means is through the "winning spirit award." This recognition is given on a monthly basis to employees who perform extraordinary deeds for

CASE IN POINT, Cont.

other people. A ceremony is held, and the honors are conveyed by Kelleher himself. He seems to enjoy this process as much as the awardees.

Service to customers is legendary. Once, a pilot who had his plane already pushed back from the gate, noticed a frantic passenger running down the jetway attempting to board the already departed aircraft. Breaking every rule in the book, he pulled the plane back to the gate so that the passenger could get on the plane. Instead of being punished for this breach of company policy, the pilot was congratulated by the executive vice president for Customers (always with a capital "C"). In another instance, a customer service agent took care of a passenger's dog for two weeks when the same agent wouldn't permit the animal aboard the plane due to its large size.[11]

It's easy for the personnel of Southwest Airlines to treat the customers well—all they have to do is model the behaviors and attitudes of their leader. Whenever Kelleher flies on his airline, he helps the flight attendants by putting ice into the drinks and serving the cockpit crew. He also tries to work in all operations of the airline on an annual basis so that he understands the inner workings of the carrier. By behaving as he wishes the employees to act and by treating the employees with respect, Kelleher, something of a "superman" himself, has created a winner!

QUESTIONS FOR DISCUSSION

1. Herb Kelleher attributes Southwest's performance to the attitudes of its employees. To what extent does the evidence support the existence of such an attitude–behavior link? Explain your answer.
2. What factors affect employee job satisfaction at Southwest Airlines? Explain.
3. How is job satisfaction related to performance at Southwest Airlines? Explain.
4. Why is employee turnover so low at Southwest Airlines?
5. Why does Southwest Airlines enjoy such a positive relationship with its unions, when so many other airlines seem to have antagonistic relations with their unions? Explain.
6. Do you think that the employees at Southwest Airlines feel committed to their organization? Support your response.

EXPERIENCING ORGANIZATIONAL BEHAVIOR

Getting What You Expect: Anticipated Compensation of Women and Men

Despite efforts to eliminate differences in pay for women and men, a gender gap persists in this respect. Currently, women's average salaries are still considerably lower than men's. Many factors probably contribute to this state of affairs. Because of past sexual discrimination, women have filled many jobs—especially higher-level ones—for shorter periods than their male counterparts. Further, women have often been encouraged to enter lower-paying fields or occupations. Yet another factor that contributes to the present gender gap is that women hold lower expectations with respect to both starting salaries and highest career salaries than men. You can demonstrate this difference for yourself by following the instructions below.

PROCEDURE

Ask five to ten classmates of each gender to answer the following questions. (To avoid bias, it would be best to work only with individuals who have *not* yet had a course in organizational behavior.)

1. What *starting salary* do you expect to receive on your first full-time job?
2. What will be the *highest salary* you will receive during your career? (Estimate in terms of current salary levels.)
3. How long will it be (in years and months) before you receive your first *major* promotion?
4. What field or occupation do you plan to enter after graduation?

POINTS TO CONSIDER

After you have collected data from all respondents, add the figures for males and females separately, and compare the means (averages) on each question. In all likelihood, you will find that females report somewhat lower expectations than males. Why? One possibility is that many females plan to enter fields offering relatively lower pay. Another possibility is that these expectations simply reflect current conditions: females recognize that they actually receive lower pay, on average, than males. Can you think of other reasons for these differences in expectations? Will they disappear in the future as efforts to eliminate sexism continue?

CHAPTER OUTLINE

SPECIAL SECTIONS

SIX

BECOMING AN ORGANIZATIONAL MEMBER: SOCIALIZATION AND CAREERS

LEARNING OBJECTIVES

After reading this chapter, you should be able to

1. *Understand the concept of socialization and identify the stages through which it develops.*
2. *Describe the various types of orientation programs designed to socialize new employees.*
3. *Explain what mentors do, and the benefits and costs of mentoring for both mentors and their protégés.*
4. *Describe the various steps through which mentoring relationships develop in organizations.*
5. *Explain the dynamics of mentoring relationships between people of the opposite sex and different races.*
6. *Understand the major considerations involved in making vocational choices.*
7. *Explain the systematic stages through which people's careers change and develop over time.*
8. *Describe the ways in which the changing composition of the workforce is affecting conflicts between work life and family life, and some of the things organizations are doing to minimize these conflicts.*

It takes twenty years to make an overnight success.

Eddie Cantor, 1892–1964
American comedian and writer
The New York Times, October 20, 1963

It doesn't matter where you start as long as you have a road map and consider every work day as training along the way.

Deborah Steelman
Associate Director,
U.S. Office of Management and Budget , 1987

PREVIEW CASE

Judith Resnick: The Path from Broke to Broker

How would you like to be 41, a single mother of two teenagers, broke, and without a day's worth of professional work experience under your belt? That was the position in which Judith Resnick found herself in 1983.

Living off the proceeds of the sale of her house, she attempted to stretch her income by making wise investments. Sadly, the broker she entrusted with her funds lost her money investing in options. Fortunately, however, she learned from the experience. "Although I was losing money, I noticed that he [the broker] was making it. I said to myself, 'Even I could do that.'" But without any experience, she was turned down for positions at one firm after another (although some were kind enough to consider her for secretarial jobs). That was until an office manager at the downtown Los Angeles branch of Drexel Burnham Lambert, saw something special in Judith, and gave her a chance as a trainee.

During her first year with the firm, Resnick called everyone she could think of and sold enough Treasury bonds and municipal bonds to net $106,000—quite remarkable for a rookie. But this was only the beginning of a meteoric rise to the top. Only two years later, Resnick was working in the Beverly Hills office, and became one of the top female brokers in the firm—grossing as much as $750,000 in a single year.

As Drexel's success mushroomed in the mid-1980s, under the leadership of Michael Milken (the "Junk Bond King," as he became known), Resnick found herself arranging trades for small institutional investors. In 1988 alone she sold bonds with a face value of $200 million.

But then things began to unravel. Milken resigned as the Securities and Exchange Commission began to investigate several irregularities and unlawful practices at the upper levels of Drexel's hierarchy. Soon afterward, Resnick was pressured into pushing bonds of doubtful quality. "I didn't think they were appropriate for my customers, so I said no. That was the day I figured it was time to go out on my own."

Judy Resnick, Chairman and CEO of Dabney/Resnick & Wagner, Inc.

Only five years after she first began looking for jobs in the investment business, Judith Resnick, now a successful, seasoned professional, was received much more warmly by those she approached for support. In fact, a local bank was willing to loan her and her partner, former Drexel salesman Neil Dabney, the funds needed to start their own brokerage firm. So, with hundreds of their former Drexel clients jumping ship along with them, Dabney/Resnick opened its doors in Beverly Hills in July 1989.

Then, just as the firm was getting started, the junk bond market collapsed. Most analysts were urging their clients to pull out, but Dabney and

Resnick recognized what bargains they were, and encouraged their clients to buy. As the market rebounded, their clients' returns—and the company's profits—were phenomenal. In fact, the firm was able to pay off its entire bank debt after only four months in business.

But the company's success has been based on more than just flukes of good luck. In 1992 alone, the firm's high-yield portfolios yielded returns as high as 39 percent (very impressive for that year), and it traded some $2.5 billion in bonds. These figures are a tribute to the company's 80 hard-working employees, and the skill and initiative of Resnick and Dabney.

If you're a woman thinking of making it big on Wall Street, Resnick has this advice: "Don't make barriers where there aren't any. Work hard, of course, but do not become one of the boys. Stay a lady." In view of her remarkable career success, this would appear to be wise advice.

If you were to conjure up an image of a successful stock broker, chances are good that it would *not* be someone like Judith Resnick. With nothing more than a healthy curiosity about the stock market going for her, she didn't match the prototype of a financial professional, and found it difficult to get started. But, once given a chance, she quickly proved her worth to the organization. This story is inspiring, to be sure, but it is certainly *not* a road map for guiding one's career. For most of us, the paths we take are much more traditional. Typically, we receive education in the field we like, and take jobs in various organizations that allow us to put our knowledge and skills to work, working our way up from lower- to higher-level jobs over the course of forty or fifty years.

Obviously, things are not always quite that simple—and if we can generalize from Resnick's case, there's more than one path to success. As you might imagine, the process of becoming an organizational member is much more complicated than meets the eye. In this chapter we will examine two key facets of this process. First we will examine **organizational socialization**—the process by which new employees learn how to become functioning members of their organizations.[1] Specifically, we will review the various stages of the socialization process as well as different types of programs, known as *employee orientation programs,* designed to formally socialize employees. We will then review the basic dimensions of organizational socialization and the impact of socialization programs on individuals and their organizations. Second, we will turn to the special, one-on-one form of socialization known as **mentoring.** Specifically, we will outline the development of mentoring relationships, as well as summarize recent research on race and gender differences in mentoring. Finally, we will turn to the topic of **careers**—the sequence of jobs, roles, and positions individuals hold during their working lives.[2] In examining how this works, we will summarize some of the factors responsible for people's job choices, the way careers tend to change and develop over time, and the special issues created by the need to balance the often conflicting demands of work life and family life.

ORGANIZATIONAL SOCIALIZATION: THE PROCESS OF JOINING UP

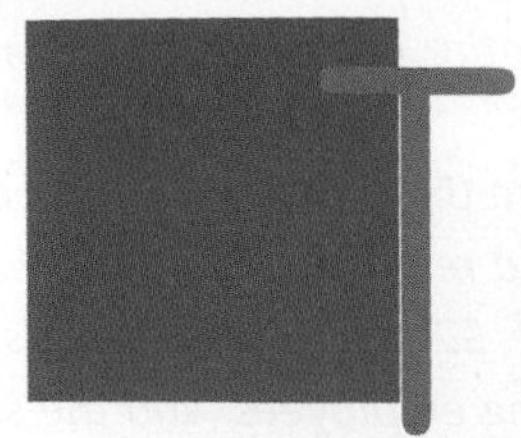

Think back over the jobs you have held in recent years. Can you recall your feelings and reactions during the first few days or weeks on each? If so, you probably remember that these were somewhat uncomfortable periods. As a new employee, you were suddenly confronted with a work environment that was different in many respects from the one you had just left. Most, if not all, of the people around you were strangers, and you had to begin the process of getting to know them—and their personal quirks—from scratch. Unless your job was identical to the one you had before, you also had to learn new procedures, skills, and operations relating to it. You had to acquire working knowledge of the policies, practices, and procedures in force in your new organization, so that you would know how to carry out your work assignments in accordance with them. In short, you had to *learn the ropes* (see Figure 6-1).

Successfully completing these complex tasks is clearly important to the future performance of virtually any new employee. In other words, the speed and ease with which individuals learn the ropes in organizations they have recently joined are crucial from both the individual's and organization's point of view. This process is known as **organizational socialization**. More formally, it can be defined as *the process through which individuals are transformed from outsiders to participating, effective members of organizations.*[3] In a sense, a career can be viewed as consisting of a series of socialization experiences as an individual moves into new organizations or new positions in his or her present one. Thus, understanding organizational socialization is important to understanding careers.

In this section, therefore, we will consider several key aspects of organizational socialization. First we will describe the basic stages of socialization—steps through which most people pass en route to becoming full members of their organization and work groups. Then we will consider various techniques used by organizations to help smooth new employees' passage through this difficult process, and some effects of these techniques.

STAGES IN THE SOCIALIZATION PROCESS

It is useful to look at organizational socialization as as a continuous process—one that starts before people arrive on the job, and proceeds for weeks or months after they begin working. The process can be divided into three basic periods described by Feldman as the stages of *getting in*, *breaking in*, and *settling in* (see Figure 6-2).[4]

cathy® — by Cathy Guisewite

FIGURE 6-1
ORGANIZATIONAL SOCIALIZATION: THE PROCESS OF LEARNING THE ROPES
To succeed, employees do many things to learn the procedures, values, and norms of the organizations in which they work. Although catching on is important, it isn't likely take the form shown here. (Cathy © 1993 Cathy Guisewite. Reprinted with permission of Universal Press Syndicate. All rights reserved.)

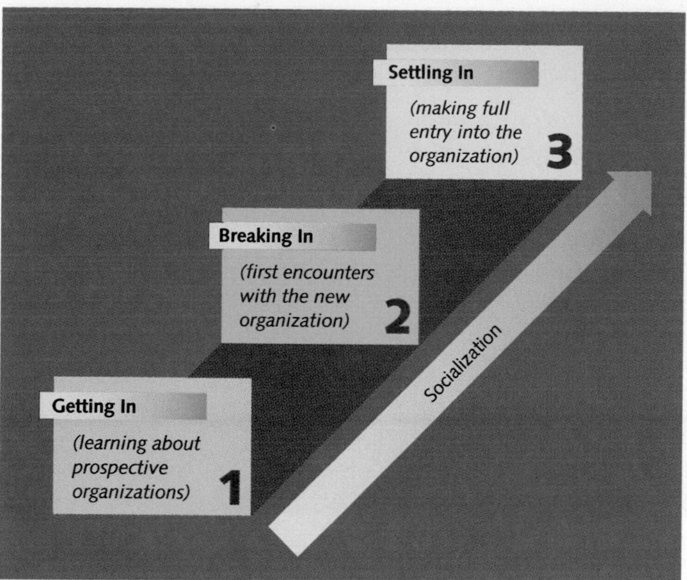

FIGURE 6-2
THE THREE BASIC STAGES OF ORGANIZATIONAL SOCIALIZATION
The process of organizational socialization usually follows the three steps summarized here: getting in, breaking in, and settling in. (Source: Based on suggestions by Feldman, 1980; see Note 4.)

GETTING IN: ANTICIPATORY SOCIALIZATION

Can you think of a specific organization in which you are interested in working someday? Why would you like to work there? What is it about that particular company that makes it such an attractive choice for you? To the extent that it is possible for you to answer these questions—even if only tentatively—you already recognize that you can know quite a bit about an organization even before you start working there. In other words, people often develop expectations about what an organization will be like in advance of actually working in it—a tendency known as *anticipatory socialization*.

Several sources of information contribute to our anticipated beliefs about an organization. First, friends or relatives who work there might tell you about their experiences, strongly coloring your perceptions and expectations as a new recruit. Second, individuals often acquire information about an organization from various formal sources, such as professional journals, magazine and newspaper articles, and corporate annual reports. Unfortunately, both of these sources of information may be biased. For example, you may only hear your friends or relatives talk about their jobs when they wish to complain and have negative things to say. Even positive statements they make may be motivated by attempts to rationalize bad situations by explaining them as being good (i.e., to resolve cognitive dissonance; see Chapter 5). Similarly, press reports of organizational activities are often reserved for sensationalistic accounts of either extremely positive news (e.g., record-breaking earnings) or negative news (e.g., violations of legal or moral standards). Thus, although we often rely on secondhand information from personal contacts and popular press accounts of organizational activities as bases for our judgments about organizations, it is important to realize that the information they provide may be questionable.

Unfortunately, sometimes the information provided directly to prospective employees by corporate recruiters is unbalanced and skewed toward the positive. Since competition for top-notch employees is often intense, successful recruitment usually involves a skilled combination of salesmanship and diplomacy. Recruiters tend to describe their companies in glowing terms, glossing over internal problems and emphasizing positive features. The result is that potential employees often receive unrealistically positive impressions of what it would be like to work in those organizations. When new employees actually arrive on the job and find that their expectations are not met, they may feel disappointment, dissatisfaction, and even resentment about being misled. Naturally, employees' reactions will not be positive. In fact, research has shown that the less employees' job expectations are met, the less satisfied and committed they are, and the more likely they are to think about quitting, and to actually do so.[5]

New employees who have the clearest expectations about what it is like to work for a particular company tend to be those who already have worked there before, and those who are referred by a present employee who believes that person would fit in well. These *inside* sources of information tend to provide more thorough and realistic information about an organization than *outside* sources, such as employ-

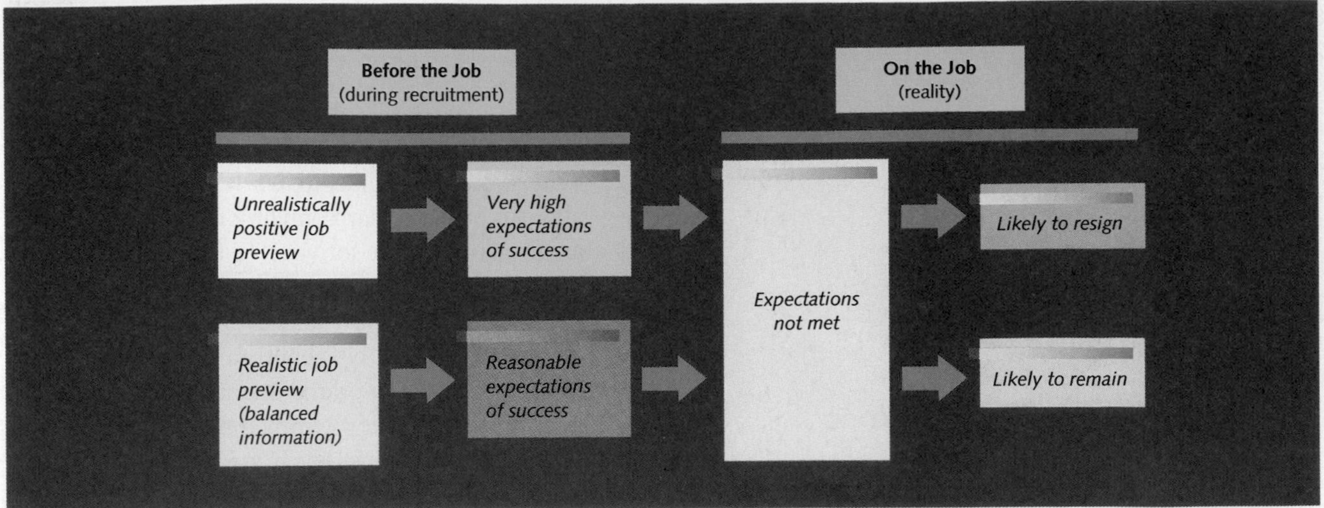

FIGURE 6-3
REALISTIC JOB PREVIEWS: AN OVERVIEW
Recruiters who give prospective employees accurate information about both the positive and negative aspects of the jobs they are likely to encounter—known as realistic job previews*—do a better job of meeting employees' expectations, and therefore preventing them from resigning.*
(Source: Based on suggestions by Wanous, 1992; see Note 1.)

ment agencies or newspaper ads. As a result, such employees experience less of what has been called **entry shock**—the strong feelings of dismay, confusion, and disillusionment stemming from not having one's employment expectations met.[6] Not surprisingly, research has shown that about 30 percent more employees survive their jobs when they are recruited by inside sources than when recruited by outside sources.[7] People recruited by inside sources tend to have more realistic expectations about their jobs when they begin work, and are more accepting of any negative aspect of the job they may encounter.

To help ensure that employees do not respond negatively when they encounter unpleasant aspects of their new jobs, some corporate recruiters go out of their way to give job candidates highly accurate descriptions—both positive and negative—of the jobs they will perform and the organizations they will enter, what has been called **realistic job previews**.[8] Growing evidence suggests that people exposed to such previews later report higher satisfaction and show lower turnover than those who receive glowing, but often unrealistic, information about the companies in question. In particular, employees given realistic job previews—information designed to counter overoptimistic *and* overpessimistic expectations—tend to be more satisfied and are less likely to quit their jobs, than those given less realistic previews.[9] By making their expectations more realistic, employees are less likely to resign when they confront negative conditions (see Figure 6-3). For this reason, it makes sense for recruiters to not only inform prospective employees about the many benefits of working for their companies (as they are already prone to do), but to supplement this information with realistic accounts of what life will be like in the organization. Painting only a positive picture will surely lead to disappointment later on.

BREAKING IN: THE ENCOUNTER STAGE

The second major stage in organizational socialization begins when individuals actually assume their new duties. During this stage, they face several key tasks. First, of course, they must master the skills required by their new jobs.[10] Second, they must become oriented to the practices and procedures of the new organization, the way things are done there. As part of this, they must learn the organization's *culture*, the shared attitudes, values, and expectations of existing organizational members (we will discuss this topic fully in Chapter 14).[11] Third, new members of an orga-

FIGURE 6-4
CORPORATE ORIENTATION PROGRAMS: A VITAL ASPECT OF SOCIALIZATION
As part of its employee orientation efforts, Union Pacific Railroad employees are fully briefed about the railroad's safety procedures. Here, Bob Morgan describes the latest techniques at the railroad's special "Safety Support Wagon" in California.

nization must establish good social relations with others. They must get to know these people, and gain their acceptance. Only when they do can they become full members of the team.

It is during the encounter stage that formal *corporate orientation programs* are conducted. As we will describe below, these are sessions designed to formally teach new employees about their organizations—not only the ways they operate, but also information about their histories, missions, and traditions (see Figure 6-4). Such programs are considered a vital part of employee training (see Chapter 2). Without them, employees are likely to find it harder to fit in and to understand what the organization is all about. Although much of what is covered in such sessions may be picked up informally over time, formal orientation programs are highly efficient ways of indoctrinating new employees and to introduce them to company officials. Of course, such efforts are merely supplements to the informal socialization between co-workers that may be expected to go on continuously. (As you might imagine, the process of breaking in involves more than just passively listening to what a company official tells you, but also the process of actively collecting information to help you do your job better. For a closer look at this process and its impact, see the Quest for Quality section on the following page.)

SETTLING IN: THE METAMORPHOSIS STAGE

Sometime after an individual enters an organization, he or she attains full-member status. Depending on the type and length of the orientation program used, this entry may be marked by a formal ceremony, or it may be quite informal. In the former case, individuals may attend a dinner, reception, or graduation exercise at which they exchange their temporary, provisional title (e.g., trainee or apprentice) for a more permanent one. Alternatively, they may receive a concrete sign of their new status (e.g., the key to the executive washroom or a pass to the executive dining room). In other cases, especially when training has been short or informal, full acceptance into the work group may not be marked by any specific ceremony at all. Instead, it may be acknowledged by informal actions, such as being invited to lunch by one's new co-workers.

Whatever form it takes, the settling-in phase of socialization marks important shifts both for individuals and for organizations. Employees now make permanent adjustments to their jobs (e.g., they resolve conflicting demands between their jobs and their personal lives). And organizations now treat them as if they will be long-term members of the work team rather than temporary fill-ins.

ORIENTATION PROGRAMS: EFFORTS TO SOCIALIZE EMPLOYEES

Most organizations have some type of program or procedure designed to help new employees adjust to their jobs. As you might imagine, these differ with respect to not only the forms they take but the impact they have on individuals and organizations.

INFORMATION SEEKING: A KEY TO SUCCESSFUL NEWCOMER SOCIALIZATION

Suppose it's your first day on a new job as a staff accountant. There's a lot to learn. For example, how do you use the company's software? Exactly what are you expected to do? What do you have to do to fit in and be accepted by the other employees? The sooner you can obtain good answers to such questions, the more successful you are likely to be, and the happier you will be. In short, for companies to obtain high-quality output and for individuals to enjoy a high quality of life at work, employees must become well socialized to their new surroundings. But how? Recent research suggests that the socialization process is greatly enhanced by the questions people ask, the efforts they make to fit in—a process known as *information seeking*.[12]

This process was examined in a recent study by Morrison, who administered a questionnaire to 240 newly hired staff accountants working at five accounting firms.[13] The questionnaire assessed the employees' reports of how frequently they sought information from various sources (e.g., their immediate supervisors, other new accountants, a secretary, and written materials) during the first six months of their employment. Specifically, they were asked to consider the way they attempted to gain each of five different types of information:

- *Normative information*, the behaviors and attitudes one's company values and expects
- *Technical information*, how to do one's job
- *Referent information*, what one is expected to do
- *Performance feedback*, information about how well one is doing
- *Social feedback*, the appropriateness of one's social behavior at work

Measures were also taken of several variables hypothesized to be related to information seeking, including how well they mastered their jobs, how clearly they defined their roles (i.e., what they were expected to do), and how well they fit into different social groups.

Morrison found that various types of information seeking were significantly related to these variables in an interesting pattern (see Figure 6-5). Specifically, she found that (1) the more newcomers sought technical information and performance feedback, the better they were able to do their jobs, (2) the more newcomers sought referent information and performance feedback, the clearer it was to them what they were expected to do, and (3) the more newcomers sought normative information and social feedback, the better they fit into their companies' various social groups.

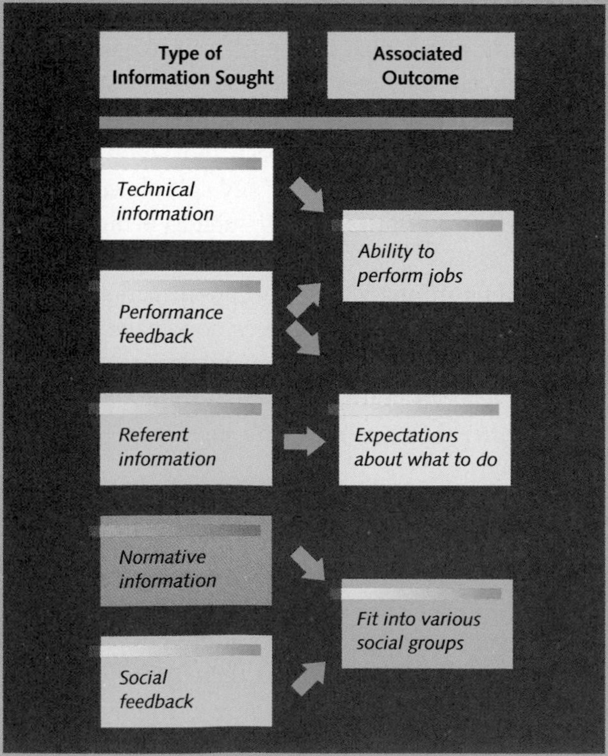

FIGURE 6-5
INFORMATION: A VITAL INGREDIENT IN SOCIALIZATION
In a recent study, Morrison found that newcomers sought specific types of information, which helped socialize them toward various aspects of their jobs. (Source: Based on data reported by Morrison, 1993; see Note 12.)

What makes these findings so interesting is that they paint a picture of the organizational newcomer not as a passive recipient of what his or her work environment has to offer, but as an active, information-seeking participant in the socialization process. In other words, people actively attempt to learn the ropes from different people in their environments. These "ropes" consist of various types of information, which ultimately help employees do a better job of working and fitting in in numerous ways. Obviously, the seeking of information is *not* a sign of weakness, but a critical aspect of learning one's job. Quality organizational performance demands that employees have a clear understanding of their job skills, and feedback is a significant ingredient in attaining such understanding.

BASIC DIMENSIONS OF ORGANIZATIONAL SOCIALIZATION

Have you ever seen ceremonies of a graduating class from a police academy? If so, then you already know that these men and women have just completed a rigorous program (often lasting several months) designed to mold them into police officers. Of course, not all orientation programs are as long or as formal. In fact, orientation programs come in many different forms. According to Van Mannen and Schein, researchers who have studied the orientation process in great detail, the differences between these efforts can be characterized with respect to the six distinct dimensions shown in Table 6-1.[14]

First, socialization programs differ with respect to whether newcomers are socialized *individually* or in *groups*. The former approach is often adopted by organizations that hire people at different times throughout the year. However, the latter approach is adopted by organizations that hire groups of workers at specific times. When this occurs, the company can efficiently orient members of the

TABLE 6-1

Basic Dimensions of Organizational Socialization

Programs of organizational socialization can vary along each of the dimensions listed here.

DIMENSION	EXPLANATION
Individual–Group	*Are newcomers socialized individually or as part of groups of trainees?*
Informal–Formal	*Is training formal or informal?*
Sequential–Nonsequential	*Do newcomers progress toward full-member status one step at a time, or do they become members as soon as orientation is over?*
Serial–Disjunctive	*Is training conducted by members of the organization or by others?*
Investiture–Divestiture	*Does training seek to affirm the self-confidence of newcomers or reduce it?*
Fixed–Variable	*Do newcomers know or not know when their probationary period will end?*

Source: *Based on suggestions by Van Maanen & Schein, 1991, see Note 14.*

incoming group all at once. If you've ever attended an orientation session for entering freshmen at your college or university, then you are probably already familiar with the group approach to socialization.

Second, socialization can be *formal,* as in the program just mentioned, or *informal*, accomplished in the absence of any structured programs. Formal programs are generally used when new employees are highly unfamiliar with their new roles or in connection with complex jobs (as in the "basic training" received in the military).[15] Informal programs are often used when employees already know much about their positions, or when their jobs are simple.

Third, socialization can be *sequential*, involving a process in which recruits obtain full membership in the organization by passing through a series of stages that represent their position in the organization (often with titles that match their position in the sequence, such as trainee, apprentice, or assistant). In contrast, socialization also can be *nonsequential*. Here, newcomers receive full-member status as soon as orientation and training are completed.

A fourth dimension involves the question of whether newcomers are trained by experienced members of the group (*serial* training) or by people who are not members of the organization itself (*disjunctive* training). In the latter type of training, professionals with special expertise are hired for this specific purpose.

Fifth, socialization programs often differ with respect to whether they are designed to affirm the ability and self-confidence of recruits (*investiture programs*) or to strip away their feelings of self-confidence so that they will be in a better state to accept new roles and patterns of behavior (*divestiture programs*). The former process is often used with high-level recruits—individuals hired because of the outstanding expertise they possess, people whom the organization does *not* wish to change. By contrast, divestiture programs are designed to strip away certain characteristics or attitudes that new recruits bring with them to the organization. Such tactics are often applied to people entering military service or college-level athletic programs. The goal is to "shake them up," so they more readily surrender any old attitudes and behaviors that may be counterproductive, and accept the new ones of the organization.

Sixth, socialization programs differ in terms of whether newcomers know in advance when their probationary period will end (fixed programs), or do not know exactly when they will gain full acceptance (variable programs).

Although these seem like a complex array of different dimensions, research has shown that they reflect only a single underlying dimension: *institutionalized socialization* versus *individualized socialization.*[16] Institutionalized socialization involves procedures in which all newcomers move through a formal, shared initiation process involving a fixed sequence of steps. Role models are provided (in the form of current employees), and socialization confirms the newcomer's identity and self-confidence (investiture). In contrast, individualized socialization is characterized by informal, individually tailored procedures, on-the-job training, and divestiture, in which newcomers' identities are disconfirmed rather than enhanced. Both types are widely used, but as we will shortly see, they have somewhat different effects on newcomers and their later performance.

THE IMPACT OF SOCIALIZATION TACTICS

As we have just noted, the procedures used by organizations to socialize new members differ in many ways. Given the scope of these differences, it seems only reasonable to expect that these contrasting tactics might yield different patterns of behavior or performance among newcomers. In fact, research by Allen and Meyer shows that this appears to be the case.[17]

These researchers suggested that the two kinds of socialization procedures described above—institutionalized versus individualized—might be related to important aspects of employees' behavior: (1) their **role orientation** with respect to their jobs—whether they adopted an *innovative* perspective in which they were willing to alter various aspects of their jobs, or a *custodial* perspective in which they were unwilling to make such alterations, and (2) their level of organizational commitment (see Chapter 5). Allen and Meyer predicted that institutionalized socialization procedures would increase organizational commitment but reduce employees' tendencies to adopt an innovative perspective. By contrast, they expected that individualized socialization practices would reduce organizational commitment, but foster an innovative perspective. Their rationale was as follows. Institutionalized socialization procedures (which expose all newcomers to shared experiences and enhance their self-confidence) increase organizational commitment to a greater extent than individualized procedures. Correspondingly, because of their fixed, formal nature, institutionalized socialization procedures foster a custodial, "don't-rock-the-boat" approach among newcomers, while individualized procedures encourage a higher level of job innovation.

To test these predictions, recent graduates of an M.B.A. program were asked to complete questionnaires describing the socialization practices used by the organizations they had recently joined, as well as to report on the extent to which they had changed procedures for doing their jobs (i.e., whether they had adopted a custodial or innovative role orientation). They also completed a measure of organizational commitment. Participants completed the last of these measures twice—six months and twelve months after graduation—to determine whether the effects of contrasting socialization practices changed over time.

Results offered clear support for both major predictions. As expected, institutionalized tactics of socialization promoted a custodial orientation among participants, whereas individualized tactics encouraged an innovative orientation (see Figure 6-6). Institutionalized tactics also were associated with higher levels of organizational commitment, whereas individualized procedures were associated with lower levels of commitment. Both effects were observed at both six and twelve months, although they were stronger on the first occasion than on the second.

These findings point to two important conclusions with practical implications for organizations. First, the socialization practices adopted by a company have important, and relatively lasting, effects on the behavior and orientation of newcomers. Second, no single type of socialization practice is best. Rather, different approaches yield contrasting outcomes that, depending on the needs of a particular organization, are more or less desirable. For example, an organization wishing to instill higher levels of commitment among its new recruits might find institutionalized practices preferable to individualized ones. In contrast, an organization wishing to foster an innovative orientation among newcomers would probably prefer individualized procedures. Of course, as Allen and

FIGURE 6-6
SOCIALIZATION TACTICS: THEIR DIFFERENTIAL IMPACT
Allen and Meyer found that individualized socialization and institutionalized socialization had different effects on organizational commitment and innovativeness. (Source: Based on data reported by Allen & Meyer, 1990; see Note 17.)

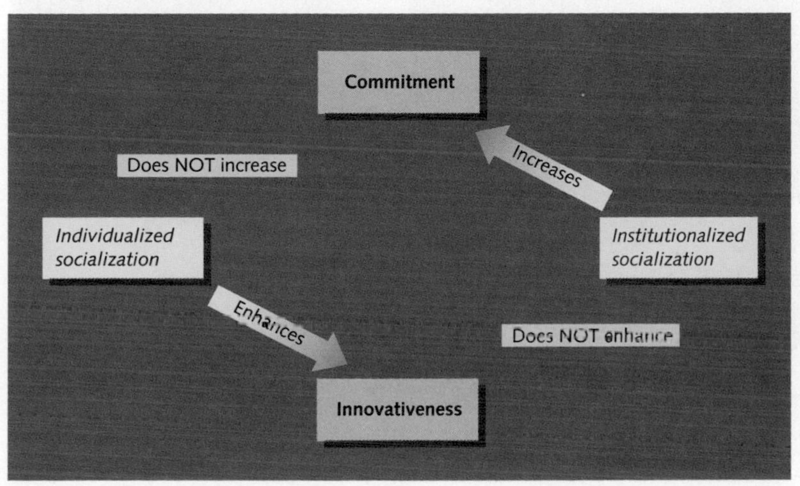

Meyer note, it may be possible to combine elements of both approaches to foster high levels of commitment *and* innovativeness. In any case, these and other findings suggest that what organizations do to teach newcomers the ropes can have lasting effects on those employees' performance and attitudes.

MENTORING: ONE-ON-ONE SOCIALIZATION

At Fu Associates Ltd. (a computer consulting firm in Arlington, Virginia), all new employees start out working directly with a mid-level manager who shows them the ropes. After a few months, Ed Fu, the owner and senior systems analyst, selects a few of the more promising new employees to work with him on important projects (see Figure 6-7). Fu describes it as "looking for talent," but his employees refer to the process as "Fu-izing."[18] The more standard term for this practice is **mentoring**, the process by which a more experienced employee—known as a **mentor**—advises, counsels, and otherwise enhances the personal development of a new employee, known as a **protégé**.[19] If you've ever had an older, more experienced person take you under his or her wing and guide you, then you probably already know how valuable mentoring can be. Indeed, research has shown that mentoring is strongly associated with career success: the more mentoring people receive, the more promotions they receive and the more highly they are compensated.[20]

In this section of the chapter we will examine various aspects of the mentoring relationship. First we will take a closer look at exactly what mentors do. Second, we will consider the benefits and costs of being involved in mentoring relationships. Third, we will review the various phases of the mentoring process. Then, finally, we will summarize important race and gender differences in mentoring relationships.

WHAT DO MENTORS DO?

Research on the nature of mentor–protégé relationships suggests that mentors do many things for their protégés.[21] For example, they provide much-needed emo-

FIGURE 6-7
MENTORING: AN IMPORTANT FORM OF SOCIALIZATION
Ed Fu, head of his own computer consulting firm, Fu Associated Ltd., believes in helping employees develop by closely mentoring them. Meeting with him are his protégés, Amy Stock (left) and Halli Kunze.

tional support and confidence for those who are just starting out and are likely to be insecure about their abilities. Mentors also help pave the way for their protégés' job success, such as by nominating them for promotions and by providing opportunities for them to demonstrate their competence. They also suggest useful strategies for achieving work objectives, typically ones that protégés might not generate for themselves. In doing all these things, they help bring the protégé to the attention of top management—a necessary first step for advancement. Finally, mentors often protect their protégés from the repercussions of errors, and help them avoid situations that may be risky for their careers.

In short, mentors do a number of things designed to help protégés in their careers. Yet, as beneficial as mentor–protégé relationships may be, not all new employees seek out mentors. Because becoming someone's protégé is so potentially valuable to one's career, you would expect that those individuals who enter into such relationships are more interested in achieving success than those who do not. Indeed, research has found this to be the case. In a questionnaire comparing the personalities of employees who were protégés with those who were not, Fagenson found that protégés had higher needs for power and achievement (see Chapter 3).[22] To the extent that those interested in becoming successful and powerful members of their organizations might seek the mentorship of more experienced employees, this finding makes a great deal of sense.

BENEFITS AND COSTS OF MENTORING

"True mentoring is a process by which you buy into another's dream," according to Ben Borne, a human resources consultant. "It is a dynamic partnering that benefits all the participants."[23] The main benefits to protégés, of course, are the various types of career support received, as noted above. But Borne is correct in implying that mentor–protégé relationships may benefit the mentor as well. Indeed, it would be misleading to depict mentors as totally selfless benefactors who seek nothing in return for their guidance.[24]

Often people become mentors because they are very appreciative of receiving such help earlier in their careers. For example, Borne recalls how senior managers at Motorola and Kaiser Aluminum helped him get started some thirty-five years ago. Knowing what it's like to have people pay attention to you, he is pleased to be in the position to offer help to junior colleagues who now need his assistance. In other words, mentors may reap psychological benefits from feeling needed, and a sense of accomplishment in helping the younger generation.

However, the gratification that comes from teaching another to become successful is not the only source of benefit for mentors. Often, in exchange for their guidance, mentors expect certain things from their protégés that help them in other ways. First, they expect their protégés to work hard at the tasks assigned to them—a way of getting a highly productive employee. Second, mentors often expect protégés to be loyal supporters within the organization. (After all, they are now members of the mentor's team!) Third, mentors may gain recognition from others in the company for their work in helping nurture young talent, and can bask in the reflected glory of any success achieved by their protégés.

This is not to say that mentor-protégé relationships are totally without any potential risks.[25] For example, protégés may find that their own success hinges on the success of their mentor. If the mentor should happen to be a falling star in the company, and suffers setbacks, the protégé's own career may be in jeopardy.

Indeed, in some cases protégés may find themselves without a job if a purge follows defeat in a political power struggle (see Chapter 12). Likewise, because the protégé's behavior reflects on the mentor, any failures on the part of the protégé may harm the mentor's reputation.

In addition, there's always the risk that a mentor's advice might not be as good as possible. This can be problematic, regardless of whether the protégé follows the bad advice (and receives a negative outcome), or does not follow it (and risks insulting the mentor). To the extent that the mentor and protégé blame each other for the poor result, their relationship is likely to develop an uncomfortable level of conflict (see Chapter 11) and break down as a result.

Finally, there's always the risk that protégés will become so highly dependent on their mentors that they will become slow to develop as self-reliant individuals. By the same token, it's possible for mentors to grow overly reliant on their protégés for help, giving them too many responsibilities that the mentors should be discharging themselves. It is, of course, one thing to help guide someone, and another to have them do too much of your work for you.

HOW DOES THE MENTORING PROCESS DEVELOP?

As you might expect, mentor–protégé relationships do not develop at random. Mentors are usually older than their protégés (by about eight to fifteen years).[26] They also tend to be individuals with considerable power and status in their companies. As a result, they can assist rising young stars without feeling threatened. On some occasions, mentor–protégé relationships are initiated by the mentor, who recognizes something impressive about the junior person. It is also possible for junior employees to approach prospective mentors about the possibility of entering into a mentoring relationship. The authors are aware that both sources of initiation occur in the case of mentor-protégé relationships with which they are very familiar—the relationship between a professor and a doctoral student. Regardless of which party initiates the relationship, for it to succeed, both must enter into it willingly—and, of course, the organization must be supportive of this association. In fact, some organizations so strongly believe in the benefits of mentoring that they are unwilling to leave the process to chance, and in recent years have formally encouraged or even required mentoring in corporate-wide programs.[27] For an overview of some of these practices, see Table 6-2.

Most human relationships develop over time, and mentorship is no exception. In fact, most mentor–protégé relationships seem to pass through several distinct phases.[28] The first, known as *initiation*, lasts from six months to a year and represents the period during which the relationship gets started and takes on importance for both parties. The second phase, known as *cultivation*, may last from two to five years. During this time, the bond between mentor and protégé deepens, and the young individual may make rapid career strides because of the skilled assistance he or she is receiving.

The third stage, *separation*, begins when the protégé feels it is time to assert independence and strike out on his or her own, or when there is some externally produced change in their roles (e.g., the protégé is promoted, or the mentor is transferred). Separation also can occur if the mentor feels unable to continue providing support and guidance to the protégé (e.g., if the mentor becomes ill). As you might imagine, this phase can be quite stressful if the mentor resents the protégé's growing independence, or if he or she feels that the mentor has withdrawn support prematurely.

TABLE 6-2

Mentorship Programs: What Some Companies Are Doing

Because the mentoring process is so very important, many companies have been unwilling to leave it to chance, and have developed formal mechanisms for bringing together mentors and protégés. Summarized here are some of these practices—many of which involve small groups devoted to mentoring.

COMPANY	DESCRIPTION
Colgate-Palmolive	*All new white-collar employees are assigned individual higher-ranking employees to serve as mentors.*
NYNEX	*Mentoring circles, consisting of six lower-ranking and two higher-ranking female employees, meet monthly to discuss work-related issues.*
Dow Jones	*Groups of four are formed consisting of a high-level mentor and three others: a white male, a woman of any race, and a minority group member of either gender.*
Chubb & Son Insurance	*In its Sponsorship Program, three protégés are assigned to each of ten different mentors.*

Source: Based on information in Granfield, 1992; see Note 27.

If this separation is successful, the relationship may enter a final stage, termed *redefinition*. Here, both persons perceive their bond primarily as one of friendship. They come to treat one another as equals, and the roles of mentor and protégé fade away completely. However, the mentor may continue to take pride in the accomplishments of his or her former protégé. Likewise, the protégé may continue to feel a debt of gratitude toward the former mentor. Although there is bound to be variation in the way mentor–protégé relationships actually develop, it is safe to say that these phases represent a relatively good picture of the generic way in which these important relationships unfold (see summary in Figure 6-8).

At this point, we note that not all mentor–protégé relationships involve intense, long-term relationships. In addition to the *primary mentoring* we have described thus far (marked by intense socialization efforts by one individual), another, less intense form known as *secondary mentoring* also exists.[29] This form of mentoring—probably more commonly found—is shorter and less intense, and tends to focus more directly on career-related issues than on personal and psychological ones. In addition, young employees may receive assistance from several different mentors rather than from only one, as is the case in primary mentoring. Still, evidence suggests that even secondary mentoring can be a highly effective tool for enhancing one's early career success.[30]

RACE AND GENDER DIFFERENCES IN MENTORING

As we have described it, mentoring is an extremely intensive form of professional involvement—one that requires a great deal of time and giving of one's energies. In view of the personal nature of the experience—the giving of guidance and emotional support—there is reason to suspect that the nature of the relationship

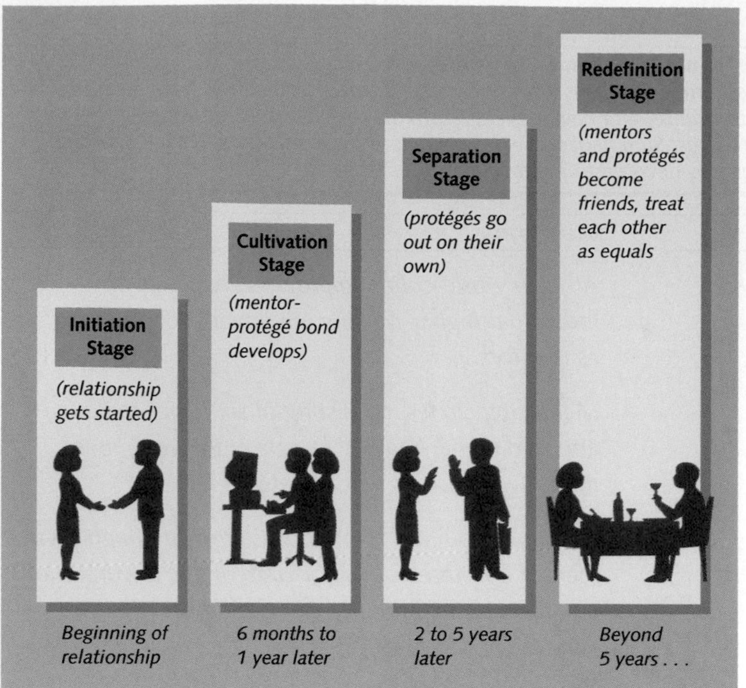

FIGURE 6-8
THE FOUR STAGES OF THE MENTORING PROCESS
Mentoring relationships generally develop following the four different stages summarized here. (Source: Based on suggestions by Kram, 1983; see Note 28.)

will depend on the level of comfort between the parties. Relationships between mentors and protégés who are different from each other might be somewhat strained. For this reason, pairings in which mentors and protégés are of the opposite gender or different races involve some special dynamics.

GENDER AND MENTORING

When one thinks of mentors, the image often comes to mind of an older male senior executive helping a younger male junior executive work his way up the corporate ladder by introducing him to the "old boy network," the small group of established, powerful people who really run an organization. By definition, any old *boy* network is sexist. And, indeed, women often seem to have less access to suitable mentors than men do.

Several factors contribute to this state of affairs.[31] First, there are simply fewer female executives available to serve as mentors for young female employees. Of course, the problem is cyclical and self-fulfilling: fewer mentors attract fewer potential protégés, leading to fewer future mentors, and so on. With this in mind, Chubb & Son has found that its Sponsorship Program has led to the promotion of over half of the company's female protégés within only two years.[32] Clearly, this one company's efforts have appeared to break the cycle.

A second reason why women may have fewer mentoring opportunities than men is that women are less willing to enter into mentoring relationships because they anticipate greater risks than men in doing so. Specifically, in a recently conducted survey women expressed more concern than men about the potential for negative exposure that might come from the increased visibility they assume because of their protégés. [33] Moreover, compared to males, women believed that they lacked the necessary qualifications to become a mentor. Interestingly, it was found that women were equally as willing as men to engage in mentoring, but perceived that there would be more drawbacks in actually doing so.

In surveying several hundred employees about their experiences in obtaining mentors, Ragins and Cotton confirmed that women perceived greater barriers to mentorship than men.[34] Specifically, compared to men, women reported having both more limited access to suitable mentors and less willingness to assume the role of mentors (see Figure 6-9). Interestingly, despite these differences, both males and females were equally successful in obtaining mentors (about 50 percent in both cases). Thus, although females face greater obstacles to obtaining mentors, they appear to exert the extra effort needed to overcome them.

RACE AND MENTORING

Unfortunately, barriers to mentoring exist not only between men and women, but also between members of different racial groups. Insofar as mentors and protégés often get together because they have similar backgrounds and share similar

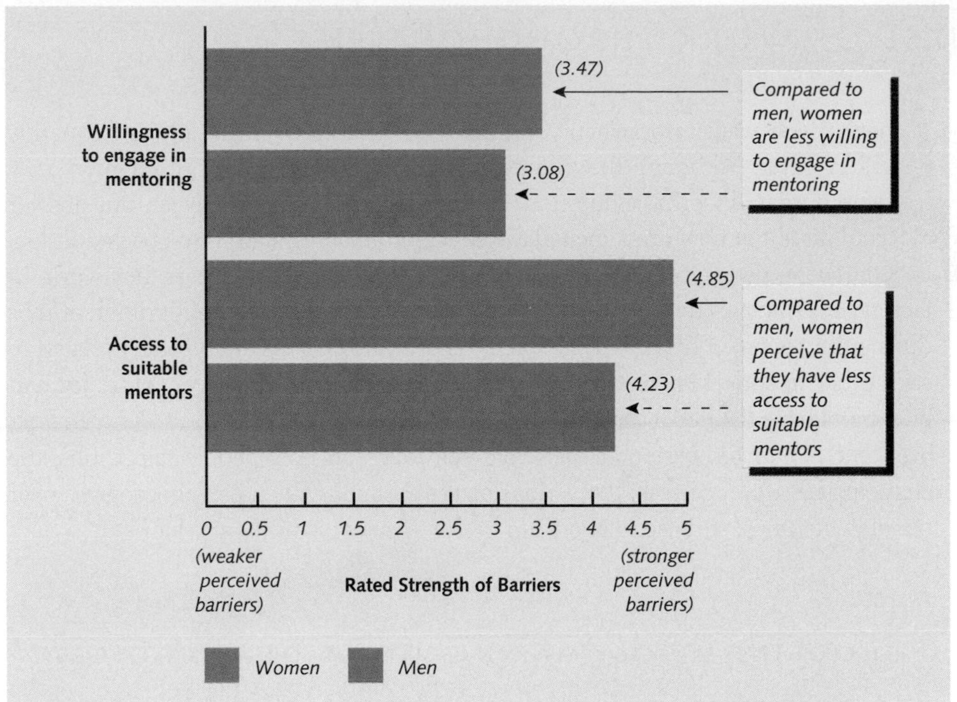

FIGURE 6-9
GENDER DIFFERENCES IN PERCEIVED BARRIERS TO MENTORING
As shown here, women perceive stronger barriers to obtaining a mentor at work than do men. Such differences exist with respect to several barriers to mentorship. (Higher numbers indicate stronger perceived barriers.) (Source: Based on data from Ragins & Cotton, 1993; see Note 32.)

attitudes, it is not surprising to find that people from different races face difficulties in their mentor-protégé relationships. To study this process, Thomas interviewed African-Americans and whites who were involved with each other in mentor–protégé relationships.[35] He found that one of the key factors linked to the success of their relationship was the parties' preferred strategies for dealing with racial differences. Specifically, two contrasting approaches were identified: *denial and suppression* (not discussing racial differences and denying that they might matter), and *direct engagement* (openly addressing racial differences and the role that they may play in their relationship).

Comparing these preferences between the whites and the African-Americans in his study, Thomas found that the nature of the mentor–protégé relationship depended on the degree to which the parties preferred similar or different strategies in dealing with their racial differences. Interestingly, neither party's preferred strategy alone was as important as the degree to which both individuals in each pair adopted the *same* strategy. Specifically, when both individuals either denied and suppressed their racial differences or when they both directly engaged each other in discussions about them, the nature of the mentoring was richer in important forms of social support than when the parties preferred different strategies. That is, the mentor not only provided instrumental guidance to the protégés about how to succeed in their careers, but they also provided psychosocial guidance and friendship. These important psychological support mechanisms were largely missing from the relationships between mentors and protégés who used different strategies in dealing with their racial differences. These findings suggest that protégés can, in fact, receive fulfilling mentoring experiences from individuals of different races, but that there is no one best way to address those differences. What matters most is that both parties agree in their strategies for dealing with them.

The fact that Thomas found the cross-race mentoring relationships to be largely successful is encouraging insofar as there are dramatic benefits to be derived for protégés who are members of minority groups. For example, Cox and Nkomo found that African-American employees who had mentors were more upwardly mobile than those who did not.[36] Anecdotal reports of various industry practices paint an equally encouraging picture. For example, at DuPont, where a formal mentoring program has been in place since 1985, the proportion of minorities in top management has risen from 10 percent to 30 percent in recent years, even as the overall number of management jobs has dropped.[37] It would appear that mentoring is a vital tool in the arsenal of those attempting to eliminate prejudicial attitudes and discriminatory behaviors toward minority groups (see Chapter 5).

CAREERS: THE COURSE OF WORK THROUGHOUT LIFE

What do you want to be when you grow up? That's a question adults frequently ask children. Although the traditional responses "nurse" and "firefighter" may seem outdated, both the question and the fact that it usually triggers any answer at all highlight how fundamental the concept of having a job is to one's adult life.

Of course, people typically have more than one job over the years they work. In fact, recent statistics reveal that the average American now holds eight different jobs during the course of his or her lifetime.[38] These various jobs are typically related to each other in some systematic way—that is, they represent a **career**. More formally, experts have defined a career as *the evolving sequence of a person's work experiences over time*.[39] Our discussion of this topic will focus on how people select jobs, the changing nature of careers, the various stages through which careers progress over people's lifetimes, and the relationship between careers and family life.

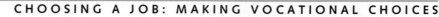

CHOOSING A JOB: MAKING VOCATIONAL CHOICES

How does someone decide what type of job to take? Although it would require a whole separate book to answer this question, we can identify several of the key factors responsible for the vocational choices people make.

To help identify the first factor, ask yourself: What kind of person becomes a doctor? How about a soldier? A car salesperson? To the extent that these job titles connote certain images to you, then it makes sense to consider the possibility that the jobs to which we are attracted may be ones that match the individual characteristics we possess. This is the idea of *person–job fit* discussed in Chapter 3. Are people prone to select jobs that match their personalities and values? Theorists, such as Holland, have claimed so, and research supports this notion.[40,41] For example, Chatman tracked the early careers of 171 entry-level auditors working in public accounting forms, and assessed the extent to which their personal values (e.g., concern about the welfare of others) matched those of the organizations in which they worked.[42] She found that the closer the fit, the more satisfied they were with their jobs, and the more interested they were in remaining there. The fit between personal and organizational values is so important, in fact, that it has been shown to be given greater weight than pay and promotional opportunities when it comes to selecting a job.[43]

Not only are people interested in selecting jobs that match their values, but they are also interested in selecting jobs that match their self-concepts—that is, their images of who they are. In other words, they attempt to match themselves to the *prototype* of a job—their belief about what the typical person who holds that job is like (see Chapter 2). So, for example, someone who sees herself as being more similar to the typical banker than the typical realtor would probably be more attracted to a career in banking than one in real estate. Testing this basic idea, Moss and Frieze asked a group of M.B.A. students to complete surveys in which they described both themselves and the typical person holding certain jobs.[44] By comparing the differences between these ratings, the researchers were able to come up with a measure of how closely people's own images matched the prototypes. Then, they asked them to rank-order their preferences for each of these jobs. When the researchers compared these rank orders to the matching scores, they found that people most preferred jobs whose prototypes closely matched their self-concepts, and least preferred those jobs in which there was less of a match. These findings suggest that people's attraction to various jobs is based, in large part, on the images they have of themselves and of the typical holder of such positions.

Not only are people generally interested in selecting jobs that match who they are, but they also may restrict their searches to jobs that are likely to be found and are believed to continue into the future. That is, people are inclined to be *rational* in their choice of jobs. There isn't much call for typesetters or blacksmiths today, so such positions may be dropped from consideration even by someone who really likes doing such work. By contrast, there are many different types of jobs that can be expected to grow in popularity, creating a wide variety of options for those who pursue them. In contrast to the traditional practice of training for a career in a certain field and expecting to work in it for a lifetime, human resources experts predict that in the years to come people will work in many jobs over their lifetimes—not because they change their minds, but because conditions will change very rapidly, eliminating the need for some jobs while creating others.[45] (For a closer look at what some of the most popular careers are likely to be in the years ahead, see the Organization of Tomorrow section below.)

THE ORGANIZATION OF TOMORROW

THE HOTTEST CAREERS FOR THE TWENTY-FIRST CENTURY

As the workplace changes, new career options appear and old ones disappear. One of the most important aspects of career planning is to keep abreast of the changing job scene, and to prepare for work in growth areas. With this in mind, experts have identified several areas in which job growth is expected to be much greater than average.[46] As you plan your own careers, you might find it useful to keep these trends in mind.

The first is *information technology*. The digital era has arrived, and jobs related to computers will be at the forefront of career growth in the years to come. Although this already has been the case for a decade, there are no signs of a slowdown. For example, the Bureau of Labor Statistics estimates that by the year 2005, there will be jobs for 317,000 additional *computer programmers*. By that same year, there also will be a 79 percent increase in the demand for specialists in the allied field of *systems analysis* (the creation of computer applications for specific business needs). We also can of expect lots of new jobs for *database managers* (people responsible for administering the systems controlling the vast amounts of information essential for business operations), *LAN administrators* (people who link together computer systems for efficient communication networks), and *telecommunications managers* (specialists in the transfer of information through telephones, modems, fax machines, voice mail, and teleconference facilities).

Another growth area for jobs, *education and training*, also reflects rapid changes in the ways companies do business. After all, as conditions change, companies need to rely on specialists who help their employees stay up-to-date. For example, *cross-cultural trainers* will become increasingly in demand as companies find themselves in need of learning about the customs of foreign nations where they do business. Also needed will be more *employee trainers* who can help individuals develop the new skills required to perform rapidly changing jobs (see Chapter 2). Because part of this job will fall into the laps of our schools as well, we also can expect a need for *school administrators* to create and evaluate changing academic curricula. Also needed will be specialists to keep up with changes in our response to the environment, such as *environmental consultants* (people who can help companies fulfill their obligations to keep the environment free of pollutants).

One of the era's most widely discussed topics for reform is *health care*, another area in which jobs are expected to continue to grow in the future. Although there are many medical specialists, there is—and will continue to be—a growing need for *family physicians*. With this, comes increased demand for allied members of the medical support team, such as *home health care nurses* (specializing in care for the sick at home), *nurse practitioners*, and *physical therapists*.

To keep organizations at the forefront of the changes they will confront, an increasing number of *managers* will be needed. These won't be run-of-the-mill general managers, but highly focused specialists. For example, there promises to be a growing demand for *diversity managers* (people who can make sure that members of a company's increasingly diverse workforce all get along), *environmental managers* (people to ensure that companies not only minimize their waste products, but also properly dispose of them), and *human resources managers* (specialists who can help organizations manage the increasingly complex issues of fair compensation, sexual harassment, and affirmative action).

As you can see from this description, there will be not only increased demand for some career choices that are currently well established (e.g., family physician), but also growth in some jobs that have developed only over the last few years (e.g., LAN administrator). In addition to these, there are also projected to be several types of jobs that are now in their infancy. Because these are so unique, we have highlighted them in Table 6-3. Of course, only time will tell for sure whether or not these prognostications will come true. But, based on the latest trends in job development, there appears to be good reason to expect that the jobs identified here will be heavily represented in tomorrow's organizations.

TABLE 6-3

Jobs Still In Their Infancy

As the nature work continues to change, several new kinds of jobs are coming into being. Here are some jobs with which you might not be familiar—at least yet—but which you can expect to hear more about in the future.

JOB	DESCRIPTION
50-Plus Marketer	*Specialists in advertising to the growing group of affluent baby-boomers, who are now turning 50.*
Managed-Care Manager	*People who help organizations manage relations with insurance companies to help find the most appropriate options for employees and rates for employers.*
Diversity Manager	*Experts who help highly diverse groups of employees work effectively in organizations; working with employers to attract and retain minority candidates, and training employees to adjust to diversity among their co-workers.*
Employee Leasing Agents	*Companies are beginning to "lease" employees from agents who make all the arrangements for insurance and taxes, and ensure compliance with legal regulations, thereby releasing employers from these responsibilities.*

Source: Based on material appearing in "The 25 hottest careers," see Note 46.

THE CHANGING NATURE OF CAREERS

As time marches on, the nature of people's jobs changes and the characteristics of organizations change—and as a result, so too do people's careers. According to Schein, these changes can be characterized as developments along three basic dimensions summarized in his *career cone* (see Figure 6-10).[47] First, careers often involve *vertical movement*—that is, promotions up an organizational hierarchy (such as from assistant manager to manager). Naturally, different people working in different settings experience vertical movement at tremendously different rates. Not only may people be prepared for advancement at different times, but also organizations may have different opportunities for promotion. In today's organizations, in which layers of management are being reduced all the time, there are fewer rungs in the organizational ladder, making opportunities for vertical movement more limited than they used to be.

FIGURE 6-10
SCHEIN'S CAREER CONE
According to Schein, careers can change along the three basic dimensions identified here: vertical movement, horizontal movement, and radial movement. (Source: Adapted from Schein, 1971; see Note 47.)

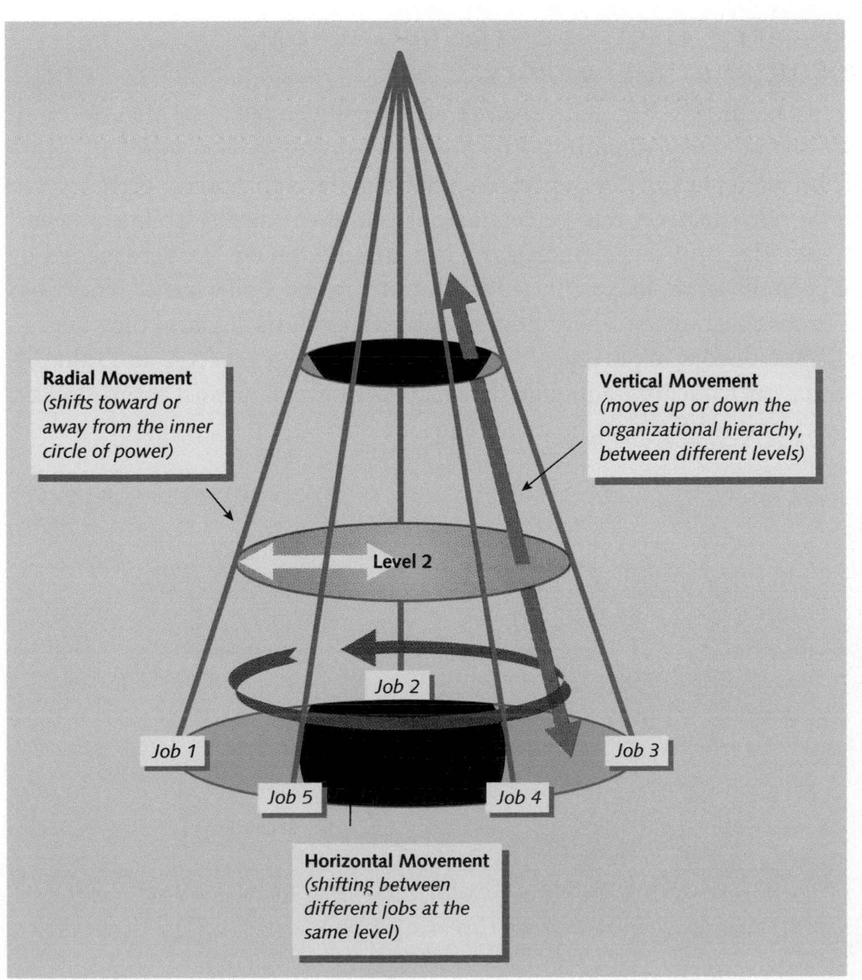

Second, careers often involve *horizontal movement*. This reflects changes in specific job functions, or sometimes, in major fields or specialties. For example, individuals who start out in marketing may move into the related field of sales. In recent years, growing numbers of people have been willing to make such horizontal moves, even though doing so may involve a considerable amount of retraining.[48] This trend may result from several sources, such as people's needs to seek fulfillment by doing different kinds of work, or by their belief that they might sooner be able to make a vertical movement by first moving horizontally into a field with greater opportunities for advancement.

Finally, careers also involve what Schein terms *radial movement*—shifts toward or away from the inner circle of management in an organization, the base of power. Such movement often follows vertical movement (i.e., promotion), but not always. For example, a manager of engineering operations for a television network, who works at its headquarters, may be promoted to the vice president of engineering (a higher rank) at one of the network's local affiliates. The promotion in this case is real, but the individual is now farther away from the organization's inner circle of power than before (both literally in terms of miles and figuratively in terms of influence).

At the same time careers develop along these three dimensions, they also seem to move through repeated cycles of stability and change.[49] Soon after an individual has been hired or promoted into a new position, a stage of *career growth* occurs. During this period, individuals consolidate their recent gains by acquiring the new skills and information needed to perform their current jobs effectively. As this process is completed, they enter a stage of *stabilization*, in which they are performing their jobs to their fullest capacity and things are on an even keel (for the time being, at least). This is followed by a period of *transition* in which individuals prepare themselves psychologically for their next move upward. During this period, they anticipate the demands of their next career stage and get ready to meet them. When the expected promotion arrives, the cycle starts over again. In short, the careers of many individuals are marked by a process in which they grow into each new position, become acclimated to it, and then begin preparations for the next step on the ladder (see Figure 6-11).

CAREER DEVELOPMENT: EARLY, MIDDLE, AND LATE STAGES

Just as people change their major life foci as they grow older (e.g., from preparing for marriage to preparing for grandchildren), so too do shifts occur in our careers. Organizational scientists often distinguish between the various issues that occur in people's careers during their *early*, *middle*, and *late* stages.

EARLY CAREER ISSUES: DEVELOPING ANCHORS AND CONFRONTING CHANGES

When people are just beginning their careers, usually in their 20s, they are faced with the issue of **career planning**—the process of deciding what jobs and activities will be attempted in the future. In selecting the appropriate path for our careers, we often rely on our perceptions of our own talents, abilities, needs, motives, attitudes, and values. Usually by our mid-30s we are strongly guided by these perceptions as we make choices about our careers. Collectively, Schein has referred to these various self-perceptions as **career anchors** because they tend to firmly attach individuals' careers to their underlying abilities, needs, and values.[50] Everyone has such anchors, although they may take several distinct forms. In fact, Schein has identified five specific career anchors.

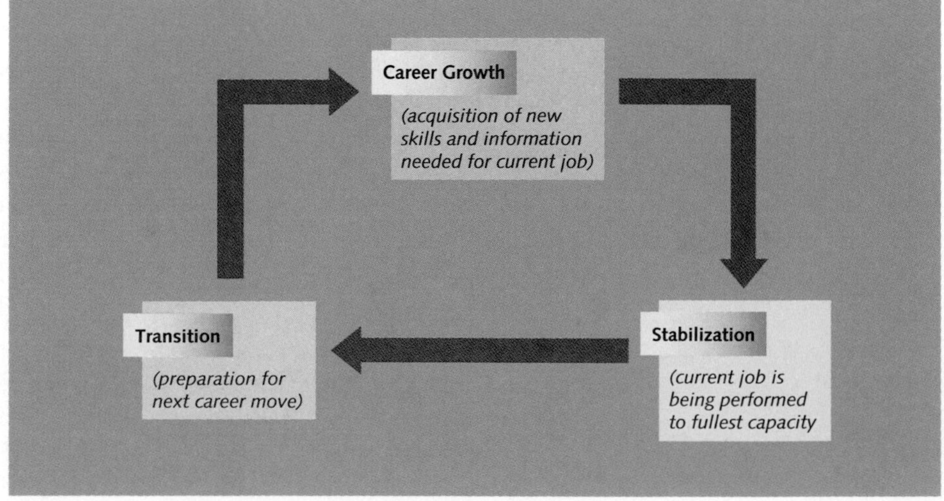

FIGURE 6-11
THE CAREER CHANGE CYCLE
Careers often move through repeated cycles of career growth, stabilization, and transition.

First, for some people career anchors are *technical* or *functional* in nature. Their primary concern in making job decisions and mapping their future careers involves the *content* of their work. Such individuals want to do certain things (e.g., cook, program computers, and so on), and plan their careers accordingly.

For a second group, career anchors emphasize not specific content areas, but *managerial competence*. People in this category want to attain high-level management positions. They like to analyze and solve difficult business problems, enjoy influencing others, and like exercising power. The career paths they choose allow them to do these things.

A third group is primarily concerned with *security* and *stability*. Their search for security often leads them to enter large, stable companies, and long-term employment with a single firm. Over the years, many people have sought positions with large companies such as IBM, AT&T, or General Motors in large part because of the security they provided. Today, however, as these companies face hard times, many individuals who looked for stability are now finding less security than they ever expected. This situation is particularly acute in Japan, where employees who toiled for lifetime security now find themselves victims of a troubled economy that threatens any hope of job security—and the viability of stability as a career anchor.[51]

In contrast, a fourth group emphasizes *creativity* or *entrepreneurship* in their career plans. Such people want to build or create a unique product or service of their own devising. They are good at starting and running small companies. But, like Steven Jobs, the founder and former head of Apple Computer, they may leave to take on new challenges once their organizations become too large. When this occurs, one's attention must turn to maintaining a large corporation instead of creating a new one. For those whose careers are anchored to more creative, entrepreneurial activities, this option may not be particularly attractive.

Finally, some individuals emphasize *autonomy* and *independence*. They want to be free of external constraints, and prefer to work at their own pace and with their own goals. Such people often seek careers in academia, or prefer to become novelists or creative artists. (See Figure 6-12 for a summary of these different career anchors.)

When people are aware of the factors that anchor their careers, it is possible for them to be more effective in searching for meaningful work. It is with this rationale in mind that Texas Instruments (TI) uses Schein's system for helping employees seek the most appropriate positions within their organizations.[52] In fact, attempts to determine people's career anchors are actively pursued at TI's Employee Development Center near Dallas. According to the company's manager for professional development, Sue Hensley, this facility was established in April 1991 "to encourage employees to take responsibility for their career development," and relies on the use of anchors as a tool to accomplish this mission.[53]

In addition to identifying the abilities, motives, and values that are important to them, people in the early stage of their careers also must confront another issue—*job changes*. Although it is often difficult to assume new positions, people often find it necessary to do so early in their careers. As people are just beginning their careers, not only might they find that certain jobs are not as attractive to them as they expected, but also that the path to upward advancement in one's chosen profession may be accelerated by taking positions in other organizations. Moreover, people are more likely to change jobs earlier in their careers rather than later because this is when they are first learning what they like and dislike about their chosen fields and discover which features they can expect to be improved at a new job, and which ones are simply typical of the profession and unlikely to change. In addition, peo-

FIGURE 6-12

CAREER ANCHORS

Individuals' perceptions of their own abilities, motives, and values often serve as career anchors. One or more of these anchors are frequently relied on as the basis for making career decisions. (Source: Based on suggestions by Schein, 1978; see Note 49.)

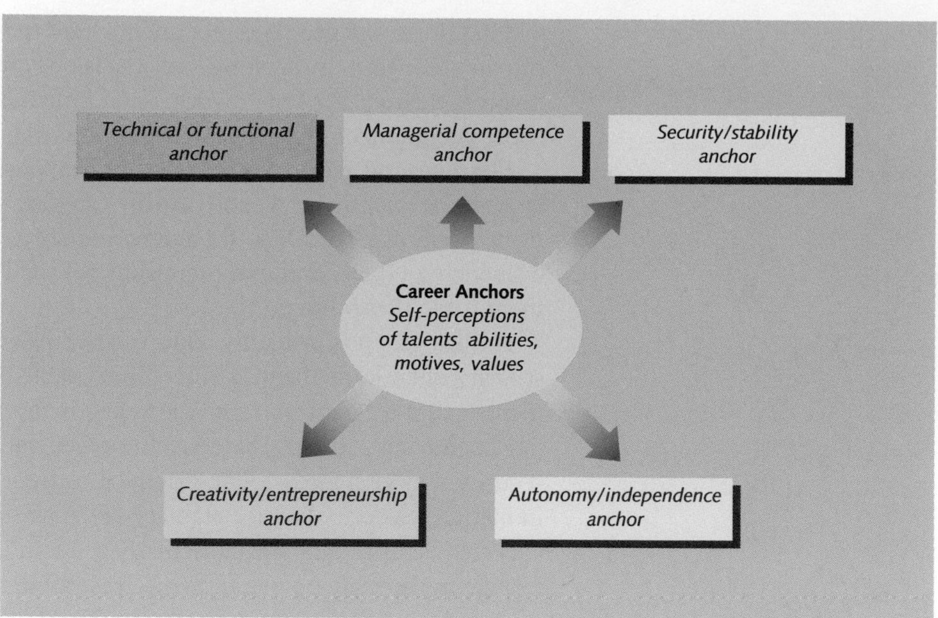

ple often find it easier to change jobs when they are younger and are more mobile than when they are older and have families to consider.

MIDDLE CAREER ISSUES: DEALING WITH THE CAREER PLATEAU

Once early career issues have been addressed, people must face the vast stretch between youth and old age—that tough period in which people confront the reality that they may not go as far as they wished, and will never fulfill their fondest career dreams.[54] At the same time, members of the 40-something crowd are likely to look ahead and see that there are fewer promotions available for them—a stage known as a **career plateau**.[55] Many people today may be reaching this point much sooner than expected because many companies are downsizing, making competition for jobs quite intense (see Chapter 16). Not only may new jobs be hard to find, but as companies confront the need for economic belt-tightening, people might find that new positions are not particularly attractive because they do not offer the increased compensation expected.[56] So, for many people, the only viable option is to stay employed at a position, even if it does not offer everything they seek. Preparing financially for their children's college expenses and their own retirement, they simply stick it out.

Because the aging of the baby boom generation has created a sizable cohort of people who are now thundering over the hill, companies are seeking ways of reinvigorating them. To help, some companies are turning to various **career development interventions**—systematic efforts designed to assist individuals in managing their careers while also helping organizations achieve their goals (for a summary of some of the specific practices used in such programs, see Table 6-4).[57] At Chevron, for example, a consultant has been employed to help its employees stay productive when incentives such as raises and promotions come much more slowly than before.[58] Many employees are counseled to simply accept the fact that they may be doing jobs that bring little gratification, and to seek stimulation outside their jobs, such as through their family life and hobbies. Consider, for example, Michael Scofield, a 42-year-old staff psychologist at AT&T, who has shifted his expectations after being repeatedly passed over for promotion. Sticking with his job by day, he now coaches his children's sports teams on evenings and weekends. "Some would say I've lowered my goals to meet reality," Scofield admits, "I say I've exchanged career goals for a vision in life."[59]

Although some simply accept the status quo, others actively attempt to change things. So, when upward moves are limited, some employees move sideways, to other departments that allow them to face new challenges. In fact, between 1991 and 1993 some 1,000 Chevron employees moved to different areas of the company. Such changes don't come cheaply. At General Motors, for example, where the white-collar workforce has been cut in half over the last few years, $10 million per year has been spent retraining some 6,100 employees, helping them find new positions where they can make a contribution to the company.[60]

For some individuals, responding to the crises of mid-career takes the form of leaving their high-level corporate jobs completely and starting their own small businesses. This phenomenon is not quite as unusual as you might think. In fact, there is a growing number of people—referred to as *corporate refugees*—who drop out of the corporate world to seek more gratifying work on their own.[61] As you might imagine, their adjustment takes some time—often about two to three years. After all, people making these changes need to learn new skills, develop a business plan, raise capital for their enterprise, and get the project going, all of which can be quite time consuming, and not at all easy. But corporate refugees are not looking for an "easy way out," rather, they see a more fulfilling existence. Take Judy Sarkozy, for example. In 1983 she was a product manager at Kellogg (in Battle Creek, Michigan) who

TABLE 6-4

Career Development Interventions: A Summary of Selected Practices

Companies often engage in systematic efforts to help employees develop their careers while at the same time helping to meet their own goals—practices known as career development interventions. Summarized here are descriptions of a few popularly used interventions, and the names of some organizations that have used them.

NAME OF INTERVENTION	DESCRIPTION	COMPANIES USING IT
Self-assessment tools	*Employees complete exercises in career manuals and take workshops before meeting with career counselors*	*Hewlett-Packard, Lawrence Livermore Laboratories*
Individualized counseling	*Meetings with trained professionals who help employees assess their personal jobs skills and abilities*	*Coca Cola, Disneyland*
Information services (e.g., job posting systems, career resource centers)	*Facilities through which employees can learn about new career options within their companies, and how to train for them*	*CBS, Merck, Aetna, General Electric*
Organizational assessment programs	*Systematic testing and counseling of employees used to learn their skills and abilities so they can be placed into the positions into which they are best suited*	*AT&T, IBM, Ford Motor Company, Shell Oil, Kodak*
Outplacement programs	*Facilities to assist terminated employees, particularly those laid off by efforts to reduce the size of the workforce*	*Alcan Company, Exxon, Mutual of New York, General Electric, Corning Glass Works*

Source: Based on material appearing in Russell, 1991, see Note 57.

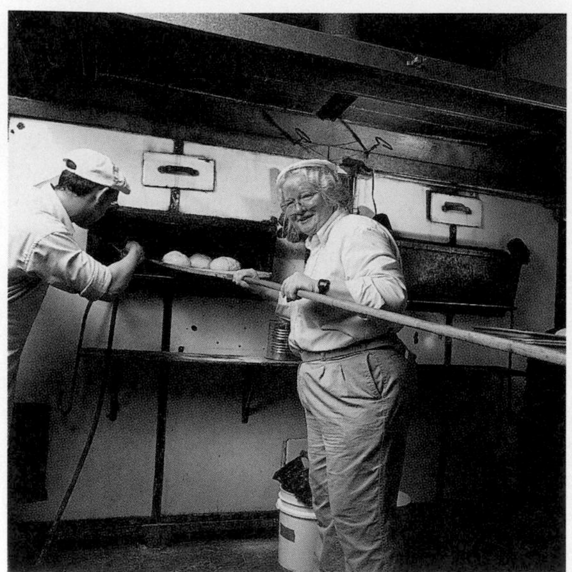

FIGURE 6-13
PORTRAIT OF A CORPORATE REFUGEE
After years of battling the bureaucracy in Battle Creek, Judy Sarkozy now finds fulfillment in running her bakery in Kalamazoo, Michigan.

became frustrated with the lack of autonomy she had in her job.[62] So, at age 51 she packed it all in for a low-tech alternative—joining her husband in opening a European-style bakery where they bake breads in a ninety-year-old brick oven (see Figure 6-13). Although there probably aren't too many high-ranking corporate managers who trade in their budget sheets for an oven, it is not at all unusual to find entrepreneurs who once held a variety of extremely different corporate posts. The growth in small business seen in recent years appears, to some extent, to reflect people's growing disenchantment with their career opportunities in the corporate arena.[63]

LATE-CAREER ISSUES: PREPARING FOR SUCCESSION AND RETIREMENT

It is often said that whatever goes up must also come down, and this adage applies as well to the course of one's career. Indeed, as people get older, they must face the fact that they may have advanced as far as they can in their careers and that they may never be able to attain their career dreams. They also must come to terms with the fact that, like their physical energies, their power and influence in the organization may be beginning to wane.

Another problem faced by older employees is that they may be the victims of negative stereotypes (see Chapter 2) and prejudicial attitudes (see Chapter 5). Typically, they are viewed as being less productive, efficient, motivated, and capable of working under pressure than younger people. Interestingly, such stereotypes persist despite strong evidence that they are inaccurate. Indeed, one recent review of previous research on the relationship between age and job performance suggests that older workers—probably because of their greater experience—are actually *more* productive than younger ones![64] Still, the stereotypes persist, a disconcerting reality for many individuals approaching the end of their careers.

Another late-career issue for many people is **job succession**—the process of identifying who will take over their positions when they retire. Few people who have spent years building up a business or department take this matter lightly. They want someone to follow in their footsteps who shares their values, will maintain the standards they have established, and will work to achieve their long-range goals. Not only might finding a successor be important to the retiring individual, but also to the organization itself. Because it is crucial to the long-term strategic success of any organization to have talented individuals available to guide it, most organizations carefully develop *succession plans* for its key personnel.[65] One popular way of identifying successors, particularly for top executive positions, is by having the outgoing individual identify and help develop a successor. Mentorship at this level not only assures the retiring executive that he or she will have a successor qualified to fill the post, but also helps prepare the successor for the job, and soothes his or her transition within the organization.

Naturally, an important issue at the late stage of one's career is preparation for retirement. This involves a gradual reorientation away from careers and work toward the leisure-time activities that will become dominant during the years ahead. In addition, it should involve careful planning to meet the special challenges faced by retired workers—a loss of social contact with many friends, reduced feelings of accomplishment, and reduced earnings, to name just a few.

Fortunately, growing evidence suggests that if individuals take the time to prepare for such changes, the end of their working years can be a new beginning.[66] It can mark entry into a period of renewed personal growth and fulfillment, rather than merely signaling decline.

CAREERS AND FAMILIES IN THE 1990s: A DELICATE BALANCING ACT

If you're currently of college age (in your late teens or early 20s), there's a good chance that your parents grew up in a household that was very different than the one in which you were raised. Twenty to thirty years ago, the typical nuclear family consisted of a husband who worked outside the home, a wife working as a homemaker, and two children. Today, however, this configuration exists in less than 4 percent of all American households.[67] In fact, in over half of all American families both spouses work outside the home (known as *dual-career couples*).[68] In addition, about twice as many children are currently being raised in single-parent families (mostly mothers) compared to 1970, and two-thirds of these single parents work outside the home.[69]

As you might imagine, these changing demographics have had considerable impact on the nature of people's careers, and organizational specialists have been highly involved in studying them.[70] When both members of married couples work outside the home, it becomes particularly challenging to be able to balance the demands of one's job (e.g., to work late to meet special projects) with the demands of one's family life (e.g., playing with the children)—what has been referred to as a *work–family conflict.* Research has shown that work–family conflicts are major sources of stress (see Chapter 7) that can have profound negative impact on people's satisfaction with both their work lives and their family lives, increasing depression and lowering overall life satisfaction.[71] In addition, because the demands of one's family life can interfere with one's work performance, job performance can suffer, and lowered income can result.[72]

In view of the changing nature of the workplace and the adjustments that people must make, many companies are working hard to resolve some of the problems of work–family conflict, and the logistic problems faced by dual-career couples.[73] Here are some of the main ways they are going about it:

- **Flextime programs:** policies that give employees some discretion over when they can arrive and leave work, thereby making it easier to adapt their work schedules to the demands of their personal lives. Typically, employees must work a common core of hours, such as 9:00 A.M. to 12 noon and 1:00 to 3:00 P.M. Scheduling of the remaining hours, within certain spans (such as 6:00 to 9:00 A.M. and 3:00 to 6:00 P.M.), is then left up to the employees themselves. Generally, such programs have been well received, and have been linked to improvements in performance and job satisfaction, as well as drops in employee turnover and absenteeism.[74] In recent years companies such as Pacific Bell and Duke Power Company have found that flexible work scheduling has helped their employees meet the demands of juggling their work and family lives.[75]

- **Family leave programs:** policies that give employees time off their jobs (often some portion of which is paid) to devote to starting a new family. At Aetna Life & Casualty, for example, a few years ago nearly one-third of the women who took maternity leave didn't return to work, causing the company to lose some of its best human resources. However, within two years after introducing a family leave program, 91 percent returned to their jobs, saving the company the considerable time and money it would have cost to replace these employees.[76]

- **Child care facilities:** sites at or near company locations where parents can leave their children while they are working. America West, for example believes so strongly in providing child care that it provides these services twenty-four hours a day, and maintained these benefits even while it was going through Chapter 11 bankruptcy proceedings (see Figure 6-14).[77]
- **Personal support policies:** practices that help employees meet the demands of their family lives, freeing them to concentrate on their work. These are often varied in nature. For example, the SAS Institute (Cary, North Carolina) not only offers its employees free, on-site Montessori child care, but also nutritious take-home dinners. The *St. Petersburg Times* advises its employees about ways to help meet the problems of elderly family members.[78] Lancaster Laboratories (Lancaster, Pennsylvania) goes one better by providing on-site *adult* day care facilities for its employees—a place where employees can bring adult family members (e.g., elderly parents) who are in need of care during working hours.[79] One company, Wilton Connor Packaging (Charlotte, North Carolina) provides even more unusual forms of support, such as an on-site laundry, high-school equivalency classes, door-to-door transportation, and a children's clothing swap center.[80]
- **Job sharing:** the practice of allowing pairs of employees to assume the responsibilities of a single job, giving them the flexibility of being able to work while having time off for family obligations. At Xerox, for example, several sets of employees share jobs, including two female employees who were sales rivals, but who joined forces to share one job when they each faced the need to reduce their working hours so they could devote time to their new families.[81]

FIGURE 6-14
CHILD CARE FACILITIES: ONE SOLUTION TO THE WORK–FAMILY CONFLICT
America West is one company that strongly believes in the wisdom of helping its employees avoid conflicts between their lives at work and their family lives by providing child care facilities. While at work, Captain Boyd Christiansen places his two children in one of the airline's child care centers.

From such *family-responsive policies*, companies derive several important benefits. First, they help retain highly valued employees—not only keeping them from competitors, but also saving the costs of having to replace them. In fact, officials at AT&T found that the average cost of letting new parents take up to a year of unpaid parental leave was only 32 percent of an employee's annual salary, compared with 150 percent to replace that person permanently.[82] Second, by alleviating the distractions of having to worry about nonwork issues, employees are freed to concentrate on their jobs and to be their most creative. Research has found that people who use the support systems their employers provide are not only more active in team problem-solving activities, but also almost twice as likely to submit useful suggestions for improvement. Commenting on such findings, Ellen Galinsky, co-president of the Families & Work Institute, said, "There's a cost to *not* providing work and family assistance."[83] A third benefit is that such policies help attract the most qualified human resources, giving companies that use them a competitive edge over those that do not.[84] (Some companies are finding it necessary to develop policies about another family-related issue: married couples working together. For a closer look at how some companies are handling this trend, see the Ethical Workplace section on the opposite page.)

THE ETHICAL WORKPLACE

MARRIED COUPLES WORKING TOGETHER: WHERE DO COMPANIES STAND?

If you work for United Parcel Service (UPS), chances are good that your spouse doesn't also work there. However, if you work at Steelcase Inc. (a furniture manufacturer in Grand Rapids, Michigan), not only your spouse, but other family members, may be working alongside you. Some might argue that it is unethical for a company to not employ a qualified individual simply because his or her spouse works there (a reverse form of nepotism). Others would counter, however, that it is in the best interest of all concerned (and therefore, highly ethical) to avoid the potential conflicts that might arise when family members work with one another. Although most companies frown on spouses supervising their mates, or even reporting to the same manager, opinions are split regarding the wisdom of simply working together.[85]

At one extreme, UPS has a written policy that discourages the hiring of relatives. Because the company relies heavily on training people for many different positions and promoting from within, it would be easy for relatives to end up working for each other. According to UPS official, Gina Ellrich, this could lead to favoritism—or even the strong suspicion of favoritism—making it difficult for managers to treat everyone fairly. At the other extreme, Steelcase goes out of its way to hire relatives, and is convinced that doing so is beneficial. For one, it helps with recruitment: long-tenured employees derive the benefit of being able to place their children in positions specifically reserved for them. Not only are the employees pleased, but this practice provides a pool of new talent that the company can tap when needed (in the past, 10 to 18 percent of new hires have been relatives of employees). And, because inside sources of information provide realistic previews of what it's like to work for a company (as you may recall from earlier in this chapter), relatives are likely to be stable employees. Besides, because Steelcase is one of the major employers in the community in which it is located, the hiring of relatives is almost unavoidable. Dan Willjenin, Steelcase's director of human resources is convinced that this practice helps the company foster the kind of family-oriented atmosphere it wishes to create.[86]

Pam and Mark Rostagno have been married for three years, but have worked at Quad/Graphics (one of Wisconsin's largest printing companies) much longer; he for thirteen years, and she for nine (see Figure 6-15). Both work in customer service and report to the same supervisor. In fact, their desks are only 20 feet apart. But at Quad, this is not unusual; over half of its employees are related to each other. According to Emily Labode, Quad's director of employee services, the company doesn't mind hiring spouses of employees. In fact, according to Pam Rostagno, "This company welcomes relatives because they usually have the same work ethic," adding, "you wouldn't recommend someone who would embarrass you by not performing well."[87] So long as performance is not a problem, the company has no problem with hiring relatives. For the Rostagnos, the main benefit of this arrangement comes from appreciating the nature of the job pressures

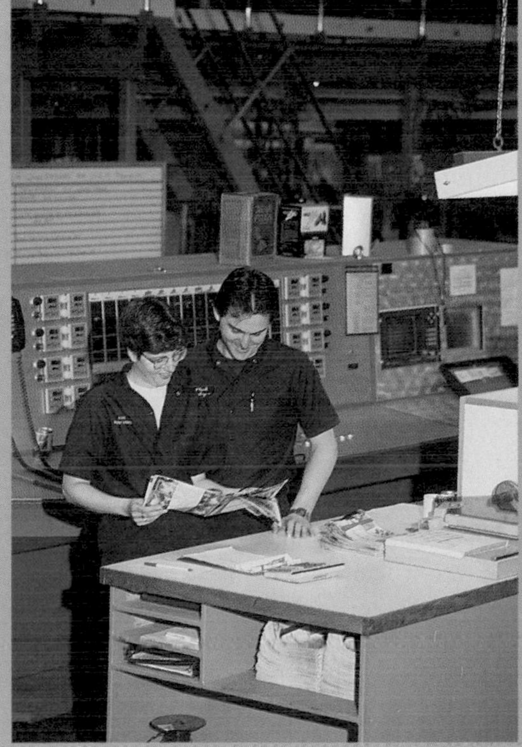

FIGURE 6-15
WORKING AT QUAD/GRAPHICS: A FAMILY AFFAIR
Although some companies frown on hiring relatives, others are content to have family members working together. Pam and Mark Rostagno, a married couple, are customer service managers at the Wisconsin printing firm, Quad/Graphics, where many employees work with their relatives.

THE ETHICAL WORKPLACE, Cont.

the other is facing. "There are no set hours for us," says Mark. "If a customer comes in, we may have to put in long hours—take them to dinner, answer their calls at 2 o'clock in the morning. The other one can understand."[88] To help relieve stress, the Rostagnos visit their young child in the company's on-site day care facility.

Other married couples who work together are similarly convinced that their relationship is enhanced because they spend time working together. Take Margaret Clark and Ralph Silverman, for example—managers with a combined total of twenty-four years working at Warren Gorham Lamont (a publishing company located in Alexandria, Virginia). According to Clark, not working together "would certainly change the ecology of our marriage."[89] In the eight years they've worked together, they have realized that work is part of the seamless web that comprises their lives, and could not imagine reliving the artificial separation of those elements that they have endured in the past, and which most other married couples experience.

This example makes it clear that we are presently in a period of transition with respect to matters of integrating work and family. Companies do not agree what to do, and there are currently widespread differences in the way they go about dealing with this issue. These range from attempts to stop married couples from working together, to openly promoting this practice. Is it ethical for companies to make personnel decisions based on one's spouse? While some debate this question, many of today's companies are taking sides by adopting work–family policies that reflect their beliefs about what's right and their experiences regarding what works best for them.

SUMMARY AND REVIEW

ORGANIZATIONAL SOCIALIZATION

The process through which newcomers learn the ropes in their organizations and become full-fledged members is known as **organizational socialization.** This process involves three distinct stages: *getting in*, *breaking in*, and *settling in*. **Realistic job previews** during the recruitment of newcomers help them avoid unrealistically optimistic or pessimistic expectations about their future jobs. There are two major types of orientation programs designed to socialize new employees. *Individualized socialization* tactics, which are informal and tailored to specific newcomers, appear to enhance an innovative perspective on jobs. In contrast, *institutionalized socialization* tactics, in which all newcomers pass through formal and identical procedures, seem to contribute to later commitment on the part of these people.

MENTORING

A one-on-one form of socialization known as **mentoring** occurs when an experienced employee (a **mentor**) advises, counsels, and aids the personal development of a new employee (a **protégé**). Mentors not only pave the way for their protégés' job success, but also provide a source of emotional support. Mentoring relationships benefit both parties, although there are also costs to each. Typically, the mentorship process has four distinct phases: *initiation*, *cultivation*, *separation*, and *redefinition*. Research has shown that compared to males, females face greater obstacles to obtaining mentors. Also, mentors tend to offer more emotional support to their protégés who belong to a different race whenever both parties follow the same strategy for addressing their racial differences (either both ignoring them or both discussing them).

CAREERS

A **career** is the evolving sequence of a person's work experiences over time. When people make vocational decisions, they often consider the extent to which their values and attitudes match those of a perspective organization (*person–job fit*), and the degree to which they see themselves as similar to the typical individual performing certain jobs (*prototypes*). People's careers can change in several ways, including *vertical movement* (up an organizational hierarchy), *horizontal movement* (different positions at the same organizational level), or *radial movement* (shifts toward or away from an organization's inner circle of power).

Careers usually develop in three distinct stages. In the *early-career* period, people form **career anchors**—perceptions of their own talents, abilities, needs, motives, attitudes, and values—and confront the prospects of frequent job changes. *Middle-career* issues involve coming to terms with the fact that all of one's hopes will not be realized, and with the possibility of a **career plateau**. *Late-career* issues involve accepting reduced power and influences, choosing one's successors, and preparing for retirement. Because there is an increasing number of *dual-career families*, people frequently face conflicts between their work lives and their family lives (*work–family conflict*). These conflicts take their toll not only on individuals (often in the form of *stress*), but also organizations (decreased productivity resulting from employees' needs to divert their attention from their jobs). A growing number of companies are introducing programs to help resolve some of these problems, including *flextime, family leave programs, child care facilities, personal support policies*, and *job sharing*.

KEY TERMS

career: The evolving sequence of a person's work experiences over time.

career anchors: Individuals' perceptions of their own abilities, motives, and values, and their efforts to choose jobs or careers consistent with these self-perceptions.

career development interventions: Systematic efforts designed to assist individuals in managing their careers while also helping organizations meet their goals.

career planning: The process of deciding what jobs one will pursue in the future.

career plateau: A point in a career from which one is unlikely to gain further promotions or receive increased job responsibility.

child care facilities: Sites at or near company locations where parents can leave their children while they are working.

entry shock: The confusion and disorientation experienced by many newcomers to an organization.

family leave programs: Policies that give employees time off their jobs (often some portion of which is paid) to devote to starting a new family.

flextime programs: Policies that give employees some discretion over when they can arrive and leave work, thereby making it easier to adapt their work schedules to the demands of their personal lives.

job sharing: The practice of allowing pairs of employees to assume the responsibilities of a single job, giving them the flexibility of being able to work while having time off for family obligations.

job succession: The process of finding and developing a new employee to take the place of one who is expected to be leaving, such as through retirement.

mentor: A more experienced employee who offers advice, assistance, and protection to a younger and less experienced one (a *protégé*).

mentoring: The process of serving as a mentor (see *mentor*).

organizational socialization: The process through which newcomers to an organization become full-fledged members who share its major values and understand its policies and procedures.

personal support policies: Practices that help employees meet the demands of their family lives, freeing them to concentrate on their work.

protégé: A less-experienced (often new) employee whose organizational socialization is facilitated by working with a mentor.

realistic job previews: Accurate information concerning the conditions within an organization or job provided to potential employees prior to their decision to join an organization.

role orientation: The extent to which employees are willing to change various aspects of their jobs (an *innovative orientation*), or are interested in keeping them the same (a *custodial orientation*).

QUESTIONS FOR DISCUSSION

1. Imagine that you are planning an orientation program for the new employees in your company. What major points would you attempt to incorporate?
2. What steps can be taken to help ensure that new employees fit in and remain in an organization?
3. Many successful businesspeople report that they have had one or more mentors over the course of their careers. In what ways might having a mentor help people become more successful in their careers?
4. Suppose you are deciding on taking a new job. What factors are you likely to take into account when making this decision?
5. What barriers do women and members of minority groups face when attempting to become successful members of organizations. What steps can be taken to help reduce these barriers?
6. Why might there be more conflicts today than ever before between people's work lives and their family lives? What effects do these conflicts have, and what can be done about them?

CASE IN POINT

SEX, SODA, AND TV: CAREER SUCCESS IN THE 1990s

Both Josie Natori and J. Bruce Llewellyn have experienced great success in their career endeavors. Natori is the 45-year-old chair of the $33 million Natori fashions house and Llewellyn, at age 65, is the chair of the Philadelphia Coca-Cola Bottling Company.[1] Although the specific businesses in which they have been involved have little to do with one another, the paths to success taken by both Natori and Llewellyn have a great deal in common.

Natori was born Josephine Alameda Cruz in Manila in the Philippines. As the oldest of six children with a very strict Catholic upbringing she was taught the importance of dedication and hard work. Her beliefs in these virtues as well as her prodigious talents as a musician led to her success in playing the piano—she was playing the classics by age 4 and gave her first solo performance with the Manila Philharmonic by age 9. Although she clearly had the opportunity to pursue a career as a professional musician, Natori leaped at the chance to attend college in the United States to study economics. She took advantage of this opportunity for two reasons. First, she had never been away from home and yearned to have some freedom. Second, she was greatly influenced by her grandmother, who owned her own business. Natori figured that by studying economics she too would be able to own her own business some day.[2]

After graduating from Manhattanville College in 1968, Natori landed a job with Merrill Lynch on Wall Street. A fast-tracker, she became its first female vice president—and, by the age of 30![3] Yet, Natori felt something was missing.[4]

To relieve her boredom and seek a new challenge, Natori started searching for a new business venture. In order to give something back to her birth country, she looked for commercial openings in the Philippines. Her search led her to the conclusion that there were opportunities to manufacture clothing. Although she began with an interest in children's apparel, a passing comment made by a fashion buyer led her to the design and production of women's lingerie.

Her company, Natori, which takes its name from her husband, is now a $33 million fashion house with boutiques throughout the United States and Japan and a mail-order catalog in Spain. Although lingerie still accounts for the bulk of the firms' revenues, apparel accounts for 14 percent of sales. The plan is for the company to expand its clothing offerings as well as other fashions in the creation of a full fashion house. Natori figures that this goal will be greatly helped by the fact that her designs were selected to appear in a fashion exhibit at New York's Metropolitan Museum of Art during the spring of 1993. Natori is delighted by the success achieved by her company. She also feels a great sense of accomplishment saying, "never in my wildest dreams did I think we'd be part of a museum exhibit. If I had to leave a legacy, I have."[5]

Despite this triumph, Natori does admit to failure and disappointment when it comes to her family. Specifically, she says that she would have liked to have more than one child but that the demands of the business precluded this choice. Similarly, she notes, "I do not have the time that we should spend as a family. I wish I could spend more time, give back to my parents. I mean, so you know, you can't have it all, but you compromise. I often thought, oh my goodness am I an unfit mother, but I don't think so."[6]

Whereas Natori's career progression from musician, to financial whiz, to owner of her own fashion company seems to have been accomplished in discrete steps, J. Bruce Llewellyn's career moved in a more seamless manner. He joined the U.S. Air Force at age 16 during World War II and learned to fly fighters. However, when the war ended there was little need for pilots, so he went to college, where he supported himself by opening a liquor store. Next he enrolled at the Columbia University business school. He followed this by completing a law degree. After all this schooling, he entered the public sector. He began work in the district attorney's office and was then appointed to the New York housing redevelopment board. Llewellyn subsequently was selected to be regional director of the Small Business Administration—a post he held for 9 years.[7]

Llewellyn became restless and longed for additional challenge and autonomy. Like Natori, he felt he wanted to contribute something to the community in which he grew up. To accomplish these goals, he decided to go into the

CASE IN POINT, Cont.

grocery business. He purchased the Fedco Foods Corporation, a chain of 10 stores in the Bronx with a $3-million loan from the Prudential.[8] In spite of the many problems in the neighborhoods in which his stores operated, he made this business into a very successful twenty-seven-store chain. After eighteen years in the grocery business, at age 55, Llewellyn searched for additional ventures. Following careful analysis, he realized that the bottling business was growing and profitable so he bought Philadelphia Coca-Cola Bottling Company. He also saw tremendous opportunities in the broadcasting industry and subsequently purchased Garden State Cablevision and Queens City Broadcasting.

Llewellyn credits his success to taking risks, hard work, and never letting anything discourage him from going after his goals and objectives. Still, with all his business success, he claims that his greatest accomplishment is his family.[9]

QUESTIONS FOR DISCUSSION

1. Use Schein's concepts of vertical, horizontal, and radial movement to describe the career progression of Natori and Llewellyn.
2. What career anchors do you think are most important to Natori and Llewellyn? What causes you to make this assessment? Do you think that their career anchors changed over time?
3. How have Natori and Llewellyn's careers progressed across the three career stages? What predictions can you make about how their careers might develop in the future?
4. Are you comfortable with the balance that both Natori and Llewellyn have developed between work and family? Why or why not? What balance do you hope to achieve between work and family? Do you expect that this might change over the course of your career?

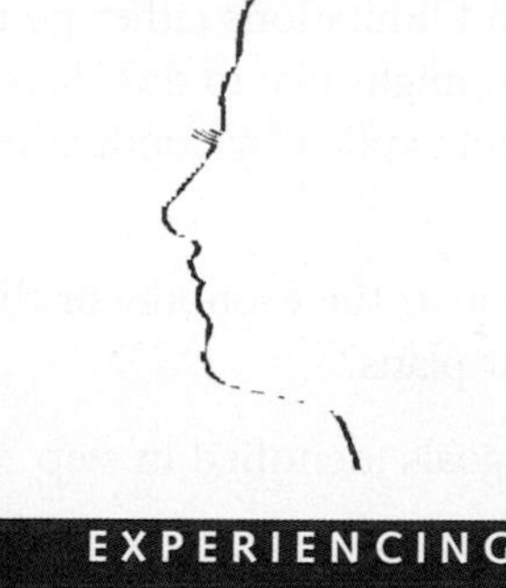

EXPERIENCING ORGANIZATIONAL BEHAVIOR

Developing a Personal Career Plan

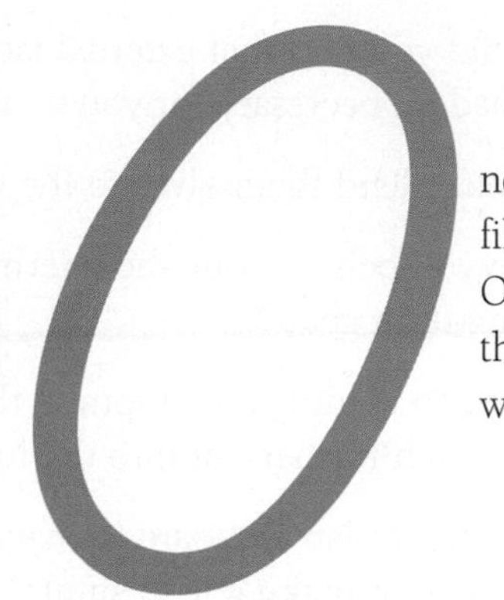

One of the most important things people can do to fulfill their career goals is to develop a **career plan**. Overall, there are five steps in this process, the first three of which you can do right now. The final two will have to wait until you're already on the job.

PROCEDURE

To complete each of the first three steps in the career-planning process, ask yourself the questions listed below and record your answers. To come up with the most accurate assessment, try to answer the questions as honestly as possible.

Step 1: Personal Assessment:

a. What special skills and aptitudes can you bring to your job?
b. What are your most serious weaknesses and limitations? (Really try to be honest on this one!)
c. What types of jobs do you like to do?
d. To what extent do the jobs you've identified in step *c* require the skills identified in step *a*? And, to what extent might they suffer from the limitations identified in step 2?

Step 2: Opportunities Analysis:

a. How has the economy affected various job prospects?
b. Is there an overabundance or a shortage of people to fill various jobs?

Step 3: Career Objectives:

a. What are your long-term goals (5–10 years)?
b. What are your intermediate goals (3–5 years)?
c. What are your short-term goals (1–3 years)?

Step 4: Implement Plan
Step 5: Revise Plan as Necessary

(Select a position. Then, after working on it, monitor your progress, solicit feedback, compare the results to your objectives, and revise your plan as needed.)

POINTS TO CONSIDER

1. Did the process of identifying your personal skills and limitations either point to, or eliminate from contention, any of the jobs you might like to do? Were you aware of these suggestions before you made them explicit by conducting this exercise?
2. To what extent did you find that external factors, such as the economy or the labor market, made it necessary for you to alter your plans?
3. Do your job choices lend themselves to the various goals identified in step 3?
4. How realistic do you believe your short-term goals are? How about your intermediate and long-term goals?
5. Is it easier for you to identify and appraise the viability of shorter-term goals than ones that stretch further out into the future? Why do you think this is?
6. How does your career plan compare to that of your classmates? What do you think is responsible for making it so similar or different?

CHAPTER OUTLINE

SPECIAL SECTIONS

SEVEN

STRESS: ITS NATURE, IMPACT, AND MANAGEMENT

LEARNING OBJECTIVES

After reading this chapter, you should be able to

1. *Understand what stress is, and is not, and how it differs from stressors and strain.*
2. *Explain the major sources of stress operating on the job, and in life in general.*
3. *Identify the ways in which stress influences various aspects of task performance.*
4. *Explain the concept of burnout, including its major causes and effects.*
5. *Describe the adverse effects of stress on personal health.*
6. *Identify various individual differences in resistance to stress, and explain how they operate.*
7. *Understand the steps people can take to minimize the adverse effects of stress, and ways that organizations can help prevent stress among its employees in the first place.*

It's better to bend than to break.

Aesop, c. 620–c. 560 B.C.
Greek fabulist
The Oak and the Reeds

Anger is momentary madness, so control your passion or it will control you.

Horace, 65–8 B.C.
Roman poet and satirist
Epistles

PREVIEW CASE

Life in the Pressure-Cooker for Nordies

At Nordstrom Stores, the Seattle-based chain of upscale department stores, live music from grand pianos fills the air, displays are packed with the latest designer fashions, and smiling sales clerks walk the marble floors lending the utmost in service to pampered customers. It sounds like a page out of some retailing fairytale, but it's quite a different picture behind the scenes—where "Nordies," as store employees call themselves, face pressures that belie the idyllic scene on the sales floors.

Signs admonishing, "Don't let us down," and "Be the Top Pacesetter" hang from the walls of the back rooms. Alongside them are graphs charting each clerk's hourly sales performance, complete with red lines distinguishing those who are safe from those who will be sent packing. For clerks who make it, success can be sweet. With their high hourly pay (about $10 per hour) and generous sales commissions, clerks may make as much as $80,000 a year!

Because a low sales-per-hour figure is grounds for dismissal, Nordies are encouraged to do a lot of their nonsales work off the clock. Restocking shelves, making customer deliveries, going to Saturday morning department meetings, and writing thank-you notes are key parts of their jobs, but ones for which they are not paid. Also to keep their figures looking good, Nordies do a lot of things to steal customers from each other ("sharking," as they call it). For example, clerks have been known to monopolize cash registers, keeping others from them, to record others' sales as their own, and even to ring up returns (deducted from sales figures) under someone else's ID code.

A Nordstrom store.

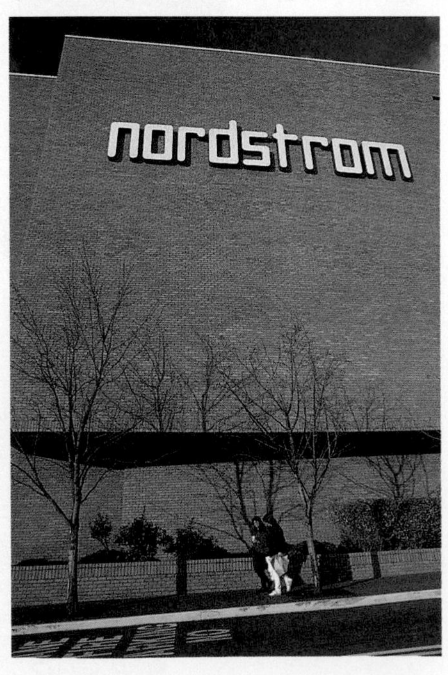

If rival salesclerks don't get you, management just might. A cosmetics manager in one of Nordstrom's California stores once wrote a memo in which she outlined a lengthy list of sales goals for cosmetics counter employees to achieve. It ended by saying, "In the next sixty days if any of these are not met to our expectations you will be terminated."

With all this going on, Nordstrom clerks might have little to smile about, but smile they must. To make sure they do, stores hire secret shoppers who monitor their demeanor. If clerks are caught frowning, they earn demerits that can lead to their termination. As a reward, those who are found smiling the most might win their store's "smiling contest," celebrated by having their picture posted on the lunchroom wall.

If you're going to smile, you have to do it for quite some time, for it is not unusual for Nordies to work twelve- to fifteen-hour days for well over a week. As tough as this is, it is completely consistent with Jim Nordstrom's beliefs that many of his clerks don't work hard enough. Indeed, official communications have indicated that even one sick day in three months is considered excessive and indicates a lack of dedication to the job.

Unfortunately, quite a few Nordstrom employees have gotten sick! These tactics have left some with ulcers, colitis, hives, and hand tremors. In the words of one longtime employee, "The girls around me were dropping like flies. Everyone was always in tears. You feel like an absolute nothing working for them." Another employee said, "Before you know it, your whole life is Nordstrom's. But you couldn't complain because then your manager would schedule you for the bad hours, your sales-per-hour would fall and the next thing you know, you're out the door." Both these employees, consistently high performers, eventually quit Nordstrom's, taking jobs with higher pay and far fewer hours—one after developing an ulcer, and the other out of sheer exhaustion.

Now, faced with pressure from unions, lawsuits, and lackluster sales, Nordstrom's is reconsidering its tactics—and, it is clear that conditions have been improving. Meanwhile, for those who have endured its pressure-cooker atmosphere, the sale is final.

Have you ever experienced a situation like that faced by Nordstrom employees—being so completely overwhelmed by the job and pressured into always performing at levels so unreasonably high that you simply cannot cope? If so, then you are already familiar with *stress*—the focus of this chapter. Although this may be an extreme case, stress is an all-too-common part of life in the 1990s, something few individuals can avoid. In fact, a nationwide survey recently conducted by a large life insurance company showed that nearly 46 percent of American workers felt that their jobs are highly stressful.[1] For 27 percent, work was the single greatest source of stress in their lives (see Figure 7-1). This same survey also found that the incidence of disabilities resulting from stress more than doubled in the last nine years alone! Growing evidence suggests that high levels of stress adversely affect physical health, psychological well-being, and many aspects of task performance.[2]

Given such effects, stress is a topic of considerable importance to the field of organizational behavior.[3] In this chapter, we will consider it in detail. First, we will examine the *basic nature* of stress—what it is and its major components. Next, we will turn to its *major causes*—factors in work settings and life in general that tend to induce high levels of stress. Third, we will examine the impact of stress—its effects on task performance, health, and other aspects of work-related behavior. Fourth, we will review individual differences in people's resistance to stress. Finally, we will examine procedures for *managing stress*—techniques that individuals and organizations can employ to help reduce stress or counter its adverse effects.

"If we hire you, you're not going to experience stress on the job, are you?"

FIGURE 7-1

STRESS: AN INEVITABLE PART OF LIFE IN ORGANIZATIONS

If he's like most people, the only promise this interviewee can live up to is that, at some time or another, he will experience stress on the job. (Cartoon by James L. Stevenson from Harvard Business Review *November–December 1992.)*

STRESS: ITS BASIC NATURE

In order to explain exactly what is meant by stress and to describe its basic nature (as well as its role in individual and organizational functioning), we need to put it into the context of other related concepts, and to distinguish it from them. With this in mind, we will now define stress, indicationg both what it is and is not.

BASIC DEFINITIONS: STRESSORS, STRESS, AND STRAIN

What do each of the following situations have in common?

- You get fired the day before you become eligible to receive your retirement pension.
- You find out that your company is about to eliminate your department.
- Your boss tells you that you are the only employee who will not be getting a raise this year.
- Your spouse is diagnosed with a terminal illness.

These are all terrible situations, of course—external events beyond our own control that create extreme demands on us. Stimuli of this type are known as **stressors**, formally defined as *any demands, either physical or psychological in nature, encountered during the course of living.*[4]

When we encounter stressors, our bodies (in particular, our sympathetic nervous systems and endocrine systems) are mobilized into action, such as through elevated heart rate, blood pressure, and respiration. According to Hans Selye, a leading expert on this topic, these physiological reactions can be divided into several distinct stages (see Figure 7-2).[5] When confronted with any threat to our safety or well-being, we experience an immediate and vigorous *alarm reaction*. Arousal rises quickly to high levels, and many physiological changes that prepare our bodies for strenuous activity (either flight or combat) take place. This initial reaction is soon replaced by a second stage known as *resistance*. Here, activation remains relatively high, but drops to levels that are more sustainable over relatively long periods of time. If the stressor persists, the body's resources may become depleted and a final stage known as *exhaustion* occurs. At this point, people's ability to cope (at least physically) decreases sharply, and severe biological damage may result. It is these patterns of responses that we have in mind when we talk about stress. Specifically, we define **stress** as *the pattern of emotional states and physiological reactions occurring in response to demands from within or outside organizations (i.e., stressors).*

As you might imagine, the mechanisms by which stressors lead to stress reactions are not direct and mechanical in nature. Rather, stress involves people's *cognitive appraisal* of the potential stressors they face.[6] In simple terms, for stress to occur people must perceive (1) that the situation they face is somehow threatening to them, and (2) that they will be unable to cope with these potential dangers or demands—that the situation is, in essence, beyond their control. In short, stress does not simply shape our thoughts; in many cases, it derives from and is strongly affected by them. To the extent that people appraise various situations as stres-

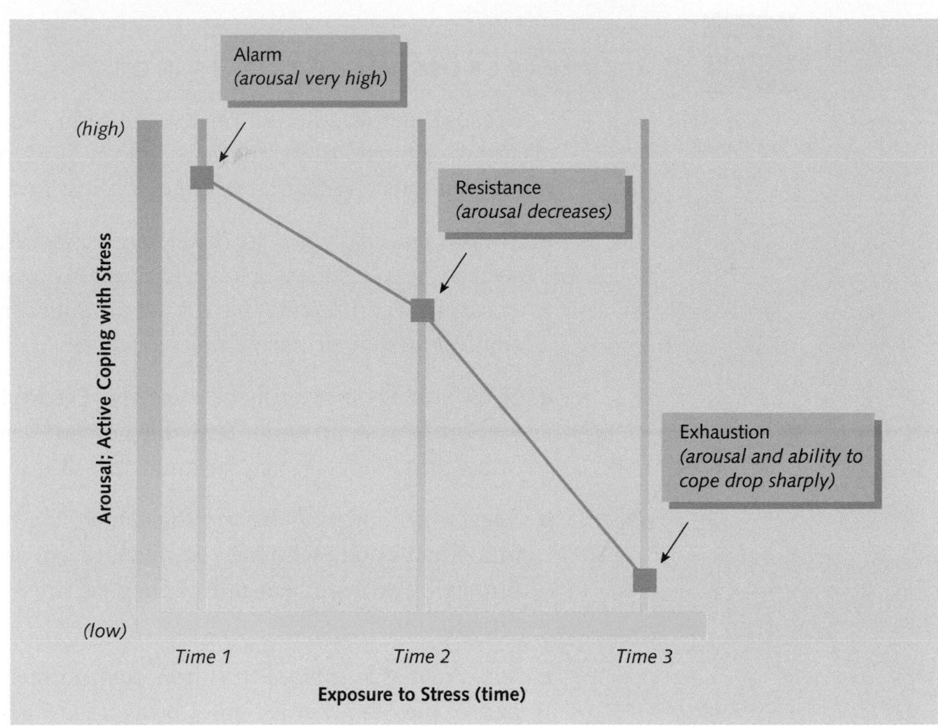

FIGURE 7-2
PHYSIOLOGICAL REACTIONS TO STRESS: THREE STAGES
When we are exposed to stress, several physiological changes occur. First we experience a vigorous alarm reaction. This is followed by a stage of resistance in which we actively seek to cope with the source of stress. Then, finally, if stress persists, exhaustion may occur. During this stage our ability to cope with stress drops to a low level. (Source: Based on suggestions by Selye, 1976; see Note 5.)

sors, they are likely to have stress reactions. Evidence of the important role of cognitive factors in the occurrence of stress is provided by Evans and Carrere in their research on stress among urban bus drivers.[7] These researchers found that as traffic volume increased, drivers reported having less control over how they performed their jobs, and at these times, they had high concentrations of adrenaline and nonadrenaline in their urine (substances known to increase during times of stress). Findings such as these provide clear evidence that people's perceptions of threatened control over work is an important determinant of their stress reactions.

As we have been suggesting, stress responses can have damaging effects on individuals. These effects can be behavioral, psychological, and/or medical in nature, and are commonly seen in the form of such conditions as insomnia, depression, and cardiovascular disease. To the extent that these responses occur, they represent a deviation from people's normal functioning, a reaction known as **strain**. Just as engineers are aware of the way physical objects become deformed (altered from their usual states) in response to the strain of physical pressure, so too are social scientists aware of strain reactions in people: *deviations from normal states of human functioning resulting from stressful events.* (For a summary of the relationships among stressors, stress, and strains, see Figure 7-3).

FIGURE 7-3
STRESSORS, STRESS, AND STRAIN: THEIR INTERRELATIONSHIPS
Stimuli known as stressors leads to stress reactions when they are cognitively appraised as threatening and beyond one's control. The deviations from normal states resulting from stress are known as strain.

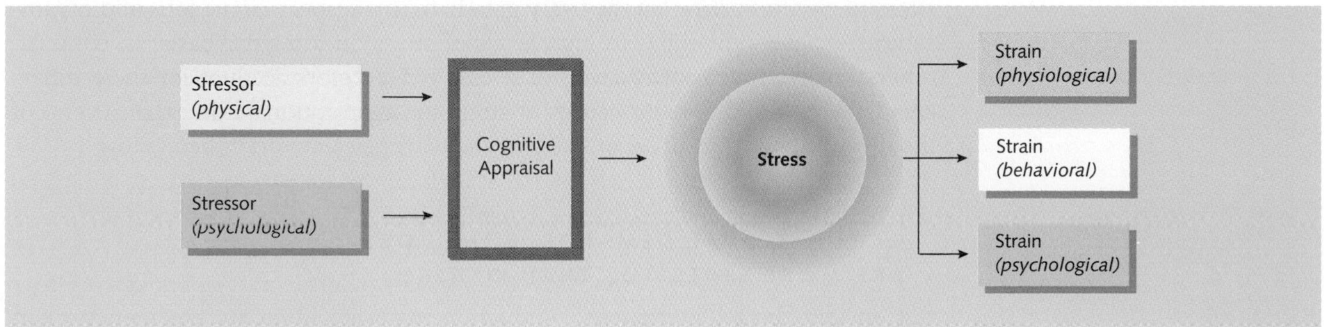

STRESS: WHAT IT IS NOT

Because people so often misuse the term *stress*, we thought it would help you clearly understand this important concept if we addressed some of these common misperceptions.[8] With this in mind, we will now consider what stress is *not*.

- *Stress is not simply anxiety or nervous tension.* Although these reactions may be seen in people suffering adverse reactions to stress, they are not the same as stress. In fact, it is possible for people suffering from stress to not exhibit any signs of anxiety or nervous tension at all.
- *Stress need not necessarily be damaging.* People frequently experience stress without any strain at all. Daily life activities, such as a rousing game of tennis, or a warm embrace, may be quite stressful, but not at all harmful.
- *Stress is not always due to overstimulation.* We usually think of the "stressed-out" individual as one who has too much to do, and cannot keep it all straight. But, as we will see later in this chapter, stress also may result from having too little to do.
- *Stress cannot be avoided.* It is important to realize that stress is an inevitable part of life, and that it cannot be avoided. What *can* be avoided, however, are the negative reactions to stress which we have described. Later in this chapter we will describe several techniques that can be used to help people cope—that is, to avoid the potentially damaging consequences of stress.

STRESS: ITS MAJOR CAUSES

What factors contribute to stress in work settings? Unfortunately, the list is a long one. As we will soon see, many different conditions play a role. Moreover, these factors are not independent in their effects. For example, the presence of one stressor may intensify reactions to one or more others. For purposes of this discussion, however, we will consider each major cause of work-related stress separately. In addition, for purposes of clarity, we will divide these factors into two major categories: those relating directly to organizations or jobs, and those relating to other aspects of individuals' lives.

WORK-RELATED CAUSES OF STRESS

As anyone who has been employed well knows, work settings are often highly stressful environments. Yet they vary greatly in this respect. Some jobs and organizations expose individuals to high levels of stress on a regular basis. In contrast, others involve much lower levels of stress. What factors account for these differences? What are the major causes of stress in organizational contexts? Several of the most important sources of stress in the workplace are described below.

OCCUPATIONAL DEMANDS: SOME JOBS ARE MORE STRESSFUL THAN OTHERS

Consider the following jobs: production manager, librarian, emergency room physician, janitor, firefighter, college professor, airline pilot. Do they differ in degree of stressfulness? Obviously, they do. Some jobs, such as emergency room physician, police officer, firefighter, and airline pilot, expose the people who hold them to high levels of stress. Others, such as college professor, janitor, and librarian, do not. This basic fact—that some jobs are much more stressful than others—has been confirmed by the results of a survey involving more than 130 different occupations.[9] The results indicated that several jobs (e.g., physician, officer manager, foreman, waitress or waiter) are quite high in stress. In contrast, others (e.g., maid, craft workers, farm laborer) are much lower in this regard. Additional research focusing on the most stressful industries has found that the overall most stressful jobs can be found in the telecommunications field (for a complete listing, see Table 7-1).[10]

What, precisely, makes some jobs more stressful than others? A partial answer is provided by a study conducted by Shaw and Riskind.[11] These researchers reviewed information about the levels of stress experienced by people holding a wide range of jobs—from executive to factory worker. Then they related this information about stressfulness to various characteristics of the jobs. Results indicated that several features of jobs are related to the levels of stress they generate. Specifically, the greater the extent to which a given job requires (1) making decisions, (2) constant monitoring of devices or materials, (3) repeated exchange of

TABLE 7-1

The Top Ten Most Stressful Industries

A study of over 1,700 employees found that jobs in some industries were more stressful than others. Here, from most to least stressful, is a listing of the top ten most stressful fields, and representative examples of jobs in each.

RANK	INDUSTRY	TYPICAL JOBS
1	*Telecommunications*	*Telephone operator, network administrator*
2	*Financial services*	*Stock trader, loan officer*
3	*Nonprofit organizations*	*Foundation administrator, church officer*
4	*Consumer products*	*Clothing sales clerk, automobile salesperson*
5	*Automobile manufacturing*	*Auto assembly worker, stamping machine operator*
6	*Gas and electric utilities*	*Natural gas drill rigger, rural electric crew chief*
7	*Health care administration*	*Claims processor, hospital director*
8	*Agricultural processing*	*Beef processing inspector, food canning operator*
9	*Management consultants*	*Management trainers, executive selection specialists*
10	*Chemical processing*	*Hazardous materials handlers, chemical safety inspector*

Source: Based on "Study Finds Most Successful Jobs," 1993; see Note 10.

- *"Unless there is the intent to harass, there is no liability."* Although this is commonly believed, it is untrue: the law does not address intent. All that matters is whether the unwanted sexually oriented activity occurred. If it did, it constitutes harassment.
- *"You can't determine guilt; it's just one person's word against another's."* There are rarely witnesses to sexual harassment, but most accused people still eventually admit their guilt, claiming ignorance of the law. Totally fabricated claims of sexual harassment are rare.
- *"They can't really do anything to us."* Quite a few companies have learned an expensive lesson about the mythical nature of this assumption. Court awards to victims in the $1 million range provide convincing evidence that "they" really *can* do something after all—and they often do!

We realize, of course, that it is far easier to identify these beliefs than to get everyone to accept them, and to respond accordingly. With this in mind, we invite you to review the suggestions listed in Table 7-2. These are some proven measures that can keep the workplace harassment-free. Organizations whose sensitivity to the problem of harassment leads them to take such steps are likely to create an enlightened environment in which all can work without confronting this potent source of stress.

TABLE 7-2

Preventing Sexual Harassment: Some Proven Measures

Although it is difficult to keep the workplace totally free of sexual harassment, several tactics have proven successful.

SUGGESTION	DESCRIPTION
■ *Develop a clear policy prohibiting sexual harassment.*	*The policy should be widely disseminated, and clearly spell out what is meant by sexual harassment (e.g., unwanted touching, advances). It should also emphasize that the company will not tolerate such offensive behavior. It should also apply to employees at every level of the organization.*
■ *Thoroughly train all employees in understanding what sexual harassment is, and how to avoid it.*	*Prevention will not come automatically. Employees require intensive training in learning how to become sensitive to the possible ways they may be offending others. (Many offenders don't even realize they are harassing!) Such efforts should be mandatory, and emphasize each employee's personal responsibility for maintining a totally harassment-free workplace.*
■ *Keep the workplace free of sexually offensive materials*	*Although photos (such as those on calendars) and slogans of a sexual nature may be innocent enough, they may offend some employees, and should not be permitted. Although it's a small step, imposing such restrictions will underscore the company's serious attitude toward eliminating the problem.*
■ *Make it clear exactly how to respond when an incident of sexual harassment occurs.*	*Sometimes employees may refrain from reporting sexual harassment because they don't know whom to talk to, or how they will be received. By clarifying the lines of internal communication, opportunities will be created to react before the problem gets worse.*
■ *Specify in advance exactly how the company intends to treat offenders, and then strictly enforce this policy.*	*Preparing a formal policy requires identifying how violators will be disciplined. The exact form of discipline (including termination, when appropriate) should be stated clearly in advance, so as to ensure fair enforcement.*

Source: Based on suggestions by Bohren, 1993; see Note 31.

such as death of a spouse, divorce, or marital separation. In contrast, smaller numbers of points were assigned to such events as change in residence, vacation, or minor violations of the law (e.g., a parking ticket).

Going further, Holmes and Rahe then related the total number of points accumulated by individuals during a single year to changes in their personal health. Their dramatic results did much to stir interest in the effects of stress among scientists in several different fields. The greater the number of "stress points" people accumulated, the greater their likelihood of becoming seriously ill. For example, in one study on this topic, Holmes and Masuda asked patients at a university medical center to report all significant life events during the past eighteen months.[34] People who experienced events totaling 300 points or more showed a much higher incidence of illness during the next nine months than those with 200 points or less (49 percent versus 9 percent).

TABLE 7-3

Stressful Life Events

When asked to assign arbitrary points (1–100) to various life events according to the degree of readjustment they required, a large group of individuals provided the values shown here. The higher the number shown, the more stressful the events listed.

EVENT	RELATIVE STRESSFULNESS
Death of a spouse	*100*
Divorce	*73*
Marital separation	*65*
Jail term	*63*
Death of a close family member	*63*
Personal injury or illness	*53*
Marriage	*50*
Fired from a job	*47*
Retirement	*45*
Pregnancy	*40*
Death of a close friend	*37*
Son or daughter leaving home	*29*
Trouble with in-laws	*28*
Trouble with boss	*23*
Change in residence	*20*
Vacation	*13*
Christmas	*12*
Minor violations of the law	*11*

Source: Based on data from Holmes & Masuda, 1974; see Note 34.

At this point, we should note that this seemingly simple relationship between stress and health is complicated by large individual differences in the ability to withstand the impact of stress. Some people suffer ill effects after exposure to a few mildly stressful events, whereas others remain healthy even after prolonged exposure to high levels of stress; they are described as being *stress-resistant* or *hardy.* We'll return to such differences later. For the moment, we merely wish to emphasize that in general, the greater the number of stressful life events experienced by individuals, the greater the likelihood that their subsequent health will suffer in some manner.

THE HASSLES OF DAILY LIFE

Traumatic life events such as the ones studied by Holmes and Rahe, although clearly very stressful, are relatively rare. Many people live for years, or even decades, without experiencing any of them. Does this mean that such individuals live their lives in a serene lake of tranquility? Hardly. Daily life is filled with countless minor irritations that seem to make up for their relatively low intensity by their high frequency of occurrence. That such *daily hassles* are an important cause of stress is suggested by the findings of several studies by Lazarus and his colleagues.[35] These researchers have developed a *Hassles Scale* on which individuals indicate the extent to which they have been "hassled" by common events during the past month. As shown in Table 7-4, items included in this scale deal with a wide range of everyday events (e.g., having too many things to do at once, shopping, concerns about money). Scores on the Hassles Scale are positively related to self-reported stress. The more hassles individuals report experiencing, the greater the stress they feel. In addition, such scores are also related to psychological symp-

TABLE 7-4

Daily Hassles as a Source of Stress

The everyday events and concerns shown here are ones many people describe as common sources of stress.

TYPE OF PROBLEM	EXAMPLES
Household hassles	*Preparing meals* *Shopping*
Time pressure hassles	*Too many things to do* *Too many responsibilities*
Inner concern hassles	*Being lonely* *Fear of confrontation*
Environmental hassles	*Neighborhood deterioration* *Noise* *Crime*
Financial responsibility	*Concerns about owing money* *Financial responsibility for someone who doesn't live with you.*

Source: Based on information in DeLongis et al., 1982; see Note 36.

toms: the more hassles people experience, the poorer their psychological well-being. Finally, scores are also linked to physical health. The more hassles people experience, the larger the number of symptoms and minor ailments they report having.[36]

In sum, although traumatic life events such as the death of a loved one or the loss of one's job are stressful and have adverse effects on health, the minor hassles of daily life—perhaps because of their frequent, repetitive nature—may be even more crucial in this respect. Whatever their relative importance, both traumatic life events and daily hassles are important sources of stress for many people. And since the stress generated off the job is often carried onto their jobs by the individuals involved, these factors are certainly worth noting.

TOTAL LIFE STRESS: THE COMBINED PICTURE

In the preceding discussion of sources of stress, we separated stressors related to work and those related to personal life events. This distinction reflects the fact that research on stressors often focuses on one or the other of these two major categories. But from the individual's point of view, work-related stress and life-related stress often combine into a seamless—and potentially overwhelming—pattern of adversity. Is work going poorly? Are there many seemingly impossible deadlines to meet? Is one's boss "acting up"? Then, it often seems, this is also the time for problems with one's children, one's relatives, or one's spouse. And it is *now*, when one is already feeling overloaded, that the furnace, car, or refrigerator begins making funny sounds—or quits working altogether!

The usefulness of adopting a broad approach in which work-related and personal causes of stress are combined into the construct of **total negative life stress** is suggested by the fact that total stress is a better predictor of negative organizational outcomes (e.g., reduced job satisfaction and organizational commitment, increased turnover intentions) than either work-related or personal stressors alone.[37] So, where stress as actually experienced by individuals is concerned, no hard-and-fast boundaries exist between what happens at work and what happens at home. On the contrary, these two spheres of life are intertwined in many ways, so that added insights into the nature and impact of stress can be gained by considering the two together as a unified whole.

STRESS: SOME MAJOR EFFECTS

By now, we're sure you are probably convinced that stress stems from many sources, and that it exerts important effects on the people who experience it. What may not yet be apparent, though, is just how powerful and far-reaching such effects can be. In fact, so widespread are the detrimental effects of stress (i.e., strain) that it has been estimated that its annual costs exceed 10 percent of the U.S. gross national product![38] Although much of this amount is accounted for by health-related effects (as illustrated in our Preview Case, where stress caused illness among Nordstrom's sales associates), research indicates that stress can influence us in other ways as well. Specifically, it can also affect our psychological well-being, our performance on many tasks, and even the accuracy of our decisions. We will now describe several of these effects in more detail.

STRESS AND TASK PERFORMANCE

Traditionally, the relationship between stress and performance on many tasks was believed to be *curvilinear*. Thus, at first, increments in stress (from none to low or moderate levels) were believed to be energizing and to lead to improved performance. Beyond some point, however, additional increments in stress were assumed to be distracting, to interfere with performance. Thus, at high or very high levels of stress, performance would actually fall.

Although this relationship may hold true under some conditions, growing evidence suggests that stress exerts mainly negative effects on task performance. In other words, performance can be disrupted even by relatively low levels of stress. Evidence pointing to this conclusion is provided in a study by Motowidlo, Packard, and Manning.[39] These researchers asked a large group of nurses to describe their own levels of work-related stress. Ratings of their actual job performance were then obtained from supervisors or co-workers. Results indicated that the higher the nurses' feelings of stress, the lower their job performance. In other words, there was no evidence for initial increments in performance as the curvilinear hypothesis suggests. These findings, and those of several other studies, indicate that in many real-life settings, performance may be reduced even by low or moderate levels of stress.

Why is this the case? Shouldn't the activation produced by moderate levels of stress facilitate performance in many situations? Although this may be the case in some situations (see below), several reasons exist for expecting even moderate levels of stress to interfere with task performance. First, even relatively mild stress can be distracting. Individuals experiencing it may focus on the unpleasant feelings and emotions stress involves rather than on the task at hand—and, as a result their performance suffers. Second, prolonged or repeated exposure to even mild levels of stress may have harmful effects on health, and this may interfere with effective performance. Finally, a large body of research indicates that as arousal increases, task performance may at first rise, but at some point begins to fall. The precise location of this *inflection point* (the point at which the direction of the function reverses) seems to depend, to an important extent, on the complexity of the task being performed. The greater the complexity, the lower the levels of arousal at which a downturn in performance occurs.

Having said all this, we must note that there are exceptions to the general rule that stress interferes with task performance. First, some individuals, at least, do seem to "rise to the occasion" and turn in exceptional performances at times of high stress. This may result from the fact that they are truly expert in the tasks being performed, making their inflection points very high. People who are exceptionally skilled at a task may cognitively appraise a potentially stressful situation as a *challenge* rather than a *threat*. And, as we noted earlier, by not cognitively appraising a situation as a threat, stress reactions are unlikely to occur.

Second, large individual differences exist with respect to the impact of stress on task performance. As your own experience may suggest, some individuals do indeed seem to thrive on stress: they actively seek arousal and high levels of sensation or stimulation. For such people, stress is exhilarating and may improve their performance. In contrast, other people react in an opposite manner. They seek to avoid arousal and high levels of sensation. Such individuals find stress upsetting, and it may interfere with their performance on many tasks.

So, taking available evidence into account, the most reasonable conclusion we can offer concerning stress and task performance is as follows: In many situations, stress can indeed interfere with performance. However, its precise effects depend on several different factors (e.g., complexity of the task being performed, personal characteristics of the individuals involved, their previous experience with this task). In view of such complexities, generalizations about the impact of stress on task performance should be made with considerable caution.

STRESS AND DECISION MAKING: SOME COSTS AND SOME BENEFITS

The mixed pattern we have presented so far also seems to apply as well to another important activity by managers—*decision making*. We will consider this topic in detail in Chapter 14, so here our interest is primarily in the impact of stress on decisions.

The *costs* referred to in the heading above refer mainly to adverse effects of stress on the quality of decision making. Existing evidence indicates that when people make decisions under high-stress conditions, they tend to make more errors than they do at other times. Moreover, the process through which decisions are reached, as well as the decisions themselves, seems to suffer. When making decisions under high levels of stress, people often tend to show *premature closure*—that is, they make their decisions before examining all available choices. Furthermore, they adopt *nonsystematic scanning*, examining the available choices in a less systematic manner than they do under lower levels of stress.[40] Clearly, then, decision making seems to suffer in several important respects when people must operate in high-stress environments.

High levels of stress also seem to exact important costs with respect to decisions by groups as well as by individuals. Several studies indicate that when organizations confront stressful conditions, they tend to centralize authority and to assign decision making to higher levels of the organization.[41] Since a lack of participation in decision making is positively related to stress and negatively related to acceptance of the decisions once they are reached, these tendencies toward centralization can prove costly. On the other side of the coin, however, high levels of stress also seem to provide certain benefits where group decision making is concerned. Research suggests that under high-stress conditions, leaders actually show greater responsiveness to inputs from subordinates, and so adopt a more egalitarian approach to decision making.

Evidence for such effects is provided by a recent study conducted by Driskell and Salas.[42] These researchers had students at a naval technical school work with a fictitious partner on a task involving visual judgments. (The partner was shown only on videotape and was not actually present.) Some students performed this task under high stress—they were told that tear gas might be introduced into the room; others performed under low stress—no mention of tear gas was made. Another aspect of the study involved students' status relative to their partners. In one condition he outranked them, and in the other they outranked him. There were no correct answers to the task, so the main question was: How would subjects respond to disagreements with their partner (programmed into the situation)? Would they change their judgments on the task to match his, or "stick to their guns"? The researchers predicted that subjects would defer to their partners when they were higher in status. However, they also predicted that high stress would increase participants' responsiveness to input from their partner, regardless of his status. This is precisely what happened: students changed their answers to agree with those of their partners more under high stress than under low stress.

What accounts for this tendency? One possibility is that people's desire for task-relevant information increases under high-stress conditions, thus increasing their tendency to accept input from others. Another is that under high stress, people's desire to diffuse responsibility—to share the blame for incorrect decisions with others—increases. This leads them to pay more careful attention to others' opinions. Whatever the process involved, it seems clear that stress can influence decision making in several different ways and that in certain contexts, at least, some of these effects can be beneficial.

BURNOUT: STRESS AND PSYCHOLOGICAL ADJUSTMENT

Most jobs involve some degree of stress. Yet, somehow, the people performing them manage to cope; they continue to function despite their daily encounters with various stressors. Some individuals, though, are not so fortunate. Over time, they seem to be worn down by repeated exposure to stress. Such people are often described as suffering from *burnout*, and they demonstrate several distinct characteristics.[43]

First, victims of burnout suffer from *physical exhaustion*. They have low energy and feel tired much of the time. In addition, they report many symptoms of physical strain such as frequent headaches, nausea, poor sleep, and changes in eating habits (e.g., loss of appetite). Second, they experience *emotional exhaustion*. Depression, feelings of helplessness, and feelings of being trapped in one's job are all part of the picture. Third, people suffering from burnout often demonstrate a pattern of *attitudinal exhaustion* (often known as *depersonalization*). They become cynical about others, tend to treat them as objects rather than as people, and hold negative attitudes toward them. In addition, they tend to derogate themselves, their jobs, their organizations, and even life in general. To put it simply, they come to view the world around them through dark gray rather than rose-colored glasses. Finally, they often report feelings of *low personal accomplishment*. People suffering from burnout conclude that they haven't been able to accomplish much in the past, and assume that they probably won't succeed in the future, either. In sum, **burnout** can be defined as a syndrome of emotional, physical, and mental exhaustion coupled with feelings of low self-esteem or low self-efficacy, resulting from prolonged exposure to intense stress. (See Figure 7-6 for a summary of the major components of the burnout syndrome.)

BURNOUT: SOME MAJOR CAUSES

What are the causes of burnout? As we have already noted, the primary factor appears to be prolonged exposure to stress. However, other variables also play a role. In particular, a number of conditions within an organization plus several personal characteristics seem to determine whether, and to what degree, individuals experience burnout.[44] For example, job conditions suggesting that one's efforts are useless, ineffective, or unappreciated seem to contribute to burnout.[45] Under such conditions, individuals develop the feelings of low personal accomplishment that are an important part of burnout. Similarly, poor opportunities for promotion and the presence of inflexible rules and procedures lead employees to feel that they are trapped in an unfair system and contribute to the development of negative views about their jobs.[46] Another important factor contributing to burnout is the *leader-*

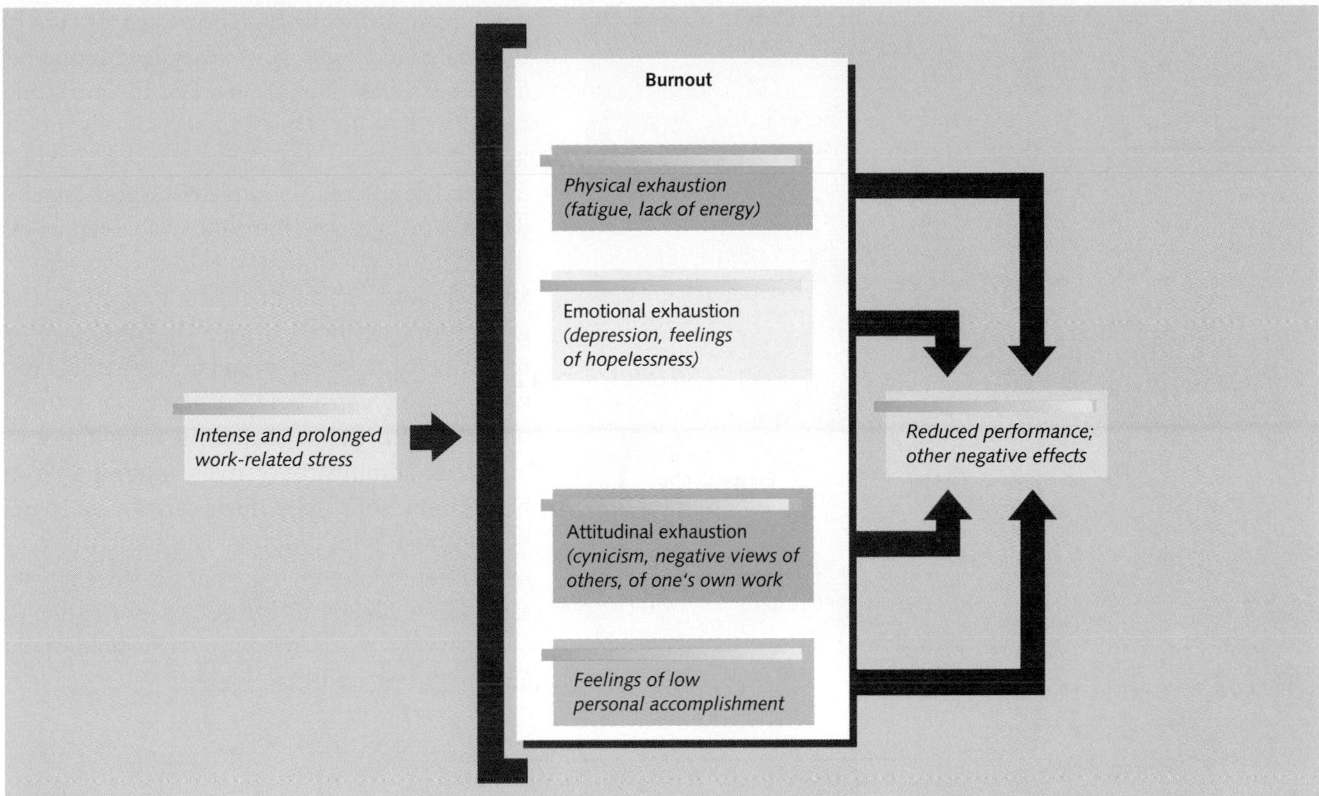

FIGURE 7-6
MAJOR COMPONENTS OF BURNOUT
When people are exposed to high levels of stress over prolonged periods of time, they may experience burnout. This syndrome involves physical, mental, and attitudinal exhaustion, plus feelings of low personal accomplishment. (Source: Based on suggestions by Maslach, 1982; see Note 43.)

ship style used by employees' supervisors. In particular, research has shown that the lower the amount of consideration demonstrated by their supervisors (i.e., the less they are concerned with employees' welfare or with maintaining friendly relations with them), the higher employees' reported levels of burnout.[47] (We will have more to say about various styles of leadership in Chapter 13.)

One of the most important factors contributing to burnout is the *coping styles* people use. Whereas some individuals are proactive and invest a great deal of energy in taking charge over events in their lives (control coping), others tend to simply react, let things happen to them, and try to avoid the consequences (*escape coping*).[48] Research has found that these different styles are related to burnout. For example, Leiter studied this issue by administering a questionnaire to a group of employees of a mental hospital.[49] Among other things, it measured their various coping behaviors, and the degree of burnout they experienced. The relationship between these measures was quite interesting. Mental health workers who used control strategies to address their difficulties at work were generally less exhausted and had more positive assessments of their personal accomplishments (two key components of burnout) than those who did not. By contrast, those who used escapist coping strategies were more prone to be exhausted emotionally and attitudinally (depersonalization) (for a summary of these relationships, see Figure 7-7). These findings make a convincing case that the way people respond to stressors in their lives can have an important effect on the likelihood of becoming a victim of burnout.

BURNOUT: ITS MAJOR EFFECTS

Whatever the precise causes of burnout, once it develops it has important individual consequences (for a summary, see Table 7-5).[50] Burnout also has important

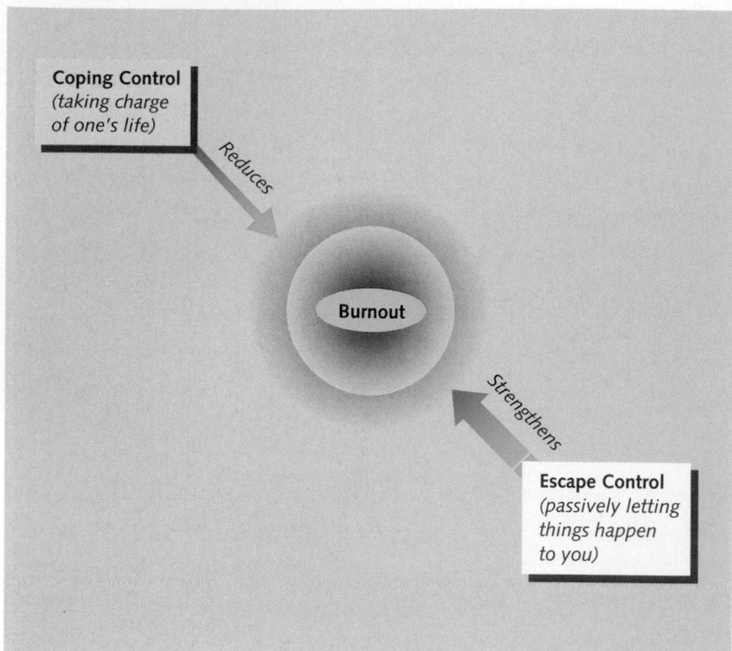

FIGURE 7-7

TWO TYPES OF COPING: THEIR EFFECTS ON BURNOUT

The way people cope with stress affects burnout. Whereas control coping has been found to reduce some symptoms of burnout, escape coping actually strengthens them. (Source: Based on suggestions by Leiter, 1991; see Note 50.)

consequences for the directions people take in their careers. Specifically, it may lead individuals to seek new jobs or careers. In one study concerned with the impact of burnout, Jackson, Schwab, and Schuler asked several hundred teachers to complete a questionnaire designed to measure burnout and to report on the extent to which they would prefer to be in another job or career.[51] As expected, the greater the teachers' degree of burnout, the more likely they were to prefer another job and to be actively considering a change of occupation. Second, people suffering from burnout may seek administrative roles where they can hide, from jobs they have grown to hate, behind huge piles of forms. Although this pattern certainly occurs, it appears to be relatively rare. Most victims of burnout seem either to change jobs or to withdraw psychologically and mark time until retirement.

BURNOUT: CAN IT BE REVERSED?

Before concluding, we should comment briefly on one final question: can burnout be reversed? Fortunately, growing evidence suggests that it can. With appropriate help, victims of burnout can recover from their physical and psychological exhaustion. If ongoing stress is reduced, if burnout victims gain added support from friends and co-workers, and if they cultivate hobbies and other outside interests, at least some people, it appears, can return to positive attitudes and renewed productivity. Such results can be attained, however, only through active efforts designed to overcome burnout and to change the conditions from which it develops.

TABLE 7-5

Symptoms of Burnout

The major signs that burnout is occurring fall into three categories: physical condition, behavioral changes, and work performance.

PHYSICAL CONDITION	BEHAVIORAL CHANGES	WORK PERFORMANCE
■ *Headaches*	■ *Increased irritability*	■ *Reduced efficiency (more time spent working, but with less productivity)*
■ *Sleeplessness*	■ *Changing moods*	■ *Dampened initiative*
■ *Weight loss*	■ *Reduced tolerance for frustration*	■ *Diminished interest in working*
■ *Gastrointestinal disturbances*	■ *Increased suspiciousness*	■ *Reduced capacity to perform effectively under stress*
■ *Exhaustion and fatigue*	■ *Greater willingness to take risks*	■ *Increased rigidity of thought (closed thinking, inflexible)*
	■ *Attempts at self-medication (use of alcohol and tranquilizers)*	

Source: Based on material reported by Moss, 1981; see Note 50.

STRESS AND HEALTH: THE SILENT KILLER

How strong is the link between stress and personal health? According to medical experts, very strong indeed. In other words, physiological strain reactions can be quite severe. In fact, some authorities estimate that stress plays a role in anywhere from 50 to 70 percent of all forms of physical illness.[52] Moreover, included in these figures are some of the most serious and life-threatening ailments known to medical science. A list of some of the more common ones is shown in Table 7-6. Even the most cursory look at this listing must leave you with the conclusion that the health-related effects of stress are not only quite widespread, but also extremely serious.

In addition to its role in the *degenerative diseases* listed, growing evidence indicates that stress also may play a major role in *infectious diseases*—diseases that are caused by the introduction into our bodies of an infectious agent such as bacteria or viruses. Many studies indicate that exposure to high levels of stress increases susceptibility to diseases such as upper respiratory infections, herpes virus infections, and various bacterial infections.[53] Some of these studies employ what is known as *prospective methodology*. In such research, the level of stress experienced by individuals at one point is related to their health at later times. Many studies of this type indicate that the rate of infectious illness increases following high-stress episodes. Still other investigations employ an approach in which healthy volunteers (emphasize the word *volunteers*) are purposely exposed to disease-causing agents, and to either stressful or nonstressful conditions. Results indicate that those exposed to stressful conditions tend to develop the illness in question more frequently.[54]

How can stress increase susceptibility to infectious disease? A model proposed by Cohen and Williamson suggests that several mechanisms may play a role. According to their conceptualization, stress may influence the immune system by affecting hormonal balance within the body or the neural mechanisms that regu-

TABLE 7-6

Health-Related Consequences of Stress

Just about any maladies you can think of have been linked to stress. The major health-related consequences fall into three categories: medical, behavioral, and psychological.

MEDICAL CONSEQUENCES	BEHAVIORAL CONSEQUENCES	PSYCHOLOGICAL CONSEQUENCES
■ *Heart disease and stroke*	■ *Smoking*	■ *Family conflict*
■ *Backache and arthritis*	■ *Drug and alcohol abuse*	■ *Sleep disturbances*
■ *Ulcers*	■ *Accident proneness*	■ *Sexual dysfunction*
■ *Headaches*	■ *Violence*	■ *Depression*
■ *Cancer*	■ *Appetite disorders*	
■ *Diabetes*		
■ *Cirrhosis of the liver*		
■ *Lung disease*		

Source: Based on material in Quick & Quick, 1984; see Note 4.

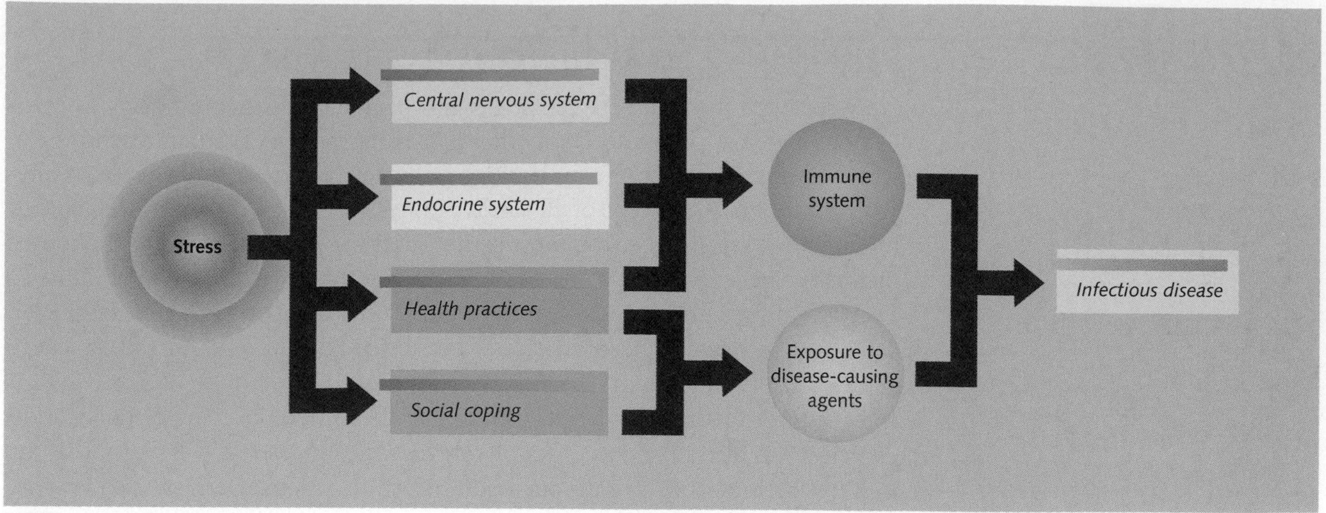

FIGURE 7-8

STRESS AND INFECTIOUS DISEASE: A MODEL

According to Cohen and Williamson, stress may increase susceptibility to infectious diseases through several different mechanisms. (Source: Based on suggestions by Cohen & Williamson, 1991; see Note 53.)

late various aspects of the immune system (e.g., production of white blood cells). Similarly, stress may influence health practices and coping through social contact; these, in turn, may alter rate of exposure to disease-causing organisms (see Figure 7-8). Whatever the precise mechanism, existing evidence suggests that stress can play a significant role in the occurrence, and course, of many infectious diseases. (Unfortunately, in extreme cases the effects of stress can be so severe that it leads to death! For a look at how this process appears to be operating in Japan, see the Global Organization section on the following page.)

INDIVIDUAL DIFFERENCES IN RESISTANCE TO STRESS

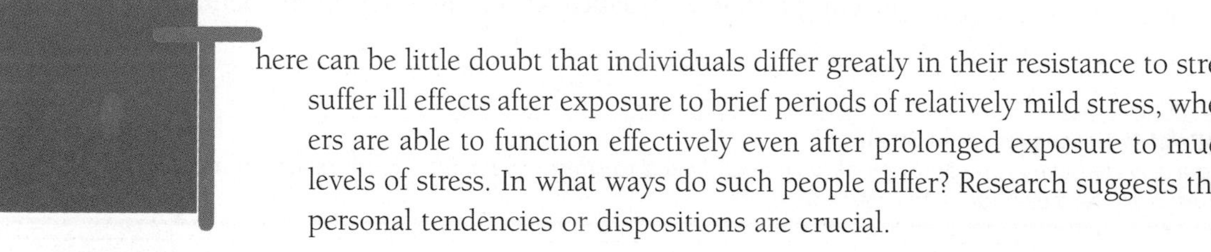

There can be little doubt that individuals differ greatly in their resistance to stress. Some suffer ill effects after exposure to brief periods of relatively mild stress, whereas others are able to function effectively even after prolonged exposure to much higher levels of stress. In what ways do such people differ? Research suggests that several personal tendencies or dispositions are crucial.

OPTIMISM: A BUFFER AGAINST STRESS

One factor that seems to play an important role in determining resistance to stress is the familiar dimension of *optimism–pessimism*. Optimists, of course, are people who see the glass as half full; they are hopeful in their outlook on life, interpret situations in a positive light, and tend to expect favorable outcomes and results. Pessimists, in contrast, are people who see the glass as half empty; they interpret many situations negatively, and expect unfavorable outcomes and results. Recent studies indicate that, as you might well guess, optimists are much more resistant to stress than pessimists. For example, optimists are much less likely than pessimists to report physical illness and symptoms during highly stressful periods, such as final exams.[58]

Additional findings help explain why. Optimists and pessimists seem to adopt sharply contrasting tactics for coping with stress. Optimists concentrate on *problem-focused coping*—making and enacting specific plans for dealing with sources of

THE GLOBAL ORGANIZATION

KAROUSHI: THE ULTIMATE EFFECT OF STRESS IN JAPAN

The "economic miracle" of modern-day Japan is well known. Following the devastation of World War II, the Japanese toiled to rebuild their country and have created a highly successful industrial power. At the root of this dramatic economic turnaround has been extremely hard work on the part of its people. For example, whereas the average American spends about 1,600 hours working per year, the comparable figure for the Japanese is 2,150 hours (see Figure 7-9).[55] For some Japanese people, working long periods without time off is not unusual (50 days straight in one case!).[56] As you might expect, this exceptionally hard work comes at a cost. For an increasing number of Japanese people, it has been a tragic one, at that—death.

The Japanese call it *karoushi*, translated as "sudden death from overwork." Although this phenomenon is relatively new, and has not been widely studied, it is popularly believed to occur soon after periods of extremely hard work. For example, in one recent case, an employee of a construction company worked 135 hours of overtime a month before he collapsed. Some nights he slept in his Tokyo office rather than spending the two hours required to return to his home in Osaka. The Nara Labor Standards Inspection Office ruled that this employee died from overwork, entitling his family to benefits.[57]

One expert, Dr. Walter Tubbs, has argued that it is not simply overwork that is killing these Japanese workers, but overwork combined with feelings of depression and helplessness. He prefers to think of *karoushi* as "stress death," because its victims not only worked very hard, but were forced to endure additional sources of stress as well (such as those listed in Table 7-3 on p. 255). A great many of the victims Tubbs studied appear to have been in jobs in which they had only minimal opportunities to control their fates, and had no chance to escape. They were caught up in a vicious cycle in which they were required to work long hours at undesirable jobs just to make ends meet. It is the resulting feeling of helplessness that Tubbs is convinced lies at the root of most *karoushi* cases, not simply the long hours themselves.

Because the evidence regarding stress death is currently quite scarce, it is difficult to say for sure whether Tubbs is correct (although his ideas appear quite plausible). It is also not entirely clear what role is played by the great importance of work in contemporary Japanese culture. Does *karoushi* occur in other cultures where working long hours is typical (such as Korea)? Or is there something unique about the cultural values or working conditions in Japan that make its people uniquely suited to becoming *karoushi* victims? Unfortunately, it is not yet possible to answer these important questions. Yet in view of the extremely serious nature of the problem, we are confident that systematic efforts to explain the stress death problem will soon provide some insight. Meanwhile, the next time you hear someone say, "Hard work never killed anyone," you may not agree.

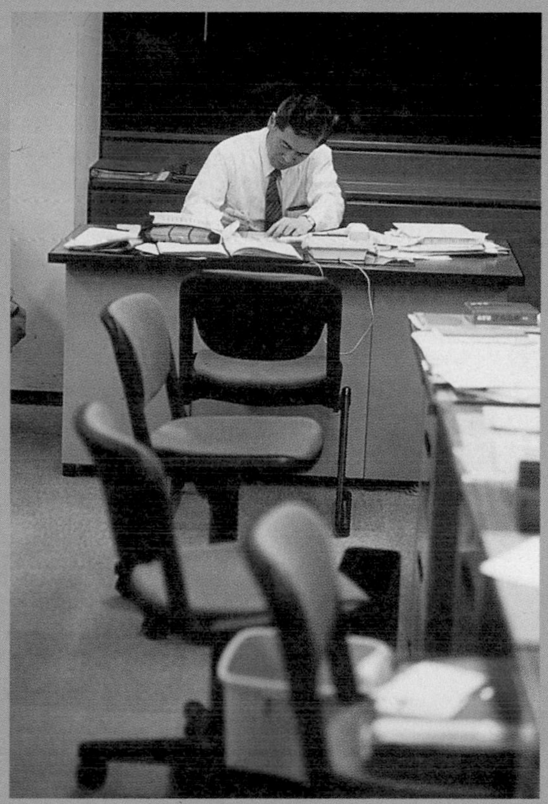

FIGURE 7-9
"HARD WORK NEVER KILLED ANYONE"—NOT SO IN JAPAN
Shigeo Shimoda puts in long hours as a manager at one of Japan's largest companies, Matsushita Electric Industrial Co. Ltd. Hopefully, he will not become a victim of karoushi—death caused by the stress of overwork under conditions of limited control.

stress. In addition, they seek *social support*—the advice and help of friends and others—and refrain from engaging in other activities until current problems are solved and stress is reduced. In contrast, pessimists tend to adopt different strategies, such as giving up in their efforts to reach goals with which stress is interfering, and denying that the stressful events have even occurred.[59] Obviously, the former strategies are often more effective than the latter.

HARDINESS: VIEWING STRESS AS A CHALLENGE

A second characteristic that seems to distinguish stress-resistant people from those who are more susceptible to its harmful effects is known as **hardiness.**[60] Actually, this term refers to a cluster of characteristics rather than just one. Hardy people seem to differ from others in three respects. They show higher levels of *commitment*, deeper involvement in their jobs and other life activities; *control*, the belief that they can, in fact, influence important events in their lives and the outcomes they experience; and *challenge*—they perceive change as a challenge and an opportunity to grow rather than as a threat to their security. Together, these characteristics tend to arm hardy people with high resistance to stress.

In a study illustrating this point, Oullette-Kobasa and Pucetti asked executives at a large public utility to complete questionnaires designed to measure their level of hardiness, the number of stressful life events they had recently experienced, and their current health.[61] Results indicated that people classified as high in hardiness did indeed report better health than those low in hardiness, even when they had recently encountered major stressful life changes. Similar results have been reported in several other studies with people from different occupations (e.g., nurses, lawyers, police officers).[62] Together, such findings suggest that hardiness is a useful concept for understanding the impact of stress.

THE TYPE A BEHAVIOR PATTERN

In Chapter 3, we noted that people who demonstrate the Type A behavior pattern (highly competitive, hard driving) respond more strongly than others to various forms of stress. Specifically, they show higher levels of arousal in the presence of stress than Type B's. Here, we note that not only do Type A's react more strongly to stress, but they also seem to actually *invite* it. Specifically, they tend to behave in ways that increase their workload and generate conditions most people would describe as stressful.

Direct evidence for such effects has been reported by Kirmeyer and Biggers, in a study of civilian radio dispatchers in police departments.[63] These researchers had seventy-two dispatchers complete a standard measure of Type A behavior, and then observed their behavior on the job during several work shifts. As predicted, these observations revealed that the higher the dispatchers scored on the Type A dimension, the more likely they were to initiate work, to engage in and complete more work, and to divide their attention between two or more simultaneous tasks. As Kirmeyer and Biggers put it, "By their actions Type A's not only constructed for themselves a highly demanding work environment but also created conditions likely to evoke a driven, time-urgent, and impatient behavioral style."[64] Clearly, this is one more reason why individuals who demonstrate the Type A pattern should take steps to modify their behavior: doing so may be extremely beneficial to their health!

TENSION DISCHARGE RATE

Nearly everyone experiences some degree of pressure or stress at work—this is a fact of life in modern organizations. However, individuals differ greatly in terms of how they handle such feelings. Some seem capable of leaving tension behind when they head for home. In contrast, others take it with them as excess psychological baggage. These individuals may be said to differ with respect to **tension discharge rate**—the rate at which individuals dissipate their job-related tensions at the end of the day (see Figure 7-10). Which group is more likely to suffer harmful effects from exposure to stress?

Research bearing on this question has shown that being able to leave one's work-related stresses at the job at the end of the day is an important determinant of how people respond to stress. In a study illustrating this phenomenon, Matteson and Ivancevich had several hundred medical technologists complete two questionnaires.[65] One measured tension discharge rate, and the other measured several aspects of personal health (e.g., the total number of health problems the technologists had experienced during the past six months). When they compared responses to these two questionnaires, the investigators found that people low in tension discharge rate (those who carried stress home with them at the end of the day) reported poorer health than those high in tension discharge rate. These findings suggest that the ability to leave one's worries behind at the end of the day can be very beneficial when it comes to resisting the harmful impact of stress.

FIGURE 7-10
TENSION DISCHARGE RATE: DISSIPATING JOB-RELATED STRESS
Whereas some people wind down soon after their work-days are over (high tension discharge rate), others tend to carry their stress home with them at the end of the day (low tension discharge rate).

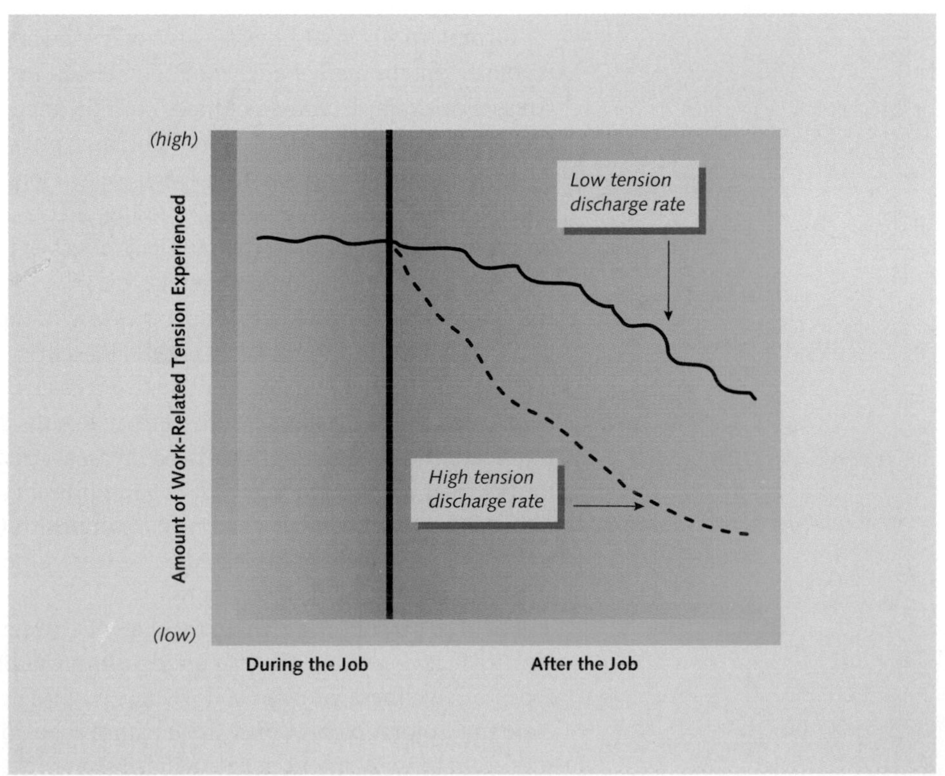

MANAGING STRESS: SOME EFFECTIVE TECHNIQUES

Stress stems from so many different factors and conditions that to eliminate it entirely from our lives is impossible. What both individuals and organizations can do, however, is take steps to reduce its intensity and minimize its harmful effects—to *cope* with stress when it occurs. Several strategies for attaining these goals exist.[66] Here, we will consider two major approaches: techniques individuals can apply themselves and interventions by organizations.

PERSONAL APPROACHES TO STRESS MANAGEMENT

What steps can people take to protect themselves against the adverse effects of stress? There are several different approaches, and these fall into four major categories: lifestyle management, physiological techniques, cognitive approaches, and behavioral changes.

LIFESTYLE MANAGEMENT: THE EFFECTS OF DIET AND EXERCISE

Today more than ever before, physicians are prescribing changes in lifestyle for their patients suffering from maladies related to stress.[67] Most popular among these are efforts at improving our diet and nutrition and increasing our physical fitness. With respect to nutrition, growing evidence indicates that reduced intake of salt and saturated fats, and increased consumption of fiber- and vitamin-rich fruits and vegetables, are steps that can greatly increase the body's ability to cope with the physiological effects of stress.[68] Although making significant changes in eating habits can be difficult—and require a large amount of willpower!—the benefits attained certainly justify such efforts.

Turning to physical fitness, existing evidence suggests that people who exercise regularly obtain many benefits closely related to resistance of the adverse effects of stress. For example, fitness reduces both the incidence of cardiovascular illness and the death rate from such diseases. Similarly, physical fitness lowers blood pressure, an important factor in many aspects of personal health. Perhaps the most convincing evidence for the stress-buffering effects of physical fitness is that reported by Brown.[69] He measured the physical fitness of college undergraduates by observing their performance on an exercise bicycle; the increase in their pulse rate after riding the bicycle provided a direct measure of the students' fitness. In addition, he obtained both self-reports of recent illnesses from participants and reports of recent stressful life events. Finally, an objective measure of their health was obtained from records at the university health center. Results indicated that for people low in physical fitness, high stress led to increased visits to the university's health center for physical illness. Among those high in physical fitness, however, increased stress did not produce a similar deterioration in health (see Figure 7-11). In sum, people who were physically fit appeared to be less vulnerable to the adverse effects of life stress than those who were less fit.

For this reason, a growing number of companies—as many as 50,000 in the United States, by one recent count—are providing exercise facilities and various types of "wellness programs" for their employees.[70] The Adolph Coors Co. (the Golden, Colorado, brewery), for example, has a separate building and full-time staff to help its employees help relieve stress by exercising and receiving counsel-

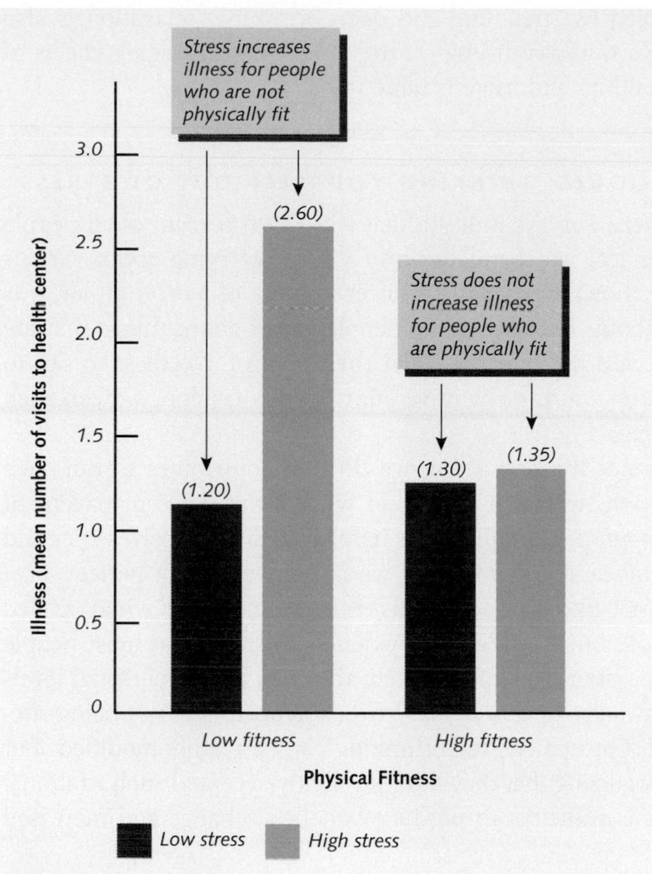

FIGURE 7-11
PHYSICAL FITNESS, RESISTANCE TO STRESS, AND PERSONAL HEALTH
Students who were physically fit showed little increase in frequency of illness when exposed to high levels of stress. In contrast, those who were not as fit showed a much larger increase in illness. (Source: Based on data from Brown, 1991; see Note 69.)

ing in nutrition.[71] The popularity of such programs is supported by evidence suggesting that physical fitness reduces absenteeism, enhances motivation and job performance (as discussed in Chapter 4), and also contributes to commitment and other positive attitudes among employees (see Chapter 5).[72]

At this point it is not entirely clear exactly what it is about the use of exercise facilities that may play a role in stress reduction.[73] Many factors appear to be involved, including the social contacts made during the course of exercising, the benefits to health and stamina, and/or the sign of commitment toward employees shown by initiating such programs. Meanwhile, while organizational researchers continue to attempt to unravel the mystery as to *why* exercise programs are effective, organizational practitioners will continue to use them.

PHYSIOLOGICAL TECHNIQUES: RELAXATION AND MEDITATION

When you think of successful executives at work, what picture comes to mind? Most of us would probably conjure up an image of someone on three phones at once, surrounded by important papers, or something similar. Probably the farthest thing from your mind would be the image of someone resting calmly in a serene setting. Yet for a growing number of today's employees, this picture is quite common. At Symmetrix (the Lexington, Massachusetts, software developer), for example, many of the company's 125 employees spend as long as 20 minutes a day behind closed office doors quietly meditating.[74] Rather than something that the company merely tolerates (after all, employees are paid to work, not rest), relaxing is a practice that it actively encourages—and has even paid consultants to teach employees to do! Moreover, this company is not unusual; others, such as Marriott, Polaroid, and The Boston Co. (an investment firm), have done the same.

What's going on in these companies *is* designed to help people become more productive, not in the traditional, stress-inducing way, but by helping them cope more effectively with stress. One technique used in this regard is **meditation**, the process of learning to clear one's mind of external thoughts, often by repeating a single syllable (known as a *mantra*) over and over again (see Figure 7-12). Essentially, meditation requires sitting quietly in a comfortable position, closing your eyes, relaxing your muscles, and breathing slowly. The trick is to not break your concentration by letting other thoughts enter your mind (if you do, experts say, you should just shrug them off and return to your mantra). Doing this once or twice a day for 10–20 minutes per session, is believed to be an effective way of enhancing one's capacity to work and to enjoy life in general.[75]

A related technique is **relaxation training**. In this method, people learn how to first tense and then relax their muscles.[76] By becoming familiar with the differences between these states, people become able to induce relaxed states whenever they feel themselves becoming tense. (An exercise explaining how to apply this technique is included at the end of this chapter; completing it may be well worth your while). When accompanied by stretching and deep breathing, relaxation is also believed to be an effective way of warding off the potentially damaging effects of stress, making people healthier and more productive.[77]

FIGURE 7-12
MEDITATION: AN EFFECTIVE WAY TO RELIEVE STRESS
Meditation involves deeply relaxing, clearing your mind of external thoughts and concentrating on a simple sound (known as a mantra). This process, when repeated on a regular basis, can be an effective means of reducing levels of stress in one's life.

COGNITIVE TECHNIQUES: THINKING YOURSELF OUT OF STRESS

Do you worry too much? Surveys indicate that almost 90 percent of all people answer yes.[78] Most of us feel we spend too much time worrying about various problems. The key issue, however, is not the sheer volume of worry; rather, it is *what* we tend to worry about. In many cases, people worry about things that are really quite unimportant and not directly under their control. Needless to say, to the extent that we can stop wasting cognitive effort in this fashion, we can each help manage our own stress.

Excessive worrying is not the only thing we do that contributes to our own stress, however. In addition, we often engage in what some stress management experts describe as *inappropriate self-talk*.[79] This involves telling ourselves over and over how horrible and unbearable it will be if we fail, if we are not perfect, or if everyone we meet does not like us. Such thoughts seem ludicrous when spelled out in the pages of a book, but considerable evidence indicates that most people entertain them at least occasionally. Unfortunately, they can add to personal levels of stress, as individuals *awfulize* or *catastrophize* over the horrors of not being successful, perfect, or loved. Fortunately, such thinking can be readily modified. For many people, merely recognizing that they have implicitly accepted such irrational and self-defeating beliefs is sufficient to produce beneficial change and increased resistance to stress.

Perhaps the guiding principle in all cognitive techniques for managing stress is this: *we can't always change the world around us, but we can change our reactions to it*. In other words, we don't have to permit ourselves to worry excessively over things we can't change or control, to allow potentially irritating situations to drive us up the wall, or to engage in hopeless quests for perfection. Instead, we can actively decide to avoid such reactions and choose not to become upset when things don't go our own way. So, for example, instead of getting upset the next time you're stuck in a bad traffic jam, it may be better to simply note that you can't do anything about it, and that the world won't come to an end if you're late. By exercising control over their own cognitive reactions, individuals can reduce the levels of stress they experience—helping themselves in many different ways.

BEHAVIORAL TECHNIQUES: LEARNING TO REACT DIFFERENTLY

Finally, several stress management techniques focus on changing people's overt behavior. When faced with events they find stressful, people can often help themselves to stem the rising tide of anxiety by adopting actions that are *incompatible* with such feelings. For example, instead of allowing our speech to become increasingly rapid and intense as we become upset, we can consciously modulate this aspect of our behavior. A reduction in arousal and tension may result. This technique is especially helpful for Type A's, whose always-in-a-hurry style tends to magnify reactions to stress in many situations.

Similarly, when confronted with rising tension, people can consciously choose to insert a brief period of delay (sometimes known as *time out*). This can involve taking a short break, going to the nearest restroom to splash cold water on one's face, or any other action that yields a few moments of breathing space. Such actions interrupt the cycle of ever-rising tension that accompanies stress, and can help to restore equilibrium and the feeling of being at least partly in control of ongoing events.

Still another behavioral technique for stress control involves building pleasure into one's life. Many people, especially Type A's, try to crowd so much into their schedules that little or no time is left for relaxation or pursuing hobbies. This is unfortunate, for even short vacations or short periods of time spent pursuing activities one really enjoys can go a long way toward alleviating the adverse effects of stress. In fact, research has shown that engaging in leisure pursuits help relieve many different symptoms of stress.[80] So, where stress is concerned, it is important for people to be kind to themselves, at least occasionally, if they wish to avoid the potential dangers of stress.

ORGANIZATION-BASED STRATEGIES FOR PREVENTING AND MANAGING STRESS

Although people may be able to increase their own resistance to stress, they cannot by themselves eliminate many of its causes from their work environments. In other words, while they may be able to help minimize its effects, they may not be able to prevent stress in the first place (see Figure 7-13). For this reason, organizations can play a key role in stress management. In particular, they can adopt changes in their internal structure and procedures, or alter the nature of jobs, to reduce stress among employees. Although such actions will certainly not eliminate stress altogether, they can go a long way toward eliminating many sources of stress in the workplace.

CHANGES IN ORGANIZATIONAL STRUCTURE AND FUNCTION

Several types of changes in organizational structure and function may be useful in preventing job-related stress. First, such benefits can sometimes be gained by *decentralization*—a process in which authority is spread more widely throughout an organization (we will describe this more thoroughly in Chapter 15). This reduces feelings of helplessness among employees—in large part, by giving them opportunities to have a voice in changing the way things are done—thereby reducing their overall level of stress. Second, steps can be taken to assure that performance appraisals and the distribution of organizational rewards are as fair as

FIGURE 7-13
INDIVIDUAL VERSUS ORGANIZATIONAL TACTICS OF STRESS MANAGEMENT
Whereas individual approaches to stress management focus on reducing the symptoms of stress (minimizing its negative impact), organizational tactics emphasize preventing the occurrence of stress in the first place.

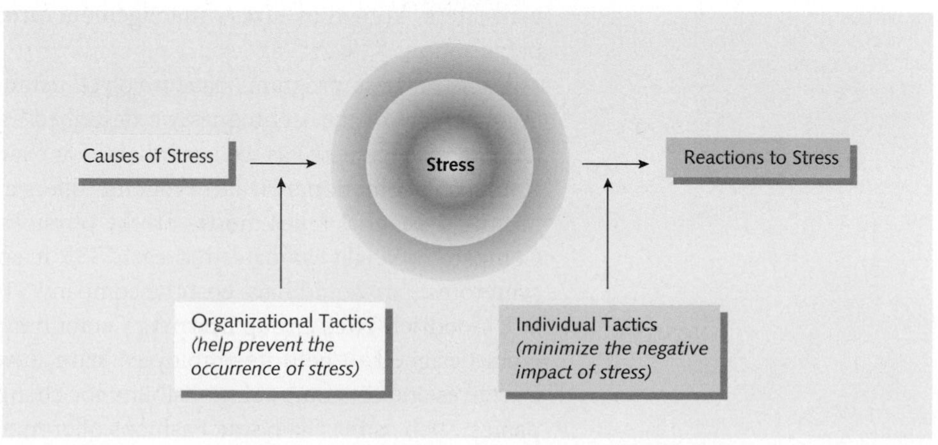

possible.[81] To the extent that individuals perceive that these matters are being handled in a reasonable fashion, the stress relating to them can be significantly reduced. Third, organizational policies should be written that help eliminate some of the uncertainties that might lead to stress.[82] These, of course, should also be widely disseminated in employee manuals and consistently followed if they are to be successful (in fact, if they are not, they may actually create stress rather than reduce it). For example, policies that clearly spell out the responsibilities of employers (e.g., statements about sick leave and vacation), and the obligations of employees (e.g., to behave ethically when conducting business) may go a long way toward eliminating some of the ambiguities that can lead to stress.

CHANGES IN THE NATURE OF JOBS

Careful attention to the nature of specific jobs can also reduce stress. For example, the stress resulting from boring, repetitive tasks can be lessened through *job enlargement*—efforts to broaden the scope of required job activities (see Chapter 4). At the very least, supervisors can try to put some variety into tasks that are by nature dull and repetitious, and to give employees opportunities to socialize with one another.

This is precisely the approach taken by Maids International, a franchised housecleaning service operating in the United States.[83] The company cannot afford the high turnover rates traditional in this industry, so they have attempted to improve conditions—and reduce stress—for employees in many different ways. As Dan Bishop, CEO of Maids International, comments, "We focused the whole concept of the company on the labor. Fatigue and boredom are what burn people out. We tried to eliminate them." To accomplish this task, the company tries to train employees in efficient ways of doing various cleaning jobs so that the amount of effort required is reduced. And time for socializing is built into the schedule during the drives between customers' houses. The result: employees stay on the job for an average of nine months, twice the industry average of under five months.

STRESS MANAGEMENT PROGRAMS

Because it is not always feasible to redesign entire organizations or individual jobs so as to prevent stress, companies are faced with having to concentrate on methods of reducing stress once it occurs. One of the most popular approaches calls for directly training employees to minimize the harmful effects of stress. Systematic efforts by organizations designed to help employees reduce and/or prevent stress, known as **stress management programs**, have been widely used in organizations.[84]

Some of these programs have involved extensive in-house training concentrating on many of the techniques we described earlier (e.g., meditation, relaxation, lifestyle management) as well as others. For example, the Equitable Life Insurance Company's "Emotional Health Program" offers a program in stress management to its employees that relies mostly on the physiological techniques described above. Company officials estimate that each $33 it spends on employees helps relieve symptoms that would have cost the company $100 in lost productivity.[85] Similarly, B. F. Goodrich Tire's Group Learning Center has prepared a nine-hour training program designed to help its employees learn how to identify the stressors in their own lives and to assume responsibility for changing their responses.[86] Other companies, such as Liz Claiborne Fashions offer much more modest, forty-five-minute sessions during lunchtime (including one entitled "Wellness and Your Funny Bone"). Finally, because many companies cannot afford to create their own stress management programs, they often rely on pre-packaged programs by outside consultants, or using widely available off-the-shelf audiovisual programs on videocassettes (even the actress Morgan Fairchild has her own: *Morgan Fairchild's Stress Management*).[87]

Companies that do not use stress management programs have other systematic ways of helping their employees. Many rely on help from their **employee assistance programs (EAPs)**—plans that provide employees with assistance in meeting various problems (e.g., substance abuse, career planning, financial, and legal problems). The Metropolitan Life Insurance Company (MetLife) is one company whose EAP has been actively involved in helping its employees reduce stress.[88] It reaches out to its 42,000 U.S. employees by providing toll-free telephone consultation for those in need of help, as well as access to on-site and external medical and psychological professionals. Although few EAPs are as extensive as MetLife's, the cost-effective nature of such programs is making them an increasingly common form of worker benefit in today's organizations.[89]

As we have shown, companies rely on many different methods for dealing with the problem of stress. The mere fact that so many organizations have been so resourceful in dealing with employee stress provides a good indication of just how critical such problems can be. (As you might imagine, such efforts are particularly important in the case of organizations whose employees are subject to high levels of stress on a regular basis—such as police officers. For a look at some of the efforts that have been taken to help control stress among people in this special group, see the Quest for Quality section below.)

THE QUEST FOR QUALITY

MANAGING STRESS AMONG POLICE OFFICERS: SOME LESSONS FROM THOSE WHO DO IT BEST

You probably don't need too much convincing that the job of police officer exposes people to far more stressors than most. The constant exposure to dangerous conditions, the uncertainties of confronting the public, pressures from peers and superiors, and the frustration of having to deal with a backlogged judicial system are the major ingredients for highly adverse stress reactions (see Figure 7-14). It's no wonder that stress-related disability claims among the half-million U.S. law enforcement personnel have been steadily on the rise.[90] It's also probably not surprising to learn that efforts have been made in many communities to help these women and men—who play such a vital role in maintaining safety for the rest of us—stay safe and healthy themselves.

Fortunately, several programs have been identified as being highly successful in helping law enforcement officers manage the high amounts of stress they confront.[91] The ones we will describe have been operating for well over a decade, and have been successful enough to continue to receive both financial and administrative support—sure signs of their value during these times of careful budget scrutiny.

One such approach is the *Health Resources Coordinator Program* (HRC) in the Palo Alto, California, police department (100 sworn officers and 60 civilian employees). Rather than simply stepping in to help after signs of a problem emerge, the HRC focuses on prevention. It does this by having a full-time psychologist available at the police station (who also can meet with officers in other locations, or by phone) to discuss the daily pressures the officers face, and to provide immediate help in dealing with them. Confidential, off-site counseling with therapists is also available to officers—and their family members, for whom life also can be highly stressful. In addition to helping people cope with stress, the program also focuses on eliminating sources of stress, whether they're specific (e.g., a supervisor whose style is causing problems) or long-standing (e.g., perceived inequities in the promotion process). HRC officials also carefully monitor conditions in the workplace (e.g., changes in workplace methods, leadership, and managerial decisions) that may have some effects on stress levels. Officers are also trained in ways to effectively communicate and solve problems with others, skills that can help avoid creating stressful situations in the future. The program is also available to help employees deal with such job-specific stressors as shootings and SWAT team activities. These, and other activities make the HRC a highly effective multipronged approach to managing stress in a stress-prone environment.

The *Psychological Services Division* (PSD) of the Prince George's County police department (a Maryland community adjacent to Washington, DC, with 1,500 sworn and civilian police employees) also provides a range of services. For example, when an officer's performance problems are believed to be based on emotional reactions (as opposed to skill deficits), he or she is referred to appropriate counseling personnel (instead of being disciplined, as might happen in other police departments). Because trauma often results from shooting incidents, a psychologist from the Critical Incident Service is called in to help the officer adjust and return to work free of stress symptoms. Another special team, the Emergency Response Service is available around the clock to help officers deal with problems they may face during emergencies, such as seeing one of their colleagues get shot. Other services are also routinely available to officers, such testing for communicable diseases, counseling for officers investigated for using excess force, individual and family-based therapy and chemical dependency treatment, training in relaxation, and special skills, such as hostage negotiation.

Although these two programs are somewhat different, they share several crucial features that make them successful. First, they are highly visible in all spheres of police activity, providing services to which officers can openly avail themselves without having to worry about appearing to be weak (a potential problem, given the "macho" culture that often prevails in police departments). Second, they are involved in the basic structure and operation of the police departments themselves (e.g., hiring and work assignment policies), not only the problems of the employees. Third, they are highly attuned to the special needs of their clients, police officers, and have custom-tailored programs especially for them. Fourth, they provide immediate, on-site attempts to deal with stressful problems before they get out of hand. Fifth, they focus on both officers and their families, recognizing the importance of family support in the lives of law enforcement agents. These important characteristics may be seen as lessons to be learned by other police departments—or any organizations, for that matter—seeking to effectively manage employee stress.

FIGURE 7-14

STRESS: A SERIOUS PROBLEM FOR LAW ENFORCEMENT OFFICIALS

Being a police officer is one of the most stressful jobs someone can have. Fortunately, several police departments have put into place highly successful programs for managing stress among their employees.

SUMMARY AND REVIEW

THE BASIC NATURE OF STRESS

We all encounter stimuli, known as **stressors**, that put physical or psychological demands on us. The pattern of emotional states and physiological reactions occurring in response to such demands is known as **stress.** People experience stress when they cognitively appraise the situations they're in as being highly threatening and beyond their control. To the extent that stress reactions cause deviations from normal states of human functioning, **strain** occurs. Stress is not simply anxiety or nervous tension, it need not necessarily be damaging, it is not always due to overstimulation, and it cannot be avoided (although negative reactions to stress *can* be avoided).

MAJOR CAUSES OF STRESS

Stress in work settings stems from many different factors. Several are directly related to jobs and organizations, and include occupational demands, conflict between work and nonwork roles, ambiguity and uncertainties on the job, underload and overload, responsibility for others, and lack of social support. An especially unsettling cause of work-related stress is **sexual harassment**—unwanted sexual contact or communication.

Stress also stems from events and situations arising outside work settings. *Stressful life events* such as divorce or death of a close relative are an important source of stress. Stress also stems from the *hassles of daily life*—milder but more frequent events that strain individuals' resources.

EFFECTS OF STRESS

Stress influences the performance of many tasks. The precise impact is difficult to predict, however, and seems to depend on the complexity of the task in question and an individual's previous experience with it. Even relatively mild levels of stress can interfere with task performance under a wide range of conditions. High levels of stress also reduce the quality or accuracy of decisions. In the case of group decisions, stress increases the responsiveness of both leaders and subordinates to input from others.

Prolonged exposure to stress can lead to **burnout**—a syndrome consisting of physical, emotional, and mental exhaustion, plus intense feelings of low personal accomplishment. Burnout is affected by several different factors, one of the most important being people's styles of coping.

Finally, stress exerts adverse effects on health. It has been linked to the occurrence of *degenerative diseases* such as heart disease, high blood pressure, hardening of the arteries, ulcers, and diabetes. Growing evidence also indicates that exposure to high levels of stress increases susceptibility to *infectious diseases*, such as upper respiratory infections and herpes virus infections.

INDIVIDUAL DIFFERENCES IN RESISTANCE TO STRESS

Considerable differences exist between people in their ability to resist the adverse effects of stress. *Optimists* are better able to cope with stress than *pessimists*. People high in **hardiness** (a combination of high commitment, feelings of personal control, and the tendency to perceive change as a challenge rather than a threat), are better able to resist the effects of stress than those low in hardiness. Type A individuals are more susceptible to the impact of stress than are Type B's, partly because they show greater physiological reactions to stress and partly because they behave in ways that expose them to high levels of stress. People who are able to leave stress at the office, those high in **tension discharge rate,** are less affected by stress than those who carry it home with them.

STRESS MANAGEMENT TECHNIQUES

Managing stress occurs at both the personal level, where individuals attempt to cope with the stress in their lives, and the organizational level, where attempts are made to eliminate the causes of stress (i.e., to prevent its occurrence). Personal approaches to managing stress include *lifestyle management*, focusing on proper diet and exercise, *physiological techniques*, such as meditation and relaxation, *cognitive techniques*, ways of rethinking potentially stressful situations, and *behavioral techniques*, learning to react differently.

Organization-based strategies for managing stress focus on prevention. They may involve changing organizational structure and function, or giving people more control over their jobs. Many organizations also rely on **stress management programs**, systematic attempts to train employees in specific ways of coping with stress. Several successful programs have been in use in various police departments.

KEY TERMS

burnout: A syndrome that results from prolonged exposure to stress. It consists of physical, emotional, and mental exhaustion, plus feelings of a lack of personal accomplishment.

employee assistance programs (EAPs): Plans that provide employees with assistance in meeting various problems (e.g., substance abuse, career planning, financial, and legal problems).

hardiness: A combination of traits (commitment to one's work, a sense of personal control, the ability to view change as a challenge rather than as a threat) that assists individuals in resisting the harmful effects of stress.

meditation: A technique for inducing relaxation in which individuals clear disturbing thoughts from their minds by repeating a single syllable (*mantra*).

qualitative overload: The belief among employees that they lack the skills or abilities needed to perform their jobs.

qualitative underload: The lack of mental stimulation that accompanies many routine, repetitive jobs.

quantitative overload: A situation in which individuals are required to do more work than they can actually accomplish in a given period of time.

quantitative underload: A situation in which individuals have so little to do that they spend much of their time doing nothing.

relaxation training: Procedures through which individuals learn to relax in order to reduce anxiety or stress.

role ambiguity: Uncertainty among employees about the key requirements of their jobs and how they should divide their time between various tasks.

role conflict: Incompatible demands made on an individual by different groups or persons.

sexual harassment: Unwanted contact or communication of a sexual nature.

strain: deviations from normal states of human functioning resulting from stressful events.

stress: The pattern of emotional states and physiological reactions occurring in response to demands from within or outside organizations (*stressors*).

stress management programs: Systematic efforts by organizations designed to help employees reduce and/or prevent stress.

stressors: Various factors in the external environment that induce stress among people exposed to them.

tension discharge rate: The rate at which individuals rid themselves of work-related tension at the end of the day. People high in *tension discharge rate* leave such tensions at the office, whereas those low in this characteristic tend to bring them home.

total negative life stress: The combined stress stemming from work-related and personal causes of stress.

QUESTIONS FOR DISCUSSION

1. Two individuals exposed to the same situation may experience sharply contrasting levels of stress. Why?
2. Suppose you are considering a new job. What factors will you examine closely to determine how stressful the new position might be?
3. Imagine that you are exposed to high levels of stress over a prolonged period of time. What effect might this have on your personal health?
4. Suppose you are faced with the task of choosing employees for a high-stress job. What personal characteristics will you seek in the people you hire? What characteristics will you try to avoid?
5. Imagine that you are faced with the task of developing a written company policy concerning sexual harassment. What points should be included in this policy?
6. What kind of things do you say silently to yourself when you are irritated or frustrated that actually increase the level of stress you experience? What different thoughts would help you better manage stress in such situations?
7. Stress-related illnesses often prove very costly to organizations in terms of employee absence and the costs of administerig health insurance plans. What steps can companies take to reduce stress among their employees?

CASE IN POINT

WORKPLACE VIOLENCE: THE NEW NATIONAL EPIDEMIC

The statistics are alarming: 750 people were murdered at work in 1992 and 110,000 acts of workplace violence occur annually.[1] In fact, murder is the third leading cause of workplace death (after motor vehicle and machinery accidents). The rise in violent acts in the workplace has prompted the Centers for Disease Control in Atlanta to classify workplace violence as a national epidemic.[2]

One institution that has been particularly hard hit by violence at work is the U.S. Postal Service (USPS). Since 1986, 38 post office employees have been killed by 10 coworkers. Unfortunately, these murders have occurred in seven different states leading one to the conclusion that violence is a systemwide problem in the USPS.[3,4]

When asked for an explanation of what might give rise to this type of fury, employees in the Oklahoma City bureau suggest that these outbursts may be a function of the nature of the job. They identify numerous tensions in the job such as the fast pace of work, the monotony of activity, the physical strain of lifting, the fast pace of activity, and the high rate of injury as elements contributing to the stress experienced by USPS employees.[5]

Furthermore, although these situations exist in many other industries, USPS employees believe that it is the combination of these physical pressures in conjunction with the psychological strains of work that have contributed to the explosion in workplace savagery. Specifically, people who work at the post office claim that "their tensions fester within an archaic, Army-like environment in which many top managers communicate by directive and front-line supervisors often hover over their charges, waiting for a mistake and timing workers' trips to the bathroom."[6]

In interviews with postal employees, Peter Kilborn found that one in every twenty with whom he spoke had personally experienced or had knowledge of another's recent clash with a supervisor. These people described their bosses as "martinets"(strict disciplinarians), and dictators. They depict the Postal Service as a quasi-military operation. This is highlighted by the military titles used (e.g., Postmaster General), the presence of U.S. and Postal Service flags, and even the time clock—calibrated in 24-hour military time.[7]

The time clock, which records seconds as well as hours and minutes, is a particular source of irritation. People are required to punch in and out when they go to lunch, to the bathroom, or simply leave their workstations. Employees report that supervisors closely scrutinize their time records. When they are a few seconds late to their posts they may be identified as "AWOL" (military term for "absent without leave"). If this occurs repeatedly, they are docked pay.[8]

In addition, discipline, in the form of suspensions and dismissals, is frequent. This would not necessarily be a problem say the Postal Service union members. However, since these actions are almost always overturned by the union grievance procedure, they are seen as arbitrary and as a result, create an atmosphere of negativism and uncertainty. One distribution and window clerk who has been fired four times and suspended more than that, has had all these incidents overturned by the resolution procedure. He says, "I'm not going to flip out, but it gets to the point where you don't sleep right, you don't eat right. Conversations become arguments."[9]

Another problem that creates pressure is that the supervisors are generally no better trained, skilled, or paid than the people they oversee. This is exacerbated by the fact that there is often one of them for every ten subordinates—a very heavy management-to-employee ratio for work that is relatively routine. Because of the large number of supervisors, they often come to think of themselves as indispensable to the accomplishment of the work to be done. Solely to prove the point that this isn't necessarily true, a four-hour meeting of all supervisors was called by a new plant manager one day. "There was no disaster," claimed one of these supervisors, who was seemingly surprised by the fact that nothing awful happened in the absence of management personnel.[10]

Sadly, workplace violence isn't limited by industry, geography, or even level of employee. Recent examples of employee killings include a teacher shooting a group of administrators in Michigan, a pizza parlor employee murdering co-workers in Colorado, a meat-packing plant employee shooting a plant manager in Boston, and a businessman bursting into the offices of his lawyers and killing seven people in San Francisco.[11,12]

CASE IN POINT, Cont.

Experts suggest both practical and psychological reasons for the rise in workplace violence. The most obvious of these "practical" explanations is the ready availability of firearms. Psychological explanations for increasing violence at work include pressure on the job or the loss, or threat of loss, of employment. In addition, the disparity between executive salaries and that of the average worker is thought to arouse anger, which is then displayed through violence. Instances in which employees feel mistreated or as "disposable commodities" also contribute to the acting out of frustration via violence.[13]

Who is most likely to commit acts of workplace terrorism? "The idea of a normal person snapping is absolutely wrong, it is also wrong to view them all as a criminal type," says Garry Mathiason, a San Francisco lawyer and expert in workplace violence.[14] Most who target the workplace for violent acts fit the profile of a white male with limited social support (e.g., few friends, limited involvement with his community) who blames others for his problems, and who is preoccupied with weapons.

Despite the seeming unpredictability of violent acts, employers can make efforts to reduce the likelihood of these outbursts. The most effective means to do this is to listen to people who make threats. It is often the case that people who engage in violent acts at work have tipped off those around them of their intentions. Confronting such employees and demanding that they take paid leave and seek help is one way to circumvent violence. Another way is to create positive work climates. Autocratic environments in which employees have little control are more likely to lead to uncontrolled emotional and physical outbursts than are positive climates in which employee contributions are solicited and valued. Finally, employers must take seriously the safety of their personnel. In places such as convenience stores, where employees are in danger of robbery and assault, employers should be sure to provide barriers (e.g., bullet-proof shielding) to such physical hazards.[15]

QUESTIONS FOR DISCUSSION

1. Do you think that working in a stressful job has anything to do with the likelihood of workplace violence?
2. Do personal qualities such as hardiness help explain who is more or less likely to commit an act of violence at work? Support your response with examples.
3. Beyond the obvious psychological and physical costs of workplace violence, what are other potential costs of workplace violence in terms of organizational attitudes and behaviors?
4. Compare and contrast workplace violence as a behavior to the behaviors typically exhibited by people experiencing burnout.
5. Explain how stress management techniques might be used to curb workplace violence.

EXPERIENCING ORGANIZATIONAL BEHAVIOR

Stressed Out? Follow This Lesson in Relaxation

One of the most effective things we can do to control our own stress levels is to relax. Relaxation helps reduce the physiological strain on the body, minimizing the long-term damage that may be caused by exposure to stressors. Although you already know how to relax, we're talking about a deeper kind of relaxation than normal. Keep an open mind, and give it a try.

PROCEDURE

As in other things, preparation is crucial. Find a quiet, comfortable place where you can be free from distractions for approximately twenty minutes. Then follow each of these steps (adapted from Quick & Quick, 1984; see Note 5):

1. Sit quietly in a comfortable position.
2. Close your eyes.
3. Starting at your feet, and working your way up toward your head, deeply relax each of your muscles. (This will take some concentration and practice.)
4. Breathe easily and naturally through your nose, concentrating on each individual breath. Each time you exhale, repeat the word "one" (or any similar simple sound) silently to yourself. (This is your *mantra.*)
5. Continue this process for about ten to twenty minutes. (It's OK to open your eyes occasionally to check the clock, but *do not use an alarm!*) After you're finished, do not jump up; remain quietly seated for a few minutes longer and then slowly rise.

Hints: Don't obsess about reaching a deep level of concentration. You probably won't be able to do so at first. But with practice, you will be able to achieve relaxation very quickly. When distracting thoughts enter your mind, simply ignore them and return to repeating your mantra. Practice this technique once or twice daily, but never within two hours after eating a meal (the process of digestion interferes with the ability to relax). It might take several weeks (or even months) to get to the point where you can relax without mental interference, so be patient.

POINTS TO CONSIDER

1. Were you skeptical about this process at first? How did trying this technique change the way you feel? Did you become a greater believer in the benefits of relaxation?

2. At first, how long did it take you to achieve deep relaxation? With practice, were you successful in reducing this time?

3. Did you find that the more you practiced this technique, the less you became distracted by outside thoughts entering your mind?

4. Did this technique to work for you? In other words, has it helped relieve stress in your life? If so, what particular sources of stress were most effectively alleviated?

5. How did your experiences with this technique compare to those of your classmates? Why do you think some were able to use the technique effectively while others were not?

PART IV

GROUP PROCESSES

CHAPTER OUTLINE

SPECIAL SECTIONS

EIGHT

GROUP DYNAMICS AND TEAMWORK IN ORGANIZATIONS

The hammers must be swung in cadence when more than one is hammering the iron.

Giordano Bruno, c. 1548–1600
Italian philosopher and astronomer
Candelaio

The path to greatness is along with others.

Baltasar Gracián, 1601–1658
Spanish priest and popular writer
Oraculo Manual

LEARNING OBJECTIVES

After reading this chapter, you should be able to

1. *Define what is meant by a group, and explain why it is not just a collection of people.*
2. *Identify different types of groups operating within organizations, and explain how they develop.*
3. *Describe the importance of norms, roles, status, and cohesiveness within organizations.*
4. *Define what teams are, and how they may be distinguished from groups in general.*
5. *Describe the various types of teams that exist in organizations, and the steps that should be followed in creating them.*
6. *Explain how individual performance in groups is affected by the presence of others (social facilitation), the cultural diversity of group membership, and the number of others with whom one is working (social loafing).*
7. *Explain the evidence regarding the effectiveness of teams in organizations.*
8. *Identify the factors responsible for the failure of some teams to operate as effectively as possible.*

PREVIEW CASE

Teaming Up for Success at XEL Communications

The telecommunications industry is populated by giants like AT&T and Northern Telecom. So, if you're a David in an ocean of Goliaths, you have to do something different from the competition—and much better—just to stay afloat. This was the situation Bill Sanko and his partners faced in the mid-1980s when they broke off from GTE and started their own 180-employee telecommunications equipment company, XEL Communications Inc.

Sanko knew that the success of his fledgling operation depended on providing speedy responses to customers' needs at reasonable prices. The custom circuit boards XEL was selling—mostly to its former parent, GTE—were taking about eight weeks to produce. This was much too long, and the company began to struggle. Customers became disgruntled, and too much money was tied up in inventory.

The problem, Sanko realized, was that it took too many individuals to get anything done, and jobs were poorly coordinated. Sanko gives this example: "If a hardware engineer needed some software to help, he'd go to his manager. The manager would say, 'Go write it up.' Then the hardware manager would take the software manager to lunch and talk about it." No wonder it took so long to get things done!

Sanko and his colleagues decided that the solution to their problem would be to eliminate the many layers of management that were slowing down the process. In its place they would substitute small teams of people responsible for getting their jobs done. So, with the help of John Puckett, XEL's vice president of manufacturing, the work floor was totally redesigned, and in 1988 work teams were created.

XEL's teams are typically composed of about a dozen members, people with individual responsibilities that are clearly identified and agreed to mutually by all team members. Teams track their own attendance, on-time deliveries, and other aspects of job performance. Banners hang high above each team's work area on the plant floor, marking their territories—and their identities.

Regularly each day, team members meet to plan their part in meeting the company's weekly schedule. All this goes on without management intervention. In fact, only once each quarter does management get involved—during a meeting in which each team makes a presentation describing what it has accomplished

A team meeting in progress at XEL Communications.

By 1993, only five years after the teams began, things dramatically had turned around at XEL. Since introducing teams, the cost of assembly dropped 25 percent, and inventory has been reduced 50 percent, all while increasing quality levels 30 percent. And that eight-week production time? It dropped to only four days—and is still falling! Importantly, sales figures reflect these dramatic improvements: between 1992 and 1993 sales jumped from $17 million to $25 million.

This success hasn't been exactly easy for XEL. For example, because team members work so closely together, adding new members has been a challenge.

Teams are so concerned about getting their jobs done that they are often impatient with newcomers, fearing that their output will suffer. As Teri Mantooth, operator of a wave-solder machine, put it, "Your first instinct is . . . we've got a new person . . . we're not going to make our numbers."

Another problem has been that in some groups, the freedom has proven to be too much. In XEL's stockroom, for example, some employees were abusing the system by cheating on their time cards. At first, problem employees were replaced, but eventually stockroom teams had to be disbanded, and replaced by full-time supervisors with disciplinary authority.

As far as Bill Sanko and his colleagues at XEL are concerned, these adjustments are a small price to pay for an approach that has worked so effectively. XEL has been so successful, in fact, that it was chosen to be featured on a video about team-based management produced by the Association for Manufacturing Excellence. Will all this success make XEL the next AT&T? Hold the line for a few years to find out.

XEL officials are convinced that its new approach—relying on teams of people working in concert instead of less committed individuals answering to several bosses—has been the key to its success. Its employees share a strong concern for the company and its goals, and everyone wants to help make it successful. The team members also clearly have a strong camaraderie. They're all interested in the company's success, and have a great deal of say in what goes on. What is it that makes groups of employees like those at XEL so successful? Are all such teams effective, or are others less successful? How should such groups be formed? How can problems, such as the ones noted at XEL, be overcome? These questions are all basic to the topics of *group dynamics* and *teamwork*, the two major foci of this chapter.

Group dynamics involves on the nature of groups—the variables governing their formation and development, their structure, and their interrelationships with individuals, other groups, and the organizations within which they exist.[1] **Teamwork** is the practice of using teams, special kinds of groups in which members are mutually committed to some goal, and share the leadership in attaining it. Given the prevalence of groups in organizations, and the growing popularity of teams, the importance of these topics in the field of organizational behavior is easy to appreciate. Because groups exist in all types of social settings, the study of group dynamics has a long history in the social sciences—including OB.[2]

In this chapter we will draw upon this work. Specifically, we will describe the nature of groups by defining what groups are, identifying various types of groups and why they form, explaining the various stages through which groups develop, and describing the dynamics of the way groups are structured. We will then describe special kinds of groups known as *teams*. Specifically, we will define teams and distinguish them from groups, describe various types of teams that exist, and identify some basic steps in creating teams. After describing the basic nature of groups and teams, we will shift our attention to how well groups and teams perform their jobs. We will describe the dynamics of individual performance in groups. Specifically, we will describe how people are affected by the presence of others, how the cultural makeup of a group affects performance, and the tendency for people to withold their individual performance under certain conditions.

Finally, we will describe the performance of teams, examining the evidence regarding team effectiveness and some of the obstacles that sometimes lead teams to fail.

GROUPS AT WORK: THEIR BASIC NATURE

To understand the dynamics of groups and their influence on individual and organizational functioning, we must begin by addressing some basic questions—namely, what is a group, what types of groups exist, and how do groups come into being?

WHAT IS A GROUP? A WORKING DEFINITION

Imagine three people waiting in line at the cashier's stand at a supermarket. Now compare them to the board of directors of a large corporation. Which collection would you consider to be a "group"? Although in our everyday language we may refer to the people waiting in line as a group, they are not a group in the same sense as the members of the board. Obviously, a group is more than simply a collection of people. But what exactly is it that makes a group a group?

Social scientists have formally defined a **group** *as a collection of two or more interacting individuals with a stable pattern of relationships among them who share common goals and who perceive themselves as being a group.*[3] To help us examine this definition more closely, we have portrayed it visually in Figure 8-1.

One of the most obvious characteristics of groups is that they are composed of *two or more people in social interaction*. In other words, the members of a group must have some influence on each other. The interaction between the parties may be either verbal (such as sharing strategies for a corporate takeover) or nonverbal (such as exchanging smiles in the hallway), but the parties must have some impact on each other to be considered a group.

Groups also must possess a *stable structure*. Although groups can change, and often do, there must be some stable relationships that keep group members together and functioning as a unit. A collection of individuals that constantly changes (e.g., the people inside an office waiting room at any given time) cannot be thought of as a group. To be a group, a greater level of stability would be required.

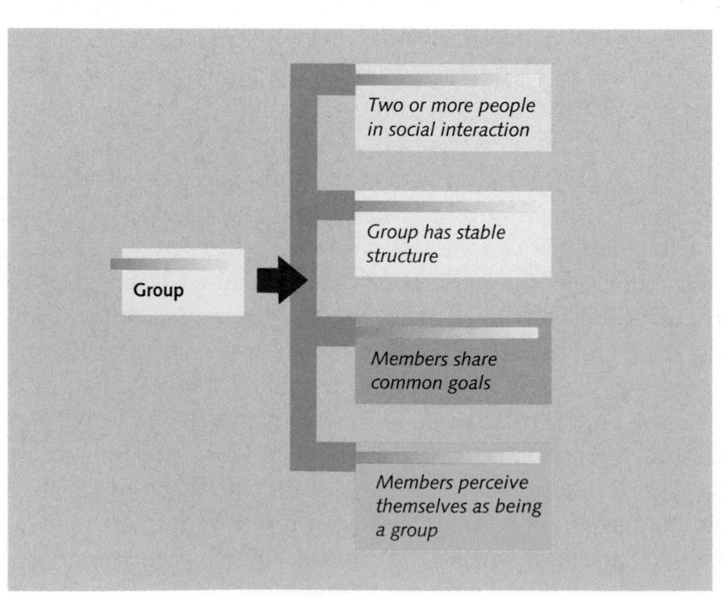

FIGURE 8-1
A GROUP: ITS DEFINING CHARACTERISTICS
To be a group, four different criteria must be met: there must be two or more people in social interaction, they also must share common goals, have a stable group structure, and perceive themselves as being a group.

A third characteristic of groups is that their *members share common interests or goals*. For example, members of a stamp-collecting club constitute a group that is sustained by the mutual interest of members. Some groups form because members with common interests help each other achieve a mutual goal. For example, the owners and employees of a sewing shop constitute a group formed around a common interest in sewing, and the common goal of making money.

Finally, to be a group, the individuals involved must *perceive themselves as a group*. Groups are composed of people who recognize each other as a member of their group and can distinguish these individuals from nonmembers. The members of a corporate finance committee or a chess club, for example, know who is in their group and who is not. In contrast, shoppers in a checkout line probably don't think of each other as being members of a group. Although they stand physically close to each other and may have passing conversations, they have little in common (except, perhaps, a shared interest in reaching the end of the line) and fail to identify themselves with the others in the line.

By defining groups in terms of these four characteristics, we have identified a group as a very special collection of individuals. As we shall see, these characteristics are responsible for the very important effects groups have on organizational behavior. To better understand these effects, we will now review the wide variety of groups that operate within organizations.

TYPES OF GROUPS AND WHY THEY FORM

What do the following have in common: a military combat unit, three couples getting together for dinner, the board of directors of a large corporation, and the three-person cockpit crew of a commercial airliner? As you probably guessed, the answer is that they are all groups. But, of course, they are very different kinds of groups, ones people join for different reasons.

FORMAL AND INFORMAL GROUPS

The most basic way of identifying types of groups is to distinguish between *formal groups* and *informal groups* (see Figure 8-2). **Formal groups** are created by the organization and are intentionally designed to direct members toward some important organizational goal. One type of formal group is referred to as a *command group*—a group determined by the connections between individuals who are a formal part of the organization (i.e., those who can legitimately give orders to others). For example, a command group may be formed by the vice president of marketing, who gathers together her regional marketing directors from around the

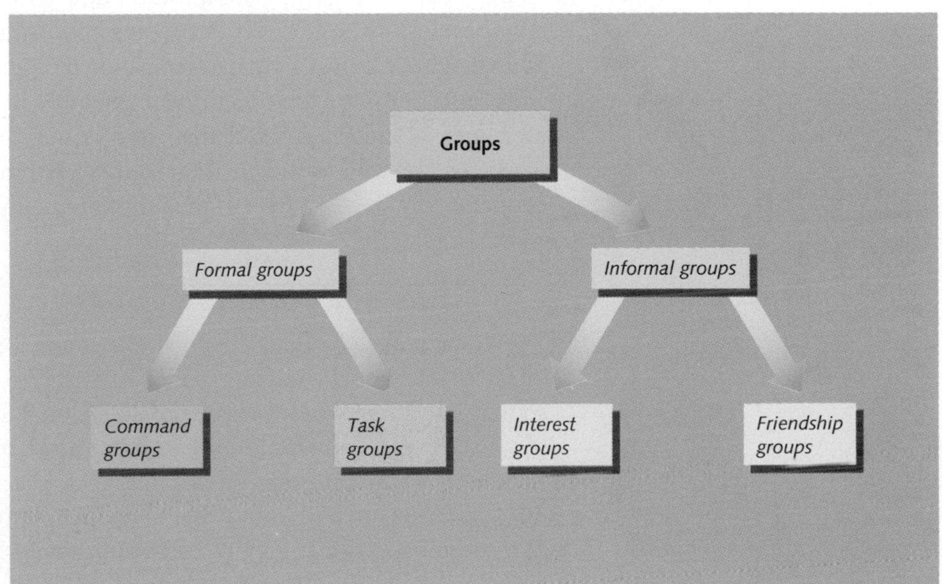

FIGURE 8-2
VARIETIES OF GROUPS IN ORGANIZATIONS
Within organizations one may find formal groups (such as command groups and task groups) and informal groups (such as interest groups and friendship groups).

country to hear their ideas about a new national advertising campaign. The point is that command groups are determined by the organization's rules regarding who reports to whom, and usually consist of a supervisor and his or her subordinates.

A formal organizational group also may be formed around some specific task. Such a group is referred to as a *task group*. Unlike command groups, a task group may be composed of individuals with some special interest or expertise in a specific area regardless of their positions in the organizational hierarchy. For example, a company may have a committee on equal employment opportunities whose members monitor the fair hiring practices of the organization. It may be composed of personnel specialists, corporate vice presidents, and workers from the shop floor. Whether they are permanent committees, known as *standing committees*, or temporary ones formed for special purposes (such as a committee formed to recommend solutions to a parking problem), known as *ad hoc committees* or *task forces*, task groups are common in organizations.

As you know, not all groups found in organizations are as formal as those we've identified. Many groups are informal in nature. **Informal groups** develop naturally among an organization's personnel without any direction from the management of the organization within which they operate. One key factor in the formation of informal groups is a common interest shared by its members. For example, a group of employees who band together to seek union representation, or who march together to protest their company's pollution of the environment, may be called an *interest group*. The common goal sought by members of an interest group may unite workers at many different organizational levels. The key factor is that membership in an interest group is voluntary—it is not forced by the organization, but encouraged by an expression of common interests.

Of course, sometimes the interests that bind individuals together are far more diffuse. Groups may develop out of a common interest in participating in sports, or going to the movies, or just getting together to talk. These kinds of informal groups are known as *friendship groups*. A group of co-workers who hang out together during lunch may also bowl or play cards together after work. Friendship groups extend beyond the workplace because they provide opportunities for satisfying the social needs of workers that are so important to their well-being (as you may recall from our discussion of Maslow's need hierarchy theory in Chapter 4).

Informal work groups are an important part of life in organizations. Although they develop without direct encouragement from management, friendship groups often originate out of formal organizational contact. For example, three employees working alongside each other on an assembly line may get to talking and discover their mutual interest in basketball, and decide to get together to shoot hoops after work. As we will see, such friendships can bind people together, helping them cooperate with each other on the job, potentially benefiting their organizations.

REASONS FOR JOINING GROUPS

We have already noted that people often join groups to satisfy their mutual interests and goals. To the extent that getting together with others allows us to achieve ends that would not be possible alone, forming groups makes a great deal of sense. In fact, organizations can be thought of as collections of groups that are focused toward achieving the mutual goal of achieving success for the company. But this is not the only motivation that people have for joining groups. There are also several additional reasons (see summary in Table 8-1).

TABLE 8-1

Why Do People Join Groups? Some Major Reasons

People become members of groups for a variety of different reasons. Any one or more of the following may explain why people join groups.

REASON	EXPLANATION
■ *To satisfy mutual interests and goals*	*By banding together, people can share their interests (e.g., hobbies) and help meet their mutual goals.*
■ *To achieve security*	*Groups provide safety in numbers, protection against a common enemy.*
■ *To fill social needs*	*Being in groups helps satisfy people's basic need to be with others.*
■ *To fill need for self-esteem*	*Membership in certain groups provides people with opportunities to feel good about their accomplishments.*

Not only do groups form for purposes of mutually achieving goals, they also frequently form for purposes of seeking protection from other groups. If you've ever heard the proverb, "There's safety in numbers," you are probably already aware that people join groups because they seek the security of group membership. Historically, for example, trade unions, such as the AFL–CIO, the UAW, and the Teamsters, have been formed by labor for purposes of seeking protection against abuses by management. Similarly, professional associations, such as the American Medical Association and the American Bar Association were created, in large part, for purposes of protecting their constituents against undesirable governmental legislation.

This is not to say that groups are always designed to promote some instrumental good; indeed, they also exist because they appeal to a basic psychological need to be social. As we already discussed in the context of Maslow's need hierarchy theory (in Chapter 4), people are social animals; they have a basic need to interact with others. Groups provide good opportunities for friendships to develop—hence, for social needs to be fulfilled.

Also as suggested by Maslow, people have a basic desire for their self-esteem needs to be filled. Group memberships can be a very effective way of nurturing self-esteem. For example, if a group to which one belongs is successful (such as a sales group that meets its quota), the self-esteem of all members (and supporters) may be boosted. Similarly, election to membership in an exclusive group (e.g., a national honor society) will surely raise one's self-esteem.

As we have shown, people are attracted to groups for many different reasons. Despite the fact that people may have different motivations for forming groups, it is interesting to note that once formed, groups develop in remarkably similar ways. We will now turn our attention to this issue.

STAGES IN THE DEVELOPMENT OF GROUPS

Just as infants develop in certain ways during their first months of life, groups also show relatively stable signs of maturation and development.[4] One popular theory identifies five distinct stages through which groups develop.[5] As we describe these below, you may want to review our summary of the five stages shown in Figure 8-3.

The first stage of group development is known as *forming*. During this stage of group development, the members get acquainted with each other. They establish the ground rules by trying to find out what behaviors are acceptable, with respect to both the job (how productive they are expected to be) and interpersonal relations (who's really in charge). During the *forming* stage, people tend to be a bit confused and uncertain about how to act in the group and how beneficial it will be to become a member of the group. Once the individuals come to think of themselves as members of a group, the forming stage is complete.

The second stage of group development is referred to as *storming*. As the name implies, this stage is characterized by a high degree of conflict within the group. Members often resist the control of the group's leaders and show hostility toward each other. If these conflicts are not resolved and group members withdraw, the group may disband. However, as conflicts are resolved and the group's leadership is accepted, the storming stage is complete.

The third stage of group development is known as *norming*. During this stage, the group becomes more cohesive, and identification as a member of the group becomes greater. Close relationships develop, shared feelings become common, and a keen interest in finding mutually agreeable solutions develops. Feelings of camaraderie and shared responsibility for the group's activities are heightened. The norming stage is complete when the members of the group accept a common set of expectations that constitutes an acceptable way of doing things.

The fourth stage is known as *performing*. During this stage, questions about group relationships and leadership have been resolved and the group is ready to work. Having fully developed, the group may now devote its energy to getting the job done—the group's good relations and acceptance of its leadership helps the group perform well.

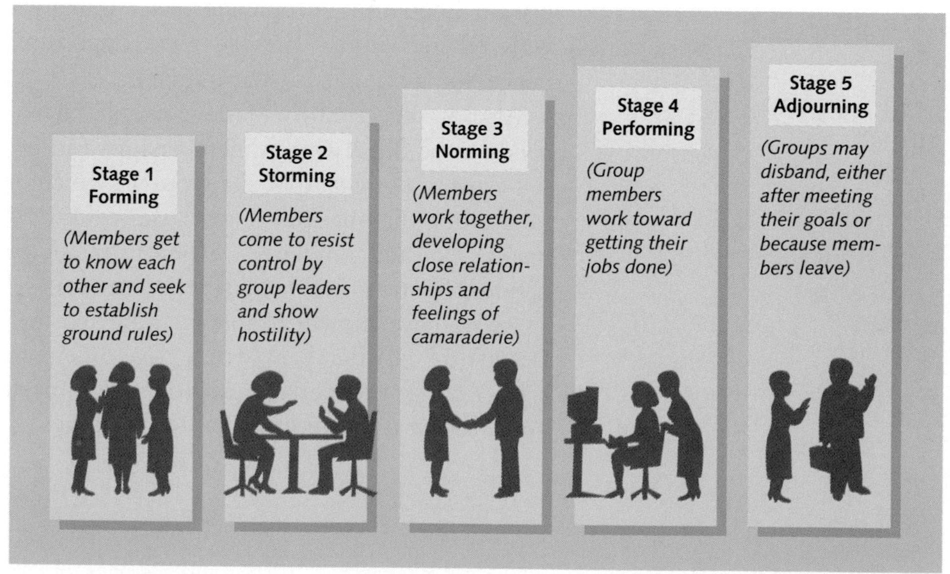

FIGURE 8-3
THE FIVE STAGES OF GROUP DEVELOPMENT
In general, groups develop according to the five stages summarized here. (Source: Based on information in Tuckman & Jensen, 1977; see Note 5.)

Recognizing that not all groups last forever, the final stage is known as *adjourning*. Groups may cease to exist because they have met their goals and are no longer needed (such as an ad hoc group created to raise money for a charity project), in which case the end is abrupt. Other groups may adjourn gradually, as the group disintegrates, either because members leave or because the norms that have developed are no longer effective for the group.

To help illustrate these various stages, imagine that you have just joined several of your colleagues on your company's newly created budget allocation committee. At first, you and your associates feel each other out: you watch to see who comes up with the best ideas, whose suggestions are most widely accepted, who seems to take charge, and the like (the forming stage). Then, as members struggle to gain influence over others (see Chapter 12), you may see a battle over control of the committee (the storming stage). Soon this will be resolved, and an accepted leader will emerge (see Chapter 13). At this stage, the group members will become highly cooperative, working together in harmony, and doing things together, such as going out to lunch as a group (the norming stage). Now it becomes possible for committee members to work together at doing their best, giving it their all (the performing stage). Then, once the budget is created and approved, the group's task is over, and it is disbanded (the adjourning stage).

It is important to keep in mind that groups can be in any one stage of development at any given time. Moreover, the amount of time a group may spend in any given stage is highly variable. In fact, some groups may fail long before they have had a chance to work together. Research has revealed that the boundaries between the various stages may not be clearly distinct, and that several stages may be combined, especially as deadline pressures force groups to take action.[6] It is best, then, to think of this five-stage model as a general framework of group formation. Although many of the stages may be followed, the dynamic nature of groups makes constant progress through the various stages in a set, predictable order unlikely.

THE STRUCTURE OF WORK GROUPS

As noted earlier, one of the key characteristics of a group is its stable structure. When social scientists use the term **group structure**, they are referring to the interrelationships between the individuals constituting a group, the characteristics that make group functioning orderly and predictable. In this section, we will describe four different aspects of group structure: the various parts played by group members (*roles*), the rules and expectations that develop within groups (*norms*), the prestige of group membership (*status*), and the members' sense of belonging (*cohesiveness*).

ROLES: THE MANY HATS WE WEAR

One of the primary structural elements of groups is members' tendencies to play specific roles in group interaction, sometimes more than one. Social scientists use the term *role* in much the same way as a director of a play would refer to the character who plays a part. Indeed, the part one plays in the overall group structure is what we mean by a role. More formally, we may define a **role** as *the typical behaviors that characterize a person in a social context.*[7]

In organizations, many roles are assigned by virtue of an individual's position within an organization. For example, a boss may be expected to give orders, and a teacher may be expected to lecture and to give exams. These are behaviors expected of the individual in that role. The person holding the role is known as a *role incumbent*, and the behaviors expected of that person are known as *role expectations*. The person holding the office of the president of the United States (the role incumbent) has certain role expectations simply because he or she currently has that post. When a new president takes office, that person assumes the same role and has the same formal powers as the previous president (see Chapter 12).

The role incumbent's recognition of the expectations of his or her role helps avoid the social disorganization that would surely result if clear role expectations did not exist. Sometimes, however, workers may be confused about the things that are expected of them on the job, such as their level of authority or their responsibility. Such *role ambiguity*, as it is called, is typically experienced by new members of organizations who have not had much of a chance to "learn the ropes," and often results in job dissatisfaction, a lack of commitment to the organization, and an interest in leaving the job.[8]

As work groups and social groups develop, the various group members come to play different roles in the social structure—a process referred to as **role differentiation**. The emergence of different roles in groups is a naturally occurring process. To illustrate this point, think of committees to which you have belonged. Was there someone who joked and made people feel better, and another member who worked hard to get the group to focus on the issue at hand? These examples of differentiated roles are typical of role behaviors that emerge in groups. Organizations, for example, often have their "office comedian" who makes everyone laugh, or the "company gossip" who shares others' secrets, or the "grand old man" who tells newcomers the stories about the company's "good old days."

Group researchers long ago found that one person may emerge who, more than anyone else, helps the group reach its goal.[9] Such a person is said to play the

TABLE 8-2

Some Roles Commonly Played by Group Members

Organizational roles may be differentiated into task-oriented, relations-oriented (or socioemotional), and self-oriented roles—each of which has several subroles. A number of these are shown here.

TASK-ORIENTED ROLES	RELATIONS-ORIENTED ROLES	SELF-ORIENTED ROLES
Initiator-contributors	**Harmonizers**	**Blockers**
Recommend new solutions to group problems	*Mediate group conflicts*	*Act stubborn and resistant to the group*
Information seekers	**Compromisers**	**Recognition seekers**
Attempt to obtain the necessary facts	*Shift own opinions to create group harmony*	*Call attention to their own achievements*
Opinion givers	**Encouragers**	**Dominators**
Share own opions with others	*Praise and encourage others*	*Assert authority by manipulating the group*
Energizers	**Expediters**	**Avoiders**
Stimulate the group into action whenever interest drops	*Suggest ways the groups can operate more smoothly*	*Maintain distance, isolate themselves from fellow group members*

Source: Based on Benne & Sheats, 1948; see Note 9.

task-oriented role. In addition, another group member may emerge who is quite supportive and nurturant, someone who makes everyone else feel good. Such a person is said to play a *socioemotional* (or *relations-oriented*) role. Still others may be recognized for the things they do for themselves, often at the expense of the group—individuals recognized for playing a *self-oriented role*. Many specific role behaviors can fall into one or another of these categories. Some of these more specific subroles are listed in Table 8-2. Although this simple distinction will help us understand some of the roles found in work groups, we should note that more complex conceptualizations have been proposed, including one that identifies as many as twenty-six different roles.[10] These efforts at understanding role differentiation, regardless of how simple or complex the distinctions may be, help make the point that similarities between groups may be recognized by the common roles members play.

NORMS: A GROUP'S UNSPOKEN RULES

One feature of groups that enhances their orderly functioning is the existence of group norms. **Norms** may be defined as *generally agreed-on informal rules that guide group members' behavior.*[11] They represent shared ways of viewing the world. Norms differ from organizational rules in that they are not formal and written. In fact, group members may not even be aware of the subtle group norms that exist and regulate their behavior. Yet they have profound effects on behavior. Norms regulate the behavior of groups in important ways, such as by fostering workers' honesty and loyalty to the company, establishing appropriate ways to dress, and dictating when it is acceptable to be late for or absent from work.

If you recall the pressures placed on you by your peers as you grew up to dress or wear your hair in certain styles, you are well aware of the profound normative pressures exerted by groups. Norms can be either *prescriptive* (dictating the behaviors that should be performed) or *proscriptive* (dictating the behaviors that should be avoided). For example, groups may develop prescriptive norms to follow their leader, or to help a group member who needs assistance. They may also develop proscriptive norms to avoid absences, or to refrain from blowing the whistle on each other. Sometimes the pressure to conform to norms is subtle, as in the dirty looks given a manager by his peers for going to lunch with one of the assembly-line workers. Other times, normative pressures may be quite severe, such as when one production worker sabotages another's work because he is performing at too high a level, making his co-workers look bad.

The question of how group norms develop has been of considerable interest to organizational researchers.[12] An insightful analysis of this process has been presented by Feldman (see summary in Table 8-3).[13] First, norms develop because of *precedents set over time*. Whatever behaviors emerge at a first group meeting will usually set the standard for how that group is to operate. Initial group patterns of behavior frequently become normative, such as where people sit, and how formal or informal the meeting will be. Such routines help establish a predictable, orderly interaction pattern.

Second, norms develop because of *carryovers from other situations*. Group members usually draw from their previous experiences to guide their behaviors in new situations. The norms governing professional behavior apply here. For example, the norm for a physician to behave ethically and to exercise a pleasant bedside manner is generalizable from one hospital to another. Such carryover norms can assist in making interaction easier in new social situations.

TABLE 8-3
Norms: How Do They Develop
This table summarizes four ways in which group norms can develop.

BASIS OF NORM DEVELOPMENT	EXAMPLE
1. Precedents set over time	*Seating location of each group member around a table*
2. Carryovers from other situations	*Professional standards of conduct*
3. Explicit statements from others	*Working a certain way because you are told "that's how we do it around here"*
4. Critical events in group history	*After the organization suffers a loss due to one person's divulging company secrets, a norm develops to maintain secrecy*

Source: Based on Feldman, 1984; see Note 13.

Third, sometimes norms also develop in *response to an explicit statement by a superior or co-worker*. Newcomers to groups quickly "learn the ropes" when someone tells them, "That's the way we do it around here." This explanation is an explicit statement of the norms; it describes what one should do or avoid doing to be accepted by the group. Often the explicit statement of group norms represents the accepted desires of more powerful or experienced group members.[14]

Fourth and finally, group norms may develop out of *critical events in the group's history*. If an employee releases an important organizational secret to a competitor, causing a loss to the company, a norm to maintain secrecy may develop out of this incident.

STATUS: THE PRESTIGE OF GROUP MEMBERSHIP

Have you ever been attracted to a group because of the prestige accorded its members? You may have wanted to join a certain fraternity or sorority because it is highly regarded by the students. Aspiring members of street gangs long for the day they can wear their gang's "colors" in the streets. No doubt, members of Super-Bowl-winning football teams proudly sport their Super Bowl rings to identify themselves as members of a championship team. Clearly, one potential reward of group membership is the status associated with being in that group. Even within social groups, different members are accorded different levels of prestige. Fraternity and sorority officers, and committee chairpersons, for example, may be recognized as more important members of their respective groups. This is the idea behind **status**—*the relative social position or rank given to groups or group members by others.*[15]

Within most organizations, status may be recognized as both formal and informal in nature. The term *formal status* refers to attempts to differentiate between the degrees of formal authority given employees by an organization. This is typically accomplished through the use of **status symbols**—*objects reflecting the position of an individual within an organization's hierarchy*. Some examples of status symbols include job titles (e.g., "Director"); perquisites, or perks (e.g., a reserved parking space); the opportunity to do desirable and highly regarded work (e.g., serving on

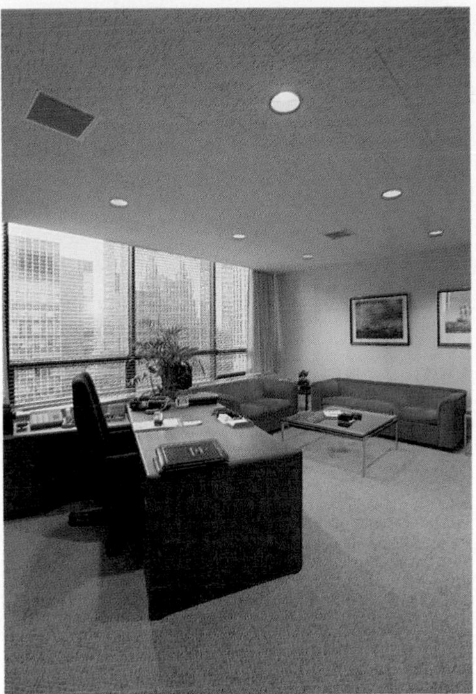

FIGURE 8-4
WORKING CONDITIONS: A SYMBOL OF ORGANIZATIONAL STATUS
A large, elegantly decorated office is a sure symbol of the occupant's high status within the organization.

important committees); and luxurious working conditions (e.g., a large, private office that is lavishly decorated) (see Figure 8-4).[16]

Status symbols help groups in many ways.[17] For one, such symbols serve to remind organizational members of their relative roles, thereby reducing uncertainty and providing stability to the social order (e.g., your small desk reminds you of your lower organizational rank). In addition, they provide assurance of the various rewards available to those who perform at a superior level (e.g., "maybe one day I'll have a reserved parking spot"). They also provide a sense of identification by reminding members of the group's values (e.g., a gang's jacket may remind its wearer of his expected loyalty and boldness). It is, therefore, not surprising that organizations do much to reinforce formal status through the use of status symbols.

Symbols of *informal status* within organizations are also widespread. These refer to the prestige accorded individuals with certain characteristics that are not formally dictated by the organization. For example, employees who are older and more experienced may be perceived as higher in status by their co-workers. Those who have certain special skills (such as the home run hitters on a baseball team) also may be regarded as having higher status than others. In some organizations, the lower value placed on the work of women and members of minority groups by some individuals—no matter how inappropriate and prejudicial—also can be considered an example of informal status in operation.[18]

One of the best-established findings in the study of group dynamics is that higher-status people tend to be more influential than lower-status people. This phenomenon may be seen in a classic study of decision making in three-man bomber crews.[19] After the crews had difficulty solving a problem, the experimenter planted clues to the solution with either a low-status group member (the tail gunner) or a high-status group member (the pilot). It was found that the solutions offered by the pilots were far more likely to be adopted than the same solutions presented by the tail gunners. Apparently, the greater status accorded the pilots (because they tended to be more experienced and hold higher military ranks) was responsible for the greater influence they wielded. Similar findings have been obtained in analyses of jury deliberations. Research in this area has shown that members of juries having high-status jobs (such as professional people) tend to exert greater influence over their fellow jurors than others holding lower occupational status.[20]

COHESIVENESS: GETTING THE TEAM SPIRIT

One obvious determinant of any group's structure is its cohesiveness. We may define **cohesiveness** as *the strength of group members' desires to remain part of their groups*. Highly cohesive work groups are ones in which the members are attracted to each other, accept the group's goals, and help work toward meeting them. In very uncohesive groups, the members dislike each other and may even work at cross-purposes.[21] In essence, cohesiveness refers to a "we" feeling, an *esprit de corps*, a sense of belonging to a group.

Several important factors have been shown to influence the extent to which group members tend to "stick together." One such factor involves the severity of initiation into the group. Research has shown that the greater the difficulty people overcome to become a member of a group, the more cohesive the group will be.[22]

To understand this, consider how highly cohesive certain groups may be that you have worked hard to join. Was it particularly difficult to "make the cut" on your sports team? The rigorous requirements for gaining entry into elite groups, such as the most prestigious medical schools and military training schools, may well be responsible for the high degree of camaraderie found in such groups. Having "passed the test" tends to keep individuals together, and separates them from those who are unwilling or unable to "pay the price" of admission.

Group cohesion also tends to be strengthened under conditions of high external threat or competition. When workers face a "common enemy," they tend to draw together. Such cohesion not only makes workers feel safer and better protected, but also aids them by encouraging them to work closely together and coordinate their efforts toward the common enemy. Under such conditions, petty disagreements that may have caused dissension within groups tend to be put aside so that a coordinated attack on the enemy can be mobilized.

Research has also shown that the cohesiveness of groups is established by several additional factors.[23] For one, cohesiveness generally tends to be greater the more time group members spend together. Obviously, limited interaction cannot help but interfere with opportunities to develop bonds between group members. Similarly, cohesiveness tends to be greater in smaller groups. Generally speaking, groups that are too large make it difficult for members to interact and, therefore, for cohesiveness to reach a high level. Finally, because "nothing succeeds like success," groups with a history of success tend to be highly cohesive. It is often said that "everyone loves a winner," and the success of a group tends to help unite its members as they rally around their success. For this reason, employees tend to be loyal to successful companies.

Although we often hear about the benefits of highly cohesive groups, the consequences of cohesiveness are not always positive. In fact, research has shown both positive and negative effects of cohesiveness (see Figure 8-5). On the positive side, people are known to enjoy belonging to highly cohesive groups. Members of closely knit work groups participate more fully in their group's activities, more readily accept their group's goals, and are absent from their jobs less often than members of less cohesive groups.[24] Not surprisingly, cohesive groups tend to work together quite well and are sometimes exceptionally productive. In fact, research has shown that high levels of group cohesiveness tend to be associated with low levels of voluntary turnover.[25] People's willingness to work together quite well and to conform to the group's norms is often responsible for their success, and their willingness to stay with the group.[26]

FIGURE 8-5
GROUP COHESIVENESS: ITS CAUSES AND CONSEQUENCES
As summarized here, several factors contribute to a group's cohesiveness. High levels of cohesiveness may have both positive and negative consequences.

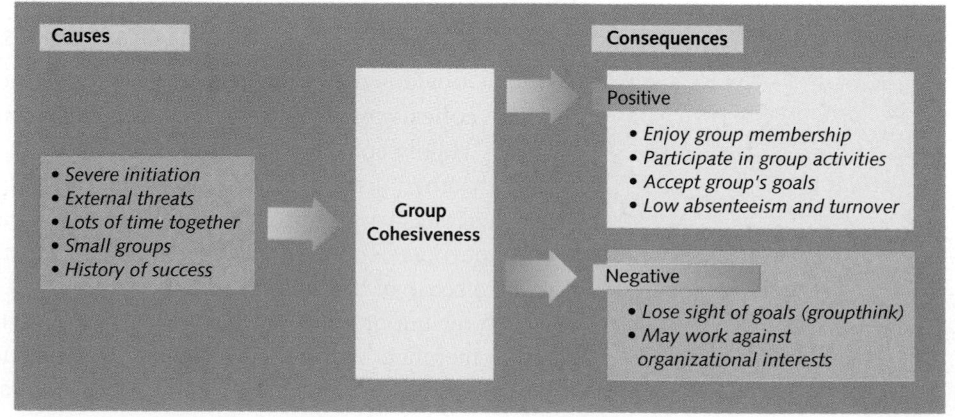

However, the tendency for members of highly cohesive groups to go along with their fellow members' wishes sometimes has negative consequences for the ultimate group product. Consider, for example, the actions of the highly cohesive Committee to Re-elect President Nixon preceding the 1972 presidential election. The Watergate conspirators were a highly cohesive group—so cohesive that they were blinded to the possibility that they were committing illegal and unethical acts. Poor decisions resulting from too high a level of cohesiveness reflect a phenomenon known as *groupthink*.[27] Groupthink occurs when a group is so cohesive that its members potentially lose sight of its ultimate goals for fear of disrupting the group itself. (Because of the negative impact of groupthink on the quality of group decisions, we will discuss this phenomenon in greater detail in the context of decision making in Chapter 10.)

Group cohesion can influence productivity in many other ways. It makes sense that after a group experiences success, its members will feel more committed to each other. Similarly, we might expect a cohesive group to work well together and to achieve a high level of success. However, a work group whose members are strongly committed to each other does not necessarily perform well within an organization.[28] For example, if a group's goals are contrary to the organization's goals, a highly cohesive group may actually do a great deal of harm to an organization, working against its interests. Highly cohesive group members who conspire to sabotage their employers are a good example. Apparently, group cohesiveness can have either positive *or* negative effects on performance .

TEAMS: SPECIAL KINDS OF GROUPS

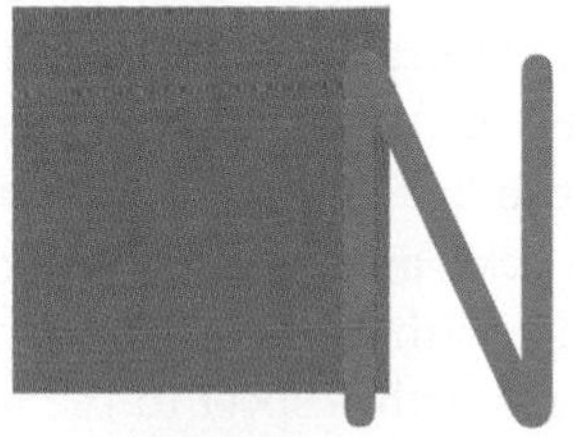

Now that you have a clear understanding of groups and how they operate, we can compare them to another type of collection of individuals known as *teams*. In this section we will define what is meant by teams and how they are different from groups. We will then describe various types of teams that may be found in organizations. Finally, we will present guidelines for creating teams in organizations.

DEFINING TEAMS AND DISTINGUISHING THEM FROM GROUPS

If you think about some of the groups we've described thus far in this chapter, such as the ones in use at XEL Communications and the corporate budget allocation committee described above, you'll probably realize that they are somehow different. Although they are each composed of several individuals working together toward common goals, the connections between the employees at XEL appear to be much deeper in scope. In essence, while the budget committee members may be interested in what they're doing, the group members at XEL seem more highly committed to their work, and are more highly involved in the way their jobs are done. This is not to say that there is necessarily anything wrong with the corporate budget committee; in fact, they would appear to be a rather typical group. The work groups at XEL, however, are examples of special kinds of groups known as *teams*. A **team** may be defined as *a group whose members have complementary skills and are committed to a common purpose or set of performance goals for which they hold themselves mutually accountable.*[29]

At this point, it is probably not entirely clear to you exactly how a team is different from an ordinary group. This confusion probably stems in part from the fact that people often refer to their groups as teams, although they are really not teams. Yet there are several important distinctions between them. First, in groups, performance typically depends on the work of individual members. The performance of a team, however, depends on both individual contributions and *collective work products*—the joint outcome of team members working in concert.

A second difference has to do with where accountability for the job lies. Typically, members of groups pool their resources to attain a goal, although it is individual performance that is taken into consideration when it comes to issuing rewards. Members of groups usually do not take responsibility for any results other than their own. By contrast, teams focus on both individual and *mutual accountability*. That is, they work together to produce an outcome (e.g., a product, service, or decision) that represents their joint contributions, and each team member shares responsibility for that outcome. The key difference is this: in groups, the supervisor holds individual members accountable for their work, whereas in teams, members hold themselves accountable.

Third, whereas group members may share a common interest goal, team members also share a *common commitment to purpose*. Moreover, these purposes typically are concerned with winning in some way, such as being first or best at something. For example, a work team in a manufacturing plant of a financially troubled company may be highly committed to making the company the top one in its industry. Another team, one in a public high school, may be committed to preparing all its graduates for the challenges of the world better than any other school in the district. Team members focusing jointly on such lofty purposes, in conjunction with specific performance goals, become heavily invested in its activities. In fact, teams are said to establish "ownership" of their purposes, and usually spend a great deal of time establishing its purpose. Like groups, teams use goals to monitor their progress. Teams, however, also have a broader purpose, which supplies a source of meaning and emotional energy to the activities performed.

Finally, in organizations teams differ from groups with respect to the nature of their connections to management. Work groups are typically required to be responsive to demands regularly placed on them by management. By contrast, once management establishes the mission for a team, and sets the challenge for it to achieve, it typically gives the team enough flexibility to do its job without any further interference. In other words, work teams are usually to some degree *self-managing*—that is, they are free to set their own goals, timing, and the approach that they wish to take, usually without management interference. Thus, many teams are described as being *autonomous* or *semiautonomous* in nature (see Figure 8-6). This is not to say that teams are completely independent of corporate management and supervision. They still must be responsive to demands from higher levels (often, higher-level teams, known as *top management teams*). For example, in the case of XEL Communications, teams regularly report their progress to management on a regularly scheduled basis.

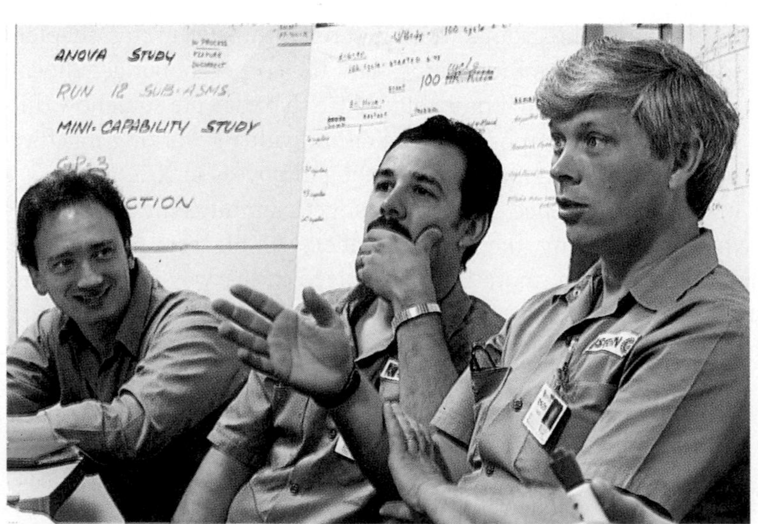

FIGURE 8-6
A WORK TEAM AT GENERAL MOTORS' SATURN ASSEMBLY PLANT
One of the largest operations using self-managing work teams is General Motors' Saturn plant in Tennessee. Teams such as the one shown here are among the most highly autonomous units in existence today. A great deal of Saturn's success has been attributed to the high quality performance of such teams.

TYPES OF TEAMS

Interesting fact: most major U.S. companies are now either using some form of teams or are seriously considering using them.[30] Although there has been a great amount of recent interest in teams, they have been around the workplace for some time. In fact, as shown in Table 8-4, many corporations have been using them for quite a few years—some, such as Procter & Gamble, well over three decades.[31]

In view of their widespread popularity, it should not be surprising to learn that there are many different kinds of teams. To help make sense out of these, Mohrman recently has categorized them into several different commonly found types.[32] According to Mohrman, teams vary along three major dimensions. The first has to do with their major *purpose or mission*. In this regard, some teams—known as *work teams*—are primarily concerned with the work done by the organization, such as developing and manufacturing new products, providing services for customers, and so on. Their principle focus is on using the organization's resources to effectively create its results (be they goods or services). (The teams at XEL Communications, described in our Preview Case, appear to be of this type.) Other teams—known as *improvement teams*—are primarily oriented toward the mission of increasing the effectiveness of the processes that are used by the organization. For example, Texas Instruments has relied on teams to help improve the quality of operations at its plant in Malaysia.[33]

A second dimension has to do with *time*. Specifically, some teams are only *temporary*, and are established for a specific project with a finite life. For example, a team set up to develop a new product would be considered temporary. As soon as its job is done, it disbands. However, other kinds of teams are *permanent*, and stay intact as long as the organization is operating. For example, teams focusing on providing effective customer service tend to be permanent parts of many organizations.

TABLE 8-4

Pioneers of Work Teams Among Major American Companies

Although many organizations are turning to work teams today, several large companies have been using them for some time. Here is a listing of some major American companies that have been the earliest adopters of work teams.

YEAR BEGAN	COMPANY
1962	*Procter & Gamble*
1973	*Cummins Engine*
1975	*General Motors*
1982	*Digital Equipment*
1982	*Ford Motor Company*
1983	*Tektronix*
1985	*General Electric*
1985	*LTV Steel*
1985	*Champion International*

Source: Adapted from Osburn, Moran, Musselwhite, & Zenger, 1990; see Note 66.

The third dimension reflects the team's connection to the organization's overall *authority structure*—that is, the connection between various formal job responsibilities (see Chapter 15). In some organizations, teams may cross over various functional units (e.g., marketing, finance, human resources, and so on), and are said to be *overlaid* (i.e., their activities are superimposed over the functioning of various organizational units). For example, a quality improvement team may be expected to get involved with the activities of several different organizational units (the mission of improving quality does not belong to any one unit working alone). As you might expect, such arrangements are often difficult because of ambiguities regarding authority. By contrast, some organizations use teams that are *intact* with respect to the existing structure of the organization. In fact, many organizations—such as General Motors and Ralston-Purina—are structured such that people work together on specific products all the time, and do not apply their specialty to a wide range of products (see Chapter 15). Within such organizations, teams can operate without the ambiguities created by having to cross functional lines.

It is important to note that the boundaries between all teams must be considered permeable. Indeed, people are frequently members of more than one team—a situation often required for organizations to function effectively. For example, members of an organization's manufacturing team must carefully coordinate their activities with members of its marketing team. To the extent that people are involved in several different kinds of teams, they may gain broader perspectives, and make more important contributions to their various teams.

MANAGERS' GUIDELINES FOR CREATING TEAMS

As you might imagine, assembling a team is no easy task. Doing so requires not only having the right combination of skilled people, but also individuals who are willing to work together with others as a team. A model proposed by Hackman provides some useful guidance on how to effectively design work teams, suggesting that the process proceeds in four distinct stages.[34] As we present this model, you may find it useful to refer to the summary in Table 8-5.

The first stage of creating an effective team is known as *prework*. One of the most important objectives of this phase is to determine whether a team should be created. A manager may decide to have several individuals working alone answer to him, or a team may be created if it is believed that it may develop the most creative and insightful ways to get things done. In considering this, it is important to note exactly what work needs to be done. The team's objectives must be established, and an inventory of the skills needed to do the job should be made. In addition, decisions should be made in advance about what authority the team should have. They may just be advisory to the manager, or they may be given full responsibility and authority for executing their task (i.e., self-regulating).

Building on this, stage 2 involves *creating performance conditions*. In this stage, organizational officials are to ensure that the team has the proper conditions under which to carry out its work. Resources necessary for the team's success should be provided. This involves both material resources (e.g., tools, equipment, and money), human resources (e.g., the appropriate blend of skilled professionals), and support from the organization (e.g., willingness to let the team do its own work as it sees fit). Unless managers help create the proper conditions for team success, they are contributing to its failure.

TABLE 8-5

Stages of Work Team Creation: A Summary

For teams to function effectively, they must be created properly. The four stages outlined here summarize how this may be accomplished.

STAGE 1: DO PREWORK
■ *Decide what work needs to be done.*
■ *Determine if a team is necessary to accomplish the task.*
■ *Determine what authority the group should have.*
■ *Decide on the team's goals.*
STAGE 2: CREATE PERFORMANCE CONDITIONS
■ *Provide all the needed materials and equipment to do the job.*
■ *Ensure that the team consists of all personnel necessary to do the job.*
STAGE 3: FORM AND BUILD THE TEAM
■ *Establish boundaries—that is, who is and is not in the team.*
■ *Arrive at an agreement regarding the tasks to be performed.*
■ *Clarify the behaviors expected of each team member.*
STAGE 4: PROVIDE ONGOING ASSISTANCE
■ *Intervene to eliminate team problems (e.g., members not doing their share).*
■ *Replenish or upgrade material resources.*
■ *Replace members who leave the team.*

Source: Based on information in Hackman, 1987; see Note 34.

Stage 3 involves *forming and building the team*. Three things can be done to help a team get off to a good start. First, managers should form boundaries—clearly establish who is and who is not a member of the team. Some teams fail simply because, membership in it is left unclear. Reducing such ambiguity can help avoid confusion and frustration. Second, members must accept the team's overall mission and purpose. Unless they do, failure is inevitable. Third, organizational officials should clarify the team's mission and responsibilities—make perfectly clear exactly what it is expected to do (but not necessarily *how* to do it). Will team members be responsible for monitoring and planning their own work? If so, such expectations should be spelled out explicitly.

Finally, once a team is functioning, supervisors should *provide ongoing assistance*. Although once teams start operating they often guide themselves, managers may be able to help by providing opportunities for the team to eliminate problems and perform even better. For example, disruptive team members may be either counseled or replaced (as was done in the case of XEL's stockroom team). Similarly, material resources may have to be replenished or upgraded. Although it may be unwise for a manager to intervene in the successful affairs of a team that has taken on its own life, it also may be unwise to neglect opportunities to help a team do even better.

As you ponder these suggestions, you will doubtless recognize the considerable managerial skill and hard work it takes to create and manage teams effectively. However, as managers learn these skills, and as individuals gain successful experiences as members of effective work teams, the deliberate steps outlined above may become second nature to all concerned. As Hackman concludes, "When that stage is reached, the considerable investment required to learn how to use work teams well can pay substantial dividends—in work effectiveness and in the quality of the experience of both managers and [team] members."[35] As we will describe later in this chapter, both the potential pitfalls and benefits of work teams can be considerable.

THE DYNAMICS OF INDIVIDUAL PERFORMANCE IN GROUPS

Now that we have reviewed the basic nature of groups and teams, we will turn to an aspect of group dynamics most relevant to the field of organizational behavior—the effects of groups on individual performance. Specifically, we will take a look at three different issues in this connection. First, we will consider how people's work performance is affected by the presence of others. Second, we will examine how the composition of groups—in particular, its racial and ethnic diversity—affects performance. Third, we will describe how performance is affected by group size.

SOCIAL FACILITATION: INDIVIDUAL PERFORMANCE IN THE PRESENCE OF OTHERS

Imagine that you have been studying drama for five years and you are now ready for your first acting audition in front of some Hollywood producers. You have been rehearsing diligently for several months, getting ready for the part. Now you are no longer alone at home with your script in front of you. Your name is announced, and silence fills the auditorium as you walk to the front of the stage. How will you perform now that you are in front of an audience? Will you freeze, forgetting the lines you studied so intensely when you practiced alone? Or will the audience spur you on to your best performance yet? In other words, what impact will the presence of the audience have on your behavior?

After studying this question for a century, using a wide variety of tasks and situations, social scientists found that the answer to this question is not straightforward.[36] Sometimes people were found to perform better in the presence of others than when alone, and sometimes they were found to perform better alone than in the presence of others. This tendency for the presence of others to enhance an individual's performance at times and to impair it at other times is known as **social facilitation**. (Although the word *facilitation* implies improvements in task performance, scientists use the term *social facilitation* to refer to both performance improvements and decrements stemming from the presence of others.) What accounts for these seemingly contradictory findings?

According to Robert Zajonc, the matter boils down to several basic psychological processes.[37] First, Zajonc explained that social facilitation was the result of the heightened emotional arousal (e.g., feelings of tension and excitement) people experience when in the presence of others. (Wouldn't you feel more tension playing the piano in front of an audience than alone?) Second, when people are aroused, they tend to perform the most dominant response—their most likely behavior in that setting. (Returning the smile of a smiling co-worker may be considered an example of a dominant act; it is a very well learned act to smile at another who smiles at you.) If someone is performing a very well learned act, the dominant response would be a correct one (such as speaking the right lines during your fiftieth performance). However, if the behavior in question is relatively novel, newly learned, the dominant response would likely be incorrect (such as speaking incorrect lines during an audition). Together, these ideas are known as Zajonc's **drive theory of social facilitation**.[38] According to this theory, the presence of others increases arousal, which increases the tendency to perform the most dominant responses. If these responses are correct, the resulting performance will be enhanced; if they are incorrect, the performance will be impaired. Based on these processes, performance may either be helped (if the task is well learned) or hindered (if the task is not well learned). (For a summary of this process, see Figure 8-7.)

A considerable amount of research has shown support for this theory: people perform better on tasks in the presence of others if that task is very well learned, but more poorly if it is not well learned. However, it is still unclear exactly *why* this effect occurs. Three positions receive a considerable amount of support. First, according to Zajonc, people become aroused simply because the others are there, what he calls their "mere presence." However, other scientists have modified Zajonc's approach, claiming that the arousal resulting from others is due to the fact not that others are simply there, but that these others can potentially evaluate the person. Their major idea, our second explanation, is that social facilitation results from **evaluation apprehension**—the fear of being evaluated or judged by another person.[39] Indeed, people may be aroused by performing a task in the presence of others because of their concern over what those others might think of them. For example, lower-level employees may suffer evaluation apprehension when they are worried about what their supervisor thinks of their work. Finally, a third explanation, known as the **distraction-conflict model** recognizes that the presence of others creates a conflict between paying attention to others and paying attention to the task at hand.[40] The conflict created by these tendencies leads to increased arousal, which in turn leads to social facilitation. If you've ever tried doing a homework assignment while your friends or family watch TV nearby, you're probably already aware of the conflict that competing demands for your attention can create.

Although many of today's scientists favor the distraction-conflict explanation of social facilitation, all three explanations provide some important insights into

FIGURE 8-7

SOCIAL FACILITATION: A DRIVE THEORY APPROACH

Zajonc's drive theory of social facilitation states that the presence of others is arousing. This, in turn, enhances the tendency to perform the most dominant (i.e., strongest) responses. If these are correct (such as if the task is well learned), performance will be improved, but if these are incorrect (such as if the task is novel), performance will suffer.

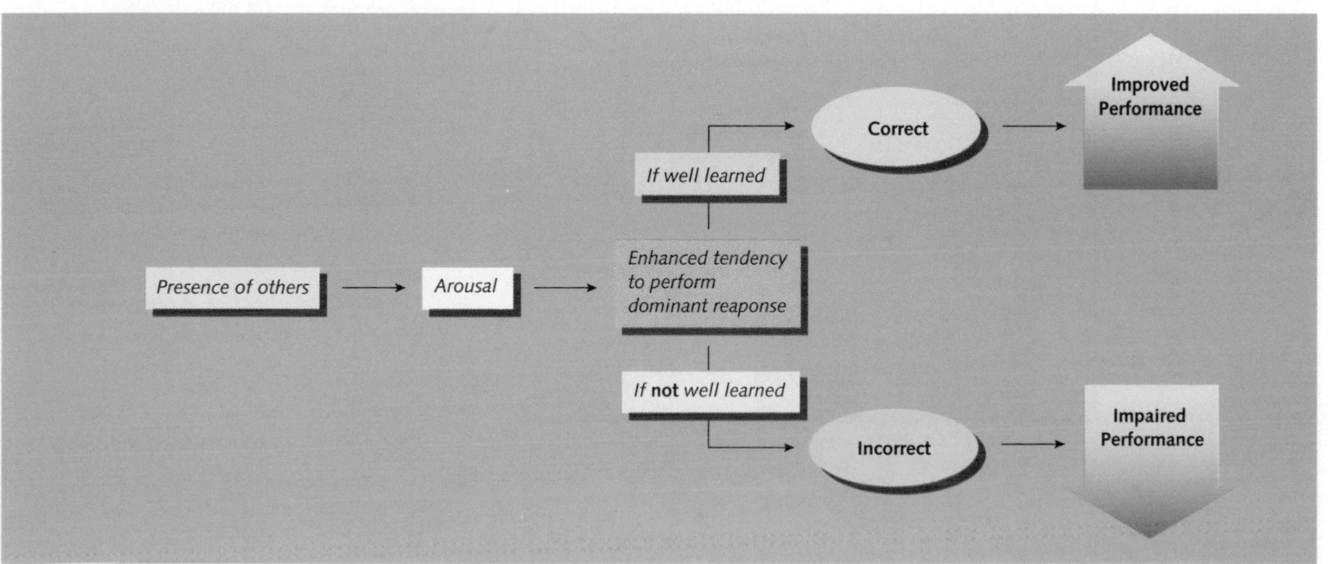

THE ORGANIZATION OF TOMORROW

COMPUTERIZED PERFORMANCE MONITORING: SOCIAL FACILITATION VIA AN "ELECTRONIC PRESENCE"

If you read George Orwell's classic book *1984*, you will recall "Big Brother," the all-knowing power that monitored people's every moves. As often happens, the science fiction of one era eventually becomes scientific fact in another. And, in the case of "Big Brother," in the workplace, at least, Orwell wasn't many years off in his predictions. The use of computers to monitor work performance today is becoming increasingly common. *Computerized performance monitoring* is already widely used in the insurance, banking, communications, and transportation industries, and it promises to become even more prevalent in tomorrow's organizations.[41] In view of this, it is important to learn about the effects of monitoring on people's job performance.

One way of understanding how computerized monitoring may influence performance is by extending our thinking about social facilitation. After all, instead of having an individual who is physically present to watch, this technique is akin to doing the same thing indirectly, by computer—an "electronic presence." Imagine, for example, that you are entering data into a computer terminal. You can be monitored in a direct physical way by an individual looking over your shoulder, or indirectly by someone checking a computerized record of the speed and accuracy of your every keystroke. If the task being performed is a complex one, social facilitation research suggests that the physical presence of an observer would lead to reduced performance. But would the same thing occur when there is only an electronic presence?

A study recently conducted by Aiello and Svec attempted to answer this question.[42] Participants in this research were college students who performed complex anagram tasks (unscrambling letters to form words) by entering their responses into a computer terminal. The conditions under which they performed this task were systematically varied by the researchers in several different ways, three of which are relevant here. One group of participants (the "control" condition) performed the task without anyone observing them work in any form. A second group (the "person-monitored" condition) was monitored by stationing two female observers immediately behind them as they performed their task in front of the computer. Finally, a third group of subjects (the "computer-monitoring" condition) was told that their performance would be monitored by people who could see their work on another

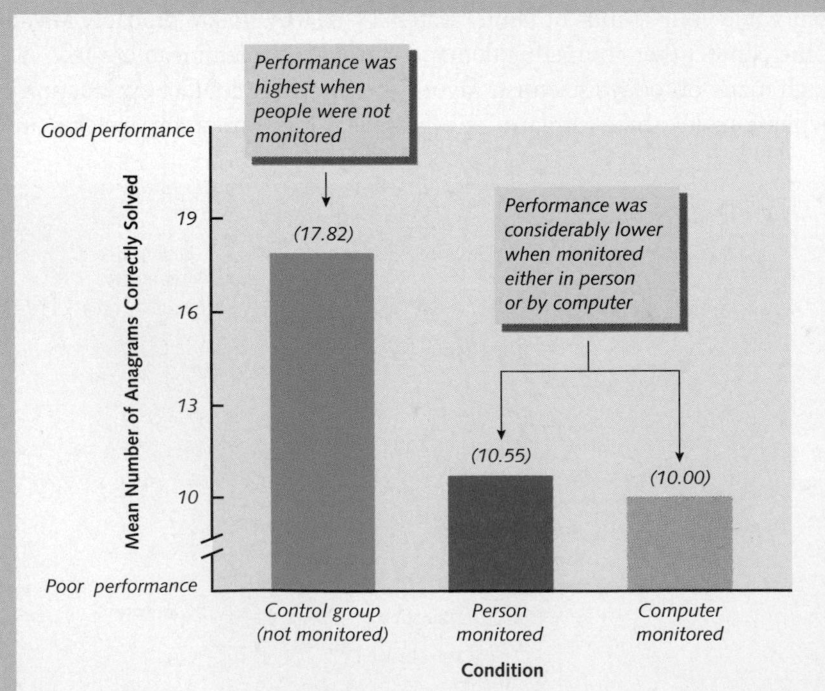

FIGURE 8-8
COMPUTER MONITORING: EVIDENCE OF ITS COUNTERPRODUCTIVE EFFECTS
Participants in a recent study performed complex tasks either alone, or while being monitored by a computer or by two other people who were physically present. Consistent with other research on social facilitation, people performed the complex task worse in the presence of others than alone. They also performed more poorly when they were monitored by the "electronic presence" of a computer. (Source: Based on data reported by Aiello & Svec, 1993; see Note 42.)

computer to which theirs was connected on a network. (To make this convincing, participants were shown the other computer equipment.) Participants performed the task for ten minutes, after which the researchers counted the number of anagrams solved correctly by people in each condition. A summary of these findings is shown in Figure 8-8.

As these data show, people performed worse when others were physically observing them (person-monitored group) than when they performed the task alone (control group). This finding is in keeping with research and theory on social facilitation, according to which performance on complex tasks is expected to suffer when in the presence of others. Even more interesting is the finding that performance also suffered when it was monitored by computer—that is, even when people were not distracted by having others looking over their shoulders. Apparently, performance can suffer even when the presence of another is known to exist, although imperceptible.

These findings support the idea that social facilitation may be due to people's concerns about being evaluated negatively by another—that is, evaluation apprehension. In the case of the task at hand, participants in the study knew that their performance could be just as easily evaluated by watching a remote computer as by watching them directly. Accordingly, opportunities for evaluation existed in both conditions, possibly accounting for the apprehension that led to the performance decrements found.

There is also a very important applied implication of these results—namely, that the act of monitoring job performance to keep levels high may actually backfire! That is, instead of causing people to improve their performance (for fear of being caught doing poorly), monitoring might actually interfere with performance (by providing a distracting source of evaluation). Because participants in Aiello and Svec's study performed their tasks for only brief periods of time, we cannot tell whether people would eventually get used to the monitoring, and improve their performance over time. However, until further research addresses this question, we must issue the following caution: using computers to monitor work performance might impair the very performance that monitoring is intended to improve. "Big Brother" just might be defeating his own purposes.

social facilitation. In other words, while the processes underlying social facilitation are somewhat unclear, the effect itself may have a profound influence on organizational behavior. (In fact, recent research has shown that those effects extend beyond the physical presence of others to their "electronic presence." For a closer look at this phenomenon, see the Organization of Tomorrow section above.)

PERFORMANCE IN CULTURALLY DIVERSE GROUPS

For many years, the task of composing work groups involved finding individuals with the right blend of skills and getting them to work together—a task that was challenging enough. Today, however, as the workplace grows increasingly diverse with respect to the racial and ethnic group composition of its members, there's a new consideration. How does a group's cultural diversity affect its task performance? Although attempts to answer this question do not have the long history of research on social facilitation, recent research has provided some good insight.

For example, considering this question, Watson, Kumar, and Michaelsen reasoned that when a culturally diverse group first forms, its members will need time to be able to adjust to the racial and ethnic differences among them.[43] To the extent that people's differing perspectives and styles may interfere with their ability to work together, then task performance may be expected to suffer. As time goes on,

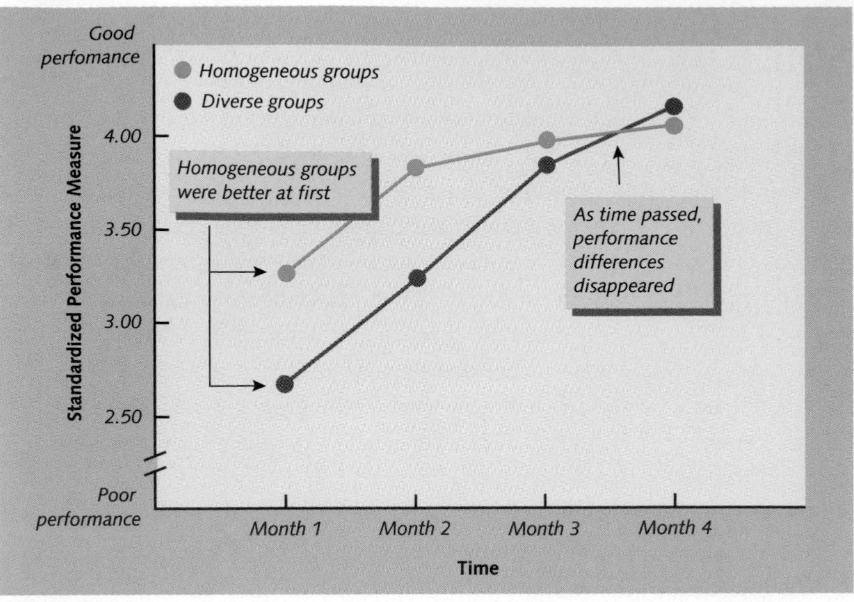

FIGURE 8-9

TASK PERFORMANCE IN CULTURALLY DIVERSE GROUPS: AN EXPERIMENTAL DEMONSTRATION

A recent experiment found that although culturally diverse groups performed worse than homogeneous groups at first, these differences disappeared over time. (Source: Based on data reported by Watson, Kumar, & Michaelsen, 1993; see Note 43.)

however, and group members learn to interact with each other despite their different backgrounds, performance differences should disappear. The researchers tested these hypotheses by assigning college students enrolled in a management class to two kinds of four-person groups. *Homogeneous groups* were composed of members from the same racial and ethnic background. *Diverse groups* were created by assembling groups consisting of one white American, one African-American, one Hispanic-American, and one foreign national. After being formed, the groups were asked to analyze business cases (a task with which management students were familiar). The groups worked on four occasions scheduled one month apart. Their analyses were then scored (using several different predetermined criteria) by experts who did not know which groups were diverse and which were homogeneous. How did following these two different recipes for group composition influence task performance? The data summarized in Figure 8-9 bear on this question.

As shown in Figure 8-9, the answer depends on the amount of time the group spent together. At first, the homogeneous group did considerably better than the diverse group. Then, during the second session, these differences grew smaller. By the third session, the differences almost completely disappeared, and by the fourth session they did (in fact, the diverse group even did slightly better than the homogeneous group). Although all groups improved their performance over time, as you would expect, the initial advantage of homogeneous groups was found to be only a temporary condition found in newly created groups. As group members had more experiences working with each other, the differences between them became less of a source of interference.

Because research on the effects of racial and ethnic group composition on task performance is just beginning, we do not yet know if these same results would hold for different kinds of tasks. We also don't know whether diverse groups would eventually perform even better than homogeneous ones. In fact, on tasks in which differing perspectives might help a group do its job, diverse groups may be expected to have an edge over heterogeneous ones. Although several key questions about the effects of diversity on group performance remain unanswered, the importance of this factor as a variable in group performance is clearly established.

SOCIAL LOAFING: "FREE RIDING" WHEN WORKING WITH OTHERS

Have you ever worked with several others helping a friend move into a new apartment, each carrying and transporting part of the load from the old place to the new one? Or how about sitting around a table with others stuffing political campaign letters into envelopes and addressing them to potential donors?

How social animals work together.

FIGURE 8-10
"MANY HANDS MAKE LIGHT THE WORK"
According to the phenomenon of social loafing, the more people involved in a group task, the less each individual will contribute to its outcome. (Source: THE FAR SIDE CARTOON by Gary Larson is reprinted by permission of Chronicle Features, San Francisco, CA. All rights reserved.)

Although these tasks may seem quite different, they actually share an important common characteristic: performing each requires only a single individual, but several people's work can be pooled to yield greater outcomes. Because each person's contributions can be added together with another's, such tasks have been referred to as **additive tasks**.[44]

If you've ever performed additive tasks—such as the ones described here—there's a good chance that you found yourself working not quite as hard as you would have if you did them alone. Does this sound familiar to you? Indeed, a considerable amount of research has found that when several people combine their efforts on additive tasks, each individual contributes less than he or she would when performing the same task alone.[45] As suggested by the old saying "Many hands make light the work," a group of people would be expected to be more productive than any one individual (see Figure 8-10). However, when several people combine their efforts on additive tasks, each individual's contribution tends to be less. Five people working together raking leaves will *not* be five times more productive than a single individual working alone; there are always some who go along for a "free ride." In fact, the more individuals who are contributing to an additive task, the less each individual's contribution tends to be—a phenomenon known as **social loafing**.[46]

This effect was first noted over sixty years ago by a German scientist named Max Ringelmann, who compared the amount of force exerted by different size groups of people pulling on a rope.[47] Specifically, he found that one person pulling on a rope alone exerted an average of 63 kilograms of force. However, in groups of three, the per-person force dropped to 53 kilograms, and in groups of eight it was reduced to only 31 kilograms per person—less than half the effort exerted by people working alone! Social loafing effects of this type have been observed in many different studies conducted in recent years.[48] The general form of the social loafing effect is portrayed graphically in Figure 8-11.

The phenomenon of social loafing has been explained by **social impact theory**.[49] According to this theory, the impact of any social force acting on a group is divided equally among its members. The larger the size of the group, the less the impact of the force on any one member. As a result, the more people who might contribute to a group's product, the less pressure each person faces to perform well—that is, the responsibility for doing the job is diffused over more people. As a result, each group member feels less responsible for behaving appropriately, and social loafing occurs.

Although feeling less responsible for an outcome is clearly one factor responsible for the social loafing phenomenon, the effect also may result from other experiences likely to arise among people performing their jobs. For example, people may engage in social loafing because they feel that the presence of others makes their contributions less needed—that is, more dispensable. Demonstrating this phenomenon, Weldon and Mustari had college students perform a judgment task (e.g., assessing the desirability of a job as the basis of describing it to potential applicants) and told them either that they were the only ones performing the task or that their judgments would be one of two or one of sixteen judgments used to make a final assessment.[50] The experimenters reasoned that people who believed their judgments would be one of many would take their jobs less seriously,

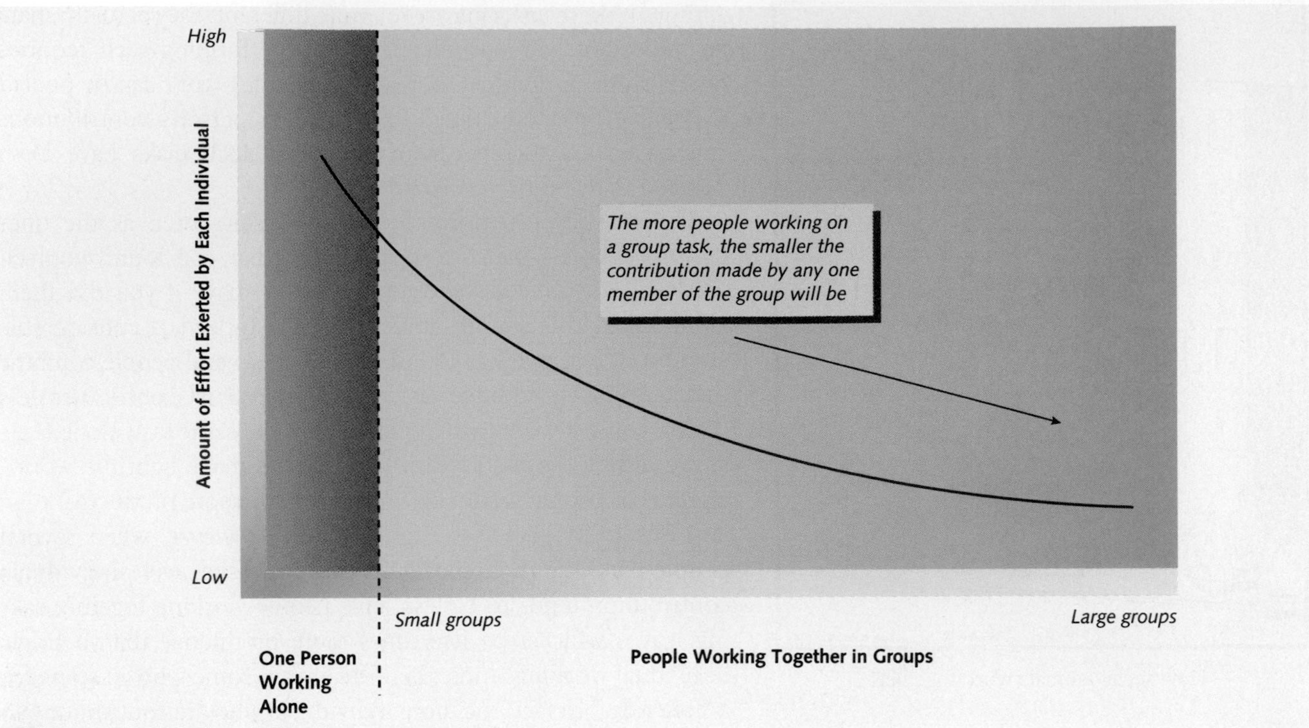

FIGURE 8-11

SOCIAL LOAFING: ITS GENERAL FORM

According to the social loafing effect, when individuals work together on an additive task, the more people contributing to the group's task, the less effort each individual exerts.

spending less time on the task and making less complex judgments. In fact, this is exactly what they found. The larger the size of the group, the more dispensable people believed their judgments were, and the less complex these judgments were found to be. These data strongly support the idea that social loafing occurs because people believe that in larger groups their contributions are less necessary than when working alone.

Obviously, the tendency for people to reduce their effort when working with others could be a serious problem in organizations. Fortunately, research has shown that there are several ways in which social loafing can be overcome. One possible antidote to social loafing is to *make each performer identifiable*. Social loafing may occur when people feel they can get away with "taking it easy"—namely, under conditions in which each individual's contributions cannot be determined. A variety of studies on the practice of "public posting" support this idea.[51] This research has found that when each individual's contribution to a task is displayed where it can be seen by others (e.g., weekly sales figures posted on a chart), people are less likely to slack off than when only overall group (or company-wide) performance is made available. In other words, the more one's individual contribution to a group effort is highlighted, the more pressure each person feels to make a group contribution. Thus, social loafing can be overcome if one's contributions to an additive task are identified: potential loafers are not likely to loaf if they fear getting caught.

Another way to overcome social loafing is to *make work tasks more important and interesting*. Research has revealed that people are unlikely to go along for a free ride when the task they are performing is believed to be vital to the organization.[52] For example, George found that the less meaningful salespeople believed their jobs were, the more they engaged in social loafing—especially when they thought their supervisors knew little about how well they were working.[53] To help in this regard, corporate officials should deliberately attempt to make jobs more intrinsically interesting to employees (perhaps, enriching them as described in Chapter 4). To

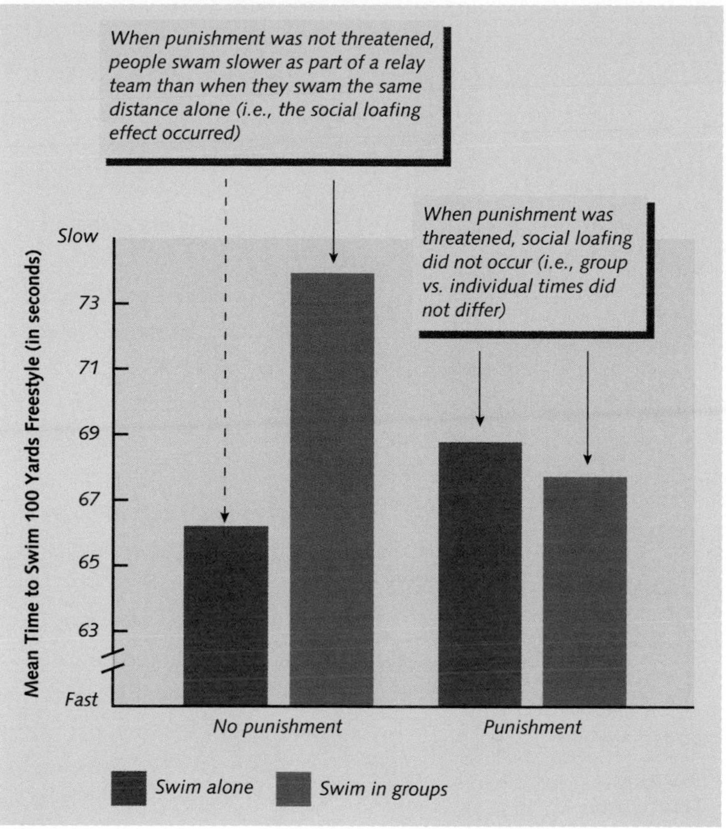
When punishment was not threatened, people swam slower as part of a relay team than when they swam the same distance alone (i.e., the social loafing effect occurred)
When punishment was threatened, social loafing did not occur (i.e., group vs. individual times did not differ)
Mean Time to Swim 100 Yards Freestyle (in seconds)
Slow
73
71
69
67
65
63
Fast
No punishment
Punishment
Swim alone
Swim in groups

FIGURE 8-12

USING PUNISHMENT THREATS TO ELIMINATE SOCIAL LOAFING: AN EXPERIMENTAL DEMONSTRATION USING SWIMMERS

High school swim team members swam 100 yards freestyle faster when they swam alone than when they swam the same distance as part of a four-person relay team. However, when they were threatened with punishment for failing to meet a prescribed time, the social loafing effect disappeared. (Source: Based on data from Miles & Greenberg, 1993; see Note 55.)

the extent that jobs are interesting, people may be less likely to loaf. It also has been suggested that managers should *reward individuals for contributing to their group's performance*—that is, encourage their interest in their group's performance.[54] Doing this (e.g., giving all salespeople in a territory a bonus if they jointly exceed their sales goal) may help employees focus more on collective concerns and less on individualistic concerns, increasing their obligations to their fellow group members. This is important, of course, in that the success of an organization is more likely to be influenced by the collective efforts of groups than by the individual contributions of any one member.

Another mechanism for overcoming social loafing is to *use punishment threats*. To the extent that performance decrements may be controlled by threatening to punish the individuals slacking off, loafing may be reduced. This effect was demonstrated in a experiment by Miles and Greenberg.[55] The participants in this study were members of high school swim teams who swam either alone or in relay races during practice sessions. In some conditions, the coach threatened the team by telling them that everyone would have to swim "penalty laps" if anyone on the team failed to meet a specified difficult time for swimming 100 yards freestyle. In a control group, no punishment threats were issued. How did the punishment threats influence task performance? As shown in Figure 8-12, people swam faster alone than as part of relay teams when no punishment was threatened, thereby confirming the social loafing effect. However, when punishment threats were made, group performance increased, thereby eliminating the social loafing effect.

Together, these findings suggest that social loafing is a potent force—and one that can be a serious threat to organizational performance. But it can be controlled in several ways that counteract the desire to loaf, such as by making loafing socially embarrassing or harmful to other individual interests. (Because different cultures have different norms about the role of work, and the acceptability of holding back work, there is reason to suspect that people in some cultures may be more willing to engage in social loafing than others. For a look at a fascinating study that examines this possibility, see the Global Organization section on the following page.)

THE GLOBAL ORGANIZATION

WHERE IN THE WORLD DOES SOCIAL LOAFING OCCUR? COMPARING CHINA, ISRAEL, AND THE UNITED STATES

A simple way of understanding social loafing is that it occurs because people are more interested in themselves (getting the most for themselves while doing the least) than their fellow group members (who are forced to do their work for them). That this phenomenon occurs in the United States is not particularly surprising insofar as American culture is highly *individualistic*—individual accomplishments and personal success are highly valued. However, there are other countries in the world where society is just the opposite—highly *collectivistic*. People in collectivistic nations, such as Israel and the People's Republic of China, place a high value on shared responsibility and the collective good of all. In collectivistic cultures, people working in groups would not be expected to engage in social loafing because doing so would have them fail in their social responsibility to the group (a responsibility that does not prevail in individualistic cultures). In fact, to the extent that people in collectivistic cultures are strongly motivated to help their fellow group members, they would be expected to be *more* productive in groups than alone. That is, not only wouldn't they loaf, but they would work especially hard!

A recent experiment by Earley tested these ideas.[56] In this research managers from the United States, Israel, and the People's Republic of China were each asked to complete an "in-basket" exercise. This task simulated the daily activities of managers in all three countries, such as writing memos, filling out forms, and rating job applicants. They were all asked to perform this task as well as

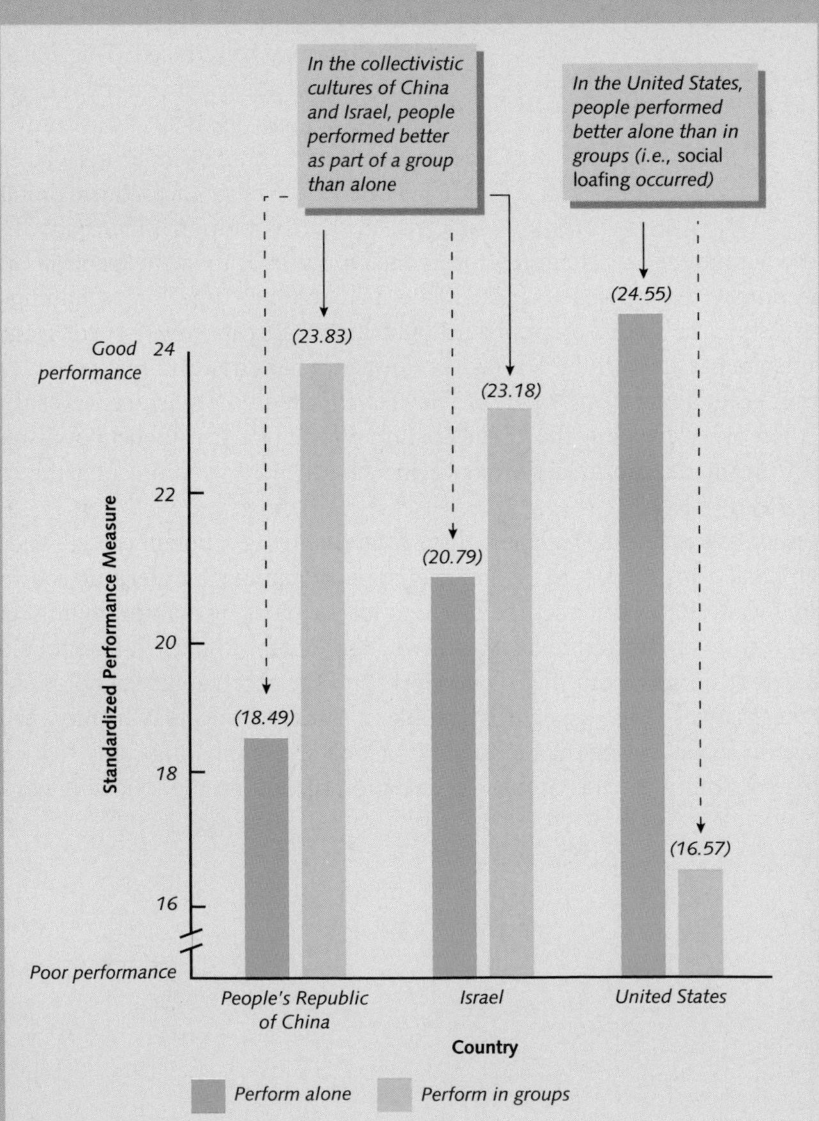

FIGURE 8-13

SOCIAL LOAFING: IS IT A UNIVERSAL PHENOMENON?

In a recent study, Earley compared the group and individual performance of people performing a managerial task in three countries: the People's Republic of China, Israel, and the United States. Although individual performance alone was lower than performance as part of a group in the United States (i.e., social loafing occurred), the opposite was found in China and Israel. The more collectivistic nature of these cultures discouraged people from letting down their fellow group members. (Source: Based on data reported by Earley, 1993; see Note 56.)

they could for a period of one hour, but under one of two different conditions: either *alone* or as part of a *group* of ten. Research participants who worked alone were simply asked to write their names on each item they completed and to turn it in. In the group condition, participants were told that their group's overall performance would be assessed at the end of the performance period. Fellow group members were not physically present, but were described as being highly similar to themselves with respect to their family and religious backgrounds as well as their interests. (Earley reasoned that groups of this type would be ones whose members people would be especially reluctant to let down by loafing.) To compare the various groups, Earley scored each participant's in-basket exercises by converting the responses to standardized performance scores.

Did social loafing occur, and in which countries? The results are summarized in Figure 8-13. These data clearly show that social loafing occurred in the United States. That is, individual performance was significantly lower among people working in groups than those working alone. However, the opposite was found in each of the two highly collectivistic cultures, Isreal and the People's Republic of China. In both these countries, individuals performed at higher levels when working in groups than when working alone. In these nations, people not only failed to loaf in groups, but they worked *harder* than they did alone. Because they strongly identified with their groups and were concerned about the welfare of its members, members of collectivistic cultures placed their group's interests ahead of their own. (It is important to note that these findings only occurred when people believed that they had strong ties to the members of their groups.)

Earley's research suggests that culture plays an important part in determining people's tendencies to engage in social loafing. Although it is tempting to think of social loafing as an inevitable aspect of human nature, it appears that the phenomenon is not as universal as you might think. Instead, loafing appears to be a manifestation of cultural values. Among cultural groups in which individualism is stressed, individual interests guide performance, but among groups in which collectivism is stressed, group interests guide performance. As more researchers explore national differences in social loafing, we expect to learn more about this important phenomenon.

EFFECTIVE TEAM PERFORMANCE

Now that we've examined the dynamics of individual performance in groups, we are prepared to appreciate the performance of teams. In this section we will examine two main questions. First, how successful are teams? And second, what are the obstacles to team success?

HOW SUCCESSFUL ARE TEAMS? A LOOK AT THE EVIDENCE

Questions regarding the effectiveness of teams in the workplace are not easy to answer. Not only are there many different kinds of teams doing different kinds of jobs operating in organizations, but their effectiveness is influenced by a wide variety of factors that go well beyond any possible benefits of teams, such as managerial support, the economy, available resources, and the like. As a result, understanding the true effectiveness of teams is a tricky business, at best. This difficulty has been fueled in recent years by cover stories in the top business periodicals touting the success of teams.[57,58] How much of this is hype stemming from the latest management fad, and how much should be accepted as valid evidence

they tell about how teams are used, and the results of using them can be quite revealing.[67] Still, there is a need for completely objective, empirical studies of team effectiveness.

Research of this type is now just beginning to be done. In one such investigation Pearson compared various aspects of work performance and attitudes of two groups of employees at a railroad car repair facility in Australia: those who were assembled into teams that could freely decide how to do their jobs, and those whose work was structured in the more traditional, non-autonomous fashion.[68] After the work teams had been in place for several months, it was found that they had significantly fewer accidents, as well as lower rates of absenteeism and turnover. Unfortunately, not all empirical studies paint such an optimistic picture of the benefits of work teams. For example, Wall, Kemp, Jackson, and Clegg examined the long-term effects of using work teams in an English manufacturing plant.[69] Although they found that employees were more satisfied with their jobs in teams compared to those in conventional work arrangements (in which individuals take orders from a supervisor), they were individually no more productive. However, because the use of teams made it possible for the organization to eliminate several supervisory positions, the company became more profitable.

These two studies do not paint a clear and convincing case for the overall effectiveness of teams. Although teams are generally well received—that is, people enjoy working in them—it is not yet apparent that they are responsible for making individuals any more productive. From an organizational perspective, teams appear to be an effective way of eliminating layers of management. When people are highly committed toward achieving excellence, it is not surprising that their companies may enjoy the results. In fact, it is precisely these types of beneficial outcomes that are being reported by the case studies we summarized above.

In view of the fact that more and more companies are turning to teams (as many as half of us will be working in teams by the end of this decade, according to one estimate), it is important to consider some things teams can do to build performance.[70] Based on the experiences of companies that have been successful with teams, several recommendations can be made for ways of building effective team performance.[71] We have summarized these in Table 8-7. As you will see when you review these tips, making teams effective is not an easy matter. They don't automatically work out simply because they are introduced. They need to be carefully cared for and maintained, such as in the ways listed, for them to accomplish their missions.

POTENTIAL OBSTACLES TO SUCCESS: WHY DO SOME TEAMS FAIL?

Although we have reported many success stories about teams, we also have hinted at several possible problems and difficulties in implementing them. After all, working in a team demands a great deal, and not everyone may be ready for them. Fortunately, we can learn from these experiences. Analyses of failed attempts at introducing teams into the workplace suggest several obstacles to team success, pitfalls that can be avoided if you know about them.

First, some teams fail because their members are *unwilling to cooperate with each other*. This is what happened recently at Dow Chemical Company's plastics group in Midland, Michigan, where a team was put into place to create a new plastic resin.[72] Some members (those in the research field) wanted to spend several

TABLE 8-7

Building Team Performance: Some Tips

Based on analyses of successful teams, it is possible to identify several things that teams can do to ensure their success. Here is a listing of some of the most important tips.

TIP	RATIONALE
• *Make the team's task urgent.*	*Team members are prone to rally around challenges that compel them to meet high performance standards.*
• *Select team members based on their skills.*	*When putting together a team, it is essential that members have the skills needed to succeed (or at least the potential to develop them).*
• *Make rules of behavior clear.*	*Effective teams have clear rules about what is and is not expected (e.g., maintain confidentiality, attendance is mandatory, give constructive criticism only).*
• *Recognize intermediate performance goals.*	*To motivate and encourage team members acknowledge goals that are met prior to the major team goals (e.g., the halfway point).*
• *Regularly challenge the team with new facts.*	*Facts are needed for teams to gauge their progress toward their goals, so bringing in new data may help provide direction.*
• *Meet regularly.*	*Members will take teamwork seriously if they are frequently reminded of their obligations.*
• *Acknowledge and reinforce vital contributions to the team.*	*Making people feel good about their contributions will encourage them to make more.*

Source: Based on information in Katzenbach & Smith, 1993; see Note 29.

months developing and testing new options, while others (those on the manufacturing end) wanted to slightly alter existing products and start up production right away. Neither side budged, and the project eventually stalled. By contrast, when team members share a common vision, and are committed to attaining it, they are generally very cooperative with each other, leading to success (see Figure 8-14).

A second reason why some teams are not effective is that they *fail to receive support from management*. Consider, for example, the experience at the Lenexa, Kansas, plant of the Puritan-Bennett Corporation, a manufacturer of respiratory equipment.[73] After seven years of working to develop improved software for its respirators, product development teams have not completed the job, despite the fact that the industry average for such tasks is only three years. According to Roger J.

FIGURE 8-14
COOPERATION: A KEY INGREDIENT TO TEAM EFFECTIVENESS
By having artists, designers, printers, and financial experts cooperating with each other as members of a new-product development team, Hallmark Cards has been highly successful in maintaining its dominance in the greeting cards market (left). Similarly, by creating teams with highly cooperative members from different fields, Thermos was able to launch its highly successful electric grill (right).

Dolida, the company's director of research and development, the problem is that management never made the project a priority, and refused to free up another key person needed to do the job. As he put it, "If top management doesn't buy into the idea . . . teams can go nowhere."[74]

A third obstacle to group success, and a relatively common one, is that *some managers are unwilling to relinquish control*. Good supervisors work their way up from the plant floor by giving orders and having them followed. However, team leaders have to build consensus and must allow team members to make decisions together. As you might expect, letting go of control isn't always easy for some to do. This problem emerged at Bausch & Lomb's sunglasses plant in Rochester, New York.[75] In 1989 some 1,400 employees were put into thirty-eight teams. By 1992 about half the supervisors had not adjusted to the change, despite receiving thorough training in how to work as part of a team. They argued bitterly with team members whenever their ideas were not accepted by the team, and eventually they were reassigned. An even tougher approach was taken at the Shelby Die Casting Company, a metal-casting firm in Shelby, Mississippi.[76] When its former supervisors refused to cooperate as co-equals in their teams, the company eliminated their jobs, and let the workers run their own teams. The result: the company saved $250,000 in annual wages, productivity jumped 50 percent, and company profits almost doubled. The message sent by both companies is clear: those who cannot adjust to teamwork are unwelcome.

Fourth, teams might fail not only because their members do not cooperate with each other, but also because they *fail to cooperate with other teams*. This problem occurred in General Electric's medical systems division when it assigned two teams of engineers, one in Waukesha, Wisconsin, and another in Hino, Japan, the task of creating software for two new ultrasound devices.[77] Shortly, teams pushed features that made their products popular only in their own countries, and duplicated each other's efforts. When the teams met, language and cultural barriers separated them, further distancing the teams from each other. Without close cooperation between teams (as well as within them!), organizations are not likely to reap the benefits they hoped for when creating teams in the first place.[78] (As you might imagine, it's a matter of not only *if* teams cooperate with each other, but precisely *how* they go about interacting with other units that will determine their effectiveness. For a description of a fascinating recent study exploring this issue, see the Quest for Quality section on the opposite page.)

THE QUEST FOR QUALITY

BOUNDARY-SPANNING STRATEGIES FOR TEAM EFFECTIVENESS: WHAT DO SUCCESSFUL TEAMS DO?

Teams rarely operate in isolation. To create quality outcomes, members must interact with other teams and individuals, both inside and outside the organizations, coordinating their activities and sharing information with them. In other words, they must span the boundaries between themselves and their external environments. But how do groups engage in *boundary spanning*, and what types of boundary-spanning tactics work best? A recent study by Ancona and Caldwell sheds light on these questions.[79]

The researchers conducted extensive interviews and administered questionnaires to members of new-product teams in several different high-tech companies. The teams were responsible for creating and developing new products that made use of their companies' technologies. As you might imagine, such a task requires a great deal of interaction with others outside the team (referred to as the *external environment*), such as gathering information about markets, pricing of materials, and production capabilities. Using the questionnaire and interview responses, teams were differentiated with respect to the major strategies they used to engage in boundary spanning activities. Four different strategies were found to be commonly used by the teams: *ambassadorial*, attempts to protect the team from outside pressures, persuade others to support the team, and lobby for resources; *technical scouting*, efforts at searching for ideas about the market, the competition, or technology, and coordinating this new information with team members; *comprehensive*, the use of ambassadorial activities while also coordinating technical information with nonteam members, and *isolationist*, engaging in few, if any, attempts at interacting with the external environment.

Ancona and Caldwell found that the particular strategy the teams used was related to some measures of how effectively the teams performed. For example, one particularly important measure for any team is the extent to which it adheres to its schedule and works within its budget. By examining company data, the researchers were able to assess these dependent variables, and combined

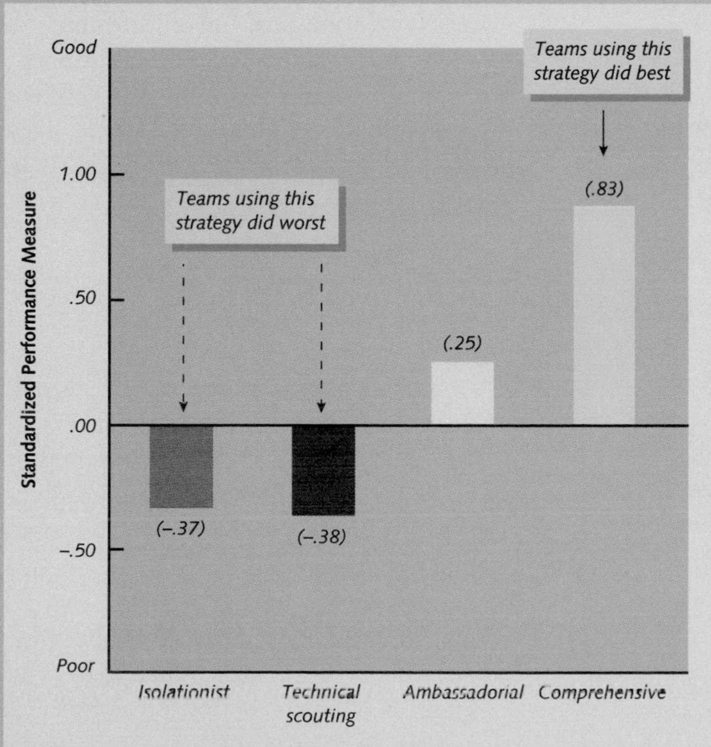

FIGURE 8-15
STRATEGY FOR SPANNING TEAMS' BOUNDARIES: ITS IMPACT ON TEAM PERFORMANCE
Ancona and Caldwell compared the task performance of teams that used different strategies for interacting with their external environments. Those that used comprehensive strategies were found to be most successful at maintaining budgets and schedules, whereas those using technical scouting and isolationist strategies were least successful. (Source: Based on data reported by Ancona and Caldwell, 1992; see Note 79.)

THE QUEST FOR QUALITY, Cont.

them to form an index. Which boundary-spanning strategies were associated with the highest scores on this important measure? As shown in Figure 8-15, teams following a comprehensive strategy did the best jobs of meeting their schedules within their budgets. Teams relying on the technical scouting and isolationist tactics were least effective in this regard.

These findings suggest that the way teams go about interacting with their external environments has some important effects on key aspects of their task performance. By actively attempting to protect themselves from outside pressures while also working hard at coordinating technical information with others, teams using comprehensive tactics were able to stay on schedule and work within their budgets. Not surprisingly, isolationist teams, ones that were less actively engaged in attempts to span the boundaries between themselves and the external environment, failed to gather the information needed to succeed on this important dimension. Ancona and Caldwell's study shows us that teams, just like individuals, have different styles of operating, and that these have important effects on their performance. As a result of this study, future researchers will be likely to focus not only on how effectively teams perform relative to other ways of working, but also on what makes some teams more successful than others.

SUMMARY AND REVIEW

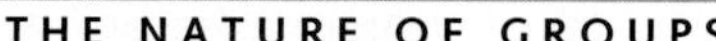

THE NATURE OF GROUPS

A **group** is defined as a collection of two or more interacting individuals with a stable pattern of relationships between them who share common goals and who perceive themselves as being a group. Within organizations, there are two major classes of groups—**formal groups** and **informal groups**. Groups often develop by going through five principal stages—*forming*, *storming*, *norming*, *performing*, and *adjourning*.

The structure of groups is determined by four key factors: **roles**, the typical pattern of behavior in a social context; **norms**, generally agreed-on informal rules; **status**, the prestige accorded group members; and **cohesiveness**, the pressures faced by group members to remain in their groups.

THE NATURE OF TEAMS

Teams are special kinds of groups, ones whose members focus on collective, rather than individual, work products, are mutually accountable to each other, share a common commitment to purpose, and are usually self-managing. Teams differ with respect to three dimensions: their *purpose or mission* (work or improvement), *time* (temporary or permanent), and *authority structure* (overlaid or intact). Creating teams involves four basic steps: prework, creating performance conditions, forming and building a team, and providing ongoing assistance.

INDIVIDUAL PERFORMANCE IN GROUPS

Individual productivity is influenced by the presence of other group members. Sometimes a person's performance improves in the presence of others (when the job he or she is doing is well learned), and sometimes performance declines in the presence of others (when the job is novel). This phenomenon is known as **social facilitation**. Not only is performance influenced by the presence of others, but by the group's racial and ethnic diversity. Performance in diverse groups is initially worse than performance in homogeneous groups, although these differences disappear with repeated involvement with the group.

On **additive tasks**, in which each member's individual contributions are combined, **social loafing** occurs. According to this phenomenon, the more people who work on a task, the less each group member contributes to it. Loafing can be reduced by making workers identifiable, making the work important and interesting, rewarding people for their group contributions, and by threatening punishment.

TEAM PERFORMANCE

In surveys, organizational officials report that teams operating in their organizations have mostly been successful. Comprehensive case studies also have found organizational productivity gains (e.g., increased outcome, improved quality, lowered costs) resulting from the use of teams. However, more objective field research has found that while employees are generally more satisfied in teams than working under traditional management, they tend to be no more productive at the individual level. Many of the organizational benefits resulting from teams appears to come from the elimination of middle-management positions.

Despite some evidence of the team successes, some teams fail. This is often because team members are unwilling to cooperate with each other, they fail to receive support from management, some managers are unwilling to relinquish control, and some teams fail to coordinate their efforts effectively with other teams.

KEY TERMS

additive tasks: Types of group tasks in which the coordinated efforts of several people are added together to form the group's product.

cohesiveness: The strength of group members' desires to remain a part of the group.

distraction-conflict model: A conceptualization explaining social facilitation in terms of the tendency for others' presence to cause a conflict between directing attention to others versus the task at hand.

drive theory of social facilitation: The theory according to which the presence of others increases arousal, which increases people's tendencies to perform the dominant response. If that response is well learned, performance will improve. But, if it is novel, performance will be impaired.

evaluation apprehension: The fear of being evaluated or judged by another person.

formal groups: Groups that are created by the organization, intentionally designed to direct its members toward some organizational goal.

group: A collection of two or more interacting individuals who maintain stable patterns of relationships, share common goals, and perceive themselves as being a group.

group dynamics: The social science field focusing on the nature of groups—the factors governing their formation and development, the elements of their structure, and their interrelationships with individuals, other groups, and organizations.

group structure: The pattern of interrelationships between the individuals constituting a group; the guidelines of group behavior that make group functioning orderly and predictable.

informal groups: Groups that develop naturally among people, without any direction from the organization within which they operate.

norms: Generally agreed-on informal rules that guide group members' behavior.

role: The typical behavior that characterizes a person in a specific social context.

role differentiation: The tendency for various specialized roles to emerge as groups develop.

CHAPTER OUTLINE

SPECIAL SECTIONS

NINE

INTERPERSONAL COMMUNICATION IN ORGANIZATIONS

The hearing ear is always found close to the speaking tongue.

Ralph Waldo Emerson, 1803–1882
American essayist and poet
Eloquence

The most immutable barrier in nature is between one man's thoughts and another's.

William James, 1842–1910
American psychologist and philosopher
Pragmatism

LEARNING OBJECTIVES

After reading this chapter, you should be able to

1. *Describe the process of communication and its role in organizations.*
2. *Identify various forms of verbal media used in organizations.*
3. *Explain what types of verbal media are most appropriate for communicating messages of different types.*
4. *Describe some of the latest high-tech methods used to communicate within and between organizations.*
5. *Explain how style of dress, and the use of time and space are used to communicate nonverbally in organizations.*
6. *Describe how the formal structure of an organization influences the nature of the communication that occurs within it.*
7. *Distinguish between centralized and decentralized communication networks with respect to their relative superiority in performing different kinds of tasks.*
8. *Describe how informal networks of communication operate within organizations.*
9. *Identify and describe concrete steps that can be taken by both individuals and organizations to improve the effectiveness of organizational communication.*

COMMUNICATION: ITS BASIC NATURE

Before we can fully appreciate the process of organizational communication, we need to address some basic issues. To begin, we will formally define what we mean by communication and then elaborate on the process by which it occurs. Following this, we will describe the important role that communication plays in organizations.

COMMUNICATION: A WORKING DEFINITION AND DESCRIPTION OF THE PROCESS

What do the following situations have in common? The district manager posts a notice stating that coffee breaks are limited to ten minutes. An executive prepares a report about the financial status of a potential corporate takeover prospect. A taxi dispatcher directs Cab 54 to pick up a fare at 1065 Cherry Drive. A foreman smiles at one of his subordinates and pats him on the back in recognition for a job well done. The answer, if you haven't already guessed it, is that each of these incidents involves some form of *communication*. Although you probably already have a good idea of what communication entails, we can better understand communication in organizations by defining it precisely and describing the nature of the communication process.

With this in mind, we define **communication** as *the process by which a person, group, or organization (the sender) transmits some type of information (the message) to another person, group, or organization (the receiver)*. To clarify this definition, and to further elaborate on how the process works, we have summarized it in Figure 9-1. You may find it helpful to follow along with this diagram as we describe the various steps in the communication process.

The communication process begins when one party has an idea that it wishes to transmit to another (either party may be an individual, a group, or an entire organization). It is the sender's mission to transform the idea into a form that can be sent to and understood by the receiver. This is what happens in the process of **encoding**—translating an idea into a form, such as written or spoken language, that can be recognized by a receiver. We encode information when we select the

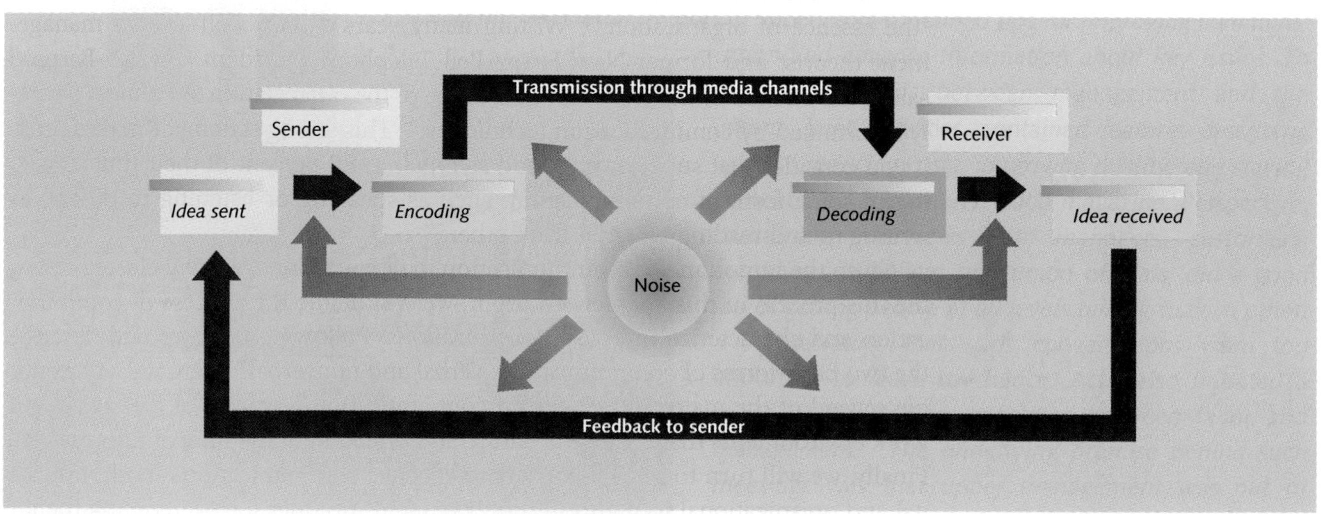

FIGURE 9-1
THE PROCESS OF COMMUNICATION
In its most basic form, communication consists of the distinct steps shown here. Senders encode *messages and* transmit *them via one or more communication channels to* receivers, *who then* decode *them. The process continues as the original receiver sends feedback to the original sender. Factors distorting or limiting the flow of information, known as* noise, *may enter into the process at any point.*

words we use to write a letter or speak to someone in person. This process is crucial if we are to clearly communicate our ideas. Unfortunately, people are far from perfect when it comes to encoding their ideas (although, as we will note later, this skill can be improved).

After a message is encoded, it is ready to be transmitted over one or more *channels of communication* to reach the desired receiver, the pathways along which information travels. Telephone lines, radio and television signals, fiber-optic cables, mail routes, and even the air waves that carry the vibrations of our voices all represent potential channels of communication. Of course, the form of encoding largely determines the way information may be transmitted. Visual information—such as pictures and written words—may be mailed, delivered in person by a courier, shipped by an express delivery service, or, with increasing popularity, sent via modems, fax machines and satellite dishes. Oral information may be transmitted over the telephone, via radio and television waves, and of course the old-fashioned way, in person. Whatever channel is used, the goal is the same: to send the encoded message accurately to a desired receiver.

Once a message is received, the recipient must begin the process of **decoding**—converting the message back into the sender's original ideas. This can involve many different subprocesses, such as comprehending spoken and written words, interpreting facial expressions, and the like. To the extent that the sender's message is accurately decoded by the receiver, the ideas understood will be the ones intended. Of course, our ability to comprehend and interpret information received from others may be imperfect (e.g., restricted by unclear messages, or by our own language skills). Thus, as in the case of encoding, limitations in our ability to decode information represent another potential weakness in the communication process—but, as we will describe later in this chapter, one that can be developed.

Finally, once a message has been decoded, the process can continue, with the receiver transmitting a new message back to the original sender. This part of the process is known as *feedback*—knowledge about the impact of messages on receivers. Receiving feedback allows senders to determine whether their messages have been understood properly. At the same time, giving feedback can help convince receivers that the sender really cares about what he or she has to say. Once received, feedback can trigger another idea from the sender, and another cycle of transferring information may begin. For this reason, we have characterized the process of communication summarized in Figure 9-1 as continuous.

Despite the apparent simplicity of the communication process, it rarely operates as flawlessly as we have described it here. As we will see, there are many potential barriers to effective communication. The name given to factors that distort the clarity of a message is **noise**. As depicted in Figure 9-1, noise can occur at any point along the communication process. For example, messages that are poorly encoded (e.g., written in an unclear way) or poorly decoded (e.g., not comprehended), or channels of communication that are too full of static (e.g., receivers' attentions are diverted from the message) may reduce communication's effectiveness. These factors, and others (e.g., time pressure, organizational politics), may contribute to the distortion of information transmitted from one party to another, and the complexity of the communication process. As you continue reading this chapter, you will come to appreciate many of the factors that make the process of organizational communication so very complex and important.

THE FUNDAMENTAL ROLE OF COMMUNICATION IN ORGANIZATIONS

When you think about people in organizations communicating with each other, what image comes to mind? A typical picture might involve one person telling another what to do. Indeed, one key purpose of organizational communication is to *direct action*, that is, to get others to behave in a desired fashion. However, communication in organizations often involves not only single efforts, but also concerted action. Thus, for an organization to function, individuals and groups must carefully coordinate their efforts and activities.[7] The waiter must take the customer's order and pass it along to the chef. The market researcher must collect information about consumers' needs and share it with the people in charge of manufacturing and advertising. Communication is the key to these attempts at coordination. Without it, people would not know what to do, and organizations would not be able to function effectively—if at all. In other words, it may be said that another key function of communication in organizations is to *achieve coordinated action*.

This function is served by the systematic sharing of information. Indeed, information—whether it's data about a product's sales performance, directions to a customer's residence, or instructions on how to perform a task—is the core of all organizational activities. It would be misleading, however, to imply that communication involves only the sharing of facts and data. There is also an interpersonal facet of organizational communication, a focus on the social relations between people.[8] For example, communication is also highly involved in such important purposes as developing friendships and building trust and acceptance. As you know, what you say and how you say it can have profound effects on the extent to which others like you. To the extent that people are interested in creating a pleasant interpersonal atmosphere in the workplace, they must be highly concerned about communication. (In some organizations, management has created an unpleasant, untrusting atmosphere by violating the confidentiality of employee communications. For a discussion of employees' rights to communication privacy on the job, see the Ethical Workplace section below.)

THE ETHICAL WORKPLACE

EMPLOYEE COMMUNICATION: NOT AS CONFIDENTIAL AS YOU THINK!

How would you feel if you found out that your boss was eavesdropping on your telephone conversations or reading the messages you sent over a computer network? Not too pleased, we suspect. However, as much as you may dislike it, not only are many companies doing this, but the practice appears to be perfectly legal![9] In recent years, for example, employees of Nissan and Epson of America caught their supervisors reading their electronic mail (e-mail).[10] When they complained, they were fired. Feeling their dismissal was unjust, the employees sued. Although the cases linger in the appeals process, thus far the courts have found for the employers.[11]

How can this be? Don't employees have a right to privacy in communication at work? Although the Fourth Amendment to the U.S. Constitution prohibits the government from "unreasonable search and seizure," it does *not* restrict your boss from rifling through the papers in your office. In recent years, laws have been enacted, such as the Electronic Communications Privacy Act of 1986, that safeguard the privacy of electronic messages sent over telephone lines. However, such laws apply only to public networks, such as CompuServe, not to private facilities, such as corporate computer systems. In the United States, attempts to enact legislation that would restrict employer's rights to eavesdrop on their employees (e.g., the proposed Privacy for Consumers and Workers Act) have been unsuccessful. The bottom line (today, at least) is clear: employers *can*, and *do*, examine their employees' communications.

Employers have argued that the practice is justified because they need to keep tabs on their employers to ensure that they are doing what they are supposed to and are being honest. Because companies own the computer systems, corporate officials feel justified accessing them whenever they wish. Indeed, a recent survey revealed that one out of five supervisors have on at least one occasion examined employees' computer files, e-mail, or voice mail, allegedly for purposes of investigating larceny or measuring performance.[12]

Somehow, the remoteness of electronic snooping makes people feel less uncomfortable than they would about breaking into an employee's file drawer. However, according to Alana Shoars, the fired Epson employee, it's a basic matter of not invading privacy: "You don't read other people's mail, just as you don't listen to their phone conversations."[13] Michael Simmons, the chief information officer at the Bank of Boston, believes otherwise. He contends that if the company owns the equipment, "it has a right to look and see if people are using it for purposes other than running the business."[14] Perhaps Simmons's views were tempered by experiences he had on a previous job. He discovered that one employee was using the company's computer system to run his own Amway business,

TABLE 9-1

A Model Employee Communication Policy

Because many organizations do not have explicit policies about communication, employees do not know what levels of privacy they can expect. The following points represent what many experts consider the basic features of a good electronic privacy communication policy.

- *Employees are entitled to reasonable expectations of personal privacy on the job.*
- *Employees know what electronic surveillance tools are used, and how management uses the collected data.*
- *Management uses electronic monitoring or searches of data files, network communications, or electronic mail to the minimum extent possible. Continuous monitoring is not permitted.*
- *Employees participate in decisions about how and when electronic monitoring or searches take place.*
- *Data are gathered and used only for clearly defined work-related purposes.*
- *Management will not engage in secret monitoring or searches, except when credible evidence of criminal activity or other serious wrongdoing comes to light.*
- *Monitoring data will not be the sole factor in evaluating employee performance.*
- *Employees can inspect, challenge, and correct electronic records kept on their activities or files captured through electronic means.*
- *Records no longer relevant to the purposes for which they were collected will be destroyed.*
- *Monitoring data that identify individual employees will not be released to any third party, except to comply with legal requirements.*
- *Employees or prospective employees cannot waive privacy rights.*
- *Managers who violate these privacy principles are subject to discipline or termination.*

Source: From "Bosses with X-ray Eyes" by Charles Piller in *MACWORLD*, July 1993, p.121. Reprinted courtesy of Macworld Communications, 501 Second St., San Francisco, CA 94107.

and another was using it to handicap horse races.

Almost 31 percent of companies responding to a recent survey indicated that they presently inform their employees that their e-mail messages might be monitored.[15] Still, some contend that simply informing employees that they might snoop does not give companies the right to actually do so. It is widely recommended that companies develop clear policies about the privacy of employee communication.[16] (For a summary of points that should be included in such a policy, see Table 9-1.) Others, such as management consultant Donn B. Parker, counter that no specific computer-related rules of conduct should be needed because "when people log onto a computer or network, they don't automatically turn off their ethical values."[17]

Experts contend that before organizations rush to eavesdrop on their employees they consider what they are communicating about their own ethical values. In other words, if organizations show disregard for the privacy of employees, they should not be surprised to find that employees are similarly tempted to test ethical boundaries.[18] To the extent that employees model the ethical standards communicated to them by company officials, the treatment of messages sent on a computer network represents a prime avenue by which organizations can project their ethical values. Meanwhile, until people can be assured that their employers are willing to respect their privacy, caution in using electronic media seems advised. As Bill Moroney, executive director of the Electronic Messaging Association, put it, "Don't put anything in writing that you wouldn't want other people to read."[19]

VERBAL COMMUNICATION: THE WRITTEN AND SPOKEN WORD

Because you are reading this book, we know you are familiar with **verbal communication**—transmitting and receiving ideas by using words. Verbal communication can be either *oral,* using spoken language in forms such as face-to-face talks, telephone conversations, tape recordings, and the like, or *written,* in forms such as memos, letters, order blanks, and electronic mail, to name just a few. Because both oral and written communications involve the use of words, they fall under the heading of verbal communication.

VARIETIES OF VERBAL MEDIA IN ORGANIZATIONS

According to Lengel and Daft, verbal media can be distinguished with respect to their capacity to convey information (see Figure 9-2).[20] Some verbal media, such as *face-to-face discussions* are considered especially *rich* insofar as they not only provide vast amounts of information, but are also highly personal in nature and provide opportunities for immediate feedback. A bit less rich are non face-to-face interactive media, such as the *telephone*. However, not all business communication requires a two-way flow of information. For example, further toward the *lean* end of the continuum are personal, but static media, such as *memos* (written messages used for communication within an organization) and *letters* (written messages used for external communication).[21] This includes one-way communications sent either physically (e.g., letter) or electronically (e.g., fax or e-mail). Finally, at the most lean end of the continuum are highly impersonal, static media, such as *flyers* and *bulletins*, written information that is targeted broadly, and not aimed at any one specific individual.

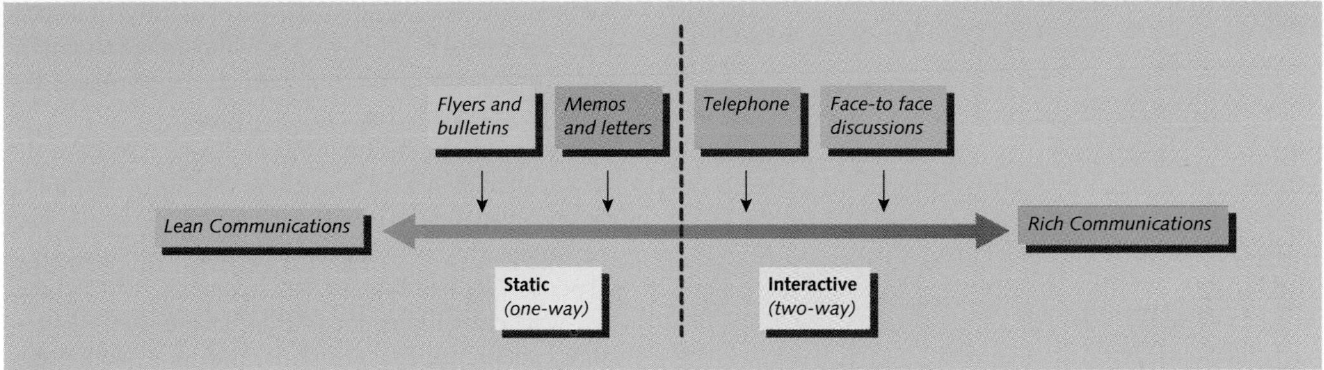

FIGURE 9-2
A CONTINUUM OF VERBAL COMMUNICATION MEDIA
Verbal communication media can be characterized along a continuum ranging from highly rich, interactive media, such as face-to-face discussions, to lean, static media, such as flyers and bulletins. (Source: Adapted from Lengel and Daft, 1988; see Note 20.)

Several types of written media deserve special mention because of the important role they play in organizations. First, although they are impersonal and aimed at a general audience, **newsletters** serve important functions in organizations, a point illustrated clearly in our Preview Case. Newsletters are regularly published internal documents describing information of interest to employees regarding an array of business and nonbusiness issues affecting them.[22] Approximately one-third of companies rely on newsletters, typically as a means of supplementing other means of communicating important information, such as group meetings.[23] McDonnell Aircraft Company, for example, relies on its newsletter as a means of communicating information about its merit pay system, a medium that has been very well received.[24] In fact, research at McDonnell Aircraft has shown that the more time its employees spend examining their company's newsletter, the more satisfied they are with their company's pay policy, and the fairer they believe it to be.[25] Newsletters appear to be effective devices in improving employees' attitudes and morale (see Chapter 5) not only because of the information they provide about matters of interest to them, but also because the mere act of publishing a newsletter sends a message that the company cares enough about its employees to communicate with them.

Another important internal publication used in organizations is the **employee handbook**—a document describing to employees basic information about the company. It is a general reference regarding the company's background, the nature of its business, and its rules.[26] Specifically, the major purposes of employee handbooks are: (1) to explain key aspects of the company's policies, (2) to clarify the expectations of the company and employees toward each other, and (3) to express the company's philosophy.[27] Handbooks are more popular today than ever before. This is not only because clarifying company policies may help prevent lawsuits, but also because corporate officials are recognizing that explicit statements about what their company stands for is a useful means of effectively socializing new employees (see Chapter 6) and promoting the company's values (see Chapter 14). As the major formal means of communicating pertinent company information to employees, employee handbooks are, in the opinion of one expert, "the most important document a company can have."[28]

USES OF ORAL AND WRITTEN COMMUNICATION: MATCHING THE MEDIUM TO THE MESSAGE

Now that we have reviewed various types of verbal communication, it makes sense to consider what types are most effective, and when. In this regard, research has shown that *communication is most effective when it uses multiple channels, such as*

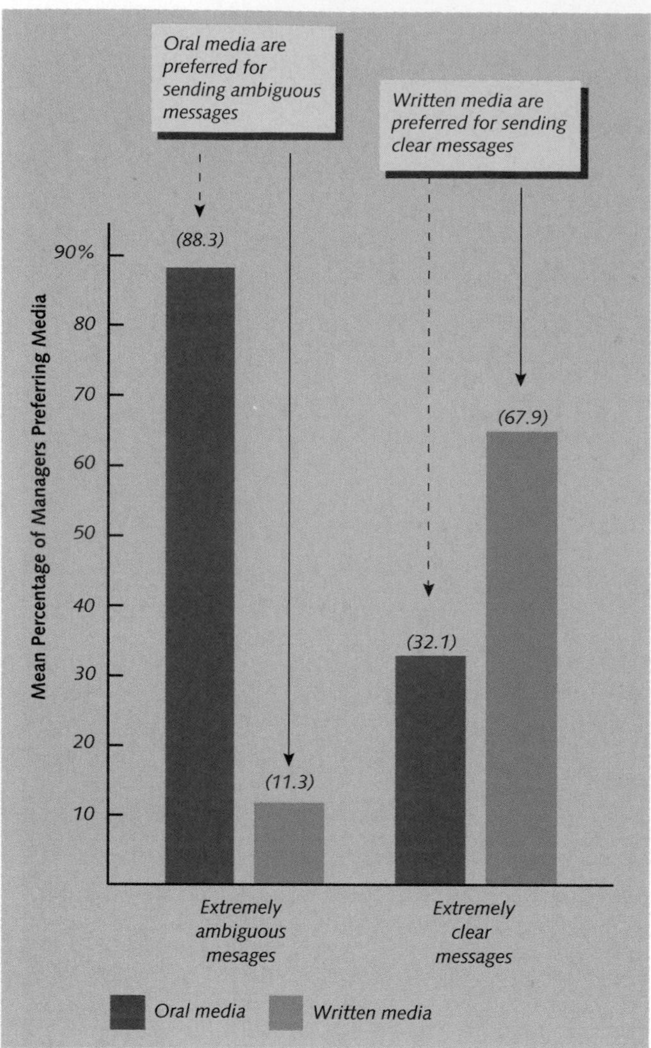

FIGURE 9-3

PREFERENCES FOR ORAL AND WRITTEN COMMUNICATION: IT DEPENDS ON THE MESSAGE

What type of communications medium do managers prefer using? The research findings reviewed here show that it depends on the degree of clarity or ambiguity of the message. Oral media (e.g., telephones or face-to-face contact) were preferred for ambiguous messages; written media (e.g., letters or memos) were preferred for clear messages. (Source: Based on data in Daft, Lengel, & Trevino, 1987; see Note 31.)

both oral and written messages.[29] Apparently, oral messages are useful in getting others' immediate attention, and the follow-up written portion helps make the message more permanent, something that can be referred to in the future. Oral messages also have the benefit of allowing for immediate two-way communication between parties, whereas written communiqués are frequently only one-way, or take too long for a response. Not surprisingly, researchers have found that two-way communications (e.g., face-to-face discussions, telephone conversations) are more commonly used in organizations than one-way communications (e.g., memos). For example, Klauss and Bass found that approximately 83 percent of the communications taking place among civilian employees of a U.S. Navy agency used two-way media.[30] In fact, 55 percent of all communications were individual face-to-face interactions. One-way, written communications tended to be reserved for more formal, official messages that needed to be referred to in the future at the receiver's convenience (e.g., official announcements about position openings). Apparently, both written and spoken communications have their place in organizational communication.

Additional research has shown that a medium's effectiveness depends on how appropriate it is for the kind of message being sent. Specifically, Daft, Lengel, and Trevino reasoned that oral media (e.g., telephone conversations, face-to-face meetings) are preferable to written media (e.g., notes, memos) when messages are ambiguous (requiring a great deal of assistance in interpreting them), whereas written media are preferable when messages are clear.[31] The researchers surveyed a sample of managers about the medium they preferred using to communicate messages that differed with respect to their clarity or ambiguity. (For example, "giving a subordinate a set of cost figures" was prejudged to be a very unambiguous type of message, whereas "getting an explanation about a complicated technical matter" was prejudged to be a very ambiguous message.) The results, summarized in Figure 9-3, show that the choice of medium was related to the clarity or ambiguity of the messages.

Specifically, the data reveal that the more ambiguous the message, the more managers preferred using oral media (such as telephones or face-to-face contact), and also that the clearer the message, the more managers preferred using written media (such as letters or memos). Apparently, most managers were sensitive to the need to use communications media that allowed them to take advantage of the rich avenues for two-way oral communications when necessary, and to use the more efficient one-way, written communications when these were adequate. Note, however, that although many managers selected media based on the pattern described here (people identified as "media sensitive"), others did not. They made their media choices almost randomly (this group was referred to as "media insensitive").

Further analysis of the data revealed that these differences were related to the managers' job performance. Those who were media sensitive were expected to be more effective than those who were media insensitive. After all, effective communication is an important part of managers' activities, and using the appropriate medium could enhance their effectiveness. Comparisons of the performance ratings of managers in the media-sensitive and media-insensitive groups supported this hypothesis. Specifically, whereas most of the media-sensitive managers (87 percent) received their company's highest performance ratings, only about half of the media-insensitive managers (47 percent) received equally high evaluations. Apparently, the skill of selecting the appropriate communications medium is an important aspect of a manager's success. Unfortunately, it is difficult to say whether the managers' choices of communications media were directly responsible for their success, or whether their media sensitivity was part of an overall set of managerial skills that together led to their success. Still, these findings highlight the importance of making appropriate media choices in successful managerial communication.

WHEN WORDS GO HIGH-TECH: SPECIAL ISSUES OF ELECTRONIC MEDIA

In recent years, advances in technology have transformed the way people engage in verbal communication. In particular, three forms of technology have revolutionized organizational communication—*video display terminals*, *electronic mail*, and *voice messaging*.

VIDEO DISPLAY TERMINALS (VDTS)

In the modern office, *video display terminals (VDTs)* linked to computers have replaced the paper-cluttered desks of office workers in the past. Although computers vastly improve office productivity, there is a hidden cost in using them. Clerical employees forced to do their work in the shadow of a computer screen all day may miss human contact, especially when they are encased in cubicles separated from others by tall partitions. In an attempt to escape such isolation, the employees in an office studied by Zuboff mischievously pried open the seam of a metal partition that separated them from their co-workers.[32] People reported feeling isolated and solitary, and longed for the kind of informal contact denied them by the design of their surroundings. When contact between managers and their subordinates is restricted, crucial opportunities to identify and solve organizational problems may be lost. Ironically, the same technology that makes people so efficient often makes interpersonal collaboration unnecessary, adding to feelings of isolation, which may undermine some of the productivity gains (a point to which we will return in Chapter 14).

ELECTRONIC MAIL (E-MAIL)

One of the primary technological advances in organizational communication in recent years has been the use of **electronic mail**, popularly referred to as **e-mail**, a system whereby people use personal computer terminals to send and receive messages between each other (see Figure 9-4). As you might imagine, such systems make communication within and between organizations easier than ever before. For large multinational operations, they're vital. Los Angeles-based Hughes Aircraft, for example, uses e-mail to connect more than 30,000 users in thirty-two different locations worldwide.[33] The electronic transmission of messages represents a

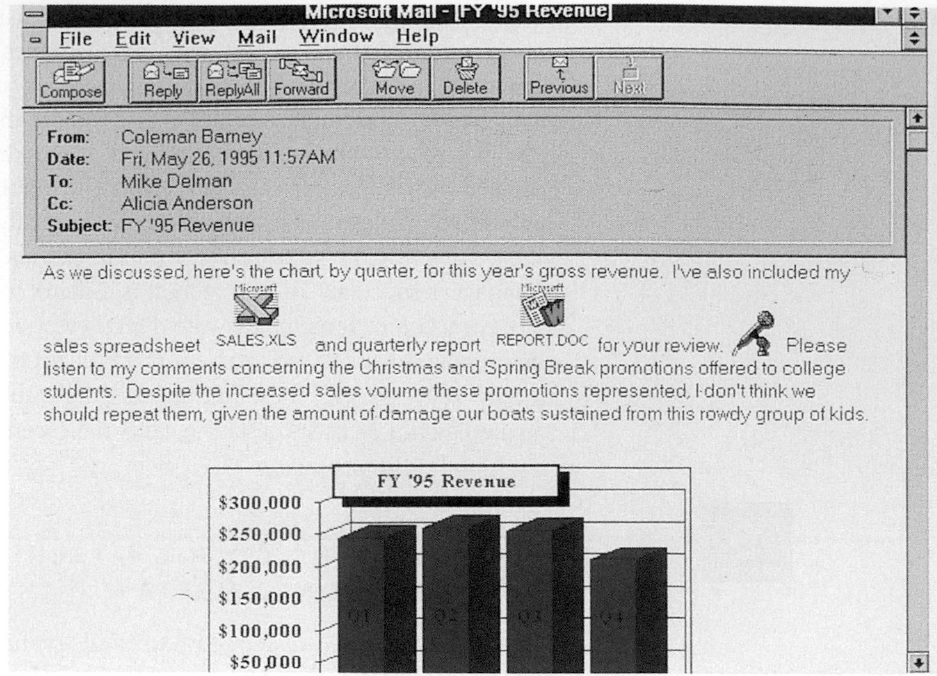

FIGURE 9-4
E-MAIL: CONNECTING PEOPLE WORLDWIDE
Electronic mail, or e-mail, is a vital tool used to communicate between individuals all over the world.

communication revolution in that it allows for the very rapid transmission of information, and the simultaneous sharing of identical information by people regardless of how widely dispersed they may be. What may be lost in terms of depth and richness of communication is more than made up for by high levels of efficiency.[34] Indeed, by using the worldwide web of 45,000 networks known as *Internet*, people from various companies and universities (some 15 million and counting) are able to communicate with each other by leaving direct messages, or by tapping into databases and electronic bulletin boards.[35] This unprecedented access to information may truly revolutionize the nature of organizational communication.

VOICE MESSAGING

Although e-mail can be very quick and efficient, it lacks the capacity to send a personal message using one's own voice. However, another recent technology known as **voice messaging** (or **voice mail)** allows for just that. Voice messaging systems use computers to convert human speech into digital information saved on a hard disk for playback any time from any touch-tone telephone. Because 76 percent of all business calls are nonimmediate in nature (i.e., they do not require instantaneous action), and 56 percent of all calls completed involve one-way communication (i.e., they either give or receive information, but not both), voice messaging is frequently very useful.[36] Voice messaging allows people to avoid wasting time playing "telephone tag," and permits the highly efficient use of voice as an information tool because it precludes the need to translate messages into written characters or keystrokes. Voice messaging systems are so efficient, in fact, that they have been credited with saving an average of $2,000 per employee annually.[37] Given its ease of use, it is not surprising that researchers have found voice mail to be generally well accepted.[38] (Video display terminals, e-mail, and voice mail—yesterday's dreams—are now commonplace ways of communicating in the modern organization. For a look at the high-tech dreams of today, and the communication tools of the not-so-distant future, see the Organization of Tomorrow section on the opposite page.)

HOW WE WILL BE COMMUNICATING IN THE TWENTY-FIRST CENTURY—IF NOT SOONER!

It wasn't so long ago that the personal computer reinvented the way we wrote. What new technologies are looming on the horizon that similarly will revolutionize the way we communicate? Although it is difficult to predict the future, advances in information technology reveal some clear images in the crystal ball.

One communication advance looming on the not-so-distant horizon is *electronic publishing*. Advances in software design (such as Adobe's "Acrobat") make it possible for newspapers and magazines to be reproduced on people's computer screens using the same exact graphics and typefaces as in the original.[39] Already, electronic editions of the *New York Times* and *Byte* magazine are being published using this technology. Even the renown L. L. Bean catalog has been testing the feasibility of electronic catalogs. As part of this revolution, textbook publishers are currently working on systems that very well may change your next textbook from a collection of bound paper (like this book), to a CD-ROM (interactive software in which audio, video, and text are stored on a compact disk).[40] Some experts foresee that by the turn of the century college texts as we now know them will give way to interactive, multimedia teaching tools stored on disk. Others claim that the revolution in publishing will take a different form. The data from which books are contained (e.g., type, pictures), they foresee, will be transmitted along networks and printed as needed at campus bookstores. Regardless of who's right, it appears certain that at least some published matter as we now know it may become a thing of the past.

Now that some of us are just getting the hang of being able to tap into databases or send messages while at the computer, word comes that we will soon be able to do the same while on the go.[41] *Wireless communication* using hand-held devices will create an office without walls (see Figure 9-5). First-generation wireless communication devices such as Apple's "Newton" and AT&T's "EO Communicator," introduced in 1993, met with only limited success but raised expectations of things to come.[42] Officials at BellSouth, a leader in the cellular business, predict that as many as 25 million Americans will be using wireless data devices by the end of this decade.[43] Among the most promising telecommunication technologies currently being developed are *personal communications networks (PCNs)*—small, inexpensive, pocket phones using "microcell" radio transmission that will eventually replace wired phones, even in homes and offices. Some companies, such as Motorola, are working on *satellite phones*—systems that ring the earth with low-orbiting satellites, making it possible to directly call anyplace on earth from anyplace else.

FIGURE 9-5

WIRELESS COMMUNICATION: INFORMATION ON THE SPOT—ANY SPOT

Using a wireless communication device, Otis Elevator's Mark Smith seeks help by tapping into his company's network.

THE ORGANIZATION OF TOMORROW, Cont.

If you think this revolution in wireless communication is really something, wait to you see what tomorrow's wired world promises to bring. In 1993 and 1994 several large companies, such as Time-Warner, Bell-Atlantic, and Sony were scrambling to be among the first to lay fiber-optic cables to construct an *information superhighway* across the United States.[44] This would be a network of cables through which homes and business would be able to access a host of *interactive entertainment and information services*. Want to watch your favorite TV show? No problem, with interactive TV you can access it at any time, not just when it's being broadcast.[45] Wondering about a batter's statistics as you watch baseball on ESPN. Just press a button to have them appear on your screen. By the year 2000, some experts predict, multimedia entertainment and information services could be a $3 trillion business.[46] Clearly, the incentive is considerable to create a world of highly entertained and informed couch potatoes.

NONVERBAL COMMUNICATION: SPEAKING WITHOUT WORDS

As we noted in Chapter 2, nonverbal cues such as smiles and glances are important sources of information influencing our impressions of people. Here we will describe other vehicles of **nonverbal communication**, the transmission of messages without the use of words. Specifically, some of the most prevalent nonverbal communication cues in organizations have to do with people's manner of dress and their use of time and space.

STYLE OF DRESS: COMMUNICATING BY APPEARANCE

If you have ever heard the expression "clothes make the man or woman," you are probably already aware of the importance of mode of dress as a communication vehicle. This is especially the case in organizations where, as self-styled "wardrobe engineer" John T. Malloy reminds us, what we wear communicates a great deal about our competence as employees.[47] In fact, research has shown that compared to people dressing inappropriately for job interviews (e.g., T-shirts and jeans), those dressing appropriately (e.g., business suits) feel more confident about themselves, and as a result, ask for higher starting salaries—on average, $4,000 higher.[48]

Despite what fashion consultants might advise, there does not exist a simple formula for exactly how to "dress for success." As you might imagine, what we communicate about ourselves by the clothing we wear is not a simple matter. Importantly, we cannot make up for the absence of crucial job skills simply by putting on the right clothes. People who are qualified for jobs, however, may communicate certain things about themselves by the way they dress. Clearly, one of the key messages sent by the clothes people wear is their understanding of the *appropriate* way of presenting themselves for the job.

Of course, what is appropriate dress for one kind of job may not be appropriate for another. For example, people working at a small software development firm may be out of place wearing a coat and tie, just as bankers would be inappropriately attired in T-shirts and jeans. As Bing Gordon, co-founder of the video game company Electronic Arts, put it, "If somebody wears a suit to work around here, it's a sure sign that he is interviewing."[49] Although the interviewee may feel obligated to dress up for an interview, even in an organization with an informal style, you can be sure that shortly after starting the job he or she will quickly adapt to its customary style of dress (a by-product of the process of socialization discussed in Chapter 6).

TIME: THE WAITING GAME

Another important mechanism of nonverbal communication in organizations is the use of time. Have you ever waited in the outer office of a doctor or dentist? Surely you have—after all, they have special "waiting rooms" just for this purpose! Why do you have to wait for such people? Mainly because they have special skills that create high demands for their services. As a result, their time is organized in a manner that is most efficient *for them*—by keeping others lined up to see them at their convenience.[50]

Medical professionals are not the only ones who make people wait to see them. In fact, individuals in high-status positions often communicate the idea that their time is more valuable than others' (and therefore that they hold higher-status positions) by making others wait to see them. This is a very subtle, but important, form of nonverbal communication. Typically, the longer you have to wait to see someone, the higher the organizational status that person has attained. This has been shown in a study by Greenberg.[51] Participants in this investigation were applicants for a job as office manager at various companies who waited to be interviewed with people of higher status (vice presidents), lower status (assistant office managers), or equal status (another office manager). As summarized in Figure 9-6, the higher the status of the person whom job candidates waited to see, the longer they had to wait. The vice president interviewers communicated their higher status to the candidates by making them wait longest. In contrast, assistant office manager interviewers communicated their lower status to candidates by being prompt—an act conveying deference and respect.

THE USE OF SPACE: WHAT DOES IT SAY ABOUT YOU?

Like time, space is another important communication vehicle. Research has shown that one's organizational status is communicated by the amount of space at one's disposal. Generally speaking, the more space one commands, the more powerful one is likely to be in an organization. For example, higher-status life insurance underwriters in one organization were found to have larger desks and larger offices than lower-status underwriter trainees.[52] Not only does the amount of space communicate organizational status, but also the way that space is arranged. For example, among faculty members at a small college, senior professors were more likely to arrange their offices so as to separate themselves from visitors with their desks, whereas junior professors were less likely to impose such physical barriers.[53] These various office arrangements systematically communicated different things about the occupants. Specifically, professors who did not distance themselves from their students by use of their desks were seen as more open and unbiased in their dealing with students than those who used their desks as a physical barrier.

The use of space appears to have symbolic value in communicating something about group interaction. Consider, for example, who usually sits at the head of a rectangular table. In most cases, it is the group leader. It is, in fact, traditional for

FIGURE 9-6
COMMUNICATING STATUS THROUGH TIME DELAYS: THE ORGANIZATIONAL WAITING GAME
Research has shown that the higher another's status relative to oneself, the more one has to wait to see that person. These findings suggest that the use of time is a nonverbal mechanism for communicating one's organizational status. (Source: Based on data reported in Greenberg, 1989; see Note 51.)

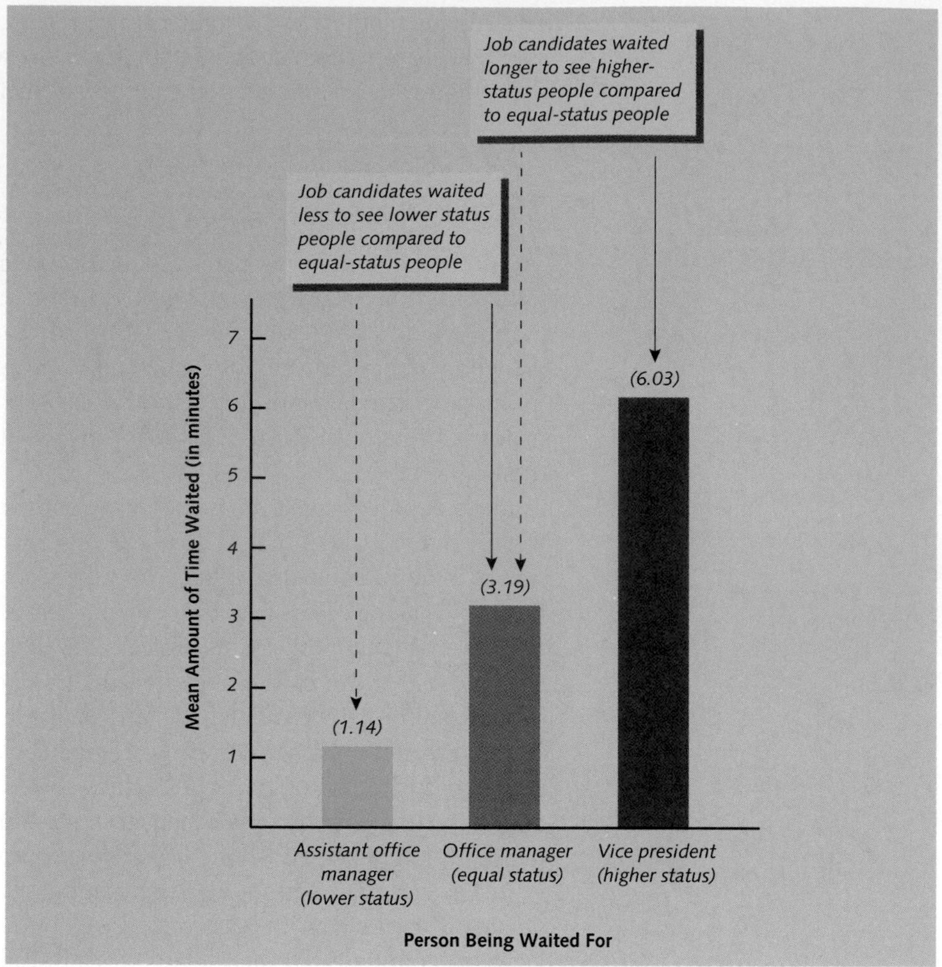

leaders to do so. But at the same time, studies have shown that people emerging as the leaders of groups tend to be ones who just happened to be sitting at the table heads.[54] Apparently, *where* a person sits influences the available communication possibilities. Sitting at the head of a rectangular table enables a person to see everyone else and to be seen by them. That leaders tend to emerge from such positions is, therefore, not surprising.

It is not only individuals who communicate something about themselves by the use of space, but organizations as well.[55] For example, according to John Sculley, former president of PepsiCo, his company's world headquarters were designed to communicate to visitors that they were seeing "the most important company in the world."[56] Similarly, by adding a second office tower to its company headquarters in Cincinnati, Procter & Gamble was said to be attempting to create a gateway-like complex that communicated the company's connection to the community.[57] As these examples suggest, organizations, as well as individuals, use space to communicate certain aspects of their identities.

In concluding this section, we note that the nonverbal mechanisms we have presented here, as important as they are, represent only a single channel of communication. Both verbal and nonverbal channels are important sources of information used in conjunction with each other in the process of communication. Thus, although we isolated the various forms of communication for purposes of presenting them to you, it is important to realize that they operate together, complementing each other in complex ways in actual practice.

MAJOR INFLUENCES ON ORGANIZATIONAL COMMUNICATION

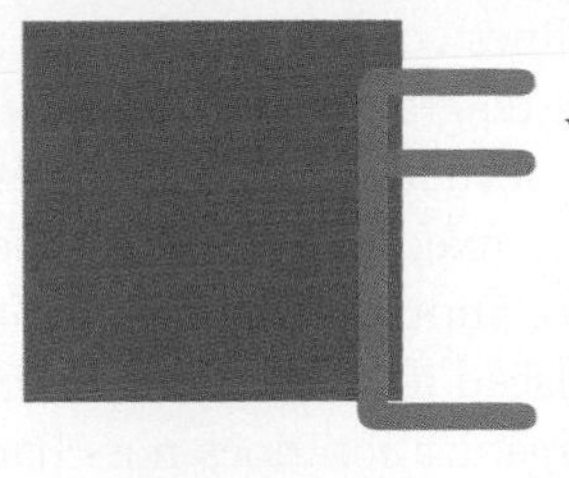

Everyone engages in communication on the job. Yet with whom we communicate and how we do so varies considerably. The communication process is influenced by many factors, including those relating to organizations (e.g., organizational structure), groups (e.g., formal networks of communication in groups), and individuals (e.g., informal networks that develop between people). We will now examine some of these key determinants of organizational communication.

ORGANIZATIONAL STRUCTURE: DIRECTING THE FLOW OF MESSAGES

Although the basic process of communication described thus far is similar in many different contexts, a unique feature of organizations has a profound impact on the communication process—namely, their structure. Organizations are often designed in ways that dictate who may and may not communicate with whom. Given this, we may ask, how is the communication process affected by the structure of an organization? The term **organizational structure** refers to *the formally prescribed pattern of interrelationships existing between the various units of an organization*. Although we will have a great deal more to say about organizational structure in Chapter 15, here we describe the many important ways in which organizational structure influences communication.

ORGANIZATIONAL STRUCTURE: ITS IMPACT ON COMMUNICATION

An organization's structure may be described using a diagram known as an **organizational chart.** Such a diagram provides a graphic representation of an organization's structure. It may be likened to an X ray showing the organization's skeleton, an outline of the planned, formal connections between its various units.[58] An organizational chart showing the structure of part of a fictitious organization is shown in Figure 9-7. (Keep in mind that this diagram represents only *one* possible

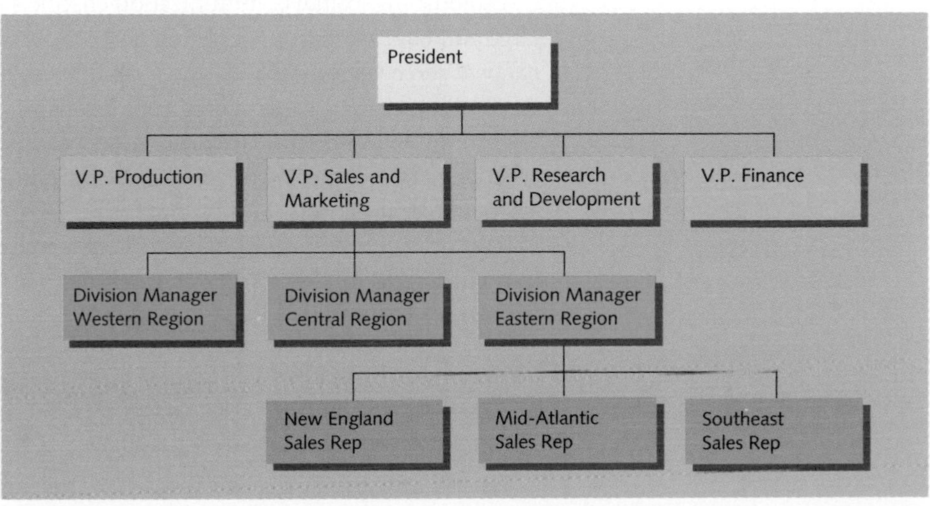

FIGURE 9-7
THE ORGANIZATIONAL CHART: A MAP OF AN ORGANIZATION'S FORMAL COMMUNICATION NETWORK
An organizational chart indicates formally prescribed patterns of communication in an organization. Shown here is a part of an organizational chart for a hypothetical company.

way of structuring an organization. Several other possibilities are described in detail in Chapter 15.)

Note the various boxes in the diagram and the lines connecting them. Each box represents a person performing a specific job. The diagram shows the titles of the individuals performing the various jobs and the formally prescribed pattern of communication between them. These are relatively fixed and defined. Each individual is responsible for performing a specified job. Should the people working in the organization leave their jobs, they must be replaced if their jobs are to be done. The key point is that the formal structure of an organization does not change just because the personnel changes. The lines connecting the boxes in the organizational chart are lines of *authority* showing who must answer to whom. Each person is responsible to (or answers to) the person at the next higher level to which he or she is connected. At the same time, people are also responsible for (or give orders to) those who are immediately below them. The boxes and lines form a sort of blueprint of an organization showing not only what people have to do, but with whom they have to communicate for the organization to operate properly.

The organizational chart in Figure 9-7 makes it clear that people may be differentiated with respect to their levels in the organization's hierarchy. Some people (e.g., the president) are higher up in terms of the formal organizational power they wield, and others (e.g., department managers) are lower down. Such differences in one's level in an organizational hierarchy may be communicated in various ways. For example, people at higher levels tend to be called by their titles (e.g., "Mr. Chairman"), and are usually addressed in a formal manner. Such individuals also may communicate their higher positions by the way they dress (e.g., formal as opposed to informal attire) and by the size and location of their offices.[59]

That individuals are connected to each other by formal lines of communication can have important effects. For example, it has been found that the more employees are integrated into an organization's formal structure, the better they adapt to using new technology.[60] This is not surprising if you consider that "being connected" to others promotes opportunities to learn. However, when formality is so great that individuals are denied opportunities to communicate their desires regarding the organization's operations, they tend to experience negative reactions such as stress, emotional exhaustion, and low levels of job satisfaction and commitment.[61] Such findings do not suggest that formal organizational structures are necessarily problematic—indeed, they are in many ways absolutely necessary for organizations to operate effectively.

Establishing formal communication channels is critical when companies are very large and have operations scattered all over the world. This is the case among *multinational corporations (MNCs)*—organizations that have operations in various countries. In some cases, these can be very extensive, such as in the case of N. V. Philips, an enormous multinational corporation headquartered in the Netherlands.[62] This company's operations require intricate communication linkages between people in many different nations. Philips, and other large multinationals, such as U.S.-based Procter & Gamble, and Japan-based Matsushita Electric, face difficult communication challenges in view of the cultural and geographic barriers that must be confronted for them to survive.

COMMUNICATING UP, DOWN, AND ACROSS THE ORGANIZATIONAL CHART

As you might imagine, the nature and form of communication vary greatly as a function of people's relative positions within an organization. Even a quick look at an organizational chart reveals that information may flow up (from lower to higher levels), down (from higher to lower levels), or horizontally (between people at the same level). However, as summarized in Figure 9-8, different types of information typically travel in different directions within a hierarchy.

Imagine that you are a supervisor. What types of messages do you think would characterize communication between you and your subordinates? Typically, *downward communication* consists of instructions, directions, and orders—messages telling subordinates what they should be doing.[63] We also would expect to find feedback on past performance flowing in a downward direction (such as when managers tell subordinates how well they have been working). A sales manager, for example, might direct members of her sales force to promote a certain product and might then congratulate them for being successful.

Despite the fact that superiors mean to communicate certain information to their subordinates, the subordinates do not always accurately perceive their superiors' messages. This phenomenon was demonstrated in a study by Schnake and his associates.[64] These researchers surveyed a large group of managers and their subordinates about the extent to which the managers communicated various things to them (e.g., goals, assignments). The study revealed considerable disagreement between what the managers thought they communicated and what the subordinates thought their managers communicated. In all cases, the managers perceived their own communications as more positive than their subordinates believed them to be. Unfortunately, these discrepancies were associated with low levels of job satisfaction; the less supervisors and subordinates were on the same wavelength, the less satisfied the subordinates were with their jobs. In short, downward communication is not always a simple matter.

Downward communication flows from one level to the next lowest one, slowly trickling down to the bottom. As a message passes through various levels, it often becomes less accurate (especially if the information is spoken). Thus, it is not surprising to find that the most effective downward communication techniques are ones directly aimed at those who are most affected by the messages—namely, small group meetings and organizational publications targeting specific groups.[65] Such methods are being used—and successfully! For example, executives at Tandem Computers hold monthly teleconferences with their employees, and as described in our Preview Case, in-person discussions and monthly newsletters are used to keep employees up to date on plant activities at General Motors' Saginaw Division. Such efforts at improving downward communication have been credited with improving productivity and reducing turnover in both companies.[66]

FIGURE 9-8

UPWARD, DOWNWARD, AND HORIZONTAL COMMUNICATION: AN OVERVIEW

The types of messages communicated within organizations tend to differ according to whether they are traveling upward (from lower to higher levels), downward (from higher to lower levels), or horizontally (across the same levels).

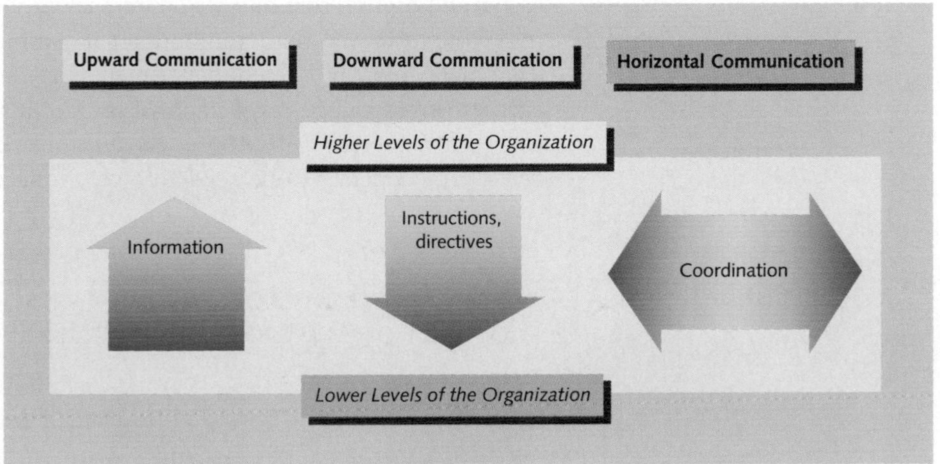

Upward communication flows from lower levels to higher levels within an organization, such as from a subordinate to his or her supervisor. Messages flowing in this direction tend to contain the information managers need to do their jobs, such as data required for decision making and the status of various projects. In short, upward communication is designed to keep managers aware of what is going on. Among the various types of information flowing upward are suggestions for improvement, status reports, reactions to work-related issues, and new ideas.

Upward communication is not simply the reverse of downward communication. The difference in status between the communicating parties makes for some important distinctions. For example, it has been established that upward communication occurs much less frequently than downward communication. In fact, one classic study found that 70 percent of assembly-line workers initiated communication with their supervisors less than once a month.[67] Further research has found that managers direct less than 15 percent of their total communication to their superiors.[68] And when people do communicate upward, their conversations tend to be shorter than discussions with their peers.[69]

Perhaps more important, upward communication often tends to suffer from serious inaccuracies. For example, subordinates frequently feel they must highlight their accomplishments and downplay their mistakes if they are to be looked on favorably.[70] Similarly, some individuals fear that they will be rebuked by their supervisors if they anticipate that their remarks will be perceived as threatening.[71] As a result, many people frequently avoid communicating bad news to their supervisors, or simply "pass the buck" for doing so to someone else.[72] This general reluctance to transmit bad news is referred to as the **MUM effect**.[73] As you might imagine, because superiors rely on information when making decisions, keeping silent about important news—even if it's bad—may be one of the worst things a subordinate can do. As one executive put it, "All of us have our share of bonehead ideas. Having someone tell you it's a bonehead idea before you do something about it is really a great blessing."[74]

Finally, we note the nature of *horizontal communication* within organizations. Messages that flow laterally (at the same organizational level) are characterized by efforts at coordination (attempts to work together). Consider, for example, how a vice president of marketing would have to coordinate her efforts to initiate an advertising campaign for a new product with information from the vice president of production about when the first products will be coming off the assembly line. Unlike vertical communication, in which the parties are at different status levels, horizontal communication involves people at the same level, and therefore tends to be easier and friendlier. Communication between peers also tends to be more casual and occurs more quickly because fewer social barriers exist between the parties. Note, however, that even horizontal communication can be problematic. For example, people in different departments may feel that they are competing against each other for valued organizational resources and may show resentment toward each other, thereby substituting an antagonistic, competitive orientation for the friendlier, cooperative one needed to get things done.[75]

COMMUNICATION NETWORKS: FORMAL CHANNELS OF INFORMATION IN GROUPS

Imagine two different work groups in the sales and marketing division of a large corporation. One consists of a team of creative writers, artists, and market researchers sitting around a table working together on developing the company's new advertising campaign. Another includes field representatives in various territories who report to regional sales managers throughout the country about consumers' preferences for various products. These people, in turn, analyze this information and report it to the vice president of sales and marketing. If you think about how these two groups differ, one key variable becomes obvious: the pattern of communication within them is not the same. Members of the creative team working on the advertising campaign can all communicate with each other at once, whereas people in the sales force speak only to those who are immediately above or below them. The patterns determining which organizational units (either people or groups) communicate to which other units are referred to as **communication networks**.

As you might imagine, there are many different possible communication networks within organizations. Do such arrangements matter? Do they make any difference in how well groups do their jobs and how satisfied group members feel? A considerable amount of research has shown that the nature of the communication linkages between group members can greatly influence group functioning.[76] So that we can appreciate these research findings, let's first consider some of the possible configurations of connections between people. Some of the most commonly studied possibilities are shown in Figure 9-9. (These various diagrams depict communication networks that have five members, although they can have any number of

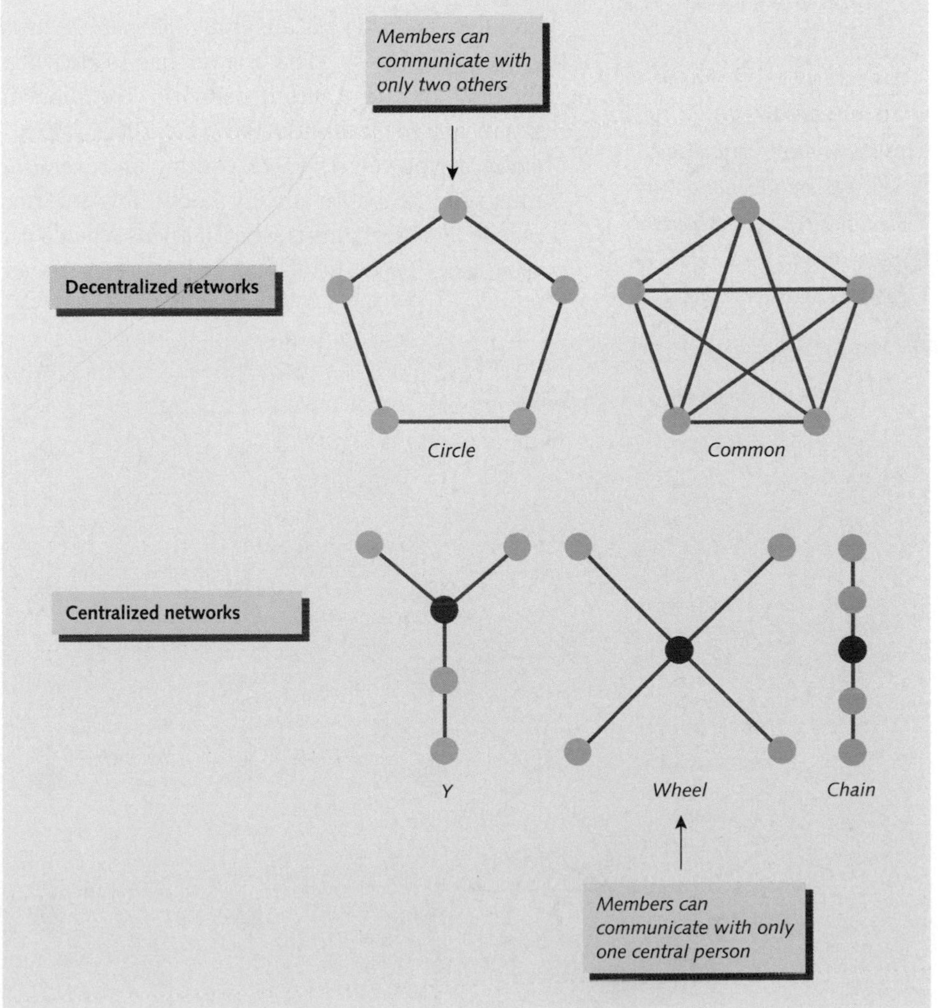

FIGURE 9-9
COMMUNICATION NETWORKS: SOME BASIC TYPES
Some examples of five-person communication networks are shown here. Networks such as the circle and comcon give all members equal opportunities to communicate with each other, and are known as decentralized networks. In contrast, networks such as the Y, wheel, and chain contain members (marked by a filled circle) through whom messages must pass to reach others.

members from three or more.) In each diagram, the circles represent individual people and the lines connecting them represent two-way lines of communication between them. (Some communication flows only in one direction, but for simplicity's sake only two-way, mutual communication flows will be used in our examples.)

As Figure 9-10 highlights, communication networks may differ with respect to a key feature: their degree of **centralization**. Briefly, this refers to the degree to which information must flow through a specific member of the network. As you can see in Figure 9-10, communication networks such as the *Y*, *wheel*, and *chain* are identified as **centralized networks**. For members of centralized networks to communicate with each other, they must go through a central person who is at the "crossroads" of the information flow. In contrast, the *circle* and *comcon* are referred to as **decentralized networks** because information can freely flow between members without going through a central person. People in decentralized networks have equal access to information, whereas those in centralized networks are unequal because the individuals at the centers have access to more information than those at the periphery.

Research has shown that these differences in communication networks are responsible for determining how effectively groups will perform various jobs. Generally speaking, it has been found that when the tasks being performed are simple, centralized networks perform better, but when the tasks are complex, decentralized networks perform better.[77] Specifically, comparing these two types of network: *centralized networks are faster and more accurate on simple tasks, whereas decentralized networks are faster and more accurate on complex tasks*.

Why is this so? The answer has to do with the pressures put on the central member of a centralized network. The more information any one member of a group has to deal with, the greater the degree of **saturation** that person experiences. If you've ever tried working on several homework assignments at the same time, you probably already know how information saturation can cause performance to suffer. This is what happens when a centralized network performs a complex task. The central person becomes so overloaded with information that the

FIGURE 9-10
COMPARING THE PERFORMANCE OF CENTRALIZED AND DECENTRALIZED COMMUNICATION NETWORKS: THE INFLUENCE OF TASK COMPLEXITY
As shown here, centralized networks are superior on simple tasks (top), and decentralized networks are superior on complex tasks (bottom).

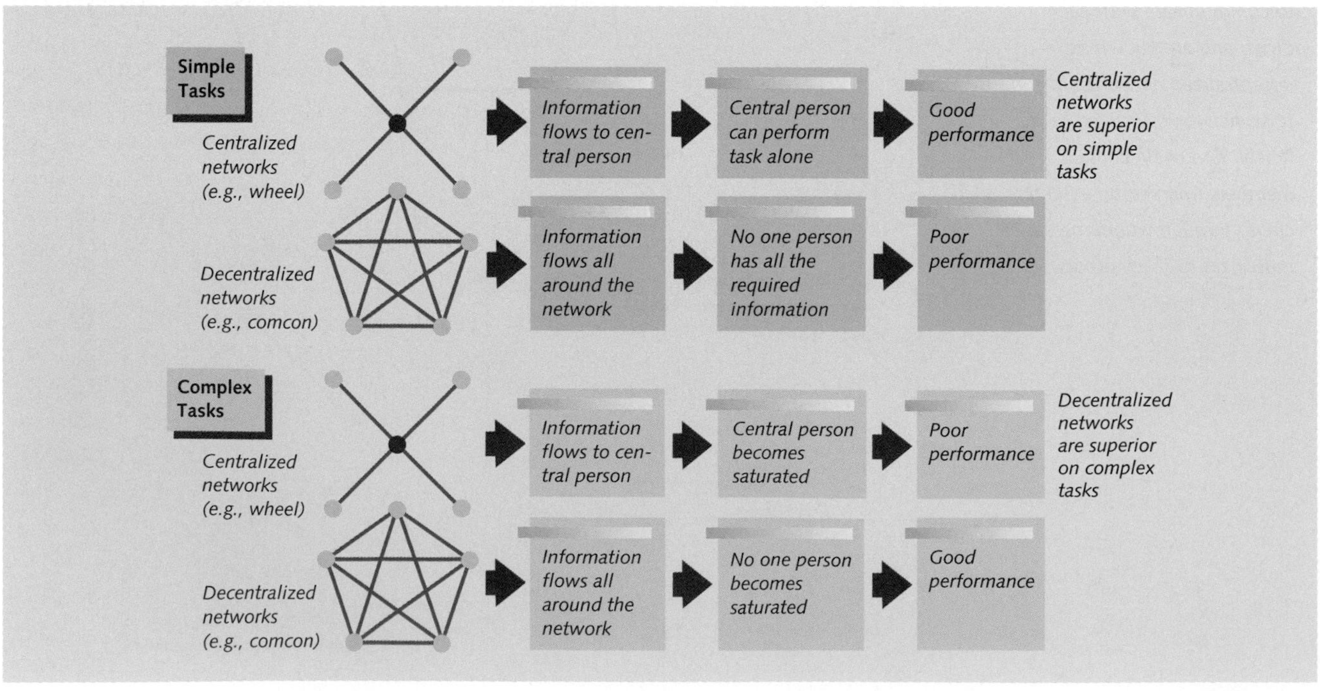

group is slowed down and many errors are made. However, when the problem is simple, the central person can easily solve it alone after receiving all the information from the other members. Decentralized networks have no one central person, so information and work demands are more evenly distributed. As a result, on simple tasks the information needed to solve the problem may be spread out over all the group members, causing delays in coming to a solution. This same feature represents an advantage, however, when tasks are highly complex because it prevents any single member from becoming saturated and lowering the group's performance. (See our summary of these processes in Figure 9-10.) In short, centralization is a double-edged sword. When tasks are simple, centralization facilitates getting the job done. However, when tasks are complex, it may cause saturation, bringing performance to a halt.

Research also shows that centralized and decentralized networks differ in terms of their members' satisfaction. Would you be more satisfied as a member of a centralized or decentralized group? Most people enjoy the greater equality in decision making that occurs in decentralized networks. Such groups give everyone involved an equal status. In contrast, as a peripheral member of a centralized network, you would be less powerful than the central member, and left out of the decision-making process. The central member controls more of the flow of information and is clearly more important, leading many peripheral members to feel that their contributions are not fully appreciated. Together, these factors combine to cause lower overall levels of satisfaction among members of centralized networks compared with those in decentralized networks.

In summary, formal communication networks clearly play an important role in organizations. However, formal communication networks may be only one of several factors responsible for organizational communication. One important consideration is that although the lines of communication between people can greatly influence their job performance and satisfaction, the various advantages and limitations of different communication networks tend to disappear the longer the groups are in operation.[78] As group members gain more experience interacting with each other, they may learn to overcome the limitations imposed by their communication networks. (For example, they may learn to send messages to specific individuals who have proven themselves in the past to be particularly competent at solving certain kinds of problems.) In other words, although the differences between various communication networks may be quite significant, they may be only temporary, accounting for the behavior of newly formed groups more than the behavior of highly experienced groups. Another important point is that any formal lines of communication operate in organizations in conjunction with widespread informal networks that also may help groups accomplish their goals. Even if formal channels impede the communication of information, informal connections between people—such as friendships, or contacts in other departments—may help the communication process. As we will describe next, the informal connections between people are extremely important in organizational communications.

INFORMAL COMMUNICATION NETWORKS: BEHIND THE ORGANIZATIONAL CHART

For a moment, think about the people with whom you communicate during the course of an average day. Friends, family members, classmates, and colleagues at work are among those with whom you may have *informal communication*—

information shared without any formally imposed obligations or restrictions. When you think about it carefully, you may be surprised to realize how widespread our informal networks can be. You know someone who knows someone else, who knows your best friend—and before long, your informal networks become very far-reaching. Informal communication networks, in part because they are so widespread, constitute an important avenue by which information flows in organizations. In fact, in a recent survey middle managers ranked informal networks as better sources of organizational information than formal networks.[79] Therefore, if an organization's formal communication represents its skeleton, its informal communication constitutes its central nervous system.[80]

ORGANIZATIONS' HIDDEN PATHWAYS

It is easy to imagine how important the flow of informal information may be within organizations. People transmit information to those with whom they come into contact, thereby providing conduits through which messages can travel. We also tend to communicate most with those who are similar to ourselves on such key variables as age and time working on the job.[81] Because we are more comfortable with similar people than with dissimilar ones, we tend to spend more time with them and, of course, communicate with them more. As a result, many informal gender-segregated networks tend to form in organizations (what among men has been referred to the *old-boys' network*). To the extent that these associations may isolate people from others in power who may be different from themselves, this practice is limiting.[82] At the same time, however, exposure to similar others with whom people feel comfortable provides valuable sources of information. For example, many African-American business leaders have formed informal networks with others of their same race so as to help them share ways of succeeding in a business world in which they constitute an ethnic minority—alliances that have been helpful to the careers of many (see our discussion of mentoring in Chapter 6).[83] This informal observation is in keeping with scientific evidence showing that the more involved people are in their organizations' communication networks, the more powerful and influential they become.[84]

The idea that people are connected informally also has been used to explain a very important organizational phenomenon—turnover. Do people resign from their jobs in ways that are random and unrelated to each other? A study by Krackhardt and Porter suggests that they do not, but that turnover is related to the informal communication patterns between people.[85] These investigators theorized that voluntary turnover (employees freely electing to resign their jobs) occurs as a result of a *snowball effect*. A snowball does not accumulate snowflakes randomly, but collects those that are in its path. Analogously, it was reasoned, patterns of voluntary turnover may not be independently distributed within a work group, but may be the result of people's influences on each other. Thus, predicting which people will resign from their jobs may be based, in large part, on knowledge of the communication patterns within groups. Someone who leaves her job for a better one in another organization may know someone who has already done so. Krackhardt and Porter found support for this snowball effect among teenagers working in fast-food restaurants. Specifically, turnover tended to be concentrated among groups of people who communicated informally with each other a great deal before they resigned. (For a suggestion regarding how this may operate, see Figure 9-11). This study provides an excellent example of the importance of informal patterns of communication in organizations.

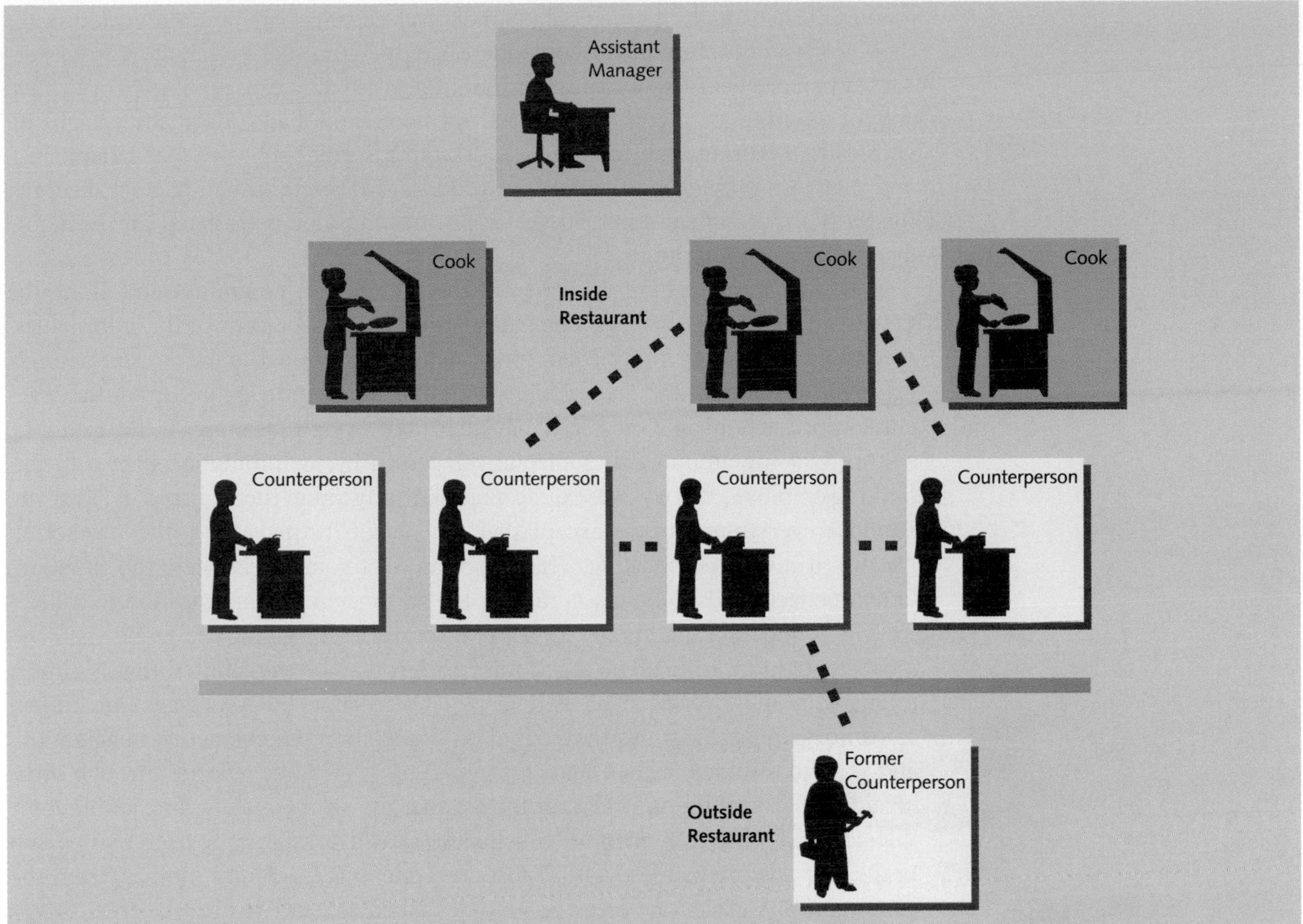

FIGURE 9-11
INFORMAL COMMUNICATION NETWORKS: A PREDICTOR OF TURNOVER PATTERNS
The informal networks of communication between people (shown in dotted lines) provide channels through which messages about better job opportunities may be communicated. Patterns of voluntary turnover have been linked to the existence of such informal networks. (Source: Based on suggestions by Krackhardt & Porter, 1986; see Note 85.)

Informal communication networks are characterized by the fact that they often are composed of individuals at different organizational levels. People can tell anyone in the network whatever informal information they wish. For example, one investigator found that jokes and funny stories tended to cross organizational boundaries, and were freely shared by those in both the managerial and nonmanagerial ranks of organizations.[86] On the other hand, it would be quite unlikely—and considered "out of line"—for a lower-level employee to communicate something to an upper-level employee about how to do the job. What flows within the pathways of informal communication is informal information, messages not necessarily related to individuals' work.

THE GRAPEVINE AND THE RUMOR MILL

When anyone can tell something informal to anyone else, it results in a very rapid flow of information along what is commonly referred to as the **grapevine**—the pathways along which unofficial, informal information travels. In contrast to a formal organizational message, which might take several days to reach its desired audience, information traveling along the organizational grapevine tends to flow very rapidly, often within hours. This is not only because informal communication can cross formal organizational boundaries (e.g., you might be able to tell a good joke to almost anyone, not just your boss or subordinates with whom you are required to communicate), but also because informal information tends to be communicated orally. As we noted earlier, oral messages are communicated faster than written ones, but may become increasingly inaccurate as they flow from person to person. Because of the confusion grapevines may cause, some people have sought to eliminate them, but they are not necessarily bad. Informally socializing with our co-workers can help make work groups more cohesive (see Chapter 8), and may also provide excellent opportunities for desired human contact, keeping the work environment stimulating. Grapevines must be considered an inevitable fact of life in organizations.[87]

It is interesting to note that most of the information communicated along the grapevine is accurate. In fact, one study found that 82 percent of the information communicated along a particular company's organizational grapevine on a single occasion was accurate.[88] The problem with interpreting this figure is that the inaccurate portions of some messages may alter their overall meaning. If, for example, a story is going around that someone got passed by for promotion over a lower-ranking employee, it may cause quite a bit of dissension in the workplace. However, suppose everything is true except that the person turned down the promotion because it involved relocating. This important fact completely alters the situation. Only one fact needs to be inaccurate for the accuracy of communication to suffer.

This problem of inaccuracy is clearly responsible for giving the grapevine such a bad reputation. In extreme cases, information may be transmitted that is almost totally without any basis in fact and usually unverifiable. Such messages are known as **rumors**. Typically, rumors are based on speculation, an overactive imagination, and wishful thinking, rather than on facts. Rumors race like wildfire through organizations because the information they present is so interesting and ambiguous. The ambiguity leaves it open to embellishment as it passes orally from one person to the next. Before you know it, almost everyone in the organization has heard the rumor, and its inaccurate message becomes taken as fact ("It must be true, everyone knows it"). Hence, even if there was, at one point, some truth to a rumor, the message quickly becomes untrue.

If you've ever been the victim of a rumor, you know how difficult they can be to quell, and how profound their effects can be. This is especially the case when organizations are the victims of rumors. For example, rumors about the possibility of corporate takeovers may not only influence the value of a company's stock, but also threaten its employees' feelings of job security. Sometimes rumors about company products can be very costly. For example, a rumor about the use of worms in McDonald's hamburgers circulated in the Chicago area in the late 1970s. Even though the rumor was completely untrue, sales dropped as much as 30 percent in some restaurants.[89] You may recall that in June 1993 stories appeared in the press stating that people across the United States found syringes in cans of Pepsi-Cola. Although the stories proved to be completely without fact, the hoax cost Pepsi plenty in terms of investigative and advertising expenses.[90]

What can be done to counter the effects of rumors? Although this is a difficult question to answer, evidence suggests that directly refuting a rumor may not always counter its effects. Although Pepsi officials denied the reports about their tainted product, the rumor was not only implausible, but was also quickly disproven by independent investigators from the Food and Drug Administration. Sometimes, however, rumors are more difficult to disprove and do not die quickly. In such cases, directly refuting the rumors only fuels the fire. When you directly refute a rumor (e.g., "I didn't do it"), you actually may help spread it among those who have not already heard about it ("Oh, I didn't know people thought that") and strengthen it among those who have already heard it ("If it weren't true, they wouldn't be protesting so much"). Directing people's attention away from the rumor may help, focusing instead on other things they know about the target of the rumor. In research studying the McDonald's rumor, for example, it was found that reminding people about other things they thought about McDonald's (e.g., that it is a clean, family-oriented place) helped counter the negative effects of the rumor.[91] If you should ever become the victim of a rumor, try immediately to refute it with indisputable facts if you can. But, if it lingers on, try directing people's attention to other positive things they already believe about you. Although rumors may be impossible to stop, their effects can, with some effort, be effectively managed.

OVERCOMING COMMUNICATION BARRIERS: TECHNIQUES FOR ENHANCING THE FLOW OF INFORMATION

Throughout this chapter we have noted the central role of communication in organizational functioning. Given this, it is easy to understand how any efforts at improving the communication process in organizations may have highly desirable payoffs for organizations as well as for the individuals and groups working in them. Several steps can be taken to obtain the benefits of effective communication.[92] In this final section, we will describe some of these techniques, including measures that can be taken by individuals, as well as tactics for improving communication that involve entire organizations.

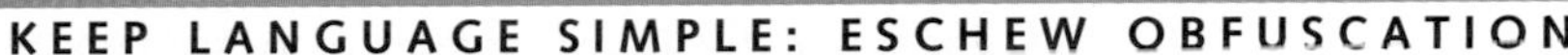

KEEP LANGUAGE SIMPLE: ESCHEW OBFUSCATION

Have you ever driven your "previously owned motor vehicle" up to an "ethyl dispensing device" and greeted by a "petroleum transfer engineer" who filled your "fuel containment module"? Or perhaps you've gone to a "home improvement center" looking for a "manually powered impact device." In either case, we wouldn't blame you if you went to another "operating entity" that had a better "customer interface capacity." You've certainly already encountered enough business double-talk without getting any more from us. Fortunately, our point can be stated simply: *using needlessly formal language may impose a serious barrier to communication.*

Keep in mind that all organizations, fields, social groups, and professions have their **jargon**—their own specialized language. Your own college or university may have a "quad," or, as a student, you may have a "roomie" who wants to go "Greek," and is interested in "rushing." These are examples of a college student's jargon. No doubt, you've encountered a lot of language in this book that may at first sound strange to you. Our point is that the use of jargon is inevitable when people within the same field or social groups communicate with each other. Some degree of highly specialized language may help communication by providing an easy way for people in the same fields to share complex ideas. Jargon also allows professionals to identify unknown others as people in their field because they "speak the same language." For example, management professors would describe this book as dealing with the field of OB, a term that would have a very different meaning to medical doctors (for whom it refers to the field of obstetrics). Obviously, within professions jargon helps communication, but it can lead to confusion when used outside the groups within which it has meaning (see Figure 9-12).

Studying the use of jargon in one large organization, Kanter noted that a COMVOC—itself a jargon term for "common vocabulary"—developed among its

FIGURE 9-12
JARGON: A BARRIER TO EFFECTIVE COMMUNICATION WITH OUTSIDERS

When people are unable express their ideas without resorting to the special language of their group—that is, jargon—the quality of their communications with others who do not share this common language is threatened. (Source: Drawing by Dana Fradon; © *1975* The New Yorker Magazine, *Inc.)*

"I can't put it into layman's language for you. I don't know any layman's language."

members.[93] For example, within some divisions there were "fast-trackers" who "shot from the hip" to go for "the big win." Unfortunately, people in other departments of the corporation who didn't understand this jargon often felt out of place, creating a communication barrier. This happened not only between various departments of the large organization studied by Kanter, but also between various employees and their family members, who, as a result, often had great difficulty understanding what their spouses or parents did on the job. In fact, the wives of male executives identified over 100 unfamiliar work-related terms and phrases that they could not understand. Accordingly, we can safely say that jargon may be an effective communication device between people within one's social or professional group, but it should be avoided when attempting to communicate with outsiders.

In addition to avoiding jargon, the clearest communicators also keep language short, simple, and to the point. Hence, it is wise to adopt the **K.I.S.S. principle** when communicating—that is, keep it short and simple.[94] People are better able to understand messages that do not overwhelm them with too much information at once than those that present more than they can absorb. A wise communicator is sensitive to this and knows how to monitor his or her audience for signs of overloading audience members' circuits with too much information. Again, although you may know what you are talking about, you may not be able to get your ideas across to others unless you package them in doses small and simple enough to be understood. When this is done effectively, even the most complex ideas can be clearly communicated.[95] (For an example of an unclear message, and how it can be simplified, see Table 9-2).

BE AN ACTIVE, ATTENTIVE LISTENER

Just as it is important to make your ideas understandable to others (i.e., sending messages), it is equally important to work at being a good listener (i.e., receiving messages). Although people do a great deal of listening, they pay attention

TABLE 9-2

A Memo That Leaves You Scratching Your Head: "What Did He Say"?

Too frequently, business communication suffers from beeing needlessly dense and difficult to interpret. Here is an example of text from an offending memo, a translation, and a suggestion for how it may be improved.

ORIGINAL MESSAGE:
"As per your subject memo, we are researching the history of Price Promotion #18B to establish why the new price sheets were not received by the sales force in advance of the effective date of the promotion. It is unclear from your memo how widespread the problem was or if it was just isolated in certain geographies. Therefore, we will need additional facts on where you think the problem occurred. As you know, we have gotten complaints from sales people in the past that they did not recieve the promotions, only to find out later that they had lost them due to their own disorganization."
TRANSLATION:
"We screwed up but are not going to admit it."
IMPROVED MESSAGE:
"Thanks for bringing the problem with this promotion to my attention. It looks like we screwed up at this end in getting the proofs to the printer on schedule. My staff and I feel badly about this and will take steps to provide better service."

Source: Reprinted, with permission of the publisher, from *Corporate Dandelions: How the Weed of Bureaucracy Is Choking America's Companies—And What You Can Do to Uproot It.*

to and comprehend only a small percentage of the information directed at them.[96] Most of us usually think of listening as a passive process of taking in information sent by others, but when done correctly the process of listening is much more active.[97] For example, good listeners ask questions if they don't understand something, and they nod or otherwise signal when they understand. Such cues provide critical feedback to communicators about the extent to which they are coming across to you. As a listener, you can help the communication process by letting the sender know if and how his or her messages are coming across to you. Asking questions and putting the speaker's ideas into your own words are helpful ways of ensuring you are taking in all the information presented.

It is also very useful to avoid distractions in the environment and concentrate on what the other person is saying. When listening to others, *avoid jumping to conclusions or evaluating their remarks*. It is important to completely take in what is being said before you respond. Simply dismissing someone because you don't like what is being said is much too easy. Doing so, of course, poses a formidable barrier to effective communication. Being a good listener also involves making sure you are aware of others' main points. What is the speaker trying to say? *Make sure you understand another's ideas before you formulate your reply*. Too many of us interrupt speakers with our own ideas before we have fully heard theirs. If this sounds like something you do, rest assured that it is not only quite common, but also correctable.

Although it requires some effort, incorporating these suggestions into your own listening habits cannot help but make you a better listener. Indeed, many organizations have sought to help their employees in this way. For example, the corporate giant Unisys has for some time systematically trained thousands of its employees in effective listening skills (using seminars and self-training cassettes). Clearly, Unisys is among those companies acknowledging the importance of good listening skills in promoting effective organizational communication.

The development of listening skills requires identifying the individual elements of listening, the separate skills that contribute to listening effectiveness. Brownell has proposed that listening effectiveness may be understood in terms of the behavioral indicators that individuals perceive as related to effective listening, skills clustered into six groups known as the **HURIER model**.[98] The term HURIER is an acronym composed of the initials of the words reflecting the component skills of effective listening: hearing, understanding, remembering, interpreting, evaluating, and responding. For a summary of these individual skills, see Figure 9-13. Although it might seem easy to do the six things needed to be a good listener, we are not all as good as we think we are in this capacity, suggesting that listening might not be as easy as it seems.

Management consultant Nancy K. Austin would agree, and explains that when you invite people to talk to you about their problems on the job, you're implicitly making a promise to listen to them.[99] Of course, when you do, you may feel hostile and defensive toward the speaker, and become more interested in speaking up and setting the record straight if you don't like what you hear. This is the challenge of listening. Good listeners should resist this temptation and pay careful attention to the speaker. When they cannot do so, they should admit the problem and schedule another opportunity to get together. Austin also advises people to "be an equal opportunity listener," that is, to pay attention not only to those whose high status commands our attention, but also to anyone at any level, and to make time to hear them all in a democratic fashion. The idea is not only that people at any job level might have something to say, but also that they may feel good about you as a manager for having shown consideration to them. Austin notes that by listening to an employee, you are saying, "You are smart and have important things to say; you are worth my time."[100] Such a message is crucial to establishing the kind of open, two-way communication essential for top management.

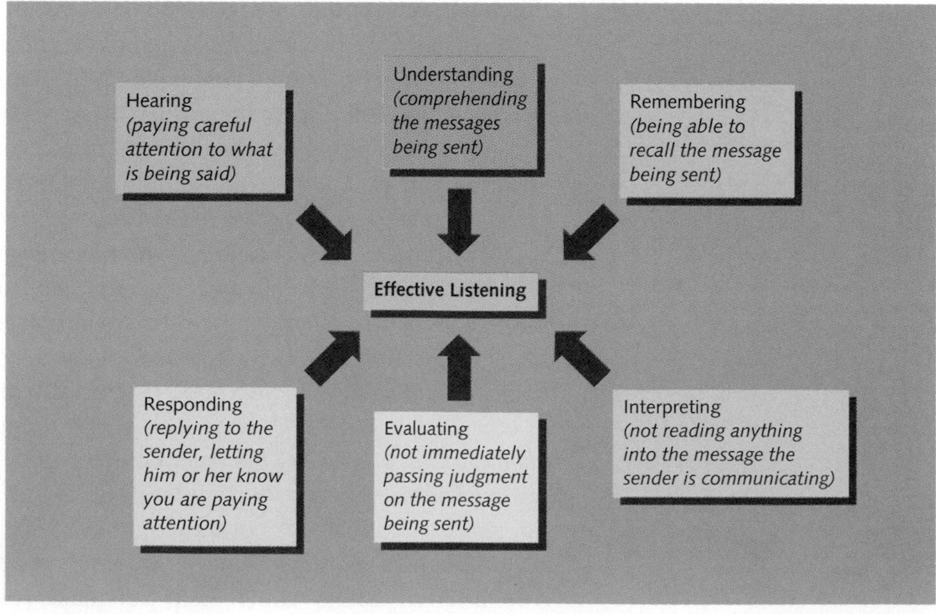

FIGURE 9-13
THE HURIER MODEL: THE COMPONENTS OF EFFECTIVE LISTENING
What makes a listener effective? Research by Brownell has shown that the six skills identified here are recognized as contributing to effective listening. (Source: Based on suggestions by Brownell, 1985; see Note 98.)

Research has confirmed the importance of listening as a management skill. In fact, it has shown that the better a person is as a listener, the more likely he or she is to rapidly rise up the organizational hierarchy[101] and to perform well as a manager.[102] Apparently, good listening skills are an important aspect of one's ability to succeed as a manager. Yet people tend to be insensitive to how others perceive their listening skills. In a survey of employees in the hospitality industry, Brownell found that almost all the managers indicated that they felt their listening skills were either "good" or "very good," although most of their subordinates did not agree.[103] Such overconfidence in one's own listening ability can be a barrier to seeking training in listening skills inasmuch as people who believe they are already good listeners may have little motivation to seek training in that area. This is unfortunate, because Brownell also found that among those who were rated as better listeners by their subordinates was a significant number of managers who had earlier been trained in listening skills. Such evidence suggests that this type of training may indeed pay off.

GAUGE THE FLOW OF INFORMATION: AVOIDING OVERLOAD

Imagine a busy manager surrounded by a tall stack of papers, with a telephone receiver in each ear and a crowd of people gathered around, waiting to talk to her. Obviously, the many demands put on this person can slow down the system and make its operation less effective. When any part of a communication network becomes bogged down with more information than it can handle effectively, a condition of **overload** is said to exist. Consider, for example, the bottleneck in the flow of routine financial information that might result when the members of the accounting department of an organization are tied up preparing corporate tax returns. (Such an overloaded condition is analogous to the experience of saturation encountered by the central members of a centralized communication network described earlier in this chapter.) Naturally, such a state poses a serious threat to effective organizational communication. Fortunately, however, several steps can be taken to manage information more effectively.

For one, organizations may employ *gatekeepers,* people whose jobs require them to control the flow of information to potentially overloaded units. For example, administrative assistants are responsible for making sure that busy executives are not overloaded by the demands of other people or groups. Newspaper editors and television news directors also may be thought of as gatekeepers, since such individuals decide what news will and will not be shared with the public. It is an essential part of these individuals' jobs to avoid overloading others by gauging the flow of information to them.

Overload also can be avoided through *queuing*. This term refers to lining up incoming information so that it can be managed in an orderly fashion. The practices of "stacking" jets as they approach a busy airport and making customers take a number (i.e., defining their position in the line) at a busy deli counter are both designed to avoid the chaos that may otherwise result when too many demands are made on the system at once. For a summary of these techniques, see Figure 9-14.

When systems are overloaded, *distortion* and *omission* are likely to result. That is, messages may be either changed or left out when they are passed from one organizational unit to the next. If you've ever played the parlor game "telephone" (in which one person whispers a message to another, who passes it on to another, and so on until it reaches the last person), you have likely experienced—or contributed

FIGURE 9-14
OVERLOAD: A PROBLEM THAT CAN BE SOLVED
Overload, *receiving too many messages at once, can seriously interfere with organizational functioning. This problem can be minimized by using* gatekeepers *(individuals who control the flow of information)* and queuing *(lining up incoming information so that it arrives in an orderly fashion).*

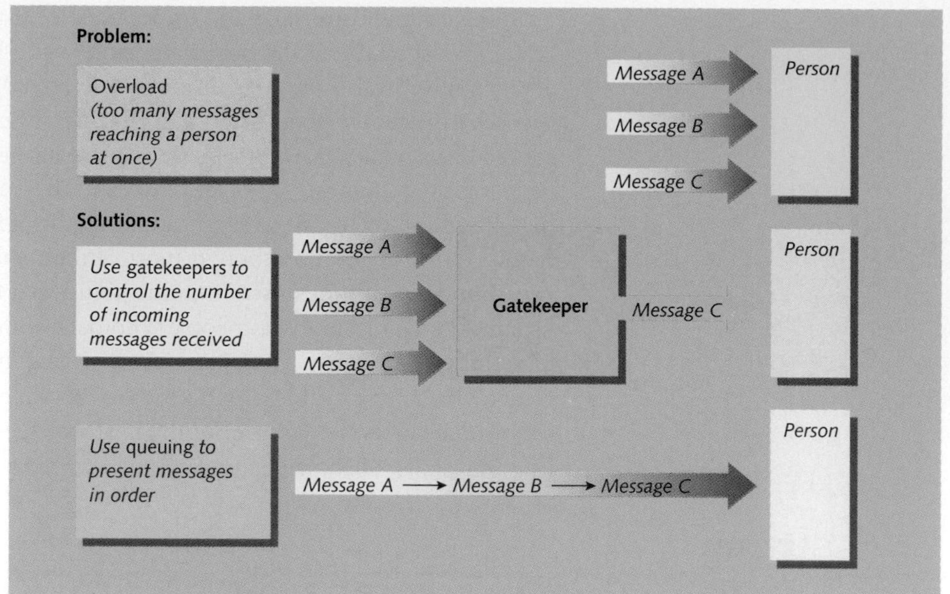

to—the ways messages get distorted and omitted. When you consider the important messages that are often communicated in organizations, these problems can be very serious. They also tend to be quite extreme. A dramatic demonstration of this was reported in a study tracing the flow of downward communication in more than a hundred organizations. The researchers found that messages communicated downward over five levels lost approximately 80 percent of their original information by the time they reached their destination at the lowest level of the organizational hierarchy.[104] Obviously, something needs to be done.

One strategy that has proven effective in avoiding the problems of distortion and omission is *redundancy*. Making messages redundant involves transmitting them again, often in another form or via another channel. For example, in attempting to communicate an important message to her subordinates, a manager may tell them the message and then follow it up with a written memo. In fact, one study has found that managers frequently encourage this practice.[105] Another practice that can help avoid distortion and omission is *verification*. This refers to making sure messages have been received accurately. Pilots use verification when they repeat the messages given them by air traffic controllers. Doing so assures both parties that the messages the pilots heard were the actual messages the controllers sent. Given how busy pilots may be during takeoffs and landings and the interference inherent in radio transmissions, coupled with the vital importance of the messages themselves, the practice of verifying messages is a wise safety measure. The practice not only is used in airline communication systems, but may be used by individual communicators as well. Active listeners may wish to verify that they correctly understood a speaker, and do so by paraphrasing the speaker's remarks within a question, asking "If I understood, you were saying. . . . "

OBTAIN FEEDBACK: OPENING UPWARD CHANNELS OF COMMUNICATION

To operate effectively, organizations must be able to communicate accurately with those who keep them running—their employees. Unfortunately, the vast majority of employees believe that the feedback between themselves and their organizations is not as good as it should be.[106] For various reasons, people are often unwilling or unable to communicate their ideas to top management. Part of the problem is the lack of available channels for upward communication and people's reluctance to use whatever ones exist. How, then, can organizations obtain information from their employees, improving the upward flow of communication?

Several techniques exist for effectively soliciting feedback (see Table 9-3). One means of facilitating upward communication in organizations is *suggestion systems*. Too often, employees' good ideas about how to improve organizational functioning fail to work their way up the organizational chart because the people with the ideas do not know how to reach the people who can implement them. Even worse, they may feel they will not be listened to even if they can reach the right person. Suggestion boxes are designed to help avoid these problems, to help provide a conduit for employees' ideas. Research has found that about 15 percent of employees use their companies' suggestion boxes, and that about 25 percent of the suggestions made are implemented.[107] Employees are usually rewarded for their successful suggestions, either with a flat monetary reward or some percentage of the money saved by implementing the suggestion.

A second method of providing important information is through *corporate hotlines*—telephone lines staffed by corporate personnel ready to answer employees' questions, listen to their comments, and the like.[108] A good example of this is the "Let's Talk" program that AT&T developed to answer its employees' questions during its 1980's antitrust divestiture. By providing personnel with easy access to information, companies benefit in several ways. Doing so not only shows employees that the company cares about them, but it also encouraged them to address

TABLE 9-3

Obtaining Employee Feedback: Some Useful Techniques

The techniques summarized here are designed to improve organizational functioning by providing top management with information about the attitudes and ideas of the workforce. They are used to promote the upward flow of information.

TECHNIQUE	DESCRIPTION
Employee surveys	*Questionnaires assessing workers' attitudes and opinions about key areas of organizational functioning, especially when results are shared with the workforce*
Suggestion systems	*Formal mechanisms through which employees can submit ideas for improving things in organizations (often by putting a note in a suggestion box); good ideas are implemented and the people who submitted them are rewarded*
Corporate hotlines	*Telephone numbers employees may call to ask questions about important organizational matters; useful in addressing workers' concerns before they become too serious*
Brown bag meetings	*Session in which subordinates and superiors meet informally over breakfast or lunch to discuss organizational matters*
Skip-level meetings	*Meetings between subordinates and superiors two or more levels above them in the organizational hierarchy*

their concerns before the issues become more serious. In addition, by keeping track of the kinds of questions and concerns voiced, top management is given invaluable insight into ways of improving organizational conditions.

A third set of techniques known as *"brown bag" meetings* and *"skip-level" meetings* are designed to facilitate communication between people who don't usually get together because they work at different organizational levels.[109] Brown bag meetings are informal get-togethers over breakfast or lunch (brought in from home, hence the term "brown bag") at which people discuss what's going on in the company. The informal nature of the meetings is designed to encourage the open sharing of ideas (eating a sandwich out of a bag is an equalizer!). Skip level meetings do essentially the same thing. These are gatherings of employees with corporate superiors who are more than one level higher than themselves in the organizational hierarchy. The idea is that new lines of communication can be established by bringing together people who are two or more levels apart, individuals who usually don't come into contact with each other.

Finally, *employee surveys* can be used to gather information about employees' attitudes and opinions about key areas of organizational operations. Questionnaires administered at regular intervals may be useful for spotting changes in attitudes as they occur. Such surveys tend to be quite effective when their results are shared with employees, especially when the feedback is used as the basis for changing the way things are done. (For a closer look at some of the ingenious ways today's organizations are surveying their employees as a means of seeking feedback, see the Quest for Quality section below.)

THE QUEST FOR QUALITY

USING SURVEY FEEDBACK TO IMPROVE ORGANIZATIONAL COMMUNICATION: WHAT SOME COMPANIES ARE DOING

The popularity of getting upward feedback from employees has grown in recent years. Companies are realizing that lower-level employees have valuable contributions to make about their operations and that it is useful to systematically gather these ideas. According to Brian Davis, a vice president at Personnel Decisions, Inc., in Minneapolis, such feedback can be a useful way of finding out how employees feel about what's going on—reactions they might not otherwise share: "Not only is it best to get feedback on leadership abilities from the subordinates who live with it daily, but upward appraisals send a message to an employee that his or her views count."[110]

Federal Express has received several awards in recognition of its efforts at soliciting upward communication from employees.[111] Its Survey–Feedback–Action (or SFA, for short) program uses a computer-administered survey to assess the reactions and suggestions of its over 68,000 employees working at 1,300 U.S. locations. The easy-to-use system has been accessed by over 10,000 employees in its first year of operation. Thus far, although relatively new, the system has been an important source of money-saving ideas for Federal Express, as well as an important morale booster. It's no wonder that the SFA system is one of the best known and most frequently emulated systems of its kind in use today.

Another company that has gone out of its way to promote upward feedback from its employees is AT&T.[112] In recent years, the company has used several different surveys to collect employees' views about management's activities. After managers are given a chance to mull over the feedback they receive, it is discussed in both one-on-one meetings (with the help of a *facilitator*, a neutral party who keeps the discussion on track) and team meetings.

Amoco Corporation uses several different employee surveys, primarily in training sessions for middle-level

THE QUEST FOR QUALITY, Cont.

managers.[113] The feedback, based on subordinates' responses to a voluntary questionnaire, is used to tell Amoco managers both *if* communication is taking place, and *how effectively* it is occurring. Interestingly, because Amoco officials were interested in comparing themselves to those in other companies, they used the same off-the-shelf questionnaires used in several other organizations instead of customized ones. Although the questionnaires have been used on a company-wide basis only since 1992, Amoco officials have been pleased with what they have learned from the feedback they provide.

Although Amoco doesn't yet hold people accountable for the feedback they receive, some offices of the professional services firm Deloitte & Touche are beginning to do just that. Feedback from subordinates, for example, is used to communicate suggestions for improvement to office managers. Survey findings are used at Deloitte & Touche as a self-counseling exercise. According to Aurora Rubin, one of the firm's partners, "It's an opportunity to assist individuals in strengthening their skills and overcoming any weaknesses."[114] Taking this feedback a step further, employees frequently use the feedback they receive as the basis for the goals they set for themselves during the coming year.

The practices profiled here are but a few of many possible examples of companies that are using surveys to nurture channels of upward communication. Although the companies gather different kinds of information in different ways, and do different things with it once collected, they all share an important element in common: an underlying belief in the importance of feedback as a tool for improving the quality of both organizational performance and individual well-being.

SUMMARY AND REVIEW

THE BASIC NATURE OF COMMUNICATION

The process of **communication** occurs when a sender of information **encodes** a message and transmits it over communication channels to a receiver, who **decodes** it and then sends **feedback**. Factors interfering with these processes are known as **noise**. Communication is used in organizations not only to direct individual action, but also to achieve coordinated action. Although the heart of communication is information, communication is also used to develop friendships and to build interpersonal trust and acceptance in organizations.

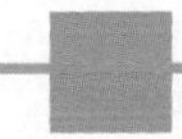

VERBAL COMMUNICATION

Communication in both oral and written forms are commonly used in organizations. Verbal media range from those that are highly personal and provide opportunities for immediate feedback, such as face-to-face discussions, to those that are impersonal and one-way, such as flyers and bulletins. **Newsletters** are important written documents used to communicate relevant news of value to employees. **Employee handbooks** are used to provide important information about a company's background, business, and rules.

Research has shown that communication is most effective when it relies on both oral and written messages. People prefer oral media to written media when messages are ambiguous, and written media to oral media when messages are clear. Furthermore, individuals who match in this manner the media they use to the ambiguity of the situations they confront tend to be more successful managers than those who do not. Communicators in modern organizations have a new array of media available to them, including **video display terminals**, **electronic mail**, and **voice messaging systems**.

NONVERBAL COMMUNICATION

People tend to have greater self-confidence when they dress appropriately for the jobs they perform, although there are widespread differences in what constitutes appropriate dress. Research has shown that people communicate their higher organizational status by requiring lower-ranking individuals to spend more time waiting for them. Status is also communicated nonverbally by the use of space: higher-status people tend to sit at the heads of rectangular tables.

MAJOR INFLUENCES ON ORGANIZATIONAL COMMUNICATION

Communication is influenced by **organizational structure**, the formally prescribed pattern of interrelationships between people in organizations. Structure dictates who must communicate with whom (as reflected in an **organizational chart**, a diagram outlining these reporting relationships) and the form that communication takes. Orders flow down an organizational hierarchy, and information flows upward. However, the upward flow of information is often distorted insofar as people are reluctant to share bad news with their superiors. Attempts at coordination characterize horizontal communication, messages between organizational members at the same level.

Formally imposed patterns of communication, called **communication networks**, influence job performance and satisfaction over brief periods of time. **Centralized networks** have certain members through whom messages must travel. In **decentralized networks**, however, all members play an equal role in transmitting information. On simple tasks, centralized networks perform faster and more accurately; on complex tasks, decentralized networks do better. Members of decentralized networks tend to be more satisfied than members of centralized networks.

Information also flows along *informal communication networks*. These informal connections between people are responsible for spreading information very rapidly because they transcend formal organizational boundaries. Informal pathways known as the **grapevine** are often responsible for the rapid transmission of partially inaccurate information known as **rumors**. Rumors may be costly to organizations as well as individuals.

OVERCOMING COMMUNICATION BARRIERS

Individuals can learn to become better communicators by keeping their messages brief, clear, and avoiding the use of **jargon** when communicating with those who may not be familiar with such specialized terms. They may also improve their *listening* skills, learning to listen actively (thinking about what is said and questioning the speaker) and attentively (without distraction).

The problem of **overload** can be reduced by using *gatekeepers* (individuals who control the flow of information to others) or by *queuing* (the orderly lining up of incoming information). The *distortion* and *omission* of messages can be minimized by making messages *redundant* and by encouraging their *verification*. At the organizational level, communication may be improved by using techniques that open upward channels of communication to employee feedback (e.g., *suggestion systems*, *corporate hotlines*, and *employee surveys*).

KEY TERMS

centralization: The degree to which information must flow through a specific central member of a communication network.

centralized networks: Communication networks that have central members through which all information must pass to reach other members (e.g., the *Y*, the *wheel*, and the *chain*).

communication: The process by which a person, group, or organization (the sender) transmits some type of information (the message) to another person, group, or organization (the receiver).

communication networks: Pre-established patterns dictating who may communicate with whom (See *centralized networks* and *decentralized networks*.)

decentralized networks: Communication networks in which all members play an equal role in the transmittal of information (e.g., the *circle* and the *comcon*).

decoding: The process by which a receiver of messages transforms them back into the sender's ideas.

electronic mail (e-mail): A system whereby people use personal computer terminals to send and receive messages among themselves.

employee handbook: A document describing to employees basic information about a company; a general reference regarding a company's background, the nature of its business, and its rules.

encoding: The process by which an idea is transformed so that it can be transmitted to, and recognized by, a receiver (e.g., a written or spoken message).

grapevine: An organization's informal channels of communication, based mainly on friendship or acquaintance.

HURIER model: The conceptualization that describes effective listening as made up of the following six components: hearing, understanding, remembering, interpreting, evaluating, and responding.

jargon: The specialized language used by a particular group (e.g., people within a profession).

K.I.S.S. principle: A basic principle of communication advising that messages should be as short and simple as possible (an abbreviation for keep it short and simple).

MUM effect: The reluctance to transmit bad news, shown either by not transmitting the message at all, or by delegating the task to someone else.

newsletters: Regularly published internal documents describing information of interest to employees regarding an array of business and nonbusiness issues affecting them.

noise: Factors capable of distorting the clarity of messages at any point during the communication process.

nonverbal communication: The transmission of messages without the use of words (e.g., by gestures, the use of space).

organizational chart: A diagram showing the formal structure of an organization, indicating who is to communicate with whom.

organizational structure: The formally prescribed pattern of interrelationships existing between the various units of an organization.

overload: The condition in which a unit of an organization becomes overburdened with too much incoming information.

rumors: Information with little basis in fact, often transmitted through informal channels (see *grapevine*).

saturation: The amount of information a single member of a communication network must handle.

verbal communication: The transmission of messages using words, either written or spoken.

voice messaging (voice mail): A system that uses a computer to convert human speech into digital information saved on a hard disk for playback later by the receiver at any time from any touch-tone telephone.

QUESTIONS FOR DISCUSSION

1. Using an example of an everyday communication in organization (e.g., a supervisor asking her assistant for the month's production schedule), describe how the communication process operates (e.g., how information is encoded, transmitted, decoded, and so on).
2. Imagine that you are a manager attempting to explain the use of a certain new computer software package to a subordinate. Should this be accomplished using written or spoken communication, or both? Explain your decision.
3. Suppose you're interviewing for a job. Describe how the way you dress, and the interviewer's use of time and space can influence what you communicate to each other.
4. What is an *organizational chart*? What does it reveal about the nature of communication within organizations?
5. Imagine that you are putting together a group of five people to evaluate proposed methods for disposing of nuclear waste. What type of communication network would be most appropriate? Why?
6. Your company is being victimized by a totally untrue rumor about a pending merger. What steps would you recommend taking to put the story to an end? Explain.
7. In Shakespeare's *Hamlet,* Polonius said, "Give every man thine ear, but few thy voice." Discuss the implications of this advice for being an active listener. What other suggestions should be followed for enhancing the effectiveness of listening?
8. Identify any two problems of organizational communication and measures that can be taken to overcome them.

CASE IN POINT

THE HEART AND SOUL OF "THE BODY SHOP"

It is not life or death, making moisturizing cream . . . We will never promote a product. . . . Malls are monuments to noncommunication that alienate humanity. . . . It is the quality of business rather than the quantity of what you make [that matters].[1]

This is a brief summary of Anita Roddick's business philosophy. This approach, though unconventional, has certainly been effective in the case of Roddick and her company, The Body Shop. Roddick launched her enterprise in 1976 as a means for her to earn a living and support her children while her husband went on a two-year horseback trip across South America.[2] Today, Body Shop stores number 1,100 in 45 countries, and have over $225 million in worldwide sales.[3,4]

Roddick's success generally has been attributed to the fact that her company sells environmentally friendly products at a time when such merchandise is extremely popular with consumers. A closer look at Roddick and her company, however, reveals a more complex explanation for this growth. Much of the Body Shop's expansion and acclaim is the result of Roddick's unusual and effective means of communication.

Within the company itself, Roddick is insistent on direct and open communication between employees of all levels. She attempts to create a climate for this by keeping the structure of the company as nonhierarchical as possible. Although the company is now too large for her to know all employees by name, she still encourages employees to contact her via phone and/or mail if they have an idea or a problem.[5]

To help encourage inspiration among the employees at Body Shop headquarters in Littlehampton, England, signs are hung throughout the lobby with messages such as "reinvent," "risk," "refuse," "resist," and "reuse."[6] Roddick believes that slogans such as these can help focus employees on the goals of the firm. Displaying these emblems in such a public place as the reception area serves Roddick by symbolically communicating to her employees the importance she places on these activities.

Information and resources are supplied to employees to reinforce Roddick's core values: helping others and caring for the planet. For example, in the waiting area at the office, stationery is provided along with instructions for a letter-writing campaign for Amnesty International (an organization dedicated to stopping abuses of human rights). Similarly, fliers are circulated asking for donations of time and money for various charitable organizations.[7] To ensure that Body Shop personnel realize Roddick's commitment to these concerns, employees are provided with paid time off to volunteer for social causes.[8]

In addition to "putting her money where her mouth is," so to speak, within her company, Roddick has cultivated nontraditional means of communicating with her customers. Unlike almost all other marketers of cosmetics, Roddick shuns advertising. She believes that her products should be good enough to sell themselves. To accomplish this, merchandise in the stores is accompanied by pamphlets and fliers describing the Body Shop philosophy as well as the products' ingredients, development, history, and use. Also, merchandise is displayed with photographs of the places from which it comes, as well as information about the people who made it. Moreover, she puts up posters in her store windows promoting environmental and human rights causes.[9]

Says Roddick,

My company has not just to do with products but the transformation of ideas, female thinking, a sense of love, self-education. Customers don't enter my store just for the products but [because they support] the company. They come in for the conversation, the link with the community.[10]

Although Roddick seems to specialize in less typical forms of communication, she is also quite adept at using traditional means of getting her message across. Intra-firm communication is buoyed by memos, reports, audits, and in-house videos.[11] In addition, Roddick has been extremely successful at marshaling the goodwill of the media. One particularly noteworthy example of this occurred soon after opening her first store. When she was threatened by a lawsuit, she went to the local newspaper and provided them a story about her struggle as a mother to support her young children. The article that ran about her situation generated so much sympathy for her that the lawsuit was dropped and many new customers streamed to her store.[12]

It sometimes seems as if Roddick herself is the target of her own messages. She once admitted to an interviewer

CASE IN POINT, Cont.

that she asks herself, "What am I doing? What have I done? What is brave? What can I do that is truly, truly remarkable?"[13] Given Roddick's passion and energy, it is likely that over the coming years she will accomplish many remarkable things. Given her style, it's unlikely that Roddick will take credit for her achievements. It's more like her to let her products speak to her success.

QUESTIONS FOR DISCUSSION

1. How does the flat hierarchy of the Body Shop contribute to encouraging communication?
2. Instead of focusing on providing information about the products sold at the Body Shop, Roddick prefers to emphasize communications about the company philosophy. What are some of the pros and cons of this approach?
3. By using the media as her main source of communicating with potential customers, what communication barriers does Roddick face?
4. What forms of verbal communication are employed by Roddick and her company?
5. What types of communication problems might you expect in a company that has operations in forty-five countries?

EXPERIENCING ORGANIZATIONAL BEHAVIOR

Becoming an Active Listener

What makes an effective communicator? Most people would probably say it's his or her ability to express ideas—to speak and write clearly. Of course these skills are important, but so too is listening. Being a good communicator requires listening carefully, picking up on others' ideas. Although we might hear others, most of us tend to be very inefficient listeners. That is, we fail to pay attention to and understand most of what others are saying. When it comes to communication in organizations, this can be quite problematic. Recognizing this, many people in organizations are trained to become more *active listeners* (see pages 354-367).

PROCEDURE

1. Review the following "do's and don'ts" of active listening.

Do	*Don't*
Show empathy; support the speaker.	Judge and draw conclusions.
Explain what you think was said.	Evaluate the ideas expressed.

2. As a class, consider how an active listener would respond to someone saying "I worked for hours on that stupid project, and the boss didn't like it. That'll be the last time I work so hard for him."

   Listening actively, it would be correct to say, "You seem disappointed that your boss didn't approve of your work." Such a response shows that you understand the speaker and encourages him or her to give more thought to the problem at hand. In contrast, it would be incorrect to say either, "You should have started that project long ago" (too judgmental) or "At least you have a good job" (no empathy).

3. The instructor should now read each of the following statements out loud. Listen actively to each one and respond to it in a way that shows you've listened actively. Discuss several students' responses relative to the guidelines for active listening noted above.

   a. I just found out my boss gave me only a 2 percent raise. If that's the kind of appreciation they show for hard work around here, they can get themselves another sucker!
   b. Why did you take Barbara's side on that budget vote? I thought you agreed with me, but apparently not. Sometimes it's tough to tell your friends from your enemies.
   c. It really sounds like a good offer. The pay is competitive, and I've always wanted to live in Crowdville.
   d. I'm really tired of those staff meetings. All we ever do is gripe. If you ask me, they're just a waste of time.

e. Try as I might, I just can't get the hand of that new computer system. Yesterday I messed with it for hours and got nowhere.

f. Being part of the Rafstone Products team is a dream come true. I just hope I can cut it around here with all those big shots.

g. Everybody's gone on vacation this week, but I have to hang around to get caught up on my work. At least that's what Mr. Nasty wanted. Sure wish I could be getting a tan like everyone else.

POINTS TO CONSIDER

1. Did it become easier for you to think of appropriate responses as you practiced more?
2. Had you not been attempting to listen actively, how would you have responded? More judgmentally?
3. What mistakes did your classmates make most commonly in responding to these statements?
4. Do you think you will be able to apply your active listening skills to your own interactions with others? Why or why not?
5. What personal benefits do you imagine will result for both speakers and listeners from using active listening techniques?
6. When do you think it would be most appropriate to use and to not use active listening in skills organizations?
7. How would you feel as the speaker if you heard the responses of your classmates?

CHAPTER OUTLINE

SPECIAL SECTIONS

TEN

DECISION MAKING IN ORGANIZATIONS

LEARNING OBJECTIVES

After reading this chapter, you should be able to

1. *Identify the steps in the traditional, analytic model of decision making and the intuitive approach of image theory.*
2. *Describe and give examples of programmed and nonprogrammed decisions.*
3. *Distinguish between the rational-economic approach and the administrative approach to decision making.*
4. *Describe the factors that dictate against high-quality decisions—both individual, cognitive biases, and organizationally-imposed barriers.*
5. *Compare the advantages and disadvantages of using groups and individuals to make decisions in organizations.*
6. *Describe the conditions under which groups make better decisions than individuals, and the conditions under which individuals make better decisions than groups.*
7. *Explain groupthink, and how it may be a barrier to effective group decisions.*
8. *Describe techniques that can be used to improve the quality of group decisions (e.g., the Delphi technique, the nominal group technique, the stepladder technique, and individual decision training).*

If you put off everything till you're sure of it, you'll get nothing done.

Norman Vincent Peale, 1898–1993
Clergyman and inspirational speaker
Reader's Digest, *January 1972*

The closeness of the decision attests the measure of the doubt.

Benjamin Nathan Cardozo, 1870–1938
U.S. Supreme Court Justice
People ex rel. Hayes v. McLaughlin (1927)

PREVIEW CASE

Chrysler's Neon: Big Decisions About a Small Car

July 31, 1990, was a lazy summer day in Detroit. No one would have suspected it would become an important date for Chrysler, and perhaps the entire American auto industry. Lee A. Iacocca, Chrysler's chief executive officer, was considering a joint venture with Italy's Fiat to build a new subcompact car, its first since the company's Dodge Omni and Plymouth Horizon in 1978.

Meeting with Robert P. Marcell, the head of Chrysler's small-car team, and a dozen engineers in a test-track garage, Iacocca heard pleas to develop the new car at home. Marcell argued that Chrysler could do it if given the chance, and that this would end the two-decades-long stream of unprofitable subcompacts rolling off Detroit assembly lines. "If we dare to be different," Marcell reasoned, "we could be the reason the U.S. auto industry survives." Iacocca was convinced, and the Fiat deal was killed. He wanted to prove that Chrysler could out-muscle the Japanese auto giants Toyota, Honda, and Nissan, who dominated the subcompact market.

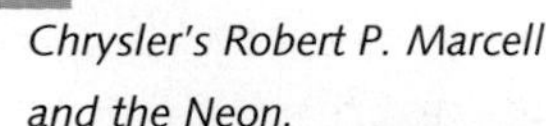

Chrysler's Robert P. Marcell and the Neon.

From this challenge was born what was to become the 1995 Chrysler Neon. Marcell, along with 600 engineers, 289 suppliers, and buses full of blue-collar workers developed the $9,000 subcompact in a speedy forty-two months, and on budget at $1.3 billion. Needing to sell an impressive 300,000 units a year to turn a profit, company officials were well aware of the need to build a quality product at an attractive price. Everyone knew that if costs weren't kept down, Chrysler would abandon the project and the dream would die. The number-three automaker couldn't afford to sell cars at a loss, as Ford was doing with its Escorts.

To save money, decisions about the Neon were made with great care. For example, it was decided to sell identical cars at both Chrysler and Dodge dealerships instead of slightly different versions as had been done at Ford, with its Ford Escort and Mercury Tracer models. The savings in engineering and tooling amounting from that decision alone came to $10 million.

Still, Chrysler executives knew that people wanted a safe and efficient car. As a result, the Neon was designed with dual air bags—the first subcompact to come with them as a standard feature. However, when it became known that using the prevailing design would have resulted in a vehicle in which the air bags constituted 10 percent of the price of the car, TRW, the supplier, was forced back to the drawing board. The result: a less expensive single impact sensor was designed to replace the three typically used.

Marcell realized that the Neon's success depended not only on such cost-saving design features, but also on the quality of the assembly process. With this in mind, he sought the help of the United Auto Workers union (UAW), soliciting suggestions from the ninety plant workers hired to assemble the first production prototypes. How could the *job be done better, plant officials asked? Answers came pouring in—some 4,000, in fact. For example, a height-adjustable assembly line was suggested to make it easier for assemblers to fasten components without making mistakes. Assembly workers also recommended ways the door installation equipment could be changed to install the window glass perfectly, minimizing wind noise and water leaks. To help the assemblers get a feel for how their efforts were paying off, they were given prototypes to test-drive—racking up some 1.5 million miles-worth of hands-on experience. Everyone working on the Neon learned an urgent message from the appeal of General Motors' Saturn: people were attracted to a well-built American car.*

Will the Neon be as successful as Marcell hopes? Will it be the vehicle to revive the troubled American auto business? Although only time will tell if Iacocca made the right decision, preliminary signs are encouraging. Despite the recall of some early Neons, Automobile magazine named the 1995 Neon its "Automobile of the Year." Editorial director David E. Davis, Jr., calls the Neon "the car the domestic [auto] industry said couldn't be built, the small car that competes successfully with the Japanese, and makes a profit." Indeed, Japanese automakers are carefully monitoring the Neon's success. Says Japan's prime minister, Morihiro Hosokowa, "The Japanese auto industry fears [it] will take a shellacking because of Neon."

Although you may not have been involved in decisions like this one—at least not yet—you can certainly appreciate the gravity of Marcell's situation. With billions of dollars at risk, not to mention the reputation of the United States as an auto-manufacturing power, there's surely a lot on the line for Chrysler. But you don't have to be a party to such a high-stakes game to relate to the pressure of making the right decision. If you've ever wrestled over decisions about what college to attend or what job to take, you probably already have a good idea of how difficult it can be to take everything into account when working through a complex problem. For Chrysler, the tastes and needs of the public, and the capacity of the competition to deliver a better product may be difficult to project. Likewise, you might not be able to tell if you made the best decision for yourself until it's already too late. This is not to say that companies and individuals cannot attempt to learn more about what the future will hold, as the basis for the decisions they make. Indeed, they often do. And despite the most careful efforts to anticipate the future and make the best possible decisions, mistakes are sometimes made. If you think about the difficulties involved in making decisions in your own life, you may appreciate how complicated and important the process of **decision making** can be in organizations, where the stakes may be considerable.

It is safe to say that decision making is one of the most important—if not *the* most important—of all managerial activities.[1] Management theorists and researchers agree that decision making represents one of the most common and most crucial work roles of executives. In fact, organizational scientist Herbert Simon, who won a Nobel prize for his work on decision making, has gone so far as to describe decision making as synonymous with managing.[2] Everyday, people in organizations make decisions about a wide variety of topics ranging from the mundane to the monumental (see Figure 10-1).[3] Understanding how these decisions are made, and how they can be improved, is an important goal of the field of organizational behavior.

FIGURE 10-1
DECISION MAKING: AN EVERYDAY ACTIVITY ON AND OFF THE JOB
People make a wide variety of decisions about many different things—some of which are more important than others. (Source: Cathy © 1988 Cathy Guisewite. Reprinted with permission of Universal Press Syndicate. All rights reserved..)

This chapter will examine theories, research, and practical managerial techniques concerned with organizational decision making. We will explore the ways individuals make decisions, and then look at the decision-making processes of groups. Specifically, we will review the basic characteristics of individual decisions and group decisions. For each, we will identify factors that may adversely affect the quality of decisions and ways of combating them—that is, techniques for improving the quality of decisions. Then we will compare the quality of individual and group decisions on a variety of tasks and note the conditions under which individuals or groups are better suited for making decisions. Finally, we will describe various techniques that can be used to improve the quality of decisions made by groups. But first we will begin by taking a closer look at the general process of decision making and the varieties of decisions made in organizations.

ORGANIZATIONAL DECISION MAKING: ITS BASIC NATURE

Given the central importance of decision making in organizations, we will begin our discussion by highlighting some of the basic steps in the decision-making process and noting the characteristics of organizational decisions. Specifically, two different approaches to decision making will be considered: the traditional orientation, which looks at decision making in terms of a continuous series of analytical steps, and a more contemporary approach, which looks at decision making as an automatic, intuitive process.

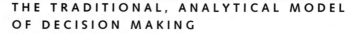

THE TRADITIONAL, ANALYTICAL MODEL OF DECISION MAKING

Traditionally, scientists have found it useful to conceptualize the process of decision making as a series of steps that groups or individuals take to solve problems.[4] A general model of the decision-making process can help us understand the complex nature of organizational decision making (see Figure 10-2).[5] This model highlights two important aspects of the decision-making process: *formulation*, the process of understanding a problem and making a decision about it, and *implementation*, the process of carrying out the decision made.[6] As we present this model, keep in mind that all decisions might not fully conform to the neat, eight-step pattern described (e.g., steps may be skipped and/or combined).[7]

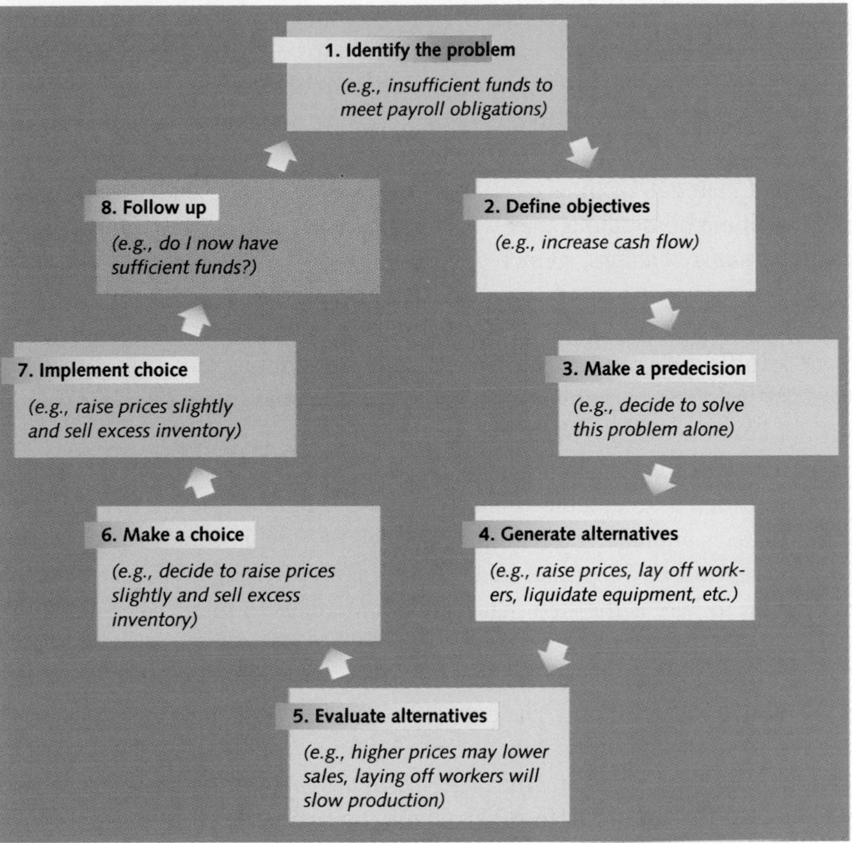

FIGURE 10-2
THE DECISION-MAKING PROCESS: THE TRADITIONAL, ANALYTICAL MODEL
The process of decision making tends to follow the eight steps outlined here. Note how each step may be applied to a hypothetical organizational problem: having insufficient funds to meet payroll obligations. (Source: Based on information in Wedley & Field, 1983; see Note 5.)

However, for the purpose of pointing out the general way the decision-making process operates, the model is quite useful.

The first step in decision making is *problem identification*. To decide how to solve a problem, one must first recognize and identify the problem. For example, an executive may identify as a problem the fact that the company cannot meet its payroll obligations. This step isn't always as easy as it sounds. In fact, research has shown that people often distort, omit, ignore, and/or discount information around them that provides important cues regarding the existence of problems.[8] You may recall from our discussion of the social perception process (see Chapter 2) that people do not always accurately perceive social situations. It is easy to imagine that someone may fail to recognize a problem if doing so makes him or her uncomfortable. Denying a problem may be the first impediment on the road to solving it!

After a problem is identified, the next step is to *define the objectives to be met in solving the problem*. It is important to conceive of problems in such a way that possible solutions can be identified. The problem identified in our example may be defined as not having enough money, or in business terms, "inadequate cash flow." By looking at the problem in this way, the objective is clear: increase available cash reserves. Any possible solution to the problem should be evaluated relative to this objective. A good solution is one that meets it.

The third step in the decision-making process is to *make a predecision*. A **predecision** is a decision about how to make a decision. By assessing the type of problem in question and other aspects of the situation, managers may opt to make a decision themselves, delegate the decision to another, or have a group make the decision. Decisions about how to make a decision should be based on research that tells us about the nature of the decisions made under different circumstances, many of which we will review later in this chapter. For many years, managers have been relying on their own intuition or empirically based information about organizational behavior (contained in books like this) for the guidance needed to make predecisions. Recently, however, computer programs have been developed that summarize much of this information in a form giving managers ready access to a wealth of social science information that may help them decide how to make decisions.[9] Such **decision support systems (DSS)**, as they are called, can only be as good as the social science information that goes into developing them. Research has shown that DSS techniques are effective in helping people make decisions about solving problems.[10] The use of decision-making technology leads to outcomes believed to be better than those made in the absence of such techniques. Moreover, computer-based DSS techniques have been found to be especially helpful in getting people to generate a higher number of alternative solutions.[11]

The fourth step in the process is *alternative generation*, the stage in which possible solutions to the problem are identified. In attempting to come up with solutions, people tend to rely on previously used approaches that might provide ready-made answers for them.[12] In our example, some possible ways of solving the revenue shortage problem would be to reduce the workforce, sell unnecessary equipment and material, or increase sales.

Because all these possibilities may not be equally feasible, the fifth step calls for *evaluating alternative solutions*. Which solution is best? What would be the most effective way of raising the revenue needed to meet the payroll? The various alternatives need to be identified. Some may be more effective than others, and some may be more difficult to implement than others. For example, although increasing sales would help solve the problem, that is much easier said than done. It is a solution, but not an immediately practical one.

Next, in the sixth step, *a choice is made*. After several alternatives are evaluated, one that is considered acceptable is chosen. As we will describe shortly, different approaches to decision making offer different views of how thoroughly people consider alternatives and how optimal their chosen alternatives are. Choosing which course of action to take is the step that most often comes to mind when we think about the decision-making process.

The seventh step calls for *implementation of the chosen alternative*. That is, the chosen alternative is carried out. The eighth and final step is *follow-up*. Monitoring the effectiveness of the decisions they put into action is important to the success of organizations. Does the problem still exist? Have any new problems been caused by implementing the solution? In other words, it is important to seek feedback about the effectiveness of any attempted solution. For this reason, the decision-making process is presented as circular in Figure 10-2. If the solution works, the problem may be considered solved. If not, a new solution will have to be attempted. (Although we have been referring to decision making as if it were a universal process, there are differences in the way people from different cultures carry out these steps. For a closer look at some fascinating cross-cultural differences in decision making, see the Global Organization section below.)

THE GLOBAL ORGANIZATION

CULTURAL VARIATIONS IN THE DECISION-MAKING PROCESS

People are people, and the process of decision making is essentially the same all over the world—right? Not exactly. Even if people were to follow the same basic steps when making decisions, there exist widespread differences in the *way* people from various cultures may go about doing so.[13] Because we tend to take for granted the way we do things in our own countries, especially such basic tasks as making decisions, some of these differences may seem quite surprising (see Figure 10-3).

For example, suppose you are managing a large construction project when you discover that one of your most important suppliers will be several months late in delivering the necessary materials. What would you do? You're probably thinking, "This is a silly question; I'd simply try to get another supplier." If you're from the United States, this is probably just what you'd do. But if you're from Thailand, Indonesia, or Malaysia, chances are good that you'd simply accept the situation as fate and allow the project to be delayed. In other words, to the American, Canadian, or western European manager, the situation may be perceived as a problem in need of a decision, whereas no such problem would be recognized by Thai, Indonesian, or Malaysian managers. Thus, as basic as it seems that decision making begins with recognizing that a problem exists, it is important to note that not all people are likely to perceive the same situations as problems.

THE GLOBAL ORGANIZATION, Cont.

Even once problems are recognized, people may be expected to focus on different types of information when making decisions. Consider, for example, the 1973 conflict in the Middle East, in which 100 million Arabs were at war with 8 million Israelis. Americans, looking at these numbers objectively, had little reason to be optimistic over the fate of the Israelis. The Israelis, however, did not use this same information to judge whether or not they could win. Basing their assessment of the situation on their vision of the future, a free Jewish state, the Israelis were far more optimistic about the outcome of their battle. Buoyed with optimism, the Israelis decided to go to war, although people from other cultures might have looked at the numbers and decided otherwise.

Cultures also differ with respect to the nature of the decision-making unit they typically employ. In the United States, for example, where people tend to be highly individualistic, individual decisions are commonly made. However, in more collectivistic cultures, such as Japan, it would be considered inconceivable for someone to make a decision without first gaining the acceptance of his or her immediate colleagues.

Similarly, there exist cultural differences with respect to *who* is expected to make decisions. In Sweden, for example, it is traditional for employees at all levels to be involved in the decisions affecting them. However, in India, where autocratic decision making is expected, it would be considered a sign of weakness for a manager to consult a subordinate about a decision.

Another cultural difference in decision making has to do with the amount of time taken to make a decision. For example, in the United States one mark of a good decision maker is that he or she is "decisive," willing to take on an important decision and make it without delay. However, in some other cultures, time urgency is downplayed. In Egypt, for example, the more important the matter, the more time the decision maker is expected to take in reaching a decision. Throughout the Middle East reaching a decision quickly would be perceived as overly hasty.

As these examples illustrate, there exist some interesting differences in the ways people from various countries go about formulating and implementing decisions. Understanding such differences is an important first step toward developing appropriate strategies for conducting business at a global level.[14]

FIGURE 10-3
CULTURE: AN IMPORTANT DETERMINANT OF DECISION MAKING
People from different cultures follow different norms with respect to making decisions. It is important to understand and accept such differences if people from culturally diverse groups are to work together effectively.

IMAGE THEORY: AN INTUITIVE APPROACH TO DECISION MAKING

If you think about it, you'll probably realize that some, but certainly not all, decisions are made following the logical steps of the traditional, analytical model of decision making. Consider Elizabeth Barrett Browning's poetic question "How do I love thee? Let me count the ways."[15] It's unlikely that one would ultimately make such a decision by carefully counting what one loves about another (although many such characteristics can be enumerated). Instead, a more intuitive-based decision making is likely, not only for matters of the heart, but for a variety of important organizational decisions as well.[16] The point is that selecting the best alternative by weighing all the options is not always a major concern when making a decision. People also consider how various decision alternatives fit with their personal standards as well as their personal goals and plans. The best decision for someone might not be the best for someone else. In other words, people may make decisions in a more automatic, intuitive fashion than is traditionally recognized. Representative of this approach is Beach and Mitchell's **image theory**.[17] This relatively new approach to decision making is summarized in Figure 10-4.

Image theory deals primarily with decisions about adopting a certain course of action (e.g., should the company develop a new product line?) or changing a current course of action (e.g., should the company drop a present product line?). According to the theory, people make adoption decisions on the basis of a simple two-step process. The first step is the *compatibility test*, a comparison of the degree to which a particular course of action is consistent with various images—particularly individual principles, current goals, and plans for the future. If any lack of compatibility exists with respect to these considerations, a rejection decision is made. If the compatibility test is passed, then the *profitability test* is carried out. That is, people consider the extent to which using various alternatives best fits their values, goals, and plans. The decision is then made to accept the best candidate. These tests are used within a certain *decision frame*—that is, with consideration of meaningful information about the decision context (such as past experiences). The basic idea is that we learn from the past and are guided by it when making decisions. The example shown in Figure 10-4 highlights this contemporary approach to decision making.

According to image theory, the decision-making process is very rapid and simple. The theory suggests that people do not ponder and reflect over decisions, but make them using a smooth, intuitive process with minimal cognitive processing. If you've ever found yourself saying that something "seemed like the right thing to do" or "something doesn't feel right," you're probably well aware of the kind of intuitive thinking that goes on in a great deal of decision making. Recent research suggests that when it comes to making relatively simple decisions, people tend to behave as suggested by image theory.[18] For example, it has been found that people decide against various options when past evidence suggests that these decisions may be incompatible with their images of the future.[19]

FIGURE 10-4

IMAGE THEORY: A SUMMARY AND EXAMPLE

According to image theory, decisions are made in a relatively automatic, intuitive fashion following the two steps outlined here. (Source: Adapted from Mitchell & Beach, 1990; see Note 16.)

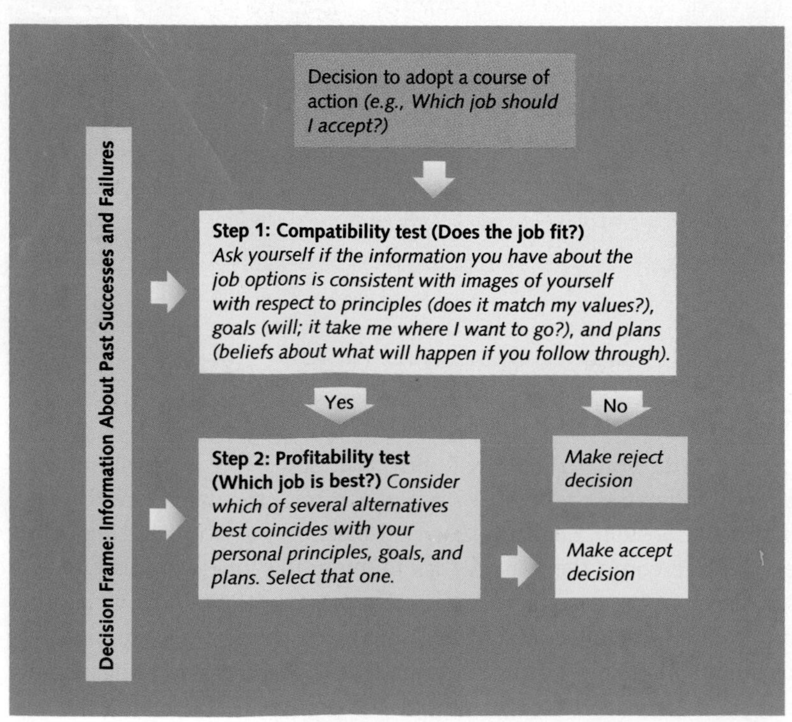
Decision Frame: Information About Past Successes and Failures
Decision to adopt a course of action (e.g., Which job should I accept?)
Step 1: Compatibility test (Does the job fit?)
Ask yourself if the information you have about the job options is consistent with images of yourself with respect to principles (does it match my values?), goals (will; it take me where I want to go?), and plans (beliefs about what will happen if you follow through).
Yes
No
Step 2: Profitability test (Which job is best?) Consider which of several alternatives best coincides with your personal principles, goals, and plans. Select that one.
Make reject decision
Make accept decision

To summarize, we have described the traditional, analytical approach to decision making, and image theory—a newer, intuitive approach to decision making. Both approaches have received support, and neither one should be seen as a replacement for the other. Instead, several different processes may be involved in decision making. Not all decision making is carried out the same way: sometimes decision making might be analytical, and sometimes it might be more intuitive. Modern organizational behavior scholars recognize the value of both approaches. As you might imagine, both of the decision-making processes just outlined may be applied to making a variety of different decisions in organizations. To better appreciate the various types of decisions that are made, we will now consider some of the basic characteristics of organizational decisions.

VARIETIES OF ORGANIZATIONAL DECISIONS

Consider, for a moment, the variety of decisions likely to be made in organizations. Some decisions have far-reaching consequences (such as Chrysler's decision to build the Neon), and others are more mundane (such as the everyday decision to reorder office supplies). People sometimes make decisions in situations in which the likely outcomes are well known (e.g., the decision to underwrite life insurance on the basis of actuarial data), whereas at other times the outcomes are much more uncertain (e.g., the decision to invade a hostile nation for purposes of freeing hostages). These examples are reflective of the two major characteristics of organizational decisions: how structured or unstructured the situation is, and how much certainty or risk is involved in the decision.

PROGRAMMED VERSUS NONPROGRAMMED DECISIONS: HOW WELL STRUCTURED IS THE DECISION SETTING?

Think of a decision that is made repeatedly, according to a pre-established set of alternatives. For example, a word processing operator may decide to make a backup diskette of the day's work, or a manager of a fast-food restaurant may decide to order hamburger buns as the supply starts to get low. Decisions such as these are known as **programmed decisions**—routine decisions, made by lower-level personnel, that rely on predetermined courses of action.

By contrast, we may identify **nonprogrammed decisions**—ones for which there are no ready-made solutions. The decision maker confronts a unique situation in which the solutions are novel. The research scientist attempting to find a cure for a rare disease faces a problem that is poorly structured. Unlike the order clerk whose course of action is clear when the supply of paper clips runs low, the scientist in this example must rely on creativity rather than pre-existing answers to solve the problem at hand.

Certain types of nonprogrammed decisions are known as **strategic decisions**.[20] These decisions are typically made by coalitions of high-level executives and have important long-term implications for the organization. Strategic decisions reflect a consistent pattern for directing the organization in some specified fashion—that is, according to an underlying organizational philosophy or mission. For example, an organization may make a strategic decision to grow at a specified yearly rate, or to be guided by a certain code of corporate ethics. Both of these decisions are likely to be considered strategic because they guide the future direction of the organization.

Table 10-1 summarizes the differences between programmed and nonprogrammed decisions with respect to three important variables. First, what is the type of task involved? Programmed decisions are made on tasks that are common and routine, whereas nonprogrammed decisions are made on unique and novel tasks. Second is the degree of reliance on organizational policies. In making programmed decisions, the decision maker can count on guidance from statements of organizational policy and procedure. However, nonprogrammed decisions require the use of creative solutions that are implemented for the first time; past solutions

TABLE 10-1

Programmed and Nonprogrammed Decisions: A Comparison

The two major types of organizational decisions—programmed decisions and nonprogrammed decisions—differ with respect to the types of task on which they are made, the degree to which solutions may be found in existing organizational policies, and the typical decision-making unit.

VARIABLE	TYPE OF DECISION	
	PROGRAMMED DECISIONS	NONPROGRAMMED DECISIONS
Type of task	*Simple, routine*	*Complex, creative*
Reliance on organizational policies	*Considerable guidance from past decisions*	*No guidance from past decisions*
Typical decision maker	*Lower-level workers (usually alone)*	*Upper-level supervisors (usually in groups)*

may provide little guidance. A final variable is the nature of the decision-making unit. Not surprisingly, nonprogrammed decisions typically are made by upper-level organizational personnel, whereas the more routine, well-structured decisions are usually relegated to lower-level personnel.[21]

CERTAIN VERSUS UNCERTAIN DECISIONS: HOW MUCH RISK IS INVOLVED?

Just think of how easy it would be to make decisions if we knew what the future held in store. Making the best investments in the stock market would simply be a matter of looking up the changes in tomorrow's newspaper. Of course, we never know exactly what the future holds, but we can be more certain at some times than others. Certainty about the factors on which decisions are made is highly desired in organizational decision making.

Degrees of certainty and uncertainty are expressed as statements of *risk*. All organizational decisions involve some degree of risk—ranging from complete certainty (no risk) to complete uncertainty, "a stab in the dark" (high risk). To make the best possible decisions in organizations, people seek to "manage" the risks they take—that is, they minimize the riskiness of a decision by gaining access to information relevant to the decision.[22]

What makes an outcome risky or not is the *probability* of obtaining the desired outcome. Decision makers attempt to obtain information about the probabilities, or odds, of certain events occurring given that other events have occurred. For example, a financial analyst may report that a certain stock has risen 80 percent of the time that the prime rate has dropped, or a meteorologist may report that the precipitation probability is 50 percent (i.e., in the past it rained or snowed half the time certain atmospheric conditions existed). These may be considered reports of *objective probabilities* because they are based on concrete, verifiable data. Many decisions are also based on *subjective probabilities*—personal beliefs or hunches about what will happen (see Figure 10-5). For example, a gambler who bets on a horse because it has a name similar to one of his children's, or a person who suspects it's going to rain because he just washed his car, is basing these judgments on subjective probabilities.

Obviously, uncertainty is an undesirable characteristic in decision-making situations. We may view much of what decision makers do in organizations as

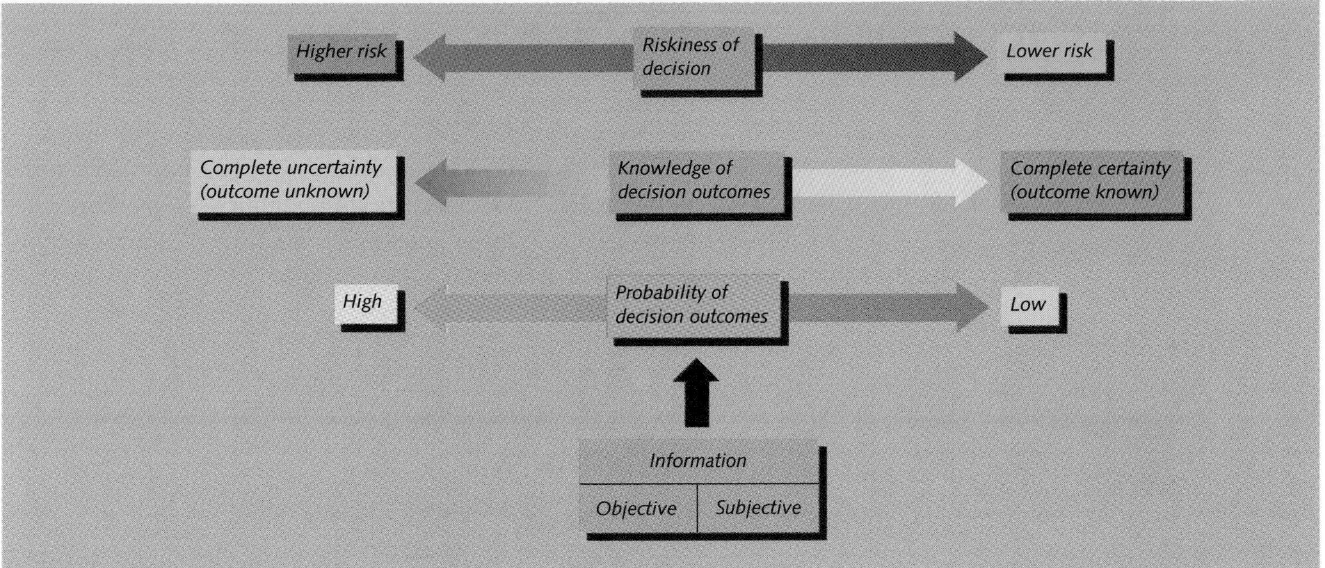

FIGURE 10-5

THE RISKINESS OF DECISIONS: A SUMMARY

Decisions differ with respect to their degree of riskiness, based on how certain (high probability) or uncertain (low probability) various outcomes may be. Information—both objective and subjective—is used as the basis for estimating the probability of a decision outcome.

attempting to reduce uncertainty so they can make better decisions. How do organizations respond when faced with highly uncertain conditions, when they don't know what the future holds for them? Studies have shown that decision uncertainty can be reduced by establishing linkages with other organizations. The more an organization knows about what another organization will do, the greater certainty it will have in making decisions.[23] This is part of a general tendency for organizational decision makers to respond to uncertainty by reducing the unpredictability of other organizations in their business environments. Those outside organizations with which managers have the greatest contact are most likely to be the ones whose actions are copied.[24]

In general, what reduces uncertainty in decision-making situations? The answer is *information*. Knowledge about the past and the present can be used to help make projections about the future. A modern executive's access to data needed to make important decisions may be as close as the nearest computer terminal. Indeed, computer technology has greatly aided people's ability to make decisions quickly, using the most accurate and thorough information available.[25] A variety of on-line information services are designed to provide organizational decision makers with the latest information relevant to the decisions they are making.

Of course, not all information needed to make decisions comes from computers. Many managerial decisions are also based on the decision maker's past experiences and intuition.[26] This is not to say that top managers rely on subjective information in making decisions (although they might), but that their history of past decisions—both successes and failures—is often given great weight in the decision-making process. In other words, when it comes to making decisions, people often rely on what has worked for them in the past. Part of the reason this strategy is often successful is because experienced decision makers tend to make better use of information relevant to the decisions they are making.[27] Individuals who have expertise in certain subjects know what information is most relevant and also how to interpret it to make the best decisions. It is therefore not surprising that people seek experienced professionals, such as doctors and lawyers who are seasoned veterans in their fields, when it comes to making important decisions. With high levels of expertise comes information relevant to assessing the riskiness of decision alternatives, and how to reduce it.

APPROACHES TO DECISION MAKING IN ORGANIZATIONS

We all like to think that we are "rational" people who make the best possible decisions. What does it mean to make a *rational* decision? Organizational scientists view **rational decisions** as ones that maximize the attainment of goals, whether they are the goals of a person, a group, or an entire organization.[28] In this section, we will present two models of decision making that derive from different assumptions about the rationality of individual decision makers: the *rational–economic model*, and the *administrative model*.

THE RATIONAL–ECONOMIC MODEL: IN SEARCH OF THE IDEAL DECISION

What would be the most rational way for an individual to go about making a decision? Economists interested in predicting market conditions and prices have relied on a rational-economic model of decision making, which assumes that decisions are perfect and rational in every way. An economically rational decision maker will attempt to maximize his or her profits by systematically searching for the optimum solution to a problem. For this to occur, the decision maker must have complete and perfect information, and be able to process all this information in an accurate and unbiased fashion.[29]

In many respects, rational-economic decisions follow the same steps outlined in the traditional, analytical model of decision making (see Figure 10-2). However, what makes the rational-economic approach special is that it calls for the decision maker to recognize *all* alternative courses of action (step 4), and to accurately and completely evaluate each one (step 5). It views decision makers as attempting to make *optimal* decisions.

Of course, the rational-economic approach to decision making does not fully appreciate the fallibility of the human decision maker. Based on the assumption that people have access to complete and perfect information and use it to make perfect decisions, the model can be considered a *normative* (also called *prescriptive*) approach—one that describes how decision makers ideally *ought* to behave so as to make the best possible decisions. It does not describe how decision makers actually behave in most circumstances. This task is undertaken by the next major approach to individual decision making, the *administrative* model (for a comparison between these two approaches, see Table 10-2.)

THE ADMINISTRATIVE MODEL: EXPLORING THE LIMITS OF HUMAN RATIONALITY

As you know from your own experience, people generally do not act in a completely rational-economic manner. To illustrate this point, consider how a personnel department might select a new receptionist. After several applicants are interviewed, the personnel manager might choose the best candidate seen so far and stop interviewing. Had the person been following a rational-economic model, he or she would have had to interview all possible candidates before deciding on the best one. However, by ending the search after finding a candidate who is just good enough, the manager is using a much simpler approach. The process used in

TABLE 10-2

The Administrative Model Versus the Rational–Economic Model: A Summary Comparison

The rational-economic model and the administrative model of individual decision making are based on a variety of different assumptions about how people make decisions.

ASSUMPTION	RATIONAL-ECONOMIC MODEL	ADMINISTRATIVE MODEL
Rationality of decision maker	*Perfect rationality*	*Bounded rationality*
Information available	*Complete access*	*Limited access*
Selection of alteratives	*Optimal choice*	*Satisfiying choice*
Type of model	*Normative (prescriptive)*	*Descriptive (proscriptive)*

this example characterizes an approach to decision making known as the **administrative model**.[30] This conceptualization recognizes that decision makers may have a limited view of the problems confronting them. The number of solutions that can be recognized or implemented is limited by the capabilities of the decision maker and the available resources of the organization. Also, decision makers do not have perfect information about the consequences of their decisions, so they cannot tell which one is best.

How are decisions made according to the administrative model? Instead of considering all possible solutions, as suggested by the rational-economic model, the administrative model recognizes that decision makers consider solutions as they become available. Then they decide on the first alternative that meets their criteria for acceptability. Thus, the decision maker selects a solution that may be just good enough, although not optimal. Such decisions are referred to as **satisficing decisions**. Of course, a satisficing decision is much easier to make than an optimal decision. In most decision-making situations, March and Simon note, satisficing decisions are acceptable and are more likely to be made than optimal ones.[31] They use the following analogy to compare the two types of decisions: *making an optimal decision is like searching a haystack for the sharpest needle, but making a satisficing decision is like searching a haystack for a needle just sharp enough with which to sew.*

As we have noted, it is often impractical for people to make completely optimal, rational decisions. The administrative model recognizes the **bounded rationality** under which most organizational decision makers must operate. The idea is that people lack the cognitive skills required to formulate and solve highly complex business problems in a completely objective, rational way.[32] It should not be surprising that the administrative model does a better job than the rational-economic model of describing how decision makers actually behave. In this respect, the approach is said to be *descriptive* (also called *proscriptive*) in nature. This interest in examining the actual, imperfect behavior of decision makers, rather than specifying the ideal, economically rational behaviors that decision makers ought to engage in, lies at the heart of the distinction between the administrative and rational-economic models. Our point is not that decision makers do not want to behave rationally, but that restrictions posed by the innate capabilities of the decision makers themselves and the social environments in which decisions are often made sometimes preclude "perfect" decisions. With this idea in mind, we will now explore some of the factors limiting optimal decisions.

IMPEDIMENTS TO OPTIMAL INDIVIDUAL DECISIONS

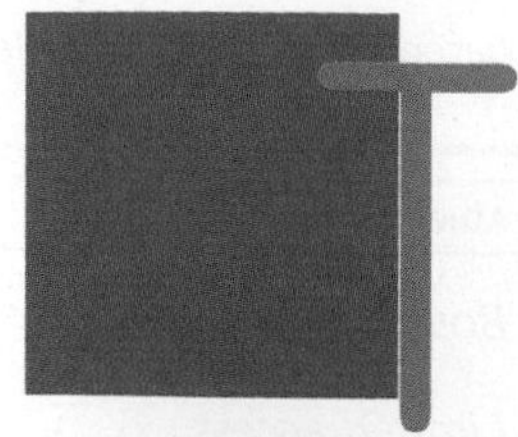

The picture of an imperfect decision maker operating in a complex world is supported by many studies that point to the seemingly confused and irrational decisions people make. The imperfections of decision makers take many forms, several of which we will review here.

COGNITIVE BIASES IN DECISION MAKING: FRAMING AND HEURISTICS

Probably the most obvious limitation on people's ability to make the best possible decisions is imposed by their restricted capacity to process information accurately and thoroughly, like a computer. For example, people often focus on irrelevant information in making decisions.[33] They also fail to use all the information made available to them.[34] Obviously, limitations in people's abilities to process complex information adversely influence their decisions. Beyond these general limitations in human information-processing capacity, we may note the existence of several systematic biases in the way people make decisions.[35]

FRAMING

One well-established decision-making bias has to do with the tendency for people to make different decisions based on how a problem is presented to them—that is, the **framing** of a problem. Specifically, Kahneman and Tversky have noted that problems framed in a manner that emphasizes the positive gains to be received tend to encourage conservative decisions (i.e., decision makers are said to be *risk averse*), whereas problems framed in a manner that emphasizes the potential losses to be suffered lead to *risk-seeking* decisions.[36] Consider the following example:

> The government is preparing to combat a rare disease expected to take 600 lives. Two alternative programs to combat the disease have been proposed, each of which, scientists believe, will have certain consequences. *Program A* will save 200 people, if adopted. *Program B* has a one-third chance of saving all 600 people, but a two-thirds chance of saving no one. Which program do you prefer?

When Kahneman and Tversky presented such a problem to people, 72 percent expressed a preference for Program A, and 28 percent for Program B. In other words, they preferred the "sure thing" of saving 200 people over the one-third possibility of saving them all. However, a curious thing happened when the description of the programs was framed in negative terms:

> *Program C* was described as allowing 400 people to die, if adopted. *Program D* was described as allowing a one-third probability that no one would die, and a two-thirds probability that all 600 would die. Now which program would you prefer?

Compare these four programs. Program C is just another way of stating the outcomes of Program A, and Program D is just another way of stating the outcomes of Program B. However, Programs C and D are framed in negative terms, which led

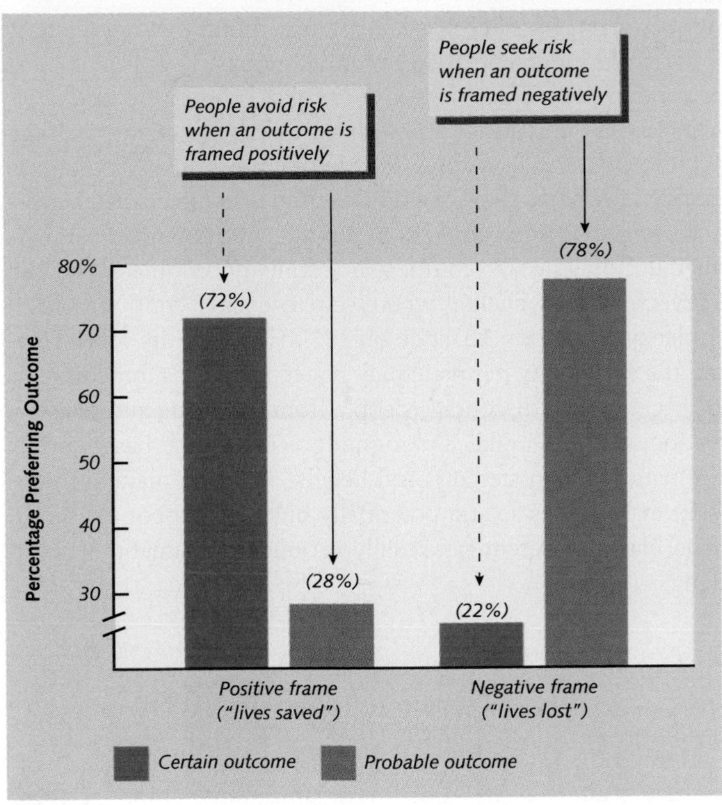

FIGURE 10-6

FRAMING EFFECTS: AN EMPIRICAL DEMONSTRATION

Research has found that differences in the framing of a problem have profound effects on the decisions individuals make. As shown here, when a problem is framed in positive terms (e.g., lives saved by a medical decision), people prefer a certain outcome, a sure thing (i.e., they avoid risk). However, when the same problem is framed in negative terms (e.g., lives lost by a medical decision), people prefer a less certain outcome (i.e., they seek risk). (Source: Based on data reported by Kahneman & Tversky, 1984; see Note 36.)

to opposite preferences: 22 percent favored Program C and 78 percent favored Program D (for a summary, see Figure 10-6). In other words, people tended to avoid risk when the problem was framed in terms of "lives saved" (i.e., in positive terms), but to seek risk when the problem was framed in terms of "lives lost" (i.e., in negative terms).

Scientists believe that such effects are due to the tendency for people to perceive equivalent situations framed differently as not really equivalent.[37] In other words, focusing on the glass as "half full" leads people to think about it differently from the way they think about it when it is presented as being "half empty," although they might recognize intellectually that the two are identical. Such findings illustrate our point that people are not completely rational decision makers, but are systematically biased by the cognitive distortions created by simple differences in the way situations are framed.

HEURISTICS

Framing effects are not the only cognitive biases to which decision makers are subjected. It also has been established that people often attempt to simplify the complex decisions they face by using **heuristics**—simple rules of thumb that guide them through a complex array of decision alternatives.[38] Although heuristics are potentially useful to decision makers, they represent potential impediments to decision making. Two very common types of heuristics may be identified.

First, the **availability heuristic** is the tendency for people to base their judgments on information that is readily available to them—even though it might not be accurate. Suppose, for example, that an executive needs to know the percentage of entering college freshmen who go on to graduate. There is not enough time to gather the appropriate statistics, so she bases her judgments on her own recollections of when she was a college student. If the percentage she recalls graduating, based on her own experiences, is higher or lower than the usual number, her estimate will be off accordingly. In other words, basing judgments solely on information that is conveniently available increases the possibility of making inaccurate decisions. Yet the availability heuristic is often used when making decisions.[39]

Second, the **representativeness heuristic** is the tendency to perceive others in stereotypical ways if they appear to be typical representatives of the category to which they belong. For example, suppose you believe that accountants are bright, mild-mannered individuals, whereas salespeople are less intelligent, but much more extraverted. Further, imagine that there are twice as many salespeople as accountants at a party. You meet someone at the party who is bright and mild-mannered. Although mathematically the odds are two-to-one that this person is a salesperson rather than an accountant, chances are you will guess that the individual is an accountant because she possesses the traits you associate with accountants. In other words, you believe this person to be representative of accountants in general—so much so that you would knowingly go against the mathematical odds in making your judgment. Research has consistently found that people tend to make this type of error in judgment, thereby providing good support for the existence of the representativeness heuristic.[40]

It is important to note that heuristics do not *always* lower the quality of decisions made. In fact, they can be quite helpful. People often use rules of thumb to help simplify the complex decisions they face. For example, architects use heuristics when deciding where to position rooms in a building, and financial planners rely on heuristics when deciding how to compose investment portfolios.[41] We also use heuristics in our everyday lives, such as when we play chess ("control the center of the board") or blackjack ("hit on 16, stick on 17"). However, the representativeness heuristic and the availability heuristic may be recognized as impediments to superior decisions because they discourage people from collecting and processing as much information as they should. Making judgments on the basis of only readily available information, or on stereotypical beliefs, although making things simple for the decision maker, does so at a potentially high cost—poor decisions. Thus, these systematic biases represent potentially serious impediments to individual decision making.

ESCALATION OF COMMITMENT: THROWING GOOD MONEY AFTER BAD

Because decisions are made all the time in organizations, some of these inevitably will be unsuccessful. What would you say is the rational thing to do when a poor decision has been made? Obviously, the ineffective action should be stopped or reversed. In other words, it would make sense to "cut your losses and run." However, people don't always respond in this manner. In fact, it is not unusual to find that ineffective decisions are sometimes followed up with still further ineffective decisions. Imagine, for example, that you have invested money in a company that appears to be failing. Rather than lose your initial investment, you may invest still more money in the hope of salvaging your first investment. The more you invest, the more you may be tempted to save those earlier investments by making later investments. That is to say, people sometimes may be found "throwing good money after bad" because they have "too much invested to quit." This is known as the **escalation of commitment phenomenon**—the tendency for people to continue to support previously unsuccessful courses of action because they have sunk costs invested in them.[42]

Although this might not seem like a rational thing to do, this strategy is frequently followed. Consider, for example, how large banks and governments may invest money in foreign governments in the hope of turning them around even though such a result becomes increasingly unlikely. Similarly, the organizers of Expo '86 in British Columbia continued pouring money into the fair long after it became apparent that it would be a big money-losing proposition.[43] Why do people do this? If you think about it, you may realize that the failure to back your own previous courses of action in an organization would be taken as an admission of failure—a politically difficult act to face in an organization. In other words, people may be very concerned about "saving face"—looking good in the eyes of others. Staw and his associates have recognized that this tendency for *self-justification* is primarily responsible for people's inclination to protect their beliefs about themselves as rational, competent decision makers by convincing themselves and others that they made the right decision all along, and are willing to back it up.[44]

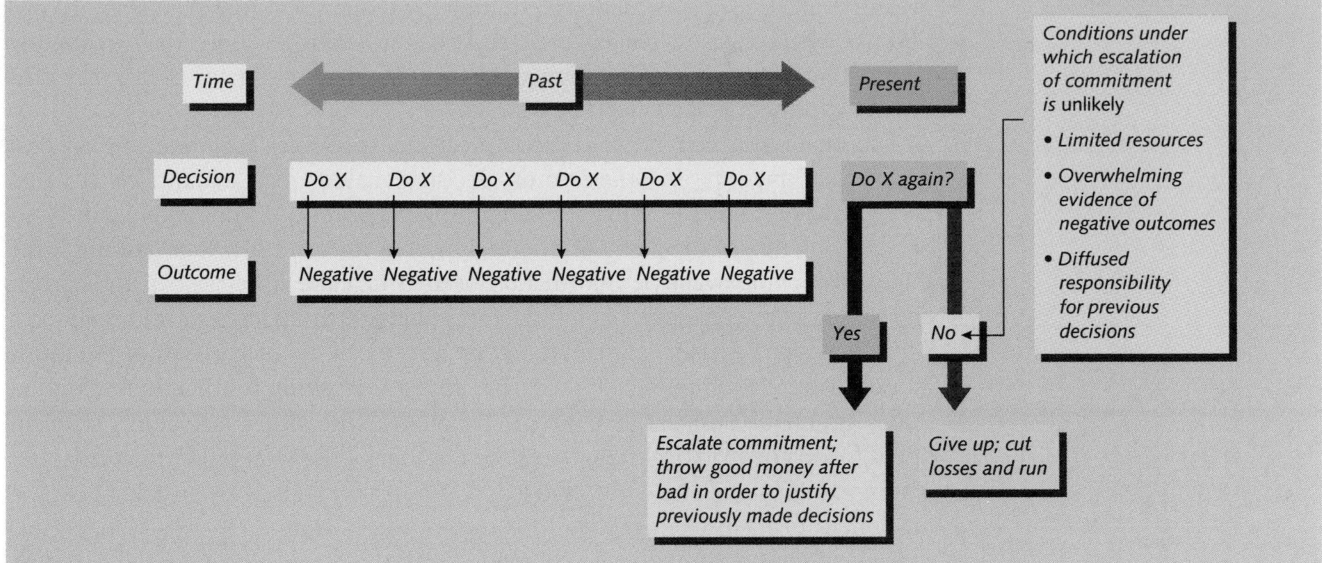

FIGURE 10-7
ESCALATION OF COMMITMENT: A SUMMARY OF THE PHENOMENON
According to the escalation-of-commitment *phenomenon, people who have repeatedly made poor decisions will continue to support those failing courses of action in order to justify their decisions. Under some conditions, summarized here, the effect will not occur.*

Although there are other possible reasons for the escalation of commitment phenomenon, research supports the self-justification explanation.[45,46] For a summary of the escalation of commitment phenomenon, see Figure 10-7.

Recently, researchers have noted several conditions under which people will refrain from escalating their commitment to a failing course of action.[47] Notably, it has been found that people will stop making failing investments under conditions in which the *available funds for making further investments are limited*, and the *threat of failure is overwhelmingly obvious*.[48] For example, when the Long Island Lighting Company decided in 1989 to abandon plans to operate a nuclear power plant in Shoreham, New York, it was in the face of twenty-three years' worth of intense political and financial pressure (a strong antinuclear movement and billions of dollars in cost overruns).[49] It also has been found that people will refrain from escalating commitment when they can *diffuse their responsibility for the earlier failing actions*. That is, the more people feel they are just one of several people responsible for a failing course of action, the less likely they are to commit to further failing actions.[50] In other words, the less one is responsible for an earlier failure, the less he or she may be motivated to justify those earlier failures by making further investments in them. To conclude, the escalation of commitment phenomenon represents a type of irrational decision making that may occur, but only under certain circumstances.

ORGANIZATIONAL BARRIERS TO EFFECTIVE DECISIONS

Thus far we have emphasized the human cognitive shortcomings and biases that limit effective decision making. However, we must not ignore several important organizational factors that also interfere with rational decisions. Indeed, the situations faced by many organizational decision makers cannot help but interfere with their capacity to make decisions.

One obvious factor is *time constraints*. Many important organizational decisions are made under severe time pressure. Under such circumstances, it is often impossible for exhaustive decision making to occur. This is particularly the case when organizations face crisis situations requiring immediate decisions. Under such conditions, when decision makers feel "rushed into" taking action, they frequently restrict their search for information and consideration of alternatives that may otherwise help them make effective decisions.[51]

The quality of many organizational decisions also may be limited by *political "face-saving" pressure*. In other words, decision makers may make decisions that help them look good to others, although the resulting decisions might not be in the best interest of their organizations. Imagine, for example, how an employee might distort the available information needed to make a decision if the correct decision would jeopardize his job. Unfortunately, such misuses of information to support desired decisions are all too common (recall our discussion of the problem of distorted communication in Chapter 9). One study on this topic reported that a group of businesspeople working on a group decision-making problem opted for an adequate—although less than optimal—decision rather than risk generating serious conflicts with their fellow group members.[52] In an actual case, a proponent of medical inoculation for the flu was so interested in advancing his pro-inoculation position that he proceeded with the inoculation program although there was only a 2 percent chance of an epidemic.[53] Apparently, people often make the decisions they need to make to cultivate the best impressions although these may not be the best ones for their organizations.

Besides the time constraints and political pressures that often limit the quality of organizational decisions, note also the limitations imposed by moral and ethical constraints—what is known as *bounded discretion*.[54] According to this idea, decision makers limit their actions to those that fall within the bounds of current moral and ethical standards.[55] So, although engaging in illegal activities such as stealing may optimize an organization's profits (at least in the short run), ethical considerations strongly discourage such actions. (As you know, it is often extremely difficult to determine whether or not a decision we are contemplating is ethical. For some suggestions as to how to make such judgments, see the Ethical Workplace section below.)

THE ETHICAL WORKPLACE

TESTING THE ETHICS OF YOUR CONTEMPLATED DECISIONS: QUESTIONS TO ASK YOURSELF

If you consider all the moral scandals that have made headlines in recent years (e.g., stock brokers accused of defrauding their customers, religious leaders accused of stealing from their ministries), it's easy to see that people often have difficulty judging what's right and behaving accordingly. Unfortunately, cheating and stealing have become more commonplace than we would like.[56] Even those of us who subscribe to high moral values are sometimes tempted to behave unethically. If you're thinking, "not me," then ask yourself: Have you ever taken home small articles of company property (e.g., pencils, tape) for personal use? Or, have you ever made personal copies on the company copier, or fudged a little on your expense account?

If the answer is "yes," you're probably thinking, "Sure, but companies *expect* employees to do these things." And, of course, taking home a pencil is not the same as making off with a $1-million payroll. Although this may be true, we cannot ignore the fact that people often attempt to justify their actions by rationalizing that they are not really unethical. For example, you may find yourself saying something like "Everybody's doing it, so it must be OK." This kind of rationalization makes it possible for us to talk ourselves into making unethical decisions, thinking that they are really not so bad. To avoid such situations—and, thereby to improve ethical decision making—it may be useful to run your contemplated decisions through an ethics test.[57] To do so, ask yourself the following questions:

1. *Does it violate the obvious "shall-nots"?* Although many people realize that "thou shall not lie, or cheat, or steal," they do it anyway. So, instead of thinking of a way around such prohibitions (e.g., by convincing yourself that "it's acceptable in this situation"), avoid violating these well-established societal rules altogether.
2. *Will anyone get hurt?* Philosophers consider an action to be ethical to the extent that it brings the greatest good to the greatest number. Thus, if someone may be harmed in any way as a result of your actions, you should probably rethink your decision; it's probably unethical.
3. *How would you feel if your decision were reported on the front page of your newspaper?* If your decision is really ethical, you wouldn't have any reason to worry about having it made public. (In fact, you'd probably be pleased to receive the publicity.) However, if you find yourself uneasy about answering this question affirmatively, the decision you are contemplating may be unethical.
4. *What if you did it 100 times?* Sometimes an unethical action doesn't seem so bad because it's done only once. In such a case, the damage might not be so bad, although the action still might not be ethical. However, if the act you're contemplating appears to be more wrong if it were done 100 times, then it's probably also wrong the first time.
5. *How would you feel if someone did it to you?* If something you are thinking of doing to another really is ethical, you would probably find it acceptable if your situations were reversed. Thus, if you have any doubts as to how you'd feel being the person affected by your decision, you may wish to reconsider.
6. *What's your gut feeling?* Sometimes things just look bad, and probably because they *are*. If your actions are unethical, you probably can tell by listening to that little voice inside your head. The trick is to listen to *that* voice and to silence the one that tells you to do otherwise—although we acknowledge that this may be easier said than done.

To be sure, considering these questions will not transform a devil into an angel. Still, they may be useful for judging the ethicalness of the decisions you may be contemplating. Your answers to these six questions may help you avoid rationalizing that unethical acts are really ethical. And once we recognize that the decisions we are thinking of making may not be ethical, we are well on the way to behaving in an ethical fashion.

GROUP DECISIONS: DO TOO MANY COOKS SPOIL THE BROTH?

Decision-making groups are a well-established fact of modern organizational life. Groups such as committees, study teams, task forces, or review panels are often charged with the responsibility for making important business decisions.[58] They are so common, in fact, that it has been said that some administrators spend as much as 80 percent of their time in committee meetings.[59] Given this, it is important to consider the strengths and weaknesses of using groups to make organizational decisions. Refer to our summary of these factors in Table 10-3.

There is little doubt that much can be gained by using decision-making groups. Several potential advantages of this approach may be identified. First, bringing people together may increase the amount of knowledge and information available for making good decisions. In other words, there may be a *pooling of resources*. A related benefit is that in decision-making groups there can be a *specialization of labor*. With enough people around to share the workload, individuals can perform only those tasks at which they are best, thereby potentially improving the quality of the group's efforts. Another benefit is that group decisions are likely to enjoy

TABLE 10-3

Group Decision Making: Pros and Cons

Should groups be used to make decisions? Both advantages and disadvantages are associated with using groups rather than individuals to make decisions.

ADVANTAGES OF GROUPS	DISADVANTAGES OF GROUPS
• *Potential pooling of resources*	• *Tendency to waste time*
• *Opportunities for specialization of labor*	• *Potential for group conflict*
• *Decisions likely to be accepted*	• *Possible intimidation by group leader*

greater acceptance than individual decisions. People involved in making decisions may be expected to understand those decisions better and be more committed to carrying them out than decisions made by someone else.[60]

Of course, there are also some problems associated with using decision-making groups. One obvious drawback is that groups are likely to *waste time*. The time spent socializing before getting down to business may be a drain on the group and be very costly to organizations. Another possible problem is that potential disagreement over important matters may breed ill will and *group conflict*. Although constructive disagreement can actually lead to better group outcomes, highly disruptive conflict may interfere with group decisions (see Chapter 11). Indeed, with corporate power and personal pride at stake, it is not at all surprising to find that lack of agreement can cause bad feelings to develop between group members. Finally, we may expect groups to be ineffective sometimes because of members' *intimidation by group leaders*. A group composed of several "yes-men" or "yes-women" trying to please a dominant leader tends to discourage open and honest discussion of solutions. In view of these problems, it is easy to understand the old adage "A camel is a horse put together by a committee."

Given the several pros and cons of using groups to make decisions, we must conclude that neither groups nor individuals are always superior. Obviously, there are important tradeoffs involved in using either one to make decisions.

COMPARING GROUP AND INDIVIDUAL DECISIONS: WHEN ARE TWO (OR MORE) HEADS BETTER THAN ONE?

Since there are advantages associated with both group and individual decision makers, a question arises as to *when* each should be used. That is, under what conditions might individuals or groups be expected to make superior decisions? Fortunately, research has addressed this important question.[61]

WHEN ARE GROUPS SUPERIOR TO INDIVIDUALS?

Imagine a situation in which an important decision has to be made about a complex problem—such as whether one company should merge with another. This is not the kind of problem about which any one individual working alone would be able to make a good decision. Its highly complex nature may overwhelm even an expert, thereby setting the stage for a group to do a better job.

Whether a group actually will do better than an individual depends on several important considerations. For one, we must consider who is in the group. Successful groups tend to be composed of *heterogeneous group members with complementary skills*. So, for example, a group composed of lawyers, accountants, real estate agents, and other experts may make much better decisions on the merger problem than would a group composed of specialists in only one field. Indeed, research has shown that the diversity of opinions offered by group members is one of the major advantages of using groups to make decisions.[62]

As you might imagine, it is not enough simply to have skills. For a group to be successful, its members must also be able to freely communicate their ideas to each other in an open, nonhostile manner (see Chapter 10). Conditions under which one individual (or group) intimidates another from contributing his or her expertise can easily negate any potential gain associated with composing groups of heterogeneous experts (see Chapter 8). After all, *having* expertise and being able to make a contribution by *using* that expertise are two different things. Indeed, research has shown that only when the contributions of the most qualified group members are given the greatest weight does the group derive any benefit from that member's presence.[63] Thus, for groups to be superior to individuals they must be composed of a heterogeneous collection of experts with complementary skills who can freely and openly contribute to their group's product.

As an example of this, Michaelsen, Watson, and Black studied the performance of 222 groups of approximately six students who worked together extensively on class projects (team learning exercises) over the course of a semester.[64] Assignments to groups were made so as to create units that were as broadly diversified as possible. The teams had to work together on answering exam questions about the material they studied. The questions were generally difficult, some requiring the ability to analyze and synthesize complex concepts. The researchers were interested in comparing the performance of the groups as a whole with that of individual members. Their findings are summarized in Figure 10-8.

As shown in Figure 10-8, the average score on the exams completed jointly by group members was not only higher than that of the average group member, but also higher than that of the best group member. In fact, of the 222 groups studied, 215 (97 percent) outperformed their best member, 4 groups tied their best member, and only 3 groups scored lower than their best member. Clearly, these findings support the idea that *on complex tasks, a benefit is derived from combining individuals into groups that goes beyond the contribution of what the best group member can do*. People can help each other solve complex problems not only by pooling their resources, but also by correcting each other's answers and assisting each other to come up with ideas. There is also likely to be an intangible *synergy* created when a group of people help each other and create a climate for success.

In contrast to complex decision tasks, imagine a situation in which a judgment is required on a simple problem with a readily verifiable answer. For example, imagine that you are asked to translate a phrase from a relatively obscure language into English. Groups might do better than individuals on such a task, but probably because the odds are increased that someone in the group knows the language and can perform the translation for the group. However, there is no reason to expect that even a large group will be able to perform such a task better than a single individual who has the required expertise. In fact, an expert working alone may do even better than a group. This is because an expert individual performing a simple task may be distracted by others and suffer from having to convince them of the correctness of his or her solution. For this reason, exceptional individuals tend

FIGURE 10-8
GROUP VERSUS INDIVIDUAL PERFORMANCE ON A COMPLEX TASK: EXPERIMENTAL EVIDENCE
Research comparing the performance of groups and individuals on a complex learning task has shown that groups as a whole performed better than either the average individual or even the best individual in the group. Such findings support the idea that the benefit of working in groups goes beyond the simple combination of individual skills. (Source: Based on data reported by Michaelsen, Watson, & Black, 1989; see Note 64.)

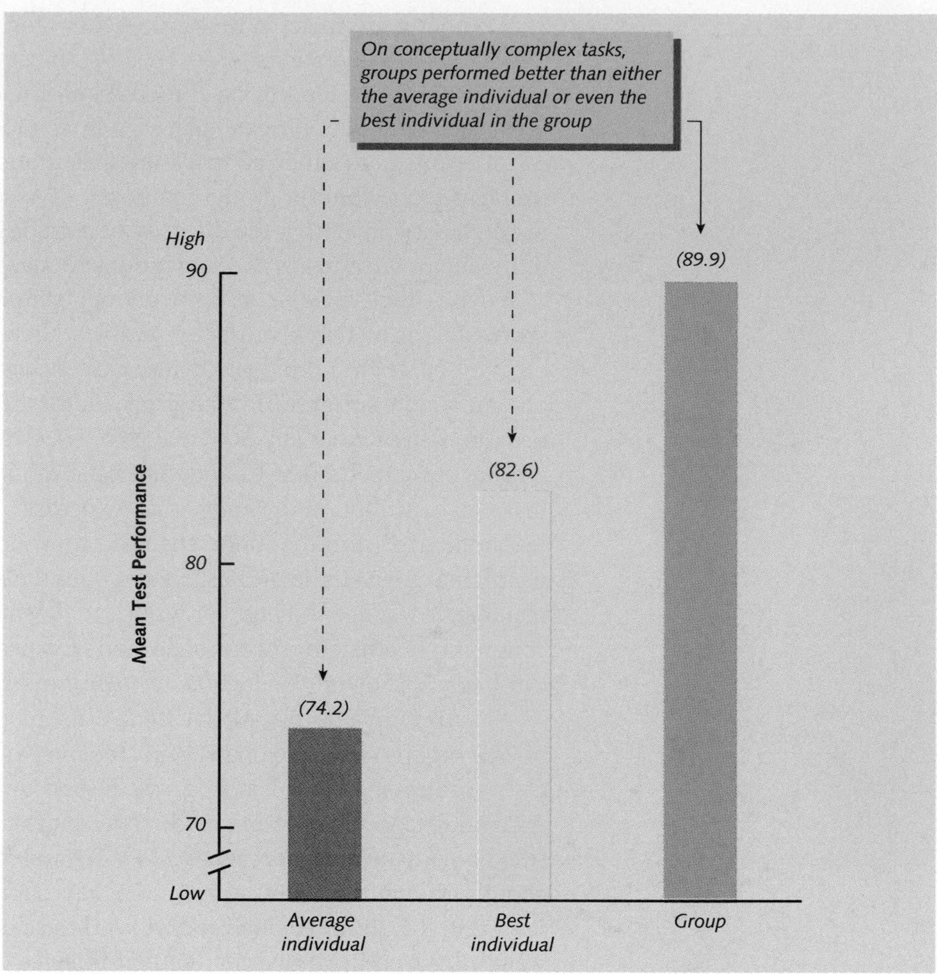

to outperform entire committees on simple tasks.[65] In such cases, for groups to benefit from a pooling of resources, there must be some resources to pool. The pooling of ignorance does not help. In other words, the question "Are two heads better than one?" can be answered this way: *on simple tasks, two heads may be better than one if at least one of those heads has enough of what it takes to succeed.*

In summary, whether groups perform better than individuals depends on the nature of the task performed and the expertise of the people involved. We have summarized some of these key considerations in Figure 10-9.

WHEN ARE INDIVIDUALS SUPERIOR TO GROUPS?

As we have described thus far, groups may be expected to perform better than the average or even the exceptional individual under certain conditions. However, there are also conditions under which individuals are superior to groups.

Most of the problems faced by organizations require a great deal of creative thinking. For example, a company deciding how to use a newly developed adhesive in its consumer products is facing decisions on a poorly structured task. Although you would expect that the complexity of such creative problems would give groups a natural advantage, this is not the case. In fact, research has shown that *on poorly structured, creative tasks, individuals perform better than groups.*[66]

An approach to solving creative problems commonly used by groups is **brainstorming**. This technique was developed by advertising executive Alex Osborn as a tool for coming up with creative, new ideas.[67] The members of brainstorming

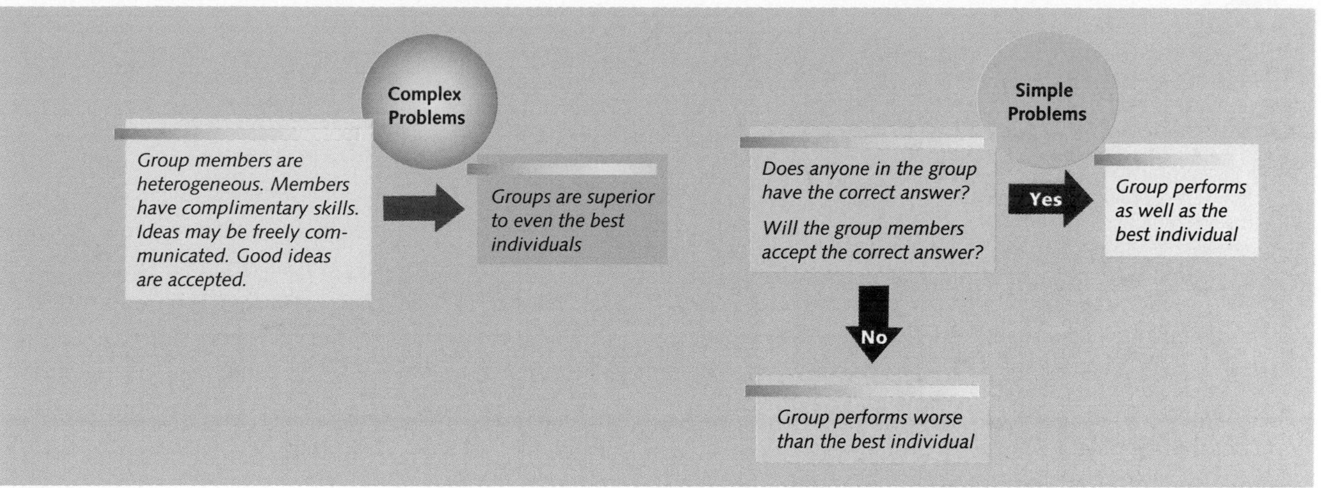
Complex
Problems
Group members are heterogeneous. Members have complimentary skills. Ideas may be freely communicated. Good ideas are accepted.
Groups are superior to even the best individuals
Simple
Problems
Does anyone in the group have the correct answer?
Will the group members accept the correct answer?
Yes
Group performs as well as the best individual
No
Group performs worse than the best individual

FIGURE 10-9
GROUP DECISIONS: WHEN ARE THEY SUPERIOR TO INDIVIDUAL DECISIONS?
When performing complex problems, groups are superior to individuals if certain conditions prevail (e.g., members have heterogeneous, complementary skills, they can freely share ideas, and good ideas are accepted). However, when performing simple problems, groups perform only as well as the best individual in the group, and then only if that person has the correct answer and that response is accepted by the group.

groups are encouraged to present their ideas in an uncritical way and to discuss freely and openly all ideas on the floor (see Figure 10-10). Specifically, members of brainstorming groups are required to follow four main rules: (1) avoid criticizing others' ideas, (2) share even far-out suggestions, (3) offer as many comments as possible, and (4) build on others' ideas to create your own.

Does brainstorming improve the quality of creative decisions? To answer this question, Bouchard and his associates conducted a study in which they compared the effectiveness of individuals and brainstorming groups working on creative problems.[68] Specifically, participants were given thirty-five minutes to consider the consequences of situations such as "What if everybody went blind?" or "What if everybody grew an extra thumb on each hand?" Clearly, the novel nature of such problems requires a great deal of creativity. Comparisons were made of the number of solutions generated by groups of four or seven people and a like number of individuals working on the same problems alone. The results were clear: individuals were significantly more productive than groups.

In summary, groups perform worse than individuals when working on creative tasks. A great part of the problem is that some individuals feel inhibited by the presence of others even though one rule of brainstorming is that even far-out ideas may be shared. To the extent that people wish to avoid feeling foolish as a result of saying silly things, their creativity may be inhibited when in groups. Similarly, groups may inhibit creativity by slowing down the process of bringing ideas to fruition. (Because brainstorming is so popular in organizations, it is useful to consider ways of minimizing these problems. For a look at one such method, see the Quest for Quality section on the following page).

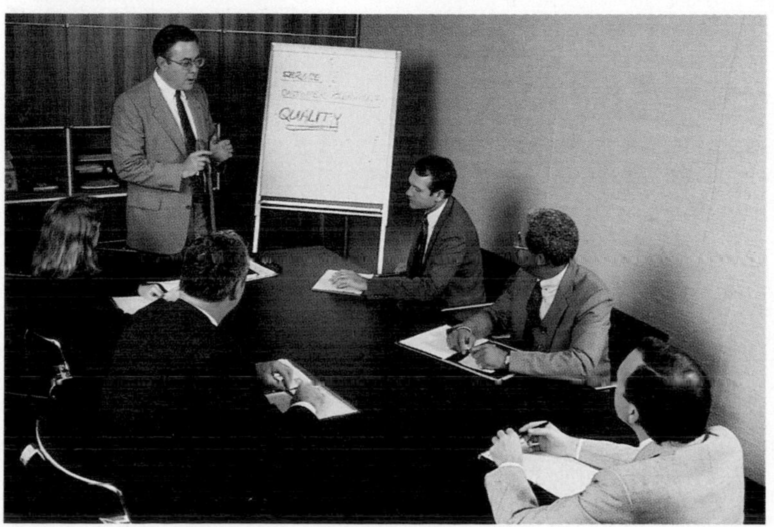
QUALITY

FIGURE 10-10
BRAINSTORMING: A POPULAR TOOL FOR MAKING CREATIVE DECISIONS
To develop the most creative solutions to problems, members of brainstorming groups are required to be uncritical of others and to freely discuss all ideas presented.

THE QUEST FOR QUALITY

ELECTRONIC BRAINSTORMING: AN EFFECTIVE MEANS OF GENERATING IDEAS

Organizations are always in need of creative new ideas. Unfortunately, many times when people put their heads together to generate them, such brainstorming comes up short.

Part of the problem with the brainstorming process is that the production of ideas is blocked by others. In other words, people may be prevented from thinking of or expressing an idea because they are required to listen to someone else and, as a result, forget what they were about to say—a problem referred to as *production blocking*. The larger the group, the more this problem is likely to be. Fortunately, through the use of technology, a way has been found to combat the inefficiency of brainstorming groups.

Specifically, organizational scientists recently have been experimenting with a technique for improving the quality of groups' creative output known as *electronic brainstorming*. In this technique, groups of people do brainstorming electronically—that is, by sitting in front of a computer terminal that allows them to simultaneously review others' suggestions while entering their own.[69] Although the group members are in different locations and cannot see each other, they can communicate with each other via anonymous messages they type that appear on the others' monitors. Does electronic brainstorming work? To find out, Gallupe and his associates compared the quality of ideas generated by groups of two, four, and six who brainstormed either electronically, or by using the traditional face-to-face method.[70] The subjects were Canadian college students asked to brainstorm about ways of improving security on their college campus and ways of attracting tourists to their small town. Did the way the brainstorming was conducted have any impact on the number of high-quality ideas generated by the groups? The data shown in Figure 10-11 suggest that the answer is clearly "yes."

These results show that as group size increased, the number of high-quality ideas generated by face-to-face brainstorming groups increased only slightly, whereas the corresponding number for electronic brainstorming groups increased dramatically. (High-quality ideas were ones

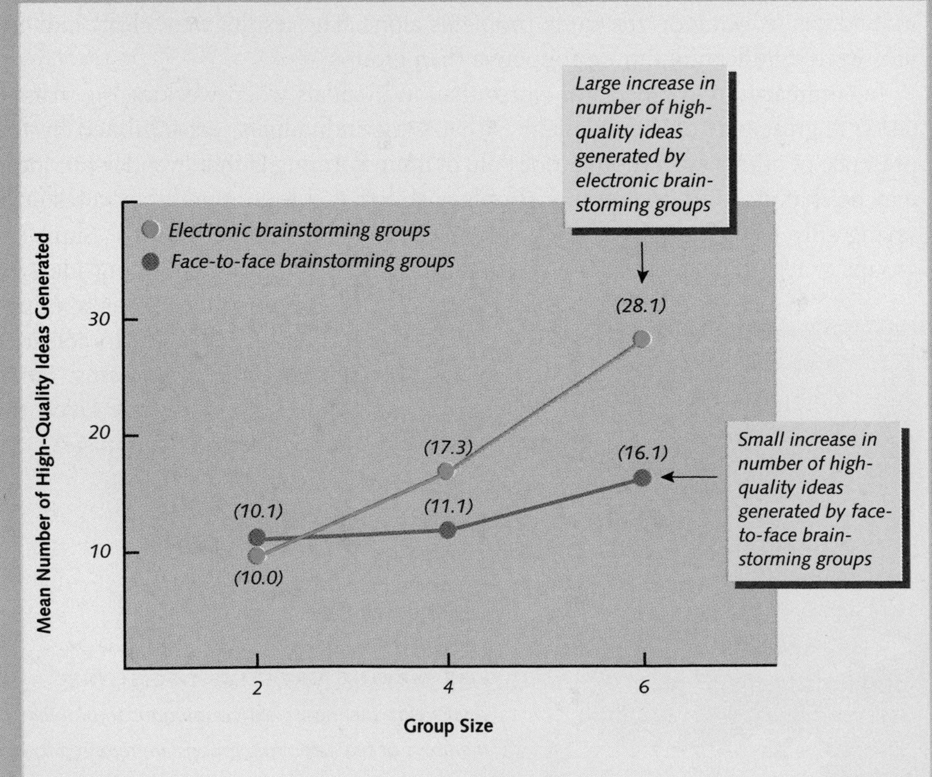

FIGURE 10-11
FACE-TO-FACE VERSUS ELECTRONIC BRAINSTORMING: AN EXPERIMENTAL COMPARISON
People in a recent experiment brainstormed creative solutions to problems in both face-to-face groups and electronic groups of either two, four, or six members. Although larger groups generated more high-quality solutions than smaller groups, the increase was far greater when electronic brainstorming was used. (Source: Based on data reported by Gallupe, Dennis, Cooper, Valacich, Bastianutti, & Nunamaker, 1993; see Note 70.)

considered both original and feasible by two expert judges.) Because the same groups did brainstorming both electronically and using the standard-face-to-face method (first using one problem and then the other), the researchers were able to dismiss the possibility that one set of groups happened to be better than the other. Instead, the researchers noted that the rate of production blocking remained at low levels for groups of all sizes during electronic brainstorming, although it increased during face-to-face brainstorming groups as the group size got larger. In other words, the computer terminals made it possible for people to express more of their ideas without interfering with others.

Gallupe and his associates also noted that as group size increased group members became more concerned about what others thought of their ideas—but only in face-to-face groups. When groups brainstormed electronically, it was not possible for people to tell who generated what ideas, thus removing the fear that an idea will be rejected. In other words, electronic brainstorming appears to have reduced the effects of *evaluation apprehension* that may well restrict people from contributing as much as they might to brainstorming groups (recall our discussion of this phenomenon in Chapter 8).

This study suggests that electronic brainstorming is an effective way of getting the most out of groups. It can be used as a means of encouraging people to share their ideas without fear of rejection while also keeping people from interfering with each other's ideas. Moreover, electronic brainstorming makes it possible for groups to engage in brainstorming although members may be physically separated from each other. Using computer technology to bring people together to "talk" to each other appears to be an effective way of getting many of the benefits of using groups that would be hoped for, while avoiding some of the key problems that hold them back.

GROUPTHINK: TOO MUCH COHESIVENESS CAN BE A DANGEROUS THING

One reason groups may fare so poorly on complex tasks lies in the dynamics of group interaction. As we noted in Chapter 8, when members of a group develop a very strong group spirit—or a high level of *cohesiveness*—they sometimes become so concerned about not disrupting the like-mindedness of the group that they may be reluctant to challenge the group's decisions. When this happens, group members tend to isolate themselves from outside information, and the process of critical thinking deteriorates. This phenomenon is referred to as **groupthink**.[71]

The concept of groupthink was proposed initially as an attempt to explain ineffective decisions made by U.S. government officials that led to fiascoes such as the Bay of Pigs invasion in Cuba and the Vietnam War.[72] Analyses of each of these cases have revealed that the president's advisers actually *discouraged* more effective decision making. An examination of the conditions under which the decision was made to launch the ill-fated space shuttle *Challenger* in January 1986 revealed that it too resulted from groupthink.[73] Post hoc analyses of conversations between key personnel suggested that the team that made the decision to launch the shuttle under freezing conditions did so while insulating itself from the engineers who knew how the equipment should function. Given that NASA had such a successful history, the decision makers operated with a sense of invulnerability. They also worked so closely together and were under such intense pressure to launch the shuttle without further delay that they all collectively went along with the launch decision, creating the illusion of unanimous agreement. For a more precise description of groupthink (and a practical guide to recognizing its symptoms), see Table 10-4.

TABLE 10-4

Groupthink: Its Warning Signals

Sometimes in highly cohesive groups the members become more concerned about maintaining positive group spirit than about making the most realistic decisions—a phenomenon known as groupthink. The major symptoms of groupthink are identified and described here.

SYMPTOM	DESCRIPTION
Illusion of invulnerability	*Ignoring obvious danger signals, being overoptimistic, and taking extreme risks*
Collective rationalization	*Discrediting or ignoring warning signals that run contrary to group thinking*
Unquestioned morality	*Believing that the group's position is ethical and moral and that all others are inherently evil*
Excessive negative stereotyping	*Viewing the opposing side as being too negative to warrant serious consideration*
Strong conformity pressure	*Discouraging the expression of dissenting opinions under the threat of expulsion for disloyalty*
Self-censorship of dissenting ideas	*Withholding dissenting ideas and counter arguments, keeping them to oneself*
Illusion of unanimity	*Sharing the false belief that everyone in the group agrees with its judgments*
Self-appointed mind guards	*Protecting the group from negative, threatening information*

Source: Adapted from Janis, 1982; see Note 71.

Groupthink occurs not only in governmental decision making, of course, but also in the private sector (although the failures may be less well publicized). For example, analyses of the business policies of large corporations such as Lockheed and Chrysler have suggested that it was the failure of top management teams to respond to changing market conditions that at one time led them to the brink of disaster.[74] The problem is that members of very cohesive groups may have considerable confidence in their group's decisions, making them unlikely to raise doubts about these actions (i.e., "the group seems to know what it's doing"). As a result, they may suspend their own critical thinking in favor of conforming to the group. When group members become fiercely loyal to each other, they may ignore potentially useful information from other sources that challenges the group's decisions. The result of this process is that the group's decisions may be completely uninformed, irrational, or even immoral.[75]

So as not to conclude on an entirely pessimistic note, we point out that several strategies can effectively combat groupthink. Here are a few proven techniques.

1. *Promote open inquiry*. Remember: groupthink arises in response to group members' reluctance to "rock the boat." Group leaders should encourage members

to be skeptical of all solutions and to avoid reaching premature agreements. It sometimes helps to play the role of *devil's advocate*, that is, to intentionally find fault with a proposed solution.[76] Research has shown that when this is done, groups make higher-quality decisions.[77] In fact, some corporate executives use exercises in which conflict is intentionally generated just so the negative aspects of a decision can be identified before it's too late.[78] This is not to say that leaders should be argumentative. Rather, raising a nonthreatening question to force both sides of an issue can be very helpful in improving the quality of decisions.

2. *Use subgroups*. Because the decisions made by any one group may be the result of groupthink, basing decisions on the recommendations of two groups is a useful check. If the two groups disagree, a discussion of their differences is likely to raise important issues. However, if the two groups agree, you can be relatively confident that their conclusions are not *both* the result of groupthink.

3. *Admit shortcomings*. When groupthink occurs, group members feel very confident that they are doing the right thing. Such feelings of perfection discourage people from considering opposing information. However, if group members acknowledge some of the flaws and limitations of their decisions, they may be more open to corrective influences. Keep in mind that no decision is perfect. Asking others to point out their misgivings about a group's decisions may help avoid the illusion of perfection that contributes to groupthink.

4. *Hold second-chance meetings*. Before implementing a decision, it is a good idea to hold a *second-chance meeting* during which group members are asked to express any doubts and propose any new ideas they may have. Alfred P. Sloan, former head of General Motors, is known to have postponed acting on important matters until any group disagreement was resolved.[79] As people get tired of working on problems, they may hastily reach agreement on a solution. Second-chance meetings can be useful devices for seeing if a solution still seems good even after "sleeping on it."

Given the extremely adverse effects groupthink can have on organizations, practicing managers would be wise to put these simple suggestions into action. The alternative—facing the consequences of groupthink—is much too serious to do otherwise.

IMPROVING THE EFFECTIVENESS OF GROUP DECISIONS: SOME TECHNIQUES

As we have made clear in this chapter, certain advantages can be gained from sometimes using individuals and sometimes using groups to make decisions. A decision-making technique that combines the best features of groups and individuals, while minimizing the disadvantages, would be ideal. Several techniques designed to realize the "best of both worlds" have been widely used in organizations. These include techniques that involve the structuring of group discussions in special ways, as well as improving the skills individuals may bring to the decision-making situation.

THE DELPHI TECHNIQUE: DECISIONS BY EXPERT CONSENSUS

According to Greek mythology, people interested in seeing what fate the future held for them could seek the counsel of the Delphic oracle. Today's organizational decision makers sometimes consult experts to help them make the best decisions as well. A technique developed by the Rand Corporation, known as the **Delphi technique**, represents a systematic way of collecting and organizing the opinions of several experts into a single decision.[80] The steps in the process are summarized in Figure 10-12.

The Delphi process starts by enlisting the cooperation of experts and presenting the problem to them, usually in a letter. Each expert then proposes what he or she believes is the most appropriate solution. The group leader compiles all these individual responses and reproduces them so they can be shared with all the other experts in a second mailing. At this point, each expert comments on the others' ideas and proposes another solution. These individual solutions are returned to the leader, who compiles them and looks for a consensus of opinions. If a consensus is reached, the decision is made. If not, the process of sharing reactions with others is repeated until a consensus is eventually obtained.

The obvious advantage of using the Delphi technique to make decisions is that it allows the collection of expert judgments without the great costs and logistical difficulties of bringing many experts together for a face-to-face meeting. However, the technique is not without limitations. As you might imagine, the Delphi process can be very time consuming. Sending out letters, waiting for everyone to respond, transcribing and disseminating the responses, and repeating the process until a consensus is reached can take quite a long time. Experts have estimated that the minimum time required to use the Delphi technique would be more than forty-four days. In one case, the process took five months to complete.[81] Obviously, the

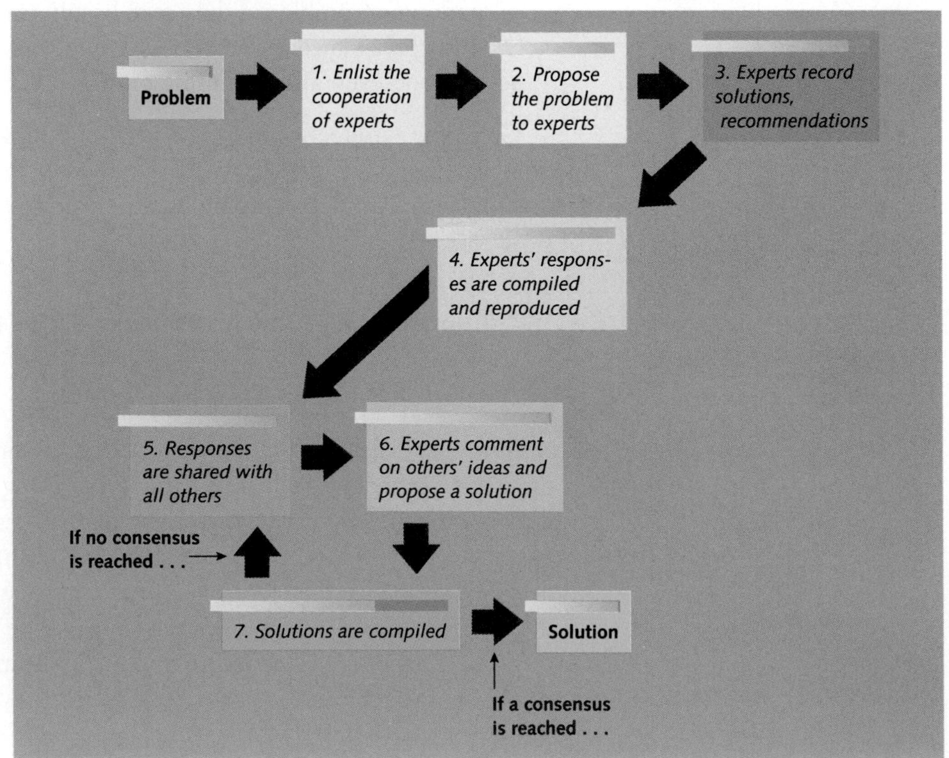

FIGURE 10-12
THE DELPHI GROUP: A SUMMARY
The Delphi technique allows decisions to be made by several experts without encountering many of the disadvantages of face-to-face group interaction.

Delphi approach would not be appropriate for making decisions in crisis situations, or whenever else time is of the essence. However, the approach has been successfully employed to make decisions such as what items to put on a conference agenda and what the potential impact of implementing new land use policies would be.[82]

THE NOMINAL GROUP TECHNIQUE: A STRUCTURED GROUP MEETING

When there are only a few hours available to make a decision, group discussion sessions can be held in which members interact with each other in an orderly, focused fashion aimed at solving problems. The **nominal group technique (NGT)** brings together a small number of individuals (usually about seven to ten) who systematically offer their individual solutions to a problem and share their personal reactions to others' solutions.[83] The technique is referred to as *nominal* because the individuals involved form a group in name only. The participants do not attempt to agree as a group on any solution, but rather vote on all the solutions proposed. For an outline of the steps in the process, see Figure 10-13.

As shown in Figure 10-13, the nominal group process begins by gathering the group members together around a table and identifying the problem at hand. Then each member writes down his or her solutions. Next, one at a time, each member presents his or her solutions to the group and the leader writes these down on a chart. This process continues until all the ideas have been expressed. Following this, each solution is discussed, clarified, and evaluated by the group members. Each

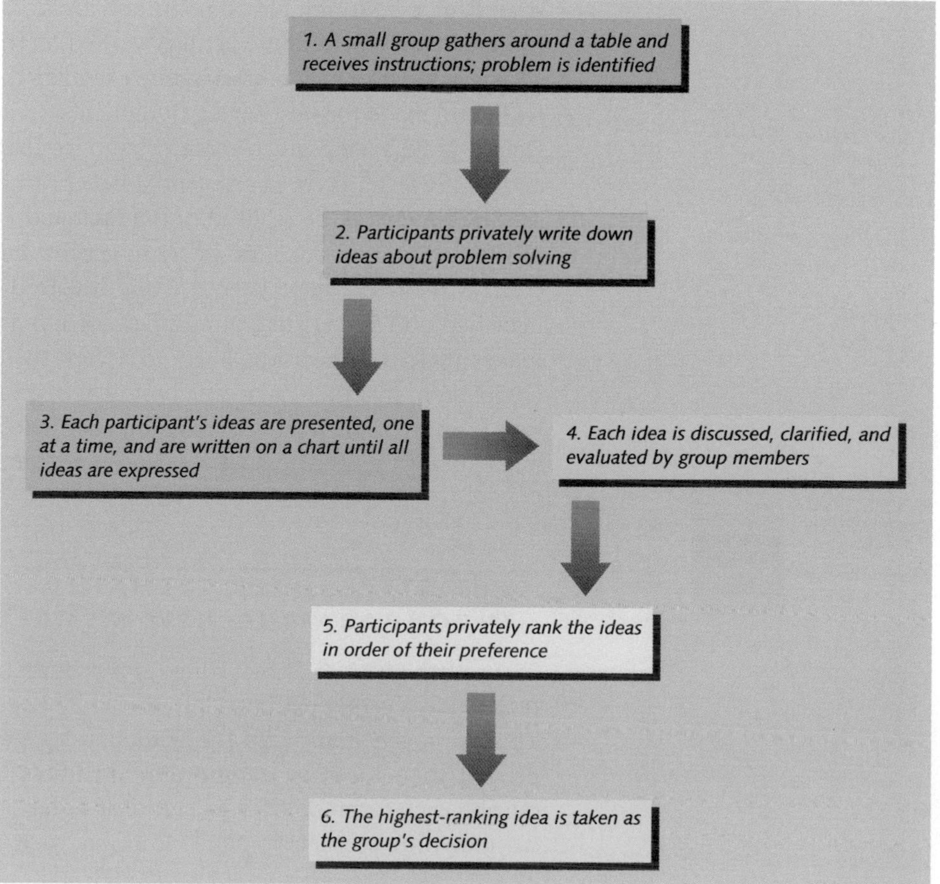
1. A small group gathers around a table and receives instructions; problem is identified
2. Participants privately write down ideas about problem solving
3. Each participant's ideas are presented, one at a time, and are written on a chart until all ideas are expressed
4. Each idea is discussed, clarified, and evaluated by group members
5. Participants privately rank the ideas in order of their preference
6. The highest-ranking idea is taken as the group's decision

FIGURE 10-13
THE NOMINAL GROUP TECHNIQUE: A SUMMARY
The nominal group technique structures face-to-face meetings in a way that allows for the open expression and evaluation of ideas.

member is given a chance to voice his or her reactions to each idea. After all the ideas have been evaluated, the group members privately rank-order their preferred solutions. The idea that receives the highest rank is taken as the group's decision.

Although nominal groups traditionally meet in face-to-face settings, advances in modern technology enable nominal groups to meet even when its members are far away from each other. Specifically, a technique known as **automated decision conferencing** has been used, in which individuals in different locations participate in nominal group conferences by means of telephone lines or direct satellite transmissions.[84] The messages may be sent either via characters on a computer monitor or images viewed during a teleconference. Despite their high-tech look, automated decision conferences are really just nominal groups meeting in a manner that approximates face-to-face contact.

The NGT has several advantages and disadvantages.[85] We have already noted that this approach can be used to arrive at group decisions in only a few hours. Another benefit of the technique is that it discourages any pressure to conform to the wishes of a high-status group member because all ideas are evaluated and the preferences are expressed in private balloting. The technique must be considered limited, however, in that it requires the use of a trained group leader. In addition, using NGT successfully requires that only one narrowly defined problem be considered at a time. So, for very complex problems, many NGT sessions would have to be run—and only *if* the problem under consideration can be broken down into smaller parts.

It is important to consider the relative effectiveness of nominal groups and Delphi groups over face-to-face interacting groups. In general, research has shown the superiority of these special approaches in many ways on a variety of decision problems.[86] For example, the effectiveness of both techniques has been demonstrated in a study by Van de Ven and Delbecq in which seven-member groups (nominal, Delphi, and interacting) worked on the task of defining the job of a dormitory counselor.[87] Nominal groups tended to be the most satisfied with their work and made the best-quality judgments. In addition, both nominal groups and Delphi groups were much more productive than interacting groups. As we noted earlier, however, there is a potential benefit to be derived from face-to-face interaction that cannot be realized in nominal and Delphi groups—that is, acceptance of the decision. Groups are likely to accept their decisions and be committed to them if members have been actively involved in making them. Thus the more detached and impersonal atmosphere of nominal and Delphi groups sometimes makes their members less likely to accept their groups' decisions. We may conclude, then, that there is no one best type of group used to make decisions. Which type is most appropriate depends on the tradeoffs decision makers are willing to make in with respect to speed, quality, and commitment.[88]

THE STEPLADDER TECHNIQUE: SYSTEMATICALLY INCORPORATING NEW MEMBERS

Another way of structuring group interaction known as the **stepladder technique** recently has been introduced by Rogelberg, Barnes-Farrell, and Lowe.[89] This approach minimizes the tendency for group members to be unwilling to present their ideas by adding new members to a group one at a time and requiring each to present his or her ideas independently to a group that already has discussed the problem at hand. To begin, each of two people works on a problem independently, and then come together to present their ideas and discuss solutions jointly. While the two-person group is working, a third person working alone also considers the problem. Then, this individual presents his or her ideas to the group and joins in a three-person discussion of a possible solution. During this period a fourth person works on the problem alone, and then presents his or her ideas to the group and joins into a four-person group discussion. After each new person has been added to the group, the entire group works together at finding a solution. (For a summary of the steps in this technique, see Figure 10-14.)

In following this procedure, it is important for each individual to be given enough time to work on the problem before they join the group. Then each person must be given enough time to present thoroughly his or her ideas to the group. Groups then must have sufficient time to discuss the problem at hand and reach a preliminary decision before the next person is added. As a last step, the final decision is made only after all individuals have been added to the group.

The rationale underlying this procedure is that by forcing each person to present independent ideas without knowing how the group has decided, the new person will not be influenced by the group, and the group is required to consider a constant infusion of new ideas. If this is so, then groups solving problems using the stepladder technique would be expected to make better decisions than conventional groups meeting all at once to discuss the same problem. In an experiment comparing both types of groups, this is exactly what Rogelberg and his associates found. Moreover, members of stepladder groups reported feeling generally more positive about their group experiences. Although the stepladder technique is new, this evidence suggests that it holds a great deal of promise as a way of enhancing the decision-making capacity of groups.

The nominal group technique, the Delphi technique, and the stepladder technique are three very useful and effective ways to improve group performance. The problem with using these techniques, however, is that they go outside the normal

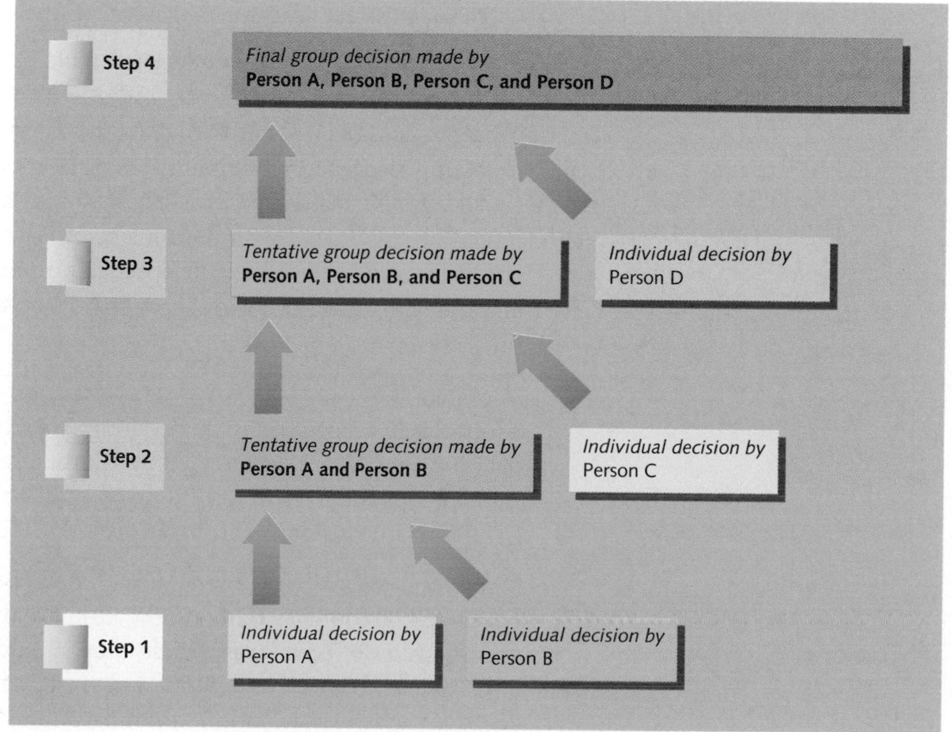

FIGURE 10-14
THE STEPLADDER TECHNIQUE: A SUMMARY
By systematically adding new individuals into decision-making groups, the stepladder technique helps increase the quality of the decisions made. (Source: Adapted from Rogelberg, Barnes-Farrell, & Lowe, 1992; see Note 89.)

decision-making channels and call for certain procedures requiring the use of specialists to run group meetings. It may not always be feasible, of course, to conduct such meetings, suggesting a need for improving the quality of group decisions on a more regular basis. What else can be done to help improve the quality of group decisions? One promising answer appears to lie in the area of training individual decision makers to work more effectively in groups.

TRAINING INDIVIDUALS TO IMPROVE GROUP PERFORMANCE

As we noted earlier in this chapter, how well groups solve problems depends in part on the composition of those groups. If at least one group member is capable of coming up with a solution, groups may benefit by that individual's expertise. Based on this reasoning, it follows that the more qualified individual group members are to solve problems, the better their groups as a whole will perform.

Bottger and Yetton found that the number of mistakes made by groups attempting to solve a creative problem was significantly reduced when members were trained to avoid several common types of errors.[90] Specifically, participants in the study were asked to be aware of and to try to avoid four common problems.

1. *Hypervigilance*. This state involves frantically searching for quick solutions to problems, going from one idea to another out of a sense of desperation that one idea isn't working and that another needs to be considered before time runs out. A poor, "last chance" solution may be adopted to relieve anxiety. This problem may be avoided by keeping in mind that it is best to stick with one suggestion and work it out thoroughly, and by reassuring the person solving the problem that his or her level of skill and education is adequate to perform the task at hand. In other words, a little reassurance may go a long way toward keeping individuals on the right track and avoiding the problem of hypervigilance.

2. *Unconflicted adherence*. Many decision makers make the mistake of sticking to the first idea that comes into their heads without more deeply evaluating the consequences. As a result, such people are unlikely to become aware of any problems associated with their ideas or to consider other possibilities. To avoid *unconflicted adherence*, decision makers are urged to (1) think about the difficulties associated with their ideas, (2) force themselves to consider different ideas, and (3) consider the special and unique characteristics of the problem they are facing and avoid carrying over assumptions from previous problems.

3. *Unconflicted change*. Sometimes people are too quick to change their minds and adopt the first new idea to come along. To avoid such unconflicted change, decision makers are encouraged to ask themselves about (1) the risks and problems of adopting that solution, (2) the good points of the first idea, and (3) the relative strengths and weaknesses of both ideas.

4. *Defensive avoidance*. Too often decision makers fail to solve problems effectively because they avoid working on the task at hand. To minimize this problem, they should do three things. First, they should attempt to *avoid procrastination*. Don't put off the problem indefinitely just because you cannot come up with a solution right away. Continue to budget some of your time on even the most

frustrating problems. Second, *avoid disowning responsibility*. It is easy to minimize the importance of a problem by saying, "It doesn't matter, so who cares?" Avoid giving up so soon. Finally, *don't ignore potentially corrective information*. It is tempting to put your nagging doubts about the quality of a solution to rest in order to be finished with it. Good decision makers would not do so. Rather, they use their doubts to test and potentially improve the quality of their ideas.

The encouraging aspect of Bottger and Yetton's findings is that merely having members of problem-solving groups consider these four potential pitfalls was an effective way of improving the quality of their groups' solutions. Apparently, how well groups perform depends to a great extent on the problem-solving skills of the individual group members. Attempting to avoid the four major pitfalls described here appears to be an effective method of improving individual decision-making skills—and hence the quality of group decisions.

SUMMARY AND REVIEW

THE NATURE OF DECISION MAKING

Traditionally, theorists have looked at **decision making** as the multistep process through which a problem is identified, solution objectives are defined, a *predecision* is made (i.e., a decision about how to make a decision), alternatives are generated and evaluated, and an alternative is chosen, implemented, and then followed up. A contemporary alternative approach recognizes that decisions are made in an automatic, intuitive fashion. Specifically, **image theory** claims that people will adopt a course of action that best fits their individual principles, current goals, and plans for the future.

The decisions made in organizations can be characterized as being either **programmed**, routine decisions made according to pre-existing guidelines, or **nonprogrammed**, decisions requiring novel and creative solutions. Decisions also differ with respect to the amount of risk involved, ranging from those in which the decision outcomes are relatively *certain* to those in which the outcomes are highly *uncertain*. Uncertain situations are expressed as statements of probability based on either objective or subjective information.

APPROACHES TO DECISION MAKING

Two major approaches to individual decision making have been identified. The rational-economic model characterizes decision makers as thoroughly searching through perfect information to make an optimal decision. This is a *normative* approach, in that it describes how decision makers ideally ought to behave to make the best possible decisions. In contrast, the administrative model is a *descriptive* approach, which describes how decision makers actually behave. It recognizes the inherent imperfections of decision makers and the social and organizational systems within which they operate. Limitations imposed by people's ability to process the information needed to make complex decisions (**bounded rationality**) restrict decision makers to making **satisfiying decisions**—solutions that are not optimal, but good enough.

IMPEDIMENTS TO OPTIMAL INDIVIDUAL DECISIONS

People make imperfect decisions due to cognitive biases. One such bias, **framing**, refers to the tendency for people to make different decisions based on how a problem is presented. For example, when a problem is presented in a way that emphasizes the positive gains to be received, people tend to make conservative, risk-averse, decisions. However, when the same problem is presented in a way that emphasizes the potential losses to be suffered, people tend to make riskier decisions. Simple rules of thumb, known as **heuristics**, also may bias decisions. For example, according to the **availability heuristic**, people base their judgments on information readily available to them, and according to the **representativeness heuristic**, people are perceived in stereotypical ways if they appear to be representatives of the categories to which they belong.

According to the **escalation-of-commitment phenomenon**, people continue to support previously unsuccessful courses of action because they have sunk costs invested in them. This occurs in large part because people need to justify their previous actions and wish to avoid having to admit that their initial decision was a mistake. Individual decisions are also limited by organizational factors, such as: time constraints, political "face-saving" pressure, and *bounded discretion* (moral and ethical restrictions imposed on decisions).

GROUP DECISION MAKING

Studies comparing the decisions made by groups and individuals reveal a complex pattern. Groups have proven superior to individual members when they are composed of a heterogeneous mix of experts who possess complementary skills. However, groups may not be any better than the best member of the group when performing a task that has a simple, verifiable answer. Compared with individuals, face-to-face **brainstorming** groups tend to make inferior decisions on creative problems. However, when brainstorming is done electronically—that is, by using computer terminals to send messages—the quality of decisions tends to improve.

Groupthink is a major obstacle to effective group decisions. The term refers to the tendency for strong conformity pressures within groups to lead to the breakdown of critical thinking and to encourage premature acceptance of potentially questionable solutions. Groupthink appears to have been responsible for major decision fiascoes, such as the United States' invasion of the Bay of Pigs in Cuba, and the decision to launch the ill-fated space shuttle *Challenger*.

TECHNIQUES FOR IMPROVING GROUP DECISIONS

The quality of group decisions can be enhanced in several different ways. First, using the **Delphi technique**, the judgments of experts are systematically gathered in writing and used to form a single joint decision. The **nominal group technique** is a method of structuring group meetings so as to elicit and evaluate the opinions of all members. The **stepladder technique** systematically adds new individuals to decision-making groups one at a time, requiring the presentation and discussion of new ideas. Finally, the quality of group decisions has been shown to improve following individual training in problem-solving skills.

KEY TERMS

administrative model: A model of decision making that recognizes the *bounded rationality* that limits the making of optimal decisions.

automated decision conferencing: A technique in which decision-making groups are formed by connecting people in different locations via satellite transmissions or telephone lines.

availability heuristic: The tendency for people to base their judgments on information that is readily available to them although it may be potentially inaccurate, thereby adversely affecting decision quality.

bounded rationality: The major assumption of the administrative model—that organizational, social, and human limitations lead to the making of *satisfiying* rather than optimal decisions.

brainstorming: A technique designed to foster group productivity by encouraging interacting group members to express their ideas in a noncritical fashion.

decision making: The process through which a problem is identified, solution objectives are defined, a *predecision* is made, alternatives are generated and evaluated, and an alternative is chosen, implemented, and followed up.

decision support systems (DSS): Computer programs in which information about organizational behavior is presented to decision makers in a manner that helps them structure their responses to decisions.

Delphi technique: A method of improving group decisions using the opinions of experts, which are solicited by mail and then compiled. The expert consensus of opinions is used to make a decision.

escalation of commitment phenomenon: The tendency for individuals to continue to support previously unsuccessful courses of action.

framing: The presentation of a problem to an individual, either in negative terms (leading to risk seeking) or positive terms (leading to risk aversion).

groupthink: The tendency for members of highly cohesive groups to so strongly conform to group pressures regarding a certain decision that they fail to think critically, rejecting the potentially correcting influences of outsiders.

heuristics: Simple decision rules (rules of thumb) used to make quick decisions about complex problems. (See *availability heuristic* and *representativeness heuristic*.)

image theory: A theory of decision making that recognizes that decisions are made in an automatic, intuitive fashion. According to the theory, people will adopt a course of action that best fits their individual principles, current goals, and plans for the future.

nominal group technique (NGT): A technique for improving group decisions in which small groups of individuals systematically present and discuss their ideas before privately voting on their preferred solution. The most preferred solution is accepted as the group's decision.

nonprogrammed decisions: Decisions made about a highly novel problem for which there is no pre-specified course of action.

predecision: A decision about what process to follow in making a decision.

programmed decisions: Highly routine decisions made according to pre-established organizational routines and procedures.

rational decisions: Decisions that maximize the chance of attaining an individual's, group's, or organization's goals.

rational-economic model: The model of decision making according to which decision makers consider all possible alternatives to problems before selecting the optimal solution.

representativeness heuristic: The tendency to perceive others in stereotypical ways if they appear to be typical representatives of the category to which they belong.

satisficing decisions: Decisions made by selecting the first minimally acceptable alternative as it becomes available.

stepladder technique: A technique for improving the quality of group decisions that minimizes the tendency for group members to be unwilling to present their ideas by adding new members to a group one at a time and requiring each to present his or her ideas independently to a group that already has discussed the problem at hand.

strategic decisions: Nonprogrammed decisions typically made by high-level executives regarding the direction their organization should take to achieve its mission.

QUESTIONS FOR DISCUSSION

1. Apply the eight-step analytical model of decision making to any decision you recently made.
2. Distinguish between programmed decisions and nonprogrammed decisions, giving an example of each in an organization with which you are familiar.
3. Describe the various barriers to effective decision making recognized by the rational-economic model. Give an example of each.
4. Identify ways in which decisions you have made may have been biased by framing, heuristics, and the escalation of commitment.
5. Suppose you were hired as a consultant to improve the decision-making skills of an organization's personnel. Outline the things you would do, and justify these measures.
6. Imagine that you are a manager facing the problem of not attracting enough high-quality personnel to your organization. Would you attempt to solve this problem alone or by committee? Explain your reasoning.
7. Groupthink is a potentially serious impediment to group decision making. Describe this phenomenon, and review some things that can be done to avoid it.
8. Suppose you find out that a certain important organizational decision has to be made by a group, but you suspect that a better decision might be made by an individual. Describe three different ways you could use groups to make a decision while at the same time avoiding many of the problems associated with groups.
9. Argue either for or against the following statement: "Individuals cannot be trained to improve the quality of group decisions."

TOMMY HILFIGER: A DESIGNER OF DECISIONS AND FASHION

Tommy Hilfiger, the founder and designer of the second-largest-selling line of men's clothing in the last ten years, is a man with a dream and a plan to accomplish it. His vision is "to represent all-American, clean cut, patriotic, classic lifestyle products of today." His plan is "to dress the customer head to toe and supply him with his lifestyle."[1]

Some might argue that these goals are very ambitious for a man who didn't attend college and began his first business, a clothing store, with only $300. Anyone who thinks this would be correct in assessing Hilfiger's ambition. But to only focus on his ambition without taking into consideration his talent, energy, and drive would result in an underestimation of Hilfiger. It would also ignore his ability to make a decision and stick to it no matter the odds against him.

Hilfiger is nothing if not direct. He always dreamed of owning his own business and designing clothes for men. Although there was nothing in his background to suggest that this was a realistic career choice, he felt that "in my heart, I could do it."[2] With extraordinary self-confidence, he has turned his dream into an empire of Tommy Hilfiger boutiques located in over 500 major retail stores, achieving sales of over $200 million per year.

The ideas for Hilfiger's designs come from the things that interest him, such as sailing, car racing, flags, and travel. He finds inspiration in these areas, which he then uses in the selection of materials and themes for his designs. A sample rack runs through his showroom from which hang thousands of articles of clothing that reflect his different ideas. Hilfiger has many interests and is very creative. In fact, he develops a new line of clothing every forty-five days!

Although he is currently successful, he has had brushes with failure. His first business, opened in 1969 at age 18, was a store selling jeans and other casual wear. This store was so prosperous that within five years he had opened nine more facilities. Unfortunately, Hilfiger was so intent on concentrating on the continued growth of his business that he made several major mistakes. He invested in too much inventory. Also, he failed to take heed of the changing economy and shifting tastes and preferences of his customers. Finally, as he says, even "when there were smoke signals that things weren't so great, I didn't want to believe it."[3] As a result of his decisions to focus on expansion and ignore the mounting evidence of problems, Hilfiger was forced to file for bankruptcy—something he found very distasteful.

Despite this setback, however, Hilfiger still believed in himself and his dream. In 1974 he headed to New York City to gain experience in the fashion industry. He landed a job with Murjani, a subsidiary of the Gloria Vanderbilt fashion empire. Within a few years, he left his employer to begin his own freelance design company. To gain attention for his products, he hired an advertising firm to develop an image for Tommy Hilfiger. The ad that resulted directly compared Hilfiger to the known greats in men's fashion—Ralph Lauren, Calvin Klein, and Perry Ellis. The decision to run this ad was quite risky in a city where taking on the world of fashion is tantamount to challenging the king. Said Hilfiger, who had already faced and survived bankruptcy, "I was not afraid because I had nothing to lose."[4]

Hilfiger's designs became so popular that in 1979 he was made an offer by Murjani International to begin the Tommy Hilfiger line of clothing. Less than ten years later, his products were so successful that he decided to buy back the company. Additional success and need for capital required that he take the company public in 1992.

Decisions about both the running of the business and design of fashions are made by Hilfiger in conjunction with his partners. He claims that all such decisions are made democratically, with no one person taking control or pushing his or her opinions on the others. According to Hilfiger, he and his partners are always in total agreement about their decisions. He claims that they never disagree because they are all "reasonably intelligent, sophisticated, prudent people," who clearly know if a decision is right or wrong.[5]

Interestingly, although Hilfiger himself did not attend college, he is often called on to speak to audiences of college students. He encourages students to stay in school because he admits that few others without a university education will have the opportunities that he did. He also advises people about their career decisions. Hilfiger says that it is crucial to "figure out exactly what you want to do and focus on it."[6] Clearly this is advice that Hilfiger has followed himself and has used to achieve much of his success.

CASE IN POINT, Cont.

QUESTIONS FOR DISCUSSION

1. How can the eight-step model of decision making be used to explain how Tommy Hilfiger decided to go into a career in fashion?
2. Do you think Hilfiger uses a rational-economic or an image theory approach to decision making? Do you think his approach may differ when making decisions about business compared to design? Explain your response.
3. According to Hilfiger, the decision to run an advertising campaign that might anger his competitors was an easy one because he "had nothing to lose." Analyze this decision in terms of the objective and subjective information Hilfiger must have used.
4. How might the concept of escalation of commitment explain why Hilfiger ignored signals that his first business was in trouble?
5. Do you think that Hilfiger and his partners may be victims of groupthink in their decision making? Why or why not? What suggestions can you make to them to keep them from falling victim to this problem?

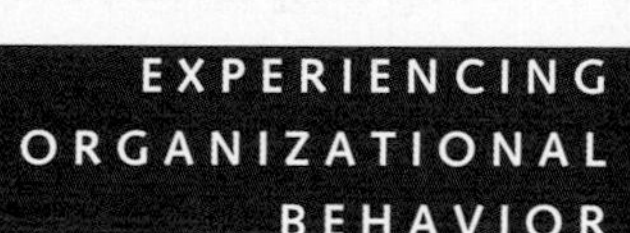

EXPERIENCING ORGANIZATIONAL BEHAVIOR

Are You a Risky Decision Maker? It Depends on Your Frame of Reference

As noted in our discussion of decision framing (see pp. 384-385), the level of risk that people are likely to take when making a decision will depend on how the decision is *framed*—that is whether it is presented in a positive manner (in terms of gains) or in a negative manner (in terms of losses). When an outcome is framed in terms of a choice between losses, people tend to see risk. However, when the same options are framed in terms of gains, people tend to avoid risk. You can demonstrate this phenomenon for yourself by considering the following situation.

PROCEDURE

Read each of the following descriptions of hypothetical situations, and answer the questions that follow.

Situation 1: Imagine that you are an executive whose policies have recently resulted in a $1 million loss for your company. Now you're considering two new projects. One of them (Alpha) will provide a definite return of $500,000. The other (Beta) will provide a fifty-fifty chance of obtaining either a $1 million return or a zero return.

Question: Which project will you select: Alpha or Beta?

Situation 2: Imagine that you are considering one of two new projects to conduct in your company. The first project (Alpha) will provide a definite return of $500,000. The other project (Beta) will provide a fifty-fifty chance of obtaining a $1 million return, or a zero return.

Question: Which project will you select: Alpha or Beta?

POINTS TO CONSIDER

In situation 1, your options follow a recent loss—a fact that causes you to frame the results of the two new options in a negative fashion (outcomes that have the effect of minimizing your losses). In other words, you can select between minimizing your loss by 50 percent (selecting Alpha) and having a fifty-fifty change of undoing the loss completely (selecting Beta). Essentially, you are choosing between two losses. In such a case, most people would make a risky decision (select Beta). Did you?

However, the opposite would occur in Situation 2. Here, most people would select the sure thing (Alpha). The difference is that this situation is viewed from a positive perspective—that is, a "positive frame" (gains received). When selecting between the sure gain (Alpha) and the chancy but larger gain (Beta), people are unwilling to risk the "bird in the hand."

If you think about it, there is no rational reason for distinguishing between these two options because they are mathematically identical. That people have strong preferences in such situations represents a bias in the way decision makers operate. Such framing effects may be responsible for many major decision failures (some of which were identified in the text). Sometimes, when decisions are framed between two losses, unusually high levels of risk are taken, resulting in failure. Some key failures in history may be seen as the result of taking high levels of risk when choosing between two apparent losses (whether or not they are recognized as such at the time). Here are a few:

- The Iran-Contra affair during the Regan administration (1980s)
- The 1986 decision to launch the space shuttle *Challenger*
- Coca-Cola's 1985 decision to change its formula
- The Iraqi invasion of Kuwait in 1990
- The Japanese attack on Pearl Harbor in 1941

Can you think of any others? For each case you identify, list the potential losses that might have been considered.

CHAPTER OUTLINE

SPECIAL SECTIONS

ELEVEN

HELPING, COOPERATION, AND CONFLICT IN ORGANIZATIONS

LEARNING OBJECTIVES

After reading this chapter, you should be able to

1. *Distinguish between prosocial behavior and altruism.*
2. *Describe some of the various forms of prosocial behavior that occur in organizations.*
3. *Describe organizational citizenship behavior and whistle-blowing, and explain what makes them forms of prosocial behavior.*
4. *Describe the basic nature of cooperation, and indicate why in organizations it is often replaced by competition.*
5. *Define conflict, and indicate how it can produce positive as well as negative effects.*
6. *Describe various styles of managing conflict, and the dimensions that underlie them.*
7. *List several interpersonal and organizational causes of conflict.*
8. *Describe both the positive and negative effects of conflict in organizations.*
9. *Identify various techniques for effectively managing conflict in organizations.*

Government and cooperation are in all things the law of life; anarchy and competition the laws of death.

John Ruskin, 1819–1900
English art critic and historian
Unto This Last

Progress flows only from struggle.

Louis Dembitz Brandeis, 1856–1941
U.S. Supreme Court Justice
Business—A Profession

PREVIEW CASE

Polishing Up the Cooperative Spirit at Johnson Wax

Cory Mason knew that customer satisfaction was everything, and also that winning customers over couldn't be done unless his company's employees first had "a spirit of cooperation." As a senior information services manager for S. C. Johnson & Son, Inc. (better known as Johnson Wax), Mason was concerned that the 100-year-old company would be unable to maintain its leadership in the household products industry unless the conflict that plagued the company could be stemmed.

The major problem, according to Mason, was that the various departments were so highly focused on their specialized responsibilities that their efforts often conflicted, limiting the company's capacity to service its customers. According to Dave Henry, a Johnson Wax vice president, "No one was really focusing on customer needs. Finance, manufacturing, distribution, sales and marketing each had a job to do and each did that job to meet its own objectives." However, Mason knew that it was essential to turn these self-interested perspectives into a unified view of what was good for the company as a whole.

Recognizing the problem and being able to do something effective are two different things, but with almost two decades of experience at the company, Mason was up to the challenge. With this in mind, he launched a program known as the Computer Integration of Customer Service Systems (CICSS) project. An important part of this initiative involved making the once independent departments dependent on each other to accomplish their work. To help, teams were created that included employees from the various departments. One of their main tasks was to create a common database that could be used to collect information about customers' needs. Doing this involved a high level of cooperation between teams working on client services and teams expert in information systems.

Unfortunately, at first, the various groups did not recognize the need to cooperate with each other—and, as a result, nothing happened. In the words of Steve Hrpcek, project supervisor, "We really couldn't bring it off because the team still wasn't singing out of the same hymnal." This failure was indicative of the very problem Mason was trying to remedy by implementing the CICSS. Fortunately, this irony was not wasted. Johnson employees realized that if they had any chance at succeeding at all, they absolutely must stop looking after their own individual interests, and start cooperating with each other.

Cory Mason of S. C. Johnson and Son

Slowly but surely, the turnaround did occur. By 1990, Johnson Wax was transformed from a group of separately functioning departments that often worked at cross-purposes to one large cross-functional unit that focused on business as a whole. Now, although there is a single unit that focuses on customer service (the customer service and logistics department), it is involved in all aspects

of the company and works to ensure a continuity of customer service throughout the company. Customer service is now everybody's business at Johnson Wax, and not an issue that can be pawned off to another department. If there is a problem, it is likely to be recognized and resolved before it comes to the customer's attention. Employees are working together to improve customer satisfaction—so much so, in fact, that the CICSS is used to track usage patterns and to anticipate customers' needs even before they occur. As vice president Dave Henry puts it, "We have the foundation in place now to be proactive."

oes it seem strange to you that a deliberate effort had to be made to get various departments at Johnson Wax to work in concert with each other? After all, you would expect employees to appreciate that they are *interdependent*: what happens to one unit affects the others. If one part of a company succeeds at the expense of another, the organization as a whole may suffer, and everyone loses. As obvious as this seems, people in organizations are not always as willing to *cooperate* with each other as you might expect. With Mason's intervention, however, employees at Johnson Wax eventually came to exchange their narrow perspectives for a vision of the common good—but reaching this point took some effort. As you might imagine, Johnson Wax is not alone in its (now former) tendency to fall short of the cooperative ideal. Instead of benevolent places filled with the spirit of mutual assistance, organizations are just as likely to be places dominated by indifference, needless competition, smoldering feuds, and even open conflict.[1]

Why is this so? What factors lead individuals and groups to work against one another when they should, by all rational standards, be cooperating? And what steps can be taken to tip the balance away from such reactions and toward higher levels of coordination? We will focus on these and related questions in this chapter. Specifically, we will examine three major processes related to the extent to which individuals or groups in an organization work with, or against, one another. The first of these is **prosocial behavior**—actions by individuals or groups that assist others without requiring the recipient to return the favor. The second is **cooperation**—mutual, two-way assistance between individuals or groups. The third, and in some ways most disturbing, is **conflict**—a process resulting from actions by groups or individuals that are perceived by others as having negative effects on their important interests.[2] We will now review current knowledge relating to each of these processes.

PROSOCIAL BEHAVIOR: HELPING OTHERS AT WORK

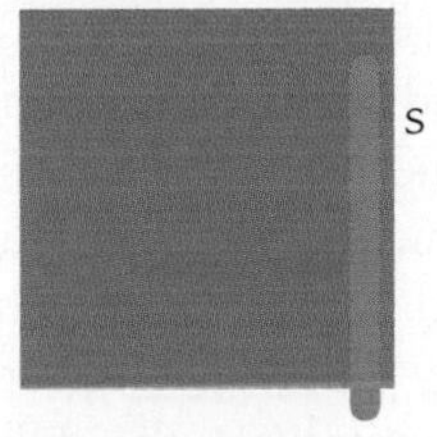

s there such a thing as pure *altruism*—actions by one person that benefit one or more others under conditions in which the donor expects nothing in return? Philosophers have long puzzled over this question. More recently, social scientists have entered the debate.[3] Disappointingly, their research casts considerable doubt on the existence of totally selfless helping (see Figure 11-1). Close examination of many instances in which individuals offer aid to others in a seemingly altruistic manner reveals that even in such cases donors anticipate some form of compensation for their assistance. This return on their investment can be quite subtle (e.g., feelings

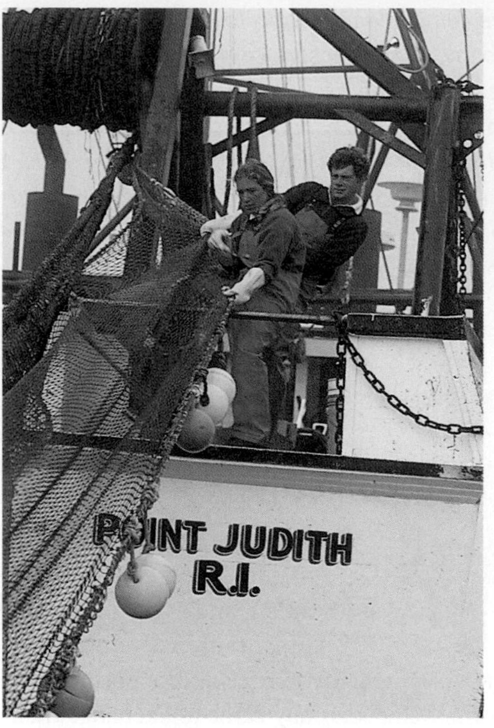

FIGURE 11-1
PROSOCIAL BEHAVIOR: NOT NECESSARILY ALTRUISTIC
People commonly help each other on the job. However, insofar as the person giving help may derive some benefit from his or her prosocial behavior (even subtle effects, such as feeling good), it cannot be said that such actions are purely altruistic.

of self-satisfaction, resulting from the knowledge that they have acted benevolently; elimination of the negative emotions produced by exposure to others in need of assistance).[4] Yet such gains are certainly real, and seem to provide at least a portion of the motivation behind seemingly altruistic acts. This is not to imply that instances of pure altruism cannot exist. A strong case can be made for the presence of such behavior in some contexts (e.g., self-sacrifice by parents for their children or by lovers for the objects of their affection). At the least, though, pure, selfless altruism seems to be far rarer and much more difficult to identify than people once assumed.

Still, it is clear that people do frequently engage in **prosocial behavior**, actions that help others in various ways. In fact, such behavior is common in work settings.[5] With this in mind, we will now attempt to characterize the widespread nature of prosocial behavior in organizations by identifying some of the various beneficiaries of prosocial actions, the targets of helping behavior. We will then describe some of the unique forms of prosocial behavior that occur in organizations.

TARGETS OF PROSOCIAL BEHAVIOR: WHO IS HELPED IN ORGANIZATIONS?

Brief and Motowidlo have identified many different ways in which helping occurs in organizations.[6] These are acts having three different beneficiaries: one's *co-workers*, *customers*, or the *organization* as a whole. For some individuals, such as counselors and corporate trainers, it is a formal part of their jobs to help others. However, people frequently assist their co-workers even if they do not have to, but simply because they want to. Because such acts—such as helping someone who has been absent catch up, and lending a helping hand to someone lifting a heavy load—go beyond one's formal requirements, they are considered *extra-role behaviors*.[7] Helping a colleague who has a personal problem, such as marital discord or emotional upset, also may be seen as extrarole forms of helping.

A recent study by Wright, George, Farnsworth, and McMahan examined the conditions under which people are willing to help a colleague in need by engaging in extra-role behaviors.[8] The subjects in their experiment were college students hired to find and correct errors systematically embedded in order forms. They were paid either a flat hourly rate regardless of how well they did, or paid a bonus only if they achieved their assigned goal. Through careful pretesting, the difficulty of these goals was systematically varied. As participants performed their task, they were joined by another person (an accomplice of the experimenter) who missed the training session and repeatedly asked the subject for assistance. Did the subjects stop what they were doing to help their co-worker? The answer depended on how costly it was to themselves to do so. Specifically, the rate of helping was lowest among participants who would only be paid if they met an extremely difficult goal (see Figure 11-2). For these individuals, the act of helping was extremely costly insofar as the time taken to help would prevent them from meeting their goal. However, in all other conditions, such as when the goal was so simple as to assure meeting it, and when payment was expected regardless of task performance, people offered significantly more help. These results suggest that people *are* in fact willing to help another, but only if doing so is not overly costly to themselves.[9]

In addition to helping one's fellow workers, people also may be prosocial in their actions toward customers. There is nothing especially prosocial about the act of helping another when doing so is a formally prescribed part of one's job, such as when a dry cleaning counter clerk takes a customer's clothes and writes up the order. However, the clerk may be acting prosocially if he or she is especially helpful, such as by finding stains in need of special attention. Sometimes people may be so helpful that they are not acting in the best interest of their organization. For example, giving customers unauthorized discounts, or dissuading them from purchasing an expensive product may fall into this category. Finally, employees may help customers in ways that are unrelated to their organization's mission. For example, they may give directions, make change needed for a phone call (or even let them use the phone), or listen sympathetically to problems—all of which are ways of helping customers.

Although it is likely that by helping one's co-workers or customers, one may be helping the organization itself, it is useful to consider ways in which people may attempt to help their organization itself directly. For example, people may help their organizations by following its rules and regulations, suggesting ways to

FIGURE 11-2
WITHHOLDING HELP WHEN THE COSTS ARE TOO GREAT: AN EXPERIMENTAL DEMONSTRATION

In a recent experiment by Wright and his associates, participants were interrupted by a co-worker in need of help (instructions about how to perform the task). The level of help given was generally high, except under conditions in which helping the other interfered with participants' own chances of success. (Source: Based on data reported by Wright, George, Farnsworth, & McMahan, 1993; see Note 8.)

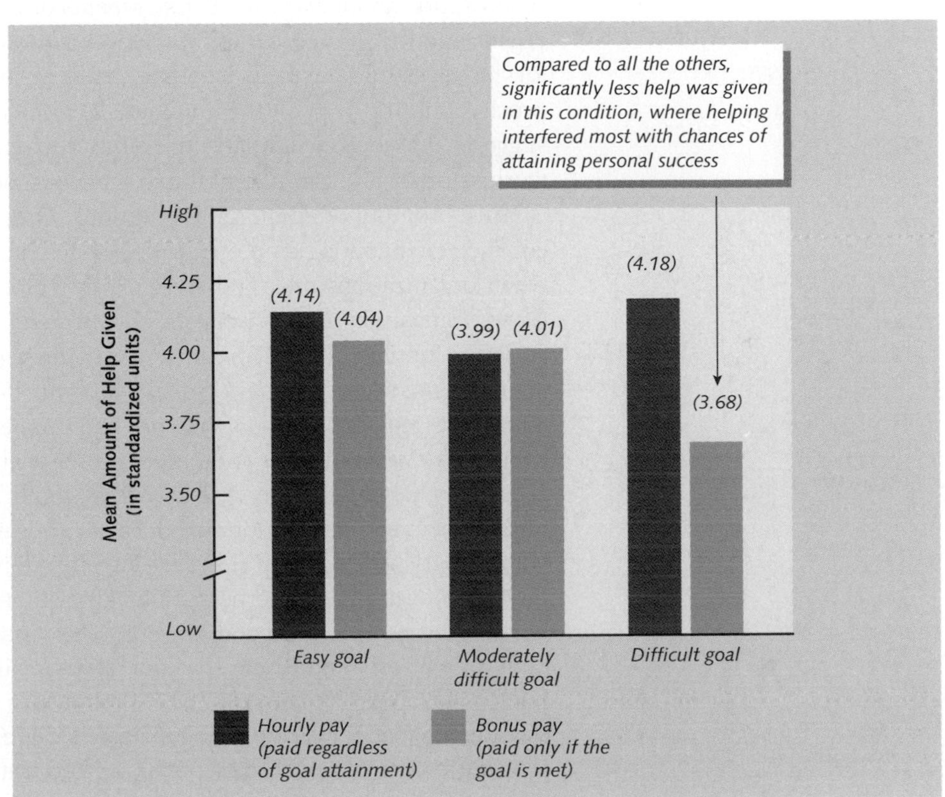

improve its operations, putting forth the effort needed to succeed, willingly accepting extra work assignments without extra pay, speaking well of the organization to outsiders, and staying loyal to the organization during times of adversity (such as during pay cuts). In conclusion, prosocial behavior is frequently directed at coworkers, customers, and the organization itself—and, such behavior takes many different forms.

SPECIAL TYPES OF PROSOCIAL BEHAVIOR: ORGANIZATIONAL CITIZENSHIP BEHAVIORS AND WHISTLE-BLOWING

In addition to the varieties of helping behaviors just described, two forms of prosocial behavior deserve special mention—*organizational citizenship behavior* and *whistle-blowing*. Not only have these topics received a considerable amount of recent attention by organizational researchers, but they are also special insofar as they are each forms of prosocial behavior that involve more than one single beneficiary.

ORGANIZATIONAL CITIZENSHIP BEHAVIORS: GOING BEYOND THE CALL OF DUTY

In Chapter 5, we noted that high levels of job satisfaction tend to promote **organizational citizenship behaviors (OCB)**, actions by individuals that are discretionary (i.e., voluntary), not related to the formal reward system of the organization, and not included in their formal job descriptions. Such behaviors include showing courtesy to others, being conscientious in work-related tasks, being a "good sport" about extra work assignments or duties, and generally protecting the organization's resources and property.[10] A central component of citizenship behaviors involves offering help to others without the expectation of immediate reciprocity on the part of the individuals receiving such aid. Growing evidence suggests that organizational citizenship behaviors enhance the pleasantness of work settings, and can contribute to increased performance and efficiency.[11]

This prompts an important question: what steps can organizations take to enhance OCB among employees? Recent research suggests that OCB is enhanced when organizations treat employees fairly.[12] Specifically, Moorman demonstrated that citizenship behaviors were strongly related to employees' perceptions of **interactional justice**—that is, the extent to which they are shown a high degree of courtesy, dignity, and interpersonal sensitivity.[13] The greater the extent to which employees felt that their supervisors had applied the formal procedures for distributing rewards in a fair and courteous manner, the greater the incidence of citizenship behavior. Obviously, employees would not be expected to "go the extra mile" to help an organization that does not appear to go out of its way to treat them with dignity and respect. However, organizations that are recognized as treating their employees in an interpersonally fair fashion tend to reap the benefits of having employees who are good citizens. This finding is consistent with a growing body of evidence indicating that interactional justice is strongly related to many kinds of behavior in organizations.[14] Fortunately, treating subordinates in a fair and considerate manner is something managers can easily do, if they try. In view of the growing evidence of the benefits associated with interactional justice, efforts at attaining it would appear to be well worthwhile.

WHISTLE-BLOWING: HELPING AN ORGANIZATION BY DISSENTING WITH IT

Sometimes employees face situations in which they recognize that their organization is behaving in an improper fashion. To right the wrong, they reveal the improper or illegal practice to someone who may be able to correct it, an action known as **whistle-blowing**.[15] Formally, whistle-blowing has been defined as *the disclosure by employees of illegal, immoral, or illegitimate practices by employers to people or organizations able to affect action.*[16]

Is this a prosocial action? From the point of view of society, it usually is. In many instances, the actions of whistle-blowers can protect the health, safety, or economic security of the general public. For example, an employee of a large bank who reports risky or illegal practices to an appropriate regulatory agency may protect thousands of depositors from considerable delay in recovering their savings. Similarly, an individual who blows the whistle on illegal dumping of toxic chemicals by his or her company may save many people from serious illness (for a summary of some cases of famous whistle-blowers, see Table 11-1).[17] As you might imagine, blowing the whistle on one's employer is likely to be a very costly act for employees, as they often find themselves facing a long, uphill battle attempting to prove the wrongdoing, and frequently face ostracism and losing their jobs in response to their disloyalty. (Although various laws prevent employers from firing people directly because they blew the whistle, organizations frequently find alternative official grounds for dismissing "troublemakers."[18]) In other words, although whistle-blowing often involves considerable cost, the importance of the action motivates many people to go through with it.

TABLE 11-1

Whistle-Blowing: A Summary of Some Cases

In recent years, whistle-blowing has occurred in a variety of different companies. Here is an overview of some famous whistle-blowers and their actions.

WHISTLE-BLOWER	ALLEGED COMPANY WRONGDOING
Charles Atchinson	*Claimed that the Comanche Park nuclear plant in Glen Rose, Texas, was unsafe*
Kermit Vandivier	*Implicated B. F. Goodrich in a scandal regarding unsafe aircraft brakes*
James Pope	*Alleged that since 1975 the U.S. Federal Aviation Administration knew of an effective device for preventing mid-air collisions, but pursued an inferior device it had a hand in developing*
Ernest Fitzgerald	*Brought to public attention enormous cost overruns on Lockheed cargo planes developed for the U.S. Air Force*
Charles Allen	*Notified the public of the U.S. government's diversion of profits from Iranian arms sales to the Nicaraguan contras*

Source: Based on information reported by Miceli & Near, 1992, see Note 14; and Newton & Ford, 1992, see Note 21.

From the point of view of the organizations involved, however, the situation is more complex. First, whether such actions are or are not prosocial in nature depends on the motivation underlying them. If a whistle-blower benefits from his or her actions while the organization suffers, or if the whistle-blower's action is part of a vendetta designed to hurt the company, the actions cannot be viewed as prosocial with respect to the organization. Second, much depends on how such whistle-blowing is carried out. If the potentially damaging information is revealed first to people in authority within the organization who can take appropriate corrective actions, whistle-blowing may be reasonably viewed as prosocial. If the information is offered first to people outside the organization, however, negative effects will probably follow, and such actions are not prosocial, at least from the organization's point of view. For example, one large brokerage house in the United States convicted of insider trading and related practices had to pay fines and damages totaling $650 million when its illegal activities were made known to the Securities and Exchange Commission.

To conclude, before a whistle-blower's actions can be regarded as prosocial in nature, they must be motivated by an underlying desire to help the organization and/or its employees—an assurance that may be difficult to come by. (Adding to this complexity is disagreement among experts as to whether or not whistle-blowing is morally defensible. For a look at this debate, see the Ethical Workplace section below.)

THE ETHICAL WORKPLACE

IS WHISTLE-BLOWING JUSTIFIABLE? AN ETHICAL DEBATE

When an employee blows the whistle, goes public about an organization's wrongdoing, it usually harms the organization (if not also the person himself or herself) and is an extreme act of disloyalty. Generally, such harmful and disloyal actions would be considered unethical. But according to some philosophers, such as Richard T. DeGeorge, there are three conditions that, if satisfied, change the moral status of whistle-blowing to completely justifiable.[19]

First, DeGeorge notes that *the organization's actions must do serious harm to the public.* The idea is that the harm done to the company must be offset by the good to the public created by the effects of the whistle-blowing. A second condition necessary for whistle blowing to be morally defensible is that *the employee should report the questionable practice to an immediate superior.* If one assumes that the organization is interested in doing the right thing (either for its own sake, or to avoid lawsuits and negative publicity), then subordinates are morally obligated to take the most expedient route to correcting the problem—usually, going to one's superior. Third, *if nothing is done to address the problem, the employee should inform progressively higher-ranking officials until all internal channels have been exhausted.* Such actions are necessary to ensure that the wrongdoing and the moral concerns are clearly recognized by organizational officials. Then, only once it is clear that the organization does not intend to right its wrong, is the whistle-blower morally justified—if not morally *obligated*—to bring the problem to the attention of outside agencies.

Others disagree with this notion. For example, Alan F. Westin has identified several reasons why whistle-blowing is not always morally defensible.[20] First, he notes that *whistle-blowing charges are frequently inaccurate.* Although whistle-blowers are sometimes correct in what they allege to be the facts about management's conduct, they also may be incorrect. In such instances, the harmful effects of whistle-blowing are certainly unwarranted. Often it is ambiguous what constitutes an unsafe or dangerous action, and until the facts are clear, it may be inappropriate to change the organization's way of operating. According to Westin, "Putting the whistle to one's lips does not guarantee that one's facts are correct."[21] Second, insofar as legislation protects employees who have

THE ETHICAL WORKPLACE, Cont.

blown the whistle on their employers from being fired, it is possible that *inadequately performing employees may blow the whistle to avoid facing justified personnel sanctions*. As such, blowing the whistle may be an inexpensive form of "antidismissal insurance" that protects poor performers. Third, Westin notes that *some whistle-blowers are not protesting unlawful or unsafe behavior, but social policies they dislike*. For example, an employee may seek negative sanctions against an employer simply because he or she doesn't approve of the company's political contributions. Of course, insofar as there is only a difference of opinion, as opposed to a clear violation of the public safety, there is no wrongdoing, and the person who blows the whistle on such occasions is protesting in an inappropriate fashion. For these reasons, Westin has argued that whistle-blowing is *not* morally justified.

For all their disagreement, both DeGeorge and Westin agree on one key point: Rather than develop laws to protect whistle-blowers from corporate retaliation, it is better to focus on making whistle-blowing unnecessary in the first place. Experts agree that executives need to act morally so that they will set high ethical standards for their organization. Leaders also should establish channels through which employees who wish to raise questions about their company's moral actions can get a fair hearing without appearing to be disloyal. These might include company ombudsmen (people who help employees solve problems), employee advocates, and committees of the board of directors.[22] In fact, DeGeorge believes that, "expressing such concerns, moreover, should be considered a demonstration of company loyalty and should be rewarded appropriately."[23]

As these arguments illustrate, and as your own experiences may tell you, whistle-blowing is a difficult choice. At what point would *you* decide that you must take action to end an evil that is being concealed? Does the value of your personal integrity outweigh the price paid for being honest? Meanwhile, as experts debate the matter, these are questions individuals must ask themselves as they make the personal decision to blow the whistle.

COOPERATION: MUTUAL ASSISTANCE IN WORK SETTINGS

Although prosocial behavior is fairly common in work settings, another pattern known as *cooperation* is probably even more widespread.[24] Here, assistance is mutual, and two or more individuals or groups work together toward shared goals. Such cooperation is a basic form of coordination in many work settings, such as when several computer experts work together to debug a new program, or when members of a special project team combine their skills to develop a new product or service (see Figure 11-3). In all these cases, the underlying principle is much the same: the individuals or groups involved coordinate their actions to reach goals or levels of performance they could not attain alone. Then, once the mutually desired goals are reached, the benefits are shared among the participants in some agreed-on manner. The result: cooperation yields positive outcomes for all concerned.

FIGURE 11-3
COOPERATION: AN ESSENTIAL INGREDIENT IN ORGANIZATIONAL SUCCESS
The medical representative and pharmacist shown here must cooperate with each other to ensure that prescription drugs are used safely and effectively by patients.

The obvious benefits of this pattern raise a basic question: Why, if it is so useful, does it often fail to develop? Why don't people seeking the same (or at least similar) goals always join forces? Although there are several factors involved, the most important one is that cooperation simply cannot develop in many situations because the goals sought by the individuals or groups involved cannot be shared. For example, two people seeking the same job or promotion cannot join forces to attain it; the reward can go to only one. Similarly, if two companies are courting the same potential merger candidate, only one can succeed; it makes little sense for them to work together to assure that a merger does in fact take place, since only one will enjoy the benefits of this transaction.

In cases such as these, an alternative form of behavior known as **competition** often develops. Here, each person, group, or unit strives to maximize its individual gains, often at the expense of others. Indeed, each side tends to view gains and losses by the other side as linked, so that their own "wins" constitute the other side's "losses," and vice versa.[25] In some contexts, competition is both natural and understandable. People and departments do have to compete for scarce organizational resources and rewards. And organizations themselves must compete in the marketplace for supplies, government contracts, customers, and market share. In many instances, however, competition is not dictated by current conditions, and cooperation might develop instead. Under what conditions will competition or cooperation occur? As we will soon describe, both individual and organizational factors play a role.

INDIVIDUAL FACTORS AND COOPERATION

Several factors affecting the tendency to cooperate function primarily through their impact on individuals. They influence the perceptions and reactions of specific people, and in this manner shape individuals' decisions with respect to cooperating or competing with others. Among the most important of these are the principle of *reciprocity*, several aspects of *communication*, and the *personal orientation* toward working with others held by individuals.

RECIPROCITY: REACTING TO OTHERS' BEHAVIOR

Throughout life, we are urged to follow the "Golden Rule"—to do unto others as we would have them do unto us. Despite such exhortations, we usually behave differently. Most people tend to treat others not as they would prefer to be treated, but rather as they have been treated in the past, either by these individuals or by others. In short, people follow the principle of *reciprocity* much of the time. This tendency to behave toward others as they have acted toward us is quite powerful. We can observe it in actions as diverse as attraction, where individuals tend to like others who express positive feelings toward them, and aggression, where "an eye for an eye and a tooth for a tooth" seems to prevail.[26] The choice between cooperation and competition is no exception to this powerful rule. When others act in a competitive manner, we usually respond with mistrust and efforts to defeat them. In contrast, if they behave cooperatively, we usually do the same.

The tendency to reciprocate cooperation is not perfect, however. In judging others' level of cooperation and adjusting our response to it, we often fall prey to the same type of self-serving bias described in Chapter 2: we perceive others' level of cooperation as lower than it really is, and our own level of cooperation as somewhat higher than it really is. The result is that in our dealings with others, we tend to undermatch the level of cooperation they demonstrate.[27]

This tendency aside, reciprocity does appear to be the guiding principle of cooperation. The key task in establishing cooperation in organizations, then, seems to be getting it started. Once individuals, groups, or units have begun to cooperate, the process may be largely self-sustaining. To encourage cooperation, therefore, managers should do everything possible to get the process under way. After it begins, the obvious benefits of cooperation, plus powerful tendencies toward reciprocity, may be expected to maintain it at high levels.

COMMUNICATION: POTENTIAL BENEFITS AND COSTS

Where cooperation could potentially develop but does not, its absence is often blamed on a "failure to communicate" (see Chapter 9). People suggest that better or more frequent contact between the individuals or groups involved might have facilitated coordination. Is this suggestion accurate? In one sense, it is. Some forms of communication do indeed seem to increase interpersonal trust, and so enhance actual cooperation. For example, an open exchange of views may convince all parties that working together is the best strategy, and that a fair division of responsibilities and rewards is possible. Similarly, unless some minimal level of communication exists, close coordination of work activities may be impossible; after all, each individual or group will have little idea of what the others are doing.

Not all types of communication yield such beneficial outcomes, however. In fact, research findings indicate that at least one type of contact between individuals or groups—communication involving the use of *threats*—can reduce rather than encourage cooperation. Threats take many different forms, but they typically involve statements suggesting that negative consequences will be delivered if the recipient does not behave in a certain manner or refrains from acting in a certain manner. For example, a manager may warn her subordinate that if he continues to tie up the phones with personal calls, his phone privileges will be revoked. Similarly, during negotiations, representatives from one company may inform those from another that they will end the current discussions unless one of their requests is met. Although the use of such tactics is tempting, they often produce mixed effects. In many cases, they anger recipients, stiffening their resolve to resist. Even when threats appear to succeed and produce immediate yielding or surrender, they may leave a residue of resentment that can return later to haunt those who issued them. And of course, threats often stimulate counterthreats and create a damaging spiral that can lead, ultimately, to open and costly conflict.

PERSONAL ORIENTATIONS AND COOPERATION

Think about the many people you have known during your life. Can you remember ones who were highly competitive—individuals who viewed most situations as contests in which they, or someone else, would triumph? In contrast, can you recall others who were highly cooperative—people who preferred to minimize differences between their own outcomes and those of others? You probably have little difficulty in bringing examples of both types to mind, for people differ greatly in their tendencies to cooperate or compete. Such differences, in turn, seem to reflect contrasting perspectives toward working with others—perspectives that individuals carry with them from situation to situation and over relatively long periods of time.[28] Both tendencies vary along continuous dimensions (from very low to very high), but research findings suggest that many, if not most, people fall into one of four distinct categories.

First, a sizable proportion are **competitors**—people whose primary motive is doing better than others—beating them in open competition. Indeed, in extreme cases competitors prefer negative outcomes that exceed those of their opponents to positive ones that are less than those attained by others. Second, some people are concerned almost exclusively with maximizing their own gains. **Individualists**, as they are called, have little interest in the outcomes of others, and don't really care whether others do better or worse than themselves. Their major focus is simply on gaining as much as possible in every situation. Third, a relatively small number of people can be classified as **cooperators**. These individuals are primarily concerned with maximizing joint outcomes—the total received by themselves and others. They want everyone they work with to be satisfied with their rewards, and do not wish to defeat them. Finally, a few people can be described as **equalizers**. Their major goal is minimizing differences between their own performance or outcomes and those of others. In short, they wish to assure that everyone they work with receives the same basic results. (See Figure 11-4 for an overview of the motives of these four types of people.)

At this point we should note that although many individuals fall into one of these categories, others demonstrate a mixture of these perspectives. For example, substantial numbers combine an individualistic orientation with a competitive one: they want to do as well as they can, but are also interested in surpassing others when possible. Similarly, some people combine an individualistic orientation with a desire for equality. They want to do as well as they can, but don't want their outcomes to get too far out of line with those of others.

How common is each of these patterns? In other words, are there more competitors or cooperators? Do mixed patterns outnumber the simple ones? A study by Knight and Dubro provides information on this issue.[29] These researchers asked a large group of individuals to complete several tasks designed to reveal their orientation toward working with others. Results indicated that substantial proportions of the participants fell into each of the categories mentioned above. However, the pattern of these preferences differed somewhat for men and women. Among males, the single largest group was competitors; fully one-third showed this orientation, whereas another 18 percent showed an individualistic pattern. In contrast, among females, the single largest group was cooperators (about 20 percent), followed closely by competitors (about 15 percent). Only a relatively small proportion of each gender could be classified as equalizers.

As you might suspect, people showing different perspectives toward working with others tend to behave quite differently.[30] Competitors frequently attempt to exploit the people around them, and cooperate only when they see no other choice. In contrast, cooperators prefer friendly ties with co-workers, and would rather work with them than against them. Individualists are flexible; they choose

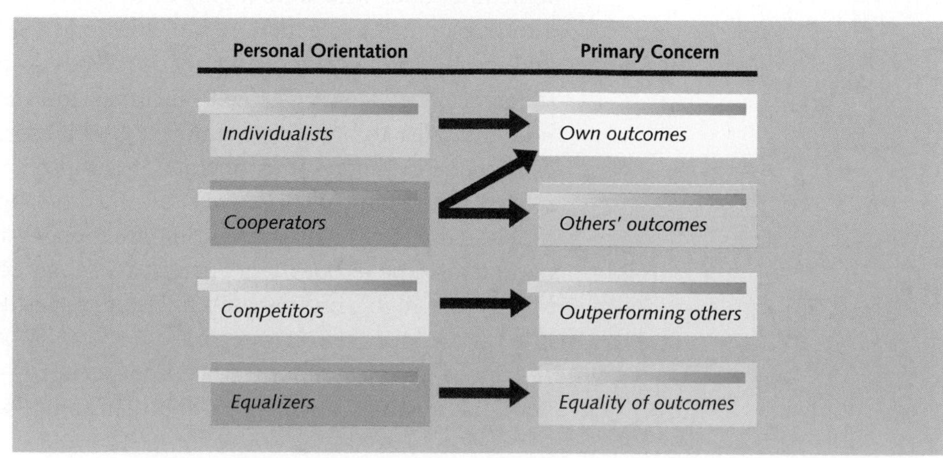

FIGURE 11-4
PERSONAL ORIENTATIONS TOWARD WORKING WITH OTHERS
As shown here, individuals with different orientations toward working with others demonstrate sharply contrasting patterns of motives. These differences, in turn, influence their behavior in a wide range of situations.

whatever strategy will succeed in a given situation. In addition, they often prefer to work alone, concentrating solely on their own outcomes rather than those of others. People with a mixed orientation are harder to predict; they often oscillate or adopt intermediate approaches in working with others.

From a practical point of view, managers should recognize the existence of these different patterns. Further, they should realize that such differences are relevant to several key personnel decisions (e.g., hiring, promotion, work assignments). For example, people with a competitive orientation may be highly effective in situations in which representatives of several organizations must compete against one another. However, they may wreak havoc in contexts requiring prolonged teamwork. In contrast, cooperators may shine as team players, but do poorly in some types of negotiations. Equalizers may excel in positions requiring the fair distribution of resources among various groups (e.g., scheduling space or equipment). But they may run into serious problems if, as managers, they must evaluate the performance of subordinates and recommend differential raises or promotions for them. In summary, individual differences with respect to such orientations are important and can affect performance in a wide range of positions.

ORGANIZATIONAL FACTORS AND COOPERATION

That organizations differ greatly in their internal levels of cooperation is obvious. Some—typically those that are quite successful—demonstrate a high degree of cooperation between their various units or departments.[31] Others—typically those that are not highly successful—show a lower level of such behavior. What accounts for these differences? Individual factors provide only a partial answer. Several factors relating to an organization's internal structure and function also play a role.

REWARD SYSTEMS AND ORGANIZATIONAL STRUCTURE

Imagine the following situation. A large insurance company has two major divisions: Consumer Underwriting (which issues policies for individuals) and Commercial Underwriting (which issues policies for businesses). The company has a bonus system in which annual bonuses are distributed to individuals in the more profitable division. This results in a high degree of competition between the units. At first glance, this might seem beneficial. However, it may lead to situations in which sales personnel from one division actively interfere with the efforts of sales personnel from the other division. For example, while working hard to win a multimillion-dollar policy with a large manufacturing concern, agents from the Commercial Underwriting division actually may discourage top management within this company from seeking individual life and property policies from their company; after all, this would contribute to the sales of their archrival, Consumer Underwriting. And the opposite pattern is true as well. Agents for the consumer division may discourage large clients from seeking policies for their businesses from the commercial division.

Although this might seem to be an extreme case, it reflects conditions that are all too common in many organizations. Reward systems are often "winner-take-all" in form. This fact, coupled with internal differentiation, tends to reduce coordination between units or divisions, as each seeks to maximize its own rewards. This is not to imply that such internal competition is necessarily bad or counterproductive—far from it. Still, managers should assure that it does not reach a level where it hinders the functioning and success of the entire organization.

INTERDEPENDENCE AMONG EMPLOYEES: THE NATURE OF SPECIFIC JOBS

Imagine two organizations. In the first, the major tasks performed by employees can be completed alone; there is no need for individuals to work closely with others. In the second, the tasks performed by employees cannot be completed alone; they must work together closely to do their jobs. In which organization will higher levels of cooperation develop? Obviously, the second. The reason for this difference, too, is apparent. The level of cooperation attained is determined by the nature of the work performed. The greater the degree of interdependence among employees, the higher cooperation among them tends to be. This relationship has been verified in research studies, so it appears to be a useful principle to keep in mind.[32]

CONFLICT: ITS NATURE, CAUSES, AND EFFECTS

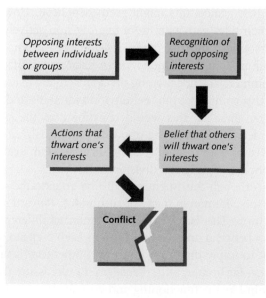

If prosocial behavior and cooperation constitute one end of a continuum describing how individuals and groups work together in organizations, **conflict** certainly lies at the other end. This term has many meanings and has been used to refer to events ranging from the inner turmoil produced by competing needs or desires (inner conflict) to open violence between entire societies (warfare). In the context of organizational behavior, however, the term *conflict* refers primarily to instances in which units or individuals within an organization work *against* rather than with one another.[33] More formally, according to one widely accepted definition, conflict is a process in which one party perceives that another party has taken some action that will exert negative effects on its major interests, or is about to take such action. In other words, the key elements in conflict seem to include (1) opposing interests between individuals or groups, (2) recognition of such opposition, (3) the belief by each side that the other will thwart (or has already thwarted) these interests, and (4) actions that actually produce such thwarting (see Figure 11-5).

Unfortunately, conflict, defined in this manner, is all too common in modern organizations. Moreover, its effects are far too costly to ignore. Practicing managers report that they spend approximately 20 percent of their time dealing with conflict and its impact.[34] And the smoldering resentment and broken relationships that are the aftermath of many conflicts can persist for months or even years, continuing to exact a major toll in precious human resources long after the situation that initiated the conflict is merely a memory. For these and related reasons, organizational conflict is an important topic for the field of OB, and one deserving of our careful attention. In the remainder of this section, we will provide an overview of current knowledge about this costly process. First we will examine two basic dimensions that underlie many forms of conflict.

FIGURE 11-5
THE NATURE OF ORGANIZATIONAL CONFLICT
Conflict involves opposing or incompatible interests between groups or individuals, recognition of these opposing interests, and the belief by both sides that their adversary has acted, or will soon act, to thwart their important interests (Source: Based on suggestions by Thomas, 1992; see Note 2.)

Second, we will describe a recent, sophisticated model of conflict. Then, finally, we will examine many causes of conflict and several of its major effects.

INTEGRATION AND DISTRIBUTION: TWO BASIC DIMENSIONS OF CONFLICT

In your dealings with other people, to what extent do you focus on your own interests, maximizing your outcomes? And to what extent do you focus on others' interests—assuring that they are treated fairly, or that the size of the available "pie" (whatever it is) is maximized for all concerned? These questions are difficult to answer accurately because most cultures have strong norms against pure selfishness—concern purely with one's own outcomes. Yet the temptation to pursue one's own interests is strong and hard to resist in many situations. Several basic models of conflict take careful note of these facts, suggesting that conflict, as an organizational or interpersonal process, can best be understood in terms of two key dimensions: **distribution**, concern with one's own outcomes; and **integration**, concern with the outcomes of others. A large body of research evidence indicates that these dimensions are important and that they are largely independent. Thus, in a given situation, it is possible to pursue actions that are high in both distribution and integration, low in both dimensions, or high in one and low in the other.[35] In fact, various combinations of these motives underlie five distinct styles of handling conflict with others: *competing*, *collaborating*, *avoiding*, *accommodating*, and *compromising*.[36]

Figure 11-6 illustrates the position of each of these styles with respect to integration and distribution. *Compromise*, which involves splitting issues down the middle, is in the middle on both dimensions; it reflects moderate degrees of concern with one's own interests and the interests of others. In contrast, *competition*

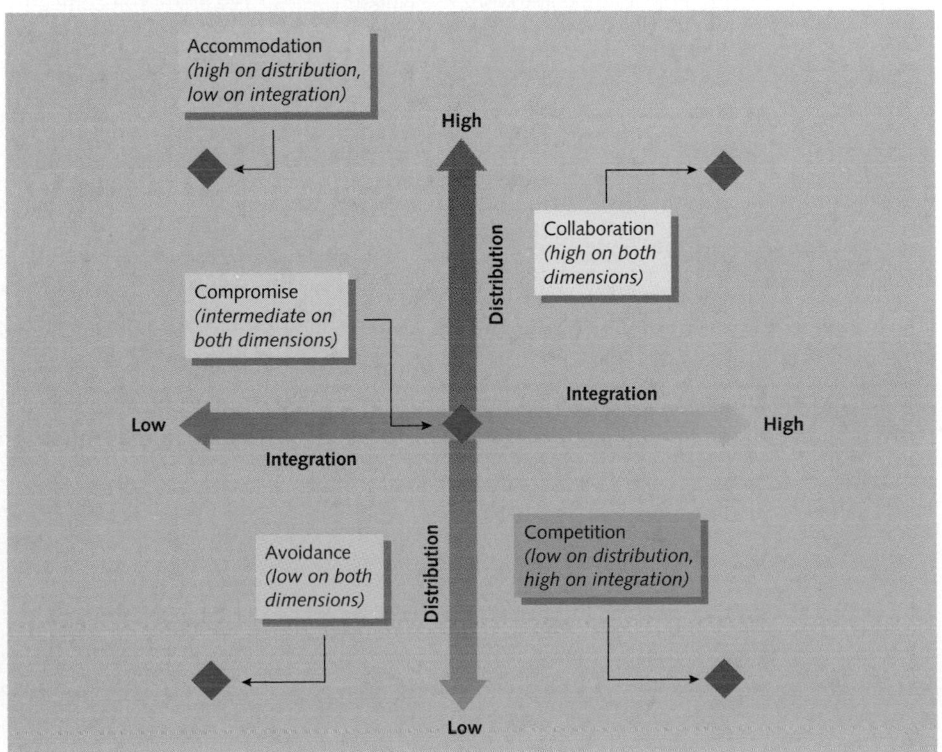

FIGURE 11-6
BASIC STYLES OF RESOLVING CONFLICT
Different approaches to resolving conflict reflect two underlying dimensions present in most conflict situations: concern with one's own outcomes (integration), and concern with the outcomes of others (distribution). The five major styles of resolving conflict reflect various positions with respect to these two dimensions.

represents a style of conflict resolution reflecting high concern with one's own interests but low concern with the interests of others. *Avoidance* reflects low standing on both dimensions, whereas collaboration—seeking maximum outcomes for both sides—is high on both dimensions. Finally, *accommodation*—giving others whatever they want—is low in distribution but high in integration. (Are these styles equally likely to occur throughout the world, or do people from various cultures prefer different styles of resolving conflicts? For an examination of this question, see the Global Organization section below.)

CONFLICT: A MODERN PERSPECTIVE

Opposing interests, it is widely agreed, lie at the core of most conflicts. Indeed, it makes little sense to use the term *conflict* in the absence of incompatible interests or aspirations. Yet conflict involves much more than this. Bitter disputes often erupt in situations where the interests of the two sides are not clearly opposed. In other cases, conflict fails to develop despite deep divisions between potential

THE GLOBAL ORGANIZATION

CULTURAL DIFFERENCES IN APPROACHES TO CONFLICT

Suppose you are visiting China or Taiwan, and observe two people attempting to resolve a conflict between them. Would you expect these individuals to behave differently from two people from the United States who are in the same situation? Research by Ting-Toomey and her associates suggests that people in Eastern cultures, such as China, Korea, Japan, Taiwan, and other Asian nations, and those in Western cultures, such as the United States and Canada, approach conflict situations quite differently.[37]

A key difference lies in the fact that Western cultures tend to be highly *individualistic*, valuing individual needs and achievement over group needs and achievement, whereas Eastern cultures tend to be highly *collectivistic*, valuing group needs and achievement over individual needs and achievement.[38] (Recall our discussion of these differences in Chapter 8.) As such, people from individualistic cultures would be expected to use more dominating strategies, when facing conflict with others. By contrast, people from individualistic cultures would be expected to face conflict by being more obliging or by avoiding conflict altogether.

To test these predictions, Ting-Toomey and her colleagues conducted a study comparing the conflict-handling tactics of people from several countries, including the United States, China, and Taiwan.[39] Participants completed surveys measuring, among other things, their preferences for various modes of conflict resolution, including dominating (defeating one's opponent), obliging, (accommodating the interests of one's opponent), and avoiding (escaping the conflict situation entirely). The researchers found significant cultural differences with respect to preferences for various modes of handling conflict. As expected, preference for dominating was highest among Americans. However, among people from China, a preference for obliging was greatest, and among people from Taiwan, the desire to avoid conflict was most strongly expressed. In contrast, the desire to be obliging and to avoid conflict were least strongly preferred by Americans.

These findings should not be taken as an indication that cultural factors are all-powerful determinants of ways of dealing with conflict. On the contrary, all individuals, regardless of their cultural background, may adopt any of several different approaches to resolving conflict depending on the nature of the situations they face. Still, it is interesting to note that people are not equally predisposed to using all approaches. Clearly, culture appears to form an important backdrop for conflict. Overlooking the role of culture would make incomplete our efforts at understanding and managing conflict between people in organizations.

adversaries. Such situations suggest that a full understanding of conflict will require much more than mere identification of opposing interests. Many other factors relating to the thoughts, feelings, and actions of the people involved enter into the picture and must be carefully considered. How, then, should we conceive of organizational conflict? A model proposed by Thomas offers one intriguing answer.[40]

According to Thomas, it is important to view conflict as a *process*—a complex series of events over time that both *reflect* external conditions and, in turn, *affect* them. More specifically, Thomas notes that conflict episodes between individuals or groups stem from preceding events and conditions, and produce results and outcomes. In other words, conflict is part of a continuing, ongoing relationship between two or more parties, not an isolated event that can be considered in and of itself. What, then, are the key elements in this continuing process? Thomas calls attention to several.

The first is awareness of the conflict. Thomas suggests that conflicts are, to a large extent, in the eyes of the beholders—they occur only when the parties involved recognize the existence of opposing interests. This, of course, is why conflict sometimes fails to emerge when outside observers notice deep divisions between potential opponents. The parties themselves do not notice (or care to notice!) these conditions, and if they do not, conflict remains only a possibility.

Second, once aware of the conflict, both parties experience emotional reactions to it and think about it in various ways. These emotions and thoughts are crucial to the course of the developing conflict. For example, if the emotional reactions of one or both sides include anger and resentment from past wrongs or from contemplated future ones, the conflict is likely to be intense. If such reactions are absent, or if other emotions (e.g., fear over the potential costs) are dominant, it may be of lower intensity and develop quite differently. Similarly, the parties' reasoning concerning the conflict can have profound effects on its form and ultimate resolution. Here, both *rational-instrumental reasoning* (e.g., thoughts concerning potential costs and benefits, the conflict's bearing on major goals) and *normative reasoning* (e.g., concerns about what is appropriate in the situation or how others would react) are important.

Third, on the basis of such thoughts and emotions, individuals formulate specific intentions—plans to adopt various strategies during the conflict. These may be quite general (e.g., plans to adopt a conciliatory, cooperative approach) or quite specific (e.g., decisions to follow specific bargaining tactics).

In the next step, such intentions are translated into actual behavior. These actions then elicit some response from the opposite side, and the process recycles. That is, the opponent's reactions affect current thoughts and feelings about the conflict, intentions concerning further behavior, and so on. (See Figure 11-7 for a summary of this process.)

Thomas's model of organizational conflict is quite sophisticated and rests on a firm base of empirical research. However, there can be little doubt that it will be modified in the years ahead as additional information about conflict and its components accumulates. Perhaps its main contribution, then, is that it calls attention to the following important facts: (1) organizational conflict is an ongoing process that occurs against a backdrop of continuing relationships and events; it is definitely not a short-term, isolated occurrence; (2) such conflict involves the thoughts, perceptions, memories, and emotions of the people involved; these must be taken into account in any complete model of organizational conflict; and (3) conflict stems from a very wide range of conditions and events—ones relating to individu-

FIGURE 11-7

CONFLICT: A MODERN VIEW

According to a framework proposed by Thomas, conflict is a complex process involving the thoughts and emotions of people, their intentions to behave in certain ways, and their overt actions. (Source: Based on suggestions by Thomas, 1992; see Note 2.)

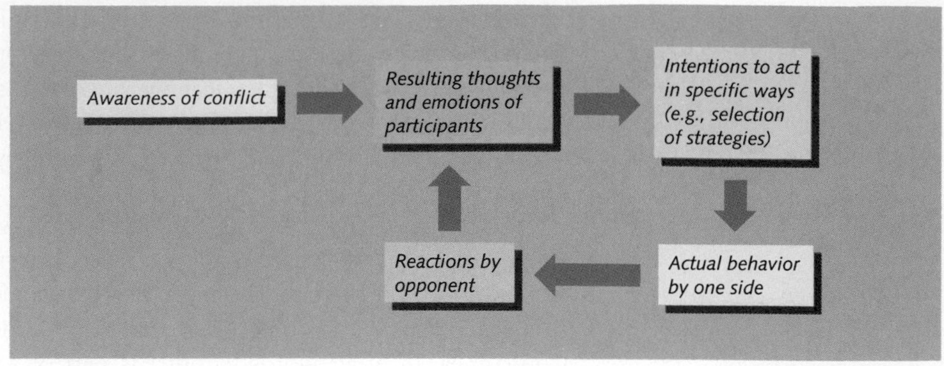

als and ones relating to the structure, norms, and functioning of organizations. It is to these factors—the major causes of conflict—that we turn next.

THE MAJOR CAUSES OF CONFLICT

As we noted above, conflict involves the presence or perception of opposing interests. Yet this condition, by itself, is neither necessary nor sufficient for the occurrence of actual conflict. Open confrontations sometimes fail to develop despite the existence of incompatible interests. And conflict sometimes emerges even when opposing interests are not present. Clearly, then, many factors and conditions contribute to the occurrence of conflict. These can be divided into two major groups: factors relating to organizational structure or functioning, and factors relating to interpersonal relations.

ORGANIZATIONAL CAUSES OF CONFLICT

Perhaps the most obvious organization-based cause of conflict is *competition over scarce resources*. No organization has unlimited resources, and conflicts often arise over the division or distribution of space, money, equipment, or personnel. Unfortunately, such conflicts are often intensified by the self-serving bias described in Chapter 2. Each side tends to inflate its contribution to the organization, and therefore its fair share of available resources. The result can be intense, prolonged conflict.

Two closely related factors are *ambiguity over responsibility* and *ambiguity over jurisdiction*. Groups or individuals within an organization are sometimes uncertain as to who is responsible for performing various tasks or duties. When this occurs, each involved party disclaims responsibility, and conflict can develop over this issue. Similarly, uncertainty frequently exists over who has jurisdiction or authority. And, as our Preview Case illustrates, disputes over this issue can be intense.

A third organizational factor that often plays a role in conflict is *interdependence* and events stemming from it. In most organizations, various units, groups, and individuals must depend on others for performance of their own jobs. They receive input from others and cannot proceed without it. When input is delayed or delivered in an incomplete or unsatisfactory form, strong conflict may result. This is hardly surprising; groups or individuals faced with this situation perceive (and rightly so) that their major goals are being blocked or interfered with by others. Little wonder that they retaliate in kind and that productive work may grind to a halt (or at least slow appreciably) in the spiraling conflict that follows.

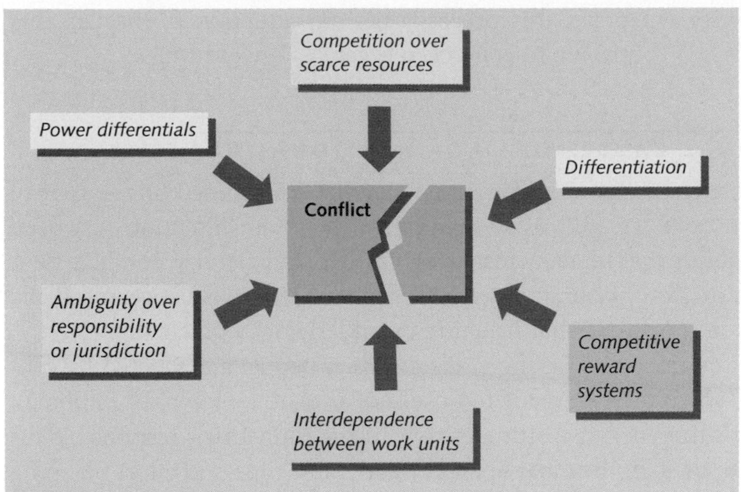

FIGURE 11-8
THE ORGANIZATIONAL CAUSES OF CONFLICT
As summarized here, several organization-based factors contribute to the occurrence of conflict in work settings.

We have already described yet another organization-based cause of conflict: *reward systems*. When such systems pit one unit or group against another (as is often the case), a degree of conflict is practically guaranteed. This is especially likely if the people involved perceive the system as somehow unfair or biased.[41,42] In such instances, the groups that fail to attain important benefits (e.g., bonuses, raises) may experience resentment, and unnecessary conflict may be the next step in the process.

Conflict is sometimes also a by-product of *differentiation* within an organization. As organizations grow and develop, many experience a trend toward an increasing number of departments or divisions (see Chapter 15). Individuals working in these groups become socialized to them, and tend to accept their norms and values. As they come to identify with these work groups, their perceptions of other organization members may change. They view people outside their units as different, less worthy, and less competent than those within it. At the same time, they tend to overvalue their own unit and the people within it. Ultimately, this process may encourage costly conflicts. After all, if individuals in each department or unit are fiercely loyal to their own turf, they may lose sight of shared organizational goals and tend to focus, instead, on pursuing their own self-interests. Increasing differentiation within an organization encourages individuals within it to divide it into "us" (members of our own group) and "them" (people outside it), and this, in turn, can be a contributing factor in the initiation of conflict. (See Figure 11-8 for a summary of the organization-based causes of conflict discussed in this section.)

Finally, as noted recently by Kabanoff, conflict can stem from *power differentials* between organization members.[43] Kabanoff states that in organizations, as in other settings, a continuous tension exists between the norms of *equity*, the belief that organization members should be rewarded in terms of their relative contributions; and *equality*, the belief that everyone should receive the same or similar outcomes, at least in certain respects. These rules are often applied to different kinds of outcomes. For example, equity is applied to raises, bonuses, and other tangible rewards. In contrast, equality is applied to such socioemotional outcomes as courteous treatment, friendliness, and so on.[44]

Kabanoff reasoned that the greater the power differential between any two organizational members, the more likely that equity will be accepted as the distributive rule governing their relationship. This is likely to occur insofar as the more powerful person is able to invoke a rule that benefits himself or herself, leaving the less powerful person to accept this situation.[45] As a result, the likelihood of overt conflict over the distribution of available rewards decreases. However, at the same time, the low-power individuals may experience feelings of frustration and decreased involvement in the relationship—reactions sometimes described as *nondirected conflict*. So, in a sense, organizations face something of a tradeoff where power differentials and conflict are concerned. High-power differentials in organizational relationships tend to minimize clear cognitions of injustice on the part of the less powerful parties, and so also reduce the likelihood of overt conflict over reward distributions. At the same time, however, such differentials give rise to a kind of smoldering discontent, which may translate into nondirected conflict.

Whatever the precise outcomes, this process calls our attention to the fact that power differentials can contribute to conflict in organizational settings.

INTERPERSONAL CAUSES OF ORGANIZATIONAL CONFLICT

In the past, most research on organizational conflict has focused on the type of organizational causes noted above. More recently, however, attention has been drawn to the possibility that in many instances, costly organizational conflicts stem as much (or perhaps more) from interpersonal factors—relations between specific individuals—as from organizational structure or underlying conflicts of interest.

First, consider the impact of lasting *grudges*. When people are angered by others, and especially when they are made to "lose face" (i.e., to look foolish publicly), they may develop strong negative attitudes toward the individuals responsible for these outcomes. As a result, they may spend considerable time and effort planning or actually seeking revenge for these wrongs. Unfortunately, such grudges can persist for years, with obvious negative effects for the organizations or work groups involved.[46]

Second, conflict often stems from (or is intensified by) *faulty attributions*—errors concerning the causes behind others' behavior (see Chapter 2). When individuals find that their interests have been thwarted by another person, they generally try to determine why this person acted the way he or she did. Was it malevolence, a desire to harm them? Or did the provoker's actions stem from factors beyond his or her control? A growing body of evidence suggests that when people reach the former conclusion, anger and subsequent conflict are more likely and more intense than when they reach the latter conclusion.[47]

For example, in one study on this issue Baron had students engage in simulated negotiations with another person (actually an accomplice).[48] Both individuals played the role of executives representing different departments within a large organization who bargained over the division of $1 million in surplus funds between their respective departments. The accomplice adopted a very confrontational stance, demanding fully $800,000 out of $1 million in available funds for his or her own department, and offered only two small concessions during the negotiations. As the bargaining proceeded, the accomplice made several statements indicating that he or she had been ordered to behave in this "tough" manner by his or her constituents. In other words, the accomplice adopted a bargaining tactic often described as the "my hands are tied" strategy. In one condition, participants received information suggesting these claims were true (the opponent appeared to be sincere in his or her statements); in another, they learned that these claims were false (the opponent appeared to be insincere). As predicted, participants reported more negative reactions to the accomplice, and stronger tendencies to avoid and compete with this person on future occasions, when they learned that he or she had misrepresented the causes behind his or her behavior.

A third interpersonal factor of considerable importance in generating organizational conflict might be termed *faulty communication*. This refers to the fact that individuals often communicate with others in a way that angers or annoys them, even though it is not their intention to do so. Faulty communication often involves a lack of clarity—for example, a manager is certain that she communicated her wishes clearly to a subordinate, but the subordinate is confused about what he is supposed to do. When the manager later finds that the task has not been completed, she is annoyed. The subordinate, in turn, is angered by what he considers unfair treatment. In other cases, conflict involves *inappropriate criticism*—negative feedback delivered in a manner that angers the recipient instead of helping this person to do a better job.

What makes criticism constructive rather than destructive? Research findings point to the factors shown in Table 11-2,[49,50] We're sure that none of the factors listed there will surprise you. After all, we all have been on the receiving end of criticism, and know that negative feedback delivered in a considerate and timely manner, does not contain threats, and does not make unflattering attributions about the causes behind our behavior or performance is far preferable to criticism that is harsh, contains threats, and so on. Although most people appreciate these basic principles, they often find it difficult to follow them in their dealings with subordinates, co-workers, friends, and family. Specifically, most people are reluctant to deliver negative feedback to others (see Chapter 9). As a result, they often say nothing at all until the problem becomes so great, or their anger and irritation becomes so strong, that they can no longer hold back. What follows is an angry outburst, unlikely to adhere to the simple rules for constructive criticism listed above.[51]

A fourth interpersonal source of conflict is *distrust*.[52] The more strongly people suspect that another party is out to get them, and likely to act without their own best interests in mind, the more likely they are to have a relationship with that party riddled with conflict. This phenomenon may be illustrated by some recent

TABLE 11-2

Constructive Versus Destructive Criticism

The factors listed here distinguish constructive criticism (negative feedback that may be accepted by the recipient and improve his or her performance) from destructive criticism (negative feedback likely to be rejected by the recipient and unlikely to improve his or her performance).

CONSTRUCTIVE CRITICISM	DESTRUCTIVE CRITICISM
Considerate—protects self-esteem of recipient	*Inconsiderate—harsh, sarcastic, biting*
Does not contain threats	*Contains threats*
Timely—occurs as soon as possible after the substandard performance	*Not timely—occurs after inappropriate delay*
Does not attribute poor performance to internal causes	*Attributes poor performance to internal causes (e.g., lack of effort, motivation, ability)*
Specific—focuses on aspects of performance that were inadequate	*General—a sweeping condemnation of performance*
Focuses on performance, not on recipient	*Focuses on the recipient—his or her personal characteristics*
Offers concrete suggestions for improvement	*Offers no concrete suggestions for improvement*
Motivated by desire to help the recipient improve	*Motivated by anger, desire to assert dominance over recipient, desire for revenge*

Sources: Based on suggestions by Weisinger, 1989, see Note 48; and Baron, 1990, see Note 49.

changes in mood among some employees at General Motors' Saturn plant in Spring Hill, Tennessee. From its inception, United Auto Workers (UAW) union officials worked closely with GM management to produce cars as a carefully orchestrated team (see Chapter 8). Recently, however, some employees have felt that UAW officials have become *too* cozy with GM management, and have not adequately represented their interests.[53] The result: a growing number of Saturn assembly workers have grown to distrust their union, and feel that their relationship with it has become strained. In general, companies that are considered great places in which to work are ones characterized by high levels of trust between people at all levels.[54]

Finally, several *personal characteristics*, too, seem to play a role in organizational conflict (see Chapter 3). For example, *Type A* individuals report becoming involved in conflict with others more frequently than *Type B* people (refer to our discussion of this characteristic in Chapter 6).[55] Conversely, people who are high in *self-monitoring* (those who are highly aware of how others are reacting to them) report resolving conflict in more productive ways (e.g., through collaboration or compromise) than those who are low in self-monitoring.[56]

In summary, considerable evidence suggests that conflict in work settings often stems from relations between individuals and from their personal characteristics, as well as from underlying structural (organization-based) factors. At first glance, this finding might appear to be quite pessimistic in its implications for the reduction or management of such conflict; after all, it adds several potential causes to those that have traditionally been viewed as important. In fact, however, it can actually be interpreted as quite optimistic. Interpersonal behavior, and even many personal characteristics, can readily be modified. Indeed, in many cases, these may be easier to change than organizational structure, and easier to modify than built-in underlying conflicts of interest. For this reason, understanding the interpersonal causes of organizational conflict may offer important, practical benefits.

THE EFFECTS OF CONFLICT: POSITIVE AND NEGATIVE

In everyday speech, the term *conflict* has strong negative connotations. It seems to imply anger, direct confrontations, and harsh, damaging behavior. In fact, however, conflict in work settings actually operates like the proverbial "double-edged sword." Depending on why it occurs and how it develops, conflict can yield beneficial as well as harmful effects.

THE NEGATIVE EFFECTS OF CONFLICT

Some of the negative effects produced by conflict are too obvious to require much comment. For example, it often produces strong negative emotions and thus can be quite stressful. Conflict frequently interferes with communication between individuals, groups, or divisions. In this way, it can all but eliminate coordination between them. Third, it diverts attention and needed energies away from major tasks and efforts to attain key organizational goals. In all these ways, conflict can seriously interfere with organizational effectiveness. And, in the case of Wemco Inc., the largest U.S. manufacturer of neckties, it did.[57] Until some changes were made in 1990, members of the Pulitzer family, owners of the company founded in 1923, quarreled so much that family members sued each other and diverted attention away from their business so often that the company's products failed to keep pace with consumers' tastes, and sales dropped considerably.

Although this is an extreme case, other negative effects of conflict are somewhat more subtle and are sometimes easily overlooked. First, it has been found that conflict between groups often encourages their leaders to shift from participative to authoritarian styles.[58] The reason for this is that groups experiencing stress require firm direction (see Chapter 13). Recognizing this fact, their leaders adopt more controlling tactics when conflict develops. As a result of such changes, groups experiencing conflict tend to provide less pleasant work environments than ones not faced with this type of stress.

Second, conflict increases the tendency of both sides to engage in negative stereotyping. As we noted earlier, the members of opposing groups or units tend to emphasize the differences between them. These differences are interpreted in a negative light, so that each side views the other in increasingly unfavorable terms.

Finally, conflict leads each side to close ranks and emphasize loyalty to their own department or group. Anyone who suggests, even tentatively, that the other side's position has some merit is viewed as a traitor and is strongly censured. As a result, it becomes increasingly difficult for opponents to take each other's perspectives—a development that sharply reduces the likelihood of an effective resolution of their differences, and increases the likelihood of *groupthink* (see Chapter 10).[59]

THE POSITIVE EFFECTS OF CONFLICT

The picture is not entirely bleak, however. Although conflict often has a disruptive impact on organizations, it can, under some conditions, also yield important benefits (for a overview of these, see Figure 11-9).[60] First, conflict serves to bring problems that have previously been ignored out into the open. And, since recognition of problems is a necessary first step to their solution, conflict can sometimes be useful in this way.

Second, conflict motivates people on both sides of an issue to know and understand each other's positions more fully. As noted by Tjosvold, this can foster open-mindedness and lead each side to incorporate aspects of the opposing views into their own.[61]

Third, conflict often encourages the consideration of new ideas and approaches, facilitating innovation and change.[62] This is so because once open conflict erupts, an organization or work unit simply cannot continue with "business as usual." The need for hard decisions, new policies, major shifts in personnel, or even a new internal structure is driven home, and appropriate change may then follow. As we will describe in Chapter 16, such change is frequently required for organizations to survive.

Fourth, growing evidence suggests that conflict can lead to better decisions. When decision makers receive information incompatible with their views—which is often the case when conflict exists—they tend to make better judgments and reach more adequate decisions than when controversy does not exist.[63] This only occurs, of course,

FIGURE 11-9
POSITIVE EFFECTS OF CONFLICT
Contrary to popular belief, conflict can produce a number of beneficial effects. The most important of these are shown here.

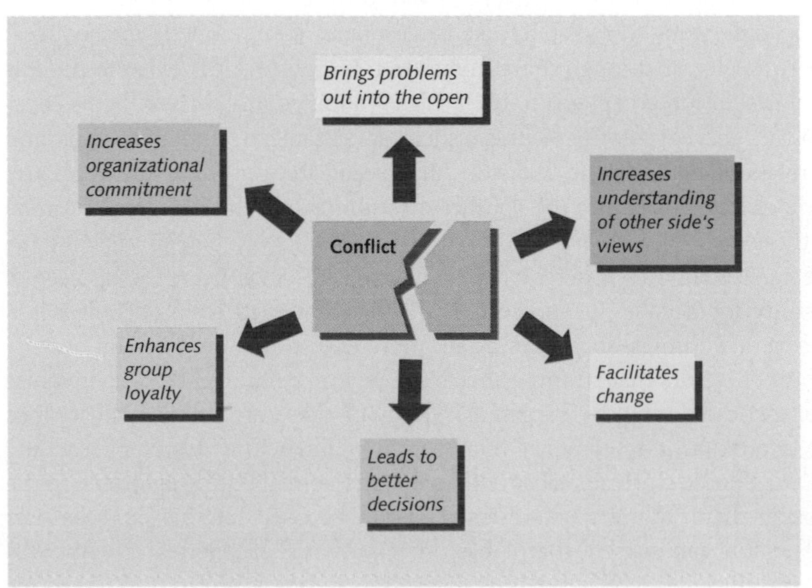

when the conflict forces people to challenge their assumptions, confront new ideas, and consider new positions. If, however, people resent having to confront different ideas, the results may be far more disruptive.[64]

Fifth, conflict enhances group loyalty, increasing motivation and performance within the groups or units involved. Each strives to attain higher levels of excellence to outdo its rival, and if not carried too far, such efforts can have beneficial effects.

Finally, recent findings indicate that conflict, especially *cognitive conflict*, in which opposing views are brought out into the open and fully discussed, can enhance organizational commitment.[65] In contrast, to the extent that such discussion is blocked and a free exchange of opposing views is not permitted to occur, job satisfaction may be reduced.[66]

In summary, conflict can actually contribute to organizational effectiveness. Note, however, that benefits occur only when conflict is carefully managed and does not get out of control. If conflict is permitted to become extreme, rationality—and the potential benefits described above—may vanish in a haze of intense negative emotions. Assuming that such dangers are avoided, however, existing evidence suggests that conflict can indeed often play a constructive role in many organizations.

EFFECTIVE CONFLICT MANAGEMENT TECHNIQUES

f conflict can indeed yield benefits as well as costs, the key task organizations face with respect to this process is managing its occurrence. In short, the overall goal should not be to eliminate conflict; instead, it should be to adopt procedures for maximizing its potential benefits while minimizing its potential costs. Fortunately, a number of approaches have been found useful in this regard. Several of these will now be reviewed.

BARGAINING: THE UNIVERSAL PROCESS

By far the most common strategy for resolving organizational conflicts, and therefore for managing them effectively, is **bargaining** or **negotiation**.[67] In this process, opposing sides to a dispute exchange offers, counteroffers, and concessions, either directly or through representatives (see Figure 11-10). If the process is successful, a solution acceptable to both sides is attained and the conflict is effectively resolved, perhaps with "extras" such as enhanced understanding and improved relations between the two sides. If, instead, bargaining is unsuccessful, costly deadlock may result and the conflict may intensify. What factors determine which of these outcomes occurs? Given the importance of bargaining, and its occurrence in virtually all spheres of life, this question has been the subject of intensive study for decades.[68] The answer that has emerged from such research would fill several volumes, so we can do no more than touch on it briefly here.

One group of factors that strongly affects the outcomes of negotiations involves the specific tactics adopted by bargainers. Many of these are designed to reduce opponents' aspirations—to convince them that they have little chance of reaching their goals and should, instead, accept offers that are actually quite favorable to the side proposing them. Many specific strategies can be used for this purpose. For example, one side can suggest that it has other potential partners and will withdraw from the current negotiations if its proposals are not accepted. Similarly, one

FIGURE 11-10

NEGOTIATION: A COMMON TACTIC FOR RESOLVING CONFLICT

In the process of negotiation, opposing sides to a dispute exchange offers and counteroffers, and make concessions until outcomes acceptable to both are attained. Fortunately, negotiators are generally not as demonstrative as the one shown here. (Source: Cartoon by Mort Gerberg, © 1991, from Harvard Business Review *September 1991.)*

"He's a very impressive negotiator—in a Mike Tyson sort of way."

party to a dispute can claim that its breakeven point is much lower than it really is—a procedure known as the "big lie" technique.[69] If the other side accepts this information, it may make sizable concessions. Third, the course of negotiations and final settlements are often strongly affected by the nature of initial offers. Relatively extreme offers seem to put strong pressure on opponents to make concessions, resulting in settlements favorable to the side adopting such positions.[70] On the other hand, if initial offers are too extreme, opponents may be angered and decide to seek other negotiating partners.

A second group of factors that determines the nature and outcomes of bargaining involves the *cognitive set* or focus adopted by negotiators. Several studies suggest that when bargainers adopt a *positive frame*—focusing on the potential benefits of negotiations and of the settlements that may result—bargaining is facilitated. In contrast, when they adopt a *negative frame*—focusing on potential losses or costs—bargaining is impaired.[71] (Recall our discussion of framing effects in the context of decision-making in Chapter 10.) In short, expectations or cognitive sets shape reality, determining the nature and course of actual bargaining.

A third aspect of negotiations that plays an important role in this process is the *perceptions* of the people involved.[72] Studies by Thompson and his colleagues reveal that negotiators often enter bargaining situations with important misperceptions. In particular, they seem to begin with the view that their own interests and those of the other side are entirely incompatible—the **incompatibility error**. This, of course, causes them to overlook interests that are actually compatible. In addition, they tend to begin with the view, often false, that the other party places the same importance or priority that they do on each issue, a tendency known as the **fixed-sum error**. Both of these assumptions are false and often prevent bargainers from obtaining an agreement that is maximally beneficial to both sides.

Fortunately, these misperceptions concerning interests and priorities often change during the course of negotiations, fading over time, often within the first few minutes of negotiations.[73] And experienced negotiators are less likely to fall prey to such errors than inexperienced ones.[74] However, many negotiators retain these false perceptions even over prolonged periods of bargaining, with the result that both parties experience lower payoffs than would otherwise be true. As might be expected, the smaller such errors in perception (i.e., the more accurate bargainers' perceptions of each other's outcomes are), the higher the joint payoffs obtained by both sides.[75] Clearly, then, steps designed to improve the accuracy of negotiators' perceptions of the situations they face and each other's interests and priorities can go a long way toward enhancing the outcomes of this process. Such steps may include training negotiators to seek information from each other during negotiations instead of clinging to their initial assumptions, and making them aware of the *fixed-sum* and *incompatibility errors* described above.

Perhaps the single most important factor determining the success of negotiations in producing settlements satisfactory to both sides, however, involves participants' overall orientation toward this process. Three decades ago, Walton and McKersie pointed out that people taking part in negotiations can approach such discussions from either of two distinct perspectives.[76] On the one hand, they can view negotiations as "win-lose" situations in which gains by one side are necessarily linked with losses for the other. On the other hand, people can approach negotiations as potential "win-win" situations—ones in which the interests of the two sides are not necessarily incompatible and in which the potential gains of both can be maximized.[77] Not all situations offer the potential for such agreements, but many that at first glance seem to involve simple head-on clashes between the two sides do, in fact, provide such possibilities. If participants are willing to explore all options carefully, and exert the effort required to identify creative potential solutions, they can attain **integrative agreements**—ones that offer greater joint benefits than simple compromise (splitting all differences down the middle).

How can such integrative agreements be attained? Pruitt and his colleagues suggest the possibilities summarized in Table 11-3.[78] As you can see, these involve several distinct tactics. In *nonspecific compensation*, one side receives certain benefits and the other is compensated for providing these in some unrelated manner (e.g., by concessions on some other issue). In *logrolling*, each side makes concessions on relatively unimportant issues to attain concessions on issues it views as more central to its needs. For example, consider a dispute between scientists and management in a research department of a large organization. The scientists want to be free

TABLE 11-3

Techniques for Reaching Integrative Agreements

Several strategies can be useful in attaining integrative agreements in bargaining. A few of the major ones are summerized here.

TYPE OF AGREEMENT	DESCRIPTION
Broadening the pie	*Available resources are broadened so that both sides can obtain their major goals.*
Nonspecific compensation	*One side gets what it wants; the other is compensated on an unrelated issue*
Logrolling	*Each party makes concessions on low-priority issues in exchange for concessions on issues that it values more highly.*
Cost cutting	*One party gets what it desires, and the costs to the other party are reduced or eliminated.*
Bridging	*Neither party gets its initial demands, but a new option that satisfies the major interests of both sides is developed.*

Source: Based on suggestions by Pruitt et al., 1983; see Note 77.

to order any equipment they want, to pursue projects they feel are important, and to do as little paperwork as possible. Management wants to hold costs to a minimum, wants the scientists to pursue only company-chosen projects, and requires many reports and forms. Under the strategy of logrolling, the scientists might agree to do more paperwork (a relatively unimportant issue to them, but one that is very important to management), and to pay more attention to costs (another issue of great importance to management). However, they would gain more freedom to pursue at least some projects of their own choosing (a central issue to the scientists).

Research findings suggest that when disputing parties strive for integrative agreements, joint outcomes do indeed increase. Moreover, the nature of their discussions changes. *Contentious tactics* such as threats or taking unyielding positions decrease, and the open exchange of accurate information between the two sides increases. Thus, not only does integrative bargaining increase the outcomes of both sides, it may enhance their relationships, too. Given these benefits, it seems clear that encouraging such an approach to negotiations is one highly effective strategy for managing real or potential conflicts.

THIRD-PARTY INTERVENTION: MEDIATION AND ARBITRATION

Despite the best efforts of both sides, negotiations sometimes deadlock. When they do, the aid of a third party, someone not directly involved in the dispute, is often sought. Such third-party intervention can take many forms, but the most common are *mediation* and *arbitration*.[79]

In **mediation**, the third party attempts, through various tactics, to facilitate voluntary agreements between the disputants. Mediators have no formal power and cannot impose an agreement on the two sides. Instead, they seek to clarify the issues involved and enhance communication between the opponents. Mediators sometimes offer specific recommendations for compromise or integrative solutions; in other cases, they merely guide disputants toward developing such solutions themselves. Their role is primarily that of *facilitator*—helping the two sides toward agreements they both find acceptable.[80]

In contrast, third-parties are more powerful during **arbitration.** Specifically, arbitrators do have the power to impose (or at least strongly recommend) the terms of an agreement. In *binding arbitration*, the two sides agree in advance to accept these terms. In *voluntary arbitration*, though, the two sides retain the freedom to reject the recommended agreement (although the personal stature and expertise of the arbitrator may make it difficult for them to do so). In *conventional arbitration*, the arbitrator can offer any package of terms he or she wishes. However, in *final-offer arbitration*, the arbitrator merely chooses between final offers made by the disputants.

Both mediation and arbitration can be helpful in resolving organizational conflicts. However, both suffer from certain drawbacks. Because it requires voluntary compliance by the disputing parties, mediation often proves ineffective. Indeed, it may simply serve to underscore the depth of the differences between the two sides. Arbitration also suffers from several potential problems. First, it may exert a *chilling effect* on negotiations, bringing voluntary progress to a halt. Since both sides know the arbitrator will resolve the dispute for them, they see little point in engaging in serious bargaining, which, after all, is hard work. Second, one or both sides may come to suspect that the arbitrator is biased. The result: disputants become increasingly reluctant to agree to arbitration. Third, a practical consideration: arbitration tends to cost more and take longer than mediation (on average, about $5,000 compared to about $500).[81] Finally, there is some indication that commitment to arbitrated settlements is weaker than that to directly negotiated ones.

In most instances, mediation and arbitration are relatively formal procedures involving the services of people from outside an organization. Are they also used by practicing managers to resolve disputes between individuals under their authority? Research by Sheppard suggests that this is not usually the case. For example, Sheppard asked a large number of practicing managers to describe how they intervened in disputes between their subordinates.[82] Careful analysis of their replies indicated that managers usually adopt one of three approaches in such situations, and none of these closely resembles traditional mediation. In the first and most common form, managers actively question both sides about the nature of the dispute and their opposing positions. Then they impose a solution that they believe will meet the needs of both sides. In a second approach, managers don't actively question both sides; they simply listen to their respective points of view and then impose a solution. Finally, in a third pattern, managers make a quick, informal diagnosis of the nature of the conflict. After doing so, they tell both sides to negotiate directly with each other and reach a solution, warning them that if they don't succeed, the manager will impose one.

Why are these approaches different from standard mediation or arbitration? Many factors probably play a role, but two seem most important. First, time constraints are often intense in such situations. Conflict between subordinates must be quickly resolved, so little opportunity exists for the institution of formal procedures. Second, managers have established relationships with the people involved. Thus, their approach to resolving conflicts between subordinates must occur within this context. Whatever the precise factors involved, it is clear that managers often seek to resolve conflicts between their subordinates in ways other than standard mediation or arbitration.

THE INDUCTION OF SUPERORDINATE GOALS

At several points in this chapter, we have noted that individuals often divide the world into two opposing camps: "us" and "them." They perceive members of their own group as quite different from, and usually better than, people belonging to other groups. These dual tendencies to magnify the differences between one's own group and others and to disparage outsiders are very powerful and are as common in organizations as in other settings.[83] Further, they seem to play a central role in many conflicts between various departments, divisions, and work groups. How can they be countered? One answer, suggested by research findings, is through the induction of **superordinate goals**—ones that tie the interests of the two sides together.[84] The basic idea behind this approach is simple: by inducing conflicting parties to focus on and work toward common objectives, the barriers between them—ones that interfere with communication, coordination, and agreement—can be weakened. When this occurs, the chances for cooperation rather than conflict are enhanced. (Sometimes people have more in common than they realize, especially when the differences between them are racial and cultural in nature. Recently, attempts to get people from diverse groups to work together in harmony have been successfully used by organizations. Such *diversity management* programs, as they are known, are described in the Quest for Quality section on the opposite page.)

THE QUEST FOR QUALITY

MANAGING CONFLICT BY MANAGING DIVERSITY: WAS ANYTHING LEARNED FROM THE LOS ANGELES RIOTS?

One of the most severe forms of conflict is a riot. And one of the most severe riots in U.S. history occurred in Los Angeles in April, 1992. When Los Angeles police officers were acquitted of beating Rodney King, despite the fact that the act was captured on home video for the world to see, the verdict ignited smoldering racial unrest, and the city erupted into several nights of intense rioting. The aftermath was enormous: 51 deaths, 1,419 injuries, 4,535 fires, 4,393 arrests, and $550 million in property damage (see Figure 11-11).[85] In an area like Los Angeles, where people from over a hundred racial and ethnic groups live and work together, interest in maintaining racial harmony, you would think, would be quite high—especially in organizations, where racial strife could be very disruptive. One also might expect that companies that were insensitive to problems of racial strife might have taken a cue from the riots and made greater efforts to maintain racial harmony among their employees. A recent study by McEnrue suggests that these expectations are not confirmed by reality.[86]

McEnrue began her study by interviewing senior managers from a wide variety of Los Angeles businesses several months before the riots occurred. Then, after the riots, she thought it would be interesting to see if the managers' answers would be any different, and reinterviewed them to find out. The interviews focused on the organizations' efforts at *managing diversity*. In general, this involves efforts directed at getting people from different racial and ethnic groups to have mutual respect for each other (see Chapter 5). At the companies surveyed, this included such activities as: training employees to accept differences between people, increasing networking with minority organizations, hiring or appointing a director of diversity, establishing scholarships and summer internships for minority group members, providing career development and mentorship assistance for minorities (see Chapter 6), and publicizing these efforts so as to attract more minorities.

Surprisingly, only one-quarter of the companies reported taking any such steps, although half indicated that they were considering doing so.[87] The remaining quarter of the sample admitted that they were not even thinking about taking any such actions. Those companies that did attempt to manage diversity within their workforce reported reaping benefits from doing so. For example, in several companies, managing diversity provided opportunities to improve the amount and quality of customer service reported. It also lowered recruiting expenses by as much as 40 percent, and significantly reduced the cost of replacing and training new hires (approximately $6,000 per person in this sample). The evidence also suggested that diversity management helped reduce workplace conflict. Specifically, it was linked to lowered levels of frustration among supervisors and reduced incidence of disciplinary actions. Diversity management efforts were also associated with improved relations between minority group subordinates and their majority group supervisors. And, in general, it decreased friction among co-workers belonging to different racial and ethnic groups.

It is easy to imagine that companies that did not give much thought to diversity issues before the riots may have

FIGURE 11-11
CONFLICT: AN EXTREME EXAMPLE
The April, 1992 Los Angeles riots are a unsettling indication of what can occur when racial tensions reach high levels. Attempts to manage diversity in the workplace are designed to minimize such tensions.

done so afterward, as top executives became more aware of the nature and extent of racial and ethnic discontent in the area. To test this possibility, McEnrue re-interviewed the same Los Angeles-based managers three months after the riots. Although many of the firms whose facilities were destroyed in the riots decided to rebuild in the area afterward (e.g., Vons supermarkets) and invested in hiring residents from this economically deprived area of the city (e.g., General Motors and its Hughes Aircraft subsidiary), none of the companies recontacted indicated that they had established new diversity management programs or expanded their existing ones.[88] In general, what the riots did was reinforce pre-existing perspectives about the value of managing diversity in the workforce. Those firms that saw it as unnecessary continued to do so; those that saw it as crucial before the riots felt even more so afterward.

Along with McEnrue, we caution that it may take some companies more time than others to become enlightened about the benefits of managing diversity in their workforces. A single instance of conflict—even one as monumental as the Los Angeles riots—is apparently not a sufficiently strong call to action for those executives who feel immune from the urban unrest occurring outside their offices. We are optimistic, however, that growing interest in reaping the benefits of managing diversity will eventually encourage a growing portion of the business community to participate. Some, we suspect, may even attempt to manage diversity simply because it is the right thing to do (see Chapter 5).

ESCALATIVE INTERVENTIONS: INTENSIFYING CONFLICTS TO RESOLVE THEM

Perhaps the most intriguing approach to managing organizational conflict suggested in recent years is one that seems, at first glance, to fly in the face of common sense. This approach, known as **escalative intervention**, seeks to intensify existing conflicts as a means of resolving them and attaining several related goals as well.[89] The reasoning behind this strategy is as follows: increasing the intensity of a conflict brings matters to a head. The underlying causes of friction or disagreement are clarified, and the motivation to search for effective, integrative solutions is increased. Then, instead of continuing to smolder beneath the surface, conflicts emerge into the open and can be resolved to the satisfaction of those involved.

According to Van de Vliert, several tactics can be used to intensify ongoing conflicts.[90] First, steps may be taken to add to the existing causes of conflict. For example, present channels of communication may be blocked, or the incompatibility of various goals can be emphasized. Similarly, various barriers to open conflict can be removed or lessened (e.g., direct contacts between the opposing sides can be increased; both sides may be urged to express negative feelings about one another). Second, the range of issues on which the conflict is based can be extended by calling attention to additional matters about which the disputants disagree. Third, additional parties can be added to the conflict, thus fueling its scope or intensity. In a fourth strategy, actions that serve to escalate the conflict can be encouraged (e.g., one side is urged to prove to the other that it is right, or to cause the other to lose face). Finally, the two sides may be encouraged to perceive hostile intentions in each other's actions, or to express strong disapproval of one another's proposals.

To the extent that such tactics succeed, ongoing conflict is intensified. Thus, strong pressures toward reaching a resolution are generated, and several benefits may follow. First, and most important, faced with mounting tension and a situa-

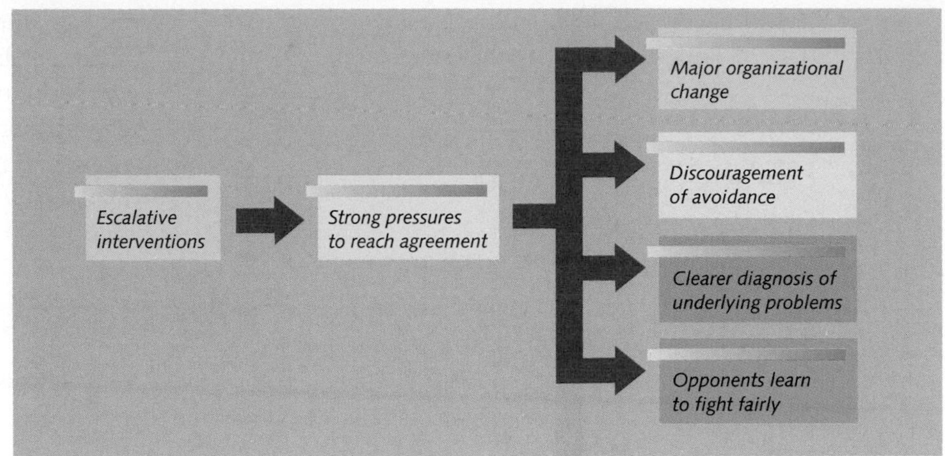

FIGURE 11-12
REDUCING CONFLICT BY INCREASING CONFLICT: ESCALATIVE INTERVENTIONS
In some instances, increasing the intensity of specific conflicts can be a useful technique for reducing overall levels of conflict. Several potential benefits of such procedures are shown here. (Source: Based on suggestions by Van de Vliert, 1985; see Note 90.)

tion that is fast becoming intolerable, the two sides may increase their efforts to reach effective, integrative agreements. In addition, other benefits, such as the stimulation of major change, discouragement of avoidance behaviors, and a clearer diagnosis of underlying problems within an organization, may also result (see Figure 11-12). However, these favorable outcomes are certainly not guaranteed. They follow only when the individuals managing such an intensification of conflict are skilled in this task and are able to direct the growing tensions and friction into constructive channels.

Is it actually possible to direct escalating conflicts in this fashion? Research evidence suggests that it is, and that escalative interventions are indeed helpful in several contexts (e.g., in marital disputes as well as organizational ones).[91] Thus, in this context, there appears to be a favorable tradeoff between controlled, temporary escalation of conflict and its effective long-term management.

SUMMARY AND REVIEW

PROSOCIAL ORGANIZATIONAL BEHAVIOR

People often engage in **prosocial behavior** in work settings, performing actions that benefit others. Beneficiaries of prosocial acts include co-workers (e.g., assisting them in doing their jobs), customers (e.g., providing extra service), and organizations (e.g., suggesting improvements). One form of helping, **organizational citizenship behaviors**—discretionary actions by individuals that aid their organization or people in it—are fostered by the individuals' feeling that they are being treated fairly by the organization. **Whistle-blowing**—disclosure by employees of illegal, immoral, or illegitimate practices to others able to right the wrong—may be considered prosocial insofar as they are intended to benefit society although they may be costly to organizations.

COOPERATION AND COMPETITION

Cooperation involves mutual assistance or coordination between two or more persons or groups. Its occurrence in work settings is affected by several factors relating to individuals (e.g., strong tendencies toward reciprocity, communication, personal orientations and preferences). It is also affected by several organizational factors (e.g., reward systems, interdependence among employees). **Competition** develops when one individual, group, or organization achieves gains at another's expense (i.e., one side's gain is the other side's loss).

CONFLICT: ITS NATURE, CAUSES AND EFFECTS

Conflict is a process that begins when one person or group perceives that another person or group has taken or is about to take some action inconsistent with the perceiver's major interests. Conflict situations involve two basic dimensions: **distribution**, concern with one's own outcomes; and **integration**, concern with others' outcomes. Contrasting styles or approaches to resolving conflict, such as *competing, collaborating, avoiding, accommodating*, and *compromising*, reflect specific points along these dimensions. Cultures vary along the **individualist–collectivist** dimension. Cultures that are relatively individualistic (e.g., the United States) emphasize the goals and rights of individuals and prefer to resolve conflicts through competitive strategies. Cultures that are collectivistic (e.g., China and Taiwan) emphasize group goals and responsibilities, and prefer to handle conflicts through accommodation and avoidance.

Modern theories of conflict emphasize that it is a process and involves the perceptions, thoughts, feelings, and intentions of all participants. **Organizational conflict** stems from both organization-based and interpersonal factors. Included in the first category are competition over scarce resources, ambiguity over responsibility or jurisdiction, interdependence, reward systems that pit people or units against one another, and power differentials. Included in the second category are attributional errors, faulty communication, and personal characteristics such as the Type A behavior pattern.

Although conflict often exerts negative effects on organizations, interfering with communication and coordination, it sometimes produces positive outcomes. These include bringing problems out into the open, enhanced understanding of each other's positions among adversaries, increased consideration of new ideas, better decisions, and increased organizational commitment.

THE MANAGEMENT OF CONFLICT

A key task with respect to conflict is managing its occurrence, deriving the benefits of conflict while minimizing its harmful effects—and *not* eliminating it entirely. Several tactics are useful in this regard. **Bargaining** or **negotiation** is the most common procedure for resolving organizational conflicts. Many factors influence the course and outcomes of bargaining, including specific tactics used by participants, their perceptions of each other's interests and priorities, and their overall approach to bargaining—"win–lose" or "win–win."

Third-party interventions such as **mediation** and **arbitration** can also prove helpful in resolving conflicts. Another approach involves the induction of **superordinate goals**—ones shared by both sides. Finally, conflict can sometimes be resolved through **escalative intervention**—actions that temporarily intensify current conflicts to resolve them more effectively. To minimize interpersonal conflict between people of different racial and ethnic groups, some companies have attempted to *manage diversity*, such as by bringing together people from different groups and allowing them to have successful work experiences.

KEY TERMS

arbitration: A form of third-party intervention in disputes in which the intervening person has the power to determine the terms of an agreement.

bargaining: A process in which two or more parties in a dispute exchange offers, counteroffers, and concessions in an effort to attain a mutually acceptable agreement.

competition: A process in which individuals or groups seek to attain desired goals at the expense of others seeking the same goals.

competitors: Individuals who are primarily concerned with exceeding the outcomes of others.

conflict: A process that begins when individuals or groups perceive that others have taken or will soon take actions incompatible with their own major interests. Conflict involves awareness of opposing interests, the thoughts and emotions of all involved parties, their strategies and intentions, and their overt actions.

cooperation: A process in which individuals or groups work together to attain shared goals.

cooperators: Individuals who are primarily concerned with maximizing joint outcomes.

distribution: A basic dimension of conflict situations, referring to the extent to which individuals show concern for their own outcomes.

equalizers: Individuals primarily concerned with assuring equality of outcomes among all people who work together on joint projects.

escalative intervention: A technique for managing conflict that seeks to increase conflict as a means of resolving it effectively.

fixed-sum error: The perception on the part of bargainers that the other party places the same importance or priority as they do on each issue.

incompatibility error: The perception on the part of bargainers that their own interests and that of the other side are completely incompatible.

individualists: People primarily concerned with maximizing their own outcomes.

integration: A basic dimension of conflict situations, the extent to which individuals show concern for others' outcomes.

integrative agreements: Agreements between negotiators that maximize the joint outcomes of all parties.

interactional justice: Perceptions of the extent to which people are shown a high degree of courtesy, dignity, and interpersonal sensitivity.

mediation: A form of third-party intervention in disputes in which the intervener does not have the authority to dictate an agreement. Mediators simply attempt to enhance communication between opposing sides and to provide conditions that will facilitate acceptable agreements.

negotiation: See *bargaining*.

organizational citizenship behaviors (OCB): Discretionary behaviors by individuals that aid their organizations and that are not related to the formal reward system or their formal job descriptions.

prosocial behavior: Actions that benefit others within an organization. Such behaviors may or may not benefit the organization as well.

reciprocity: The tendency to treat others as they have treated us in the past.

superordinate goals: Goals shared by the parties in a conflict or dispute.

whistle-blowing: Calling attention to actions or practices that are inconsistent with established organizational norms or policies.

QUESTIONS FOR DISCUSSION

1. What kinds of organizational citizenship behaviors have you observed in your own work experiences? Why, if individuals receive no direct benefit for engaging in such actions, do they ever perform them?
2. What are the ethical issues one must consider when deciding whether or not to blow the whistle on an organization suspected of some wrongdoing?
3. Under what conditions does communication enhance cooperation? Under what conditions does it interfere with cooperation?
4. For what kind of jobs would highly competitive people be best? For what kind of jobs would very cooperative people be a better choice?
5. Do you think that consistent individual differences exist with respect to the preferred mode of resolving conflicts? In other words, do some people consistently prefer competition, others collaboration, still others avoidance, and so on?
6. "Conflict doesn't exist until it is recognized by the parties involved." Do you agree with this statement? Why or why not?
7. The negative side of conflict is obvious, but growing evidence indicates that it has a positive side as well. Have you ever experienced positive results from a conflict? If so, why do you think such effects occurred?
8. Many people approach bargaining as a "win–lose" situation. Why is a "win–win" approach often better?
9. If people in your organization are frequently in conflict with each other, what might you do? Describe steps that may be taken to minimize the potentially harmful effects that may result from such conflict while simultaneously enhancing any potential benefits.

MAKING THE SKIES FRIENDLY AGAIN

During the winter and early spring of 1989, business magazines and newspapers were filled with reports of a head-on clash between two exceptional and unbending adversaries: Frank Lorenzo, CEO of Texas Air, the parent company of Eastern Airlines, and Charlie Bryan, the head of Eastern's powerful International Association of Machinists (IAM). Both men claimed that they wanted to see Eastern, the center of this storm of conflict, survive.[1] Yet both took actions that, looking back, seemed to doom the airline to its eventual fate: a place in the dustbin of failed corporations.

The conflict between Eastern's unions (particularly the IAM) and its management had a long history. In fact, the conflict had grown so intense during the time Frank Borman was Eastern's CEO, that the union was instrumental in calling for the sale of the troubled airline to Texas Air. Following the deal, Borman was replaced as CEO by Lorenzo.[2]

Lorenzo had quite a reputation in the airline industry. His holding company, Texas Air Corporation, owned not only Eastern but also Continental, and what were formerly Frontier Airlines, New York Air, and People Express. He received a great deal of publicity when, in 1983, he took Continental into bankruptcy, canceled its union contracts, and slashed fares. Lorenzo is described by colleagues and enemies alike as brilliant, pragmatic, and crafty.[3] He admits that he wants to be in control, and often acts in a manner designed to assure that he gets his way. The long-standing dispute with Eastern's unions finally came to a boil when Lorenzo requested that the machinists take a 28 percent pay cut and agree to work rule reforms including cross-utilization of employees as well as hiring part-time personnel.[4] The unions' outraged response brought the conflict to a crisis, and moved Eastern rapidly along the road to corporate oblivion.

Bryan, head of the IAM, also developed a well-known reputation. He is described as extremely stubborn, cautious—and above all, mistrustful of management. He strongly believed that he had his union's best interests at heart and that by sticking to his plan—no givebacks or rules changes—he would win the final victory.[5]

During the dispute, both Lorenzo and Bryan used numerous ploys to get the other side to "see the light." Lorenzo engaged in a great deal of financial maneuvering. He halted service to fourteen cities and slashed 4,000 jobs. He sold Eastern's reservation system to Texas Air for $100 million. Then, he negotiated the sale of Eastern's prize property, its Shuttle, for $365 million. It was widely believed that with this money and profits from Texas Air, Lorenzo planned to accumulate almost $1 billion with which to fight off the unions.[6] Meanwhile, Bryan steadfastly refused to agree to pay cuts. He tried to raise support from Eastern's other unions, and his success in gaining the cooperation of its pilots was instrumental in bringing the airline to its knees. Bryan also helped launch a safety campaign that resulted in the FAA's review of Eastern's fleet and operations. Although the FAA ultimately gave Eastern a clean bill of health, the publicity surrounding the investigation created a great deal of consumer distrust and defection. Partly as a result of this series of events, both Lorenzo and Bryan filed numerous lawsuits against each other's units.

As history now records, this contentious climate gave way to a lengthy strike that ultimately saw the carrier enter into bankruptcy and cease operations after sixty-two years.[7] However, a new chapter to this sad story is being written by many former Eastern employees. These people, led by forty-six former pilots, have launched a new airlines—Kiwi International Airlines (KIA). The main management philosophy at Kiwi has been formed from the collapse of Eastern. Specifically, at KIA they believe that cooperation is much more healthy and useful than conflict. As Robert Iverson, the president and CEO of the company says, "We strive for a warm service atmosphere. Service to each other and our customers is our motto."[8]

To help reinforce the spirit of cooperation, everyone at Kiwi must invest in the enterprise. Pilots must put up $50,000 and all others must purchase $5,000 of stock in the entirely employee-owned and operated company. Another means of fostering cooperation is that most employees work in many different types of jobs, thereby gaining an appreciation of the work of their colleagues. This policy is enhanced by the fact that the new carrier is organized in such a way as to take advantage of the 20–30 years of experience of its many employees.[9]

CASE IN POINT, Cont.

Kiwi's emphasis on a spirit built on participation seems to be effective—at least thus far. In its first year of operations—September 1, 1992, to September 1, 1993—the company grew from leasing two aircraft to eight, and increased revenues from zero to $10 million per month. The number of cities served has increased from four to seven.

The owners and operators of Kiwi feel strongly about their belief in cooperation. After all, almost all of them lived through the demise of their former organization due to conflict gone awry. They claim that their new airline is managed "the way it should be done." As CEO Iverson says, "Cooperation is necessary. We can't fail each other."[10] This message is all the more poignant when the meaning of the name "Kiwi" is known. The Kiwi is a bizarre-looking New Zealand bird that cannot fly![11] The people at KIA clearly hope that through the spirit of cooperation and participation they can keep their big birds in the air.

QUESTIONS FOR DISCUSSION

1. Why is it necessary for labor unions and management to cooperate with one another?
2. Using Thomas's conflict model, explain the positions taken by Lorenzo and Bryan.
3. How can the concepts of reciprocity, communication, and personal orientation explain the positions taken by Lorenzo and Bryan?
4. Do you expect that there will be conflicts at Kiwi International Airlines in the future? If so, how do you imagine these might be handled?
5. Are there any problems arising from too much cooperation that might be faced at KIA? If so, how might these be avoided?

EXPERIENCING ORGANIZATIONAL BEHAVIOR

Personal Styles of Conflict Management

Conflict among people is a common and inescapable part of life. Given this fact, it is important for all of us to *manage* conflict effectively when it arises. How do *you* deal with such situations? What is your preferred mode of handling disagreements and conflicts with others? The following exercise is designed to give you some insights into this important issue.

PROCEDURE

First, recall three events in which you have experienced conflict with others. On a sheet of paper, describe each briefly, and then answer each of the five following questions with respect to each. (It may help to make three copies of the questionnaire.)

1. To what extent did you try to resolve this conflict through *avoidance*—sidestepping the issue, withdrawing from the situation?

Did Not Do This						Did Do This
1	2	3	4	5	6	7

2. To what extent did you try to resolve this conflict through *accommodation*—trying to win, standing up for your rights or views?

Did Not Do This						Did Do This
1	2	3	4	5	6	7

3. To what extent did you try to resolve this conflict through *competition*—trying to win, standing up for your rights or views?

Did Not Do This						Did Do This
1	2	3	4	5	6	7

4. To what extent did you try to resolve this conflict through *compromise*—finding the middle ground between your position and the other person's?

Did Not Do This						Did Do This
1	2	3	4	5	6	7

5. To what extent did you try to resolve this conflict through *collaboration*—working with the other person to find some solution that would satisfy both of your basic needs or concerns?

Did Not Do This						Did Do This
1	2	3	4	5	6	7

POINTS TO CONSIDER

Now examine your reactions in all three situations. Do you notice any consistencies? Did you tend to prefer one basic mode of resolving conflict over the others? Research on this topic suggests that many people possess relatively clear preferences in this regard: they tend to approach many conflict situations in a similar manner. Although such preferences are understandable, they can cause serious difficulties. Each conflict situation we encounter is, to some extent, unique. Thus, the most adaptive approach is probably the one emphasizing *flexibility:* choosing the approach that best fits the current circumstances. Keeping this point firmly in mind may help you manage conflicts more effectively.

PART V

INFLUENCING OTHERS

CHAPTER OUTLINE

SPECIAL SECTIONS

TWELVE

INFLUENCE, POWER, AND POLITICS IN ORGANIZATIONS

Authority intoxicates.

Samuel Butler, 1612–1680
English poet
Miscellaneous Thoughts

A friend in power is a friend lost.

Henry Brooks Adams, 1838–1918
American writer and historian
The Education of Henry Adams

LEARNING OBJECTIVES

After reading this chapter, you should be able to

1. *Distinguish among influence, power, and politics in organizations.*
2. *Characterize the major varieties of social influence that exist.*
3. *Describe the conditions under which social influence is used.*
4. *Identify the five major bases of individual social power and alternative types of individual power.*
5. *Characterize the conditions under which power is used.*
6. *Explain the two major approaches to the development of subunit power in organizations (the resource-dependency model and the strategic contingencies model).*
7. *Describe when and where organizational politics is likely to occur and the forms it is likely to take.*
8. *Explain the major ethical issues surrounding the uses of power and political behavior in organizations.*

PREVIEW CASE

The Prescription for a Chronic Power Abuser at Abbott Laboratories

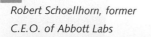

Most people have heard of Murine eye and ear drops and Selsun Blue dandruff shampoo. Their manufacturer, Abbott Laboratories, is also a major player in the pharmaceuticals business. The $8 billion company is now fully recovered after the antics of its former chief executive officer (CEO), Robert Schoellhorn, almost left it on the critical list.

Schoellhorn joined Abbott in 1973, after working for one of its major competitors, American Cyanamid, for twenty-six years. Diligent and hardworking, Schoellhorn developed an impressive record as a manager and in 1979 was promoted to CEO. During the early part of his reign, Schoellhorn helped Abbott chalk up impressive profits. As time went on, he lost sight of the contributions of the company's tens of thousands of dedicated employees, and began to think of the company's success as solely the result of his leadership. To Schoellhorn, Abbott was his private fiefdom to run as he pleased regardless of what others thought.

Because of his powerful position, Schoellhorn's presence and advice were sought by his fellow CEOs. Such attention only strengthened his delusion that he was solely responsible for Abbott's success. By the mid-1980s it was clear that Schoellhorn became so taken with his powerful position that he spent considerable time doing things to reinforce his image. He was away from the office three-quarters of the time—not vacationing, but being a "statesperson," enhancing his own fame and fortune. In 1985 he divorced his wife and married his former secretary, someone who accepted his power and enjoyed basking in its reflection. Together they spent millions of the company's dollars buying not one, but two corporate jets (dubbed "his and hers" by corporate officials) used exclusively by the Schoellhorns to take them wherever they wished.

Abbott executives allege that Schoellhorn's primary agenda was preserving his own power and eliminating his competition. Drunk with power and interested in protecting his position, Schoellhorn surrounded himself with yes-men. Three top-ranking Abbott executives who dared to challenge him were immediately fired, including three presidents in eight years.

Unfortunately for the company, Schoellhorn should have listened when financial signals turned red. But, being more interested in maintaining his image as a leader than ensuring the long-term viability of the company, Schoellhorn took some dangerous financial steps—among them, shoring up company earnings by cutting its considerable research and development budget.

But it was not mortgaging the company's future in this way that finally ended Schoellhorn's reign—rather, it was a social faux pas. When Mrs. Schoellhorn hired a stripper to perform at her husband's sixtieth birthday party, Abbott executives and their spouses were outraged. Combined with his other antics, the board of directors had had enough, and fired Schoellhorn in March 1990, just months before he was scheduled to retire.

Robert Schoellhorn, former C.E.O. of Abbott Labs

A fighter, Schoellhorn didn't take the ouster lying down. He sued his former company, and eventually received a $5.2 million out-of-court settlement. This is a lot of money, to be sure, but in the minds of Abbott's board members, it was a small price to pay to rid the company of its "iron-fisted" chief executive. Experts note that unjust dismissal suits by top executives are extremely unusual—but then again, so too is Mr. Schoellhorn.

Although Schoellhorn's activities are rather extreme, such abuses of power are not as unusual as you might think. In fact, this case illustrates a basic fact of life in organizations: people seek to control the actions of others and try to successfully influence their behavior. This occurs whether we're talking about a dispatcher asking the newspaper delivery person to complete the route more quickly, or the board of directors pressuring a company president to make the company more profitable. Efforts to get others to behave as desired, known as **social influence**, are commonplace in all social settings, especially organizations. A large part of this process, as illustrated by Schoellhorn's behavior, is an interest in **power**—the formal capacity to influence others and/or the company. In this case, Schoellhorn was strongly focused on cultivating a grand image of himself and protecting his self-interest, efforts known as **organizational politics.**

Because the processes of influence, power, and politics play key roles in organizational functioning, we will devote this chapter to examining them. Specifically, we will describe the tactics used to influence others in organizations. Then we will examine how power is attained—both by individuals and by organizational subunits—and how that power is used. Following this, we will examine the political mechanisms used to gain power—what they are and when they occur. We also will pay special attention to the ethical aspects of power and politics; activities of this nature may be of questionable morality due to their potentially adverse effects on others. Before turning to these topics, however, we will begin by carefully distinguishing among the concepts of influence, power, and politics.

ORGANIZATIONAL INFLUENCE, POWER, AND POLITICS: SOME KEY DISTINCTIONS

Imagine that you are a supervisor heading a group of a dozen staff members working on an important new project for your company. Tomorrow is the day you're supposed to make a big presentation to company officials, but the report isn't quite ready. If only several staff members will work a few hours extra, the job will be done on time. Unfortunately, a company party is scheduled for tonight and nobody wants to work late. Question: What can you do to persuade some of your staff to work late and complete the job? In other words, how will you attempt to influence their behavior?

The concept of **social influence** refers to *attempts (whether successful or unsuccessful) to affect another in a desired fashion*. It may be said that we have influenced someone to the extent that our behavior has had an effect—even if unintended—on that person. Although we may attempt to affect another's behavior in a certain fashion, our attempts may be unsuccessful. This would not mean, however, that we did not influence the person, just that we did not influence him or her successfully. To illustrate this point, let's return to our example of a boss needing people to work overtime on party night. Imagine that you see the boss coming out of her office, and you expect her to ask you to work overtime. Uninterested in doing so, you walk away from your desk in the hope that the boss has not seen you and will ask someone else instead. In this case, can we say that the boss influenced you? Although she was unsuccessful, she clearly *did* have an effect on you (after all, you ran away from her). Thus, we can say that the boss influenced you. However, we *cannot* say that the boss influenced your behavior as desired. For that to be true, the boss would have to be successful in bringing about the intended effects—in this case, getting you to stay and work overtime.

Where do power and politics fit in? As illustrated in the center portion of Figure 12-1, **Power** refers to the potential to influence another. More formally, it is *the capacity to change the behavior or attitudes of another in a desired fashion.*[1] In contrast with social influence (actions that affect others), the related concept of power refers to the *capacity* to have a desired effect on others. As we will detail in the next section, there are several different sources of such power. For now, however, assume that the boss has power over you by virtue of her access to considerable resources that enable her to reward you with raises (in exchange for being cooperative) or punish you by not supporting your promotion (if you refrain from pitching in). These represent the formal actions the supervisor can take to attempt to influence you successfully; they are the sources of her power.

Often, when people exercise their power, they take into account their own individual interests. For example, the supervisor in our story may be motivated by an interest in promoting—or at least saving—her own career by making sure that the report gets done on time. This is not to say that she might not also recognize the value of the report to the company. It's just that her actions are motivated primarily by her own selfish concerns. The actions taken to satisfy these concerns reflect **organizational politics**. This term refers to *uses of power that enhance or protect one's own or one's group's personal interests.*[2] Later in this chapter, we will describe many varieties of political actions; people can use their power in a number of ways to protect their personal interests in organizations.

Now that we have clarified the distinctions between social influence, power, and politics (see summary in Figure 12-1) we are in a good position to take a closer look at the social influence process in organizations. In the next section, we will examine some of the most widely used social influence techniques and review some of the ways influence is used in organizations. (Although most of us think of the social influence process as being universal in nature, it appears that there exist reliable cultural differences in people's willingness to accept others' power and influence. For a closer look at this phenomenon, see the Global Organization section on the opposite page.)

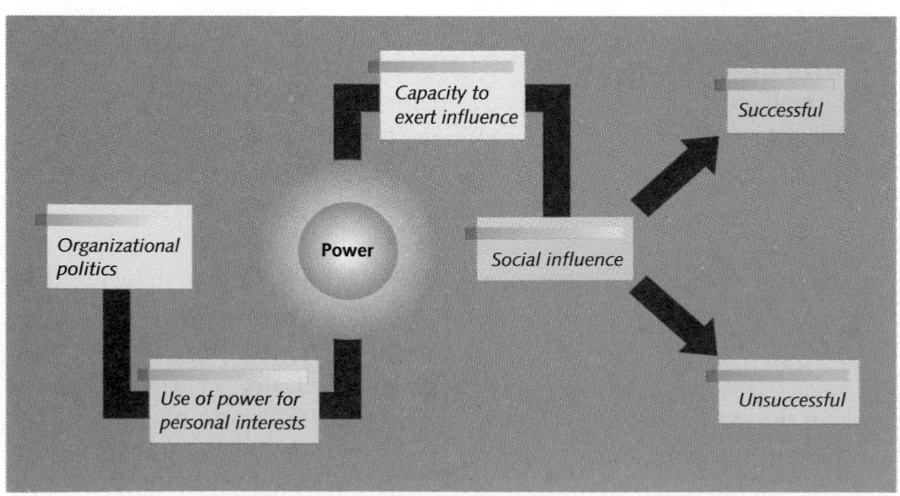

FIGURE 12-1
RELATIONSHIP AMONG SOCIAL INFLUENCE, CONTROL, POWER, AND POLITICS
When someone attempts to get another to act in a desired fashion, that person is seeking to influence the other. The capacity to exert influence over another is known as power. *Uses of power that enhance or protect one's self-interest are known as* organizational politics.

THE GLOBAL ORGANIZATION

NATIONAL DIFFERENCES IN ACCEPTANCE OF UNEQUAL AUTHORITY: POWER DISTANCE

It is usually the case that power tends to be unequally distributed among people in organizations; some have more of it, and others have less. Although this is generally true within organizations all over the world, people from different countries are not equally accepting of this situation. The extent to which less powerful members of organizations accept the authority of more powerful members is known as **power distance**. Large-scale studies have found that in some countries power distance tends to be quite high, whereas in others it is quite low (see Table 12-1).[3]

In high power distance countries, people tend to believe that the boss is right simply because he or she is the boss, and that they should do what the boss wants because that's what's requested. For example, in the Philippines, Venezuela, and India, to go over the head of one's superior is considered taboo. By contrast, in low power distance countries, people are only likely to accept the boss's influence if they believe this person knows what he or she is doing and can offer good advice. For example, in Israel and Denmark employees would give little thought to bypassing their supervisor if that's what it takes to get the job done.[4]

Understanding such differences, although difficult, is important for those who hope to conduct business abroad successfully. For example, if one is attempting to negotiate with an organizational representative of a high power distance country, it would be wise to send a representative with a title equivalent to or higher than one's counterpart in the host nation. This is because titles, status, and formality are considered very important in high power distance countries.

Illustrating this phenomenon, Adler describes an incident involving an American executive who went to London to manage his company's British office.[5] After a few weeks on the job, he noticed that visitors were never sent directly to his office. Instead, they would first have to speak with the receptionist, then the secretary, then the office manager, and only then would the person be sent to him. The American, feeling this practice was a waste of time, spoke to his British colleagues about it, but to no avail—visitors continued to be routed to him after running the gauntlet of successively higher-ranking personnel. Slowly the executive came to accept the fact that in Britain, there is a greater emphasis placed on formality and respect for one's position in an organizational hierarchy than there is in the United States.

Adler describes another incident that further illustrates the importance of power distance in organizations. A young representative from one of Canada's leading banks hosted a dinner and reception for a Chinese delegation, and decided to share the organizing chores with one of the Chinese. Although the event was carefully planned to respect the dietary preferences of the Chinese, it was

TABLE 12-1

Power Distance: Countries at the Extremes of the Continuum

The extent to which people accept the authority of more powerful others is known as power distance. *As summarized here, people in some countries tend to be high in* power distance*—accepting others' authority because of their positions. However, people in other countries tend to be low in power distance—not necessarily accepting others' authority simply because of their positions.*

LOW POWER DISTANCE COUNTRIES	HIGH POWER DISTANCE COUNTRIES
Austria	*Philippines*
Israel	*Venezuela*
Denmark	*Mexico*
New Zealand	*Yugoslavia*
Ireland	*Singapore*
Great Britain	*India*

Source: Based on information in Hofstede, 1980; see Note 3.

strained, innocently enough, by the *way* the arrangements were handled. First, the Chinese were confused about having two people share the hosting. Who was really in charge? Second, because the Canadian host was much younger than his Chinese counterpart, the Chinese were insulted. It was considered inappropriate for them to have a young person work with a higher-status, senior person. These misunderstandings, although they may seem trivial, cost the Canadians in their business dealings with their visitors. Had the low power distance Canadians understood in advance the concerns of their high power distance associates in the Chinese delegation, the event would have been more successful.

Although it may be tempting to dismiss these incidents as trivial, this would be unwise. Misunderstandings between people related to differences in power distance can be important sources of strain between people in organizations, and no one can afford to drive a wedge between themselves and their business associates. It is important to realize that differences in power distance are deeply ingrained elements of culture, and that understanding and accepting them is critical to the success of cross-national business ventures.

SOCIAL INFLUENCE: HAVING AN IMPACT ON OTHERS

By what means do you persuade others to fulfill your wishes? Are you straightforward and tell people what you want them to do, or are you more inclined to emphasize why they should do what you say and what will happen to them if they do not do so? Is it your style to pressure people, or to convince them to do what you want by getting them to like you? Regardless of your answers, you are confronting the challenge of *social influence*—getting others to do what you want.

It is widely acknowledged that successful managers are those who are quite adept at influencing others.[6] We will summarize the social influence techniques used, and then review when and how people use their influence over others.

TACTICS OF SOCIAL INFLUENCE

In recent years, researchers have examined the tactics people use to influence each other in organizations. Specifically, they have questioned people on the job about how they get others—bosses, peers, and subordinates—to do what they want them to do.[7] Investigations by Yukl and his associates found that nine major tactics are used.[8] These are identified and summarized in Table 12-2.

Research has shown that these various tactics are used differently based on whether one is attempting to influence another who is at a higher, lower, or equivalent organizational level.[9,10] In general, the most popularly used techniques to influence people at all levels were consultation, inspirational appeal, and rational persuasion. Each of these techniques involve getting someone else to accept a request as being highly desirable, and they are socially acceptable for influencing people at all levels. It is therefore not surprising that people who use these techniques are believed to be highly effective in carrying out their responsibilities.

By contrast, the more socially undesirable forms of influence, pressure and legitimating, were much less frequently used. In fact, pressure, when it was used, was more likely to be relied on as a follow-up technique than as a tool for one's initial

TABLE 12-2

Tactics of Social Influence: A Summary

Research by Yukl and his associates has found that people use the nine different tactics of social influence summarized here.

TACTIC	DESCRIPTION
Rational persuasion	*Using logical arguments and facts to persuade another that a desired result will occur*
Inspirational appeal	*Arousing enthusiasm by appealing to one's values and ideals*
Consultation	*Asking for participation in decision making or planning a change*
Ingratiation	*Getting someone to do what you want by putting her in a good mood or getting her to like you*
Exchange	*Promising some benefits in exchange for complying with a request*
Personal appeal	*Appealing to feelings of loyalty and friendship before making a request*
Coalition	*Persuading by seeking the assistance of others, or by noting the support of others*
Legitimating	*Pointing out one's authority to make a request, or verifying that it is consistent with prevailing organizational policies and practices*
Pressure	*Seeking compliance by using demands, threats, or intimidation*

Source: Adapted from Yukl & Tracey, 1992; see Note 9.

influence attempt—and then, only for subordinates. It is important to note that some techniques, such as ingratiation, coalition, personal appeal, and exchange, are more likely to be used in combination with other techniques than alone. Clearly, people attempt to influence different others using a wide variety of different combinations of techniques. However, as a general rule, more open, consultative techniques are believed to be more appropriate than more coercive techniques.[11]

PUTTING INFLUENCE TACTICS TO WORK

As you might imagine, when people decide to use a certain influence tactic they take into account the reaction they anticipate from the person being influenced. Specifically, research findings indicate that people attempting to influence their bosses used inspirational appeals and ingratiation when they believed their bosses were inclined to be highly authoritarian, but used rational persuasion when they believed their bosses were highly participative.[12] These findings make sense if you imagine that influence requires a highly coercive action (such as appealing to one's superior) to influence an authoritarian boss, whereas a participative boss might be more amenable to learning about a rational argument. These findings are important because they suggest that people's use of power is a function not simply of their own characteristics, but also of their beliefs about the likely effects of their actions.

The social influence tactics we've been discussing can be effective in changing people's behavior. Often, these techniques are helpful in bringing about behavior that is adaptive to oneself and helpful to the organization. Returning to our "overtime" example, it certainly would be helpful to your boss and the organization as a whole for you to work overtime. Doing so also would benefit you to the extent that you are credited for your last-minute contribution (indeed, a good manager would remember and reward you for your good organizational citizenship; see Chapter 11). However, because people are typically part of many different social groups, they may confront several conflicting sources of social power—including some that may be quite negative. For instance, adolescents' use of alcohol and tobacco is directly linked to the extent to which they are influenced by their peers.[13] This is both because they are directly affected by peers who pressure them into using these substances and because they already believe that the majority of their peers use them. Obviously, peer influence can exert powerful effects on behavior.

INDIVIDUAL POWER: A BASIS FOR INFLUENCE

s defined earlier, *power* involves the potential to influence others—both the things they do and the ways they feel about something. In this section, we will focus on the individual bases of power—that is, factors that give people the capacity to influence others successfully. It is an inevitable fact of organizational life that some individuals can boast a greater capacity to influence people successfully than others. Within organizations, the distribution of power is typically unequal. Why is this so? What sources of power do people have at their disposal?

FIVE BASES OF INDIVIDUAL POWER

Answers to these questions are provided in a classic framework developed by French and Raven.[14] This work identifies five different bases of social power derived from the characteristics individuals possess and the nature of the relationships between individuals with and without power. As we describe each of these interpersonal sources of power, it may be useful to refer to the summary presented in Table 12-3.

REWARD POWER: CONTROLLING VALUED RESOURCES

Imagine a supervisor in charge of twenty-five employees in a department of a large organization. As part of her job, she is free to hire staff members, set pay raises, control work assignments, and prepare budgets for department projects. How this kind of control over desired resources can provide a source of power for this supervisor is easy to see. The resources at her disposal—access to jobs and money, in this case—are highly desired. Individuals with the capacity to control the rewards workers will receive are said to have **reward power** over them. Subordinates often comply with their superiors' wishes in hopes of receiving the valuable rewards they control.

TABLE 12-3

Individual Power: Five Major Bases

Power in organizations may be derived from any of the sources identified and described here.

TYPE OF POWER	DESCRIPTION OF BASE
Reward power	*Based on the ability to control valued organizational rewards and resources (e.g., pay, information)*
Coercive power	*Based on control over various punishments (e.g., suspensions, formal reprimands)*
Legitimate power	*Based on the belief that an individual has the recognized authority to control others by virtue of his or her organizational position (e.g., the person is a high-ranking corporate official)*
Referent power	*Based on liking of the power holder by subordinates (e.g., the superior is friends with a subordinate)*
Expert power	*Based on the accepted belief that the individual has a valued skill or ability (e.g., expert medical skills)*

Source: Based on French & Raven, 1959; see Note 14.

The rewards at a manager's disposal may be tangible, such as raises, promotions, and time off, or intangible, such as praise and recognition. In either case, access to these resources often forms a source of individual power in organizations. Indeed, managers have been known to complain that the inability to control any important resources in their organizations leaves them powerless figureheads. This is especially likely in the case of first-line supervisors, who often find themselves responsible for the actions of others but severely restricted by the incentives they can offer others for following their orders.[15]

Keep in mind (based on our discussion of the concepts of *reinforcement* in Chapter 2 and *valence* in Chapter 4) that resources may enhance one's power only to the extent that they are actually desired by the recipients. You also may recall from Chapter 2 that to be effective in changing people's behavior, rewards must be closely tied to the desired behavior. Thus, whereas access to valued resources may enhance a manager's power base, the manager must administer rewards properly to be effective. Having resources at one's disposal and using them appropriately are obviously two different things.

COERCIVE POWER: CONTROLLING PUNISHMENTS

In addition to controlling desired resources, managers often control the punishments others receive—a capacity known as **coercive power**. Subordinates may do what their superior desires because they fear the superior will punish them if they do not. Punishments may include pay cuts, demotions, suspension without pay, formal reprimands, undesirable work assignments, and the like. As in the case of reward power, punishments are effective only if used properly. In Chapter 2, we noted that punishments may have undesirable side effects if they are too harsh or inconsistently administered (in extreme cases, employees may even rebel against an overly harsh supervisor by organizing their colleagues in protest or by quitting their jobs).[16] Regardless, the capacity to administer punishment represents an important source of power in organizations.

LEGITIMATE POWER: RECOGNIZED ORGANIZATIONAL AUTHORITY

What would happen in your class if you learned that one of your classmates would be making the decisions about the final course grades instead of your instructor? Someone might stand up and question this, asking, "Who is *he* to make those decisions?" If so, the speaker would be challenging the legitimacy of that individual's power. However, if the professor announced that she would be determining the final grades herself, no one would raise any questions. The difference between these two situations has to do with **legitimate power**—the recognized right of individuals to exercise authority over others because of their position in an organizational hierarchy. Students recognize the accepted authority of professors to determine their grades (i.e., professors have legitimate power in this regard), but reject as illegitimate the power of their classmates to make these same decisions.

Usually, legitimate power is derived from an individual's formal rank or position. Organizational members are likely to accept attempts to influence their behavior based on the fact that one has a higher position (see Figure 12-2). This does not mean, however, that the higher-ranking individual can legitimately control all aspects of others' behavior. Managers have authority over only those aspects of others' behavior that fall under their accepted areas of organizational responsibility. For example, whereas secretaries may recognize the legitimate authority of their bosses to ask them to file and prepare office correspondence, they may reject as illegitimate a boss's request to type his son's homework papers. Similarly, a plant manager may accept the authority of a vice president of production who directs him to increase inventories of certain items, but may question the authority of the very same order voiced by the vice president of finance. The key point is that legitimate authority applies only to the range of behaviors that are recognized and accepted as legitimate by the parties involved.

FIGURE 12-2
LEGITIMATE POWER: CONTROL BASED ON FORMAL AUTHORITY
One source of social power, legitimate power, is based on the idea that members of an organization recognize and accept the formal authority of individuals who have higher-ranking positions within the organizational hierarchy.

REFERENT POWER: CONTROL BASED ON ADMIRATION

"Joe, we go back over twenty years in this company, and I consider you a good friend. I'm in kind of a bind right now, and I could sure use your help. You see, what happened is. . . ." Joe is most certainly being set up to help the speaker, who is relying on the fact that he and Joe have a long-standing friendship. Out of his allegiance to that relationship and his liking and admiration for the speaker, Joe probably feels obligated to go along with whatever is being asked. Individuals who are liked and respected by others can get them to alter their actions in accord with their directives—a type of influence known as **referent power**. Senior managers who possess desirable qualities and good reputations may find that they have referent power over younger managers who identify with them and wish to emulate them. Similarly, sports heroes and popular movie stars often have referent power over their admiring fans (a fact advertisers often capitalize on when they employ these individuals as spokespeople to endorse their products).

EXPERT POWER: CONTROL BASED ON SKILLS AND KNOWLEDGE

If a foreman tells one of his machine shop workers to readjust the settings on a certain piece of equipment, that person may well do it because he believes that the foreman is expert in the operation of the machine. To the extent that a subordinate recognizes a superior's advanced skill or knowledge and follows his orders because he realizes that the superior knows what's best, that superior is said to have **expert power**. The running of organizations often relies on experts who must be consulted frequently, and whose advice must be followed if an organization is to survive.

The power of various experts is usually very narrowly defined, limited to the scope of their expertise. Accountants may have expert power when it comes to corporate taxes and investments, whereas market researchers may have expert power when it comes to deciding what type of advertising to use for a new product. Research has revealed that within teams of health care professionals (e.g., nurses, occupational therapists), the physician tends to hold the most power—in part a result of the high level of professional expertise they are believed to possess.[17]

Expert power can be a very successful way of influencing others in organizations. After all, it would be difficult to justify not following the directives of a trained professional who is better equipped than you are to know what to do. Thus, problems often develop when younger, less experienced employees are given responsibility for a work crew. Until they prove themselves with a record of success, many employees find it difficult to exercise power over others. By the same token, the recognized expertise of many managers and the extreme power they wield as a result makes them highly sought after as employees.

MEASURING INDIVIDUAL POWER BASES AND AN ALTERNATIVE CONCEPTUALIZATION

How can researchers tell what kinds of power people use? The answer in general is: they ask them. But, asking questions about the kinds of power people use is easier said than done. In fact, scientists have criticized the way power has been measured in several previous studies.[18] A questionnaire developed by Hinkin and Schriesheim appears to have improved on the limitations of the previous efforts.[19] People completing their scale are asked to describe how closely various statements describe their own supervisors' behaviors. Four items measure each of the five bases of power identified by French and Raven. Participants complete the scale by indicating how much they agree that each item describes the way their supervisors treat their subordinates. The questionnaire is then scored by summing the degrees of agreement with the four items reflecting each scale. By collecting several such measures for a particular supervisor, we can gauge the relative degree to which that supervisor is recognized by his or her subordinates for using various types of power. For a look at items similar to those developed by Hinkin and Schriesheim, see Table 12-4.

By design, questionnaire items such as these tap French and Raven's five bases of social power. Unfortunately, this conceptualization, although frequently cited, has not been subject to much empirical verification. Are there, in fact, really only five bases of social power that people use? An exploratory study by Yukl and Falbe reveals that although evidence exists for the five bases of power already identified, there appear to be three more, for a total of eight.[20] What's more, these bases of power reflect two basic underlying dimensions. Refer to the summary of this alternative view of power in Figure 12-3 as we describe it in more detail below.

TABLE 12-4

What Kinds of Power Do You Use?

Scientists use tests similar to this one to measure people's beliefs about their supervisors' power. To complete the test, follow the directions below. To score, add your responses to numbers 1 and 3. This measures your beliefs about your supervisor's reward power. The sum of numbers 2 and 4 measures coercive power. The sum of numbers 5 and 7 measures legitimate power. The sum of numbers 6 and 9 measures expert power. Finally, the sum of numbers 8 and 10 measures referent power. Although the questionnaire is incomplete and items presented are not exactly the same as the ones actually used, this will give you a good idea of how social scientists measure individual power in organizations.

Directions: Indicate how strongly you agree or disagree that each of the following statements accurately describes your supervisor. Answer by using the following numbers: 1 = strongly disagree; 2 = disagree; 3 = neither agree nor disagree; 4 = agree; 5 = strongly agree.

My supervisor can

__________ *1. See that I get a raise*

__________ *2. Give me jobs I dislike*

__________ *3. Make sure I get the promotion I desire*

__________ *4. Make my work life miserable*

__________ *5. Explain my responsibilities*

__________ *6. Give me good advice on getting the job done*

__________ *7. Understand the tasks I have to accomplish*

__________ *8. Make me feel good*

__________ *9. Give me the benefit of his or her technical know-how*

__________ *10. Get me to feel important*

Source: Based on Hinkin & Schriesheim, 1989; see Note 19.

One broad dimension, referred to as **position power**, has to do with power based on one's formal position in an organization. It includes three of the five bases of power we've identified so far—legitimate power, reward power, and coercive power—and a new one, **information power**. This refers to the extent to which a supervisor provides a subordinate with the information needed to do the job.

The other broad dimension is known as **personal power**. This refers to the power that one derives because of his or her individual qualities or characteristics. It includes two of the French and Raven power bases—expert power and referent power—plus two more, persuasive power and charisma. **Persuasive power** refers to the ability to use facts and logic to present a case persuasively. In contrast, **charisma** is more elusive—namely, an attitude of enthusiasm and optimism that is contagious. (Note that this use of the term is similar to the way it will be used to refer to a characteristic of a leader in Chapter 13.)

This alternative approach is obviously a bit more thorough and complex than the original conceptualization proposed by French and Raven more than thirty-five years ago. Although the evidence is promising that it provides a very thorough and accurate view of the types of power that exist within organizations, it is still too

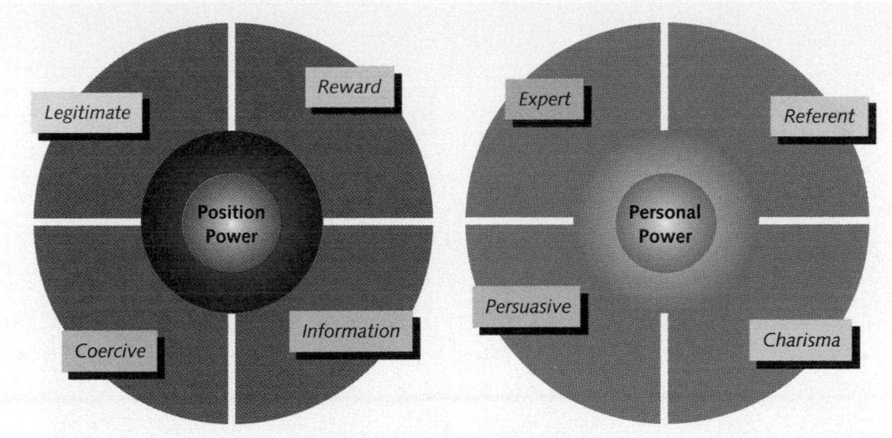

FIGURE 12-3
AN ALTERNATIVE CONCEPTUALIZATION OF SOCIAL POWER
Yukl and Falbe have noted that individual power is best conceptualized as having two major dimensions—position power and personal power—each of which has four distinct power bases. This conceptualization builds on and extends French and Raven's original view of five power bases. (Source: Based on Yukl & Falbe, 1991; see Note 20.)

soon to tell whether this approach is really any better than the original. If you think more about the conceptualization, you may realize that a clearer distinction is needed between the somewhat similar notions of referent power and charisma, as well as between expert power and information power. Similarly, position power and legitimate power also appear to be closely related. Given how important these notions are in explaining behavior in organizations, efforts at clarifying distinctions between various sources of power would prove worthwhile. Fortunately, because researchers are actively investigating this topic, conceptual clarification and evidence regarding the value of various approaches to understanding individual power bases will probably be forthcoming.

INDIVIDUAL POWER: HOW IS IT USED?

As researchers take on the challenge of distinguishing among the various bases of individual power, one consideration facing them is the widespread overlap in the ways people use power. Only sometimes is a single source of power used; indeed, it is recognized that the various power bases are closely related to each other.[21] For example, consider that the more someone uses coercive power, the less that person will be liked, and hence, the lower his or her referent power will be. Similarly, managers who have expert power are also likely to have legitimate power because their directing of others within their field of expertise is accepted. In addition, the higher someone's organizational position, the more legitimate power that person has, which is usually accompanied by greater opportunities to use reward and coercion.[22] Clearly, then, the various bases of power should not be thought of as completely separate and distinct from each other. They are often used together in varying combinations.

What bases of power do people prefer to use? Although the answer to this question is quite complex, research has shown that people most prefer using expert power and least prefer using coercive power.[23] These findings are limited to the power bases we've identified thus far. However, when we broaden the question and ask people to report exactly what sources of power they have on their jobs, a fascinating picture emerges. Figure 12-4 depicts the results of a survey in which 216 CEOs of American corporations were asked to rank-order the importance of a series of specific sources of power.[24] The figures indicate the percentage of executives who included that source of power among their top three choices. These findings indicate not only that top executives rely on a broad range of powers, but

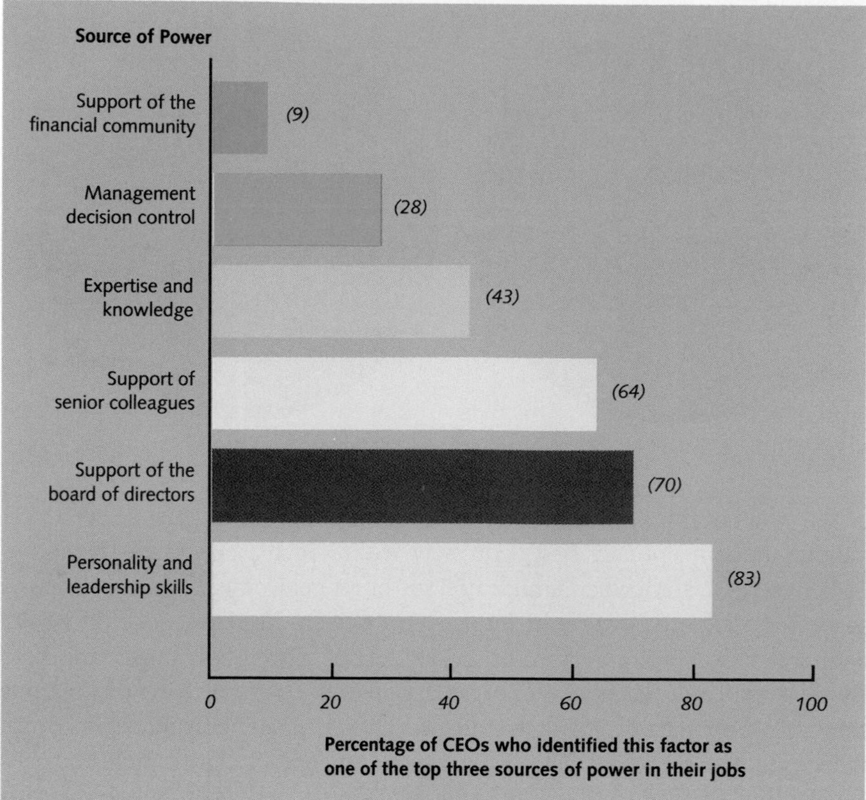

FIGURE 12-4
AMERICAN CEOs: WHAT ARE THEIR POWER BASES?
A survey of more than 200 American CEOs revealed that they obtained their power primarily through the support of others at different levels throughout the organization. (Source: Based on data appearing in Stewart, 1989; see Note 24.)

also that they base these powers on support from people located in a host of other places throughout their organizations. Interestingly, when asked about how much power they currently had compared to ten years ago, only 19 percent said they now had more power. Thirty-six percent indicated that they had the same amount of power, and the largest group, 42 percent, indicated that they had less power.

Although many different forms of power tend to be used to influence subordinates, research has shown that expert power is the preferred form used to influence peers and superiors.[25] After all, it is almost always appropriate to try to get others to go along with you if you justify your attempt on the basis of your expertise. In contrast, coercive tactics tend to be frowned on in general, and are especially inappropriate when one is attempting to influence a higher-ranking person.[26] Influencing superiors is tricky because of the *counterpower* they have. When attempting to influence another who is believed to have no power at his or her disposal, one doesn't have to worry about retaliation. When dealing with an individual with considerably greater power, however, one can do little other than simply comply with that more powerful person.

However, the situation is complicated by the fact that one party may have higher power on one dimension, and another party may have higher power on another dimension. Consider, for example, the case of some secretaries who have acquired power because they have been with their companies for many years. They know the ropes and can get things done for you if they want, or they can get you hopelessly bogged down in red tape. Their expert knowledge gives them a great sense of power over others. Although they may lack the legitimate power of their executive bosses, secretaries' expertise can be a valuable source of counterpower over those with more formal powers. In a growing number of offices, administrative assistants are likely to have considerable power to operate however they think best, with little intervention from their superiors. Individuals who have been given such opportunities are said to have been **empowered**. (For a closer look at the empowerment process, and its implications for the future of the manager's job as we know it, see the Organization of Tomorrow section on the opposite page.)

THE ORGANIZATION OF TOMORROW

WHAT WILL BECOME OF MANAGERIAL POWER IN THE AGE OF THE EMPOWERED EMPLOYEE?

There's no mistaking the trend: a growing number of middle managers are being laid off.[27] Why should a group that represents only 5 percent of the workforce represent almost a quarter of those whose jobs are eliminated? One of the key reasons is that managers aren't as necessary as they once were. In part, this is because a key aspect of managers' jobs—information handling—can now be easily performed by anyone operating a computer. But there's more to it than that.

In a growing number of today's organizations, power is shifting out of the offices of managers and into the hands of lower level employees. Many of today's workers are not being "managed" in the traditional, authoritarian styles that have been used by managers of generations past. Instead, power is often shared by a team of workers empowered to make decisions themselves. As a result, the new breed of managers are less likely to be "bosses" who push people around (using coercive power) and more likely to serve as teachers, or "facilitators," who guide their teams by using their knowledge and experience (i.e., their expert power). In the words of John Ring, the director of Okidata (the Tokyo-based maker of printers and other office tools), "to influence people you have to prove you're right."

Whereas traditional managers usually told people what to do and how and when to do it, new-style managers are more inclined to ask questions to get people to solve problems and make decisions on their own. Consider, for example, the job of Dee Zalentatis, the information group manager at a Hudson, Massachusetts, division of America's largest printer, R. R. Donnelley & Sons (see Figure 12-5). Since her division began using self-managed teams (see Chapter 8), Zalentatis found that her job has become one of teaching, cajoling, and comforting forty others until they feel confident enough to do handle many of her responsibilities. She sees her job now as being more of a temporary, internal consultant than a permanent, traditional manager. In fact, she says, "I'd like to manage my way out of my current job in two years."[28]

Clearly, the key to successful managing in the future will be the sharing of expert information and not the hoarding or information, as it has been in the past. Tomorrow's "managers"—or whatever they will be called—are likely to be more open than ever before. As such, they are likely to empower employees by widely disseminating information, allowing better decisions to be made. For example, at NeXT Computer, chief executive officer Steven Jobs (best known as one of the co-founders of Apple Computer) strongly believes that employees must be privy to vital information about sales and profits, and such, for them to appreciate the work they do. In fact, Jobs goes so far as to make available a list of each employee's pay. When questions arise as to why someone

FIGURE 12-5
MANAGING THE EMPOWERED WORK TEAM
Although she's formally a manager at the large printing company, R. R. Donnelley & Sons, Dee Zalentatis considers herself as more of an internal consultant who teaches the highly empowered members of her work team than as a traditional boss who tells subordinates what to do and how to do it.

else may be getting paid more, Jobs uses that occasion to explain what he sees as the differences between their contributions. Such information, he believes, helps cultivate the impression that company management is being straight with them and has nothing to hide—in other words, that it's not abusing its power.

If the practices we've been describing here don't square with your experiences, we're not surprised. The empowered employee is still in the minority in the vast majority of today's organizations—but a change in that direction is coming, and fast. According to management consultant James Champey, "We won't see them in great numbers for another five to ten years. But corporate American is definitely moving in that direction."[29] If this prediction is correct, as we believe it is, we can look forward to significant changes in the way people will use power in organizations.

GROUP OR SUBUNIT POWER: STRUCTURAL DETERMINANTS

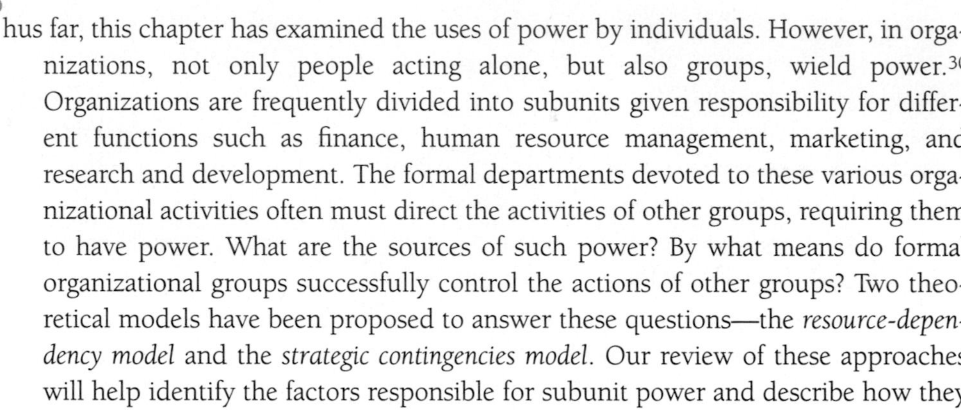

Thus far, this chapter has examined the uses of power by individuals. However, in organizations, not only people acting alone, but also groups, wield power.[30] Organizations are frequently divided into subunits given responsibility for different functions such as finance, human resource management, marketing, and research and development. The formal departments devoted to these various organizational activities often must direct the activities of other groups, requiring them to have power. What are the sources of such power? By what means do formal organizational groups successfully control the actions of other groups? Two theoretical models have been proposed to answer these questions—the *resource-dependency model* and the *strategic contingencies model*. Our review of these approaches will help identify the factors responsible for subunit power and describe how they operate.

THE RESOURCE-DEPENDENCY MODEL: CONTROLLING CRITICAL RESOURCES

It is not difficult to think of an organization as a complex set of subunits that are constantly exchanging resources with each other. By this, we mean that formal organizational departments may be both giving to and receiving from other departments such valued commodities as money, personnel, equipment, supplies, and information. These critical resources are necessary for the successful operation of organizations.

Various subunits often depend on others for such resources. To illustrate this point, imagine a large organization that develops, produces, and sells its products. The sales department provides financial resources that enable the research and development department to come up with new products. Of course, it cannot do so effectively without information from the marketing department about what consumers are interested in buying and how much they would be willing to pay. The production department has to do its part by manufacturing the goods on time, but only if the purchasing department can supply the needed raw materials—and at a price the finance department accepts as permitting the company to turn a profit. It is easy to see how the various organizational subunits are involved in a complex set

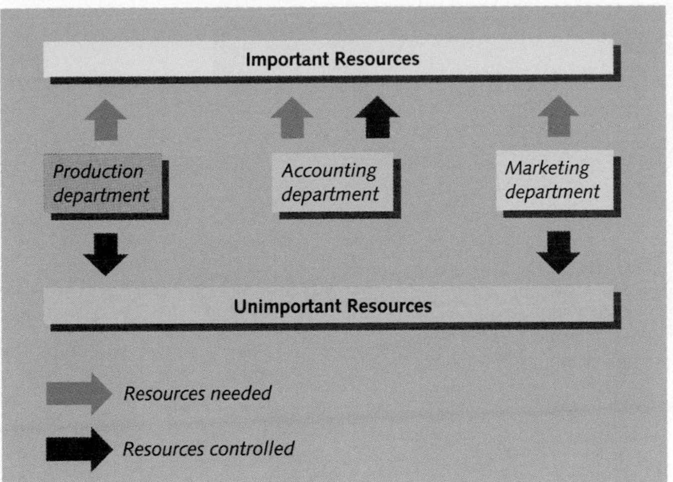

FIGURE 12-6
POWER BETWEEN SUBUNITS: THE RESOURCE-DEPENDENCY MODEL
The resource-dependency model of organizational power explains that subunits acquire power when they control critical resources needed by other subunits. In the example shown here, the accounting department would be considered more powerful than either the production department or the marketing department.

of interrelationships with others. To the extent that one subunit controls the resources on which another subunit depends, it may be said to have power over it. After all, controlling resources allows groups to successfully influence the actions of other groups. Subunits that control more resources than others may be considered more powerful in the organization. Indeed, such imbalances, or *asymmetries*, in the pattern of resource dependencies occur normally in organizations. The more one group depends on another for needed resources, the less power it has (see Figure 12-6).

In proposing their **resource-dependency model**, Pfeffer and Salancik note that a subunit's power is based on the degree to which it controls the resources required by other subunits.[31] Thus, although all subunits may contribute something to an organization, the most powerful ones are those that contribute the most important resources. Controlling the resources other departments need puts a subunit in a better position to bargain for the resources it requires. To illustrate this point, let's consider an important study by Salancik and Pfeffer.[32] Within a university, the various academic departments may be very unequal with respect to the power they possess. For example, some may have more students, be more prestigious in their national reputation, receive greater grant support, and have more representatives on important university committees than others. As such, they would be expected to have greater control over valued resources. This was found to be the case within the large state university studied by Salancik and Pfeffer. The more powerful departments proved to be those that were most successful in gaining scarce and valued resources from the university (e.g., funds for graduate student fellowships, faculty research grants, and summer faculty fellowships). As a result, they became even more powerful, suggesting that within organizations, the rich subunits get richer.

A question that follows from this conclusion is: How do various organizational subunits come to be more powerful to begin with? That is, why might certain departments come to control the most resources when an organization is newly formed? Insight into this question is provided by Boeker's fascinating study of the semiconductor industry in California.[33] Boeker used personal interviews, market research data, and archival records as the main sources of data for this investigation. Results indicated that two main factors accounted for how much power an organizational subunit had: (1) the period within which the company was founded, and (2) the background of the entrepreneur starting the company. For example, because research and development functions were crucial among the earliest semiconductor firms (founded 1958–1966, when semiconductors were new), this department had the most power among the oldest firms. Hence, the importance of the area of corporate activity at the time the company began dictated the relative power of that area years later (in 1985, when the study was done). It also was found that the most powerful organizational subunits tended to be those that represented the founder's area of expertise (see Figure 12-7). Thus, for example, the marketing and sales departments of companies founded by experts in marketing and sales tended to have the greatest amounts of power. This research provides an important missing link in our understanding of the attainment of subunit power within organizations.

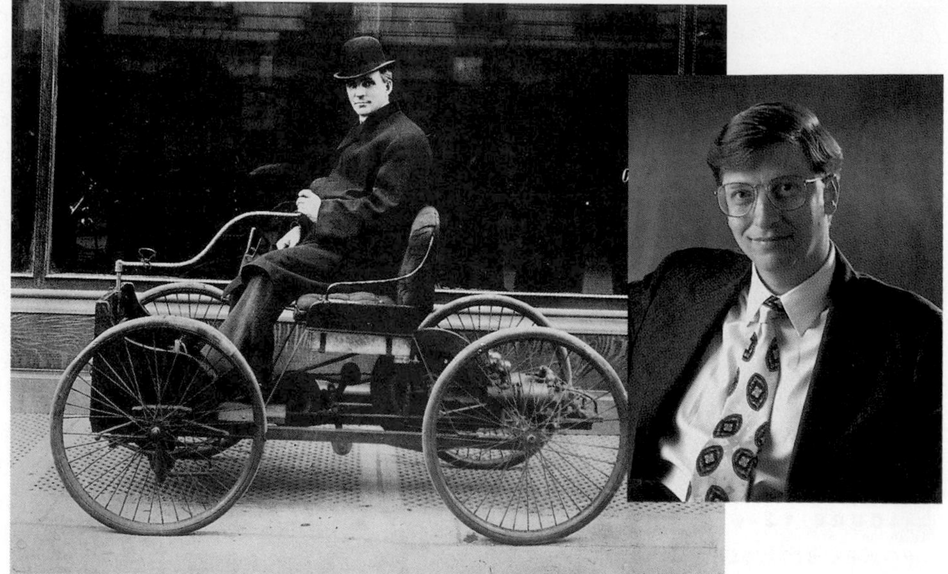

FIGURE 12-7
COMPANY FOUNDERS: IMPORTANT INFLUENCES ON SUBUNIT POWER
Research has shown that the functional areas within which company founders specialize tend to be the ones that have the most power. For example, Henry Ford, the founder of the Ford Motor Company (left), was a specialist in manufacturing technology—still a powerful department at Ford. William Gates, the founder of Microsoft (right), is a specialist in developing computer software products—still a powerful department at Microsoft.

The resource-dependency model suggests that a key determinant of subunit power is the control of valued resources. However, as we will now illustrate, it is not only control over resources that dictates organizational power, but also control over the activities of other subunits.

THE STRATEGIC CONTINGENCIES MODEL: POWER THROUGH DEPENDENCE

The accounting department of a company might be expected to have responsibility over the approval or disapproval of funds requested by various departments. If it does, its actions greatly affect the activities of other units, who depend on its decisions—that is, other departments' operations are *contingent* on what the accounting department does. To the extent that a department is able to control the relative power of various organizational subunits by virtue of its actions, it is said to have control over *strategic contingencies*. For example, if the accounting department consistently approved the budget requests of the production department but rejected the budget requests of the marketing department, it would be making the production department more powerful.

Where do the strategic contingencies lie within organizations? In a classic study, Lawrence and Lorsch found out that power was distributed in different departments in different industries.[34] They found that within successful firms, the strategic contingencies were controlled by the departments that were most important for organizational success. For example, within the food-processing industry, where it was crucial for new products to be developed and sold, successful firms had strategic contingencies controlled by the sales and research departments. In the container manufacturing field, where the timely delivery of high-quality goods is a crucial determinant of organizational success, successful firms placed most of the decision-making power in the sales and production departments. Thus, successful firms focused the control over strategic contingencies within the subunits most responsible for their organization's success.

What factors give subunits control over strategic contingencies? The **strategic contingencies model** of Hickson and his associates suggests several key consider-

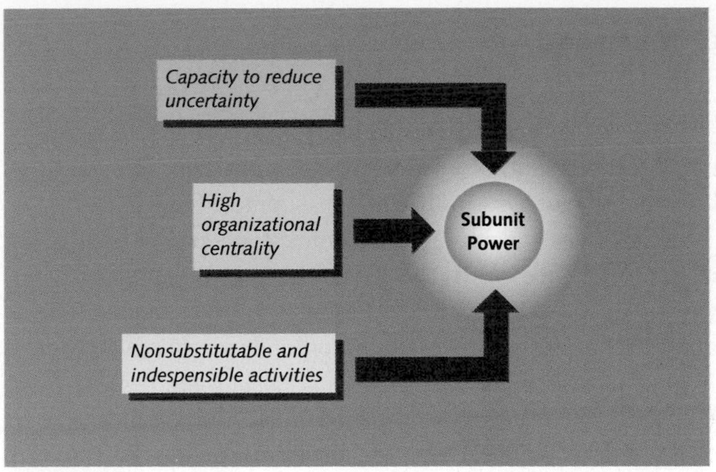

FIGURE 12-8
STRATEGIC CONTINGENCIES MODEL: IDENTIFYING SOURCES OF SUBUNIT POWER
The strategic contingencies model explains intraorganizational power in terms of the capacity of some subunits to control the actions of others. Subunit power may be enhanced by the factors shown here.

ations.[35] Refer to the summary of these factors in Figure 12-8.

Power may be enhanced by subunits that can help reduce the levels of uncertainty faced by others. Any department that can shed light on the uncertain situations organizations may face (e.g., those regarding future markets, government regulation, availability of needed supplies, financial security) can be expected to wield the most organizational power. Accordingly, the balance of power within organizations may be expected to change as organizational conditions change. Consider, for example, changes that have taken place over the years in public utility companies. Studying the strategic contingencies in such organizations, Miles noted that a shift has occurred.[36] When public utilities first began, the engineers tended to wield the most power. But now that these companies have matured and face problems of litigation and governmental regulation (particularly over nuclear power), the power has shifted to lawyers. A similar shift toward the power of the legal department has occurred in recent years in the area of human resource management, where a complex set of laws and governmental regulations have created a great deal of uncertainty for organizations. Powerful subunits are those that can help reduce organizational uncertainty.

That more powerful subunits are ones that have *a high degree of centrality in the organization* also has been established. Some organizational subunits perform functions that are more central, and others, more peripheral. For example, some departments—such as accounting—may have to be consulted by most others before any action can be taken, giving them a central position in their organizations. Centrality is also high when a unit's duties have an immediate effect on an organization. For example, the effects would be much more dramatic on an auto manufacturer if the production lines stopped than if market research activities ceased. The central connection of some departments to organizational success dictates the power they wield.

Third, a subunit controls power when its *activities are nonsubstitutable and indispensable*. If any group can perform a certain function, subunits responsible for controlling that function may not be particularly powerful. In a hospital, for example, personnel on surgical teams are certainly more indispensable than personnel in the maintenance department because fewer individuals have the skills needed to perform their unit's duties. Because an organization can easily replace some employees with others either within or outside it, subunits composed of individuals who are most easily replaced tend to wield very little organizational power.

The strategic contingencies model has been tested and supported in several organizational studies.[37] For example, one investigation conducted in several companies found that a subunit's power within an organization was higher when it could reduce uncertainty, occupied a central place in the work flow, and performed functions that other subunits could not perform.[38] The strategic contingencies model should be considered a valuable source of information about the factors that influence the power of subunits within organizations.

ORGANIZATIONAL POLITICS: POWER IN ACTION

Our discussion of power focused on the potential to influence others successfully. When this potential is realized, put into action to accomplish desired goals, we are no longer talking about power, but **politics**.[39] It is quite easy to imagine situations in which someone does something to accomplish his or her own goals, which do not necessarily agree with the goals of the organization (Mr. Schoellhorn's behavior described in our Preview Case is a good example). This is what **organizational politics** is all about—*actions not officially sanctioned (approved) by an organization taken to influence others to meet one's personal goals*.[40]

If you think we're describing something that is a bit selfish and appears to be an abuse of organizational power, you are correct. Organizational politics *does* involve placing one's self-interests above the interests of the organization. Indeed, this element of using power to foster one's own interests distinguishes organizational politics from uses of power that are approved and accepted by organizations.[41]

ORGANIZATIONAL POLITICS: WHERE DOES IT OCCUR?

Although organizational politics is widespread, political activity is not equally likely to occur throughout all parts of organizations.[42] Specifically, a survey by Gandz and Murray found that the most likely areas of political activity were those in which clear policies were nonexistent or lacking, such as interdepartmental coordination, promotions and transfers, and delegation of authority.[43] However, when it came to organizational activities that had clearly defined rules and regulations, such as hiring and disciplinary policies, political activities were lowest.

A survey of organizational political practices by Allen and his associates revealed similar findings.[44] Specifically, organizational politics was perceived to be greatest in subunits (such as boards of directors and members of the marketing staff) that followed poorly defined policies, whereas political activity was perceived to be lowest in areas (such as production and accounting) in which clearly defined policies existed. Similarly, because of the inherently high levels of ambiguity associated with human resource management tasks (such as personnel selection and performance appraisal), political behavior is likely to occur when these functions are being performed.[45] Together, these findings help make an important point: *political activity is likely to occur in the face of ambiguity*. When there are clear-cut rules about what to do, it is unlikely that people will be able to abuse their power by taking political action. However, when people face highly novel and ambiguous situations in which the rules guiding them are unclear, it is easy to imagine how political behavior results.

Where in the organization is the political climate most active? In other words, at what organizational levels do people believe the most political activities are likely to occur? As shown in Figure 12-9, Gandz and Murray found that organizations were perceived as more political at the higher levels, and less political at the lower managerial and nonmanagerial levels of the organization.[46] Apparently, politics is most likely to occur at the top, where, of course, the stakes are highest and power may corrupt.

FIGURE 12-9
ORGANIZATIONAL POLITICS: MORE LIKELY AT THE TOP
Survey research has shown that employees believe political activity is more likely to occur at higher organizational levels (where the guiding rules are more ambiguous and the stakes are higher) than at lower levels. (Source: Based on data reported by Gandz & Murray, 1980; see Note 43.)

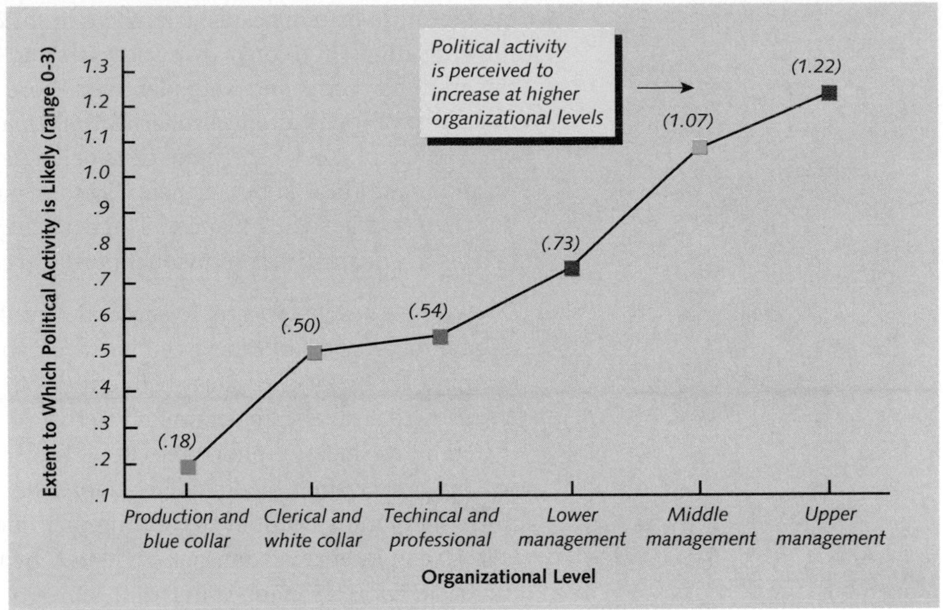

POLITICAL TACTICS: GAINING THE POWER ADVANTAGE

To understand organizational politics, one must recognize the various forms political behavior can take in organizations. In other words, what are the techniques of organizational politics? When this question was asked of a group of managers surveyed by Allen and his associates, five techniques were identified as being used most often.[47]

1. *Controlling access to information.* As we noted in Chapter 10, information is the lifeblood of organizations. Therefore, controlling who knows and doesn't know certain things is one of the most important ways to exercise power in organizations. Although outright lying and falsifying information may be used only rarely in organizations (in part because of the consequences of getting caught), there are other ways of controlling information to enhance one's organizational position. For example, you might (1) withhold information that makes you look bad (e.g., negative sales information), (2) avoid contact with those who may ask for information you would prefer not to disclose, (3) be very selective in the information you disclose, or (4) overwhelm others with information that may not be completely relevant. These are all ways to control the nature and degree of information people have at their disposal. Such information control can be critical. An analysis of the organizational restructuring of AT&T's Phone Stores revealed that control was transferred through the effective manipulation, distortion, and creation of information.[48] A vice president's secret plan to feed incomplete and inaccurate information to the CEO was responsible for that vice president's winning control over the stores.

2. *Cultivating a favorable impression.* People interested in enhancing their organizational control commonly engage in some degree of image building—an attempt to enhance the goodness of their impressions on others. Such efforts may take many forms, such as (1) "dressing for success" (as will be discussed in Chapter 13), (2) associating oneself with the successful accomplishments of

others (or, in extreme cases, taking credit for others' successes), or (3) simply drawing attention to one's own successes and positive characteristics.[49] With this in mind, Ferris and King identified those who worked hard to fit into their organizations as *organizational chameleons*.[50] Such individuals figure out what behaviors they believe are considered generally appropriate in their organization, and then go out of their way to make sure that others are aware that they behaved in such a manner. These are all ways of developing the "right image" to enhance one's individual power in organizations.

3. *Developing a base of support.* To successfully influence people, it is often useful to gain the support of others within the organization. Managers may, for example, lobby for their ideas before they officially present them at meetings, ensuring that others are committed to them in advance and thereby avoiding the embarrassment of public rejection. They also may "scatter IOUs" throughout the organization by doing favors for others who may feel obligated to repay them in the form of supporting their ideas. The norm of *reciprocity* is very strong in organizations, as evidenced by the popular phrases "You scratch my back, and I'll scratch yours" and "One good turn deserves another." After all, when someone does a favor for you, you may say, "I owe you one," suggesting that you are aware of the obligation to reciprocate that favor. "Calling in" favors is a well-established and widely used mechanism for developing organizational power.

4. *Blaming and attacking others.* One of the most popularly used tactics of organizational politics involves blaming and attacking others when bad things happen. A commonly used political tactic is finding a *scapegoat*, someone who could take the blame for some failure or wrongdoing. A supervisor, for example, may explain that the failure of a sales plan she designed was based on the serious mistakes of one of her subordinates—even if this is not entirely true. Explaining that "it's his fault"—that is, making another "take the fall" for an undesirable event—gets the real culprit "off the hook" for it.

FIGURE 12-10
SCAPEGOATING: A FUNDAMENTAL POLITICAL TACTIC
The practice of blaming another for one's own failures, or scapegoating, *is a widely used political tactic despite its dubious ethical nature. (Source: Copyright © 1991 by Nick Downes; from* Harvard Business Review, *May–June 1992 issue.)*

"The report was just released, sir. Isn't it a bit early for finger pointing?"

Finding a scapegoat can allow the politically astute individual to avoid (or at least minimize) association with the negative situation. For example, research has found when corporate performance drops, powerful chief executives often resort to placing the blame onto lower-ranking individuals, protecting themselves from getting fired while their subordinate gets the axe.[51] Despite the obvious ethical questions that may be raised about the practice of unjustly pointing the finger at someone else, it occurs in organizations more than you might imagine (see Figure 12-10).

5. *Aligning oneself with more powerful others.* One of the most direct ways to gain power is by connecting oneself with more powerful others. There are several ways to accomplish this. For example, a lower-power person may become more powerful if she has a very powerful mentor, a more powerful and

better-established person who can look out for and protect her interests (recall our discussion of mentor–protégé relationships in Chapter 6). As another example, people may also agree in advance to form *coalitions*—groups that band together to achieve some common goal (e.g., overthrowing a current corporate CEO).[52] Research has shown that the banding together of relatively powerless groups is one of the most effective ways they have to gain organizational power.[53] Two relatively powerless individuals or groups may become stronger if they agree to act together, forming a coalition. People may also align themselves with more powerful others by giving them "positive strokes" in the hope of getting more powerful people to like them and help them—a process known as *ingratiation*.[54] Agreeing with someone more powerful may be an effective way of getting that person to consider you an ally. Such an alliance, of course, may prove indispensable when you are looking for support within an organization. To summarize, having a powerful mentor, forming coalitions, and using ingratiation are all potentially effective ways of gaining power by aligning oneself with others.

The techniques of organizational politics noted here are just some of the many available means of gaining power in organizations.[55] That there are so many techniques has led organizational scientists to view political behavior as a collection of games going on in a multiring circus. The idea is that many people or groups may be trying to influence many other people or groups simultaneously—as in playing a game. What, then, are the political games that unfold in organizations?

PLAYING POLITICAL GAMES IN ORGANIZATIONS

One expert in the field of organizational power and politics, Henry Mintzberg, has identified four major categories of political games.[56] As we describe them here, refer to our summary in Table 12-5.

1. *Authority games*. Some games, known as *insurgency games*, are played to resist authority. Others, known as *counterinsurgency games*, are played to counter such resistance to authority. Insurgency can take forms ranging from quite mild (such as intentionally not doing what is asked) to very severe (such as organizing workers to mutiny or sabotage their workplaces).[57] Companies may try to fight back with counterinsurgency moves. One way they may do so is by invoking stricter authority and control over subordinates. Often unproductive for both sides, such games frequently give way to the more adaptive techniques of bargaining and negotiation discussed in Chapter 11.

2. *Power base games*. These games are played to enhance the degree and breadth of one's organizational power. For example, the *sponsorship game* is played with superiors. It involves attaching oneself to a rising or established star in return for a piece of the action. A relatively unpowerful subordinate, for example, may agree to help a more established person (such as his boss) by loyally supporting him in exchange for getting advice and information from him, as well as some of his power and prestige. Both benefit as a result. Similar games may be played among peers, such as the *alliance game*. Here, workers at the same level agree in advance to mutually support each other, gaining strength by increasing their joint size and power.

TABLE 12-5

Political Games: A Summary of Some Examples

Many political games are played in organizations, each involving different individuals playing for different political goals.

GAME	TYPICAL MAJOR PLAYERS	PURPOSE
Authority Games		
Insurgency game	*Lower-level managers*	*To resist formal authority*
Counterinsurgency game	*Upper-level managers*	*To counter resistance to formal authority*
Power Base Games		
Sponsorship game	*Any subordinate employee*	*To enhance base of power with superiors*
Alliance game	*Line managers*	*To enhance base of power with peers*
Empire building	*Line managers*	*To enhance base of power with subordinates*
Rivalry Games		
Line versus staff game	*Line managers and staff personnel*	*To defeat each other in the quest for power*
Rival camps game	*Any groups at the same level*	*To defeat each other in the quest for power*
Change Games		
Whistle-blowing game	*lower-level managers*	*To correct organizational wrongdoings*
Young Turks game	*Upper-level managers*	*To seize control over the organization*

Source: Adapted from Mintzberg; see Note 6.

One of the riskiest power base games is known as *empire building*. In this game, an individual or group attempts to become more powerful by gaining responsibility for more and more important organizational decisions. Indeed, a subunit may increase its power by attempting to gain control over budgets, space, equipment, or any other scarce and desired organizational resource.

3. *Rivalry games*. Some political games are designed to weaken one's opponents. For example, in the *line versus staff game* managers on the "line," who are responsible for the operation of an organizational unit, clash with those on "staff," who are supposed to provide needed advice and information. For example, a foreman on an assembly line may attempt to ignore the advice from a corporate legal specialist about how to treat one of his production workers, thereby rendering the staff specialist less powerful. (We will have more to say about the distinction between "line" and "staff" positions in Chapter 15.)

   Another rivalry game is the *rival camps game*, in which groups or individuals with differing points of view attempt to reduce each other's power. For example, an organization's production department may favor the goals of stability and efficiency, whereas the marketing department may favor the goals of growth and customer service. The result may be that each side attempts to cultivate the favor of those allies who can support it and who are less sensitive to the other side's interests. Of course, because organizational success requires the various organizational subunits to work in concert with each other, such rivalries are considered potentially disruptive to organizational functioning.

Regardless of which side wins, the organization is sure to lose when the rival camps game is played.

4. *Change games*. Several different games are played to create organizational change. For example, in the *whistle-blowing game* an organizational member secretly reports some organizational wrongdoing to a higher authority in the hope of righting the wrong and bringing about change. (Recall our discussion of whistle-blowing in Chapter 11).

   A game played for much higher stakes is known as the *young Turks game*. In it, camps of rebel workers seek to overthrow the existing leadership of an organization—a most extreme form of insurgency. The change sought by people playing this game is not minor, but far-reaching and permanent. In government terms, they are seeking a coup d'état.

Some political activities may readily coexist with organizational interests (e.g., the sponsorship game), whereas others are clearly antagonistic to organizational interests (e.g., the young Turks game). As such games are played out, it becomes apparent that although political activity may sometimes have little effect on organizations, more often it is quite harmful.[58] Now that we know what types of behavior reflect political activity in organizations, we are prepared to consider the conditions under which such behaviors take place.

WHEN DOES POLITICAL ACTION OCCUR?

Imagine the following situation. You are the director of a large charitable organization that administers funds supporting many worthy projects (e.g., saving endangered animals, providing shelter to the homeless). A wealthy philanthropist dies, and his will leaves your organization $10 million to be spent in any desired manner. Hearing of this generous bequest, the directors of the various charitable groups are all interested in obtaining as much of this money as possible to support their projects. Several aspects of this situation make it liable to trigger political activity.[59]

First, this situation is fraught with uncertainty; it is not obvious where the money should be spent. If the organization has no clearly prescribed priorities about how to spend its funds, various groups might very well try to get their share by any means possible. Second, this is clearly a matter in which there is an important decision involving large amounts of scarce resources. If the size of the gift were much smaller, say $500, or if it involved something trivial or readily available, such as paper clips, the incentive for political action would probably be weak.

The different groups in our example each have conflicting goals and interests. The save-our-wildlife group is intent on serving its interests; the shelter-for-the-homeless group has very different interests. These differing goals make political activity likely. Finally, note that the potential for political activity in this situation is great because the different charitable groups are all approximately equal in power. If there were a highly asymmetrical balance of power (with one group having a lot more control over resources than the others), political action would be futile because the most powerful group would simply make the decision.

In summary, political behavior is likely to occur when (1) uncertainty exists, (2) large amounts of scarce resources are at stake, (3) organizational units (individuals or groups) have conflicting interests, or (4) the parties involved have approximately equal power.

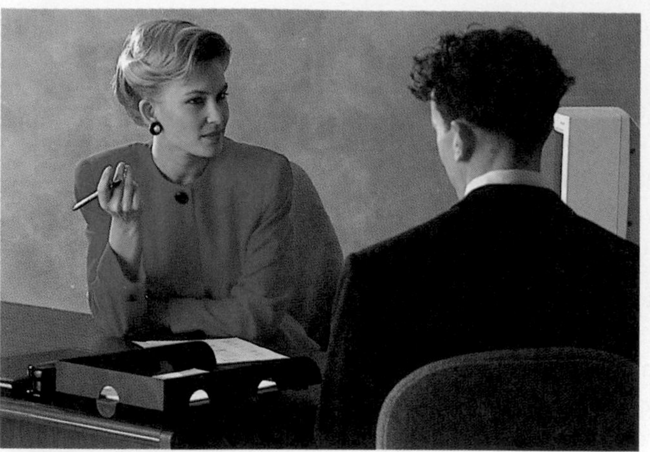

FIGURE 12-11
PERSONNEL DECISIONS: OFTEN POLITICAL IN NATURE
When making decisions about the hiring and promotion of others people are likely to take into account not only the effects of these decisions on the organization, but also their impact on their own careers.

POLITICS IN HUMAN RESOURCE MANAGEMENT

If you think about these conditions, you won't be surprised that political behavior often centers around key human resource management activities such as performance appraisal, personnel selection, and compensation decisions.[60] For example, given that there is often a certain amount of ambiguity associated with evaluating another's performance, and that such evaluations might cultivate certain images of oneself, it follows that performance ratings may be recognized as more of a reflection of the rater's interest in promoting a certain image of himself than an interest in accurately evaluating another's behavior.[61,62] Similarly, when making personnel decisions, people are at least as much concerned about the implications of their hires for their own ideal careers (e.g., will this person support me or make me look bad?) as they are concerned about doing what's best for the organization (see Figure 12-11).[63]

Finally, pay raise decisions have been shown to be politically motivated. Specifically, in a management simulation exercise, Bartol and Martin found that managers gave the highest raises to individuals who threatened to complain if they didn't get a substantial raise, particularly if it were known that these people had political connections within the organization.[64] Taken together, these findings suggest that the very nature of human resource management activities in organizations makes them prime candidates for activities within which organizational politics are likely to be activated.

POLITICS AND THE ORGANIZATIONAL LIFE SPAN

The conditions leading to political activities are likely to differ as a function of the stage of an organization's life. Hence, contrasting degrees and types of political activity are expected. Organizations can be distinguished quite simply as those that are just being started by entrepreneurs (the *birth and early growth* stage), those that are fully developed (the *maturity* stage), and those that face decline and dissolution (the *decline* or *redevelopment* stage). As Gray and Ariss explain, different types of political activity are likely to occur during these various stages of an organization's life.[65]

When an organization is newly begun, it may have little or no structure and be guided by the philosophy of the founder. During this stage, the entrepreneur gains political power by presenting his or her ideas as rational to the employees, who accept this person's image of the corporate mission. The founder usually has complete access to information and makes decisions based on his or her own values. Explaining these decisions to subordinates is a way of inculcating these values to others in the organization, and thereby exercising power over them. Political activity is not particularly likely during this stage.

However, as organizations mature and become more complex, they tend to grow and to departmentalize, creating conditions in which the vested interests of different groups are likely to conflict. Political means may be used to gain an advantage in such a situation. Indeed, it is likely that the full range of political activities noted earlier will be employed when organizations are mature (e.g., forming coalitions, using information). It is particularly interesting to note that when organizations begin to decline, subunits may be quite insecure and the need for political action may be great as people and groups compete for the power to control (and perhaps turn around) the organization. A period of decline reflects a time of great uncertainty, and thus a period in which political activity is likely to be quite intense. For example, Hannan and Freeman found that staff members employed in California school districts experiencing decline tended to have more intense competitive interactions and were at odds with each other more than members of similar organizations during periods of growth.[66] Clearly, the use of political practices in organizations is likely to be affected by its degree of maturity.

COPING WITH ORGANIZATIONAL POLITICS: SOME TECHNIQUES

Given how fundamental the need for power appears to be among people, and how differences in power between employees are basic to organizations, it is safe to say that organizational politics is inevitable. This is not good news, however, as many of the effects of organizational politics are quite negative. Indeed, lowered corporate morale and diversion from key organizational goals (as employees pay closer attention to planning their attacks on others than to doing their jobs) are expected to result from political activity. The more organizational politics is recognized as going on, the less trust and more alienation people are likely to feel.[67]

In view of this, managers must consider ways to minimize the effects of political behavior. Although it may be impossible to abolish organizational politics completely, managers can do several things to limit its effects.

1. *Clarify job expectations*. You will recall that political behavior is nurtured by highly ambiguous conditions. To the extent that managers help reduce uncertainty, they can minimize the likelihood of political behavior. For example, managers should give very clear, well-defined work assignments. They should also clearly explain how work will be evaluated. Employees who know precisely what they are supposed to do and what level of performance is acceptable will find political games to assert their power unnecessary. Under such conditions, recognition will come from meeting job expectations, instead of from less acceptable avenues.

2. *Open the communication process*. People have difficulty trying to foster their own goals at the expense of organizational goals when the communication process is open to scrutiny by all. Compare, for example, a department manager who makes budget allocation decisions in a highly open fashion (announced to all) and one who makes the same decisions in secret. When decisions are not openly shared and communicated to all, conditions are ideal for unscrupulous individuals to abuse their power. Decisions that can be monitored by all are unlikely to allow any one individual to gain excessive control over desired resources.

3. *Be a good role model*. It is well established that higher-level personnel set the standards by which lower-level employees operate. As a result, any manager who is openly political in her use of power is likely to create a climate in which her subordinates behave the same way. Engaging in dirty political tricks teaches subordinates not only that such tactics are appropriate, but also that they are the desired way of operating within the organization. Managers will certainly find it difficult to constrain the political actions of their subordinates

unless they set a clear example of honest and reasonable treatment of others in their own behavior.

4. *Do not turn a blind eye to game players.* Suppose you see one of your subordinates attempting to gain power over another by taking credit for that individual's work. Immediately confront this individual, and do not ignore what he did. If the person believes he can get away with it, he will try to do so. What's worse, if he suspects that you are aware of what he did, but didn't do anything about it, you are indirectly reinforcing his unethical political behavior—showing him that he can get away with it.

In conclusion, it is important for practicing managers to realize that because power differences are basic to organizations, attempts to gain power advantages through political maneuvers are to be expected. However, a critical aspect of a manager's job is to redirect these political activities away from any threats to the integrity of the organization. Although expecting to eliminate dirty political tricks would be unrealistic, we believe the suggestions offered here provide some useful guidelines for minimizing their impact.

THE ETHICAL IMPLICATIONS OF ORGANIZATIONAL POLITICS

Probably one of the most important effects of organizational power is that it invites corruption. Indeed, the more power an individual has at his or her disposal, the more tempted that person is to use that power toward some immoral or unethical purpose.[68] Obviously, then, the potential is quite real for powerful individuals and organizations to abuse their power and to behave unethically. Because such behaviors are negatively regarded, the most politically astute individuals—including politicians themselves—often attempt to present themselves in a highly ethical manner.

Unfortunately, the potential to behave unethically is too frequently realized. Consider, for example, how greed overtook concerns about human welfare when the Manville Corporation suppressed evidence that asbestos inhalation was killing its employees, or when Ford failed to correct a known defect that made its Pinto vulnerable to gas tank explosions following low-speed rear-end collisions.[69] Companies that dump dangerous medical waste materials into our rivers and oceans also appear to favor their own interests over public safety and welfare. Although these examples are better known than many others, they do not appear to be unusual. In fact, the story they tell may be far more typical than we would like, as one expert estimates that about two-thirds of the 500 largest American corporations have been involved in one form of illegal behavior or another.[70] Given the scope of the problems associated with unethical organizational behaviors, we will focus on the ethical aspects of politics in this final section of this chapter.

POLITICAL BEHAVIOR: WHAT MAKES IT ETHICAL?

Although there are no clear-cut ways to identify whether a certain organizational action is ethical, Velasquez and his associates suggest some useful guidelines.[71] For a summary of the central questions associated with assessing the ethics of political behavior, see Figure 12-12.

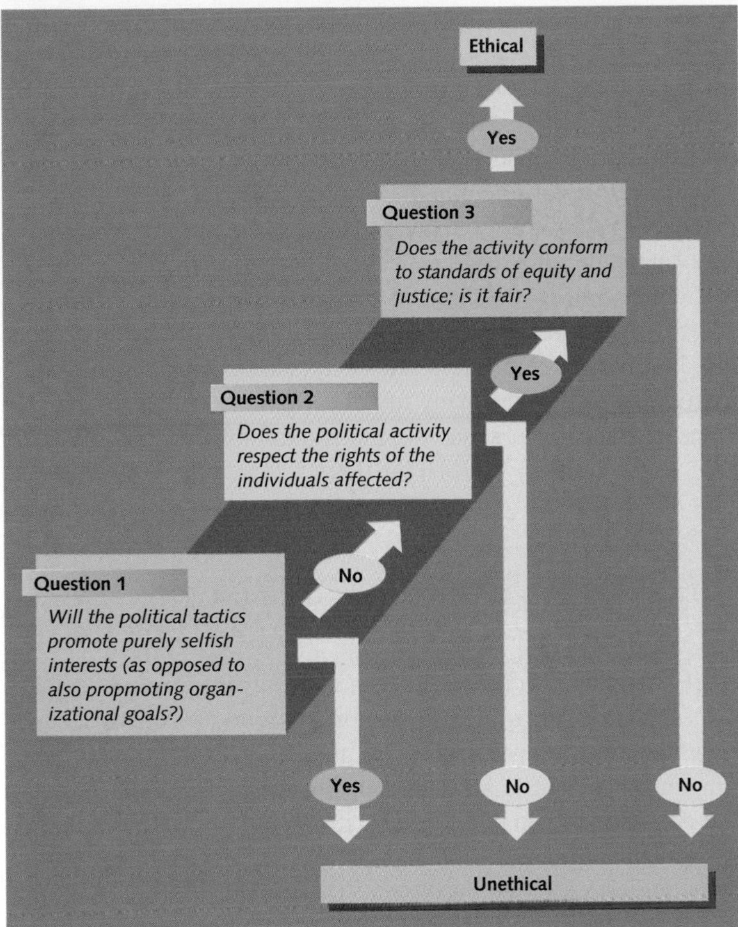

FIGURE 12-12
GUIDELINES FOR DETERMINING ETHICAL ACTION
Although assessing the ethicality of a behavior is a complex matter, answers to the three questions shown here can provide a good indication. This flowchart shows the path that must be taken to achieve ethical action. (Source: Based on suggestions by Velasquez, Moberg, & Cavanaugh, 1983; see Note 71.)

As a first consideration, we may ask: *Will the political tactics promote purely selfish interests, or will they also help meet organizational goals?* If only one's personal, selfish interests are nurtured by a political action, it may be considered unethical. Usually, political activity fails to benefit organizational goals, but not always. Suppose, for example, that a group of top corporate executives is consistently making bad decisions that are leading the organization down the road to ruin. Would it be unethical in such a case to use political tactics to try to remove the power holders from their positions? Probably not. In fact, political actions designed to benefit the organization as a whole (as long as they are legal) may be justified as appropriate and highly ethical. After all, they are in the best interest of the entire organization.

A second question in considering the ethics of organizational politics is: *Does the political activity respect the rights of the individuals affected?* Generally speaking, actions that violate basic human rights are, of course, considered unethical. For example, dirty political tricks that rely on espionage techniques (such as wiretapping) are not only illegal, but also unethical in that they violate the affected individual's *right to privacy*. However, as you may know, police agencies are sometimes permitted by law to use methods that violate privacy rights under circumstances in which the greater good of the community at large is at stake. It is not easy, of course, to weigh the relative benefits of an individual's right to privacy against the greater societal good. Indeed, making such decisions involves a potential misuse of power in itself. It is because of this that society often entrusts such decisions to high courts charged with the responsibility for considering both individual rights and the rights and benefits of the community at large.

Velasquez and his associates also identified a third consideration in assessing the ethics of political action: *Does the activity conform to standards of equity and justice; is it fair?* Any political behavior that unfairly benefits one party over another may be considered unethical. Paying one person more than another similarly qualified person is one example (as you may recall from our discussion of equity theory in Chapter 4). Standards regarding the fair treatment of individuals are often unclear. Not surprisingly, more powerful individuals often use their power to convince others (and themselves!) that they are taking action in the name of justice. That is, they seek to implement seemingly fair rules that benefit themselves at the expense of others.[72] This, of course, represents an abuse of power.

However, we must sometimes consider instances in which violating standards of justice may be considered appropriate. For example, it has been found that managers may sometimes give poorly performing employees higher pay than they deserve in the hope of stimulating them to work at higher levels.[73] Although the principle of equity is violated in this case (i.e., people should be paid in proportion to their job contributions), the manager may argue that the employee and the organization benefit as a result. Of course, the result may be considered unfair to the other individuals who are not so generously treated. Obviously, we will not be able to settle this complex issue here. Our point is that although ethical behavior involves adhering to standards of justice, there may be instances in which violations of these standards may be considered ethically acceptable.

As you can probably tell by now, most matters involving the resolution of moral and ethical issues are quite complex. Each time a political strategy is considered, its potential effects should be evaluated in terms of the questions outlined here. If the practice appears to be ethical based on these considerations, it may be acceptable in that situation. If ethical questions arise, however, alternative actions should be seriously considered. Unfortunately, many unethical political practices are followed in organizations despite their obvious violations of moral standards. We will now consider some of the underlying reasons for this.

WHY DOES UNETHICAL BEHAVIOR OCCUR IN ORGANIZATIONS? PREVAILING POLITICAL NORMS

As noted earlier in this chapter, unethical organizational practices are embarrassingly commonplace.[74] It is easy to define as morally wrong practices such as dumping chemical wastes into rivers, insider trading on Wall Street, and overcharging the government for Medicaid services. Yet these and many other unethical practices go on almost routinely in many organizations. Why is this so? In other words, what accounts for the unethical actions of people within organizations?

One answer to this question is based on the idea that *organizations often reward behaviors that violate ethical standards*. Consider, for example, how many business executives are expected to deal in bribes and payoffs, and how good corporate citizens blowing the whistle on organizational wrongdoings may fear being punished for their actions (see Chapter 11). Jansen and Von Glinow explain that organizations tend to develop *counternorms*—accepted organizational practices that are contrary to prevailing ethical standards.[75] Some of these are summarized in Figure 12-13.

The top of Figure 12-13 identifies being open and honest as a prevailing ethical standard. Indeed, governmental regulations requiring full disclosure and freedom of information reinforce society's values toward openness and honesty. Within organizations, however, it is often considered not only acceptable, but desirable, to be much more secretive and deceitful. The practice of *stonewalling*—willingly hiding relevant information—is quite common. One reason is that organizations may actually punish those who are too open and honest. Consider, for example, the disclosure that B. F. Goodrich rewarded employees who falsified data on the quality of aircraft brakes so as to win certification.[76] Similarly, it has been reported that executives at Metropolitan Edison encouraged employees to withhold information from the press about the Three Mile Island nuclear accident.[77] In both incidents, the counternorms of secrecy and deceitfulness were accepted and supported by the organization.

As you can see from Figure 12-13, many other organizational counternorms promote morally and ethically questionable practices. That these practices are commonly rewarded and accepted suggests that organizations may be operating within a world that dictates its own set of accepted rules. This reasoning suggests a second answer to the question of why organizations act unethically—namely,

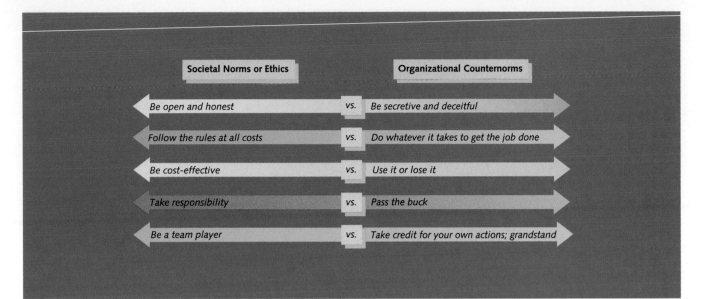

Societal Norms or Ethics		Organizational Counternorms
Be open and honest	vs.	Be secretive and deceitful
Follow the rules at all costs	vs.	Do whatever it takes to get the job done
Be cost-effective	vs.	Use it or lose it
Take responsibility	vs.	Pass the buck
Be a team player	vs.	Take credit for your own actions; grandstand

FIGURE 12-13
SOCIETAL NORMS VERSUS ORGANIZATIONAL COUNTERNORMS: AN ETHICAL CONFLICT
Although societal standards of ethics and morality dictate the appropriateness of certain actions, counternorms that encourage and support opposite practices often develop within organizations. (Source: Based on suggestions by Jansen & Von Glinow, 1985; see Note 75.)

because *managerial values exist that undermine integrity*. In a recent analysis of executive integrity, Wolfe explains that managers have developed some ways of thinking (of which they may be quite unaware) that foster unethical behavior.[78]

One culprit is referred to as the **bottom-line mentality**. This line of thinking supports financial success as the only value to be considered. It promotes short-term solutions that are immediately financially sound, despite the fact that they cause problems for others within the organization or for the organization as a whole. It promotes an unrealistic belief that everything boils down to a monetary game. As such, rules of morality are merely obstacles, impediments along the way to immediate financial gain.

Wolfe also notes that managers tend to rely on an **exploitative mentality**—a view that encourages "using" people in a way that promotes stereotypes and undermines empathy and compassion. This highly selfish perspective sacrifices concern for others in favor of benefits to one's own immediate interests. In addition, there is a **Madison Avenue mentality**—a perspective suggesting that anything is right if the public can be convinced that it's right. The idea is that executives may be more concerned about their actions appearing ethical than about their legitimate morality—a public relations-guided mentality. This kind of thinking leads some companies to hide their unethical actions (by dumping their toxic wastes under cover of night, for instance) or to otherwise justify them by attempting to explain them as completely acceptable.

Recognizing the problems associated with these various orientations is not difficult. Their overemphasis on short-term monetary gain may lead to decisions that not only hurt individuals in the long run, but also threaten the very existence of organizations themselves. Although an organization may make an immediate profit by cutting corners, exploiting people, and convincing others that they have behaved appropriately, it is questionable whether such practices are in the long-term best interest of organizations. Just as people are learning that they cannot continue to exploit their natural environments forever without paying a cost (e.g., depletion of natural resources, hazards allegedly caused by openings in the earth's ozone layer), the same may apply to business environments as well. Indeed, society appears to be increasingly less tolerant of organizations that continue to violate moral standards in the name of short-term profits.[79]

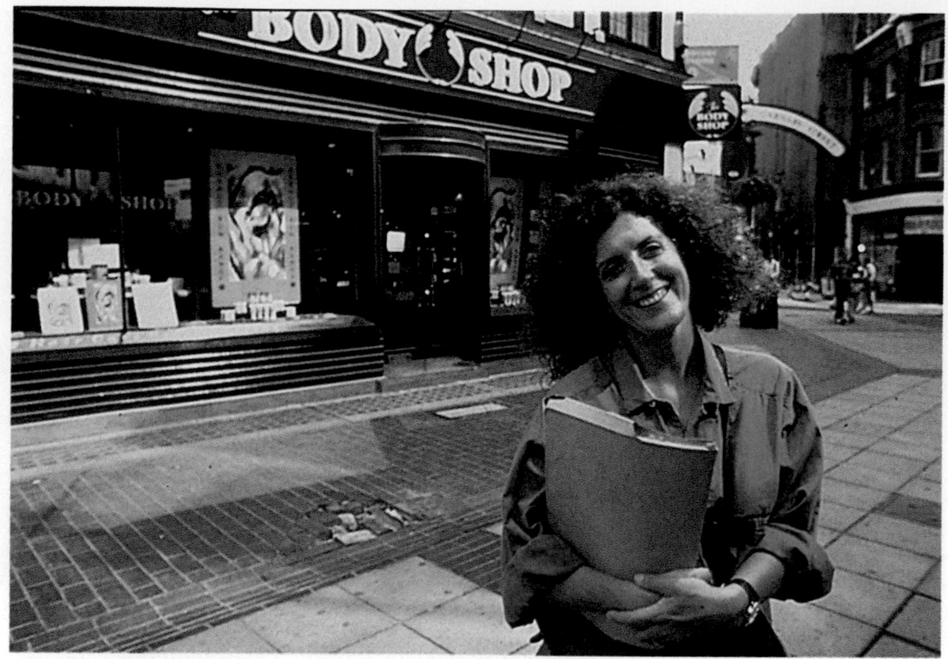

FIGURE 12-14
ONE ORGANIZATION WITH HIGH ETHICAL PRINCIPLES
Anita Roddick's worldwide chain of cosmetics stores, the Body Shop, is widely known for its socially responsible policies toward people, animals, and the physical environment. Consumers have supported the Body Shop in large part because they endorse the ethical principles by which it conducts business.

It has even been argued that when organizations continue to behave unethically, they may actually find that doing so is unprofitable in the long run. Consumers who find the well-publicized unethical actions of various companies objectionable may cast their votes for greater social responsibility by not patronizing those organizations.[80] In contrast, a growing number of organizations—such as the Body Shop (see Figure 12-14) and Tom's of Maine, to name only two—have long engaged in highly ethical practices with respect to the treatment of living beings and the environment, and have prospered in great part because of consumers' appreciation of these policies.[81,82] Although it appears that companies are becoming increasingly concerned about behaving ethically, it must be cautioned that such trends are difficult to assess. (One effective means of tracking ethical values in organizations is to conduct surveys tapping perceptions of ethical practices in organizations. According to the results of a recent survey, self-serving, political pressures appear to be responsible for many of the most unethical practices within organizations. For a review of these findings, see the Ethical Workplace section on the opposite page.)

POLITICAL ANTICS TOP THE "MOST UNETHICAL" LIST

A sure sign of someone's authority in an organization is the capacity to "pull strings," to get things done in a manner that goes outside normal organizational channels. Consider, for example, someone who may tell you, "I have a friend at that company who owes me a favor, so I'll get him to hire you for that job you want." Although such practices are not uncommon, survey research has shown that hiring decisions made to fulfill a favor are considered unethical because they are not based on job performance.

More than a thousand professionals in the field of human resources management were surveyed concerning their feelings about the ethics of various managerial practices.[83] Interestingly, among the ethical situations considered most serious were several practices that dealt with political activities reflecting an abuse of power. These included practices such as "making personnel decisions based on favoritism instead of job performance," and "basing differences in pay on friendship." In fact, these were the two most frequently cited types of unethical

FIGURE 12-15

MOST SERIOUS ETHICAL SITUATIONS: SURVEY RESULTS

Among the most widely reported sources of unethical behaviors noted in a survey of human resources managers are those dealing with political behaviors—actions that benefit oneself as opposed to the organization. (Source: Based on data reported by the Commerce Clearing House, 1991; see Note 83.)

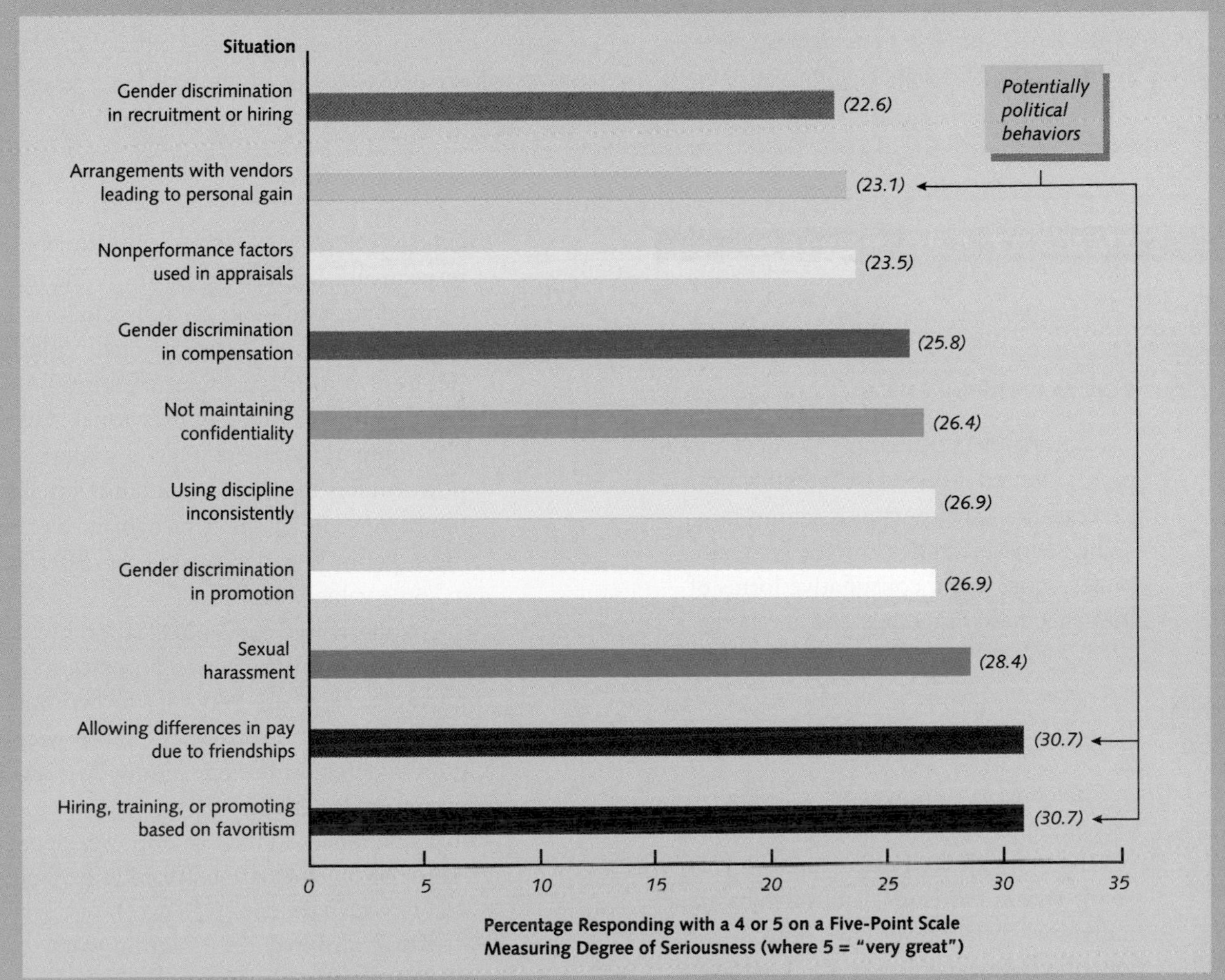

situations faced by human resource managers (with almost 31 percent of the sample indicating that each was among *the* most serious violations).

Another type of unethical political behavior (indicated as being most serious by over 23 percent of the sample) was "making arrangements with vendors leading to personal gain." As shown in Figure 12-15, these actions are in addition to various other types of unethical behavior that represent bias, but that are not so clearly self-serving as to constitute political acts.

Given that so many critical ethics violations appear to be politically motivated, self-serving actions, it is not surprising that these happened to be the very behaviors that managers had the greatest difficulty addressing. In fact, only about half of the managers surveyed reported having any success in minimizing a problem such as hiring based on favoritism. The very fact that such behaviors benefit oneself makes them difficult to eliminate. In contrast, it is easier to combat unethical behaviors based on insensitivity (e.g., lack of attention to privacy) because these serve no beneficial functions for the person doing the violating.

Managers tend to be relatively unaware of the political biases underlying their unethical actions, however. Instead, they attribute their actions to the attitudes and behaviors of senior management. Specifically, whereas only 10 percent of the participants attributed unethical behaviors to political pressures, 56 percent attributed unethical behaviors to the attitudes and behaviors of senior management. They blamed top management most frequently for instances of unethical behavior, but they also recognized that top management of organizations tends to be committed to ethical conduct. Despite such commitment, company officials tend to overlook the capacity of human resources managers to help promote their company's ethical values. Too often, they tend to concentrate on using human resources managers for maintaining up-to-date legal information about personnel matters. But ethics goes well beyond mere compliance with the law, and society expects companies to go well beyond the ethical minimums. For these reasons—not to mention the long-term success of companies themselves—it is essential for human resources officials to help institute policies that encourage basing personnel-related decisions on job performance instead of favoritism.

SUMMARY AND REVIEW

SOCIAL INFLUENCE

When someone attempts to affect another in a desired fashion—whether or not successfully—that person is said to be using **social influence**. People generally prefer to use open, consultative forms of influence rather than coercive methods.

ORGANIZATIONAL POWER

The concept of **power** refers to the capacity to change the behavior or attitudes of others in a desired manner. Power may reside within individuals, and five bases of individual social power have been identified. **Reward power** and **coercive power** refer to an individual's capacity to control valued rewards and punishments, respectively. **Legitimate power** is the recognized authority that an individual has by virtue of his or her organizational position. **Referent power** is a source of control based on the fact that an individual is liked and admired by others. Finally, **expert power** refers to the power an individual has because he or she is recognized as having superior knowledge, skill, or expertise in some valued area.

An alternative conceptualization of power distinguishes between **position power** (power based on one's formal organizational position) and **personal power** (power derived from one's individual qualities or characteristics). Research has shown that differences in the use of power depend on the specific situations faced (e.g., facing others who have counterpower).

Power also may reside within work groups, or subunits. The **resource-**

dependency model asserts that power resides within the subunits that control the greatest share of valued organizational resources. The **strategic contingencies model** explains power in terms of a subunit's capacity to control the activities of other subunits. Such power may be enhanced by the capacity to reduce the level of uncertainty experienced by another unit, having a central position within the organization, or performing functions that other units cannot perform.

ORGANIZATIONAL POLITICS

Behaving in a manner that is not officially approved by an organization to meet one's own goals by influencing others is known as **organizational politics**. Such activities typically occur under ambiguous conditions (such as in areas of organizational functioning in which clear rules are lacking). Political tactics may include blaming and attacking others, controlling access to information, cultivating a favorable impression, developing an internal base of support, and aligning oneself with more powerful others. This may involve the playing of political games, such as asserting one's authority, enhancing one's power base, attacking one's rivals, and trying to foster organizational change.

Such actions typically occur under conditions in which organizational uncertainty exists, important decisions involving large amounts of scarce resources are made, and the groups involved have conflicting interests but are approximately equal in power. Specifically, political activity is expected to be high when it comes to matters of human resource management and during an organization's mature stage of development (as opposed to its early and declining stages). The effects of organizational politics can be limited by practices such as clarifying job expectations, opening the communication process, being a good role model, and not turning a blind eye to game players.

THE ETHICAL IMPLICATIONS OF ORGANIZATIONAL POLITICS

Although there are exceptions, political behavior may be considered ethical to the extent that it fosters organizational interests over individual greed, respects the rights of individuals, and conforms to prevailing standards of justice and fair play. Unethical behavior occurs in organizations for several reasons. For one, organizations develop *counternorms* that reward individuals for behaving in ways that are not considered ethical in the outside world (e.g., being secretive and stonewalling instead of being open and honest with others). In addition, managerial values exist that undermine integrity, such as the **bottom-line mentality** (a focus on short-term profit maximization), the **exploitative mentality** (selfishly using others for one's advantage), and the **Madison Avenue mentality** (convincing others that one's unethical actions are actually moral).

KEY TERMS

bottom-line mentality: The view that places the greatest importance on short-term financial gains of an organization. It considers ethics and morality as obstacles in the path of financial gain.

charisma: An attitude of enthusiasm and optimism that is contagious; an aura of leadership.

coercive power: The individual power base derived from the capacity to administer punishment to others.

empowerment: Giving people the opportunity to have control over the way they do their jobs.

expert power: The individual power base derived from an individual's recognized superior skills and abilities in a certain area.

exploitative mentality: The selfish view that sacrifices concern for others in favor of an individual's own immediate interests.

information power: The extent to which a supervisor provides a subordinate with the information needed to do the job.

legitimate power: The individual power base derived from one's position in an organizational hierarchy; the accepted authority of one's position.

Madison Avenue mentality: The view suggesting that anything is right if others can be convinced that it's right; a public relations-guided morality.

organizational politics: Actions not officially approved by an organization, taken to influence others in order to meet one's personal goals.

personal power: The power that one derives because of his or her individual qualities or characteristics.

persuasive power: The ability to use facts and logic to present a case persuasively.

politics: See *organizational politics*.

position power: Power based on one's formal position in an organization.

power: The capacity to change the behavior or attitudes of others in a desired manner.

referent power: The individual power base derived from the degree to which one is liked and admired by others.

resource-dependency model: The view that power resides within subunits that are able to control the greatest share of valued organizational resources.

reward power: The individual power base derived from a person's capacity to administer valued rewards to others.

social influence: Attempts to affect another in a desired fashion.

strategic contingencies model: A view explaining power in terms of a subunit's capacity to control the activities of other subunits. A subunit's power is enhanced when (1) it can reduce the level of uncertainty experienced by other subunits, (2) it occupies a central position in the organization, and (3) its activities are highly indispensable to the organization.

QUESTIONS FOR DISCUSSION

1. Suppose your professor asks you to redo a homework assignment. Explain the various bases of individual social power he or she may use to influence your behavior in this situation.
2. Using the resource-dependency model and the strategic contingencies model as the basis for your analysis, describe the relative power differences between groups in any organization with which you are familiar.
3. Suppose you are a corporate official on the lookout for places within your organization where political behavior is likely to occur. What places and conditions would you look for? Explain your answer.
4. Describe the political tactics and tricks that one person may use to gain a power advantage over another in an organization.
5. Although it might not be possible to completely eliminate organizational politics, it might be possible to effectively manage political activity. Describe some of the things that can be done to cope with organizational politics.
6. Suppose you're the manager of a human resources department. Are political activities more likely or less likely to take place in your department compared to other departments? Why? What form might these actions be expected to take?
7. Explain why an organization's ethical norms may differ from ethical standards existing in the outside world.
8. Argue for or against this statement: "The use of power in organizations is unethical."

CASE IN POINT

THE MOST POWERFUL MAN IN SPORTS

What do Arnold Palmer, Jack Nicklaus, Andre Agassi, Martina Navratilova, the Mayo Clinic, the Nobel Foundation, and the World Ski Federation have in common? Each of these people and institutions has hired the International Management Group (IMG), to help them promote their products or services and/or to manage their careers.[1] Even the Vatican has hired IMG! In this case, the company was called on to help coordinate the merchandising of the official souvenirs of Pope John Paul II's visit to the United Kingdom in 1982.[2]

IMG has 61 offices in twenty-two countries, and revenues of nearly $1 billion.[3] Although the company has recently branched out to include the management of models and musicians as well as institutions, they developed their expertise in marketing and management through the world of sports. They create, promote, produce, and consult to sporting events such as the Olympics, Wimbledon, the major golf tournaments, the Virginia Slims Tennis Tournaments, and "The Skins" games.[4] The company also represents the interests of athletes in negotiating their endorsements and managing their careers. Not only does IMG manage the athletes and the events, they develop more hours of sports programming for television than any other company. In fact, IMG is so intricately involved in the marketing of sports that *Sports Illustrated* has called the company founder, chairman, and CEO, Mark McCormack, "the most powerful man in sports."[5]

McCormack serves as an example of a businessman who was in the right place, at the right time, with a good idea. Through his interest in golf, he became friends with Arnold Palmer in the early 1960s. As he was thinking of a way to stay close to the game after completing Yale Law School, he suggested to Palmer that he check over his contracts and serve as his general business manager. Soon thereafter, he took over the management of Gary Player and Jack Nicklaus—neither of whom had won any tournaments at this time. As McCormack notes, all of them then started "winning everything in sight."[6] With the major expansion in television coverage of sports and the age of jet travel beginning to explode, McCormack was in the position to create the entire industry of sports marketing.

McCormack's success stems from many different talents but probably none so important as his expertise in dealing with, understanding, and relating to people. He clearly excels in listening to others to determine what their needs and wishes are so that he can offer solutions that meet their interests. In this way he gains additional business as well as increasing status as the company comes to represent more and more world-reknown personalities.

McCormack is also very aware of the power of friendship. As he says, "All things being equal, people will do business with a friend. All things being not equal, they will still do business with a friend."[7] To cultivate friendships, McCormack takes a genuine interest in the success of the people his firm represents. He attempts to generate enthusiasm and commitment by appealing to the winning and competitive values of his clients. In addition, he shows support by attending many of the events in which his company represents the stars. Similarly, he always provides advice in his clients' best interests—never pushing an athlete, for example, to appear in an event that may damage his or her career standing even if it would make money for IMG.[8]

The size, power, and scope of IMG and the various activities in which it is involved has led some critics to charge that the firm has the potential for abuse. This is because the company not only represents the athletes, but also may create and sponsor the event in which they participate, as well as produce the television coverage and sell the broadcast rights. Although McCormack admits that this situation provides the opportunity for unethical coercion of the various parties involved, he claims that his company has not done this because it would not be in the long-term interest of all involved. He does admit, however, that just like any big business, his firm uses its power in the marketplace to most favorably position their events and clientele.[9] This, of course, is its job.

Because IMG is a privately held company and McCormack is the founder as well as majority owner, he has a great deal of command over the ways in which the company operates. Although it would be impossible for him to keep his hands on all aspects of management throughout the world, he creates the impression that he is in control of practically everything. He does this by maintaining a killer schedule. He gets up each day at 4:00 a.m. After reading for an hour, he makes international phone calls to take advantage of the different time zones in which people with whom he needs to communicate may be located. Next, starting between 5:30 and 6:00 A.M., he dictates correspondence to his secretary for an hour and a half. Following this, he prepares for the rest of his day. These days often involve travel, as McCormack attends nearly a thousand events each year! In order to meet all his commitments, he keeps such tight management of his schedule that he doesn't allow activities to go more than seven minutes past their allotted times.[10]

Not only does McCormack find time and energy to direct his company, he has written eight books on management. The most commercially successful of these, *What They Don't Teach You at Harvard Business School*,[11] solidified his reputation as a man very knowledgeable about the people side of business. This has further enhanced his ability to market his own expertise to the business community.

McCormack, a powerhouse in his industry, has learned a great deal from the sports champions he represents. He suggests that winners have three qualities: (1) the killer instinct and desire to win, (2) the ability to "peak" at the right time, and (3) the determination to continue improving no matter how good they are or how much they achieve. In becoming "the most powerful man in sports," McCormack clearly has demonstrated that he has mastered these attributes.[12]

QUESTIONS FOR DISCUSSION

1. Which tactics of social influence does McCormack appear to use most frequently?
2. What bases of power does McCormack have relative to the management of his business? Are these the same bases of power he has in his personal relationships? Explain your response.
3. Although McCormack wants to believe that his company does not use undue coercion toward its athletes, do you think that the money involved may provide a subtle pressure on the stars? How might this operate?
4. McCormack is friends with many famous people. Do you think that this influences other stars and businesspeople in their dealings with him?

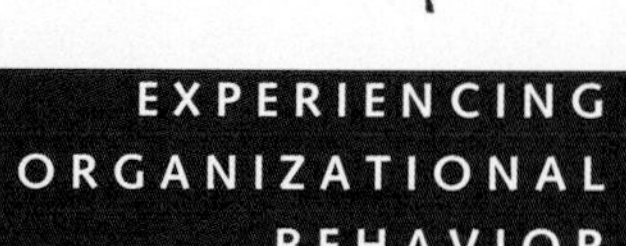

EXPERIENCING ORGANIZATIONAL BEHAVIOR

Occupational Differences in the Use of Power

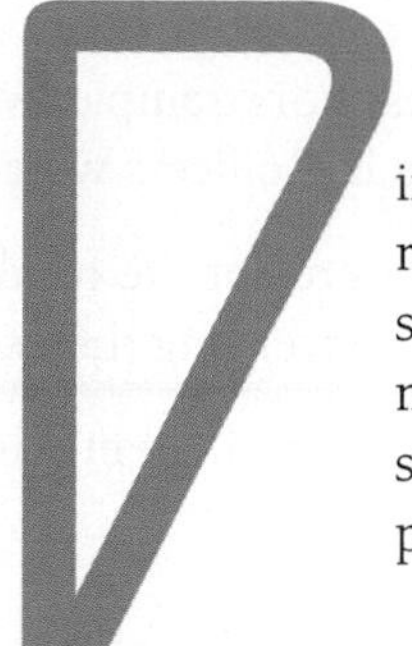

Different individual predispositions and work situations are responsible for the ways people use power. If one assumes some commonalties among people in various professions, it may follow that people in the same profession use power similarly and that people within different professions use power differently. This exercise explores such a possibility.

PROCEDURE

1. Based on class discussion, identify members of various professions whom students in the class know well enough to survey. Try to find different professions whose members can be approached by several different class members (about five different professions whose members can be surveyed by 10 different students would be ideal). For example, several class members may have access to people working in church organizations or the military, or to teachers or nurses.

2. Type and copy the questionnaire shown in Table 12-4 (on page 464). Have each student in the class give the questionnaire to people in the assigned groups, specifying that they are to describe their immediate supervisors. (Make sure that all local Institutional Review Board permissions are granted and that students have permission from appropriate organizational officials to administer the questionnaire. It usually helps to have students ask permission of an official of an organization whom they already know.)

3. When students return to class with their questionnaires, tabulate the uses of each of the five sources of power by people in each profession tapped. It would help to summarize the data as follows (adding as many professions as needed):

Types of Power	*Profession 1*	*Profession 2*	*Profession 3*
Reward			
Coercive			
Referent			
Legitimate			
Expert			

In each cell, insert the mean scores (following the scoring directions) for that type of power within that profession, using the data collected by all students who surveyed individuals in that profession.

POINTS TO CONSIDER

1. Did people from different professions use power differently? For each profession, what type of power was highest and lowest? For each type of power, what professions scored highest and lowest?
2. Were there any logical connections between the use of power and the stereotypes of the professions? For example, were kindergarten teachers higher in reward power, whereas law officers were higher in coercive power?
3. Discuss the possible reasons for the results. For example, are the stereotypes consistent with reality concerning the use of power?
4. What could have been done differently to improve this demonstration?

CHAPTER OUTLINE

SPECIAL SECTIONS

THIRTEEN

LEADERSHIP: ITS NATURE AND IMPACT IN ORGANIZATIONS

LEARNING OBJECTIVES

After reading this chapter, you should be able to

1. *Define leadership, and indicate why leading and managing are not always the same.*
2. *Describe several traits that distinguish leaders from other people.*
3. *Describe various forms of participative and autocratic leader behavior.*
4. *Distinguish between the two basic forms of leader behavior: person-oriented behavior and production-oriented behavior.*
5. *Explain what the leader–member exchange (LMX) model says about the relationships between leaders and followers*
6. *Describe the role of attribution in the leadership process.*
7. *Describe the nature of transformational or charismatic leadership.*
8. *Explain the general nature of contingency theories of leader effectiveness.*
9. *Summarize the basic nature of five different contingency theories: LPC contingency theory, situational leadership theory, path–goal theory, substitutes for leadership theory, and normative decision theory.*

To lead the people, walk behind them.

Lao-Tzu, c. 604–c. 531 B.C.
Chinese philosopher
and founder of Taoism
Tao Te Ching

Leadership is not manifested by coercion, even against the resented.

Margaret Chase Smith
U.S. Senator
Address to National
Republican Women
April 16, 1962

PREVIEW CASE

Mary Kay Ash: Leadership That Is Not Merely Cosmetic

There are "rags-to-riches stories," and then there's Mary Kay Ash, the founder of the successful Mary Kay Cosmetics empire. At age 45 she became disenchanted with the limited opportunities for women in business in the early 1960s, and with only the help of her children she gambled her life savings of $5,000 on a cosmetics business. Some three decades later this investment has grown into a giant corporation with annual sales over $613 million and a sales force some 300,000 strong. Not surprisingly, the woman behind all this has been considered one of the best business leaders in the United States.

Many attribute the company's success in large part to the fact that Mary truly cares about her employees, almost all of whom are women. By giving them opportunities to succeed and recognizing their success, she motivates and inspires them. At its annual "Seminar" in Dallas, for example, Mary Kay representatives are awarded such forms of recognition as pink Cadillacs (some $90 million worth have been given away already), first-class trips abroad, gold bracelets studded in diamonds spelling out "$1,000,000" (for selling that amount of cosmetics), and lapel pins and ribbons denoting other sales milestones. These lavish forms of recognition are matched only by the opulent, Las Vegas-style productions in which they are presented—fêtes that take on the noise level and excitement of political conventions.

One of the things Mary Kay executives pride themselves in doing is helping women become financially successful and feel good about themselves. "Give me a hard-working waitress," says Shirley Hutton, "and in a year I'll turn her into a director making $35,000." Many do better—much better. Indeed, seventy-four sales consultants have earned commissions of over $1 million during their careers. The national sales director, Shirley Hutton of Minneapolis earned approximately that amount in 1993 alone!

Mary Kay is recognized for her sincerity and concern for her consultants' well-being. According to Gloria Hilliard Mayfield, a relatively new sales consultant, she is surprisingly approachable. "You wouldn't just walk over to, say, John Akers [CEO of IBM]," she explains. "But Mary Kay calls you her daughter and looks you dead in the eye. She makes you feel you can do anything. She's sincerely concerned about your welfare." When Hutton's daughter was ill, for example, Mary Kay called her several times to cheer her up. Such expressions of personal interest are contagious: many beauty consultants treat their customers the same way—sending them birthday cards and showing they're interested in them. This, they are convinced, sells makeup!

Recognition from Mary is considered the ultimate form of recognition. At each year's seminar, she personally crowns four "Queens of Seminar" in recognition of their sales accomplishments. She kisses them, gives them roses, and pats their hands. This personal touch is so important that one year, when she was ill, she made an appearance from her sickbed via a closed-circuit television hookup—just to make her presence felt.

Mary Kay Ash of Mary Kay Cosmetics

What will happen to Mary Kay, the company, after Mary Kay Ash, the woman, is gone? "There will be a flood of tears unlike anything you've ever seen," says the husband of a sales consultant. "I'd love to have the tissue concession." But no one doubts that the company will continue without its inspirational leader—her legacy is too strong to not be felt.

There are very few individuals who have been as successful as Mary Kay Ash, and who have changed the lives of so many with their leadership. John D. Rockefeller at Standard Oil, Lee Iacocca at Chrysler, Tom Watson at IBM, and Alfred Sloan at General Motors also come to mind as some of the most visible examples of business leaders whose achievements have been well publicized (see Figure 13-1). But these well-known leaders simply mirror the accomplishments of thousands of unsung leaders who toil in the trenches of businesses both large and small on a daily basis. If you asked 100 executives to name the single most important factor in determining organizational success, chances are good that many would reply, "effective leadership." This answer reflects the general belief in the world of business that **leadership** is a key ingredient in corporate effectiveness. And this view is by no means restricted to organizations; leadership also plays a central role in politics, sports, and many other human activities.

Is this view justified? Do leaders really play such a crucial role in shaping the fortunes of organizations? Almost a century of research on this topic suggests that they do.[1] Effective leadership, it appears, is indeed a key factor in organizational success.[2] Given this fact and its relevance to the field of organizational behavior, it seems appropriate for us to consider the topic of leadership in some detail. In this chapter, therefore, we will summarize current information about this complex process. One review of research on leadership published a few years ago cited more than 10,000 separate articles and books on this topic.[3] Not surprisingly, leadership is considered the most studied concept in the social sciences.[4]

Obviously, there is quite a lot of ground to cover. To make the task of summarizing this wealth of information more manageable, we will proceed as follows. First, we will consider some basic points about leadership—what it is and why being a leader is not necessarily synonymous with being a manager. Second, we will examine views of leadership focusing on the traits of leaders, and another focusing primarily on their behaviors. Third, we will examine several major theories of leadership that focus on the relationship between leaders and their followers. Finally, we will review several contrasting theories dealing with the conditions under which leaders are effective or ineffective in their important role.

FIGURE 13-1
TWO FAMOUS BUSINESS LEADERS
Although Lee Iacocca of Chrysler Corporation (left) and Thomas J. Watson, Jr. of IBM (right) are two well-known leaders of large corporations, there are also many less visible leaders making important contributions to their organizations on a daily basis.

LEADERSHIP: ITS BASIC NATURE

In one sense, at least, leadership resembles love: it is something most people feel they can recognize, but often find difficult to define. What, precisely, is it? And how does being a leader differ from being a manager? We will now focus on these questions.

LEADERSHIP: A WORKING DEFINITION

Imagine that you have accepted a new job and entered a new work group. How would you recognize its **leader**? One possibility, of course, is through the formal titles and assigned roles each person in the group holds. In short, the individual designated as department head or project manager would be the one you would identify as the group's leader. But imagine that during several staff meetings, you noticed that this person was really not the most influential. Although she or he held the formal authority, these meetings were actually dominated by another person, who, ostensibly, was the top person's subordinate. What would you conclude about leadership then? Probably that the real leader of the group was the person who actually ran things—not the one with the fancy title and the apparent authority.

In many cases, of course, the disparity we have just described does not exist. The individual possessing the greatest amount of formal authority is also the most influential. In some situations, however, this is not so. And in such cases, we typically identify the person who actually exercises the most influence over the group as its leader. These facts point to the following working definition of **leadership**—one accepted by many experts on this topic: *the process whereby one individual influences other group members toward the attainment of defined group or organizational goals.*[5]

Note that according to this definition, leadership is primarily a process involving influence—one in which a leader changes the actions or attitudes of several group members or subordinates. As we saw in Chapter 12, many techniques for exerting such influence exist, ranging from relatively coercive ones (in which one has little choice but to do what is requested) to relatively noncoercive ones (in which one can choose to accept or reject the influence offered). In general, leadership refers to the use of relatively noncoercive influence techniques. This characteristic distinguishes a leader from a *dictator.* Whereas dictators gets others to do what they want by using physical coercion or by threats of physical force, leaders do not.[6] As Mao Zedong (founder of the People's Republic of China) put it, "Power grows out of the barrel of a gun." This may be true with respect to the power of dictators, but not the power of leaders. The point is that leadership rests, at least in part, on positive feelings between leaders and their subordinates. In other words, subordinates accept influence from leaders because they respect, like, or admire them—not simply because they hold positions of formal authority.[7]

The definition presented above also suggests that leadership involves the exercise of influence for a purpose—to attain defined group or organizational goals. In other words, leaders focus on altering those actions or attitudes of their subordinates that are related to specific goals; they are far less concerned with altering actions or attitudes that are irrelevant to such goals.

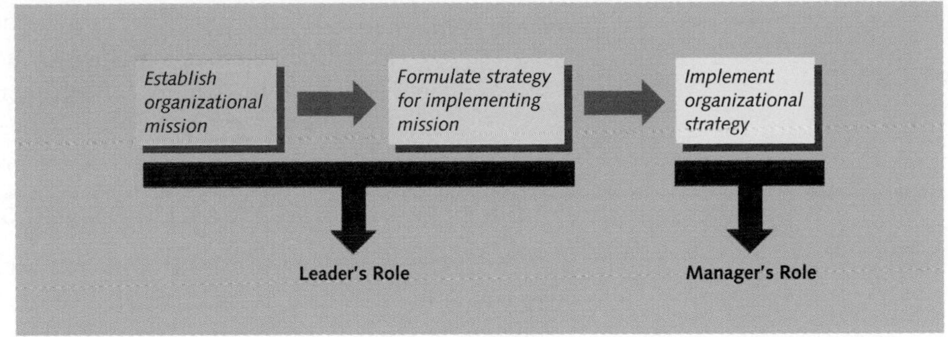

FIGURE 13-2
LEADERS AND MANAGERS: DISTINGUISHING THEIR ROLES
Whereas leaders are primarily responsible for establishing an organizational mission and formulating a strategy for implementing it, managers are responsible for the actual implementation of that strategy. In many cases, however, these distinctions are blurred in actual practice.

Finally, note that our definition, by emphasizing the central role of influence, implies that leadership is really something of a two-way street. Although leaders do indeed influence subordinates in various ways, leaders are also influenced by their subordinates. In fact, it may be said that leadership exists only in relation to followers. After all, one cannot lead without followers!

LEADERS VERSUS MANAGERS: A KEY DISTINCTION—AT LEAST IN THEORY

In everyday speech, the terms *leader* and *manager* are often used almost interchangeably. Although we understand the temptation to do so, the two terms need to be clearly distinguished. According to Kotter, the primary function of a leader is to create the essential purpose or mission of the organization and the strategy for attaining it. By contrast, the job of the manager is to implement that vision. He or she is the means of achieving the end, the vision created by the leader (see Figure 13-2).[8]

The confusion between these two terms rests in the fact that the distinction between establishing a mission and implementing it is often blurred in practice. This is because many leaders, such as top corporate executives, are frequently called on not only to create a vision, but also to help implement it. Similarly, managers are often required to lead those who are subordinate to them while at the same time carrying out their leader's mission. Some have observed that too many so-called leaders get bogged down in the managerial aspects of their job, creating organizations that are "overmanaged and underled."[9]

In summary, although some managers are indeed leaders, others are not, making no clear link between these two roles. For this reason, we will distinguish carefully between these two terms throughout this chapter.

LEADER TRAITS AND BEHAVIORS

At one time or another, most people have daydreams about being a leader. They fantasize about taking charge of large groups and being viewed with great awe and respect. Despite the prevalence of such daydreams, however, relatively few individuals convert them into reality by becoming leaders. Further, among these, only a small proportion are considered effective in this role. This fact raises an intriguing question: what sets effective leaders apart from most others? Why, in short, do some people, but not others, become effective leaders? Many answers have been proposed, but two have received the most attention. These perspectives suggest, respectively, that effective leadership is largely a function of either the traits possessed by individuals, or the patterns of behavior they demonstrate.[10,11]

THE TRAIT APPROACH: HAVING THE "RIGHT STUFF"

Are some people born to lead? Common sense suggests that this is so. Great leaders of the past such as Alexander the Great, Queen Elizabeth I, and Abraham Lincoln do seem to differ from ordinary human beings in several respects. For example, they all seem to have possessed high levels of ambition coupled with clear visions of precisely where they wanted to go. To a lesser degree, even leaders lacking in such history-shaping fame seem different from their followers. Top executives, some politicians, and even sports heroes or heroines often seem to possess an aura that sets them apart from others. On the basis of such observations, early researchers interested in leadership formulated a view known as the **great person theory**. According to this approach, great leaders possess key traits that set them apart from most other human beings. Further, the theory contends that these traits remain stable over time and across different groups. Thus, it suggests that all great leaders share these characteristics regardless of when and where they lived, or the precise role in history they fulfilled.

Certainly, these are intriguing suggestions, and seem to fit quite well with our own informal experience. You will probably be surprised to learn, therefore, that they have not been strongly confirmed. Decades of active research (most conducted prior to 1950) failed to yield a short, agreed-on list of key traits shared by all leaders.[12] A few consistent findings did emerge (e.g., leaders tend to be slightly taller and more intelligent than their followers), but these were hardly dramatic in nature or in scope.[13] Indeed, the overall results of this persistent search for traits associated with leadership were so disappointing that most investigators gave up in despair and reached the following conclusion: leaders simply do not differ from followers in clear and consistent ways.

Until quite recently, this conclusion was widely accepted as true. Now, however, it has been called into question by a growing body of evidence indicating that leaders *do* actually differ from other people in several important—and measurable—respects. After reviewing a large number of studies on this issue, Kirkpatrick and Locke recently reached the conclusion that traits *do* matter—that certain traits, together with other factors, contribute to leaders' success in business settings.[14] What are these traits? A listing and description of those identified as most important by Kirkpatrick and Locke is presented in Table 13-1. You will readily recognize and understand most of these characteristics (drive, honesty and integrity, self-confidence). However, others seem to require further clarification.

Consider, first, what Kirkpatrick and Locke term **leadership motivation**. This refers to leaders' desire to influence others and—in essence—to lead. Such motivation, however, can take two distinct forms. On the one hand, it may cause leaders to seek power as an end in itself. Leaders who demonstrate such *personalized power motivation* wish to dominate others, and their desire to do so is often reflected in an excessive concern with status. In contrast, leadership motivation can cause leaders to seek power as a means to achieve desired, shared goals. Leaders who evidence such *socialized power motivation* cooperate with others, develop networks and coalitions, and generally work with subordinates rather than trying to dominate or control them. Needless to say, this type of leadership motivation is usually far more adaptive for organizations than personalized leadership motivation.

With respect to *cognitive ability*, it appears that effective leaders must be intelligent and capable of integrating and interpreting large amounts of information. However, mental genius does not seem to be necessary and may, in some cases, prove detrimental.[15] A final characteristic, *flexibility,* refers to the ability of leaders to recognize what actions are required in a given situation and then to act accordingly. Evidence suggests that the most effective leaders are not prone to behave in the same ways all the time, but to be adaptive, matching their style to the needs of followers and the demands of the situations they face.[16]

In summary, recent evidence seems to necessitate some revision in the widely accepted view that leaders do not differ from other people with respect to specific traits. As noted by Kirkpatrick and Locke,

> Regardless of whether leaders are born or made . . . it is unequivocally clear that *leaders are not like other people*. Leaders do not have to be great men or women by being intellectual geniuses or omniscient prophets to succeed, but they do need to have the "right stuff" and this stuff is not equally present in all people. Leadership is a demanding, unrelenting job with enormous pressures and grave responsibilities. It would be a profound disservice to leaders to suggest that they are ordinary people who happened to be in the right place at the right time . . . . In the realm of leadership (and in every other realm), the individual does matter.[17]

Supplementing the idea that various traits distinguish effective leaders from others (that is, *who leaders are*) is the idea that leaders also may be distinctive with respect to the way they behave (in other words, *what leaders do*).

TABLE 13-1

Characteristics of Successful Leaders

Research findings indicate that successful leaders demonstrate the traits listed here.

TRAIT OR CHARACTERISTIC	DESCRIPTION
Drive	*Desire for achievement; ambition; high energy; tenacity; initiative*
Honesty and integrity	*Trustworthy; reliable; open*
Leadership motivation	*Desire to exercise influence over others to reach shared goals*
Self-confidence	*Trust in own abilities*
Cognitive ability	*Intelligence; ability to integrate and interpret large amounts of information*
Knowledge of the business	*Knowledge of industry, relevant technical matters*
Creativity	*Originality*
Flexibility	*Ability to adapt to needs of followers and requirements of situation*

PARTICIPATIVE VERSUS AUTOCRATIC LEADERSHIP BEHAVIORS

Think about the different bosses you have had in your life or career. Can you remember one who wanted to control virtually everything—someone who made all the decisions, told people precisely what to do, and wanted, quite literally, to run the entire show (see Figure 13-3)? In contrast, can you recall a boss or supervisor who allowed employees greater freedom and responsibility—someone who invited their input before making decisions, was open to suggestions, and allowed them to carry out various tasks in their own way? If so, you already have firsthand experience with two sharply contrasting styles of leadership: **autocratic** and **participative**.

In the past, these styles were viewed as endpoints along a single continuum. However, as noted by Muczyk and Reimann, they actually seem to involve two separate dimensions.[18] The first is the extent to which leaders permit subordinates to take part in decisions; this is the *autocratic-democratic* dimension. The second involves the extent to which leaders direct the activities of subordinates and tell them how to carry out their jobs; this is the *permissive–directive* dimension. Combining these two variables yields four possible patterns, which Muczyk and Reimann label (1) directive autocrat, (2) permissive autocrat, (3) directive democrat, and (4) permissive democrat. (These patterns are summarized in Table 13-2.) Although any attempt to divide human beings into discrete categories raises thorny issues, these patterns do seem to make good sense; many managers adopt a leadership style that fits, at least roughly, within one.

FIGURE 13-3
AUTOCRATIC LEADERS: THEY *DO* MAKE THE RULES
The autocratic leader shown here may be contrasted with his participative counterpart, who would allow group members to participate in making the rules. (Source: Drawing by Leo Cullum; © 1986 The New Yorker Magazine, *Inc.)*

"I was just going to say 'Well, I don't make the rules.' But, of course, I do make the rules."

But given that leaders differ along these two dimensions and can, as a result, be classified as falling into one of the four patterns listed above, do any of them have a clear-cut edge? In short, is one pattern superior to the others in many, if not most, situations? Existing evidence suggests that this is doubtful. All four styles seem to involve a mixed pattern of advantages and disadvantages. Moreover—and this is the crucial point—the relative success of each depends heavily on conditions existing within a given organization and its specific stage of development. For example, consider managers who might be described as *directive autocrats*. Such people make decisions without consulting subordinates and supervise subordinates' work activities very closely. It is tempting to view such a pattern as undesirable (it runs counter to the value of personal freedom), but this approach may actually be highly successful in some settings—such as when employees are inexperienced or underqualified for their jobs, or when subordinates adopt an adversarial stance toward management and must be closely supervised.

In contrast, consider the case of *permissive autocrats*—leaders who combine permissive supervision with an autocratic style of making decisions. This pattern may be useful in dealing with employees who have a high level of technical skill and want to be left alone to manage their own jobs (e.g., scientists, engineers, computer programmers), but who have little desire to participate in routine decision

TABLE 13-2

Contrasting Styles of Leadership

According to Muczyk and Reimann, leaders tend to adopt any of four distinct styles described here.

Are subordinates told exactly how to do their jobs?	Are subordinates permitted to participate in making decisions?	
	Yes *(democratic)*	**No** *(autocratic)*
Yes *(directive)*	**Directive democrat** *(makes decisions participatively; closely supervises subordinates)*	**Directive autocrat** *(makes decisions unilaterally; closely supervises subordinates)*
No *(permissive)*	**Permissive democrat** *(makes decisions participatively; gives subordinates latitude in carrying out their work)*	**Permissive autocrat** *(makes decisions unilaterally; gives subordinates latitude in carrying out their work)*

Source: Based on suggestions by Muczyk & Reimann, 1987; see Note 18.

making. The remaining two patterns (directive democrat and permissive democrat) are also most suited to specific organizational conditions. The key task for leaders, then, is to match their own style to the needs of their organization, and to change as these needs shift and evolve. What happens when leaders in organizations lack such flexibility?

Actual events in one former company—People Express Airlines—are instructive.[19] Don Burr, the founder and CEO of this airline, had a very clear managerial style: he was a highly permissive democrat. He involved employees in many aspects of decision making, and emphasized autonomy in work activities. Indeed, he felt that everyone at People Express should be viewed as a "manager." This style worked well while the company was young, but as it grew and increased in complexity, such practices created mounting difficulties. New employees were not necessarily as committed as older ones, so permissive supervision was ineffective with them. And as decisions increased in both complexity and number, a participative approach became less and less appropriate. Unfortunately, top management was reluctant to alter its style; after all, it seemed to have been instrumental in the company's early success. This poor match between the style of top leaders and changing external conditions seems to have contributed (along with many other factors) to People Express's mounting problems. Losses rose until finally the company was purchased by Texas Air, whose CEO, Frank Lorenzo, favored a much more directive leadership style.

To conclude, no single leadership style is best under all conditions and in all situations.[20] However, recognizing the importance of differences in this respect can be a constructive first step toward assuring that the style most suited to a given set of conditions is, in fact, adopted.

PERSON-ORIENTED VERSUS PRODUCTION-ORIENTED LEADERS

Think again about all the bosses you have had in your career. Divide these into two categories: those who were relatively effective and those who were relatively ineffective. How do the two groups differ? If you think about this issue carefully, your answers are likely to take one of two forms. First, you might reply, "My most effective bosses helped me to get the job done. They gave me advice, answered my questions, and let me know exactly what was expected of me. My most ineffective bosses didn't do this." Second, you might answer, "My most effective bosses seemed to care about me as a person. They were friendly, listened to me when I had problems or questions, and seemed to help me toward my personal goals. My ineffective bosses didn't do this."

A large body of research, much of it conducted in the 1950s at the University of Michigan and at the Ohio State University suggests that leaders do differ greatly along these dimensions.[21,22] Those at the high end of the first dimension, known as **initiating structure**, are mainly concerned with production and focus primarily on getting the job done. They engage in actions such as organizing work, inducing subordinates to follow rules, setting goals, and making leader and subordinate roles explicit. In contrast, other leaders are lower on this dimension and show less tendency to engage in these actions.

Leaders at the high end of the second dimension, known as **consideration**, are primarily concerned with establishing good relations with their subordinates and being liked by them. They engage in actions such as doing favors for subordinates, explaining things to them, and assuring their welfare. Others, in contrast, are low on this dimension and don't really care much about how they get along with subordinates.

At first glance, you might assume that initiating structure and consideration are linked such that people high on one of these dimensions are automatically low on

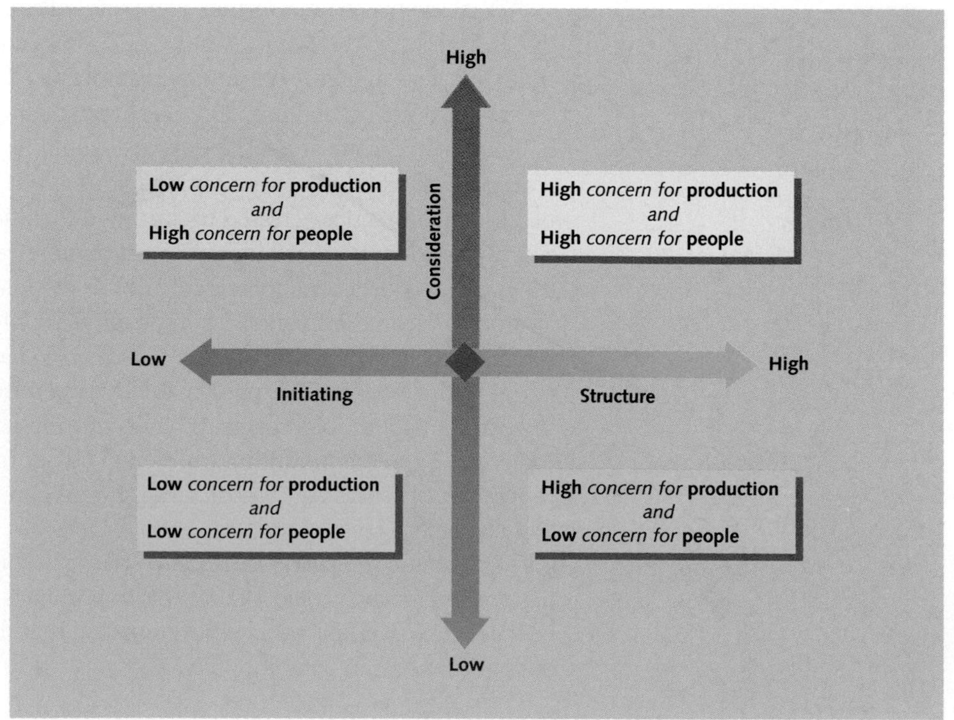

FIGURE 13-4
LEADER BEHAVIOR: ITS BASIC DIMENSIONS
Leaders' behavior can vary from low to high with respect to consideration *(person orientation) and* initiating structure *(task orientation). Patterns of leader behavior produced by variations along these two dimensions are illustrated here.*

the other. In fact, this is not the case. The two dimensions actually seem to be largely independent.[23] Thus, a leader may be high on both concern with production and concern for people, high on one of these dimensions and low on the other, moderate on one and high on the other, and so on (see Figure 13-4).

Is any one of these possible patterns best? Careful study indicates that this is a complex issue; production-oriented and people-oriented leadership behaviors both offer a mixed pattern of pluses and minuses. With respect to showing consideration (high concern with people and human relations), the major benefits are improved group atmosphere and morale.[24] However, since leaders high on this dimension are reluctant to act in a directive manner toward subordinates and often shy away from presenting them with negative feedback, productivity sometimes suffers. Regarding initiating structure (high concern with production), efficiency and performance are indeed sometimes enhanced by this leadership style. If leaders focus entirely on production, however, employees may soon conclude that no one cares about them or their welfare. Then work-related attitudes such as job satisfaction and organizational commitment may suffer.

Having said all this and pointed out the complexities, we add that one specific pattern may indeed have an edge in many settings. This is a pattern in which leaders demonstrate high concern with both people *and* production.[25] (As we will see in Chapter 16, encouraging such an approach is the goal of a popular form of organizational development, known as *grid training*.[26]) Indeed, research has shown that high amounts of concern with people (showing consideration) and concern with productivity (initiating structure) are not incompatible. Rather, skillful leaders can combine both of these orientations into their overall styles to produce favorable results. Thus, although no one leadership style is best, leaders who combine these two concerns may often have an important edge over leaders who show only one or the other. (These conclusions are all based on research conducted in the United States. However, it is logical to expect that different cultural norms existing in other countries might contribute to the ways leaders act. For a closer look at this possibility, see the Global Organization section below.)

THE GLOBAL ORGANIZATION

NATIONALITY AND LEADER BEHAVIOR: IS THERE A WORLD OF DIFFERENCE?

Concern with people (or consideration) and concern with production (or initiating structure) are the two main categories of leader behavior that have been indentified in several different theories of leadership. Despite this consistency, it is important to note that because all the theories were developed and tested in the United States it is uncertain how generalizable these basic dimensions of leadership really are. The question arises: Are these, in fact, basic dimensions of leaderhip behavior found all over the world? To answer this question, it is necessary to do cross-cultural leadership research. One such study, conducted by Smith, Misumi, Tayeb, Peterson, and Bond, provides important insight into the generalizability of the two basic leadership dimensions.[27]

These researchers administered questionnaires to several hundred members of work teams in electronics assembly plants located in each of four countries—Great Britain, the United States, Hong Kong, and Japan. The questionnaires required employees to indicate the extent to which they believed their superiors engaged in each of several different kinds of behaviors. These dealt with both person-oriented behaviors (e.g., "Does your superior try to understand your viewpoint?") and production-oriented behaviors (e.g., "To what extent does your superior give you instructions and orders?").

Overall, based on sophisticated statistical tests, it was found that the person-orientation and production-orientation dimensions did, in fact, constitute the two main types of leader behaviors exhibited in all four countries. In several cases, in fact, the same specific behaviors were exhibited. For example, in all countries a person-oriented leader was described as showing sympathy to a team member with personal difficulties, and willing to spend time discussing career plans with them. Similarly, a production-oriented leader in all countries was likely to talk about progress in relation to a work schedule and to share information required to do the job.

However, insofar as different cultures may make different types of behavior more or less acceptable, the researchers expected—and found—that concerns for people and concerns for production also were exhibited in different ways in the various countries. First let's examine concerns about people. In each country there was at least one form of this behavior that was uniquely exhibited. In Great Britain, for example, concern about people was demonstrated by showing employees how to use new equipment and helping them accept change. American employees demonstrated their concern for people by not sending written memos, and not talking about work-related problems. Among people from Hong Kong, concern for others was often expressed by spending social time together. Finally, in Japan, the most distinctive ways of expressing concern for others included speaking about subordinates' problems with others in their absence, and by teaching new job skills.

Differences also were found with respect to the specific ways people in each country showed their concern for production. Specifically, in Great Britain, this was done by voicing dissatisfaction when employees arrived late. In the United States, it took the form of addressing superiors using formal language. In Hong Kong, concern for production frequently involved meeting with subordinates and encouraging communication with others. Finally, in Japan, concern for production was expressed by checking work quality and by helping people complete their work.

Together, these findings lead to two important conclusions about the role of culture in leadership—at least with respect to the four cultures studied by Smith and his associates. First, they demonstrate that concern for people and concern for production are, in fact, universal dimensions of leadership behavior. Second, people are likely to express their concerns about people and production very differently in different cultures. The particular behaviors used to demonstrate these concerns are guided by the cultural traditions of the countries in which the employees are operating.[28] Based on this idea, we caution that interpreting leadership behavior in cultures other than one's own requires firmly understanding the norms and traditions of the people in those cultures.

LEADERS AND FOLLOWERS

Thus far throughout this chapter, we have focused on leaders—their traits and their behaviors. Followers, by and large, have been ignored. But note: in a crucial sense, followers are the essence of leadership. Without them, there really is no such thing as leadership. As Lee put it, "Without followers leaders cannot lead. . . . Without followers, even John Wayne becomes a solitary hero, or, given the right script, a comic figure, posturing on an empty stage."[29]

The importance of followers, and the complex, reciprocal relationship between leaders and followers, is widely recognized by organizational researchers. Indeed, major theories of leadership, such as those we will consider in this section note—either explicitly or implicitly—that leadership is really a two-way street. We will now consider three such approaches: the *leader–member exchange model*, the *attribution approach* to leadership, and the *transformational (or charismatic) approach* to leadership.

THE LEADER–MEMBER EXCHANGE (LMX) MODEL: THE IMPORTANCE OF BEING IN THE "IN-GROUP"

Do leaders treat all their subordinates in the same manner? Informal observation suggests that, clearly, they do not. Yet many theories of leadership ignore this fact. They discuss leadership behavior in terms that suggest similar actions toward all subordinates. The importance of potential differences in this respect is brought into sharp focus by the **leader–member exchange (LMX) model** developed by Graen and his associates.[30]

This theory suggests that for various reasons leaders form different kinds of relationships with various groups of subordinates. One group, referred to as the *in-group* is favored by the leader. Members of in-groups receive considerably more attention from the leader and larger shares of the resources they have to offer (such as time and recognition). By contrast, other subordinates fall into the *out-group*. These individuals are disfavored by leaders. As such, they receive fewer valued resources from their leaders. Leaders distinguish between in-group and out-group members very early in their relationships with them—and on the basis of surprisingly little information. Sometimes perceived similarity with respect to personal characteristics such as age, gender, or personality is sufficient to categorize followers into a leader's in-group. Similarly, a particular follower may be granted in-group status if the leader believes that person to be especially competent at performing his or her job.[31]

According to LMX theory, members of in-groups are expected to perform their jobs better, and to hold more positive attitudes toward their jobs than members of out-groups. In general, research has supported this prediction. For example, Deluga and Perry have found that in-group members were more satisfied with their jobs and more effective in performing them than out-group members.[32] Research also has supported the idea that leaders favor members of their in-groups. For example, in a recent study Duarte, Goodson, and Klich found that supervisors inflated the ratings they gave poorly performing employees when these individuals were members of the in-group, but not when they were members of the out-group.[33]

Together, these studies provide good support for the LMX model. Such findings suggest that attention to the relations between leaders and their followers can be very useful. The nature of such relationships can strongly affect the morale, commitment, and performance of employees. Helping leaders to improve such relations, therefore, can be extremely valuable in several respects.

THE ATTRIBUTION APPROACH: LEADERS' EXPLANATIONS OF FOLLOWERS' BEHAVIOR

As we have just noted, leaders' relationships with individual subordinates can play an important role in determining the performance and satisfaction of these individuals. One specific aspect of such exchanges serves as focus of another contemporary perspective on leadership—the **attribution approach**.[34] This theory emphasizes the role of leaders' attributions concerning the causes behind followers' behavior—especially, the causes of their job performance (see Chapter 2).

Leaders observe the performance of their followers and then attempt to understand why this behavior met, exceeded, or failed to meet their expectations. Since

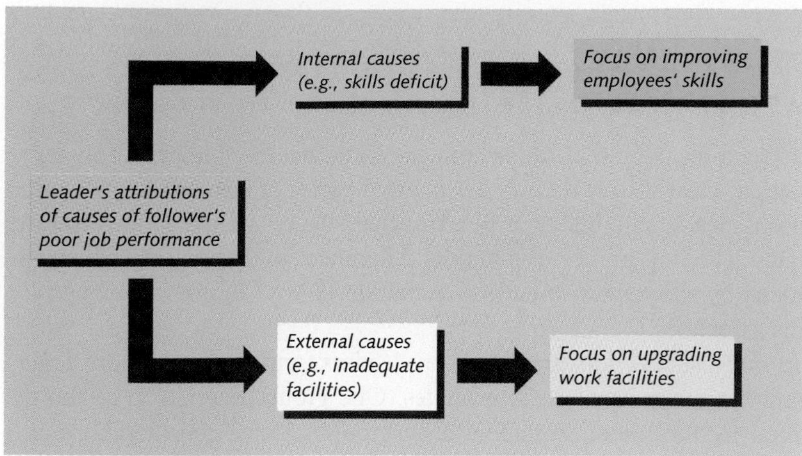

FIGURE 13-5
LEADERS' ATTRIBUTIONS OF FOLLOWERS' POOR PERFORMANCE
The way leaders respond to their followers depends on the attributions they make regarding the causes of followers' performance. In the example presented here, attributions made about the causes of subordinates' poor performance direct them to take completely different actions.

poor performance often poses greater difficulties than effective performance, leaders are more likely to engage in a careful attributional analysis when confronted with the former. When they do, they examine the three kinds of information described in Chapter 2 (consensus, consistency, and distinctiveness), and on the basis of such information form an initial judgment as to whether followers' performance stemmed from internal causes (e.g., low effort, commitment, or ability) or external causes (factors beyond their control, such as faulty equipment, unrealistic deadlines, or illness). Then, on the basis of such attributions, they formulate specific actions designed to change the present situation and perhaps improve followers' performance. Attribution theory suggests that such actions are determined, at least in part, by leaders' explanations of followers' behavior. For example, if they perceive poor performance as stemming from a lack of required materials or equipment, they may focus on providing such items. If, instead, they perceive poor performance as stemming mainly from a lack of effort, they may reprimand, transfer, or terminate the person involved (for a summary example, see Figure 13-5).

Evidence for the accuracy of these predictions has been reported in several studies.[35] In perhaps the best known of these, Mitchell and Wood presented nursing supervisors with brief accounts of errors committed by nurses.[36] The incidents suggested that the errors stemmed either from internal causes (e.g., lack of effort or ability) or from external causes (e.g., overdemanding work environment). After reading about the incidents, supervisors indicated what kind of action they would be likely to take in each situation. Results showed that they were more likely to direct corrective action toward the nurses (e.g., showing them how to do something) when they perceived the errors as stemming from internal causes, but more likely to direct action toward the environment (e.g., changing schedules or improving facilities) when they perceived the errors as stemming from external factors.

In summary, the attribution approach suggests that leaders' behavior often reflects their attributions concerning the actions and performance of followers. Leadership, then, lies as much in the perceptions of the people who exercise such influence as in the perceptions of those who confer the right to wield it over them.

TRANSFORMATIONAL LEADERSHIP: LEADERS WITH CHARISMA

In the darkest days of the Depression, the United States seemed poised on the brink of social chaos. With millions out of work and the economy in an apparently endless decline, despair was, seemingly, out of control. Through his inspiring speeches ("The only thing we have to fear is fear itself . . .") and vigorous actions, President Franklin D. Roosevelt pulled the nation back from the brink of disaster and saved the grand American experiment in political democracy.

In the 1970s, Chrysler Corporation was being written off by many analysts of the automobile industry with a single word: "terminal." One man, however,

FIGURE 13-6
CHARISMATIC LEADERS THROUGH HISTORY
Over the centuries, some highly charismatic leaders—such as Martin Luther King, Jr., and John F. Kennedy—have exerted a profound impact on their own societies, and even the entire world.

refused to accept this economic verdict. Instead, Lee Iacocca launched a concerted campaign to win government loan guarantees for Chrysler, and so continued survival for the company. Through example—his famous $1 salary—and exhortation, he rallied Chrysler's tens of thousands of employees to unheard-of levels of effort and sacrifice, and saved the day. Chrysler survived, prospered, and paid back all its loans, thus establishing a new chapter in the annals of government–industry cooperation in the United States.

World history and the history of organizations are replete with similar examples. Through the ages, some leaders have had extraordinary success in generating profound changes in the beliefs, perceptions, values, and actions of their followers (see Figure 13-6). Indeed, it is not extreme to suggest that such people have often served as key agents of social change, transforming entire societies through their words and actions.[37] Individuals who accomplish such feats have been referred to as **charismatic** or **transformational leaders**, and the terms seem fitting.[38] They do indeed transform social, political, or economic reality; and they do seem to possess unusual and special skills that equip them for this task. (The word *charisma* means "gift" in Greek.) What personal characteristics make certain leaders charismatic? How do such leaders exert their profound effects on many other people? Systematic research on this issue has begun to yield some intriguing answers to these and related questions.

THE BASIC NATURE OF CHARISMA

At first glance, it is tempting to assume that transformational or charismatic leaders are special by virtue of the traits they possess. In other words, such leadership might be understood as an extension of the great person theory described earlier in this chapter.[39] Although traits may play a role in transformational leadership, the belief that it makes more sense to view such leadership as involving a special type of relationship between leaders and their followers is growing.[40] Within this framework, charismatic leadership rests more on specific types of reaction by followers than on traits possessed by leaders. Such reactions include (1) levels of performance beyond those that would normally be expected,[41] (2) high levels of devotion, loyalty, and reverence toward the leader,[42] (3) enthusiasm for and excitement about the leader and the leader's ideas, and (4) a willingness on the part of subordinates to sacrifice their own personal interests for the sake of a larger collective goal.[43] In short, transformational or charismatic leadership involves a special kind of leader–follower relationship, in which the leader can, in the words of one author, "make ordinary people do extraordinary things in the face of adversity."[44]

THE BEHAVIOR OF TRANSFORMATIONAL LEADERS

What, precisely, do transformational or charismatic leaders do to generate this kind of relationship with their subordinates? Studies designed to answer this question point to the following general conclusion: such leaders gain the capacity to exert profound influence over others through many different tactics.

First, and perhaps most important, transformational leaders *articulate a vision*. They describe, usually in vivid, emotion-provoking terms, an image of what their nation, group, or organization could—and should—become. Mary Kay Ash, described in our Preview Case operates in this fashion, providing a stirring vision that engaged the energies and enthusiasm of many people in her company. An even more dramatic example is provided by the words of Martin Luther King, Jr., in his famous "I Have a Dream" speech:

> So I say to you, my friends, that even though we must face the difficulties of today and tomorrow, I still have a dream. It is a dream deeply rooted in the American dream that one day this nation will rise up and live out the true meaning of its creed—we hold these truths to be self-evident, that all men are created equal. This will be the day when all of God's children will be able to sing with new meaning 'My country 'tis of thee, sweet land of liberty. . . .'

But transformational leaders do not simply describe a dream or vision; they *provide a plan for attaining their vision*. In other words, they provide a roadmap for their followers showing, in straightforward terms, how to get from here to there. This too seems crucial, for a vision that appears perpetually out of reach is unlikely to motivate people to try to attain it (see the discussion of goal setting in Chapter 4).

Third, transformational leaders engage in what Conger terms *framing*: they define the purpose of their movement or organization in a way that gives meaning and purpose to whatever actions they are requesting from followers.[45] Perhaps the nature of framing is best illustrated by the well-known tale of two stonecutters working on a cathedral in the Middle Ages. When asked what they are doing, one replies, "Why, cutting this stone, of course." The other replies, "Building the world's most beautiful temple to the glory of God." Which person would be more likely to expend greater effort? The answer is obvious. In the business world, transformational leaders frame the activities of their organizations in ways that give them added meaning and that tie them closely to the accepted values of society. Once again, consider the charisma of Mary Kay Ash, who in describing her company once said, "My objective was just to help women. It was not to make a tremendous amount of sales. I want women to earn money commensurate with men. I want them to be paid on the basis of what they have between their ears and their brains and not because they are male or female."

Imagine if, instead, she had stated, "My objective was to increase our sales by 25 percent annually, so that in five years we'd become the third- or fourth-largest company in the business. In that way, we'd provide an excellent return to shareholders and build the value of our company's stock." Would you, as a Mary Kay representative, work as hard for these goals and this vision as for the one Ash actually expressed? We suspect not.

In addition, transformational leaders often show greater-than-average *willingness to take risks* and engage in unconventional actions to reach their stated goals. To help thwart the coup that threatened the budding democracy of his nation, Boris Yeltsin rushed to the Russian Parliament, where he stood on top of a tank and pleaded with troops sent there by the new hard-liners to withdraw. By this high-risk behavior, he demonstrated his deep commitment to the forces of reform.

Other qualities shown by transformational leaders include expressing high levels of self-confidence; showing a high degree of concern for their followers' needs; demonstrating excellent communication skills, such as the ability to "read" others' reactions quickly and accurately; and a stirring personal style. Finally, transformational leaders are often masters of impression management, engaging in tactics that enhance their attractiveness and appeal to others (see Chapter 2).

When these forms of behavior are added to the captivating and exciting visions they propound, the tremendous impact of transformational or charismatic leaders begins to come sharply into focus. Their influence, it appears, does not stem from the possession of any magical traits; rather, it is a logical result of a complex cluster of behaviors and techniques. In the final analysis, however, the essence of transformational leadership does appear to rest on the ability of such people to inspire others, through their words, their vision, and their actions. As Conger put it, "If you as a leader can make an appealing dream seem like tomorrow's reality, your subordinates will freely choose to follow you."[46]

THE EFFECTS OF CHARISMATIC LEADERSHIP

As you might imagine, charismatic leaders can have dramatic effects on the behavior of their followers. Indeed, several studies have shown that charismatic leadership is positively correlated with job performance and satisfaction.[47,48] It is easy to imagine how charismatic leaders may inspire their followers to achieve high levels of performance. And because these leaders are perceived as being so heroic, followers are very pleased with them—satisfaction that generalizes to perceptions of the job itself. In short, people enjoy working for charismatic leaders, and do well under their guidance. On a larger scale, research by House and his associates has found that U.S. presidents believed to be highly charismatic (as suggested by biographical accounts of their personalities and their reactions to world crises) received higher ratings by historians of their effectiveness as president.[49] In short, evidence suggests that charismatic leadership can have some very positive effects. (Although we have been referring to charismatic leaders as individuals who use their visions to create good, unfortunately, this is not always the case. For a discussion of both the positive and negative sides of charismatic leadership, see the Ethical Workplace section on the following page.)

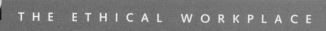

THE TWO FACES OF CHARISMATIC LEADERS

When we think of charismatic leaders we tend to picture larger-than-life heroes celebrated for turning around ailing companies and launching new enterprises—dynamic forces for change and improvement. However, as Howell and Avolio have pointed out recently, there is also a dark side to some charismatic leaders.[50] Such individuals use their charisma to promote dangerous values, building blind fanaticism to serve their passions for power.

Based on surveys and firsthand interviews with various business leaders, as well as analyses of leaders appearing in the popular press, Howell and Avolio distinguished between two groups of charismatic leaders—those who used their charisma to advance ethical ends, and those who did just the opposite. Leaders in the first group, referred to as *ethical charismatics*, go out of their way to promote the collective interests of employees by incorporating their followers' hopes and dreams into their visions. "These leaders develop creative, critical thinking in their followers, provide opportunities for them to develop, welcome positive and negative feedback, recognize the contributions of others, share information with followers, and have moral standards that emphasize collective interests of the group, organization, or society."[51] By contrast, *unethical charismatics* are primarily interested in pursuing their own personal visions. These individuals control and manipulate their followers to promote their own selfish interests, doing what's best for themselves rather than their organizations.

Specifically, ethical and unethical charismatics differ with respect to several major dimensions. First, with respect to exercising power, unethical charismatics use power in dominant and authoritarian ways for their personal gain, showing insensitivity to followers' needs. However, ethical charismatics use power to serve others, and show considerable concern for others, such as by coaching and supporting them as needed. Second, charismatic leaders differ with respect to how they create and express their visions. Whereas ethical charismatics align their visions with their followers' needs and aspirations, unethical charismatics promote their own selfish visions. A third difference has to do with the way the leaders communicate with their followers. Ethical charismatics consider their followers' ideas and learn from them, using two-way communication. They stimulate their followers to think independently and to question their leaders' views. Unethical charismatics are just the opposite: they censure critical or opposing views, use one-way communication, and demand that their own decisions be accepted without question.

When you consider the impact on followers, the double-edged sword of charismatic leadership becomes most apparent. Whereas ethical charismatics convert followers into leaders, encouraging them to think on their own, unethical charismatics "enslave" their followers, undermining their ability to work independently. For

TABLE 13-3

Creating Ethical Charismatic Leaders: Some Recommendations

What can top management do to help build ethical charismatic leaders? Based on interviews with corporate leaders, Howell and Avolio recommend the six actions summarized here.

- *Show commitment to a code of ethics that is continually enforced*
- *Recruit, select, and promote only individuals with the highest moral standards*
- *Create performance standards that emphasize respect for people*
- *Train leaders how to respect and integrate diverse viewpoints*
- *Train leaders in ethical values and develop their skills in this area*
- *Identify as heroes or heroines individuals who show exemplary moral conduct*

Source: Based on suggestions by Howell & Avolio, 1992; see Note 50.

example, by empowering employees to make decisions, the late Sam Walton was highly effective at nurturing leaders within Wal-Mart.[52] By contrast, Michael Milken, former head of the brokerage firm Drexel Burnham Lambert (later arrested for illegal stock trading), amassed a body of loyal disciples who supported his actions, regardless of how illegal or immoral they were.[53] He was highly charismatic, to be sure, but just as dangerous.

In view of these considerations, what can companies do to create and sustain ethical charismatic leaders? Howell and Avolio make six recommendations summarized in Table 13-3. As you might imagine, building internal ethical standards in leaders is a serious challenge, but one that must be undertaken for organizations to avoid being strangled by unethical charismatics. Moreover, when you consider all the good that can be done by ethical charismatics (such as Mary Kay Ash described in our Preview Case), it is easy to make a strong case for paying careful attention to these suggestions.

CONTINGENCY THEORIES OF LEADER EFFECTIVENESS

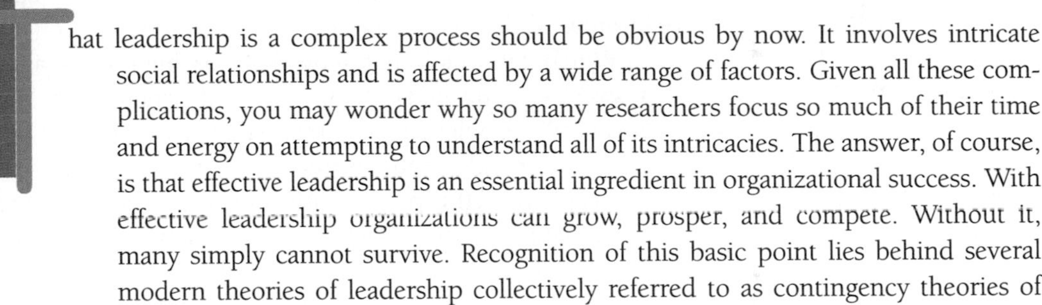

That leadership is a complex process should be obvious by now. It involves intricate social relationships and is affected by a wide range of factors. Given all these complications, you may wonder why so many researchers focus so much of their time and energy on attempting to understand all of its intricacies. The answer, of course, is that effective leadership is an essential ingredient in organizational success. With effective leadership organizations can grow, prosper, and compete. Without it, many simply cannot survive. Recognition of this basic point lies behind several modern theories of leadership collectively referred to as contingency theories of leader effectiveness.

As will soon be clear, these theories differ sharply in their content, terminology, and scope. Yet all are linked by two common themes. First, all adopt a *contingency approach*—they recognize that there is no single preferred style of leadership, and that the key task of organizational behavior researchers is determining which leadership styles will prove most effective under which specific conditions. Second, all are concerned with the issue of *leader effectiveness*. They seek to identify the conditions and factors that determine whether, and to what degree, leaders will enhance the performance and satisfaction of their subordinates. Yukl and Van Fleet have identified several theories in this category.[54] Among these are five that we will describe here: *LPC contingency theory*, *situational leadership theory*, *path–goal theory*, *substitutes for leadership theory*, and *normative decision theory*.

LPC CONTINGENCY THEORY: MATCHING LEADERS AND TASKS

Leadership does not occur in a social or environmental vacuum. Rather, leaders attempt to exert their influence on group members within the context of specific situations. Since these can vary greatly along many different dimensions, it is reasonable to expect that no single style or approach to leadership will always be best. Rather, as we have already noted, the most effective strategy will probably vary from one situation to another.

ESSENTIALS OF THE THEORY

Acceptance of this fact lies at the core of the **LPC contingency theory** developed by Fiedler.[55] The *contingency* aspect of the theory is certainly appropriate, for its central assumption is that a leader's contribution to successful performance by his or her group is determined both by the leader's traits and by various features of the situation. To fully understand leader effectiveness, both types of factors must be considered.

With respect to characteristics possessed by leaders, Fiedler identifies *esteem (liking) for least-preferred co-worker* (**LPC** for short) as most important. This refers to a leader's tendency to evaluate in a favorable or unfavorable manner the person with whom she or he has found it most difficult to work. Leaders who perceive this person in negative terms (low LPC leaders) are primarily concerned with attaining successful task performance. In contrast, those who perceive their least-preferred co-worker in a positive light (high LPC leaders) are mainly concerned with establishing good relations with subordinates. (As you can see, this dimension is related to two aspects of leader behavior described previously: initiating structure and showing consideration.) It is important to note that Fiedler considers LPC to be fixed—an aspect of an individual's leaderhip style that cannot be changed. As we will explain below, this has important implications for applying the theory so as to improve leaders' effectiveness.

Which type of leader—low LPC or high LPC—is more effective? Fiedler's answer is: it depends. And what it depends on is several situational factors. Specifically, Fiedler suggests that whether low LPC or high LPC leaders are more effective depends on the degree to which the situation is favorable to the leader—that is provides this person with control over subordinates. This, in turn, is determined largely by three factors: (1) the nature of the leader's relations with group members (the extent to which he or she enjoys their support and loyalty), (2) the degree of structure in the task being performed (the extent to which task goals and subordinates' roles are clearly defined), and (3) the leader's position power (his or her ability to enforce compliance by subordinates). Combining these three factors, the leader's situational control can range from very high (positive relations with group members, a highly structured task, high position power) to very low (negative relations, an unstructured task, low position power).

To return to the central question: when are different types of leaders most effective? Fiedler suggests that low LPC leaders (ones who are task oriented) are superior to high LPC leaders (ones who are people oriented) when situational control is either very low or very high. In contrast, high LPC leaders have an edge when situational control falls within the moderate range (refer to Figure 13-7).

The reasoning behind these predictions is as follows: under conditions of low situational control, groups need considerable guidance and direction to accomplish their tasks. Since low LPC leaders are more likely to provide structure than high LPC leaders, they usually will be superior in such cases. Similarly, low LPC leaders are also superior under conditions that offer the leader a high degree of situational control. Here, low LPC leaders realize that conditions are very good, and that successful task performance is virtually assured. As a result, they turn their attention to improving relations with subordinates, and often adopt a relaxed, "hands off" style. Subordinates appreciate such treatment, and performance and morale are both enhanced. In contrast, high LPC leaders, feeling that they already enjoy good relations with their subordinates, may shift their attention to task performance. Their attempts to provide guidance may then be perceived by subordinates as needless meddling, with the result that performance is impaired.

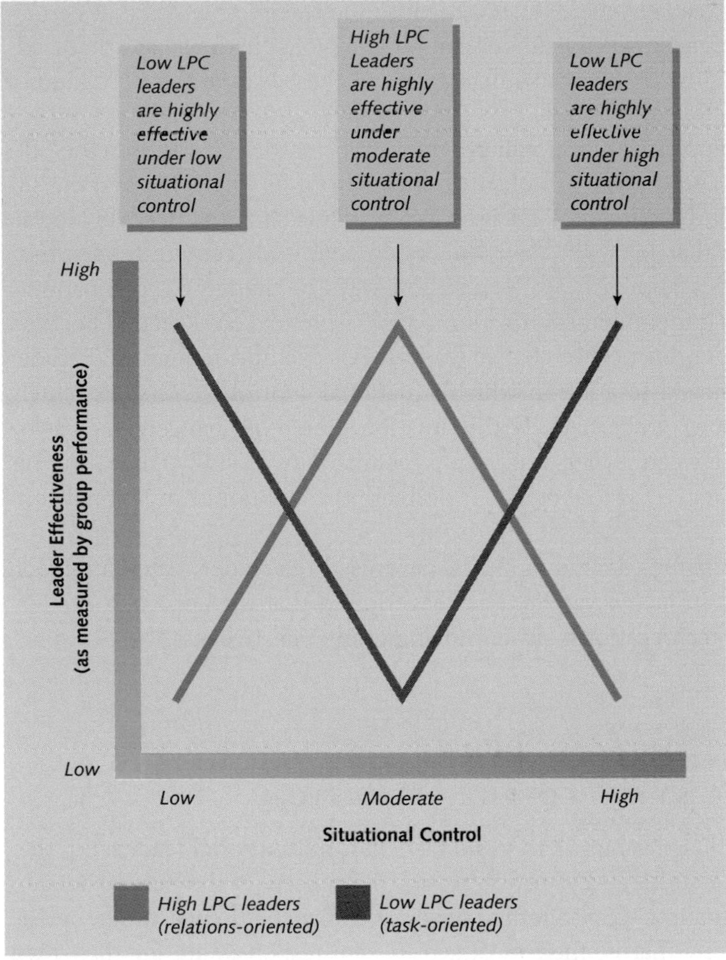

FIGURE 13-7
LPC CONTINGENCY THEORY: ITS BASIC PREDICTIONS
Fiedler's LPC contingency theory predicts that low-LPC leaders (ones who are primarily task oriented) will be more effective than high-LPC leaders (ones who are primarily people oriented) when situational control is either very low or very high. The opposite is true when situational control is moderate.

Turning to situations offering the leader moderate situational control, conditions are mixed, and attention to good interpersonal relations is often needed. High LPC leaders, with their interest in people, often have an important advantage in such cases. In contrast, low LPC leaders, who tend to focus on task performance, may become even more autocratic and directive. The negative reactions of subordinates to such behaviors may then have detrimental effects on performance.

To repeat: Fiedler's theory predicts that low LPC (task-oriented) leaders will be more effective than high LPC (relations-oriented) leaders under conditions of either low or high situational control. In contrast, high LPC leaders will have an edge under conditions in which situational control is moderate. Because it directs attention to characteristics of leaders, situational factors, and reactions among subordinates, Fiedler's theory is fully consistent with the modern view of leadership described earlier.

RESEARCH STATUS OF THE THEORY

Where any scientific theory is concerned, the ultimate question must be "How does it fare when put to actual test?" For the contingency theory, the answer appears to be "moderately well." One review of more than 170 studies undertaken to test various aspects of Fiedler's theory indicates that most obtained at least some positive results.[56] Although the results of many studies are encouraging and lend support to the theory (particularly laboratory studies), not all findings have been consistent with it. In particular, field investigations (carried out within existing groups operating in a wide range of contexts) generally have not been as favorable.[57]

Such investigations have sometimes yielded results contrary to what contingency theory would predict. In addition, the theory has been criticized on several important grounds. For example, a degree of ambiguity exists with respect to classifying specific situations along the dimension of situational control. Unless situations can be accurately classified as very low, low, moderate, and so on in this regard, predictions concerning leader effectiveness are difficult to make. Similarly, some critics have questioned the adequacy of the questionnaire used to assess leaders' standing on the LPC dimension. In particular, the reliability of this measure does not seem to be as high as that of other widely used tests (see Chapter 3).[58] Thus, although LPC contingency theory has added to our understanding of leadership effectiveness, several questions about its accuracy remain.

APPLYING THE THEORY

Despite the fact that research testing LPC contingency theory has yielded mixed results, practitioners have found it to be quite useful when it comes to suggesting ways of enhancing leaders' effectiveness. Because the theory assumes that certain kinds of leaders are most effective under certain kinds of situations, and that leadership style is fixed, the best way to enhance effectiveness is to fit the right kind of leaders to the situations they face.

This involves completing questionnaires that can be used to assess both the LPC score of the leader and the amount of situational control he or she faces in the situation. Then, using these indexes, a match can be made such that leaders are put into the situations that best suit their leadership styles—a technique known as **leader match.**[59] This approach also focuses on ways of changing the situational control variables—leader–member relations, task structure, and leader position power—when it is impractical to change leaders. For example, a high-LPC leader either should be moved to a job in which situational control is either extremely high or extremely low, or alternatively, the situation should be changed (such as by altering relations between leaders and group members, or raising or lowering his or her position power) so as to increase or decrease the amount of situational control encountered.

Quite a few companies, including Sears, have used the leader match approach with some success. In fact, several studies have found that the approach is effective—on at least some occasions—in improving group effectiveness.[60,61]

SITUATIONAL LEADERSHIP THEORY: ADJUSTING LEADERSHIP STYLE TO THE SITUATION

Another theory of leadership, Hersey and Blanchard's **situational leadership theory**, is considered a contingency theory because it focuses on the best leadership style for a given situation.[62] Specifically, Hersey and Blanchard concentrate on the *maturity* of followers—that is, their readiness to take responsibility for their own behavior. This includes both their job knowledge and skills, as well as their willingness to work without taking direction from others. Effective leaders are, according to this theory, able to adjust their styles to accommodate their followers' need for guidance and direction (*task behavior*) as well as their need for emotional support (*relationship behavior*). As shown in Figure 13-8, these two dimensions are independent.

By combining high and low levels of each dimension, four different types of situations are identified, each of which is associated with a leaderhip style that is most effective. Starting in the lower left corner of Figure 13-8 are situations in which followers need very little in the way of emotional hand holding and guidance with respect to how to do their jobs. In this situation, *delegating* is the best way to treat followers—that is, turning over to followers the responsibility for making and implementing decisions. Then, in the upper left corner of the diagram is a situation in which followers are able, but unwilling to do their jobs, and require high amounts of supportive behavior to motivate them. A *participating* style of leadership works well in this situation because it allows followers to share their ideas, enhancing their desire to perform. In the next situation followers are unable, and unwilling to do their jobs, and require both task direction and emotional support. The style known as *selling* is most appropriate here. This involves explaining decisions and providing opportunities for clarification. Finally, in the lower right corner are situations in which followers are unable but willing to take responsibility for their actions. They are motivated, but lack the appropriate skills. The practice of *telling* followers what to do is most useful in such situations—that is, giving them specific instructions and closely supervising their work.

FIGURE 13-8

SITUATIONAL LEADERSHIP THEORY: ITS BASIC DIMENSIONS

Hersey and Blanchard's situational leadership *theory specifies that the most appropriate leadership style depends on the amount of emotional support required (i.e., followers' willingness to do the job) in conjunction with the amount of guidance required (i.e., followers' capacity to do the job).*

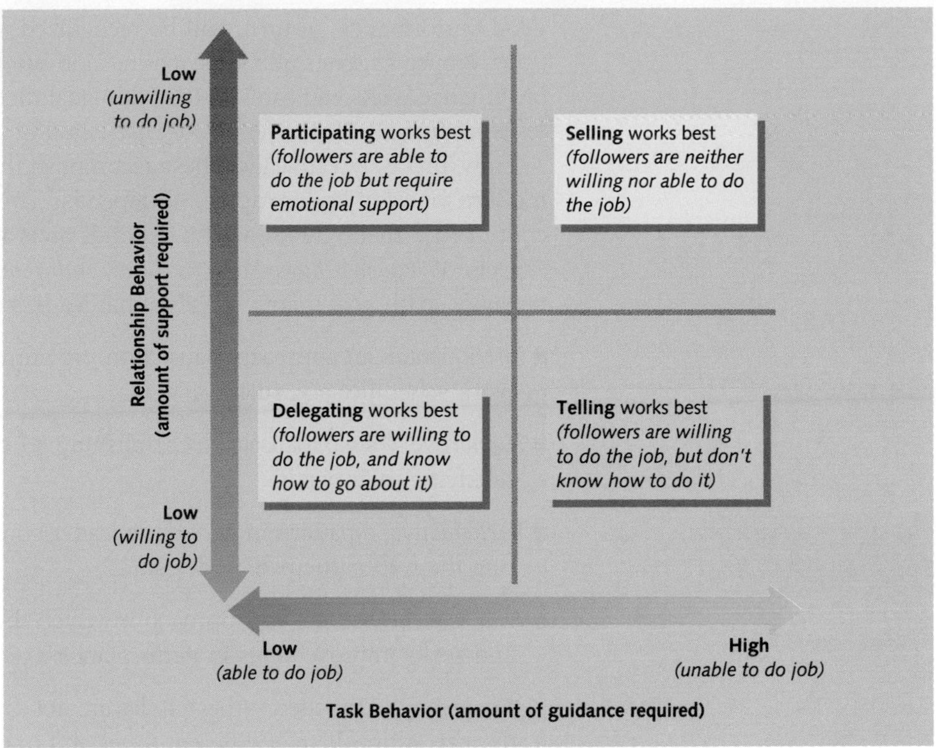

According to this conceptualization, leaders must be able to (1) diagnose the situations they face, (2) identify the appropriate behavioral style, and then (3) implement that response. Because the situations leaders face may change all the time, leaders must constantly reassess them, paying special attention to their followers' needs for guidance and emotional support. To the extent that they do so, they are likely to be effective.

Because situational leadership theory is quite new, little evidence about it currently exists. The handful of studies that have been conducted to test the theory generally have been supportive, although not comprehensive.[63,64] Still, practitioners have found the approach to be quite useful. In fact, it has been widely used to train leaders such corporate giants as Xerox, Mobil Oil, and Caterpillar, and in the U.S. military services as well.[65]

PATH–GOAL THEORY: LEADERS AS GUIDES TO VALUED GOALS

Suppose you conducted an informal survey in which you asked a hundred people to indicate what they expect from their leaders. What kind of answers would you receive? Although they would vary greatly, one common theme you might uncover would be "I expect my leader to *help*—to assist me in reaching goals I feel are important." This basic idea plays a central role in House's **path–goal theory** of leadership.[66] In general terms, the theory contends that subordinates will react favorably to a leader only to the extent that they perceive this person as helping them progress toward various goals by clarifying actual paths to such rewards. More specifically, the theory contends that actions by a leader that clarify the nature of tasks and reduce or eliminate obstacles will increase perceptions on the part of subordinates that working hard will lead to good performance and that good performance, in turn, will be recognized and rewarded. Under such conditions, House suggests, job satisfaction, motivation, and actual performance will all be enhanced. (As you can see, the path–goal theory of leadership is closely related to expectancy theory; refer to our discussion of this theory in Chapter 4.)

How, precisely, can leaders best accomplish these tasks? The answer, as in other modern views of leadership, is, "it depends." (In fact, that's how you can tell it is a contingency theory.) And what it depends on is a complex interaction between key aspects of *leader behavior* and certain *contingency* factors. With respect to leader behavior, path-goal theory suggests that leaders can adopt four basic styles:

- *Instrumental*: an approach focused on providing specific guidance, establishing work schedules and rules
- *Supportive:* a style focused on establishing good relations with subordinates and satisfying their needs
- *Participative*: a pattern in which the leader consults with subordinates, permitting them to participate in decisions
- *Achievement-oriented*: an approach in which the leader sets challenging goals and seeks improvements in performance

According to the theory, these styles are not mutually exclusive; in fact, the same leader can adopt them at different times and in different situations. Indeed, showing such flexibility is one important aspect of an effective leader.

Which of these contrasting styles is best for maximizing subordinates' satisfaction and motivation? The answer depends on the contingency factors mentioned above. First, the style of choice is strongly affected by several characteristics of subordinates. For example, if followers have great ability, an instrumental style of leadership may be unnecessary; instead, a less structured, supportive approach may be preferable. On the other hand, if subordinates have little ability, the opposite may be true; people with poor ability need considerable guidance to help them attain their goals. Similarly, people high in need for affiliation (that is, those desiring close, friendly ties with others) may strongly prefer a supportive or participative style of leadership. Those high in the need for achievement may strongly prefer an achievement-oriented leader.

Second, the most effective leadership style also depends on several aspects of the work environment. For example, path–goal theory predicts that when tasks are unstructured and nonroutine, an instrumental approach by the leader may be best; much clarification and guidance are needed. However, when tasks are structured and highly routine, such leadership may actually get in the way of good performance, and may be resented by subordinates who think the leader is engaging in unnecessary meddling. (See Figure 13-9 for an overview of all these aspects of path–goal theory.)

FIGURE 13-9

PATH-GOAL THEORY: AN OVERVIEW

According to House's path–goal theory, *perceptions among employees that leaders are helping them reach valued goals enhance both employees' motivation and job satisfaction. Such perceptions, in turn, are encouraged when a leader's style is consistent with the needs and characteristics of subordinates (e.g., their level of experience) and aspects of the work environment (e.g., requirements of the tasks being performed). (Source: Based on suggestions by House & Baetz, 1978; see Note 66.)*

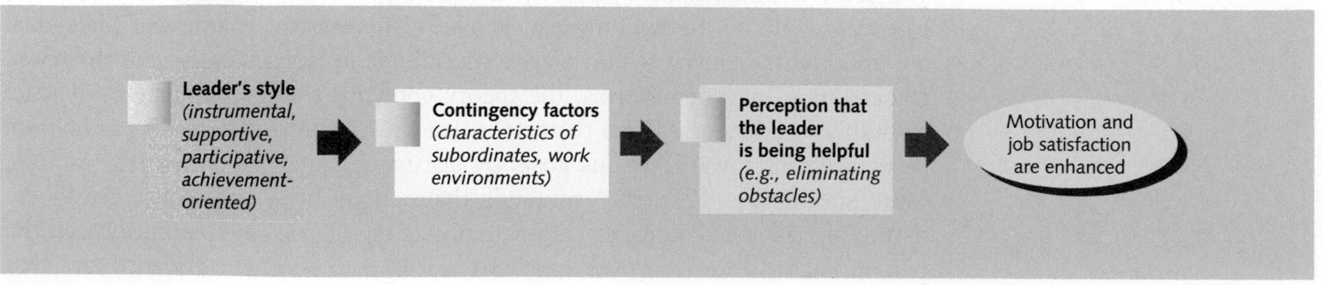

Path–goal theory has been subjected to empirical testing in several studies.[67] In general, results have been consistent with major predictions derived from the theory, although not uniformly so. Thus, at present, path–goal theory appears to be another framework offering valuable insights into leadership and the many factors that determine the degree to which individual leaders are successful in this role.

SUBSTITUTES FOR LEADERSHIP THEORY: WHEN LEADERS ARE SUPERFLUOUS

Throughout this chapter, we have emphasized that leaders are important. Their style, actions, and degree of effectiveness all exert major effects on subordinates and, ultimately, on organizations. In many cases, this is certainly true. Yet almost everyone has observed or been part of groups in which the designated leaders actually had little influence—groups in which these people were mere figureheads with little impact on subordinates. One explanation for such situations involves the characteristics of the leaders in question: they are simply weak and unsuited for their jobs. Another, and in some ways more intriguing, possibility is that in some contexts, other factors may actually substitute for a leader's influence, making it superfluous. Kerr and Jermier propose this idea formally in their **substitutes for leadership theory**.[68]

According to this framework, many different variables can produce such effects. Thus, we may ask: Under what conditions are leaders expected to have limited impact on task performance? The answers fall into three different categories. First, leadership may be unnecessary because of various individual characteristics. For example, a high level of knowledge, commitment, or experience on the part of subordinates may make it unnecessary for anyone to tell them what to do or how to proceed. Second, leadership may be unnecessary because jobs themselves may be structured in ways that make direction and influence from a leader redundant. For example, highly routine jobs require little direction, and jobs that are highly interesting also require little in the way of outside leadership stimulation. Third, various characteristics of organizations may make leadership unnecessary. For example, various work norms and strong feelings of cohesion among employees may directly affect job performance and render the presence of a leader unnecessary. Similarly, the technology associated with certain jobs may strongly determine the decisions and actions of people performing them, and so leave little room for input from a leader.

Evidence for these assertions has been obtained in several studies.[69] For example, in a recent investigation Podsakoff, Niehoff, MacKenzie, and Williams examined the work performance and attitudes of a broad sample of workers (including building service employees, administrative and clerical employees, and managers) who completed scales measuring their perceptions of the extent to which various leadership behaviors and substitutes for leadership were exhibited on their jobs.[70] Consistent with the theory, they found that job performance and attitudes were more strongly associated with the various substitutes than with the leadership behaviors themselves.

If leaders are superfluous in many situations, why has this fact often been overlooked? One possibility, suggested by Meindl and Ehrlich, is that we have a strong tendency to *romanticize* leadership—to perceive it as more important and more closely linked to performance in many contexts than it actually is.[71] To test this suggestion, they presented M.B.A. students with detailed financial information about an imaginary firm, including a paragraph describing the firm's key operating strengths.

The content of this paragraph was varied so that four different groups of subjects received four different versions. These attributed the firm's performance either to its top-level management team, the quality of its employees, changing patterns of consumer needs and preferences, or federal regulatory policies, respectively.

After reading one of these paragraphs and examining other information about the firm, subjects rated two aspects of its overall performance: profitability and risk. Meindl and Ehrlich reasoned that because of the tendency to overestimate the importance of leadership, subjects would rate the firm more favorably when its performance was attributed to top-level management than when it was attributed to any of the other factors. As you can see in Figure 13-10, this was precisely what occurred. The imaginary company was rated as higher in profitability and lower in risk when subjects had read the management-based paragraph than when they had read any of the others.

These findings, plus others obtained by the same researchers, help explain why leaders are often viewed as important and necessary even when, to a large degree, they are superfluous. Note: this in no way implies that leaders are usually unimportant. On the contrary, they often do play a key role in work groups and organizations. However, because this is not always so, their necessity should never be taken for granted.

NORMATIVE DECISION THEORY: THE RIGHT TIME FOR EMPLOYEE PARTICIPATION

As we discussed in Chapter 10, one of the major tasks performed by leaders is making decisions. Indeed, one defining characteristic of leadership positions is that

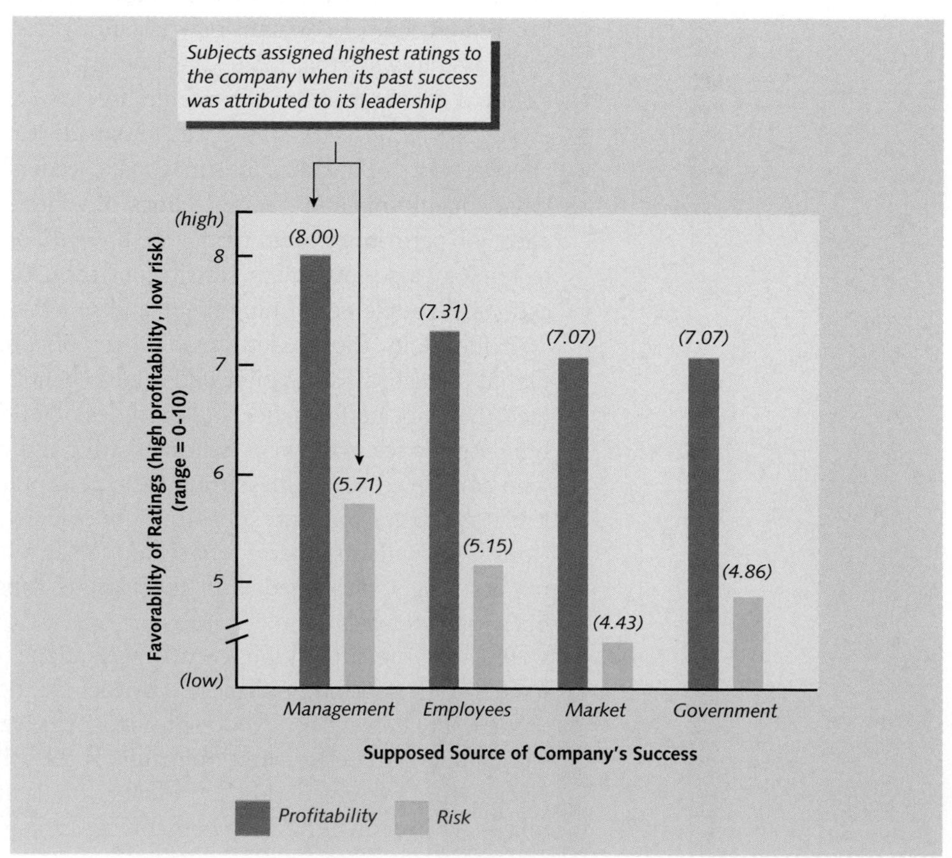

FIGURE 13-10
LEADERSHIP: EVIDENCE OF OUR TENDENCY TO OVERESTIMATE ITS IMPORTANCE

People who received information suggesting that an imaginary company's past success was attributable to its top management rated the company more favorably (higher in profitability, lower in risk) than those who received information suggesting that the identical record resulted from other causes. These findings suggest that people romanticize leadership, overestimating its impact in many situations. (Source: Based on data from Meindl & Ehrlich, 1987; see Note 71.)

they are where "the buck finally stops" and concrete actions must be taken. Since the decisions reached by leaders often have far-reaching effects on their subordinates, one major determinant of leader effectiveness clearly is the adequacy with which they perform this key task. Leaders who make good decisions will be more effective in the long run than leaders who make bad ones. But how should they go about making decisions? Specifically, how much participation should leaders invite from them? As we noted earlier, participation in decision making is an important variable in many organizational settings—one with implications for job satisfaction, stress, and productivity. Thus, the manner in which leaders handle this issue can be crucial in determining their effectiveness.

But how much participation in decisions by subordinates should leaders allow? Perhaps the most useful answer to this question is provided by the **normative decision theory** developed by Vroom and Yetton.[72] After careful study of available evidence, these researchers concluded that leaders often adopt one of five distinct methods for reaching decisions. These are summarized in Table 13-4, and as you can see, they cover the entire range—from decisions made solely by the leader in a totally autocratic manner through ones that are fully participative.

Are any of these approaches strongly preferable to the others? Vroom and Yetton suggest not. Just as there is no single best style of leadership, there is no single best strategy for making decisions. Each pattern offers its own mixture of benefits and costs. For example, decisions reached through participative means stand a better chance of gaining support and acceptance among subordinates. However, such decisions require a great deal of time—often more time than a leader or organization can afford. Similarly, decisions reached autocratically (by the leader alone) can be made more rapidly and efficiently. But such an approach can generate resentment among followers and encounter difficulties with respect to actual implementation. According to Vroom and Yetton, then, a major task faced by leaders is selecting the specific decision-making approach that will maximize potential benefits but minimize potential costs. How can this be done? Again, they offer specific suggestions.

TABLE 13-4

Potential Strategies for Making Decisions

According to Vroom and Yetton, leaders making decisions often adopt one of the five basic strategies described here.

DECISION STRATEGY	DESCRIPTION
AI (autocratic)	*Leader solves problem or makes decision unilaterally, using available information.*
AII (autocratic)	*Leader obtains necessary information from subordinates but then makes decision unilaterally.*
CI (consultative)	*Leader shares the problem with subordinates individually, but then makes decision unilaterally.*
CII (consultative)	*Leader shares problem with subordinates in group meeting but then makes decision unilaterally.*
GII (group decision)	*Leader shares problem with subordinates in a group meeting; decision is reached through discussion to consensus.*

Source: Based on suggestions from Vroom & Yetton, 1973; see Note 72.

Vroom and Yetton propose that leaders should attempt to select the best approach (or at least eliminate ones that are not useful) by answering several basic questions about the situations in which they find themselves. These relate primarily to the *quality of the decision*—the extent to which it will affect important group processes such as communication or production; and to *acceptance of the decision*—the degree of commitment among subordinates needed for its implementation. For example, with respect to decision quality, a leader should ask questions such as: "Is a high-quality decision required? Do I have enough information to make such a decision? Is the problem well structured?" With respect to decision acceptance, he or she should ask: "Is it crucial for effective implementation that subordinates accept the decision? Do subordinates share the organizational goals that will be reached through solution of this problem?"

TABLE 13-5

Decision Rules in Normative Decision Theory

By applying the rules shown here, leaders can eliminate decision-making strategies that are likely to prove ineffective in a given situation, and select those likely to be most effective.

RULES DESIGNED TO PROTECT DECISION QUALITY	
Leader Information Rule	*If the quality of the decision is important and you do not have enough information or expertise to solve the problem alone, eliminate an autoctratic style.*
Goal Congruence Rule	*If the quality of the decision is important and subordinates are not likely to make the right decision, rule out the highly participative style.*
Unstructured Problem Rule	*If the quality of the decision is important but you lack sufficient information, and expertise and the problem is unstructured, eliminate the autocratic leadership styles.*
RULES DESIGNED TO PROTECT DECISION ACCEPTANCE	
Acceptance Rule	*If acceptance by subordinates is crucial for effective implementation, eliminate the autocratic styles.*
Conflict Rule	*If acceptance by subordinates is crucial for effective implementation, and they hold conflicting opinions over the means of achieving some objective, eliminate autocratic styles.*
Fairness Rule	*If the quality of the decision is unimportant but acceptance is important, use the most participatory style.*
Acceptance Priority Rule	*If acceptance is critical and not certain to result from autocratic decisions, and if subordinates are not motivated to achieve the organization's goals, use a highly participative style.*

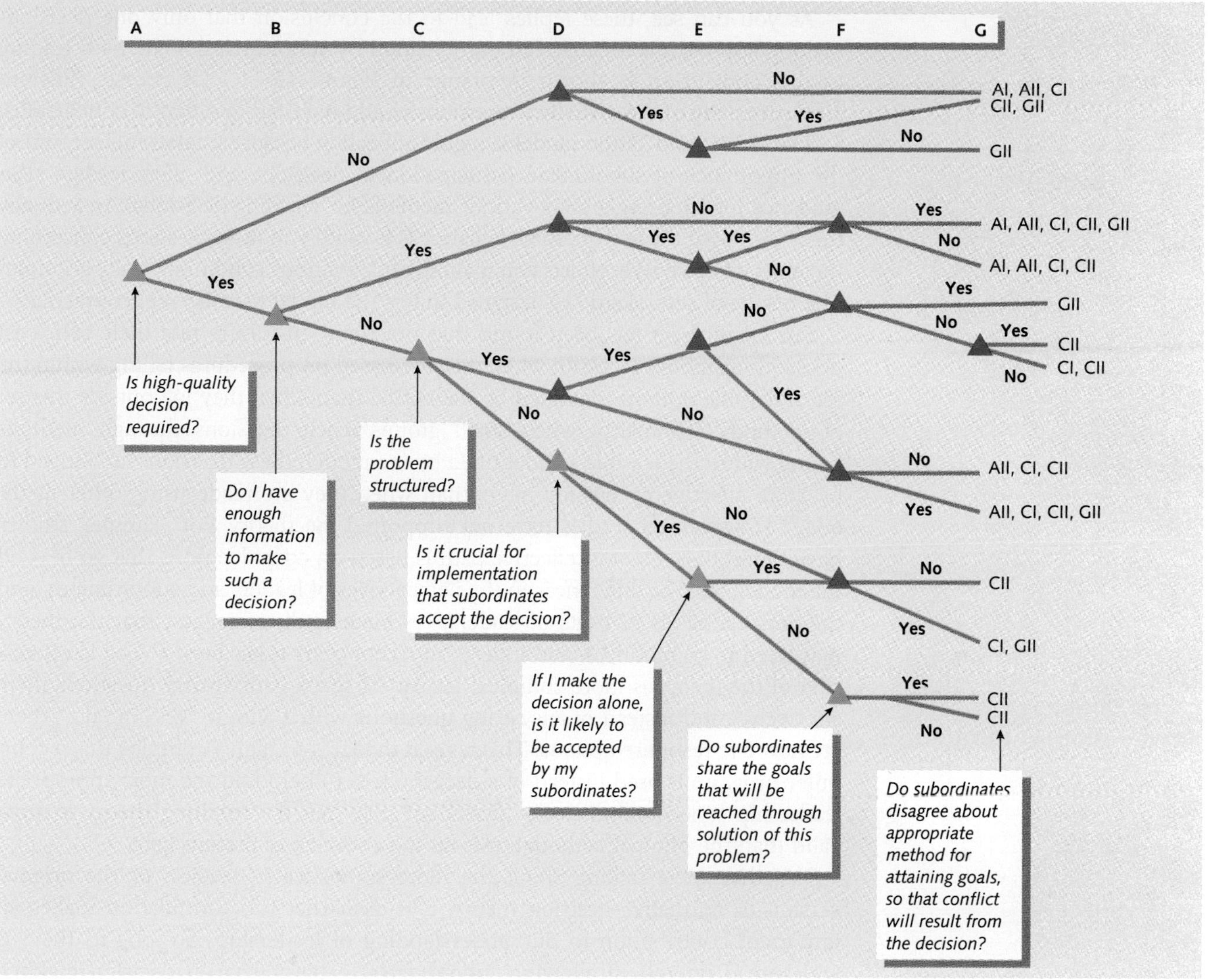
A
B
C
D
E
F
G
Is high-quality decision required?
Do I have enough information to make such a decision?
Is the problem structured?
Is it crucial for implementation that subordinates accept the decision?
If I make the decision alone, is it likely to be accepted by my subordinates?
Do subordinates share the goals that will be reached through solution of this problem?
Do subordinates disagree about appropriate method for attaining goals, so that conflict will result from the decision?
Yes
No
AI, AII, CI
CII, GII
GII
AI, AII, CI, CII, GII
AI, AII, CI, CII
GII
CII
CI, CII
AII, CI, CII
AII, CI, CII, GII
CII
CI, GII
CII
CII

FIGURE 13-11
NORMATIVE DECISION THEORY: SELECTING THE MOST EFFECTIVE DECISION-MAKING STRATEGY
By answering the questions listed here and tracing a path through this decision tree, leaders can identify the most effective approaches to making decisions in a specific situation. Note: the path suggested by the answers to questions A through G (see this page) is shown by the orange-colored triangles. (Source: Based on suggestions by Vroom & Yetton, 1973; see Note 72.)

According to normative decision theory, answering such questions, and applying specific rules such as those shown in Table 13-5, eliminates some of the potential approaches to reaching a given decision. Those that remain constitute a feasible set that can, potentially, be used to reach the necessary decision.

To simplify this process, Vroom and Yetton recommend using a decision tree such as the one shown in Figure 13-11. To apply this diagram, a manager begins on the left side and responds, in turn, to the questions listed under each letter (A, B, C, and so on). As the manager replies to each question, the set of feasible approaches narrows. For example, imagine that the manager's answers are as follows:

Question A: Yes—a high-quality decision is needed.
Question B: No—the leader does not have sufficient information to make a high quality decision alone.
Question C: No—the problem is not structured.
Question D: Yes—acceptance by subordinates is crucial to implementation.
Question E: No—if the leader makes the decision alone, it may not be accepted by subordinates.
Question F: No—subordinates do not share organizational goals.
Question G: Yes—conflict among subordinates is likely to result from the decision.

As you can see, these replies lead to the conclusion that only one decision-making approach is feasible: full participation by subordinates. (The path leading to this conclusion is shown in orange in Figure 13-11.) Of course, different answers to any of the seven key questions would have led to different conclusions.

The Vroom and Yetton model is highly appealing because it takes full account of the importance of subordinate participation in decisions and offers leaders clear guidance for choosing among various methods for reaching decisions. As with any theory, though, the key question remains: Is it valid? Are its suggestions concerning the most effective style of decision making under various conditions really accurate? The results of several studies designed to test the model have been encouraging.

For example, it has been found that practicing managers rate their own past decisions as more successful when they are based on procedures falling within the set of feasible options identified by the model than when they fall outside this set of methods.[73] Similarly, when small groups reach decisions through methods falling within the feasible set identified by the model, these decisions are judged to be more effective by outside raters than when they are made using other methods.[74] However, all studies have not supported the theory. For example, studies have found that the most effective path is based on considerations that go beyond the model, such as differences in the perspectives of leaders and subordinates, and the personal skills or traits of leaders.[75,76] Such findings suggest that the theory may need to be modified, and indeed, in recent years it has been.[77] The latest version of the theory is more complex: instead of seven contingency questions there are twelve, and instead of answering questions with a simple "yes" or "no," there are now five response options. This revised model is so highly complex that a computer program is used instead of a decision tree to help find the most appropriate leadership style. Preliminary evidence suggests that the resulting theory is more valid than the original, although it is far too complex to present here.

Whether we're talking about the more sophisticated version or the original version of normative decision theory, it is clear that this formulation makes an important contribution to our understanding of leadership. So long as there is widespread interest in allowing subordinates to participate in decision making, normative decision theory is useful insofar as it gives leaders clear guidance as to when such a move may be expected to improve task performance. (Although leaders often encourage their subordinates to be actively involved in decisions, the advent of work teams takes this practice one step further. For a look at the special considerations involved in leading work teams, see the Quest for Quality section below.)

THE QUEST FOR QUALITY

ACHIEVING SUCCESS AS A TEAM LEADER: SOME GUIDELINES

When most people think of leaders, they tend to think of individuals who make strategic decisions on behalf of followers, who are responsible for carrying them out. In many of today's organizations, however, where the movement toward *work teams* predominates (see Chapter 8), it is less likely than ever that leaders are responsible for getting others to implement their orders to help fulfill their visions. Instead, team leaders may be called on to provide special resources to groups empowered to implement their own missions in their own ways (see Figure 13-12). This suggests that the role of team leader is clearly very different from the traditional, supervisory leadership role we have been discussing in this chapter.[78] Hierarchical leadership approaches are doomed to failure in team-oriented environments. With this in mind, here are a few guidelines that may be followed to achieve success as a team leader.

First, instead of directing people, team leaders work at *building trust and inspiring teamwork*. One way this can be done is by encouraging interaction between all members of the team as well as between the team and its customers and suppliers. Another key is to take initiatives to make things better. Instead of taking a reactive, "If it ain't broke, don't fix it" approach, teams may be led to success by individuals who set a good example for improving the quality of their team's efforts.

Second, instead of focusing simply on training individuals, effective team leaders concentrate on *expanding team capabilities*. In this connection, team leaders function primarily as coaches, helping team members by providing all members with the skills needed to perform the task, removing barriers that might interfere with task success, and finding the necessary resources required to get the job done. Likewise, team leaders work at building the confidence of team members, cultivating their untapped potential.

Third, instead of managing one-on-one, team leaders attempt to *create a team identity*. In other words, leaders must help teams understand their missions and recognize what they're doing to help fulfill it. In this connection, team leaders may help the group set goals—pointing out ways they may adjust their performance when they do not meet them, and planning celebrations when team goals are attained.

Fourth, although traditional leaders have worked at preventing conflict between individuals, team leaders are encouraged to *make the most of team differences*. Without doubt, it is a considerable challenge to meld a diverse group of individuals into a highly committed and productive team, but doing so is important. This can be done by building respect for diverse points of view, making sure that all team members are encouraged to present their views, and respecting these ideas once they are expressed.

Fifth, unlike traditional leaders who simply react to change, team leaders should *foresee and influence change*. To the extent that leaders recognize that change is inevitable (a point we will emphasize more fully in Chapter 16), they may be better prepared to make the various adaptations required. Effective team leaders continuously scan the business environment for clues as to changes that appear to be forthcoming and help teams decide how to be responsive to them.

In conclusion, leading teams is a far cry from leading individuals in the traditional directive (or even a participative) manner. The special nature of teams makes the leader's job very different. Although appreciating these differences is easy, making the appropriate adjustments may be extremely challenging—especially for individuals who are well practiced in the ways of traditional leadership. However, given the prevalence of teams in today's work environment, the importance of making the adjustments cannot be overstated. Leading new teams using old methods is a surefire formula for failure.

FIGURE 13-12

KODAK'S "TEAM ZEBRA": A SUCCESSFULLY LED WORK TEAM

Leaders of high-quality work teams are typically more like coaches, and are much less directive than leaders of groups with more traditional hierarchical structures. This fact is well appreciated by the leaders of Kodak's "Team Zebra," its highly successful black-and-white film-manufacturing unit.

SUMMARY AND REVIEW

LEADERSHIP: SOME BASIC ISSUES

Leadership is the process whereby one individual influences other group members toward the attainment of defined group or organizational goals. Leaders generally use noncoercive forms of influence and are influenced, in turn, by their followers. Whereas *leaders* create the group's or organization's mission and outline the strategy for attaining it, *managers* are responsible for implementing that mission. In practice, however, many leaders are also responsible for managerial tasks. Thus, although there is a distinction between leaders and managers, it is often blurred in practice.

LEADER TRAITS AND BEHAVIORS

Early efforts to identify key traits that set leaders apart from other people—the **great person theory**—generally failed. However, recent evidence suggests that leaders do, in fact, differ from followers in certain respects. They are higher in leadership motivation, drive, honesty, self-confidence, and several other traits. In addition, successful leaders appear to be high in *flexibility*—the ability to adapt their style to the followers' needs and to the requirements of specific situations.

Leaders differ greatly in their style or approach to leadership. One key dimension involves the extent to which leaders are *directive* or *permissive* toward subordinates. Another involves the extent to which they are **participative** or **autocratic** in their decision making. Leaders also vary along two other key dimensions: concern with, and efforts to attain, successful task performance (**initiating structure**) and concern with maintaining favorable personal relations with subordinates (**consideration**). Research shows that although these basic dimensions appear to be universal, many of the specific behaviors reflecting each one tend to be uniquely associated with the leader's culture.

LEADERS AND FOLLOWERS

Three approaches to leadership focus on the relationships between leaders and their followers. Graen's **leader–member exchange (LMX) model** specifies that leaders favor members of some groups—referred to as in-groups—more than others—referred to as out-groups. As a result, in-groups perform better than out-groups.

The **attributional approach** focuses on leaders' attributions of followers' performance—that is, its underlying causes. When leaders perceive that their subordinates' poor performance is caused by internal factors, they react by helping him or her to improve. However, when poor performance is attributed to external sources, leaders direct their attention toward changing aspects of the work environment believed to be responsible for the poor performance.

Some leaders—known as **transformational** or **charismatic** leaders—exert profound effects on the beliefs, perceptions, and actions of their followers. Such leaders have a special relationship with their followers, in which they can inspire exceptionally high levels of performance, loyalty, and enthusiasm. An important factor in the impressive influence of transformational leaders over others involves their proposal of an emotion-provoking vision. Other actions by transformational leaders involve *framing*—defining the purpose of their movement or organization in highly meaningful terms—and the willingness to take risks and engage in unconventional actions to reach stated goals. Although many leaders use their charisma for ethical purposes, others do not.

CONTINGENCY THEORIES OF LEADER EFFECTIVENESS

Contingency theories of leadership assume that there is no one best style of leadership, and that the most effective style of leadership depends on the specific conditions or situations faced. For example, Fiedler's **LPC contingency theory** suggests that both a leader's characteristics and situational factors are crucial. Task-oriented leaders (termed high-LPC leaders) are more effective than people-oriented leaders (termed low-LPC leaders) under conditions in which the leader has either high or low control over the group in question. In contrast, people-oriented leaders are more effective under conditions where the leader has moderate control.

The **situational leadership theory** proposed by Hersey and Blanchard suggests that the most effective style of leadership—delegating, participating, selling, or telling—depends on the extent to which followers require guidance and direction, and emotional support. Effective leaders are required to diagnose the situations they face and implement the appropriate behavioral style for that situation.

House's **path–goal theory** of leadership suggests that leaders' behavior will be accepted by subordinates and will enhance their motivation only to the extent that it helps them progress toward valued goals and provides guidance or clarification not already present in work settings.

The **substitutes for leadership** approach suggests that leaders are unnecessary in situations in which other factors can have just as much influence. For example, leaders are superfluous when (1) subordinates have exceptionally high levels of knowledge and commitment, (2) jobs are highly structured and routine, and (3) the technology used strongly determines individuals' behavior.

Finally, Vroom and Yetton's **normative decision theory** focuses on decision making as a key determinant of leader effectiveness. According to this theory, different situations call for different styles of decision making (e.g., autocratic, consultative, participative) by leaders. Decisions about the most appropriate style of decision making for a given situation are made on the basis of answers to questions regarding the quality of the decision required and the degree to which it is important for followers to accept and be committed to the decisions made. Complex decision trees are used to guide managers to the most appropriate styles of leadership.

KEY TERMS

attribution approach (to leadership): The approach to leadership that focuses on leaders' attributions of followers' performance—that is, their perceptions of its underlying causes.

autocratic (leadership style): A style of leadership in which the leader makes all decisions unilaterally.

charismatic leaders: Leaders who exert powerful effects on their followers and to whom special traits are attributed (e.g., possession of an idealized vision or goal, willingness to engage in unconventional behaviors to reach it).

consideration: Actions by a leader that demonstrate concern with the welfare of subordinates and establish positive relations with them. Leaders who focus primarily on this task are often described as demonstrating a person-oriented style.

contingency theories (of leadership): Any of several theories that recognize that certain styles of leadership are more effective in some situations than others.

great person theory: The view that leaders possess special traits that set them apart from others, and that these traits are responsible for their assuming positions of power and authority.

initiating structure: Activities by a leader designed to enhance productivity or task performance. Leaders who focus primarily on these goals are described as demonstrating a task-oriented style.

leader: An individual within a group or an organization who wields the most influence over others.

leader match: The practice of matching leaders (based on their LPC scores) to the groups whose situations best match those in which they are expected to be most effective (according to LPC contingency theory).

leader–member exchange (LMX) model: A theory suggesting that leaders form different relations with various subordinates and that the nature of such dyadic exchanges can exert strong effects on subordinates' performance and satisfaction.

leadership: The process whereby one individual influences other group members toward the attainment of defined group or organizational goals.

leadership motivation: The desire to influence others, especially toward the attainment of shared goals.

LPC: Short for "esteem for least-preferred coworker"—a personality variable distinguishing between individuals with respect to their concern for people (high LPC) and their concern for production (low LPC).

LPC contingency theory: Fiedler's theory suggesting that leader effectiveness is determined both by characteristics of leaders (see their LPC scores) and by the level of situational control they are able to exert over subordinates.

normative decision theory: A theory of leader effectiveness focusing primarily on strategies for choosing the most effective approach to making decisions.

participative (leadership style): A style of leadership in which the leader permits subordinates to take part in decision making, and also permits them a considerable degree of autonomy in completing work activities.

path–goal theory: A theory of leadership suggesting that subordinates will be motivated by a leader only to the extent they perceive this individual as helping them to attain valued goals.

situational leadership theory: A theory suggesting that the most effective style of leadership—either: delegating, participating, selling, or telling—depends on the extent to which followers require guidance, direction, and emotional support.

substitutes for leadership theory: The view that high levels of skill among subordinates or certain features of technology and organizational structure sometimes serve as substitutes for leaders, rendering their guidance or influence superfluous.

transformational leaders: See *charismatic leaders*.

QUESTIONS FOR DISCUSSION

1. What are the major differences among leaders, dictators, and managers?
2. It has often been said that "leaders are born, not made." Do you agree? If so, why? If not, why?
3. Argue for or against the following statement: "The best leaders encourage participation from their subordinates."
4. Under what conditions are people-oriented leaders more effective than task-oriented leaders and vice versa?
5. Most people prefer to be involved in decisions concerning their jobs. Is such partici-

pative decision making always preferable to a more directive approach?

6. In your experience, do most leaders have a small in-group? If so, what are the effects of this clique on other group members?
7. Explain how the process of attribution is involved in organizational leadership.
8. Consider all the people who have been president of the United States (or leaders of whatever country you live in) during your lifetime. Which of these (if any) would you describe as charismatic? Why?
9. Describe the conditions under which different types of leadership are most and least effective, noting the theories that make these claims.
10. Concern for people and concern for production are two recurring themes in the study of leadership. Describe the way they manifest themselves in various theories of leadership.

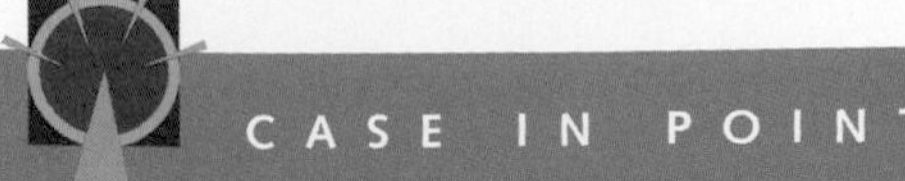

MAKING DREAMS COME TRUE

He takes a creative approach to resources. . . . He is not detail oriented but instead is people oriented. . . . He is a great communicator and communicates enthusiasm.[1]

These are a few of the things that have been said about Steve Bacque, founder of A.S. Bacque Enterprises and one of *Inc.* magazine's regional entrepreneurs of the year for 1992. These comments might just as well refer to Fernando Mateo, the founder of Carpet Fashions, a company with annual sales of $5 million—and an interesting mission.

Bacque's company clearly reflects the values and needs of its founder and owner. The company manufactures western-type cowboy toys. He was attracted to these products based on his upbringing in Texas, where cowboys were revered. The one type of toy he won't make, however, is guns. Bacque doesn't believe in violence.

Bacque's company is dedicated to the memory of his first child. His decision about whom to employ also follows from his personal experience. As an adult enrolled in a college program, Bacque discovered that he was dyslexic. He was told that he should curb his ambitions due to his disability. This aroused a great desire in him to be successful and to help create meaningful employment for others who are physically and mentally challenged. As a result, his all-American workforce is comprised almost entirely of people facing such challenges.

Employing the "disabled" (a label Bacque regards with contempt) has been a boon to all involved. The employees produce good-quality merchandise, are paid good wages (equal to those of nondisabled personnel), and are extremely loyal. Bacque gives to the community by employing people who might not otherwise work, and they, in turn, contribute to the community by paying taxes.

Bacque's belief that people should be utilized to their fullest potential is one of the bases for his selection of employees. This also pushed him to become active in working with students from a local community college. The students put into use the knowledge they gain from their business classes to advise Bacque about how to manage his company. He refers to these students as his "volunteer management consultants." To reach his fullest potential as an entrepreneur, Bacque utilizes all the services offered by the U.S. Small Business Administration, absorbing information "like a sponge."[2]

Fernando Mateo also believes in the importance of achieving one's full potential. To help accomplish this, he founded the "Mateo Institute of Technology" (MIT for short) to teach people in jail the trade of carpet installation so they will have a skill on which to rely when they get out of prison. As he explains to these individuals, "the limits you place on yourself can become more confining than the prison bars."[3] His message and teachings clearly have been very successful to date. After only two years of this program, twenty-nine of the thirty inmates who completed the training under Mateo have found work in the community and have remained crime free.

Mateo's success may come as something of a surprise to people familiar with his background. He grew up in a rough neighborhood in New York City and dropped out of high school at age 15. His father, none too pleased at this turn of events, nevertheless helped him by giving him the money necessary to learn a trade. The trade he learned was carpet installation—an activity for which his passion is extraordinary.

It is this passion that Mateo credits for his business success. He says that he was inspired by a man he worked for who taught him to "sell a product because you believe in it and to always only sell the best."[4] By following this advice Mateo, who began his operations with limited education, no business experience, and only $2,000, has built his company into a firm with annual sales of $5 million and a client roster that includes the likes of large banks, consulting firms, and the Democratic National Convention.

Mateo is not only the sole owner of Carpet Fashions, he is the soul of the organization as well.[5] In the year in which he spent a great deal of time away from the business working on the establishment of the "MIT," his company lost money for the only time in its eighteen-year history. Mateo takes full responsibility for this turn of events, saying that he knows that a company does not run effectively when the owner is not present.[6] He realizes this belief may make others think he is a "control freak"—a quality he readily admits. However, even though he likes to be available to provide direction to his employees, he feels that his role is more like that of a consultant. "I work side-by-side with my employees, and when there are problems I work for my employees helping to find solutions," he says.[7]

Mateo feels very strongly that it is his obligation to be socially responsible and to pay back the community that helped him achieve his success. He asserts that institutions today want to do business with companies where there is knowledge, skill and social responsibility. Interestingly, Mateo's dream is to be like Bill Gates (the founder and chairman of Microsoft and the richest man in the United States). The reason for this is that Mateo feels someone like Gates has the opportunity to positively impact millions of lives—a mission about which Mateo feels very strongly.[8]

Mateo also feels strongly about taking personal responsibility for his actions. He recognizes that he may have lost business opportunities on occasion because of his Hispanic background. However, he believes that if he doesn't make a sale, it must be because he didn't do a good enough job of selling his capabilities and services.[9]

Both Mateo and Bacque have had to take great personal risks to establish their companies. Bacque put up $45,000 of his own money—everything he had. Mateo, at age 19, with no money of his own, literally begged (on his hands and knees) a carpet distributor for a line of credit. This show of humility and energy so impressed the businessman that the credit was extended. Both also risked family relations. Bacque borrowed money against his wife's earnings, and Mateo employed two of his siblings. Both men also rose to the challenge of accomplishing something that had not been done before. They each had a dream and pursued it to their limits.

QUESTIONS FOR DISCUSSION

1. Are Steve Bacque and Fernando Mateo managers, leaders, or both. Explain your answer.
2. What leadership traits are exemplified by Bacque and Mateo?
3. What styles of leadership do Bacque and Mateo appear to use. On what do you base this assessment?
4. Do you think that Steve Bacque is a high-LPC or low-LPC leader? Why is this effective or ineffective in his company?
5. Are Bacque and/or Mateo transformational leaders? On what evidence do you base this claim?
6. Do you think that you could ever be passionate about carpet or children's toys? Why or why not? What products or services do you feel strongly about?
7. Both Mateo and Bacque have taken many risks in starting their businesses. Do you think that it is necessary for a leader to take risks in order to be successful? Explain.

EXPERIENCING ORGANIZATIONAL BEHAVIOR

In Search of Great Leaders

This is a group exercise, so enlist the aid of two or three friends. Then, work together as described below. Your task is to identify *three great leaders.* These leaders can be historical figures from out of the past, or they can be people alive now. You can select your great leaders from any sphere of human activity, such as: politics, military, sports, business, science or medicine, or religion.

After your group has agreed on three leaders, do the following.

PROCEDURE

1. Indicate why each leader can be considered great—what did each do, what did he or she accomplish? Note: *great* does not necessarily mean good.

   Leader 1:

   Leader 2:

   Leader 3:

2. Now indicate whether you think these people would have been great leaders at any time in history, in any culture, and in the face of any set of circumstances. Defend your decision.

   Leader 1:

   Leader 2:

   Leader 3:

POINTS TO CONSIDER

1. Do the leaders you identified as being great have any traits or characteristics in common? The chances are good that they do, for as noted earlier in this chapter, all transformational or charismatic leaders do seem to share some key characteristics.
2. Assuming such traits or skills are crucial for effective leadership, do you think they can be trained? In other words, can almost any individual be taught, through appropriate procedures, to be a great leader?

PART VI

ORGANIZATIONAL PROCESSES

CHAPTER OUTLINE

SPECIAL SECTIONS

FOURTEEN

THE WORK ENVIRONMENT: CULTURE AND TECHNOLOGY

LEARNING OBJECTIVES

After reading this chapter, you should be able to

1. *Define organizational culture, and describe the role it plays in organizational functioning.*
2. *Distinguish between dominant cultures and subcultures as they may exist within organizations.*
3. *Identify various mechanisms by which organizational culture is created.*
4. *Describe and give examples of various techniques used to transmit organizational culture.*
5. *Summarize the effects of organizational culture on both organizational and individual performance.*
6. *Explain why and how organizational culture is likely to change.*
7. *Identify the four major types of technology identified by Perrow.*
8. *Define and give examples of automation, and explain how people are affected by the use of automation in the organizations within which they work.*
9. *Describe how technology can be used in organizations for purposes of assisting people with disabilities, monitoring job performance, and improving the quality of customer service.*

Diffused knowledge immortalizes itself.

James Mackintosh, 1765–1832
Scottish physician, judge, and historian
Vindiciae Gallicae

Any sufficiently advanced technology is indistinguishable from magic.

Arthur C. Clarke
English science fiction writer and scientist
Peers, 1,001 Logical Laws
(Doubleday, 1979)

PREVIEW CASE

Putting the "Service" Back into United Parcel Service: UPS Now Really Delivers

When you've been in business almost ninety years, it's understandable that you might begin to feel comfortable, and set in your ways. This is the position in which United Parcel Service (UPS) found itself only a few years ago—a situation that slowed domestic growth during the late 1980s and early 1990s, while some aggressive competitors, notably Roadway Package Systems (RPS) and Airborne Express, were increasing volume by 30 to 40 percent. One of UPS's problems was that its pricing and service policies were highly rigid.

For example, at Eastman Kodak Co., officials such as Terrance M. Golomb, manager of worldwide transportation services, had become so frustrated with UPS's inflexibility that they almost dropped UPS. This "we-know-what's best" approach prevailed at UPS for many years. That was until 1990, when Kent C. "Oz" Nelson, UPS's chief executive officer overhauled the company's underlying philosophy, transforming it from an aloof and rigid approach to a highly flexible one. As Nelson put it, "If we can't satisfy users, then rigid methodologies . . . lose their importance." This orientation reflects a whole new way of doing business. UPS now has a full-time service representative in place at Kodak who helps reduce shipping expenses. Instead of dropping UPS, Kodak increased its business by 15 percent—shipping some 50,000 packages with UPS a week!

Although UPS saved Kodak from defecting to the competition, the highly aggressive RPS was successful in luring some UPS customers with volume pricing and innovative ways of tracing and billing shipments. UPS has been a long-time believer in a single-price formula. Now, however, volume shippers get price breaks. This policy was largely the result of Nelson's interest in listening to customers to find out what their needs are and how UPS might meet them.

Kent C. "Oz" Nelson, CEO of United Parcel Service

To ensure that UPS's corporate customers remained satisfied—and loyal—Nelson appointed a panel of senior executives to study the company's problems. With this in mind, 25,000 UPS customers were interviewed to find out what new services they required. From this effort several new innovations were launched, including a new three-day guaranteed delivery service introduced in February 1993. This product was aimed at customers who wanted assured delivery, but who didn't need overnight or second-day deliveries, and who were attracted by the 20 percent lower price. Other changes merely required suspending rigid policies. For example, although customers used to be told when they had to have their packages ready, high-volume shippers can now get customized pickup and delivery times.

Listening to its customers, UPS also invested heavily—some $2 billion since 1987 and $3 billion more planned by 1997—in the latest technology needed to pinpoint all shipments in the system. UPS underwent a fundamental overhaul in its technology. To track pack-

ages, drivers now carry handheld computers using an advanced bar code system that took five years and $300 million to develop. Using cellular technology inside UPS's 50,000 package vans, drivers transmit delivery information back to the company's central computers. The result: if you call about your package, UPS can tell you exactly where it is. Although Federal Express customers were used to this service for some time, the stodgier UPS was behind the times when it came to using the latest technology to improve its tracking service. Now, however, UPS's system is so sophisticated that in 1993 it won the annual Excellence in Technology Award presented by The Conference Board and the Gartner Group.

As you might imagine, overhauling the company's indifference toward its customers didn't come about simply because Nelson snapped his fingers and declared it so. The change took some time to gain acceptance, as employees had to perceive that company officials were really very serious about the new approach. UPS was so serious, in fact, that it sent over 500 managers to Michigan State University for week-long seminars in customer service. The company's commitment to customer service is also reflected in its intensive involvement in community service activities. Believing that being in tune with customers is important, UPS executives are regularly pulled off their jobs and pressed into service as interns in various charitable service projects.

The fact that people commonly talk about "FedEx-ing," instead of "UPS-ing" their shipments suggests that UPS may have lost the undisputed dominance in the delivery business it had only a decade ago. But with the changes it has made, it is apparent that "Big Brown," as it is often called, will keep on delivering—and profitably. Indeed, it is still considered a formidable competitor in the delivery business.

It's hard to imagine that a company whose presence has been so strong (who doesn't recognize those boxy brown trucks?) may have been so out of touch with the demands of the marketplace—and, for such a long time, at that. The well-established UPS, set in its ways, was late to realize its customers' desires for improved service and flexible pricing, creating needs that its many competitors were only too glad to fill. Although UPS was able to rebound, it was not due to a slight adjustment here and there, but a major shift in the company's central values. Until Nelson read the handwriting on the wall, the prevailing corporate orientation was "We'll do it our way, and you'll adjust." Then, realizing that this philosophy was eroding the company's customer base, Nelson began teaching UPS employees a new tune: "Be flexible in pricing, and provide the service customers need." This represents a fundamentally different approach to conducting business, an attempt to alter the shared beliefs, expectations, and core values of people in the organization—a change in what is known as **organizational culture.**[1]

As you might imagine, an organization's culture can be so deeply imbedded within the way it operates that its effects can be quite profound. In the case of UPS, several aspects of its culture threatened the bottom line, at least before Nelson began the process of changing it. Other companies—such as McDonald's, MCI, and the Walt Disney Company—have exceptionally strong and effective cultures that have been credited for contributing to their longevity and corporate success. If you go to work at Disney World, for example, you are thoroughly trained in the "guest-driven," wholesome, family-oriented culture that Walt Disney created in 1955 when he opened Disneyland (see Figure 14-1).[2]

FIGURE 14-1
ORGANIZATIONAL CULTURE: THE MAGIC BEHIND THE "MAGICAL KINGDOM"
Part of the magic at Disney World is created by the strong organizational culture of the Walt Disney Company, with its wholesome, family values, and commitment to guest relations.

Although the effects of organizational culture clearly can be quite profound, it would be misleading to suggest that culture operates in a vacuum. Indeed, whereas culture influences organizations from inside, the external environments within which organizations operate also have considerable impact on their functioning. For example, economists tell us how economic forces affect corporate performance, lawyers consider the impact of legal rulings and governmental regulations, and marketers investigate the effects of competition and product demand. Specialists in organizational behavior are also sensitive to the effects of the external environmental forces acting on organizations, particularly the use of **technology**—that is, the organization's methods for transforming raw materials (whether physical entities, such as iron ore, or abstract ones, such as ideas) into various goods or services.[3] UPS was affected by not only signals of problems in its culture, but also the availability of technology to keep track of shipments. Driven by the need to shift to a more customer-oriented corporate culture, high-tech digital telecommunications equipment was brought into use to help the company's operations. In other words, the response to competition at UPS involved both the company's internal work environment (organizational culture) as well as a strong external force (technology).

Because these two aspects of the work environment are so vital to organizational functioning, they will be the focus of this chapter.[4] Specifically, we will begin by describing the basic nature of organizational culture, including the role it plays in organizations. Then, we will describe the processes through which organizational culture is formed and maintained. Next, we will review the effects of organizational culture on individual and organizational functioning, and examine when and how culture is subject to change. Following this, we will shift our attention to technology. In this regard, we will examine the role of technology in organizations, focusing especially on the way people respond to automation. Finally, we will review various ways technology is used today to improve both employees' quality of life and the effectiveness of organizational functioning.

ORGANIZATIONAL CULTURE: ITS BASIC NATURE

To more fully understand organizational culture, we will begin by exploring three very fundamental issues. First we will formally define organizational culture. Second, we will examine the role that culture plays in organizations. Finally, we will consider a key issue relevant to understanding culture: whether there is only one or many different cultures operating within organizations.

ORGANIZATIONAL CULTURE: A DEFINITION

Anyone who has worked in several different organizations knows that each is unique. Even organizations concerned with the same activities or that provide similar products or services can be very different places in which to work. For example, in the world of retailing, Wal-Mart employees are encouraged to be agents for the customer, focusing on service and satisfaction.[5] By contrast, employees of Sears Roebuck & Co. allegedly have been pressured into meeting sales quotas, pushing customers to make unnecessary purchases.[6]

How can such similar businesses be so very different in their approaches? It's tempting to speculate that because people have different personalities, the organizations in which they work are likely to be different from each other as well. However, when you consider that entire organizations are often so consistently different from each other, it's apparent that there's more involved than simply differences in the personalities of the employees. In fact, in many organizations, employees are a constantly changing cast of characters—old ones frequently leave and new ones join. Despite such shifts, however, the organizations themselves alter slowly, if at all. In fact, it is often the new employees who themselves change rather than their organizations. In a sense, then, organizations have a stable existence of their own, quite apart from the unique combination of people of which they are composed at any given time.

What accounts for such stability? To a great extent, the answer involves the impact of **organizational culture**—*a cognitive framework consisting of attitudes, values, behavioral norms, and expectations shared by organization members.*[7,8] Once established, these beliefs, expectancies, and values tend to be relatively stable and exert strong influences on organizations and those working in them.

At the root of any organization's culture is a set of core characteristics that are collectively valued by members of an organization. Although several such characteristics may be involved, Martin suggests that four are especially important (see Table 14-1).[9] First, organizations differ with respect to their *sensitivity to the needs of customers and employees*. For example, while the old culture at UPS was relatively rigid and inflexible with respect to customer needs, its new culture places a high value on customer service and satisfaction. Second, organizations differ with respect to their *interest in having employees generate new ideas*. Walt Disney Co. employees—or "cast members," as they are called—undergo lengthy orientation programs to ensure that they know exactly what to say and how to behave toward guests.[10] By contrast, people working at MCI are encouraged to be unique, and to bring fresh ideas to their work.[11] (In fact, company founder Bill McGowan is so adamant about this that procedure manuals are nowhere to be found at MCI.)

Third, companies also differ with respect to the *value placed on taking risks*.[12] For example, whereas Bank of America is very conservative, making only the safest investments, buyers at The Limited are discouraged from making too many "safe" choices. The fourth value has to do with the *openness of available communication*

TABLE 14-1

Core Organizational Values Reflected in Culture

Organizations may be distinguished with respect to their basic values, such as the very fundamental ones summarized here.

- *Sensitivity to needs of customers and employees*
- *Freedom to initiate new ideas*
- *Willingness to tolerate taking risks*
- *Openness to communication options*

Source: Based on suggestions by Martin, 1992; see Note 90.

options. In some companies, such as DuPont and Tandem Computers, employees are expected to freely make decisions and to communicate with whomever is needed to get the job done.[13] At IBM, however, the tradition has been to work within the proper communication channels and to vest power in the hands of only a few key individuals (although this appears to be changing).[14] These examples clearly illustrate different sets of core values that are reflected in the cultures of organizations.

CULTURE'S ROLE IN ORGANIZATIONS

As you read about the various cultural values that make organizations special, it probably strikes you that culture is an intangible force, but one with far-reaching consequences. Indeed, culture plays several important roles in organizations. Most obviously, an organization's culture provides a *sense of identity* for its members. The more clearly an organization's shared perceptions and values are defined, the more strongly people can associate themselves with their organization's mission, and feel a vital part of it. For example, employees at Southwest Airlines feel special because of their company's emphasis on having fun and joking around on the job (a widespread practice initiated by founder, Herb Kelleher).[15] Southwest's employees feel strongly associated with the company, that they belong there. As a result, they only infrequently resign to take other positions in the airline industry.

This example also illustrates a second important function of culture, generating *commitment to the organization's mission* (see Chapter 5). Sometimes it's difficult for people to go beyond thinking of their own interests: how will this affect me? However, when there is a strong, overarching culture, people feel that they are part of that larger, well-defined whole, and involved in the entire organization's work. Bigger than any one individual's interests, culture reminds people of what their organization is all about.

A third important function of culture is that it serves to *clarify and reinforce standards of behavior*. While this is essential for newcomers, it is also beneficial for seasoned veterans. In essence, culture guides employees' words and deeds, making it clear what they should do or say in a given situation. In this sense, it provides stability to behavior, both with respect to what one individual might do at different times, but also what different individuals may do at the same time. For example, in a company with a culture that strongly supports customer satisfaction, employees will have clear guidance as to how they are expected to behave: doing whatev-

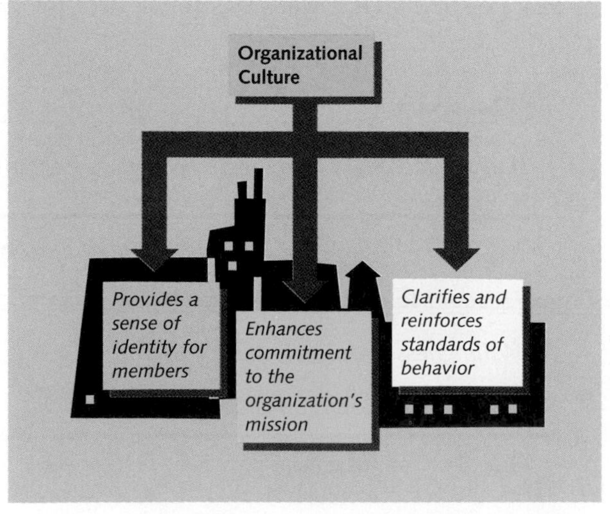

FIGURE 14-2
THE BASIC FUNCTIONS OF ORGANIZATIONAL CULTURE
Organizational culture serves the three major functions summarized here.

er it takes to please the customer (a topic we will discuss in more detail later in this chapter). By serving these three important roles, it is clear that culture is an important force influencing behavior in organizations (for a summary, see Figure 14-2).

CULTURES WITHIN ORGANIZATIONS: ONE OR MANY?

Our discussion thus far has implied that each organization has only a single, uniform culture—one set of shared values, beliefs, and expectations. In fact, this is rarely the case. Instead, organizations—particularly large ones—typically have *several* cultures operating within them.[16]

In general, people tend to have more attitudes and values in common with others in their own fields or work units than they do with those in other fields or other parts of the organization. These various groups may be said to have several different **subcultures**—cultures existing within parts of organizations rather than entirely through them. These typically are distinguished with respect to either functional differences (i.e., the type of work done) or geographic distances (i.e., the physical separation between people). Indeed, research suggests that several subcultures based on occupational, professional, or functional divisions usually exist within any large organization.[17]

This is not to say, however, that there also may not be a **dominant culture**, a distinctive, overarching "personality" of an organization—the kind of culture to which we have been referring. An organization's dominant culture reflects its core values, dominant perceptions that are generally shared throughout the organization. Typically, while members of subcultures may share additional sets of values, they generally also accept the core values of their organizations as a whole (see Figure 14-3).[18] Thus, subcultures should not be thought of as a bunch of totally separate cultures, but rather "mini" cultures operating within a larger, dominant culture.

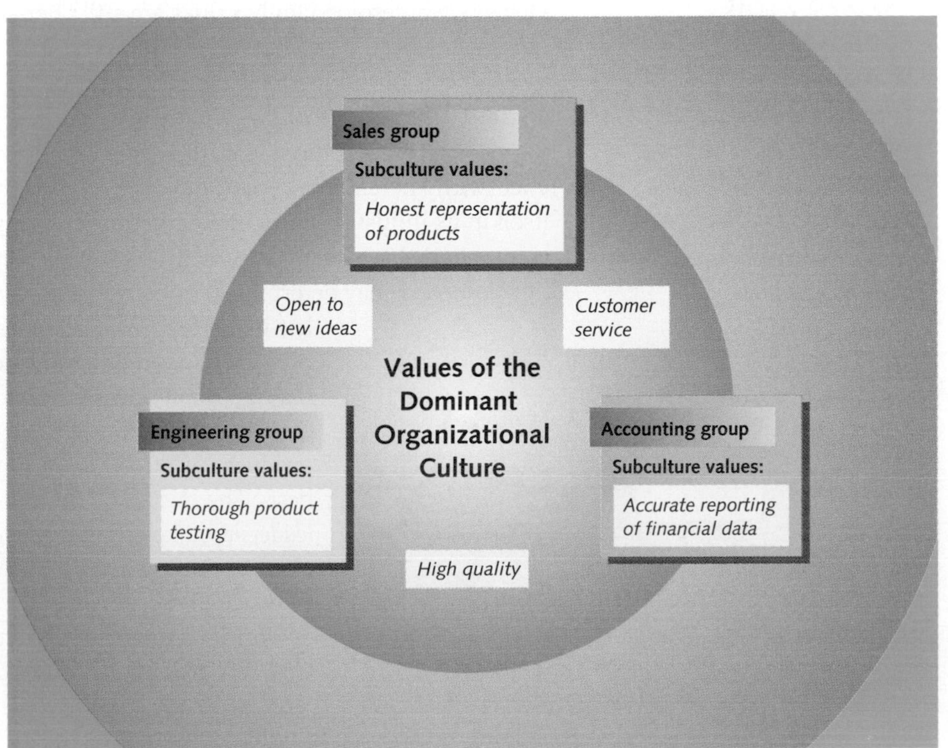

FIGURE 14-3
VALUES OF THE DOMINANT ORGANIZATIONAL CULTURE AND SUBCULTURES
The dominant culture of an organization includes values shared by people in the entire organization. In addition, there are frequently unique sets of values shared by members of various subcultures that supplement the dominant culture. The values of three hypothetical subcultures are shown in this example.

THE FORMATION AND MAINTENANCE OF ORGANIZATIONAL CULTURE

Now that we have described what organizational culture is and how it operates, we are prepared to consider two more important issues: how culture is initially created, and how it is sustained—that is, what keeps it going once it is created.

HOW IS ORGANIZATIONAL CULTURE CREATED?

Why do many individuals within an organization share basic attitudes, values, and expectations? Several factors contribute to this state of affairs, and hence, to the emergence of organizational culture.

First, organizational culture may be traced, at least in part, to the founders of the company.[19] These individuals often possess dynamic personalities, strong values, and a clear vision of how the organization should operate. Since they are on the scene first, and play a key role in hiring initial staff, their attitudes and values are readily transmitted to new employees. The result: these views become the accepted ones in the organization, and persist as long as the founders are on the scene. For example, the culture at Microsoft calls for working exceptionally long hours, in large part because that's what co-founder Bill Gates has always done. Sometimes, founders' values can continue to drive an organization's culture even after that individual is no longer with the organization. For example, the late Ray Kroc founded the McDonald's restaurant chain on the values of good food at a good value served in clean, family-oriented surroundings—key cultural values that persist today (see Figure 14-4). Likewise, although he's no longer with us, Walt Disney's wholesome family values are still cherished at the company that bears his name—in large part because employees ask themselves, "What would Walt think?"[20] These individuals' values continue to permeate their entire companies and are central parts of their dominant cultures.

FIGURE 14-4
RAY KROC: THE FOUNDER OF McDONALD'S
Although Ray Kroc died in 1984, the values of high quality, good service, and cleanliness live on in the culture he created in his McDonald's restaurant chain.

Second, organizational culture often develops out of an organization's experience with the external environment.[21] Every organization must find a niche for itself in its industry and in the marketplace. As it struggles to do so in its early days, it may find that some values and practices work better than others. For example, one company may determine that delivering defect-free products is its unique market niche; by doing so, it can build a core of customers who prefer it to competing businesses. As a result, the organization may gradually acquire a deep, shared commitment to high quality. In contrast, another company may find that selling products of moderate quality, but at attractive prices, works best. The result: a dominant value centering around *price leadership* takes shape. In these and countless other ways, an organization's culture is shaped by its interaction with the external environment.

Third, organizational culture develops out of contact between groups of individuals within an organization. To a large extent, culture involves shared interpretations of events and actions on the part of organization members.[22] In short, organizational culture reflects the fact that people assign similar meaning to various events and actions—that they come to perceive the key aspects of the world, those relevant to the organization's work, in a similar manner (refer to our discussion of perception in Chapter 2). But does repeated interaction between organization members actually lead them to share perceptions or interpretations of the external world?

A study conducted by Rentsch provides direct evidence for this view.[23] In this investigation, members of an accounting firm were first interviewed and asked to describe their organization—what events take place in it, why these events occur, and so on. On the basis of these interviews, fifteen frequently occurring events were identified (e.g., account executives allocate billable work to team members; staff and partners are to be reviewed every six months), as were nine sets of adjectives to describe them (e.g., *professional–nonprofessional*, *stressful–relaxed*). Participants then completed questionnaires in which they indicated the extent to which the fifteen events were similar to one another, and rated each event in terms of the nine adjective dimensions. They also indicated the extent to which they personally interacted with all other members of the organization. This last set of data was used to identify various *interaction groups*—groups of people within the organization who interacted regularly with one another. Rentsch's major predictions were straightforward: people belonging to various interaction groups would perceive organizational events in a similar manner to a greater extent than people belonging to different interaction groups. In other words, people who interacted with one another on a regular basis would come to perceive key aspects of their working world in similar terms, whereas those who did not interact regularly would come to perceive the same events differently. Results offered strong support for these predictions (see Figure 14-5).

These findings suggest that shared meanings or interpretations—a key ingredient in organizational culture—derive, at least in part, from shared experiences and from the experience of working together. Moreover, this same process seems to play a role in the development of organizational subcultures, as groups of employees who usually work together develop views somewhat different from those of other groups of employees about what is happening in their company and of the meaning of such events.

There are several practical applications suggested by these findings. First, because different groups within an organization have somewhat different cultures, interventions designed to change job performance or work-related attitudes through shifts in culture should be customized for each important group.[24] Second, if shared expectations and values are desired across an organization, steps should be taken to increase contact and interaction between various groups. Finally, Rentsch's findings point to the fact that sometimes seemingly small events can carry big messages. For example, one of the events described most frequently by members of the organization studied was "Partners sometimes play golf in the afternoon." Senior partners in the company were shocked to discover that this activity, which they viewed as relatively trivial, received so much attention from others. In retrospect, however, they realized that it conveyed important meanings to other

FIGURE 14-5
ORGANIZATIONAL CULTURE AS SHARED MEANINGS
Organizational members who interacted with one another on a regular basis came to share interpretations of organizational events. Those who did not interact with one another did not share such interpretations. According to Rentsch (1991; see Note 23), such shared meanings or interpretations are an important component of organizational culture.

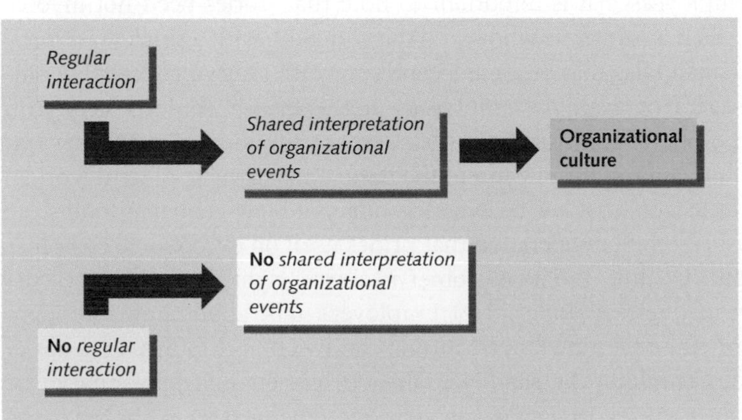

employees—meanings such as "Only senior partners have any privileges around here" or "Whatever people say, status is really important." We will return to this point in our discussion of efforts to change organizational culture. For now, we simply note that where organizational culture is concerned, actions, as they say, do indeed "speak louder than words."

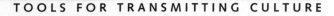

TOOLS FOR TRANSMITTING CULTURE

How are cultural values transmitted between people? In other words, how do employees come to learn about their organization's culture? Research has shown that there are several key mechanisms involved—most importantly, *symbols*, *stories*, *jargon*, *ceremonies*, and *statements of principle*.[25]

SYMBOLS: OBJECTS THAT SAY MORE THAN MEETS THE EYE

First, organizations often rely on **symbols**—material objects that connote meanings that extend beyond their intrinsic content.[26] For example, some companies use impressive buildings to convey the organization's strength and significance, signifying that it is a large, stable place.[27] Other companies rely on slogans, such as General Electric's "Progress is our most important product" or Ford's "Quality is job 1," to symbolize their values. Corporate cars (or even jets!) are also used to convey information about an organization's culture, such as who wields power (see Chapter 12).

In an interesting study, Ornstein showed drawings of company reception areas to people and then asked them to evaluate what the companies pictured were like.[28] It was found that different types of symbols projected different images of the organizations' likely cultures. For example, firms in which there were lots of plants and flower arrangements were judged to have friendly, person-oriented cultures, whereas those in which waiting areas were adorned with awards and trophies were believed to be highly interested in achieving success. These findings suggest that material symbols are potent tools for sending messages about organizational culture.

STORIES: "IN THE OLD DAYS, WE USED TO . . ."

Organizations also transmit information about culture by virtue of the stories that are told in them, both formally and informally.[29] Stories illustrate key aspects of an organization's culture, and telling them can effectively introduce or reaffirm those values to employees.[30] It is important to note that stories need not involve some great event, such as someone who saved the company with a single wise decision, but may be small tales that become legends because they so effectively communicate a message. For example, employees at the British confectionery firm Cadbury are purposely told stories about the company's founding on Quaker traditions to get them to appreciate and accept the basic Quaker value of hard work.[31]

Consider this little story that has become legendary at Stew Leonard's food store in Connecticut, a $100 million operation that prides itself on exceptional customer service.[32] (Its motto is "Rule 1: The customer is always right. Rule 2: If the customer is ever wrong, re-read Rule 1."[33]) Employees talk about how president Stewart J. Leonard, Jr., once unwrapped a tuna sandwich and found a packet of mayonnaise inside. Thinking the sandwich already had enough mayonnaise, he told the deli manager to stop inserting these packets. The next week, however, he ordered another tuna sandwich and once again found a packet of mayonnaise. When he looked into the situation, he got this reply from the clerk who made the sandwiches: "Sorry, Stew, the customers want the extra mayo, so I'm packing it again."[34] The fact that a low-level employee would directly disobey an order from the president in order to please the customers is a story told to establish how very seriously the company is committed to customer satisfaction.

JARGON: THE SPECIAL LANGUAGE THAT DEFINES A CULTURE

Even without telling stories, the everyday language used in companies helps sustain culture. For example, the slang or *jargon* that is used in a company helps its employees define their identities as members of an organization (see Chapter 9). For example, for many years employees at IBM referred to disk drives as "hard files" and circuit boards as "planar boards," nonstandard terms that defined the insulated nature of their culture.[35] Someone who works in a human resources department may be found talking about the FMCS (Federal Medication and Conciliation Service), ERISA (the Employee Retirement Income Security Act), BFOQs (bona fide occupational qualifications), RMs (elections to vote out a union), and other acronyms that sound odd to the uninitiated. Over time, as organizations—or departments within them—develop unique language to describe their work, their terms, although strange to newcomers, serve as a common factor that brings together individuals belonging to a corporate culture or subculture.

To illustrate this point, consider the following personal anecdote. Several years ago, one of the authors served as the director of a division of a large federal agency in Washington, DC—a job requiring him to learn some 200 different acronyms! So essential was this knowledge to being able to work within the agency's culture that he was tested on his knowledge of these acronyms before he was permitted to begin the job. Clearly, this agency was not taking any chances that its new director would be unable to use the language that kept its unique culture alive.

CEREMONIES: SPECIAL EVENTS THAT COMMEMORATE CORPORATE VALUES

Organizations also do a great deal to sustain their cultures by conducting various types of *ceremonies*. Indeed, ceremonies may be seen as celebrations of an organization's basic values and assumptions.[36] Just as a wedding ceremony symbolizes a couple's mutual commitment and a presidential inauguration ceremony marks the beginning of a new presidential term, various organizational ceremonies also celebrate some important accomplishment. For example, one accounting firm celebrated its move to much better facilities by throwing a party, a celebration signifying that it "has arrived" or "made it to the big time."[37] Such ceremonies convey meaning to people inside and outside the organization. As Deal and Kennedy put it, "Ceremonies are to the culture what the movie is to the script . . . values that are difficult to express in any other way."[38]

STATEMENTS OF PRINCIPLE: DEFINING CULTURE IN WRITING

A fifth way in which culture is transmitted is via the direct *statements of principle*. Some organizations have explicitly written their principles for all to see. For example, Forrest Mars, the founder of the candy company M&M Mars, developed his "Five Principles of Mars," which still guide his company today: quality (everyone is responsible for maintaining quality), responsibility (all employees are responsible for their own actions and decisions), mutuality (creating a situation in which everyone can win), efficiency (most of the company's forty-one factories operate continuously), and freedom (giving employees opportunities to shape their futures).[39] Some companies have chosen to make explicit the moral aspects of their cultures by publishing **codes of ethics**—specific statements of a company's ethical values. According to Hershey Foods chief executive officer, Richard Zimmerman, this is an effective device: "[O]ften, an individual joins a firm without recognizing the type of environment in which he will place himself and his career. The loud and clear enunciation of a company's code of conduct . . . [allows] that employee to determine whether or not he fits that particular culture."[40] (For an example of how an important cultural element expressed in one company's ethical code helped guide it through a crisis, see the Ethical Workplace section below.)

THE ETHICAL WORKPLACE

HOW CODIFYING ETHICAL VALUES SAVED JOHNSON & JOHNSON: THE TYLENOL CASE

September 28, 1982, was a tragic day in greater Chicago. That's when twelve year-old Mary Kellerman was found dead in her home. A few miles away, Adam Janus collapsed and died, and later that same evening, so did his brother Stanley. Only a few days later Stanley's wife, Theresa also died, as did three others from the Chicago area. Autopsies revealed that the deaths were the result of cyanide poisoning.[41] The source of the cyanide? Intensive investigations, and a little luck, revealed that all the victims had taken Extra Strength Tylenol capsules.

Immediately after this discovery, the makers of Tylenol, McNeil Consumer Products, and its parent company, Johnson & Johnson, had to act quickly to stop further deaths. And so, although Tylenol was the largest revenue-generating product for Johnson & Johnson, company officials made a tough decision, but the only one it could make under the circumstances: it immediately withdrew Tylenol capsules from the market and urged people not to use any they had on hand. In fact, the company actively participated in attempts to notify the public about the poisonings (e.g., running television commercials, creating telephone hotlines, sending mailgrams to doctors and retailers), and fully cooperated with efforts to investigate the incident. Rather than being defensive, as some might be under such circumstances, officials from McNeil and Johnson & Johnson assisted in helping find the source of the tainted products (later found to be tampering), offering a $100,000 reward for information leading to the arrest of the culprit.[42] Press reports praised Johnson & Johnson for its swift and effective action. Consider, for example, this opinion expressed in the *Washington Post*:

> *Though the hysteria and frustration generated by random murder have often obscured the company's actions, Johnson & Johnson has effectively demonstrated how a major business ought to handle a disaster . . . . From the day the deaths were linked to the poisoned Tylenol . . . Johnson & Johnson has succeeded in portraying itself to the public as a company willing to do what's right regardless of cost.*[43]

Although companies don't always put the welfare of the public ahead of their own profits (especially when the company is itself a victim), this is precisely what Johnson & Johnson did. What led company officials to act in such a socially responsible manner? According to James E. Burke, Johnson & Johnson's chairman and chief executive officer, "The guidance of the Credo played the single most important role in our decision making . . . . The Credo was tested—and it worked."[44] The "Credo" to which Mr. Burke refers is a statement of the company's responsibilities originally authored by Gen. Robert Wood Johnson in 1947 (although it has been modernized several times since), a document that has defined Johnson & Johnson's culture for some thirty-five years before it was put to the test in a crisis. In particular, the opening lines of the Credo state that the company's *first* responsibility is to those who use its products (see Figure 14-6). Company officials credited this statement with helping them decide what to do at a time when there was no time to gather all the information and weigh all the options. In Burke's words, "We believe the consistency of our overall performance as a corporation is due to . . . our adherence to the ethical principles embodied in our Credo," adding, "This decision [regarding Tylenol] stems from our management philosophy. [Such decisions] are difficult and costly, but we haven't the slightest doubt that they are in the best long-term interests of our stockholders."[45]

As you might imagine, the Tylenol crisis cost Johnson & Johnson plenty—some $50 million, according to the company's 1982 annual report.[46] Potentially, the most devastating cost resulted from lost public confidence, causing defection to competing pain relief products. However, Johnson & Johnson did not give up, and battled hard to regain the public confidence. In fact, only six weeks after it had withdrawn all Tylenol capsules from the market (31 million bottles with a retail value of over $100 million), the company reintroduced the product in tamper-proof packages, as are used in all of today's pharmaceutical products. Amazingly, Tylenol very shortly thereafter regained 95 percent of the market share it had before the crisis.[47]

This classic case illustrates how very well a company can be served by a statement of principles. Because the Credo was not just a document prepared for public relations purposes filed away in a drawer, but a vivid reflection of Johnson & Johnson's dominant culture, it guided officials in making extremely difficult decisions. And, because these decisions represented the best interests of the public, it rewarded the company by expressing its regained confidence in the form of sales. It should be considered no coincidence that the aftermath of the Tylenol incident brought not only tamper-proof packages to drug store shelves, but also codes of ethical conduct to the office shelves of business executives everywhere.[48]

Our Credo

We believe our first responsibility is to the doctors, nurses and patients,
to mothers and fathers and all others who use our products and services.
In meeting their needs everything we do must be of high quality.
We must constantly strive to reduce our costs
in order to maintain reasonable prices.
Customers' orders must be serviced promptly and accurately.
Our suppliers and distributors must have an opportunity
to make a fair profit.

We are responsible to our employees,
the men and women who work with us throughout the world.
Everyone must be considered as an individual.
We must respect their dignity and recognize their merit.
They must have a sense of security in their jobs.
Compensation must be fair and adequate,
and working conditions clean, orderly and safe.
We must be mindful of ways to help our employees fulfill
their family responsibilities.
Employees must feel free to make suggestions and complaints.
There must be equal opportunity for employment, development
and advancement for those qualified.
We must provide competent management,
and their actions must be just and ethical.

We are responsible to the communities in which we live and work
and to the world community as well.
We must be good citizens – support good works and charities
and bear our fair share of taxes.
We must encourage civic improvements and better health and education.
We must maintain in good order
the property we are privileged to use,
protecting the environment and natural resources.

Our final responsibility is to our stockholders.
Business must make a sound profit.
We must experiment with new ideas.
Research must be carried on, innovative programs developed
and mistakes paid for.
New equipment must be purchased, new facilities provided
and new products launched.
Reserves must be created to provide for adverse times.
When we operate according to these principles,
the stockholders should realize a fair return.

FIGURE 14-6
THE JOHNSON & JOHNSON CREDO
This statement of values is credited with guiding the decisions of Johnson & Johnson officials during the Tylenol crisis. (Reprinted by permission of Johnson & Johnson.)

ORGANIZATIONAL CULTURE: ITS CONSEQUENCES AND CAPACITY TO CHANGE

f you are beginning to think that organizational culture can play an important role in the functioning of organizations, you are right. To make this point explicit, we will now examine the various ways in which organizational culture has been found to affect organizations and the behavior of individuals in them. Because some of these effects might be undesirable, organizations are sometimes interested in changing their cultures. Accordingly, we will also consider why and how organizational culture might be changed.

THE EFFECTS OF ORGANIZATIONAL CULTURE

Organizational culture exerts many effects on individuals and organizational processes—some dramatic, and others more subtle. Culture generates strong pressures on people to go along, to think and act in ways consistent with the existing culture.[49] Thus, if an organization's culture stresses the importance of product quality and excellent service, its customers will generally find their complaints handled politely and efficiently. If, instead, the organization's culture stresses high output at any cost, customers seeking service may find themselves on a much rockier road. An organization's culture can strongly affect everything from the way employees dress (e.g., the white shirts traditionally worn by male employees of IBM) and the amount of time allowed to elapse before meetings begin, to the speed with which people are promoted.

Turning to the impact of culture on organizational processes, considerable research has focused on the possibility of a link between culture and performance.[50] One view is that in order to influence performance, organizational culture must be strong. In other words, approval or disapproval must be expressed to those who act in ways consistent or inconsistent with the culture, respectively, and there must be widespread agreement on values among organizational members.[51] Only if these conditions prevail, researchers believe, will a link between organizational culture and performance be observed. Some evidence supports this contention. For example, Dennison found that corporations with cultural values favoring participation by employees in activities such as decision making generate a return on investment twice as great as that of corporations lacking this value.[52] Similarly, in their best-selling book of a decade ago, *In Search of Excellence*, Peters and Waterman reported that the most effective companies had certain cultural characteristics in common (e.g., a bias for action, employee involvement).[53]

Although it is an intriguing idea that there are certain types of organizational cultures that are better than others, the evidence is not all that compelling.[54] In fact, some of the firms Peters and Waterman classified as having the best cultures, such as Wang Laboratories and Texas Instruments, have suffered serious financial difficulties since their book was published.[55] It makes sense that the financial profitability of a company is linked to so many different factors (e.g., the economy, governmental regulation, the existence of competitors) that a single force alone, even a potent one such as organizational culture, may have only limited impact on a company's financial status. In other words, the idea that some cultures are more strongly associated with successful organizational performance than others must be considered questionable at this time.

This does not mean that organizational culture cannot have considerable effects on individuals' attitudes and performance. Indeed, it appears that people are more willing to work in some types of cultures than others. Demonstrating this idea, Sheridan compared the voluntary survival rates (how long employees stay with the company before resigning) of over 900 new employees at several different public accounting firms over a six-year period.[56] Based on responses to a questionnaire, the cultures of the firms were distinguished between those that primarily emphasized the value of hard work and those that emphasized the value of pleasant interpersonal relationships. As shown in Figure 14-7, survival rates among the new employees differed according to the cultures of the organizations in which they worked. Although voluntary turnover was nonexistent within the first year of employment, differences emerged over time. Specifically, employees survived longer in firms whose cultures stressed pleasant interpersonal relationships than those whose cultures emphasized the value of hard work—14 months longer, on average. Although people stay with jobs for various reasons, it is clear that the nature of the organization's culture is an important consideration.

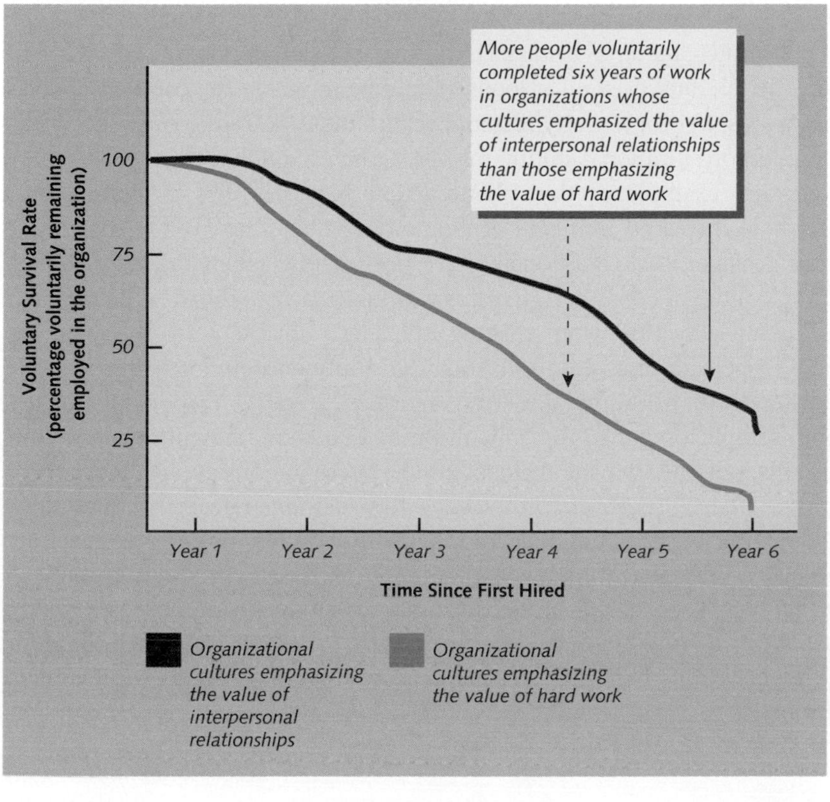

Additional research suggests that to understand the effects of organizational culture, we should consider not just the nature of an organization's culture alone, but also the extent to which the values held by employees match those of their organizations. The better this fit, the more effectively employees should be able to operate on their jobs. To test this idea, O'Reilly, Chatman, and Caldwell conducted a study in which they first asked hundreds of individuals from eight different organizations to complete a questionnaire designed to measure the values of their companies (e.g., orientation toward outcomes or results, attention to detail, innovation, and risk taking).[57] Next, the same participants reported the extent to which similar values were important to them personally. Finally, the researchers assessed how closely individuals' personal values coincided with their organizations (i.e., *person–organization fit*; see Chapter 6), and compared this to various attitudinal and behavioral measures over a two-year period (e.g., organizational commitment, job satisfaction, intentions to leave, and records of actual turnover). It was found that the closer the person–organization fit, the more satisfied people were with their jobs, and the less interested they were in quitting (see Chapter 5). In fact, when participants were divided into groups with relatively high and low person–organization fit, those for whom fit was high were indeed less likely to quit their jobs over a two-year period than those for whom fit was low.

These findings have important implications both for individuals and for organizations. First, they suggest that people seeking employment should examine carefully the prevailing culture of an organization before deciding to join it. If they don't, they run the risk of finding themselves in a situation where

FIGURE 14-7

VOLUNTARY SURVIVAL: ITS CONNECTION TO ORGANIZATIONAL CULTURE

Sheridan examined the voluntary survival rate of new employees of public accounting firms over a six-year period. On average, employees worked longer for firms whose cultures emphasized pleasant interpersonal relationships than those whose cultures emphasized hard work. [Source: Adapted from Sheridan, 1992; see Note 56.]

their own values and those of their company clash. Second, these findings also suggest that organizations should focus on attracting individuals whose values match their own. This involves identifying key aspects of organizational culture, communicating these to prospective employees, and selecting those for whom the person–organization fit is best. Considerable effort may be involved in completing these tasks. Given that high levels of person–organization fit can contribute to commitment, satisfaction, and low rates of turnover among employees, however, the effort appears to be worthwhile.

WHY AND HOW DOES ORGANIZATIONAL CULTURE CHANGE?

Our earlier comments about the relative stability of organizational culture may have left you wondering about the following questions: If culture tends to be so stable, why and how does it ever change? Why isn't it simply passed from one generation of organizational members to the next in a totally static manner? The basic answer, of course, is that the world in which all organizations operate constantly changes (a point we will fully explain in Chapter 16). External events such as shifts in market conditions, new technology, altered government policies, and many other factors change over time, necessitating changes in an organization's mode of doing business—and hence its culture.

COMPOSITION OF THE WORKFORCE

Over time, the people entering an organization may differ in important ways from those already in it, and these differences may impinge on the existing culture of the organization. For example, people from different ethnic or cultural backgrounds may have contrasting views about various aspects of behavior at work. For instance, they may hold dissimilar views about style of dress, the importance of being on time (or even what constitutes "on time" behavior), the level of deference one should show to higher-status people, and even what foods should be served in the company cafeteria. In other words, as people with different backgrounds and values enter the workplace, changes in organizational culture may be expected to follow.

An interesting example of this phenomenon may be seen at Ford Motor Company, where increased numbers of women are now employed in positions, such as auto designer, that traditionally have been held by men.[58] Until recently, the prevailing culture of Ford's design teams was insensitive to the idea that women may have special concerns when picking out a car—overlooking the fact that women buy 49 percent of all cars sold today, and influence almost 80 percent of the purchasing decisions. Mimi Vandermolen, a Ford designer responsible for the 1993 Probe, sought to change the subculture of Ford's traditionally male design unit. To do this, not only did she make countless presentations about the needs of women in car design, she even produced a film demonstrating the difficulties women had getting in and out of vehicles. The culture of Ford's design team is now more attuned to the concerns of women than ever. As a result, the Probe was redesigned with such features as upholstery that won't snag pantyhose, glove box latches that allow for long fingernails, and pedals that are designed at just the right angle for drivers wearing high heels. These small redesigned elements, which make the new Probe friendlier to women, are concrete evidence of changes in a subculture of one large organization.

MERGERS AND ACQUISITIONS

Another, and even more dramatic, source of cultural change is mergers and acquisitions, events in which one organization purchases or otherwise absorbs another.[59] When this occurs, there is likely to be a careful analysis of the financial and material assets of the acquired organization. However, it is rare that any consideration is given to the acquired organization's culture. This is unfortunate, insofar as there have been several cases in which the merger of two organizations with incompatible cultures leads to serious problems, commonly referred to as *culture clashes* (see Table 14-2).

A classic example is provided by the 1988 merger of Nabisco, Inc. (a producer of cookies and other baked goods famous for such brands as Fig Newtons and Oreos), with RJ Reynolds, Inc. (a major producer of tobacco products), to become RJR Nabisco.[60] Nabisco was headquartered in New York, and its executives were known for a fast-paced life in which perks such as corporate jets, penthouse apartments, and lavish parties featured prominently. Yet company employees prided themselves on the "American-as-apple-pie" image of Nabisco, and valued the high degree of autonomy in performing their jobs that Nabisco management permitted. Several hundred miles away, RJ Reynolds, headquartered in Winston-Salem, North Carolina, had a strikingly different culture. It was characterized by a strong work ethic, much less autonomy for employees, and a deep commitment to its local community and to philanthropic activities. Corporate jets, penthouse apartments, and lavish parties were definitely *not* features of corporate life at RJ Reynolds.

TABLE 14-2

Mergers and Acquisitions: A Potential Source of Culture Clashes

When organizations with incompatible cultures merge, the potential for friction is high. Summarized here are some cases in which cultures clashed so much that various indications of performance suffered.

ACQUIRING COMPANY	ACQUIRED COMPANY	RESULT
RJ Reynolds Tobacco	*Nabisco*	*Internal feuds resulted when RJ Reynolds executives, with highly controlling cultures, worked together with Nabisco executives used to having more autonomy.*
Waterford Crystal	*Wedgwood China*	*Entirely different accounting practices and management styles led to poor morale, lowered quality, and declining financial performance.*
Bank of America	*Charles Schwab & Co.*	*The aggressive, flashy style of Schwab employees didn't fit in with the highly conservative style of Bank of America, leading Schwab to buy his company back after four difficult years together.*

Sources: Based on material in Burrough & Helyar (1990), see Note 60; Cartwright & Cooper (1993), see Note 62; Smith (1993), see Note 12; Walter (1985), see Note 59.

When the two companies merged, sparks flew. Nabisco executives chafed under the tighter controls imposed by Tylee Wilson, chief executive officer of Reynolds.[61] As some put it, "You have to raise your hand to go to the bathroom!" The fact that their company was not afforded the level of independence within the new corporation promised before the merger upset many Nabisco employees. The result: within a year, bitter internal feuds erupted. These resulted in a takeover of the new company by Ross Johnson, CEO of Nabisco. Once in power, he quickly purged the company of virtually all former Reynolds executives and moved the merged company headquarters to a neutral location, Atlanta. Now, years later, the merged organization still suffers from decreased productivity in some units, increased turnover, and strong internal divisions. Clearly, when organizational cultures collide, the changes that follow can be wrenching.

In a recent analysis of culture clashes resulting from organizational mergers, Cartwright and Cooper lament the fact that in too many cases the larger, more powerful, acquiring company attempts to dominate the smaller, acquired company, based on the mistaken belief that it knows best—a situation they liken to a traditional marriage.[62] In such instances, clashes can result when the two merging organizations have certain combinations of cultures. For example, when each is heavily autocratic, neither group will be interested in giving up its ways, resulting in considerable conflict. Similarly, when the dominant culture is highly autocratic and the culture of the acquired organization is highly person–oriented, neither side may see the wisdom of the other's approach. Rather than jumping into a marriage that may be conflict ridden, Cartwright and Cooper recommend handling mergers the way it has been done in Japan—by first working collaboratively on a joint venture and merging only after it is clear that the company's cultures can coexist. For example, the successful partnership between Sony and CBS was preceded by years of experience with each other. In short, just as the marriage of two people requires keen attention to their individual personalities, so too does the marriage of two companies suggest the need to be sensitive to their different organizational cultures.

PLANNED ORGANIZATIONAL CHANGE

Finally, even if an organization doesn't change by acquiring another, cultural change still may result from other planned changes, such as conscious decisions to alter the internal structure or the basic operations of an organization (see Chapter 15). Once such decisions are reached, many practices in the company that both reflect and contribute to its culture may change. For example, the company may adopt different criteria for recruiting newcomers or promoting current employees. Similarly, managers may be directed to focus their attention on different goals from those in the past. As these shifts take place, new norms governing preferred or acceptable behavior emerge, and attitudes and values supporting these norms may take shape. The result may be a considerable shift in existing culture.

A good example of this can be seen in IBM in recent years.[63] In response to staggering losses IBM realized that one of its problems was that it was heavily bureaucratic, making it difficult for lower-level people to make on-the-spot decisions. As a result, IBM changed the nature of its corporate structure from one in which there was a steep hierarchy with many layers of management to a "delayered" one with far fewer managers. As you might imagine, the newly "rightsized" IBM developed a new corporate culture.[64] Once known for a highly rigid, autocratic culture in which decision making was centralized in the hands of just a few, the reorganized company is now much more open and democratic in its approach than ever before.

To conclude, it is clear that although organizational culture is generally stable, it is not immutable. In fact, culture often evolves in response to outside forces (e.g., changes in workforce composition) as well as deliberate attempts to change the design of organizations (e.g., through mergers, and corporate restructuring; see Chapters 15 and 16). One important outside force that affects culture—and is affected by culture—is *technology*, the topic to which we will now turn.

TECHNOLOGY: ITS ROLE IN ORGANIZATIONS

What image comes to mind when you think of technology? An enormous industrial robot arm? Space shuttle astronauts repairing an orbiting telescope? The latest piece of advanced office equipment (see Figure 14-8)? Indeed, technology can be all these things—plus more. For all these sophisticated images, the definition of technology is deceptively simple. Specifically, **technology** refers to *the physical and mental processes used to transform inputs into usable outputs.*[65] Simply put, technology deals with the activities, equipment, and knowledge used to get things done. Although robots, spacecraft, and automated office equipment are examples of technological devices—as is the digital signature pad used by UPS in our Preview Case—it is important to note that technology also can take on abstract forms, such as ideas and formulas. Indeed, Procter & Gamble's recipe for a new household detergent is every bit as much an example of technology as the elaborate computer-controlled equipment used to manufacture it.[66]

In just the past few years, technology has advanced at a staggering pace. The compact disc has replaced the phonograph record, word processors have replaced typewriters, and in many libraries, computer terminals have replaced card catalogs. Why are we concerned about these things in the field of OB? The answer is simple: *technology affects the behavior of people on the job as well as the effective functioning of organizations*. After all, technology helps individuals work differently (e.g., they may use a teleconference instead of a face-to-face meeting, or they may operate a machine that performs heavy, dangerous work instead of doing that work themselves). It also is used to help companies gain a competitive advantage over others, such as by finding a more effective way to produce products or deliver services better and less expensively.[67] Indeed, keeping abreast of the latest technology is often needed just to not fall behind the competition (e.g., it's almost impossible to function today without computers and fax machines). In other words, sometimes using technology doesn't give one an advantage; it merely keeps

FIGURE 14-8
TECHNOLOGY: A VITAL ASPECT OF OFFICE OPERATIONS
Increasingly sophisticated technology has brought levels of efficiency to new highs, especially in the office. Before long, perhaps, copiers will be able to empty the trash—although we hope they don't talk back! (Source: Reprinted by permission, Tribune Media Services.)

one in the game! Clearly, technology represents a potent external force to which all organizations must be responsive. It is, therefore, not surprising that top management scholars such as Peter F. Drucker have asserted that technology holds the key to managing tomorrow's organizations.[68]

We will now turn our attention to the matter of how technology affects individual and organizational functioning. Given how wide-reaching this topic is, it shouldn't be surprising to you that we already have had occasion to describe the effects of technology elsewhere in this book—such as in the context of communication (Chapter 9) and decision making (Chapter 10), and that we will do so again later—notably, in connection with organizational structure and design (Chapter 15). Here, we will concentrate on the more general aspects of technology. Specifically, we will begin by reviewing the basic dimensions of technology. Following this, we will explore a critical issue involving technology in today's organizations—the way people respond to automation.

CLASSIFYING TECHNOLOGY'S BASIC DIMENSIONS

Although many organizational theorists have described the various types of technologies that exist, the most comprehensive scheme has been suggested by Charles Perrow.[69] This system is useful for categorizing the technologies of both manufacturing and service organizations.

Perrow begins by distinguishing between two basic dimensions. The first is *exceptions*, the degree to which an organization makes use of standard inputs to turn out standard outputs (i.e., makes few exceptions) or encounters many nonroutine situations (i.e., has to make many exceptions in the way it operates). Perrow's second dimension is known as *problems*—the degree to which the situations encountered are either easy to analyze, allowing for programmed decisions, or complex and difficult to analyze, requiring nonprogrammed decision making (recall the distinction between programmed and nonprogrammed decisions made in Chapter 10). By dichotomizing both dimensions and overlaying them onto each other, Perrow identified four distinct technological types. The resulting **matrix of technologies** is summarized in Table 14-3.

The first technological type is known as **routine technology**. It includes operations with highly standardized inputs and outcomes and problems that are easy to analyze. Examples include assembly-line manufacturing and vocational training, both cases in which the product or service is clearly defined. But when exceptions occur—such as when new products are to be produced, or new subjects are to be taught—the appropriate reaction is readily apparent. Perrow's second technological type, **craft technology**, involves operations in which inputs and outcomes are also standardized, but problems are more difficult to analyze. For example, cabinet makers always use wood and laminated products to create finished furniture products. Similarly, public schools focus their attention on ways of teaching the average student. In either case—such as when a special order is placed, or a student with a learning disability is encountered—the appropriate response is not entirely clear. Organizations of this type are simply not set up to handle exceptional cases where the most appropriate decisions are not clearly specified in advance.

In contrast, Perrow's final two technological types involve industries that are better prepared to handle exceptions. For example, organizations using **engineering technology**, such as those in heavy machinery construction, and health and fitness clubs, expect to encounter many exceptions in inputs or outputs, but these can be

TABLE 14-3

Perrow's Matrix of Technologies

By combining two levels of exceptions (few and many) with two levels of problems (easy to analyze and difficult to analyze), Perrow identified the four technological types identified here.

EXCEPTIONS	PROBLEMS	TECHNOLOGICAL TYPE (AND EXAMPLES)
Few	*Easy to analyze*	*Routine technology (e.g., assembly-line manufacturing, vocational training)*
	Difficult to analyze	*Craft technology (e.g., cabinet making, public schools)*
Many	*Easy to analyze*	*Engineering technology (e.g., heavy machinery construction, health and fitness club)*
	Difficult to analyze	*Nonroutine technology (e.g., research unit, psychiatric hospital)*

Source: Perrow, 1967; see Note 69.

dealt with in standardized ways. For example, people come to health and fitness facilities in different physical condition and with different goals. Some may be trying to lose weight, others may be trying to regain strength and agility after an injury, and still others may be training for a major body-building contest. Although different types, amounts and difficulty levels of exercise may be dictated on a case-by-case basis, the decision regarding exactly what the client should do to achieve his or her goal is relatively straightforward, and based on pre-established information about the effectiveness of different exercise regimes. Other industries also face exceptions, but more difficult decisions as well. Such organizations are said to employ **nonroutine technology**. For example, research units, by their very existence, are created to tackle difficult, exceptional situations. Psychiatric hospitals also fit into this category. Not only do they encounter a wide variety of people with unique histories and combinations of mental and physical problems, but the appropriate treatment is not always obvious. Despite widespread advances in psychiatric diagnoses, treatment decisions are extremely complex and far from routine.

HUMAN RESPONSES TO AUTOMATION

Traditionally, using technology on the job involved the manual or mechanical manipulation of things. People at work used chains and pulleys to help them lift heavy items and maneuver them from one place to another. Although work of this type still goes on, today's workplace is making increasing use of **high technology**, an advanced form of technology employing tools that are electronic in nature, usually relying on the use of microprocessor chips. For example, typesetters used to have to move together pieces of metal type on wooden blocks to create plates from which documents were printed. Today, this process goes on invisibly, as compositors simply enter letters onto a keyboard, just as you do word processing at home. Clearly, technology has changed the fundamental nature of work for many people.[70] Some examples of high technology used by today's organizations include

- **Advanced manufacturing technology (AMT)**—manufacturing in which the various processes are guided by computers
- **Computer-integrated manufacturing (CIM)**—manufacturing processes that go beyond AMT by using computers to gather information, and using this information to make decisions about ways in which the manufacturing process needs to be altered
- **Computer-aided design and engineering (CAD/CAE)**—the processes of using computers to build and simulate the characteristics of products, and to test their effectiveness
- **Industrial robotics (IR)**—computer-controlled machines that manipulate materials and perform complex functions

The economics of automation are simple. As competition (frequently from foreign firms) drives prices down, companies are forced to improve quality and reduce labor costs, and so they turn to more efficient modes of operation, **automation**—the process of using machines to perform tasks that might otherwise be done by people. Evidence of automation is all around us. Just think of automated call menu devices that route your phone calls to the appropriate person (if not to another computer!), and automated teller machines that dispense currency. Such equipment has certainly reduced the need for human involvement in many activities. By substituting machines programmed to execute actions faster, more accurately, and more consistently than human beings, today's organizations are seeking the same kinds of increased efficiency that factory owners sought a century ago when they introduced machines driven by steam-powered engines onto their shop floors. Not surprisingly, the growth of automation has been referred to as "the second industrial revolution."[71]

Indeed, evidence suggests that today's automation vastly improves industrial efficiency. Specifically, surveys have shown that companies using various forms of automation have reported reductions in lead time, unit cost, inventories, and labor expense, as well as improvements in quality.[72] For example, after General Electric introduced computer-integrated manufacturing in its St. Louis dishwasher factory, productivity jumped 30 percent, and warranty calls were reduced by half, boosting its market share by 12 percentage points.[73]

Executives reviewing this evidence should exercise caution before rushing out and automating their operations. For one, automation is expensive—the General Electric dishwasher plant described earlier cost $600 million, IBM spent $350 million on an automated typewriter plant in Kentucky, and a robotized General Motors auto assembly plant in Michigan cost $500 million—figures that leave some corporate accountants questioning the wisdom of their investments.[74] But as we've been saying throughout this book, there's more to organizations than money and machines—there's also people. Our examples show that as a result of using high technology in organizations, the kind of work people do is different, as is the nature of the demands on them.[75] According to the U.S. Office of Technology Assessment, one of the main impediments to using technology effectively rests in its impact on people.[76]

One obvious effect is that automation makes people so highly efficient that it eliminates the need for some positions, leading to unemployment. Indeed, the flip side of the effectiveness described above is the human cost: automation is designed to eliminate jobs, and the more it does so, the more effective it is considered to be. Not surprisingly, many labor unions have been less than enthusiastic about automation despite the fact that it usually allows people to work in safer, cleaner, and healthier conditions while avoiding the tedious and repetitive aspects of many jobs (a dangerous, boring job may be better than none at all). Fearing that automation may make its members obsolete, some labor unions have insisted on agreements with management that prohibit laying off employees or transferring them to lower-paying jobs.[77] Statistics suggest that such fears are not unfounded. Specifically, today's companies are using high-tech tools to get more work out of a smaller workforce than ever before.[78] Not only might fewer people be needed to do the job, but it is often the case that only those companies that can afford to invest in high-tech equipment will be able to conduct business profitably. As a result, we often see shakeouts in which many smaller companies—and their employees—find themselves casualties of the high tech revolution. For example, as computer-controlled machines are being used to mill lumber, only a few people are needed to flip switches and monitor logs on video screens. Such mills operate so efficiently that smaller mills—ones that cannot afford the $15 million or more startup costs—are often driven out of the market and forced to close their doors.[79]

Although some people are being replaced by machines, to be sure, it is frequently the case that people work along *with* machines to help get their jobs done—and better than ever before. The once-popular vision of the workerless factory in which only white-coated technicians walked the floor to check up on the machines, as hordes of displaced factory workers walked the unemployment line, has never materialized. More typical is the situation in which people work side by side with robots, each doing what it does best. For example, although robots play a large part in the production of automobiles, such as General Motors' Saturn, company officials acknowledge that the technology only works because of the people (see Figure 14-9).[80] Advanced technology alone won't build a successful car. In the words of the Japanese industrialist Jaruo Shimada, "Only people give wisdom to the machines."[81] The idea is that people and machines are really complementary aspects of any organization.

If people and machines are to work together as cooperating elements of an organization's technology, however, it is essential that the nature of the work performed by people remains highly motivating (see Chapter 4). This tends to be a problem

FIGURE 14-9
ROBOTS: AN IMPORTANT PART OF AUTOMOBILE PRODUCTION
By performing the boring, repetitive, and dangerous tasks, robots free auto assemblers to do more interesting and creative work.

in situations in which automation so severely simplifies, or "dumbs up," a job that the worker becomes bored and alienated, leading to lowered quality performance. After all, why should anyone really care about doing a good job when all one has to do is stand around and watch machines doing the job, on the off chance that one will break down?

It would be misleading, however, to imply that automation leaves only routine and boring jobs for people to perform. Indeed, new jobs created by the introduction of robots are often considered more demanding than the old jobs. In the words of one employee describing his response to a robot in his manufacturing plant, "The job now requires more skills. . . . You have to learn how to program the robot and run it. . . . The job is more sophisticated."[82] Indeed, automation frequently frees people to do more interesting work (see Figure 14-10). For example, the use of automatic teller machines frees human bank tellers to play more of a problem-solving role in dealing with bank customers. Just because opportunities may arise for people to do interesting work, while leaving the boring work to the machinery, doesn't necessarily ensure that this will happen. To make sure, when introducing automation, some companies go out of their way to make the remaining human jobs as involving as possible. For example, at its heavily automated Grand Rapids, Michigan, furniture plant, Westinghouse has an elaborate network of committees and taskforces in operation that encourages employees to be highly involved in the facility's decision making (see Chapter 10).[83] Autonomous work teams have been used in some organizations to ensure that employees keep interested in their jobs when the jobs have changed in response to automation (see Chapter 8).[84]

In other words, if people don't lose their jobs in response to automation, jobs certainly may change. Automation creates new jobs as growing numbers of people are needed to program and service the high-tech equipment (in fact, consider all the new careers becoming available in high tech fields noted in Chapter 6). Thus, automation may be seen as causing a shift in the *kinds* of jobs people do. According to an official at National Semiconductor Corporation, "We will be upgrading jobs through automation. I think we will be changing all our collars to white over the next few years."[85] Changes of this type indicate a need for employee training if automation is to be successful (see Chapter 2). With this in mind, Chrysler Corporation invested some 900,000 person-hours in training its employees before

FIGURE 14-10
THE IMPACT OF AUTOMATION
As summarized here, the economics of automation has a key effect on people in organizations. By making workers so efficient, automation reduces the need for as many people to perform routine jobs. As a result, jobs are either eliminated (leading to unemployment), or changed into new jobs, a few of which may be boring (e.g., monitoring machines), but many of which will be even more challenging (e.g., programming and maintaining the machines).

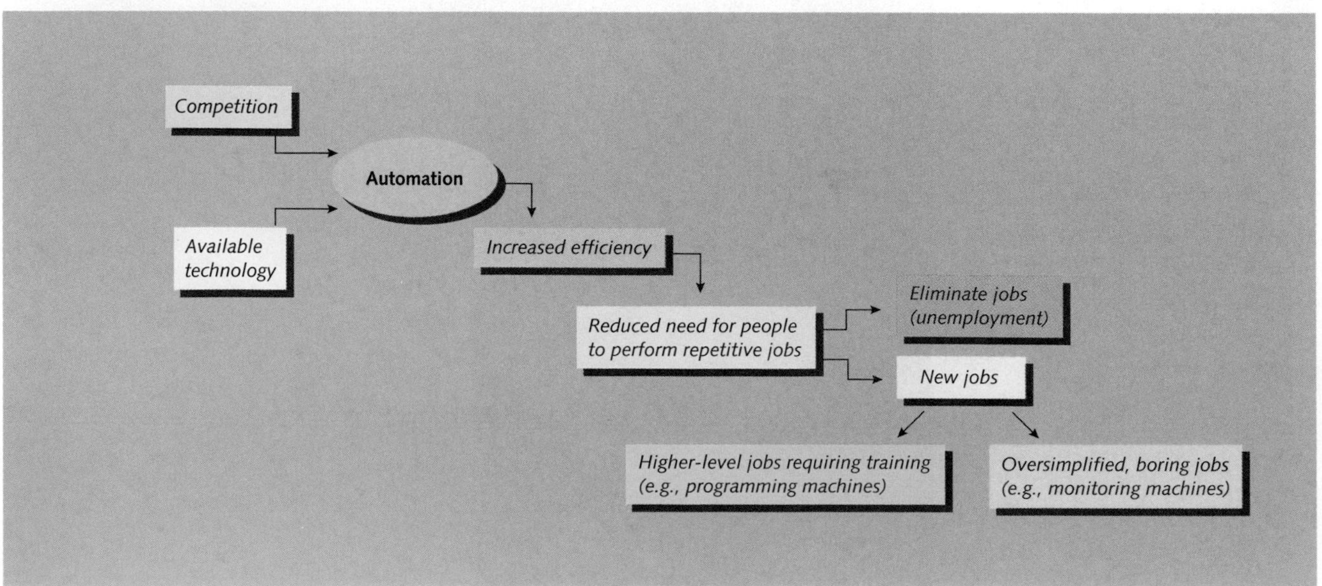

opening the futuristic factory used to manufacture some of its latest models.[86] Chrysler is not alone in this regard. Many other companies also have been working diligently at upgrading their employees' skills, keeping their skills from becoming obsolete.[87] After all, if a company is going to invest millions in equipment, it certainly may be expected to make the needed investment in the people needed to run it. (Thanks to high-tech advances, one area in which people may have to be retrained is in the flow of information between offices. For a closer look at this fast-growing trend, see the Organization of Tomorrow section below.)

THE ORGANIZATION OF TOMORROW

WORKFLOW AUTOMATION: TOWARD THE PAPERLESS OFFICE

Suppose your company is developing a marketing plan for one of its new products. Typically, the marketing manager approves the plan submitted by the person championing the product. This individual then approves the budget for the research. The researchers gather the necessary data from the database, and the product champion writes a first draft. This document is then reviewed by a manager, edited, revised, and rewritten. New data may have to be collected before the proposal is rewritten, and on and on and on the process goes. Through how many steps does the document have to flow before it is finally approved and implemented? Ten, twenty, or even more? And, how long does this process take—and at what cost to the organization? Surely, moving papers from one person's out-box to another's in-box can be very time consuming, especially when the ultimate path a document must travel is a long one—not even including the inevitable delays caused by lost or misdirected documents. In fact, according to some experts, the time spent gathering and transferring paper documents takes as much as *90 percent* of the time needed to complete typical office tasks![88]

Enter **workflow automation**—an advance in automating the flow of information in offices that is beginning to take off. This approach is guided by software that automatically directs the appropriate parts of documents, business forms, and other types of information (typically scanned and stored on optical disks) over computer networks to the terminal of the next most appropriate person.[89] Such systems, are expected to be able to interconnect not only personal computers, but also telephones, copiers, fax machines, printers, and the newly popular hand-held devices known as "personal digital assistants."

Implementing such a system requires that organizations analyze the current paths taken by information and pinpoints bottlenecks and unnecessary procedures that only slow down the flow of information. (This process alone can be very beneficial—and quite an eye-opener!) Then, once new routes for effectively transmitting information between people have been identified, software is installed that automatically sends the document to the right desk regardless of the form its in—be it a digital image of a contract or an electronic mail comment from a customer (see Chapter 9). The basic idea behind workflow automation is quite simple: by substituting a computer network for the mail cart, information can more rapidly flow between the appropriate parties, allowing for more timely and efficient action. For workflow automation to work, not only must information be entered and stored digitally (today's computers can store just about any kind of information, be it sound or pictures), but the system also must be programmed with the correct routing, even if it's a complex decision rule (e.g., if the check is for over $1,000, it must go to Mary for approval, but if it's under $1,000, it can go to Lillian). (For a summary of a hypothetical workflow diagram, see Figure 14-11).

Experts estimate that American corporations are currently spending approximately $710 million per year on workflow automation. About one-third of this amount is for consulting services, and the balance is for software. With a market this large, it is not surprising that it has attracted such industry giants as Microsoft (with its "At Work" package), Xerox (with its "InConcert" package), and Word Perfect (which has incorporated workflow features into its word processing package). Some smaller firms, such as FileNet Corp. of Costa Mesa, California, have been selling turnkey workflow automation systems, complete with workstations and its own "Work-Flo" software.

Aetna Health Plans (a division of Aetna Life Insurance Company) has been among the first companies to jump on the workflow automation bandwagon. According to Mary Schramke, leader of Aetna's workflow automation pilot project, "Installing a workflow system makes you ask: 'What do you really want to do?'" What Aetna wanted to do was simple (at least to describe!): speed up processing of claims. In one Aetna office, one particular task was slashed from twenty-seven steps down to only five. The slowdown was indeed the processing of paper; the mail room only sent claim forms to their next destination after stacks of fifty had accumulated. When you process some 80 million claims annually, you certainly don't need to slow things down any more than necessary!

Industry analysts generally agree that workflow automation will catch on. One writer for *Business Week* says that it is "bound to become ubiquitous," adding that it will "become the backbone of many computer networks."[90] John B. Dykeman, associate publisher of *Managing Office Technology*, wrote in a recent editorial that workflow automation "could significantly influence your future ideas of how traditional office devices can or will be integrated with computer systems."[91] Workflow automation is an advance that takes us one step closer to the paperless office. However, just how soon this vision will come to reality is hard to tell. For today, there's still lots of paper in most offices—more than ever, in fact. Tomorrow, however, is anybody's guess.

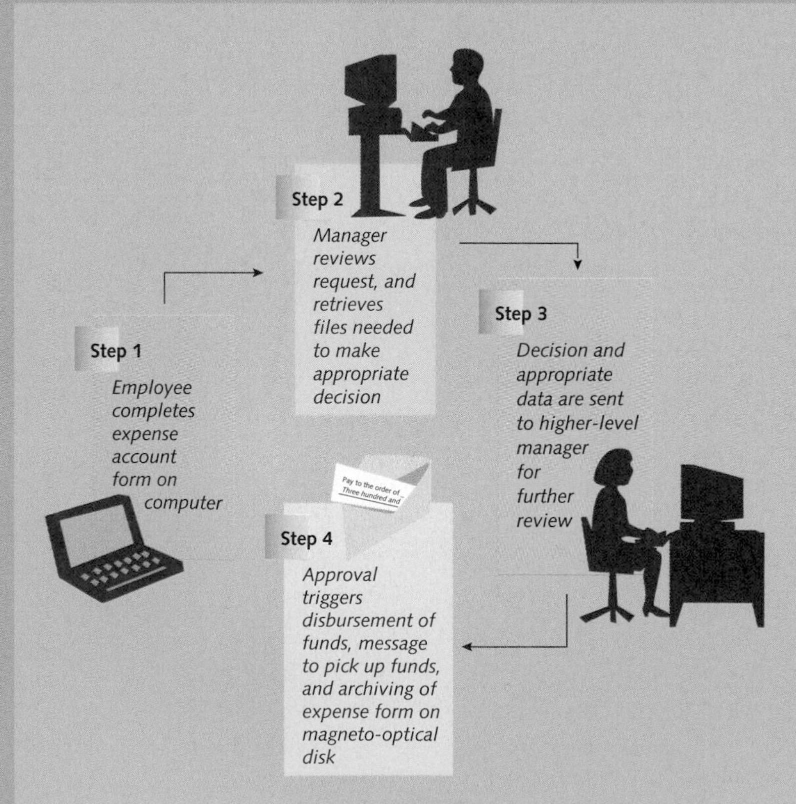
Step 1
Employee completes expense account form on computer
Step 2
Manager reviews request, and retrieves files needed to make appropriate decision
Step 3
Decision and appropriate data are sent to higher-level manager for further review
Step 4
Approval triggers disbursement of funds, message to pick up funds, and archiving of expense form on magneto-optical disk
Pay to the order of
Three hundred and

FIGURE 14-11
WORKFLOW AUTOMATION: A SUMMARY
As information is stored in computers, workflow management systems can automate its movement between people at computerized workstations. The example summarized here involves processing an employee's expense reimbursement request. [Source: Adapted from Verity, 1993; see Note 88.]

USING TECHNOLOGY IN MODERN ORGANIZATIONS

People use technology in various ways while performing many different jobs. In this section of the chapter we will consider several of the latest ways in which technology is being used in organizations today. Specifically, we will focus on three contemporary uses of technology. First, we will describe *assistive technology*—devices that help people with disabilities take advantage of their work skills so they can be fully functioning, productive members of their organizations. Second, we will present a controversial technology that allows company officials to observe—or, some would say, "snoop" on—their employees, a practice known as *computerized performance monitoring*. Finally, we present ways in which computer-based technology—often criticized for being cold and impersonal—is being used to improve and personalize the quality of customer service delivered in today's organizations.

ASSISTIVE TECHNOLOGY: HELPING PEOPLE WITH DISABILITIES WORK PRODUCTIVELY

If you've ever seen public telephones with volume controls, elevator signs with floor markings in Braille, and cutaway curbs on sidewalks, you are already familiar with the fact that things can be done to enable people with various handicaps to function effectively in society. However, these accommodations are just a small part of the picture when it comes to using technology to assist disabled people. In today's organizations, technology is widely used to make it possible for skilled people to perform their jobs although they may be challenged by some form of physical or mental condition. (For examples of technological advances used for these purposes, refer to Table 14-4.) As a result of this technology, it is possible for people who only a few years ago could not have done so to perform mainstream jobs today. Such technology is referred to as **assistive technology**—devices and other solutions that help individuals with physical or mental problems perform the various actions needed to do their jobs.[92]

Beside the fact that it is just "the right thing to do," there are several good reasons why assistive technology is in such widespread use today. For one, the workplace is so competitive that employers simply cannot afford to overlook qualified employees just because adjustments need to be made to the way they do their jobs. According to the Job Accommodation Network, a clearinghouse of information on ways to help people with disabilities, this process need not be expensive. In fact, they claim that about half the accommodations that need to be made cost under $50, and almost one-third are without any cost whatsoever.[93] For example, instead of investing in new plumbing to lower a drinking fountain so a person in a wheelchair could use it, a much cheaper alternative is possible: simply provide a dispenser for drink cups.

A second reason why assistive technology is in such widespread use is because of the simple demographic fact that the workforce is aging and people are living longer.[94] As people get older, even the healthiest are likely to suffer impairments in their hearing, vision, and manual dexterity. If such individuals, who are likely to be highly experienced and knowledgeable, are to leave their jobs, it would likely be prohibitively expensive, and possibly impossible, to replace them. Making the adjustments necessary to help these individuals perform their jobs makes good business sense.

TABLE 14-4

Assistive Technology: Some Examples

Technology can be used to assist people with various disabilities function effectively on the job. Here are examples of devices—some sophisticated and some simple—applied to this purpose.

DEVICE	DESCRIPTION
Telephone handset amplifier	*Mechanism for raising the volume of telephone earpiece, enabling hearing-impaired people to use the telephone.*
Voice-activated computer	*Software that allows people to input words into a computer by speaking. IBM's "Speech Server" series has a 32,000-word vocabulary, and the capacity to enter 70 words per minute.*
Reading machine	*Hardware using simulated speech to read to visually impaired people (such as the portable unit introduced by Xerox's Kurzweil Business Unit).*
Sight devices	*Portable sensory guides and closed-circuit TV monitors with magnification that enable people with visual impairments to navigate their physical environments.*
Mouthpicks	*Stylus-like tools that quadriplegics can use to operate computers.*
Gooseneck telephones	*Adjustable telephone headsets that can be used by people with limited physical dexterity.*

Sources: Tompkins, 1993, see Note 92; Anonymous, 1993, see Note 94.

Another reason—and, for some, the major reason—why technology is being widely used to help people perform their jobs is that they are required to do so by law: specifically, the recently enacted *Americans with Disabilities Act* (*ADA*). According to this law, U.S. employers must make "reasonable accommodations" for disabled people who are otherwise qualified to perform their jobs so long as this can be done without imposing an undue financial burden on the company or causing a direct threat to anyone's safety. As companies attempt to comply with ADA requirements, many new technologies have been developed, including, for wheelchair users, cartop carriers for carrying their wheelchairs, and desktops that are high enough to accommodate them while working.[95] With an eye toward publicizing the latest in assistive technology, a cable-TV network called "America's Disability Channel" headquartered in San Antonio, Texas, has gone on the air.

To help companies comply with the ADA, the federal government of the United States has several initiatives to encourage private companies to develop suitable assistive technologies. For example, the Disabled Access Credit Act gives small businesses a tax credit for investing in ways of meeting ADA requirements. Tax laws also provide credits for companies attempting to make their facilities accessible to people with disabilities, and for hiring new employees with disabilities referred by state employment services.[96]

So intensive have been efforts to use technology to help mainstream disabled employees, that specific new positions have been created—*assistive technology coordinators*, people who help businesses and educational institutions find ways of accommodating individuals with disabilities. Laura Micklus at the Center for Independent Living of Southwestern Connecticut, in Stratford, Connecticut, is one person who holds such a job.[97] Micklus has noted that the same highly automated equipment and computers earlier described as making it easier for able-bodied people to perform their jobs is often the difference between working and not working for people with disabilities. When she says this, Micklus, herself a cerebral palsy patient, knows what she's talking about. She relies on $10,000 worth of computer equipment in her office to retrieve information from a national database of ways people with handicaps can be accommodated on the job. This is not to say that Micklus is desk bound. Making use of still more assistive technologies, she sometimes finds herself traveling to job sites around the country to analyze jobs and recommend modifications or appropriate equipment that can be used to help disabled people perform their jobs. Clearly, Micklus is proof that this can be done!

COMPUTERIZED PERFORMANCE MONITORING: MANAGEMENT BY REMOTE CONTROL

One of the most popular uses of technology in the workplace today comes in the form of using computers to collect, store, analyze, and report information about the work people are doing—a practice known as **computerized performance monitoring (CPM).**[98] (You may recall that we already introduced this topic in the context of social facilitation in Chapter 8.) As this definition implies, CPM refers to a broad range of procedures that enable supervisors to "look in" on employees doing their jobs (see Figure 14-12). CPM makes it possible for employees' work to be observed and quantified—particularly those who work at computer terminals (e.g., phone sales agents, data entry and word processing personnel, airline reservation agents, and telephone operators). Not all CPM systems are the same. In some, employees are monitored all the time as work is carried out; in others, observation occurs only sometimes, although the software keeps a detailed record of their work.[99] Regardless of differences between systems, all make it possible for job performance to be observed in a constant, unblinking fashion.

Within the past decade CPM systems have grown in popularity. Recent estimates are that more than 10 million employees are monitored in over 70,000 companies in the United States, representing an investment in equipment of over $1 billion.[100] As one California vendor of networking software advertises, their CPM system provides a simple solution to supervisors interested in closely watching many employees at once, all from one convenient spot: "Look in on Sue's computer screen . . . In fact, Sue doesn't even know you're there! Hot key again and off you go on your rounds of the company. Viewing one screen after another, helping some, watching others. All from the comfort of your chair."[101] Clearly, CPM changes the basic nature of the supervisor–subordinate relationship.[102]

Not surprisingly, the use of CPM has been the subject of considerable debate.[103] Some have argued that it represents an invasion of employees' privacy, creates an atmosphere of distrust, and can be a source of work-related stress (see Chapter 7).[104] In fact, the U.S. Congress is considering legislation that would require employers to notify employees of their intent to monitor their performance and to somehow signal when monitoring is occurring. Proponents have countered, however, that CPM makes it possible for supervisors to gather more objective information about performance, providing a valuable source of feedback and information useful for planning training programs and workloads.[105]

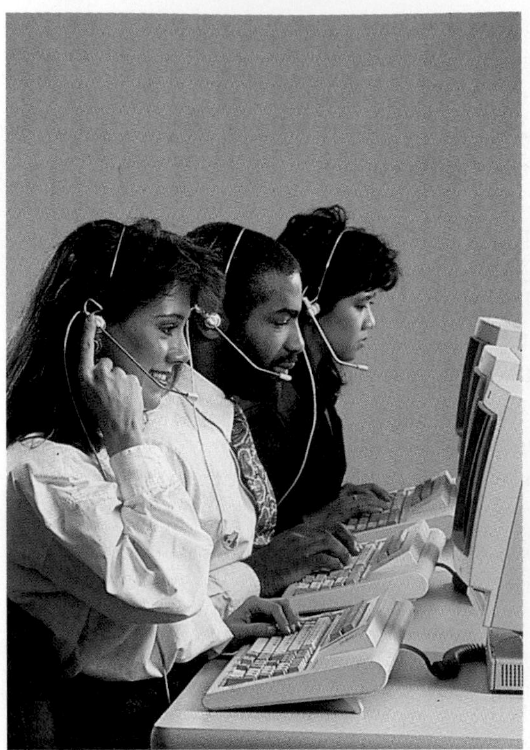

FIGURE 14-12
COMPUTERIZED PERFORMANCE MONITORING: AN INVASION OF PRIVACY?
Computer networks and special software make it possible for supervisors to observe and record the work of employees at computer terminals. Although computerized performance monitoring, *as it is known, can be used to provide valuable developmental feedback to employees, many see it as an unwarranted invasion of privacy.*

What does the scientific evidence have to say about these arguments? Although there has been only limited research on the effects of CPM, what little work has been done has suggested that to some degree *both* perspectives are correct. For example, research comparing monitored and nonmonitored employees found that monitored employees were, in fact, more productive on simple tasks. However, as we described in Chapter 8, monitoring lowers performance on complex tasks. (Both findings are consistent with the idea of social facilitation, discussed in Chapter 8.) However, even if performance on simple tasks increases in response to monitoring, CPM also leads people to experience higher levels of stress and lower levels of job satisfaction.[106] Part of the problem seems to be that working in front of video display terminals all day contributes to feelings of isolation and loneliness, unpleasant conditions that are associated with stress (see Chapter 7).[107]

It is important to note that employees who are monitored with respect to specific aspects of their performance might be expected to work hard to improve those performance measures, even if doing so comes at the expense of other, possibly more important, aspects of performance. For example, Aiello reports an incident in which telephone operators were monitored by supervisors who checked to see that they did not spend longer than twenty-two seconds on each call.[108] The result: operators almost always met the standard—but some, as many as 25 percent, admitted that they did so by "cheating." In instances in which customers required more than twenty-two seconds to help, such as when they had strong accents or hearing impediments, operators simply disconnected such callers so they could be rewarded for meeting their goal. Even those who didn't take such drastic measures lamented that they could not take the time to be as pleasant and friendly as they wanted.

Not only do employees dislike being monitored, evidence also shows that many supervisors dislike the added workload that comes from having to review constantly incoming data about employees' work performance. The problem is that monitoring raises expectations that supervisors will have to "say something" to employees about their performance, holding them to a standard that their busy schedules may not permit.[109] However, when employee performance appears to be unexpectedly poor, supervisors are able to rely on computerized records of performance as the basis for making accurate assessments of the problem.[110] Under such conditions, supervisors will surely benefit from having accurate information at their disposal to help them diagnose the problem at hand.

To summarize, it appears that although there may be some benefits associated with CPM, this particular use of technology has a long way to go before it gains widespread acceptance. By creating a whole new dynamic between superiors and subordinates, CPM—like many other new technologies that have been introduced in the workplace—appears threatening. But will it ever be completely accepted? We suspect that the answer resides in how the technique is used—or abused—in practice. If used as a tool to help improve performance, we believe CPM has a valuable role in organizations. However, if it is misused—such as for close surveillance of nonwork activities, such as bathroom trips—such invasions of privacy are sure to be rejected. In conclusion, it is not necessarily the technology itself that is either useful or harmful in practice, but the way in which people use it.

TECHNOLOGICAL AIDS TO CUSTOMER SERVICE

Have you ever heard someone grumble that the service received today is "not like it was in the good old days"? For the most part, such complaints are well founded. Through the early 1950s, it was not unusual for businesses to provide high levels of courteous, personalized service. You could phone in your order to Mr. Smith's corner store, and his son would deliver your groceries to your table after school, and charge them to your account. You also could go to the corner "service" station, where Gus would pump your gas, clean your windshield, check your oil, and even install a new muffler or set of tires on your car. Today, however, Smith's place more than likely has given way to a huge, twenty-four-hour supermarket, and Gus has been replaced by a pay-at-the-pump, self-serve operation (see Figure 14-13). Experts tell us that the depersonalization of service came about as a result of several forces. The automobile led to suburban sprawl, cities grew, and markets expanded. Increasing competition led to reduced profit margins, and the need to standardize goods and services. The result: Mom's diner surely delivered more personalized service than McDonald's, but given its economic disadvantage (e.g., the higher per-unit cost of producing on a small scale), it simply couldn't afford to compete. As standardization became more feasible than individual attention, personal service became a casualty.

Analyzing this state of affairs, Ives and Mason have pointed out that technology is now being used to revitalize customer service (an interest stimulated in great part to companies' growing concern with improving quality; see Chapter 16).[111] They note that this is occurring in three distinct ways. First, many of today's organizations are employing technology to help them deliver more *personalized service*. Doing so involves noting the individual requirements of each client and delivering service as needed. At Scandinavian Airlines (SAS), for example, this comes in the form of a seat assignment system that allows gate agents the opportunity to reassign passengers to certain seats as needed (e.g., a particularly tall passenger may be reassigned to a seat with greater leg room).[112] Computerized systems are also used to give the most appropriate coupons to shoppers who make certain purchases at their supermarket. Systems are in use in many chains in which in-store coupons

FIGURE 14-13
CUSTOMER SERVICE: OLD AND NEW
Although intense competition has made it economically impractical for companies to offer personal service as they did forty or more years ago, technology has created new ways in which customer service can be revitalized. Although the personal service of yesterday's "full-service" gasoline station (left) has all but vanished, today's self-serve customers enjoy a broad range of new conveniences (right).

are printed on the backs of register receipts (or, in some systems, on separate printers). These coupons are customized to fit the customer's profile of purchases. For example, purchasers of one brand of breakfast cereal may be given a coupon to induce them to try another brand. Or purchasers of peanut butter may be given coupons for products that might go with it, such as bread or jelly. Although these practices are not "personalized" in the same sense as Mr. Smith taking your grocery order and delivering it to your door, they do represent forms of personalization that capitalize on the computer technology available today.

A second way in which technology is being used to help revitalize service is by *augmenting service*. This refers to the practice of providing customers with additional support related to the product or service. How can technology be used to help provide "something extra"? Several companies have been fairly ingenious in this regard. Sometimes, the additional service is small—but quite helpful. For example, Hertz pioneered systems by which rental car customers are guided to their vehicles by signs displaying their names, and hand-held devices that agents use to check-in returned vehicles and print customer receipts on the spot—practices that eliminated check-in and check-out lines. This customer-friendly technology helped Hertz attract considerable business. American Hospital Supply is another company whose business also grew because of the technology they used to help customers. Their strategy was to install terminals in the offices of clients, devices that could be used to order any of 135,000 products directly from the company at any time with just a few simple keystrokes. Both examples represent extra services made available through technology that add to the benefits customers receive from dealing with those companies.

Finally, Ives and Mason note that technology can help by *transforming business*—that is, developing entirely new practices that better satisfy customers' needs. Specifically, today's advanced computer information systems make it possible for customized goods to be made with almost the same efficiency as standardized goods. For example, Benjamin Moore Paints uses a photospectrometer to identify the color of a customer's fabric sample and tells the computer how to match it by appropriately mixing the company's paints. In-store displays also exist today to help Hallmark customers create greeting cards personalized with the name and message specified by the purchaser. Similarly, Warner Brothers has a system in which customers can mail-order music cassettes containing their favorite songs selected from a menu of available titles. As a final example, printing technology has made it possible for magazine publishers to tailor their advertisements and editorials to different readers. As a result, swine farmers in Iowa who subscribe to the *Farm Journal* are sent a somewhat different magazine from that sent to dairy farmers in Vermont. All these examples represent ways in which today's companies are using technology to transform their businesses so as to provide improved customer service.

Although some technology has led to the depersonalization of service, the above examples make it clear that technology also can be used—and, in fact, *is* being used—to vastly improve customer service. While we shouldn't look anytime soon for Mr. Smith to return to his corner grocery, or Gus to return to his service station, we can expect technology to be used to improve customer service in these, and all businesses, in a variety of different forms. (Some companies are bringing new levels of customer service to their clients by arming their salespeople with laptop computers that can tap into their companies' information networks. For a closer look at this process, see the Quest for Quality section on the opposite page.)

THE QUEST FOR QUALITY

LAPTOP COMPUTERS: A KEY TO IMPROVING THE SALES PROCESS

For most, the image of a salesperson is probably not unlike Willy Loman, the lead character in Arthur Miller's classic play "Death of a Salesman," found toting a case of samples from location to location. Today, however, we're more likely to see modern-day Willies carrying their laptop computers instead. Not only do computers make the salesperson's job easier, but they also help them do a better job of providing the services the customer needs.[113]

For example, consider Ascom Timeplex Inc., a telecommunications equipment firm headquartered in Woodcliff Lake, New Jersey. As far as its customers and over 200 salespeople are concerned, the company's location is immaterial. All that matters is that its computer network is only a modem call away. To learn more about the company's history with clients, salespeople can review all the information they want by dialing into the company's database from their computers. Salespeople seated across the desk from clients can look at their Apple PowerBooks and review the latest price lists, the status of previous orders, and other vital information. Then, when agreements have been reached, the same computer is used not only to enter the data, but to double-check it for errors and transmit it to the company's main order center, where it interfaces with yet another computer.

Before making the move to laptops, the sales process at Timeplex was a paper chase, as it is in most companies. According to Peter Cammick, the company's director of sales, it used to take about two weeks to get quotes and proposals typed up and faxed to customers. Now price quotes are typically available in only two hours! Then, once an order was placed it took as long as ten days to process. With the computerized system, not only has processing time been cut to four days, but there are also 25 percent fewer errors. (For a summary comparison of the typical sales process both before and after the use of computers, see Figure 14-14.)

Other companies also use computers in ways that make salespeople more efficient. Representatives of the heavy equipment company John Deere used to spend several days "mining for data" in the company's unfriendly

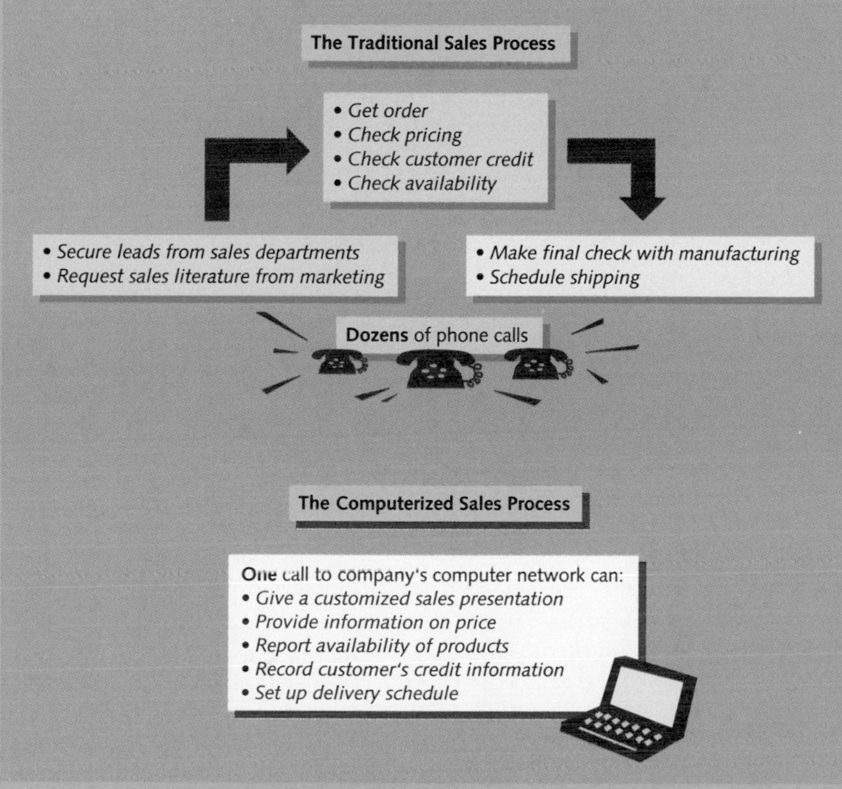

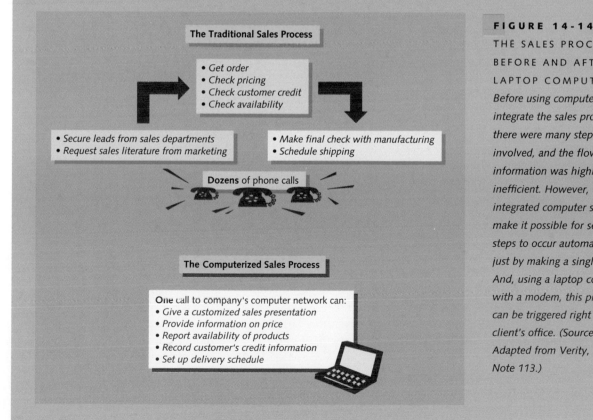

FIGURE 14-14
THE SALES PROCESS: BEFORE AND AFTER LAPTOP COMPUTERS
Before using computers to integrate the sales process, there were many steps involved, and the flow of information was highly inefficient. However, today's integrated computer systems make it possible for several steps to occur automatically just by making a single call. And, using a laptop computer with a modem, this process can be triggered right from the client's office. (Source: Adapted from Verity, 1993; see Note 113.)

mainframe computer to prepare for sales calls. Now, by providing the same information by making a single call from a portable laptop computer to the company's network, salespeople have managed to trim about two days off the process—time that competitors sometimes spent beating Deere to the deal.

Not only do computers improve the quality of the sales process, but also the quality of the service received by customers. For example, CWC Inc., of Mankato, Minnesota, developed a computer graphics system that allows truck manufacturers to work with customers to determine exactly what features they want. As sales reps and customers sit down together, they can look at a computer screen and select from a menu of hardware and color options. Not only do customers get an advance peek at what their rigs will look like, the program also keeps a running tab of the price, making it easy to tailor a package that fits the customer's transportation and financial needs. Then, when the final decisions have been made, the same computer can run through various financing plans as well.

Taken to the extreme, a company will not need a sales office—just a team of salespeople with laptops and a database stored on the home office's main computer. Such *virtual offices*, as they are called, are already a reality for at least one company—Perkin-Elmer Corp., a maker of analytic instruments. Without an office to check into, salespeople are free to live and work wherever they wish, so long as they are only a phone call away.[114] Quite obviously, technology is changing the way salespeople work as well as the quality of the services they can deliver—and, in both cases, for the better.

SUMMARY AND REVIEW

ORGANIZATIONAL CULTURE: ITS BASIC NATURE

Organizational culture is a cognitive framework consisting of attitudes, values, behavioral norms, and expectations shared by organization members. It serves several different functions, including providing members with a sense of identity, generating commitment to the organization's mission, and clarifying and reinforcing standards of behavior. Typically, organizations consist of both a **dominant culture**, reflecting the organization's overall values, and various **subcultures**, separate cultures existing within selected parts of the dominant culture.

THE FORMATION AND MAINTENANCE OF ORGANIZATIONAL CULTURE

The emergence of organizational culture can be traced to several different factors. Among these are the influence of founders, the organization's experiences with the external environment, and contact between various people within the organization. Culture is transmitted via various mechanisms, including *symbols*, *stories*, *jargon*, *ceremonies*, and *statements of principle* (including **codes of ethics**).

ORGANIZATIONAL CULTURE: ITS CONSEQUENCES AND CAPACITY TO CHANGE

Although it is popularly believed that certain types of organizational culture are associated with more successful organizational performance, scientific evidence does not support this claim. However, the voluntary turnover of individuals is related to organizational culture: people remain employed longer in cultures that stress pleasant interpersonal relationships than in those emphasizing hard work. Turnover is also lower among individuals whose personal values more closely match those of the organizations in which they are employed than those for whom personal and organizational values are less closely matched.

Organizational culture is likely to change due to a variety of factors. Among these are: changes in the composition of the workforce (over time, different people bring different values into the organization), mergers and acquisitions (adjustments have to be made to accommodate the "marriage" between companies), and planned change (deliberate decisions to alter the organization's structure or its basic operations).

THE ROLE OF TECHNOLOGY IN ORGANIZATIONS

Technology is the physical and mental processes used to transform inputs into usable outputs. According to Perrow's **matrix of technologies**, four different classes of technology may be identified: *routine technology*, *craft technology*, *engineering technology*, and *nonroutine technology*. Today's organizations frequently rely on the use of such *high-technology* tools as **automation**—the process of using machines to perform tasks that might otherwise be done by people. Not only is automation extremely expensive to employ, but it sometimes also leads to high levels of unemployment. When people remain employed in automated work environments, their work is typically either extremely dull (e.g., monitoring machines that do all the work), or highly challenging and involving a great deal of training (e.g., programming and maintaining the machines). Economic competition is making the shift to automation a reality in a growing number of manufacturing and service organizations.

MODERN USES OF TECHNOLOGY

Technology is used in many different ways in today's organizations. For example, **assistive technology** focuses on the task of helping people with handicaps perform their jobs. Such efforts are stimulated both by law (e.g., the *Americans with Disabilities Act*), and economic forces (e.g., the need to keep qualified employees who happen to be disabled). Technology known as **computerized performance monitoring (CPM)** is used to observe and record the performance of employees, particularly those working at computer terminals. Although this practice may lead to performance improvement, it is also very stress-provoking, and generally disliked by employees. Finally, technology is also frequently used to improve customer service. Computers are being used in various ways to deliver not only more personalized service, but also to add new and improved services to those currently performed.

KEY TERMS

advanced manufacturing technology (AMT): Manufacturing in which the various processes are guided by computers.

assistive technology: Devices and other solutions that help individuals with physical or mental problems perform the various actions needed to do their jobs.

automation: The process of using machines to perform tasks that might otherwise be done by people.

codes of ethics: Explicit statements describing a company's ethical principles and values.

computer-aided design and engineering (CAD/CAE): The processes of using computers to build and simulate the characteristics of products, and to test their effectiveness.

computer-integrated manufacturing (CIM): Manufacturing processes that go beyond *advanced manufacturing technology* by using computers to gather information, and using this information to make decisions about ways in which the manufacturing process needs to be altered.

computerized performance monitoring (CPM): The practice of using computers to collect, store, analyze and report information about the work people are doing.

craft technology: Technology involving highly standardized inputs and outputs, and problems that are difficult to analyze (e.g., cabinet makers and public schools). (See *matrix of technologies*.)

dominant culture: The overall culture of an organization, reflected by core values that are shared throughout the organization.

engineering technology: Technology involving many exceptions in inputs or outputs, and problems that are easy to analyze (e.g., heavy machinery construction and health and fitness clubs). (See *matrix of technologies*.)

high technology: The kind of technology that is electronic in nature, usually relying on the use of microprocessor chips.

industrial robotics (IR): Computer-controlled machines that manipulate materials and perform complex functions.

matrix of technologies: Perrow's system of categorizing technologies based on two dimensions: *exceptions*, the degree to which an organization makes use of standard inputs to turn out standard outputs, and *problems*, the degree to which the situations encountered are either easy or difficult to analyze.

nonroutine technology: Technology involving many exceptions in inputs or outputs, and problems that are difficult to analyze (e.g., research units and psychiatric hospitals). (See *matrix of technologies.*)

organizational culture: A cognitive framework consisting of attitudes, values, behavioral norms, and expectations shared by organization members.

routine technology: Technology involving highly standardized inputs and outputs, and problems that are easy to analyze (e.g., assembly lines and vocational training). (See *matrix of technologies.*)

subcultures: Cultures existing within parts of organizations rather than entirely through them. Members of subcultures share values in addition to the core values of their organization as a whole.

symbols: Material objects that connote meanings extending beyond their intrinsic content.

technology: The physical and mental processes used to transform inputs into usable outputs.

workflow automation: A technique for automating the flow of information in offices using software to automatically guide data and information to the most appropriate individual.

QUESTIONS FOR DISCUSSION

1. Characterize the culture of any organization with which you may be familiar by describing the core characteristics collectively valued by its members.
2. Argue for or against the following statement: "Because organizations consist of so many different kinds of people, they are likely to have more than one culture."
3. Suppose you are starting a new company. Describe how you might either intentionally or unintentionally affect its culture.
4. Long after the founder of a company has left, his or her influence on organizational culture may still be felt. How does this work? Through what means are cultural values transmitted in organizations?
5. Describe the kinds of events that might be responsible for the changing of organizational culture. Explain why these events are likely to be so influential.
6. Using Perrow's system for classifying technology, categorize the types of technology employed by the major businesses closest to where you live.
7. It may be said that automation may lead to unemployment on the one hand, and new opportunities for employment, on the other. Explain how this can be.
8. Explain various ways technology can be used to improve: (a) work opportunities for people with physical handicaps, and (b) the quality of customer service delivered.
9. Do you think the practice of computerized performance monitoring (CPM) is ethical? Why or why not? What benefits and costs may be expected from using CPM?

QUALITY SUPPORTED BY TECHNOLOGY AND CULTURE

One of the oldest manufacturing industries in the United States—the world, in fact—is the making of textiles for use in clothing and home furnishing and decoration. The mills that once populated New England towns, however, have moved to areas such as the Carolinas and more recently have been relocated abroad to countries such as Mexico and Taiwan. An Italian company, Loro Piana Textiles, is attempting to reverse this trend with their purchase and rehabilitation of the Warren of Stafford mill in Stafford, Connecticut.

Loro Piana Textiles is a family-owned and -operated Italian company in business for 180 years as a maker of high-quality, luxury textile products. Four generations of legendary weavers have created a reputation for Loro Piana as a maker of extremely high-quality luxury woolens and cashmere. The company has sold its products in the United States for many years, but has only recently begun production here. The reason for establishing a manufacturing facility in Connecticut is to provide Loro Piana customers in the United States with the best-quality, best-value woven materials.

To achieve the level of quality expected by the owners and managers of this firm, the mill where the textiles are manufactured underwent a major renovation. Not only were changes made to the plant's architecture, as well as ventilation and communication systems, but complete new technology was installed by which to make the products. This technology relies heavily on computers as well as state-of-the-art machinery for spinning fibers from raw materials.

The company owners were aware of the fact that the former mill employees might not be accustomed to their way of doing things. As a result, they invested heavily in a training program to teach their personnel how to use the equipment. For master weavers, this involved spending up to six months at the facility in Italy. Others were trained locally for a period of two months.

The owners of Loro Piana also recognized that the use of technology was not the only thing with which employees in the mill would have to become familiar. They also would have to learn to understand and appreciate the Loro Piana culture that places a premium on quality. In addition, the owners were aware of the concern in the community of Stafford that people were fearful of being displaced by an Italian way of management. The owners of the firm tried to counter this fear with a focus on their passion for their product. They hoped that by showing their new employees how much they cared for quality that their values would be contagious. They also hoped that they could convince their new personnel that by doing things the Loro Piana way that the firm would grow and that new jobs would be created.[1]

The Loro Piana culture is somewhat quiet, understated, and elegant (much like the products). This works well for the company because of its niche in the textile industry and the fact that it only has two manufacturing facilities (the one in Italy and the other in Connecticut), employing fewer than 600 people.

As you might expect, larger firms with more diverse locations in different markets may have other means of communicating their values to their employees. For example, Wal-Mart—that most quintessential of American companies—is anything but quiet in reinforcing its corporate values and culture.

The most distinguishing feature of the Wal-Mart culture is its emphasis on the worth of its employees—a value that is communicated from Day 1 of their employment. On the top of every page of the employee manual (which is called the *Associates Handbook*) appears a smiling face and the greeting "We're glad you're here." At the bottom of each page, employees are reminded that "Our PEOPLE make the difference."[2] Reminders such as these also appear in the workplace plastered on the walls in the employee break rooms and over the front doors of the stores. All meetings end with the Wal-Mart cheer ("Give me a "W," give me an "A," etc.). Associates' concerns and complaints are voiced annually at a grassroots meeting where people are specifically gathered to share ideas. There is also an open-door policy so that any employee can go to their boss (who is known as a "coach") or even, if they so desire, to corporate headquarters if they "are not happy with what they are getting and what is going on in the store."[3]

The other main cultural value that the company emphasizes is customer satisfaction. In fact, Wal-Mart is so well known for this that their customer service is legendary. When a shopper asked a manager about a product that the store did not carry (it was only sold on television), the manager ordered the item and had it sent to the person's home as a gesture of goodwill.[4] Just as there is a Wal-Mart cheer, there is also a pledge "to greet every customer within ten feet, so help me, Sam."[5]

In order to administer an empire that stretches from coast to coast, including over 2,000 stores and close to 400,000 employees, the managers at Wal-Mart rely on the latest in technology. Regional vice presidents use the company's fifteen aircraft to fly all over their territories, typically visiting twelve stores in any given week. A television satellite system links all the stores to headquarters so that training programs, store data, and other information can be shared virtually instantaneously. Important messages from the weekly top management meeting held at headquarters in Bentonville, Arkansas, can be placed on videotape and then distributed throughout the country to share ideas with store personnel. Similarly, voice mail and electronic mail are used to communicate with people throughout the far-flung empire of Wal-Mart.

Although Loro Piana and Wal-Mart are about as different as can be in terms of their origins, histories, markets, and size, they both share a central concern with their employees and their customers. Both companies emphasize training their employees so that they can provide the best-quality service or products available. Similarly, they both respect their customers and try to please them by providing products and services that they desire. Finally, both firms rely on the latest in technology to accomplish their mission of customer satisfaction.

QUESTIONS FOR DISCUSSION

1. Do you think that the cultures at Loro Piana and Wal-Mart will be any different in the future when newer technology replaces that which is currently available? Support your response.
2. In what ways might the cultures at Wal-Mart and Loro Piana differ as a result of the different countries in which they were founded?
3. Do you suspect that the company culture at the Loro Piana factory in Connecticut is different from that at the facility in Italy? Do you think that the Wal-Mart culture differs across regions of the United States? Explain your answers.
4. How is corporate culture transmitted at Loro Piana and Wal-Mart? Do you think one culture is "stronger" than the other? Why?

EXPERIENCING ORGANIZATIONAL BEHAVIOR

Assessing Organizational Culture

It is often difficult to recognize the culture of an organization without carefully assessing it. Typically, this is done by administering a questionnaire to large numbers of people working within an organization, and then averaging together all their answers. This simple questionnaire is designed to assess only a single aspect of culture—concern for people. More complex questionnaires would address several different aspects of organizational culture.

PROCEDURE

Because it may be impractical for you to distribute a questionnaire in the organization in which you work, you can begin to think about the culture of your organization by completing the following questionnaire yourself. Respond to each question by using the following rating scale: 1 = strongly disagree, 2 = disagree, 3 = neither agree nor disagree, 4 = agree, 5 = strongly agree.

_____ 1. My boss is concerned about how I feel about my work.

_____ 2. The people I work with are truly interested in my ideas about things.

_____ 3. We believe in giving the best possible service to our customers.

_____ 4. My co-workers are likely to give me a hand when I need it.

_____ 5. Whenever possible, we get together to socialize outside the job.

_____ 6. My boss does not misrepresent things when talking to us.

_____ 7. The suggestions I make are taken seriously.

_____ 8. When one of us has a birthday, the others all pitch in for a gift.

_____ 9. Top management treats us with dignity and respect.

_____ 10. When I'm having trouble with a job, my boss is likely to help without making me feel bad.

To score yourself, add up your answers. They will range between 10 to 50. The higher they are (40 or above), the more you believe the culture of your organization values concern for the well-being of people. Lower scores (20 or below) reflect less of a concern for people permeating the culture of your organization.

POINTS TO CONSIDER

1. Your scores represent *your own* perceptions of your organization's culture. How do you think others would complete the questionnaire? Would your responses be typical or atypical? Why?
2. Do you think this questionnaire did a good job of measuring concern for people as an element of your organization's culture? How might it be changed to do a better job? In particular, what additional items might need to be added to reflect the unique nature of your particular organization?
3. Because this questionnaire measured only a single aspect of culture, it is not complete. What additional aspects of culture may be assessed? What would questions look like that could be used to measure perceptions of these other aspects of culture?
4. What did this questionnaire tell you about your organization's culture that you didn't realize before completing it?
5. How do you think your organization's culture, as measured by this questionnaire, compares to the cultures of other organizations? How do the cultures of the organizations rated by your classmates compare to yours? Why do you think they may be different?
6. If you were to complete this questionnaire by thinking of your *ideal* organization, how would it differ from the way you just completed it here?

CHAPTER OUTLINE

SPECIAL SECTIONS

FIFTEEN

ORGANIZATIONAL STRUCTURE AND DESIGN

LEARNING OBJECTIVES

After reading this chapter, you should be able to

1. *Explain the basic characteristics of organizational structure revealed in an organization chart (hierarchy of authority, division of labor, span of control, line versus staff, and decentralization).*
2. *Describe different approaches to departmentalization—functional organizations, product organizations, and matrix organizations.*
3. *Distinguish between classical and neoclassical approaches to organizational design.*
4. *Explain how the contemporary approach to organizational design differs from the classical and neoclassical approaches.*
5. *Describe how an organization's design is influenced by the environment within which it operates.*
6. *Distinguish between mechanistic organizations and organic organizations, and describe the conditions under which each is most appropriate.*
7. *Describe the five organizational forms identified by Mintzberg: simple structure, machine bureaucracy, professional bureaucracy, divisional structure, and adhocracy.*
8. *Characterize two forms of intraorganizational design—conglomerates and joint ventures.*
9. *Describe the relationship between organizational design and structure identified in the Woodward studies and the Aston studies.*
10. *Explain the implications of interdependence on organizational structure.*

The difference between "structure" and "stricture" is "I."

Marlene Solomon
Publisher, Magna Magazine
Sales meeting, February 17, 1988

Hierarchies remain; our belief in their efficacy does not.

John Naisbitt
Chairman, Naisbitt Group
Megatrends *(Warner, 1984)*

PREVIEW CASE

Johnson & Johnson: Separate Companies Under One Umbrella

Band-Aid bandages, Johnson's Baby Oil, Mylanta, Reach toothbrushes, Retin-A acne cream, and Tylenol are all well-known products found in medicine cabinets around the world. Chances are good that you know them all. What you might not know is that all these and many other products come from the same company—Johnson & Johnson (J&J). More precisely, they come from any of 166 companies belonging to J&J.

Starting in the 1930s, under the guidance of longtime chairman and son of one of the co-founders, Robert Wood Johnson, J&J went out of its way to keep the various businesses independent of each other. Believing that the companies would be more manageable and more responsive to their markets if they remained smaller, self-governing units, Johnson resisted pressures to merge them, fearing an enormous bureaucracy. According to J&J's chief executive, Ralph S. Larsen, this approach helps create a sense of ownership and responsibility.

At the same time, Larsen realizes that these benefits must be weighed against the costs—namely, excessive expenses due to redundancies. For example, at 41 percent of sales, J&J's overhead is considerably greater than its competitors Merck & Co. and Bristol-Meyers Squib Co., whose overhead figures run no more than 30 percent of sales. Another cost comes in the area of customer service. Large retailers, such as Wal-Mart and Kmart are increasingly interested in streamlining their contacts with suppliers, and are growing impatient with sales calls from dozens of different J&J companies.

Ralph S. Larsen, CEO of Johnson & Johnson

To meet these realities, J&J is taking measures to centralize some of its operations. For example, under Larsen's guidance, J&J has been pooling various administrative functions, such as payroll and benefits processing, computer services, purchasing, and accounts payable. So too are companies being merged—creating, for example, Ortho-McNeil Pharmaceuticals, a new drug company formed from two formerly separate companies. An innovation, code-named "Pathfinder," united customer service and credit functions that used to reside in four different departments in various companies. Now a single phone call can handle all these needs. Streamlining J&J operations meant trimming the workforce by 3,000 in 1993, leading to an annual savings of $100 million.

Not all J&J insiders have agreed with Larsen's consolidation plans. In fact, one top executive, William C. Egan, III, quit J&J after seventeen years because he so strongly disagreed with Larsen's approach. The straw that broke the camel's back in this case was the decision to merge the Baby Products Company with several others to form the Johnson & Johnson Consumer Products Company. (J&J also has many companies specializing in medical and surgical supplies, such as sutures and anesthesia drugs.) What bothered Egan was that the decentralization he came to know at J&J was being dismantled.

Larsen believes he is simply righting an imbalance in J&J's corporate structure. For example, considering only the professional segment of the company's European business, J&J had twenty-eight separate units, which he has recently pared down to eighteen. Allaying the fears of those worried he will take things too far, Larsen cautions, "We will never give up the principle of decentralization, which is to give our operating executives ownership of a business." Indeed, things continue to work this way at J&J, where business strategy flows not from the top down, but from the bottom up—that is, initiatives come from the individual companies themselves, and are not set by executives in some distant corporate headquarters. In fact, although J&J employs some 84,000 people worldwide (including 40,000 in the United States), only 1,000 work at the company's headquarters in New Brunswick, New Jersey.

Larsen likens his job to an orchestra conductor. He gives the players direction while assuring them creative freedom to use their talents. And given the company's average annual profit gains—19 percent since 1980, including recent annual earnings of over $1.5 billion—there's no doubt that he has J&J making beautiful financial music.

As this case illustrates, J&J has been making some changes in the way it is organized. Traditionally a group of independently operating companies, pressures to eliminate waste and duplication has forced J&J officials to combine some basic business functions so as to cut costs to remain competitive. But not all recognize the wisdom behind such a move; critics have countered that smaller companies can function more effectively. Which side is right? Posing the question more generally, how should companies organize themselves into separate units, such as departments or divisions, so as to be most effective? This question is a venerable one in the world of business—and, as we shall see, a very important one.

OB researchers and theorists have provided considerable insight into the matter by studying what is called **organizational structure**—the way individuals and groups are arranged with respect to the tasks they perform—and **organizational design—**the process of coordinating these structural elements in the most effective manner. As you probably suspect, finding the best way to structure and design organizations is not a simple matter. However, because understanding the structure and design of organizations is essential to fully appreciate their functioning, organizational scientists have devoted considerable energy to this topic. We will describe these efforts in this chapter.

To begin, we will identify the basic building blocks of organizations, which can be identified by the *organizational chart,* a useful pictorial way of depicting key features of organizational structure. Following this, we will examine how these structural elements can be most effectively combined into productive organizational designs. Finally, we will discuss the role of technology as a cause—and a consequence—of organizational design. In so doing, we will be highlighting some basic facts regarding the role of the environment on organizational design.

ORGANIZATIONAL STRUCTURE: THE BASIC DIMENSIONS OF ORGANIZATIONS

Think about how a simple house is constructed. It is composed of a wooden frame positioned atop a concrete slab covered by a roof and siding materials. Within this basic structure are separate systems operating to provide electricity, water, and telephone services. Similarly, the structure of the human body is composed of a skeleton surrounded by various systems of organs, muscle, and tissue serving bodily functions such as respiration, digestion, and the like. Although you may not have thought about it much, we also can identify the structure of an organization in a similar fashion.

Consider, for example, the college or university you attend. It is probably composed of various groupings of people and departments working together to serve special functions. Individuals and groups are dedicated to tasks such as teaching, providing financial services, maintaining the physical facilities, and so on. Of course, within each group even more distinctions can be found among the jobs people perform. For example, it's unlikely that the instructor for your organizational behavior course is also teaching seventeenth-century French literature. You also can distinguish between the various tasks and functions people perform in other organizations. In other words, an organization is not a haphazard collection of people, but a meaningful combination of groups and individuals working together purposefully to meet the goals of the organization.[1] The term **organizational structure** refers to *the formal configuration between individuals and groups with respect to the allocation of tasks, responsibilities, and authority within organizations.*[2]

Strictly speaking, one cannot see the structure of an organization; it is an abstract concept. However, the connections between various clusters of functions of which an organization is composed can be represented in the form of a diagram known as an **organizational chart**. In other words, an organizational chart can be considered a representation of an organization's internal structure (see Figure 15-1). As you might imagine, organizational charts may be recognized as useful tools for avoiding confusion within organizations regarding how various tasks or functions are interrelated. By carefully studying organizational charts, we can learn

"Clearly, someone's not holding up his end."

FIGURE 15-1
THE ORGANIZATIONAL CHART: A VALUABLE GUIDE TO ORGANIZATIONAL STRUCTURE
Organizational charts provide useful information about the interrelationships between various organizational units and the basic structural elements of organizations. (Source: Copyright © 1992 by Nick Downes; from Harvard Business Review.*)*

about some of the basic elements of organizational structure. With this in mind, we will now turn our attention to the five basic dimensions of organizational structure that can be revealed by organizational charts.

ORGANIZATIONAL CHARTS: WHAT DO THEY REVEAL ABOUT ORGANIZATIONAL STRUCTURE?

Organizational charts provide information about the various tasks performed within an organization and the formal lines of authority between them. For example, look at the chart depicting part of a hypothetical manufacturing organization shown in Figure 15-2. Each box represents a specific job, and the lines connecting them reflect the formally prescribed lines of communication between the individuals performing those jobs (see Chapter 9). To specialists in organizational structure, however, such diagrams reveal a great deal more.

HIERARCHY OF AUTHORITY: UP AND DOWN THE ORGANIZATIONAL LADDER

In particular, the organizational chart also provides information about who reports to whom—what is known as **hierarchy of authority**. The diagram reveals which particular lower-level employees are required to report to which particular individuals immediately above them in the organizational hierarchy. In our hypothetical example in Figure 15-2, the various regional sales managers (at the bottom

FIGURE 15-2
ORGANIZATIONAL CHART OF A HYPOTHETICAL MANUFACTURING FIRM
An organizational chart, such as this one, identifies pictorially the various functions performed within an organization and the lines of authority between people performing those functions.

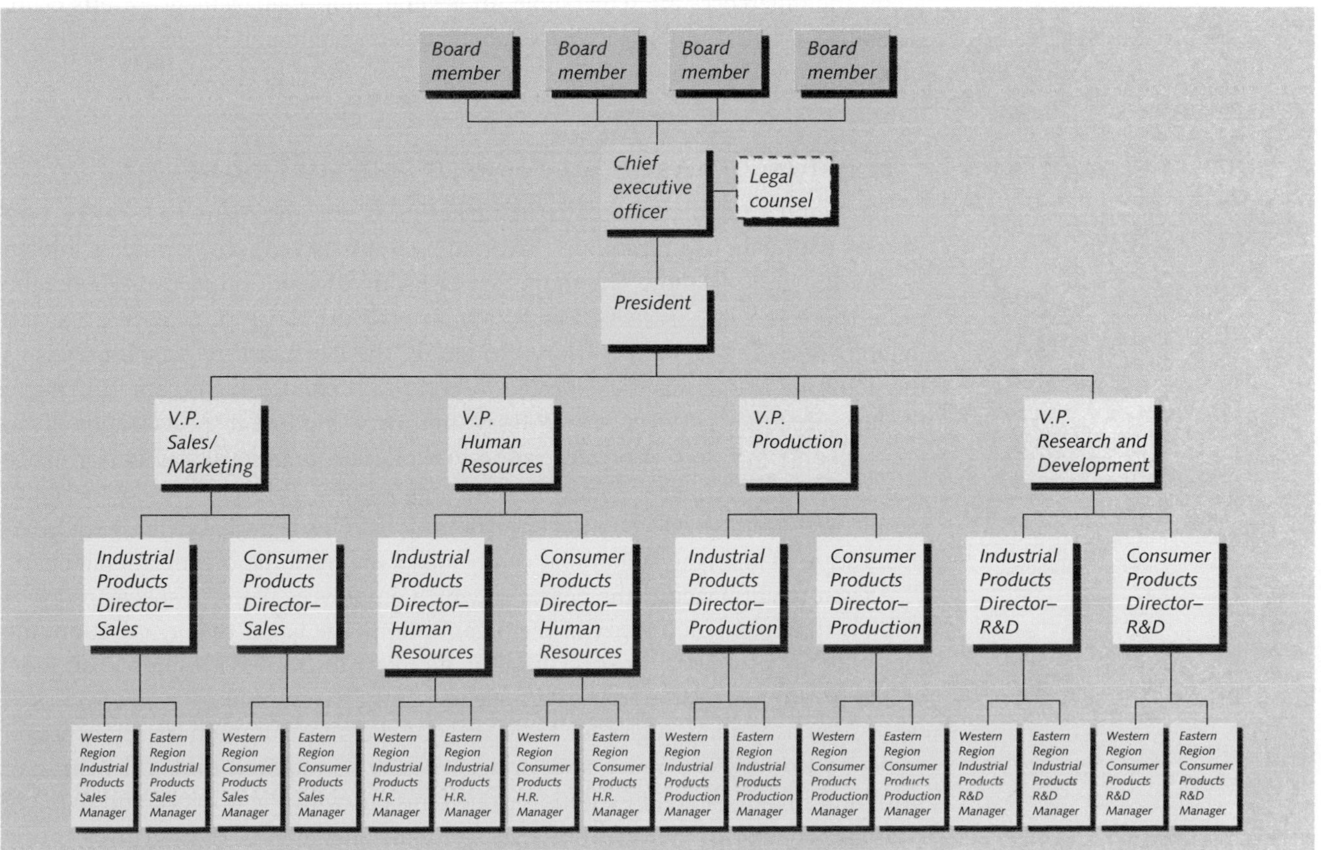

of the hierarchy and the bottom of the diagram) report to their respective regional sales directors, who report to the vice president of sales, who reports to the president, who reports to the chief executive officer, who reports to the members of the board of directors. As we trace these reporting relationships, we work our way up the organization's hierarchy. In this example, only six levels are identified (although there are likely to be even more layers of hierarchy at lower ranks). Organizations may have many levels, in which case their structure is considered *tall*, or only a few, in which case their structure is considered *flat*.

In recent years, a great deal has appeared in the news about organizations restructuring their workforces by flattening them out.[3] Although it has not been uncommon for large companies to lay off people in low-level assembly-line jobs, these days middle managers and executives, long believed to be secure in their positions, find themselves unemployed as companies "downsize," "rightsize," "delayer," or "retrench" by eliminating entire layers of organizational structure (we will discuss this trend, and its impact, in more detail in Chapter 16).[4] In fact, it has been estimated that during the 1980s one-quarter of middle-management jobs were eliminated in American companies.[5] In 1990 alone, nearly one million managers of American companies with annual salaries over $40,000 lost their jobs due to the flattening of organizational hierarchies.[6] And the trend continues today.

The underlying assumption behind all these changes is that fewer layers reduce waste and enable people to make better decisions (by moving them closer to the problems at hand), thereby leading to greater profitability. Consider an example from the auto industry. Whereas Ford has seventeen layers of management between its CEO and its employees on the factory floor, and GM has as many as twenty-two, the more profitable Toyota has only seven.[7] Although this is hardly conclusive evidence of the benefits of reducing the size of an organizational hierarchy, the differences are remarkable. In general, most management experts claim that although hierarchy is necessary, too many layers of hierarchy can be hazardous to a company's bottom line.[8]

DIVISION OF LABOR: CARVING UP THE JOBS DONE

The standard organizational chart makes clear that the many tasks to be performed within an organization are divided into specialized jobs, a process known as the **division of labor**. The more that tasks are divided into separate jobs, the more those jobs are *specialized* and the narrower the range of activities that job incumbents are required to perform. In theory, the fewer tasks a person performs, the better he or she may be expected to perform them, freeing others to perform the tasks that they perform best. (We say "in theory" because if specialization is too great, people may lose their motivation to work at a high level and performance may suffer; see Chapter 4.) Taken together, an entire organization is composed of people performing a collection of specialized jobs. This is probably the most obvious feature of an organization that can be observed from the organizational chart.

As you might imagine, the degree to which employees perform specialized jobs is likely to depend on the size of the organization. The larger the organization, the more the opportunities for specialization are likely to exist. For example, an individual working in a large advertising agency may get to specialize in a very narrow field, such as writing jingles for radio and TV spots for automobiles. By contrast, someone working at a much smaller agency may be required to do all writing of print and broadcast ads in addition to helping out with the artwork and meeting with the clients. Obviously, the larger company might be expected to reap the benefits of efficiently using the talents of employees (a natural result of an extensive division of labor). As companies downsize, however, many managerial jobs become less specialized. For example, at General Electric, quite a few middle-management positions have been eliminated in recent years. As a consequence, the remaining managers must perform a wider variety of jobs, making their own jobs less specialized.[9] You can see this relationship in our summary in Table 15-1.

SPAN OF CONTROL: BREADTH OF RESPONSIBILITY

Over how many individuals should a manager have responsibility? The earliest management theorists and practitioners alike (even the Roman legions) addressed this question.[10] When you look at an organizational chart, the number of people formally required to report to each individual manager is immediately clear. This number constitutes what is known as a manager's **span of control**. Those responsible for many individuals are said to have a *wide* span of control, whereas those responsible for fewer are said to have a *narrow* span of control. In our organizational chart (Figure 15-2), the CEO is responsible for only the actions of the president, giving this individual a narrower span of control than the president himself or herself, who has a span of control of four individuals. Sometimes, when organization leaders are concerned that they do not have enough control over lower-level employees, they restructure their organizations so that managers have responsibility over smaller numbers of subordinates. This is the case at Canada's largest bank, Royal Bank, where a team of top managers recently recommended that area managers reduce the number of branches under their control to between seven and twelve.[11]

When a manager's span of control is wide, the organization itself tends to have a flat hierarchy. In contrast, when a manager's span of control is narrow, the organization itself tends to have a tall hierarchy. This is demonstrated in Figure 15-3. The diagram at the top shows a *tall* organization—one in which there are many layers in the hierarchy, and the span of control is relatively narrow (i.e., the number of people supervised is low). In contrast, the diagram at the bottom of Figure 15-3 shows a *flat* organization—one in which there are only a few levels in the hierarchy, and the span of control is relatively wide. Note that both organizations depicted here have the same number of positions, but these are arranged differently.

The organizational chart may not reflect perfectly a manager's actual span of control. Other factors not immediately forthcoming from the chart itself may be involved. For example, managers may have additional responsibilities that do not appear on the chart—notably, assignments on various committees. Moreover, some subordinates (e.g., new people to the job) might require more attention than others. Also, the degree of supervisory control needed may increase (e.g., when jobs

TABLE 15-1

Division of Labor: A Summary

Low and high levels of division of labor can be characterized with respect to the dimensions shown here.

DIMENSION	DIVISION OF LABOR: LOW	HIGH
Degree of specialization	*General tasks*	*Highly specialized tasks*
Typical organizational size	*Small*	*Large*
Economic efficiency	*Inefficient*	*Highly efficient*

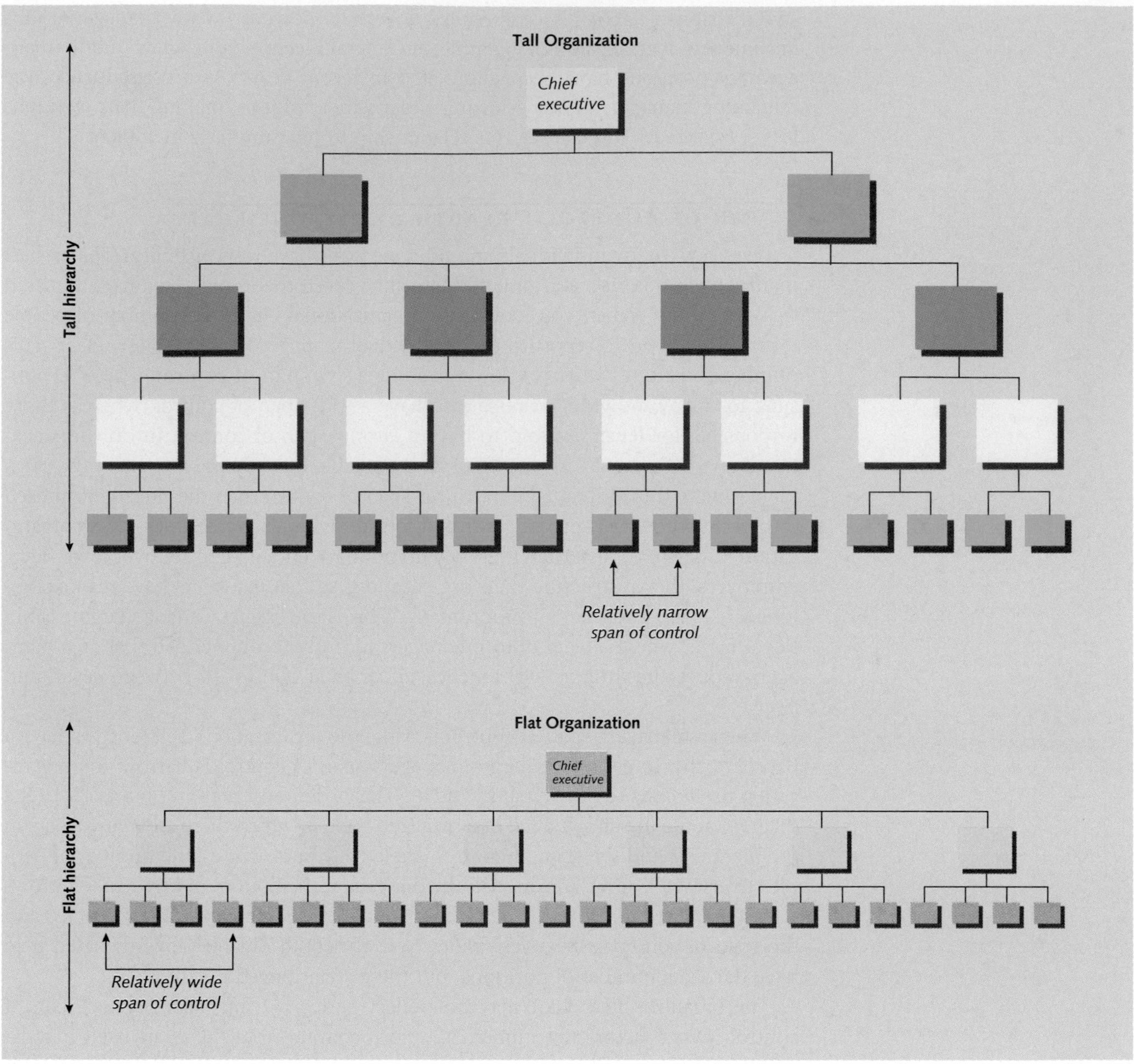

FIGURE 15-3

TALL VERSUS FLAT ORGANIZATIONS: A COMPARISON

In tall organizations, the hierarchy has many layers and managers have a narrow span of control (i.e., they are responsible for few subordinates). However, in flat organization the hierarchy has few layers and managers have a wide span of control (i.e., they are responsible for many subordinates). Each of the organizations depicted here have thirty-one members, although each one is structured differently.

change), or decrease (e.g., when subordinates become more proficient). In fact, it is not readily possible to specify the "ideal" span of control that should be sought. Instead, it makes better sense to consider what form of organization is best suited to various purposes. For example, because supervisors in a military unit must have tight control over subordinates and get them to respond quickly and precisely, a narrow span of control is likely to be effective. As a result, military organizations tend to be extremely tall. In contrast, people working in a research and development lab must have an open exchange of ideas and typically require little managerial guidance to be successful. Units of this type tend to have very flat structures.

LINE VERSUS STAFF POSITIONS: DECISION MAKERS VERSUS ADVISERS

The organizational chart shown in Figure 15-2 reveals an additional distinction that deserves to be highlighted—that between **line positions** and **staff positions**. People occupying *line positions* (e.g., the various vice presidents and managers) have decision-making power. However, the individual shown in the dotted box—the legal counsel—cannot make decisions, but provides advice and recommendations to be used by the line managers. Such individuals are said to hold *staff positions*. For example, the legal counsel may help corporate officials decide whether a certain product name can be used without infringing on copyright restrictions. However, he or she will only make recommendations, but will not make any key decisions. In many of today's organizations, human resources managers may be seen as occupying staff positions because they may provide specialized services regarding testing and interviewing procedures as well as information about the latest laws on personnel discrimination. However, the ultimate decisions on personnel selection might be made by more senior managers in specialized areas—that is, staff managers.

Differences between line and staff personnel are not unusual. Such differences may be conflict arousing, or even may be used to create intentional sources of conflict. For example, when Harold Green was the CEO of ITT Corporation, staff specialists in the areas of planning and strategy were regularly brought in from headquarters to challenge the decisions made by line managers in an attempt to "keep them on their toes."[12] Sociologists have noted that staff managers tend to be younger, better educated, and more committed to their fields than to the organizations employing them.[13] Line managers might feel more committed to their organizations not only because of the greater opportunities they have to exercise decisions, but also because they are more likely to perceive themselves as part of a company rather than as an independent specialist (whose identity lies primarily within his or her specialty area).

DECENTRALIZATION: DELEGATING POWER DOWNWARD

During the first half of the twentieth century, as companies grew larger and larger, they shifted power and authority into the hands of a few upper-echelon administrators—executives whose decisions influenced the many people below them in the organizational hierarchy. In fact, it was during the 1920s that Alfred P. Sloan, Jr., then the president of General Motors, introduced the notion of a "central office," the place where a few individuals made policy decisions for the entire company.[14] As part of Sloan's plan, decisions regarding the day-to-day operation of the company were pushed lower and lower down the organizational hierarchy, allowing those individuals who were most affected to make the decisions. This process of delegating power from higher to lower levels within organizations is known as **decentralization**. It is the opposite, of course, of *centralization*, the tendency for just a few powerful individuals or groups to hold most of the decision-making power (see Chapter 10).

Recent years have seen a marked trend toward greater decentralization. As a result, organizational charts might show fewer staff positions, as decision-making authority is pushed farther down the hierarchy. Many organizations have moved toward decentralization to promote managerial efficiency and to improve employee satisfaction (the result of giving people greater opportunities to take responsibility for their own actions). For example, in recent years, thousands of staff jobs have been eliminated at companies such as 3M, Eastman Kodak, AT&T, and GE as these companies have decentralized.[15]

Decentralization is not always an ideal step for organizations to take. In fact, for some types of jobs, it actually may be a serious hindrance to productivity. Consider production-oriented positions, such as assembly-line jobs. In a classic study, Lawrence and Lorsh found that decentralization improved the performance on some jobs—notably, the work of employees in a research lab—but interfered with the performance of people performing more routine, assembly-line jobs.[16] These findings make sense once you consider that people working in research and development positions are likely to enjoy the autonomy to make decisions that decentralization allows, whereas people working on production jobs are likely to be less interested in taking responsibility for decisions and may enjoy not having to take such responsibility (as noted in Chapter 4). With this in mind, many of today's companies heavily involved in research and development—including parts of Hewlett-Packard, Intel Corporation, Philips Electronics, and AT&T's Bell Laboratories—have shifted to more decentralized designs.[17,18]

In contrast, under some conditions, such as when only a few individuals are in a position to judge what's best for the company, highly centralized authority makes the most sense. For instance, at Delta Airlines, CEO Ronald W. Allen must personally approve every expenditure over $5,000 (except jet fuel).[19] By so doing, he can very carefully monitor the company's expenses and keep it afloat during difficult times. Despite the possible benefits likely to result from relieving Allen of these chores, he believes that it is necessary to tightly enforce the decisions made at times when the margin for error is small. To conclude, although the potential exists to derive considerable benefits from decentralization, the process should be avoided under certain conditions (see the summary in Table 15-2).

The five elements of structure described thus far—hierarchy of authority, division of labor, span of control, line versus staff positions, and decentralization—are the building blocks of organizational structure. They represent key dimensions along which organizations differ.

APPROACHES TO DEPARTMENTALIZATION: VARIOUS WAYS OF STRUCTURING ORGANIZATIONS

Thus far, we have been talking about "the" organizational chart of an organization. Typically, such charts, like the one shown in Figure 15-2, divide an organiza-

TABLE 15-2

Decentralization: Benefits When Low and When High

Various benefits are associated with low decentralization (high centralization) and high decentralization (low centralization) within organizations.

LOW DECENTRALIZATION (HIGH CENTRALIZATION)	HIGH DECENTRALIZATION (LOW CENTRALIZATION)
Eliminates the additional responsibility not desired by people performing routine jobs	*Can eliminate levels of management, making a leaner organization*
Permits crucial decisions to be made by individuals who have the "big picture"	*Promotes greater opportunities for decisions to be made by people closest to problems*

tion according to the various functions performed. However, as we will explain in this section, this is only one option. Organizations can be divided up not only by function, but also by product or market, and by a special blend of function and product or market known as the *matrix* form. We will now take a closer look at these various ways of breaking up organizations into coherent units—that is, the process of **departmentalization**.

FUNCTIONAL ORGANIZATIONS: DEPARTMENTALIZATION BY TASK

Because it is the form organizations usually take when they are first created, and because it is how we usually think of organizations, the **functional organization** can be considered the most basic approach to departmentalization. Essentially, functional organizations departmentalize individuals according to the nature of the functions they perform, with people who perform similar functions assigned to the same department. For example, a manufacturing company might consist of separate departments devoted to basic functions such as production, sales, research and development, and finance and accounting (see Figure 15-4).

Naturally, as organizations grow and become more complex, additional departments are added or deleted as the need arises. Consider, for example, what is beginning to happen at Johnson & Johnson, as described in our Preview Case. As certain functions become centralized, resources can be saved by avoiding duplication of effort, resulting in a higher level of efficiency. Not only does this form of organizational structure take advantage of economies of scale (by allowing employees performing the same jobs to share facilities and not duplicating functions), but in addition, it allows individuals to specialize, thereby performing only those tasks at which they are most expert. The result is a highly skilled workforce, a direct benefit to the organization.

Partly offsetting these advantages, however, are several potential limitations. The most important of these stems from the fact that functional organizational structures encourage separate units to develop their own narrow perspectives, and to lose sight of overall organizational goals. For example, in a manufacturing company, an engineer might see the company's problems in terms of the reliability of its products, and lose sight of other key considerations, such as market trends, overseas competition, and so on. Such narrow-mindedness is the inevitable result of functional specialization—the downside of people seeing the company's operations through a narrow lens. A related problem is that functional structures discourage innovation because they channel individual efforts toward narrow, functional areas and do not encourage coordination and cross-fertilization of ideas between areas. As a result, functional organizations are slow to respond to the challenges and opportunities they face from the environment (such as the need for new products and services). In summary, although functional organizations are certainly logical in nature and have proven useful in many contexts, they are by no means the perfect way to departmentalize people in organizations.

FIGURE 15-4
FUNCTIONAL ORGANIZATION OF A TYPICAL MANUFACTURING FIRM
Functional organizations are ones in which departments are formed on the basis of common functions performed. In the hypothetical manufacturing firm shown in this chart, four typical functional departments are identified. In specific organizations, the actual functions may differ.

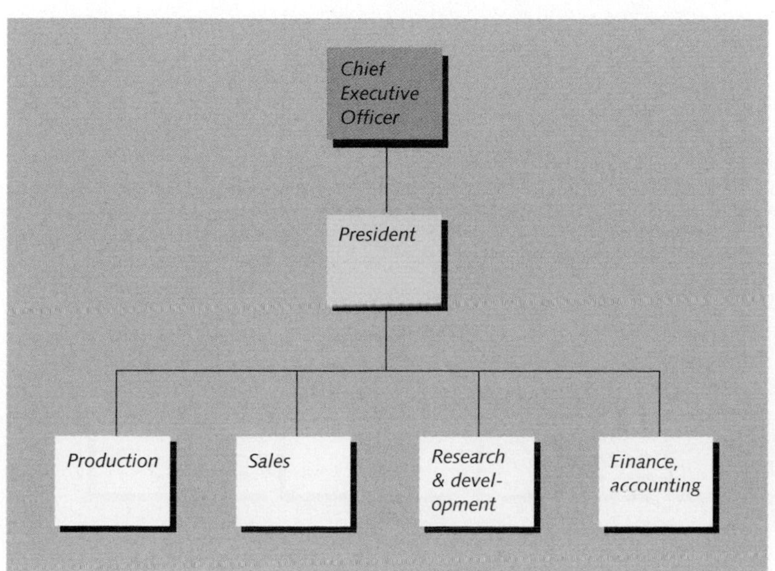

PRODUCT ORGANIZATIONS: DEPARTMENTALIZATION BY TYPE OF OUTPUT

Organizations—at least successful ones—do not stand still; they constantly change in size and scope. As they develop new products and seek new customers, they might find that a functional structure doesn't work as well as it once did. Manufacturing a wide range of products using a variety of different methods, for example, might put a strain on a manufacturing division of a functional organization. Similarly, keeping track of the varied tax requirements for different types of business (e.g., restaurants, farms, real estate, manufacturing) might pose quite a challenge for a single financial division of a company. In response to such strains, a **product organization** might be created. This type of departmentalization creates self-contained divisions, each of which is responsible for everything to do with a certain product or group of products. (For a look at the structure of a product organization, see Figure 15-5.)

When organizations are departmentalized by products, separate divisions are established, each of which is devoted to a certain product or group of products. Each unit contains all the resources needed to develop, manufacture, and sell its products. The organization is composed of separate divisions, operating independently, the heads of which report to top management. Although some functions might be centralized within the parent company (e.g., human resource management or legal staff), on a day-to-day basis each division operates autonomously as a separate company or, as accountants call them, "cost centers" of their own.

Consider, for example, how separate divisions of General Motors are devoted to manufacturing cars, trucks, locomotives, refrigerators, auto parts, and the like. The managers of each division can devote their energies to one particular business. Product organizations may be beneficial from a marketing perspective as well. Consider, for example, Honda's 1987 introduction of its line of luxury cars, Acura.[20] By creating a separate division, manufactured in separate plants and sold by a separate network of dealers, the company made its higher-priced cars look special, and avoided making its less expensive cars look less appealing by putting them together with superior products on the same showroom floors. Given Honda's success with this configuration, it is not surprising that Toyota and Nissan followed suit when they introduced their own luxury lines, Lexus and Infiniti, in 1989.

FIGURE 15-5
AN EXAMPLE OF A PRODUCT ORGANIZATION
In a product organization, separate units are established to handle different products or product lines. Each of these divisions contains all the departments necessary for operating as an independent unit.

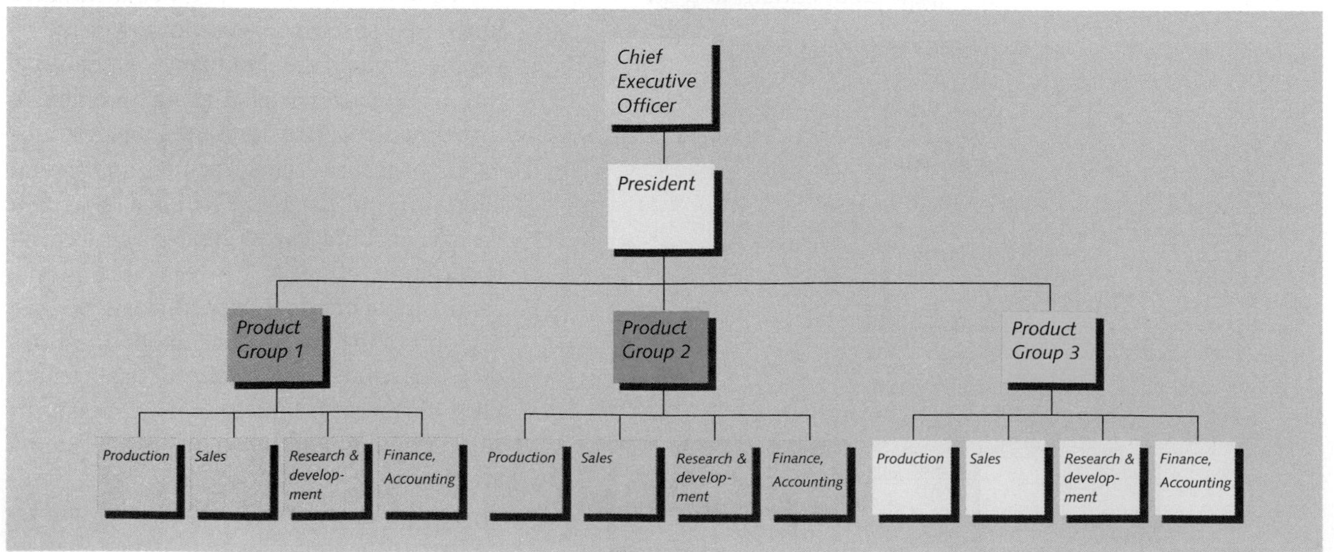

This is not to say that product organizations do not have limitations. Indeed, they have several drawbacks. The most obvious of these is the loss of economies of scale stemming from the duplication of various departments within operating units. For example, if each unit carries out its own research and development functions, the need for costly equipment, facilities, and personnel may be multiplied. Another problem associated with product designs involves the organization's ability to attract and retain talented employees. Since each department within operating units is necessarily smaller than a single combined one would be, opportunities for advancement and career development may suffer. This, in turn, may pose a serious problem with respect to the long-term retention of talented employees. Finally, problems of coordination across product lines may arise. In fact, in extreme cases, actions taken by one operating division may have adverse effects on the outcomes of one or more others.

A clear example of such problems is provided by Hewlett-Packard, a major U.S. manufacturer of computers, printers, and scientific test equipment. During most of its history, Hewlett-Packard adopted a product design. It consisted of scores of small, largely autonomous divisions, each concerned with producing and selling certain products. As it grew in size and complexity, the company found itself in an increasingly untenable situation in which sales representatives from different divisions sometimes attempted to sell different lines of equipment, often to be used for the same basic purposes, to the same customers! To deal with such problems, top management at Hewlett-Packard decided to restructure the company into sectors based largely on the markets they served (such as business customers, and scientific and manufacturing customers). In short, Hewlett-Packard switched from a fairly traditional product organization to an internal structure driven by market considerations.[21] Although it's too soon to determine whether the effects of this reorganization will be as positive as top management hopes, initial results, at least, are promising.

The Hewlett-Packard case points out a particular variation on the basic theme of market departmentalization. Self-contained operating units can also be established on the basis of specific geographic regions or territories, and even customers, rather than different products. So, for example, a large retail chain might develop separate divisions for different regions of the country (e.g., Macy's New York and Macy's California), or for different customer bases (e.g., Bloomingdale's by Mail and Bloomingdale's Retail). Similarly, a large record company (itself likely a division of a larger entertainment company) may establish independent divisions (each with its own labels) to sign, develop, produce, and promote recordings of interest to people in different markets (e.g., children, classical, Latin, pop). By departmentalizing in this fashion, having separate companies within a large company (e.g., MCA or CBS), a company can give artists the attention they would expect from a smaller company, and the specialization and economies of scale they would expect from a large company. Regardless of the exact basis for departmentalizing—be it product, region, market, or customer group—the basic rationale remains the same: divide the organization's operations in a way that enhances efficiency.

MATRIX ORGANIZATIONS: DEPARTMENTALIZATION BY BOTH FUNCTION AND PRODUCT

When the aerospace industry was first developing, the U.S. government demanded that a single manager in each company be assigned to each of its projects so that it was immediately clear who was responsible for the progress of each project. In response to this requirement, TRW established a "project leader" for each project, someone who shared authority with the leaders of the existing functional departments.[22] This temporary arrangement later evolved into what is called a **matrix organization**, the type of organization in which an employee is required to report to both a functional (or division) manager and the manager of a specific project (or product). In essence, they developed a complex type of organizational structure that combines both the function and product forms of departmentalization.[23] Recently, matrix organizational forms have been used in many organizations.[24] To better understand matrix organizations, let's take a closer look at the organizational chart shown in Figure 15-6.

Employees in matrix organizations have two bosses (or, more technically, they are under *dual authority*). One line of authority, shown by the vertical arrows on Figure 15-6, is *functional*, managed by vice presidents in charge of various functional areas. The other, shown by the horizontal arrows, is *product* (or it may be a specific project or temporary business), managed by specific individuals in charge of certain products (or projects).

In matrix designs, there are three major roles. First, there is the *top leader*—the individual who has authority over both lines (the one based on function and the one based on product or project). It is this individual's task to enhance coordination between functional and product managers and to maintain an appropriate balance of power between them. Second, there are the *matrix bosses*—people who head functional departments or specific projects. Since neither functional managers nor project managers have complete authority over subordinates, they must

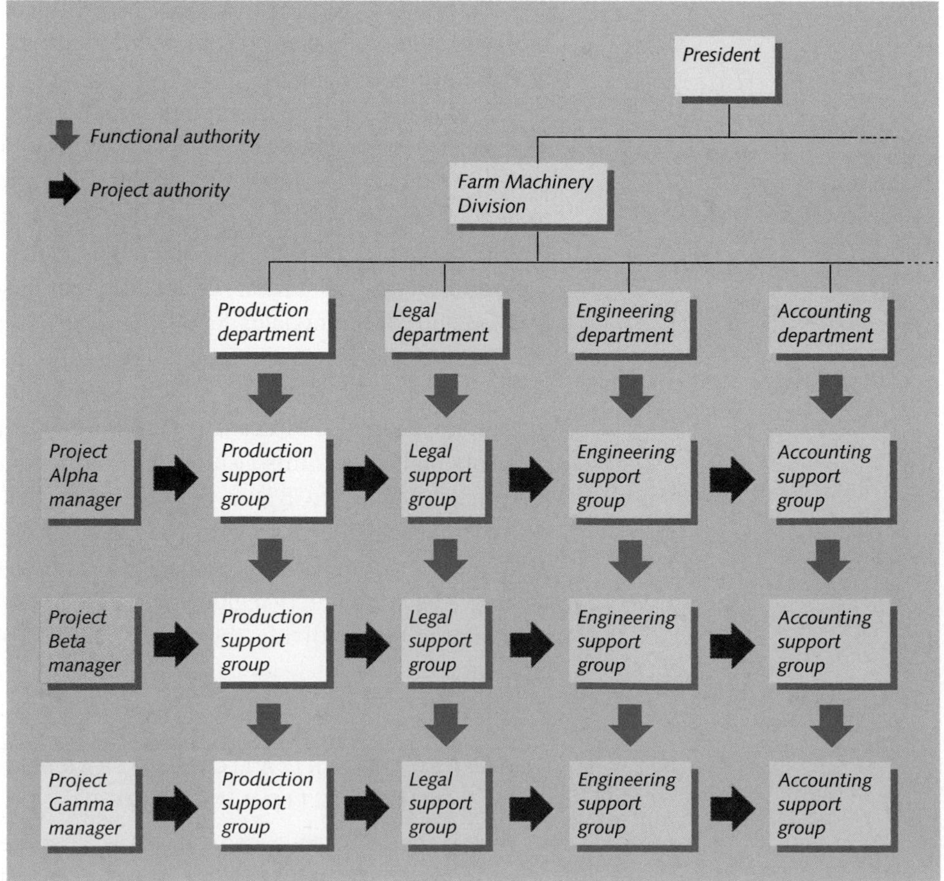

FIGURE 15-6
A TYPICAL MATRIX ORGANIZATION
In a matrix organization, a product structure is superimposed on a basic functional structure. This results in a dual system of authority in which some managers report to two bosses—a project (or product) manager, and a functional (departmental) manager.

work together to assure that their efforts mesh rather than conflict. In addition, they must agree on issues such as promotions and raises for specific people working under their joint authority. Finally, there are *two-boss managers*—people who must report to both product and functional managers, and attempt to balance the demands of each.

Not all organizations using the matrix structure do so on a permanent basis. Several partial, or temporary, types of matrix designs have been identified.[25] First, the *temporary overlay* is a form of matrix structure in which projects are crossed with functions on a special, short-term basis. This is in contrast to a *permanent overlay*, in which project teams are kept going after each project is completed. Finally, there are *mature matrix organizations*, those in which both the functional lines and the product lines are permanent, and equally strong within the organization.

With a matrix organization that has been in effect for over twenty years, Dow Corning is an example of a mature matrix organization.[26] At this company, each functional representative reports to the leaders of his or her own department, while also contributing to the design and operation of the particular product line for which he or she is responsible. Because people working in this fashion have two bosses, they must have sufficient freedom to attain their objectives. As you might imagine, a fair amount of coordination, flexibility, openness, and trust is essential for such a program to work, suggesting that not everyone adapts well to such a system.

Organizations are most likely to adopt matrix designs when they confront certain conditions. These include a complex and uncertain environment (one with frequent changes), and the need for economies of scale in the use of internal resources. Specifically, a matrix approach is often adopted by medium-size organizations with several product lines that do not possess sufficient resources to establish fully self-contained operating units. Under such conditions, a matrix design provides a useful compromise. Some companies that have adopted this structure, at least on a trial basis, are TRW Systems Group, Liberty Mutual Insurance, and Citibank.[27]

Key advantages offered by matrix designs have already been suggested by our discussion so far.[28] First, they permit flexible use of an organization's human resources. Individuals within functional departments can be assigned to specific products or projects as the need arises and then return to their regular duties when this task is completed. Second, matrix designs offer medium-size organizations an efficient means of responding quickly to a changing, unstable environment. Third, such designs often enhance communication among managers; indeed, they literally force matrix bosses to discuss and agree on many matters.

Disadvantages of such designs include the frustration and stress faced by two-boss managers in reporting to two different supervisors, the danger that one of the two authority systems (functional or product) will overwhelm the other, and the consistently high levels of cooperation required from the people involved for the organization to succeed.[29] As we noted in Chapter 10, this is sometimes far easier to imagine than to achieve! In situations where organizations must stretch their financial and human resources to meet challenges from the external environment or take advantage of new opportunities, however, matrix designs can often play a useful role. (Traditionally, matrix organizations, like functional and product organizations, distinguish between people on the basis of their positions on a corporate hierarchy. In the future, however, organizations are expected to pay less attention to corporate ladders and more attention to effective ways of getting the job done. For a description of this trend, see the Organization of Tomorrow section on the following page.)

THE ORGANIZATION OF TOMORROW

FORGET THE HIERARCHY, HERE COMES THE HORIZONTAL ORGANIZATION: STRUCTURING BY PROCESS INSTEAD OF FUNCTION

If the experts are right, we are in store for a new way of structuring work in tomorrow's organizations—one that means more than just tinkering with the boxes on an organizational chart. Enter the **horizontal organization**, an approach advocated by many organizational experts, and touted by consultants from the firm McKinsey & Co, as "the first real, fundamentally different, robust alternative" to the functional organization.[30]

The essence of the idea is simple. Instead of organizing jobs in the traditional, vertical fashion, by having a long chain of groups or individuals perform parts of a task (e.g., one group that sells the advertising job, another that plans the ad campaign, and yet another that produces the ads), horizontal organizations have flattened hierarchies.[31] That is, they arrange autonomous work teams (see Chapter 8) in parallel, each performing many different steps in the process (e.g., members of an advertising team may bring different skills and expertise to a single team responsible for all aspects of advertising). Essentially, organizations are structured around *processes* instead of tasks. Performance objectives are based on customers' needs, such as lowered cost or improved service. Once the core processes that meet these needs (e.g., order generation, new product development) have been identified, they become the company's major components—instead of the traditional departments such as sales or manufacturing (for a summary, see Figure 15-7).

According to consultant Michael Hammer, "In the future, executive positions will not be defined in terms of collections of people, like head of the sales department, but in terms of processes, like senior-VP-of-getting-stuff-to-customers, which is sales, shipping, billing. You'll no longer have a box on an organization chart. You'll own part of a process map."[32] Envision it as a whole company lying on its side, and organized by process. An ardent believer in this approach, Lawrence Bossidy, CEO of Allied Signal, says, "Every business has maybe six basic processes. We'll organize around them. The people who run them will be the leaders of the business."[33] In an industrial company, for example, these processes might include things like new product development, flow of materials, and the order–delivery–billing cycle. Individuals will constantly move into and out of various teams as needed, drawing from a directory of broadly skilled in-house corporate experts available to lend their expertise.

The horizontal organization is already a reality in at least parts of several of today's organizations—including AT&T (network systems division), Eastman Chemical (a division of Kodak), Hallmark Cards, and Xerox. Consider, for example, General Electric's factory in Bayamón, Puerto Rico. The 172 hourly workers, 15 salaried "advisers," plus a single manager manufacture "arresters" (surge protectors that guard power stations from lightning). That's the entire workforce; there are no support staff and no supervisors—only about half as many people as you'd find in a conventional factory. Bayamón employees are formed into

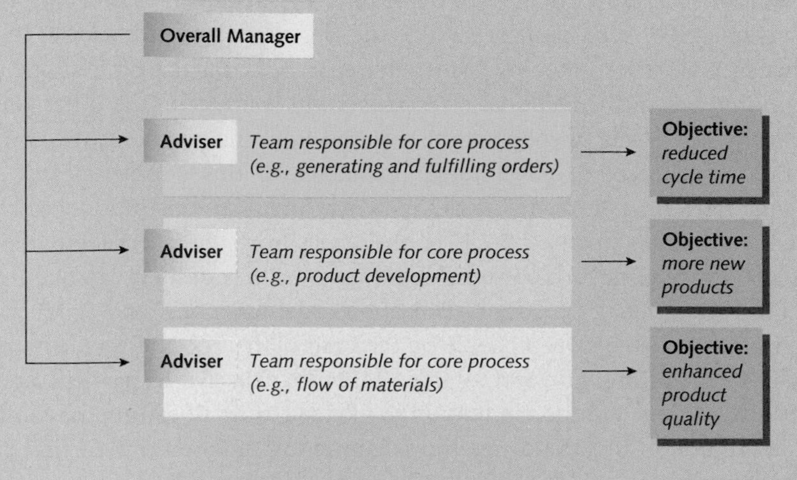

FIGURE 15-7
THE HORIZONTAL ORGANIZATION: FORMAL USE OF TEAMS
In the horizontal organization, *teams of employees with diverse skills, led by advisers, are created to meet objectives relating to various core processes that must be performed.*

separate teams of approximately 10 widely skilled members who "own" such parts of the work as shipping and receiving, assembly, and so on. For the most part, the teams do whatever is required to get the job done; the advisers get involved only when needed.

Although it is difficult to directly assess the impact of this new approach without carefully controlled experiments (which have not yet been conducted), those who have used it are convinced of its effectiveness. One top McKinsey consultant, for example, claims that this new approach to organizational design can help companies cut their costs by at least one-third. Some of their clients, they boast, have done even better. Will the horizontal organization replace the traditional pyramid of the hierarchical organization? Only time will tell. Meanwhile, those who have turned to horizontal organizational structures appear to be glad they did.

ORGANIZATIONAL DESIGN: COORDINATING THE STRUCTURAL ELEMENTS OF ORGANIZATIONS

We began the first major section of this chapter by likening the structure of an organization to the structure of a house. Now we are prepared to extend that analogy for purposes of introducing the concept of organizational design. Just as a house is designed in a particular fashion by combining its structural elements in various ways, so too can an organization be designed by combining its basic elements in certain ways. Accordingly, **organizational design** refers to *the process of coordinating the structural elements of organizations in the most appropriate manner.*

As you might imagine, this is no easy task. Although we might describe some options that sound neat and rational on the next few pages, in reality this is hardly ever the case. Even the most precisely designed organizations will face the need to change at one time or another, adjusting to the realities of technological changes, political pressures, accidents, and so on. Organizational designs might also be changed purposely in an attempt to improve operating efficiency, such as the promise by some recent U.S. presidents to streamline the huge federal bureaucracy. Our point is simple: because organizations operate within a changing world, their own designs must be capable of changing as well. Those organizations that are either poorly designed or inflexible cannot survive. If you consider the large number of banks and airlines that have gone out of business in the last few years because of their inability to deal with rapid changes brought about by deregulation and a shifting economy (see Figure 15-8), you'll get a good idea of the ultimate consequences of ineffective organizational design.

FIGURE 15-8

FAILURE TO ADAPT TO A CHANGING ENVIRONMENT: SOME EXTREME EXAMPLES

The changing environments within which organizations operate require that their designs are capable of changing so as to properly adapt. When airlines and banks became less heavily regulated by the U.S. government, many found themselves unable to change rapidly enough to survive.

CLASSICAL AND NEOCLASSICAL APPROACHES: THE QUEST FOR THE ONE BEST DESIGN

The earliest theorists interested in organizational design did not operate out of awareness of the point we just made regarding the need for organizations to be flexible. Instead, they approached the task of designing organizations as a search for "the one best way." Although today we are more attuned to the need to adapt organizational designs to various environmental and social conditions, theorists in the early and middle part of the twentieth century sought to establish the ideal form for all organizations under all conditions—the universal design.

In Chapter 1, we described the efforts of organizational scholars such as Max Weber, Frederick Taylor, and Henri Fayol. These theorists believed that effective organizations were ones that had a formal hierarchy, a clear set of rules, specialization of labor, highly routine tasks, and a highly impersonal working environment. You may recall that Weber referred to this organizational form as a *bureaucracy*. This **classical organizational theory** has fallen into disfavor because it is insensitive to human needs and is not suited to a changing environment. Unfortunately, the "ideal" form of an organization, according to Weber, did not take into account the realities of the world within which it operates. Apparently, what is ideal is not necessarily what is realistic.

In response to these conditions, and with inspiration from the Hawthorne studies (see Chapter 1), the classical approach to the bureaucratic model gave way to more of a human relations orientation. Organizational scholars such as McGregor, Argyris, and Likert attempted to improve on the classical model—which is why their approach is labeled **neoclassical organizational theory**—by arguing that economic effectiveness is not the only goal of an industrial organization, but also employee satisfaction.

Specifically, Douglas McGregor was an organizational theorist who objected to the rigid hierarchy imposed by Weber's bureaucratic form because it was based on negative assumptions about people—primarily that they lacked ambition and wouldn't work unless coerced (the *Theory X* approach).[34] In contrast, McGregor argued that people desire to achieve success by working and that they seek satisfaction by behaving responsibly (the *Theory Y* approach) (see Chapter 1). Another neoclassical theorist, Chris Argyris, expressed similar ideas.[35] Specifically, he argued that managerial domination of organizations blocks basic human needs to express oneself and to successfully accomplish tasks. Such dissatisfaction, he argues, would encourage turnover and lead to poor performance.

Another neoclassical theorist, Rensis Likert, shared these perspectives, arguing that organizational performance is enhanced not by rigidly controlling people's actions, but by actively promoting their feelings of self-worth and their importance to the organization.[36] An effective organization, Likert proposed, was one in which individuals would have a great opportunity to participate in making organizational decisions—what he called a *System 4 organization*. Doing this, he claimed, would enhance employees' personal sense of worth, motivating them to succeed. (Although this assumption appears a bit naive in view of the more complex approaches to motivation we examined in Chapter 4, the same basic idea is inherent in even more sophisticated, contemporary approaches. Accordingly, rather than dismissing these approaches because of their simplicity, it makes more sense to applaud them for their insight and foresight.) Likert called the opposite type of organization *System 1*, the traditional form in which organizational power is distributed in the hands of a few top managers who tell lower-ranking people what to do. (*System 2* and *System 3* are intermediate forms between the System 1 and System 4 extremes.)

The organizational design implications of these neoclassical approaches are clear. In contrast to the classical approach, calling for organizations to be designed with a rigid, tall hierarchy, with a narrow span of control (allowing managers to maintain close supervision over their subordinates), the neoclassical approach argues for designing organizations with flat hierarchical structures (minimizing managerial control over subordinates), and a high degree of decentralization (encouraging employees to make their own decisions). Indeed, such design features may well serve the underlying neoclassical philosophy.

Like the classical approach, the neoclassical approach also may be faulted on the grounds that it is promoted as "the one best approach" to organizational design. Although the benefits of flat, decentralized designs may be many, to claim that this represents the universal, ideal form for all organizations would be naive. In response to this criticism, more contemporary approaches to organizational design have given up on finding the one best way to design organizations in favor of finding designs that are most appropriate to various circumstances and contexts within which organizations operate.

THE CONTEMPORARY APPROACH: DESIGN CONTINGENT ON ENVIRONMENTAL CONDITIONS

The idea that the best design for an organization depends on the nature of the environment in which the organization is operating lies at the heart of the modern **contingency approach** to organizational design. We use the term *contingency* here in a manner similar to the way we used it in our discussion of leadership (Chapter 13) (i.e., the most effective leadership style depends on the situation). But rather than considering the best approach to leadership for a given situation, we are considering the best way to design an organization given the environment within which the organization functions.

THE EXTERNAL ENVIRONMENT: ITS CONNECTION TO ORGANIZATIONAL DESIGN

It is widely assumed that the most appropriate type of organizational design depends on the organization's *external environment*. In general, the external environment is the sum of all the forces impinging on an organization with which it must deal effectively if it is to survive.[37] These forces include general work conditions, such as the economy, geography, and national resources, as well as the specific task environment within which the company operates—notably, its competitors, customers, workforce, and suppliers.

Let's consider some examples. Banks operate within an environment that is highly influenced by the general economic environment (e.g., interest rates and government regulations) as well as a task environment sensitive to other banks' products (e.g., types of accounts) and services (e.g., service hours, access to account information by computers and/or telephone), the needs of the customer base (e.g., direct deposit for customers), the availability of trained personnel (e.g., individuals suitable for entry-level positions), as well as the existence of suppliers providing goods and services (e.g., automated teller equipment, surveillance equipment, computer workstations) necessary to deliver requisite services.

FIGURE 15-9
ENVIRONMENTAL FORCES ON INDUSTRY: ONE EXAMPLE
The changing environment affects the automobile industry in many ways. For example, as fuel prices increase, consumer demand for small, fuel-efficient cars increases and the demand for larger, gas guzzlers decreases. Governmental regulations restricting foreign trade, requiring enhanced safety features, demanding increased fuel efficiency, and limiting levels of air pollution, have had dramatic influences on the automobile industry.

Analogous examples can be found in other industries as well. For example, think about the environmental forces faced by the airlines, the computer industry, and automobile manufacturers (see Figure 15-9). It's easy to recognize the features of their environments that must be taken into account when considering how organizations in these industries could be designed.

Although many features of the environment may be taken into account when considering how an organization should be designed, a classic investigation by Burns and Stalker provides some useful guidance.[38] They interviewed people in twenty industrial organizations in the United Kingdom to determine the relationship between managerial activities and the external environment. In so doing, they distinguished between organizations that operated in highly *stable*, unchanging environments, and those that operated in highly *unstable*, turbulent environments. For example, a rayon company in their sample operated in a highly stable environment. The environmental demands were predictable, people performed the same jobs in the same ways for a long time, and the organization had clearly defined lines of authority that helped get the job done. In contrast, a new electronics development company in their sample operated in a highly turbulent environment. Conditions changed on a daily basis, jobs were not well defined, and no clear organizational structure existed.

Burns and Stalker noted that many of the organizations studied tended to be described in ways that were appropriate for their environments. For example, when the environment is stable, people can do the same tasks repeatedly, allowing them to perform highly specialized jobs. However, in turbulent environments, many different jobs may have to be performed, and such specialization should not be designed into the jobs. Clearly, a strong link exists between the stability of the work environment and the proper organizational form. It was Burns and Stalker's conclusion that two different approaches to management existed and that these are largely based on the degree of stability within the external environment. These two approaches are known as **mechanistic organizations** and **organic organizations**.

MECHANISTIC VERSUS ORGANIC ORGANIZATIONS: DESIGNS FOR STABLE VERSUS TURBULENT CONDITIONS

If you've ever worked at a McDonald's, you probably know how highly standardized each step of the most basic operations must be.[39] Boxes of fries are to be stored two inches from the wall in stacks one inch apart. Making those fries is another matter—one that requires nineteen distinct steps, each clearly laid out in a training film shown to new employees. The process is the same, whether it's done in Moscow, Idaho, or in Moscow, Russia. This is an example of a highly mechanistic task. Organizations can be highly mechanistic when conditions don't change. Although the fast-food industry has changed a great deal in recent years (with the introduction of new, healthier menu items, competitive pricing, and the like), the making of fries at McDonald's has not changed. The key to using mechanization is the lack of change. If the environment doesn't change, a highly mechanistic organizational form can be very efficient.

An environment is considered stable whenever there is little or no unexpected change in product, market demands, technology, and the like. Have you ever seen an old-fashioned-looking bottle of E. E. Dickinson's witch hazel (a topical astringent used to cleanse the skin in the area of a wound)? Because the company has been making the product following the same distillation process since 1866, it appears to be operating in a relatively stable manufacturing environment.[40] As we described earlier, stability affords the luxury of high employee specialization. Without change, people can easily specialize. When change is inevitable, specialization is impractical.

Mechanistic organizations can be characterized in several additional ways (for a summary, see Table 15-3). Not only do mechanistic organizations allow for a high degree of specialization, but they also impose many rules. Authority is vested in a few people located at the top of a hierarchy who give direct orders to their subordinates. Mechanistic organizational designs tend to be most effective under conditions in which the external environment is stable and unchanging.

Now think about high-technology industries, such as those dedicated to computers, aerospace products, and biotechnology (see Chapter 14). Their environmental conditions are likely to be changing all the time. These industries are so prone to change that as soon as a new way of operating could be introduced into one of them, it would have to be altered. It isn't only technology, however, that makes an environment turbulent. Turbulence also can be high in industries in which adherence to rapidly changing regulations is essential. For example, times were turbulent in the hospital industry when new Medicaid legislation was passed, and times were turbulent in the nuclear power industry when governmental regulations dictated the introduction of many new standards that had to be followed. With the dominance of foreign automobiles in the United States, the once-stable American auto industry has faced turbulent times of late. Unfortunately, in this case, the design of the auto companies could not rapidly accommodate the changes needed for more organic forms (since the American auto industry was traditionally highly mechanistic).

The pure organic form of organization may be characterized in several different ways (see Table 15-3). The degree of job specialization possible is very low; instead, a broad knowledge of many different jobs is required. Very little authority is exercised from the top. Rather, self-control is expected, and an emphasis is placed on coordination between peers. As a result, decisions tend to be made in a highly democratic, participative manner. Be aware that the mechanistic and organic types of organizational structure described here are ideal forms. The mechanistic-organic distinction should be thought of as opposite poles along a continuum rather than as completely distinct options. Certainly, organizations can be relatively organic or relatively mechanistic compared with others, but may not be located at either extreme.

TABLE 15-3

Mechanistic Versus Organic Designs: A Summary

Mechanistic and organic designs differ along several key dimensions identified here. These represent extremes; organizations can be relatively organic, relatively mechanistic, or somewhere in between.

	STRUCTURE	
DIMENSION	MECHANISTIC	ORGANIC
Stability	*Change unlikely*	*Change likely*
Specialization	*Many specialists*	*Many generalists*
Formal rules	*Rigid rules*	*Considerable flexibility*
Authority	*Centralized in a few top people*	*Decentralized, diffused throughout the organization*

Finally, note that research supports the idea that organizational effectiveness is related to the degree to which an organization's structure (mechanistic or organic) is matched to its environment (stable or turbulent). In a classic study, Morse and Lorsch evaluated four departments in a large company—two of which manufactured containers (a relatively stable environment) and two of which dealt with communications research (a highly unstable environment).[41] One department in each pair was evaluated as being more effective than the other. It was found that for the container-manufacturing departments, the more effective unit was the one structured in a highly mechanistic form (roles and duties were clearly defined). In contrast, the more effective communications research department was structured in a highly organic fashion (roles and duties were vague). In addition, the other, less effective departments were structured in the opposite manner; that is, the less effective manufacturing department was organically structured, and the less effective research department was mechanistically structured (see Figure 15-10). Taken together, the results made it clear that departments were most effective when their organizational structures fit their environments. This notion of "which design is best under which conditions?" lies at the heart of the modern orientation—the contingency approach—to organizational structure. Rather than specifying *which* structure is best, the contingency approach specifies *when* each type of organizational design is most effective.

MINTZBERG'S FRAMEWORK: FIVE ORGANIZATIONAL FORMS

Although the distinction between mechanistic and organic designs is important, it is not terribly specific with respect to exactly how organizations should be designed. Filling this void, however, is the work of contemporary organizational

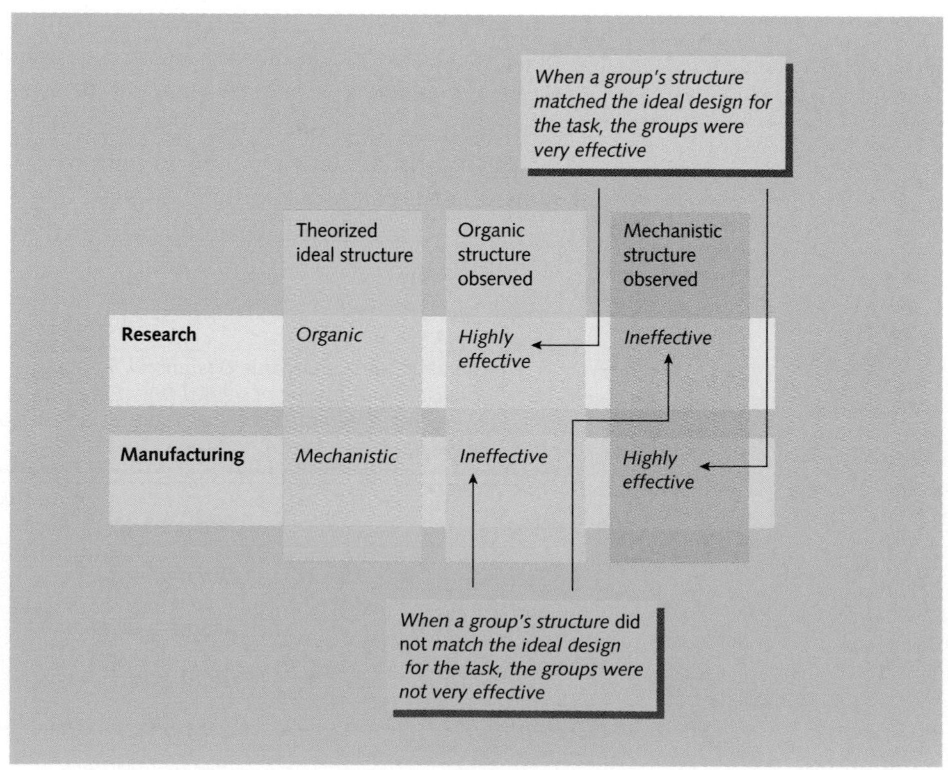

FIGURE 15-10
MATCHING ORGANIZATIONAL DESIGN AND INDUSTRY: THE KEY TO EFFECTIVENESS
In a classic study, Morse and Lorsch evaluated the performance of four departments in a large company. The most effective units were ones in which the way the group was structured (mechanistic or organic) matched the most appropriate form for the type of task performed (i.e., organic for research work, and mechanistic for manufacturing work). (Source: Based on suggestions by Morse & Lorsch, 1970; see Note 41.)

theorist, Henry Mintzberg.[42] Specifically, Mintzberg claims that organizations are composed of five basic elements, or groups of individuals, any of which may predominate in an organization. The one that does will determine the most effective design in that situation. The five basic elements are

- *The operating core:* Employees who perform the basic work related to the organization's product or service. Examples include teachers (in schools) and chefs and waiters (in restaurants).
- *The strategic apex*: Top-level executives responsible for running the entire organization. Examples include the entrepreneur who runs her own small business, and the general manager of an automobile dealership.
- *The middle line*: Managers who transfer information between the strategic apex and the operating core. Examples include middle managers, such as regional sales managers (who connect top executives with the sales force) and the chair of an academic department in a college or university (an intermediary between the dean and the faculty).
- *The technostructure*: Those specialists responsible for standardizing various aspects of the organization's activities. Examples include accountants and auditors, and computer systems analysts.
- *The support staff*: Individuals who provide indirect support services to the organization. Examples include consultants on technical matters, and corporate attorneys.

What organizational designs best fit under conditions in which each of these five groups dominate? Mintzberg has identified five specific designs: *simple structure*, *machine bureaucracy*, *professional bureaucracy*, the *divisionalized structure*, and the *adhocracy* (see summary in Table 15-4).

TABLE 15-4

Mintzberg's Five Organizational Forms: A Summary

Mintzberg has identified five distinct organizational designs, each of which is likely to occur in organizations in which certain groups are in power.

DESIGN	DESCRIPTION	DOMINANT GROUP	EXAMPLE
Simple structure	*Simple, informal, authority centralized in a single person*	*Strategic apex*	*Small, entrepreneurial business*
Machine bureaucracy	*Highly complex, formal environment with clear lines of authority*	*Technostructure*	*Government offices*
Professional bureaucracy	*Complex, decision-making authority is vested in professionals*	*Operating core*	*Universities*
Divisionalized structure	*Large, formal organizations with several separate divisions*	*Middle line*	*Multidivision businesses such as General Motors*
Adhocracy	*Simple, informal, with decentralized authority*	*Support staff*	*Software development firm*

Source: Based on suggestions by Mintzberg, 1983; see Note 42.

SIMPLE STRUCTURE

Imagine that you open up an antique shop and hire a few people to help you out around the store. You have a small, informal organization in which there is a single individual with the ultimate power. There is little in the way of specialization or formalization, and the overall structure is organic in nature. The hierarchy is quite flat, and all decision-making power is vested in a single individual—you. An organization so described, simple in nature, with the power residing at the strategic apex, is referred to by Mintzberg as having a **simple structure**. As you might imagine, organizations with simple structure can respond quickly to the environment and be very flexible. For example, the chef-owner of a small, independent restaurant can change the menu to suit the changing tastes of customers whenever needed, without first consulting anyone else. The downside of this, however, is that the success or failure of the entire enterprise is dependent on the wisdom and health of the individual in charge. Not surprisingly, organizations with simple structure are risky ventures.

MACHINE BUREAUCRACY

If you've ever worked for your state's department of motor vehicles, you probably found it to be a very large place, with numerous rules and procedures for employees to follow. The work is highly specialized (e.g., one person gives the vision tests, and another completes the registration forms), and decision making is concentrated at the top (e.g., you need to get permission from your supervisor to do anything other than exactly what's expected). This type of work environment is highly stable, and does not have to change. An organization so characterized, where power resides with the technostructure, is referred to as a **machine bureaucracy**. Although machine bureaucracies can be highly efficient at performing standardized tasks, they tend to be dehumanizing, and very boring for the employees (see Chapter 1).

PROFESSIONAL BUREAUCRACY

Suppose you are a doctor working at a large city hospital. You are a highly trained specialist with considerable expertise in your field. You don't need to check with anyone else before authorizing a certain medical test or treatment for your patient; you make the decisions as they are needed, when they are needed. At the same time, the environment is highly formal (e.g., there are lots of rules and regulations for you to follow). Of course, you do not work alone; you also require the services of other highly qualified professionals such as nurses and laboratory technicians. Organizations of this type—and these include universities, libraries, and consulting firms, as well as hospitals—maintain power with the operating core, and are called **professional bureaucracies**. Such organizations can be highly effective because they allow employees to practice those skills for which they are best qualified. However, sometimes specialists become so overly narrow that they fail to see the "big picture," leading to errors and potential conflict between employees (see Chapter 11).

DIVISIONAL STRUCTURE

When you think of large organizations, such as General Motors, DuPont, Xerox, and IBM, the image that comes to mind is probably closest to what Mintzberg describes as **divisional structure**. Such organizations consist of a set of autonomous units coordinated by a central headquarters (i.e., they rely on departmental structure based on products, as described on pages 588–589). In such organizations, because the divisions are autonomous (e.g., a General Motors employee at Buick does not have to consult with another at Chevrolet to do his or her job) division managers (the *middle line* part of Mintzberg's basic elements) have considerable control. Such designs preclude the need for top-level executives to think about the day-to-day operations of their companies, and free them to concentrate on larger-scale, strategic decisions. At the same time, companies organized into separate divisions frequently tend to have high duplication of effort (e.g., separate order-processing units for each division). Having operated as separate divisions for the past seventy years, General Motors is considered the classic example of divisional structure.[43] Although the company has undergone many changes during this time—including the addition of the Saturn Corporation—it has maintained its divisional structure. IBM is another company that has had a divisional structure that has changed many times.[44] For a look at its most recent divisional structuring, see Figure 15-11.

FIGURE 15-11
IBM'S LATEST DIVISIONALIZED STRUCTURE
In 1992 IBM reorganized into thirteen major divisions, nine of which are based on product lines (left side), and four of which are based on geographic region (right side). (Source: Based on suggestions by Kirkpatrick, 1992; see Note 44.)

ADHOCRACY

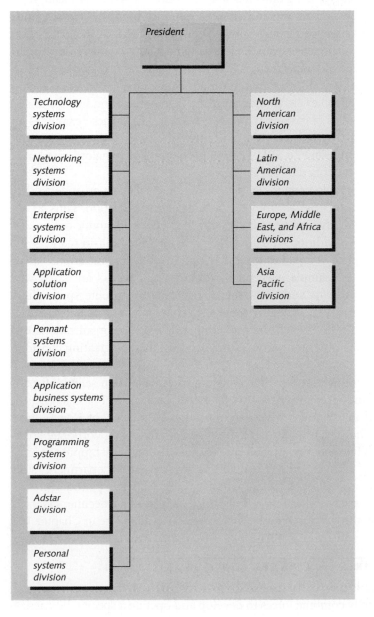

After graduating from college, where you spent years learning how to program computers, you take a job at a small software company. Compared to your friends who found positions at large accounting firms, your professional life is much less formal. You work as a member of a team developing a new time-management software product. There are no rules, and schedules are made to be broken. You all work together, and although there is someone who is "officially" in charge, you'd never know it. Using Mintzberg's framework, you work for an **adhocracy**—an organization in which power resides with the support staff. Essentially, this is the epitome of the organic structure identified earlier. Specialists coordinate with each other not because of their shared functions (e.g., accounting, manufacturing), but as members of teams working on specific projects. The primary benefit of the adhocracy is that it fosters innovation. Some large companies, such as Johnson & Johnson (see this chapter's Preview Case), nest within their formal divisional structure units that operate as adhocracies. In the case of J&J, it's the New Products Division, a unit that has been churning out an average of forty products per year during recent years.[45] As in the case of all other designs, there are disadvantages. In this case, the most serious limitations are their high levels of inefficiency (they are the opposite of machine bureaucracies in this regard), and the greatest potential for disruptive conflict.

INTERORGANIZATIONAL DESIGNS: GOING BEYOND THE SINGLE ORGANIZATION

All the organizational designs we have examined thus far have concentrated on the arrangement of units within an organization—what may be termed *intraorganizational designs*. However, sometimes at least some parts of different organizations must operate jointly. To coordinate their efforts on such projects, organizations must create *interorganizational designs*, plans by which two or more organizations come together. Two such designs are commonly found: *conglomerates* and *strategic alliances*.

CONGLOMERATES: DIVERSIFIED "MEGACORPORATIONS"

When an organization diversifies by adding an entirely unrelated business or product to its organizational design, it may be said to have formed a **conglomerate**. Some of the world's largest conglomerates may be found in Asia. For example, in Korea companies such as Samsung and Hyundai produce home electronics, automobiles, textiles, and chemicals in large, unified conglomerates known as *chaebols*.[46] These are all separate companies overseen by the same parent company leadership. In Japan, the same type of arrangement is known as a *keiretsu*.[47] A good example of a *keiretsu* is the Matsushita Group.[48] This enormous conglomerate consists of a bank (Asahi Bank) and a consumer electronics company (Panasonic), and has ties to several insurance companies (e.g., Sumitomo Life, Nippon Life). These examples are not meant to suggest that conglomerates are unique to Asia. Indeed, many large U.S.-based corporations, such as IBM and Tenneco, are also conglomerates, as is Johnson & Johnson, described in our Preview Case.

Companies form conglomerates for several reasons. First, as an independent business, the parent company can enjoy the benefits of diversification. Thus, as one industry languishes, another may excel, allowing for a stable economic outlook for the parent company. In addition, conglomerates may provide built-in markets and access to supplies, since companies typically support other organizations within the conglomerate. For example, General Motors cars and trucks are fitted with Delco radios, and Ford cars and trucks have engines with Autolite spark plugs, separate companies that are owned by their respective parent companies. In this manner, conglomerates can benefit by providing a network of organizations that are dependent on each other for products and services, thereby creating considerable advantages.

In recent years, however, many large conglomerates have been selling off parts of themselves in a move to concentrate on their core business.[49] For example, the giant Korean *chaebol*, Hyundai (which accounts for 10 percent of Korea's gross national product), has recently dismantled parts of its sprawling corporate structure, selling controlling interests in its heavy manufacturing and shipping companies, and severing all ties with its hotel, insurance, and department store companies.[50] In other words, compared to the 1960s, which was a period of growth for many conglomerates, the 1990s appears to be a period of decline. (We will describe more fully the general trend for organizations to downsize in Chapter 16.)

JOINT VENTURES: ALLIANCES FOR MUTUAL BENEFIT

A **joint venture** is a type of organizational design in which two or more separate companies legally combine forces to develop and operate a specific business.[51]

The goal of a joint venture is to provide benefits to each individual organization that could not be attained if they operated separately.[52]

Frequently, companies form joint ventures with foreign firms to gain entry into that country's market. The company in the host country also may benefit by the influx of foreign expertise and capital. For example, Florida's Orlando Helicopter Airway Company and China's Guangdung No. 3 Machine Tools Factory formed a joint venture in 1986 to make the first helicopters available in Guangdung Province, China.[53] Joint ventures also may allow for an exchange of technology and manufacturing services. For example, Korea's Daewoo receives technical information and is paid to manufacture automobiles for companies with which it has entered into joint venture agreements, such as General Motors, as well as Germany's Opel and Japan's Isuzu and Nissan.[54] Some companies, such as the telecommunications giant MCI, are actively involved in several joint ventures, including one in Canada and several in New Zealand.[55]

In addition to the financial incentives (circumventing trade and tariff restrictions) and marketing benefits (access to internal markets) associated with joint ventures, direct managerial benefits also are associated with extending one company's organizational chart into another's. These benefits primarily come from improved technology and greater economies of scale (e.g., sharing functional operations across organizations). For these benefits to be derived, a high degree of coordination and fit must exist between the parties, each delivering on its promise to the other. Finally, it is noteworthy that joint ventures with companies in nations with transforming economies (such as China and eastern Europe) provide good opportunities for those nations' economies to develop.[56] Given the rapid move toward globalization of the economy, we may expect to see many companies seeking joint ventures in the future as a means for gaining or maintaining a competitive advantage.[57] (Sometimes, limited joint ventures develop into more sustained alliances. For a look at a carefully planned legal alliance between two European automakers with complementary needs, see the Global Organization section on the following page.)

TECHNOLOGY: A MAJOR CAUSE—AND CONSEQUENCE—OF DESIGN

Organizations differ tremendously with respect to **technology**—the means by which they transform inputs into outputs (see Chapter 14). These can vary from the simplest of tools used by single individuals to huge machines and complex, automated equipment. Clearly, the technology employed by a given organization is closely linked to the work it performs and the major tasks it seeks to accomplish. But growing evidence indicates that this relationship, too, is something of a two-way street. Organizations not only choose the technology they will employ; they are also affected by such tools once they are selected. In short, just as the design of a specific building reflects the activities that take place within it, the structure of many organizations, too, tends to mirror the technologies they employ. In the discussion that follows, we will describe several major studies that point to this conclusion. As you will soon see, these investigations classify technology in contrasting ways and focus on a wide range of issues. Thus, their findings are often difficult to compare in a simple or direct manner. Generally, though, all point to the same basic conclusion: technology plays an important role in shaping both the design and performance of many organizations.

THE GLOBAL ORGANIZATION

"DO YOU, VOLVO, TAKE THEE, RENAULT . . . ?": AN ALLIANCE ON WHEELS

Although vows may not have been spoken and rice thrown, the 1990 alliance between Volvo and Renault, according to Rick Dowden, president and CEO of Volvo of North America, "is intended to be a marriage."[58] As in the marriage of two people, the marriage of two companies, is not taken lightly; each has some idea of what it is looking for in a partner.

Because Volvo manufactures only 400,000 cars a year, and its competitors produce millions, it was looking for a partner to help it stay competitive in the world market. Specifically, it wanted an alliance with a company that understood its business, could complement it, and was not so large that it would dominate the relationship. After its successful joint venture in the realm of engine manufacturing with Renault, Volvo felt comfortable with Renault. And Renault met Volvo's criteria: it was another auto manufacturer, but with strengths in different areas (e.g., Renault is strong in small cars and diesel engines, with developed markets in southern Europe and Latin America, whereas Volvo is strong in larger cars and gasoline technology, with strong markets in northern Europe and North America) (see Figure 15-12).

Importantly, the top executives involved, Volvo's Chairman Pehr Gellenhammar, and Renault's then-chairman Raymond Levy, held similar views about what they wanted to do and how they wanted to do it. As Dowden put it, "These were two people who knew and respected each other and had common goals and aspirations for their companies," adding, "if the people don't work together, I don't care how much the numbers seem to work, you won't get that [spirit] of cooperation."[59]

Like most marriages, the decision to formalize the relationship between Renault and Volvo came only after serious consideration of how it would work out. Various groups were formed to study how functions such as product design, research and development, and purchasing would be accomplished. After much careful study, it was concluded that Renault and Volvo would each benefit from the alliance, with enhanced competitiveness and long-term profitability. And so, in February 1990, their alliance was officially announced—an arrangement viewed as a permanent one that kept the parties separate in some ways, but brought them together in many others. To create a financial interdependence between the two companies, each bought a large portion of the other's stock.

Also like marriages between people, Volvo and Renault have had to work hard at making sure that the differences between them do not become a sore point. For example, Volvo has traditionally been a very decentralized company,

FIGURE 15-12
VOLVO AND RENAULT: SEPARATE BUT TOGETHER
After several successful joint ventures, officials from the European automakers Volvo and Renault decided to enter into a long-term alliance through which they would share resources so as to strengthen the position of each in the market.

vesting considerable power in the individual employees, whereas Renault has been—and remains—highly centralized. However, by setting up joint work groups to administer different parts of the industrial system, the companies have learned to work together and compromise their very different approaches.

Completing our marriage analogy, Volvo and Renault are planning to be loyal to each other, and to not enter into any other major alliances with other companies. Each company fully expects to benefit from its connection with the other and is unwilling to risk the success of its relationship by becoming too cozy with another. Will Volvo and Renault "live happily ever after," or will they end up in divorce court? To find out how this particular marriage works out, keep an eye on the financial pages, instead of the gossip column, of your local newspaper.

TECHNOLOGY AND STRUCTURE IN MANUFACTURING COMPANIES: THE WOODWARD STUDIES

Perhaps the best-known study on the effects of technology is one conducted in England during the 1960s by Woodward and her associates.[60] To determine the relationship between various structural characteristics (e.g., span of control, decentralization) and organizational performance (e.g., profitability, market share), these investigators gathered data about 100 manufacturing firms. In keeping with the classical view of management (described on page 594), they initially expected that organizations classified as highly successful would share similar structural characteristics, and those classified as relatively unsuccessful would share other characteristics. Surprisingly, this was not the case. Instead, various aspects of organizational structure appeared to be just as common in successful and unsuccessful companies. Thus, there was little if any support for the accuracy of universal principles of management.

Instead, Woodward and her colleagues found that the organization's success depended on the degree to which it was structured in the most appropriate way given the technology used. Specifically, they compared organizations using each of three different types of technology in popular use at the time. In the first, labeled **small-batch production**, custom work was the norm. Capital equipment (machinery) was not highly mechanized, and the companies involved typically produced small batches of products to meet specific orders from customers. Employees were either skilled or unskilled, depending on the tasks they performed. Firms included in this category made items such as specialized construction equipment or custom-ordered electronic items. Other examples include dressmaking and printing.

Companies in the second category, known as **large-batch** or **mass production**, used basic assembly-line procedures. These organizations typically engaged in long production runs of standardized parts or products. Their output then went into inventory from which orders were filled on a continuous basis. Employees were mainly unskilled or semiskilled, with a sprinkling of research and engineering personnel. The third category, known as **continuous process production**, was the most technologically complex. Here, there was no start and no stop to production, which was automated and fully integrated. Employees were skilled workers or engineers. Among the organizations employing such advanced technology were oil-refining and chemical companies.

When companies using these various types of technology were compared, important differences were noted. First, as expected, they demonstrated contrasting internal structures. For example, the span of control (of first-level supervisors) and centralization were higher in companies employing mass production than in ones using small-batch or continuous process technologies. Similarly, chains of command were longest in organizations using continuous-process production, and shortest in those using small-batch methods. In short, the type of technology employed in production appeared to be an important variable in shaping organizational structure. As Woodward herself put it, "Different technologies imposed different kinds of demands on individuals and organizations, and those demands had to be met through an appropriate structure."[61]

Perhaps even more important than these findings was the fact that the characteristics distinguishing highly successful from unsuccessful companies also varied with technology. At the low and high ends of the technology dimension described above, an *organic* management approach seemed best; companies showing this strategy were more successful than those demonstrating a *mechanistic* approach. In contrast, in the middle of the technology dimension (large-batch, or mass production), the opposite was true. Here, companies adopting a mechanistic approach tended to be more effective (see Figure 15-13). Another finding was that successful firms tended to have structures suited to their level of technology. Specifically, those with above-average performance showed structural characteristics similar to most other firms using the same type of production methods; in contrast, those with below-average records tended to depart from the median structure shown by companies in the same technology category. In summary, the results of Woodward's study indicated that important links exist between technology and performance.

FIGURE 15-13
THE WOODWARD STUDIES: THE RELATIONSHIP BETWEEN TECHNOLOGY AND DESIGN
In a classic study, Woodward found that organic organizations were most effective when performing small-batch production and continuous batch production jobs, whereas mechanistic organizations were most effective when performing large-batch production jobs. (Source: Based on findings by Woodward, 1965; see Note 60.)

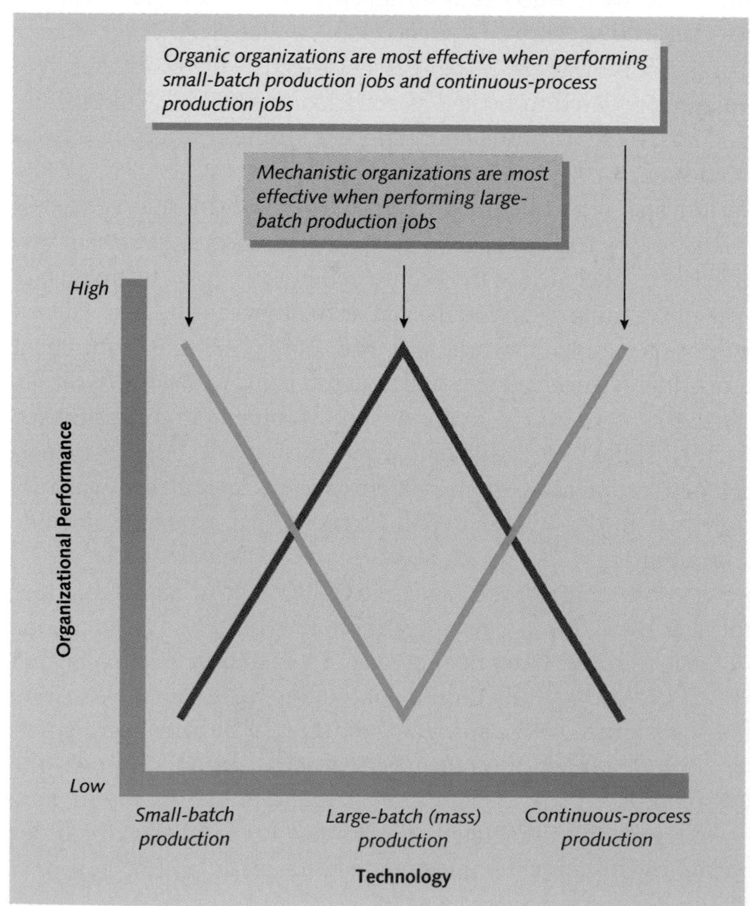

Additional support for these conclusions was later obtained in several other studies. For example, in a project involving fifty-five U.S. firms Zwerman found that organizations employing small-batch or continuous process technology tended to adopt an organic management approach.[62] Those employing mass production generally showed a mechanistic approach. In general, research has shown that the more sophisticated technology is used, the greater are the opportunities for organizations to thrive when authority is decentralized (in essence, because the "smart" technology is making the decisions, eliminating the need for some people in the hierarchy).[63] Woodward's findings are valuable because they were among the first that recognized the value of the contemporary contingency approach to organizational structure.

As you might imagine, we have learned a great deal about organizational design since Woodward's time—if for no other reason than technology has changed so much. In addition to the three types of technology studied by Woodward, today some organizations produce highly customized, high-performance products in relatively small runs. However, because these products are technologically advanced and complex, they are produced by highly automated, computer-controlled equipment. Moreover, the people involved in their manufacture often must possess a high level of professional or technical knowledge. In short, such companies share some characteristics with the traditional small-batch firms studied by Woodward, but share others with the technologically advanced continuous process firms at the other end of her continuum.

What type of internal structure do such technical batch organizations demonstrate? Evidence on this issue has been provided by Hull and Collins.[64] These researchers examined the internal structure of 110 separate companies operating in the United States. On the basis of careful examination of their methods of production, Hull and Collins divided these organizations into four categories—traditional batch, technical batch, mass production, and process production. Then they compared the companies' internal structures along several key dimensions (e.g., supervisory span of control, occupational specialization, decentralization, and formalization). As the data in Figure 15-14 show, the types differed in various ways. As predicted, organizations classified as traditional batch or technical batch in their methods of production showed contrasting structure in several respects. For example, the traditional batch companies possessed a larger supervisory span of control. In contrast, the technical batch companies showed a greater degree of occupational specialization and more decentralization. Further, and perhaps most important, the technical batch companies showed a much higher level of innovative activity (e.g., a higher percentage of employees involved in research and development activities).

In summary, expanding Woodward's original categories to reflect recent developments in methods of production yielded additional evidence for the powerful impact of technology on internal structure. Additional research along similar lines may help us to sharpen our knowledge of this important relationship still further.

FIGURE 15-14

TECHNOLOGY AND STRUCTURE: EVIDENCE OF LINKAGES

Organizations employing technical batch technology differ in several respects from those employing traditional batch technology. (Source: Based on data from Hull & Collins, 1987; see Note 64.)

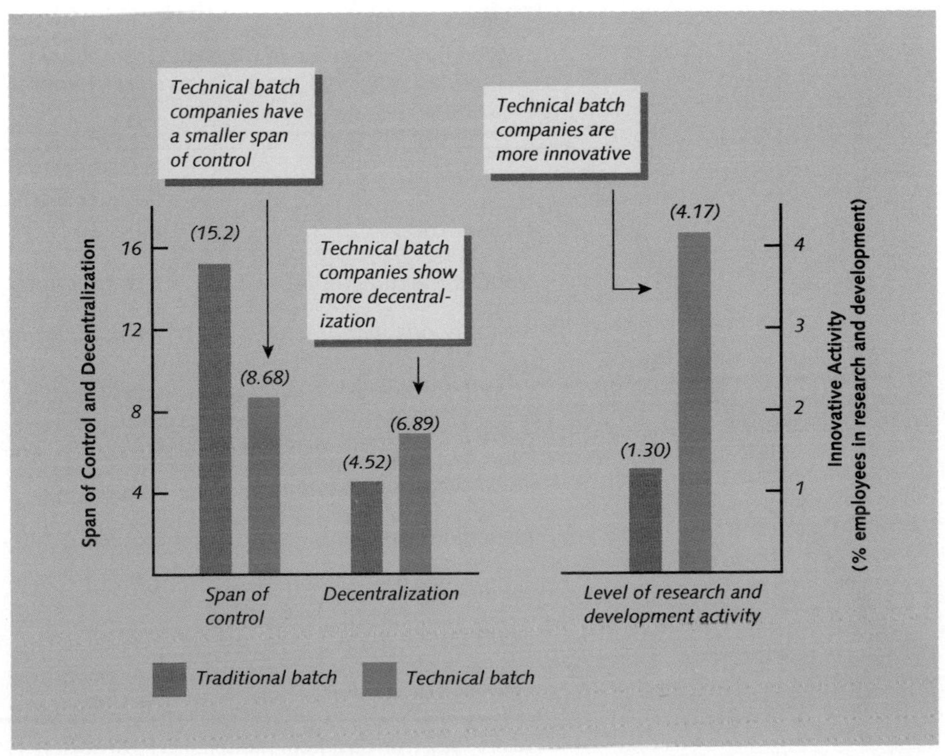

WORKFLOW INTEGRATION: THE ASTON STUDIES

As the heading of the preceding section suggests, Woodward's project, and several subsequent investigations, focused primarily on the links between technology and structure in manufacturing companies. Thus, as thorough as this work was, it left a basic issue unresolved: would similar findings be observed in other types of companies as well?

Evidence on this question was provided by another team of British researchers affiliated with the University of Aston.[65] After studying a wide range of both manufacturing and service organizations (e.g., savings banks, insurance companies, department stores), these researchers concluded that technology can be described in terms of three basic characteristics: *automation of equipment*, the extent to which work activities are performed by machines; *workflow rigidity*, the extent to which the sequence of work activities is inflexible; and *specificity of evaluation*, the degree to which work activities can be assessed by specific, quantitative means. Since these three factors appeared to be highly associated, they were combined into a single scale labeled **workflow integration**. The higher an organization's score on this scale, the more likely it was to employ automation, rigid task sequences, and quantitative measurement of its operations. The workflow integration scores obtained by various companies are shown in Table 15-5. As you can see from this table, manufacturing firms generally scored higher than those whose primary output was service.

When workflow integration was related to structural characteristics in the organizations studied, no strong or general links were uncovered. Thus, at first glance findings seemed contradictory to those reported by Woodward. Closer analysis of the data obtained, however, revealed that technological complexity *was* related to structural features in at least some ways. For example, as workflow integration increased, so did specialization, standardization, and decentralization of authority.

TABLE 15-5

Workflow Integration in Different Organizations

Manufacturing firms generally score higher on workflow integration than do service organizations (e.g., banks, stores).

ORGANIZATION	CLASSIFICATION (MANUFACTURING OR SERVICE)	WORKFLOW INTEGRATION SCORE
Vehicle manufacturer	*Manufacturing*	17
Metal goods manufacturer	*Manufacturing*	14
Tire manufacturer	*Manufacturing*	12
Printer	*Service*	11
Local water department	*Service*	10
Insurance company	*Service*	7
Savings bank	*Service*	4
Department stores	*Service*	2
Chain of retail stores	*Service*	1

Source: Based on data from Hickson, Pugh & Pheysey, 1969; see Note 65.

The magnitude of these findings was small, and they seemed to involve mainly those aspects of structure closely connected to actual workflow. Moreover, *size* exerted stronger effects on several aspects of structure than technology.

These findings, plus those obtained in later studies, point to two conclusions. First, although technology does indeed seem to affect the internal structure of organizations, it is only one of several influences. As a result, the so-called *technological imperative*—the view that technology always has a compelling influence on organizational structure—clearly overstates the case.[66] Second, technology probably exerts stronger effects on structure in small organizations, where such characteristics impinge directly on workflow, than in large ones, where structure is complex and often far removed from actual production. In any case, taken as a whole, the findings of the Aston studies can be interpreted as indicating that the impact of technology on organizational structure is not restricted to manufacturing concerns. Under certain conditions, it can be observed in other types of companies as well.

TECHNOLOGY AND INTERDEPENDENCE: THOMPSON'S FRAMEWORK

Another aspect of technology with important implications for organizational structure is **interdependence**. This refers to the extent to which individuals, departments, or units within a given organization depend on each other in accomplishing their tasks. Under conditions of low interdependence, each person, unit, or group can carry out its functions in the absence of assistance or input from others. Under high interdependence, in contrast, such coordination is essential. A framework proposed by Thompson helps clarify the various types of interdependence possible in organizations, and also the implications of this factor for effective structural design.[67]

The lowest level within this framework is known as **pooled interdependence**. Under such conditions, departments or units are part of an organization, but work does not flow between them. Rather, each carries out its tasks independently. One example of pooled interdependence is provided by the branch stores of a clothing retailer in many large shopping malls. Each contributes to the total earnings of the parent company, but there is little, if any, contact or coordination between them.

The next higher level suggested by Thompson is **sequential interdependence**. Here, the output of one department or subunit becomes the input for another. For example, the marketing department of a food company cannot proceed with promotional campaigns until it receives information about new products from the product development unit. Similarly, in a company that manufactures electronic toys, final assemblers cannot perform their jobs unless they receive a steady supply of component parts from other work units or outside suppliers. Note that in sequential interdependence, information, products, and components flow in one direction. Thus, units farther along the chain of production are dependent on ones that precede them, but the reverse is not true.

The highest level in Thompson's model is known as **reciprocal interdependence**. Here, the output of each department or unit serves as the input for other departments or units in a reciprocal fashion. Thus, the output of department A provides input for department B, and the output of department B serves as the input for department A. An example of such reciprocal interdependence is provided by the operations of the marketing and production departments of many companies. Marketing, by using appropriate surveys, may develop a profile of new products or product innovations attractive to potential customers. This serves as input for production, which considers the feasibility of actually making such products and suggests modifications. The appeal of these modifications is then assessed by marketing, and the results obtained serve as the basis for further planning by production. This process may be repeated until a plan for product innovations acceptable to both units is devised (see Figure 15-15).

These three forms of interdependence require varying levels of coordination between the units involved. The need for coordination is quite low under conditions of pooled interdependence, since each of the departments involved is relatively independent. Rules and standard operating procedures usually suffice. In contrast, sequential interdependence requires substantially greater coordination. Here formal meetings and vertical communication are often needed. Finally, reciprocal interdependence calls for concerted efforts at coordination, including many meetings and a high level of horizontal communication.[68]

The level of interdependence existing between various units within an organization also has important implications for internal structure. Special attention should be directed in organizational design to departments or units that are reciprocally interdependent. These should be grouped together so that they can engage in continuous, mutual adjustment (e.g., they should be close to each other physically and should fall under the authority of the same person). Further, specific mechanisms for assuring a high degree of coordination between them (e.g., daily meetings, the creation of special liaison positions) should be developed. Although top priority in devising internal structure should be given to reciprocal interdependence, efforts to establish effective communication between units that are sequentially interdependent are important, too. These should have ready access to one another so that workflow between them can proceed in a smooth and orderly manner.

In summary, the kind of work activities performed within an organization, and the specific technologies it employs, often determine the level of interdependence between its various units. Such interdependence, in turn, should be taken into careful account when planning internal structure. (You may have noticed that the various theories linking technology and structure have failed to address the most modern technologies—those used in many of today's high-tech firms. For a discussion of the special organizational design considerations relevant to such firms, see the Quest for Quality section on the opposite page.)

FIGURE 15-15
RECIPROCAL INTERDEPENDENCE: AN EXAMPLE
Under conditions of reciprocal interdependence, the output of two or more departments serves as the input for each other in a reciprocal fashion. (Source: Based on suggestions by Thompson, 1967; see Note 56.)

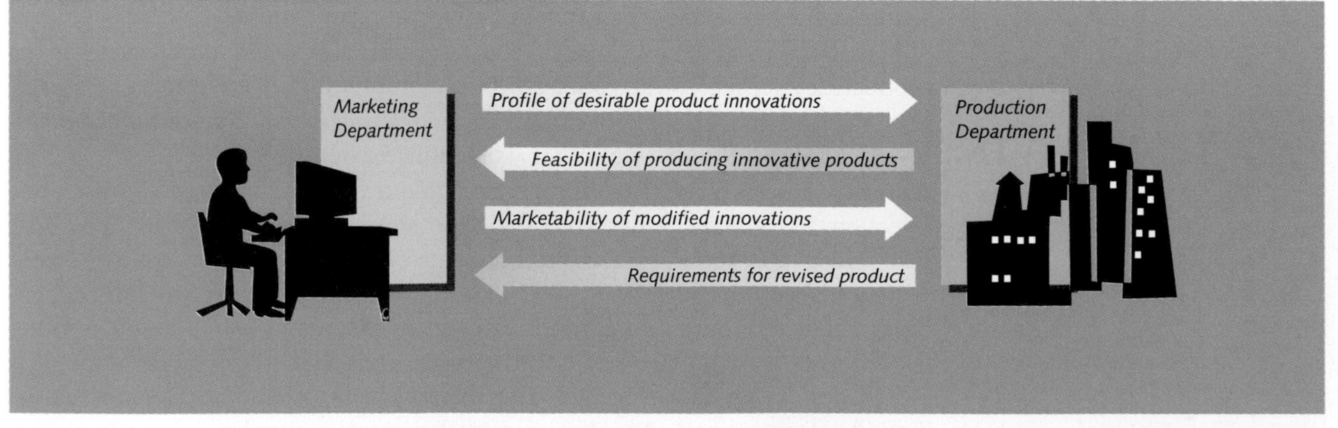

THE QUEST FOR QUALITY

FLEXIBILITY: THE KEY TO DESIGNING SUCCESSFUL HIGH-TECH ORGANIZATIONS

As we described in several places throughout this text (e.g., Chapters 6 and 14), most of today's job growth lies in high-tech fields, such as telecommunications, hardware and software design, and systems analysis. Organizations specializing in these and other high-tech areas have been springing up throughout the country. In many ways, these are not your ordinary organizations. The products they produce have extremely short life cycles (how long did you have your computer before it was replaced with a more powerful—and less expensive—model?), new products are introduced very rapidly, markets change very rapidly and narrow windows of opportunity must be met. A successful product can bring rapid growth, but it can be eclipsed by a technical breakthrough by a competitor. As a result, today's successful company can be tomorrow's bankruptcy case. In this "boom or bust" world, the idea of orderly growth and carefully considered organizational designs is just a dream. Instead, today's well-designed high-tech firm is sporting *flexibility*, and plenty of it.

From an organizational design perspective, how can high tech firms be characterized? Based on an analysis of 37 high-tech firms in California's Silicon Valley, Bahrami has identified several key characteristics.[69]

First, high-tech firms tend to be extremely flat, and have *little or no vertical hierarchy*. Because their world moves so rapidly, there is no time for the slow responses associated with seeking decisions from higher up. Instead, high-tech firms are akin to a *federation* or *constellation* of independent business units that rely on each other for expertise, and a core leadership that orchestrates a broad strategic vision. As one executive of a high-tech firm described management's mission, it is "to support our business units in fulfilling their business goals, and perform the truly corporate services in an effective and cost-efficient manner."[70] This idea that management operates as a service to the employees is typical in many high-tech firms—even very large ones, such as Apple Computer.

Second, in high-tech firms *organizational designs change quite frequently*. A design that works when a company is small and makes a few products, might be less effective when it is larger and makes several. As a case in point, consider ROLM, a telecommunications company that operated as an independent company from 1969 to 1984, when it was acquired by IBM. During its fifteen years of existence, this company had four different organizational designs, including functional (in 1973, when revenues were only $3.6 million), divisional (in 1977 when revenues were $30 million), and various combinations of these and other designs (in the 1980s, when revenues were in the hundreds of millions of dollars). ROLM's ever-changing size and technology necessitated a bewildering evolution of design structures that made the company quite a different place to work over its lifetime.

Third, competitive pressures to reduce costs have *blurred the distinction between line and staff functions*. Thus, instead of having some specialists who merely give advice (the traditional staff function) and others who have the power to make decisions based on that advice (the traditional line function), the use of teams in many high-tech work groups is putting decision-making power into the hands of those individuals who need to take action.

Fourth, instead of dividing jobs into specific predetermined roles and formal hierarchical relationships, many high-tech firms are characterized by *informal networks and relationships*. Continuous changes makes institutionalized roles and positions impractical. Instead, informal groupings of people based on the knowledge and skills they bring to the task at hand determines how people work together and what they do. Employees are required to be highly versatile, and many companies, the Intel Corporation being a prime example, go out of their way to ensure that they are exposed to a broad variety of experiences.[71]

High-quality performance in today's high-tech firms—or even their mere existence, for that matter—demands previously unheard-of levels of flexibility, agility, and versatility. Key among the adjustments required to succeed in this environment is a willingness to change one's traditional thinking about organizational design. In this rapidly changing, "anything goes" environment, any company that ties its employees to a traditional, rigid organizational form goes is likely to suffer.

SUMMARY AND REVIEW

ORGANIZATIONAL STRUCTURE

The formal configuration between individuals and groups with respect to the allocation of tasks, responsibilities, and authority within organizations is known as **organizational structure**, an abstract concept that can be represented by an **organizational chart**. Such diagrams represent five different elemental building blocks of organizational structure: **hierarchy of authority** (a summary of reporting relationships), **division of labor** (the degree to which jobs are specialized), **span of control** (the number of individuals over which a manager has responsibility), **line** versus **staff positions** (jobs permitting direct decision-making power versus jobs in which advice is given), and **decentralization** (the degree to which decisions can be made by many lower-ranking employees as opposed to only a few higher-ranking individuals).

Within organizations, groups of people can be combined into departments in various ways. The most popular approach is the **functional organization**, organizations created by combining people in terms of the common functions they perform (e.g., sales, manufacturing). An alternative approach is to departmentalize people by virtue of the specific products for which they are responsible, known as the **product organization**. Another form of **departmentalization** combines both of these approaches into a single form known as the **matrix organization**. In such organizations, people have at least two bosses; they are responsible to a superior in charge of the various functions and a superior in charge of the specific product. Employees also may have to answer to high-ranking people responsible for the entire organization, the top leaders.

ORGANIZATIONAL DESIGN

The process of coordinating the structural elements of organizations in the most appropriate manner is known as **organizational design**. **Classical organizational theorists** (such as Weber, with his notion of bureaucracy) believed that one universally best way to design organizations exists, an approach based on high efficiency. **Neoclassical organizational theorists** (such as McGregor, Argyris, and Likert) also believe that there is one best way to design organizations, although their approach emphasizes the need to pay attention to basic human needs to succeed and express oneself.

In contrast, the contemporary, **contingency approach** to organizational design is predicated on the belief that the most appropriate way to design organizations depends on the external environments within which they operate. Specifically, a key factor has to do with the degree to which the organization is subject to change: a stable environment is one in which business conditions do not change, whereas a turbulent environment is one in which conditions change rapidly. Research has shown that when conditions are stable, a **mechanistic organization** is effective. A mechanistic organization is one in which people perform specialized jobs, many rigid rules are imposed, and authority is vested in a few top-ranking officials. When conditions are turbulent, an **organic organization** is effective. These are organizations in which jobs tend to be very general, there are few rules, and decisions can be made by low-level employees. The mechanistic and organic forms are pure types, and organizations can be located in between these two extremes.

Five specific organizational forms have been identified by Mintzberg. Organizations with **simple structure** are small and informal, and have a single powerful individual, often the founding entrepreneur, who is in charge of everything (e.g., a small retail store owned by a sole proprietor). In a **machine bureaucracy**, work is highly specialized, decision making is concentrated at the top, and the work environment is not prone to change (e.g., a government office). In **professional bureaucracies**, such as hospitals and universities, there are lots of rules to follow, but employees are highly skilled and free to make decisions on their own. **Divisional structure** characterizes many large organizations (such as General Motors) in which separate autonomous units are created to deal with entire product lines, freeing top management to focus on larger-scale, strategic decisions. Finally, the **adhocracy** is a highly informal, organic organization in which specialists work in teams, coordinating with each other on various projects (e.g., many software development companies).

Other organizational designs represent ways of combining more than one organization. Such interorganizational designs include the **conglomerate** (large corporations that diversify by getting involved in unrelated businesses), and the **joint venture** (organizations combining forces to operate a specific business).

TECHNOLOGY AS A FACTOR IN ORGANIZATIONAL DESIGN

The technology employed by an organization often affects its internal structure. Companies employing **small-batch**, **large-batch (mass) production**, and **continuous process** technologies often differ with respect to their internal structure. In recent years, companies employing small-batch production coupled with a high-level technology have emerged. The internal characteristics of such companies are different from those of traditional small-batch organizations, which typically employ simpler means of production.

Organizations vary with respect to the level of **interdependence** between departments or other work units. The higher such interdependence, the greater the need for structural components that enhance coordination.

KEY TERMS

adhocracy: A highly informal, organic organization in which specialists work in teams, coordinating with each other on various projects (e.g., many software development companies).

classical organizational theory: Approaches assuming that there is a single most effective way to design organizations.

conglomerate: A form of organizational diversification in which an organization (usually a very large, multinational one) adds an entirely unrelated business or product to its organizational design.

contingency approach: The contemporary approach that recognizes that no one approach to organizational design is best, but that the best design is the one that best fits with the existing environmental conditions.

continuous process production: A highly automated form of production that is continuous in nature and highly integrated in terms of component steps and processes.

decentralization: The extent to which authority and decision making are spread throughout all levels of an organization rather than being reserved for top management (centralization).

departmentalization: The process of breaking up organizations into coherent units.

divisional structure: The form used by many large organizations, in which separate autonomous units are created to deal with entire product lines, freeing top management to focus on larger-scale, strategic decisions.

division of labor: The process of dividing the many tasks performed within an organization into specialized jobs.

functional organization: The type of departmentalization based on the activities or functions performed (e.g., sales, finance).

hierarchy of authority: A configuration of the reporting relationships within organizations; that is, who reports to whom.

horizontal organization: A new organizational design in which teams are created to focus on the various core processes necessary for the organization to do its work.

interdependence: The extent to which the units or departments within an organization depend on each other to accomplish tasks.

joint venture: A type of organizational design in which two or more separate companies legally combine forces to develop and operate a specific business.

large-batch (mass) production: Technology based on long production runs of standardized parts or products.

line positions: Positions in organizations in which people can make decisions related to doing its basic work.

machine bureaucracy: An organizational form in which work is highly specialized, decision making is concentrated at the top, and the work environment is not prone to change (e.g., a government office).

mass production: See *large-batch production*.

matrix organization: The type of departmentalization in which a product or project form is superimposed on a functional form.

mechanistic organization: An internal organizational structure in which people perform specialized jobs, many rigid rules are imposed, and authority is vested in a few top-ranking officials.

neoclassical organizational theory: An attempt to improve on the classical organizational theory that argues that economic effectiveness is not only the goal of organizational structure but also employee satisfaction.

organic organization: An internal organizational structure in which jobs tend to be very general, there are few rules, and decisions can be made by lower-level employees.

organizational chart: A diagram representing the connections between the various departments within an organization; a graphic representation of organizational design.

organizational design: The process of coordinating the structural elements of an organization in the most appropriate manner.

organizational structure: The formal configuration between individuals and groups with respect to the allocation of tasks, responsibilities, and authorities within organizations.

pooled interdependence: A relatively low level of interdependence in which units within an organization operate in a largely independent manner.

product organization: The type of departmentalization based on the products (or product lines) produced.

professional bureaucracy: An organization in which there are lots of rules to follow, but employees are highly skilled and free to make decisions on their own (e.g., hospitals and universities).

reciprocal interdependence: A high level of interdependence in which the output of each unit within an organization serves as the input for others, and vice versa.

sequential interdependence: An intermediate level of interdependence in which the output of one unit serves as input for another.

simple structure: An organization characterized as being small and informal, with a single powerful individual, often the founding entrepreneur, who is in charge of everything.

small-batch production: A technology in which products are custom-produced in response to specific customer orders.

span of control: The number of subordinates in an organization who are supervised by managers.

staff positions: Positions in organizations in which people make recommendations to others, but are not themselves involved in making decisions concerning the organization's day-to-day operations.

technology: The knowledge, tools, and procedures used by an organization to perform its major work.

workflow integration: A measure of technology that takes account of the degree of automation, workflow rigidity, and specificity of evaluation within an organization.

QUESTIONS FOR DISCUSSION

1. How are the various elements of organizational design likely to be related to each other?
2. As organizations grow and become more complex, their designs are likely to change. Describe the various ways in which size may influence organizational design. How are these changes likely to influence individuals?
3. Describe the difficulties you believe will result from implementing a matrix organization.
4. In what ways may classical and neoclassical organizational designs be considered naive when it comes to describing the behavior of people in organizations?
5. Can you identify any examples of contemporary organizations that are relatively mechanistic or relatively organic? To what extent is each characterized by stable or turbulent environments as predicted by the contingency approach to organizational design?
6. Give an example of a specific company you know that fits each of the five organizational forms identified by Mintzberg: *simple structure*, *machine bureaucracy*, *professional bureaucracy*, *divisional structure*, and *adhocracy*. On what grounds does each qualify as an example?
7. Using an example of an organization you know, describe how its prevailing technology is related to its organizational design.

THE "UPSIDE-DOWN" ORGANIZATION

We turned the organization upside-down and now the president reports to me.[1]

You might guess that this claim is a bit exaggerated. Perhaps you think that this was suggested by a vice president at the company in question. In fact, however, this boast was made by Cherie Porter, a customer service representative at the Matthew Thornton Health Plan, one of the oldest health maintenance organizations (HMOs) in the United States. Happily, Marsha Marsh, the president of this company, agrees with this assessment.

Why was the company so radically reorganized? First, the HMO itself realized that it was poorly structured to conduct business in the increasingly competitive health care marketplace. The company recognized that it could not grow as fast as the need for their services demanded. Similarly, they realized that their customers were unhappy with the benefits provided by the HMO. The company, located in New Hampshire, also identified that they were not serving many people in need of medical services in the rural areas of the state. Internally, the employees of the HMO were also displeased with the bureaucracy that had been established to manage their everyday work activities.

As a result, the top management at Matthew Thornton Health Plan recognized that a major restructuring was necessary. The decision to make such radical change was made after the leadership attended a seminar on the topic of reorganization. To identify the form of the reorganization necessary, top management began by asking the question "What do people pay us to do?"[2]

In response to this query, management began by completely restructuring their arrangement of departments and supervisors. These had been organized like most health care institutions—that is, by medical departments such as internal medicine, pediatrics, orthopedics, radiology, and so on. Each department had its own administrative staff to handle patient records and billing as well as the organization and management of physicians. After carefully studying the needs of their customers, medical staff, and other administrative personnel, the HMO was reorganized into five units. These are (1) customer service and education; (2) medical management; (3) developing quality network providers; (4) claims, processing, and payments; and (5) customer acquisition.

The unit focusing on the development of quality network providers was a completely new idea. It grew out of the companies' identification of the fact that many potential customers of the HMO were not purchasing this type of health coverage because none of the health plan's providers were located in the rural areas in which these people lived. To remedy this situation, this new area was developed so that high-quality doctors could be located throughout the state and encouraged to join the HMO. As a result of this focus and other changes made at the HMO, the number of customers enrolled in their programs increased from approximately 63,500 to 90,000 in two years.

There are two main management philosophies underlying this pattern of organization. One is that the customers tell the HMO what its problems are and how to fix them. The members of the company take very seriously the ideas and suggestions of their client base. They believe that by listening to their consumers they will provide better products and services in the most time- and cost-efficient manner. The second principle underlying this type of reorganization is known as the creation of "process owners." This refers to the idea that each employee is empowered to complete activities as if running his or her own business. By establishing this atmosphere, all individuals act responsibly by making suggestions for improvement and working in as efficient a manner as possible.

Certainly, Matthew Thornton Health Plan believes that this type of restructuring has been crucial to its continued survival. It also expects that it will need to continue to make changes and restructure its delivery systems or else face being left behind by the chaotically changing health care marketplace.

Improvements of this scope and magnitude aren't limited to small service-providing companies such as an HMO. The Union Carbide Company has used a similar approach to reduce fixed costs by $400 million in just three years. Similarly, GTE has redesigned the way in which its telephone operations are provided resulting in increases in productivity of between 20 and 30 percent. At Blue Cross of Washington and Alaska, the insurance claims-processing division increased its productivity by 20 percent in fifteen months.

In order for extensive organizational redesign to work properly and realize these types of improvements, however, it needs to be carefully implemented. Says Thomas H. Davenport, head of research for Ernst & Young, "This hammer is incredibly powerful, but you can't use it on everything."[3] Redesigning organizations works best when a company is in an industry that is experiencing a great deal of change and a burst in market competitiveness. This is why, for example, it worked so well at Matthew Thornton. The providers of health care have been facing a great increase in competition as insurers enter the HMO field and as hospitals merge to reduce capacity and increase service provisions. This process is only successful when introduced and championed by top management. Again, at this HMO the president strongly believed in the necessity of restructuring. Interestingly, however, although this process must begin at the top, it must be carried out by employees from the bottom up. This is because they are the people who know the most about the positions and are in the greatest day-to-day contact with the customers. This process was followed at the HMO with great success. In fact, it was this type of employee involvement that led Cherie Porter, the customer service representative, to remark that the company had been turned upside-down.

QUESTIONS FOR DISCUSSION

1. Construct an organization chart for Matthew Thornton Health Plan. Be prepared to defend your placement of the various entities.
2. In an organization such as Matthew Thornton, how might the span of control and distinction between line and staff positions change as the design of the organization changes?
3. Describe the nature of departmentalization at Matthew Thornton both before and after the redesign of the organization.
4. Is the newly designed company more mechanistic or more organic in nature? Explain your response.
5. Do you think that the relationship between technology and design as described by the Woodward studies will apply as well to tomorrow's organizations? Why or why not?

EXPERIENCING ORGANIZATIONAL BEHAVIOR

Mechanistic Versus Organic Organizations: Which Do You Prefer?

As we have described mechanistic and organic organizations, each is likely to be most effective under different sets of conditions. Several well-known studies cited in the chapter support this idea. Extending this work, it is an intriguing possibility that the effectiveness of each form is related to how the employees feel about that type of organization. After all, the conditions one can expect to experience in mechanistic and organic organizations are likely to be quite different—and people might not be equally comfortable with those conditions. This quiz is designed to be a self-assessment tool that helps you learn about your own preferences for each type of organization and, in doing so, learn about the various organizational forms themselves.

PROCEDURE

Each of the following questions deals with your preferences for various conditions that may exist where you work. Answer each one by checking the one alternative that best describes your feelings.

1. When I have a job-related decision to make, I usually prefer to

    ______ a. make the decision myself

    ______ b. have my boss make it for me

2. I usually find myself more interested in performing

    ______ a. a highly narrow, specialized task

    ______ b. many different types of tasks

3. I prefer to work in places in which working conditions

    ______ a. change a great deal

    ______ b. generally remain the same

4. When a lot of rules are imposed on me, I generally feel

    ______ a. very comfortable

    ______ b. very uncomfortable

5. I believe that governmental regulation of industry is

    ______ a. usually best for all

    ______ b. rarely good for anyone

Score your responses by giving yourself one point each time you answered as follows: question 1, b; question 2, a; question 3, b; question 4, a; question 5, a. The resulting score is your preference for *mechanistic organizations*. Now, subtract this score from 6. The result is your preference for *organic organizations*. Higher scores (i.e., closer to 5) reflect stronger preferences; lower scores (i.e., closer to 0) reflect weaker preferences.

POINTS TO CONSIDER

1. How did you score? In other words, which type of organization does this quiz indicate you prefer?
2. Think back at organizations in which you've worked. Can you identify some that were mechanistic and others that were organic in design? (Although your information may not be perfect, base your judgment on the descriptions appearing in the text as closely as you can.)
3. How did your own preferences fit in with the nature of the organizations? Generally, was there a match (i.e., you preferred the type of organizations within which you usually worked) or mismatch (i.e., you did not prefer the type of organizations within which you usually worked)?
4. Although it might be difficult to answer this question in an unbiased way, please give it careful thought: How were your work performance and attitudes related to any matches or mismatches? In other words, did you perform better and enjoy the job more when you worked in the type of organization you preferred? Or, did this not really make any difference?
5. Consider some of the factors that might account for your responses to question 4 above. Given that we *could* assess your job performance and attitudes (although these are not being carefully measured here), why would you expect them to be related or not related to a match between the type of organization that exists and the type of organization that is preferred?
6. What could be done to improve this questionnaire? What other items might be added, or how could the items be rewritten to better measure one's preferences for each type of organizational design?

CHAPTER OUTLINE

SPECIAL SECTIONS

SIXTEEN

ORGANIZATIONAL CHANGE AND DEVELOPMENT

LEARNING OBJECTIVES

After reading this chapter, you should be able to

1. *Identify the major forces responsible for organizational change.*
2. *Describe the primary targets of organizational change efforts.*
3. *Identify the conditions under which organizational change is likely to occur.*
4. *Explain the major factors making people resistant to organizational change—and some ways of overcoming them.*
5. *Describe the major techniques of organizational development.*
6. *Evaluate the effectiveness of organizational development efforts.*
7. *Debate the idea that organizational development is inherently unethical.*
8. *Describe current managerial practices directed at improving quality in organizations.*

Only the wisest and the stupidest of men never change.

Confucius, c. 551 B.C.–c. 479 B.C.
Chinese philosopher and teacher
Analects

To improve is to change; to be perfect is to change often.

Winston Churchill, 1874–1965
English Prime Minister,
writer and soldier
Speech, House of Commons, 1925

PREVIEW CASE

Keeping Boeing Flying High

It's impossible to escape the desperate concern for survival expressed by Boeing Co. president Philip M. Condit, when he says, "We want to make sure we're in the phone book 10 years from now." Although it would be a long journey from being one of the world's largest manufacturers of commercial jet aircraft to a crash landing in bankruptcy court, signs of a tailspin are unmistakable. In recent years, production was cut 35 percent, almost 40,000 jobs were eliminated, and losses have averaged some $3 billion a year in the United States alone for the past three years.

Boeing's problem is that its customers, the world's major airlines, have suffered unprecedented losses, taking a heavy toll on orders for new airplanes. As if this isn't bad enough, the threat of new competition looms large. Toyota, for example, has expressed interest in entering the airplane business—a prospect that has struck fear into the hearts of all who work at Boeing's Seattle headquarters. According to Dean D. Thornton, president of Boeing's Commercial Airplane Group, the company is dedicated to avoiding what other big companies have done—getting to the top and then resting on its laurels.

The result: Boeing is radically reinventing itself. Under the leadership of CEO Frank A. Shrontz, the entire process of designing and building an airplane is changing. For example, breaking with its long-standing tradition of keeping its design process top secret (customers used to refer to it as "the Kremlin"), Boeing now works side by side with its customers to better anticipate their needs. As tangible evidence, the new 777 jetliner is designed so that airline mechanics can locate galleys and lavatories almost anywhere in the cabin with just a few hours work.

This customer focus paid off when Boeing convinced United Parcel Service to choose its freighter over those from McDonnell Douglas or the French company, Airbus Industrie. The deal was closed when Boeing promised to build and design the new plane in only twenty-eight months—fully ten months quicker than usual—and at a very attractive price. Boeing is committed to maintaining 1992 prices through 1997. But how can this be done? To fulfill this promise meant radically altering the methods used in manufacturing. This was accomplished, in part, by moving to a "just-in-time" manufacturing process—one in which parts are received at the factory immediately before they are needed, thereby saving considerable money on inventory.

Philip M. Condit, President of Boeing Co.

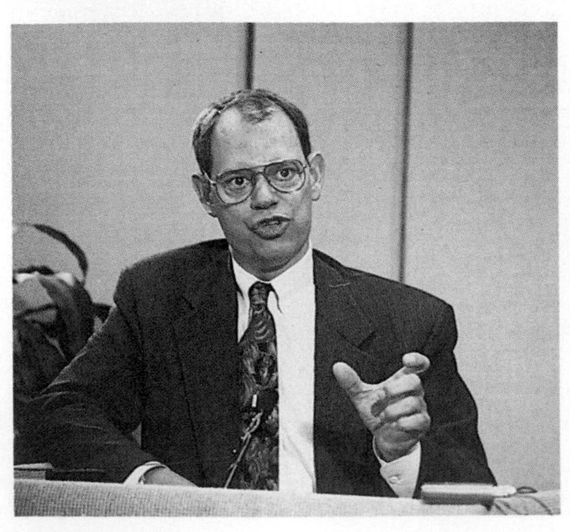

Inspired by knowledge picked up by touring factories of Japan's most productive companies (e.g., Toyota, NEC, and Komatsu), Shrontz set up a training program to get all Boeing employees to become more innovative and efficient. For example, by revising the production processes, the time taken to paint a wide-body jet was cut from seven days down to three. As a result of such improvements, the production time for a 737 jetliner was sliced in half—from almost thirteen months to about six! Despite these successes, many of Boeing's employees are growing tired of the constant pressure to keep working as efficiently as possible. In fact, some

union officials fear that workers might become so efficient that they just may put themselves out of a job.

For Boeing officials, it's not the loss of 1 or 2, or even 30,000 jobs they're most worried about, but the long-term survival of the entire company. Some industry analysts fear that no matter how much Boeing—or its competitors—find ways to cut expenses while making their products better and cheaper, airlines still will be unable to afford them. Recognizing the seriousness of this economic threat, experts have predicted that single airline companies will be a thing of the past by the year 2010. Instead, multicompany teams of engineers on three continents may design aircraft, using parts made in eight different countries. Boeing would very much like to be part of this future.

When you picture an organization fighting for its existence, you probably don't think of a large, well-established business like Boeing. Yet, confronting strong forces—many of which are beyond its control—Boeing's future is uncertain. Faced with economic pressures and the threat of competition, Boeing radically changed its manufacturing process and now provides a better product at a better price than ever before. Whether these efforts prove to be too little too late or a new beginning for Boeing, one thing is for certain: a great deal of *change* has occurred. The pressure for change is enormous, and not just at Boeing. Think of the changes you may have seen in recent years in the way businesses operate. The prices of many fast food items have dropped, some auto dealerships have adopted no-haggle pricing policies, accommodations for people with handicaps have appeared, and just about everything you can imagine has become computerized. If you think about it, signs of the impact of **organizational change** can be found everywhere (see Figure 16-1). Examining both the causes and consequences of change is one of the key missions of this chapter.

Most people have difficulty accepting that they may have to alter their work methods. After all, if you're used to working a certain way, a sudden change can be very unsettling. Fortunately, social scientists have developed various methods, known collectively as **organizational development** techniques, that are designed to implement needed organizational change in a manner that both is acceptable to

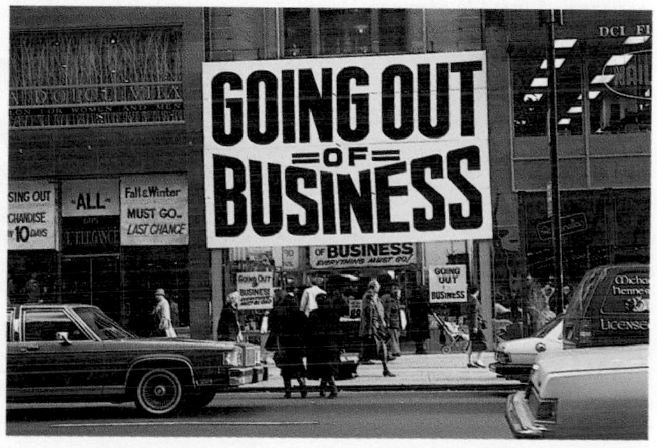

FIGURE 16-1
SIGNS OF THE TIMES: SIGNALS OF ORGANIZATIONAL CHANGE
Signs such as these provide a good indication of changing environmental conditions that influence organizational functioning. Organizational growth places demands on the pool of available human resources (left), sometimes compensating for increased supply generated by organizational decline elsewhere (right).

employees and enhances the effectiveness of the organizations involved.[1] We will examine these techniques and their effectiveness in this chapter, including strategies focusing on improving organizational quality that are in popular use today. Before doing so, however, we will take a closer look at the organizational change process by chronicling different forces for change acting on organizations. Then we will explore some major issues involved in the organizational change process, such as what is changed, when change will occur, why people are resistant to change, and how this resistance can be overcome.

ORGANIZATIONAL CHANGE: SOME DETERMINING FACTORS

A century ago, advances in machine technology made farming so highly efficient that fewer hands were needed to plant and reap the harvest. The displaced laborers fled to nearby cities, seeking jobs in newly opened factories, opportunities created by some of the same technologies that sent them from the farm (see Chapter 14). The economy shifted from agrarian to manufacturing, and the *Industrial Revolution* was under way. With it came drastic shifts in where people lived, how they worked, how they spent their leisure time, how much money they made, and how they spent it. Today's business analysts claim that we are currently experiencing *another* industrial revolution—one driven by a new wave of economic and technological forces.[2] As one observer put it, "This workplace revolution . . . may be remembered as a historic event, the Western equivalent of the collapse of communism."[3]

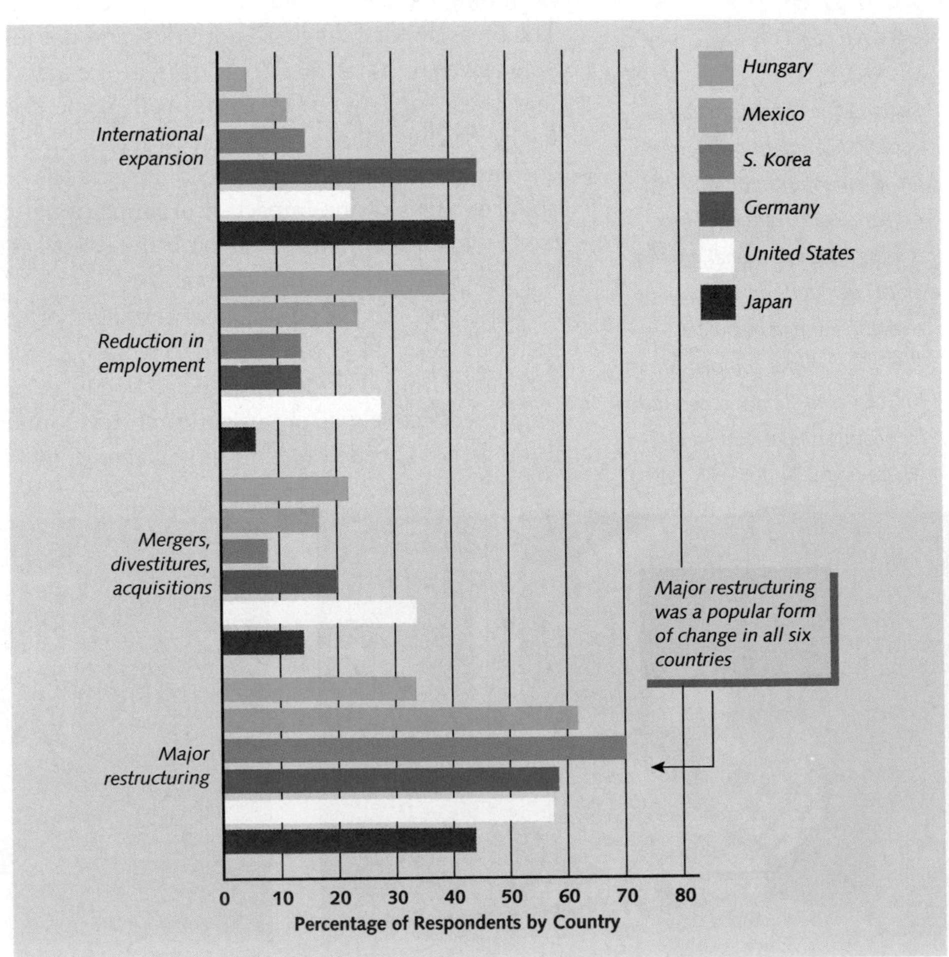

FIGURE 16-2
ORGANIZATIONAL CHANGE: AN INTERNATIONAL PHENOMENON
A large cross-national survey found that various forms of organizational change are reported to occur throughout the world. Shown here are the percentages of respondents in six countries indicating that each of four different forms of change occurred in organizations within their country in the past two years. Major restructuring was found to be the most widely encountered form of change in most countries. (Source: Based on data reported by Kanter, 1991; see Note 4.)

Interestingly, the forces for organizational change are not isolated to the United States; they appear to be global in nature. To illustrate this point, consider the findings of a survey of 12,000 managers in twenty-five different countries conducted just a few years ago.[4] When asked to identify the changes they've experienced in the past two years, respondents reported that major restructurings, mergers, divestitures and acquisitions, reductions in employment, and international expansion had occurred in their nations. Figure 16-2 shows the percentage reporting each of these activities in six selected nations. Although some forms of change were more common in some countries than others, organizations in all countries were actively involved in each of these change efforts—especially major restructurings. Clearly, the evidence suggests that organizational change is occurring throughout the world.

In recent years, just about all companies, large and small, have made adjustments in the ways they operate, some more pronounced than others. Citing the most publicized examples from recent years, General Electric, Allied Signal, Ameritech, and Tenneco have radically altered the way they operate, their culture, the technology they use, their structure, and the nature of their relations with employees.[5] With so many companies making such drastic changes, the message is clear: *either adapt to changing conditions or shut your doors.*

Unfortunately, many companies fail to change when required and find themselves out of business as a result.[6] In fact, fully 62 percent of new ventures fail to last as long as five years, and only 2 percent make it for fifty years.[7] Amazingly, however, some American companies have beaten the odds—so soundly, in fact, that they have remained in business for well over two hundred years (see Table 16-1 for a summary of these "corporate Methuselahs").[8] As you might imagine, these companies have undergone *many* changes during their years of existence. For example, the United States' oldest company, J. E. Rhoads & Sons, now makes conveyer belts, although it originally started out in 1702 making buggy whips. Another company,

TABLE 16-1

The Ten Oldest Companies in America

Very few companies continue to exist as long as the ones shown here. As you might expect, all have undergone considerable changes in their 200 to 300 years.

RANK	YEAR FOUNDED	NAME	CURRENT BUSINESS
1	1702	J. E. Rhoads & Sons	Conveyer belts
2	1717	Covenant Life Insurance	Insurance
3	1752	Philadelphia Contributionship	Insurance
4	1767	Dexter	Adhesives and coatings
5	1784	D. Landreth Seed	Seeds
6	1784	Bank of New York	Banking
7	1784	Mutual Assurance	Insurance
8	1784	Bank of Boston	Banking
9	1789	George R. Ruhl & Sons	Bakery supplies
10	1790	Burns & Russell	Building materials

Source: "The Ten Oldest Companies in America" from *Fortune*, July 26, 1993.

Dexter, in Windsor Locks, Connecticut, began in 1767 as a grist mill. As you might imagine, it no longer does that; now it makes adhesives and coatings for aircraft. Earlier, it manufactured specialty papers for stationery and for tea bags. Obviously, this company is very willing to change. According to Dexter spokesperson Ellen Cook, "We have no traditions, whatsoever. None."[9]

Obviously, ever-changing conditions pose a formidable challenge to organizations, which must learn to be flexible and adapt to them. However, not all organizational changes are the result of unplanned, externally imposed factors. Some organizational changes are planned, and quite intentional. The large variety of determinants of organizational change—forces dictating change—can be organized into four major categories. These categories are created by combining two key distinctions: (1) whether the organizational change is *planned* or *unplanned* by the organization, and (2) whether it derives from factors *internal* or *external* to the organization. The taxonomy that results from combining these two dimensions—planned internal change, planned external change, unplanned internal change, and unplanned external change—will be used to summarize our presentation of the major determinants of organizational change.

PLANNED INTERNAL CHANGE

A great deal of organizational change comes from the strategic decision to alter the way an organization does business or the very nature of the business itself. Three examples of planned organizational change can be identified—changes in products or services, changes in administrative systems, and changes in organizational size and structure.

CHANGES IN PRODUCTS OR SERVICES

Imagine that you and a friend begin a small janitorial business. The two of you divide the duties, each doing some cleaning, buying supplies, and performing some administrative work. Before long, the business grows and you expand, adding new employees, and really begin "cleaning up." Many of your commercial clients express interest in window cleaning, and so you and your partner think it over and decide to expand into the window-cleaning business as well. This decision to take on a new direction to the business, to add a new, specialized service, will require a fair amount of organizational change. Not only will new equipment and supplies be needed, but also new personnel will have to be hired and trained, new insurance will have to be purchased, and new accounts will have to be secured. In short, the planned decision to change the company's line of services necessitates organizational change.

This is exactly the kind of change that Federal Express encountered in 1989 when it sought to expand its package delivery service, formerly limited exclusively to North America, to international markets, or that Citicorp, a longtime leader in consumer banking, encountered when it attempted to become an international leader in corporate banking.[10,11] As you are undoubtedly aware, the rash of new products and services offered to consumers each year is staggering. Unfortunately, many of these are unsuccessful; only about one out of every eight ever becomes profitable. In fact, both Federal Express and Citicorp have experienced difficult financial battles in their attempts to expand their service markets beyond their traditional boundaries.

CHANGES IN ADMINISTRATIVE SYSTEMS

Although an organization may be forced to change its policies, reward structure, goals, and management style in response to outside competition, governmental regulation, and economic changes (as we will note later), it is also quite common for changes in administrative systems to be strategically planned in advance. Such changes may stem from a desire to improve efficiency, to change the company's image, or to gain a political power advantage within the organization (see Chapter 12).[12] As an example of this, let's consider the decision by PepsiCo to structurally reorganize.[13] For many years, PepsiCo had a separate international food service division, which included the operation of sixty-two foreign locations of the company's Pizza Hut and Taco Bell restaurants. Because of the great profit potential of these foreign restaurants, PepsiCo officials decided to reorganize, putting these restaurants directly under the control of the same executives responsible for the successful national operations of Pizza Hut and Taco Bell. This type of departmentalization allows the foreign operations to be managed under the same careful guidance as the national operations (see Chapter 15).

Typically, the pressure to bring about changes in the administration of organizations (e.g., to coordinate activities, set goals and priorities) comes from upper management—that is, from the top down. In contrast, pressure to change the central work of the organization (i.e., the production of goods and services) comes from the technical side of the organization, from the bottom upward.[14] This is the idea behind the **dual-core model** of organizations. Many organizations, especially medium-size ones, may be characterized by potential conflicts between the administrative and the technical cores—each faction wishing to change the organization according to its own vested interests. Which side usually wins? Research suggests that the answer depends on the design of the organization in question (refer to Chapter 15). Organizations that are highly *mechanistic* as opposed to *organic* in their approach (i.e., ones that are highly formal and centralized) tend to be more successful in introducing administrative changes.[15] The high degree of control wielded by the administrative core paves the way for introducing administrative change.

CHANGES IN ORGANIZATIONAL SIZE AND STRUCTURE

Just as organizations change their products, services, or administrative systems to stay competitive, so too do they alter the size and basic configurations of their organizational charts—that is, they *restructure*. In many cases, this has meant reducing the number of employees needed to operate effectively—a process known as **downsizing**.[16] Typically, this involves more than just laying off people in a move to save money. It is directed at adjusting the number of employees needed to work in newly designed organizations, and is therefore also known as **rightsizing**.[17] Whatever you call it, the bottom line is painfully clear: many organizations need fewer people to operate today than in the past—sometimes far fewer.

The statistics tell a sobering tale. Since 1979 *Fortune* 500 companies have eliminated a quarter of the jobs they once provided, some 4.4 million positions.[18] One recent survey found that some degree of downsizing has been occurring in about half of all U.S. companies—especially in the middle management and supervisory ranks.[19] In fact, figures for the first half of 1993 showed that 2,389 Americans lost their jobs each working day.[20] Although layoffs have been occurring across the board in the United States and other major countries, some industries have felt the brunt of it more than others. Table 16-2 presents the number of layoffs announced by various American industries from January through July 1993. Boeing's woes,

TABLE 16-2

Layoffs: Where Are They Occurring Most?

During the first seven months of 1993 millions of jobs were eliminated. The greatest numbers of layoffs were announced in the five industries shown here. As noted, the job axe cut particularly deep in some companies.

INDUSTRY	TOTAL NUMBER OF LAYOFFS ANNOUNCED (JANUARY–JULY 1993)	COMPANIES MOST AFFECTED
Aerospace	*89,890*	*28,000 jobs lost at Boeing*
Computers	*86,257*	*60,000 jobs lost at IBM*
Retailing	*62,090*	*50,000 jobs lost at Sears*
Food processing, consumer goods	*23,504*	*13,000 jobs lost at Procter & Gamble*
Transportation	*12,073*	*Jobs eliminated by most airlines*
Communications	*10,329*	*6,200 jobs lost at GTE, 1,400 jobs lost at AT&T*

Source: Based on information reported in Richman, 1993; see Note 20.

described in our Preview Case, are typical of those found in the aerospace business, the industry with the dubious distinction of topping this list.

Another way organizations are restructuring is by completely eliminating parts of themselves that focus on noncore sectors of the business, and hiring outside firms to perform these functions instead—a practice known as **outsourcing**.[21] For example, companies like ServiceMaster, which provides janitorial services, and ADP, which provides payroll processing services, make it possible for organizations to concentrate on the business functions most central to their mission, thereby freeing them from these peripheral support functions.

In some cases, the only way people can tell that their part of the organization no longer exists is that they receive paychecks from someone else. For example, Xerox has taken over all the internal service functions of Bankers Trust (e.g., mailroom, print shop, employee record keeping, payroll, telephone switchboard), employing in many cases, the same individuals who used to perform these functions while working for Bankers Trust.[22] Ironically, some businesses providing outsourcing services, such as EDS, a data-processing firm with $8.2 billion in annual sales, have become so large that they may outsource some services themselves while providing outsourcing services to their clients.[23]

Some critics fear that outsourcing represents a "hollowing out" of companies—a reduction of functions that weakens organizations by making them more dependent on others.[24] Others counter that outsourcing makes sense when the work that is outsourced is not crucial to competitive success (e.g., janitorial services), or when it is so crucial that the only way to succeed requires outside assistance.[25] For example, when Apple Computer introduced its first notebook computer, the Macintosh Powerbook 100, it subcontracted its manufacturing to Sony, enabling it to speed entry into the market.[26] Although this practice may sound unusual, it isn't. In fact, one industry analyst has estimated that 30 percent of the largest American industrial firms outsource over half their manufacturing.[27] (Sometimes, instead of eliminating entire organizational functions and buying them back through outside service providers, organizations are eliminating individual jobs and hiring people to perform them on an as-needed basis. For a closer look at this practice, see the Organization of Tomorrow section below.)

THE ORGANIZATION OF TOMORROW

THE CONTINGENCY WORKFORCE: PERMANENT TEMPORARY EMPLOYEES

For most people, the thought of temporary employment probably brings to mind the image of someone wrapping packages at a department store at Christmas, or an income tax preparer working from February 1 through April 15. But, how about a senior executive? Believe it or not, a growing number of companies have been hiring executives from temporary-employment firms such as Imcor (located in Stamford, Connecticut), which specializes in providing companies with temporary senior executives.[28] Such "throwaway executives" have been hired to come in and make hard decisions—such as firing certain individuals—that those hoping to keep their jobs might shy away from (see Figure 16-3).

Although there's little chance that most companies will be turning in their full-time, experienced top executives anytime soon, there has been a sustained growth in what has been called the **contingency workforce**—people hired to perform temporary work caused by unexpected or temporary challenges faced by organizations. The contingency workforce includes not only the traditional part-time employees, such as department store Santas, but also freelancers, subcontractors, and independent professionals. In fact, the contingent workforce is so large that Manpower, the biggest temporary employment agency in the United States, is also the country's largest employer: some 600,000 people are on its payroll—200,000 more than General Motors.[29]

The trend toward corporate restructuring has caused many companies to keep their staff sizes so small that they must frequently draw on the services of Manpower, or any other of the nation's 7,000 temporary employment firms for help. In fact, some analysts predict that by the year 2000, just a few years from now, half of all working Americans—some 60 million people—will be working on a part-time or freelance basis. Specifically, British consultant Charles Handy has described the organization of the future as being more like an apartment than a home for life, "an association of temporary residents gathered together for mutual convenience."[30] Although others believe this prospect is far-fetched, it is clear that a growing number of people are seeking the freedom and variety of temporary employment rather than facing repeated layoffs from ever-downsizing corporations. They are opting for permanent impermanence in their jobs, so to speak.

There are, of course, downsides to temporary employment, both for employees and employers. Benefits, which

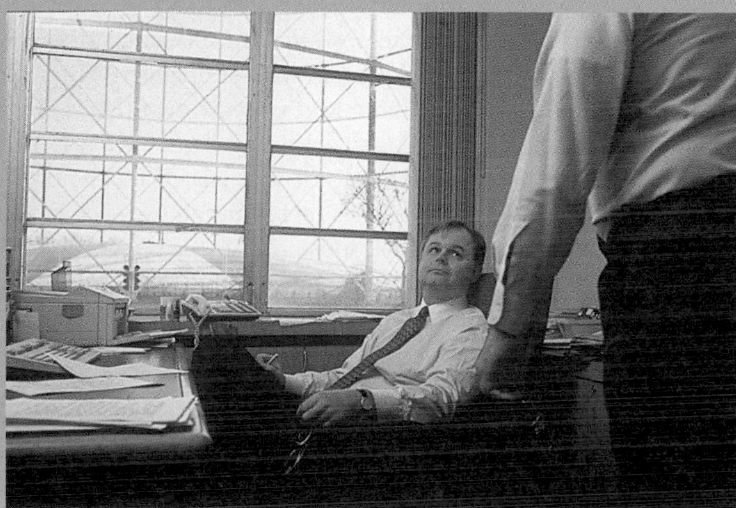

FIGURE 16-3
THE "DISPOSABLE" SENIOR EXECUTIVE: A NEW BREED
Matthew Harrison, 49, is the head of a manufacturing company in Queens, New York, a position he holds only temporarily. In fact, this is one of four such executive posts he has held during the past seven years. A growing number of companies are using temporary employees, even at high organizational levels.

make up about 30 percent of a full-time employee's wages, are typically lacking, and wages are often lower. Moreover, some "unwilling contingent workers" consider their temporary work too stressful, and would prefer full-time employment—*if* they could find it. Meanwhile the daily availability of temporary workers is at an all-time high of approximately 2 million, providing a boon to companies seeking their talents. Kolmar Laboratories, a Port Jervis, New York, maker of cosmetics, has filled as many as half of its 600 assembly-line jobs with temporary workers. Unfortunately, so much conflict erupted between the temporary employees (paid $5.60 per hour without benefits) and the permanent employees (paid $9 per hour plus benefits) that the expenses of having to rework products and recruit and train new employees offset the savings in wages.

Many corporate officials strongly adhere to the belief that quality performance depends on the kind of skill and commitment to the organization that temporaries cannot offer. Says Georgia-Pacific's CEO, Pete Correll, "Our manufacturing facilities need operators who are well trained and who understand the quality requirements of the job. You can't just drop someone into that. We want workers who will buy into our dream...."[31] Thus, although there may be a growing number of contingency employees, either by choice or by happenstance, the permanent employee is in no danger of extinction—although the size of the herd is most certainly dwindling.

PLANNED EXTERNAL CHANGE

In addition to planning changes in the ways organizations are run, it is often possible to plan which change variables originating outside the organization will be incorporated into it. Introductions of new technology and advances in information processing and communication fall into this category. Both of these advances typically originate outside the organization and are introduced into it in some planned fashion.

INTRODUCTION OF NEW TECHNOLOGIES: FROM SLIDE RULES TO COMPUTERS

As described in Chapter 14, advances in technology have produced changes in the way organizations operate. Senior scientists and engineers, for example, can probably tell you how their work was drastically altered in the mid-1970s, when their ubiquitous plastic slide rules gave way to powerful pocket calculators. Things changed again only a decade later, when calculators were supplanted by powerful desktop microcomputers, which have revolutionized the way documents are prepared, transmitted, and filed in an office. Manufacturing plants have also seen a great deal of growth recently in the use of computer-automated technology and robotics (see Chapter 14). Each of these examples represents an instance in which technology has altered the way people do their jobs.

The use of computer technology has been touted as one of the major revolutions occurring in the business world today. Not only are personal computers found in 30 percent of American homes, but they also are used by people in practically every job you can think of, from agricultural agent to zookeeper.[32] During the earliest years in which computers were used in the workplace, they failed to fulfill the promise of increased productivity that was used to usher them in. The hardware and software technology was not only too primitive, but also the users were too unprepared. Today, however, this has finally changed. According to William Wheeler, a consultant at Coopers & Lybrand, "For the first time the computer is an enabler of productivity improvement rather than a cause of lack of productivity."[33]

ADVANCES IN INFORMATION PROCESSING AND COMMUNICATION

Although we now easily take for granted everyday events such as television transmissions and long-distance telephone calls, these things were merely exotic dreams not too many years ago. If you've ever seen an old western film in which the Pony Express rider struggled through uncharted territories to deliver messages to people in distant western cities, you are well aware of the difficulties that people faced communicating over long distances. Of course, with today's sophisticated satellite transmission systems, fiber-optic cables crisscrossing the planet, fax machines, portable telephones, teleconferencing facilities and the like, it is easier than ever for businesses to communicate with each other and with their clients (see Chapters 9 and 14). Our main point is that as such communication systems improve, opportunities for organizational growth and improvement follow.[34]

One key to success is to selectively incorporate advances in technology that allow organizations to share vast amounts of information faster and more widely than ever before. For example, as recently as 1987 General Electric Lighting had thrity-four warehouses and twenty-five customer service centers. Today, using a vast computer network linked to a database, the company needs only eight warehouses and one customer service center to do the same amount of work even more efficiently. Indeed, information technology is reducing the need for expensive investments in physical assets such as factories and warehouses. Seeing this handwriting on the wall, companies are now investing more money on equipment to manage information (e.g., computers and telecommunications hardware) than on such traditional capital expenses as industrial equipment.[35]

UNPLANNED INTERNAL CHANGE

Not all forces for change are the result of strategic planning. Indeed, organizations must often be responsive to changes that are unplanned—especially those derived from factors internal to the organization. Two such forces are changes in the demographic composition of the work force, and performance gaps.

CHANGING EMPLOYEE DEMOGRAPHICS

It is easy to see, even within your own lifetime, how the composition of the workforce has changed. Consider these illustrative statistics and projections for the American workforce as the twentieth century draws to a close.

- The percentage of women in the American workforce is greater than ever before. In 1976, women accounted for 40.5 percent of the adult workforce, a figure that had increased to 45 percent by 1988 and is projected to rise to 47.3 percent by 2000.[36]
- The American workforce is getting older. People aged 35 to 54 constituted 38 percent of the workforce in 1985, but they will be 51 percent of the workforce by the year 2000.[37]
- The American workforce is becoming more culturally diverse. In 1980,

African-Americans made up 10 percent of the workforce and Hispanic-Americans made up 6 percent. By the year 2000, African-Americans are expected to represent 12 percent of the workforce, Hispanic-Americans will account for 10 percent, and Asian-Americans, 4 percent.[38]

These statistics represent only some of the major demographic changes that have been occurring in the American labor force. To people concerned with the long-term operation of organizations, these are not simply curious sociological trends, but shifting conditions that will force organizations to change. Questions regarding the number of people who will be working, what skills they will bring to their jobs, and what new influences they will bring to the workplace are of key interest to human resources managers. In the words of Frank Doyle, corporate vice president for external and industrial relations at General Electric, the impending changes in workforce demographics "will turn the professional human resources world upside down."[39] Indeed, some companies such as American Express have already responded to these changes by educating their supervisors on how to manage a changing, increasingly diversified workforce.[40]

PERFORMANCE GAPS

If you've ever heard the phrase "If it's not broken, don't fix it," you already have a good feel for one of the most potent sources of unplanned internal changes in organizations—*performance gaps*. A product line that isn't moving, a vanishing profit margin, a level of sales that isn't up to corporate expectations—these are examples of gaps between real and expected levels of organizational performance. Few things force change more than sudden and unexpected information about poor performance. Organizations usually stay with a winning course of action and change in response to failure; in other words, they follow a *win–stay/lose–change rule*. Indeed, several studies have shown that a performance gap is one of the key factors providing an impetus for organizational innovation.[41] Those organizations that are best prepared to mobilize change in response to unexpected downturns are expected to be the ones that succeed.

UNPLANNED EXTERNAL CHANGE

One of the greatest challenges faced by an organization is its ability to respond to changes from the outside world over which it has little or no control. As the environment changes, organizations must follow suit. Research has shown that organizations that can best adapt to changing conditions tend to survive.[42] Two of the most important unplanned external factors are governmental regulation and economic competition.

GOVERNMENT REGULATION

One of the most commonly witnessed unplanned organizational changes results from government regulations. In the late 1980s, restaurant owners in the United States had to alter the way they report the income of waiters and waitresses to the federal government for purposes of collecting income taxes. In recent years, the U.S. federal government has been involved in both imposing and eliminating regulations in industries such as commercial airlines (e.g., mandating inspection schedules, but no longer controlling fares) and banking (e.g., restricting the

FIGURE 16-4
GOVERNMENT REGULATION: WILL IT MAKE CRAB FISHING SAFER?
With a death rate of 660 per 100,000 workers—close to one hundred times the national average—crab fishing is the most lethal job in America. Governmental regulations have focused on changing the way this industry operates so as to increase safety.

amount of time checks can be held before clearing, but no longer regulating interest rates). Such activities have greatly influenced the way business is conducted in these industries.

An excellent example of how government activities drive organizational change is provided by the 1984 divestiture of AT&T. A settlement of antitrust proceedings dramatically rearranged the activities of almost a million employees of the Bell System. Among other things, the agreement led to the creation of seven new independent companies. At Southwestern Bell, CEO Zane Barnes remarked that the divestiture forced them to "rethink the functions of some 90,000 employees," a process likened to "taking apart and reassembling a jumbo jet while in flight."[43] Not surprisingly, the company relied on its expertise in satellite and communications technology to provide information about the change process to its employees in fifty-seven locations.

Government regulations are often imposed on organizations following some crisis of public health or safety. For example, following the March 22, 1990, sinking of a crab-fishing boat, the *Aleutian Enterprise*, off the coast of Alaska, the National Transportation Safety Board stiffened regulations regarding the condition of ships and the procedures used to bring in the catch (see Figure 16-4).[44] Similarly, following the 1979 accident at Three Mile Island, the Nuclear Regulatory Commission imposed safety standards on all nuclear power plants.[45]

ECONOMIC COMPETITION IN THE GLOBAL ARENA

It happens every day: someone builds a better mousetrap—or at least a cheaper one. As a result, companies often must fight to maintain their share of the market, advertise more effectively, and produce products more inexpensively. This kind of economic competition not only forces organizations to change, but also demands that they change effectively if they are to survive. On some occasions, competition can become so fierce that the parties involved would actually be more effective if they dropped their swords and joined forces. It was this "If you can't beat 'em, join 'em" reasoning that was responsible for the announced alliance between arch rivals IBM and Apple Computer in the summer of 1991, an alliance dubbed "the deal of the decade" by one financial analyst.[46]

Although competition has always been crucial to organizational success, today competition comes from around the globe. As it has become increasingly less expensive to transport materials throughout the world, the industrialized nations have found themselves competing with each other for shares of the international marketplace. This is especially the case since markets have opened up to the new capitalist nations of eastern Europe and the former Soviet Union, creating an ever-growing global marketplace. This situation is made more complex by the newly developing economic powers of the Third World (e.g., Mexico, South Korea), nations that are rapidly developing their own corporate giants ready to compete in the world market.[47]

This extensive globalization presents a formidable challenge to all organizations wishing to compete in the world economy. The primary challenge is to meet the ever-present need for change, to be innovative. For example, consider how the large American automobile manufacturers suffered by being unprepared to meet the world's growing demand for small, high-quality cars—products their Japanese competitors were only too glad to supply to an eager marketplace. Today, the same countries that posed threats for American-made products now provide markets. Global competition has accelerated so rapidly that between 1987 and 1992 the value of U.S. direct foreign investment abroad rose 35 percent (to $776 billion) and the value of foreign investment in the United States doubled (to $692 billion). With this rapidly changing growth in globalization, one thing is certain: only the most adaptive organizations can survive.

As we have been describing in this part of the chapter, organizations change in many ways and for many reasons. For a summary of these sources of organizational change, see Table 16-3.

THE PROCESS OF ORGANIZATIONAL CHANGE: SOME BASIC ISSUES

As you might imagine, the process of changing organizations is not haphazard; rather, it proceeds according to some well-established, orderly fashion. It is well known, for example, what the targets of organizational change efforts may be. Under which conditions organizational change is likely to occur, and when people will be most likely to resist making such changes, are also known. We will address these basic issues in this section.

TARGETS OF ORGANIZATIONAL CHANGE: WHAT IS CHANGED?

Imagine that you are an engineer responsible for overseeing the maintenance of a large office building. The property manager has noted a dramatic increase in the

TABLE 16-3

Varieties of Organizational Change: A Summary

Organizational changes may be either planned or unplanned, and based on either internal or external forces. Some examples of changes within each of the four categories are listed here.

IS THE CHANGE BASED ON INTERNAL OR EXTERNAL FORCES?	IS THE CHANGE PLANNED OR UNPLANNED? PLANNED CHANGE	UNPLANNED CHANGE
Internal change	■ *Changes in products or services*	■ *Changing employee demographics*
	■ *Changes in administrative systems*	■ *Performance gaps*
	■ *Changes in organizational size or structure (e.g., downsizing, outsourcing)*	
External change	■ *Introduction of new technologies*	■ *Government regulations*
	■ *Advances in information processing and communication*	■ *External competition*

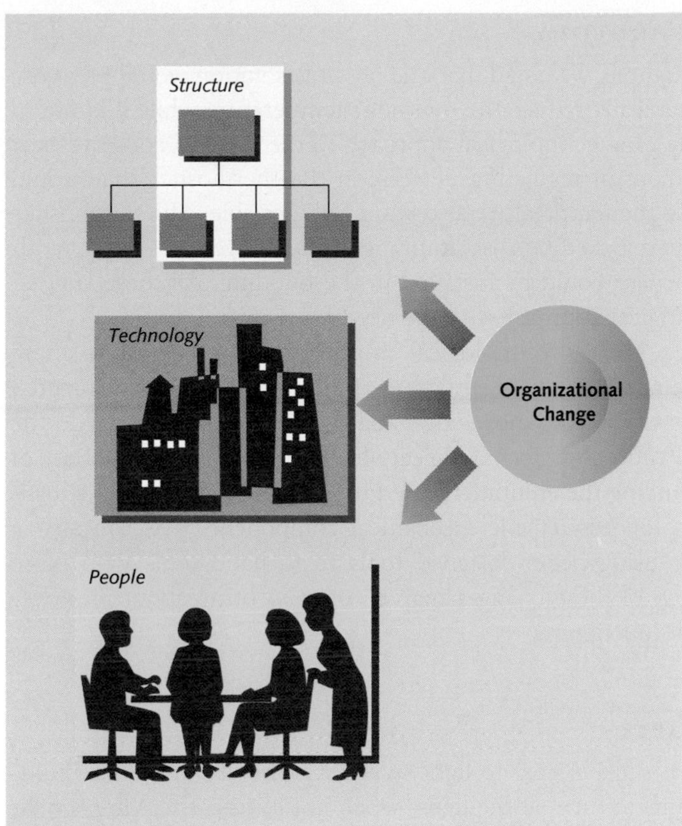

FIGURE 16-5
ORGANIZATIONAL CHANGE TARGETS: STRUCTURE, TECHNOLOGY, PEOPLE
To create change in organizations, one can rely on altering organizational structure, technology, and/or people. Changes in any one of these areas may necessitate changes in the others.

use of heat in the building, causing operating costs to skyrocket. In other words, a need for change exists—specifically, a reduction in the building's heat usage. You cannot get the power company to lower its rates, so you realize you must bring about changes in the use of heat. But how? One possibility is to rearrange job responsibilities so that only maintenance personnel are permitted to adjust thermostats. Another option is to put timers on all thermostats so that the building temperature is automatically lowered during periods of nonuse. Finally, you consider the idea of putting stickers next to the thermostats, requesting that occupants do not adjust them. These three options represent good examples of the three potential targets of organizational change we will consider—changes in *organizational structure*, *technology*, and *people* (see Figure 16-5).

CHANGES IN ORGANIZATIONAL STRUCTURE

In Chapter 15 we described the key characteristics of organizational structure. Here, we note that altering the structure of an organization may be a reasonable way of responding to a need for change. In the above example, a structural solution to the heat regulation problem came in the form of reassigning job responsibilities. Indeed, modifying rules, responsibilities, and procedures may be an effective way to manage change. Changing the responsibility for temperature regulation from a highly decentralized system (whereby anyone can make adjustments) to a centralized one (in which only maintenance personnel may do so) is one way of implementing organizational change in response to a problem. This particular structural solution called for changing the power structure (i.e., who was in charge of a particular task).

Different types of structural changes may take other forms.[48] For example, changes can be made in an organization's span of control, altering the number of employees for which supervisors are responsible. Structural changes also may take the form of revising the basis for creating departments—such as from product-based departments to functional departments (see Chapter 15). Other structural changes may be much simpler, such as clarifying someone's job description or the written policies and procedures followed.

Structural changes are not uncommon in organizations. Consider, for example, some changes reported in recent years at the huge consumer products company Procter & Gamble.[49] In response to growing competition, the company was forced to make a number of changes that streamlined its highly bureaucratic organizational structure. For example, the decision-making process used to be so centralized that many decisions that could have been made at lower levels were being made by top corporate personnel—such as the color of the cap on the can of decaffeinated instant Folger's coffee! Now decentralized business teams have been instituted and are permitted to make all the decisions about developing, manufacturing, and marketing products.

CHANGES IN TECHNOLOGY

In our thermostat example, we noted that one possible solution would be to use thermostats that automatically reduce the building's temperature while it is not in use. This is an example of a technological approach to the need to conserve heat in the building. Placement of regulating devices on the thermostats that would thwart attempts to raise the temperature also would be possible. The thermostats also could be encased in a locked box, or simply removed altogether. A new, modern, energy-efficient furnace could be installed in the building. All these suggestions represent technological approaches to the need for change.

The underlying idea is that technological improvements can lead to more efficient work (a theme addressed in Chapter 14). Indeed, if you've ever prepared a term paper on a typewriter, you know how much more efficient it is to do the same job using a word processor. Technological changes may involve a variety of alterations, such as changing the equipment used to do jobs (e.g., robots), substituting microprocessors for less reliable mechanical components (e.g., on airline equipment), or simply using better-designed tools (e.g., hand tools with more comfortable grips). Each of these changes may be used to bring about improvements in organizational functioning.

CHANGES IN PEOPLE

You've probably seen stickers next to light switches in hotels and office buildings asking the occupants to turn off the lights when not in use. These are similar to the suggestion in our opening example to affix signs near thermostats asking occupants to refrain from adjusting the thermostats. Such efforts represent attempts to respond to the needed organizational change by altering the way people behave. The basic assumption is that the effectiveness of organizations is greatly dependent on the behavior of the people working within them.

As you might imagine, the process of changing people is not easy—indeed, it lies at the core of most of the topics discussed in this book. However, theorists have identified three basic steps that summarize what's involved in the process of changing people.[50,51] The first step is known as *unfreezing*. This refers to the process of recognizing that the current state of affairs is undesirable and in need of change. Realizing that change is needed may be the result of some serious organizational crisis or threat (e.g., a serious financial loss, a strike, a major lawsuit), or simply becoming aware that current conditions are unacceptable (e.g., antiquated equipment, inadequately trained employees).

In recent years, some executives have gotten employees to accept the need to change while things are still good, by creating a sense of urgency. They introduce the idea that there is an impending crisis although conditions are, in fact, currently acceptable—an approach referred to as *doomsday management*.[52] This process effectively unfreezes people, stimulating change before it's too late to do any good. Before rejecting this practice, consider this analogy. People usually switch to healthier diets only after they've suffered heart attacks, although they may have been able to prevent them altogether had their doctors emphasized the urgency of adopting a healthier lifestyle beforehand. An analagous approach is sometimes used to instigate positive changes in organizational behavior.

After unfreezing, *changing* may occur. This step occurs when some planned attempt is made to create a more desirable state for the organization and its members. Change attempts may be quite ambitious (e.g., an organization-wide restructuring) or only minor (e.g., altering a training program). (A thorough discussion of such planned change techniques will be presented in the next major part of this chapter.)

Finally, *refreezing* occurs when the changes made are incorporated into the employees' thinking and the organization's operations (e.g., mechanisms for rewarding behaviors that maintain the changes are put in place). Hence, the new attitudes and behaviors become a new, enduring aspect of the organizational system. For a summary of these three steps in the individual change process, please see Figure 16-6. Despite the simplicity of this model, it does a good job of identifying some of the factors that make people willing to change their behavior—thereby potentially improving organizational effectiveness.

READINESS FOR CHANGE: WHEN WILL ORGANIZATIONAL CHANGE OCCUR?

As you might imagine, there are times when organizations are likely to change, and times during which change is less likely. Even if the need for change is high and resistance to change is low (two important factors), organizational change does not automatically occur. Other factors are involved, and we have summarized some of the key variables in Figure 16-7.[53]

As Figure 16-7 summarizes, change is likely to occur when the people involved believe that the benefits associated with making a change outweigh the costs involved. The factors contributing to the benefits of making a change are (1) the amount of dissatisfaction with current conditions, (2) the availability of a desirable alternative, and (3) the existence of a plan for achieving that alternative. Theorists have claimed that these three factors combine multiplicatively to determine the benefits of making a change.[54] Thus, if any one of these factors is zero, the benefits of making a change, and the likelihood of change itself, are zero.

If you think about it, this should make sense to you. After all, people are unlikely to initiate change if they are not at all dissatisfied, or if they don't have any desirable alternative in mind (or any way of attaining that alternative, if they do have one in mind). Of course, for change to occur, the expected benefits must outweigh the likely costs involved (e.g., disruption, uncertainties). Professionals in the field of organizational development pay careful attention to these factors before they attempt

FIGURE 16-6
CHANGING PEOPLE: SOME BASIC STEPS
The process of changing people involves the three basic steps outlined here: unfreezing, changing, and refreezing. (Sources: Based on suggestions by Lewin, 1951; see Note 50; and Schein, 1968; see Note 37.)

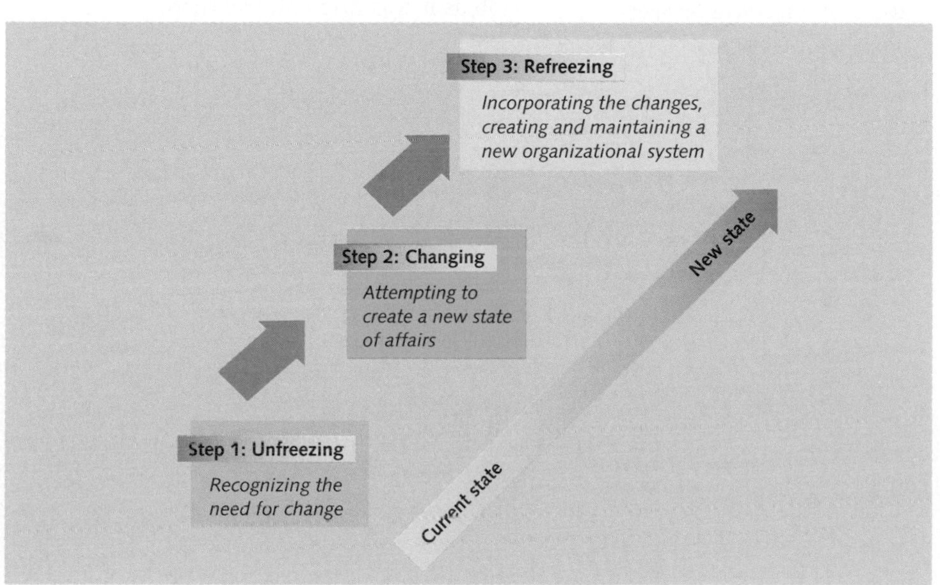

to initiate any formal, ambitious organizational change programs. Only when the readiness for change is high will organizational change efforts be successful.

RESISTANCE TO CHANGE: WILL ORGANIZATIONAL CHANGE BE ACCEPTED?

Although people may be unhappy with the current state of affairs confronting them in organizations, they may be afraid that any changes will be potentially disruptive and will only make things worse. Indeed, fear of new conditions is quite real and it creates unwillingness to accept change. Organizational scientists have recognized that **resistance to change** stems from both individual and organizational variables.

INDIVIDUAL BARRIERS TO CHANGE

Researchers have noted several key factors that are known to make people resistant to change in organizations.[55]

1. *Economic insecurity*. Because any changes on the job have the potential to threaten one's livelihood—by either loss of job or reduced pay—some resistance to change is inevitable.
2. *Fear of the unknown*. Employees derive a sense of security from doing things the same way, knowing who their co-workers will be, and whom they're supposed to answer to from day to day. Disrupting these well-established, comfortable patterns creates unfamiliar conditions, a state of affairs that is often rejected.
3. *Threats to social relationships*. As people continue to work within organizations, they form strong bonds with their co-workers. Many organizational changes (e.g., the reassignment of job responsibilities) threaten the integrity of friendship groups that provide valuable social rewards.
4. *Habit*. Jobs that are well learned and become habitual are easy to perform. The prospect of changing the way jobs are done challenges people to develop new job skills. Doing this is clearly more difficult than continuing to perform the job as it was originally learned.

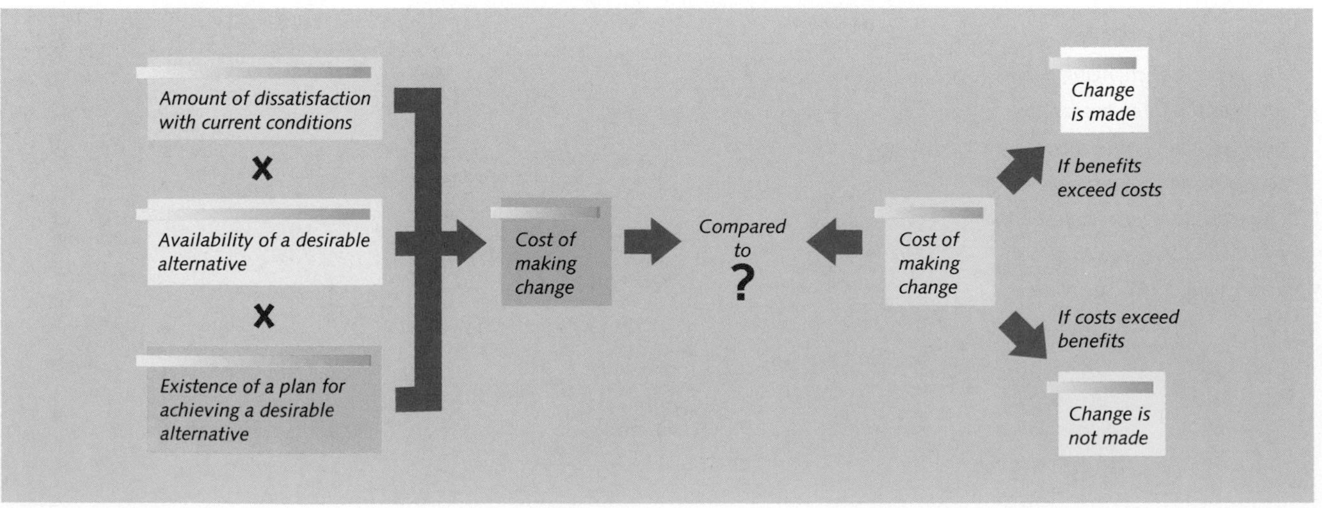

FIGURE 16-7
ORGANIZATIONAL CHANGE: WHEN WILL IT OCCUR?
Whether or not an organizational change will be made depends on people's beliefs regarding the relative benefits and costs of making the change. The benefits are reflected by three considerations reviewed here. (Source: Based on suggestions by Beer, 1980; see Note 54.)

5. *Failure to recognize need for change.* Unless employees can recognize and fully appreciate the need for changes in organizations, any vested interests they may have in keeping things the same may overpower their willingness to accept change.

ORGANIZATIONAL BARRIERS TO CHANGE

Resistance to organizational change also from conditions associated with organizations themselves.[56] Several such factors may be identified.

1. *Structural inertia.* Organizations are designed to promote stability. To the extent that employees are carefully selected and trained to perform certain jobs, and rewarded for doing them well, the forces acting on individuals to perform in certain ways are very powerfully determined—that is, jobs have **structural inertia**.[57] Thus, because jobs are designed to have stability, it is often difficult to overcome the resistance created by the forces that create stability.

2. *Work group inertia.* Inertia to continue performing jobs in a specified way comes not only from the jobs themselves but also from the social groups within which people work—**work group inertia.** Because of the development of strong social norms within groups (see Chapter 8), potent pressures exist to perform jobs in certain ways. Introducing change disrupts these established normative expectations, leading to formidable resistance.

3. *Threats to existing balance of power.* If changes are made with respect to who's in charge, a shift in the balance of power between individuals and organizational subunits is likely to occur (see Chapter 12). Those units that now control the resources, have the expertise, and wield the power may fear losing their advantageous positions resulting from any organizational change.

4. *Previously unsuccessful change efforts.* Anyone who has lived through a past disaster understandably may be reluctant to endure another attempt at the same thing. Similarly, groups or entire organizations that have been unsuccessful in introducing change in the past may be cautious about accepting further attempts at introducing change into the system.

Over the past decade, General Electric (GE) has been undergoing a series of widespread changes in its basic strategy, organizational structure, and relationship with employees.[58] In this process, it experienced several of the barriers just identified.[59] For example, GE managers had mastered a set of bureaucratic traditions that kept their habits strong and their inertia moving straight ahead. The prospect of doing things differently was scary for those who were so strongly entrenched in doing things the "GE way." In particular, the company's interest in globalizing triggered many fears of the unknown. Resistance to change at GM was also strong because it threatened to strip power from those units that traditionally possessed most of it (e.g., the power systems and lighting division). Changes also were highly disruptive to GE's "social architecture"; friendship groups were broken up and scattered throughout the company. In all, GE has been a living example of many different barriers to change all rolled into a single company.

Having summarized some of the barriers to organizational change, we will now outline some of the major methods used to overcome this resistance. After all, unless these barriers can be overcome, any attempts to systematically change organizations may be doomed to failure.

OVERCOMING RESISTANCE TO ORGANIZATIONAL CHANGE: SOME GUIDELINES

Because organizational change is inevitable, managers should be sensitive to the barriers to change so that resistance can be overcome. This, of course, is easier said than done. However, several useful approaches have been suggested, and the key ones are summarized here.[60,61]

1. *Shape political dynamics.* In Chapter 12 we described the important role of organizational politics in achieving desired goals. Politics is also involved in getting organizational changes accepted. Politically, resistance to change can be overcome by winning the support of the most powerful and influential individuals. Doing so builds a critical internal mass of support for change. Demonstrating clearly that key organizational leaders endorse the change is an effective way to get others to go along with it—either because they share the leader's vision or because they fear the leader's retaliation. Either way, the political support will facilitate acceptance of change.
2. *Educate the workforce.* Sometimes, people are reluctant to change because they fear what the future has in store for them. Fears about economic security, for example, may be put to rest by a few reassuring words from power holders. As part of educating employees about what organizational changes may mean for them, top management must show a considerable amount of emotional sensitivity. Doing so makes it possible for the people affected by change to become instrumental in making it work. Some companies have found that simply answering the question "what's in it for me?" can help allay a lot of fears. For example, sales reps at New Jersey-based Sandoz Pharmaceuticals balked at first when laptop computers were introduced as a means for compiling and transmitting sales reports.[62] Then, once it was explained how this new technology would free them from the cumbersome job of writing weekly sales reports (a task that used to consume much of their weekend time), the computers were not only accepted, but embraced.
3. *Involve employees in the change efforts.* It is well established that people who participate in making a decision tend to be more committed to the outcomes of that decision than are those who are not involved.[63] Accordingly, employees who are involved in responding to unplanned change, or who are made part of the team charged with planning a needed organizational change, may be expected to have very little resistance to change. Organizational changes that are "sprung" on the workforce with little or no warning might be expected to encounter resistance simply as a knee-jerk reaction until employees have a chance to assess how the change affects them. In contrast, employees who are involved in the change process are better able to understand the need for change, and are therefore less likely to resist it. Says Duane Hartley, general manager of Hewlett-Packard's microwave instruments division, "I don't think people really enjoy change, but if they can participate in it and understand it, it can become a positive [experience] for them."[64] It is precisely these kinds of efforts at participative management that are credited with the successful changes in Southwestern Bell after the breakup of AT&T.[65]
4. *Reward constructive behaviors.* One rather obvious, and quite successful, mechanism for facilitating organizational change is rewarding people for behaving in the desired fashion. Changing organizational operations may necessitate

changing the kinds of behaviors that need to be rewarded by the organization. This is especially critical when an organization is in the transition period of introducing the change. For example, employees who are required to learn to use new equipment should be praised for their successful efforts. Feedback on how well they are doing not only provides a great deal of useful assurance to uncertain employees, but also goes a long way toward shaping the desired behavior (see Chapter 2).

Although these four suggestions may be easier to state than to implement, any effort to follow them will be well rewarded. Given the many forces that make employees resistant to change, managers should keep these guidelines in mind. If organizational change is to be beneficial, all employees must work toward accepting the change rather than using it as a rallying point around which conflict and dissension may focus.

ORGANIZATIONAL DEVELOPMENT: THE IMPLEMENTATION OF PLANNED ORGANIZATIONAL CHANGE

Now that we have shed some light on the basic issues surrounding organizational change, we are ready to look at planned ways of implementing it—collectively known as techniques of **organizational development** (**OD**). More formally, we may define organizational development as *a set of social science techniques designed to plan and implement change in work settings for purposes of enhancing the personal development of individuals and improving the effectiveness of organizational functioning.*[66] By planning organization-wide changes involving people, OD seeks to enhance organizational performance by improving the quality of the work environment and the attitudes and well-being of employees.[67]

Over the years, many different strategies for implementing planned organizational change (referred to as *OD interventions*) have been used by specialists attempting to improve organizational functioning (referred to as *OD practitioners*).[68] All too often, some such techniques are merely managerial fads that do not stand the test of time.[69] However, several well-established OD techniques have been developed over the years, and we will begin this section by summarizing them. Following this, we will examine their effectiveness, addressing the question "do they work?"

ORGANIZATIONAL DEVELOPMENT INTERVENTIONS: MAJOR TECHNIQUES

All the major methods of organizational development attempt to produce some kind of change in individual employees, work groups, and/or entire organizations. This is the goal of the six well-known OD techniques we will review—*survey feedback, sensitivity training, team building, grid training, quality of work life programs*, and *management by objectives*.

SURVEY FEEDBACK: INDUCING CHANGE BY SHARING INFORMATION

For effective organizational change to occur, employees must understand their organization's current strengths and weaknesses. That's the underlying rationale behind the **survey feedback** method.

This technique follows the three steps summarized in Figure 16-8.[70] First, data are collected that provide information about matters of general concern to employees, such as organizational climate, leadership style and job satisfaction. This may take the form of intensive interviews or structured questionnaires, or both. Because it is important that this information be as unbiased as possible, employees providing feedback should be assured that their responses will be kept confidential. For this reason, this process is usually conducted by outside consultants.

The second step calls for reporting the information obtained back to the employees during small group meetings. Typically, this consists of summarizing the average scores on the attitudes assessed in the survey. Profiles are created of feelings about the organization, its leadership, the work done, and related topics. Discussions also focus on why the scores are as they are, and what problems are revealed by the feedback. The final step involves analyzing problems dealing with communication, decision making, and other organizational processes to make plans for dealing with them. Such discussions are usually most effective when they are carefully documented and a specific plan of implementation is made, with someone put in charge of carrying it out.

Survey feedback is a widely used organizational development technique.[71] This is not surprising in view of the advantages it offers. It is efficient, allowing a great deal of information to be collected relatively quickly. Also, it is very flexible and can be tailored to the needs of different organizations facing a variety of problems. However, the technique can be no better than the quality of the questionnaire used—it must measure the things that really matter to employees. Of course, to derive the maximum benefit from survey feedback, it must have the support of top management. Specifically, the plans developed by the small discussion groups must be capable of being implemented with the full approval of the organization. When these conditions are met, survey feedback can be a very effective OD technique.

SENSITIVITY TRAINING: DEVELOPING PERSONAL INSIGHT

The method by which small, face-to-face group interaction experiences are used to give people insight into themselves (e.g., who they are, the way others respond to them) is known as **sensitivity training**. Developed in the 1940s, sensitivity training groups (also referred to as *encounter groups*, *laboratory groups*, or *T-groups*) were among the first organizational development techniques used in organizations (such as Standard Oil and Union Carbide).[72] The rationale behind sensitivity training is that people are usually not completely open and honest with each other, a condition that thwarts insights into oneself and others. However, when people are placed in special situations within which open, honest communication is allowed and encouraged, personal insights may be gained. To do this, small groups (usual-

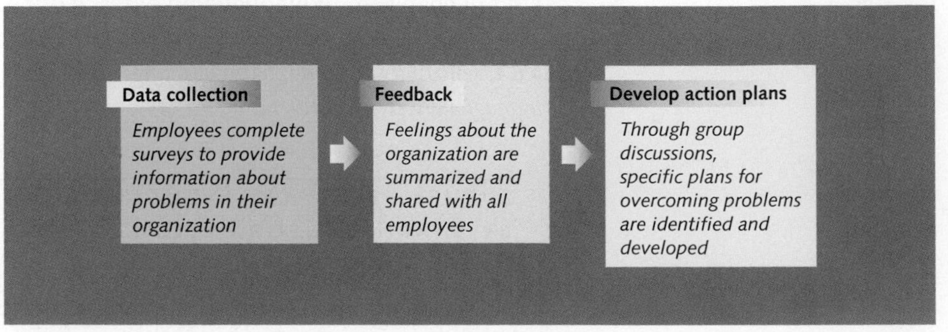
Data collection
Employees complete surveys to provide information about problems in their organization
Feedback
Feelings about the organization are summarized and shared with all employees
Develop action plans
Through group discussions, specific plans for overcoming problems are identified and developed

FIGURE 16-8
SURVEY FEEDBACK: AN OVERVIEW
The survey feedback technique of organizational development follows the three steps outlined here: collecting data, giving feedback, and developing action plans.

ly about eight to fifteen in number) are created and meet away from the pressures of the job site for several days. An expert trainer (referred to as the *facilitator*) guides the group at all times, helping assure that the proper atmosphere is maintained.

The sessions themselves are completely open with respect to what is discussed. Often, to get the ball rolling, the facilitator will frustrate the group members by not getting involved at all, appearing to be passively goofing off. As members sit around and engage in meaningless chit-chat, they begin to feel angry at the change agent for wasting their time. Once these expressions of anger begin to emerge, the change agent has created the important first step needed to make the session work—he or she has given the group a chance to focus on a current event. At this point, the discussion may be guided into how each of the group members expresses his or her anger toward the others. They are encouraged to continue discussing these themes openly and honestly, and not to hide their true feelings as they would often do on the job. So, for example, if you think someone is relying too much on you, this is the time to say so. Participants are encouraged to respond by giving each other *immediate feedback* to what was said. By doing this, it is reasoned, people will learn more about how they interrelate with others, and will become more skilled at interpersonal relations. These are among the major goals of sensitivity groups.

It probably comes as no surprise to you that the effectiveness of sensitivity training is difficult to assess. After all, measuring insight into one's own personality is clearly elusive. Even if interpersonal skills seem to be improved, people will not always be able to successfully transfer their newly learned skills when they leave the artificial training atmosphere and return to their jobs.[73] As a result, sensitivity training tends not to be used extensively by itself for OD purposes. Rather, as we will see, it is often used in conjunction with, or as part of, other OD techniques.

TEAM BUILDING: CREATING EFFECTIVE WORK GROUPS

The technique of **team building** applies the techniques and rationale of sensitivity training to work groups. The approach attempts to get members of a work group to diagnose how they work together, and to plan how this may be improved.[74] Given the importance of group efforts in effective organizational functioning, attempts to improve the effectiveness of work groups are likely to have profound effects on organizations. If one assumes that work groups are the basic building blocks of organizations, it follows that organizational change should emphasize changing groups instead of individuals.[75]

Team building begins when members of a group admit that they have a problem and gather data to provide insight into it. The problems that are identified may come from sensitivity training sessions, or more objective sources, such as production Figures or attitude surveys. These data are then shared, in a *diagnostic session*, to develop a consensus regarding the group's current strengths and weaknesses. From this, a list of desired changes is created, along with some plans for implementing these changes. In other words, an *action plan* is developed—some task-oriented approach to solving the group's problems as diagnosed. Following this step, the plan is carried out, and its progress is evaluated to determine whether the originally identified problems remain. If the problems are solved, the process is completed and the team may stop meeting. If not, the process should be restarted. (See Figure 16-9 for a summary of these steps.)

Work teams have been used effectively to combat a variety of important organizational problems.[76] For these efforts to be successful, however, all group members must participate in the gathering and evaluating of information as well as the plan-

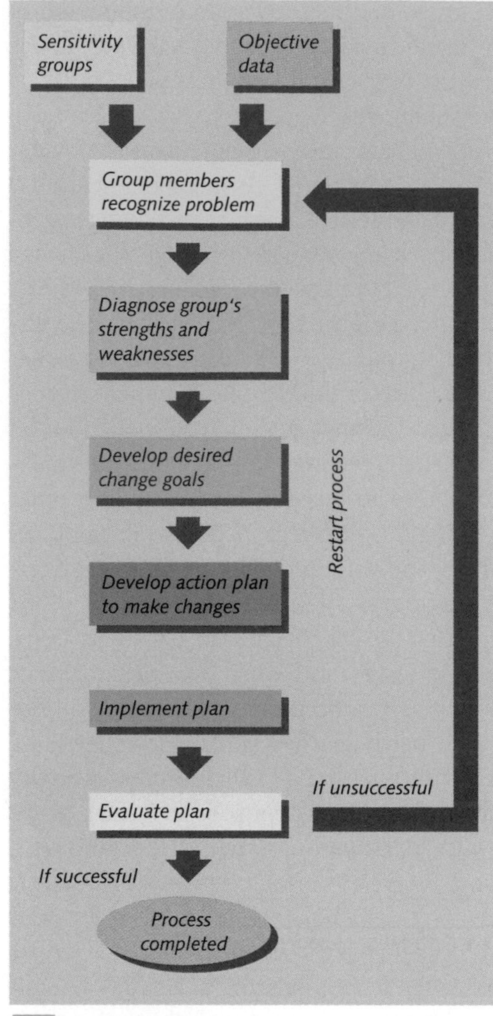

FIGURE 16-9
TEAM BUILDING: ITS BASIC STEPS
Team building, a popular technique of organizational development, follows the steps outlined here.

ning and implementing of action plans. Input from group members is also especially crucial in evaluating the effectiveness of team building.[77] Keep in mind that because the team-building approach is highly task-oriented, interpersonal problems between group members may be disruptive and need to be neutralized by an outside party. With interpersonal strain out of the way, the stage is set for groups to learn to effectively solve their own problems. However, this does not happen overnight. To be effective, team building should *not* be approached as a one-time exercise undertaken during a few days away from the job. Rather, it should be thought of as an ongoing process that takes several months (or even years) to develop. Given the great impact effective teams can have on organizational functioning (see Chapter 8), efforts to build effective work teams seem quite worthwhile.

A successful team-building program has been in use at the France-based multinational corporation, Groupe Bull.[78] Instead of using team-building exercises exclusively among top leaders (who presumably have already bought into the company's philosophies), lower-level executives and managers from companies on several different continents are brought together for several two- to three-week sessions in which they try to solve problems of mutual interest.

Some techniques used in team-building exercises for attaining high levels of interpersonal trust are a bit more unorthodox. For example, as part of many team-building exercises, group members are put into highly challenging real-life situations that are metaphors for how they have to pull together to meet challenges on the job. The idea is that by facing these difficult off-the-job challenges successfully, they will develop the skills needed for working together effectively on the job. Groupe Bull executives so strongly believe in this idea that their team-building exercises have taken them on an adventurous white-water rafting trip in the swirling waters of the river Spey in the mountains of Scotland.[79] Other companies have sent their executives off on such challenges as mountain-climbing expeditions and dog sled trips.[80]

Why the exotic adventures? In theory, learning to work together on navigating the treacherous river while staying afloat can help team members recognize how they interact with each other while navigating the rough waters of international business. But does it work? Obviously, the effectiveness of such an approach depends on the extent to which participants come away from the experience with the type of insight desired and translate these new-found ideas into meaningful work-related activities (see Figure 16-10). By itself, some rafting or mountain-climbing expedition is not likely to make executives become a cohesive team. However, such adventures can be an effective part of an ongoing program of regular team development.

GRID TRAINING: IMPROVING MANAGERIAL EFFECTIVENESS

Improving the total organization on a long-term basis is the goal of **grid training**. This approach, developed by Blake and Mouton, seeks to promote organizational excellence by fostering concern for both production and people.[81] Working on the premise that most organizational problems stem from poor communication and inadequate planning, Blake and Mouton proposed a multistep process for improving organizations by attempting to cultivate these skills.

FIGURE 16-10

PHYSICAL CHALLENGES: DO THEY HELP WITH TEAMWORK ON THE JOB?

Some team-building exercises put people in physically challenging conditions. The rationale is that learning to overcome these obstacles will teach team members how to work together cooperatively. The value of the exercises is realized only when the principles of teamwork learned during the training are applied back on the job. (Source: © Leo Cullum 1994.)

"We rafted dangerous rapids together. We scaled sheer rock walls tied together by a skinny rope, and now you won't back me in this proposal? I wonder if you got anything at all out of our summer program."

The initial step consists of a *grid seminar*—a session in which an organization's line managers (who have been previously trained in the appropriate theory and skills) help organization members analyze their own management styles. This is done using a specially designed questionnaire that allows managers to determine how they stand with respect to two important dimensions of effective management—their *concern for production* and their *concern for people* (recall similar dimensions identified in several approaches to leadership discussed in Chapter 13). Each participant's approach on each dimension is scored using a number ranging from 1 (low) to 9 (high). Managers who score low on both concern for production and concern for people are scored 1,1—evidence of *impoverished management*. A manager who is highly concerned about production but shows little interest in people, the *task management* style, scores 9,1. In contrast, ones who show the opposite pattern—high concern with people but little concern with production—are described as having a *country club* style of management; they are scored 1,9. Managers scoring moderately on both dimensions, the 5,5 pattern, are said to follow a *middle-of-the-road* management style. Finally, there are individuals who are highly concerned with both production and people, those scoring 9,9. This is the most desirable pattern, representing what is known as *team management*. These various patterns are represented in a diagram like that shown in Figure 16-11, known as the *managerial grid®*.

After a manager's position along the grid is determined, training begins to improve concern over production (planning skills) and concern over people (communication skills) to reach the ideal, 9,9 state. This training consists of organization-wide team training aimed at helping people interact more effectively with each other. Then, training is expanded to reducing conflict between groups that work with each other. Additional phases of training include efforts to identify the extent to which the organization is meeting its strategic goals and then comparing this performance to an ideal. Next, plans are made to meet these goals, and these plans are implemented in the organization. Finally, progress toward the goals is continuously assessed, and problem areas are identified.

FIGURE 16-11

THE MANAGERIAL GRID®: KEY DIMENSIONS OF MANAGEMENT

*A manager's standing along two basic dimensions—*concern for production *and* concern for people*—can be illustrated by means of a diagram such as this one, known as the managerial grid®. Blake and Mouton, the developers of the popular organizational development technique* grid training, *suggest that organizational effectiveness results when managers are trained to score high on both dimensions. (Source: Based on suggestions by Blake & Mouton, 1969; see Note 81.)*

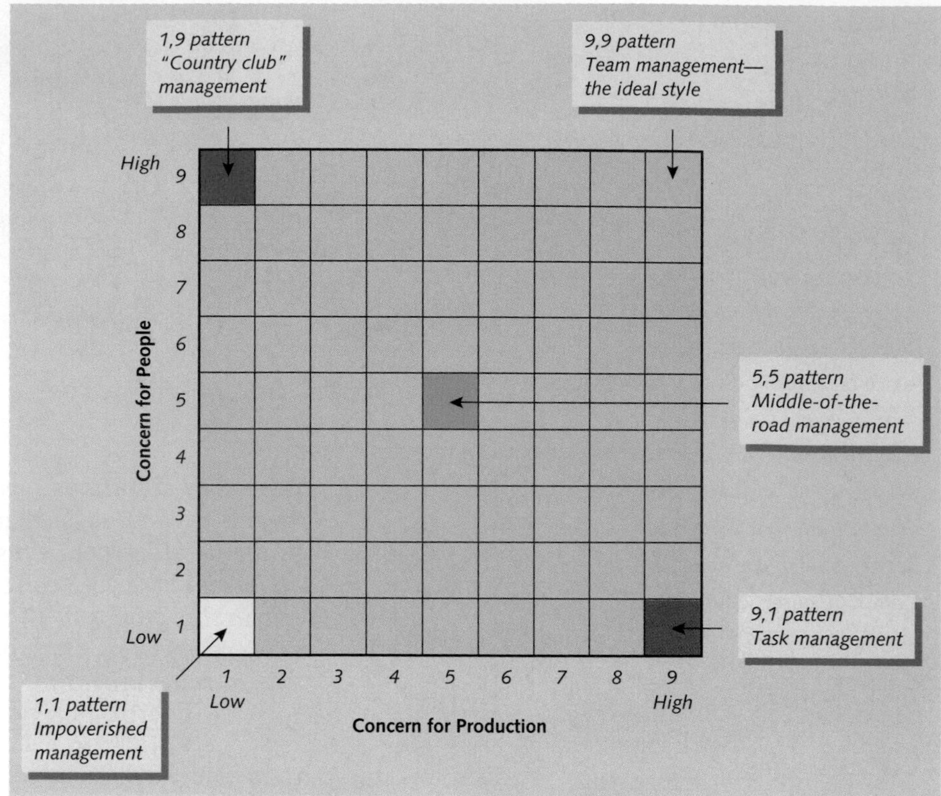

As you can tell, full implementation of grid training involves many changes, making it difficult to tell which individual aspects are responsible for improved organizational functioning. Some skeptics argue that because grid training is designed to be used in all organizations, it may not meet the special development needs of any particular organization. Specifically, it always assumes that being concerned about both people and production is the best management style. However, as described in Chapter 13, there are situations in which effective leadership requires more of one of these skills than the other. Regardless, the technique has been identified as a successful mechanism for implementing planned organizational change in several studies.[82] Because the grid approach trains managers to train their co-workers, it has been widely used—allowing several hundred thousand people to reap its benefits.

QUALITY OF WORK LIFE PROGRAMS: HUMANIZING THE WORKPLACE

When you think of work, do you think of drudgery? Although many people believe these two terms go together naturally, it has grown increasingly popular to systematically improve the quality of life experienced on the job. As more people demand satisfying and personally fulfilling places to work, OD practitioners have attempted systematically to create work situations that enhance employees' motivation, satisfaction, and commitment—factors that may contribute to high levels of organizational performance. Such efforts are known collectively as **quality of work life** (**QWL**) programs. Specifically, such programs are ways of increasing organizational output and improving quality by involving employees in the decisions that affect them on their jobs. Typically, QWL programs support highly democratic treatment of employees at all levels and encourage their participation in decision making. Although many approaches to improving the quality of work life exist, they all share a common goal: humanizing the workplace.[83]

One popular approach to improving the quality of work life involves *work restructuring*—the process of changing the way jobs are done to make them more interesting to workers.[84] If this sounds familiar to you, it is because we already discussed several such approaches to redesigning jobs—including *job enlargement*, *job enrichment*, and the *job characteristics model*—in our discussion of motivation in Chapter 4. In the present context, note that such techniques also represent effective ways of improving the quality of work life for employees.

Another approach to improving the quality of work life is **quality circles (QCs)**. These are small groups of volunteers (usually around ten) who meet regularly (usually weekly) to identify and solve problems related to the quality of the work they perform, and the conditions under which people do their jobs.[85] An organization may have several QCs operating at once, each dealing with a particular work area about which it has the most expertise. To help them work effectively, the members of the circle usually receive some form of training in problem solving. Large companies such as Westinghouse, Hewlett-Packard, and Eastman Kodak, to name only a few, have included QCs as part of their QWL efforts.[86] Groups have dealt with issues such as how to reduce vandalism, how to create safer and more comfortable working environments, and how to improve product quality. Research has shown that although quality circles are very effective at bringing about short-term improvements in quality of work life (i.e., those lasting up to eighteen months), they are less effective at creating more permanent changes.[87]

As you might imagine, a variety of benefits (even if short-term ones) might result from QWL programs. These fall into three major categories.[88] The most direct benefit is usually increased job satisfaction, organizational commitment, and reduced turnover among the workforce.[89,90] A second benefit is increased productivity. In fact, a recent study comparing the performance of employees who participated in a QC program with a control group (an equivalent group that had not participated in such a program) revealed that in the year following the group involvement, those who had participated received higher job performance ratings and were more likely to get promoted than those who had not participated in the QC program.[91] Related to these first two benefits is a third—namely, increased organizational effectiveness (e.g., profitability, goal attainment). Many companies, including industrial giants such as Ford, General Electric, and AT&T, have active QWL programs and are reportedly quite pleased with their results.[92]

Achieving these benefits is not automatic, however. Two major potential pitfalls must be avoided for QWL programs to be successfully implemented. First, both management and labor must cooperate in designing the program. Should any one side believe that the program is really just a method of gaining an advantage over the other, it is doomed to fail. Second, the plans agreed to by all concerned parties must be fully implemented. It is too easy for action plans developed in QWL groups to be forgotten amid the hectic pace of daily activities.[93] It is the responsibility of employees at all levels—from the highest-ranking manager to the lowest-level laborer—to follow through on their part of the plan.

MANAGEMENT BY OBJECTIVES: CLARIFYING ORGANIZATIONAL GOALS

In Chapter 4 we detailed the positive motivational benefits of setting specific goals. As you might imagine, not only individuals, but entire organizations stand to benefit from setting specific goals. For example, an organization may strive to "raise production" and "improve the quality" of its manufactured goods. These goals, noble and well intentioned though they may be, may not be as useful to an organization as more specific ones, such as "increase production of widgets by 15 percent" or "lower the failure rate of widgets by 25 percent." After all, as the old saying goes, "It's usually easier to get somewhere if you know where you're going." Peter Drucker, consulting for General Electric during the early 1950s, was well aware of this idea and is credited with promoting the benefits of specifying clear organizational goals—a technique known as **management by objectives (MBO)**.[94]

The MBO process, summarized in Figure 16-12, consists of three basic steps. First, goals are selected that employees should try to attain to best serve the needs of the organization. The goals should be selected by managers and their subordinates together. The goals must be set mutually, not imposed on subordinates by their managers. Further, these goals should be directly measurable and have some time frame attached to them. Goals that cannot be measured (e.g., "make the company better"), or that have no time limits, are useless. As part of this first step, it is crucial that managers and their subordinates work together to plan ways of attaining the goals they have selected—what is known as an *action plan*.

Once goals are set and action plans have been developed, the second step calls for *implementation*—carrying out the plan and regularly assessing its progress. Is the plan working? Are the goals being approximated? Are there any problems being encountered in attempting to meet the goals? Such questions need to be considered while implementing an action plan. If the plan is failing, a mid-course correction may be in order—changing the plan, the way it's carried out, or even the goal itself. Finally, after monitoring progress toward the goal, the third step may be instituted: *evaluation*—assessing goal attainment. Were the organization's goals reached? If so, what new goals should be set to improve things still further? If not, what new plans can be initiated to help meet the goals? Because the ultimate assessment of the extent to which goals are met helps determine the selection of new goals, MBO is a continuous process.

MBO represents a potentially effective source of planning and implementing strategic change for organizations. Individual efforts designed to meet organizational goals get the individual employee and the organization itself working togeth-

FIGURE 16-12
MANAGEMENT BY OBJECTIVES: DEVELOPING ORGANIZATIONS THROUGH GOAL SETTING
The organizational development technique of management by objectives *requires managers and their subordinates to work together on setting and trying to achieve important organizational goals. The basic steps of the process are outlined here.*

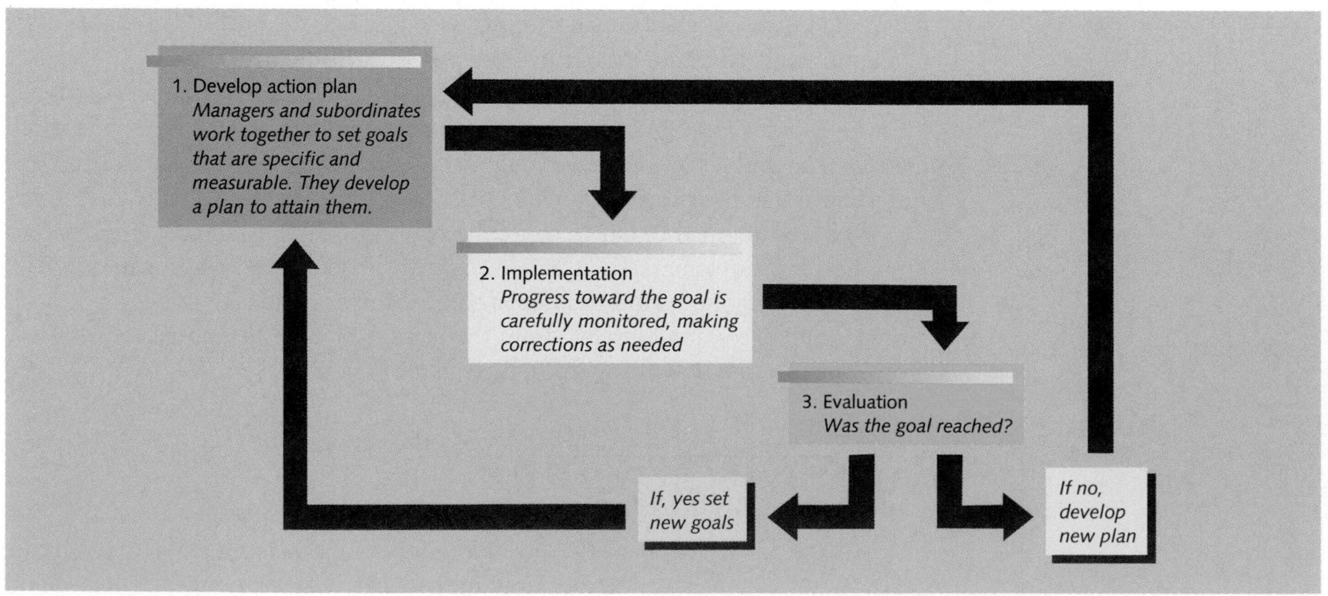
1. Develop action plan
Managers and subordinates work together to set goals that are specific and measurable. They develop a plan to attain them.
2. Implementation
Progress toward the goal is carefully monitored, making corrections as needed
3. Evaluation
Was the goal reached?
If, yes set new goals
If no, develop new plan

er toward common ends. Hence, systemwide change results. Of course, for MBO to work, everyone involved has to buy into it. Because MBO programs typically require a great deal of participation by lower-level employees, top managers must be willing to accept and support the cooperation and involvement of all. Making MBO work also requires a great deal of time—anywhere from three to five years.[95] Hence, MBO may be inappropriate in organizations that do not have the time to commit to making it work.

Despite these considerations, MBO has become one of the most widely used techniques for affecting organizational change in recent years. It not only is used on an ad hoc basis by many organizations, but also constitutes an ingrained element of the organizational culture in some companies, such as Hewlett-Packard and IBM. An MBO program was used effectively by Northwest Airlines in 1989 to help improve various areas of performance in its Atlanta-based crew.[96] Figure 16-13 shows part of a Northwest Airlines internal document listing the key objectives sought. The program was reportedly effective in meeting these and other vital goals, thereby helping to improve Northwest's overall safety and performance record. Given the success MBO has experienced, its widespread use is not surprising.[97]

THE EFFECTIVENESS OF ORGANIZATIONAL DEVELOPMENT: DOES IT REALLY WORK?

Thus far, we have described some of the major techniques used by OD practitioners to improve organizational functioning. As is probably clear, carrying out these techniques requires a considerable amount of time, money, and effort. Accordingly, it is appropriate to ask if the investment in implementing OD interventions is worth it. In other words, does OD really work? Given the growing popularity of OD in organizations, the question is more important than ever.[98]

Research has revealed that the answer is a qualified "yes." In other words, although many studies have revealed beneficial effects associated with OD programs, the findings are far from unanimous. Consider, for example, research on quality circles. Although many researchers have found that QCs help reduce organizational costs and improve employees' attitudes, other studies reported no such beneficial effects.[99] Mixed results also have been obtained in many studies assessing the effectiveness of sensitivity training programs. For example, whereas such programs often lead to temporary differences in the way people interact with others, the results tend to be short-lived on the job, and are not related to permanent

FIGURE 16-13
MANAGEMENT BY OBJECTIVES AT NORTHWEST AIRLINES
As part of an MBO program at Northwest Airlines, this document (only part of which is shown here) was prepared to remind employees of some of the key objectives sought for Atlanta-based employees in 1989. (Source: Based on material in Midas & Devine, 1991; see Note 96. Reprinted with permission from National Productivity Review, *10(3), Summer, 1991. Copyright © 1991 John Wiley & Sons, Inc.)*

NORTHWEST AIRLINES—ATLANTA
1989 CONTINUOUS IMPROVEMENT
The Year of the Customer . . . External and Internal

1989 Strategic Objectives for the Atlanta Base

1. A 50 percent reduction in number of on-the-job injuries.
2. JT8D engine turn time of 43 work days.
3. DC-9 check average turn time of 10 days—nonpaint; 14 days—with paint.
4. Component shops turn 90 percent of the rotable–repairable in 14 days.
5. Metal finishing turn 98 percent of the units in 20 days.
6. 98 percent of M & E personnel receive 40 hours of training.
7. 95 percent on-time Atlanta launch departures.

changes in the way people behave.[100] Thus, whereas OD may have many positive effects, not all desired outcomes may be realized.

A review by Porras and Robertson compared the results of forty-nine OD studies published between 1975 and 1986.[101] Among the different types of OD interventions studied were those we described: grid training, MBO, QWL, survey feedback, sensitivity groups, and team building. The investigators categorized the research with respect to whether they found the effects of the interventions to be beneficial, harmful, or nonexistent. The outcomes studied were both individual (e.g., job satisfaction) and organizational (e.g., profit, productivity) in nature. The results, summarized in Figure 16-14, reveal that a sizable percentage of the studies found effects of the various interventions beneficial. However, these beneficial results were not as impressive for individual outcomes (where the vast majority of the studies demonstrated no effects of any of the interventions) as they were for organizational outcomes (where many studies found positive effects). Clearly, the benefits of OD techniques are more firmly established with respect to improving organizational functioning than with respect to improving individuals' job attitudes.

We hasten to add that any conclusions about the effectiveness of OD should be qualified in several important ways. First, research has shown that OD interventions tend to be more effective among blue-collar employees than among white-collar employees.[102] Second, it has been found that the beneficial effects of OD can be enhanced by using several techniques instead of just one. Specifically, studies in which four or more OD programs were used together yielded positive findings more frequently than those in which fewer techniques were used.[103] Thus, it appears that the effectiveness of OD efforts can be enhanced by relying not on any one single technique, but rather on a combination of several.[104] Finally, research has shown that the effectiveness of OD techniques depends on the degree of support they receive from top management: the more programs are supported from the top, the more successful they tend to be.[105]

Despite the importance of attempting to evaluate the effectiveness of OD interventions, a great many of them go unevaluated. Although there are undoubtedly many reasons for this, one key factor is the difficulty of assessing change. Because many factors can cause people to behave differently in organizations, and because

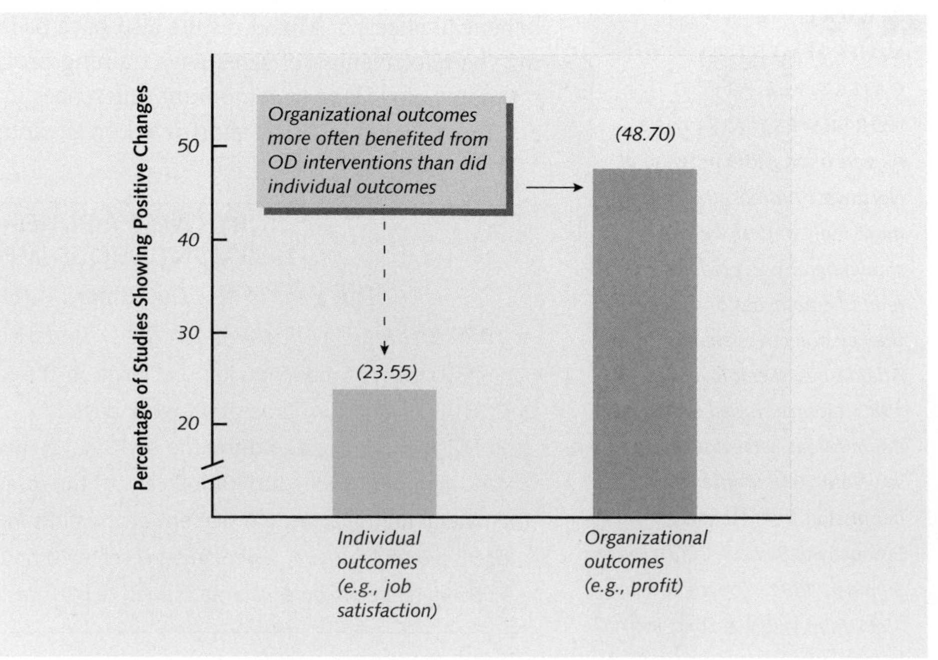

FIGURE 16-14

ORGANIZATIONAL DEVELOPMENT: HOW EFFECTIVE IS IT?

In reviewing forty-nine studies using organizational development techniques, Porras and Robertson found a greater percentage reporting improvement among organizational outcomes (e.g., productivity) than individual outcomes (e.g., job satisfaction). (Source: Based on data reported by Porras & Robertson, 1992; see Note 101.)

such behaviors may be difficult to measure, many OD practitioners avoid the problem of measuring change altogether. In a related vein, political pressures to justify OD programs may discourage some OD professionals from honestly and accurately assessing their effectiveness. After all, in doing so, one runs the risk of scientifically demonstrating one's wasted time and money (a similar point was made in Chapter 2 regarding the assessment of organizational training programs).

In cases where the effects of OD have been studied, however, the research is more often than not conducted in a manner that leaves its conclusions seriously open to question.[106] In particular, it is often very difficult to isolate exactly which aspects of an organizational intervention were responsible for the changes noted. Also, because OD practices are a novelty to most employees, they may have a tendency to produce temporary improvements (recall our discussion of the Hawthorne effect in Chapter 1).[107] In other words, serious questions may be raised about the true effectiveness of organizational development efforts as revealed in existing research.

We may conclude that despite some limitations, organizational development is an approach that shows considerable promise in its ability to benefit organizations and the individuals working within them. (These benefits notwithstanding, some have raised questions about the ethics of OD practice. For a discussion of this controversy, see the Ethical Workplace section below.)

THE ETHICAL WORKPLACE

IS ORGANIZATIONAL DEVELOPMENT INHERENTLY UNETHICAL? A DEBATE

By its very nature, OD applies powerful social science techniques in an attempt to change attitudes and behavior. From the perspective of a manager attempting to accomplish various goals, such tools are immediately recognized as very useful. However, if you think about it from the perspective of the individual being affected, several ethical issues arise.

For example, it has been argued that OD techniques impose the values of the organization on the individual without taking the individual's own attitudes into account.[108] OD is a very one-sided approach, reflecting the imposition of the more powerful organization on the less powerful individual. A related issue is that the OD process does not provide any free choice on the part of the employees.[109] As a result, it may be seen as *coercive* and *manipulative*. When faced with a "do it or else" situation, employees tend to have little free choice, and are forced to allow themselves to be manipulated, a potentially degrading prospect.

Another issue is that the unequal power relationship between the organization and its employees makes it possible for the true intent of OD techniques to be misrepresented. As an example, imagine that an MBO technique is presented to employees as a means of allowing greater organizational participation, whereas in reality it is used as a means for holding individuals responsible for their poor performance and punishing them as a result. Although such an event might not happen, the potential for abuse of this type does exist, and the potential to misuse the technique—even if not originally intended—might later prove to be too great a temptation.

Despite these considerations, many professionals do not agree that OD is inherently unethical. Such a claim, it has been countered, is to say that the practice of management is itself unethical. After all, the very act of going to work for an organization requires one to submit to the organization's values and the overall values of society at large.[110] One cannot help but face life situations in which others' values are imposed. This is not to say that organizations have the right to impose patently unethical values on people for the purpose of making a profit (e.g., stealing from customers). Indeed, because they have the potential to abuse their power (such as in the MBO example above), organizations have a special obligation to refrain from doing so.

Although abuses of organizational power are all too

common (see Chapter 12), OD itself is not necessarily the culprit. Indeed, like any other tool (even a gun!), OD is not inherently good or evil. Instead, *whether the tool is used for good or evil will depend on the individual using it.* With this in mind, the ethical use of OD interventions will require that they be supervised by professionals in an organization that places a high value on ethics. To the extent that top management officials embrace ethical values and behave ethically themselves, norms for behaving ethically are likely to develop in organizations. When an organization has a strong ethical culture, it is unlikely that OD practitioners would even think of misusing their power to harm individuals. The need to develop such a culture has been recognized as a way for organizations to take not only moral leadership in their communities, but financial leadership as well.

After considering both sides of this issue, you will probably wish to draw your own conclusions about this matter. The only thing we can be sure about here is that the debate is not settled, and it is likely to remain a key question for years to come. One reason the issue might not be put to rest anytime soon is that executives are becoming increasingly concerned about the importance of ethics in their organizations. Given corporations' ongoing concerns about being competitive, it is also likely that OD interventions will remain popular in the years to come.

IMPROVING ORGANIZATIONAL QUALITY: CURRENT PRACTICES

In recent years, a great deal of energy has been focused on changing organizations in a certain way—by improving the quality of the goods manufactured and/or the services provided.[111] Although these efforts have taken many forms, two approaches have received the most widespread attention—*reengineering*, and *total quality management (TQM)*.

REENGINEERING: STARTING OVER AGAIN

Recent articles in the popular business press have referred to *reengineering* as "the hottest trend in management,"[112] noting that "if this radical idea . . . hasn't landed at your company, it's probably on its way."[113] Pioneered by consultants Michael Hammer and James Champy, **reengineering** is defined as *the fundamental rethinking and radical redesign of business processes to achieve drastic improvements in performance.*[114]

Reengineering does not involve fixing anything—rather, as the term implies, it means starting over from scratch about the fundamental way things are done. Organizations that use reengineering forget all about how work was performed in the past and start all over with a clean sheet of paper, thinking about how things can be done best right now—hence the word *radical* in the definition. The main focus of reengineering is the customer. Everything that is done starts with the idea of adding value for the customer: improving service, raising quality, and lowering costs. Practices are eradicated simply because they are traditional, or convenient for the company if they don't otherwise help the customer. Doing this involves organizing around process rather than function (see Chapter 15). That is, work is arranged according to the processes needed to get the job done most effectively (for this reason, reengineering is also known as *process innovation*). For example, in many companies the simple process of order fulfillment is frequently chopped up

FIGURE 16-15
BELL ATLANTIC: ONE COMPANY THAT BENEFITED BY REENGINEERING
This team at Bell Atlantic reengineered the process used to hook up telephone service to customers. Faster service with fewer errors was the result.

into single tasks performed by people in many different departments although customers may be better served by assigning it to a single unit responsible for the entire process.

As an example of reengineering in action, consider changes made at IBM Credit Corp., a subsidiary responsible for financing IBM's hardware and software.[115] Before reengineering, the task of processing a credit application was cumbersome and very slow—so slow, in fact, that it frequently cost the company sales. A credit request would come in by phone and would be logged on a piece of paper. Then the paper went on a long journey from credit checkers, to pricers (who determined what interest rate to charge), to many others who also performed single, specialized functions. Often applications were bounced back and forth between departments before they were properly completed. Total processing time ranged from six days to two weeks.

Out of curiosity, some IBM senior managers decided one day to walk a financing request through the process, taking it from department to department asking personnel in each office to put aside whatever they were doing to process this request in the normal fashion, only without the delay. They learned from this demonstration that the actual process took only *90 minutes*; the remaining days or weeks were consumed by handing the form off between departments. Enlightened by this eye-opening demonstration, IBM Credit reengineered its operations by replacing a series of specialists with generalists. Now, one person processes an entire application from beginning to end without handing it off to others. (Essentially, this is a form of *job enrichment* described in Chapter 4.) Did it work? In the newly reengineered jobs, credit approval takes only about four hours. Furthermore, the number of applications processed has increased a hundred-fold—and using *fewer* employees than before. Other companies, such as Ford, Kodak, Hallmark, Taco Bell, and Bell Atlantic (see Figure 16-15) also have used reengineering successfully. Union Carbide claims to have reduced its fixed costs by $400 million in just three years by using reengineering.[116] Don't let all these big names mislead you; small companies also have been using reengineering to achieve success.[117]

Although it is too early to predict the long-term benefits of reengineering, there is good reason to suspect that it will continue to be quite effective—and popular. Because it combines effective principles of job design and job enrichment (Chapter 4) and organizational design (Chapter 15), we are optimistic that this burgeoning approach will not soon become tomorrow's outdated fad.

TOTAL QUALITY MANAGEMENT: A COMMITMENT TO CUSTOMERS

If reengineering is the buzzword of the 1990s, then **total quality management (TQM)** was the buzzword of the 1980s. However, if the amount of attention given to this topic in the popular business press is any indication, the buzz is still being heard today.[118] So what's the uproar all about? In a word, *quality,* as the name implies. Total quality management may be defined as *an organizational strategy of commitment to improving customer satisfaction by developing techniques to carefully manage output quality.*[119] TQM is not so much a special technique as a well-ingrained aspect of corporate culture—a way of life demonstrating a strong commitment to improving quality in everything that is done.[120] In this regard, TQM is similar to reengineering. The difference, however, lies in the fact that whereas reengineering questions the basic need for what an organization may be doing, TQM assumes that what it is doing is necessary, although it can be improved.

According to W. Edwards Deming, the best-known advocate of TQM, successful TQM requires that everyone in the organization—from the lowest-level employee to the chief executive officer—must be fully committed to making whatever innovations are necessary to improve quality.[121] This involves both carefully measuring quality (through elaborate statistical procedures) and taking whatever steps are necessary to improve it. Typically, this requires continuously improving the manufacturing process in ways that make it possible for higher quality to result. For example, in developing its Lexus LS 400, Toyota purchased competing cars from Mercedes, and BMW, disassembled them, examined the parts, and developed ways of building an even better car. (This process of comparing one's own products or services with the best from others is known as *benchmarking.*) Spending some $500 million in this process, Toyota was clearly dedicated to creating a superior product.[122] And given the recognition that Lexus has received among customers for its high quality, it appears as if Toyota's TQM efforts have paid off.

Another key ingredient of TQM is incorporating concern for quality into all aspects of organizational culture (see Chapter 14). At Rubbermaid, for example, concern for quality is not only emphasized in the company's manufacturing process, but also its concern for cost, service, speed, and innovation.[123] Realizing that it is often difficult to create a quality-focused culture, Deming has offered several suggestions; the key ones are summarized in Table 16-4.[124] As you review this list, keep in mind that the basic idea is to keep everyone focused on creating and maintaining sustained levels of extremely high quality.

To assure that it is meeting quality standards, many companies conduct *quality control audits*—careful examinations of how well it is meeting its standards. For example, companies such as PepsiCo and Federal Express regularly interview their clients to find out what problems they may be having. These responses are then taken very seriously in making whatever improvements are necessary to avoid them in the future.[125] (Some companies have been so very successful at achieving high quality in all respects that they have been honored for their accomplishments. For a description of this special recognition, see the Quest for Quality section on page 656.)

TABLE 16-4

Deming's Suggestions for Improving Quality

W. Edwards Deming, one of the pioneers of total quality management, *made the following recommendations for incorporating quality into organizational culture.*

SUGGESTION	EXPLANATION
■ *Create a constancy of purpose for improving goods and services.*	*Instead of focusing on making money, focus on constantly improving and innovating. When this is done, the money will follow.*
■ *Change your tolerance for poor quality.*	*Too many people are tolerant of poor workmanship and service. Mistakes should be considered unacceptable.*
■ *Stop relying on mass inspection.*	*Instead of relying on one person to make products and another to inspect them, organize the process so that people making products also inspect them, and are responsible for the results.*
■ *Don't award business only on the basis of the lowest bid.*	*Buyers should seek the best possible quality instead of the lowest possible price.*
■ *Make improvements constantly.*	*Rather than thinking of improvement as a one-time effort, continually look for ways to raise quality.*
■ *Provide training.*	*Quality work can only result when people know exactly how to do their jobs. Formal training can be very helpful.*
■ *Institute leadership.*	*Supervisors shouldn't only manage, but also lead employees—sharing their visions for success and showing them ways to do a better job.*
■ *Eliminate fear from the workplace.*	*Too many employees are afraid to ask questions. Unless people are encouraged to ask questions (and are not ridiculed for doing so), they will continue to make mistakes.*
■ *Break down barriers between staff functions.*	*Departments must be made to cooperate with each other as a single team, rather than compete with each other.*
■ *Avoid introducing slogans.*	*These won't help. Let people develop their own slogans.*
■ *Eliminate numerical quotas.*	*Focusing on numerical quotas only encourages people to meet the numbers, often at the expense of quality.*
■ *Eliminate barriers to quality workmanship.*	*Faulty equipment and materials interfere with people's interest in doing a good job. These barriers should be removed.*
■ *Educate the entire workforce.*	*Everyone must be thoroughly educated in the techniques essential to create high-quality goods and services.*
■ *Take action to make the transformation.*	*It is essential for top managers to develop an action plan for carrying out the mission of developing sustained high quality.*

Source: Adapted from Walton, 1990; see Note 121.

THE BALDRIDGE AWARD: RECOGNIZING THE BEST IN QUALITY

In 1987 the U.S. Congress established the Malcom Baldridge Quality Award (named after President Reagan's late secretary of commerce) to recognize American companies that practice effective quality management and make significant improvements in the quality of their goods and services.[126] Up to two companies are given the award each year in each of three categories: manufacturing, service, and small business (any independent company with fewer than 500 full-time employees). For a listing of each year's winners by category, see Table 16-5. (A description of one recent winner, the Ames Rubber Co., appears in the Case-in-Point at the end of this chapter.)

Companies interested in being considered for the award complete a detailed application (running as long as seventy-five pages) in which they thoroughly document their quality achievements. Winners are determined by a board of examiners at the National Institute of Standards and Technology, currently composed of approximately 250 quality experts. The board reviews each written application, and then visits the sites of companies that have scored high enough to be in contention. Scores are given on each of seven different criteria, totaling 1,000 points. The criteria—and their approximate maximum point values (these change slightly each year)—are as follows:

TABLE 16-5

The Baldridge Award: A List of Winners

The Malcom Baldridge Quality Award has been given each year since 1988 to U.S. companies whose practices reflect the highest standards of quality in all aspects of their operations. Here is a listing of the winners through 1993 in each of the three categories in which an award can be made—manufacturing, small business, and service.

YEAR	MANUFACTURING CATEGORY	SMALL BUSINESS CATEGORY	SERVICE CATEGORY
1988	*Motorola, Inc.*	*Globe Metallurgical, Inc.*	*(none)*
	Commercial Nuclear Fuel Division of Westinghouse Electric		
1989	*Miliken & Company*	*(none)*	*(none)*
	Xerox Business Products and Systems		
1990	*Cadillac Motor Car Company*	*Wallace Co., Inc.*	*Federal Express Corporation*
1991	*Solectron Corporation*	*Marlowe Industries*	*(none)*
	Zytec Corporation		
1992	*AT&T Network Systems Group*	*Granite Rock Co.*	*AT&T Universal Card Services*
	Texas Instruments, Inc.		*The Ritz-Carlton Hotel Co.*
1993	*Eastman Chemical Company*	*Ames Rubber Company*	*(none)*

Source: Information provided by the National Institute of Standards and Technology.

THE QUEST FOR QUALITY, Cont.

- *Senior executive leadership* (90 points). Judges look at both a dedicated symbolic commitment to quality by top management as well as active commitment to quality on a daily basis by senior staff.
- *Information and analysis* (80 points). An exceptionally thorough system for collecting and analyzing the quality of performance is needed.
- *Strategic quality planning* (60 points). To win a Baldridge, companies have to show that they have planned for quality by establishing two or three specific goals and establish in detail how effectively they met them.
- *Human resource development and management* (150 points). Not only must companies show quality in attaining performance goals, but also in tapping the potential of its employees. Of particular interest is the extent to which employees are empowered to make decisions (see Chapter 12).
- *Management of process quality* (140 points). Award-winning companies demonstrate their appreciation for the critical processes that flow across traditional business functions (see Chapter 15).
- *Quality and operational results* (180 points). Judges must find clear evidence that improvement in critical company operations has been steadily improving for at least three years.
- *Customer focus and satisfaction* (300 points). Consideration is given to evidence of customer satisfaction, taking into account the number of different sources of information (e.g., customer surveys, sales calls, hotlines, etc.) and their objectivity. Because judges consider this to be the most important category (following from the basic ideas of TQM and reengineering), this category is the most heavily weighted in picking a winner.

The major goal of the award is to promote quality achievement by recognizing those companies that deliver continually improving value to customers while maximizing their overall productivity and effectiveness. To ensure that all companies can benefit from the winners' experiences, winning companies are expected to share their successful quality strategies with other American firms. This has been done in the form of personal presentations, books, and cases presented on videotape.[127] In the case of IBM, preparing its application for the Baldridge caused it to so carefully examine itself that benefits came not only from the recognition it received by winning (in 1990), but the detailed process of preparing the application itself.[128]

SUMMARY AND REVIEW

DETERMINANTS OF ORGANIZATIONAL CHANGE

Changes in organizations may be either planned or unplanned, and they may be based either internal or external to the organization. Planned internal changes may include changes in products or services, changes in administrative systems, or changes in organizational size and structure. Decisions to engage in **downsizing** (reorganizing the structure of an organization in a manner that reduces the number of employees needed) and **outsourcing** (eliminating peripheral organizational functions and purchasing them from outside the organization) fall into this category. Planned external changes include the introduction of new technologies and advances in information processing and communication. Unplanned internal changes include shifts in the demographic characteristics of the workforce and responses to performance gaps. Unplanned external change may result from governmental regulation as well as from economic competition.

THE PROCESS OF ORGANIZATIONAL CHANGE

Organizations may change with respect to their organizational structure (responsibilities and procedures used), the technology used on the job, and the people who perform the work. Change is likely to occur whenever the benefits associated with making a change (i.e., dissatisfaction with current conditions, the availability of desirable alternatives, and the existence of a plan for achieving that alternative) outweigh the costs involved. In general, people are resistant to change because of individual factors (e.g., economic insecurity, fear of the unknown) and organizational factors (e.g., the stability of work groups, threats to the existing balance of power). However, **resistance to change** can be overcome in several ways, including educating the work force about the effects of the changes and involving employees in the change process.

TECHNIQUES OF ORGANIZATIONAL DEVELOPMENT

Techniques for planning organizational change in order to enhance personal and organizational outcomes are collectively known as **organizational development (OD)** practices. For example, **survey feedback** uses questionnaires and/or interviews as the basis for identifying organizational problems, which are then addressed in planning sessions. **Sensitivity training** is a technique in which group discussions are used to enhance interpersonal awareness and reduce interpersonal friction. **Team building** involves using work groups to diagnose and develop specific plans for solving problems with respect to their functioning as a work unit. **Grid training** focuses on efforts to improve managers' concern for people and their concern for production by training them in communication skills and planning skills. **Quality of work life** programs attempt to humanize the workplace by involving employees in the decisions affecting them (e.g., through quality circle meetings) and by restructuring the jobs themselves. Finally, **management by objectives** focuses on attempts by managers and their subordinates to work together at setting important organizational goals and developing a plan to help meet them. The rationale underlying all six of these techniques is that they may enhance organizational functioning by involving employees in identifying and solving organizational problems.

The effectiveness of most organizational development programs is not systematically assessed in practice, and the few studies that have attempted to measure the success of such programs were not carefully conducted. However, those studies that have systematically evaluated organizational development programs generally find them to be successful in improving organizational functioning and, to a lesser degree, individual satisfaction. Some have argued that OD is unethical for several reasons, most notably because it has the potential to be used for illegitimate purposes. However, others counter that OD is just a tool and that it is people who are at fault for using it inappropriately.

IMPROVING ORGANIZATIONAL QUALITY: CURRENT PRACTICES

Many of today's organizations engage in efforts directed at improving the quality of the goods produced or services provided. One of these approaches, **reengineering**, is the fundamental rethinking and radical redesign of business processes to achieve drastic improvements in performance. It encourages executives to totally reconsider the best processes to use to accomplish the organization's goals. Another approach, **total quality management**, is an organizational strategy for improving customer satisfaction by developing techniques to carefully manage output quality. It focuses heavily on measuring and maintaining quality standards in addition to making a commitment to quality a key part of the organization's culture. The Baldridge award is given each year to companies in recognition of their accomplishments in attaining truly outstanding quality in all areas.

KEY TERMS

contingency work force: The growing group of people who, either willingly or unwillingly, hold a series of temporary jobs instead of permanent jobs.

downsizing: The process of reducing the size of a company's workforce in response to changes in structure that eliminates the need for some employees (sometimes used interchangeably with *rightsizing*).

dual-core model: The theory recognizing that changes in the administration of organizations come from upper management (i.e., from the top down), whereas changes in the work performed come from the technical specialists within organizations (i.e., from the bottom up).

grid training: The OD technique designed to strengthen managers' communication skills (their concern for people) and their planning skills (their concern for production).

management by objectives (MBO): The technique by which managers and their subordinates work together to set, and then meet, organizational goals.

organizational change: Alterations in the operations of organizations that are either planned or unplanned, and are a result of either internal or external influences.

organizational development (OD): A set of social science techniques designed to plan change in organizational work settings, for purposes of enhancing the personal development of individuals and improving the effectiveness of organizational functioning.

outsourcing: The process of completely eliminating parts of organizations that focus on noncore aspects and hiring outside firms to perform these functions instead.

quality circles (QCs): An approach to improving the quality of work life, in which small groups of volunteers meet regularly to identify and solve problems related to the work they perform and the conditions under which they work.

quality of work life (QWL): An OD technique designed to improve organizational functioning by humanizing the workplace, making it more democratic, and involving employees in decision making.

reengineering: The fundamental rethinking and radical redesign of business processes to achieve drastic improvements in performance.

resistance to change: The tendency for employees to be unwilling to go along with organizational changes, either because of individual fears of the unknown, or organizational impediments (such as structural inertia).

rightsizing: The process of making adjustments in the size of a company's workforce in response to restructuring (sometimes used interchangeably with *downsizing*).

sensitivity training: An OD technique that seeks to enhance employees' understanding of their own behavior and its impact on others. Such changes, it is believed, will reduce the interpersonal conflicts that interfere with organizational effectiveness.

structural inertia: The organizational forces acting on employees, encouraging them to perform their jobs in certain ways (e.g., training, reward systems), thereby making them resistant to change.

survey feedback: An OD technique in which questionnaires and interviews are used to collect information about issues of concern to an organization. This information is shared with employees and is used as the basis for planning organizational change.

team building: An OD technique in which employees discuss problems related to their work group's performance. On the basis of these discussions, specific problems are identified and plans for solving them are devised and implemented.

total quality management (TQM): An organizational strategy of improving customer satisfaction by developing techniques to carefully manage output quality. TQM relies on measuring and maintaining quality standards in addition to making a commitment to quality a key part of the organization's culture.

work group inertia: Forces operating within work groups, such as norms, that discourage organizational change.

QUESTIONS FOR DISCUSSION

1. Some changes in organizations are unplanned, whereas others are the result of deliberate, planned actions. Give examples of each of these varieties of change, and explain their implications for organizational functioning.
2. Suppose you are having difficulty managing a small group of subordinates who work in an office 1,000 miles away from your home base. What kinds of changes in structure, technology, and people can be implemented to more closely supervise these distant employees?
3. Under what conditions will people be most willing to make changes in organizations? Explain your answer and give an example.
4. Suppose that you are a top executive of a large organization about to undertake an ambitious restructuring involving massive changes in job responsibilities for most employees. Explain why people might be resistant to such changes and what steps could be taken to overcome this resistance.
5. Imagine that you are supervising ten employees who are not getting along. Their constant fighting is interfering with their job performance. Identify any two different organizational development techniques that might be employed to address this problem. Explain why they may help. Describe the steps required to implement these techniques.
6. Overall, how effective is organizational development in improving organizational functioning? With respect to what factors does it work or not work?
7. Argue for or against the following statement: "Organizational development is inherently unethical and should not be used."
8. Some have claimed that reengineering and total quality management are not really new, and represent the repackaging of older, well-established OB concepts. Do you agree? If so, what OB ideas would you say are incorporated into these practices?

CHANGING AHEAD OF THE COMPETITION

Ames Rubber Corporation of Hamburg, New Jersey, is not the kind of company people typically associate with innovation. This is because the company has been in business for over fifty years making products that are neither glamorous, new, nor high-tech. This firm operates in a mature industry making equipment used by the manufacturers of office machinery. In fact, Ames Rubber is the world's largest manufacturer of rubber rollers used in office machines such as copiers.[1] The company has been profitable and well managed throughout its history.

Despite all these standards of success, in 1986, even when the company was delivering high-quality products to satisfied customers, the firm embarked on a major organizational change. The purpose: to be able to compete successfully in the future. In this case, the change involved the development and implementation of a total quality management (TQM) system. Interestingly, this successful company was so effective in developing this programmatic change that in 1993 they won the Malcolm Baldrige National Quality Award for excellence in quality management for small businesses (see Table 16-5 on page 656).[2]

The president of Ames Rubber, Joel Marvel, believed that it was crucial for his company to go out and look for ways to change so that they could improve their productivity to remain competitive throughout the 1990s. According to Marvel, any manufacturing company that does not embrace TQM will not be viable throughout the rest of the decade.[3]

Fortunately, Marvel understood the magnitude of the change he was seeking at his company. He knew that the implementation of a TQM system would be extremely time consuming and costly. Similarly, he realized that without getting the buy-in of all employees—not just top management—the change he coveted would be doomed. He also recognized that he would have to be the champion of the TQM effort for the change to be taken seriously and for it to be given the resources and energy necessary for success.

To begin the change process, Marvel and the Ames Rubber executive committee selected the brightest and most talented managers and asked for their input on how best to reorganize the company around functional processes.[4] He also encouraged his top management to set strategy and direction and then listened to input from all his employees. No doubt, part of the reason this change to a TQM system was so successful was that Marvel and his management team spent eight months gathering input and studying the TQM changes they thought might be effective.[5]

The first step in this data-gathering stage was to analyze the company's internal and external customers. In this case, a customer was defined as any person, group, or institution that uses the output of others. An example of internal customers was the people further down the assembly line who worked on the product. External customers were defined as all people who used the product.

After the customers and their needs were identified, management and employees worked together to develop systems that allowed these needs to be satisfied. Although this required that managers give up some degree of control, they went along with this program because they believed that it was in the best interest of the company. One outcome of this process was that all employees can now decide to stop the manufacturing process at any point when they think there is a quality problem that needs to be corrected.

Next, employee teams were formed. The purpose of these groups was for their members to support and help one another.

To understand and implement the changes required by the TQM system. These units were further reinforced by the fact that all employees of Ames Rubber, from the president to the "people who sweep the floor"[6] were given twenty-four hours of education in the new ways of production and TQM philosophies. In addition, managers were provided with training about how to best serve as resources for their subordinates and how to communicate effectively with them.[7] One hoped-for benefit of this effort was that it would help all the people who worked at Ames Rubber to share a common understanding about the company goals.

If the employees are to be believed, this common goal has actually been achieved. Many employees report that they feel much more committed to the organization now that the TQM system has been adopted. They claim that they know they are important in making a good product. Also, they appreciate that their ideas are listened to. According to Marvel, the sharing of a common goal of high quality has generated a great deal of enthusiasm and a sense of energy and purpose among the employees of Ames Rubber.[8]

The evidence of the effectiveness of the careful development and implementation of a TQM plan at Ames Rubber are very impressive. Sales rose by 48 percent between 1989 and 1992. Similarly, profits soared by over 100 percent. Ideas generated by employees have saved the company and its customers over $3 million between 1987 and 1992. It is estimated that in 1993 these savings averaged $2,700 for each of the company's 445 employees! Clearly, these financial indications demonstrate that Ames' focus on quality has been profitable. The statistics indicating the extent of the improvement in quality, however, are even more astounding than the profits. The company has reduced the number of defective parts that reach its customers from 30,000 to 11 parts per million, an increase in quality of almost 3,000 percent! Ames has also extended its TQM beliefs to its suppliers, requiring them to share the company's quality values and commitment to continuous improvement. In so doing, Ames has reduced the number of suppliers, on which its relies from 42 to 19, and increased their quality performance to 99 percent.[9]

QUESTIONS FOR DISCUSSION

1. What are the elements in the planned change implemented by Ames Rubber?
2. In what ways did the implementation of the TQM process change the structure, people, and technology at Ames Rubber Corporation?
3. How might have training and teamwork contributed to the effectiveness of unfreezing, change, and refreezing?
4. How did Marvel and Ames Rubber Corporation's management work to overcome organizational resistance to change?
5. Critics suggest that TQM is just the latest management fad. How do you think the management at Ames Rubber might respond to this assertion?

EXPERIENCING ORGANIZATIONAL BEHAVIOR

Facing Up to Organizational Change

If there's any one constant in the world, it's that things change, and the same truism applies to organizations. As technology advances, the composition of the workforce shifts, and new markets evolve, people must confront the reality of organizational change. Such changes are often quite threatening to people, and pose serious challenges to managers attempting to implement the changes needed for organizations to survive. This exercise will help you appreciate the resistance to change that many supervisors encounter and to consider some ways to overcome it.

PROCEDURE

Listed below are two situations involving organizational change. For each one, list some of the impediments that are likely to arise on the part of employees, and things that managers can do to overcome this resistance.

Situation A: Members of a secretarial staff very familiar with using typewriters must now face using a word processing system.

Impediments to Change	*Ways to Overcome Impediments*
1.	1.
2.	2.
3.	3.

Situation B: An older, well-liked supervisor is retiring and will be replaced by a younger person hired from outside the company.

Impediments to Change	*Ways to Overcome Impediments*
1.	1.
2.	2.
3.	3.

POINTS TO CONSIDER

1. For each of the different situations described, were the impediments to change similar or different?
2. For each of the different situations described, were the ways of overcoming these impediments similar or different?
3. In what ways do you think the nature of the organizational change situation may dictate the types of change barriers likely to be encountered and the ease with which these may be overcome?

NOTES

CHAPTER 1

PREVIEW CASE SOURCE

Taylor, A., III (1993, May 17). Why GM leads the pack in Europe. *Fortune*, pp. 83–84, 86–87.

TEXT

1. Greenberg, J. (Ed.). (1994). *Organizational behavior: The state of the science*. Hillsdale, NJ: Erlbaum.

2. Elden, M., & Chisholm, R. F. (1993). Emerging varieties of action research: Introduction to the special issue. *Human Relations, 46*, 121–142.

3. Case, J. (1993, April). A company of businesspeople. *Inc.*, pp. 79–84, 86–87, 90, 92–93.

4. McGregor, D. (1960). *The human side of enterprise*. New York: McGraw-Hill.

5. Katz, D., & Kahn, R. (1978). *The social psychology of organizations*. New York: Wiley.

6. Kiechel, W., III. (1993, May 17). How we will work in the year 2000. *Fortune*, pp. 38–46, 48, 52.

7. Boyett, J. H., & Conn, H. P. (1992). *Workplace 2000*. New York: Plume.

8. Sherman, S. (1993, January 25). A brave new Darwinian workplace. *Fortune*, pp. 50–52, 56. (quote, p. 51)

9. Anonymous. (1993, June). Catching up on homework. *Home Office Computing*, p. 16.

10. See Note 6.

11. Case, J. (1993, April). A company of businesspeople. *Inc.*, pp. 79–84, 86–87, 90, 92–93. (quote, p. 83)

12. See Note 6.

13. Pennings, J. M. (1992). Structural contingency theory: A reappraisal. In B. M. Staw & L. L. Cummings (Eds.), *Research in organizational behavior* (Vol. 14, pp. 267–310). Greenwich, CT: JAI Press.

14. Jackson, S. E., & Alvarez, E. B. (1992). Working through diversity as a strategic imperative. In S. E. Jackson (Ed.), *Diversity in the workplace* (pp. 13–29). New York: Guilford Press.

15. Fierman, J. (1990, July 30). Why women still don't hit the top. *Fortune*, pp. 40–46, 50–56, 57, 59–60.

16. Towers Perrin, & Hudson Institute. (1990). *Workforce 2000: Competing in a seller's market*. Valhalla, NY: Towers Perrin.

17. Maruyama, M. (1992). Changing dimensions in international business. *Academy of Management Executive, 6*, 88–96.

18. Pucik, V., Tichy, N. M., & Barnett, C. K. (1993). *Globalizing management*. New York: Wiley.

19. Ricks, D. A., Toyne, B., & Martinez, Z. (1990). Recent developments in international management research. *Journal of Management, 16*, 219–253.

20. Fernandez, J. P., & Barr, M. (1993). *The diversity advantage*. New York: Lexington Books.

21. Ivancevich, J. M., DeFrank, R. S., & Gregory, P. R. (1992). The Soviet enterprise director: An important resource before and after the coup. *Academy of Management Executive, 6*, 42–55. (quote, p. 46)

22. See Note 21.

23. Lawrence, P. R., & Vlashoutsicos, C. A. (1990). *Behind the factory walls*. Boston: Harvard Business School Press.

24. DeFrank, R. S., Ivancevich, J. M., & Schweiger, D. M. (1988, Winter). Job stress and mental well–being: Similarities and differences among American, Japanese, and Indian managers. *Behavioral Medicine*, 160–170.

25. Feller, G. (1993, June). Kaliningrad: Western gateway to Russian business. *Management Review*, pp. 46–49.

26. Kennedy, C. (1991). *Instant management*. New York: William Morrow and Company.

27. Taylor, F. W. (1947). *Scientific management*. New York: Harper & Row.

28. Drucker, P. F. (1974). *Management: Tasks, responsibilities, practices*. New York: Harper & Row.

29. Münsterberg, H. (1913). *Psychology and industrial efficiency*. New York: Houghton Mifflin.

30. Metcalf, H. & Urwick, L. F. (Eds.) (1942). *Dynamic administration: The collected papers of Mary Parker Follett*. New York: Harper & Row.

31. Bedian, A. (1976, June). Finding the one best way: An appreciation of Frank B. Gilbreth, the father of motion study. *Conference Board Record*, pp. 37–39.

32. Gotcher, J. M. (1992). Assisting the handicapped: The pioneering efforts of Frank and Lillian Gilbreth. *Journal of Management, 18*, 5–13.

33. Gilbreth, F. B., & Gilbreth, L. M. (1917, April 28). The problem of the crippled soldier: How to put him on the payroll. *Scientific American Supplement, 83*, pp. 260–261. (quote, p. 261)

34. Mayo, E. (1933). *The human problems of an industrial civilization*. London: Macmillan.

35. Roethlisberger, F. J., & Dickson, W. J. (1939). *Management and the worker*. Cambridge, MA: Harvard University Press.

36. Baron, R. A., Rea, M. S., & Daniels, S. G. (1992). Lighting as a source of environmentally-generated positive affect in work settings: Impact on cognitive tasks and interpersonal behavior. *Motivation and Emotion, 15*, 1–34.

37. Fayol, H. (1949). *General and industrial management*. London: Pittman.

38. Weber, M. (1921). *Theory of social and economic organization*. (A. M. Henderson & T. Parsons, Trans.). London: Oxford University Press.

39. Flexner, S. B. (1976). *I hear America talking*. New York: Van Nostrand Reinhold.

40. Lawrence, P. R. (1987). Historical development of organizational behavior. In J. W. Lorsch (Ed.), *Handbook of organizational behavior* (pp. 1–9). Englewood Cliffs, NJ: Prentice Hall.

41. Gardner, B., & Moore, G. (1945). *Human relations in industry*. Homewood, IL: Irwin.

42. See Note 38.

43. Gordon, R. A., & Howell, J. E. (1959). *Higher education for business*. New York: Columbia University Press.

44. Porter, L. W., & McKibbin, L. L. (1988). *Management education and development: Adrift or thrust into the 21st century*. New York: McGraw-Hill.

45. Blood, M. (1994). The role of organizational behavior in the business school curriculum. In J. Greenberg (Ed.), *Organizational behavior: The state of the science* (pp. 207–220). Hillsdale, NJ: Lawrence Erlbaum Associates.

46. Cooper, H., & Hedges, L. V. (1994). *The handbook of research synthesis*. New York: Russell Sage Foundation.

47. Van Mannen, J., Dabbs, J. M., Jr., & Faulkner, R. R. (1982). *Varieties of qualitative research*. Newbury Park, CA: Sage Publications.

48. Greenberg, J., & Folger, R. (1988). *Controversial issues in social research methods*. New York: Springer-Verlag.

49. Eisenhardt, K. M. (1989). Building theories from case study research. *Academy of Management Review, 14*, 532–550.

CASE IN POINT: THE LIFE AND TIMES OF ED WAX

1. CNN. *Pinnacle*, Saatchi and Saatchi, September 15, 1991.

2. Rabinovitz, J. (1991, August 3). "Management team at Saatchi revamped." *New York Times*, p. 35.

3. See Note 1.

4. Donaton, S. (1993, April 26). Agencies being left behind by technology. *Advertising Age*, pp. 3, 48.

5. Wells, M. (1993, February 1). Saatchi, WPP set new pay plans. *Advertising Age*, p. 35.

6. Wentz, L. (1991, June 3). Saatchi thinks global with "int'l bonuses." *Advertising Age*, p. 49.

7. Garcia, S. (1993, April 12). Saatchi California shops to rethink their structuring, *Adweek*, p. 5.

8. Levin, G. (1992, September 14). Saatchi, Euro RSCG build new agencies: Mergers link CME, KHBB, Della Femina, Messner. *Advertising Age*, pp. 4, 47.

9. See Note 1.

CHAPTER 2

PREVIEW CASE SOURCE

Salwen, K.G. (1993, April 19). German-owned maker of power tools finds job training pays off. *Wall Street Journal*, pp. A1, A4.

TEXT

1. Schiffmann, H. R. (1993). *Sensation and perception* (4th ed.). New York: Wiley.

2. Murphy, K. R., Jako, R. A., & Anhalt, R. L. (1993). Nature and consequences of halo error: A critical analysis. *Journal of Applied Psychology, 78*, 218–225.

3. Pulakos, E. D., & Wexley, K. N. (1983). The relationship among perceptual similarity, sex, and performance ratings in manager-subordinate dyads. *Academy of Management Journal, 26*, 129–139.

4. Turban, D. B., & Jones, A. P. (1988). Supervisor-subordinate similarity: Types, effects, and mechanisms. *Journal of Applied Psychology, 73*, 228–234.

5. Srull, T. K., & Wyer, R. S. (1988). *Advances in social cognition*. Hillsdale, NJ: Lawrence Erlbaum Associates.

6. Weiss, D. H. (1991). *Fair, square, and legal*. New York: American Management Association.

7. Brenner, O. C., Tomkiewicz, J., & Schein, V. E. (1989). The relationship between sex role stereotypes and requisite management characteristics revisited. *Academy of Management Journal, 32*, 662–669.

8. Schein, V. E., & Mueller, R. (1992). Sex role stereotyping and requisite management characteristics: A cross cultural look. *Journal of Organizational Behavior, 13*, 439–447.

9. Medcof, J. W. (1990). PEAT: An integrative model of attribution processes. In M. P. Zanna (Ed.), *Advances in experimental social psychology* (Vol. 23, pp. 111–209). San Diego, CA: Academic Press.

10. Jones, E. E., & McGillis, D. (1976). Correspondent inferences and the attribution cube: A comparative reappraisal. In J. H. Harvey, W. J. Ickes, & R. F. Kidd (Eds.), *New directions in attribution research* (Vol. 1, pp. 389–420). Hillsdale, NJ: Lawrence Erlbaum Associates.

11. Fiske, S. T., & Taylor, S. E. (1991). *Social cognition* (2nd ed.). Reading, MA: Addison-Wesley.

12. Hansen, R. D. (1980). Common sense attribution. *Journal of Personality and Social Psychology, 39*, 996–1009.

13. Mullen, B., & Riordan, C. A. (1988). Self-serving attributions for performance in naturalistic settings: A meta-analytic review. *Journal of Applied Social Psychology, 18*, 3–22.

14. Moussavi, F., & Evans, D. A. (1993). Emergence of organizational attributions: The role of a shared cognitive schema. *Journal of Management, 19*, 79–95.

15. Fletcher, C. (1989). Impression management in the selection interview. In R. A. Giacalone & P. Rosenfeld (Eds.), *Impression management in the organization* (pp. 269–282). Hillsdale, NJ: Lawrence Erlbaum Associates.

16. Giacalone, R. A., & Rosenfeld, P. (1989). *Impression management in the organization*. Hillsdale, NJ: Lawrence Erlbaum Associates.

17. Greenberg, J. (1990). Looking fair vs. being fair: Managing impressions of organizational justice. In B. M. Staw & L. L. Cummings (Eds.), *Research in organizational behavior* (Vol. 12, pp. 111–157). Greenwich, CT: JAI Press.

18. Fiske, S. T., & Neuberg, S. L. (1990). A continuum of impression formation, from category-based to individuating processes: Influences of information and motivation on attention and interpretation. In M. P. Zanna (Ed.), *Advances in experimental social psychology* (Vol. 23, pp. 1–74). San Diego, CA: Academic Press.

19. Feldman, D. C., & Klich, N. R. (1991). Impression management and career strategies. In R. A. Giacalone & P. Rosenfeld (Eds.), *Applied impression management: How image–making affects managerial decisions* (pp. 67–80). Newbury Park, CA: Sage.

20. Wayne, S. J., & Kacmar, K. M. (1991). The effects of impression management on the performance appraisal process. *Organizational Behavior and Human Decision Processes, 48*, 70–88.

21. Wayne, S. J., & Ferris, G. R. (1990). Influence tactics, affect, and exchange quality in supervisor-subordinate interactions: A laboratory experiment and field study. *Journal of Applied Psychology, 75*, 487–499.

22. Fandt, P. M., & Ferris, G. M. (1990). The management of information and impressions: When employees behave opportunistically. *Organizational Behavior and Human Decision Processes, 45*, 140–158.

23. Ashford, S. J., & Northcraft, G. B. (1992). Conveying more (or less) than we realize: The role of impression-management in feedback-seeking. *Organizational Behavior and Human Decision Processes, 53*, 310–334.

24. Garbett, T. (1988). *How to build a corporation's identity and project its image*. Lexington, MA: Lexington Books.

25. Gatewood, R. D., Gowan, M. A., & Lautenschlager, G. J. (1993). Corporate image, recruitment image, and initial job choice decisions. *Academy of Management Journal, 36*, 414–427.

26. Mohrman, A. M., Jr., Resnick-West, S. M., & Lawler, E. E., III. (1989). *Designing performance appraisal systems*. San Francisco: Jossey-Bass.

27. Ilgen, D. R., Major, D. A., & Tower, S. L. (1994). The cognitive revolution in organizational behavior. In J. Greenberg (Ed.), *Organizational behavior: The state of the science* (pp. 1–22). Hillsdale, NJ: Lawrence Erlbaum Associates.

28. Hogan, E. A. (1987). Effects of prior expectations on performance ratings: A longitudinal study. *Academy of Management Journal, 30*, 354–368.

29. Heneman, R. L., Greenberger, D. B., & Anonyuo, C. (1989). Attributions and exchanges: The effects of interpersonal factors on the diagnosis of employee performance. *Academy of Management Journal, 32*, 466–476.

30. Mitchell, T. R., Green, S. G., & Wood, R. S. (1982). An attributional model of leadership and the poor performing subordinate: Development and validation. In B. M. Staw & L. L. Cummings (Eds.), *Research in organizational behavior* (Vol. 3, pp. 197–234). Greenwich, CT: JAI Press.

31. Wick, C. W., & Leon, L. S. (1993). *The learning edge: How smart managers and smart companies stay ahead*. New York: McGraw-Hill.

32. Atkinson, R. C., Herrnstein, R. J., Lindzey, G., & Luce, R. D. (Eds.), (1988). *Stevens' handbook of experimental psychology (2nd ed.)* (Vol. 1, pp. 218–266). New York: Wiley.

33. Thorndike, E. L. (1911). *Animal intelligence*. New York: Macmillan.

34. Skinner, B. F. (1969). *Contingencies of reinforcement*. New York: Appleton-Century-Crofts.

35. Daniels, A. C. (1994). *Bringing out the best in people*. New York: McGraw-Hill.

36. Scott, W. E., & Podsakoff, P. M. (1985). *Behavioral principles in the practice of management*. New York: Wiley.

37. Bandura, A. (1986). *Social foundations of thought and action*. Englewood Cliffs, NJ: Prentice Hall.

38. Harrison, J. K. (1992). Individual and combined effects of behavior modeling and the cultural assimilator in cross-cultural management training. *Journal of Applied Psychology, 77*, 962.

39. Goldstein, I. L. (1991). Training in work organizations. In M. D. Dunnette & L. M. Hough (Eds.), *Handbook of industrial and organizational psychology (2nd ed.)* (Vol. 2, pp. 507–620). Palo Alto, CA: Consulting Psychologists Press.

40. Schnake, M. E. (1986). Vicarious punishment in a work setting. *Journal of Applied Psychology, 71*, 343–345.

41. O'Reilly, C. O., III, & Puffer, S. (1989). The impact of rewards and punishment in a social context: A laboratory and field experiment. *Journal of Occupational Psychology, 25*, 467–483.

42. Trevino, L. K., & Ball, G. A. (1992). The social implications of punishing unethical behavior: Observers' cognitive and affective reactions. *Journal of Management, 18*, 751–768.

43. Carnevale, A. P., & Gainer, L. J. (1989). *The learning enterprise*. Alexandria, VA: American Society for Training and Development.

44. Del Valle, C. (1993, April 26). From high schools to high skills. *Business Week*, pp. 110, 112.

45. O'Reilly, B. (1993, April 5). How execs learn now. *Fortune*, pp. 52–54, 58.

46. Bolt, J. F. (1993, May). Achieving the CEO's agenda: Education for executives. *Management Review*, pp. 44–48.

47. Webster, J., & Martocchio, J. J. (1993). Turning work into play: Implications for microcomputer software training. *Journal of Management, 19*, 127–146.

48. Gist, M. E., Stevens, C. K., & Bavetta, A. G. (1991). Effects of self-efficacy and post-training intervention on the acquisition and maintenance of complex interpersonal skills. *Personnel Psychology, 44*, 837–861.

49. Impoco, J. (1992, July 13). Basic training Sanyo style. *U.S. News & World Report*, pp. 46–48.

50. Argyris, C. (1991, May–June). Teaching smart people how to learn. *Harvard Business Review, 69*(3), 99–109.

51. Weiss, H. M. (1990). Learning theory in industrial/organizational psychology. In M. D. Dunnette & L. M. Hough (Eds.), *Handbook of industrial and organizational psychology (2nd ed.)* (Vol. 1, pp. 171–222). Palo Alto, CA: Consulting Psychologists Press.

52. Baldwin, T. T., & Ford, J. K. (1988). Transfer of training: A review and directions for future research. *Personnel Psychology, 41,* 63–105.

53. Ford, J. K., Quiñones, M. A., Sego, D. J., & Sorra, J. S. (1992). Factors affecting the opportunity to perform trained tasks on the job. *Personnel Psychology, 45,* 511–527.

54. Tziner, A., Haccoun, R. R., & Kadish, A. (1991). Personal and situational characteristics influencing the effectiveness of transfer of training improvement strategies. *Journal of Occupational Psychology 64,* 167–177.

55. Ilgen, D. R., & Moore, C. F. (1987). Types and choices of performance feedback. *Journal of Applied Psychology, 72,* 401–406.

56. Henkoff, R. (1993 August 18). Companies that train best. *Fortune,* pp. 62–64, 68, 73–75.

57. Miller, L. (1978). *Behavior management.* New York: Wiley.

58. Hamner, W. C., & Hamner, E. P. (1976). Behavior modification on the bottom line. *Organizational Dynamics, 4*(4), 8–21.

59. Frederiksen, L. W. (1982). *Handbook of organizational behavior management.* New York: Wiley.

60. Anonymous. (1985, May 15). Hot 100: A million dollar incentive plan. *Business Week,* p. 52.

61. See Note 59.

62. Morin, W. J., & Yorks, L. (1990). *Dismissal.* New York: Drake Beam Morin.

63. Miner, J. B., & Brewer, J. F. (1976). The management of ineffective performance. In M. D. Dunnette (Ed.), *Handbook of industrial and organizational psychology* (pp. 995–1029). Chicago: Rand McNally.

64. Beyer, J. M., & Trice., H. M. (1984). A field study of the use and perceived effects of discipline in controlling work performance. *Academy of Management Journal, 27,* 743–754.

65. Oberle, R. J. (1978). Administering disciplinary actions, *Personnel Journal, 18*(3), 30–33.

66. Arvey, R. D., & Jones, A. P. (1985). The use of discipline in organizational settings: A framework for future research. In L. L. Cummings & B. M. Staw (Eds.), *Research in organizational behavior* (Vol. 7, pp. 367–408). Greenwich, CT: JAI Press.

67. Kiechell, W., III. (1990, May 7). How to discipline in the modern age. *Fortune,* pp. 179–180 (quote, p. 180).

68. Arvey, R. E., & Icancevich, J. M. (1980). Punishment in organizations: A review, propositions, and research suggestions. *Academy of Management Review, 5,* 123–132.

69. Trevino, L. K. (1992). The social effects of punishment in organizations: A justice perspective. *Academy of Management Review, 17,* 647–676.

70. Lussier, R. H. (1990, August), A discipline model for increasing performance. *Supervisory Management,* pp. 6–7.

71. Kerr, S. (1975). On the folly of rewarding "A" while hoping for "B." *Academy of Management Journal, 18,* 769–783.

CASE IN POINT: DIFFERENCES IN UNDERSTANDING

1. McCarthy, M. J. (1988, June 14). Supreme Court to rule on sex-bias case. *Wall Street Journal,* p. 37.

2. Weisel, M. S. (1989, October). Sexual stereotyping in partnership decisions: The second stage. *The Woman CPA,* p. 7.

3. See Note 1, p. 37.

4. See Note 2, p. 35.

5. Yu, W. (1985, September 11). Asian-Americans charge prejudice slows climb to management ranks. *Wall Street Journal,* p. 36.

6. See Note 5, p. 35.

7. Power, J. (1994, January 9). The myth of the model minority. *The Boston Globe Magazine,* pp. 8, 9 24–29, 35–36.

8. See Note 5.

9. See Note 5.

CHAPTER 3

PREVIEW CASE SOURCES

Bleakley, F.R. (1993, July 27). Who's news: American Express's Chenault is likely to get high post at lead unit TRS. *Wall Street Journal,* p. B7. Harrington, J. (1993, August 2–8). AmEx taps Chenault. *Crain's New York Business.* p. 26. Morgan, J. (1992, December 7). Credit card wars: It's getting ugly out there. *New York Newsday,* sec. 1, p. 27. Nathans, L., Holland, K., & Lewyn, M. (1993, September 13). The American Express card: Don't shuffle papers without it? *Business Week,* p. 36. Stodghill, R., III (1993, September 13). Eyes on the prize at AMEX. *Business Week,* pp. 59–60, 62.

TEXT

1. Carver, C. S., & Scheier, M. F. (1993). *Perspectives on personality.* Boston: Allyn & Bacon.

2. Mischel, W. (1973). Toward a cognitive social learning reconceptualization of personality. *Psychological Review, 80,* 252–283.

3. Davis–Blake, A., & Pfeffer, J. (1989). Just a mirage: The search for dispositional effects in organizational research. *Academy of Management Review, 14,* 385–400.

4. Costa, P. T., & McCrae, R. R. (1988). Personality in adulthood: A six-year longitudinal study of self-reports and spouse ratings on the NEO Personality Inventory. *Journal of Personality and Social Psychology, 54,* 853–863.

5. Bouchard, T. J., Jr. (1984). Twins reared apart and together: What they tell us about human diversity. In S. Fox (Ed.), *The chemical and biological bases of individuality* (pp. 147–184). New York: Plenum.

6. Pervin, L. A. (1985). Personality: Current controversies, issues, and directions. *Annual Review of Psychology, 36,* 83–114.

7. Schneider, B. (1987). $E = f(P,B)$: The road to a radical approach to person-environment fit. *Journal of Vocational Behavior, 31,* 353–361.

8. Chatman, J. A. (1989). Improving interactional organizational research: A model of person-organization fit. *Academy of Management Review, 14,* 333–349.

9. Osipow, S. H. (1990). Convergence in theories of career choice and development: Review and prospect. *Journal of Vocational Behavior, 36,* 122–131.

10. Caldwell, D. F., & O'Reilly, C. A., III. (1990). Measuring person-job fit with a profile-comparison process. *Journal of Applied Psychology, 75,* 648–657.

11. Allport, G. W., & Odbert, H. S. (1936). Trait names: A psycholexical study. *Psychological Monographs, 47,* 211–214.

12. Goldberg, L. R. (1990). An alternative "description of personality": The big five factor structure. *Journal of Personality and Social Psychology, 59,* 1216–1229.

13. Tett, R. P., Jackson, D. N., & Rothstein, M. (1991). Personality measures as predictors of job performance: A meta-analytic review. *Personnel Psychology, 44,* 703–741.

14. Cortina, J. M., Doherty, M. L., Schmitt, N., Kaufman, G., & Smith, R. G. (1992). The big five personality factors in the IPI and MMPI: Predictors of police performance. *Personnel Psychology, 45,* 119–140.

15. Barrick, M. R., & Mount, M. K. (1991). The big five personality dimensions and job performance: A meta–analysis. *Personnel Psychology, 44,* 1–26.

16. Barrick, M. R., & Mount, M. K. (1993). Autonomy as a moderator of the relationships between the big five personality dimensions and job performance. *Journal of Applied Psychology, 78,* 111–118.

17. Murphy, K. R. (1993). *Honesty in the workplace.* Pacific Grove, CA: Brooks/Cole.

18. Collins, J. M., & Schmidt, F. L. (1993). Personality, integrity, and white collar crime: A construct validity study. *Personnel Psychology, 46,* 295–311.

19. Richardson, J. E. (1993). *Annual editions: Business ethics 93/94.* Guilford, CT: Dushkin.

20. George, J. M., & Brief, A. P. (1992). Feeling good—doing good: A conceptual analysis of the mood at work-organizational spontaneity relationship. *Psychological Bulletin, 112,* 310–329.

21. Isen, A. M., & Baron, R. A. (1991). Positive affect as a factor in organizational behavior. In B. M. Staw & L. L. Cummings (Eds.), *Research in organizational behavior* (Vol. 13, pp. 1–54). Greenwich, CT: JAI Press.

22. Staw, B. M., Sutton, R. I., & Pelled, L. H. (1993). Employee positive emotion and favorable outcomes at the workplace. *Organization Science, 3,* 124–137.

23. Staw, B. M., & Barsade, S. G. (1993). Affect and managerial performance: A test of the sadder-but-wiser vs. happier-and-smarter hypotheses. *Administrative Science Quarterly, 38,* 304–331.

24. George, J. M. (1990). Personality, affect, and behavior in groups. *Journal of Applied Psychology, 75,* 107–116.

25. Schneider, B. (1987). The people make the place. *Personnel Psychology, 40,* 437–453.

26. Friedman, M., & Rosenman, R. H., (1974). *Type A behavior and your heart.* New York: Knopf.

27. Jenkins, C. D. (1965). *The Jenkins activity survey for health predictions*. Chapel Hill, NC: Author.

28. Lee, C., Ashford, S. J., & Jamieson, L. F. (1993). The effects of Type A behavior dimensions and optimism on coping strategy, health, and performance. *Journal of Organizational Behavior, 14*, 143–157.

29. Glass, D. C., (1977). *Behavior patterns, stress, and coronary disease*. Hillsdale, NJ: Lawrence Erlbaum Associates.

30. Holmes, D. S., McGilley, B. M., & Houston, B. K. (1984). Task-related arousal of Type A and Type B persons: Level of challenge and response specificity. *Journal of Personality and Social Psychology, 46*, 1322–1327.

31. Jamal, M., & Baba, V. V. (1991). Type A behavior, its prevalence and consequences among women nurses: An empirical examination. *Human Relations, 44*, 1213–1228.

32. Lee, M., & Kanungo, R. (1984). *Management of work and personal life*. New York: Praeger.

33. Holmes, D. S., & Will, M. J. (1985). Expression of interpersonal aggression by angered and nonangered persons with the Type A and Type B behavior patterns. *Journal of Personality and Social Psychology, 48*, 723–727.

34. Baron, R. A. (1989). Personality and organizational conflict: Effects of the Type A behavior pattern and self–monitoring. *Organizational Behavior and Human Decision Processes, 44*, 281–297.

35. Bandura, A. (1986). *Social foundations of thought and action: A social-cognitive view*. Englewood Cliffs, NJ: Prentice Hall.

36. Gist, M. E., & Mitchell, T. R. (1992). Self-efficacy: A theoretical analysis of its determinants and malleability. *Academy of Management Review, 17*, 183–211.

37. Vasil, L. (1992). Self-efficacy expectations and causal attributions for achievement among male and female university faculty. *Journal of Vocational Behavior, 41*, 259–269.

38. Wood, R., Bandura, A., & Bailey, T. (1990). Mechanisms governing organizational performance in complex decision-making environments. *Organizational Behavior and Human Decision Processes, 46*, 181–201.

39. Eden, D., & Aviram, A. (1993). Self-efficacy training to speed reemployment: Helping people to help themselves. *Journal of Applied Psychology, 78*, 352–360.

40. Shamir, B. (1986). Self–esteem and the psychological impact of unemployment. *Social Psychology Quarterly, 49*, 61–72.

41. Brockner, J. (1988). *Self-esteem at work*. Lexington, MA: Lexington Books.

42. Ellis, R. A., & Taylor, M. S. (1983). Role of self-esteem within the job search process. *Journal of Applied Psychology, 68*, 632–640.

43. Turban, D. B., & Keon, T. L. (1993). Organizational attractiveness: An interactionist perspective. *Journal of Applied Psychology, 78*, 184–193.

44. Pierce, J. L., Gardner, D. G., Dunham, R. B., & Cummings, L. L. (1993). Moderation by organization-based self-esteem of role condition-employee response relationships. *Academy of Management Journal, 36*, 271–288.

45. Levy, P. E. (1993). Self–appraisal and attributions: A test of a model. *Journal of Management, 19*, 51–62.

46. Brockner, J., & Guare, J. (1983). Improving the performance of low self-esteem individuals: An attributional approach. *Academy of Management Journal, 36*, 642–656.

47. Blitzer, R. J., Petersen, C., & Rogers, L. (1993, February). How to build self-esteem. *Training & Development*, pp. 58–60.

48. Snyder, M. (1987). *Public appearances/private realities: The psychology of self-monitoring*. New York: W. H. Freeman.

49. Jenkins, J. M. (1993). Self-monitoring and turnover: The impact of personality on intent to leave. *Journal of Organizational Behavior, 14*, 83–91.

50. Caldwell, D. F., & O'Reilly, C. A., III. (1982). Boundary spanning and individual performance: The impact of self-monitoring. *Journal of Applied Psychology, 67*, 124–127.

51. Larkin, J. E., (1987). Are good teachers perceived as high self-monitors? *Personality and Social Psychology Bulletin, 23*, 64–72.

52. Fandt, P. M., & Ferris, G. M. (1990). The management of information and impressions: When employees behave opportunistically. *Organizational Behavior and Human Decision Processes, 45*, 140–158.

53. Deutsch, M. (1990). Sixty years of conflict. *International Journal of Conflict Management, 1*, 237–263.

54. Friedman, H. S., & Miller-Herringer, T. (1991). Nonverbal display of emotion in public and private: Self monitoring, personality, and expressive cues. *Journal of Personality and Social Psychology, 61*, 766–775.

55. Christie, R., & Geis, F. L. (1970). *Studies in Machiavellianism*. New York: Academic Press.

56. Schultz, C. J., II. (1993). Situational and dispositional predictors of performance: A test of the hypothesized Machiavellianism x structure interaction among sales persons. *Journal of Applied Social Psychology, 23*, 478–498.

57. McClelland, D. C. (1985). *Human motivation*. Glenview, IL: Scott, Foresman.

58. See Note 43.

59. McClelland, D. C. (1977). Entrepreneurship and management in the years ahead. In C. A. Bramlette, Jr. (Ed.), *The individual and the future of organizations* (pp. 12–29). Atlanta, GA: Georgia State University.

60. Miller, D., & Droge, C. (1986). Psychological and traditional determinants of structure. *Administrative Science Quarterly, 31*, 539–560.

61. McClelland, D. C. (1961). *The achieving society*. Princeton, NJ: Van Nostrand.

62. McClelland, D. C. (1962). Business drive and national achievement. *Harvard Business Review, 40*, 99–102.

63. de Vos, G. (1968). Achievement and innovation in culture and personality. In E. Norbeck, D. Price-Williams, & W. McCord (Eds.), *The study of personality: An interdisciplinary appraisal* (pp. 348–370). New York: Holt, Rinehart and Winston. (quote, p. 359)

64. Imai, M. (1986). *Kaizen: The key to Japan's competitive success*. New York: McGraw-Hill.

65. Holpp, L. (1989, October). Achievement motivation and kaizen. *Training and Development Journal*, pp. 53–63.

66. McClelland, D. C., & Boyatzis, R. E. (1982). Leadership motive pattern and long-term success in management. *Journal of Applied Psychology, 67*, 737–743.

67. Robinson, J. P., Shaver, P. R., & Wrightsman, L. S. (1991). *Measures of personality and social psychological attitudes*. San Diego, CA: Academic Press.

68. McClelland, D. C. (1961). *The achieving society*, Princeton, NJ: Van Nostrand.

CASE IN POINT: RICHARD BRANSON—NOT YOUR AVERAGE MILLIONAIRE

1. Cohen, R. (1993, February 28). How did I get to be so rich? *New York Times*, p. F1.

2. PBS. "At the Helm: Styles of Leadership," *Taking the lead: The management revolution*. November, 1993.

3. Shifren, C.A. (1993, January 18). BA settles libel suit with Virgin Atlantic. *Aviation Week and Space Technology*, p. 33.

4. McKenna, J.T. (1993, March 15) Growing at Virgin. *Aviation Week and Space Technology*, p. 21.

5. See Note 2.

6. CNN. "Richard Branson," *Inside Business*, July 18, 1992.

7. See Note 2, p. 8.

8. See Note 1.

9. Richard Branson, over $1 billion. (1993, July 5) *Forbes*, p. 99.

10. See Note 1.

11. See Note 9.

12. See Note 1.

13. See Note 1.

14. See Note 2, p. 9.

CHAPTER 4

PREVIEW CASE SOURCES

Caldwell, M. (1994, April). Personal communication. United Electric Control. Hyatt, J. (1991, May). Ideas at work. *Inc.*, pp. 59–66.

TEXT

1. Kanfer, R. (1990). Motivational theory and industrial and organizational psychology. In M. D. Dunnette & L. M. Hough (Eds.), *Handbook of industrial and organizational psychology* (2nd ed., Vol. 1, pp. 75–170). Palo Alto, CA: Consulting Psychologists Press.

2. Katzell, R., & Thompson, D. (1990). Work motivation: Theory and practice. *American Psychologist, 45*, 144–153.

3. Blau, G. (1993). Operationalizing direction and level of effort and testing their relationships to individual job performance. *Organizational Behavior and Human Decision Processes, 55*, 152–170.

4. Furnham, A. (1989). *The Protestant work ethic: The psychology of work beliefs and behaviours*. London: Routledge.

5. Grant, M. (1960). *The world of Rome*. London: Weidenfeld and Nicolson. (quote, p. 112)

6. *Newsweek* (1971, October 18), p. 31.

7. Nord, W. R., Brief, A. P., Atieh, J. M., & Doherty, E. M. (1988). Work values and the conduct of organizational behavior. In B. M. Staw & L. L. Cummings (Eds.), *Research in organizational behavior* (Vol. 10, pp. 1–42). Greenwich, CT: JAI Press.

8. Work still a labor of love. (1981, April 20). *The Columbus Dispatch*, p. 1.

9. Elizur, D., Borg, I., Hunt, R., & Beck, I. M. (1991). The structure of work values: A cross cultural comparison. *Journal of Organizational Behaviour, 12*, 21–38.

10. Maslow, A. H. (1970). *Motivation and personality* (2nd ed.). New York: Harper & Row.

11. Mudrack, P. E. (1992). "Work" or "leisure"? The Protestant work ethic and participation in an employee fitness program. *Journal of Organizational Behaviour, 13*, 81–88.

12. Miller, A., & Springen, K. (1988, October 31). Forget cash, give me the TV. *Newsweek*, p. 58.

13. Porter, L. W. (1961). A study of perceived need satisfaction in bottom and middle management jobs. *Journal of Applied Psychology, 45*, 1–10.

14. Betz, E. L. (1982). Need fulfillment in the career development of women. *Journal of Vocational Behavior, 20*, 53–66,

15. Wahba, M. A., & Bridwell, L. G. (1976). Maslow reconsidered: A review of research on the need hierarchy theory. *Organizational Behavior and Human Performance, 15*, 212–240.

16. Alderfer, C. P. (1972). *Existence, relatedness, and growth*. New York: Free Press.

17. Salancik, G. R., & Pfeffer, J. (1977). An examination of need-satisfaction models of job satisfaction. *Administrative Science Quarterly, 22*, 427–456.

18. Miller, A., & Bradburn, E. (1991, July 1). Shape up—or else! *Newsweek*, pp. 42–43.

19. Cronin, M. P. (1993, September). Easing workers' savings woes. *Inc.*, p. 29.

20. Leana, C. R., & Feldman, D. C. (1992). *Coping with job loss*. New York: Lexington Books.

21. Schwartz, E. L. (1991, June 17). Hot dogs, roller coasters, and complaints. *Business Week*, p. 27.

22. Jaffe, C. A. (1990, January). Management by fun. *Nation's Business*, pp. 58–60.

23. Gunsch, D. (1991). Award programs at work. *Personnel Journal, 23* (4), 85–89.

24. Miller, A., & Springen, K. (1988, October 31). Forget cash, give me the TV. *Newsweek*, p. 58.

25. Wood, R. A., & Locke, E. A. (1990). Goal setting and strategy effects on complex tasks. In B. M. Staw & L. L. Cummings (Eds.), *Research in organizational behavior* (Vol. 12, pp. 73–110). Greenwich, CT: JAI Press.

26. Locke, E. A., & Latham, G. P. (1990). *A theory of goal setting and task performance*. Englewood Cliffs, NJ: Prentice Hall.

27. Mento, A. J., Locke, E. A., & Klein, H. J. (1992). Relationship of goal level to valence and instrumentality. *Journal of Applied Psychology, 77*, 395–405.

28. Klein, H. J. (1991). Further evidence on the relationship between goal setting and expectancy theories. *Organizational Behavior and Human Decision Processes, 49*, 230–257.

29. Gellatly, I. R., & Meyer, J. P. (1992). The effects of goal difficulty on physiological arousal, cognition, and task performance. *Journal of Applied Psychology, 77*, 694–704.

30. Wright, P. M. (1992). An examination of the relationships among monetary incentives, goal level, goal commitment, and performance. *Journal of Management, 18*, 677–693.

31. Earley, P. C., & Litucy, T. R. (1991). Delineating goal and efficacy effects: A test of three models. *Journal of Applied Psychology, 76*, 81–98.

32. Latham, G. P., & Lee, T. W. (1986). Goal setting. In E. A. Locke (Ed.), *Generalizing from laboratory to field settings* (pp.100–117). Lexington, MA: Lexington Books.

33. Latham, G., & Baldes, J. (1975). The practical significance of Locke's theory of goal setting. *Journal of Applied Psychology, 60*, 122–124.

34. Locke, E. A., & Latham, G. P. (1984). *Goal setting: A motivational technique that works!* Englewood Cliffs, NJ: Prentice Hall.

35. Locke, E. A., & Latham, G. P. (1984). *Goal setting for individuals, groups, and organizations*. Chicago: Science Research Associates.

36. Bernstein, A. (1991, April 29). How to motivate workers: Don't watch 'em. *Business Week*, p. 56.

37. Stedry, A. C., & Kay, E. (1964). *The effects of goal difficulty on task performance*. General Electric Company, Behavioral Research Service.

38. Latham, G. P., Erez, M., & Locke, E. A. (1988). Resolving scientific disputes by the joint design of crucial experiments by the antagonists: Application to the Erez–Latham dispute regarding participation in goal setting. *Journal of Applied Psychology, 73*, 753–772.

39. Pritchard, R. D., Jones, S. D., Roth, P. L., Stuebing, K. K., & Ekberg, S. E. (1988). Effects of group feedback, goal setting, and incentives on organizational productivity. *Journal of Applied Psychology, 73*, 337–358.

40. Kulik, C. T., & Ambrose, M. L. (1992). Personal and situational determinants of referent choice. *Academy of Management Review, 17*, 212–237.

41. Greenberg, J. (1987). A taxonomy of organizational justice theories. *Academy of Management Review, 12*, 9–22.

42. Adams, J. S. (1965). Inequity in social exchange. In L. Berkowitz (Ed.), *Advances in experimental social psychology* (Vol. 2, pp. 267–299). New York: Academic Press.

43. Greenberg, J. (1989). Cognitive re-evaluation of outcomes in response to underpayment inequity. *Academy of Management Journal, 32*, 174–184.

44. Greenberg, J. (1990). Organizational justice: Yesterday, today, and tomorrow. *Journal of Management, 16*, 399–432.

45. Pritchard, R. D., Dunnette, M. D., & Jorgenson, D. O. (1972). Effects of perceptions of equity and inequity on worker performance and satisfaction. *Journal of Applied Psychology 57*, 75–94.

46. Harder, J. W. (1992). Play for pay: Effects of inequity in a pay–for–performance context. *Administrative Science Quarterly, 37*, 321–335.

47. Bretz, R. D., Jr., & Thomas, S. L. (1993). Perceived equity, motivation, and final–offer arbitration in major league baseball. *Journal of Applied Psychology, 77*, 280–287.

48. Greenberg, J. (1993). Stealing in the name of justice: Informational and interpersonal moderators of theft reactions to underpayment inequity. *Organizational Behavior and Human Decision Processes, 54*, 81–103.

49. Martin, J. E., & Peterson, M. M. (1987). Two-tier wage structures: Implications for equity theory. *Academy of Management Journal. 30*, 297–315.

50. Ross, I. (1985, April 29). Employers win big on the move to two-tier contracts. *Fortune*, pp. 82–92.

51. See Note 50.

52. Lawler, E. E., III. (1967). Secrecy about management compensation: Are there hidden costs? *Organizational Behavior and Human Performance, 2*, 182–189.

53. Greenberg, J. (1990). Looking fair vs. being fair: Managing impressions of organizational justice. In B. M. Staw & L. L. Cummings (Eds.), *Research in organizational behavior* (Vol. 12, pp. 265–301). Greenwich, CT: JAI Press.

54. Greenberg, J. (1993). The social side of fairness: Interpersonal and informational classes of organizational justice. In R. Cropanzano (Ed.), *Justice in the workplace: Approaching fairness in human resource management* (pp. 79–103), Hillsdale, NJ: Lawrence Erlbaum Associates.

55. Greenberg, J. (1994). Using socially fair treatment to promote acceptance of a work site smoking ban. *Journal of Applied Psychology, 79*, 288–297.

56. Vroom, V. H. (1964). *Work and motivation*. New York: Wiley.

57. Porter, L. W., & Lawler, E. E., III. (1968). *Managerial attitudes and performance*. Homewood, IL: Irwin.

58. Mitchell, T. R. (1983). Expectancy-valence models in organizational psychology. In N. Feather (Ed.), *Expectancy, incentive, and action* (pp. 293–314). Hillsdale, NJ: Lawrence Erlbaum Associates.

59. Schuster, J. R., & Zingheim, P. K. (1992). *The new pay: Linking employee and organizational performance*. New York: Lexington Books.

60. Perry, N. J. (1992, May 4). Talk about pay for performance! *Fortune*, p. 77.

61. Stern, J. M., & Stewart, G. B., III. (1993, June). Pay for performance: Only the theory is easy. *HRMagazine*, pp. 48–49.

62. "Flexible-benefit plans grow." (1989, March 21). *USA Today*, p. C1.

63. Zippo, M. (1982). Flexible benefits: Just the beginning. *Personnel Journal*, 17(4), 56–58.

64. Ehrenfeld, T. (1993, July). Cashing in. *Inc.*, pp. 69–70.

65. Griffin, R. W., & McMahan, G. C. (1994). Motivation through job design. In J. Greenberg (Ed.),

Organizational behavior: The state of the science (pp. 23–44). Hillsdale, NJ: Lawrence Erlbaum Associates.

66. Rigdon, J. E. (1992, May 26). Using lateral moves to spur employees. *Wall Street Journal*, pp. B1, B9.

67. Campion, M. A., & McClelland, C. L. (1991). Interdisciplinary examination of the costs and benefits of enlarged jobs: A job design quasi-experiment. *Journal of Applied Psychology*, *76*, 186–198.

68. Campion, M. A., & McClelland, C. L. (1993). Follow-up and extension of the interdisciplinary costs and benefits of enlarged jobs. *Journal of Applied Psychology*, *78*, 339–351.

69. Gellenhammar, P. G. (1977). *People at work*. Reading, MA: Addison-Wesley.

70. Luthans, F., & Reif, W. E. (1974). Job enrichment: Long on theory, short on practice. *Organizational Dynamics*, 2(2), 30–43.

71. Steers, R. M., & Spencer, D. G. (1977). The role of achievement motivation in job design. *Journal of Applied Psychology*, *62*, 472–479.

72. Goldman, R. B. (1976). *A work experiment: Six Americans in a Swedish plant*. New York: Ford Foundation.

73. Winpisinger, W. (1973, February). Job satisfaction: A union response. *AFL–CIO American Federationist*, pp. 8–10.

74. Hackman, J. R., & Oldham, G. R. (1980). *Work redesign*. Reading, MA: Addison-Wesley.

75. Graen, G. B., Scandura, T. A., & Graen, M. R. (1986). A field experimental test of the moderating effects of growth need strength on productivity. *Journal of Applied Psychology*, *71*, 484–491.

76. Hackman, J. R., & Oldham, G. R. (1976). Motivation through the design of work: Test of a theory. *Organizational Behavior and Human Performance*, *16*, 250–279.

77. Johns, G., Xie, J. L., & Fang, Y. (1992). Mediating and moderating effects in job design. *Journal of Management*, *18*, 657–676.

78. Orpen, C. (1979). The effects of job enrichment on employee satisfaction, motivation, involvement, and performance: A field experiment. *Human Relations 32*, 189–217.

79. Ropp, K. (1987, October). Candid conversations. *Personnel Administrator*, p. 49.

80. Hackman, J. R. (1976). Work design In J. R. Hackman & J. L. Suttle (Eds.), *Improving life at work* (pp. 96–162). Santa Monica, CA: Goodyear.

81. Magnet, M. (1993, May 3). Good news for the service economy. *Fortune*, pp. 46–50, 52.

82. Callari, J. J. (1988, June). You can be a better motivator. *Traffic Management*, pp. 52–56.

83. Finegan, J. (1993, July). People power. *Inc.*, pp. 62–63.

84. See Note 83.

85. See Note 83.

86. See Note 83.

CASE IN POINT: HOG WILD WITH ENTHUSIASM AT HARLEY-DAVIDSON

1. Slutsker, G. (1993, May 24). Hog wild. *Forbes*, pp. 45–46.

2. Peak, M.H. (1993, June). Harley Davidson: Going whole hog to provide stakeholder satisfaction. *Management Review*, p. 53.

3. CNN. The empowered worker. *Work in Progress*.

4. See Note 3.

5. See Note 2.

6. See Note 2, p. 55.

7. See Note 1.

8. See Note 1.

9. Milbank, D. (1993, September 9). Telephone sales reps do unrewarding jobs that few can abide. *Wall Street Journal*, pp. 1, 10.

10. See Note 9, p. 10.

CHAPTER 5

PREVIEW CASE SOURCE

Rogers, B. (1993, March). Clarifying the choices. *HRMagzine*, pp. 40–43.

TEXT

1. Quarstein, V. A., McAfee, R. B., & Glassman, M. (1992). The situational occurrences theory of job satisfaction. *Human Relations*, *45*, 859–873.

2. Hulin, C. L. (1991). Adaptation, persistence, and commitment in organizations. In M. D. Dunnette & L. M. Hough (Eds.), *Handbook of industrial and organizational psychology (2nd ed.)* (Vol. 2, pp. 445–506). Palo Alto, CA: Consulting Psychologists Press.

3. Stone, E. F., Stone, D. L., & Dipboye, R. L. (1991). Stigmas in organizations: Race, handicaps, and physical unattractiveness. In K. Kelley (Ed.), *Issues, theory, and research in industrial/organizational psychology* (pp. 385–457). Amsterdam: Elsevier Science Publishers.

4. McGuire, W. J. (1985). Attitudes and attitude change. In G. Lindzey & E. Aronson (Eds.), *Handbook of social psychology (3rd ed.)* (Vol. 2, pp. 233–346). New York: Random House.

5. Festinger, L. (1957). *A theory of cognitive dissonance*. Evanston, IL: Row, Peterson.

6. Petty, R. E., & Cacioppo, J. T. (1984). *Attitudes and persuasion: Central and peripheral routes to persuasion*. New York: Springer-Verlag.

7. Miller, N., Maruyama, G., Beaber, R. J., & Valone, K. (1976). Speed of speech and persuasion. *Journal of Personality and Social Psychology*, *34*, 615–624.

8. Moscovici, S. (1985). Social influence and conformity. In G. Lindzey & E. Aronson (Eds.), *Handbook of social psychology (3rd ed.)* (Vol. 2, pp. 347–412). New York: Random House.

9. See Note 4.

10. Bateman, T. S., Sakano, T., & Fujita, M. (1992). Roger, me, and my attitude: Film propaganda and cynicism toward corporate leadership. *Journal of Applied Psychology*, *77*, 768–771.

11. Locke, E. A. (1976). The nature and causes of job satisfaction. In M. D. Dunnette (Ed.), *Handbook of industrial and organizational psychology* (pp. 1297–1350). Chicago: Rand McNally.

12. Thornburg, L. (1992, July). When violence hits business. *HRMagazine*, pp. 40–45.

13. Page, N. R., & Wiseman, R. L. (1993). Supervisory behavior and worker satisfaction in the United States, Mexico, and Spain. *Journal of Business Communication*, *30*, 161–180.

14. Quinn, R. P., & Staines, G. L. (1979). *The 1977 quality of employment survey*. Ann Arbor, MI: Institute for Social Research.

15. Weaver, C. N. (1980). Job satisfaction in the United States in the 1970s. *Journal of Applied Psychology*, *65*, 364–367.

16. Eichar, D. M., Brady, E. M., & Fortinsky, R. H. (1991). The job satisfaction of older workers. *Journal of Organizational Behaviour*, *12*, 609–620.

17. Bedian, A. G., Ferris, G. R., & Kacmar, K. M. (1992). Age, tenure, and job satisfaction: A tale of two perspectives. *Journal of Vocational Behavior*, *40*, 33–48.

18. Lambert, S. L. (1991). The combined effect of job and family characteristics on the job satisfaction, job involvement, and intrinsic motivation of men and women workers. *Journal of Organizational Behaviour*, *12*, 341–363.

19. Staw, B. M., & Ross, J. (1985). Stability in the midst of change: A dispositional approach to job attitudes. *Journal of Applied Psychology*, *70*, 56–77.

20. Gutek, B. A., & Winter, S. J. (1992). Consistency of job satisfaction across situations: Fact or framing artifact? *Journal of Vocational Behavior*, *41*, 61–78.

21. Agho, A. O., Price, J. L., & Mueller, C. W. (1992). Discriminant validity of measures of job satisfaction, positive affectivity and negative affectivity. *Journal of Occupational and Organizational Psychology*, *65*, 185–196.

22. Smith, P. C., Kendall, L. M., & Hulin, C. L. (1969). *The measurement of satisfaction in work and retirement*. Chicago: Rand McNally.

23. Weiss, D. J., Dawis, R. V., England, G. W., & Loftquist, L. H. (1967). *Manual for the Minnesota Satisfaction Questionnaire* (Minnesota Studies on Vocational Rehabilitation, Vol. 22). Minneapolis, MN: Industrial Relations Center, Work Adjustment Project, University of Minnesota.

24. Heneman, H. G., III, & Schwab, D. P. (1985). Pay satisfaction: Its multidimensional nature and measurement. *International Journal of Psychology*, *20*, 129–141.

25. Judge, T. A. (1993). Validity of the dimensions of the Pay Satisfaction Questionnaire: Evidence of differential prediction. *Personnel Psychology*, *46*, 331–355.

26. Smith, B. (1993, July). FedEx's key to success. *Management Review*, pp. 23–24.

27. Sutton, R. I., & Callahan, A. L. (1987). The stigma of bankruptcy: Spoiled organizational image and its management. *Academy of Management Journal*, *30*, 405–436.

28. Herzberg, F. (1966). *Work and the nature of man*. Cleveland: World.

29. Machungaws, P. D., & Schmitt, N. (1983). Work motivation in a developing country. *Journal of Applied Psychology*, *68*, 31–42.

30. Landy, F. J. (1985). *Psychology of work behavior (3rd ed.)*. Homewood, IL: Dorsey.

31. Locke, E. A. (1984). Job satis-

faction. In M. Gruenberg & T. Wall (Eds.), *Social psychology and organizational behavior* (pp. 93–117). London: Wiley.

32. McFarlin, D. B., & Rice, R. W. (1992). The role of facet importance as a moderator in job satisfaction processes. *Journal of Organizational Behaviour, 13*, 41–54.

33. Miceli, M. P., & Lane, M. C. (1991). Antecedents of pay satisfaction: A review and extension. In K. Rowland & G. R. Ferris (Eds.), *Research in personnel and human resources management* (Vol. 9, 235–309). Greenwich, CT: JAI Press.

34. Berkowitz, L., Fraser, C., Treasure, F. P., & Cochran, S. (1987). Pay equity, job gratifications, and comparisons in pay satisfaction. *Journal of Applied Psychology, 27*, 544–551.

35. Barber, A. E., Dunham, R. B., & Formisano, R. A. (1992). The impact of flexible benefits on employee satisfaction: A field study. *Personnel Psychology, 45*, 55–75.

36. Trempe, J., Rigny, A. J., & Haccoun, R. R. (1985). Subordinate satisfaction with male and female managers: Role of perceived supervisory influence. *Journal of Applied Psychology, 70*, 44–47.

37. Callan, V. J. (1993). Subordinate-manager communication in different sex dyads: Consequences for job satisfaction. *Journal of Occupational and Organizational Psychology, 66*, 13–27.

38. Locke, E. A., & Schweiger, D. M. (1979). Participation in decision-making: One more look. In B. M. Staw & L. L. Cummings (Eds.), *Research in organizational behavior* (Vol. 1, pp. 265–339). Greenwich, CT: JAI Press.

39. Curry, J. P., Wakefield, D. S., Price, J. L., & Mueller, C. W. (1986). On the causal ordering of job satisfaction and organizational commitment. *Academy of Management Journal, 29*, 847–858.

40. Wright, P. L. (1990). Teller job satisfaction and organization commitment as they relate to career orientations. *Human Relations, 43*, 369–381.

41. Hackman, J. R., & Oldham, G. R. (1976). Motivation through the design of work: Test of a theory. *Organizational Behavior and Human Performance, 16*, 250–279.

42. Sundstrom, E. (1986), *Workplaces*. New York: Cambridge University Press.

43. See Note 11.

44. Day, D. V., & Bedian, A. G. (1991). Work climate and Type A status as predictors of job satisfaction: A test of the interactional perspective. *Journal of Vocational Behavior, 38*, 39–52.

45. Scheier, M. F., Weintraub, J. K., & Carver, C. S. (1986). Coping with stress: Divergent strategies of optimists and pessimists. *Journal of Personality and Social Psychology, 51*, 1257–1264.

46. Near, J. P., Smith, C. A., Rice, R. W., & Hunt, R. G. (1984). A comparison of work and non-work predictors of life satisfaction. *Academy of Management Journal, 27*, 33–42.

47. Fricko, M. A. M., & Beehr, T. A. (1992). A longitudinal investigation of interest congruence and gender concentration as predictors of job satisfaction. *Personnel Psychology, 45*, 99–117.

48. Judge, T. A., & Watanabe, S. (1993). Another look at the job-life satisfaction relationship. *Journal of Applied Psychology, 78*, 939–948.

49. Rain, J. S., Lane, I. M., & Steiner, D. D. (1991). A current look at the job satisfaction/life satisfaction relationship: Review and future considerations. *Human Relations, 44*, 287–307.

50. Tait, M., Padgett, M., & Baldwin, T. T. (1989). Job and life satisfaction: A reevaluation of the strength of the relationship and gender effects as a function of the date of the study. *Journal of Applied Psychology, 74*, 502–507.

51. Dalton, D. R., & Todor, W. D. (1993). Turnover, transfer, absenteeism: An interdependent perspective. *Journal of Management, 19*, 193–219.

52. Porter, L. W., & Steers, R. M., (1973). Organizational work and personal factors in employee turnover and absenteeism. *Psychological Bulletin, 80*, 151–176.

53. "No–Shows: A Costly Trend," (1993, August). *Executive Management Forum*, p. 3.

54. Tett, R. P., & Meyer, J. P. (1993). Job satisfaction, organizational commitment, turnover intention, and turnover: Path analyses based on meta-analytic findings. *Personnel Psychology, 46*, 259–293.

55. Judge, T. A. (1993). Does affective disposition moderate the relationship between job satisfaction and voluntary turnover? *Journal of Applied Psychology, 78*, 395–401.

56. Mobley, W. H., Horner, S. O., & Holingsworth, A., T. (1978). An evaluation of precursors of hospital employee turnover. *Journal of Applied Psychology, 63*, 408–414.

57. Carsten, J. M., & Spector, P. E. (1987). Unemployment, job satisfaction, and employee turnover: A meta-analytic test of the Murchinsky model. *Journal of Applied Psychology, 72*, 374–381.

58. Ostroff, C. (1992). The relationship between satisfaction, attitudes and performance: An organizational level analysis. *Journal of Applied Psychology, 77*, 963–974.

59. Iaffaldano, M. T., & Murchinsky, P. M. (1985). Job satisfaction and job performance: A meta-analysis. *Psychological Bulletin, 97*, 251–273.

60. Porter, L. W., & Lawler, E. E., III. (1968), *Managerial attitudes and performance*. Homewood, IL: Dorsey Press.

61. Schnake, M. (1991). Organizational citizenship: A review, proposed model, and research agenda. *Human Relations, 44*, 735–759.

62. Moorman, R. H. (1993). The influence of cognitive and affective based job satisfaction measures on the relationship between satisfaction and organizational citizenship behavior. *Human Relations, 46*, 759–776.

63. Vandenberg, R. J., & Lance, C. E. (1992). Examining the causal order of job satisfaction and organizational commitment. *Journal of Management, 18*, 153–167.

64. Becker, T. E., & Billings, R. S. (1993). Profiles of commitment: An empirical test. *Journal of Organizational Behaviour, 14*, 177–190.

65. Reichers, A. E. (1985). A review and reconceptualization of organizational commitment. *Academy of Management Review, 10*, 465–476.

66. Becker, H. S. (1960). Notes on the concept of commitment. *American Journal of Sociology, 66*, 32–40.

67. Porter, L. W., Steers, R. M., Mowday, R. T., & Boulian, P. V. (1974). Organizational commitment, job satisfaction, and turnover among psychiatric technicians. *Journal of Applied Psychology, 59*, 603–609.

68. Mathieu, J. E., & Zajoc, D. M. (1990). A review and meta-analysis of the antecedents, correlates, and consequences of commitment. *Psychological Bulletin*, 108, 171–194.

69. Meyer, J. P., Allen, N. J., & Gellatly, I. R. (1990). Affective and continuance commitment to the organization: Evaluation of measures and analysis of concurrent and time-lagged relations. *Journal of Applied Psychology, 75*, 710–720.

70. Meyer, J. P., & Allen, N. J. (1991). A three-component conceptualization of organizational commitment. *Human Resource Management Review, 1*, 61–89.

71. Hackett, R. D., Boycio, P., & Hausdorf, P. A. (1994). Further assessments of Meyer and Allen's (1991) three-component model of organizational commitment. *Journal of Applied Psychology, 79*, 15–23.

72. McGee, G. W., & Ford, R. C. (1987). Two (or more?) dimensions of organizational commitment: Reexamination of the affective and continuance commitment scales. *Journal of Applied Psychology, 72*, 638–641.

73. Whitener, E. M., & Waltz, P. M. (1993). Exchange theory determinants of affective and continuance commitment and turnover. *Journal of Vocational Behavior, 42*, 265–281.

74. Allen, N. J., & Meyer, J. P. (1990). The measurement and antecedents of affective, continuance, and normative commitment to the organization. *Journal of Occupational Psychology, 63*, 1–18.

75. Curry, J. P., Wakefield, D. S., Price, J. L., & Mueller, C. W. (1986). On the causal ordering of job satisfaction and organizational commitment. *Academy of Management Journal, 29*, 847–858.

76. Mathiew, J. E., & Hamel, K. (1989). A causal model of the antecedents of organizational commitment among professionals and nonprofessionals. *Journal of Vocational Behavior, 34*, 299–317.

77. Thompson, C. A., Kopelman, R. E., & Schriesheim, C. A. (1992). Putting all one's eggs in the same basket: A comparison of commitment and satisfaction among self- and organizationally-employed men. *Journal of Applied Psychology, 77*, 738–743.

78. Florkowski, G. W., & Schuster, M. H. (1992). Support for profit sharing and organizational commitment: A path analysis. *Human Relations, 45*, 507–523.

79. Greenberg, J. (1990). Looking fair vs. being fair: Managing impressions of organizational justice. In B. M. Staw & L. L. Cummings (Eds.), *Research in organizational behavior* (Vol. 12, pp. 111–157). Greenwich, CT: JAI Press.

80. Caldwell, D. F., Chatman, J. A., & O'Reilly, C. A. (1990). Building organizational commitment: A multifirm study. *Journal of Occupational Psychology, 63,* 245–261.

81. See Note 65.

82. Gregersen, H. B. (1992). Commitments to a parent company and a local work unit during repatriation. *Personnel Psychology, 45,* 29–54.

83. Gregersen, H. B., & Black, J. S. (1992). Antecedents of commitment to a parent company and a foreign operation. *Academy of Management Journal, 35,* 65–90.

84. Bruning, N. A., & Snyder, R. A. (1983). Sex and position as predictors of organizational commitment. *Academy of Management Journal, 26,* 485–491.

85. Tsui, A. S., Egan, T. D., & O'Reilly, C. A., III. (1992). Being different: Relational demography and organizational attachment. *Administrative Science Quarterly, 37,* 549–579.

86. See Note 86. (quote, p. 575)

87. Randall, D. M. (1990). The consequences of organizational commitment: A methodological investigation. *Journal of Organizational Behavior, 11,* 361–378.

88. Shore, L. M., & Martin, H. J. (1989). Job satisfaction and organizational commitment in relation to work performance and turnover intentions. *Human Relations, 42,* 625–638.

89. Lee, T. W., Ashford, S. J., Walsh, J. P., & Mowday, R. T. (1992). Commitment propensity, organizational commitment, and voluntary turnover: A longitudinal study of organizational entry processes. *Journal of Management, 18,* 15–32.

90. Randall, D. M., Fedor, D. P., & Longenecker, C. O. (1990). The behavioral expression of organizational commitment. *Journal of Vocational Behavior, 36,* 210–224.

91. Romzek, B. S. (1989). Personal consequences of employee commitment. *Academy of Management Journal, 39,* 641–661.

92. Stephan, W. G. (1985). Intergroup relations. In G. Lindzey & E. Aronson (Eds.), *Handbook of social psychology (3rd ed.)* (Vol. 2, pp. 599–658). New York: Random House.

93. Fernandez, J. P., & Barr, M. (1993). *The diversity advantage.* New York: Lexington Books.

94. Malone, M. S. (1993, July 18). Translating diversity into high-tech gains. *New York Times,* p. B2.

95. Yang, C. (1993, June 21). In any language, it's unfair: More immigrants are bringing bias charges against employers. *Business Week,* pp. 110–112.

96. Hawkins, C. (1993, June 28). Denny's: The stain that isn't coming out: Can a pact with the NAACP help it overcome charges of bias? *Business Week,* pp. 98–99.

97. Mason, J. C. (1993, July). Knocking on the glass ceiling. *Management Review,* p. 5.

98. Solomon, C. M. (1992, July). Keeping hate out of the workplace. *Personnel Journal,* 30–36.

99. See Note 93.

100. Ornstein, S. L., & Sankowsky, D. (1994). Overcoming stereotyping and prejudice: A framework and suggestions for learning from groupist comments in the classroom. *Journal of Management Education, 18,* 80–90.

101. Boyett, J. H., & Conn, H. P. (1992). *Workplace 2000.* New York: Plume.

102. Overman, S. (1993, June). Myths hinder hiring of older workers. *HRMagazine,* pp. 51–52.

103. Lawrence, B. S. (1988). New wrinkles in the theory of age: Demography, norms, and performance ratings. *Academy of Management Journal, 31,* 309–337.

104. See Note 3.

105. Yang, C., & Forest, S. A. (1993, April 12). Business has to find a new meaning for "fairness": The Disabilities Act means some workers get special treatment. *Business Week,* p. 72.

106. See Note 105.

107. See Note 105.

108. Martinez, M. N. (1993, June). Recognizing sexual orientation is fair and not costly. *HRMagazine,* pp. 66–68, 70, 72.

109. Williamson, A. D. (1993, July–August). Is this the right time to come out? *Harvard Business Review,* pp. 18–20, 22, 24, 26, 28.

110. See Note 109.

111. See Note 108.

112. See Note 108.

113. See Note 108.

114. See Note 93.

115. See Note 95.

116. See Note 95. (quote, p. 111)

117. See Note 95.

118. Lander, M. (1992, June 8). Corporate women. *Business Week,* pp. 74, 76–78.

119. Steinberg, R., & Shapiro, S. (1982). Sex differences in personality traits of female and male master of business administration students. *Journal of Applied Psychology, 67,* 306–310.

120. Greenberg, J., & McCarty, C. (1990). Comparable worth: A matter of justice. In G. R. Ferris & K. M. Rowland (Eds.), *Research in personnel and human resources management* (Vol. 8, pp. 265–301). Greenwich, CT: JAI Press.

121. McCarty, P. A. (1986). Effects of feedback on the self–confidence of men and women. *Academy of Management Journal, 29,* 840–847.

122. Wilkerson, I. (1991, September 15). A remedy for old racism has a new kind of shackles. *New York Times,* p. A1.

123. Heilman, M. E., Block, C. J., & Lucas, J. A. (1992). Presumed incompetent? Stigmatization and affirmative action efforts. *Journal of Applied Psychology, 77,* 536–544.

124. Thomas, R. R., Jr. (1992). Managing diversity: A conceptual framework. In S. E. Jackson (Ed.), *Diversity in the workplace* (pp. 306–317). New York: Guilford Press.

125. Murray, K. (1993, August 1). The unfortunate side effects of "diversity training." *New York Times,* pp. E1, E3.

126. Gottfredson, L. S. (1992). Dilemmas in developing diversity programs. In S. E. Jackson (Ed.), *Diversity in the workplace* (pp. 279–305). New York: Guilford Press.

127. Sessa, V. I. (1992). Managing diversity at the Xerox Corporation: Balanced workforce goals and caucus groups. In S. E. Jackson (Ed.), *Diversity in the workplace* (pp. 37–64). New York: Guilford Press.

128. Roberson, L., & Gutierrez, N. C. (1992). Beyond good faith: Management diversity at Pacific Bell. In S. E. Jackson (Ed.), *Diversity in the workplace* (pp. 65–88). New York: Guilford Press.

129. Walker, B. A., & Hanson, W. C. (1992). Valuing differences at Digital Equipment Corporation. In S. E. Jackson (Ed.), *Diversity in the workplace* (pp. 119–137). New York: Guilford Press.

130. See Note 129. (quote, p. 120)

131. See Note 126.

132. See Note 125.

133. See Note 126.

134. S. E. Jackson (Ed.), *Diversity in the workplace.* New York: Guilford Press.

CASE IN POINT: "KILLER" ANTICS AT SOUTHWEST AIRLINES

1. (1988, June 6). Swim the friendly skies. *Time,* p. 59.

2. Woodbury, R. (1993, January 25). Prince of midair. *Time,* p. 55

3. Teitelbaum, R. S. (1993, October 30). Keeping promises. *Fortune,* pp. 32, 34.

4. Barrett, C. (1993, April) Pampering customers on a budget. *Working Woman,* pp. 19, 22.

5. Chakravarty, S. N. (1991, September 16). Hit 'em hardest with the mostest. *Forbes,* p. 48.

6. Southwest Air's gain noted. (1993, May 13) *New York Times,* p. D12.

7. See Note 3.

8. Teitelbaum, R. S. (1992, August 24). Where service flies right. *Fortune,* pp. 115–116.

9. See Note 7, p. 115.

10. See Note 4, p. 51

11. See Note 3.

CHAPTER 6

PREVIEW CASE SOURCE

Morgenson, G. (1993, March 15). "I didn't know I was oppressed." *Forbes,* pp. 140–141.

TEXT

1. Wanous, J. P. (1992). *Organizational entry: Recruitment, selection, orientation, and socialization.* Reading, MA: Addison-Wesley.

2. Ornstein, S., & Isabella, L. A. (1993). Making sense of careers: A review 1989–1992. *Journal of Management, 19,* 243–267.

3. Feldman, J. C. (1976). A contingency theory of socialization. *Administrative Science Quarterly, 21,* 433–452.

4. Feldman, J. C. (1980). A socialization process that helps new recruits succeed. *Personnel, 57,* 11–23.

5. Wanous, J. P., Poland, T. D., Premack, S. L., & Davis, K. S. (1992). The effects of met expectations on newcomer attitudes and behaviors: A review and meta-analysis. *Journal of Applied Psychology, 77,* 288–297.

6. Louis, M. R. (1980). Surprise and sense making: What newcomers experience in entering unfamiliar organizational settings. *Administrative Science Quarterly, 25,* 226–251.

7. See Note 1.

8. Wanous, J. P., & Coella, A.

(1989). Organizational entry research: Current status and future directions. In G. Ferris & K. Rowland (Eds.), *Research in personnel and human resources management* (Vol. 7, pp. 59–120). Greenwich, CT: JAI Press.

9. Meglino, B. M., DeNisi, A. S., Youngblood, S. A., & Williams, K. J. (1988). Effects of realistic job previews: A comparison using an enhancement and a reduction preview. *Journal of Applied Psychology, 73*, 259–266.

10. Morrison, R. F., & Brantner, T. M. (1992). What enhances or inhibits learning a new job? A basic career issue. *Journal of Applied Psychology, 77*, 926–940.

11. Harrison, J. R., & Carroll, G. R. (1991). Keeping the faith: A model of cultural transmission in formal organizations. *Administrative Science Quarterly, 36*, 552–582.

12. Morrison, E. W. (1993). Newcomer information seeking: Exploring types, modes, sources, and outcomes. *Academy of Management Journal, 36*, 557–589.

13. Morrison, E. W. (1993). Longitudinal study of the effects of information seeking on newcomer socialization. *Journal of Applied Psychology, 78*, 173–183.

14. Van Mannen, J., & Schein, E. H. (1991). Toward a theory of organizational socialization. In B. Staw (Ed.), *Research in organizational behavior* (Vol. 1, pp. 209–264). Greenwich, CT: JAI Press.

15. Nebeker, D. M. (1994). I/O and OB in the military services: Past, present, and future. In J. Greenberg (Ed.), *Organizational behavior: The state of the science* (pp. 245–274). Hillsdale, NJ: Lawrence Erlbaum Associates.

16. Jones, G. R. (1986). Socialization tactics, self-efficacy, and newcomers' adjustments to organizations. *Academy of Management Journal, 29*, 262–279.

17. Allen, N. J., & Meyer, J. P. (1990). Organizational socialization tactics, self-efficacy, and newcomers' adjustments to organizations. *Academy of Management Journal, 29*, 262–279.

18. Rothman, H. (1993, April). The boss as mentor. *Nation's Business*, pp. 66–67. (quote, p. 66)

19. Kram, K. E. (1985). *Mentoring at work: Developmental relationships in organizational life*. Glenview, IL: Scott, Foresman.

20. Whitely, W., Dougherty, T. W., & Dreher, G. F. (1991). Relationship of career mentoring and socioeconomic origin to managers' and professionals' early career progress. *Academy of Management Journal, 34*, 331–351.

21. Olian, J., Carroll, S., Giannantonio, & Feren, D. (1988). What do protégés look for in a mentor? Results of three experimental studies. *Journal of Vocational Behavior, 33*, 15–37.

22. Fagenson, E. A. (1992). Mentoring—who needs it? A comparison of protégés' and nonprotégés' need for power, achievement, affiliation, and autonomy. *Journal of Vocational Behavior, 41*, 48–60.

23. See Note 18. (quote, p. 66)

24. Burke, R. J. (1984). Mentors in organizations. *Group and Organization Studies, 9*, 353–372.

25. Hurley, D. (1988, May). The mentor mystique. *Psychology Today*, pp. 38–43.

26. Kram, K. (1988). Mentoring in the workplace. In D. T. Hall (Ed.), *Career development in organizations* (pp. 160–201). San Francisco: Jossey-Bass.

27. Granfield, M. (1992, November). '90s mentoring: Circles and quads. *Working Woman*, p. 15.

28. Kram, K. E. (1983). Phases of the mentor relationship. *Academy of Management Journal, 26*, 608–625.

29. Zey, M. (1984). *The mentor connection*. Homewood, IL: Dow Jones-Irwin.

30. See Note 20.

31. Noe, R. A. (1988). Women and mentoring: A review and research agenda. *Academy of Management Review, 13*, 65–78.

32. Ragins, B. R., & Cotton, J. L. (1991). Easier said than done: Gender differences in perceived barriers to gaining a mentor. *Academy of Management Journal, 34*, 939–951.

33. Ragins, B. R., & Cotton, J. L. (1993). Gender and willingness to mentor in organizations. *Journal of Management, 19*, 97–111.

34. See Note 32.

35. Thomas, D. A. (1993). Racial dynamics in cross–race developmental relationships. *Administrative Science Quarterly, 38*, 169–194.

36. Cox, T., & Nkomo, S. (1986). Differential performance appraisal criteria: A field study of black and white managers. *Group and Organization Studies, 11*, 101–119.

37. See Note 27.

38. Collins, G. (1993, July). Career survival, *Star Trek* style. *Working Woman*, p. 80.

39. Arthur, M. B., Hall, D. T., & Lawrence, B. S. (1989). Generating new directions in career theory: The case for a transdisciplinary approach. In M. B. Arthur, D. T. Hall, & B. S. Lawrence (Eds.), *Handbook of career theory* (pp. 7–25). New York: Cambridge University Press.

40. Holland, J. L. (1985). *Making vocational choices: A theory of vocational personalities and work environments*. Englewood Cliffs, NJ: Prentice Hall.

41. Meier, S. T. (1991). Vocational behavior, 1988–1990: Vocational choice, decision-making, career development interventions, and assessment. *Journal of Vocational Behavior, 39*, 131–181.

42. Chatman, J. A. (1991). Matching people and organizations: Selection and socialization in public accounting forms. *Administrative Science Quarterly, 36*, 459–484.

43. Judge, T. A., & Bretz, R. D., Jr. (1992). Effects of work values on job choice decisions. *Journal of Applied Psychology, 77*, 261–271.

44. Moss, M. K., & Frieze, I. H. (1993). Job preferences in the anticipatory socialization phase: A comparison of two matching models. *Journal of Vocational Behavior, 42*, 282–297.

45. Hines, A. (1993, April). Transferable skills land future jobs. *HRMagazine*, pp. 55–56.

46. "The 25 hottest careers." (1993, July). *Working Woman*, pp. 41–51.

47. Schein, E. H. (1971). The individual, the organization, and the career: A conceptual scheme. *Journal of Applied Behavioral Science, 7*, 401–426.

48. Overman, S. (1993, October). Retraining our workforce. *HRMagazine*, pp. 40–44.

49. Schein, E. H. (1978). *Career dynamics: Matching individual and organizational needs*. Reading, MA: Addison-Wesley.

50. See Note 49.

51. Powell, B., & Takayama, H. (1993, March 22). Who's better off? *Newsweek*, pp. 54–57, 59–60.

52. Overman, S. (1993, March). Weighing career anchors. *HRMagazine*, p. 56, 58.

53. See Note 52. (quote, p. 56)

54. Dalton, G. W., Thompson, P. H., & Price, R. (1977). Career stages: A model of professional careers in organizations. *Organizational Dynamics, 14*, 19–42.

55. Ference, T. P., Stoner, J. A. F., & Warren, E. K. (1977). Managing the career plateau. *Academy of Management Review*, 2, 602–612.

56. Fierman, J. (1993, September 6). Beating the midlife career crisis. *Fortune*, pp. 52–54, 58, 60, 62.

57. Russell, J. E. (1991). Career development interventions in organizations. *Journal of Vocational Behavior, 38*, 237–287.

58. See Note 56.

59. See Note 56. (quote, p. 60)

60. See Note 56.

61. Nussbaum, B., Cuneo, A., Carlson, B., & McWilliams, G. (1993, April 12). Corporate refugees. *Business Week*, pp. 58–62, 64–65.

62. See Note 61.

63. O'Neal, M. (1993). Just what is an entrepreneur? *Business Week/Enterprise*, pp. 104–105, 108, 112.

64. Waldman, D. A., & Avolio, B. J. (1986). A meta-analysis of age differences in job performance. *Journal of Applied Psychology, 71*, 33–38.

65. Borwick, C. (1993, May). Eight ways to assess succession plans. *HRMagazine*, pp. 109–110, 112, 114.

66. Waldman, D. A., & Avolio, B. J. (1993). Aging and work performance in perspective: Contextual and developmental considerations. In G. Ferris (Ed.), *Research in personnel and human resources management* (Vol. 11, pp. 133–162). Greenwich, CT: JAI Press.

67. London, M., & Greller, M. M. (1991). Demographic trends and vocational behavior: A twenty year retrospective and agenda for the 1990s. *Journal of Vocational Behavior, 38*, 125–164.

68. Boyett, J. H., & Vonn, H. P. (1992). *Workplace 2000*. New York: Plume.

69. Goff, S. J., Mount, M. K., & Jamison, R. L. (1990). Employer supported child care, work/family conflict, and absenteeism: A field study. *Personnel Psychology, 43*, 793–810.

70. Swanson, J. L. (1992). Vocational behavior, 1989–1991: Life-span career development and reciprocal interaction of work and nonwork. *Journal of Vocational Behavior, 41*, 101–161.

71. Higgins, C. A., Duxbury, L. E., & Irving, R. H. (1992). Work-family conflict in the dual-career family. *Organizational Behavior and Human Decision Processes*, *51*, 51–75.

72. Schneer, J. A., & Reitman, F. A. (1993). Effects of alternate family structures on managerial career paths. *Academy of Management Journal*, *36*, 830–843.

73. Collins, R., & Magid, R. Y. (1990). Work and family: How managers can make a difference. *Personnel*, *67*(7), 14–19.

74. Cohen, A. R., & Gadon, H. (1978). *Alternative work schedules*. Reading, MA: Addison-Wesley.

75. Galen, M., Palmer, A. T., Cuneo, A., & Maremont, M. (1993, June 28). Work & family. *Business Week*, pp. 80–84, 86, 88.

76. Herchenroether, S. (1992, January). Family leave, without labor pains. *Working Woman*, pp. 27–28.

77. Mason, J. C. (1993, July). Working in the family way. *HRMagazine*, pp. 25–28.

78. Martinez, M. N. (1993). Family support makes business sense. *HRMagazine*, pp. 38–43.

79. Fenn, D. (1993, July) Bottoms up. *Inc.*, pp. 57–60.

80. See Note 80.

81. Meier, L., & Meagher, L. (1993, September). Teaming up to manage. *Working Woman*, pp. 31–32, 108.

82. See Note 75.

83. See Note 75.

84. See Note 79.

85. Thornburg, L. (1993, June). Workplace couples face mixed reactions. *HRMagazine*, pp. 43–46.

86. See Note 85.

87. See Note 85. (quote, p. 46)

88. See Note 85. (quote, p. 46)

89. See Note 85. (quote, p. 46)

CASE IN POINT: SEX, SODA, AND TV: CAREER SUCCESS IN THE 1990S

1. *Who's Who in America* (1994).

2. CNN. House of Natori. *Pinnacle*. September 29, 1991.

3. See Note 1.

4. See Note 2.

5. Dobrzynski, D. H. (1993, April 5). The Metropolitan's Natorious display. *Business Week*, p. 64.

6. See Note 1.

7. CNN. J. Bruce Llewellyn, Chairman, Coca-Cola. *Pinnacle*, September 26, 1992.

8. (1989, June). J. Bruce Llewellyn: In search of a blockbuster deal. *Black Enterprise*, p. 304.

9. See Note 7.

CHAPTER 7

PREVIEW CASE SOURCE

Faludi, S. C. (1990, February 20). At Nordstrom Stores, service comes first—But at a big price. *Wall Street Journal*, pp. A1, A16.

TEXT

1. Northwestern National Life Insurance Company. (1991). *Employee burnout: America's newest epidemic*. Minneapolis, MN: Author.

2. Quick, J. C., Murphy, L. R., & Hurrell, J. J., Jr. (1992). *Stress and well-being at work*. Washington, DC: American Psychological Association.

3. Kahn, R. L., & Byosiere, P. (1992). Stress in organizations. In M. D. Dunnette & L. M. Hough (Eds.), *Handbook of industrial and organizational psychology (2nd ed.)* (Vol 3, pp. 571–650). Palo Alto, CA: Consulting Psychologists Press.

4. Quick, J. C., & Quick, J. D. (1984). *Organizational stress and preventive management*. New York: McGraw-Hill.

5. Selye, H. (1976). *Stress in health and disease*. Boston: Butterworths.

6. Lazarus, R. S., & Folkman, S. (1984). *Stress, appraisal, and coping*. New York: Springer-Verlag.

7. Evans, G. W., & Carrere, S. (1991). Traffic congestion, perceived control, and psychophysiological stress among urban bus drivers. *Journal of Applied Psychology*, *76*, 658–663.

8. See Note 4.

9. See Note 5 (quote, p. 20).

10. "Study Finds Most Stressful Jobs." (1993, April). *HRMagazine*, supplement p. 3.

11. Shaw, J. B., & Riskind, J. H. (1983). Predicting job stress using data from the Position Analysis Questionnaire. *Journal of Applied Psychology*, *68*, 253–261.

12. Fox, M. L., Dwyer, D. J., & Ganster, D. C. (1993). Effects of stressful job demands and control on physiological and attitudinal outcomes in a hospital setting. *Academy of Management Journal*, 36, 289–318.

13. Raggat, P. T. F. (1991). Work stress among long–distance coach drivers: A survey and correlational study. *Journal of Organizational Behaviour*, *12*, 565–579.

14. Schaubroeck, J., & Ganster, D. C. (1993). Chronic demands and responsivity to challenge. *Journal of Applied Psychology*, *78*, 73–85.

15. O'Driscoll, M. P., Ilgen, D. R., & Hildreth, K. (1992). Time devoted to job and off–job activities, interrole conflict, and affective experiences. *Journal of Applied Psychology*, *77*, 272–279.

16. Cooke, R., & Rousseau, D. (1984). Stress and strain from family roles and work-role expectations. *Journal of Applied Psychology*, *69*, 252–260.

17. Williams, K. J., Suls, J., Alliger, G. M., Learner, S. M., & Choie, K. W. (1991). Multiple role juggling and daily mood states in working mothers: An experience sampling study. *Journal of Applied Psychology*, *76*, 664–674.

18. Newton, T. J., & Keenan, A. (1987). Role stress reexamined: An investigation of role stress predictors. *Organizational Behavior and Human Decision Processes*, *40*, 346–368.

19. McGrath, J. E. (1976). Stress and behavior in organizations. In M. D. Dunnette (Ed.), *Handbook of industrial and organizational psychology* (pp. 1351–1398). Chicago: Rand McNally.

20. Schaubroeck, J., Ganster, D. C., Sime, W. E., & Ditman, D. (1993). A field experiment testing supervisory role clarification. *Personnel Psychology*, *46*, 1–25.

21. French, J. R. P., & Caplan, R. D. (1972). Organizational stress and individual strain. In A. J. Morrow (Ed.), *The failure of success* (pp. 68–84). New York: Amacom.

22. See Note 12.

23. McClean, A. A. (1980). *Work stress*. Reading, MA: Addison-Wesley.

24. Oullette-Kobasa, S. C., & Pucetti, M. C. (1983). Personality and social resources in stress resistance. *Journal of Personality and Social Psychology*, *45*, 839–850.

25. Storm, S. (1991, October 20). Harassment rules often not pushed. *New York Times*, pp. A1, A22.

26. Fisher, A. B. (1993, August 23). Sexual harassment: What to do. *Fortune*, pp. 84–86, 88.

27. Kolbert, E. (1991, October 10). Sexual harassment at work is pervasive. *New York Times*, pp. A1, A17.

28. Segal, T., Kelly, K., & Solomon, A. (1992, November 9). Getting serious about sexual harassment. *Business Week*, pp. 78, 82.

29. Gutek, B., Nakamura, C. Y., Ganart, M., Handschumacher, J. W., & Russell, D. (1980). Sexuality and the workplace. *Basic and Applied Social Psychology*, *1*, 255–265.

30. Terpstra, D. E., & Baker, D. S. (1992). Outcomes of federal court decisions on sexual harassment. *Academy of Management Journal*, *35*, 181–190.

31. Bohren, J. (1993). Six myths of sexual harassment. *Management Review*, pp. 61–63.

32. George, J. M. (1990). Personality, affect, and behavior in groups. *Journal of Applied Psychology*, *75*, 107–116.

33. Nelson, D. L., & Sutton, C. (1990). Chronic work stress and coping: A longitudinal study and suggested new directions. *Academy of Management Journal*, *33*, 859–869.

34. Holmes, T. H., & Rahe, R. H. (1967). Social readjustment rating scale. *Journal of Psychosomatic Research*, *11*, 213–218.

35. Lazarus, R. S., & Folkman, S. (1984). *Stress, appraisal, and coping*. New York: Springer-Verlag.

36. DeLongis, A., Coyne, J. C., Dakof, G., Folkman, S., & Lazarus, R. S. (1982). Relationships of daily hassles, uplifts and major life events to health status. *Health Psychology*, *1*, 119–136.

37. Bhagat, R. S., McQuaid, S. J., Lindholm, H., & Segovis, J. (1985). Total life stress: A multimethod validation of the construct and its effects on organizationally valued outcomes and withdrawal behaviors. *Journal of Applied Psychology*, *70*, 202–214.

38. Sullivan, S. E., & Bhagat, R. S. (1992). Organizational stress, job satisfaction, and job performance: Where do we go from here? *Journal of Management*, *18*, 353–374.

39. Motowidlo, S. J., Packard, J. S., & Manning, M. R. (1986). Occupational stress: Its causes and consequences for job performance. *Journal of Applied Psychology*, *71*, 618–629.

40. Keinan, G. (1987). Decision making under stress: Scanning of alternatives under controllable and uncontrollable threats. *Journal of Personality and Social Psychology*, 52, 638–644.

41. Staw, B. M., Sandelands, L. E., & Dutton, J. E. (1983). Threat-

rigidity effects in organizational behavior: A multi-level analysis. *Administrative Science Quarterly*, *26*, 501–524.

42. Driskell, J. E., & Salas, E. (1991). Group decision making under stress. *Journal of Applied Psychology*, *76*, 473–478.

43. Maslach, C. (1982). *Burnout: The cost of caring*. Englewood Cliffs, NJ: Prentice Hall.

44. Golombiewski, R. T., Ninzenrider, R. F., & Stevenson, J. G. (1986). *Stress in organizations: Toward a phase model of burnout*. New York: Praeger.

45. Pines, A. M., Aronson, E., & Kafru, D. (1981). *Burnout: From tedium to personal growth*. New York: W. H. Freeman.

46. Gaines, J., & Jermeier, J. M. (1983). Emotional exhaustion in high stress organizations. *Academy of Management Journal*, *31*, 567–586.

47. Stelzer, J., & Numerof, R. E. (1986). Supervisory leadership and subordinate burnout. *Academy of Management Journal*, *31*, 439–446

48. Latack, J. C. (1986). Coping with job stress: Measures and future directions for scale development. *Journal of Applied Psychology*, *71*, 377–385.

49. Leiter, M. P. (1991). Coping patterns as predictors of burnout: The function of control and escapist coping patterns. *Journal of Organizational Behaviour*, *12*, 123–144.

50. Moss, L. (1981). *Management stress*. Reading, MA: Addison-Wesley.

51. Jackson, S. E., Schwab, R. L., & Schuler, R. S. (1986). Toward an understanding of the burnout phenomenon. *Journal of Applied Psychology*, *71*, 630–640.

52. Frese, M. (1985). Stress at work and psychosomatic complaints: A causal interpretation. *Journal of Applied Psychology*, *70*, 314–328.

53. Cohen, S., & Williamson, G. M. (1991). Stress and infectious disease in humans. *Psychological Bulletin*, *109*, 5–24.

54. Totman, R., Kiff, J., Reed, S. E., & Craig, H. W. (1980). Predicting experimental colds in volunteers from different measures of recent live stress. *Journal of Psychosomatic Research*, *24*, 155–163.

55. No real sense of affluence. (1989, January 15). *Mainichi Daily News*, p. 23.

56. Tubbs, W. (1993). *Karoushi*: Stress-death and the meaning of work. *Journal of Business Ethics*, *12*, 869–877.

57. See Note 56.

58. Scheier, M. F., & Carver, C. S. (1985). Optimism, coping, and health: Assessment and implications of generalized outcome expectancies. *Health Psychology*, *4*, 219–247.

59. Scheier, M. F., & Weintraub, J. K., & Carver, C. S. (1986). Coping with stress: Divergent strategies of optimists and pessimists. *Journal of Personality and Social Psychology*, *51*, 1257–1264.

60. Kobasa, S. C. (1982). The hardy personality: Toward a social psychology of stress and health. In G. E. Sanders & J. Suls (Eds.), *Social psychology of health and illness* (pp. 215–255). Hillsdale, NJ: Lawrence Erlbaum Associates.

61. See Note 24.

62. Rich, V. L., & Rich, A. R. (1985, August). *Personality hardiness and burnout in female staff nurses*. Paper presented at the annual meeting of the American Psychological Association, Los Angeles.

63. Kirmeyer, S. L., & Biggers, K. (1988). Environmental demand and demand engendered behavior: An observational analysis of the Type A pattern. *Journal of Personality and Social Psychology*, *54*, 997–1005.

64. See Note 63. (quote, p. 1003)

65. Matteson, M. T., & Ivancevich, J. M. (1983). Note on tension discharge rate as an employee health status predictor. *Academy of Management Journal*, *26*, 540–545.

66. Latack, J. C., & Havlovic, S. J. (1992). Coping with job stress: A conceptual evaluation framework for coping measures. *Journal of Organizational Behavior*, *13*, 479–508.

67. Editors of Consumer Reports. (1993). *Mind/body medicine*. Fairfield, OH: Consumer Reports Books.

68. See Note 21.

69. Brown, J. D. (1991). Staying fit and staying well: Physical fitness as a moderator of life stress. *Journal of Personality and Social Psychology*, *60*, 555–561.

70. Falkenberg, L. E. (1987). Employee fitness programs: Their impact on the employee and the organization. *Academy of Management Review*, *12*, 511–522.

71. Dunkin, A. (1993, May 10). Meditation, the new balm for corporate stress. *Business Week*, pp. 86–87.

72. Shephard, R. J., Cox, M., & Corey, P. (1981). Fitness program: Its effects on workers' performance. *Journal of Occupational Medicine*, *23*, 359–363.

73. Kirkcalady, B. D., & Cooper, C. L. (1993). The relationship between work stress and leisure style: British and German managers. *Human Relations*, *46*, 669–680.

74. See Note 69.

75. Sobel, D. (1993, May). Outsmarting stress. *Working Woman*, pp. 83–84, 101.

76. Benson, H. (1975). *The relaxation response*. New York: William Morrow.

77. Reynolds, S., Taylor, E., & Shapiro, D. A. (1993). Session impact in stress management training. *Journal of Occupational and Organizational Psychology*, *66*, 99–113.

78. Roskies, E. (1987). *Stress management for the healthy Type A*. New York: Guilford.

79. Weisinger, H. (1985). *Anger workout book*. New York: Quill.

80. Kirkcalady, B. D., Furnham, A., & Lynn, R. (1992). Cultural differences in work attitudes: Germany and U.K. *European Work and Organizational Psychologist*, *2*, 81–102.

81. Greenberg, J. (1986). Determinants of perceived fairness of performance evaluations. *Journal of Applied Psychology*, *71*, 340–342.

82. Falsey, T. A. (1989). *Corporate philosophies and mission statements*. New York: Quorum Books.

83. Stewart, T. A. (1990, October 22). Do you push your people too hard? *Fortune*, pp. 121, 124, 128.

84. Reynolds, S., & Shapiro, D. A. (1991). Stress reduction in transition: Conceptual problems in the design, implementation, and evaluation of worksite stress management interventions. *Human Relations*, *44*, 717–733.

85. See Note 4.

86. See Note 4.

87. Martin, E. V. (1992). Designing stress training (pp. 207–224). In J. C. Quick, L. R. Murphy, & J. J. Hurrell, Jr. (1992). *Stress and well–being at work*. Washington, DC: American Psychological Association.

88. Philips, S. B., & Mushinski, M. H. (1992). Configuring an employee assistance program to fit the corporation's structure: One company's design (pp. 317–328). In J. C. Quick, L. R. Murphy, & J. J. Hurrell, Jr. (1992). *Stress and well–being at work*. Washington, DC: American Psychological Association.

89. Roman, P. M., & Blum, T. C. (1989). Alcohol problem intervention in the workplace: Data on present status and future implications. *Alcohol Health and Research World*, *13*, 375–380.

90. Kirschman, E. (1983). Wounded heroes: A case study and systems analysis of job related stress and emotional dysfunction in three police officers. *Dissertation Abstracts International*, *44*, 1279B (University Microfilms No. 83–19, 921).

91. Kirschman, E., Scrivner, E., Ellison, K., & Marcy, C. (1992). Work and well-being: Lessons from law enforcement (pp. 178–192). In J. C. Quick, L. R. Murphy, & J. J. Hurrell, Jr. (1992). *Stress and well-being at work*. Washington, DC: American Psychological Association.

CASE IN POINT: WORKPLACE VIOLENCE: THE NEW NATIONAL EPIDEMIC

1. Fields, G. (1993, December 17). In '92, 750 were slain on the job. *USA Today*, p. 3A.

2. WCVB. (1993, December 17). *News at 6* broadcast.

3. Kilborn, P. T. (1993, May 17). Inside post offices, the mail is only part of the pressure. *New York Times*, pp. 1, 15.

4. Solomon, J., & King, P. (1993, July 19). Waging war in the workplace. *Newsweek*, pp. 30–31, 34.

5. See Note 3.

6. See Note 3, p. 1.

7. See Note 3.

8. See Note 3.

9. See Note 3, p. 15.

10. See Note 3, p. 15.

11. Field, G. (1993, December 17). Lethal week at the workplace. *USA Today*, p. 3A.

12. See Note 4.

13. See Note 4.

14. See Note 4, p. 31.

15. See Note 4.

CHAPTER 8

PREVIEW CASE SOURCE

Case, J. (1993, September). What the experts forgot to mention. *Inc.*, pp. 66–68, 70, 72, 76, 78.

TEXT

1. Cartwright, D., & Zander, A. (1968). Origins of group dynamics. In D. Cartwright & A. Zander (Eds.), *Group dynamics: Research and theory* (pp. 3–21). New York: Harper & Row.

2. Bettenhausen, K. L. (1991). Five years of groups research: What we have learned and what needs to be addressed. *Journal of Management, 17*, 345–381.

3. Forsyth, D. L. (1983). *An introduction to group dynamics*. Monterey, CA: Brooks/Cole.

4. Long, S. (1984). Early integration in groups: "A group to join and a group to create." *Human Relations, 37*, 311–332.

5. Tuckman, B. W., & Jensen, M. A. (1977). Stages of small group development revisited. *Group and Organization Studies, 2*, 419–427.

6. Gersick, C. J. G. (1988). Time and transition in work teams: Toward a new model of group development. *Academy of Management Journal, 31*, 9–41.

7. Biddle, B. J. (1979). *Role theory: Expectations, identities, and behavior*. New York: Academic Press.

8. Jackson, S. E., & Schuler, R. S. (1985). A meta-analysis and conceptual critique of research on role ambiguity and role conflict in work settings. *Organizational Behavior and Human Decision Processes, 36*, 16–78.

9. Benne, K. D., & Sheats, P. (1948). Functional roles of group members. *Journal of Social Issues, 4*, 41–49.

10. Bales, R. F. (1980). *SYMLOG case study kit*. New York: Free Press.

11. Hackman, J. R. (1992). Group influences on individuals in organizations. In M. D. Dunnette & L. M. Hough (Eds.), *Handbook of industrial and organizational psychology (2nd ed.)* (Vol. 3, pp. 199–268). Palo Alto, CA: Consulting Psychologists Press.

12. Bettenhausen, K., & Murnighan, J. K. (1985). The emergence of norms in competitive decision-making groups. *Administrative Science Quarterly, 30*, 350–372.

13. Feldman, D. C. (1984). The development and enforcement of group norms. *Academy of Management Review, 9*, 47–53.

14. Wanous, J. P., Reichers, A. E., & Malik, S. D. (1984). Organizational socialization and group development: Toward an integrative perspective. *Academy of Management Review, 9*, 670–683.

15. Wilson, S. (1978). *Informal groups: An introduction*. Englewood Cliffs, NJ: Prentice Hall.

16. Greenberg, J. (1988). Equity and workplace status: A field experiment. *Journal of Applied Psychology, 73*, 606–613.

17. Stryker, S., & Macke, A. S. (1978). Status inconsistency and role conflict. In R. H. Turner, J. Coleman, & R. C. Fox (Eds.), *Annual review of sociology* (Vol. 4, pp. 57–90). Palo Alto, CA: Annual Reviews.

18. Jackson, L. A., & Grabski, S. V. (1988). Perceptions of fair pay and the gender wage gap. *Journal of Applied Social Psychology, 18*, 606–625.

19. Torrance, E. P. (1954). Some consequences of power differences on decision making in permanent and temporary three-man groups. *Research Studies: Washington State College, 22*, 130–140.

20. Greenberg, J. (1976). The role of seating position in group interaction: A review, with applications for group trainers. *Group and Organization Studies, 1*, 310–327.

21. Hare, A. P. (1976). *Handbook of small group research (2nd ed)*. New York: Free Press.

22. Aronson, E., & Mills, J. (1959). The effects of severity of initiation on liking for a group. *Journal of Abnormal and Social Psychology, 59*, 177–181.

23. See Note 3.

24. Cartwright, D. (1968). The nature of group cohesiveness. In D. Cartwright & A. Zander (Eds.), *Group dynamics: Research and theory (3rd ed.)* (pp. 91–109). New York: Harper & Row.

25. George, J. M., & Bettenhausen, K. (1990). Understanding prosocial behavior, sales performance, and turnover: A group-level analysis in a service context. *Journal of Applied Psychology 75*, 698–709.

26. Shaw, M. E. (1981). *Group dynamics: The dynamics of small group behavior (3rd ed.)*. New York: McGraw-Hill.

27. Janis, I. L. (1982). *Groupthink: Psychological studies of policy decisions and fiascoes (2nd ed.)*. Boston: Houghton Mifflin.

28. Douglas, T. (1983). *Groups: Understanding people gathered together*. New York: Tavistock.

29. Katzenbach, J. R., & Smith, D. K. (1993, March–April). The discipline of teams. *Harvard Business Review, 71*(2), 111–120.

30. Manz, C. C., & Sims, H. P., Jr. (1993). *Business without bosses*. New York: John Wiley & Sons.

31. Hoerr, J. (1989, July 10). The payoff from teamwork. *Business Week*, p. 58–62.

32. Mohrman, S. A. (1993). Integrating roles and structure in the lateral organization. In J. R. Galbraith & E. E. Lawler, III (Eds.), *Organizing for the future* (pp. 109–141). San Francisco: Jossey-Bass.

33. See Note 4.

34. Hackman, J. R. (1987). The design of work teams. In J. W. Lorsch (Ed.), *Handbook of organizational behavior* (pp. 315–342). Englewood Cliffs, NJ: Prentice Hall.

35. See Note 34. (quote, p. 338)

36. Geen, R. (1989). Alternative conceptualizations of social facilitation. In P. B. Paulus (Ed.), *Psychology of group influence (2nd ed.)* (pp. 15–51). Hillsdale, NJ: Lawrence Erlbaum Associates.

37. Zajonc, R. B. (1965). Social facilitation. *Science, 149*, 269–274.

38. Zajonc, R. B. (1980). Compresence. In P. B. Paulus (Ed.), *Psychology of group influence* (pp. 35–60). Hillsdale, NJ: Lawrence Erlbaum Associates.

39. Geen, R. B., Thomas, S. L., & Gammill, P. (1988). Effects of evaluation and coaction on state anxiety and anagram performance. *Personality and Individual Differences, 6*, 293–298.

40. Baron, R. S. (1986). Distraction/conflict theory: Progress and problems. In L. Berkowitz (Ed.), *Advances in experimental social psychology* (Vol. 19, pp. 1–40). New York: Academic Press.

41. Kulik, C. T., & Ambrose, M. L. (1993). Category-based and feature-based processes in performance appraisal: Integrating visual and computerized sources of performance data. *Journal of Applied Psychology, 78*, 821–830.

42. Aiello, J. R., & Svec, C. M. (1993). Computer monitoring of work performance: Extending the social facilitation framework to electronic presence. *Journal of Applied Social Psychology, 23*, 537–548.

43. Watson, W. E., Kumar, K., & Michaelsen, K. K. (1993). Cultural diversity's impact on interaction process and performance: Comparing homogeneous and diverse task groups. *Academy of Management Journal, 36*, 590–602.

44. Steiner, I. D. (1972). *Group processes and productivity*. New York: Academic Press.

45. Shepperd, J. A. (1993). Productivity loss in performance groups: A motivation analysis. *Psychological Bulletin, 113*, 67–81.

46. Latané, B., Williams, K., & Harkins, S. (1979). Many hands make light the work: The causes and consequences of social loafing. *Journal of Personality and Social Psychology, 37*, 822–832.

47. Kravitz, D. A., & Martin, B. (1986). Ringelmann rediscovered: The original article. *Journal of Personality and Social Psychology, 50*, 936–941.

48. Karau, S. J., & Williams, K. D. (1993). Social loafing: A meta-analytic review and theoretical integration. *Journal of Personality and Social Psychology, 65*, 681–706.

49. Latané, B., & Nida, S. (1980). Social impact theory and group influence: A social engineering perspective. In P. B. Paulus (Ed.), *Psychology of group influence* (pp. 3–34). Hillsdale, NJ: Lawrence Erlbaum Associates.

50. Weldon, E., & Mustari, E. L. (1988). Felt dispensability in groups of coactors: The effects of shared responsibility and explicit anonymity on cognitive effort. *Organizational Behavior and Human Decision Processes, 41*, 330–351.

51. Nordstrom, R., Lorenzi, P., & Hall, R. V. (1990). A review of public posting of performance feedback in work settings. *Journal of Organizational Behavior Management, 11*, 101–123.

52. Bricker, M. A., Harkins, S. G., & Ostrom, T. M. (1986). Effects of personal involvement: Thought-provoking implications for social loafing. *Journal of Personality and Social Psychology, 51*, 763–769.

53. George, J. M. (1992). Extrinsic and intrinsic origins of perceived social loafing in organizations. *Academy of Management Journal, 35*, 191–202.

54. Albanese, R., & Van Fleet, D. D. (1985). Rational behavior in groups: The free-riding tendency. *Academy of Management Review, 10*, 244–255.

55. Miles, J. A., & Greenberg, J. (1993). Using punishment threats to attenuate social loafing effects among swimmers. *Organizational Behavior and Human Decision Processes*, *56*, 246–265.

56. Earley, P. C. (1993). East meets West meets Mideast: Further explorations of collectivistic and individualistic work groups. *Academy of Management Journal*, *36*, 19–348.

57. Dumaine, B. (1990, May 7). Who needs a boss? *Fortune*, pp. 52–60.

58. See Note 31.

59. Ilgen, D. R., Major, D. A., Hollenbeck, & Sego, D. J. (1993). Team research in the 1990s. In M. M. Chemers & R. Ayman (Eds.), *Leadership theory and research* (pp. 245–270). San Diego: Academic Press.

60. Lawler, E. E., III, Mohrman, S. A., & Ledford, G. E., Jr. (1992). *Employee involvement and total quality management*. San Francisco: Jossey–Bass.

61. Hackman, J. R. (Ed.) (1990). *Groups that work (and those that don't)*. San Francisco: Jossey-Bass.

62. See Note 30.

63. See Note 30.

64. Katzenbach, J. R., & Smith, D. K. (1993). *The wisdom of teams*. Boston: Harvard Business School Press.

65. Wellins, R. S., Byham, W. C., & Wilson, J. M. (1991). *Empowered teams*. San Francisco: Jossey-Bass.

66. Osburn, J. D., Moran, L., Musselwhite, E., & Zenger, J. H. (1990). *Self-directed work teams*. Burr Ridge, IL: Irwin.

67. See Note 30.

68. Pearson, C. A. L. (1992). Autonomous workgroups: An evaluation at an industrial site. *Human Relations*, *45*, 905–936.

69. Wall, T. D., Kemp, N. J., Jackson, P. R., & Clegg, C. W. (1986). Outcomes of autonomous workgroups: A long-term field experiment. *Academy of Management Journal*, *29*, 280–304.

70. See Note 31.

71. See Note 30.

72. Stern, A. (1993, July 18). Managing by team is not always as easy as it looks. *New York Times*, p. B14.

73. See Note 72.

74. See Note 72.

75. See Note 72.

76. See Note 72.

77. See Note 72.

78. Maginn, M. D. (1994). *Effective teamwork*. Burr Ridge, IL: Business One Irwin.

79. Ancona, D. G., & Caldwell, D. G. (1992). Bridging the boundary: External activity and performance in organizational teams. *Administrative Science Quarterly*, *37*, 634–655.

CASE IN POINT: TEAM SATURN: THE OTHERWORDLY WAY TO MAKE CARS

1. Woodruff, D. (1992, August 17). Saturn. *Business Week*, pp. 86–91.

2. Woodruff, D. (1992, October 23). Where employees are management. *Business Week*, p. 66.

3. Solomon, C. M. (1991, June). Behind the wheel at Saturn. *Personnel Journal*, *70*, 72–75.

4. See Note 1, p. 89.

5. See Note 2.

6. See Note 1, p. 90.

7. See note 1, p. 88.

8. See Note 2, p. 66.

9. See Note 1.

10. Chappell, L. (1993, November 1). LeFauve won't rush plant's progress. *Automotive News*, p. 43.

11. See Note 1, p. 90.

CHAPTER 9

PREVIEW CASE SOURCE

McKeand, P. J. (1990, November). GM division builds a classic system to share internal information. *Public Relations Journal*, pp. 24–26, 41.

TEXT

1. Fulk, J. (1993). Social construction of communication technology. *Academy of Management Journal*, *36*, 921–950.

2. Scudder, J. N., & Guinan, P. J. (1989). Communication competencies as discriminators of superiors' ratings of employee performance. *Journal of Business Communication*, *26*, 217–229.

3. Roberts, K. H. (1984). *Communicating in organizations*. Chicago: Science Research Associates. (quote, p. 4)

4. Weick, K. E. (1987). Theorizing about organizational communication. In F. M. Jablin, L. L. Putnam, K. H. Roberts, & L. W. Porter (Eds.), *Handbook of organizational communication* (pp. 97–122). Newbury Park, CA: Sage.

5. Barnard, C. I. (1938). *The functions of the executive*. Cambridge, MA: Harvard University Press.

6. Mintzberg, H. (1973). *The nature of managerial work*. New York: Harper & Row.

7. Baskin, O. W., & Aronoff, C. E. (1980). *Interpersonal communication in organizations*. Santa Monica, CA: Goodyear.

8. Quinn, R. E., Hildebrandt, H. W., Rogers, P. S., & Thompson, M. P. (1991). A competing values framework for analyzing presentational communication in management contexts. *Journal of Business Communication*, *28*, 213–232.

9. Smith, L. (1993, August 9). What your boss knows about you. *Fortune*, pp. 88–93.

10. Rifkin, G. (1991, December 8). Do employees have a right to electronic privacy? *New York Times*, p. F8.

11. Anonymous. (1993, July). Who's reading your e-mail? *Information Management Forum*, pp. 1, 4.

12. Piller, C. (1993, July). Bosses with x-ray eyes. *Macworld*, pp. 118–123.

13. See Note 10.

14. See Note 10.

15. See Note 12.

16. See Note 10.

17. See Note 10.

18. Petit, J. D., Jr., Vaught, B., & Pulley, K. J. (1990). The role of communication in organizations: Ethical considerations. *Journal of Business Communications*, *27*, 233–249.

19. Kantrowitz, B., & McKay, B. (1993, December 20). Who holds the key to the e-mailbox? *Newsweek*, p. 108.

20. Lengel, R. H., & Daft, R. L. (1988). The selection of communication media as an executive skill. *Academy of Management Executive*, *2*, 225–232.

21. Yates, J., & Orlikowski, W. J. (1992). Genres of organizational communication: A structurational approach to studying communication and media. *Academy of Management Review*, *17*, 299–326.

22. Szwergold, J. (1993, June). Employee newsletters help fill an information gap. *Management Review*, p. 8.

23. Sibson and Company, Inc. (1989). *Compensation planning survey, 1989*. Princeton, NJ: Author.

24. Heneman, R. L. (1992). *Merit pay*. Reading, MA: Addison-Wesley.

25. Killian, C. M. (1993). *Using a corporate newsletter to communicate information about pay: A study of pay fairness*. Unpublished doctoral dissertation, The Ohio State University, Columbus.

26. Brady, T. (1993, June). Employee handbooks: Contracts or empty promises? *Management Review*, pp. 33–35.

27. Anonymous. (1993, November). The (handbook) handbook. *Inc.*, pp. 57–64.

28. See Note 27. (quote, p. 64)

29. Level, D. A. (1972). Communication effectiveness: Methods and situation. *Journal of Business Communication*, *28*, 19–25.

30. Klauss, R., & Bass, B. M. (1982). *International communication in organizations*. New York: Academic Press.

31. Daft, R. L., Lengel, R. H., & Trevino, L. K. (1987). Message equivocality, media selection, and manager performance: Implications for information systems. *MIS Quarterly*, *11*, 355–366.

32. Zuboff, S. (1988). *In the age of the smart machine*. New York: Basic Books.

33. Medina, D. (1991, June 24). Management's e-mail message. *Information Week*, p. 60.

34. Ritchie, L. D. (1991). Another turn of the information revolution. *Communication Research*, *18*, 412–427.

35. Schwartz, E. I. (1993, October 11). The Cleavers enter cyberspace. *Business Week*, p. 142.

36. Johnson, B. (1988, November–December). Streamlining corporate communications through voice imaging technology. *The Professional Communicator*, pp. 19–20.

37. See Note 36.

38. Reinsch, N. L., Jr., & Beswick, R. W. (1990). Voice mail versus conventional channels: A cost minimization analysis of individuals' preferences. *Academy of Management Journal*, *33*, 801–816.

39. Schwartz, E. (1993, June 28). This magazine could be on your PC screen. *Business Week*, p. 56.

40. Cox, M. (1993, June 1). Technology threatens to shatter the world of college textbooks. *Wall Street Journal*, pp. A1, A5.

41. Ziegler, B. (1993, December 6). Going on-line when you're off the beaten path. *Business Week*, p. 170.

42. Ziegler, B., Lewyen, M., Hof, R. D., & Therrien, L. (1993, April 5). Building a wireless future. *Business Week*, pp. 56–60.

43. Kupfer, A. (1993, December 13). Look, Ma! No wires! *Fortune*, pp. 147–148, 150, 152, 154.

44. Reynolds, L. (1993, July). Speeding toward the information superhighway. *Management Review*, pp. 61–63.

45. Coy, P. (1993, November 1). There'll be a heaven for couch potatoes, by and by. *Business Week*, p. 38.

46. Landler, M, Grover, R., Ziegler, B., & Hawkins, C. (1993, July 12). Media mania. *Business Week*, pp. 110–113, 116, 118–119.

47. Malloy, J. T. (1990). *Dress for success*. New York: Warner Books.

48. Solomon, M. R. (1986, April). Dress for effect. *Psychology Today*, pp. 20–28.

49. Saporito, B. (1993, September 20). Unsuit yourself: Management goes informal. *Fortune*, pp. 118–120. (quote, p. 118)

50. Schwartz, G. (1976). *Queuing and waiting*. Chicago: University of Chicago Press.

51. Greenberg, J. (1989). The organizational waiting game: Time as a status-asserting or status-neutralizing tactic. *Basic and Applied Social Psychology*, *10*, 13–26.

52. Greenberg, J. (1988). Equity and workplace status: A field experiment. *Journal of Applied Psychology*, *73*, 606–613.

53. Zweigenhaft, R. L. (1976). Personal space in the faculty office: Desk placement and student-faculty interaction. *Journal of Applied Psychology*, *61*, 629–532.

54. Greenberg, J. (1976). The role of seating position in group interaction: A review, with applications for group trainers. *Group and Organization Studies*, *1*, 310–327.

55. Capowski, G. S. (1993, June). Designing a corporate identity. *Management Review*, pp. 37–40.

56. Scully, J. (1987). *Odyssey: Pepsi to Apple . . . a journey of adventure, ideas, and the future*. New York: Harper & Row.

57. Carstairs, E. (1986, February). No ivory tower for Procter & Gamble. *Corporate Design and Reality*, pp. 24–30.

58. Argyris, C. (1974). *Behind the front page: Organizational self–renewal in a metropolitan newspaper*. San Francisco. Jossey-Bass.

59. Hogarty, D. B. (1993, June). Who goes where? A new look at office design. *Management Review*, p. 9.

60. Papa, M. J. (1990). Communication network patterns and employee performance with new technology. *Communication Research*, *17*, 344–368.

61. Miller, K. I., Ellis, B. H., Zook, E. G., & Lyles, J. S. (1990). An integrated model of communication, stress, and burnout in the workplace. *Communication Research*, 17, 300–326.

62. Ghoshal, S., & Bartlett, C. A. (1990). The multinational corporation as an interorganizational network. *Academy of Management Review*, *15*, 603–625.

63. Hawkins, B. L., & Preston, P. (1981). *Managerial communication*. Santa Monica, CA: Goodyear.

64. Schnake, M. R., Dumler, M. P., Cochran, D. S., & Barnett, T. R. (1990). Effects of differences in superior and subordinate perceptions on superiors' communication practices. *Journal of Business Communication*, *27*, 37–50.

65. Szilagyi, A. (1981). *Management and performance*. Glenview, IL: Scott, Foresman.

66. Kiechell, W., III. (1986, January 6). No word from on high. *Fortune*, pp. 19, 26.

67. Walker, C. R., & Guest, R. H. (1952). *The man on the assembly line*. Cambridge, MA: Harvard University Press.

68. Luthans, F., & Larsen, J. K. (1986). How managers really communicate. *Human Relations*, *39*, 161–178.

69. Kirmeyer, S. L., & Lin, T. (1987). Social support: Its relationship to observed communication with peers and superiors. *Academy of Management Journal*, *30*, 138–151.

70. Read, W. (1962). Upward communication in industrial hierarchies. *Human Relations*, *15*, 3–16.

71. Glauser, M. J. (1984). Upward information flow in organizations: Review and conceptual analysis. *Human Relations*, *37*, 613–643.

72. Lee, F. (1993). Being polite and keeping MUM: How bad news is communicated in organizational hierarchies. *Journal of Applied Social Psychology*, *23*, 1124–1149.

73. Tesser, A., & Rosen, S. (1975). The reluctance to transmit bad news. In L. Berkowitz (Ed.), *Advances in experimental social psychology* (Vol. 8, pp. 192–232). New York: Academic Press.

74. Kiechel, W., III. (1990, June 18). How to escape the echo chamber. *Fortune*, pp. 129–130. (quote, p. 130)

75. Rogers, E. M., & Rogers, A. (1976). *Communication in organizations*. New York: Free Press.

76. Shaw, M. E. (1978). Communication networks fourteen years later. In L. Berkowitz (Ed.), *Group processes* (pp. 351–361). New York: Academic Press.

77. Forsyth, D. R. (1983). *An introduction to group dynamics*. Monterey, CA: Brooks/Cole.

78. Burgess, R. L. (1968). Communication networks: An experimental reevaluation. *Journal of Experimental Social Psychology*, *4*, 324–327.

79. Harcourt, J., Richerson, V., & Waitterk, M. J. (1991). A national study of middle managers' assessment of organization communication quality. *Journal of Business Communication*, *28*, 348–365.

80. Krackhardt, D., & Hanson, J. R. (1993, July–August). Informal networks: The company behind the chart. *Harvard Business Review*, pp. 104–111.

81. Zenger, T. R., & Lawrence, B. S. (1989). Organizational demography: The differential effects of age and tenure distributions on technical communication. *Academy of Management Journal*, *32*, 353–376.

82. Ibarra, H. (1992). Homophily and differential returns: Sex differences in network structure and access in an advertising firm. *Administrative Science Quarterly*, *37*, 422–447.

83. Lesley, E., & Mallory, M. (1993, November 29). Inside the black business network. *Business Week*, pp. 70–72, 77, 80–81.

84. Brass, D. J. (1985). Men's and women's networks: A study of interaction patterns and influence in an organization. *Academy of Management Journal*, *28*, 327–343.

85. Krackhardt, D., & Porter, L. W. (1986). The snowball effect: Turnover embedded in communication networks. *Journal of Applied Psychology*, *71*, 50–55.

86. Duncan, J. W. (1984). Perceived humor and social network patterns in a sample of task-oriented groups: A reexamination of prior research. *Human Relations*, *37*, 895–907.

87. Baskin, O. W., & Aronoff, C. E. (1989). *Interpersonal communication in organizations*. Santa Monica: Goodyear.

88. Walton, E. (1961). How efficient is the grapevine? *Personnel*, *28*, 45–49.

89. Thibaut, A. M., Calder, B. J., & Sternthal, B. (1981). Using information processing theory to design marketing strategies. *Journal of Marketing Research*, *18*, 73–79.

90. Lesley, E., & Zinn, L. (1993, July 5). The right moves, baby. *Business Week*, pp. 30–31.

91. See Note 88.

92. Alessanddra, T., & Hunksaker, P. (1993). *Communicating at work*. New York: Fireside.

93. Kanter, R. M. (1977). *Men and women of the corporation*. New York: Basic Books.

94. Borman, E. (1982). *Interpersonal communication in the modern organization (2nd ed.)*. Englewood Cliffs, NJ: Prentice Hall.

95. Cantoni, C. J. (1993). *Corporate dandelions*. New York: AMACOM.

96. Rowe, M. P., & Baker, M. (1984, May–June). Are you hearing enough employee concerns? *Harvard Business Review*, pp. 127–135.

97. Burley-Allen, M. (1982). *Listening: The forgotten skill*. New York: John Wiley & Sons.

98. Brownell, J. (1985). A model for listening instructions: Management applications. *ABCA Bulletin*, *48*(3), 39–44.

99. Austin, N. K. (1991, March). Why listening's not as easy as it sounds. *Working Woman*, pp. 46–48.

100. See Note 99.

101. Seyper, B. D., Bostrom, R. N., & Seibert, J. H. (1989). Listening, communication abilities, and success at work. *Journal of Business Communication*, *26*, 293–303.

102. Penley, L. E., Alexander, E. R., Jernigan, I. E., & Henwood, C. I. (1991). Communication abilities of managers: The relationship to performance. *Journal of Management*, *17*, 57–76.

103. Brownell, J. (1990). Perceptions of effective listeners: A management study. *Journal of Business Communication*, *27*, 401–415.

104. Nichols, R. G. (1962, Winter). Listening is good business. *Management of Personnel Quarterly*, p. 4.

105. See Note 29.

106. McCathrin, Z. (1990, Spring). The key to employee communication: Small group

meetings. *The Professional Communicator*, pp. 6–7, 10.

107. Vernyi, B. (1987, April 26). Institute aims to boost quality of company suggestion boxes. *Toledo Blade*, p. B2.

108. Taft, W. F. (1985). Bulletin boards, exhibits, hotlines. In C. Reuss & D. Silvis (Eds.), *Inside organizational communication (2nd ed.)* (pp. 183–189). New York: Longman.

109. See Note 106.

110. Romano, C. (1993, December). Fear of feedback. *Management Review*, pp. 38–41.

111. Smith, B. (1993, July). FedEx's key to success. *Management Review*, pp. 23–24.

112. See Note 110.

113. See Note 110.

114. See Note 110. (quote, p. 41)

CASE IN POINT: THE HEART AND SOUL OF "THE BODY SHOP"

1. Conlin, J. (1994, February). Survival of the fittest. *Working Woman*, p. 29.

2. CNN (1991, October 27). Inside business: Environmentally friendly cosmetics.

3. Conlin, J. (1994, February) Survival of the fittest. *Working Woman*, pp. 29–31, 68–69, 72–73.

4. Chatzky, J. S. (1992, March 2). Changing the world. *Forbes*, pp. 83, 87.

5. See Note 2.

6. See Note 3.

7. See Note 3.

8. See Note 2.

9. See Note 3.

10. See Note 3.

11. See Note 3, p. 30.

12. See Note 3.

13. See Note 3, p. 73.

CHAPTER 10

PREVIEW CASE SOURCES

Anonymous. (1993, November 29). Automobile magazine names Chrysler's Neon Automobile of the Year. *PR Newswire*, Financial News Section. Cook, W. J. (1994, February 28). Chrysler's star keeps rising. *U.S. News & World Report*, pp. 51–56. McWhirter, W. (1993, December 13). Back on the fast track. *Time*, pp. 62–65. Woodruff, D., & Miller, K.L. (1993, May 3). Chrysler's Neon: Is this the small car Detroit couldn't build? *Business Week*, pp. 116–119, 122, 124, 126. Vettraino, J. P. (1993, September 27). Global positioning. *AutoWeek*, pp. 12–14.

TEXT

1. Mintzberg, H. J. (1988). *Mintzberg on management: Inside our strange world of organizations*. New York: Free Press.

2. Simon, H. (1977). *The new science of management decisions (2nd ed.)*. Englewood Cliffs, NJ: Prentice Hall.

3. Allison, S. T., Jordan, A. M. R., & Yeatts, C. E. (1992). A cluster-analytic approach toward identifying the structure and content of human decision making. *Human Relations*, *45*, 49–72.

4. Harrison, E. F. (1987). *The managerial decision-making process (3rd ed.)*. Boston: Houghton Mifflin.

5. Wedley, W. C., & Field, R. H. G. (1984). A predecision support system. *Academy of Management Review*, *9*, 696–703.

6. Nutt, P. C. (1993). The formulation process and tactics used in organizational decision making. *Organization Science*, *4*, 226–251.

7. Nutt, P. (1984). Types of organizational decision processes. *Administrative Science Quarterly*, *29*, 414–450.

8. Cowan, D. A. (1986). Developing a process model of problem recognition. *Academy of Management Review*, *11*, 763–776.

9. Dennis, T. L., & Dennis, L. B. (1988). *Microcomputer models for management decision making*. St. Paul, MN: West.

10. Fulk, J., & Boyd, B. (1991). Emerging theories of communication in organizations. *Journal of Management*, *17*, 407–446.

11. Sainfort, F. C., Gustafson, D. H., Bosworth, K., & Hawkins, R. P. (1990). Decision support systems effectiveness: Conceptual framework and empirical evaluation. *Organizational Behavior and Human Decision Processes*, *45*, 232–252.

12. Stevenson, M. K., Busemeyer, J. R., & Naylor, J. C. (1990). Judgment and decision-making theory. In M. D. Dunnette & L. M. Hough (Eds.), *Handbook of industrial and organizational psychology (2nd ed.)* (Vol. 1, pp. 283–374). Palo Alto, CA: Consulting Psychologists Press.

13. Adler, N. J. (1991). *International dimensions of organizational behavior*. Boston: PWS-Kent.

14. Roth, K. (1992). Implementing international strategy at the business unit level: The role of managerial decision-making characteristics. *Journal of Management*, *18*, 769–789.

15. Browning, E. B. (1850/1950). *Sonnets from the Portuguese*. New York: Ratchford and Fulton.

16. Mitchell, T. R., & Beach, L. R. (1990). ". . . Do I love thee? Let me count . . ." Toward an understanding of intuitive and automatic decision making. *Organizational Behavior and Human Decision Processes*, *47*, 1–20.

17. Beach, L. R., & Mitchell, T. R. (1990). Image theory: A behavioral theory of image making in organizations. In B. M. Staw and L. L. Cummings (Eds.), *Research in organizational behavior* (Vol. 12, pp. 1–41). Greenwich, CT: JAI Press.

18. Hollenbeck, J. R., Ilgen, D. R., Phillips, J. M., & Hedlund, J. M. (1994). Decision risk in dynamic two-stage contexts: Beyond the status quo. *Journal of Applied Psychology*.

19. Dunegan, K. J. (1993). Framing, cognitive modes, and image theory: Toward an understanding of a glass half full. *Journal of Applied Psychology*, *78*, 491–503.

20. Hill, C. W., & Jones, G. R. (1989). *Strategic management*. Boston: Houghton Mifflin.

21. See Note 4.

22. Amit, R., & Wernerfelt, B. (1990). Why do firms reduce business risk? *Academy of Management Journal*, *33*, 520–533.

23. Provan, K. G. (1982). Interorganizational linkages and influence over decision making. *Academy of Management Journal*, *25*, 443–451.

24. Galaskiewicz, J., & Wasserman, S. (1989). Mimetic processes within an interorganizational field: An empirical test. *Administrative Science Quarterly*, *34*, 454–479.

25. Parsons, C. K. (1988). Computer technology: Implications for human resources management. In G. R. Ferris & K. M. Rowland (Eds.), *Research in personnel and human resources management* (Vol. 6, pp. 1–36). Greenwich, CT: JAI Press.

26. Simon, H. A. (1987). Making management decisions: The role of intuition and emotion. *Academy of Management Executive*, *1*, 57 64.

27. Kirschenbaum, S. S. (1992). Influence of experience on information-gathering strategies. *Journal of Applied Psychology*, *77*, 343–352.

28. Linstone, H. A. (1984). *Multiple perspectives for c* New York: North-

29. Simon, H. A. (1 decision making in o *American Economic Rev* 493–513.

30. March, J. G., & Simon, H. A. (1958). *Organizations*. New York: John Wiley & Sons.

31. See Note 30.

32. Simon, H. A. (1957). *Models of man*. New York: John Wiley & Sons.

33. Gaeth, G. J., & Shanteau, J. (1984). Reducing the influence of irrelevant information on experienced decision makers. *Organizational Behavior and Human Performance*, *33*, 263–282.

34. Ginrich, G., & Soli, S. D. (1984). Subjective evaluation and allocation of resources in routine decision making. *Organizational Behavior and Human Performance*, *33*, 187–203.

35. Abelson, R. P., & Levi, A. (1985). Decision-making and decision theory. In G. Lindzey & E. Aronson (Eds.), *Handbook of social psychology (3rd ed.)* (Vol. 1, pp. 231–309). Reading, MA: Addison-Wesley.

36. Kahneman, D., & Tversky, A. (1984). Choices, values, and frames. *American Psychologist*, *39*, 341–350.

37. Frisch, D. (1993). Reasons for framing effects. *Organizational Behavior and Human Decision Processes*, *54*, 399–429.

38. Nisbett, R. E., & Ross, L. (1980). *Human inference: Strategies and shortcomings of social judgment*. Englewood Cliffs, NJ: Prentice Hall.

39. See note 35.

40. Kahneman, D., & Tversky, A. (1973). On the psychology of prediction. *Psychological Review*, *80*, 251–273.

41. See note 35.

42. Conlon, D. E., & Garland, H. (1993). The role of project completion information in resource allocation decisions. *Academy of Management Journal*, *36*, 402–413.

43. Ross, J., & Staw, B. M. (1986). Expo '86: An escalation prototype. *Administrative Science Quarterly*, *31*, 274–297.

44. Staw, B. M. (1981). The escalation of commitment to a course of action. *Academy of Management Review*, *6*, 577–587.

45. Brockner, J. (1992). The escalation of commitment to a failing course of action: Toward theoreti-

_al progress. *Academy of Management Review*, *17*, 39–61.

46. Whyte, G. (1993). Escalating commitment in individual and group decision making: A prospect theory approach. *Organizational Behavior and Human Decision Processes*, *54*, 430–455.

47. Simonson, I., & Staw, B. M. (1992). Deescalation strategies: A comparison of techniques for reducing commitment to losing courses of action. *Journal of Applied Psychology*, *77*, 419–426.

48. Garland, H., & Newport, S. (1991). Effects of absolute and relative sunk costs on the decision to persist with a course of action. *Organizational Behavior and Human Decision Processes*, *48*, 55–69.

49. Ross, J., & Staw, B. M. (1993). Organizational escalation and exit: Lessons from the Shoreham nuclear power plant. *Academy of Management Journal*, *36*, 701–732.

50. Whyte, G. (1991). Diffusion of responsibility: Effects on the escalation tendency. *Journal of Applied Psychology*, *76*, 408–415.

51. Tjosvold, D. (1984). Effects of crisis orientation on managers' approach to controversy in decision making. *Academy of Management Journal*, *27*, 130–138.

52. Johnson, R. J. (1984). Conflict avoidance through acceptable decisions. *Human Relations*, *27*, 71–82.

53. Neustadt, R. E., & Fineberg, H. (1978). *The swine flu affair: Decision making on a slippery disease*. Washington, DC: U.S. Department of Health, Education and Welfare.

54. Shull, F. A., Delbecq, A. L., & Cummings, L. L. (1970). *Organizational decision making*. New York: McGraw-Hill.

55. Sonnenberg, F. K. (1994). *Managing with a conscience*. New York: McGraw-Hill.

56. Patterson, J., & Kim, P. (1991). *The day America told the truth*. New York: Plume.

57. Dubrin, A. J. (1994). *Contemporary applied management (4th ed.)*. Burr Ridge, IL: Irwin.

58. Davis, J. H. (1992). Introduction to the special issue on group decision making. *Organizational Behavior and Human Decision Processes*, *52*, 1–2.

59. Delbecq, A. L., Van de Ven, A. H., & Gustafson, D. H. (1975). *Group techniques for program planning*. Glenview, IL: Scott, Foresman.

60. Murninghan, J. K. (1981). Group decision making: What strategies should you use? *Management Review*, *25*, 56–62.

61. Hill, G. W. (1982). Group versus individual performance: Are N + 1 heads better than one? *Psychological Bulletin*, *91*, 517–539.

62. Wanous, J. P., & Youtz, M. A. (1986). Solution diversity and the quality of group decisions. *Academy of Management Journal*, *29*, 149–159.

63. Yetton, P., & Bottger, P. (1983). The relationships among group size, member ability, social decision schemes, and performance. *Organizational Behavior and Human Performance*, *32*, 145–149.

64. Michaelsen, L. K., Watson, W. E., & Black, R. H. (1989). A realistic test of individual versus group consensus decision making. *Journal of Applied Psychology*, *74*, 834–839.

65. See Note 61.

66. See Note 61.

67. Osborn, A. F. (1957). *Applied imagination*. New York: Scribner's.

68. Bouchard, T. J., Jr., Barsaloux, J., & Drauden, G. (1974). Brainstorming procedure, group size, and sex as determinants of the problem-solving effectiveness of groups and individuals. *Journal of Applied Psychology*, *59*, 135–138.

69. Gallupe, R. B., Bastianutti, L. M., & Cooper, W. H. (1991). Unblocking brainstorms. *Journal of Applied Psychology*, *76*, 137–142.

70. Gallupe, R. B., Dennis, A. R., Cooper, W. H., Valacich, J. S., Bastianutti, L. M., & Nunamaker, J. F. (1992). Electronic brainstorming and group size. *Academy of Management Journal*, *35*, 350–369.

71. Janis, I. L. (1982). *Groupthink: Psychological studies of policy decisions and fiascoes (2nd ed.)*. Boston: Houghton Mifflin.

72. Aldag, R. J., & Fuller, S. R. (1993). Beyond fiasco: A reappraisal of the groupthink phenomenon and a new model of group decision processes. *Psychological Bulletin*, *113*, 533–552.

73. Morehead, G., Ference, R., & Neck, C. P. (1991). Group decision fiascoes continue: Space shuttle *Challenger* and a revised groupthink framework. *Human Relations*, *44*, 539–550.

74. Janis, I. L. (1988). *Crucial decisions: Leadership in policy making and crisis management*. New York: Free Press.

75. Morehead, G., & Montanari, J. R. (1986). An empirical investigation of the groupthink phenomenon. *Human Relations*, *39*, 399–410.

76. Schweiger, D. M., Sandberg, W. R., & Ragan, J. W. (1986). Group approaches for improving strategic decision making: A comparative analysis of dialectical inquiry, devil's advocacy, and consensus. *Academy of Management Journal*, *29*, 51–71.

77. Schweiger, D. M., Sandberg, W. R., & Rechner, P. L. (1989). Experiential effects of dialectical inquiry, devil's advocacy, and consensus approaches to strategic decision making. *Academy of Management Journal*, *32*, 745–772.

78. Cosier, R. A., & Schwenk, C. R. (1990). Agreement and thinking alike: Ingredients for poor decisions. *Academy of Management Executive*, *4*, 69–74.

79. Sloan, A. P., Jr. (1964). *My years with General Motors*. New York: Doubleday.

80. Dalkey, N. (1969). *The Delphi method: An experimental study of group decisions*. Santa Monica, CA: Rand Corporation.

81. Van de Ven, A. H., & Delbecq, A. L. (1971). Nominal versus interacting group processes for committee decision making effectiveness. *Academy of Management Journal*, *14*, 203–212.

82. See Note 81.

83. Gustafson, D. H., Shulka, R. K., Delbecq, A., & Walster, W. G. (1973). A comparative study of differences in subjective likelihood estimates made by individuals, interacting groups, Delphi groups, and nominal groups. *Organizational Behavior and Human Performance*, *9*, 280–291.

84. Taylor, R. N. (1984). *Behavioral decision making*. Glenview, IL: Scott, Foresman.

85. Ulshak, F. L., Nathanson, L., & Gillan, P. B. (1981). *Small group problem solving: An aid to organizational effectiveness*. Reading, MA: Addison-Wesley.

86. Willis, R. E. (1979). A simulation of multiple selection using nominal group procedures. *Management Science*, *25*, 171–181.

87. Van de Ven, A. H., & Delbecq, A. L. (1974). The effectiveness of nominal, Delphi, and interacting group decision making processes. *Academy of Management Journal*, *17*, 605–621.

88. Stumpf, S. A., Zand, D. E., & Freedman, R. D. (1979). Designing groups for judgmental decisions. *Academy of Management Review*, *4*, 589–600.

89. Rogelberg, S. G., Barnes-Farrell, J. L., & Lowe, C. A. (1992). The stepladder technique: An alternative group structure facilitating effective group decision making. *Journal of Applied Psychology*, *77*, 730–737.

90. Bottger, P. C., & Yetton, P. W. (1987). Improving group performance by training in individual problem solving. *Journal of Applied Psychology*, *72*, 651–657.

CASE IN POINT: TOMMY HILFIGER: A DESIGNER OF DECISIONS AND FASHION

1. CNN. (1993, September 19). Pinnacle: Tommy Hilfiger.

2. See Note 1.

3. See Note 1.

4. See Note 1.

5. See Note 1.

6. See Note 1.

CHAPTER 11

PREVIEW CASE SOURCES

Pantages, A. (1990, March 15). The new order at Johnson Wax. *Datamation*, pp. 103–106. Personal interview with C. Mason, March 1994.

TEXT

1. Deutsch, M. (1990). Sixty years of conflict. *International Journal of Conflict Management*, *1*, 237–263.

2. Thomas, K. W. (1992). Conflict and negotiation processes in organizations. In M. D. Dunnette & L. M. Hough (Eds.), *Handbook of industrial and organizational psychology (2nd ed.)* (Vol. 3, pp. 651–718). Palo Alto, CA: Consulting Psychologists Press.

3. Eisenberg, N. (1985). *Altruistic emotion, cognition, and behavior*. Hillsdale, NJ: Lawrence Erlbaum Associates.

4. Dovidio, J. F., Allen, J. L., & Schroeder, D. A. (1990). Specificity of empathy-induced helping: Evidence for altruistic motivation. *Journal of Personality and Social Psychology*, *59*, 249–26.

5. Kanunga, R. N., & Conger, J. A. (1993). Promoting altruism as a corporate goal. *Academy of Management Executive*, *7*, 34–48.

6. Brief, A. P., & Motowidlo, S. J. (1986). Prosocial organizational behaviors. *Academy of Management Review*, *11*, 710–725.

7. Katz, D. (1964). The motivational basis of organizational behavior. *Behavioral Science, 9*, 131–146.

8. Wright, P. M., George, J. M., Farnsworth, S. R., & McMahan, G. C. (1993). Productivity and extra-role behavior: The effects of goals and incentives on spontaneous helping. *Journal of Applied Psychology, 78*, 374–381.

9. Latané, B., & Darley, J. M. (1970). *The unresponsive bystander: Why doesn't he help?* New York: Appleton-Century-Crofts.

10. Organ, D. W. (1988). *Organizational citizenship behavior: The good soldier syndrome*. Lexington, MA: Lexington Books.

11. Organ, D. W. (1990). The motivational basis of organizational citizenship behavior. In B. M. Staw & L. L. Cummings (Eds.), *Research in organizational behavior* (Vol. 12, pp. 43–72). Greenwich, CT: JAI Press.

12. Greenberg, J. (1993). Justice and organizational citizenship: A commentary on the state of the science. *Employee Responsibilities and Rights Journal, 6*, 245–260.

13. Moorman, R. H. (1991). Relationship between organizational justice and organizational citizenship behaviors: Do fairness perceptions influence employee citizenship? *Journal of Applied Psychology, 76*, 845–855.

14. Greenberg, J. (1993). The social side of fairness: Interpersonal and informational classes of organizational justice. In R. Cropanzano (Ed.), *Justice in the workplace: Approaching fairness in human resource management* (pp. 79–103). Hillsdale, NJ: Lawrence Erlbaum Associates.

15. Miceli, M. P., & Near, J. P. (1992). *Blowing the whistle*. New York: Lexington Books.

16. Near, J. P., & Miceli, M. P. (1985). Organizational dissidence: The case of whistle–blowing. *Journal of Business Ethics, 4*, 1–16.

17. Glazer, M. P., & Glazer, P. M. (1989). *The whistle blowers: Exposing corruption in government and industry*. New York: Basic Books.

18. See Note 15.

19. DeGeorge, R. T. (1994). *Business ethics*. New York: Macmillan.

20. Westin, A. F. (1992). What can and should be done to protect whistle blowers in industry? In L. H. Newton & M. M. Ford (Eds.) *Taking sides: Clashing views on controversial issues in business ethics and society (2nd ed.)* (pp. 105–107). Guilford, CT: Dushkin Publishing Group.

21. See Note 20, p. 105.

22. Newton, L. H., & Ford, M. M. (1993). *Taking sides: Clashing views on controversial issues in business ethics and society (2nd ed.)*. Guilford, CT: Dushkin Publishing Group.

23. See Note 19, p. 109.

24. Forsyth, D. R. (1983). *An introduction to group dynamics*. Monterey, CA: Brooks/Cole.

25. Tjosvold, D. (1986). *Working together to get things done*. Lexington, MA: Lexington Books.

26. Gouldner, A. W. (1960). The norm of reciprocity: A preliminary statement. *American Sociological Review, 25*, 161–178.

27. Youngs, G. A., Jr. (1986). Patterns of threat and punishment reciprocity in a conflict setting. *Journal of Personality and Social Psychology, 51*, 541–546.

28. Knight, G. P., & Dubro, A. F. (1984). Cooperative, competitive, and individualistic social values: An individualized regression and clustering approach. *Journal of Personality and Social Psychology, 46*, 98–105.

29. See Note 28.

30. Weingart, L. R., Bennett, R. J., & Brett, J. M. (1993). The impact of consideration of issues and motivational orientation on group negotiation processes and outcome. *Journal of Applied Psychology, 78*, 504–517.

31. Peters, T. J., & Waterman, R. H., Jr. (1982). *In search of excellence: Lessons from America's best-run companies*. New York: Warner Books.

32. Cheng, J. L. (1983). Interdependence and coordination in organizations: A role-system analysis. *Academy of Management Journal, 26*, 156–162.

33. See Note 2.

34. Thomas, K. W., & Schmidt, W. H. (1976). A survey of managerial interests with respect to conflict. *Academy of Management Journal, 10*, 315–318.

35. Walton, R. E., & McKersie, R. B. (1965). *A behavioral theory of labor negotiations: An analysis of a social interaction system*. New York: McGraw-Hill.

36. Thomas, K. W. (1976). Conflict and conflict management. In M. D. Dunnette (Ed.), *Handbook of industrial and organizational psychology* (pp. 889–935). Chicago: Rand McNally.

37. Ting-Toomey, S., Gao, G., Trubisky, P., Yang, Z., Kim, H. S., Lin, S. L., & Nishids, T. (1991). Culture, face maintenance, and styles of handling interpersonal conflict: A study in five cultures. *International Journal of Conflict Management, 2*, 275–296.

38. Hofstede, G. (1980). *Culture's consequences: International differences in work-related values*. Beverly Hills, CA: Sage.

39. Ting-Toomey, S. (1988). Intercultural conflict styles: A face-negotiation theory. In Y. Kim & W. Gudykunst (Eds.), *Theories in intercultural communication* (pp. 213–235). Newbury Park, CA: Sage.

40. See Note 2.

41. Schuster, J. R., & Zingheim, P, K. (1992). *The new pay*. New York: Lexington.

42. Sitkin, S. B., & Bies, R. J. (1993). Social accounts in conflict situations: Using explanations to manage conflict. *Human Relations, 46*, 349–370.

43. Kabanoff, B. (1991). Equity, equality, power, and conflict. *Academy of Management Review, 16*, 416–441.

44. Greenberg, J. (1982). Approaching equity and avoiding inequity in groups and organizations. In J. Greenberg & R. L. Cohen (Eds.), *Equity and justice in social behavior* (pp. 389–435). New York: Academic Press.

45. Cohen, R. L. (1986). Power and justice in intergroup relations. In H. W. Bierhoff, R. L. Cohen, & J. Greenberg (Eds.) *Justice in interpersonal relations* (pp. 65–860). New York: Plenum.

46. Sprouse, M. (1992). *Sabotage in the American workplace*. San Francisco: Pressure Drop Press.

47. Johnson, T. E., & Rule, B. G. (1986). Mitigating circumstance information, censure, and aggression. *Journal of Personality and Social Psychology, 50*, 537–542.

48. Baron, R. A. (1988). Attributions and organizational conflict: The mediating role of apparent sincerity. *Organizational Behavior and Human Decision Processes, 41*, 111–127.

49. Weisinger, H. (1989). *The critical edge*. Boston: Little, Brown.

50. Baron, R. A. (1990). Countering the effects of destructive criticism: The relative efficacy of four potential interventions. *Journal of Applied Psychology, 75*, 235–245.

51. Shapiro, D. L., Buttner, E. H., & Barry, B. (1994). Explanations: What factors enhance their perceived adequacy? *Organizational Behavior and Human Decision Processes, 58*, 346–368.

52. Pescarella, P. (1993, February 1). 15 ways to win people's trust. *Nation's Business*, pp. 47–51.

53. Woodruff, D. (1993, February 8). Saturn: Labor's love lost? *Business Week*, pp. 122, 124.

54. Levering, R., & Moskowitz, M. (1993). *The 100 best companies to work for in America*. New York: Currency Doubleday.

55. Baron, R. A. (1989). Personality and organizational conflict: Effects of the Type A behavior pattern and self-monitoring. *Organizational Behavior and Human Decision Processes, 44*, 281–297.

56. See Note 55.

57. Poole, C. (1993, April 26). Family ties. *Forbes*, pp. 124–126.

58. Fodor, E. M. (1976). Group stress, authoritarian style of control and use of power. *Journal of Applied Psychology, 61*, 313–318.

59. Blake, R. R., & Mouton, J. S. (1984). *Solving costly organizational conflicts*. San Francisco: Jossey-Bass.

60. Baron, R. A. (1991). Positive effects of conflict: A cognitive perspective. *Employee Responsibilities and Rights Journal, 4*, 25–36.

61. Tjosvold, D. (1985). Implications of controversy research for management. *Journal of Management*, 11, 21–37.

62. Robbins, S. P. (1974). *Managing organizational conflict: A nontraditional approach*. Englewood Cliffs, NJ: Prentice Hall.

63. Schwenk, C. R., & Cosier, R. A. (1980). Effects of the expert, devil's advocate, and dialectical inquiry methods of prediction performance. *Organizational Behavior and Human Performance, 26*, 409–424.

64. See Note 46.

65. Cosier, R. A., & Dalton, D. R. (1990). Positive effects of conflict: A field assessment. *International Journal of Conflict Management, 1*, 81–92.

66. See Note 65.

67. Lewicki, R. J., & Litterer, J. A. (1985). *Negotiation*. Homewood, IL: Irwin.

68. Lewicki, R. J., Weiss, S. E., & Lewin, D. (1992). Models of conflict, negotiation and third party intervention: A review and synthesis. *Journal of Organizational Behavior, 13*, 209–252.

69. Chertkoff, J. M., & Baird, S. L. (1971). Applicability of the big lie technique and the last clear change doctrine to bargaining. *Journal of Personality and Social Psychology, 20,* 298–303.

70. Chertkoff, J. M., & Conley, M. (1967). Opening offer and frequency of concessions as bargaining strategies. *Journal of Personality and Social Psychology, 7,* 181–185.

71. Huber, V. L., Neale, M. A., & Northcraft, G. G. (1987). Decision bias and personnel selection strategies. *Organizational Behavior and Human Decision Processes, 40,* 136–147.

72. Thompson, L., & Hastie, R. (1990). Social perception in negotiation. *Organizational Behavior and Human Decision Processes, 47,* 98–123.

73. See Note 72.

74. Thompson, L. (1990). An examination of naive and experienced negotiators. *Journal of Personality and Social Psychology, 59,* 82–90.

75. Thompson, L., & Hastie, R. (1990). Judgment tasks and biases in negotiation. In B. H. Sheppard, M. H. Bazerman, & R. J. Lewicki (Eds.), *Research on negotiation in organizations* (Vol. 2, pp. 77–102). Greenwich, CT: JAI Press.

76. See Note 35.

77. Tjosvold, D. (1991). *The conflict-positive organization.* Reading, MA: Addison-Wesley.

78. Pruitt, D. G., Carnevale, J. D., Ben-Yoav, O., Nochajski, T. H., & Van Slyck, M. R. (1983). Incentives for cooperation in integrative bargaining. In R. Tietz (Ed.), *Aspiration levels in bargaining and economic decision making* (pp. 118–149). New York: Springer-Verlag.

79. Thomas, K. W. (1992). Conflict and conflict management: Reflections and update. *Journal of Organizational Behavior, 13,* 265–274.

80. Overman, S. (1993). Why grapple with the cloudy elephant? *HRMagazine,* pp. 60–65.

81. See Note 80.

82. Sheppard, B. H. (1984). Third party conflict intervention: A procedural framework. In B. Staw & L. Cummings (Eds.), *Research in organizational behavior* (Vol. 6, pp. 141–190). Greenwich, CT: JAI Press.

83. Fiske, S. T., & Taylor, S. E. (1984). *Social cognition.* Reading, MA: Addison-Wesley.

84. Sherif, M., Harvey, O. J., White, B. J., Hood, W. E., & Sherif, C. W. (1961). *Intergroup conflict and cooperation: The Robbers Cave experiment.* Norman, OK: Institute of Group Relations.

85. McEnrue, M. P. (1993). Managing diversity: Los Angeles before and after the riots. *Organizational Dynamics, 21*(3), 18–29.

86. See Note 85.

87. See Note 85.

88. See Note 85.

89. Van de Vliert, E. (1984). Conflict: Prevention and escalation. In P. J. D. Drenth, H. Thierry, P. J. Willems, & C. J. de Wolff (Eds.), *Handbook of work and organizational psychology* (pp. 276–311). New York: John Wiley & Sons.

90. Van de Vliert, E. (1985). Escalative intervention in small-group conflicts. *Journal of Applied Behavioral Science, 21,* 19–36.

91. See Note 90.

CASE IN POINT: MAKING THE SKIES FRIENDLY AGAIN

1. Stockton, W. (1998, November 6). Tearing apart Eastern Air Lines. *New York Times Magazine,* pp. 36–39, 82–87.

2. Engardio, P. & Bernstein, A. (1998, November 21). Charlie Bryan has ideas—and Lorenzo is listening. *Business Week,* pp. 88–93.

3. See Note 1, p. 38.

4. See Note 1.

5. See Note 2.

6. See Note 1.

7. Kolcum, E. H. (1991, January 28). Airline mainstay Eastern stops flying after 62 years. *Aviation Week and Space Technology,* pp. 64-65.

8. CNN. (1993, November 14). Managing with Lou Dobbs, Kiwi International Airlines.

9. See Note 7.

10. See Note 7.

11. Linden, D. W. (1992, September 14). Can this kiwi fly? *Forbes,* pp. 426–427.

CHAPTER 12

PREVIEW CASE SOURCES

Anonymous. (1990, March 10). Abbott board fires chairman, sparks legal row. *United Press International,* Financial Section. Anonymous. (1990, March 19). Abbott boardroom dispute erupts into a court suit. *Chemical Marketing Reporter,* p. 3. Byrne, J.A., Symonds, W. C., & Siler, J. F. (1991, April 1). CEO disease. *Business Week,* 52-60. Morris, S. (1990, March 13). Abbott boss's suit points to a trend. *Chicago Tribune,* Business Section, p. 1. Oloroso, A., Jr. (1990, March 19). Abbott fight will get messier. *Crain's Chicago Business,* p. 3

TEXT

1. Cobb, A. T. (1984). An episodic model of power: Toward an integration of theory and research. *Academy of Management Review, 9,* 482–493.

2. Mayes, B. T., & Allen, R. T. (1977). Toward a definition of organizational politics. *Academy of Management Review, 2,* 672–678.

3. Hofstede, G. (1990, Summer). Motivation, leadership, and organization: Do American theories apply abroad? *Organizational Dynamics,* 42–63.

4. Adler, N. J. (1991). *International dimensions of organizational behavior (2nd ed.).* Boston: PWS-Kent.

5. See Note 4.

6. Mintzberg, H. (1983). *Power in and around organizations.* Englewood Cliffs, NJ: Prentice Hall.

7. Schriesheim, C. A., & Hinkin, T. R. (1990). Influence tactics used by subordinates: A theoretical and empirical analysis and refinement of the Kipnis, Schmidt, and Wilkinson subscales. *Journal of Applied Psychology, 75,* 246–257.

8. Yukl, G., & Tracey, J. B. (1992). Consequences of influence tactics used with subordinates, peers, and the boss. *Journal of Applied Psychology, 77,* 525–535.

9. Yukl, G., Falbe, C. M., & Youn, J. Y. (1993). Patterns of influence behavior for managers. *Group & Organization Management, 18,* 5–28.

10. Falbe, C. M., & Yukl, G. (1992). Consequences for managers of using single influence tactics and combinations of tactics. *Academy of Management Journal, 35,* 638–652.

11. Offermann, L. R. (1990). Power and leadership in organizations. *American Psychologist, 45,* 179–189.

12. Ansari, M. A., & Kapoor, A. (1987). Organizational context and upward influence tactics. *Organizational Behavior and Human Decision Processes, 40,* 39–49.

13. Graham, J. W., Marks, G., & Hansen, W. B. (1991). Social influence processes affecting adolescent substance abuse. *Journal of Applied Psychology, 76,* 291–298.

14. French, J. R. P., & Raven, B. (1959). The bases of social power. In D. Cartwright (Ed.), *Studies in social power* (pp. 150–167). Ann Arbor, MI: Institute for Social Research, University of Michigan.

15. Kanter, R. M. (1979). Power failure in management circuits. *Harvard Business Review, 57,* 65–75.

16. Arvey, R. E., & Jones, A. P. (1985). The use of discipline in organizational settings: A framework for future research. In L. L. Cummings & B. M. Staw (Eds.), *Research in organizational behavior* (Vol. 7, pp. 367–408). Greenwich, CT: JAI Press.

17. Fiorelli, J. S. (1988). Power in work groups: Team member's perspective. *Human Relations, 41,* 1–12.

18. Schriesheim, C. A., Hinkin, T. R., & Podsakoff, P. M. (1991). Can ipsative and single-item measures produce erroneous results in field studies of French and Raven's (1959) five bases of power? An empirical investigation. *Journal of Applied Psychology, 76,* 106–114.

19. Hinkin, T. R., & Schriesheim, C. A. (1989). Development and application of new scales to measure the French and Raven (1959) bases of social power. *Journal of Applied Psychology, 74,* 561–567.

20. Yukl, G., & Falbe, C. M. (1991). Importance of different power sources in downward and lateral relations. *Journal of Applied Psychology, 76,* 416–423.

21. Podsakoff, P. M., & Schriesheim, C. A. (1985). Field studies of French and Raven's bases of power: Critique, re-analysis, and suggestions for future research. *Psychological Bulletin, 97,* 387–411.

22. Huber, V. L. (1981). The sources, uses, and conservation of managerial power. *Personnel,* 51(4), 62–67.

23. Kipnis, D., Schmidt, S. M., Swaffin-Smith, C., & Wilkinson, I. (1984, Winter). Patterns of managerial influence: Shotgun managers, tacticians, and bystanders. *Organizational Dynamics,* 58–67.

24. Stewart, T. (1989, November 6). CEOs see clout shifting. *Fortune,* p. 66.

25. Kahn, R. L., Wolfe, D. M., Quinn, R. P., Snoek, J. D., & Rosenthal, R. A. (1964). *Organizational stress: Studies in role conflict and ambiguity.* New York: John Wiley & Sons.

26. See Note 21.

27. Dumaine, B. (1993, February 22). The new non-manager managers. *Fortune,* pp. 80–84.

28. See Note 27.

29. See Note 27.

30. Gresov, C., & Stephens, C. (1993). The context of interunit influence attempts. *Administrative Science Quarterly*, *38*, 252–276.

31. Pfeffer, J., & Salancik, G. (1978). *The external control of organizations*. New York: Harper & Row.

32. Salancik, G., & Pfeffer, J. (1974). The bases and uses of power in organizational decision-making. *Administrative Science Quarterly*, *19*, 453–473.

33. Boeker, W. (1989). The development and institutionalization of subunit power in organizations. *Administrative Science Quarterly*, *34*, 388–410.

34. Lawrence, P. R., & Lorsch, J. W. (1967). *Organization and environment*. Cambridge, MA: Harvard University Press.

35. Hickson, D. J., Astley, W. G., Butler, R. J., & Wilson, D. C. (1981). Organization as power. In L. L. Cummings & B. M. Staw (Eds.), *Research in organizational behavior* (Vol. 4, pp. 151–196). Greenwich, CT: JAI Press.

36. Miles, R. H. (1980). *Macro organizational behavior*. Glenview, IL: Scott, Foresman.

37. Saunders, C. S., & Scarmell, R. (1982). Intraorganizational distributions of power: Replication research. *Academy of Management Journal*, *25*, 192–200.

38. Hinings, C. R., Hickson, D. J., Pennings, J. M., & Schneck, R. E. (1974). Structural conditions of intraorganizational power. *Academy of Management Journal*, *19*, 22–44.

39. See Note 2.

40. Drory, A., & Romm, T. (1990). The definition of organizational politics: A review. *Human Relations*, *43*, 1133–1154.

41. Ferris, G. R., & Kacmar, K. M. (1992). Perceptions of organizational politics. *Journal of Management*, *18*, 93–116.

42. Ferris, G. R., & King, T. R. (1991). Politics in human resources decisions: A walk on the dark side. *Organizational Dynamics*, *20*, 59–71.

43. Gandz, J., & Murray, V. V. (1980). The experience of workplace politics. *Academy of Management Journal*, *23*, 237–251.

44. Allen, R. W., Madison, D. L., Porter, L. W., Renwick, P. A., & Mayes, B. T. (1979). Organizational politics: Tactics and characteristics of its actors. *California Management Review*, *22*, 77–83.

45. See Note 42.

46. See Note 43.

47. Mulder, M., de Jong, R. D., Koppelaar, L., & Verhage, J. (1986). Power, situation, and leaders' effectiveness: An organizational field study. *Journal of Applied Psychology*, *71*, 566–570.

48. Feldman, S. P. (1988). Secrecy, information, and politics: An essay in organizational decision making. *Human Relations*, *41*, 73–90.

49. Greenberg, J. (1990). Looking fair vs. being fair: Managing impressions of organizational justice. In B. M. Staw & L. L. Cummings (Eds.), *Research in organizational behavior* (Vol. 12, pp. 111–157). Greenwich, CT: JAI Press.

50. See Note 42.

51. Boeker, W. (1992). Power and managerial dismissal: Scapegoating at the top. *Administrative Science Quarterly*, *37*, 400–421.

52. Cobb, A. T. (1991). Toward the study of organizational coalitions: Participant concerns and activities in a simulated organizational setting. *Human Relations*, *44*, 1057–1079.

53. Feldman, S. P. (1988). Secrecy, information, and politics: An essay in organizational decision making. *Human Relations*, *41*, 73–90.

54. Liden, R. C., & Mitchell, T. R. (1988). Ingratiatory behaviors in organizational settings. *Academy of Management Review*, *13*, 572–587.

55. Vredenburgh, D. J., & Maurer, J. G. (1984). A process framework for organizational politics. *Human Relations*, *37*, 47–66.

56. See Note 6.

57. Sprouse, M. (1992). *Sabotage in the American workplace*. San Francisco: Pressure Drop Press.

58. Madison, D. L., Allen, R. W., Porter, L. W., Renwick, P. A., & Mayes, B. T. (1980). Organizational politics: An exploration of managers' perceptions. *Human Relations*, *33*, 79–100.

59. Pfeffer, J. (1992). *Managing with power*. Boston: Harvard Business School.

60. See Note 41.

61. Wayne, S. J., & Ferris, G. R. (1990). Influence tactics, affect, and exchange quality in supervisor-subordinate interactions. *Journal of Applied Psychology*, *75*, 487–499.

62. Greenberg, J. (1991). Motivation to inflate performance ratings: Perceptual bias or response bias? *Motivation and Emotion*, *15*, 81–98.

63. See Note 42.

64. Bartol, K. M., & Martin, D. C. (1990). When politics pays: Factors influencing managerial compensation decisions. *Personnel Psychology*, *43*, 599–614.

65. Gray, B., & Ariss, S. S. (1985). Politics and strategic change across organizational life cycles. *Academy of Management Review*, *10*, 707–723.

66. Hannan, M. T., & Freeman, J. H. (1978). Internal politics of growth and decline. In M. W. Meyer (Ed.), *Environment and organizations* (pp. 177–199). San Francisco: Jossey-Bass.

67. Kumar, P., & Ghadially, R. (1989). Organizational politics and its effects on members of organizations. *Human Relations*, *42*, 305–314.

68. Kipnis, D. (1976). *The powerholders*. Chicago: University of Chicago Press.

69. Buchholz, R. A. (1989). *Fundamental concepts and problems in business ethics*. Englewood Cliffs, NJ: Prentice Hall.

70. Gellerman, S. W. (1986, July–August). Why "good" managers make bad ethical choices. *Harvard Business Review*, pp. 85–90.

71. Velasquez, M., Moberg, D. J., & Cavanaugh, G. F. (1983). Organizational statesmanship and dirty politics: Ethical guidelines for the organizational politician. *Organizational Dynamics*, *11*, 65–79.

72. See Note 49.

73. Greenberg, J. (1982). Approaching equity and avoiding inequity in groups and organizations. In J. Greenberg & R. L. Cohen (Eds.), *Equity and justice in social behavior* (pp. 389–435). New York: Academic Press.

74. Ferrell, O. C., & Fraedrich, J. (1994). *Business ethics (2nd ed.)*. Boston: Houghton Mifflin.

75. Jansen, E., & Von Glinow, M. A. (1985). Ethical ambivalence and organizational reward systems. *Academy of Management Review*, *10*, 814–822.

76. Vandevier, K. (1978). The aircraft brake scandal. A cautionary tale in which the moral is unpleasant. In A. G. Athos & J. J. Babarro (Eds.), *Interpersonal behavior: Communication and understanding relationships* (pp. 529–540). Englewood Cliffs, NJ: Prentice Hall.

77. Gray, M., & Rosen, I. (1982). *The warning*. New York: Norton.

78. Wolfe, D. M. (1988). Is there integrity in the bottom line: Managing obstacles to executive integrity. In S. Srivastava (Ed.), *Executive integrity: The search for high human values in organizational life* (pp. 140–171). San Francisco: Jossey-Bass.

79. See Note 69.

80. Murray, K. B., & Montanari, J. R. (1986). Strategic management of the socially responsible firm: Integrating management and marketing theory. *Academy of Management Review*, *11*, 815–827.

81. Roddick, A. (1991). *Body and soul*. New York: Crown.

82. Chappell, T. (1993). *The soul of a business*. New York: Bantam.

83. Commerce Clearing House. (1991, June 26). *1991 SHRM/CCH survey*. Chicago: Author.

CASE IN POINT: THE MOST POWERFUL MAN IN SPORTS

1. McCormack, M. (1984). *What they don't teach you at Harvard Business School*. New York: Bantam.

2. Butler, C. (1992, January). On the mark. *Successful Meetings*, pp. 52–54, 73.

3. CNN. (1993, May 26). Pinnacle. Mark McCormack.

4. See Note 3.

5. See Note 3.

6. See Note 4.

7. See Note 3.

8. See Note 3.

9. See Note 3.

10. See Note 3.

11. See Note 1.

12. See Note 3.

CHAPTER 13

PREVIEW CASE SOURCES

Mary Kay Cosmetics. (March 1994) Farnham, A. (1993, September 20). Mary Kay's lessons in leadership. *Fortune*, pp. 68–69, 71, 74, 76–77.

TEXT

1. Yukl, G., & Van Fleet, D. D. (1992). Theory and research on leadership in organizations. In M. D Dunnette & L M. Hough (Eds.), *Handbook of industrial and organizational psychology (2nd ed.)* (Vol. 3, pp. 147–197). Palo Alto, CA: Consulting Psychologists Press.

2. House, R. J., & Podsakoff, P. M. (1994). Leadership effectiveness:

Past perspectives and future directions for research. In J. Greenberg (Ed.), *Organizational behavior: The state of the science* (pp. 45–82). Hillsdale, NJ: Lawrence Erlbaum Associates.

3. Bass, B. M. (1990). *Bass and Stogdill's handbook of leadership (3rd ed.)*. New York: Free Press.

4. Bennis, W. G., & Nanus, B. (1985). *Leaders: The strategies for taking charge*. New York: Harper & Row. (quote, p. 4)

5. Yukl, G. A. (1989). *Leadership in organizations (2nd ed.)*. Englewood Cliffs, NJ: Prentice Hall.

6. Locke, E. A. (1991). *The essence of leadership*. New York: Lexington Books.

7. Cialdini, R. B. (1988). *Influence (2nd ed.)*. Glenview, IL: Scott, Foresman.

8. Kotter, J. P. (1990). *A force for change*. New York: Free Press.

9. See Note 4.

10. Geier, J. G. (1969). A trait approach to the study of leadership in small groups. *Journal of Communication*, *17*, 316–323.

11. See Note 3.

12. See Note 5.

13. See Note 3.

14. Kirkpatrick, S. A., & Locke, E. A. (1991). Leadership: Do traits matter? *Academy of Management Executive*, *5*, 48–60.

15. Lord, R. G., DeVader, C. L., & Alliger, G. M. (1986). A meta-analysis of the relation between personality traits and leadership perceptions: An application of validity generalization procedures. *Journal of Applied Psychology*, *61*, 402–410.

16. Zaccaro, S. J., Foti, R. J., & Kenny, D. A. (1991). Self-monitoring and trait-based variance in leadership: An investigation of leader flexibility across multiple group situations. *Journal of Applied Psychology*, *76*, 308–315.

17. See Note 14. (quote, p. 58)

18. Muczyk, J. P., & Reimann, B. C. (1987). The case for directive leadership. *Academy of Management Review*, *12*, 637–647.

19. Chen, C. C., & Meindl, J. R. (1991). The construction of leadership images in the popular press: The case of Donald Burr and People Express. *Administrative Science Quarterly*, *36*, 521–551.

20. Stogdill, R. M. (1963). *Manual for the leader behavior description questionnaire, form XII*. Columbus, OH: Ohio State University, Bureau of Business Research.

21. Likert, R. (1961). *New patterns in management*. New York: McGraw-Hill.

22. See Note 3.

23. Weissenberg, P., & Kavanagh, M. H. (1972). The independence of initiating structure and consideration: A review of the evidence. *Personnel Psychology*, *25*, 119–130.

24. Vroom, V. H. (1976). Leadership. In M. D. Dunnette (Ed.), *Handbook of industrial-organizational psychology* (pp. 1527–1552). Chicago: Rand-McNally.

25. See Note 3.

26. Blake, R. R., & Mouton, J. S. (1985). *The new managerial grid*. Houston: Gulf.

27. Smith, P. B., Misumi, J., Tayeb, M., Peterson, M., & Bond, M. (19890. On the generality of leadership style measures across cultures. *Journal of Occupational Psychology*, *62*, 97–109.

28. Misumi, J., & Peterson, M. F. (1985). The performance-maintenance (PM) theory of leadership: Review of a Japanese research program. *Administrative Science Quarterly*, *30*, 198–223.

29. Lee, C. (1991). Followership: The essence of leadersip. *Training*, 28, 27–35.

30. Graen, G. B., & Scandura, T. A. (1987). Toward a psychology of dyadic organizing. In L. L. Cummings & B. M. Staw (Eds.), *Research in organizational behavior* (Vol. 9, pp. 175–208). Greenwich, CT: JAI Press.

31. Dunegan, K. J., Duchon, D., & Uhl-Bien, M. (1992). Examining the link between leader-member exchange and subordinate performance: The role of task analyzability and variety as moderators. *Journal of Management*, *18*, 59–76.

32. Deluga, R. J., & Perry, J. T. (1991). The relationship of subordinate upward influencing behaviour, satisfaction and perceived superior effectiveness with leader-member exchanges. *Journal of Occupational Psychology*, *64*, 239–252.

33. Duarte, N. T., Goodson, J. R., & Klich, N. R. (1993). How do I like thee? Let me appraise the ways. *Journal of Organizational Behavior*, *14*, 239–249.

34. Lord, R. G., & Maher, K. (1989). Perceptions in leadership and their implications in organizations. In J. Carroll (Ed.), *Applied social psychology and organizational settings* (Vol. 4, pp. 129–154). Hillsdale, NJ: Lawrence Erlbaum Associates.

35. Heneman, R. L., Greenberger, D. B., & Anonyuo, C. (1989). Attributions and exchanges: The effects of interpersonal factors on the diagnosis of employee performance. *Academy of Management Journal*, *32*, 466–476.

36. Mitchell, T. R., & Wood, R. E. (1980). Supervisors' responses to subordinate poor performance: A test of an attribution model. *Organizational Behavior and Human Performance*, *25*, 123–138.

37. Bass, B. M. (1985). *Leadership and performance beyond expectations*. New York: Free Press.

38. See Note 37.

39. See Note 5.

40. House, R. J., Spangler, W. D., & Woycke, J. (1991). Personality and charisma in the U.S. presidency: A psychological theory of leader effectiveness. *Administrative Science Quarterly*, *36*, 364–396.

41. See Note 37.

42. House, R. J. (1977). A 1976 theory of charismatic leadership. In J. G. Hunt & L. L. Larson (Eds.), *Leadership: The cutting edge* (pp. 189–207). Carbondale, IL: Southern Illinois University Press.

43. See Note 42.

44. Conger, J. A. (1991). Inspiring others: The language of leadership. *Academy of Management Executive*, *5*, 31–45.

45. See Note 44.

46. See Note 44. (quote, p. 44)

47. Keller, R. T. (1992). Transformational leadership and the performance of research and development project groups. *Journal of Management*, *18*, 489–501.

48. Howell, J. M., & Avolio, B. J. (1993). Transformational leadership, transactional leadership, locus of control, and support for innovation: Key predictors of consolidated-business-unit performance. *Journal of Applied Psychology*, *78*, 891–902.

49. See Note 40.

50. Howell, J. M., & Avolio, B. J. (1992). The ethics of charismatic leadership: Submission or liberation? *Academy of Management Executive*, *6*, 43–54.

51. See Note 50. (quote, p. 44)

52. Smith, S. (1990, January 29). Leaders of the most admired. *Fortune*, pp. 46–48, 50, 52.

53. Mayer, M. (1993). *Nightmare on Wall Street*. New York: Simon & Schuster.

54. Fiedler, F. E. (1978). Contingency model and the leadership process. In L. Berkowitz (Ed.), *Advances in experimental social psychology* (Vol. 11, pp. 60–112). New York: Academic Press.

55. See Note 54.

56. Strube, M. J., & Garcia, J. E. (1981). A meta-analytic investigation of Fiedler's contingency model of leadership effectiveness. *Psychological Bulletin*, *90*, 307–321.

57. Peters, L. H., Hartke, D. D., & Pohlman, J. T. (1985). Fiedler's contingency theory of leadership: An application of the meta-analytic procedures of Schmidt and Hunter. *Psychological Bulletin*, *97*, 274–385.

58. Ashour, A. S. (1973). The contingency model of leadership effectiveness: An evaluation. *Organizational Behavior and Human Performance*, *9*, 339–355.

59. Fiedler, F. E., Chemers, M. M., & Mahar, L. (1976). *Improving leadership effectiveness: The leader match concept*. New York: John Wiley & Sons.

60. Fiedler, F. E., & Mahar, L. (1979). The effectiveness of contingency model training: A review of the validation of leader match. *Personnel Psychology*, *32*, 45–62.

61. Fiedler, F. E., Garcia, J. E., Bell, C. H., Chemers, M. M., & Patrick, D. (1984). Increasing mine productivity and safety through management training and organization development: A comparative study. *Basic and Applied Social Psychology*, *5*, 1–18.

62. Hersey, P., & Blanchard, K. H. (1988). *Management of organizational behavior*. Englewood Cliffs, NJ: Prentice Hall.

63. Hambleton, R. K., & Gumpert, R. (1982). The validity of Hersey and Blanchard's theory of leader effectiveness. *Group and Organization Studies*, *7*, 225–242.

64. Vecchio, R. P. (1987). Situational leadership theory: An examination of a prescriptive theory. *Journal of Applied Psychology*, *72*, 444–451.

65. See Note 62.

66. House, R. J., & Baetz, M. L. (1979). Leadership: Some empirical generalizations and new research directions. In B. M. Staw (Ed.), *Research in organizational behavior* (Vol. 1, pp. 341–424). Greenwich, CT: JAI Press.

67. Milbank, D. (1990, March 5).

Managers are sent to "Charm Schools" to discover how to polish up their acts. *Wall Street Journal*, pp. A14, B3.

68. Kerr, S., & Jermier, J. M. (1978). Substitutes for leadership: Their meaning and measurement. *Organizational Behavior and Human Performance*, *22*, 375–403.

69. Sheridan, J. E., Vredenburgh, D. J., & Abelson, M. A. (1984). Contextual model of leadership influence in hospital units. *Academy of Management Journal*, *27*, 57–78.

70. Podsakoff, P. M., Niehoff, B. P., MacKenzie, S. B., & Williams, M. L. (1993). Do substitutes for leadership really substitute for leadership? An empirical examination of Kerr and Jermier's situational leadership model. *Organizational Behavior and Human Decision Processes*, *54*, 1–44.

71. Meindl, J. R., & Ehrlich, S. B. (1987). The romance of leadership and the evaluation of organizational performance. *Academy of Management Journal*, *30*, 91–109.

72. Vroom, V. H., & Yetton, P. W. (1973). *Leadership and decision making*. Pittsburgh: University of Pittsburgh Press.

73. Vroom, V. H., & Jago, A. G. (1978). On the validity of the Vroom-Yetton model. *Journal of Applied Psychology*, *63*, 151–162.

74. Field, R. H. (1982). A test of the Vroom-Yetton normative model of leadership. *Journal of Applied Psychology*, *67*, 532–537.

75. Heilman, M. E., Hornstein, H. A., Cage, J. H., & Herschlag, J. K. (1984). Reactions to prescribed leader behavior as a function of role perspective: The case of the Vroom-Yetton model. *Journal of Applied Psychology*, *69*, 50–60.

76. Crouch, A., & Yetton, P. (1987). Manager behavior, leadership style, and subordinate performance: An empirical extension of the Vroom-Yetton model. *Journal of Applied Psychology*, *69*, 50–60.

77. Vroom, V. H., & Jago, A. G. (1988). *The new leadership: Managing participation in organizations*. Englewood Cliffs, NJ: Prentice Hall.

78. Zenger, J. H., Musselwhite, E., Hurson, K., & Perrin, C. (1994). *Leading teams: Mastering the new role*. Homewood, IL: Business One Irwin.

CASE IN POINT: MAKING DREAMS COME TRUE

1. CNN. (1993, August 7). Managing with Lou Dobbs.

2. See Note 1.

3. CNN. (1993, August 29). Pinnacle. Fernando Mateo.

4. See Note 3.

5. See Note 3.

6. See Note 3.

7. See Note 3.

8. See Note 3.

9. See Note 3.

CHAPTER 14

PREVIEW CASE SOURCES

Anonymous. (1993, June 3). Freight carriers' technology tune: We've only just begun. *Purchasing*, p. 37. Fitzgerald, M. (1993, November 29). UPS delivers new bar-code system to public domain. *ComputerWorld*, p. 38. Hawkins, C., & Oster, P. (1993, May 31). After a U-turn, UPS really delivers. *Business Week*, pp. 92–93. Laabs, J. J. (1993, October). Community service helps UPS develop managers. *Personnel Journal*, pp. 90–92, 94, 96, 98. Margolis, N. (1993, March 1). UPS head launched for IS use. *ComputerWorld*, p. 65. Pastore, R. (1993, December 15). A measured success. *CIO*, pp. 40–45.

TEXT

1. Schneider, B. (1990). *Organizational climate and culture*. San Francisco: Jossey-Bass.

2. Johnson, R. (1991, September/October). A strategy for service—Disney style. *Journal of Business Strategy*, pp. 38–43.

3. Pennings, J. M., & Buitendam, A. (1987). *New technology as organizational innovation*. Cambridge, MA: Ballinger.

4. Zammuto, R. F. (1992). Gaining advanced manufacturing technologies' benefits: The role of organization design and culture. *Academy of Management Review*, *17*, 701–728.

5. Saporito, B. (1992, August 24). A week aboard the Wal-Mart express. *Business Week*, pp. 77–81, 84.

6. Flynn, J., Del Valle, C., & Mitchell, R. (1992, August 3). Did Sears take other customers for a ride? *Business Week*, pp. 24–25.

7. Weinfield, A. H., & Tiggemann, M. (1990). Employment status and psychological well-being: A longitudinal study. *Journal of Applied Psychology*, *75*, 455–459.

8. Schein, E. H. (1985). *Organizational culture and leadership*. San Francisco: Jossey-Bass.

9. Martin, J. *Cultures in organizations*. New York: Oxford University Press.

10. See Note 2.

11. Andrews, E. L. (1989, December). Out of chaos. *Business Month*, p. 33.

12. Smith, R. C. (1993). *Comeback*. Boston: Harvard Business School Press.

13. Dumaine, B. (1990, January 15). Creating a new company culture. *Fortune*, pp. 127–128, 130–131.

14. Dobrzynski, J. H. (1993, April 12). "I'm going to let the problems come to me." *Business Week*, pp. 32–33.

15. Labich, K. (1994, May 2). Is Herb Kelleher America's best CEO? *Fortune*, pp. 44–47, 50, 52.

16. Martin, J., & Meyerson, D. (1988). Organizational cultures and the denial, channeling, and acknowledgment of ambiguity. In L. R. Pondy, R. J. Boland, Jr., & H. Thomas (Eds.), *Managing ambiguity and change* (pp. 93–125). New York: John Wiley & Sons.

17. Schein, E. H. (1985). How culture forms, develops, and changes. In R. H. Kilmann, M. J. Saxton, & R. Serpa (Eds.), *Gaining control of corporate culture* (pp. 17–43). San Francisco: Jossey-Bass.

18. Sackmann, S. A. (1992). Cultures and subcultures: Analysis of organizational knowledge. *Administrative Science Quarterly*, *37*, 140–161.

19. Martin, J., Sitkin, S. B., & Boehm, M. (1985). Founders and the elusiveness of a cultural legacy. In P. J. Frost, L. F. Moore, M. R. Louis, C. C. Lundberg, & J. Martin (Eds.), *Organizational culture* (pp. 99–124). Beverly Hills, CA: Sage.

20. See Note 13.

21. See Note 17.

22. Weick, K. E. (1985). The significance of corporate culture. In P. J. Frost, L. F. Moore, M. R. Louis, C. C. Lundberg, & J. Martin (Eds.), *Organizational culture* (pp. 381–390). Beverly Hills, CA: Sage.

23. Rentsch, J. R. (1991). Climate and culture: Interaction and qualitative differences in organizational meanings. *Journal of Applied Psychology*, *75*, 668–681.

24. Lundberg, C. C. (1985). On the feasibility of cultural intervention in organizations. In P. J. Frost, L. F. Moore, M. R. Louis, C. C. Lundberg, & J. Martin (Eds.), *Organizational culture* (pp. 169–186). Beverly Hills, CA: Sage.

25. Ott, J. S. (1989). *The organizational culture perspective*. Chicago: Dorsey.

26. Dandridge, T. C. (1985), The life stages of a symbol: When symbols work and when they can't. In P. J. Frost, L. F. Moore, M. R. Louis, C. C. Lundberg, & J. Martin (Eds.), *Organizational culture* (pp. 141–154). Beverly Hills, CA: Sage.

27. Walton, T. (1988). *Architecture and the corporation*. New York: Macmillan.

28. Ornstein, S. L. (1986). Organizational symbols: A study of their meanings and influences on perceived psychological climate. *Organizational Behavior and Human Decision Processes*, *38*, 207–229.

29. Neuhauser, P. C. (1993). *Corporate legends and lore: The power of storytelling as a management tool*. New York: McGraw-Hill.

30. Martin, J. (1982). Stories and scripts in organizational settings. In A. Hastorf & A. Isen (Eds.), *Cognitive social psychology* (pp. 255–306). New York: Elsevier-North Holland.

31. Rowlinson, M., & Hassard, J (1993). The invention of corporate culture: A history of the histories of Cadbury. *Human Relations*, *46*, 299–326.

32. Richman, T. (1990, January). The master entrepreneur. *Inc.*, p. 50.

33. Deal, T. E., & Kennedy, A. A. (1982). *Corporate cultures*. Reading, MA: Addison-Wesley.

34. See Note 29. (quote, p. 19)

35. Lewis, G. (1993, April 12). One fresh face at IBM may not be enough. *Business Week*, p. 33.

36. See Note 25.

37. See Note 25.

38. See Note 33. (quote, p. 63)

39. Brenner, J. G. (1992, April 19). The world according to planet Mars. *Dallas Morning News*, pp. 1H, 2H, 7H.

40. Manley, W. W., II. (1991). *Executive's handbook of model business conduct codes*. Englewood Cliffs, NJ: Prentice Hall. (quote, p. 5).

41. Falsey, T. A. (1989). *Corporate philosophies and mission statements*. New York: Quorum.

42. Waldholz, M. (1982, October 4). Johnson & Johnson officials

take steps to end more killings linked to Tylenol. *Wall Street Journal*, p. 16.

43. See Note 41. (quote, p. 25)

44. See Note 41. (quote, p. 26)

45. Foster, L. G. (1983, Spring). The Johnson & Johnson Credo and the Tylenol crisis. *New Jersey Bell Journal*, *6*(1), 7.

46. Buchholz, R. (1989). *Fundamental concepts and problems in business ethics*, Englewood Cliffs, NJ: Prentice Hall.

47. Waldholz, M. (1982, December 24). Tylenol regains most of no. 1 market share amazing doomsayers. *Wall Street Journal*, p. 1.

48. See Note 40.

49. Hatch, M. J. (1993). The dynamics of organizational culture. *Academy of Management Review*, *18*, 657–693.

50. Weiner, Y. (1988). Forms of value systems: A focus on organizational effectiveness and cultural change and maintenance. *Academy of Management Review*, *13*, 534–545.

51. Saffold, G. S., III. (1988). Culture traits, strength, and organizational performance: Moving beyond "strong" culture. *Academy of Management Review*, *13*, 546–558.

52. Dennison, D. (1984). Bringing corporate culture to the bottom line. *Organizational Dynamics*, *13*, 5–22.

53. Peters, T., & Waterman, R. H. (1982). *In search of excellence*. New York: Harper & Row.

54. Siehl, C., & Martin, J. (1988). *Organizational culture: A key to financial performance?* Research Paper Series No. 998. Stanford, CA: Stanford University, Graduate School of Business.

55. Hitt, M. A., & Ireland, R. D. (1987). Peters and Waterman revisited: The unended quest for excellence. *Academy of Management Executive*, *1*, 91–98.

56. Sheridan, J. E. (1992). Organizational culture and employee retention. *Academy of Management Journal*, *35*, 1036–1056.

57. O'Reilly, C. A., III, Chatman, J., & Caldwell, D. F. (1991). People and organizational culture: A profile comparison approach to assessing person-organization fit. *Academy of Management Journal*, *34*, 487–516.

58. Vandermolen, M. (1992, November). Shifting the corporate culture. *Working Woman*, pp. 25, 28.

59. Walter, G. A. (1985). Culture collisions in mergers and acquisitions. In P. J. Frost, L. F. Moore, M. R. Louis, C. C. Lundberg, & J. Martin (Eds.), *Organizational culture* (pp. 301–314). Beverly Hills, CA: Sage.

60. Byrbem J. A., Symonds, W. C., & Siler, J. F. (1991, April 1). CEO disease. *Business Week*, pp. 52–60.

61. Burrough, B., & Helyar, J. (1990). *Barbarians at the gate*. New York: Harper Collins.

62. Cartwright, S., & Cooper, C. L. (1993). The role of culture compatibility in successful organizational marriage. *Academy of Management Executive*, *7*, 57–70.

63. Carroll, P. (1993). *Big blues: The unmaking of IBM*. New York: Crown.

64. Boyett, J. H., Schwartz, S., Osterwise, L., & Bauer, R. (1993). *The quality journey*. New York: Dutton.

65. Hulin, C. L., & Roznowski, M. (1985). Organizational technologies: Effects on organizations' characteristics and individuals' responses. In L. L. Cummings & B. M. Staw (Eds.), *Research in organizational behavior* (Vol. 7, pp. 39–86). Greenwich, CT: JAI Press.

66. Swasy, A. (1993). *Soap opera: The inside story of Procter & Gamble*. New York: Times Books.

67. Porter, M. E. (1985). *Competitive advantage*. New York: Free Press.

68. Drucker, P. F. (1992). *Managing for the future*. New York: Truman Talley Books/Dutton.

69. Perrow, C. (1967). A framework for the comparative analysis of organizations. *American Sociological Review*, *32*, 194–208.

70. Katzell, R. (1994). Contemporary meta-trends in industrial and organizational psychology. In. H. C. Triandis, M. D. Dunnette, & L. M. Hough (Eds.), *Handbook of industrial and organizational psychology (2nd ed.)* (Vol. 4, pp. 1–89). Palo Alto, CA: Consunting Psychologists Press.

71. Dean, J. W., Yoon, S. J., & Susman, G. I. (1992). Advanced manufacturing technology and organization structure: Empowerment or subordination? *Organization Science*, *3*, 203–229.

72. Ettlie, J. E. (1988). *Taking charge of manufacturing*. San Francisco: Jossey-Bass.

73. Valery, N. (1988). Factory of the future. In J. Gibson, J. Ivancevich, & J. Donnelly, Jr. (Eds.), *Organizations close-up* (pp. 274–301). Plano, TX: Business Publications.

74. See Note 73.

75. Weick, K. (1990). Technology as equivoque: Sensemaking in new technologies. In P. S. Goodman & L. S. Sproull (Eds.), *Technology and organizations* (pp. 1–44). San Francisco: Jossey-Bass.

76. Office of Technology Assessment. (1985). *Automation of American offices, 1985–2000*. Washington, DC: Author.

77. Solomon, J. S. (1987, Fall). Union responses to technological change: Protecting the past or looking into the future? *Labor Studies Journal*, pp. 51–65.

78. Farnham, A. (1993, Autumn). Making high tech work for you. *Fortune (Special Issue)*, p. 1.

79. Bayless, A. (1986, October 16). Technology reshapes North America's lumber plants. *Wall Street Journal*, p. 6.

80. Sherman, J. (1994). *In the rings of Saturn*. New York: Oxford University Press.

81. Neff, R. (1987, April 20). Getting man and machine to live happily ever after. *Business Week*, pp. 61–63.

82. Argote, L., Goodman, P. S., & Schkade, D. (1983, Spring). The human side of robots: How workers react to a robot. *Sloan Management Review*, pp. 31–42.

83. See Note 81.

84. Katzenbach, J. R., & Smith, D. K. (1993). *The wisdom of teams*. Boston: Harvard Business School Press.

85. Carstairs, J. F. (1988, March 28). America rushes to high tech for growth. *Business Week*, pp. 84–86, 88, 90.

86. See Note 73.

87. See Note 78.

88. Verity, J. W. (1993, June 21). Getting work to go with the flow. *Business Week*, pp. 156, 161.

89. See Note 87.

90. See Note 87. (p. 161)

91. Anonymous. (1993, October). The paperless office—again? *Information Management Forum*, p. 1.

92. Tompkins, N. C. (1993, April). Tools that help performance on the job. *HRMagazine*, pp. 84, 87, 89–91.

93. See Note 92.

94. Anonymous. (1993, September). New technology and the disabled. *Information Management Forum*, pp. 1, 4.

95. See Note 92.

96. See Note 92.

97. See Note 92.

98. U.S. Congress, Office of Technology Assessment. (1987). *The electronic supervisor: New technology, new tensions* (OTA-CIT-333). Washington, DC: U.S. Government Printing Office.

99. Aiello, J. R. (1993). Computer-based work monitoring: Electronic surveillance and its effects. *Journal of Applied Social Psychology*, *23*, 499–507.

100. See Note 98.

101. Bylinsky, G. (1991, November). How companies spy on employees. *Fortune*, pp. 131–133, 136, 138, 140. (quote, p. 136).

102. Kipnis, D. (1991). The technological perspective. *Psychological Science*, *2*, 62–69.

103. Marx, G. T., & Sherizen, S. (1986), Monitoring on the job: How to protect privacy as well as property. *Technology Review*, *89*, 62–72.

104. See Note 99.

105. Kulik, C. T., & Ambrose, M. L. (1993). Category-based and feature-based processes in performance appraisal: Integrating visual and computerized sources of performance data. *Journal of Applied Psychology*, *78*,, 821–830.

106. Irving, R. H., Higgins, C. A., & Safayeni, F. R. (1986). Computerized performance monitoring systems: Use and abuse. *Communications of the ACM*, 29, 794–801.

107. See Note 99.

108. See Note 99.

109. Chalykoff, J., & Kochan, T. A. (1989). Computer-aided monitoring: Its influence on employee satisfaction and turnover. *Personnel Psychology*, *40*, 807–834.

110. Fenner, D. B., Lerch, F. J., & Kulik, C. T. (1993). The impact of computerized performance monitoring and prior performance knowledge on performance evaluation. *Journal of Applied Social Psychology*, 23, 572–601.

111. Ives, B., & Mason, R. O. (1990). Can information technology revitalize your customer service? *Academy of Management Executive*, *4*, 52–69.

112. Carlzon, J. (1987). *Moments of truth*. Cambridge, MA: Ballinger.

113. Verity, J. W. (1993, October 23). Taking a laptop on a call. *Business Week*, pp. 124–125.

114. Churbuck, D. C., & Young, J. S. (1992, November 23). The vir-

tual workplace. *Forbes*, pp. 184, 18–188, 190.

CASE IN POINT: QUALITY SUPPORTED BY TECHNOLOGY AND CULTURE

1. CNN. (1993, October 31). Managing with Lou Dobbs. Loro Piana Textiles.

2. Levering, R., & Moskowitz, M. (1993). *The 100 best companies to work for in America*. New York: Currency Doubleday. (quote, p. 476)

3. See Note 2, p. 477.

4. Saporito, B. (1992, August 24). A week aboard the Wal-Mart Express. *Fortune*, pp. 77–81, 84.

5. See Note 4, p. 77.

CHAPTER 15

PREVIEW CASE SOURCES

Anonymous. (1993, August 16). Johnson & Johnson cuts 3,000 jobs world-wide. *Chemical Marketing Reporter*, p. 5. Tanouye, E. (1993, August 12). Another job reduction set in drug industry. *Wall Street Journal*, p. A4. Weber J. (1992, May 4). A big company that works. *Business Week*, pp. 124–127, 130, 132.

TEXT

1. Miller, D. (1987). The genesis of configuration. *Academy of Management Review*, 12, 686–701.

2. Galbraith, J. R. (1987). Organization design. In J. W. Lorsch (Ed.), *Handbook of organizational behavior* (pp. 343–357). Englewood Cliffs, NJ: Prentice Hall.

3. Hendricks, C. F. (1992). *The rightsizing remedy*. Homewood, IL: Business One Irwin.

4. Swoboda, F. (1990, May 28–June 3). For unions, maybe bitter was better. *Washington Post National Weekly Edition*, p. 20.

5. Weber, J. (1990, December 10). Farewell, fast track. *Business Week*, pp. 192–200.

6. See Note 3.

7. Treece, J. B. (1990, April 9). Will GM learn from its own role models? *Business Week*, pp. 62–64.

8. Lawler, E. E. (1988, Summer). Substitutes for hierarchy. *Organizational Dynamics*, pp. 5–6, 15.

9. Speen, K. (1988, September 12). Caught in the middle. *Business Week*, pp. 80–88.

10. Urwick, L. F. (1956). The manager's span of control. *Harvard Business Review*, *34*(3), 39–47.

11. Charan, R. (1991). How networks reshape organizations—for results. *Harvard Business Review*, *69*(5), 10.

12. Green, H., & Moscow, A. (1984). *Managing*. New York: Doubleday.

13. Dalton, M. (1950). Conflicts between staff and line managerial officers. *American Sociological Review*, *15*, 342–351.

14. Chandler, A. (1962). *Strategy and structure*. Cambridge, MA: MIT Press.

15. Mitchell, R. (1987, December 14). When Jack Welch takes over: A guide for the newly acquired. *Business Week*, p. 93–97.

16. Lawrence, P., & Lorsch, J. (1967). *Organization and environment*. Boston: Harvard University.

17. Pitta, J. (1993, April 26). It had to be done and we did it. *Forbes*, pp. 148–152.

18. For best results, decentralize R&D. (1993, June 28). *Business Week*, p. 134.

19. Dumaine, B. (1990, November 5). How to manage in a recession. *Fortune*, pp. 72–75.

20. Toy, S. (1988, April 25). The Americanization of Honda. *Business Week*, pp. 90–96.

21. Uttal, B. (1985, June 29). Mettle test time for John Young. *Fortune*, pp. 242–244, 248.

22. Mee, J. F. (1964). Matrix organizations. *Business Horizons*, *7*(2), 70–72.

23. Bartlett, C. A., & Ghoshal, S. (1990). Matrix management: Not a structure, a frame of mind. *Harvard Business Review*, *68*(3), 138–145.

24. Wall, W. C., Jr. (1984). Integrated management in matrix organizations. *IEEE Transactions on Engineering Management*, *20*(2), 30–36.

25. Davis, S. M., & Lawrence, P. R. (1977). *Matrix*. Reading, MA: Addison-Wesley.

26. Goggin, W. (1974). How the multidimensional structure works at Dow Corning. *Harvard Business Review*, *56*(1), 33–52.

27. See Note 24.

28. Ford, R. C., & Randolph, W. A. (1992). Cross-functional structures: A review and integration of matrix organization and project management. *Journal of Management*, *18*, 267–294.

29. See Note 28.

30. Stewart, T. A. (1992, May 18). The search for the organization of tomorrow. *Fortune*, pp. 93–98. (quote, p. 93)

31. Byrne, J. A. (1993, December 20). The horizontal corporation. *Business Week*, pp. 76–81.

32. See Note 30. (quote, p. 96)

33. See Note 30. (quote, p. 96)

34. McGregor, D. (1960). *The human side of enterprise*. New York: McGraw-Hill.

35. Argyris, C. (1964). *Integrating the individual and the organization*. New York: John Wiley & Sons.

36. Likert, R. (1961). *New patterns of management*. New York: McGraw-Hill.

37. Duncan, R. (1979, Winter). What is the right organization structure? *Organizational Dynamics*, pp. 59–69.

38. Burns, T., & Stalker, G. M. (1961). *The management of innovation*. London: Tavistock.

39. Deveney, K. (1986, October 13). Bag those fries, squirt that ketchup, fry that fish. *Business Week*, pp. 57–61.

40. Kerr, P. (1985, May 11). Witch hazel still made the old-fashioned way. *New York Times*, pp. 27–28.

41. Morse, J. J., & Lorsch, J. W. (1970). Beyond Theory Y. *Harvard Business Review*, *48*(3), 61–68.

42. Mintzberg, H. (1983). *Structure in fives: Designing effective organizations*. Englewood Cliffs, NJ: Prentice Hall.

43. Livesay, H. C. (1979). *American made: Man who shaped tie American economy*. Boston: Little, Brown.

44. Kirkpatrick, D. (1992, July 27). Breaking up IBM. *Fortune*, pp. 44–49, 52–54, 58.

45. Weber, J. (1992, May 4). A big company that works. *Business Week*, pp. 124–127, 130, 132.

46. Nakarmi, L., & Einhorn, B. (1993, June 7). Hyundai's gutsy gambit. *Business Week*, p. 48.

47. Gerlach, M. L. (1993). *Alliance capitalism: The social organization of Japanese business*. Berkeley, CA: University of California Press.

48. Miyashita, K. & Russell, D. (1994). *Keiretsu: Inside the Japanese conglomerates*. New York: McGraw-Hill.

49. Lubove, S. (1992, December 7). How to grow big yet stay small. *Forbes*, pp. 64–66.

50. See Note 46.

51. Hayden, C. L. (1986). *The handbook of strategic expertise*. New York: Free Press.

52. Ernst, D., & Bleeke, J. (1993). *Collaborating to compete: Using strategic alliances and acquisitions in the global marketplace*. New York: John Wiley & Sons.

53. Fletcher, N. (1988, December 10). U.S., China form joint venture to manufacture helicopters. *Journal of Commerce*, p. 58.

54. Bransi, B. (1987, January 3). South Korea's carmakers count their blessings. *The Economist*, p. 45.

55. Mason, J. C. (1993, May). Strategic alliances: Partnering for success. *Management Review*, pp. 10–15.

56. Newman, W. H. (1992). Focused joint ventures in transforming economies. *The Executive*, *6*, 67–75.

57. Lewis, J. (1990). *Partnerships for profit: Structuring and managing strategic alliances*. New York: Free Press.

58. Mason, J. C. (1993, May). The marriage of Volvo and Renault. *Management Review*, p. 12.

59. See Note 58.

60. Woodward, J. (1965) *Industrial organization: Theory and practice*. London: Oxford University Press.

61. See Note 60. (quote, p. 58)

62. Zwerman, W. L. (1970). *New perspectives on organizational theory*. Westport, CT: Greenwood.

63. Huber, G. P. (1990). A theory of the effects of advanced information technologies on organizational design, intelligence, and decision making. *Academy of Management Review*, *15*, 47–71.

64. Hull, F. M., & Collins, P. D. (1987). High-technology batch production systems: Woodward's missing type. *Academy of Management Journal*, *30*, 786–797.

65. Hickson, D., Pugh, D., & Pheysey, D. (1969). Operations technology and organization structure: An empirical reappraisal. *Administrative Science Quarterly*, *26*, 349–377.

66. Singh, J. V. (1986). Technology, size and organization structure: A reexamination of the Okayama study data. *Academy of Management Journal*, *29*, 800–812.

67. Thompson, J. D. (1967). *Organizations in action*. New York: McGraw-Hill.

68. Daft, R. L. (1986). *Organizational theory and design (2nd ed.)*. St. Paul, MN: West.

69. Bahrami, H. (1992). The emerging flexible organization: Perspectives from Silicon Valley. *California Management Review*, *34*(4), 33–52.

70. See Note 69. (quote, p. 38)

71. See Note 69.

CASE IN POINT: THE "UPSIDE-DOWN" ORGANIZATION

1. CNN. (1993, August 14). *Managing with Lou Dobbs*.

2. See Note 1.

3. Stewart, T. A. (1993, August 23). Reengineering: The hot new management tool. *Fortune*, p. 42.

CHAPTER 16

PREVIEW CASE SOURCES

Anonymous. (1993, November 9). Taking off: Boeing. Financial World, pp. 53–54. Anonymous. (1994, February 18). Boeing: Back on course. *Financial World*, pp. 22, 24. Condit, P. M. (1994) Focusing on the customer: How Boeing does it. *Research-Technology Management*, 37(1), 33–37. Major, M. J. (1993, December). Candor helps Boeing handle massive layoffs. *Public Relations Journal*, pp. 20–21. Ott, J. (1993, November 22). Cutting costs key to recovery. *Aviation Week & Space Technology*, pp. 42–43, 45–47. Proctor, P. (1993, November 22). Boeing meets competition with "six-month" airplane. *Aviation Week & Space Technology*, pp. 63–64. Proctor, P. (1993, December 6). Boeing develops new tool to analyze aircraft costs. *Aviation Week & Space Technology*, p. 43. Witt, C. E. (1993, September). Boeing's smooth approach to landing business. *Material Handling Engineering*, pp. 46–51. Yang, D. J., & Rothman, A. (1993, March 1). Reinventing Boeing: Radical changes amid crisis. *Business Week*, pp. 60–63.

TEXT

1. Woodman, R. W. (1989). Organizational change and development: New arenas for inquiry and action. *Journal of Management*, *15*, 205–228.

2. Stewart, T. A. (1993, December 13). Welcome to the revolution. *Fortune*, pp. 66–68, 70, 72, 76, 78.

3. Sherman, S. (1993, December 13). How will we live with the tumult? *Fortune*, pp. 123–125.

4. Kanter, R. M. (1991, May–June). Transcending business boundaries: 12,000 world managers view change. *Harvard Business Review*, pp. 151–164.

5. A master class in radical change. (1993, December 13). *Fortune*, pp. 82–84, 88, 90.

6. Haveman, H. A. (1992). Between a rock and a hard place: Organizational change and performance under conditions of fundamental environmental transformation. *Administrative Science Quarterly*, 37, 48–75.

7. Nystrom, P. C., & Starbuck, W. H. (1984, Spring). To avoid organizational crises, unlearn. *Organizational Dynamics*, 44–60.

8. Reese, J. (1993, July 26). Corporate Methuselahs. *Fortune*, pp. 14–15.

9. See Note 8. (quote, p. 18)

10. Calonius, E. (1990, December 3). Federal Express's battle overseas. *Fortune*, pp. 137–140.

11. Daft, R. L. (1992). *Organization theory and design (4th ed.)*. St. Paul, MN: West.

12. Cobb, A. T., & Marguiles, N. (1981). Organizational development: A political perspective. *Academy of Management Review*, *6*, 49–59.

13. McCarty, M. (1990, October 30). PepsiCo to consolidate its restaurants, combining U.S. and foreign operations. *Wall Street Journal*, p. A4.

14. Daft, R. L. (1982). Bureaucratic versus nonbureaucratic structure and the process of innovation and change. In S. B. Bachrach (Ed.), *Research in the sociology of organizations* (Vol. 1, pp. 56–88). Greenwich, CT: JAI Press.

15. Gaertner, G. H., Gaertner, K. N., & Akinnusi, D. M. (1984). Environment, strategy, and implementation of administrative change: The case of civil service reform. *Academy of Management Journal*, 27, 525–543.

16. Tomasko, R. M. (1990). *Downsizing: Reshaping the corporation for the future*. New York: AMACOM.

17. Hendricks, C. F. (1992). *The rightsizing remedy*. Homewood, IL: Business One Irwin.

18. Fierman, J. (1994, January 24). The contingency work force. *Fortune*, pp. 30–34, 36.

19. Szwergold, J. (1993, December). Downsizing: Down, but not out. *Management Review*, p. 6.

20. Richman, L. S. (1993, September 20). When will the layoffs end? *Fortune*, pp. 54–56.

21. Tomasko, R. M. (1993). *Rethinking the corporation*, New York: AMACOM.

22. See Note 21.

23. Lusk, A. (1992, May). New business from old clients. *Working Woman*, pp. 26, 28.

24. Bettis, R. A., Bradley, S. P., & Hamel, G. (1992). Outsourcing and industrial decline. *Academy of Management Review*, *6*, 7–22.

25. Haapaniemi, P. (1993, Winter). Taking care of business. *Solutions*, pp. 6–8, 10–13.

26. See Note 21.

27. Stewart, T. A. (1993, December 13). Welcome to the revolution. *Fortune*, pp. 66–68, 70, 72, 76, 78.

28. See Note 18.

29. See Note 18.

30. Handy, C. (1994). *The age of paradox*. New York: Morrow.

31. See Note 18. (quote, p. 36)

32. See Note 27.

33. See Note 27. (quote, p. 70)

34. Keen, P. G. W. (1988). *Competing in time: Using telecommunications for competitive advantage (rev. ed.)*. Cambridge, MA: Ballinger.

35. See Note 27.

36. Miller, W. A. (1991, May 6). A new perspective for tomorrow's workforce. *Industry Week*, pp. 7–8, 17.

37. Johnson, W. R., & Packer, A. H. (1987). *Workforce 2000*. Indianapolis: Hudson Institute.

38. Kiplinger, A. A., & Kiplinger, K. A. (1989). *America in the global '90s*. Washington, DC: Kiplinger Books.

39. See Note 36.

40. See Note 36.

41. Wheelen, T. L., & Hunger, J. D. (1989). *Strategic management and business policy (3rd ed.)*. Reading, MA: Addison-Wesley.

42. Singh, J. V., House, R. J., & Tucker, D. J. (1986). Organizational change and mortality. *Administrative Science Quarterly*, *31*, 587–611.

43. Barnes, Z. E. (1987). Change in the Bell System. *Academy of Management Executive*, *1*, 43–46. (quote, p. 43.)

44. Saporito, B. (1993, May 31). The most dangerous job in America. *Fortune*, pp. 130–132, 134, 136, 138, 140.

45. Marcus, A. A. (1988). Implementing externally induced innovations: A comparison of rule-bound and autonomous approaches. *Academy of Management Journal*, *31*, 235–256.

46. Powell, B., & Stone, J. (1991, July 15). The deal of the decade. *Newsweek*, p. 40.

47. Kilmann, R. H., & Covin, T. J. (1987). *Corporate transformation: Revitalizing organizations for a competitive world*. San Francisco: Jossey-Bass.

48. Glueck, W. F. (1979). *Personnel: A diagnostic approach*. Dallas: Business Publications.

49. Swasy, A. (1993). *Soap opera: The inside story of Procter & Gamble*. New York: Times Books.

50. Lewin, K. (1951). *Field theory in social science*. New York: Harper & Row.

51. Schein, E. H. (1968). Organizational socialization and the profession of management. *Industrial Management Review*, *9*, 1–16.

52. Dumaine, B. (1993, June 28). Times are good? Create a crisis. *Fortune*, pp. 123–124, 126, 130.

53. Armenakis, A. A., Harris, S. G., & Mossholder, K. W. (1993). Creating readiness for organizational change. *Human Relations*, *46*, 681–703.

54. Beer, M. (1980). *Organizational change and development: A systems view*. Glenview, IL: Scott, Foresman.

55. Nadler, D. A. (1987). The effective management of organizational change. In J. W. Lorsch (Ed.), *Handbook of organizational behavior* (pp. 358–369). Englewood Cliffs, NJ: Prentice Hall.

56. Katz, D., & Kahn, R. L. (1978). *The social psychology of organizations (2nd ed.)*. New York: John Wiley & Sons.

57. Hannan, M. T., & Freeman, J. (1984). Structural inertia and organizational change. *American Sociological Review*, *49*, 149–164.

58. Tichy, N. M. (1993). *Control your destiny or someone else will*. New York: Doubleday Currency.

59. Tichy, N. M. (1993, December 13). Revolutionize your company. *Fortune*, pp. 114–115, 118.

60. Kotter, J. P., & Schlesinger, L. A. (1979, March–April). Choosing strategies for change. *Harvard Business Review*, pp. 106–114.

61. See Note 55.

62. Farber, S. (1989, September).

When employees ask: "What's in it for me?" *Business Month*, p. 79.

63. Pasmore, W. A., & Fagans, M. R. (1992). Participation, industrial development, and organizational change: A review and synthesis. *Journal of Management, 18*, 375–397.

64. Huey, J. (1993, April 5). Managing in the midst of chaos. *Fortune*, pp. 38–41, 44, 46, 48.

65. See Note 43.

66. Porras, J. I., & Robertson, P. J. (1992). Organization development: Theory, practice, and research. In M. D. Dunnette & L. M. Hough (Eds.), *Handbook of industrial and organizational psychology (2nd ed.)* (Vol. 3, pp. 719–822). Palo Alto, CA: Consulting Psychologists Press.

67. Sanzgiri, J., & Gottlieb, J. Z. (1992). Philosophic and pragmatic influences on the practice or organization development, 1950–2000. *Organizational Dynamics, 21*(2), 57–69.

68. Huse, E. F., & Cummings, T. G. (1985). *Organization development and change (3rd ed.)*. St. Paul, MN: West.

69. Abrahamson, E. (1991). Managerial fads and fashions: The diffusion and rejection of innovations. *Academy of Management Review, 16*, 586–612.

70. See Note 68.

71. Franklin, J. L. (1978, May–June). Improving the effectiveness of survey feedback. *Personnel*, pp. 11–17.

72. Golombiewski, R. T. (1972). *Reviewing organizations: A laboratory approach to planned change*. Itasca, IL: Peacock.

73. Campbell, J. P., & Dunnette, M. D. (1968). Effectiveness of T-group experiences in managerial training and development. *Psychological Bulletin, 70*, 73–104.

74. See Note 54.

75. See Note 54.

76. Beckhard, R. (1972, Summer). Optimizing team building efforts. *Journal of Contemporary Business*, pp. 23–32.

77. Vicars, W. M., & Hartke, D. D. (1984). Evaluating OD evaluations: A status report. *Group and Organization Studies, 9*, 177–188.

78. McClenahen, J. S. (1990, October 15). Not fun in the sun. *Industry Week*, pp. 22–24.

79. See Note 78.

80. Fisher, L. (1992, January 12). The latest word on teamwork? "Mush." *New York Times*, p. B16.

81. Blake, R. R., & Mouton, J. S. (1969). *Building a dynamic corporation through grid organizational development*. Reading, MA: Addison-Wesley.

82. Porras, J. I., & Berg, P. O. (1978). The impact of organization development. *Academy of Management Review, 3*, 249–266.

83. Burke, W. W. (1982). *Organization development: Principles and practices*. Boston: Little, Brown.

84. Hackman, J. R., & Oldham, G. R. (1980). *Work redesign*. Reading, MA: Addison-Wesley.

85. Munchus, G. (1983). Employer-employee based quality circles in Japan: Human resource implications for American firms. *Academy of Management Review, 8*, 255–261.

86. Meyer, G. W., & Scott, R. G. (1985, Spring). Quality circles: Panacea or Pandora's box? *Organizational Dynamics*, 34–50.

87. Griffin, R. W. (1988). Consequences of quality circles in an industrial setting: A longitudinal assessment. *Academy of Management Journal, 31*, 338–358.

88. Suttle, J. L. (1977). Improving life at work—problems and prospects. In J. R. Hackman & J. L. Suttle (Eds.), *Improving life at work: Behavioral science approaches to organizational change* (pp. 1–29). Santa Monica, CA: Goodyear.

89. Fields, M. W., & Thacker, J. W. (1992). Influence of quality of work life on company and union commitment. *Academy of Management Journal, 35*, 439–450.

90. Buch, K. (1992). Quality circles and employee withdrawal behaviors: A cross-organizational study. *Journal of Applied Behavioral Science, 28*, 62–73.

91. Buch, K., & Spangler, R. (1990). The effects of quality circles on performance and promotions. *Human Relations, 43*, 573–582.

92. Jick, T. D., & Ashkenas, R. N. (1985). Involving employees in productivity and QWL improvements: What OD can learn from the manager's perspective. In D. D. Warrick (Ed.), *Contemporary organization development: Current thinking and applications* (pp. 218–230). Glenview, IL: Scott, Foresman.

93. Deutsch, C. H. (1991, May 26). A revival of the quality circle. *New York Times*, p. E4.

94. Drucker, P. (1954). *The practice of management*. New York: Harper & Row.

95. Kondrasuk, J. N., Flager, K., Morrow, D., & Thompson, R. (1984). The effect of management by objectives on organization results. *Group and Organization Studies, 9*, 531–539.

96. Midas, M. T., Jr., & Devine, T. E. (1991, Summer). A look at continuous improvement at Northwest Airlines. *National Productivity Review, 10*, 379–394.

97. Kondrasuk, J. N. (1981). Studies in MBO effectiveness. *Academy of Management Review, 6*, 419–430.

98. French, W. L., Bell, C. H., Jr., & Zawacki, R. A. (1989). *Organization development: Theory, practice, and research (3rd ed.)*. Homewood, IL: BPI/Irwin.

99. Steel, R. P., & Shane, G. S. (1986). Evaluation research on quality circles: Technical and analytical implications. *Human Relations, 39*, 449–468.

100. See Note 73.

101. See Note 66.

102. Nicholas, J. M. (1982). The comparative impact of organization development interventions on hard criteria measures. *Academy of Management Review, 7*, 531–542.

103. See Note 82.

104. Neuman, G. A., Edwards, J. E., & Raju, N. S. (1989). Organizational development interventions: A meta-analysis of their effects on satisfaction and other attitudes. *Personnel Psychology, 42*, 461–483.

105. Rodgers, R., Hunter, J. E., & Rogers, D. L. (1993). Influence of top management commitment on management program success. *Journal of Applied Psychology, 78*, 151–155.

106. Roberts, D. R., & Robertson, P. J. (1992). Positive-findings bias, and measuring methodological rigor, in evaluations of organization development. *Journal of Applied Psychology, 6*, 918–925.

107. White, S. E., & Mitchell, T. R. (1976). Organization development: A review of research content and research design. *Academy of Management Review, 1*, 57–73.

108. Schaffer, R. H., & Thomson, H. H. (1992, January–February). Successful change processes begin with results. *Harvard Business Review*, pp. 80–91.

109. Cobb, A. T. (1986). Political diagnosis: Applications in organizational development. *Academy of Management Review, 11*, 482–496.

110. White, L. P., & Wotten, K. C. (1983). Ethical dilemmas in various stages of organizational development. *Academy of Management Review, 8*, 690–697.

111. Port, O., & Smith, G. (1992, November 30). Quality: Small and midsize companies seize the challenge—not a moment too soon. *Business Week*, pp. 66–70, 72, 74–75.

112. Stewart, T. A. (1993, August 23). Reengineering: The hot new managing tool. *Fortune*, pp. 40–43, 46, 48.

113. The promise of reengineering. (1993, May 3). *Fortune*, pp. 94–97.

114. Hammer, M., & Champy, J. (1993). *Reengineering the corporation*. New York: Harper Business.

115. See Note 114.

116. See Note 112.

117. Barrier, M. (1994, February). Re-engineering your company. *Nation's Business*, pp. 16–22.

118. Rothman, H. (1994, February). Quality's link to productivity. *Nation's Business*, pp. 33–34.

119. Sashkin, M., & Kiser, K. J. (1991). *Total quality management* Seabrook, MD: Ducouchon Press.

120. Lawler, E. E., III. (1994). Total quality management and employee involvement: Are they compatible? *Academy of Management Executive, 8*, 68–76.

121. Walton, M. (1990). *The Deming management method at work*. New York: Perigree.

122. Hunt, D. V. (1992). *Quality in America*. Homewood, IL: Business One Irwin.

123. Jacob, R. (1993). TQM: More than a dying fad? *Fortune*, pp. 66–68, 72.

124. See Note 121.

125. Bank, J. (1992). *The essence of total quality management*. Englewood Cliffs, NJ: Prentice Hall.

126. Hart, C. W. L., & Bogan, C. E. (1992). *The Baldridge*. New York: McGraw-Hill.

127. Hodgetts, R. M. (1993). *Blueprints for continuous improvement: Lessons from the Baldridge winners*. New York: AMACOM.

128. Boyett, J. H., Schwartz, S., Osterwise, L., & Bauer, R. (1993). *The quality journey: How winning the Baldridge sparked the remaking of IBM*. New York: Dutton.

CASE IN POINT: CHANGING AHEAD OF THE COMPETITION

1. (1993, November 1). 1993 winners of the Baldridge Quality Award: Eastman Chemical Co. and Ames Rubber Corp. *Business America*, pp. 20–21.

2. CNN. (1993, November 7). Managing with Lou Dobbs. Ames Rubber Corp.

3. See Note 1.

4. Shelton, J. (1992, November). Putting TQM on line. *Manufacturing Engineering*, pp. 12.

5. See Note 1.

6. See Note 2.

7. See Notes 2 and 4.

8. See Note 2.

9. See Note 1.

COMPANY INDEX

NAMES INDEX

SUBJECT INDEX

N

O

P

U

V

W

Y